THE ROUTLEDGE COMPANION TO
FEMINIST PHILOSOPHY

The Routledge Companion to Feminist Philosophy is an outstanding guide and reference source to the key topics, subjects, thinkers, and debates in feminist philosophy. Fifty-six chapters, written by an international team of contributors specifically for the *Companion*, are organized into five sections: (1) Engaging the Past; (2) Mind, Body, and World; (3) Knowledge, Language, and Science; (4) Intersections; (5) Ethics, Politics, and Aesthetics. The volume provides a mutually enriching representation of the several philosophical traditions that contribute to feminist philosophy. It also foregrounds issues of global concern and scope; shows how feminist theory meshes with rich theoretical approaches that start from transgender identities, race and ethnicity, sexuality, disabilities, and other axes of identity and oppression; and highlights the interdisciplinarity of feminist philosophy and the ways that it both critiques and contributes to the whole range of subfields within philosophy.

Ann Garry is Professor Emerita of Philosophy at California State University, Los Angeles. Her work in feminist philosophy ranges from applied ethics to intersectionality and feminist philosophical methods.

Serene J. Khader is Jay Newman Chair in Philosophy of Culture at Brooklyn College and Associate Professor at the CUNY Graduate Center. Her research in feminist philosophy focuses on global gender justice.

Alison Stone is Professor of European Philosophy at Lancaster University, UK. She specializes in feminist philosophy and post-Kantian European philosophy in the nineteenth and twentieth centuries.

D1597944

Routledge Philosophy Companions

Routledge Philosophy Companions offer thorough, high quality surveys and assessments of the major topics and periods in philosophy. Covering key problems, themes and thinkers, all entries are specially commissioned for each volume and written by leading scholars in the field. Clear, accessible and carefully edited and organized, *Routledge Philosophy Companions* are indispensable for anyone coming to a major topic or period in philosophy, as well as for the more advanced reader.

The Routledge Companion to Free Will
Edited by Kevin Timpe, Meghan Griffith, and Neil Levy

The Routledge Companion to Sixteenth Century Philosophy
Edited by Benjamin Hill and Henrik Lagerlund

The Routledge Companion to Philosophy of Social Science
Edited by Lee McIntyre and Alex Rosenberg

The Routledge Companion to Feminist Philosophy
Edited by Ann Garry, Serene J. Khader, and Alison Stone

—

For a full list of published *Routledge Philosophy Companions*, please visit www.routledge.com/series/PHILCOMP.

Forthcoming

The Routledge Companion to Seventeenth Century Philosophy
Edited by Dan Kaufman

The Routledge Companion to Thought Experiments
Edited by James Robert Brown, Yiftach Fehige, and Michael T. Stuart

The Routledge Companion to Medieval Philosophy
Edited by Richard Cross and JT Paasch

The Routledge Companion to Philosophy of Race
Edited by Paul C. Taylor, Linda Martín Alcoff, and Luvell Anderson

The Routledge Companion to Environmental Ethics
Edited by Benjamin Hale and Andrew Light

The Routledge Companion to Philosophy of Technology
Edited by Joseph Pitt and Ashley Shew Helfin

The Routledge Companion to Philosophy of Psychology, Second Edition
Edited by Sarah Robins, John Symons, and Paco Calvo

The Routledge Companion to Shakespeare and Philosophy
Edited by Craig Bourne and Emily Caddick Bourne

The Routledge Companion to the Frankfurt School
Edited by Axel Honneth, Espen Hammer, and Peter Gordon

The Routledge Companion to Philosophy of Physics
Edited by Eleanor Knox and Alastair Wilson

THE ROUTLEDGE COMPANION TO FEMINIST PHILOSOPHY

Edited by
Ann Garry, Serene J. Khader,
and Alison Stone

LONDON AND NEW YORK

First published 2017 by Routledge

2 Park Square, Milton Park, Abingdon, Oxfordshire OX14 4RN
52 Vanderbilt Avenue, New York, NY 10017

Routledge is an imprint of the Taylor & Francis Group, an informa business

First issued in paperback 2019

Library of Congress Cataloging in Publication Data
Names: Garry, Ann, editor.
Title: The Routledge companion to feminist philosophy / edited by
Ann Garry, Serene J. Khader, and Alison Stone.
Description: 1 [edition]. | New York : Routledge, 2017. |
Series: Routledge philosophy companions | Includes
bibliographical references and index.
Identifiers: LCCN 2016046368 | ISBN 9781138795921 (hardback)
Subjects: LCSH: Feminist theory.
Classification: LCC HQ1190 .R68 2017 | DDC 305.4201—dc23
LC record available at https://lccn.loc.gov/2016046368

ISBN: 978-1-138-79592-1 (hbk)
ISBN: 978-0-367-25798-9 (pbk)

Typeset in Goudy Oldstyle Std
by Swales & Willis Ltd, Exeter, Devon, UK

CONTENTS

CONTENTS

CONTENTS

CONTENTS

NOTES ON CONTRIBUTORS

Alia Al-Saji is Associate Professor of Philosophy at McGill University. She works on phenomenology, French philosophy, feminist theory, and critical philosophy of race. She has published in *Continental Philosophy Review*, *Philosophy and Social Criticism*, and *Research in Phenomenology*, and co-directs the Society for Phenomenology and Existential Philosophy.

Edwina Barvosa is an Associate Professor of Social and Political Theory in the department of Feminist Studies at UC Santa Barbara. Her interdisciplinary work focuses on the multiplicity of the self and implicit bias as they impact democratic governance. She is the author of *Wealth of Selves: Mestiza Consciousness, Multiple Identities and the Subject of Politics* (2008).

Christine Battersby is Reader Emerita in Philosophy and Associate Fellow of the Centre for Research in Philosophy, Literature, and the Arts at the University of Warwick, UK. Her publications include *The Sublime, Terror and Human Difference* (2007), *The Phenomenal Woman* (1998), and *Gender and Genius* (1989).

Talia Mae Bettcher is Professor of Philosophy and Department Chair at California State University, Los Angeles. Some of her articles include "Evil Deceivers and Make-Believers: Transphobic Violence and the Politics of Illusion" (*Hypatia* 2007) and "Trapped in the Wrong Theory: Re-thinking Trans Oppression and Resistance" (*Signs* 2014).

Tanella Boni is Full Professor at the University of Cocody, Ivory Coast. What started as work on the idea of life in Aristotle at the University of Paris IV-Sorbonne culminated in *Que vivent les femmes d'Afrique?* (2008). She is also a novelist and poet, who has won numerous literary prizes.

Tina Fernandes Botts is Assistant Professor of Philosophy at California State University, Fresno. With doctoral degrees in both law and philosophy, she specializes in philosophy of law, philosophy of race, and feminism. She is the editor of *Philosophy and the Mixed Race Experience* (2016).

Susan J. Brison, Eunice and Julian Cohen Professor for the Study of Ethics and Human Values at Dartmouth, has written *Aftermath: Violence and the Remaking of a Self* (2002), co-written *Debating the Ethics of Pornography: Sex, Violence, and Harm* (forthcoming), and published numerous articles on free speech theory and on gender-based violence.

Jacqueline Broad is an Australian Research Council Future Fellow in the Philosophy department at Monash University, Melbourne. Her main area of expertise is early modern philosophy, with a particular focus on women philosophers of the seventeenth and eighteenth centuries.

Adriana Cavarero is an Italian philosopher and feminist thinker. She teaches at the University of Verona and focuses on philosophy, politics, and literature. Her books in English include *Horrorism* (2009), *For More Than One Voice* (2005), *Stately Bodies* (2002), *Relating Narratives* (2000), and *In Spite of Plato* (1995).

Clare Chambers is University Senior Lecturer in Philosophy at the University of Cambridge. She is the author of *Sex, Culture, and Justice* (2008) and, with Phil Parvin, *Teach Yourself Political Philosophy* (2012), as well as numerous articles. Her next book, *Against Marriage*, is forthcoming.

Sin Yee Chan is an Associate Professor of Philosophy at the University of Vermont. Her research interests include Confucianism, comparative philosophy, feminism and moral psychology. Her recent papers discuss the concept of desires in Mencius and why homosexuality is compatible with Confucianism.

Tina Chanter is Professor of Philosophy and Gender, and Head of the School of Humanities at Kingston University. Her books include *Rancière, Art, and Politics: Broken Perceptions* (2016) and *Whose Antigone? The Tragic Marginalization of Slavery* (2011).

Beverley Clack is Professor of Philosophy of Religion at Oxford Brookes University, UK. Her publications include *Freud on the Couch* (2013), *Philosophy of Religion: A Critical Introduction*, co-authored with Brian R. Clack (second edition 2008), and *Sex and Death* (2002). She co-edited *Feminist Philosophy of Religion: Critical Readings* (2004).

Claire Colebrook is Edwin Erle Sparks Professor of English at Penn State University. She has written books and articles on literary theory, literary history, contemporary European philosophy, feminist theory, queer theory, and Gilles Deleuze. She has just completed a book on *Fragility* (2017, forthcoming).

Robin S. Dillon is William Wilson Selfridge Professor of Philosophy at Lehigh University, and a founder and long-time director of Women's, Gender, and Sexuality Studies. She works in normative ethics, moral psychology, feminist ethics, and Kantian ethics, and has written on self-respect, respect, arrogance, humility, and critical character theory.

Kristie Dotson, an Associate Professor of Philosophy at Michigan State University, researches in epistemology and Black feminism. Dotson has edited a special issue of *Hypatia*, published numerous articles, and is writing a monograph on epistemic oppression for Oxford University Press.

Carla Fehr holds the Wolfe Chair in Scientific and Technological Literacy in the Philosophy Department at the University of Waterloo in Ontario, Canada. She works in philosophy of biology, feminist epistemology, and socially relevant philosophy of Science.

Leslie P. Francis, PhD, JD, is Distinguished Professor of Philosophy and Law at the University of Utah. She served as President of the American Philosophical Association, Pacific Division and is former Vice President of the International Association of Philosophy of Law and Social Philosophy. She writes on justice, disability, and bioethics.

Elizabeth Frazer is Head of Department, Politics and International Relations, University of Oxford, and Fellow in Politics, New College, Oxford. She is the author of books and articles on the themes of normative ideals of politics, political education, and the relationship between politics and violence in political thought and theory.

Miranda Fricker is Professor of Philosophy at the City University of New York. Her research is in moral philosophy and social epistemology. Her publications include *Epistemic Injustice* (2007) and several co-edited works, including *The Cambridge Companion to Feminism in Philosophy* (2000). She is an Associate Editor of the *Journal of the American Philosophical Association*.

Ann Garry is Professor of Philosophy Emerita at California State University, Los Angeles. Her writing ranges from feminist issues in bioethics, pornography, and philosophy of law to intersectionality, analytic feminist epistemology, and philosophical method. She co-edits the Feminist Philosophy section of the *Stanford Encyclopedia of Philosophy*.

Moira Gatens is Challis Professor of Philosophy at the University of Sydney. She teaches early modern philosophy (especially Spinoza), political philosophy, and philosophy and literature. Two lectures about her recent work on Spinoza and George Eliot were published as *Spinoza's Hard Path to Freedom* (2011).

Trish Glazebrook is Professor of Philosophy at Washington State University. She publishes on science and technology, Heidegger, ecofeminism, international development, gender, and climate change. She currently researches women subsistence farmers' climate change adaptations in Ghana, and oil development in Africa.

Heidi Grasswick is the George Nye and Anne Walker Boardman Professor of Mental and Moral Science in the Department of Philosophy at Middlebury College and is affiliated with the Gender, Sexuality, and Feminist Studies Program. Her research spans questions of feminist epistemology, social epistemology, and the connections between the epistemic and the ethical.

Kim Q. Hall is Director of Gender, Women's, and Sexuality Studies and Professor of Philosophy at Appalachian State University. Recent publications include her guest edited *New Conversations in Feminist Disability Studies*, a 2015 special issue of *Hypatia: A Journal of Feminist Philosophy*.

Sandra Harding is a Distinguished Research Professor at UCLA. She is the author or editor of seventeen books, including *Objectivity and Diversity* (2015), *The Postcolonial Science and Technology Studies Reader* (2011), and *Sciences From Below* (2008). She co-edited *Signs: Journal of Women in Culture and Society* (2000–2005).

Sally Haslanger is Ford Professor of Philosophy and Women's and Gender Studies at MIT. She specializes in metaphysics, epistemology, feminist theory, and critical race theory. Her book *Resisting Reality: Social Construction and Social Critique* (2012) collects seventeen of her papers.

Patrice Haynes is a Senior Lecturer in Philosophy at Liverpool Hope University. She publishes in continental philosophy of religion and feminist philosophy. Her first book is *Immanent Transcendence: Reconfiguring Materialism in Continental Philosophy* (2012).

Sara Heinämaa is Professor of Philosophy at the University of Jyväskylä and Director of the "Subjectivity, Historicity, Communality" research group, University of Helsinki. Her publications include "Phenomenologies of Mortality and Generativity" in *Birth, Death, and Femininity*, ed. Robin May Schott (2010) and *Toward A Phenomenology of Sexual Difference* (2003).

Kimberly Hutchings is Professor of Politics and International Relations, Queen Mary University of London. Among her works are *Hegel and Feminist Philosophy* (2003) and *Beyond Antigone* (2010). She is currently collaborating with Elizabeth Frazer on a series of papers on the relationship between violence and politics within the history of political thought.

V. Denise James is Associate Professor of Philosophy at the University of Dayton. She researches and writes about the politics of geography, identity, and social justice. She has published essays on the intersections of classical American pragmatism and black feminism.

Alison M. Jaggar is College Professor of Distinction at the University of Colorado, Boulder. She holds a joint appointment with Philosophy and with Women and Gender Studies and is affiliated with the Department of Ethnic Studies. Jaggar is also a Distinguished Research Professor at the University of Birmingham, UK.

Katharine Jenkins is Assistant Professor of Philosophy at the University of Nottingham. Her main interests are social ontology, feminist philosophy, and the critical philosophy of race. Her publications include "Amelioration and Inclusion: Gender Identity and the Concept of *Woman*" in *Ethics* (2016).

Jean Keller is Professor of Philosophy at the College of St. Benedict/St. John's University. She co-edited *Feminist Interventions in Ethics and Politics* (2005) and *Envisioning Plurality: Feminist Perspectives on Pluralism in Ethics, Politics, and Social Theory* (2013). Her writing has focused on feminist ethics, relational autonomy, mothering, and adoption.

Serene J. Khader is Jay Newman Chair at Brooklyn College and Associate Professor at the CUNY Graduate Center. She works in moral psychology, ethics, and political philosophy. She is the author of *Adaptive Preferences and Women's Empowerment* (2011) and is currently writing a book on transnational feminist solidarity.

Eva Feder Kittay is Distinguished Professor of Philosophy at Stony Brook University/ SUNY. Her publications include *Love's Labor: Essays on Women, Equality, and Dependency* (1999); *Cognitive Disability and the Challenge to Moral Philosophy* (2010); *Blackwell Guide to Feminist Philosophy* (2006); *The Subject of Care: Theoretical Perspectives on Dependency* (2002); and *Women and Moral Theory* (1987).

Janet A. Kourany, Associate Professor of Philosophy and Gender Studies at the University of Notre Dame, does research in philosophy of science, science and social values, philosophy of feminism, and ignorance studies. She is working on a book, *Forbidden Knowledge: The Social Construction and Management of Ignorance*.

Susanne Lettow does research at the Institute for Philosophy, Free University Berlin. She specializes in feminist theory and continental philosophy, critical theory, philosophy of the life sciences, and biopolitics. She edited *Reproduction, Race and Gender in Philosophy and the Early Life Sciences* (2014) and a special issue of *Hypatia* on Emancipation.

Noëlle McAfee is a Professor of Philosophy at Emory University. Her books include *Democracy and the Political Unconscious* (2008); *Julia Kristeva* (2004); and *Habermas, Kristeva, and Citizenship* (2000). Her current book project is titled *Democracy Otherwise: Politics, Psychoanalysis, and the Work of Mourning*.

Catriona Mackenzie is Professor of Philosophy and Associate Dean (Research) in the Faculty of Arts at Macquarie University, Sydney. She has published widely on relational autonomy and other topics in moral psychology, ethics, applied ethics, and feminist philosophy.

Ishani Maitra is an Associate Professor of Philosophy at the University of Michigan at Ann Arbor. Her main areas of research interest are philosophy of language, feminist philosophy, and philosophy of law. She has published articles on silencing, the right to free speech, assertion, contextualism, and testimony.

Anna Malavisi was a development worker and program manager in NGOs in Bolivia before completing a Philosophy PhD. She has published on development ethics in *The Development Bulletin* (2001) and the *Journal of Global Ethics* (2014) and is currently writing a book, *Global Development and Its Discontents*.

Mimi Marinucci serves as Professor of Philosophy and Women's and Gender Studies at Eastern Washington University. Marinucci is the author of *Feminism Is Queer* (2nd ed. 2016), which explores the social and political aspects of the production of knowledge regarding sex, sexuality, and gender.

Mari Mikkola is Professor of Practical Philosophy at the Humboldt-Universität in Berlin. She works mainly in feminist philosophy, especially feminist metaphysics and pornography. Additionally, she has research interests in social ontology and is an editor of the *Journal of Social Ontology*.

Elaine P. Miller is Professor of Philosophy at Miami University of Ohio. She is the author of *Head Cases: Julia Kristeva on Philosophy and Art in Depressed Times* (2014) and *The Vegetative Soul: From Philosophy of Nature to Subjectivity in the Feminine* (2002), and co-edited *Returning to Irigaray: Feminist Philosophy, Politics, and the Question of Unity* (2007).

Monica Mookherjee is Senior Lecturer in Political Philosophy at Keele University, UK. She authored *Women's Rights as Multicultural Claims* (2009) and edited *Democracy, Religious Pluralism and the Liberal Dilemma of Accommodation* (2010). Her research interests span feminism, multiculturalism, cosmopolitanism, human rights, and the politics of recognition.

Johanna Oksala is Academy of Finland Research Fellow in the Department of Philosophy, History, Culture and Art Studies at the University of Helsinki. She is the author of five monographs, including *Feminist Experiences* (2016) and *Foucault on Freedom* (2005), and more than fifty journal articles and book chapters in political philosophy and feminist theory.

Amy A. Oliver is Associate Professor and Chair in the Department of Philosophy and Religion and Associate Professor in Spanish and Latin American Studies, American University. Her areas of specialization are Spanish and Latin American philosophy, women's studies, and philosophy of literature.

Kelly Oliver is W. Alton Jones Professor of Philosophy at Vanderbilt University. She is the author of thirteen books, including most recently *Hunting Girls: Sexual Violence from The Hunger Games to Campus Rape* (2016) and *Earth and World: Philosophy After the Apollo Missions* (2015). Her best known work is *Witnessing: Beyond Recognition* (2001).

Serena Parekh is an Associate Professor of Philosophy at Northeastern University in Boston, where she is the Director of the Politics, Philosophy, and Economics Program. She is editor of the *American Philosophical Association Newsletter on Feminism and Philosophy*.

Gertrude Postl is Professor of Philosophy and Women's and Gender Studies at Suffolk County Community College in Selden, New York. Her work focuses on feminist theories of language and the body, aesthetics, and philosophy and literature. Her most recent publication is a co-edited volume in German on Hélène Cixous.

Janice Richardson is Associate Professor of Law at Monash University, Australia. Her publications include *Law and the Philosophy of Privacy* (2015), *The Classic Social Contractarians: Critical Perspectives from Feminist Philosophy and Law* (2009), and *Selves, Persons, Individuals: Philosophical Perspectives on Women and Legal Obligations* (2004).

Wendy A. Rogers is Professor of Clinical Ethics at Macquarie University, Sydney. Her research interests include feminist bioethics, the ethics of evidence-based medicine, research ethics, vulnerability, and overdiagnosis. She is a founding member of the Editorial Board of the *International Journal of Feminist Approaches to Bioethics*.

Phyllis Rooney, Professor of Philosophy at Oakland University, has interests in feminist philosophy, epistemology, philosophy of science, and logic and argumentation theory. She publishes on rationality, gender, and cognition, feminism and argumentation, values in science, and the connections among feminist, pragmatist, and naturalized epistemology.

Falguni A. Sheth is Associate Professor in the Department of Women's, Gender, and Sexuality Studies at Emory University. Her research is in the areas of continental and political philosophy, legal and critical race theory and philosophy of race, post-colonial theory, and sub-altern and gender studies.

Alison Stone is Professor of European Philosophy at Lancaster University, UK. She has published books on Hegel, Irigaray, motherhood, and the aesthetics of popular music, as well as *An Introduction to Feminist Philosophy* (2007) and many articles on nineteenth- and twentieth-century continental philosophy.

Anita Superson is Professor of Philosophy at the University of Kentucky. Her research is in ethics and feminism, particularly practical moral skepticism, feminist moral psychology, and sexism in the academy. She is working on a book defending the right to bodily autonomy.

Theresa W. Tobin is Associate Professor of Philosophy at Marquette University. She researches and teaches in theoretical and practical ethics with particular interests in moral justification, philosophical methodology, and practical ethical issues related to violence, spirituality, and gender.

Robin R. Wang is Professor of Philosophy and Director of Asian Pacific Studies at Loyola Marymount University, LA, and President of the Society for Asian and Comparative Philosophy (2016–2018). Her publications include *Yinyang: The Way of Heaven and Earth in Chinese Thought and Culture* (2012).

Sara Weaver is a philosophy doctoral student at the University of Waterloo. She works mainly in feminist and non-feminist philosophy of science. Her doctoral work is supported by the Social Science and Humanities Council of Canada Joseph Armand-Bombardier Canada Graduate Scholarship.

Allison Weir is Research Professor in Social and Political Philosophy and Gender Studies in the Institute for Social Justice at the Australian Catholic University in Sydney. She is the author of *Identities and Freedom* (2013) and *Sacrificial Logics: Feminist Theory and the Critique of Identity* (1996).

Shay Welch is Assistant Professor of Philosophy at Spelman College. She specializes in feminist political philosophy, feminist ethics, and Native American philosophy. Her recent publications include *Existential Eroticism: A Feminist Ethics Approach to Women's Oppression-Perpetuating Choices* (2015).

Alison Wylie teaches philosophy at the University of Washington and Durham University. As a philosopher of social science her primary interest is in understanding how we know what we think we know, especially in archaeology and feminist social science. Recent work includes *Material Evidence* (2015) and *Evidential Reasoning in Archaeology* (2016).

Ewa Plonowska Ziarek is Julian Park Professor of Comparative Literature, University of Buffalo. Her books include *Feminist Aesthetics and the Politics of Modernism* (2012) and *An Ethics of Dissensus* (2001). Her research interests include feminist political theory, modernism, feminist philosophy, ethics, and critical race theory.

INTRODUCTION

Ann Garry, Serene J. Khader, and Alison Stone

Aims of this Companion

Feminist philosophy is a substantial and vibrant area of contemporary philosophy. Feminist philosophers critique and also contribute to traditional areas of philosophy such as philosophy of language, epistemology, metaphysics, philosophy of mind, philosophy of science, ethics, political philosophy, and aesthetics. One notable feature of feminist philosophy is its interdisciplinarity. Dialogues between feminist philosophy and other disciplines concern not only gender but also the various forms of oppression and identity that surround race and ethnicity, sexuality, disability, class and economic inequities, and the relations between humanity and non-human animals and the natural environment.

Insofar as it originated in feminist politics, feminist philosophy included from the start discussion of feminist political issues and positions—such as the influential taxonomy and evaluation of liberal, Marxist, radical, and socialist feminism in Alison Jaggar's *Feminist Politics and Human Nature* (1983). Feminist philosophers began to expose sexist biases running through the various branches of philosophy, including its historical canon, as we discuss in more detail below. Feminists then began work to construct new positions and approaches to combat the sexist assumptions they had identified. Initially moral and political philosophy drew much of the critical and reconstructive attention, but kindred feminist projects have unfolded in almost every area of philosophy: epistemology, philosophy of science, philosophy of language, metaphysics, philosophy of mind, aesthetics, and history of philosophy. However, non-feminist philosophers were often slow to recognize the philosophical character of what feminists were doing. For instance, there have long been feminists including women of color working on identity, such as María Lugones and Gloria Anzaldúa, but it has not always been recognized that in doing this work they were making important contributions to philosophy of mind (see Chapter 17).

A multi-faceted dilemma arises, though, when we seek as in this volume to trace how feminist philosophical debates have evolved into their current forms. The voices of white, Western feminists, often those working in "analytic" or Anglo-American philosophy, have prevailed within these debates. Often debates have taken shape around these women's contributions rather than those of women of color, from outside the West, or working in more marginalized traditions. For example, there has been extensive discussion over the years of Catharine MacKinnon's theory of gendered power relations, according to which women are subordinated to men through their social construction as sexual objects against men as sexual agents. But the focus of this theory is the subordination of women in general, a focus that directs our attention away from power differences among women, and the different ways in which women experience their gender in concert with their race, class, or other social divisions. That said, there have long been feminists who have argued that gender cannot rightly be considered in isolation from other social divisions, such as the Combahee River Collective in the 1970s and their nineteenth-century foremothers such as Anna Julia Cooper, Maria Stewart, and Sojourner Truth (see Chapters 10, 28, and 29). Yet these arguments have far too rarely been fully integrated into feminist philosophy.

The dilemma, then, is that in tracing the development of feminist debates one may remain focused on those more privileged or powerful voices that have particularly influenced these debates. Although there is no single solution to this dilemma, different contributors to this volume address it in a range of ways: re-inserting relatively neglected voices into these debates; introducing new debates and challenging the terms of existing debates; critiquing the power relations to which feminist thought has been subject despite itself; and reflecting on the concept of intersectionality itself, that is, the idea that gender is always intersected by other social power relations and that women are never simply women but always, inextricably, white women or women of color, middle- or working-class women, and so on. We have also endeavored as editors to design this volume in a way that responds to these dilemmas, as we will now explain.

We have divided this volume into five sections: (1) Engaging the Past; (2) Mind, Body, and World; (3) Knowledge, Language, and Science; (4) Intersections; (5) Ethics, Politics, and Aesthetics. This organization is designed to facilitate several different kinds of diversity. First, we wish to ensure a mutually enriching representation of both the Anglo-American (or analytic) and continental European philosophical traditions. We have therefore designed each section to include chapters on both "continental" and "analytic" themes and to put distinct approaches into dialogue (for example, by pairing chapters on analytic and continental feminist approaches to philosophy of language). This said, some chapters have a more analytic and others a more continental orientation while others fall in between or take different stances altogether, ones that are more interdisciplinary or are guided by non-Western traditions. To facilitate discussion between continental and analytic traditions we have organized all chapters thematically. An effect of this topic-based organization is that some figures, such as Simone de Beauvoir, Judith Butler, Kimberlé Crenshaw and Iris Marion Young come up across many sections—which evidences the breadth and impact of their thought.

Our second aim is to foreground issues of global concern and scope. Particularly in "Ethics, Politics, and Aesthetics," we have centralized global issues and asked authors to address general themes in a global setting. For instance, in discussing care ethics (Chapter 43) Jean Keller and Eva Kittay address global concerns such as the transnational migration of care workers and the global "chains of care" whereby care flows overall from the global south to the north and from the disempowered to the more powerful. Nonetheless, the focus of this companion remains feminist philosophy as it exists today in the Western world, in critical interaction with Western philosophical and related intellectual traditions. By and large, then, Western approaches provide the framework through which global issues will be addressed. This returns us to one of the dilemmas noted earlier: that tracing how feminist debates in ethics and politics have developed entails focusing largely on the West, even though the predominance of Western voices is a product of the unequal global power relations of which many feminists are critical.

While we focus largely on the West, we have included chapters on non-Western philosophical approaches—Daoism, African feminism, and Confucianism—and approaches that might be classed as "Western" in purely geographical terms—namely Native American and Latin American traditions—although these are not "Western" taking "the West" to be a political rather than narrowly geographical entity. While very far from comprising an exhaustive treatment of non-Western traditions, these chapters are designed to enable readers to identify points of connection and contrast with other essays in the volume. This helps to counter narrower views that non-Western traditions such as Daoism or Confucianism are not properly philosophical at all (e.g., for those who believe that philosophy began in ancient Greece). Such views are problematic, partly in presuming that we all know what is and isn't philosophy. We do not want to follow mainstream Western philosophy in restricting philosophy to the West. Nonetheless, due to space constraints we have had to cover a small selection of non-Western approaches, which are intended to be indicative rather than representative.

Third, the "Intersections" section includes several kinds of diversity. We focus on the ways in which feminist theory meshes with rich theoretical approaches that start from transgender identities, race and ethnicity, sexuality, and disabilities. In addition, chapters cover some of feminist philosophy's disciplinary intersections with development studies, religious diversity, and ecological and environmental studies. We have deliberately avoided treating intersectional work as an afterthought or as something separate from the rest of feminist philosophy. Instead we have designed this volume so that, throughout, there is space for our authors to attend to intersecting nodes among power relations—for example, in the ways that the aesthetic tradition has tended to be exclusive not only of white women's artistic and cultural contributions but equally those of people of color.

Finally, reflecting the variety of approaches to feminist philosophy, there is diversity in the styles of writing adopted by different chapter authors, and in the extent to which they provide original interpretations or arguments regarding their topic or, alternatively, explain the positions already taken by others on this topic. Having explained how we conceive the overall purpose and organization of this volume, we now want to introduce the aims and structure of each of its five sections.

Engaging the Past

Early work in feminist history of philosophy concentrated on criticizing the philosophical canon, not only targeting the explicit sexism of many of the figures in this canon but also arguing that more pervasive sexist biases often shape entire philosophical frameworks. For example, Genevieve Lloyd (1984) argued that Descartes's mind/body dualism implicitly ranks the "female" body below the "male" mind even though Descartes himself does not associate women with the body, because in Western thought the body has ingrained historical associations with the female. In this context, dividing mind from body works to the detriment of "the female" and by extension actual women. One conclusion drawn by some feminist historians of philosophy was that a whole series of hierarchical or "binary" oppositions runs through the history of philosophy and Western culture more broadly: mind/body, reason/emotion, culture/nature, action/passion, self/other, and so on—generally with these contrasts lined up with male/female. But must such concepts as *mind* and *reason* be *necessarily* linked to *maleness*, or are these associations merely contingent, so that these concepts in themselves pose no problems for feminists? Among the range of feminist answers to this question, one possible answer is this: the links are not exactly necessary, but the associations have been made so deeply and pervasively across history that we cannot just set them aside, but instead need to rethink the concepts *mind, reason*, etc. Thus, critiques of the canon helped to motivate the positive feminist projects of re-thinking ethics, epistemology, and other fields in a feminist light.

Since those critiques of the canon were articulated, though, there have been considerable shifts in orientation within feminist history of philosophy—shifts to move beyond the established canon and rediscover previously forgotten or neglected women philosophers and philosophers of color, or to recognize them as contributing to philosophy and not only, e.g., to politics. For instance, there has been a rediscovery of historical philosophers who used Descartes's ideas in a feminist or proto-feminist way (see Chapter 6). So, as Moira Gatens puts it (in Chapter 1), building on Eileen O'Neill's work, it is not so much that there were no women in philosophy in the past but rather that we have insufficient memory of the women who were in it. The problem may be not so much philosophy's actual history but our selective narratives of that history. Another development is to remain with canonical figures but re-read their work positively or as containing positive elements despite their authors' overt wishes (for example, in Chapter 2 Adriana Cavarero takes this kind of approach to Plato).

We hope that this volume shows some ways in which feminist discussions of the history of philosophy intersect with work that has a more contemporary focus. For example, feminist re-thinkings of fields such as aesthetics and embodiment are often informed by critical appreciation of the work of past figures such as Descartes and Kant (as with Chapters 15 and 37, among others). And such historical traditions as phenomenology, pragmatism and Black feminist thought all run forward from nineteenth-century roots into the present day, again indicating that there is no sharp divide between past and present (see Chapters 10–12).

Mind, Body, and World

From its outset feminist philosophy has addressed issues in philosophy of mind and metaphysics, particularly concerning the relations between body and mind, between selves and others, and the nature of identity. Thinking about the sex/gender distinction has been central to the first of those issues. Early on in English-speaking second-wave feminist thought, the distinction was drawn between the biological body and social gender in order to make the point that the ways men and women are understood and expected to behave, and the ways they come to experience and identify themselves in light of these expectations, are matters of social norms and pressures rather than direct causal effects of biology. However, this early discussion did not take into account biological variations of sexual development such as intersex or the full spectrum of genders, including trans.

4

There are other problems with the sex/gender distinction too. First, what about our bodies as we experience and live them, in light of cultural meanings? This seems to belong neither with sex nor gender. This aspect of the body—as lived and not merely biological—has been explored by phenomenologists and psychoanalytic theorists (see Chapters 12 and 15). Second, perhaps gender norms and the expectation that everyone should be either masculine or feminine shape our categorization of bodies into two sexes all along, where alternative ways of categorizing human bodies are equally possible and might be preferable. Further questions arise about what it means for gender to be socially constructed (see Chapter 13), and in what way, if any, all women count as women, especially if there are no common properties or experiences that all women share (the question of "essentialism," discussed in Chapter 14). In turn, feminist thinking about the body has led to broader reflection on matter and materiality (Chapter 16).

There has also been much feminist attention to identity and the self, especially in light of debates about identity politics. But these discussions have not always been recognized as contributing to philosophy of mind, partly because feminists tend to eschew the highly abstract and de-contextualized approach to personal identity and the mind which is common in contemporary Anglophone philosophy. Attention among feminist philosophers has been more to identities in the plural, in different contexts, and with more attention to actual experiences (for instance, of undergoing sexual assault), in contrast to traditional philosophy's preoccupation with the unity of the self and to the focus on thought experiments in much Anglophone philosophy of mind (see Chapter 18). Feminists have considered how relations with individual others, and social situations, figure into our identities such that selves are not self-contained—as with hybrid, including mestiza, identities, in which different social locations and related senses of self co-exist, perhaps antagonistically, within a single person (see Chapter 17). Some feminist philosophers have also turned to psychoanalysis to analyse how external social relations become internalized into our mental processes and how these processes, in turn, shape the social realm (see Chapter 19).

Knowledge, Language, and Science

Both the practices of science and our everyday lives lead us to converging insights about the value of feminist philosophy concerning topics of objectivity, reason, trust, knowledge, meaning and their connections to values, power, and gender. Most feminist philosophers have little desire to reject key concepts in theory of knowledge and philosophy of science such as reason, knowledge, truth, and objectivity. Instead they want to reconstruct them in ways that are more reflective of our actual epistemic situations, which are more richly conducive to social justice, and that better enable us to avoid past errors such as power-laden, gender-linked dichotomies (the hierarchical, binary oppositions discussed above: male = rational versus female = emotional) (see Chapter 20). Feminist philosophers attest that knowledge is "situated"; they try to provide complex analyses of the patterns and systems that structure the way we come to know what we do. This means that purely abstract analyses of knowledge or allegedly value-free analyses are not adequate to the tasks at hand. Instead, most feminists use forms of "social epistemology" that incorporate concrete facts about knowers and institutional (power-filled) structures. This means that we can discuss whose word ("testimony") is likely to be under- or overvalued on the basis of prejudice or implicit bias, or what groups may not even have adequate concepts to describe their own experience authoritatively; we can also look into what it means to have the virtue of being epistemically trustworthy both as a speaker and as a listener (see Chapters 21 and 22). Traditional philosophers, including those working in non-feminist social epistemology or virtue epistemology, have come very late to discovering the importance of discussing epistemic injustice, ignorance, and their relation to trust.

Feminist philosophers of science have found many opportunities for analysis both of the practices of science and in the philosophy of science. Over the decades feminist philosophers, along with feminists in other disciplines, have exposed sexism and andro-centric biases in the conduct of scientific research, the topics chosen for study, misunderstandings of the roles of values in science, and ways that power is unjustly manifested in science—to name a few. One of the most important insights to emerge from feminist philosophers of science—whether they focus on the physical, biological or social sciences—is that standards of scientific rationality and objectivity in fact become more stringent when feminist or egalitarian values are at their base (see Chapters 25, 26, and 27). Related to the high standard for objectivity is "standpoint epistemology," the view that favors starting research from the lives/positions of those who are marginalized rather than dominant. Although this approach was originally adapted from Marx's views, it has been broadened in the past few decades so that one of its core insights—that the position of the knower/investigator matters to the reliability of the knowledge produced—has been incorporated by feminist philosophers from many methodological backgrounds (see Intemann 2010; Wylie, Chapter 27).

Both continental and analytic feminist philosophers have critically analyzed language for several decades. The two strands have developed in different directions although they share concerns—initially about sexism in language, which leads to women's invisibility and reinforces unjust imbalances of power (consider "Man bears his young"), and more recently in their use of "speech act theory" (for example, Judith Butler's (1990) performative analysis of gender and analytic feminists' discussion of unjust silencing of women). From continental, specifically "French feminist," perspectives, language is seen as a symbolic system embodying various kinds of gender biases that can be built into grammar as well as concrete forms of language use. Gertrude Postl explores this in Chapter 24: continental feminists' concern with feminine writing (écriture féminine) and their analyses at a psychoanalytic level. Ishani Maitra, in Chapter 23, illustrates analytic feminists' use of speech act theory as she analyzes various kinds of linguistic injustices in terms of the ways women are silenced, even as they are speaking.

Intersections

As noted earlier, one of our aims is to foreground the importance of intersectional analysis for feminist philosophy. By "intersectional analyses" we mean approaches to issues that reflect the complex interactions among multiple structures and axes of oppression and privilege that are salient in our social identities, for example, race/ethnicity, gender, class, sexual orientation, and ability differences. Although many authors throughout the entire volume utilize intersectional thinking, this section begins by providing historical and critical analysis of the concept of intersectionality itself, especially as it has developed out of critical race theory, since the intersections between gender and race have been a particular focus of thinking about intersectionality (see Chapters 28 and 29).

Understanding intersecting axes of oppression in social reality requires both attending to the details of people's lives and drawing upon distinct bodies of theory that have arisen around each of the axes. Several chapters in this section focus upon the interactions among these bodies of theory (Chapters 29, 30, 31, 32, and 33). For instance, in critical response to the oppression of people such as lesbians and gay men on the basis of their sexuality, queer theory and critical sexuality studies have formed. Thinking about the close relations between gender and sexuality-based oppression has often involved cooperation between feminist philosophy and these areas of thought (and has contributed to the development of both). The chapters in this section highlight some salient cases where these theoretical intersections—for example, with critical race theory, queer theory, trans theory, disability studies, and Native American metaphysics—shed light on the multiple intersecting social structures that manifest themselves in our everyday lives. Also included here are chapters on global development, ecological thought and environmentalism, and feminist engagement with religious diversity, which pertain to further problematic sets of power relations—those of the global economic system, human exploitation and degradation of the natural world, and intolerance of religious diversity (Chapters 34, 35, and 36).

Ethics, Politics, and Aesthetics

As we have seen, feminists both argue that oppressive values have shaped the content and methods of academic philosophy and advocate for philosophy informed by feminist values. Engagement with values is thus not limited to the subfields of philosophy traditionally described as "value theory," i.e., moral and political philosophy and aesthetics. Part of the feminist contribution to philosophy has been to reveal the importance of value inquiry across philosophical domains. For instance, some feminist philosophers of science argue that prevalent ideals of objectivity arbitrarily value intellectual virtues that are culturally coded as masculine. They claim that value-laden approaches that recover a broader range of intellectual virtues may produce better science. Feminist epistemologists also emphasize that just political contexts, and partly political virtues, such as epistemic justice, are important to knowledge acquisition and legitimation.

Within ethics and aesthetics—two traditional philosophical subfields explicitly focused on values—feminist philosophers argue for shifts in what we valorize and in methods of evaluative justification. Early feminist interventions in value theory revealed how notions of the good, the just, and the beautiful served the interests of men and other dominant groups. One way traditional conceptions of value served the dominant, according to feminist philosophers, was by arbitrarily assigning positive value to masculine traits. For example, autonomy has historically been assigned a high value in Western moral and political thought. Kant argues that moral action is defined by autonomy of the will, and many contemporary liberal thinkers claim that respect-worthy conceptions of the good must be autonomously chosen. Early feminist moral philosophers claimed that Western philosophy downgraded culturally feminine traits, such as interdependence and empathy. The ultimate aim of these early feminist arguments was normative; they did not merely claim that women had been socialized to value differently from men, but also that androcentric bias had produced a distorted view of which ends in human life were worth pursuing.

In addition to claiming that traditional philosophical approaches had wrongly preferred "masculine" to "feminine" traits, goals, and values, early feminist ethics and aesthetics argued that androcentrism had problematically narrowed the *scope* of worthy evaluative questions. In both aesthetics and ethics, questions that seemed salient from the perspectives of people in dominant groups had eclipsed other important questions. To give some examples: Aesthetic theories focused on analyzing beauty in "fine art" rather than craft practices such as weaving, quilting, and cooking that have been pursued in the domestic sphere. Despite the fact that all human beings are born dependent and the result that human societies are inevitably faced with allocating caring labor, most moral and political philosophies were silent on topics such as dependency work, interpersonal trust, and relations of vulnerability. Although liberal political philosophy had devoted significant attention to analyzing economic inequality, it had fewer tools for diagnosing other forms of marginalization, such as sexism, racism, homophobia, ableism—and intersections among these forms.

Feminism has always integrated such critical projects with positive ones, but positive projects in moral and political philosophy and aesthetics have flourished in the last fifteen years. Care ethics, initially discussed primarily in terms of its contrast to more mainstream approaches, has now developed into a distinct family of moral approaches. In the 1990s, care ethics was described primarily in contrast to ethics of justice and rights, and a debate emerged as to whether feminists should eschew justice altogether (see Chapter 43). Today, some care ethicists hold that care is a comprehensive moral perspective from within which the value of concepts like rights can be explained. Others attempt to subsume care into a virtue ethics, and still others argue that care ethics and Confucianism can be incorporated into a single perspective (see Chapter 44). Similarly, the body of feminist scholarship criticizing the philosophical tendency to treat the self as atomistic and downplay the effects of social construction has now produced a rich feminist literature on autonomy. Relational accounts, discussed at length by Wendy Rogers (Chapter 46) and Catriona Mackenzie (Chapter 41), define autonomy in ways that highlight the autonomy-enhancing qualities of the right types of relationships and social conditions. They also emphasize the role social *structures* play in both limiting and enabling autonomy. For instance, some accounts define autonomy so that oppressive socialization is a paradigmatic case of autonomy restriction. Other accounts, especially within bioethics, are constitutively relational—suggesting that an agent cannot be fully autonomous if she lacks certain opportunities. As Mackenzie notes, the question of whether oppressive socialization is incompatible with autonomy has provoked decades of debate about whether feminist ethicists should take the content of agents' beliefs and values as central to determining the autonomy of their choices.

More broadly, many positive ethical and aesthetic projects develop tools for evaluating the impacts of social structures on our individual and collective lives. Liberalism has been the dominant tradition in Western political philosophy for decades, and liberals have tended to focus on injustices perpetrated by identifiable agents, such as individuals and governments. Even as issues about sexism and racism have become more mainstream within philosophy, a number of feminists have noted the disproportionate tendency to focus on the implicit biases of individual actors, rather than the networks of material forces that reward and implant these biases. A significant contribution of feminist philosophy in the last two decades has been to develop theoretical tools for identifying and responding to injustices that occur because of habits and patterns of action that cannot be easily said to originate in an actor. A number of feminists have criticized the current philosophical preoccupation with attributing sexism and racism to implicit bias. As Serena Parekh notes here, such structural injustices raise particularly vexing questions about responsibility, both because their consequences are often invisible to those involved in them, and because it is difficult to attribute causation to any individual agent. Feminist philosophers, such as Iris Marion Young, have developed forward-looking models of political responsibility that address difficulties attributing responsibility for structural injustice. Similarly, as the chapters by Sandra Harding and Anna Malavisi (Chapter 34), Serene Khader (Chapter 48), and Serena Parekh (Chapter 49) all note, feminists are renewing attention to the concept of exploitation, especially to analyse the use of women's unpaid and undervalued labor to subsidize "development."

Feminist philosophy, as we have noted earlier, has always been shaped by an engagement with political movements. Non-ideal theory has gained much attention in mainstream moral and political philosophy in recent years, but feminists have emphasized non-ideal approaches for at least the last thirty years. Non-ideal approaches suggest that, rather than imagining just social institutions, political thought should focus on identifying existing injustices and developing normative principles and concepts that help us to move beyond them. Nearly all of the essays in ethics and political philosophy take this as a methodological starting point; for example, Wendy Rogers's essay on bioethics begins from attention to existing healthcare disparities (Chapter 46), and Clare Chambers assumes that responsiveness to sexist oppression is a desideratum of liberalism (Chapter 52). Drawing on Onora O'Neill's work, Charles Mills (2005) argues that non-ideal approaches are attentive to the dangers of idealizing the agents who make normative judgments and the contexts in which they are made. An insistence that agents charged with making evaluative judgments are shaped by, and operate within, unjust social contexts cuts across the majority of essays on ethics, politics, and aesthetics in this volume. As Margaret Urban Walker famously put this point, "philosophers are in the plane of morality, not hovering above or perched outside it" (2007: 28). Alison Jaggar and Theresa Tobin argue in Chapter 40 that the pervasiveness of epistemic injustice, that is, conditions of knowledge production that harm marginalized people, offers a reason to reject the ideal of a single, universalizable method of moral justification. Allison Weir (Chapter 53) states that conceptions of freedom from colonized peoples reach beyond some key impasses in Western political thought, which connects with Shay Welch's chapter on indigenous metaphysics (Chapter 30). Although the ideal/non-ideal distinction is not a topic in aesthetics, Tina Chanter's essay in this volume (Chapter 37) shows how racial aperspectivalism infects not only moral judgments but also judgments about beauty.

Engagement with political movements has also caused the subject matter of feminist philosophy to shift along with changes in real-world political landscapes. It is unsurprising, then, that this volume is more transnational in scope than earlier compilations on feminist philosophy. Monica Mookherjee's essay on postcolonialism and multiculturalism (Chapter 47) raises concerns about ethnic and religious minority communities within Western liberal states. Amy Oliver's essay on Latin American feminist ethics (Chapter 50) highlights the role of women's philosophical inquiry in responding to political violence in Latin America. Tanella Boni's essay (Chapter 4) discusses political challenges particular to the sub-Saharan African context, such as navigating worldviews that attach women's worth to their capacity to biologically procreate and acknowledging the intersectional effects of gender and age in determining social status.

The essays on transnational feminisms, care ethics, and bioethics all emphasize the increasing importance of developing theoretical responses to gender and racial impacts of neoliberalism. Trish Glazebrook's essay on ecofeminism (Chapter 35) addresses issues such as climate change and the privatization of the global food supply.

In conclusion, we hope that this volume showcases the breadth and depth of feminist thinking across a wide range of philosophical traditions and topics, while featuring feminist perspectives that challenge and reconsider the history and contours of feminist thinking on these topics up to the present day. In this way we hope both to introduce the reader to the shape of feminist philosophy so far and also to provide a new set of original interventions with which current and future scholars and students will want to engage.

Some Thanks and a Note about Usage

A number of people deserve our deepest thanks. Routledge Philosophy Editor, Andrew Beck, who commissioned the volume; Routledge Production Editor Sarah Adams and Editorial Assistant Vera Jane Lochtefeld as well as Swales & Willis Production Editor Laura Christopher and Copy Editor Kelly Derrick; anonymous reviewers who improved its structure; and Alyssa Colby who contributed careful editing as well as general advice and support, funded by the Jay Newman Fund at Brooklyn College. Lancaster University provided Alison Stone with a term of sabbatical leave to expedite her editorial work. Finally, sixty-two authors made time in their densely packed and sometimes trauma-filled lives to write and revise the wonderful chapters you read here. We have enjoyed working with them and with each other.

Note: We left it to the discretion of individual authors whether or not to capitalize "Black" when referring to people with African ancestry.

References

Butler, Judith (1990) *Gender Trouble*, New York: Routledge.

Intemann, Kristen (2010) "25 Years of Feminist Empiricism and Standpoint Theory: Where Are We Now?" *Hypatia* 25(4): 778–796.

Jaggar, Alison (1983) *Feminist Politics and Human Nature*, Lanham, MD: Rowman & Littlefield.

Lloyd, Genevieve (1984) *The Man of Reason: "Male" and "Female" in Western Philosophy*, London: Routledge.

Mills, Charles (2005) "Ideal Theory as Ideology," *Hypatia* 20(3): 165–184.

Walker, Margaret Urban (2007) *Moral Understandings: A Feminist Study in Ethics*, New York: Oxford University Press.

Part I

ENGAGING THE PAST

1

FEMINIST METHODS IN THE HISTORY OF PHILOSOPHY, OR, ESCAPE FROM COVENTRY

Moira Gatens

This chapter addresses the various forms taken by feminist enquiry into the relationship between women and the history of philosophy. It will focus mostly on philosophy from the early modern and modern period, and on feminist work produced in Europe, Australia, and North America (for Ancient and non-Anglophone approaches see the other chapters in this section). The chapter subtitle intentionally evokes the idea that the historical exclusion of women from philosophy has involved a kind of interdiction or exile from which women have only relatively recently, and even then only partially, escaped. This chapter closes with a brief consideration of the work of the writer, George Eliot (1819–1880), who may be seen as someone who metaphorically as well as literally escaped from Coventry, and who provides a fine example of a woman who was excluded from institutional contexts of knowledge but nevertheless produced outstanding philosophical thought although in a non-traditional format.

Second-wave feminism—roughly from the 1960s to the 1980s—raised the question: Why are there no female philosophers in the history of philosophy? Why do Christine de Pisan, Mary Wollstonecraft, and Simone de Beauvoir stand out as the apparently isolated exceptions who serve to prove the rule? What follows is a sketch of four influential methodologies developed by feminist thinkers in their attempt to answer the puzzle of women's absence from philosophy. As will be shown, feminist responses to the question of women's relation to philosophy have developed into a series of exciting and creative developments in philosophical thought. Critical readings of key works in the history of philosophy have often resulted in the generation of entirely new ways of conceptualizing traditional philosophical problems. This feminist philosophical scholarship, begun in earnest in the last quarter of the twentieth century, opened up many unexpected and productive lines of inquiry, including care ethics (Gilligan 1982; Noddings 1984), standpoint epistemology (Harding 1991), ontologies of embodied difference (Bordo 1993; Crenshaw 1989), sexual and racial contract theory (Mills 1997; Pateman 1988), and numerous other approaches.

My exegesis of the path breaking thought that served to prepare the ground in which these innovative philosophies took root will favor work that responded critically to then prevalent dogmatic philosophical assumptions about women, such as the claim that the family and relations between men and women do not change across time or place. The idea that women and the family are ahistorical, simply part of nature rather than created in and through cultural practices, is common in the history of philosophical thought. For example, in *Emile* (1979 [1762]) Jean-Jacques Rousseau referred to the family and to men's relation to women as aspects of invariant nature. This erroneous view was echoed in Beauvoir's otherwise challenging study, *The Second Sex* (1953), when she asserted that women have no history. One of the most important challenges for feminist philosophers is to understand and change these kinds of powerful, destructive, and entrenched dogmas of thought that associate women with nature, the body, and emotion.

The Philosophical Imaginary and the Héloïse Complex

Michèle Le Dœuff made an early and influential contribution to the task of dismantling destructive philosophical conceptions of women. Her pioneering interpretation of the relationship between women and philosophy centered on the proposition that philosophical thought deploys an extensive repertoire of metaphors and images, including images of irrational, emotional, and objectified women. In *The Philosophical Imaginary* (1989), Le Dœuff shows that contrary to philosophy's self-conception as a master discipline based in truth and reason, one finds that the canonical texts are replete with images of trees, clocks, islands, storms, horses, donkeys, and so on. Certain aspects of the philosophical imaginary—for example, the Baconian image of nature as a woman that science must conquer and penetrate if her secrets are to be known—conspire against associating women with reason, culture, and knowledge. Sexed associations between dichotomous values (e.g. reason–emotion, subjective–objective) are endemic to philosophical thought and philosophy has played a major role in defining what it means to be male (e.g., rational, objective) or female (e.g., emotional, subjective). It is partly for this reason that Le Dœuff argues that what turns women away from the practice of philosophy is intrinsic to philosophy, at least as it is presently conceived and practiced. How could I, a woman, join the Baconian quest for knowledge if that venture is imagined in terms of the sexual subjection of women? Of course, an alternative kind of philosophical practice may not need to project negative values onto women or exclude them from the privilege of being recognized as subjects capable of reason. This type of non-totalizing philosophy, Le Dœuff muses, would be capable of accepting the necessarily incomplete and provisional nature of all thought. Le Dœuff writes about this approach to philosophical thought as "operative," open-ended, and as "thinking on the move." Her engagement with philosophy and its history is not only critical but also constructive and productive of new, more inclusive ways of engaging in philosophical thinking. An inclusive approach to philosophy would acknowledge its imaginary component and accept responsibility for re-engaging that imaginary in order to shift it onto new, more equitable, ground. An inclusive approach would also need to lift the ban on the participation of certain kinds of persons in the philosophical conversation, including women.

In "Women and Philosophy" (1977) Le Dœuff introduced the idea of the "Héloïse complex" in order to explain why even those few privileged women in the past who managed to gain access to philosophical thought were nevertheless prevented from becoming philosophers. The historical person from whom the complex takes its name is Héloïse d'Argenteuil, who was the lover-student of the famous medieval philosopher Peter Abelard. The Héloïse complex describes an "erotico-theoretical transference" that takes place between a female pupil and a male philosopher, who are often, but not always, lovers. The female pupil looks up to the philosopher as "the one who knows." The male philosopher finds such adoration satisfying because it protects him against self-doubt and the lack in knowledge that drives philosophical enquiry. In a subtle argument, Le Dœuff develops the idea that the transference on the female side, when coupled with women's exclusion from institutions of learning, results in women's access to philosophy amounting to mere appearance. In actual fact, this type of relation between pupil and master amounts to a ban, a "cunning prohibition" on women's ability to philosophize, and condemns them to the role of acolyte. This is because insofar as women's access to philosophy is mediated through a male lover-philosopher it amounts to access to only a particular kind of philosophy—*his* philosophy. This prevents women from developing their own independent relation to thought and so blocks their capacities to create philosophies that would represent their own perspectives and ways of knowing. Hence, she argues, this situation amounts to a surreptitious prohibition on women becoming philosophers. Although Le Dœuff does not deny the existence of an erotico-theoretical transference between male pupils and masters, she insists that there was not an *in principle* reason that prevented male pupils from becoming masters in turn because, unlike women, they enjoyed a formal status in institutions of learning. For males, the institution is able to function as a third term that mediates the intense dyadic relation between teacher and pupil and so can deflect the transferential relation onto other teachers or, indeed, onto the institution itself.

In addition to Héloïse and Abelard, Le Dœuff offers examples of other couples caught in the complex, including Hipparchia (c.350 BC) and Crates, Princess Elisabeth of Bohemia and René Descartes, and Beauvoir and Jean-Paul Sartre. Le Dœuff refined and sometimes revised elements of this argument in her later work, including in *Hipparchia's Choice: An Essay Concerning Women, Philosophy, Etc.* (1991) and *The Sex of Knowing* (2003). As feminist research into the work of past female philosophers increased in scope, and their writings became more widely available, it became clear that women in the history of philosophy had a great deal more autonomy than had appeared at first sight. For example, Héloïse enjoyed high standing as a Classics scholar before she became Abelard's student, and after their sexual relation ended she continued to study and compose works. Le Dœuff revised her view of women's relation to philosophy in stages, and her more mature view is that women *did* produce philosophy, *did* engage in autonomous philosophical thought, but that often they did so in clandestine ways and through genres atypical for philosophical work such as letters, novels, poetry, and plays. In other words, she suggests, they wrote philosophy "on the sly." Le Dœuff was one of the first second-wave feminists to put the names of neglected historical female philosophers in print and thereby helped to stimulate curiosity in works such as the letters of Héloïse and Abelard and the correspondence between Princess Elisabeth and Descartes, and Le Dœuff's sustained engagement with the life and writings of Beauvoir reinvigorated study of Beauvoir's contributions to feminism and philosophy.

The Man of Reason

Like Le Dœuff, Genevieve Lloyd stressed the importance of the fact that one of the oldest set of values in Western thought, the Pythagorean table of opposites, associates women with the table's negative values—e.g. left, dark, bad, formless—and men with the table's positive values—e.g., right, light, good, form. In her landmark text first published in 1984, *The Man of Reason: "Male" and "Female" in Western Philosophy* (1993), Lloyd's aim was not to study the values of actual historical male philosophers but rather to attend to the symbolic and metaphorical aspects of canonical texts in the history of philosophy. She sought to demonstrate that the maleness of the "man of reason" cannot be reduced to a mere linguistic bias. Rather, reason has historically been defined in opposition to femininity and those qualities with which femininity is especially associated—emotion, the body.

Of course there is a link between philosophy's power to describe and define "male" and "female" and the experience of actual empirical men and women. Hence, women in the past (and perhaps in the present too) experienced not only exclusion from institutions of learning, illiteracy, domestic confinement, and so on, but they also experienced a discursive or symbolic dissonance between the practice of philosophy and their lived womanhood. In agreement with Le Dœuff, then, Lloyd's analysis of philosophy from the Greeks to the twentieth century shows that even when women have had access to philosophy such access is constrained by the mismatch between philosophy's highest values and the values associated with being a woman. In Lloyd's view, philosophy is, in part, grounded in the conceptual exclusion of "woman," and femininity as lived by women has been partially constituted by philosophical discourses. Reason defines itself against femininity and emotion and then burdens woman with the excluded terms. The difficult task of critical feminist philosophy, then, is to break this self-confirming circle of women's supposed incapacity to reason.

Lloyd's analysis is subtle and open to misinterpretation. Indeed, in the second edition of *The Man of Reason* (1993), Lloyd refined her stance in response to some of the ways in which her thesis had been misconstrued. She insists that her claim is not that women cannot, or do not, reason. Nor is it that they have their own feminine type of reason. Rather, the so-called maleness of reason should, Lloyd says, be understood in metaphorical terms. However, the power of metaphor should not be underestimated and the dissonance felt by women who study and practice philosophy, even today, may help to explain women's massive underrepresentation in professional philosophy (see Haslanger 2008). Furthermore, the existence of an ideal sex-neutral reason to which we should all aspire is doubtful. Traditional philosophical ideals of reason were developed in contexts of gross inequalities—between men and women, colonizers and colonized, enslavers and enslaved—that distort human capacities and potentials. As Lloyd remarks "if there is a Reason genuinely common to all, it is something to be achieved in the future, not celebrated in the present" (1993: 107).

Both Le Dœuff and Lloyd made early contributions to the attempt to understand the complex historical relationship between women and philosophy, and part of that contribution has involved the development of new ways of practicing philosophy. Consistent with Le Dœuff's view of philosophy as "operative" and open-ended, Lloyd too recommends feminist work that engages with traditional philosophy not only in order to expose its exclusions but also as an appropriable resource for enriching our understanding of the present (Lloyd 2000). This constructive approach to joining the conversation of philosophy, including "conversations" with historical figures, is bolstered by the steadily increasing amount of feminist scholarship on women philosophers of the past (for example by Shapiro, Green, Broad, O'Neill; see also the Penn State Press series

"Re-Reading the Canon"). Not only are women philosophers, in the present, creating new philosophical approaches, but it also turns out that there is much more extant work by women philosophers of the past than was first thought.

Written in Invisible Ink

Eileen O'Neill's influential paper "Disappearing Ink: Early Modern Women Philosophers and their Fate in History" asks why "almost all trace of women's published contributions to early modern theoretical knowledge" (1998: 19) has disappeared, as if it were written in invisible ink. In a significant departure from the starting points of Le Dœuff and Lloyd, O'Neill describes women's past philosophical work as "extant but lost to sight" (1998: 19). Hence, the feminist puzzle to be addressed has shifted from women's *exclusion* from philosophy to their invisibility in or *erasure* from philosophy. This difference is important because in the former case the idea is that women were prevented from producing philosophy, whereas in the later case they produced work but that work was excised from our historical record. How might this be explained? O'Neill's argument is that between the seventeenth century, on the one hand, and the eighteenth and nineteenth centuries, on the other, certain events transpired that resulted in the expurgation of many women philosophers from the standard history of philosophy anthologies. This had the catastrophic effect of severing nineteenth-century women thinkers from their intellectual legacy.

O'Neill's explanation for this excision is multifaceted, and all that can be offered here is a brief summary of her extensive scholarship under four points (but see O'Neill 1998; 2005; 2007). First, she reiterates the standard feminist claim that "anon" was a woman. Eighteenth-century ideals of feminine modesty and diffidence did not encourage women writers to claim their works and so they often published their work anonymously (anon.). Writing anonymously, or under a male pseudonym, may also have given the work a better chance of receiving a fair or unbiased reception. Second, O'Neill notes that at the end of the eighteenth and the beginning of the nineteenth centuries philosophy underwent a process of "purification" that involved the separation of works deemed properly philosophical from works considered theological or religious, such as sermons, tracts of faith, or spiritual meditations. The removal of the latter types of work, *ipso facto*, included the writings of many women philosophers.

Third, the underlying episteme favored by some early modern women philosophers—notably, Scholasticism and Neo-Platonism—did not emerge victorious from the struggle of ideas. O'Neill finds puzzling the way in which these superseded epistemic worldviews then came to be associated with femininity. The reason for this association does not seem to be that some women favored the discarded views but rather because such views were contrasted with the emerging empirical, scientific approach to philosophy that was associated with masculinity. The old episteme was associated with femininity insofar as it was viewed as "weak," "degenerate," or "passive." What O'Neill calls the "slippage" between the work that came to be coded as "feminine" and the work produced by women likely served to add to the erasure of female philosophers from the canon. A *locus classicus* of the way in which these feminine and masculine associations came to be inscribed in philosophy is the Kantian idea that philosophy itself is "masculine," whereas he associates the receptive arts, such as poetry and literature, with women and femininity. The tendency of philosophy to sex its values has important consequences for how we understand the gendering of genres. As Catherine Gardner has shown in *Women Philosophers: Genre and the Boundaries of Philosophy* (2003), if one wishes to find women philosophers in the history of philosophy one must sometimes look to genres of writing other than those found in traditional philosophy. Consider, for example, Catharine Macaulay, who wrote several volumes on the history of England as well as letters, Mary Wollstonecraft, who wrote novels and travelogues as well as philosophical treatises, and George Eliot, who wrote novels, essays, and poetry. How and why in the twentieth century the dominant genre for professional Anglo-American philosophy has developed into the twenty-page journal article needs to be considered alongside the disappearance of women's writings from the philosophical canon.

The fourth and final explanation for the disappearance of women from our historical record in the eighteenth century is what O'Neill calls the "oxymoron problem." This is the idea that a woman philosopher is a kind of an unnatural hybrid: like a hyena in petticoats (as the Whig politician, Horace Walpole, said of Mary Wollstonecraft)? Or, like a bearded woman? (Kant commented that a woman who would learn Greek or debate mechanics might as well grow a beard.) According to O'Neill, it is during the late eighteenth century and especially the nineteenth century that the image of the female author comes to represent a huge threat to social and political life, and the woman author who dared to pick up her pen in order to write philosophy became a target of especially virulent attacks. O'Neill asserts that the "dramatic disappearance of women from the histories of philosophy in the nineteenth century can be fully understood only against the political backdrop of the aftermath of the French Revolution" (1998: 37). This assertion about women's erasure from philosophy leans heavily on Geneviève Fraisse's account of the crisis precipitated in French culture by the threat to masculine hegemony that was presented by the spectre of a genuinely universal democratic polity.

Women, Reason, and Democracy

Fraisse's *Reason's Muse: Sexual Difference and the Birth of Democracy* (1994) makes a distinctive contribution to the question of women's relation to philosophy by considering the issue of the "slippage" between the concepts "feminine" and "woman" in a particular historical and political context, namely, late eighteenth-century Europe. Fraisse argues that the construction of woman during this era as being incapable of reason, and so incapable of philosophy, constituted a powerful mechanism to justify their exclusion from the public sphere and from politics. On her account, the feminization of the French salons served to create a barrier between women and the public sphere. The question that drives her monograph is disturbing. She asks: is there "a necessary link between founding a democracy and excluding women?" (Fraisse 1994: 2) If the traditional religious story about women's divinely ordained obligation to obey loses traction, then those who would retain political and domestic power must find another narrative to justify women's subordination to men. The notion that women have a natural incapacity for theoretical reason is suited to the task. The convenient corollary to the proposition that women lack reason is that women who engage in theoretical reason are therefore "unnatural"; they are not real women. (Of course, the possession of practical reason, necessary in order to raise a family and function as man's helpmeet, was granted to women.)

Fraisse's analysis points to the acute anxiety of eighteenth- and nineteenth-century philosophers concerning the instability of sexual difference and the "fear of confusing the sexes" (1994: 193). Her monograph offers a close and scholarly reading of key texts by Rousseau, Charles Fourier, and J. S. Mill, which together provide an outline of the shape of the debates that raged around the question of woman's proper place in the emerging democracies of Europe. This debate came to be known as "the Woman Question." One part of the complexity of that debate is captured in the view of marriage of the naturalist Julien-Joseph Virey (1823): "Violence only produces a slave whereas consent produces a helpmeet" (quoted in Fraisse 1994: 93). J. S. Mill's vocal and strident objection to the suite of rights that English law conferred upon husbands shows that some male philosophers saw the situation differently. Both Mill and Harriet Taylor—the woman who, after a long friendship, became his wife—argued for women's education and emancipation and Mill felt compelled to renounce, in writing, all the rights over Taylor's person and property legally conferred by her "consent" to marry him.

Fraisse's argument raises many important issues for feminist scholarship. Her fundamental thesis is that access to reading, and especially to writing, were jealously guarded in the eighteenth century because they were taken to be the paradigmatic activities of rational beings. If the newly crafted claim of the "right of man" to self-governance is based in reason, then it is not surprising that the desire to restrict the scope of that right involved denying that certain kinds of beings—women, the colonized, people of color—possess the capacity to reason. The denial of reason to women, and others, justifies the retention of men's traditional powers over women in a context where traditional norms and extant laws were undergoing radical change. In the late eighteenth and nineteenth century, Fraisse maintains, the "woman question" becomes a question about woman's social, economic, and political emancipation. In this sense, she is concerned with a very specific historical moment in which the debate over women's nature and potential centered on challenges to, and justifications for, traditional norms and laws. It is only in the nineteenth century that the question of woman's relation to reason, and so woman's relation to philosophy, becomes an overtly political issue and begins to take the shape of a "democratic debate" (Fraisse 1994: 181). This is an important claim to consider because it illustrates that "woman," "femininity," "reason," and "nature" are not static or fixed concepts that render women's exclusion or erasure from the history of philosophy an unchanging feature of philosophical discourse. On the contrary, Fraisse's analysis allows us to see clearly that these concepts are dynamic and responsive to historical conditions.

The four methodologies treated here converge in a significant way. Le Dœuff, Lloyd, O'Neill, and Fraisse all respond to the puzzle of women's absence or erasure from philosophy by attending to the connections between women's treatment in the history of philosophy and the specific historical contexts in which such treatments emerged. Although much second-wave feminist research began as a critique of the misogyny of philosophy, it has developed into a much more complex set of questions and concerns. As the chapters in this volume amply demonstrate, feminist philosophers have appropriated and transformed traditional philosophical problems and issues. Some feminist philosophers are engaged in what might be called a retrieval project where the erased work of women philosophers is being put into conversation with past and present philosophical thought. This ongoing process of retrieval continues to generate immensely interesting and innovative research questions about the contribution of past thought to the formation of contemporary social and political values—e.g., freedom and equality—and institutions—e.g., law and Parliament. It is in the continuing generation of these kinds of questions that the future of a more inclusive philosophy is to be found.

So, have contemporary women philosophers escaped from Coventry? I indicated in the first paragraph of this chapter that my subtitle is meant to convey something of the sense of exile experienced by many women in philosophy, a sense captured by the playground punishment of being "sent to Coventry." Although women's representation in professional philosophy has improved over the last few decades, it still hovers around 25 percent in many Western universities. Philosophy remains a discipline with one of the lowest participation rates of women in all the humanities (e.g., see APA 2016 online data: women in philosophy). Recent research on the exceptionally low rates of citation of work by female philosophers offers more hard evidence of women's continuing exclusion from the philosophical conversation (see Healy 2015).

My opening paragraph also promised to close my contribution with a sketch of a woman philosopher who instantiates many aspects of the exclusions and erasures of women from philosophy, namely, George Eliot. Even a brief consideration of a historical woman who had to deal with the exclusions and erasures that have been catalogued by feminist scholarship can serve to remind us that the history of philosophy is not only about abstract concepts and ideas but had—and continues to have—palpable effects on living persons.

Eliot's birth name was Mary Ann Evans and she was raised in Nuneaton, a small town near Coventry in England. She was well schooled for a woman of her class and time, in part because her family and teachers recognized her genius for languages, science, and philosophy. Her formal schooling ceased when she was sixteen and she became her father's housekeeper (her mother had died). Even for someone extraordinarily gifted, there were very few paths in life open to women. Accepting a position as a governess, living with a male member of her family in a housekeeping role, or marriage, would have more or less exhausted Eliot's options. But the woman who was to become George Eliot had other ideas. She had already acquired a taste for philosophy through her wide reading and her translation of David Strauss's *Life of Jesus* (later she translated Feuerbach's *The Essence of Christianity* and Spinoza's *Ethics*). After the death of her father, when she was thirty years old, she travelled in Europe and then moved to London where she became the clandestine editor of the *Westminster Review*, a journal founded by Jeremy Bentham and other so-called Philosophical Radicals. She was romantically involved with the naturalist Herbert Spencer and the philosopher, George Henry Lewes, both of whom influenced but did not dominate her philosophical views. In some ways she was caught in the Héloïse complex but, like Héloïse, she also enjoyed independence of thought.

Although clearly a philosophical thinker, Eliot never claimed the title of "philosopher" or wrote in the genres typical of philosophy. Much of her non-fiction writing appeared as "anon" in the various journals in which she published. She wrote her novels under a male pseudonym in order that they would be read as serious literature rather than as "ladies' novels." Although she certainly was socially ostracized for a time because of the unorthodox nature of her relationship with her partner in life, George Henry Lewes, (they were unmarried) she was not accused of lacking femininity or of growing a beard. Almost all commentators on her life, however, feel obliged to mention her physical unattractiveness. Through her novels and poetry Eliot offered exceptionally astute and deeply philosophically informed analyses of religion, the vicissitudes of male–female sexual relations, nature versus nurture, the difficulty of gaining self-knowledge, evolution (*The Mill on Floss*), and anti-Semitism (*Daniel Deronda*). She treated complex moral problems, including infanticide (*Adam Bede*), alcoholism, and domestic violence (*Janet's Redemption*); and she dissected arguments for and against the education of women (*Middlemarch*), the franchise for the working man (*Felix Holt*), and the proper roles of church and state (*Romola*). In other words, although she wrote across the entire gamut of philosophical topics she never composed a single philosophical treatise, as such. This is not say, however, that she allowed herself to be excluded from the conversation of philosophy. (One of the earliest issues of the philosophy journal, *Mind*, contains an extended appreciation by James Sully of Eliot's art and her astute grasp of human psychology.) Her escape from Coventry lay in her power to initiate a new conversation. Indeed, her writings did much to keep aspects of the thought of philosophers such as Feuerbach and Spinoza alive in nineteenth-century Europe (and not simply through her translations of their works). George Eliot was a woman who suffered from many of the sexual discriminations and exclusions that have been the subject of this chapter. However, she also may be taken as an exemplar of the ingenuity of thought, and resilience of spirit, which characterize women's historical relation to philosophical thought and practice.

Further Reading

Broad, Jacqueline (2014) "Women on Liberty in Early Modern England," *Philosophy Compass* 9(2): 112–122.

Gatens, Moira (Ed.) (2009) *Re-Coupling Gender and Genre*, Special issue of *Angelaki: Journal of the Theoretical Humanities* 13(2): 1–139.

Green, Karen (2015) "A Moral Philosophy of Their Own? The Moral and Political Thought of Eighteenth-Century British Women," *The Monist* 98(1): 89–101.

O'Neill, Eileen (2005) "Early Modern Women Philosophers and the History of Philosophy," *Hypatia* 20(3): 185–197.

—— (2007) "Justifying the Inclusion of Women in Our Histories of Philosophy: The Case of Marie de Gournay," in Linda Alcoff and Eva Feder Kittay (Eds.) *The Blackwell Guide to Feminist Philosophy*, Oxford: Blackwell, 17–42.

Shapiro, Lisa (1999) "Princess Elizabeth and Descartes: The Union of Soul and Body and the Practice of Philosophy," *British Journal for the History of Philosophy* 7(3): 503–520.

Waithe, Mary Ellen (1987) *A History of Women Philosophers*, Volumes I–IV. Dordrecht: Kluwer.

Related Topics

Feminist engagement with Judeo-Christian religious traditions (Chapter 5); early modern feminism and Cartesian philosophy (Chapter 6); feminism and the enlightenment (Chapter 8); feminist engagements with nineteenth-century philosophy (Chapter 9).

References

APA Committee on the Status of Women (2016) *Data on Women in Philosophy* American Philosophical Association [online]. Available from: www.apaonlinecsw.org/data-on-women-in-philosophy.

Beauvoir, Simone de (1953) *The Second Sex*, trans. H. M. Parshley, Harmondsworth: Penguin.

Bordo, Susan (1993) *Unbearable Weight: Feminism, Western Culture and the Body*, Berkeley, CA: University of California Press.

Crenshaw, Kimberlé (1989) "Demarginalizing the Intersection of Race and Sex," *The University of Chicago Legal Forum* 140: 139–167.

Fraisse, Geneviève (1994) *Reason's Muse: Sexual Difference and the Birth of Democracy*, Chicago, IL: University of Chicago Press.

Gardner, Catherine Villanueva (2003) *Women Philosophers: Genre and the Boundaries of Philosophy*, Boulder, CO: Westview Press.

Gilligan, Carol (1982) *In a Different Voice*, Cambridge, MA: Harvard University Press.

Harding, Sandra (1991) *Whose Science? Whose Knowledge?* Milton Keynes, UK: Open University Press.

Haslanger, Sally (2008) "Changing the Ideology and Culture of Philosophy: Not by Reason (Alone)," *Hypatia* 23(2): 210–223.

Healy, Keiran (2015) "Gender and Citation in Four General-Interest Philosophy Journals, 1993–2013" [online]. Available from: http://kieranhealy.org/blog/archives/2015/02/25/gender-and-citation-in-four-general-interest-philosophy-journals-1993-2013.

Le Doeuff, Michèle (1977) "Women and Philosophy," *Radical Philosophy* 17(Summer): 2–11.

—— (1989) *The Philosophical Imaginary*, trans. C. Gordon, London: Athlone.

—— (1991) *Hipparchia's Choice: An Essay Concerning Women, Philosophy, Etc.*, trans. Trista Selous, Oxford: Blackwell.

—— (2003) *The Sex of Knowing*, trans. Kathryn Hamer and Lorraine Code, London: Psychology Press.

Lloyd, Genevieve (1993 [1984]) *The Man of Reason: "Male" and "Female" in Western Philosophy*, 2nd ed., London: Methuen.

—— (2000) "Feminism in History of Philosophy: Appropriating the Past," in Miranda Fricker and Jennifer Hornsby (Eds.) *The Cambridge Companion to Feminism in Philosophy*, Cambridge: Cambridge University Press, 245–263.

Mills, Charles W. (1997) *The Racial Contract*, Ithaca, NY: Cornell University Press.

Noddings, Nel (1984) *Caring*, Berkeley, CA: University of California.

O'Neill, Eileen (1998) "Disappearing Ink: Early Modern Women Philosophers and their Fate in History," in Janet A. Kourany (Ed.) *Philosophy in a Feminist Voice: Critiques and Reconstructions*, Princeton, NJ: Princeton University Press, 17–62.

—— (2005) "Early Modern Women Philosophers and the History of Philosophy," *Hypatia* 20(3): 185–197.

—— (2007) "Justifying the Inclusion of Women in Our Histories of Philosophy: The Case of Marie de Gournay," in Linda Alcoff and Eva Feder Kittay (Eds.) *The Blackwell Guide to Feminist Philosophy*, Oxford: Blackwell, 17–42.

Pateman, Carole (1988) *The Sexual Contract*, Cambridge: Polity Press.

Rousseau, Jean-Jacques (1979 [1762]) *Emile, or on Education*, trans. Allan Bloom, New York: Basic Books.

2

FEMINISM AND ANCIENT GREEK PHILOSOPHY

Adriana Cavarero
Translated by Robert Bucci

Binary Logic

Describing the birth of the universe, Plato stated in the *Timaeus* (Plato 1997: 1245, 42b) that, as human nature was of two kinds, the superior race would hereafter be called *man* and the inferior race *woman*. More precisely, according to him, woman was created when the prototype of man, having lived an unrighteous life, passed into another, lesser life and returned as a woman. After having defined man as *zoon logon echon*—a rational animal— Aristotle affirmed in the *Politics* (Aristotle 1988: 19, 1260a) that, while the slave is wholly lacking the deliberative element of *logos*, the female has it but that it lacks authority: that is, women lack rationality. These are two significant examples of the various sexist and misogynistic aspects that characterize ancient philosophy and expose it as an expression of a patriarchal society in which the human being, broadly understood, is modeled on the male sex only. Consequently the female sex is characterized as a kind of being that is not fully human and that is deficient, inferior, and for this reason subordinate.

Scholars in feminist and gender studies have long drawn attention to the patriarchal stain of ancient culture by insisting above all, with regard to the field of philosophy, on the positions of its two greatest representatives, Plato and Aristotle. Having intensified during the 1990s in important edited collections on Plato and Aristotle (Bar On 1994; Tuana 1994; Ward 1996; Freeland 1998), numerous feminist essays have had the merit of showing how, in the works of the two greatest philosophers of antiquity, the conception of sexual difference—far from being the simple and naïve reception of a sexist stereotype—intersects with Plato's and Aristotle's thought in profound and complex ways, often influencing their theoretical frameworks. As much as it is interesting and curious, the mere exercise of unmasking the misogynist prejudices that span the ancient philosophers' work risks, in fact, being an exercise that sets out to discover the obvious. With rare and rather problematic exceptions, philosophy—like other forms of knowledge—cannot but reflect and reproduce the overtly patriarchal culture of the time. Feminist criticism has therefore taken on the particular task of delving into the texts of the ancient philosophers in order to demonstrate how the treatment of sexual difference and of gender stereotypes falls back on the overall construction of their philosophical systems and often places them in crisis. Above all, these systems are characterized by a binary logic—by an oppositional, dual, and hierarchical structure—which, starting from the man–woman dichotomy, constructs a series of oppositions: mind/body, spirit/matter, public/private, active/passive, etc. In these the first terms, considered positive and dominant, coincide with the masculine pole, while the second terms, considered instead negative and subordinate, coincide with the feminine pole.

It is not at all surprising that the patriarchal stain, easily observable in the entire history of philosophy as in the history of culture in general, already characterizes the thought of ancient Greece, in which philosophy had its origin. In recent decades feminist studies of ancient philosophy have, first and foremost, been inserted into the wider horizon of studies, which—from diverse disciplinary perspectives—have revisited almost the whole production of classical antiquity in light of the concepts of sexual difference, sex and gender, sexuality and sexual desire, or sexual orientation. From epic to tragedy, from mythology to poetry, from art to politics, from medicine to cosmogony, reflections on these themes now constitute a vast and fertile field of research. Exemplary in this respect is feminist scholars' particular and constant attention to Antigone, the character from Greek tragedy who has never ceased to interest philosophy, from Hegel onward (see, e.g., Söderbäck 2010). Also notable, though, is the attention given to feminine figures from myth—Demeter, Athena, Medea, and many others—to whom, in the 1980s, the French historian Nicole Loraux dedicated seminal books that marked a radical innovation in classical studies by opening the way to a different reading of the relationship between politics and sexual identity (Loraux 1991; 1998).

The intermingling of the various disciplinary perspectives and multiple styles of thought that re-examine classical culture through recent categories of sexual difference and gender is a distinctive feature of feminist interpretation of ancient philosophy, which contributes to the originality of this field. The fact that it deals with recent categories that are bound to the historical origins and current developments of feminist theory constrains interpretative work to engage with at least two methodological questions. On one level the work is to examine the problematic nature of applying the concept of sexual difference to ancient texts, and, even more so, of applying the current although controversial distinction between sex and gender. On another level the work recognizes that the fundamental starting point for a genealogical reconstruction of the same ideas of sex and gender, if not of sexual difference, is in classical antiquity (Sandford 2010; Holmes 2012). The first question concerns the terminological and conceptual layout of feminist theory, while the second evokes the theme of the origin of philosophy that always presents itself when we speak of the Greeks.

Terminology and the Question of Origin

Feminist interpretations of ancient philosophy are affected by the various vicissitudes that, in the feminism of the last decades, have seen the term *gender* placed side by side, sometimes polemically and at other times in a conciliatory fashion, with that of *sexual difference*. Prevalent in the English-speaking world, the category of gender alludes to a culturally and socially constructed representation of female and of male, a representation that is distinct from the biological category of sex. Having spread throughout international feminism together especially with the texts of the French philosopher Luce Irigaray, sexual difference is instead employed as a critical concept that calls on the intersecting web of symbolic and material structures in order to re-think the feminine radically and free it from the logic of the patriarchal order. In general, with the term "patriarchal," the language of feminist theory refers to a cultural system, a discursive register, a regime of truth—more simply, a vision of the world—structured by a binary logic. That logic defines the human being by modeling it on a single masculine subject, reserving a subordinate role for women, who, not being men, are thus imperfect or inferior humans. Along with the term "patriarchal," which alludes to the power of fathers, feminist criticism in recent decades has elaborated other terms that express the same concept or approach it in greater depth. These include "androcentric" (centered on man), "phallologocentric" (centered on the phallus and on the *logos*), and "phallogocentric" (a simplification of the preceding term that underlines the identity, almost the inseparable fusion, between the phallus and the *logos*). Because philosophy, at least since the pre-Socratic thinkers Parmenides and Heraclitus, has been a reflection on *logos*—whose fundamentally untranslatable meaning ranges from "speech" to "language," from "thought" to "reason"—many feminist interpreters tend to privilege the term "phallogocentric" in order to denounce the masculine stain of the philosophical tradition. This allows us to pass to the second question mentioned above, that of the historical origin of philosophy.

As the Western tradition understands it, philosophy was born in the Greek world during the seventh century BC, and was established, as a form of knowledge with its own precise disciplinary charter, under Plato and Aristotle. In particular, it is Plato who used the term *philosophia* (love of wisdom) in a technical sense and who underlined the superiority of this new method for reaching knowledge of truth compared to other discursive or performative registers such as epic, poetry, rhetoric, and tragedy. Proudly declaring its innovative character, philosophy is constructed polemically and antagonistically ever since its historical origin with Plato. All the terminological baggage that comes from Plato's writings and that passes to the philosophical tradition— primarily *idea*, *theory*, *epistemology*, and so forth—is inserted into a system of discourse that proclaims itself to be different, more powerful, and more valid—as well as the only exact, true, and correct system—in comparison to the other discursive regimes that dominate the culture of the time. It is a battle of *logos* in the name of a superior *logos*, a philosophical *logos* that reflects upon itself in order to discover its universal truth and, more precisely, the method by which to reach that truth. It is worth noting that the term "method" is a Greek word that means the way, the path (*odos*), through (*metà*) which discourse must proceed in order to know truth. The famous myth of the cave, at the beginning of Book VII of Plato's *Republic*, describes this path. It recounts how the philosopher must turn his back on the Athens of his time—which is depicted as a dark cave where rhetoricians, Sophists, poets, and artists manipulate public attention with their deceptive discourses. The philosopher must turn his back on this in order to adopt the method that leads to the incontrovertible clarity of the philosophical discourse on ideas, and—no less important, as the second part of the myth narrates—to assume the order of ideas as the model for designing the optimal city, *kallipolis*, to be governed by the philosophers who are its "guardians." From a feminist perspective, the theme of the guardians of the *kallipolis* is particularly interesting because, in a well-known passage in the *Republic* (Plato 1997: 1078–1079, 450c–451e), it results in stirring up a sort of enigma. In this passage, Plato makes a proposal that seems to retract the thesis of the inferiority of women that he sustains in the entirety of his work: surprisingly, through the mouth of Socrates, he declares in fact that there is no reason not to admit women into the role of the city's guardians. A question can therefore be posed: Was Plato a feminist?

Was Plato a Feminist?

In the field of ancient philosophy, just as in every other field of knowledge, feminist studies are a very rich constellation, articulated in many theoretical perspectives and multiple styles of thought, which cannot be traced to a simple framework. The afore-mentioned important lexical variation between gender and sexual difference signals the development of two conceptual currents, from whose mixing further trends arise. To the latter one can add, at a minimum, the position of liberal and socialist feminism, which is based on the history of the emancipation of women and therefore insists on the principle of equality. In fact, even if the denunciation of the misogynistic version of the differences between the sexes in the Western tradition is shared by almost all feminists, a vast and articulated area of contemporary critical feminist theory holds that sexual difference is to be retrieved and re-signified in a new context that values the otherness of the female by removing it from patriarchal binary logic. The area of liberal and socialist feminism, on the other hand, holds that the modern principle of equality between men and women must prevail over their difference. Even though the criticism of androcentric binarism is shared, in the first case the outcome is the radical rethinking of difference, while in the second case the outcome is instead the resolution of difference in equality. One should therefore not be at all surprised that, from the lat-ter perspective, Plato's proposal in the *Republic* on the equality between the sexes proves to be particularly interesting.

Plato's proposal does not pertain to all citizens but rather only to the two superior classes of the guardians into which the *kallipolis* is organized: the warriors who defend the city and the philosophers who govern it. Overlooking his frequent declarations of the natural inferiority of women, Socrates argues that the difference between the sexes in regard to the reproductive act—"the female bears and the male mounts" (Plato 1997: 1081, 454e)—is inconsequential with respect to the political and military work of the guardians. Tellingly, so convinced is Socrates of an egalitarianism between the sexes that was completely unacceptable and scandalous at the time that he expects a "great wave" to beat down on him and crush him in reaction to his proposal.

Despite highlighting some aspects of Plato's egalitarian proposition and its disruptiveness in respect to the prejudices of the time, the greater part of feminist philosophers have stressed that Plato cannot be considered a proto-feminist and that his thesis does not anticipate the entirely modern question of the rights of women (Annas 1976). In particular, it has been observed that Plato's thesis of equality between the sexes is symptomatically inscribed in a political and social project that, for the guardian classes, abolishes the family and thus the domestic role of care and service, a role traditionally taken on by women, which is instead relegated to the class of the other citizens, who are the most numerous (Moller Okin 1979: 15–50). In order to render women equal to men in the government of the polis, Plato therefore turns women into de-sexed and unnatural females (Saxonhouse 1996: 147–157). In the *Republic*, the admission of women to the class of the guardians is realized in the context of a "communism" before its time, which was based on the customs of ancient Sparta and has unsettling eugenic aspects. This "communism" replaces the family with the political program of sexual unions for a reproductive purpose whose results—that is, children—are raised collectively and who call all the women and men who carry out the role of guardians their mothers and fathers.

Although interesting in terms of an archaeology of the emancipationist idea in the West, the Platonic proposal on the equality of the sexes is very complex and involves themes that concern the institutional engineering of the philosopher and his so-called utopia. The extensive critical literature that feminist scholars have dedicated to the argument reflects this complexity (Kochin 2002; McKeen 2006; Brill 2013). The fact remains that the sexist prejudices that Plato expresses in other passages of the *Republic* and in all his work also, inevitably, appear during the speech in which he states his egalitarian thesis. At the same point that Socrates holds that men and women have the same nature for education and employment, he says that the guardians share women and children in common, thus leaving it to be understood that men remain the true subjects of this revolutionary social order.

Plato's Cave and the *Chora*

There is another passage in the *Republic* on which feminist philosophers have focused their attention: the myth of the cave. Constructed by Plato in a polystratified manner, and marked by an overabundant symbolic density, the myth has generated an infinite series of interpretations throughout the centuries. We owe one of these interpretations to Luce Irigaray. In her book *Speculum of The Other Woman*, published in French in 1974 and translated into English in 1985, Irigaray breaks away from the canons of the interpretative traditions, rereads the myth in the light of sexual difference, and furnishes an interpretation that has become an obligatory reference for all successive feminist considerations of Plato's cave (Irigaray 1985: 243–364). It is important to note the dates of publication and of translation of Irigaray's book because Julia Kristeva's book, translated into English in 1984 as *Revolution in Poetic Language*, was also published in French in 1974, a work that has also had considerable influence on feminist studies dedicated to Plato. Interdisciplinary thinkers who work between philosophy, psychoanalysis, and linguistics, Irigaray and Kristeva, although in different ways, are two central figures of the current of thought that bears the name "French Feminism," which has been very popular with contemporary feminist studies in general and, in particular, with those studies relating to Plato. Both scholars treat an enigmatic category in the *Timaeus*, the *chora*, which—together with the myth of the cave—constitutes one of the principal points on which feminist interpreters of Plato focus their attention.

Imagine a subterranean cave, says Socrates in the *Republic* (Plato 1997: 1132, 514a), where men sit who, "since childhood, fixed in the same place, with their necks and legs fettered, able to see only in front them," observe a sequence of shadows on the wall before them. So begins the myth of the cave. The story proceeds to narrate how one of the prisoners frees himself from the chains, gets on his feet, turns around, and walks in ascent through the narrow tunnel that leads toward the entrance to the cave. Outside there are fields, trees, lakes; a landscape illuminated by the midday sun. Drawn by the light—and after having discovered that the shadows on the cave's wall were produced by strange mechanisms of projection and formed but a deception of poetic and sophistic discourses—the prisoner, now free and in the open, can turn his eyes to the sun and contemplate it (*theorein*) as the bright and fertile source of all that is and is knowable. Socrates sketches an analogy between the sun and the Idea of the Good, and he calls them respectively "son" and "father." Full of political and ethical significance, the myth is an allegory that illustrates the educational and formative itinerary—the *paideia*—of whoever practices philosophy. The *methodos* allows the prisoner to rise from the darkness into the light, from false and misleading discourses to the true discourse, or rather to the knowledge of what truly is: the realm of ideas, eternal and unchanging forms, the originals of which the shadows in the cave are copies of copies. Exiting the cave, the philosopher is born and is constructed by Plato as solitary and immobile, a "vertically erect" contemplator of the phallogocentric order of ideas (Cavarero 2013). High up and very bright, the truth without shadows, Plato states, recalls the figure of the father.

Luce Irigaray notes in *Speculum* that the cave is a uterus and that the labor undergone in order to come out of the cave, through a narrow cervix, mimics childbirth. This is not, however, a naïve, naturalistic imitation. Although the term "mother" does not appear in the text, the account has a precise structure and is, first and foremost, constructed around the polarity between a father/sun, guarantor of truth and knowledge, and a mother/cave, the seat of sensory deception and ignorance. At first glance, here as in all of Western tradition, the design is part of what Irigaray herself calls a binary economy. This is a system of dual oppositions in which the basic element of coming into the world sexed male or female, or rather the fact of sexual difference, is translated into a symbolic order in which man occupies an essential, founding, and dominant position, whereas woman holds a subordinate role often characterized by negativity and spite.

Upon closer inspection, as clarified by Irigaray and others, Plato's allegory has very interesting manifestations of instability with regard to sexual difference. Beyond operating as the female pole of the binary economy, the cave/uterus also functions as a screen—material that is given and not representable—on which the philosopher projects and represents his gnosiological and educational journey toward the bright truth of the father. This means that philosophy or, if one wants, Platonic metaphysics, as the outcome of a process of the disincarnation, abstraction, and verticalization of the rational subject, is built on the mother/matrix that, precisely because it serves as the material for representation—as a screen for the system's projection—cannot be represented and therefore exceeds the system itself. Elsewhere in the *Timaeus*, Plato calls this material *chora*, an untranslatable term that is essentially characterized by not having any form, indeed by being shapeless, the amorphous matter on which the forms and ideas of the father are imprinted.

It is interesting to connect the myth of the cave and the passage on the *chora* in the *Timaeus*. On the one hand, the recourse to the metaphor of sexual difference in the *Timaeus* is much more explicit, and on the other hand that explicitness is part of a "family romance"—mother, father, and son are named—that involves a clear allusion to the sexual act. The theme of the *Timaeus* is cosmogony, the generation of the perceivable world: the *cosmos*. Indicated by Plato as the son, the cosmos is at once the copy and the product of the intelligible model, corresponding to the father, which generates it; the father imprints his forms, namely his ideas, in the shapeless, inert, and passive *chora*, which carries out the role of mother. It is worth insisting on the amorphous character of the *chora* and on the difficulties of conceptualizing it, something that Plato himself exposes. Resorting to a metaphorical, varying, and imprecise language, he calls it "mother," "receptacle," "wet nurse," thus taking advantage, for the most part, of the polyvalence of the term *chora*, which in Greek oscillates between the meanings of "space," "abundance," and "place."

As the third element necessary for the "family romance" of the generation of the cosmos, and placed to the side of the son that corresponds to the cosmos itself, and the begetting father that is its intelligible model, the *chora* is variously defined by Plato in the *Timaeus*. He calls it "an invisible and formless being which receives all things" (50a), or "a receptacle, in the manner of a nurse, of all generation" (49a), or "like the mother and receptacle of generated things which are visible and fully perceivable" (50a), or yet again as "the natural recipient of all impressions" (50c) (Plato 1997: 1251–1253). Far from showing the richness of Plato's imagination, this variety of expressions exposes the philosopher's confusion with respect to something that eludes conceptual grasp, something that escapes the sphere of intelligible forms, which, not by chance, is reserved for the father. In other words, there is an element that is necessary for generation and for knowledge, the *chora*, which remains outside the hold of discourse, of *logos* as a conceptual system and rational model, but that discourse itself, wanting nevertheless to name it, calls *mother* and other names that allude to the female. *Logos*, in its desire to say everything, to understand everything, and to place everything in the rigid, vertical order of ideas, is forced to recognize the existence of something irreducible—unconceptualizable, uncontrollable, unintelligible—that is described as maternal, as feminine.

In the final analysis, in the Platonic philosophy that emerges from the *Republic*'s myth of the cave and from the passage on the generation of the cosmos in the *Timaeus*, the female therefore assumes a double face and ambiguously occupies two different positions. On the one hand, the less problematic of the two, we find the female inside the binary logic of the system. Opposed to man and subordinate to him, woman performs a precise role in the domestic setting and within social organization as wife and mother. On the other hand, much more problematically, having been crucially named as mother/matter, woman is outside of the system and elusive to it, but she is nonetheless necessary so that the system can be built and can function. The cave is necessary for the games of projection that lead to the philosophical journey to the light of the father; the *chora* is indispensable in order that the father's *logos* can create the cosmos.

One can maintain that, at least beginning with Luce Irigaray's *Speculum*, the problem of the relationship between these two types of representation of the female—the domestic and domesticated woman inside the system's binary economy, and the undomesticated woman, irreducible to the system—becomes a decisive theme for a large part of feminist critical philosophy. Rather than focus on searching for and unmasking stereotypes of the female inside of the patriarchal binary, many feminist philosophers work to make the most of and to give new meaning to that irreducible female—the *feminine other*—which the patriarchal order itself, starting with Plato, recognizes as unsettling, unclassifiable, and therefore potentially subversive. The strategy is not only that of a thinking of sexual difference, but also to give rise to a different thinking in which the feminine other defines a camp of radical alterity that can extend to welcome all who are excluded from the system, that is, those subjects that the binary system casts into its constitutive outside: gays, lesbians, queers, or what has been called "the abject" (Butler 1995). The binary economy that characterizes ancient metaphysics and is inherited by Western tradition is in fact also a normative device that establishes, inside itself, what is normal as it rejects that which, not fitting into these norms, is abnormal, monstrous. Indeed, Plato's discourse in the *Timaeus* illustrates the tension between these two types of movement: one that is normative and assuaging, that places the *chora* within the binary opposition form/matter, and another that is expulsive and worrisome, that recognizes the strange and horrific, the inexpressible and unconceptualizable character of the *chora*.

The experimental richness of Irigaray's engagement with ancient philosophy and Greek intellectual tradition cannot be stressed enough (Tzlepis and Athanasiou 2010). Her exemplary manner of tracing that feminine other, which eludes the binary economy in ancient philosophy, and of transforming it into the fulcrum of a different thinking, is fruitfully harnessed by various feminist strategies that insist on revisiting Plato's *chora*. They highlight the *chora*'s anarchic and disruptive but also fluid, dynamic, and vital character, the source of a universe that is becoming and in perpetual change, which contrasts to the rigid and lethal fixity of the realm of ideas.

As I have already stated, the interest of feminist philosophers in the *chora* has also been influenced by the analysis of Julia Kristeva in *Revolution in Poetic Language*. Kristeva identifies the *chora* in what she calls the "semiotic," the bodily element of language, associated with rhythms, movement, and tones, which opposes but permeates the symbolic, understood as the realm of the denotative meaning of words. By engaging with Lacan's vocabulary, Kristeva primarily calls on the *chora* as the feminine locus of subversion of the paternal law. However, the *chora*'s subversive effect, on which most contemporary feminist philosophers insist, unveils the problematic core of Plato's philosophy even more directly and deeply. On the one hand, if we assume that the *chora* is the bodily and rhythmical realm of the vocal, made up of plural voices communicating their incarnate uniqueness, then this very *chora/voice* becomes the perfect contrast to the abstract universality of *logos*, that *logos* that Plato in the *Sophist* (1997: 287, 263e) describes as the soundless thought of which the spoken discourse is a simple sonorization (Cavarero 2005). On the other hand, in as much as the *chora* alludes to the bond between the material and the maternal, between matter and mother, crucial questions arise about Plato's notoriously ambiguous relationship to the issue of maternity.

In this regard feminists have spoken of "symbolic matricide." In Plato, there is an explicit mimesis of maternal power when philosophy—and, above all, the Socratic method, which is compared to that of a midwife—is described as a work of *logos* for ensuring that the souls of young men may give birth to the ideas with which they are pregnant. Together with the topic of love (*eros*), the issue is developed in "Diotima's speech" (Irigaray 1993: 20–34). We read in Plato's *Symposium* (1997: 491–493, 209b–210d) that, pregnant in soul, men bring to birth many beautiful, even magnificent, words and thoughts in a love of wisdom, while women, pregnant only in body, give birth to human and mortal children. It is a woman, Diotima, who says these words. Plato decides to place in the mouth of a woman the definition of philosophy as the method that, on the one hand, mimetically takes on childbirth as a feminine characteristic, and that, on the other, debases childbirth as the production of mere mortal children, a product incomparable to the immortal thoughts born of philosophers. The rhetorical device of having a woman offer a speech that claims maternal power but at the same time degrades it functions, therefore, as a symbolic matricide.

Diotima is an ambiguous character who underscores the typical difficulty of the Platonic system with respect to a female who enters into the binary economy and, at the same time, exceeds it. From one point of view, breaking every stereotype of the domestic woman, Diotima is presented by Plato as the wise priestess and teacher of Socrates. From the other, she formulates a definition of philosophy that imitates and dispossesses maternity. Symptomatically, a mimesis of childbirth that raises crucial questions is also present in the allegory of the cave/uterus and in the figure of the *chora*. In the writings of Plato, maternity functions as a sign of a metaphysics that is not yet perfectly structured, as a theme that supports but concurrently puts into question the hierarchical verticality of the system.

Aristotle

With Aristotle the organization of philosophical writing becomes more systematic and takes the form of the treatise, which will later become customary. Feminist scholars who reread Aristotle have often noted that his misogynistic canon is more explicit and less problematic than Plato's. "The male is by nature superior, and the female inferior; and the one rules, and the other is ruled," Aristotle states in the *Politics* (1988: 7, 1254b13–15). One of the essential aspects of Platonism's binary logic, the dichotomy between mind and body—respectively identified within the limits of the masculine and of the feminine—is not only confirmed by Aristotle but also revisited in terms of a separation between the public and the private. Systematizing the customs of his society and at the same time furnishing a model of gender roles that would endure up until modernity, Aristotle maintains that free men—that is to say, those who are not slaves—belong to the sphere of politics while women belong to the domestic sphere: two separate and distinct settings, one public and the other private, where each of the two sexes best fulfills its nature (Cavarero 1992; Elshtain 1993).

When Aristotle formulates the famous definition of man as an animal equipped with *logos*, a rational animal (*zoon logon echon*), and therefore also a political animal (*zoon politikon*), he models the paradigm of the human on a single male subject, giving that subject a universal valence at the same time. It is worth recalling that this universalization of the masculine, definitively put in place by Aristotle, is a typical expression of the androcentric foundation of the whole of Western tradition and is also reflected at the level of language. Still today, in modern languages just as in Greek, the term "man" denotes, at the same time, the human being universally understood and those humans of the male sex, something that does not occur with the word "woman." With all coherence, Aristotle argues in *Politics* that, since they do not fully possess *logos*, women are not political animals but, rather, domestic animals, inferior and imperfect humans destined, along with slaves, to tend to caretaking—which is necessary for corporeal life—in the setting of the home. Exemplary in each of its details, the Aristotelian model also foresees that, within the domestic setting, it is again the man who is master of the house—indicated in Greek with the revealing name of *despotes*, despot, who commands women and slaves. Binary logic here finds a quintessential expression.

Feminist studies dedicated to Aristotle have shown how sexist binary logic, which emerges from his political writings and characterizes all of his work, finds an additional foundation in his biological writings. These are very complex texts in which he undertakes a detailed examination of sexual reproduction within the teleological process of nature (Lange 1983; Nielsen 2008). In the *Generation of Animals* (1942: 109–111, 729a) Aristotle claims that in the production of embryos the male semen supplies the form of the potential child, while woman supplies the matter, consisting of menstrual blood. Moreover, the embryo, according to Aristotle, is always of the male sex, turned into the female sex when the maternal matter fails to function properly. Thus the uterus works as a little oven that, depending on its good or bad performance, produces the perfect male child that the father deposited in it in the form of a male embryo, or the imperfect female child as the unfortunate outcome of the functioning of a defective womb. Yet, although the female offspring is the result of a material mishap—although, as Aristotle argues in the *Generation of Animals*, a deviation from nature takes place "when a female is formed instead of a male"—nonetheless, "this indeed is a necessity required by nature, since the races of creatures" can only be perpetuated through the copulation of the two sexes (1942: 401, 767b7–9). Thus a deviation from nature that produces the female as a deformed male—but also produces some further peculiar monstrosities, depending on the matter/mother's unpredictable and aleatory, errant status—ends up endorsing the final purpose (*telos*) of nature. There is a speculative turbulence in Aristotle's biology, a "feminine symptom," which destabilizes the structural coherence of the text. Obscure site of unaccountable movements, deviations, deformations, and even potential creative revolutions, the Aristotelian matter (*hyle*) perhaps has much more in common with Plato's *chora* than is generally acknowledged (Bianchi 2014).

Although there are feminist scholars who appreciate the Aristotelian texts and develop a positive reading of them (Homiak 1996; Witt 2011), Aristotle is certainly the ancient philosopher who, more than others, succeeds in providing a solid, speculative foundation for the gender stereotypes present in his society and inherited by tradition. One need only think of the success of the oppositional couples public/private and active/passive in subsequent literature on the natural subordination of women to men. Nevertheless, just like the works of Plato especially when they thematize and strain to rationalize the issue of matter/mother, Aristotle's texts also reveal some symptoms of instability and deep anxiety. In the final analysis, feminist criticism finds it more interesting to reflect on these symptoms and to take advantage of their disruptiveness rather than to denounce the obvious phallogocentrism of the Aristotelian system.

In Conclusion

Although the innovative contribution of feminism to studies on Aristotle is noteworthy, it is not a coincidence that feminist scholars have focused their attention largely on Plato, producing experimentally dense and original interpretations. Organized in the form of a dialogue, and able to blend the definitional attitude of philosophy with narrative digressions, allegorical accounts, and inventions of myths, Plato's philosophy—unlike Aristotle's—is not constructed as a treatise, a potentially closed system. Instead Plato develops an experimental, discontinuous, incomplete, and substantially open composition. There are unsutured knots in the fabric of Plato's writing that can be retrieved, decoded, and resituated within a feminist horizon that changes their meaning. There are female figures who can be extracted, "stolen" from context and re-thought in light of sexual difference (Cavarero 1995). A large part of the feminist consideration dedicated to Plato excavates his texts, along its fissures, interstices, caesuras, and fault lines, in order both to deconstruct patriarchal metaphysics and to think the feminine other differently. In tune with Plato's experimental practice of thought, the result is not so much an academic revisiting of ancient philosophy as it is a way of philosophizing that, free and unprejudiced once again, confronts the conceptual and lexical structures of the entire philosophical tradition with the texts in which they have their origin.

Further Reading

Blundell, Sue (1995) *Woman in Ancient Greece*, Cambridge, MA: Harvard University Press.

Duvergès, Blair Elena (2012) *Plato's Dialectic on Woman: Equal, Therefore Inferior*, New York: Routledge.

Lovibond, Sabina (2000) "Feminism in Ancient Philosophy: The Feminist Stake in Greek Rationalism," in Fricker, Miranda, and Jennifer Homsby (Eds.) *The Cambridge Companion to Feminism in Philosophy*, Cambridge: Cambridge University Press, 10–28.

Rabinowitz, Nancy and Richlin, Amy, Eds. (1993) *Feminist Theory and the Classics*, New York: Routledge.

Zajko, Vanda and Leonad, Miriam, Eds. (2008) *Laughing with Medusa: Classical Myth and Feminist Thought*, Oxford: Oxford University Press.

Related Topics

Feminist methods in the history of philosophy (Chapter 1); Dao becomes female: a gendered reality, knowledge, and strategy for living (Chapter 3); embodiment and feminist philosophy (Chapter 15); materiality: sex, gender and what lies beneath (Chapter 16); psychoanalysis, subjectivity and feminism (Chapter 19); rationality and objectivity in feminist philosophy (Chapter 20); language, writing and gender differences (Chapter 24).

References

Annas, Julia (1976) "Plato's *Republic* and Feminism," *Philosophy* 51(197): 307–321.

Aristotle (1942) *Generation of Animals*, trans. A. L. Peck, London: Heinemann.

——(1988) *The Politics*, Ed. Stephen Everson, Cambridge: Cambridge University Press.

Bar On, Bat-Ami, Ed. (1994) *Engendering Origins: Critical Feminist Readings in Plato and Aristotle*, Albany, NY: State University of New York Press.

Bianchi, Emanuela (2014) *The Feminine Symptom: Aleatory Matter in The Aristotelian Cosmos*, New York: Fordham University Press.

Brill, Sara (2013) "Plato's Critical Theory," *Epoché* 17(2): 233–248.

Butler, Judith (1995) *Bodies That Matter*, New York: Routledge.

Cavarero, Adriana (1992) "Equality and Sexual Difference: Amnesia in Political Thought," in Gisela Bock and Susan James (Eds.) *Beyond Equality and Difference: Citizenship, Feminist Politics, and Female Subjectivity*, London: Routledge, 32–47.

——(1995) *In Spite of Plato: A Feminist Rewriting of Ancient Philosophy*, trans. Serena Anderlini-D'Onofrio and Aine O'Healy, Cambridge: Polity.

——(2005) *For More Than One Voice: Toward a Philosophy of Vocal Expression*, trans. Paul A. Kottman, Stanford, CA: Stanford University Press.

——(2013) "Rectitude: Reflexions on Postural Ontology," *Journal of Speculative Philosophy* 27(3): 220–235.

Elshtain, Jean Bethke (1993) *Public Man, Private Woman*, Princeton, NJ: Princeton University Press.

Freeland, Cynthia, Ed. (1998) *Feminist Interpretations of Aristotle*, University Park, PA: Pennsylvania State University Press.

Homiak, Marcia (1996) "Feminism and Aristotle's Rational Ideal," in Julie K. Ward (Ed.) *Feminism and Ancient Philosophy*, New York: Routledge, 118–139.

Holmes, Brooke (2012) *Gender: Antiquity and Its Legacy*, Oxford: Oxford University Press.

Irigaray, Luce (1985) *Speculum of the Other Woman*, trans. Gillian C. Gill, Ithaca, NY: Cornell University Press.

——(1993) *An Ethics of Sexual Difference*, trans. Carolyn Burke and Gillian C. Gill, Ithaca, NY: Cornell University Press.

Kochin, Michael S. (2002) *Gender and Rhetoric in Plato's Political Thought*, Cambridge: Cambridge University Press.

Lange, Lydia (1983) "Woman Is Not a Rational Animal: On Aristotle's Biology of Reproduction," in Sandra Harding and Merrill B. Hintikka (Eds.) *Discovering Reality: Feminist Perspectives on Epistemology, Metaphysics, Methodology and Philosophy of Science*, Dordrecht: Reidel, 1–16.

Loraux, Nicole (1991) *Tragic Ways of Killing a Woman*, trans. Anthony Forster, Cambridge, MA: Harvard University Press.

——(1998) *Mothers in Mourning*, trans. Corinne Pache, Ithaca, NY: Cornell University Press.

McKeen, Catherine (2006) "Why Women Must Guard and Rule in Plato's Kallipolis," *Pacific Philosophical Quarterly* 87: 527–548.

Moller Okin, Susan (1979) *Women in Western Political Thought*, Princeton, NJ: Princeton University Press.

Nielsen, Karen M. (2008) "The Private Parts of Animals: Aristotle on the Teleology of Sexual Difference," *Phronesis* 53(4–5): 373–405.

Plato (1997) *Complete Works*, John M. Cooper (Ed.) Indianapolis, IN: Hackett.

Saxonhouse, Arleen W. (1996) *Fear of Diversity: The Birth of Political Science in Ancient Greek Thought*, Chicago, IL: University of Chicago Press.

Söderbäck, Fanny, Ed. (2010) *Feminist Readings of Antigone*, Albany, NY: State University of New York Press.

Sandford, Stella (2010) *Plato and Sex*, Cambridge: Polity.

Tuana, Nancy, Ed. (1994) *Feminist Interpretations of Plato*, University Park, PA: Pennsylvania State University Press.

Tzelepis, Elena and Athanasiou, Athena, Eds. (2010) *Rewriting Difference: Luce Irigaray and "the Greeks,"* Albany, NY: State University of New York Press.

Ward, Julie K., Ed. (1996) *Feminism and Ancient Philosophy*, New York: Routledge.

Witt, Charlotte (2011) *The Metaphysics of Gender*, New York: Oxford University Press.

3

DAO BECOMES FEMALE

A Gendered Reality, Knowledge, and Strategy for Living

Robin R. Wang

Introduction

Laozi's *Daodejing* or *Classics of Way and Its Power* is traditionally assigned to the sixth century BCE, but possibly dates from as recently as the third century BCE. It has only about 5,250 Chinese characters in eighty-one brief sections or paragraphs, yet is known as the foundation of Daoism (or Taoism). The term *Dao* 道 appears seventy-three times in the text and has a complicated and multilayered meaning. Throughout Chinese history, *Dao* has been cherished by all schools of thought and has generally been taken to be the ultimate origin, source, and principle of the universe and of the myriad things. There is no existence, or literally no-thing, beyond *Dao*.

Daoism, a *Dao* based and inspired teaching and practice, has been considered to be the philosophy of yielding in Chinese intellectual history. One important aspect of yielding is being *rou* 柔—soft, gentle, supple—which the *Daodejing* couples with the feminine. Not surprisingly, then, the female and femininity have enormous significance for Laozi and Daoism. To highlight this unique philosophical aspect of Daoism, this chapter will place femininity/the feminine/the female center stage to investigate Daoist thought and its possible contribution to feminist thought in a contemporary global setting. In this chapter I promote a somewhat female consciousness of *Dao*, or a Daoist female consciousness, which may expand, support, or alter feminist assumptions about femininity/the feminine/the female. The overarching focal point of this understanding lies in a depiction of the female and femininity as a cosmic force, a way of knowing, and a strategy for leading a flourishing life. The main points are that *Dao* does not govern actually existing gender relations—or, at least, that the social and political reality of gender relations is not modeled on *Dao*, because the patriarchy is not *Dao*. Highlighting the female or feminine aspect of *Dao*, or *Dao* as becoming female, is a feminist intervention, using resources from within classical Daoist thought in order to re-imagine or reconfigure gender for our time.

Dao as Cosmic Mother and Female Body

All phenomena in nature or, in classical Chinese terminology, "all things under heaven" (*tian xia* 天下) can be distinguished according to their characteristics as either *yin* or *yang*, and man/male/masculinity and woman/female/femininity are naturally identified with this yinyang matrix (Wang 2012). Unlike other interpretations of the *yin/yang* complementarity in Chinese thought, the *Daodejing* suggests the primordiality, indeed the superior power, of *yin* in general and the female and femininity in particular. From the perspective of the *Daodejing* the female/femininity is not excluded, shunned, frozen out, disadvantaged, rejected, unwanted, abandoned, dislocated, or otherwise marginalized. Its basic identity as a cosmic potentiality and a necessary part of any and every generative process is highly valued and celebrated. Actually, the spontaneous potency of *Dao* is female, or is becoming female. *Dao* is associated with the female body, which is a common metaphor for *Dao* in the *Daodejing*. This metaphor reveals not just the importance of *yin* and its generative capacity, but also designates a *yin* origin that is hidden, implicit, or empty.

This is how the *Daodejing* begins:

As to a Dao—

if it can be specified as a Dao,

it is not a permanent Dao.

As to a name—

if it can be specified as a name,

it is not a permanent name.

Having no name

is the beginning of the ten thousand things.

Having a name,

is the mother of the ten thousand things.

(Moeller 2007: 3)

Here the mother is designated as the beginning of all things or the name of all things. In chapter 52 we encounter this mother again:

The world has a beginning:

it is considered the Mother of the world. 天下有始、以爲天下母

(Moeller 2007: 123)

In chapter 25, the *Daodejing* defines *Dao*:

There is a thing—

it came to be in the undifferentiated,

it came alive before heaven and earth.

What stillness! What emptiness!

Alone it stands fast and does not change.

It can be mother to heaven and earth.

(Moeller 2007: 123)

The *Daodejing* explains that the first way to describe the *Dao* is *mu*母, "mother." The word *mu* has a broader range of meanings than merely "biological mother." It is expanded to mean the source of heaven and earth and the myriad things in them. *Dao*/mother is responsible for the origin of all things, is with all things, and provides the patterns that one should follow. This basic philosophical commitment reflects a view that the cosmos and world are generated, not created, through a multiplicative process. The terms used in classical Chinese texts for the origin of the myriad things incorporate a sense of "life" and "birth," both of which are encompassed in the Chinese term *sheng* 生 (generation). This link between generation and the mother naturally leads to the priority of female energy. It is generation or transformation, not a substance or Being, which builds up the Chinese philosophical landscape or horizon.

In chapter 42, the *Daodejing* gives a specific account of the origination of the world:

Dao generates oneness,

oneness generates twoness,

twoness generates threeness,

and threeness generates the ten thousand things.

(Moeller 2007: 107)

The concrete world originates from a unitary but indistinct source, *Dao*. The movement from that source toward the tangible world is again a process of specification and differentiation, from one to two to three and to the myriad things, literally the "ten thousand things" (*wanwu* 萬物). Thus, *Dao* disseminates a gendered lens through which to perceive the world and reality. As a result this lens is one of change, uncertainty, body, and sexuality. The source of the variable and changing lies in the intrinsic femininity of *Dao*. Interestingly, there are no "male" images of *Dao*, such as father or son; nor are traditionally male traits, like force, strength, or aggression, linked to *Dao*. This gendered world is different from Aristotle's male–female cosmos in which the masculine *telos* takes precedence, and is a prime mover upon the feminine, passive matter (Bianchi 2014: 2). The Daoist feminine is also different from the ancient Greek and Roman goddesses who are powerful when they possess male power rather than through their own powers of fertility:

The goddesses Diana and Minerva become the symbol of these women [philosophers]. These Roman goddesses, borrowed from the Ancient Greeks, as Diana or Artemis symbolises the tradition of virginity and independence of males, the other . . . Athene/Minerva [is] the goddess of wisdom and war.

(Hagengruber 2010: 11)

In addition to the word *mu* (mother), the *Daodejing* incorporates two other sets of terms in relation to femininity, *pin* 牝 appearing three times and *ci* 雌 appearing twice. It is important to highlight the fact that these terms are different from *nu* 女 (woman in contemporary Chinese) or *fu* 婦 (woman in classical Chinese). The notion of *nu* or *fu* refers to woman in a social relationship. This social construction of woman does not appear in the *Daodejing* at all. Both *pin* and *ci* have been translated as "female"; in fact *pin* refers to female animals in general and *ci* refers specifically to hens, as opposed to *xiong*, which refers to roosters (for more discussion of these two pairs, see Ryden 1997: 29–36). *Pin* and *ci* are ways to demonstrate a natural supremacy and potency of the feminine.

We read in *Daodejing* chapter 6:

> The spirit of the valley does not die—
>
> This is called mysterious femininity [*pin*].
>
> The gate of mysterious femininity [*pin*]—
>
> This is called the root of heaven and earth.

(Moeller 2007: 17)

Here the *pin* is mysterious, the root of heaven and earth, an unlimited resource. This gendered source without beginning or end, persisting in perpetuity, is the realm of becoming. The character for spirit, *gu* 谷, originally meant generation, and is equated with *sheng* (part of the character for gender and nature or tendencies), and its shape is often taken to represent the female genitals.

With respect to "mysterious femininity," one can notice two interesting directions. On the one hand, there is what we might call the horizontal level in which femininity/yin and masculinity/yang are counterparts, both of which are embedded in the myriad things. On the other hand, there is a vertical level in which masculinity/yang refers to the things before us, while femininity/yin refers to the origin that is hidden, implicit, or empty.

In this context, let us consider the pairing of *you* 有 and *wu* 無. *You* literally means "to have," whereas *wu* means "to lack." To say that something exists in classical Chinese is literally to say that it "is had," whereas to say it does not exist is to say it is not had or possessed. By extension, these terms come to denote something like "being" and "non-being" or "presence" and "absence." *You* corresponds with yang/masculinity, and *wu* with yin/femininity.

There are inherent connections between the pairings having (*you*)/not having (*wu*) or fullness (*shi*)/void (*xu*). Excavated versions of the *Daodejing* support this unity. In the received version, chapter 40 says that the myriad things come from being (*you*) and being comes from non-being (*wu*). In other words, the myriad things form simultaneously from *you* and *wu*, the foreground and background, yin and yang. The contemporary Chinese scholar Liu Xuyi (刘绪义) explains the importance of this version of *Daodejing* chapter 40:

> The myriad things are generated in *you* (having or to have) and *wu* (nothing). Here *you* (having) and *wu* (nothing) are not connected in a sequence, one leading to [the] other but rather they are parallel, *Dao* generates *you* and also generates *wu*. *You* and *wu* exist at the same time. *You* refers to a general existence that has a form in the formless. Yet *wu* is formless, independent and unchanging. *Wu* is a part of *you*.

(Liu 2009: 5)

Liu illustrates this with the example of a young girl and a mother. A young girl has not given birth, so she is *wu*; however, she still has the potential to exercise her reproductive ability to become *you*, or a mother (Liu 2009: 287) So this description of *Dao* follows the biological ability and development of a female body. A young girl becoming a mother is the way of *Dao*; Laozi's *Dao* is the mother of all myriad things. This is representative of *Dao*'s unity of *you* and *wu*.

Dao's tendency towards reproduction results in an association between metaphysical and ontological origins and biological reproduction. This connection, of course, appears in other cultures as well. For example, Diotima in Plato's *Symposium* says, "All of us are pregnant . . . both in body and in soul" (Plato 1993: xix). One of her definitions of love is the desire to give birth in beauty. *Dao* as the source of generation and reproduction in the world is based on such a biological model, with concrete things being born through the interplay of *you* and *wu*, *yin* and *yang*. More importantly, the *Daodejing* invites us to share in *Dao*, that is, to be with *Dao*, to be female and to accept femininity as a rhythm of our nature and the way of our life. The becoming female of *Dao* and the rhythm of femininity are accessible by all humans or all beings, irrespective of their sexed bodies or gender roles. *Dao* becoming female develops a radically altered consciousness of femininity, and this consciousness-raising might provide a unique and diverse conceptual resource for contemporary feminist thought, one that assumes no rigid division or opposition between femininity and masculinity.

Femininity as a Way to Know *Dao*

The *Daodejing* arguably designates one model of thinking about the feminine character of nature. The female is not just portrayed and acclaimed as the *yin*, soft (*rou*) force of the world, but also resonates with the mystical meanings of *Dao*. Other traditionally feminine characteristics such as being "empty," "returning," "low," "soft," and "yielding" are attributes of *Dao*. Thus, there is a robust association between the knowing of a female and the knowing of *Dao*. To come to a female consciousness of *Dao* is to problematize a way of thinking and knowing. The feminine as a value in the *Daodejing* conveys a cognitive style and an epistemological stance.

Daodejing chapter 40 says that:

> Reversal [returning, *fan*] is the movement of the *Dao*,
>
> Weakness [softening, *rou*] is the usefulness [function] of *Dao*. (反者道之動,弱者道之用)
>
> The things of the world are generated from presence [*you*].
>
> Presence is generated from nonpresence [*wu*].
>
> (Moeller 2007: 97)

Returning and reversal as the movement of *Dao* illustrates a waxing and waning of change in *time*, just as the yinyang symbol of two curved, interlocking geometric shapes depicts a rotating, self-creating cycle. The softening function of *Dao* elucidates a great multi-dimensional *space* in which an unseen potentiality is a necessary part of all existence. This characteristic of non-presence or emptiness is what permits or creates the efficacy of *Dao*. It is noteworthy that the softness of *Dao* is identified with the empty, the void or non-presence of *Dao*.

According to the *Hanshu*漢書 *(The Book of Han*, AD 111) "*xu*"—emptiness—and *wu*—no-presence—are the foundation of Daoist method:

> The Daoist School is about not doing [*wuwei*] 無為, but leaving nothing undone. Its theory is easy to practice but its expression in words is hard to know. Its method takes emptiness and nonexistence as its root and takes following along as its function [道家無為, 又曰無不為, 其實易行, 其辭難知. 其術以虛無為本, 以因循為用].
>
> (Ban 1962: 2713)

The *Daodejing* uses the word *wu* (no-presence/nothingness) 101 times. In the oracle bones (turtle shells used for divinations in ancient China) *wu* is the symbol for dancing. In fact, there are three closely related characters with the same pronunciation: *wu* 無, meaning nothingness, *wu* 舞, meaning to dance, and *wu* 巫, meaning a female shaman. The earliest comprehensive dictionary of Chinese characters, the *Shuowen Jiezi* (說文解字) by the Han scholar Xu Shen 許慎 (58–147 CE), explicates the link: *wu* 巫 (shamans) are women who can perform service to *wu* 無 (the shapeless) and make the spirits come down by *wu* 舞 (dancing). Dancing was the way to communicate with and know *shen* 神 (spirits) (Xu 1981: 201). However, these spirits are unseen and formless; only through dancing activities can one communicate with *shen*. *Wu*'s dancing is something present, yet they are working (*shi* 事) with *wu* (non-presence). In its origin, *wu* (nothingness) is the undifferentiated source of potency and growth that lets things function, much as the empty spaces between joints and muscles are what allows Cook Ding to cut with such ease in the famous story from the *Zhuangzi* (Ziporyan 2009: 34). More importantly, this non-presence is always a part of femininity's presence.

Femininity/*yin* emphasizes background and hidden structures while masculinity/*yang* specifies what is prevailing, exposed, and at front. This mindfulness of the background is found in the *Daodejing* statement in chapter 42: "All the myriad things *fu yin bao yang* (負陰抱陽) [carry (embody) *yin* and embrace *yang*]" (Moeller 2007: 103). Here *yin*/femininity and *yang*/masculinity are woven into the condition of the myriad things. *Bao* (抱) means to embrace, and literally refers to putting your arms around something, often in a sense of holding something valuable, as in "to *bao* your child." The myriad things all embrace or wrap their arms around the *yang*, which is in front of them, i.e. apparent or masculine. The idea of *bao yang* is derived from the sun: one faces south and embraces direct sunlight. Another extension is confronting what is in front and seeing what is present (*you* 有).

The word *fu* (負), translated above as "embody," has more than twenty meanings in the classical Chinese dictionary *Shuowen Jiezi*. One of the main meanings of *fu* is to carry or bear something on your back, that is, not in front of you but behind or in the background. Thus, this word *fu* in the *Daodejing* can be taken as *bei*背 (on your back). *Fuyin* (負陰) then refers to things that are not confronted, or not seen, but still carried along, something feminine. It is carrying something unseen or non-present. The *fuyin* always predicates a set of situations, a unique way of being with the world. Taken together, *fuyin* and *baoyang* reveal awareness of two aspects of reality: a feminine, the hidden underlying structure, and a masculine, the explicit presence in front of us. Although *baoyang* and *fuyin* are inseparable, the *Daodejing* argues that our natural tendency is to look more at what stands before us, which is *yin*/masculine, and to ignore *yin*/feminine. The *Daodejing* counteracts this tendency with a focus on *yin*/feminine. The feminine should be guarded (*shou* 守) and protected (*bao* 保). One should remember to "stay at the front by keeping to the rear" (Moeller 2007: 158).

As *Daodejing* chapter 16 explains:

To reach emptiness [虛 *xu*]—

This is the utmost.

To keep stillness [靜 *jing*]—

This is control.

The ten thousand things occur along with each other:

So I watch where they turn.

The things in the world are manifold,

they all return again to their root: stillness.

Stillness—this is what return to the mandate is called.

The return to the mandate—this is permanence.

To know permanence –this is clarity [illumination, 明 *ming*].

(Moeller 2007: 41)

Here the *Daodejing* necessitates a specific meditation method to attain the stage of *xu* and *jing*. This will stabilize the mind and enable us to attain *ming* (illumination). This conceptual formulation has later been developed into a specifically female Daoist practice of body cultivation. For example, female Daoist Cao Wenyi 曹文逸 (1039–1119) was regarded as the "master of tranquility and human virtue and the perfection of the Dao." Another female Daoist Sun Buer 孫不二 (1119–1182) is one of the most prominent female masters in Daoist history, the only female figure among the seven patriarchs of the Northern School of Daoism in the Song dynasty. Her work is the foundation of the School of Purity and Stillness 清靜 (*Qingjing*), which advocates concentrating one's heart or mind on the *Daodejing*'s concepts of emptiness and quietness.

This understanding of *xu* and *jing* is rooted in natural phenomena. According to classical Chinese thought, everything emerges from the dark ground and hidden places. A plant comes from a seed that has been hidden in the depths of the earth. The power of growing and nourishment below the surface allows it to spring up and be displayed. In the same way that the soil provides nourishment for the seed, the mother provides a nourishing condition that allows the child to grow and flourish, just as the female body supplies all nutrients for a fetus to survive and develop. When the male's sperm meets the female's egg, the former's function in the process of creating new life can be completed. The female, however, works slowly, nourishing the fetus for nine months. The power and uniqueness of the female's slower effort should be recognized. Thus femininity is *xu* because it can offer a space for a thing to grow. Femininity is *jing* (stillness) because it exemplifies the potency of nourishing. This female ability wins the *Daodejing*'s philosophical recognition and admiration. It is called "dark efficacy" (mysterious virtue).

> The Dao generates them;
>
> The De [efficacy] nourishes them;
>
> As things they are formed; And as utensils they are completed.
>
> Therefore, the ten thousand things honor the Dao
>
> and cherish the De [efficacy].
>
> Honoring the Dao,
>
> cherishing the De.
>
> The Dao generates them,
>
> Nourishes them,
>
> Lets them grow,
>
> Accompanies them,
>
> Rests them,
>
> Secures them,
>
> Fosters them,
>
> Protects them.
>
> Generating without possessing,
>
> Acting without depending,
>
> Rearing without ordaining:
>
> This is called "dark efficacy." [玄德 *xuande*]
>
> (Moeller 2007: 121)

The importance of this feminine knowing brings out an epistemic assumption underlying thinking: any given point of knowing, like the male/masculine or the female/feminine, is only a small knot in a giant and coherent gendered web. Any knowing contains infinite unknowing, because the known discloses only a part of the unknown. Nonetheless, because we naturally focus on what is present and available, masculinity/*yang*, we pay great attention to the foreground and often ignore the background, femininity/*yin*. Farmers exemplify the *Daodejing*'s point: they do not simply see what will grow out of the soil, but also make an effort to cultivate the soil, that is, they attend to the background. A seed is embraced in the depths of the earth, where it will grow and be nourished, which will allow it to spring up and be on display to the world. And farming is very similar to mothering, as special attention is needed in the cultivation and growth of a child.

Clearly this Daoist gendered knowing is not structured according to a Pythagorean dichotomy between a heavenly order of rationality and a terrestrial disorder of irrationality.

There are not two qualitatively different realms—one the calculable order of heaven that appeals to our thought, the other a variety of earthly shapes and events impinging upon our observation and sensual experience. The world of the senses is pervasive throughout the interplay of cosmic forces, which rule the stars in the heaven, the seasons on the earth, and the smallest elements in human beings.

This Daoist view challenges the gender asymmetry that has been pervasive in the history of Western philosophy, in which the masculine poses as a disembodied universality while the feminine gets constructed as a disavowed corporeality. But the femininity of Daoism is not based in an exclusion of the masculine; nor is the masculine taken to be a rejection of the feminine. There is no feminine outside of the masculine, and there is no masculine outside of the feminine. This prescribes a developmental and dynamic process that defines an original fullness of the ultimate reality and of human being.

Basically, this female Daoist thinking is grounded in the value of the body. There is no dualistic dichotomy that separates reason from emotion and excludes femininity, the body, and engagement from rationality and knowing. As *Daodejing* chapter 13 claims:

> Thus, if you esteem taking care of your body (*sheng* 身) more than you do taking care of the world,
>
> Then you can be entrusted with the world;
>
> if you love your body as if it were the world,
>
> then the world can be handed over to you.
>
> (Moeller 2007: 33)

The Female Mode: The Ultimate Power and Strategy

In a general sense, throughout much of human history and across many cultures, the masculine has been associated with power, control, and dominance, whereas the feminine has been associated with yielding, flexibility, and submissiveness. The *Daodejing* inverts the values of these aspects, pointing out the power of the feminine. Traditionally, however, that inversion went against mainstream views, particularly those of the Confucians who dominated social and political institutions. The *Daodejing* started a full-fledged campaign to put greater pressure on the sages' leadership ability, moral character, and actions. This calling rippled through the fabric of Chinese culture. Sages—who were traditionally men—must have a capacity for fostering femininity.

Scholars have articulated two gendered animal sets for evaluating human actions in early China. The cow and bull correlate with categories of things (e.g. Earth and Heaven) and actions (e.g. receiving and giving). The hen and rooster expound a type of behavior (e.g. humility and arrogance). *Xiongjie* 雄節—rooster mode—invariably leads to fighting and destruction while *cijie* 雌節—hen mode—inevitably generates peace and prosperity. As some scholars write, "Interestingly, the parallel structure inferred in the phrasing for cock mode indicates that hen mode promises to fulfill all the classic goals touted throughout pre-modern Chinese social orders: wealth, health, and progeny" (Ryden 1997: 40). The *Daodejing* exemplifies this emphasis and promotes the "hen mode," which is the path to be with *Dao* and gains the power that defeats the great and hard.

Daodejing 10 asks: "When heaven's gate opens and closes, can you become female [*ci*]?" (Moeller 2007: 25). Chapter 28 suggests: "Know *xiong* (male) and maintain *ci* (female), be the world's river" (Moeller 2007: 71). The *Daodejing* accentuates the greater power of the feminine, as in chapter 61: "A large state is low lying waters, the female [*pin*] of the world, the connection of the world. The female [*pin*] overcomes the male by constant stillness. Because she is still, she is therefore fittingly underneath" (Moeller 2007: 141). The *Daodejing* also uses water as a metaphor for intrinsic feminine power and resilience in chapter 8:

> The best is like water.
>
> The goodness of water consists in
>
> Being beneficial to the ten thousand things,
>
> And in that it, when there is contention, takes on the place that the mass of the people detest.
>
> (Moeller 2007: 21)

Chapter 78 reads:

> Nothing in the world is smoother and softer than water;
>
> but nothing surpasses it in tackling the stiff and the hard,
>
> because it is not to be changed.
>
> That water defeats the solid,
>
> That the soft defeats the hard:
>
> No one in the world who does not know this,
>
> But still no one is able to practice it.
>
> (Moeller 2007: 181)

Daodejing chapter 76 also makes a simple observation to confirm the significance of softness:

> When alive, men are supple and soft.
>
> When dead, they are, stretched out and reaching the end, hard and rigid.
>
> When alive, the ten thousand things and grassed and trees are supple and pliant.
>
> When dead, they are dried out and brittle.
>
> Therefore it is said:
>
> The hard and the rigid are the companions of death.
>
> The supple and the soft the delicate and the fine are the companions of life.
>
> (Moeller 2007: 177)

Another key factor in this feminine power is a strategy of *yin* 因. In contemporary Western terminology, this *yin* is similar to the idea of resourcefulness. In the *Lüshi Chunqiu* of 239 BCE, the notion of relying on (因 *yin*) has great importance: "By employing the techniques of 'relying' [yin], the poor and lowly can vanquish the rich and noble and the small and weak can control the strong and big" (Knoblock and Reigel 2000: 358). "Relying" is a technique or strategy for success. On what does one rely?

"The wise invariably rely on the right timing or opportunity. But there is no guarantee that the timing or opportunity will come, so one must also rely on ability, just like making use of a boat or a cart" (Knoblock and Reigel 2000: 360). What one relies on is the natural propensity of things, such as water's power or the tendencies of the human heart. The *Lüshi Chunqiu* articulates this ability to be resourceful through examples:

> When those who scrutinize the sky recognize the four seasons by examining the zodiac constellations, this is an instance of relying on the natural state of things. When those who keep the calendars know when the first and last days of the month will occur by observing the movements of the moon, this is a case of relying on the natural state of things [yin 因].
>
> (Knoblock and Reigel 2000: 367)

The uniqueness of a sage is found, at least partly, in this ability. Another passage illuminates further:

> The true kings of antiquity acted less on their own and more by "relying on." The person of relying on has the art/technique of a sovereign; action is the way of ministers. Acting by oneself entails disturbance; reliance on others will have quiescence. Relying on winter creates cold; relying on summer creates heat— what need is there for the sovereign to act in that matter? Thus, it is said, the *Dao* of the lord is not knowing and not acting. Yet because it is worthier than knowing and acting, it attains the truth.
>
> (Knoblock and Reigel 2000: 416)

As a strategy, "relying" shifts the focus away from one's own actions and powers and instead emphasizes what is already available in a given situation. In different conditions, one needs to figure out what kinds of things can be relied on. What are the resources available? There can be different kinds of relying under different circumstances, but everything must have something to rely on for its own existence. This belief also makes clear why *guanxi* (關係)—social connections—permeates all aspects of Chinese social life even up today.

Relying, as a form of non-action or *wuwei* (無為), or appearing soft, indicates the importance of trusting the rhythm, patterns, timing, and opportunities that have an inherent tendency to unfold in a given moment. This relying is different from a causal relationship that articulates a linear sequence between events. Relying is embedded in complexity; it is relying on the context of associations. What sages rely on are the yin/feminine factors: yin emphasizes background and hidden structures, whereas yang specifies what is dominant, open, and in front. Thus *Liezi* says,

> If you want to be hard (gang 剛), you must guard it with softness (rou 柔); if you want to be strong, you must protect it with weakness (ruo 弱). Hardness that is accumulated in softness will be necessarily hard and strength that is accumulated in weakness will be necessarily strong.
>
> (Graham 1990: 83)

The necessity of considering *yin* factors arises on several different levels, most of which we have already addressed in more abstract terms. Emptiness (*xu* 虛) and nothingness (*wu* 無) are always intertwined with fullness (*shi* 實) and being (*you* 有). Consider, for example, a vessel or container (*qi* 器), as discussed in the *Daodejing*. A vessel only serves its purpose because of its emptiness. Thus, concrete things themselves always exist through an element of emptiness. Non-presence is embedded in presence. While we might say that both are equally important, our tendency to see only the present and the difficulty of addressing the non-present suggests a deliberate strategy for focusing on the unseen.

Final Remarks

The *Daodejing* makes a philosophical imaginary of the feminine into a privileged locus and relies on the feminine as a way of thinking, knowing, experiencing, and desiring. This study of the *Daodejing* can proffer a useful framework for raising female consciousness in Daoist contexts. Neither women nor men should reject their important aspects of femininity; rather, both should cultivate their femininity to achieve effective results. However, femininity as the *Daodejing* conceives it was situated in a particular cultural and historical context, so that the text was not intended to change women's social and political position in China. It does not promote the kind of gender equality that Western feminists fight for. The *Daodejing* has not been used politically, socially, and economically to advance women's interests and benefits.

The historical relations between Daoism and patriarchy are both conceptually and practically complex. Daoism values female power and femininity conceptually because it takes them to be a cosmic potent force. To do this, however, is neither to respect women as social beings nor to justify the patriarchal system. Daoism (*daojia*) as a school of teaching does not fight to better women's social and political conditions. But Daoism (*daojiao*) as a religious practice has offered an alternative way for women to live and to redefine those restrictive social expectations and roles. In particular, Daoism as religious practice does not have fixed restrictions on what women can or cannot do in terms of religious leadership. Many Daoist religious masters in China today are women. Thus, Daoism does not make a political critique of the mainstream of Confucian patriarchy, yet it does not fully support that mainstream either.

Nonetheless, a Daoist feminism might use Daoist femininity to challenge sexist patriarchy and cultivate a different value system. China today greatly needs an injection of feminist thought to truly assist women's living conditions. There are at least two conceptual issues we might take from the ancient Chinese Daoist philosophy of femininity. First, this philosophy can help us to rethink the very notions of man/male/masculinity and woman/female/femininity, which are constructed through gendered terminology. The original concepts of female and male in the *Daodejing* were articulated to capture the dynamic rhythm of nature, the world, and human life. They have little to do with contemporary Western constructions of the social gender of women or men. The *Daodejing* would agree with many Western feminists when they take the view that gender is not natural and that there is nothing essentially fixed about gender roles. The gender identification of women with femininity and men with masculinity implies a predestined biological and social fate. Women and men have internalized those gender-biased social expectations and standards to surrender to a social system. Furthermore, gender as system of social categorization is performative and is culturally taught, cognitively framed, and implemented by individuals. In contrast, the original concepts of female and male in the *Daodejing* describe the ebb and flow of everything in existence as a sustained dance of *wu* and *you*, *yin* and *yang*.

Second, the Daoist conception of femininity reminds us that feminine and masculine constructions must be situated in the rhythm of interactions and mutual integration. Daoism values fluidity, not solidity. Like *yin* and *yang* classifications of the human body, the same element can be *yin*/female in a certain relation but *yang*/male in another, and one can talk about *yin*/female within a *yang*/male, or *yang*/male within a *yin*/female. Moreover, like the yinyang distinction in the human body the division between the male and female in social life should be highly dynamic and fluid . . . more like using chopsticks rather than a fork and knife. The latter require two hands, while the former constitutes more of a singular harmonious action, with one hand negotiating the utensils. Therefore, using chopsticks is a kind of harmony in action. They must be used in concert with one another. Similar to classifications of femininity and masculinity, the chopsticks' exact position or classification may vary, but only within a rhythmical and interrelated framework—an ongoing dance of mutually engaged and nurturing equals. This is the manifestation of the cosmic forces *yin* and *yang*. Thus, instead of fixating on gender roles as a determining aspect of one's identity, they can be viewed as aspects of the situation with which one can choose to go along. However, they are not decisive for one's identity. A person can "play" or move between different characteristics, be male or female, depending on the situation. One is not limited to what society prescribes.

Finally, the *Daodejing* affirms the remarkable female power contained in *Dao*. Daoism becomes the philosophy most amenable to female influence, glorifying the latent force of the female water element, illuminating the potency of the mother, and prescribing the Daoist sovereign to cleave to the role of the female. We have much to learn from this ancient wisdom!

Further Reading

Allan, Sarah (1997) *The Way of Water and the Sprouts of Virtue*, Albany, NY: SUNY Press.
Bokenkamp, Stephen (1997) *Early Daoist Scriptures*, Berkeley, CA: University of California Press.
Despeux, Catherine, and Kohn, Livia (2005) *Women in Daoism*, Cambridge, MA: Three Pines Press.
Moeller, Hans-Georg (2006) *Philosophy of The Daodejing*, New York: Columbia University Press.
Wang, Robin R. (2003) *Images of Women in Chinese Thought and Culture: Writings from the Pre-Qin Period to the Song Dynasty*, Indianapolis, IN: Hackett.

Related Topics

Feminist methods in the history of philosophy (Chapter 1); feminism and ancient Greek philosophy (Chapter 2); language, writing, and gender differences (Chapter 24); Native American chaos theory and the politics of difference (Chapter 30); Confucianism and care ethics (Chapter 44); multicultural and postcolonial feminisms (Chapter 47).

References

Ban Gu 班固 (1962) *Hanshu* 漢書 [*The Book of Han*], Beijing: Chinese Press.
Bianchi, Emanuela (2014) *The Feminine Symptom: Aleatory Matter in The Aristotelian Cosmos*, New York: Fordham University Press.

Graham, Angus C. (trans.) (1990) *The Book of Lieh-tzu: A Classic of Tao*, New York: Columbia University Press.

Hagengruber, Ruth (2010) "Von Diana zu Minerva: Philosophierende Aristokratinnen des 17. und 18. Jahrhunderts und ihre Netzwerke," in Ruth Hagengruber and Ana Rodriguez (Eds.) *Von Diana zu Minerva*, Munich: Oldenbourg Akademie-Verlag, 11–32.

Knoblock, John, and Reigel, Jeffrey (trans.) (2000) *The Annals of Lü Buwei: A Complete Translation and Study*, Stanford, CA: Stanford University Press.

Liu Xuyi 刘绪义 (2009) *The World of Heaven and Human Being: A Study of Origin of Pre-Qin Schools*, Beijing: People's Press.

Moeller, Hans-Georg (trans.) (2007) *Daodejing: A Complete Translation and Commentary*, Chicago, IL and La Salle, IL: Open Court.

Plato (1993) *The Symposium*, trans. R. E. Allen, New Haven, CT: Yale University Press.

Ryden, Edmund (trans.) (1997) *The Yellow Emperor's Four Canons: A Literary Study and Edition of the Text from Mawangdui*, Taipei: Guangqi Press.

Shen Xu 許慎 (1981) *Shouwen Jiezi* 說文解字 [*Explanation of Patterns*], Ed. Duan Yucai 段玉裁, Shanghai: Shanghai Guji Press.

Wang, Robin R. (2012) *Yinyang: The Way of Heaven and Earth in Chinese Thought and Culture*, Cambridge: Cambridge University Press.

Ziporyn, Brook (trans.) (2009) *Zhuangzi: The Essential Writings with Selections from Traditional Commentaries*, Indianapolis. IN: Hackett.

4

FEMINISM, PHILOSOPHY, AND CULTURE IN AFRICA

Tanella Boni
Translated from French by Eva Boodman

Introduction: Contextualizing Theories and Practices

African feminisms emerge out of a heterogeneous context. Because Africa's globalization has been ongoing for centuries now, African women pay a steep price for it, all while the patriarchal order remains firmly in place.

But what is Africa? "Africa" as a designation refers to a dynamic geographical, political, military, economic, social, familial, historical, linguistic, cultural and religious context. The African context—continental, but also diasporically dispersed and transatlantic—is marked by complexity and multiplicity. Borders were drawn onto the African continent on the goodwill of the European leaders rallied around Bismarck at the Berlin Conference of November 1884 to February 1885. For this reason, Africa is not one but many broken-up Africas that have undergone slavery, colonization and racial segregation, as in the case of South African Apartheid. In spite of the way that these Africas are differentiated by their languages, educational systems, and cultures, the Venus Hottentot, whose body was instrumentalized and dehumanized by whites at the beginning of the nineteenth century, continues to be a strong symbol of the way that African women's rights have been violated because of the color of their skin, the shape of their bodies, and their gender.

Today's difficult postcolonial situations—and the challenges of living in them—are the result of having been subject to different forms of colonization. The feminisms that emerge in this kind of context ask real questions that cannot be fully treated by academic research or "development" activism. And yet, the challenge of a plural Africa must be faced here, too, and not just by men, around whom revolve constructions of virility and masculine dominance. Women represent half of the African population. Irrespective of their age or multiple identities, these women continue to struggle against the real and imaginary barriers that must be deconstructed in order for them to have the right to a full and complete existence. There are many African feminist movements: some based on industry, some transdisciplinary or transnational. These movements work, in theory and practice, to transform social and political realities. But these feminisms— which sometimes reject the term "feminism" to adopt another, like "womanism," for example—are plagued by the question of their culturalist or universalist position, the question of how to enter into dialogue with other feminisms. And on top of all of this, there is a linguistic gap that these feminisms must find ways to overcome.

Feminism as Engagement

For a long time, like the African writers discussed by Susan Arndt (Arndt 2000), I refused to be called a "feminist" even if my novels and poems showcased the violence done to women and the subtleties of the patriarchal order. To reject the word "feminist" does not mean that one is not concerned with feminism. Today, I ask myself whether "feminism" is indeed a doctrine, that is to say, a set of determinate concepts that form a system. I think, rather, that it is a life philosophy in which the subordination of women and the injustices done to them are explained through concepts, including that of "gender." To effect an "epistemological break" of my own, I asked myself whether I, too, should use the concept of "gender." But first I needed to test it, and not reject it out of hand, as other African women have done. All around me, gender was the explanation for everything: in Africanist discourses, but also in those of development agencies and even universities. Non-governmental organizations (NGOs) talked about "gendered approaches" in their grant applications. As soon as there were a few women on a team made up of many men, a project was thought to have used such an "approach" and to have satisfied the requirements of the granting agency! The instrumentalization of the word "gender" is so striking, in fact, that one no longer feels the need to ask what the word means or what the concept refers to.

The many African feminisms, however, cannot be boiled down to "gender" or a "gendered approach," since that word does not mean much if it isn't being applied to a set of facts. Indeed, it seems to me that "gender" serves to unravel the causes of the inequalities, injustices and harms that women must face. Once these causes are perceived, one asks how the situation can be improved. In this way, "gender" is both a tool for thought and a method of social transformation.

I was trying to find the justification for things needing to be done better, with less injustice, more rights, and responsibilities shared equally between men and women. I was asking myself loads of questions in a philosophy department where for twenty years I was the only woman professor. Today, fortunately, there are ten or so women teaching in that department. I don't know whether they worry about "gender" or whether they choose freely the authors they would like to teach.

As far I'm concerned, my salutary break came, in the first instance, out of the discipline from which women were notably absent. I was teaching the history of philosophy, which had nothing to do with my lived reality. Thinkers from other regions of the world, and Africa in particular, had no place in a curriculum modeled on the teaching priorities of French universities. Women philosophers were practically invisible, with rare exceptions like Hannah Arendt, Simone Weil or Simone de Beauvoir. But in my own work, I found I had to limit myself to a few ancient philosophers. My research ended up focusing on negative representations of the female sex as an equivalent to "matter" in Aristotle's biology (Aristotle 2002). The male sex was the beautiful sex, active and superior. I understood that Western philosophy supplied all the elements needed to justify sexual hierarchy, the inferiority of women and their exclusion from public debate, with some exceptions. In reproduction, males had a "natural" power over females. In this way, the philosophy that I was teaching, which was far from "African," gave me the material to think about my own situation and that of other women. This alien philosophy, so far away from my own experience, gave me a theoretical arsenal.

In the social, political, cultural and academic world where I lived, inequality and injustice were law. I understood that a man and a woman with equal competence did not have equal chances of being listened to or taken seriously in the realm of knowledge production or scholarly debate. Something broke in me; I would never be able to see the world in the same way. From that moment onward, I allowed myself to imagine my environment as a world of walls and obstacles that become visible and audible only when one develops an awareness of them.

It was not in philosophy, however, that I was first able to express the inequality and violence that I was experiencing and observing, but in literature, which I believed to be a space of freedom. (The problems I continue to encounter with publishing are other barriers in the so-called Francophone world. Age, subject matter, language of publication (French), and the laws of the free market have to be taken into account along with an author's sex to understand what is at work in a publication, which is not free of constraint, in spite of the invention of the web.) But I needed to go further, theoretically, to understand this world structured like a network with different orders of interconnected levels. In the twenty-first century, women have not been the only ones subject to patriarchal programming; so are all humans whose bodies or sexualities do not conform to the moral, political, cultural and religious norms of patriarchal society. So to reject the word "feminist," as I did, following in the footsteps of many other African women, wasn't to reject a mere label, nor was it to surrender in the face of the struggle.

For these reasons, up until 2008, I was reluctant to characterize my own theoretical research as "feminist." "Feminism?" I would say; "I'm more interested in discussing 'the woman question,' since, philosophically speaking, it really is a question" (Boni 2008). Even if it is a philosophical question, there is a vast gulf between the word "woman" and the word "feminist." What separates the two is not the quest for a definition of the category of women; it is, rather, a form of engagement. It is, on the one hand, a cold, dispassionate question that can be dissected externally and can give rise to all kinds of interpretations and discussions, just like any philosophical question. But on the other hand, it is an involved engagement, an approach that comes from our body and soul and maybe even our gut, where there is anger, revolt and determination. All feminisms seem to me to be of this order, and feminisms related to Africa to an even greater degree.

African feminism's unofficial history could be told in this way, before it made any reference to academic research or treatises on violence against women, their place in "development" or their rights and duties as citizens. On an individual level, then, I would say that one doesn't get into feminism in the way that one does a religion, that is, by choice. Rather, we become feminists because we have no choice. We struggle and resist so that we can "find" ourselves, take responsibility, have a place in the world, and we do this by supporting and caring for ourselves and our loved ones. In this way, concern for self and others is a step prior to all reasoning and activism we might want to qualify as "feminist." When novelist Chimamanda Ngozi Adichie (Adichie 2012; 2014) writes about running up against the language, facts, and gestures that underscore the power of patriarchal domination, she doesn't learn about it in books: it is an experienced reality. What gives her the right to speak it, however, is the authority that comes from being an internationally renowned author. In this way, creative writing, art, song and cinema are all materials that show us that before all theorization and all activism, we have our own experience. Engagement starts, then, with the clear recognition that what is wrong, and affects us so closely, must change.

We see, then, that when we engage ourselves, we break with what seems natural in the eyes of most. But does this mean that we must engage ourselves alone? With others? This depends on our own experiences, the kinds of encounters we have, and the kind of dialogue we maintain with other feminists from Africa and elsewhere. It also depends on our understanding, at each stage of our lives, of the fundamental questions that, paradoxically, can separate us from other women, all while bringing us closer in many ways.

The State of Affairs: A Brief Overview

The questions of identity, colonization and postcolonialism—and even imperialism and globalization—are grafted onto African feminism. While there is, among African women, a desire to throw off the colonial yoke by thinking of ourselves through the paradigms of a pre-colonial past, it is also worrisome that theoretical reflection is often too far away from the situations in which most African women find themselves. These situations are characterized by urgent matters such as war and violence, diseases like AIDS, the militarization of African societies, and the non-application of international laws and conventions (most notably CEDAW, the Convention on the Elimination of all Forms of Discrimination against Women, UN General Assembly, 1979).

But how are we to name what is happening when the situation of women's lives is so complex? What are the locations that give rise to, and are points of transmission for, feminist research and activism in Africa?

Since the 1970s, big international conferences, like those organized in Mexico (1975), Copenhagen (1980), Nairobi (1985), and all those that followed, have been occasions for African women to express their concerns. With these conferences came an unprecedented activism that developed along many different institutional lines: through the academy (Imam, Mama, and Sow 1997) and international institutions like the UN and the World Bank, within religious institutions, or through more independent initiatives like NGOs and women's associations fighting for economic, social and cultural rights. From the point of view of the state, "Ministries of Women's Affairs" or of "The Status of Women" made notable appearances in several West African countries. An example of such state-organized feminism are the activities of every 8th of March, meant to raise consciousness about women's issues like excision in the regions where it is practiced. Theory, especially from a "gender and development" perspective, followed closely behind political practice and activism, and took several orientations: gender and politics, gender and economics, gender and reproductive health, HIV-AIDS, sexuality and violence, etc. (Bennett 2010). Little by little, research centers and institutes in Gender and Women's Studies were born. In Dakar, CODESRIA (the Council for the Development of Social Science Research in Africa) created, in the 1990s, a new series of publications dedicated to gender, guided by the following statement:

> CODESRIA's series on gender expresses the need to challenge the forms of masculinity that are the basis for the repression of women. The goal of the series is to undertake and sustain social science research through discerning inquiry and debate that challenges the conventional knowledge, structures and ideologies narrowly informed by the centrality of masculinity.
>
> (CODESRIA, www.codesria.org)

Today, the African Gender Institute and Gender and the Department of Women's Studies for Africa's transformation (GWS) at the University of Cape Town have a journal, *Feminist Africa*, with an editorial policy that is summarized in this way:

> *Feminist Africa* is a continental gender studies journal produced by the community of feminist scholars. It provides a platform for intellectual and activist research, dialogue and strategy. *Feminist Africa* attends to the complex and diverse dynamics of creativity and resistance that have emerged in postcolonial Africa, and the manner in which these are shaped by the shifting global geopolitical configurations of power.
>
> (*Feminist Africa*, http://agi.ac.za/journals)

Since the beginning of the 2000s, the journal has published around twenty thematic issues that are available online. In 2013, on the occasion of the fiftieth anniversary of the creation of the African Union, the journal published an issue devoted to "Pan-Africanism and Feminism." The issue commemorated the not insignificant role played by women in war, conflict and liberation struggle: in Uganda, Guinea-Bissau, and Sudan, but also in the continental and transatlantic Pan-African struggle. Another journal, *JENDA: A Journal of Cultural and African Women's Studies*, created in the early 2000s, articulated its goals in this way:

> Our conceptualization of *JENDA: A Journal of Culture and African Women Studies* was guided by two main objectives: the first is to create a space from which to theorize our experiences, presently marginalized in today's global context of unequal economic relations; and the second is to wrest ourselves from the mould of stereotypical assumptions in which this international economic order and its attendant culture of hierarchy have cast us.
>
> (www.jendajournal.com/nzegwu1.html)

This journal, which has received much recognition, is published through Binghamton University.

While in most Francophone countries feminist research seems not to be a priority, given that it is absent from many research and teaching programs, in the Anglophone world things are happening. Anglophone feminist thinking has been moving forward for several decades now, and has a long tradition of debate on women and gender, masculinity and femininity, as well as lesbian, gay, bisexual, transgender, and intersex (LGBTI) rights.

With this in mind, in November of 2006 a forum of African feminists was organized in Accra by the African Women's Development Fund (AWDF). The forum brought together 100 participants, mostly Anglophone, to adopt a "Charter of Feminist Principles for African Feminists." The Charter states: "Africa has a long tradition of resistance to patriarchy. We claim henceforth the right to formalize our actions, to write for ourselves, to formulate our own strategy, and to do this ourselves as African feminists" (AWDF 2006: 11). The question of women's rights is doubly evoked in the charter: It is a matter of being citizens in the fullest sense, to be free to make this kind of demand, to have freedom of speech and thought; but it is also a matter of being free to meet the challenge of taking care of one's own problems without leaving that task to be undertaken by others, and especially actors from "the West." To work together, all that is needed is agreement on principles, methods and actions to carry out. The question of language, however, is yet another difficulty that blocks the flow of ideas.

The Language Gap

A language barrier separates African feminists from one another. We cannot say it enough: the languages in which we express ourselves do not enable debate, even when English speakers, French speakers, Portuguese speakers and Arabic speakers are brought together at big conferences. What can be talked about? Must each of them wait until their own words are translated from one language to another? In this way, the language gap is a parameter to take into account in understanding the exclusion of African women and their lack of visibility on the playing field of serious debate. They are even less audible when they do not express themselves or write in English, the dominant language. One might think that official languages bring feminists closer to one another in serving as unifying vehicles across a multiplicity of local languages. One only needs to consult a bibliography of feminist research or gender studies in Africa to be convinced of this: English, the dominant language, is the language of publication for most single-author essays, co-authored reports, and feminist movement publications. English is also the language in which a number of concepts were invented, including womanism, stiwanism, nego-feminism and many others. Where "womanism" is a term used by Alice Walker (Walker 1984 [1983]), Chikwenye Okonjo Ogunyemi's thought is to be differentiated from the Walkerian conception of womanism, and indeed, from Western feminism on the whole (Ogunyemi 1985). According to Ogunyemi, "womanists" account for culture, race, politics and economics in such a way that gender no longer occupies a central role in Walker's theory. Molara Ogundipe-Leslie's stiwanism takes STIWA (social transformation including women in Africa) to be the starting place for understanding the role of women in society. In the case of Obioma Nnaemeka's nego-feminism, feminism is taken to be a "negotiation without ego," where theory informs practice and vice versa (Nnaemeka 2004). These different concepts articulated by Nigerian activists and theorists, however, have yet to unite all the African feminisms.

As long as *francophonie*—the Francophone world as a political and cultural realm—allows some African countries to become linked to Western countries like France and Canada, then there will be some spaces (like colloquia, for example) where debates can take place and experiences can be exchanged. But one has to ask what place African feminist philosophy has in these Francophone debates, since it seems to be practically non-existent. For that matter, at meetings that aim to bring together French, Quebecois, Belgian, Swiss, and African Francophones (Sow 2009), the questions most important to Anglophone feminists received little attention or were entirely absent. Do Francophone African feminists, who find themselves preempted or supported by other feminists, really need to ask themselves the question of Western dominance?

Gender Alone Cannot Explain All Injustice

The majority of theorists and activists, regardless of what languages they speak, do not disregard gender's connections with class, age, social and family position, not to mention a number of other elements that have to be taken into consideration when biological sex is discussed. There is, in fact, no undefined "woman" without reference to a situation. I'm tempted to say that one is born a girl—that one is certainly someone's girl, even when one is "fatherless"—but one becomes woman, which is a long-term undertaking. One becomes a mother, which society expects us to do in addition to many other things. Motherhood is, without a doubt, a concept to clarify, and a point of difference between African women and other feminists who claim Simone de Beauvoir for her account of motherhood as alienation of the female body (Beauvoir 1949). What many African cultures have in common is a conception of sterility as a great tragedy for a woman who cannot bear children, as well as a dishonor for the husband (Kourouma 1970). This is a reference to the idea that the female body is made to bear children and to preserve the honor of her husband. However, a mother is not only the one who gives life; her role is also to provide food, care and education. There are nourishing mothers, spiritual mothers and protective mothers, and in this way, they are powerful and have both men and women under their control. Mothers-in-law can rule entire families. Relationships of brotherhood and sisterhood, moreover, are not always horizontal, but are hierarchized. Sisterhood is, for African women, a point of integration and stability in the family. The concept of family, then, needs to be revisited and adapted to local realities; it does not correspond to ideas of family that come from elsewhere. The notion of "couple" also needs to be rethought. To what does "couple" refer? The question is worth asking when, in certain situations, polygamy is at play in its most insidious forms, and even among educated men and women aware of their rights. One asks, then, how to account for these complex situations that seem to be socially acceptable while also being in contradiction with written laws. What recourse is available to women whose rights are violated if written laws do not protect them, and oral and traditional laws do not recognize the injustices they are made to endure? (Boni 2011)

In this way, the individual lives of African women are marked by a long and paradoxical history of violence. The violence begins in the family. I'm talking here about life, because it's where everything begins: there can be no emancipation, no freedom, no justice if we do not first have the right to life. And this right is threatened when one is born a girl. Does the role of a boy not have more value than that of a girl? Many African women who want a son, and not just those in rural areas, undergo multiple pregnancies, often under difficult conditions, until the desired child with the male sex is born. The desire for a male child is, in my view, an internalization of patriarchal principles by women themselves, who unwittingly participate in its reproduction. If a family happens to accept the birth of a girl anyway, is it not because, from the moment of her birth, she has already entered into the framework of a symbolic exchange? The girl will marry, and this will be of great economic benefit to her parents.

And so, everything does seem to be built around biological sex, motherhood, but also symbolic relationships—which can also be monetary (and it should be noted that not all forms of sexual expression are tolerated). We continue to think that female genital mutilation is part of the "feminization" of the body. And what if this, too, were only another expression of the dominance of patriarchal power in the regions where it is practiced? However, it was this view of the practice that offended many African feminists at the Copenhagen Conference in 1980, an occasion when suspicion took hold between Africans, Europeans, and Americans (Sow 1998). Nonetheless, the urgency was clear: tools were needed to understand and discuss our own reality.

Women's Silence and the Reproduction of Patriarchal Ideology

If theoretical discourse and radical activist strategy use "gender" in connection with other concepts to analyze the place of women "in development," concrete lives must also benefit from the illumination of the concept. And this is the rub. In private life, the patriarchal order, the principles of which are anchored into ways of thinking, continues to reign unabated. In this way, life trajectories—which I call biographies—are of great importance, and not just the activities one performs. Who African women are is just as important as what they do. In fact, human activities are never disembodied; it is precisely bodies and souls who undertake them, human beings who imagine, think, work and speak. Speech, then, or rather its absence, is a key element on which the violence driven by the prejudice of patriarchal ideology is exercised. From this point of view, we see that one of the survival strategies adopted by African women is to act as though everything is fine, to never speak from the place that hurts the most. Only writing and other art forms can attempt to break this wall of silence (D'Almeida 1994). In "Francophone" literature, novelist Mariama Bâ (2001 [1979]) was one of the first to discuss internal states and intimacy in relation to gender, sexual relationships, social organization, religion, and polygamy. Silence overtakes the sense of revolt that boils up in us; and this is why most African women refuse to call themselves "feminist," as if all feminisms were a danger to be avoided.

On reflection, the refusal to call oneself "feminist" reveals the existence of a dominant multi-secular system that thinks of itself as holding the standard of truth. Other forms of discrimination and violence graft themselves onto this system, imposing their diktats in men's or women's voices: through family education, public space, the workplace, schools and universities, indeed, every public or private space. Women are efficient conduits in their reproducing and transmitting the values of the patriarchal order. A time comes, however, when women open their eyes and see what is around them. They finally accept that they can conceive of their own world, their own history, their own relationships with other worlds, their place and their future on the chessboard of globalization, by and for themselves. Indeed, thinking for oneself, when one is an African woman, is in the first place to break with a number of prejudices; it is to want things to change. It isn't to think against "man," or to reject concepts made elsewhere, but to think with one's own faculties and to imagine the world with one's own sensibilities, by trying to find one's own place among other humans and living things, animals and plants. This is what the Kenyan political activist and ecologist Wangari Maathai—who disappeared in 2011—did (Maathai 2006).

Conclusion

The act of being an African feminist is a challenge one gives to oneself. In fact, cultures, traditions, and all sorts of particulars show us that "gender" doesn't designate a relationship of domination comprised of only two poles: the woman in the inferior position, and the man in the superior position. Relationships of domination reproduce themselves and are interconnected; to know this, one only needs to ask what a family is. What is a mother? What is a father? Does "the couple" exist? What is sexuality? Why are fathers so often physically absent when all family, social, spiritual, and intellectual life is organized in their name? Fundamental philosophical questions show us the degree to which the word "gender" merits being questioned. It could be that women themselves are at the center of the development of informal economic life, though this remains to be proven. Should gender be understood from the standpoint of exclusive ethnicities in a plural Africa that includes thousands of "ethnic groups," languages, religions, and cultures? Though there may be many types of domination, patriarchal ideology defends the interests of men, irrespective of their situation. Whether it is a matter of relationships between individuals in a family or in a state context—and at state summits there are mothers and fathers in attendance, just like in the family—everything revolves around the organization of masculinities that must remain infallible, virile and powerful. We understand, too, why LGBTI-identified people have so few rights in many African countries and are hounded by public and political opinion, and moral, social and religious law. Is being a feminist not, then, in the end, to disrupt the order built by patriarchal ideology that reproduces itself at every level of sociality in the name of normality?

In African philosophical discourse, the word "feminism" is quite rare. Other disciplines like sociology, anthropology, ethnology, history, geography, economics, and literary studies tend to recognize feminist concerns well before any African woman philosopher—a phrase that always makes one smile—could give herself permission to think through the realities of most immediate concern to her. For a long time now, Western thinkers have analyzed the lives of African men and women, their cultures, societies, and religions. My impression of the current situation is that the thought produced by African women does not exist in philosophy, and especially not in francophone African countries. Women professors and researchers in philosophy do exist, however, in universities. They must struggle to include topics related to gender, intersectionality, and women's lives, knowledge and thought into research and teaching programs—efforts that do not always succeed. It is an arduous task, because one must have a voice in the first place, that is, some kind of power to change the way philosophy sees itself. African philosophy textbooks are rarely used in francophone countries, since Western philosophy is taken to be primary, and texts by African authors are virtually absent. This is the legacy of colonialism but also of the postcolonial situation in which the patriarchal system remains in place. Research on African philosophers yields only limited results in specialized publications or on the Internet.

The debate on African philosophy in the 1970s—the result of which was a diversification of African philosophies—did not include a single feminist dimension among its concerns. The philosophers who took part in this debate are men, and those who continue to be cited today are also men. From this point of view, invisibility is a problem that every African woman philosopher must have on her mind, before ever calling herself a feminist, since there is a great risk that her words will remain unheard.

Because public opinion cannot, on its own, imagine philosophers as women (even if women philosophy professors do exist in universities), the only remaining path is to publish philosophical essays that take women, men, gender, and sexualities into account, all while thinking through political, economic, social, and cultural particularities. Feminist philosophers have a duty to make their thinking known. It's first of all a matter of thinking alongside the first feminist thinkers in the social and human sciences, without forgetting that philosophy is one's specialization. To be able to change imaginaries programmed by patriarchal ideology that cannot see women in philosophy (or philosophy in women), is in the first place to write and publish. In francophone countries, this resembles the process of "squaring a circle": one must be able to find editors interested in the writing of women philosophers, but one must also find a way for these books to be read by students as well as the general public—the latter being an entire battle on its own. But to write in French, a language within easy reach, is already to take the first step.

Further Reading

Bennett, Jane (2010) "Circles and Circles: Notes on African Feminist Debates around Gender and Violence in the C 2," *Feminist Africa* 14: 21–47. (A discussion of contemporary debates in African feminist movements.)

Nnaemeka, Obioma (Ed.) (1998) *Sisterhood, Feminism and Power in Africa: From Africa to the Diaspora*, Trenton: African Word Press. (Relationships between feminism and womanism.)

—— (2005) "African Women, Colonial Discourses and Imperialist Interventions: Female Circumcision as Impetus," in Nnaemeka, Obioma (Ed.) *Female Circumcision and the Politics of Knowledge: African Women in Imperialist Discourses*, Westport: Praeger, 27–45. (Who has the right to pontificate on female circumcision in Africa?)

Oyewumi, Oyeronke (1997) *The Invention of Women: Making an African Sense of Western Gender Discourses*, Minneapolis, MN: University of Minnesota Press. (Can we speak of gender in pre-colonial Africa?)

Thiam, Awa (1978) *La Parole aux Négresses*, Paris: Denoël-Gonthier (African women bear witness to patriarchal violence.)

Related Topics

Introducing Black feminist philosophy (Chapter 10); the sex/gender distinction and the social construction of reality (Chapter 13); the genealogy and viability of the concept of intersectionality (Chapter 28); women, gender, and philosophies of global development (Chapter 34); moral justification in an unjust world (Chapter 40); postcolonial and multicultural feminisms (Chapter 47); feminism and freedom (Chapter 53).

References

Adichie, Chimamanda Ngozi (2012) *We Should All Be Feminists* [Transcript of Lecture for TEDxEuston, December 2012], London: Fourth Estate.

——(2014) *We Should All Be Feminists*, London: Harper Collins.

African Women's Development Fund (AWDF) (2006) [online]. Available at: http://awdf.org/charter-of-feminist-principles-for-african-feminists/.

Aristotle (2002) *Génération des Animaux* [Generation of Animals], Paris: Belles-Lettres.

Arndt, Susan (2000) "Who Is Afraid of Feminism? Critical Perspectives on Feminism in Africa and African Feminism," *Palabres* III: 35–61.

Bâ, Mariama (2001 [1979]) *Une Si Longue Lettre* [So Long a Letter], Paris: Serpent à plumes.

Bennett, Jane (2010) "'Circles and Circles': Notes on African Feminist Debates Around Gender and Violence in the Twenty-First Century," *Feminist Africa* 14: 21–47.

Beauvoir, Simone de (1949) *Le Deuxième Sexe* [The Second Sex], Paris: Gallimard.

Boni, Tanella (2008) "Femme et Etre Humain: Autonomisation et Réalisation de Soi [Woman and Human Being: Autonomization and Self-Realization]," *Africultures* 75: 27–37.

—— (2011) *Que Vivent les Femmes d'Afrique?* [What Is the Lived Experience of African Women?], Paris: Karthala.

D'Almeida, Irene (1994) *Francophone African Writers: Destroying the Emptiness of Silence*, Gainesville, FL: University Press of Florida.

Iman, Ayesha, Mama, Amina, and Sow, Fatou (Eds.) (1997) *Engendering African Social Sciences*, Dakar: CODESRIA.

Kourouma, Ahmadou (1970) *Les Soleils des Indépendances* [*The Suns of Independence*], Paris: Seuil.

Maathai, Wangari (2006) *Unbowed: A Memoir*, New York: Knopf.

Nnaemeka, Obioma (2004) "Nego-Feminism: Theorizing, Practicing and Pruning Africa's Way," *Signs* 29(2): 357–385.

Ogunyemi, Chikwenye Okonjo (1985) "Womanism: The Dynamics of the Contemporary Black Female Novel in English," *Signs* 11: 63–80.

Sow, Fatou (1998) "Mutilations Génitales Féminines et Droits Humains en Afrique [Female Genital Mutilation and Human Rights in Africa]," *Afrique en Développement* XXIII(3): 9–27.

—— (Ed.) (2009) *La Recherche Féministe Francophone: Langue, Identités et Enjeux* [*Francophone Feminist Research: Language, Identities Issues*], Paris: Karthala.

Walker, Alice (1984 [1983]) *In Search of Our Mothers' Gardens: Womanist Prose*, London: Women's Press.

5

FEMINIST ENGAGEMENT WITH JUDEO-CHRISTIAN RELIGIOUS TRADITIONS

Beverley Clack

A Brief History of Feminist Religious and Theological Critique

When considering the feminist engagement with Judeo-Christian religious and theological traditions, it is tempting to offer a straightforward "history of ideas." This would describe the various ways in which these religious traditions have been critiqued, deconstructed, and reconstructed by feminist scholars.

Adopting such an approach, we might begin with the critique of God conceived as Father offered by Mary Daly (1985 [1973]). For Daly, it is this notion that lies at the heart of patriarchal ideologies, reifying political systems based upon an implicit belief in the superiority of the male. Daly's famous remark that "if God is male, then the male is God" offers a pithy description of the effect that patriarchal religion has on the construction of social structures (1985 [1973]: 19). Theology is not an esoteric practice, divorced from the world of social relationships: it both supports and shapes political ideology. Daly's *The Church and the Second Sex* (1968) paved the way for this conclusion, exposing the way in which theological formulations and religious practices shape misogyny. Rosemary Radford Ruether (1974), among others, built upon Daly's arguments to further expose the use of religious ideas to support sexism. Nearly fifty years on, there is no room for complacency, Daly's evocative description of the social effect of masculinist theological language continuing to resonate in a contemporary context where women's representation—both political and religious—remains a contested issue.

From Daly's groundbreaking work, our intellectual history might go on to detail the direction taken by feminists like Carol Christ (1979; 1998) who concluded that patriarchal religions cannot escape their formation in patriarchal history and are thus incapable of supporting the well-being of women. As a result, Christ, with others (Goldenberg 1979), preferred to construct new forms of feminist spirituality based on the ancient religious traditions of the Goddess (Raphael 1999).

Noting this *thea*-logical shift, we might then consider approaches that resist such a move. Ruether's response, for example, is to develop a critical feminist liberation theology by identifying a "Golden Thread" concerned with liberation, which, she claims, runs through the Hebrew Bible and the New Testament (Ruether 1983; 1998). Galatians 3: 28 might be held up as a text that exemplifies this radical message of equality and freedom from oppression: "There is neither Jew nor Greek, there is neither slave nor free, there is no male and female, for you are all one in Christ Jesus."

The positive reclamation of religious tradition has been furthered by figures such as Janet Martin Soskice (1984; 2007) and Sarah Coakley (1996), who argue that there are good reasons not to discard religious traditions that have emerged from a history defined by male domination. For Coakley, the self-giving or *kenosis* of the Christian God offers a radical way of reformulating ideas of vulnerability. For Soskice, the plethora of images offered in the Hebrew Bible and the New Testament is rich enough to challenge the patriarchal models that have disproportionately shaped Christian theory and practice.

Our history of Western feminist religious thought might then consider more recent examples of feminists such as Amy Hollywood (2001) and Ellen Armour (1999; 2006) who apply critical theory to the development of radical new feminist religious positions. We might, in similar vein, consider Melissa Raphael's blending of Goddess spirituality with her Jewish faith (2003). This approach shows that feminist commitments need not be defined by an acceptance of an implicit dualism in which it is a simple case of deciding for one or other side of a dualistic construction of belief systems.

It would also be vital when detailing the richness of feminist thinking to consider the critique made of "white feminist" theology by Womanist theologians such as Dolores Williams (2005). For Womanists, feminist theology has avoided tackling the issue of race, thereby enabling racial oppression to go unchallenged. A self-critical feminist theology must engage with this powerful critique if it is not to speak only to the concerns of a few women rather than the need of all women to be affirmed in their full humanity. In what follows, the importance of this feminist intellectual history will be present, if not foregrounded, for its variety bears witness to the creativity of this area of feminist enquiry.

My intention is not, however, to offer a straightforwardly descriptive account of the history of feminist attempts to engage with the Judeo-Christian religious past, creative as such attempts undoubtedly are. What will shape my narrative is a rather different concern: *Why* might radically different feminist scholars with radically different concerns have felt compelled to shape their ideas through an engagement with that religious past? For, rather than ditch the whole area of religious enquiry as hopelessly outmoded, they have sought to develop religious positions that take seriously women's lives and experiences, maintaining the value of religious perspectives for the pursuit of human flourishing.

The Attraction of Religion: Michèle Le Doeuff on Possibilities and Pitfalls

A comment made by the French philosopher Michèle Le Doeuff can illuminate the reasons for continuing to engage with religious ideas. Towards the end of her reflections on the exclusion of women from the history of philosophy (1989), Le Doeuff describes the pull of the religious perspective for those who, like her, are attempting to shape an alternative feminist philosophy:

Still confused, I now open Pascal—and I suddenly see why, however foreign the religious concepts of his work are to me, I feel more "at home" in the *Pensées* than in any of the other classic texts. It is because the religious perspective hints at this penumbra of unknowledge (a penumbra which has nothing to do with the limits of reason), which metaphysics has denied. Here is a form of writing which does not claim to reconstruct and explain everything, which slides along the verge of the unthought, develops only by grafting itself on to another discourse, and consents to be its tributary.

(1989: 127)

Why this turn to religion from someone who is not religious? It is worth tracing Le Doeuff's route to this point, for it helps to clarify the continuing attraction of religious perspectives for feminist thinkers. It also, perhaps, challenges Tina Beattie's (1999) claim that all too often feminist theologians have felt like Cinderellas excluded from the secular feminist ball.

Le Doeuff's comments arise as she considers the kind of method that is possible if one rejects masculinist constructions of what it is to do philosophy. She begins by considering reasons why women might have been excluded from the practice of philosophy, and cautions against simplistic accounts that claim women have been excluded "from time immemorial" (1989: 100). As she notes, women have always managed to become philosophers, but invariably they have felt compelled to position their thoughts in relation to the thinking of a man. Consider, Le Doeuff says, the relationship of Abelard and Héloïse. Just as Héloïse came to frame her thoughts in relation to Abelard's theology, so other women have been similarly nervous about developing their own ideas unshackled from the constricting frame of discipleship. A troubling example of this tendency is provided by Simone de Beauvoir's startling acceptance of Sartre's conclusion that she was *not* a philosopher, analysed by Le Doeuff in *Hipparchia's Choice* (2007 [1990]: Third Notebook). Given Beauvoir's position as the mother of contemporary feminism—a status recently reclaimed for her by Susan Hekman (2014)—her unwillingness to claim the title "philosopher" is both perplexing and unsettling for those women who are attempting to do so.

The temptation to give way before the supposed brilliance of the "male master" mirrors the theological temptation to align oneself overly closely with the thought of either a particular man, or, indeed, with a specific patriarchal religious history. While post-Christians have challenged the status of the "man who is God" for their Christian sisters, they have not been able to escape entirely from the organizing pull of the male thinker. Daphne Hampson (2002) uses Schleiermacher to construct her post-Christian God, while Carol Christ (2003) appropriates Charles Hartshorne for her process thealogy of the Goddess. In order not to ignore my own duplicity, my attempt to shape a psychoanalytic account of religion does so by reclaiming aspects of Freud's critique (Clack 2013). It is not surprising that so many make this move to anchor their thoughts in the ideas of a male master. As Daly notes, barring relocating to the moon, which she does imaginatively in her autobiography, it is almost impossible to escape a patriarchal past that is, sadly, a universal feature of human society (1993: 337–345).

Le Doeuff's solution to this problem is to shift the understanding of philosophy away from discipleship towards practice. As she develops this position, she appropriates a key feature of the religious perspective that seems to accommodate the openness she seeks for her framing of philosophy.

Le Doeuff turns her attention to the implicit gendering of philosophical practice. With Grace Jantzen (1995: 31–32), Le Doeuff notes the significance of Pythagoras' (*c*.570–495 BCE) dualistic framing of reality, itself a defining moment in the history of philosophical method. Pythagoras aligns the female with that which is infinite and multiple, and the male with limit and unity (Le Doeuff 1989: 113). The implications of this dualistic construction for an ideal of "the philosopher" cannot be underestimated. That which is boundless—the female—must be constrained by the force of the limiting male. Social control and method mesh, philosophical practice coming to reflect the primacy of establishing limits and creating unity as its practitioners pursue watertight arguments and final conclusions. Philosophy is constructed as a closed system, where debate is directed towards the final goal of "true knowledge" (Le Doeuff 1989: 117).

Absolutism in thinking lends itself with some ease to the quest for a master who has the one, true answer. Le Doeuff resists this construction, arguing that there is never an end to philosophical practice: it is simply what we do. It is "an unfinished philosophical discourse, never closed and never concluded," an incomplete practice that involves "the abandonment of any totalizing aim" (1989: 126–127). To accept her vision is to reject the model of the lone philosopher seeking "the truth." The subject of the enterprise that is philosophy is

> no longer a person—or, better still, if each person involved in the enterprise is no longer in the position of being the subject of the enterprise but in that of being a worker, engaged in and committed to an enterprise which is seen from the outset as collective—it seems to me that the relationship to knowledge—and to gaps in knowledge—can be transformed.
>
> (Le Doeuff 1989: 127)

Rejecting the role of the master, Le Doeuff argues for a collective form of philosophical engagement, where the practice of critical thinking challenges and shapes both individual behavior and, crucially, the public sphere. Anne-Marie Mulder, in her recent attempt to frame an ethical philosophy of religion, makes a similar point when she argues for a philosophical practice which "develop[s] and maintain[s] horizontal relations between subjects" (2010: 299). For Le Doeuff, critical thought has the power to establish this possibility, challenging habitual ways of behaving through the application of rigorous philosophical critique. For both Mulder and Le Doeuff, philosophical practice is not divorced from the public sphere, having the power to enable better ways of living together.

Framing a Practical Feminist Philosophy of Religion

How to frame this practical philosophy? While cautious of the theological acceptance of "mystery," Le Doeuff recognizes the value of a perspective that sees incompleteness as fundamental to human experience. Religious perspectives allow for the recognition that not all can be known. Similarly, to adopt a religious perspective is to engage in the kind of un-knowing that gets us to think about the world differently. Human knowledge is not a closed system; it is not incapable of challenge and change. Enshrining not-knowing in this way is useful for Le Doeuff's framing of philosophical practice as it suggests a way of thinking by which "a relationship to the unknown and the unthought is at every moment reintroduced" (1989: 128).

Importantly, such a perspective cultivates openness, although it also does more than this. Openness is not openness for its own sake: it is important because it provides the basis for a different kind of life together, in which the complexity of communal life is not evaded, but celebrated. As Western societies increasingly seem willing to accept the claim that "There Is No Alternative" to their dominant economic and social system (the so-called TINA doctrine), the stance that Le Doeuff advocates allows precisely for such alternatives to emerge. There is always the possibility of change, always the possibility of finding and enacting ways of living more conducive to the flourishing of all, not just a few. One is reminded of Hannah Arendt's vision of the healthy political space as one in which a plethora of positions is acknowledged and accepted (Arendt 1998 [1958]). Something even more fundamental characterizes Le Doeuff's position, for she returns feminist philosophy to the defining feature of feminism: it is a political movement concerned with liberation.

Thinking Again About Religion and Feminism

And so we return to religion. There are, of course, many possible pitfalls if one recognizes the pull of the religious dimension. One might become enmeshed in repeating the historical formulations of the fathers; one might reject openness in favor of accepting the dogmatic formulations of a particular tradition. As feminist liberation theologian Lisa Isherwood notes, we do well to remember that religious doctrine can all too easily become a bar to creative thinking, acting as "the fossilisation of people's original reflections of the nature of the divine in their lives" (2008: 202).

There is danger, but there is also possibility. Religious space, as Le Doeuff identifies it, provides an open place for creative reflection. At the heart of this space is a willingness to accept the uncertainties that attend to the experience of being mutable beings in a changing world. Accepting uncertainty is no easy thing, for it demands giving up on the idea that human beings are in control of every aspect of their lives. The kind of philosophical practice that Le Doeuff rejects might be seen in this context. The philosophical obsession with pinning things down can be traced back to an anxiety about the precariousness of life in this world, its methods offering a false sense of security by eschewing the things that have historically been identified with the female: nature, desire, physicality, change. Le Doeuff's approach to this problem is subtle. Resisting the move to enshrine and validate feminine difference articulated by feminists like Luce Irigaray (1985 [1977]), Le Doeuff maintains the significance of critical reflection, while going beyond simply reclaiming rationality for the female. Instead, her method recognizes the ambiguity inherent in human experience, and the need to transform binary accounts of rationality.

Accepting, rather than rejecting, ambiguity suggests common ground between Le Doeuff's reworking of philosophical method and the practices of feminist theo/alogians. For thealogians, the divinity of the body is enshrined in their formulation of the Goddess who reflects and shapes experience of the female body (Raphael 1996). Those remaining in the Christian tradition similarly challenge dualistic constructions of mind and body. Here, the Christian idea of Incarnation is reworked, Christ revealing the radical possibilities of proclaiming a God made flesh. Isherwood captures the radical nature of this formulation as she reflects on the emergence of her theology from her roots in the Welsh landscape:

64

> As a Celt my landscape begs me to question the hierarchy of worlds; as the mists lie low over the mountaintops it is easy to understand the gap between the human and the divine is ruah, a breath—or one small step into uncertainty.
>
> (2008: 203)

To be religious is not to find certainty but to embrace uncertainty. Isherwood's image of mist on mountaintops suggests a way of thinking religiously that is conducive to the sense of openness that Le Doeuff seeks. Religion need not be framed as providing easily accessible answers to existential or metaphysical questions, but rather as a space that makes possible deeper thinking about humanity and our place in the world.

To think of religion in this way may sound strange. After all, the notion of religion as a means of providing answers to the questions of existence is long-lived and extremely attractive in a world of chance and change. But in feminist theo/alogical thought, religion offers a different way of engaging with that reality, providing stories and images capable of opening up rather than closing down the engagement with such a world. If Pythagoras makes a connection between Woman, the infinite and that which is without limit, we might, in the manner of Luce Irigaray (1993 [1984]), embrace rather than reject this characterization (see Jantzen 1998). In feminist philosophy of religion, this possibility has been taken seriously, with feminist practitioners challenging the habitual construction of the discipline as the practice by which the rational grounds for religious belief can be determined. Twentieth-century philosophy of religion has been defined as the attempt to establish "the coherence of theism," to appropriate the title of Richard Swinburne's book on the subject (1977). But feminist philosophers of religion have challenged the implication that we should reject whatever lies outside of these philosophical constraints on a rational religious perspective.

We might pause, however, before rejecting out of hand the method that Swinburne advocates. There may be good reasons for directing the cool eye of reason to an area of life that can all too easily be co-opted to hateful or violent behavior. We have, after all, already noted the role of religious tradition in promoting misogynistic attitudes and behaviors (see also Clack 1999a). Kant, famously, was suspicious of religious enthusiasm because of the potentially destructive emotions it elicits. And he was suitably dismissive of claims that Abraham was told by God to sacrifice Isaac, for to accept such a conclusion would mean that God could do that which is immoral in human eyes, a claim Kant stoutly rejects (Kant 1998 [1793]). Yet to approach religion critically need not mean rejecting the possibility of using it to engage creatively with the world.

Adopting this strategy might take us in surprising directions: Elizabeth Stuart's (2008) revisiting of the belief in life after death offers an example. While Stuart notes the ease with which feminists reject the notion of continued life after death (Plumwood 1993; Jantzen 1998: 137–141; Clack 1999b), she argues that no theme should be foreclosed to feminists. Indeed, she makes a strong case for maintaining such a belief in a world of injustice and pain. We might disagree with her conclusions but, for Stuart, feminist thinking must be defined by the willingness to reject the easy closing down of debates, resisting the temptation to establish new orthodoxies that constrain creative thinking.

Religious Plurality and Feminist Flourishing

A plethora of positions are possible, then, for religious thinking when claims for uncertainty are taken seriously. It is difficult not to be reminded of Nietzsche's use of the open sea as a metaphor for the time after the death of god (2001 [1881]: §343). As he notes, this openness can be experienced as liberating, but it can also be experienced as inducing seasickness as we realize the loss of any obvious anchor for thought and action (2001 [1881]: 119–120).

Nietzsche's approach emphasizes the loneliness of the *Übermensch* who alone has the strength to embrace this open future, boldly embarking on the transvaluation of all values. Feminists need not tread a similarly lonely path. A different move is possible for a feminism that takes seriously its roots as a political movement, and, moreover, as a movement concerned to create a more just and equal society. As a movement, we do not encounter openness or uncertainty alone but together. The feminist philosopher is not modelled like Descartes, dependent on the servant girl "who lit the fire in [his] stove" (Jantzen 1998: 33), thereby enabling his philosophical isolation. As we saw, for Le Doeuff, philosophical activity has to be re-visioned as a joint activity of mutual endeavour. Relationship becomes the context for generating ideas, but also acts as the focus for that philosophizing: how best to create a society where we are able to live well together?

The focus, then, shifts to the question of what makes for human flourishing. When Pamela Sue Anderson (1998) and Grace Jantzen (1998) produced the first works dedicated to developing a feminist approach to philosophy of religion, they both understood flourishing to be at the heart of feminist thinking. Rather different starting points shape their approaches: Anderson offers an explicitly Kantian approach, while Jantzen applies psychoanalytic categories to uncover the role of the unconscious. Yet for both what matters is developing an ethical philosophy of religion.

Jantzen's work is the most telling for an account that attempts to understand the usefulness of religious frameworks for feminist philosophers. She offers critical reflections on the effects of patriarchal religion on women and marginalized others, but this does not stop her thinking about the kinds of religious sensibility that might help to create healthy communities (Jantzen 1998: 204–226). The divine horizon that she appropriates from Irigaray's work helps Jantzen to develop an alternative to patriarchal religion that provides the space for creative thinking and—crucially—for better ways of living.

Religion can be viewed, then, as providing space for the kind of playfulness necessary for shaping alternative visions of how we might live. Perhaps it is not surprising that Jantzen should adopt aspects of psychoanalytic theory in order to do this, her work prompting thoughts of Donald Winnicott's (1971) location of religion in the space opened up between self and other by play. Religion emerges in the place between two people or positions where relationship is created. As Julia Kristeva notes, relationship *requires* this space between self and other (1987 [1985]). Thinking of religion as located in the spaces between selves is to adopt a model rather different from that which imagines it as a form of pseudo science, attempting to fill in the gaps in human knowledge. Instead, religion can be seen as providing a space in which we share in the creative imagining of the world.

What does it mean to commit oneself to creating communities capable of sustaining the flourishing of individuals and, indeed, the planet? For it is worth noting that Jantzen takes on board the concerns of ecofeminists as she explores what makes for a flourishing world (1998: 156–170). Flourishing is difficult to define: what makes *me* flourish might be different from—indeed, in tension with—what *you* require. It is this complexity that brings into play the quality necessary for flourishing that, at the same time, has rarely been considered worthy of "serious" philosophical investigation: love.

Feminist philosophers have understood the importance of attending to love (see Anderson 2008). Kristeva finds religious stories useful for considering love's nature. Love, of all concepts and emotions the most difficult to pin down, reveals the weaknesses of the philosopher's desire for control. As Kristeva notes, when philosophers try to "settle a score with theology" they forget that "in this respect one had to consider our loves—that with which theology, for its part, had the cunning to concern itself" (1987 [1985]: 279). For Kristeva, then, religious ideas provide a valuable way of engaging with the messiness of the experience of love, in all its myriad forms.

The most dramatic example of this appropriation of religious stories is found in Kristeva's essay "Stabat Mater," in which reflection on the grieving Mary at the foot of her son's cross is used to explore the sometimes painful experiences of motherhood (Kristeva 2001 [1977]: 112–138). Love, in all its joyful and sorrowful manifestations, is made through relationship, without which we are incapable of flourishing as human beings. We might also note Andrei Rublev's icon of the Trinity, which has become a popular way of envisaging the Trinity: three androgynous figures sit at a table eating, an image that suggests the need for communion with each other, expressed here in a relational depiction of the divine.

Feminists have used relational depictions of the God-In-Three-Persons to explore what makes for good relationships. Sallie McFague (1982) explores the nature of friendship as she models God as Friend. Similarly, Beverly Harrison (1985) makes love the basis for theology and community. For our purposes, pursuing Le Doeuff's co-option of religion for philosophical method, the idea of God *as* conversation makes possible good philosophical practice. Good conversation grounds friendship. There is no end point to the conversation between friends, just an ever-open discourse that shapes and reflects the relationship itself.

It is not necessary to hold to the doctrine of the Trinity in order to recognize relationship as fundamental to what it means to be human. Aristotle's definition of the human being as a "*zoon politikon*" ("social animal") suggests a similar recognition of our need for one another. But there is something about the religious desire to connect with others and the world—arguably the desire that lies at the root of that much-debated word "*religare*"—that enables the anchoring of human flourishing in social relationships. We cannot flourish alone.

This is one of the reasons why feminist theo/alogies are orientated towards the ethical. What makes for good community demands not just theory but practical steps to live that theory out. Similarly, Le Doeuff's work is peppered with examples drawn from her experience as a feminist activist. Feminist philosophy as she conceives it draws its power from the practical work of community building. In this way, we come to know whether our philosophy has a positive or negative effect on the lives of others; whether it helps or hinders the cultivation of places conducive to the well-being of all, including those who are marginalized (Le Doeuff 2003: 82–83).

The work of creating societies capable of supporting human flourishing requires both the work of deconstruction and reconstruction: activities that have marked the history of feminist religious thought. We need to identify the things that hinder as well as the things that enable human flourishing. This may take us beyond the usual parameters of feminist thought. We might, for example, need to embark on far-reaching critiques of the dominant neoliberal discourse that suggests that "the market" and the desires of individuals are the only determinants of value. Locating our philosophies in such a context may well necessitate a return to the question of truth, for it is not without importance for establishing the kind of values that support the flourishing of all. As Harriet Harris (2001) notes, a critical feminist philosophy of religion will do well to remember that the striving for truth is not without ethical import. Openness does not mean the rejection of that critical striving, and Harris' work challenges us to consider the effect of our philosophies and theologies on those with whom we share this world.

Conclusion

We return to the questions posed at the outset. Why is the engagement with religion important for feminists? What does a religious perspective add to Le Doeuff's desire for an open form of philosophical practice?

The variety of feminist religious and theological perspectives suggests something of the ways in which religious ideas and stories enable new ways of engaging with the world and with others. Religions emerged as attempts to make sense of the world in which human beings found themselves. Through providing frameworks for thinking, they shaped human community. They have not always done this successfully, and history is replete with examples of the destructive effects of religious traditions that have sought to force their view of the world on others. But religions have also borne witness to the creative impulse of human beings, and the desire to express that creativity in community.

In feminist philosophy of religion there is the possibility of anchoring philosophy in life. In the uncertainty to which religions bear witness, there is the possibility of allowing for a new openness in the way in which we engage with each other, meeting the other person as someone who is also struggling to find a way through the complex and often painful experience of life in this world. Feminist philosophy, thus located, becomes a form of liberating practice. As Patrice Haynes notes: "feminist philosophy of religion must advance a form of critical thinking that can serve as the basis for social transformation" (2010: 281). Feminism returns to its roots as a political movement, which demands that its followers live out its concern with liberation in personal relationships and political action. To do that we need rich and colorful stories to think again about the things that really matter in life. In their ability to generate these stories, religious traditions offer a helpful way forward.

Further Reading

Anderson, Pamela Sue (2010) *New Topics in Feminist Philosophy of Religion*, London: Springer.
Hampson, Daphne (2002) *After Christianity*, 2nd ed. London: SCM.
Le Doeuff, Michèle (1989) "Long Hair, Short Ideas," in Michèle Le Doeuff, *The Philosophical Imaginary*, London: Athlone, 100–128.
Radford Ruether, Rosemary (2011) *Women and Redemption: A Theological History*, 2nd ed., Minneapolis, MN: Fortress Press.

Related Topics

Feminist methods in the history of philosophy (Chapter 1); feminist intersections with environmentalism and ecological thought (Chapter 35); encountering religious diversity (Chapter 36); aesthetics and the politics of gender: on Arendt's theory of narrative and action (Chapter 38); feminism and power (Chapter 54).

References

Anderson, Pamela Sue (1998) *A Feminist Philosophy of Religion: The Rationality and Myths of Religious Belief*, Oxford: Wiley.

—— (2008) "Liberating Love's Capabilities: On the Wisdom of Love," in Norman Wirzba and Bruce Ellis Benson (Eds.) *Transforming Philosophy and Religion*, Indianapolis, IN: Indianapolis University Press, 201–226.

Arendt, Hannah (1998 [1958]) *The Human Condition*, Chicago, IL: Chicago University Press.

Armour, Ellen (1999) *Deconstruction, Feminist Theology and the Problem of Difference*, Chicago, IL: University of Chicago Press.

—— (2006) *Bodily Citations: Judith Butler and Religion*, New York: Columbia University Press.

Beattie, Tina (1999) "Global Sisterhood or Wicked Stepsisters? Why Don't Girls with God-Mothers Get Invited to the Ball?" in Deborah Sawyer and Diane M. Collins (Eds.) *Is There a Future for Feminist Theology?* Sheffield: Sheffield Academic Press, 115–125.

Christ, Carol (1979) "Why Women Need the Goddess," in Judith Plaskow (Ed.) *Womanspirit Rising*, London: Harper & Row.

—— (1998) *Rebirth of the Goddess*, London: Routledge.

—— (2003) *She Who Changes*, London: Palgrave Macmillan.

Clack, Beverley (1999a) *Misogyny in the Western Philosophical Tradition*, London: Routledge.

—— (1999b) "Revisioning Death: A Thealogical Approach to the 'Evils' of Mortality," *Feminist Theology* 22: 67–77.

—— (2013) *Freud on the Couch*, Oxford: OneWorld.

Coakley, Sarah (1996) "Kenosis and Subversion: On the Repression of Vulnerability in Christian Feminist Writing," in Daphne Hampson (Ed.) *Swallowing a Fishbone?* London: SPCK, 82–111.

Daly, Mary (1968) *The Church and the Second Sex*, Boston, MA: Beacon Press.

—— (1985 [1973]) *Beyond God the Father*, Boston, MA: Beacon Press.

—— (1993) *Outercourse: The Be-Dazzling Voyage*, London: Women's Press.

Goldenberg, Naomi (1979) *Changing of the Gods: Feminism and the End of Traditional Religion*, Boston, MA: Beacon Press.

Hampson, Daphne (2002) *After Christianity*, 2nd ed., London: SCM Press.

Harris, Harriet (2001) "Struggling for Truth," *Feminist Theology* 28: 40–56.

Harrison, Beverly (1985) *Making the Connections*, Boston, MA: Beacon Press.

Hekman, Susan (2014) *The Feminine Subject*, Cambridge: Polity Press.

Hollywood, Amy (2001) *Sensible Ecstasy*, Chicago, IL: University of Chicago Press.

Irigaray, Luce (1985 [1977]) *This Sex Which Is Not One*, trans. Catherine Porter and Carolyn Burke, Ithaca, NY: Cornell University Press.

—— (1993 [1984]) *An Ethics of Sexual Difference*, trans. Carolyn Burke and Gillian C. Gill, London: Athlone Press.

Isherwood, Lisa (2008) "Jesus Past the Posts: An Enquiry into Post-Metaphysical Christology," in Lisa Isherwood and Kathleen McPhillips (Eds.) *Post-Christian Feminisms*, Aldershot: Ashgate, 201–210.

Jantzen, Grace (1995) *Power, Gender and Christian Mysticism*, Cambridge: Cambridge University Press.

—— (1998) *Becoming Divine: Towards a Feminist Philosophy of Religion*, Manchester: Manchester University Press.

Kant, Immanuel (1998 [1793]) *Religion Within the Boundaries of Mere Reason*, Cambridge: Cambridge University Press.

Kristeva, Julia (1987 [1985]) *In the Beginning Was Love*, New York: Columbia University Press.

—— (2001 [1977]) "Stabat Mater," in Morny Joy, Kathleen O'Grady and Judith L. Poxon (Eds.) *French Feminists on Religion: A Reader*, London: Routledge, 112–138.

Le Doeuff, Michèle (1989) *The Philosophical Imaginary*, London: Athlone Press. University Press.

—— (2003) *The Sex of Knowing*, London: Routledge.

—— (2007 [1990]) *Hipparchia's Choice*, New York: Columbia

McFague, Sallie (1982) *Metaphorical Theology*, London: SCM.

Mulder, Anne-Marie (2010) "An Ethics of the In-Between," in Pamela Sue Anderson, (Ed.) *New Topics in Feminist Philosophy of Religion*, London: Springer, 297–318.

Nietzsche, Friedrich (2001 [1887]) *The Gay Science*, Cambridge: Cambridge University Press.

Plumwood, Val (1993) *Feminism and the Mastery of Nature*, London: Routledge.

Raphael, Melissa (1996) *Thealogy and Embodiment*, London: Continuum.

—— (1999) *Introducing Thealogy: Discourse on the Goddess*, Sheffield: Sheffield Academic Press.

—— (2003) *The Female Face of God in Auschwitz*, London: Routledge.

Ruether, Rosemary Radford (Ed.) (1974) *Religion and Sexism*, New York: Simon & Schuster.

—— (1983) *Sexism and God-Talk*, London: SCM.

—— (1998) *Introducing Redemption in Christian Feminism*, London: Continuum.

Soskice, Janet Martin (1984) *Metaphor and Religious Language*, Oxford: Oxford University Press.

—— (2007) *The Kindness of God*, Oxford: Oxford University Press.

Stuart, Elizabeth (2008) "The Return of the Living Dead," in Lisa Isherwood and Kathleen McPhillips (Eds.) *Post-Christian Feminisms*, Aldershot: Ashgate, 211–222.

Swinburne, Richard (1977) *The Coherence of Theism*, Oxford: Clarendon Press.

Williams, Dolores (2005) *Sisters in the Wilderness: The Challenge of Womanist God-Talk*, Maryknoll, NY: Orbis.

Winnicott, Donald (1971) *Playing and Reality*, London: Psychology Press.

6

EARLY MODERN FEMINISM AND CARTESIAN PHILOSOPHY

Jacqueline Broad

Introduction

In early modern Europe (c.1500–1700) it was a common perception that men and women had different bodily qualities: men's bodies were hot and dry, while women's were cold and moist; men were strong and active, while women were weak and passive. According to French physician Marin Cureau de la Chambre, these different bodily temperaments gave rise to different dispositions in the minds of men and women. On account of being hot, a man was naturally inclined to be courageous, magnanimous, sincere, liberal, merciful, just, and grateful. Because he was dry, a man was also capable of having a strong resolve, and of being constant, patient, modest, faithful, and judicious. By contrast, on account of being cold, a woman was:

> *Weak*, and consequently *Fearfull, Pusillanimous, Jealous, Distrustfull, Crafty*, apt
> to *Dissemble, Flatter, Lie*, easily *Offended, Revengefull, Cruel* in her revenge,
> *Unjust, Covetous, Ungratefull, Superstitious*. And from her being *moist*, it follows
> that she should be *Unconstant, Light, Unfaithfull, Impatient*, easily *Perswaded,
> Compassionate, Talkative*.
>
> (Cureau 1670: 26, italics in original)

A woman's mind was especially susceptible to impressions from outside: it was credulous, changeable, and fickle. Though Cureau and others insisted that these inclinations were proper and natural to the female sex—and thus constituted a woman's "perfection" (when held in equilibrium)—it was generally thought that women *compared to men* were defective by nature, and that women were inherently lacking in the moral and intellectual competence of the male sex.

While these were popular views of the time, however, they were by no means uncontested or uncontroversial. The seventeenth century bore witness to a number of arguments in favor of the moral and intellectual equality of the sexes (for helpful overviews, see Clarke 2013; O'Neill 2011). Such arguments can be found in the works of Marie le Jars de Gournay, François Poullain de la Barre, Anna Maria van Schurman, Bathsua Makin, Margaret Cavendish, Mary Astell, Judith Drake, Gabrielle Suchon, Mary Chudleigh, and Damaris Masham, among others.

In this chapter I examine the influence of Cartesian philosophy on feminist thought of the seventeenth century. More specifically, I outline the impact of Cartesian epistemological, metaphysical, and ethical ideas on the arguments of the French thinker François Poullain de la Barre (1647–1723) and the English philosopher Mary Astell (1666–1731). My purpose is to highlight those aspects of Cartesian philosophy that were central to their feminist thought. In doing so, I propose to elaborate on—and, to some extent, sharpen and refine—previous statements on the subject of Cartesianism and feminism.

In the scholarly literature to date, it is an accepted view that Descartes' method of doubt provided significant inspiration for early modern feminists. This is the famous method whereby Descartes doubted every belief that he could possibly doubt in order to obtain clear and certain knowledge. By analogy, he reasoned, it was better to demolish an old house built on weak foundations and construct a new building rather than try to repair the old one piece by piece. His process of "demolition" or universal doubt famously came to an end with one certain and indubitable truth: that "*I am, I exist,* is necessarily true whenever it is put forward by me or conceived in my mind" (Descartes 1984: 17). This insight, now known as the *cogito*, provided Descartes with a criterion of truth and certainty—"clarity and distinctness"—from which to re-build knowledge on secure foundations.

Though Descartes' method was never intended to cast doubt on political or religious authority, its anti-authoritarian implications were obvious to a number of his near contemporaries (see Israel 2001). Ruth Perry observes that Cartesian method enabled early modern feminists to call into question the aforementioned prejudices and preconceptions concerning female moral and intellectual inferiority. By gaining a familiarity with this radical method, and engaging in a "willful doubting of all previous knowledge," Perry says (1985: 479), women became critically minded toward oppressive gender stereotypes of their time. The method of doubt thus provided a "powerful and revolutionary" mechanism by which women could be liberated (Perry 1985: 475).

Scholars also claim that Descartes' philosophy of mind provided crucial support for the idea that "the mind has no sex." According to Descartes, the mind is essentially a thinking substance. Simply by looking within myself, I can know that the essence of my mind is to think. I can also deduce that the essence of my body, a material thing, is to be extended in length, breadth, and depth. Furthermore, I can clearly and distinctly conceive of my mind, a purely thinking, non-extended thing, existing apart from my body, a purely extended, non-thinking thing. In Descartes' view, it follows that the mind and body are two distinct substances, capable of existing independently of one another.

Perry notes that in this period, "Once mind was separated from body, and elevated, nothing could be argued from physiology," and that "women's reproductive capacity could no longer be held against them if all minds were created equal and rationality was the cardinal virtue" (1985: 473). Catharine Gallagher likewise points out that: "Many seventeenth-century women writers were inspired by Descartes' dualism to assert their intellectual equality with men; for if, as Descartes argued, mind has no extension, then it also has no gender" (1988: 34). In her view, Cartesian philosophy instituted a "clean break" between mind and body (Gallagher 1988: 34). Erica Harth adds that "the mind has no sex" is a "rallying cry" for feminists in the period (1992: 81), and Marcelle Maistre Welch likewise asserts that "the mind has no sex" is "the bedrock of modern feminist philosophy" in this era, one that owes its origins to Descartes' "dualism of mind and body" (Poullain 2002: 82, n. 27).

These common generalizations about Cartesianism and feminism face certain difficulties and limitations, however. First, it must be noted that in the context of Descartes' wider project the method of doubt is, strictly speaking, a skeptical tool: it is an instrument to annihilate opinions rather than establish positive truths (Descartes' doubting comes to an *end* with the *cogito*). So while the method of doubt is useful for the purposes of negative feminist critique, by itself it is unable to establish certain positive truths about women's mental competence, or to suggest normative reasons why women should not be treated differently to men. To form the basis of a full-blooded feminist theory, this method requires supplementation with a theory of mind and an ethical or political standpoint.

Second, the supposedly Cartesian idea that "the mind has no sex" is hard to reconcile with Descartes' explicit claim that the living human being is *a mind–body composite* (on this point, see O'Neill 1999: 240). In his *Meditationes de prima philosophiae* [*Meditations on First Philosophy*] (first published 1641), following an argument for the real distinction between mind and body, Descartes states: "I am not merely present in my body as a sailor is present in a ship" (1984: 56). To some extent, of course, he concedes that I *am* like a sailor in a ship: I can steer my body this way and that, and I can make certain choices and perform certain actions that prevent my vessel from coming to harm. But in other respects, I am *not* like a sailor: when a sailor's boat hits the rocks, he does not intimately experience the damage. But when *my body* hits the rocks, I feel the impact deep within me: I am discomposed by sensations of pain, I experience the passions of fear and dread, and I am unable *not* to feel the pounding of my heart and the shortness of my breath. Such feelings and sensations overwhelm my ability to think clearly and rationally. As Descartes explains in his final work *Les Passions de l'âme* [*The Passions of the Soul*] (1649), the body influences the mind's thought processes in disturbing and confusing ways. Cartesian philosophy does not therefore institute a "clean break" between mind and body, or posit a "separation" between the two substances. It holds that for any living human being, a mind will always be united to, and closely intermingled with, a particular body. For Descartes, then, the human mind *does* have a sex: it is tied, fused, joined, united, and closely connected to either a male or a female physiology.

In light of these points, several puzzles and questions arise about the Cartesian influence on feminist thought in this period. In particular, it is difficult to see how the mere assertion of a sexless mind could have mounted an effective challenge to the prevailing sexism of the times. In Cureau's view, a woman's natural temperament made her a slave to her bodily passions: it rendered her weak, feeble, inconstant, easily persuaded, and generally mentally incompetent. In her correspondence with Descartes about the mind–body union, Princess Elisabeth of Bohemia expresses a similar view about the immaterial mind's inability to overcome her female bodily temperament. "I have a body imbued with a large part of the weaknesses of my sex," she says, "so that it is affected very easily by the afflictions of the soul and has none of the strength to bring itself back into line" (Elisabeth and Descartes 2007: 88). She raises a pertinent point: if women's minds could still be so strongly influenced by their bodies, it is not clear that with the rise of Cartesianism, "nothing could be argued from physiology" or that "women's reproductive capacity could no longer be held against them" as Perry says (1985: 473).

In the following discussion, I propose to address these difficulties by highlighting other influential aspects of Cartesian philosophy for feminist thought, such as

Descartes' views concerning error and judgment, his philosophy of the passions, and his ethical ideas concerning virtue. I suggest that the writings of Poullain and Astell are valuable for giving us a strong appreciation of the philosophical sophistication of Cartesian feminism in this era.

Poullain

François Poullain de la Barre is significant for being one of the first writers to follow through on the socio-political implications of Descartes' philosophy. From 1673 to 1675, in three anonymous French works—De L'Égalité des deux sexes [On the Equality of the Two Sexes] (1673), De L'Éducation des dames [On the Education of Ladies] (1674), and De L'Excellence des hommes [On the Excellence of Men] (1675)—Poullain argues in favor of the equality of the sexes. Using Cartesian method, he challenges the prevailing prejudice that women are naturally morally and intellectually inferior and therefore ought to be treated as social inferiors to men. Significantly, he does not attempt a general demolition of opinions or a "willful doubting of all previous knowledge," as Descartes does in the Meditations. Rather, in On the Education of Ladies, Poullain defines a state of general doubt as a "frame of mind, a state of impartiality or of objectivity in which we lean neither to one side nor the other, suspending our judgment until doubt has been allayed" (2002: 175). In this respect, his method bears a resemblance to Descartes's method of avoiding error, or his way of "rightly conducting one's reason," in his Discours de la méthode [Discourse on the Method] (1637) and the Fourth Meditation of the Meditations (both cited in Poullain 2002: 237). Poullain also emulates the methodological approach of Descartes' followers Antoine Arnauld and Pierre Nicole in their 1662 work La Logique, ou l'art de penser [Logic, or the Art of Thinking] (cited in Poullain 2002: 237).

In the aforementioned texts, each author recommends following certain useful rules of thinking in order to find truth. According to Descartes, error is the result of a dysfunctional relationship between the two mental faculties of the will and the understanding. The understanding is a passive faculty of perceiving ideas in the mind, whereas the will is an active faculty of affirming or denying, rejecting or accepting, whatever is presented to it. Error comes about when the intellect presents me with certain ideas, and my will leaps in and rashly affirms those ideas as true or false, without taking time for proper reflection. Error, in other words, is a result of hasty judgments. It is an outcome of the will "getting the jump on" the understanding, so to speak, rather than waiting for the understanding to determine its assent. To avoid error, I must attentively follow the right method of thinking: I must suspend or withhold my judgments about confused and obscure perceptions, and my will must affirm only those ideas that are clear and distinct (Descartes 1984: 40–41).

Along the same lines, in On the Equality, Poullain subjects certain sexist assumptions to "the rule of truth": he resolves to "accept nothing as true unless it is supported by clear and distinct ideas" (2002: 50). This method enables him to challenge ill-founded prejudices—rash judgments, that is, "made without examination" (Poullain 2002: 49, n. 2). Poullain critically examines the common prejudice that women have a native feebleness, that they do not have an aptitude for learning and study in the sciences, and that they are necessarily incapable of virtue due to their inconstancy, timidity, and credulity. In his view, these judgments fail to pass the test of verity. He allows that in early modern society, women are in a state of subjection to men. They are psychologically, intellectually, and financially dependent on men, and they are barred from access to all higher education and any public position that requires a sophisticated level of intelligence and skill. Consequently, as a matter of contingent fact, he says, women exhibit a certain dependence of mind, a seeming intellectual deficiency, and a timidity and reserve in their manner. But in his opinion, this is neither a natural nor a necessary state of affairs.

To demonstrate this point, Poullain highlights the fact that uneducated women often show more common sense than learned men. In their everyday lives, he says, ordinary women give countless examples that they are capable of reasoning about complicated things. History, moreover, has shown us that some women have been the supreme leaders of nations; others have acted as magistrates in various courts of law; and many have shown remarkable valor, bravery, and resolution in defense of their religion (Poullain 2002: 77). In short, he argues that popular generalizations about female incompetence can be readily contradicted by empirical evidence, and that women are perfectly capable of occupying public positions in society. If we were to judge that women's current condition in society is natural or right merely because it *happens* to be the case, then this would be a hasty and potentially erroneous judgment. In keeping with Cartesian method, we must suspend or withhold such judgments.

For Poullain, Cartesian method is not only a negative tool of critique: the method of right thinking also features strongly in his arguments for the claim that women's intellectual deficiencies can be overcome. To deduce the truth, he says, requires only that the mind have a capacity for judgment; anyone who can exercise this capacity in one sphere of inquiry can easily apply it in another. In order to think clearly, a woman has only to apply her mind seriously to the objects before her, "to form clear and distinct ideas of them, to apprehend all aspects of them and their different relationships, and to pass judgment only on what is obviously verifiable" (Poullain: 2002: 85). Like Elisabeth, Poullain shows a keen awareness that a woman's bodily temperament might impede her capacity for reflective judgment, and so he is careful to explain the role of the body in the search for truth. To see this, we need only look to the original context of Poullain's famous marginal note, "l'esprit n'a point de sexe" (literally, "the mind has no sex whatsoever"; see Stuurman 2004: 94). In the passage in question, he aims to show that women are as capable as men of advanced learning. Toward that end, he says:

> It is easy to see that the difference between the two sexes is limited to the body, since that is the only part used in the reproduction of humankind. Since the mind merely gives its consent, and does so in exactly the same way in everyone, we can conclude that it has no sex.
>
> (Poullain 2002: 82)

Shortly thereafter, Poullain affirms that, "A woman's mind is joined to her body, like a man's, by God himself, and according to the same laws" (2002: 82). A woman's mind is intermingled with her body—a woman is thus subject to those feelings, sensations, and imaginings that are a natural consequence of the close association between these two substances. But in this respect, Poullain emphasizes, a woman is no different to a man. In fact, apart from their reproductive organs, men and women have almost no relevant bodily differences: they have the same anatomy, the same brain functions, and the same sensory organs (2002: 83). According to his Cartesian physiology, the life, motion, and sensations of both sexes can be explained by the same mechanical principles (for details, see Stuurman 2004: 105–109).

Since the differences between men and women do not lie in their minds and bodies, Poullain says, the differences must be attributed to outside causal factors, such as education, religion, and other environmental effects. If a woman is to improve her mind, she must come to understand the contribution that her body—and the causal influences *on* that body—make to her perceptions and volitions. More specifically, Poullain proposes that the method of avoiding error can help women to overcome the confusing and disturbing influence of *their passions*. For Poullain, an understanding of the passions is the key to attaining self-knowledge and virtue. The passions are those feelings and emotions—such as wonder, love, hate, sadness, joy, and desire—that occur in the soul as a result of its intimate ties with the body. In the Fourth Conversation in *On the Education*, Poullain's mouthpiece Stasimachus tells us to pay attention to "what our interest is in the objects that excite our passions and what is the basis of this interest" (2002: 217). Once we have recognized those causes that excite our passions, we are in a better position to evaluate their worth and significance. Following such judgments, we might either move towards what is good for us, or turn away from what is bad. Likewise, in *On the Equality*, Poullain affirms that with experience and training we might learn "how we can yoke our will to them [i.e., the causes that excite our passions] or dissociate it from them" (2002: 84).

This last remark problematizes Martina Reuter's claim that Poullain rejects Descartes' notion of free will in favor of a concept of the free intellect (Reuter 2013: 66, 80). Here, like Descartes, Poullain suggests that agents are capable of overcoming the influence of their bodies through the exercise of free will: they might either "yoke" their will to the causes of their passions or "dissociate" it from them. The problem for women is that they are taught to accept everything they are told without question, and so their minds are "too easily carried away by appearances or custom or some other gushing stream" (Poullain 2002: 163). To counteract this, Poullain recommends that, for once in their lives, women stop to examine things seriously, to reflect carefully on their beliefs and desires, and to use their natural capacity for judgment to accept or reject those beliefs and desires accordingly:

> Examine everything, judge everything, reason about everything—about what has been done, what is being done, and what you foresee will be done. But in all cases, don't let yourself be influenced by mere words nor by hearsay. You possess the power of reasoning: use it, and don't sacrifice it blindly to anyone.
> (Poullain 2002: 238)

To resist the mental slavery of custom, an agent must recognize that she herself is responsible for her chains, and that she submits of her "own *free will*" to her subjugation (Poullain 2002: 182; my emphases).

Astell

In the late seventeenth century, strikingly similar ideas and arguments can be found in the writings of Mary Astell. There is no hard evidence that Astell had read Poullain's works, but it's possible that she was familiar with translated excerpts in a popular English periodical, *The Gentleman's Journal*. In May 1692 and October 1693, this journal featured select passages from Poullain's works, titled "The Equality of Both Sexes, asserted by new Arguments" and "An Essay to Prove, that Women May Apply Themselves to Liberal Arts and Sciences." Following in Poullain's footsteps, Astell's first work, *A Serious Proposal to the Ladies* of 1694, is a call for the education of women so that they might become useful members of society; and in her 1697 sequel to this work, she puts forward a method whereby women might improve their minds through critical reasoning. Toward this end, Astell recommends Descartes' *Principia philosophiae* [*Principles of Philosophy*] (1644) and his *Passions of the Soul* (Astell 2002: 172, 218; see also 82) as well as Arnauld and Nicole's *Logic, or the Art of Thinking* (Astell 2002: 166, 184, 189).

Several views abound about the precise nature of Astell's intellectual debt to Descartes. Ruth Perry and Hilda Smith trace Astell's critique of male tyranny back to the Cartesian method of doubt. Perry says that "the key to Astell's [feminist] radicalism is radical doubt, not radical politics" (1986: 332), and Smith links Astell's feminist program with "a strong attachment to Cartesian doubt" (2007: 204) and "a philosophical doubt about all knowledge" (1982: 119). I think that these scholars are right to highlight Astell's deep mistrust of prejudices and preconceptions. In the second part of her *Proposal*, she advises her readers "not [to] give credit to any thing any longer because we have once believ'd it, but because it carries clear and uncontested Evidence along with it" (2002: 133). She suggests that we must "generously . . . disengage our selves from the deceptions of sense," reject those ideas that do not stand "the Test of a Severe Examination and sound Reason," and remove "those Prejudices and Passions which are in our way" (2002: 136, 137, 191).

These remarks, however, must be placed in context. In Astell's wider schema, they are not part of a skeptical annihilation of opinions or a process of hyperbolic doubt, but rather a positive program for the moral and intellectual advancement of women. Like Poullain, Astell claims that women's intellectual deficiencies might be corrected through study and training. Unlike Poullain, however, she rarely points to empirical evidence or to counterexamples that undermine ill-grounded prejudices about women's abilities. Appealing to introspection rather than sensory observation, she simply asserts that "all may *Think*, may use their own Faculties rightly, and consult the Master who is within them" (2002: 168). In her longest work of philosophy, *The Christian Religion* (1705), Astell says that she is:

> A woman who has not the least reason to imagine that her understanding is any better than the rest of her sex's. All the difference, if there be any, arising only from her application, her disinterested, unprejudiced love to truth, and unwearied pursuit of it, notwithstanding all discouragements, which are in every woman's power as well as in hers.
>
> (2013: §401)

To establish that they are likewise capable of attaining truth, Astell urges her fellow women to look within themselves. She suggests that they familiarize themselves with their own natural logic. "I call it natural," she says, "because I shall not send you further than your Own Minds to learn it" (2002: 166). If they are unable to discern this natural capacity, then—sadly—they must be ranked among "the Fools and Idiots," or perhaps even among "the Brutes" (2002: 202, 81). But before they give up in despair, women should reflect again: can they reason about the management of a household, the course of a romance, or the design of a dress? If so, then this is adequate performative evidence of their ability to reason. If we look carefully enough, Astell assures her readers, we will see that truth can be found "in our own Breasts" (2002: 167).

Patricia Springborg has referred to this last remark as Astell's "restatement" of Descartes' *cogito* (see Astell 2002: 167, n. 5). It is not clear, however, that it plays the same role as Descartes's assertion that "*I am, I exist*" is true whenever it is put forward by me or entertained in my mind. For Astell, the claim that "we all *think*, needs no proof" (2013: §229) is not the endpoint of a systematic doubt, or the hallmark of clarity and distinctness; it is the intuitive, self-evident starting point from which to show that women are capable of attaining virtue and knowledge. Astell further differs from Descartes by claiming that "we can't Know the Nature of our Souls Distinctly" (2002: 173). In this respect, she follows the lead of her unorthodox Cartesian contemporaries Nicolas Malebranche and John Norris (see Broad 2015: 64–65). Instead of affirming a clear and distinct idea of the soul, Astell simply points to an internal awareness or immediate consciousness of a certain power or capacity in the mind—more specifically, its capacity for judgment.

Like Descartes, Astell also attributes false or erroneous judgments to the "headstrong and rebellious" will (Astell 2002: 130). Instead of dutifully suspending its assent and regulating its actions according to the understanding, she says, the will rushes forward and hastily affirms ideas as true or false, without proper examination. She allows that her fellow women are particularly prone to making poor judgments. But this failing is due to custom and a limited education—it is an acquired rather than a natural defect. Women might correct this defect by following the Cartesian rules for thinking: by ridding themselves of prejudices, by thinking carefully in an orderly manner, from the simplest ideas to the most complex, and by learning to suspend their judgments until clarity and distinctness win them over (Astell 2002: 135, 137, 159, 164). This is the context in which mistrust, doubt, and skepticism play an important role in Astell's work. "[I]f we would judge to purpose," she says, "we must free ourselves from prejudice and passion, must examine and prove all things, and not give our assent till forced to do so by the evidence of truth" (Astell 2013: §4). Women will benefit from recognizing that they have this "Natural Liberty" within them—a power of judging for themselves—which makes them capable of checking ill-grounded opinions, and adhering only to the truth (Astell 2002: 201).

What role, if any, does the body play in Astell's search for truth? Cynthia Bryson asserts that Astell was attracted to Descartes because "he clearly separates the gendered body from the nongendered 'disembodied mind,' which Astell identifies as the true 'self'" (Bryson 1998: 54). Nevertheless, while it is correct that, for Astell, the mind is the true self and that the mind and body are distinct substances (see Astell 2013: §274, 229), like Descartes she too emphasizes that the mind and body are intimately joined in the human person. "Human nature is indeed a composition of mind and body," she says, "which are two distinct substances having different properties, and yet make but one person. The certainty of this union is not to be disputed, for everyone perceives it in himself" (2013: §272). Following Descartes, Astell allows that in this lifetime the mind can never attain complete *separation* from the body or the bodily influences of the sensations, passions, and appetites (see Atherton 1993: 30; Broad 2015: 85; O'Neill 1999: 242).

In addition, Astell emphasizes that the body might be of "great service" in the search for truth, provided that we know how to employ it (2013: §305). One concern, of course, is that the bodily passions incline women to make poor moral judgments: "we are hurried on to sin and folly," she says, "by rash judgments arising from our passions" (2013: §248). The passions can thus prevent women from arriving at the true and the good. Even in the grip of strong and violent passions, however, women are never completely powerless; there is always some course of action they can take. A woman might permit the passion to continue until it has dissipated, for example, or she might divert it to another object: "tho we may find it difficult absolutely to quash a Passion that is once begun," Astell says, "yet it is no hard matter to transfer it" (2002: 223). Over time, by cultivating her natural capacity for judgment, and regulating the will according to the intellect, a woman might obtain dominion over the passions—she might develop a habitual disposition to direct her passions in accordance with reason. This habitual disposition constitutes *virtue*, according to Astell. Virtue consists in the mind governing the body and directing its passions to worthy objects, in the right "pitch" or intensity, according to reason (2002: 214).

Astell's approach to virtue and the passions strongly resembles that of Descartes in his *Passions of the Soul*. In this book, Descartes, too, advises that we can gain mastery over the passions, and meliorate their discomposing effects, by learning to judge what is truly good and truly evil. For him, the pursuit of virtue consists in a strong resolution always to do what we judge the best. Once we have learnt habitually to regulate our wills in accordance with reason, he says, we will come to direct our passions at the right objects in the right measure; we will attain virtue (for details, see Shapiro 2008). Poullain echoes these same points. In *On the Equality*, he says that virtue consists in a "firm and steadfast resolve to do what one thinks best, depending on the different situations" (2002: 108). In his view, women's minds are more than capable of this steadfast resolve—their bodily differences to men are irrelevant in this respect. "The body," he points out, "is merely the organ and instrument of this resolve, like a sword held ready for attack and defense" (Poullain 2002: 108).

More than this, however, Poullain goes beyond Descartes' ethical ideas to develop a nascent theory of women's *rights*. He argues that happiness is the natural goal of all human actions, and so we all have a right to the means of achieving it. But true happiness cannot be achieved without clear and distinct knowledge about where that happiness lies: that is, in the pursuit of virtue. It follows that, for the sake of their virtue and happiness, women have "an equal right to truth" or a "right to the same knowledge" as men and should therefore be granted access to study and learning (Poullain 2002: 91, 94). "Since both sexes are capable of the same happiness," he says, "they have the same right to all the means of achieving it" (Poullain 2002: 92).

Astell derives similar conclusions from her appropriation of Cartesian ethics. In particular, she holds that the exercise of freedom is a necessary precondition for the attainment of virtue and happiness. For her, true liberty "consists not in a power to do what we will, but in making a right use of our reason, in preserving our judgments free, and our integrity unspotted" (Astell 2013: §249). True liberty is a liberty of judgment—an act of the will in combination with the understanding—rather than the mere freedom to do as we will. This kind of liberty is a vital condition for moral responsibility. To be truly responsible for their choices and actions, women must identify with their choices and actions *as their own*, and not those that others have foisted upon them. On behalf of women, then, Astell defends "that most valuable privilege, and indefeasible right, of judging for ourselves" (2013: §256), and the "just and natural" right of women "to abound in their own sense" (2013: §3).

In sum, these Cartesian feminists mounted a sophisticated and surprisingly modern challenge to common sexist assumptions of their time. There is clearly some truth to the claim that Poullain and Astell, like other feminists of their era, used Cartesian method and the Cartesian concept of the mind to argue against the view that women's bodies necessarily rendered them morally and intellectually incompetent. It is an over-simplification, however, to say that their core feminist insights owe their origins to the method of doubt or to the idea that "the mind has no sex." Poullain and Astell both appropriate Cartesian method for feminist purposes, but for them it is Descartes's method of right thinking, or of avoiding error, that is most salient. And while these thinkers embrace Descartes' notion of the mind as a non-extended thinking substance, they do not overlook the crucial role of the body in the avoidance of error. Their feminism is built on the insight that although minds and bodies are intimately conjoined, women nevertheless have the capacity to gain mastery over the disturbing influence of the bodily passions. For them, the equality of men and women does not lie in the fact that "the mind has no sex," but rather in the claim that men and women equally possess that crucial power or capacity needed to attain knowledge and virtue—the capacity for judgment.

Further Reading

Broad, Jacqueline (2002) *Women Philosophers of the Seventeenth Century*, Cambridge: Cambridge University Press.

Clarke, Stanley (1999) "Descartes's 'Gender,'" in Susan Bordo (Ed.) *Feminist Interpretations of René Descartes*, University Park, PA: Pensylvania State University Press, 82–102.

O'Neill, Eileen (1998) "Disappearing Ink: Early Modern Women Philosophers and Their Fate in History," in Janet A. Kourany (Ed.), *Philosophy in a Feminist Voice: Critiques and Reconstructions*, Princeton, NJ: Princeton University Press, 17–62.

Reuter, Martina (1999) "Questions of Sexual Difference and Equality in Descartes' Philosophy," *Acta Philosophica Fennica* 64: 183–208.

Related Topics

Feminist methods in the history of philosophy (Chapter 1); feminism and the enlightenment (Chapter 8); embodiment and feminist philosophy (Chapter 15); rationality and objectivity in feminist philosophy (Chapter 20); feminism and freedom (Chapter 53).

References

Astell, Mary (2002) *A Serious Proposal to the Ladies, Parts I and II*, Ed. Patricia Springborg, Peterborough, ON: Broadview Press.

——(2013) *The Christian Religion, as Professed by a Daughter of the Church of England*, Ed. Jacqueline Broad, Toronto, ON: Centre for Reformation and Renaissance Studies and Iter Publishing.

Atherton, Margaret (1993) "Cartesian Reason and Gendered Reason," in Louise M. Antony and Charlotte Witt (Eds.) *A Mind of One's Own: Feminist Essays on Reason and Objectivity*, Boulder, CO: Westview Press, 19–34.

Broad, Jacqueline (2015) *The Philosophy of Mary Astell: An Early Modern Theory of Virtue*, Oxford: Oxford University Press.

Bryson, Cynthia (1998) "Mary Astell: Defender of the Disembodied Mind," *Hypatia: A Journal of Feminist Philosophy* 13(4): 40–62.

Clarke, Desmond M. (2013) "Introduction," in Desmond M. Clarke (Ed. and trans.) *The Equality of the Sexes: Three Feminist Texts of the Seventeenth Century*, Oxford: Oxford University Press, 1–53.

Cureau de la Chambre, Marin (1670) *The Art How to Know Men*, trans. John Davies, London: Thomas Basset.

Descartes, René (1984) "Meditations on First Philosophy," in *The Philosophical Writings of Descartes*, vol. 2, trans. John Cottingham, Robert Stoothoff, and Dugald Murdoch, Cambridge: Cambridge University Press.

Elisabeth, Princess of Bohemia, and René Descartes (2007) *The Correspondence between Princess Elisabeth of Bohemia and René Descartes*, trans. and Ed. Lisa Shapiro, Chicago, IL: University of Chicago Press.

Gallagher, Catherine (1988) "Embracing the Absolute: the Politics of the Female Subject in Seventeenth-Century England," *Genders* 1(1): 24–39.

Harth, Erica (1992) *Cartesian Women: Versions and Subversions of Rational Discourse in the Old Regime*, Ithaca, NY: Cornell University Press.

Israel, Jonathan I. (2001) *Radical Enlightenment: Philosophy and the Making of Modernity 1650–1750*, Oxford: Oxford University Press.

O'Neill, Eileen (1999) "Women Cartesians, 'Feminine Philosophy,' and Historical Exclusion," in Susan Bordo (Ed.) *Feminist Interpretations of René Descartes*, University Park, PA: Pennsylvania State University Press, 232–257.

—— (2011) "The Equality of Men and Women," in Desmond M. Clarke and Catherine Wilson (Eds.) *The Oxford Handbook of Philosophy in Early Modern Europe*, Oxford: Oxford University Press, 445–474.

Perry, Ruth (1985) "Radical Doubt and the Liberation of Women," *Eighteenth-Century Studies* 18(4): 472–93.

—— (1986) *The Celebrated Mary Astell: An Early English Feminist*, Chicago, IL: University of Chicago Press.

Poullain de la Barre, François (2002) *Three Cartesian Feminist Treatises*, introduction and annotations by Marcelle Maistre Welch, trans. Vivien Bosley, Chicago, IL: University of Chicago Press.

Reuter, Martina (2013) "Freedom of the Will as the Basis of Equality: Descartes, Princess Elisabeth and Poullain de la Barre," in Quentin Skinner and Martin van Gelderen (Eds.) *Freedom and the Construction of Europe*, vol. 2, Cambridge: Cambridge University Press, 65–83.

Shapiro, Lisa (2008) "Descartes's Ethics," in Janet Broughton and John Carriero (Eds.) *A Companion to Descartes*, Malden, MA: Wiley-Blackwell, 445–463.

Smith, Hilda L. (2007) "'Cry Up Liberty': The Political Context of Mary Astell's Feminism," in William Kolbrener and Michal Michelson (Eds.) *Mary Astell: Reason, Gender, Faith*, Aldershot, UK: Ashgate, 193–204.

—— (1982) *Reason's Disciples: Seventeenth-Century English Feminists*, Urbana, IL: University of Illinois Press.

Stuurman, Siep (2004) *François Poulain de la Barre and the Invention of Modern Equality*, Cambridge, MA: Harvard University Press.

7

FEMINIST ENGAGEMENTS WITH SOCIAL CONTRACT THEORY

Janice Richardson

Introduction

The idea of a social contract is employed in both political and ethical philosophy. In early modern political philosophy, in the seventeenth and eighteenth centuries, the social contract was part of a conjectural history or political idea, mainly associated with the work of Hobbes, Locke, Rousseau, and Kant. They used it in order to justify obedience to the law based only upon the consent of the governed. Each author told a story about the transition from the state of nature to that of civil society, a state with a sovereign and laws, which took place as a result of a social contract. All viewed the political organization of society as something that is constructed by human beings, rejecting the previous assumptions that there is a natural hierarchy between men and that sovereigns rule as an expression of God's will. However, there is an inconsistency in these progressive stories with regard to women, whom the classic theorists—with the possible exception of Hobbes—continued to view as natural subordinates to men.

Classic social contract theorists actually wrote about women. It was only later that discussions about the sexes became marginalized as irrelevant to political philosophy and earlier feminist arguments ignored. Social contract theory went into abeyance but, when it regained popularity after Rawls published *A Theory of Justice* in 1971, it continued this later trend of depoliticizing the position of women. Feminist theory therefore marks a radical shift by forcing mainstream political theorists to recognize that women's subordination is a *political* problem. In her groundbreaking attack on social contract theory, Carole Pateman (Brennan and Pateman 1979; Pateman 1988; 1989) analyses the political assumptions that come to light when the position of women is considered. In the second section below, I will detail Pateman's arguments, including her view that it is through contract that subordination is created and managed in modernity (on which, see also Chapter 52 in this volume).

Turning from politics to ethics, in her essay "Feminist Contractarianism," Jean Hampton produces an ethical theory of the social contract. Hampton distinguishes between two types of contract: one derived from Hobbes and the other from Kant. As a Kantian, Hampton characterizes the Hobbesian position as only mimicking morality

(Hampton 2007: 13). Hobbes claims that it is prudent to appear to treat people with respect and to maintain contracts (so long as others do the same). This "advice to the fool" who would betray the trust of others (Hobbes 1994: chap. XV, 90) has been taken up by game theorists, in particular David Gauthier (1987) and also a few feminists (Dimock 2008). Hobbesian "morality" is based upon self-interest, in contrast to Kant's position in which persons are to be respected as having equal intrinsic worth.

Kant himself was dubious as to whether women could be classed as moral persons (1960: 79–81 [2: 229–231]). Nevertheless, Hampton (2002; 2007) employs the Kantian idea of a contract to ask of a heterosexual relationship (with marriage in mind): "would free and equal persons agree to this relationship?" and she does not accept any false sense of duty, or emotional ties on behalf of the wife, to justify exploitation. Again, this involves a major shift in thinking as she highlights a moral problem that arises when women are taught always to prioritize the interests of others at the expense of their own needs. In the third section I will detail the implications of Hampton's use of the social contract as a test for fairness in heterosexual relationships.

There are areas in which the distinction between the political and ethical divide in social contract theory blurs. Pateman is critical of the way that social contract theory in the twentieth century, under the influence of Rawls (1999), diminishes political philosophy by situating it as moral philosophy:

> Political philosophy has been turned into moral philosophy . . . Moreover, theories of original contracts are not about moral reasoning . . . they are about the creation and justification of specific forms of political order; they are about the creation of the modern state and structures of power, including sexual and racial power.
>
> (Pateman and Mills 2007: 20)

Hampton (2007: 8) points out that philosophy is often influenced by a mental picture, even if philosophers are loathe to admit it. Liberal social contract theorists envisage free and equal persons sitting around a table, and ask what they would agree to. While Hampton employs this question as a test for fairness in heterosexual relationships, Rawls employs it to attempt to justify liberal principles by asking what persons would agree to if they were asked what sort of society they would join, without knowing their position within it—that is, deciding under a "veil of ignorance" (Rawls 1999). The aim of these thought experiments is to prompt fairness. This is not achieved by relying upon the hypothetical contract functioning as an actual agreement. It is to focus the mind on the position of the worst off in a society.

It now seems remarkable that Rawls was initially blind to the position of women. In his thought experiment in the original A Theory of Justice published in 1971, he envisaged male "heads of household" who were to decide the principles of a society, without recognizing that there was (and still is) a conflict of interest within the traditional heterosexual family. It is important to remember the possibility of this type of blindness to an area of subordination years after Susan Moller Okin (1989) pointed out this deficiency in Rawls' thought experiment. She employs Rawls' Kantian image of free and equal persons, turning it to feminist ends by prompting the reader to ask: Would free and equal persons agree to be women in our society? How would you like it?

Feminist philosophy often challenges the usual ways in which philosophy is categorized. The question of what free and equal persons would agree to, as a test of equal worth, has been employed by feminist theorists from very different traditions. Continental philosopher and lawyer Drucilla Cornell (1995: ch. 1) adopts this question in a manner that shares some similarities with Hampton. Both treat the question as an evocative test that is to be repeatedly asked in certain circumstances, in contrast to Rawls' one-off posing of the question in his thought experiment. For Hampton, the question functions as a way of consciousness-raising, to focus upon whether a heterosexual relationship is one in which the extent of inequality indicates a lack of respect for the equal worth of the parties. In contrast, Cornell proposes that the question is to be employed whenever common law judges or legislators make a legal decision. In other words, these legal decisions are to be underpinned by the principles of equality by employing the question of whether free and equal persons could agree to them. If judges allow their stereotyped images of women to influence their judgement, then this indicates that they are being unreasonable and thereby failing in their public duty.

Cornell (2000) also develops her position to support rights in terms of race. Similarly, Charles Mills (1997) has drawn from Pateman, Okin, and Hampton to argue for the political usefulness of thinking of a racial contract. Like Rawls and Okin, Mills employs the thought experiment of free and equal persons deciding on the principles of a society, under the veil of ignorance. Whereas Okin (1989) points out that the participants should be viewed as not knowing their gender, prompting the question of whether free and equal persons would agree to be female in our society, Mills asks this question with regard to race. Mills' aim is to speak to Rawlsians in their own terms and to produce a "subversive social contract," akin to that of Okin on gender, Rousseau on class, and, Mills argues, Pateman. However, Pateman resists this characterization of her work, as I will discuss in detail below. In addition to adopting the idea of a social contract to highlight racism, there have been diverse arguments on the relationship between the social contract and disability (Becker 2005) and lesbians (Wittig 1989).

I will now consider in more detail, first, the classic social contract theorists; second, Pateman's political analysis; and third, Hampton's ethics. In the fourth and final section I will draw out the differences in the main feminist positions on social contract theory, both in its political and ethical forms.

The Classic Social Contract Theorists

Hobbes' *Leviathan*, published in 1651, was radical in starting with an image of human beings as naturally free and equal in a state of nature and arguing that political arrangements are socially constructed. In this conjectural history, Hobbes describes a transition from the state of nature to a civil society with laws. The reason for this transition is based upon the need to escape the state of nature in which life is "solitary, poor, nasty brutish and short" (Hobbes 1994: ch. XIII [9], 149). It is a cautionary tale, influenced by the English civil war, that warns of what would happen without a sovereign. Hobbes' arguments are based upon his images of humanity: as selfish, acquisitive, competing individuals, who are also rational enough to recognize the benefits of a social contract and to create a sovereign, whose role is to enforce law—and hence contractual agreements—by the use of force.

In our natural state, without marriage contracts, there would be no assumption that the man would be the head of a family. As usual, Hobbes is practical. Given that the woman would be the only one who may know the identity of the father of her child and could choose not to tell him: "the right of dominion over the child dependeth upon her will, and is consequently hers" (Hobbes 1994: ch. XX [5], 129). Further, in any dispute between men and women, Hobbes does not assume that men will win:

> And whereas some have attributed the dominion to the man only, as being of the more excellent sex, they misreckon in it. For there is not always that differ-ence of strength or prudence between the man and the woman as that the right can be determined without war.
>
> (Hobbes 1994: ch. XX [4], 128)

Pateman therefore highlights an inconsistency in Hobbes' otherwise rigorously told story: why should women, who are not subordinate in a state of nature, join a social contract as a result of which—in Hobbes' time—marriage laws would be enacted that would render them subordinate to men? I will discuss this further below.

In contrast, Locke views as natural a family form in which wives are subordinate to their husbands (1988a: ch. V §27, 174). Locke's conjectural history is a story of natural property owners who are also able to use money. However, in a state of nature, indi-viduals have the right to enforce justice against anyone who wrongs them and many are biased in their own cause. Male heads of household are therefore motivated to enter into a social contract to have a sovereign to guarantee impartial justice and preserve property rights. Locke's justification for private property (1988b: ch. V) is the origin of "property in the person," which is central to Pateman's critique of contract, to be discussed below. Locke's move of viewing male dominance in the family as natural is central to Rousseau's strongly misogynist understanding of women and the sentimental family, as described in his story of the transition from the state of nature to civil society (see for example, Okin 2002).

Kant's social contract theory differs from those of Hobbes, Locke, and Rousseau in that Kant does not speculate on life in a state of nature. Instead, Kant describes the social contract as an idea that we have as a result of our ability to reason,

> [The social contract] is in fact merely an *idea* of reason, which nonetheless has undoubted practical reality; for it can oblige every legislator to frame his laws in such a way that they could have been produced by the united will of a whole nation and regard each subject, in so far as he can claim citizenship, as if he had consented to the general will.
>
> (Kant 1991: 79 [8: 35–42])

Kant draws a distinction between the faculties of reason and understanding that differs from previous uses by Plato and Aristotle. As an "idea of reason," the social contract can be distinguished from a concept of the understanding. The idea of a social contract is therefore similar to ideas of God or freedom. It does not relate to objects of experi-ence (which we can understand), but nevertheless it can be thought and is related to morality. As the above quotation illustrates, Kant employs the idea of the social contract as a test for legitimacy of laws. For example, he argues against enactment of hereditary privilege on the grounds that free and equal persons could not agree to such laws (Kant 1996: 139 [6: 329]).

The Political Social Contract: Carole Pateman

Pateman's *The Sexual Contract* (1988) marks a decisive moment in feminist critique of the social contract. She asks why a progressive political argument against natural hierarchy, in the seventeenth and eighteenth centuries, did not include women. She shows the inter-relationship between different areas of subordination and is practical in her analysis of freedom, providing a theoretical basis in support of greater workplace democracy and a basic income. Pateman adds a fiction of her own to the social contract stories. She points to a "sexual contract" between men that allows them access to women's sexual and other labour and that perpetuates and manages women's subordination. In civil society, the sovereign passes laws, including marriage laws that—at the time that the classic social contract theorists were writing—included the doctrine of coverture, under which women were effectively civil slaves to their husbands. Without an assumption that women's subordination is natural, social contract theorists cannot explain why women in their stories would enter into a social contract that, through marriage laws, would render them subordinate to men. In this way, Pateman also draws a link between the social contract and the marriage contract.

Pateman's analysis of the meaning of "contract" in modernity brings together the social contract with marriage contracts and employment contracts in an unusual way. It allows her to take the imaginative step of examining the position of the weaker party in a "contract" as envisaged in both political theory and in legal practice. She thereby invites us to compare the relationships between sovereign and subject alongside those of employer and employee *and* traditional husband and wife. In each case the contract *creates* a weaker party, who supposedly freely consents to obey the other party. The fact that they do not expect to have their voices heard undermines the possibility of participative democracy.

Pateman examines and problematizes the idea of the consent of the weaker parties in these contracts. All are viewed as exchanging "property in the person," which acts as a political and legal fiction to "justify" subordination. The type of "property in the person" envisaged cannot be separated from the human body and so involves a relationship based upon obedience. In the classic social contract theories individuals are envisaged as giving up their right of self-government to different degrees, depending upon the theorist. Similarly, as Marx points out, in the employment contract employees' exchange of their labour power for a wage means that they expect to be told what to do within the workplace (1976: 280). In the traditional marriage contract—which Pateman situates as having its "heyday" between 1840 and 1970 (1996: 204)—the wife was expected to provide *consortium* (sex and housework). Unlike employees, she was not treated as owning her own labour power, and her labour in the home was unlimited in time and was exchanged for financial support rather than a wage. Divorce remained blocked by law well after workers gained the right to leave their employer, leaving aside the financial and other "exit costs" that both suffer. By attacking the myth of the consent of the governed, in the widest sense of the phrase, Pateman also undermines the image of liberal individuals whose reasons for acting are viewed as deriving from their own free will rather than being socially situated.

Hence Pateman draws from, but importantly extends, Macpherson's (1962) criticism of social contract theories. Pateman argues that whereas in feudalism there were clear hierarchies based upon the idea of natural status, in modernity hierarchical relations are created (and governed) by contracts that involve the exchange of property in the person. Pateman provides the other neglected side of Macpherson's analysis, which focuses only upon citizens and employees. Even in the twentieth century, the welfare state assumed the model of a husband/breadwinner and wife, and the courts employed the fiction of "implied contractual terms" in marriage to women's detriment. ("Implied terms" are contractual terms that a court will assume to be part of contracts even though they are not stated. They are employed to allow courts to regulate contracts.) One implied term was that women's consent to marriage was also consent to have sex with her husband at any time. The effect was to place husbands beyond the reach of the criminal rape law in the UK and Australia until 1991. The use of this legal fiction also regulates employment contracts. For example, there is an implied term that workers are expected to obey reasonable orders.

Today contract law courses still only focus upon one-off transactions rather than contracts that create and broadly regulate relationships. It still appears to be odd to link the social contract—a story of individuals' agreement to create a sovereign to rule them—with employment contracts and marriage contracts. Yet all of these contracts are used to explain and, through law, to regulate obedience, and all envisage relationships that endure through the fictional exchange of property in the person.

Pateman traces the history of early modern political theory to highlight differences between social contract theories in ways that are still relevant today. She argues that:

> Hobbes was too revealing about civil society. The political character of the conjugal right was expertly concealed in Locke's separation of what he called "paternal" power from political power and, ever since, most political theorists, whatever their views about other forms of subordination, have accepted that powers of husbands derive from nature and hence are not political.
>
> (Pateman 1989: 462)

For Pateman, Locke closes down an argument in support of women's natural equality that arose when Hobbes' political analysis started with individuals rather than the traditional heterosexual family. Ironically, Locke holds a politically progressive position but ultimately excludes women. In the first part of the *Two Treatises of Government* Locke (1988a) argues against Filmer's support for the divine right of kings to rule based upon paternal power. Pateman points out that Locke's discussion of paternal power—the power of fathers over their children—occludes his additional assumption that husbands naturally exercise power over their wives: "When paternal power is seen as paradigmatic of natural subjection, critical questions about the designation of sexual and conjugal rights as natural are all too easily disregarded" (Pateman 1988: 92).

Locke draws an insidious distinction between male power within the traditional family and *political* power. It is this division of power into two types—one to be exercised within the household and the other in the state—that explains Locke's inconsistency regarding women. It allows him to reject the naturalness of male hierarchy while dismissing women's subordination within the household as falling outside of politics. This idea of women's natural subordination to men within marriage was subsequently continued in the form of the claim that women's "place in the home" was natural and not properly discussed as part of political philosophy.

Pateman's use of the "sexual contract" in her analysis has been criticized on the grounds that it "rests on an unspecified and unwarranted essentialist conception of historical development that makes it impossible to alter institutions and practices without first rooting out their historical foundations" (Schochet 2007: 241). In response to this line of argument, Pateman points out that she did not aim to produce an origin story herself (Pateman and Mills 2007). The fictional "sexual contract" is employed to illustrate a point, as part of an analysis of the origin stories of the classic social contractarians. The classic social contract tales work "as if" there were also a sexual contract.

In addition to questioning Pateman's dismissal of contract for feminist ends, Okin (1990: 666) argues that Pateman moves ambiguously between a critique of liberal social contract theory and of libertarianism in her analysis of contract. However, as Okin recognizes, one of Pateman's central concerns is the fiction that we can exchange or commodify human abilities. This fiction is relied upon in both liberal and neo-liberal societies, being the basis of the institution of employment as well as traditional marriage.

The Ethical Social Contract: Jean Hampton

Whereas Pateman is critical of the social contract, Hampton applies the Kantian/Rawlsian idea of asking what individuals would agree to, if given the choice. In her paper, "Feminist Contractarianism," she describes the test of fairness in relationships in the following terms:

> Given the fact that we are in this relationship, could both of us reasonably accept the distribution of costs and benefits (that is, the costs and benefits that are not themselves side effects of any affective or duty-based tie between us) if it were the subject of an informed, unforced agreement in which we think of ourselves as motivated solely by self-interest?
>
> (Hampton 2007: 21)

Hampton bases her test question on Kant's claim that we all have equal moral worth. Her work reminds women that this involves treating *themselves* as equal. When they perceive themselves as owing a "false duty" to look after others to such an extent that they are exploited, then they fail in their duty to treat themselves as being of equal moral worth. What I am calling a "false duty" can therefore function just like "emotional ties," by prompting women to maintain exploitative heterosexual relationships in which they are treated as having lower moral worth than their male partner. If these areas of leverage are not excluded then the husband is effectively saying: you put more into this relationship because it is your role as a woman or because you love me more.

Similarly, in the Hobbesian version of contractarian morality, the adoption of "non-tuism" has been argued to be necessary for women to avoid exploitation (Dimock 2008). Non-tuism is the assumption that individuals must be treated as disinterested in the other parties' preferences when asking what individuals would agree to in a hypothetical contract. This is not because human beings are actually disinterested in each other—as their *preferences* themselves may prioritize others' welfare—but because as Gauthier puts it,

> [T]he contractarian sees sociability as enriching human life; for him, it becomes a source of exploitation if it induces persons to acquiesce in institutions and practices that but for their fellow-feelings would be costly to them. Feminist thought has surely made this, perhaps the core form of human exploitation, clear to us.
>
> (Gauthier 1987: 11)

While claiming that the basis for her test is that of equal moral worth (and hence moral realism) rather than that of exploitation per se, Hampton has also explained that she finds evocative Hobbes' claim that "we are not under any obligation to make ourselves prey to others" (Hampton and Pyle 1999: 236; Hobbes 1994: ch. XIV [5] 80). However, it should be stressed that her test serves simply to demonstrate when a relationship is so one-sided as to indicate a lack of respect for equal worth (that one is making oneself the prey of another) and is *not* the same as the Hobbesian contract position of considering what would be the best possible deal available. This is what separates Hampton's Kantian use of contract ("contractualism") from the Hobbesian one ("contractarianism"). The implication of Hampton's Kantianism is that if there were no marriages that would allow her to respect herself as of equal worth then she should not marry, because of her duty to herself. In contrast, for Hobbesians, you make the best deal possible, given that one's worth is nothing more than one's price (Hobbes 1994: ch. X [16] 51).

Like Pateman, Hampton focuses upon subordination. For Hampton, exploitation (as indicated in the hypothetical contract by the fact that the woman would not agree to the basis of the marital relationship if not for leverage as a result of falsely perceived duty and affection) indicates that she is being treated as having unequal moral worth and hence as a subordinate. In contrast, Pateman traces the history of different types of subordination, which facilitate exploitation. With regard to this aspect of their work, Hampton, as a liberal, is reframing Rawls but Pateman, in part, extends and refocuses Marx.

Hampton also employs her Kantian contractualist analysis to understand the criminal law and to address the question of when forgiveness is acceptable. This is based upon the view of crime as occurring when the criminal holds himself (or herself) above the victim in terms of moral worth. (In terms of Hampton's test for unfairness in relationships it would be at the extreme end of failure.) Criminal law judges are therefore under a duty to make a public statement, by the punishment, that the criminal was wrong to hold himself (or herself) above the victim. This is not achieved if, for example, the penalty for rape, or for hate crimes generally, is derisory. From within her critique of classic social contract theory, Pateman (1979) approaches the same problem—that of gaining justice for female victims under criminal law—when she points out that some citizens do not receive the same advantages as others from living in a state and yet receive more burdens.

Feminists whose work promotes an ethic of care are major critics of any use of social contract theory, specifically criticising Hampton. Virginia Held (1987), for example, argues that the paradigmatic image of these contracting individuals is that of economic man, characterized as selfish and individualistic. Hampton's response is that she derives an objective morality from her Kantian position from which to claim justice for women, and that whether the images of the parties to the contract appear to be male because of our empirical practices is irrelevant to this normative position. In response, Held argues that it is individualism, implicit within the use of a hypothetical contract, as a *moral ideal* that is the subject of her critique. There have also been criticisms of Kantian personhood in the feminist continental philosophical tradition. For example, Irigaray argues that, by "adding in" women to the conception of the Kantian person, the possibility of sexual difference is closed down, to women's detriment (Irigaray 1985; see also Battersby 1998).

Held's concern that the individual envisaged within the hypothetical contract is unencumbered, and stereotypically male, is consistent with Pateman's historically situated analysis of the emergence and interaction of different forms of subordination in relation to women and class (and race in her later analysis of the white settler contract in Pateman and Mills 2007). Held cites Pateman approvingly when Pateman complains that, "One of the most striking features of the last two decades is the extent to which the assumptions of liberal individualism have permeated the whole of social life" (Pateman 1985: 182–183; cited in Held 1987: 111). This raises questions about the extent to which different feminist responses to social contract theory are compatible and about the areas of debate between these theorists.

Are Feminist Perspectives on the Social Contract Compatible?

In his conversation with Pateman, Mills argues that Pateman's work is compatible with that of Hampton; that Pateman's analysis does not undermine the Kantian idea of equal worth (Pateman and Mills 2007). This repeats a point made by Okin (1989). It leads Mills to argue that Pateman's "sexual contract" could be viewed as a non-ideal, subversive contract, within the social contract tradition itself. Pateman resists this positioning of her work. I will now consider this debate before comparing Cornell's framework with that of Hampton and then Pateman (see Richardson 2009).

Pateman claims that Hampton "lets the cat out of the bag" because Hampton does not require a reference to a hypothetical contract to make her arguments based on equal moral worth (Pateman and Mills 2007: 22). Mills agrees and—on this basis—argues that Pateman's criticism of social contract theory has no bite against Hampton's use of it. However, Pateman's central concern is that subordination is perpetuated and participatory democracy is undermined by a particular type of contract involving the fictional exchange of property in the person. Therefore it is unsurprising that she resists the unnecessary legitimation of the idea of contract as symbolic of fairness in a thought experiment. While Mills finds the idea of the "subversive contract" a useful way to respond to Rawlsian liberals in their own language, Pateman simply rejects their approach to political philosophy.

Similarly, Pateman argues that Okin's re-reading of Rawls—to ask if free and equal persons, beneath the veil of ignorance, would agree to be women in our patriarchal society—is also unnecessary. Okin's arguments regarding injustice in the traditional family do not depend upon it (Pateman and Mills 2007: 22). Pateman goes on to explain why such a contractual procedure is not only unnecessary but distracts from truly political questions: "The pertinent question for me is what policies may be feasible and have a reasonable chance of moving things in a more democratic direction. And that also requires an analysis of what is wrong at present" (Pateman and Mills 2007: 22).

What of the continental theorist Drucilla Cornell? I will compare her work with that of Hampton then Pateman. Cornell draws from Kant's idea of the agreement of free and equal persons to make a claim against judges and the legislature. However, she distinguishes her position from that of Hampton (Cornell 1995: 242, fn16). Cornell refuses to be classified as a "contractarian" to the extent that this means employing the contract as a "moral or justice proof procedure" (1995: 242, fn16). However, as discussed above, Hampton's position only depends upon equal moral worth, not the hypothetical contract per se. Where Cornell and Hampton really differ, aside from their uses of the hypothetical contract, is in terms of Cornell's position on selfhood and our use of imagination. She argues that in order to have a democracy, it is necessary to have people who are able to *become* citizens, and she holds an anti-humanist position in which the process of individuation—of becoming an individual separate from others—is itself a problem.

Hampton supports her own analysis by showing how boys are brought up to have a greater sense of entitlement than girls. For Cornell, adopting a Lacanian psychoanalytic view, self-development does not end with childhood. Instead we continually struggle to become "persons," capable of citizenship. As a result, Cornell argues that free and equal persons would not agree to laws that would undermine their "project of becoming a person" in the first place. This "project" is threatened by sexual harassment, for example, because it can interfere with someone's *imago*, or ideal self-image. As a lawyer, Cornell extends that move to argue for specific laws and an underpinning of legal decisions by repeating the question of what free and equal persons would agree to, whereas Hampton's test is to detect injustice in relationships.

Turning to the contrast between Cornell and Pateman, Pateman also asks what it takes to produce citizens (1970: 24–25). In contrast to Cornell's use of Lacan, Pateman draws from Rousseau (1968). She argues that participative democracy can only occur if prospective citizens expect to have their voices heard in their everyday lives, rather than imagining that they exchange or sell parts of themselves in the traditional home and the workplace. The necessary skills and confidence to participate in citizenship are learned when we have the opportunity to negotiate and say what we agree to *in practice*, as in workplace democracy. Pateman, as a political philosopher, details the history of subordination through contract to support her contemporary arguments for a basic income and in favour of a participative democracy. While Cornell may be sympathetic with these claims, she argues for the basis of law to be formulated in terms of equal respect for moral worth.

Feminist philosophers' engagements with social contract theory are rich and diverse. A major divide lies between critics of social contract theory and those who try to use it for feminist ends; those who view the tradition as political, and those who view it as producing techniques for thinking about ethics and for game theory. The extent to which these positions are compatible depends upon theorists' wider political analyses and their conceptions of what it is to be human.

Further Reading

Abbey, Ruth (Ed.) (2013) *Feminist Interpretations of John Rawls*, University Park, PA: Pennsylvania State University Press.

Carver, Terrell and Chambers, Samuel A. (2013) *Carole Pateman: Democracy, Feminism, Welfare*, Hoboken, NJ: Taylor & Francis.

Cudd, Ann (2013) "Contractarianism," in Edward N. Zalta (Ed.) *The Stanford Encyclopedia of Philosophy*, Winter 2013 edition. Available from: http://plato.stanford.edu/archives/win2013/entries/contractarianism/.

Hirschmann, Nancy J. and Wright, Joanne Harriet (Eds.) (2012) *Feminist Interpretations of Thomas Hobbes*, University Park, PA: Pennsylvania State University Press.

O'Neill, Daniel I., Shanley, Mary Lyndon, and Young, Iris Marion (Eds.) (2008) *Illusion of Consent: Engaging with Carole Pateman*, Pennsylvania, PA: Pennsylvania State University Press.

Richardson, Janice (2007) "Contemporary Feminist Perspectives on Social Contract Theory," *Ratio Juris* 20(3): 402–423.

Sample, Ruth J. (2002) "Why Feminist Contractarianism?" *Journal of Social Philosophy* 33(2): 257–281.

Related Topics

Feminist methods in the history of philosophy (Chapter 1); feminism and the Enlightenment (Chapter 8); critical race theory, intersectionality, and feminist philosophy (Chapter 29); feminist metaethics (Chapter 42); feminism, structural injustice, and responsibility (Chapter 49); feminism and liberalism (Chapter 52); feminism and freedom (Chapter 53); feminist philosophy of law, legal positivism, and non-ideal theory (Chapter 56).

References

Battersby, Christine (1998) *The Phenomenal Woman: Feminist Metaphysics and the Patterns of Identity*, London: Routledge.

Becker, Lawrence C. (2005) "Reciprocity, Justice, and Disability," *Ethics* 116(1): 9–39.

Brennan, Teresa and Pateman, Carole (1979) "'Mere Auxiliaries to the Commonwealth': Women and the Origins of Liberalism," *Political Studies* 27(2): 183–200.

Cornell, Drucilla (1995) *The Imaginary Domain: Abortion, Pornography and Sexual Harassment*, London: Routledge.

——(2000) "Spanish Language Rights: Identification, Freedom, and the Imaginary Domain," in *Just Cause: Freedom, Identity, and Rights*, Lanham, MD: Rowman & Littlefield, 129–154.

Dimock, Susan (2008) "Why All Feminists Should Be Contractarians," *Dialogue: Canadian Philosophical Review/Revue Canadienne de Philosophie* 47(2): 273–290.

Gauthier, David P. (1987) *Morals by Agreement*, new ed., Oxford: Clarendon.

Hampton, Jean (2002) "Feminist Contractarianism," in Louise M. Antony and Charlotte Witt (Eds.) *A Mind of One's Own: Feminist Essays on Reason and Objectivity*, Boulder, CO: Westview Press, 337–368.

—— (2007) "Feminist Contractarianism," in David Farnham (Ed.) *The Intrinsic Worth of Persons: Contractarianism in Moral and Political Philosophy*, Cambridge: Cambridge University Press, 1–38.

Hampton, Jean, and Pyle, Andrew (1999) "Jean Hampton," in Andrew Pyle (Ed.) *Key Philosophers in Conversation*, London: Routledge, 231–239.

Held, Virginia (1987) "Non-Contractual Society: A Feminist View," *Canadian Journal of Philosophy* 17(supplement 1): 111–137.

Hobbes, Thomas (1994) *Leviathan: With Selected Variants from the Latin Edition of 1668*, Edwin Curley (Ed.) Indianapolis, IN: Hackett.

Irigaray, Luce (1985) *Speculum of the Other Woman*, trans. Gillian C. Gill, Ithaca, NY: Cornell University Press.

Kant, Immanuel (1960) *Observations on the Feeling of the Beautiful and Sublime*, trans. John T. Goldthwait, Berkeley, CA: University of California Press.

—— (1991) "An Answer to the Question: 'What Is Enlightenment?'" in H. S. Reiss (Ed.) *Kant: Political Writings*, 2nd ed., Cambridge: Cambridge University Press, 54–60.

—— (1996) *The Metaphysics of Morals*, Roger J. Sullivan (Ed.), trans. Mary J. Gregor, 2nd revised ed., Cambridge: Cambridge University Press.

Locke, John (1988a) "First Treatise," in Peter Laslett (Ed.) *Locke: Two Treatises of Government*, Cambridge: Cambridge University Press.

—— (1988b) "Second Treatise," in Peter Laslett (Ed.) *Locke: Two Treatises of Government*, Cambridge: Cambridge University Press.

Macpherson, Crawford Brough (1962) *The Political Theory of Possessive Individualism: Hobbes to Locke*, Oxford: Clarendon Press.

Marx, Karl (1976) *Capital: Volume 1: A Critique of Political Economy*, trans. Ben Fowkes, London: Penguin.

Mills, Charles W. (1997) *The Racial Contract*, Ithaca, NY: Cornell University Press.

Okin, Susan Moller (1989) "Justice as Fairness: For Whom?" in *Justice, Gender, and the Family*, New York: Basic Books, 89–109.

—— (1990) "Feminism, the Individual, and Contract Theory," *Ethics* 100(3): 658–69.

—— (2002) "The Fate of Rousseau's Heroines," in Lydia Lange (Ed.) *Feminist Interpretations of Jean-Jacques Rousseau*, University Park, PA: Penn State University Press, 89–112.

Pateman, Carole (1970) *Participation and Democratic Theory*, Cambridge: Cambridge University Press.

—— (1979) *The Problem of Political Obligation: A Critique of Liberal Theory*, Chichester: Wiley.

—— (1985) *The Problem of Political Obligation: A Critique of Liberal Theory*, Berkeley, CA: University of California Press.

—— (1988) *The Sexual Contract*, Cambridge: Polity Press.

—— (1989) "'God Hath Ordained to Man a Helper': Hobbes, Patriarchy and Conjugal Right," *British Journal of Political Science* 19(4): 445–463.

—— (1996) "A Comment on Johnson's Does Capitalism Really Need Patriarchy," *Women's Studies International Forum* 19(3): 203–205.

Pateman, Carole and Mills, Charles W. (2007) *Contract and Domination*, Cambridge: Polity Press.

Rawls, John (1999) *A Theory of Justice*, 2nd ed., Oxford: Oxford University Press.

Richardson, Janice (2009) *The Classic Social Contractarians*, London: Ashgate.

Rousseau, Jean-Jacques (1968) *The Social Contract*, trans. Maurice Cranston, London: Penguin.

Schochet, Gordon J. (2007) "Models of Politics and the Place of Women in Locke's Political Thought," in Nancy J. Hirschmann and Kirstie Morna McClure (Eds.) *Feminist Interpretations of John Locke*, University Park, PA: Penn State University Press, 131–154.

Wittig, Monique (1989) "On the Social Contract," *Feminist Issues* 9(1): 3–12.

8

FEMINISM AND THE ENLIGHTENMENT

Susanne Lettow

The Enlightenment and its legacies are highly controversial among contemporary feminist philosophers. Since the eighteenth century, the notions of reason, equality, and human rights have played an important role in denouncing and resisting domination and exploitation. To a great extent, feminists have articulated critiques of gender hierarchies in the language of the Enlightenment. At the same time, feminist philosophers have explored and criticized the structural limitations of Enlightenment discourse, and have argued that—far from being truly universal—the notions of equality, reason, progress, tolerance, and human rights foster prejudice, exclusion, and domination. In many respects, feminist critiques that explore the "dark" side of these "bright" concepts converge with other critical perspectives, in particular from postcolonial studies, poststructuralism, critical Marxism, and the early Frankfurt School, which have all—in one way or the other—exposed the dialectics of Enlightenment. Accordingly, the Enlightenment claim to scrutinize all forms of authority and power and to conceive of society based on the principle of equality is understood as being structurally intertwined with multiple forms of domination in terms of gender, race, class, and empire.

The question open for discussion is whether feminist critiques of the Enlightenment still need to build on and re-enact the legacy of the Enlightenment, or whether a new theoretical language that overcomes the discourse of the Enlightenment as it emerged in eighteenth-century Europe has to be shaped. A close look at the philosophical interventions made by feminists in the historical period of the Enlightenment itself, i.e. the eighteenth century, is certainly helpful for a better understanding of this problem, since it makes clear that "the Enlightenment" has always been a contested discursive space, where a wide variety of arguments and interventions were formulated, and where feminists sought to challenge established gender hierarchies.

The Plurality of the Enlightenment

Many feminist scholars argue that the monolithic understanding of the Enlightenment that has long prevailed in the history of ideas needs to be replaced with a more open and plural understanding that allows one to conceive of the Enlightenment as a collection of "disparate and often contradictory phenomena" (DeLucia 2015: 9). Such a view focuses on debates, controversies, and intellectual networks and practices through which certain ideas came to circulate in the eighteenth century, rather than on fixed concepts. "Enlightenment," as Sarah Knott and Barbara Taylor argue, "was a living world where ideas were conveyed not only through 'high' philosophical works but also through novels, poetry, advice literature, popular theology, journalism, pornography, and that most fluid of eighteenth-century genres, the 'miscellaneous essay'" (Knott and Taylor 2005: xvii). Women's contributions to the discourse of Enlightenment took many different forms, most prominently letter writing and the management of "salons." In order to fully grasp how women's intellectual contributions helped to shape Enlightenment discourse, it is important to note that in the eighteenth century no clear boundaries existed between science, literature, philosophy, letter writing, journalism, etc., and that the invention of new intellectual practices was a major concern for Enlightenment thinkers. In fact, assessing the philosophical impact of women and feminist thought requires one to challenge a narrow, disciplinary, and anachronistic notion of philosophy and endorse a broader understanding of philosophical activity.

Not only was the Enlightenment constituted through a wide range of theoretical practices, but also this intellectual movement took different shapes in the various European countries and regions. Debates were loosely connected through the transnational circulation of ideas, books, and persons, so that similarities as well as differences between the multiple Enlightenments exist. In France, the institution of the salon flourished in the second half of the eighteenth century and became the paradigmatic institution of the Enlightenment. It "upheld both reciprocal exchange and the principle of governance by substituting a female *salonnière* for a male king as the governor of its discourse" (Goodman 1994: 5). Guided by women such as Marie-Thérèse Geoffrin, Anne-Catherine de Lignville Helvétuis, Julie de Lespinasse, and Suzanne Necker, the salon constituted a "mixed-gender sociability" (Goodman 1994: 5). In this context, the social meaning of "femininity" and of gender relations became major issues of philosophical debate. Intellectuals such as Voltaire or Buffon claimed that civilization and politeness manifest themselves in gender equality, and that women were a "civilizing force on which depended the 'gentleness of society'" (Buffon, quoted in Goodman 1994: 7).

Female intellectuals often also endorsed such a positive view of cultivated femininity, although Jean-Jacques Rousseau converted this ambivalent ideal of femininity into a hierarchical model of gender complementarity. In particular, in his treatise *Emile, or On Education*, Rousseau developed an understanding of femininity according to which women are "naturally" disposed towards pleasing men, while at the same time regulating their own and—indirectly—their husband's desires. The sentimental arrangement of the sexes of which Rousseau conceives clearly builds on an imbalance of power. While Sophie, the female figure that Rousseau introduces in chapter 5 of the book as a companion for Emile, is mainly educated to serve the cultivation of Emile, the ideal that governs Emile's education is autonomy. It therefore comes as no surprise that, as Karen Green notes, the "earliest female responses to Rousseau were fundamentally negative" (Green 2014: 167). However, intellectuals such as Germaine de Staël or Louise Keralio-Robert at least partly endorsed his idea of femininity, according to which "any tender bourgeois mother and competent housekeeper could aspire to govern her husband for the greater social good, through the bonds of sexual desire and love" (Green 2014: 169). By the end of the century, though, Olympe de Gouges formulated a powerful plea for gender equality in France as did Mary Wollstonecraft in England, rejecting any essentialist notion of gender difference.

In England and Scotland, the Bluestockings circle had a significant impact on the development of Enlightenment thought during the 1760s and 1770s. This circle "grew out of activities of a number of intellectually compatible female friends, who encouraged each other's literary endeavors" (Green 2014: 132). They also helped to shape a new vision of women's moral mission in the development of society. Sarah Scott, "the most articulate political theorist of the group," envisioned

> a utopian community, set up by women where they take in and educate young girls whose families cannot provide for them, and which provides a sheltered environment, in which the disabled and disadvantaged poor can work and contribute to their own upkeep.
>
> (Green 2014: 134)

According to Scott, enlightened women should work to transform society "into 'a state of mutual confidence, reciprocal services, and correspondent affections' grounded in Christian virtue" (Green 2014: 141).

A similar notion of the "civilizing" role of women can be found in the writings of Elizabeth Montagu who received many of the male protagonists of the Scottish Enlightenment in her salon. Recently, JoEllen DeLucia has argued that "the conversations in the Bluestocking's salons . . . acted as a laboratory for the theories of sociability and sentiment developed by Scottish literati such as Adam Smith and James [John] Millar" (DeLucia 2015: 6). In particular the idea that

> social progress is a gendered continuum that moves from masculine "undifferentiated primal energy," a state of barely controlled individual passions, to a "refined" and "feminized" modernity in which emotions are tempered by a feminine desire to reflect on the needs and feelings of others,

echoes the Bluestockings' understanding of women's role in society (DeLucia 2015: 8). It also set the agenda for later modernization theories and their ambivalent, often colonialist, attitude towards the social organization of gender relations in "non-Western" societies.

While France, England, and Scotland certainly witnessed the most sophisticated debates about the role of women in society and about the meaning of gender difference, as well as critiques of the legal, political, and cultural subordination of women, debates about women's education, gender equality, and difference also developed in other European countries. In Spain the most outspoken feminist position was formulated by Josefa Amar y Borbón who pleaded for women's "right to happiness" (Franklin Lewis 2004: 18). In her *Discourse in Defense of the Talent of Women, and of Their Aptitude for Governing and Other Positions in Which Men Are Employed* (1786), Amar developed "a plan to procure that happiness for future generations of women" (Franklin Lewis 2004: 18). Elizabeth Franklin Lewis compares Amar's *Discourse* to Mary Wollstonecraft's *Vindication of the Rights of Woman*, which appeared three years later, and stresses that Amar opposed the newly emerging understanding of gender differences in terms of nature and physiology.

Like many of her contemporaries, Amar repeatedly referred to slavery in order to decry the restrictions of women's social and legal situation. However, in contrast to the French and English writers, Amar's opposition to "slavery" did not refer to transatlantic slavery and the abolitionist movement but to Muslim societies. While Muslim women are enslaved, the argument goes, "in the Western world . . . women experience a more subtle kind of slavery, which appears to be veneration" (Franklin Lewis 2004: 32). As Amar put it: "In one part of the world they are slaves, in the other women are dependents" (Amar, quoted in Franklin Lewis 2004: 32). This intercultural comparison nevertheless construed Muslim societies as an "abject" or negative Other to which enlightened societies should not fall back.

In the German speaking territories, a new model of the "learned woman" emerged in the eighteenth century, with Louise Gottsched (née Kalmus) being the most prominent example. In contrast to the French *salonnières*, these women who were mostly trained by their academic fathers "viewed their intellectual labor as a more 'professional,' if supportive activity" (Goodman 1999: 239). Among them were Christiane Mariana von Ziegler, Hedwig Sidonia Zäunemann, and Dorothea Schlözer, the first woman to earn a doctorate in Germany. Only the end of the century, however, witnessed the anonymous publication of a political treatise claiming equal rights and the admission of women to all public institutions. The author was Theodor Gottlieb von Hippel, the "city president" of Königsberg and a frequent guest at Kant's lunch table. The title of Hippel's essay *On the Civil Improvement of Women* (1792) referred to *On the Civil Improvement of the Jews* (1781), an essay by Christian Wilhelm Dohm, who argued for the legal and political emancipation of the Jews. Hippel thus constructed parallel egalitarian claims, made in favor of religious freedom and civil equality, and lamented the failure of the French Revolution, which did not succeed in extending human and civil rights to women.

Equality, Difference, and Human Rights: Olympe de Gouges and Condorcet

This extension had been the project of Olympe de Gouges in her *Declaration of the Rights of Woman and the Female Citizen*, which is a unique document of feminist political philosophy. De Gouges, born Marie Gouze, never received a formal education. She published several theater plays and political pamphlets, and in October 1789, right at the beginning of the revolutionary process in France, she submitted "a reform program to the National Assembly which encompassed legal sexual equality, admission for women to all occupations, and the suppression of the dowry system through a state provided alternative" (Landes 1988: 124). In 1791, de Gouges published her reformulation of the *Declaration of the Rights of Man and Citizen* that had first been issued by the National Assembly in 1789. De Gouges was sent to the Guillotine in November 1793 for "plastering the walls of Paris with posters urging that a federalist system replace Jacobin centralized rule" (Scott 1992: 114). Associated with the Girondist faction, de Gouges nonetheless proposed to defend the king in his trial before the National Convention, and, also in 1791, published a *Declaration of the Rights of Woman*, "dedicated to the Queen." Some scholars therefore depict de Gouges as a monarchist. But this view neglects the fact that she endorsed the revolutionary political principles of egalitarianism and human rights as they were articulated in the *Declaration of Rights of Man and Citizen* and as they correlated with an understanding of society and the political opposed to that of the *ancien régime*.

97

De Gouges' *Declaration of the Rights of Women and the Female Citizen* introduces two areas of concern that today are still central concerns of feminist political philosophy. These are first the dialectics of equality and difference, or universalism and particularism, and second the extension of the bourgeois notion of the political. The first is already present in the title of the *Declaration*, which points out that the "rights of man" are, in fact, tailored to the male part of humanity only, and do not encompass those rights that are required if women, too, are to be regarded as equals. However, de Gouges does not only reclaim equality—claiming that "all female and male citizens, being equal . . . have to be equally admissible to all dignities, public offices and employments according to their abilities" (Gouges 1986: 103; translations follow Hunt 1996). Also, de Gouges makes clear that when abstract human rights are adapted to the concrete lifeworld of women, those rights acquire a new meaning. Such is the case with the right to freedom of speech. De Gouges translates it into the right of a woman to name, under any circumstances, the father of her child, so that she and the child would receive means of subsistence and public recognition. "Every female citizen," she declares, should be able "to speak frankly: I am the mother of a child which belongs to you, without any barbarian prejudice forcing her to dissimulate the truth" (Gouges 1986: 104). This right, if applied, would obviously have had a huge impact on women's possibilities to shape sexual and familial relations according to their needs and desires. Not least of all, it would have enabled them to escape the restrictions of marriage—"the tomb of trust and love," according to de Gouges (quoted in Scott 1992: 110).

Clearly, de Gouges' *Declaration* is an attempt to overcome the exclusions that are produced or at least continued through the language of human rights and equality. Her theoretical strategy to include those who have previously been excluded from the language of universalism thereby reflects the problem of particularism that until today haunts every critique of universalism. When de Gouges claims that women are "the superior sex in terms of beauty, like in terms of courage of maternal suffering" (Gouges 1986: 102), she obviously subscribes to an essentialist understanding of difference. Joan Scott has termed this "the paradox of an embodied equality," highlighting the fact that "de Gouges never escaped the ambiguity of feminine identity, the simultaneous appeal to and critique of established norms" (Scott 1992: 106). However, the "paradoxes" that de Gouges' text displays are not merely intellectual shortcomings: they expose constitutive problems of Enlightenment thought and modern political philosophy. First and foremost, they reveal that there is a problem of how to recognize difference without falling back on particularism and essentialism. In addition, the *Declaration*, although only implicitly, also suggests a way out of this impasse, namely the politicization of difference. As Scott states, de Gouges' "addition of Women" is "disruptive because it implies the need to think differently about the whole question of rights" (Scott 1992: 110). In contrast to other articulations of the relation between equality and difference, de Gouges' text works towards questioning the limits of the political.

A year before de Gouges published the *Declaration*, Condorcet's *On the Admission of Women to the Rights of Citizenship* (1790) appeared. The Marquis de Condorcet, a member of the abolitionist *Société des Amis des Noirs* and a Girondist like de Gouges, contended that women should receive the full rights of citizenship and be admitted to all public institutions. The "principle of the equality of rights" (Condorcet 1996: 119), he argued, does not allow any exception:

Either no individual of the human species has any true rights, or all have the same; and he or she who votes against the rights of another, whatever may be his or her religion, colour, or sex, has by that fact abjured his own.

(Condorcet 1996: 120)

Condorcet's famous essay also refers to the opposition of equality and difference but, in contrast to de Gouges' essay, he does not treat it as a "disruptive" paradox. Condorcet instead establishes a notion of equality that includes difference by way of subordination, treating it as a specification of the general. Condorcet argues that "women are not governed . . . by the reason (and experience) of men; they are governed by their own reason (and experience)" (1996: 120). This distinction resonates with his understanding of the distinctive "private" duties, for which—Condorcet responds to his opponents—women "would only be better fitted" if they become equal citizens.

As Joan Landes has remarked, Condorcet, "at this point in his argument, appears to bow to masculinist prejudices of republican doctrine—specifically to the increasingly popular notion that women's domesticity can be made to service the wider polity" (Landes 1988: 114). Moreover, in Condorcet's essay a certain model of women's emancipation emerges that has informed much of subsequent politics and political theory, liberal and socialist alike. According to this model, women are to be treated as equals in the public sphere and within the market economy while leaving the power relations of the private sphere intact. De Gouges' *Declaration*, in contrast, points in a different direction as it undermines "the possibility of any meaningful opposition between public and private" (Scott 1992: 111). In fact, when de Gouges introduces "woman" into the discourse of human rights, she subverts the underlying notion of the political as a distinctive sphere in which autonomous subjects meet. So even if the rights she refers to are the same as in the *Declaration of the Rights of Man and Citizen*, these rights now constitute the non-political—relations of kinship, reproduction, and sexual desire—as political.

In addition, de Gouges' *Declaration* hints at the fact that the opposition between equality and difference is not stable. Differences proliferate. What is at stake is not only the difference between men and women, but also differences among women, for example women of rich and of poor families for whom the same laws do not have the same effects, as de Gouges explains in the *Postambule* to the *Declaration*. In addition, the question that looms at the margins of her text concerns the interrelations between gendered and racialized forms of oppression, in particular slavery. De Gouges extends her egalitarian view to those enslaved and colonized: "Man everywhere is equal" (*L'homme partout est égal*), she states in her 1788 *Reflections on Black Men* (*Réflexions sur les hommes nègres*; Gouges 1986). She also deconstructs the "black–white" dichotomy: "Men's colour is nuanced, like all the animals that nature has produced, as well as the plants and minerals. . . . All is varied and this is the beauty of nature" (quoted in Scott 1992: 113). If, one could argue, the extension of the language of universal human rights and equality to the colonized and enslaved evokes the dialectics of equality and universalism in a similar way to the feminist perspective, then the question emerges of how these forms of critique interfere with each other.

Education, Equality, and Independence: Mary Wollstonecraft in Context

Mary Wollstonecraft (1759–1798) is certainly the most prominent feminist Enlightenment thinker. In defense of the early French Revolution she published *A Vindication of the Rights of Men*, the first reply to Edmund Burke's *Reflections on the French Revolution*, in which she heavily criticized Burke's aristocratic views. In this book, though, she did not reflect upon the situation of women as she had already done in her first book *Thoughts on the Education of Daughters* (1786) and as she continued to do up to her last novel *Maria, or the Wrongs of Women* (1798), published posthumously by William Godwin, her husband and the father of her daughter Mary Shelley.

The *Vindication of the Rights of Women* (1792), her most important publication, is a plea for gender equality through equal education. Wollstonecraft's "central organizing principle, through which she expresses her observations about the oppression and domination of women" (Coffee 2014: 908), and thus her leading ethical ideal, is "independence." In the dedication to Talleyrand, who Wollstonecraft wishes to convince of the necessity of women's equal education, she stresses: "Independence I have long considered as the grand blessing of life, the basis of every virtue" (Wollstonecraft 1989: 65). The main precondition for gaining independence—including economic independence—is, according to Wollstonecraft, for every being "the exercise of its own reason" (1989: 90). In the present state of society, she diagnoses, women are systematically hindered in this with fatal consequences for the female habitus. Education is thus meant to initiate a "revolution in feminine manners" and to change women's subaltern forms of behavior, which Wollstonecraft critically exposes again and again throughout the *Vindication* (1989: 114). Indeed, education was a major topic in Enlightenment discourse, as a wide range of authors considered it the central means for improving the individual and society alike. In line with this, Wollstonecraft reflects upon the correlation between the transformation of society and the transformation of subjectivity, or the need of women's "reforming themselves to reform the world" (1989: 114). She thereby introduces an understanding of emancipation that has had an enormous impact on feminist notions of the political as starting from and indispensably including a politics of subjectivity and self-transformation.

Wollstonecraft, who "seems to have read very few of the earlier women writers on her sex, radical or conservative" (Ferguson and Todd 1984: 61), and who did not have any connection to the Bluestockings circle, was deeply impressed by Catherine Macauley's *Letters on Education*. Wollstonecraft reviewed the book enthusiastically upon its appearance in 1790, and as Moira Ferguson and Janet Todd highlight, "In all essential ideas on women Wollstonecraft and Macauley agree—politics, religion, and pedagogy" (1984: 61). Macauley, too, advocated the equal education of boys and girls and argued that "differences that actually subsist between the sexes" might be altered through education (1996: 204). She engaged in a kind of deconstruction of sexual difference and argued heavily against Rousseau's ideal of complementarity. For Macauley, Rousseau's account of girls' education, which he gives in chapter 5 of his *Emile, or On Education*, in which he introduces the figure of Sophie, is "blinded by his pride and sensuality" (Macauley 1996: 213). His ideal of femininity, which requires that a woman "cultivate her agreeable talents, in order to please her future husband," must, in Macauley's view, be compared to the ideal Circassian slave, who "cultivates hers [i.e. her agreeable talents] to fit her for the harem of an eastern bashaw" (1996: 213). This orientalist theme also runs through Wollstonecraft's criticism of women's oppression and her critique of Rousseau.

Wollstonecraft's relation to Rousseau is complex. Certainly, she was critical of Rousseau's idea of gender complementarity, which many of her contemporaries endorsed.

Her "quarrel with the depiction of women in Emile" was, however, by no means a "wholesale repudiation of his ideas" (Taylor 2002: 115). On the contrary, Wollstonecraft shared his critique of how inequality distorts society and has led to degeneration. Her attempt is to "extend" his argument "to women, and confidently assert that they have been drawn out of their sphere by false refinement" (Wollstonecraft 1989: 90). As a consequence, Wollstonecraft argues that women "must return to nature and equality" instead of "degrading themselves" (1989: 90). Wollstonecraft's statement that Rousseau's construction of femininity "appears to me grossly unnatural" (1989: 93) is thus completely in line with her interpretation of Rousseau. While Wollstonecraft acknowledges some gender differences—"women, I allow, may have different duties" (1989: 120)—her overall claim is that different tasks do not constitute differences on the level of moral principles. "They are *human* duties," she contends, "and the princi-ples that should regulate the discharge of them, I sturdily maintain, must be the same" (1989: 120). In the last instance, it is the "authority of reason" that should govern all human behavior (1989: 120).

Among twentieth and twenty-first century feminist philosophers, this rational-ist commitment, together with Wollstonecraft's harsh critique of sensuality and her "astringent attitude to heterosexual love," (Taylor 2002: 112) have attracted much crit-icism. Authors such as Cora Kaplan and Mary Poovey have argued that Wollstonecraft adopted a masculine ideal of reason, which led to a neglect of the body and a "denial of female sexuality" (Kaplan 2002: 258). In a similar way, Joan Landes has argued that Wollstonecraft endorsed "the implicitly masculine values of the bourgeois sphere" and repudiated the "female position" (Landes 1988: 135).

Vivian Jones, however, has challenged these readings by highlighting the "innovative quality" of Wollstonecraft's views on sex education (Jones 2005: 145). Wollstonecraft extensively read the medical literature of her day and engaged in the so-called "botany controversy" that surrounded the eroticized depictions of plants in the poems of Erasmus Darwin. Wollstonecraft took sides, Jones argues, with "a language of sexual instruction based on rational ideals of openness and transparency" (Jones 2005: 146). Accordingly, Wollstonecraft's refusal of feminine sensuality should not be misunderstood as a nega-tion of bodily pleasures but as a critique of imposed subaltern subjectivity.

Another controversial issue is how far Wollstonecraft reflects on the intersection-ality of domination. Of particular interest here are her relation to abolitionism and the references that she makes to slavery in order to decry the subordination of women. Like other radical egalitarians such as de Gouges and Condorcet, Wollstonecraft also advocated the abolition of slavery. In particular, the abolitionist movement and the revolution of Black slaves in the French colony of Saint-Domingue impacted on Wollstonecraft's understanding of slavery. "Formerly, in all forms of discourse throughout the eighteenth century, conservative and radical women alike railed against marriage, love, and education as forms of slavery perpetrated upon women by men and by the conventions of society at large" (Ferguson 1996: 126). In the wake of the French and the Haitian Revolutions, "slavery" was "recontextualized in terms of colonial slavery" (Ferguson 1996: 126).

Moira Ferguson credits Wollstonecraft with having "been the first writer to raise issues of colonial and gender relations so tellingly in tandem" (1996: 131). Indeed the *Vindication of the Rights of Women* on many occasions decries colonial slavery. However, the more conventional, metaphorical reference to "slavery" also runs through the text, invoking a supposed moral superiority of the European nations. Penelope Deutscher, in her account of Wollstonecraft's use of analogies, therefore hints at the problematic, yet unthought aspects of the complex analogies that her text displays.

> For when the claim that women are like animals and slaves (not to mention children and savages) serves the interests of women's claim to a better status, what links the analogy with the analogy of the analogy is the hinge of what may be named an indirect, aspirational, analogical subordination of those whom it would . . . be degrading for women to be "like."
>
> (Deutscher 2014: 204)

An equally unsolved problem that only surfaces in Wollstonecraft's late writings, the *Letters from Sweden* and *Maria, or the Wrongs of Woman*, is the interference of gender and class domination. In her last novel Wollstonecraft portrays "with sympathy the peculiar horror suffered by women of the laboring class" (Ferguson and Todd 1984: 85). But Wollstonecraft does not engage in theoretical reflection about that horror.

Feminist Engagements with the Enlightenment

From the second half of the twentieth century onward, feminist philosophers have engaged with the Enlightenment in various ways. Methodologically two strategies can be distinguished: re-readings of Enlightenment authors and debates about the legacy of the Enlightenment for present feminist theory.

The first strategy worked, on the one hand, against the neglect of the theoretical contributions of female authors. Prior to the feminist wave of the 1960s and 1970s, de Gouges, for example, had been more or less "forgotten" while Wollstonecraft was largely recalled because of her biography and her personal struggle for independence. In this respect Emma Goldman and Virginia Woolf paid tribute to her, but scholarship and serious engagement with her theoretical positions only date from the last decades of the twentieth century. On the other hand, the masculine canon of philosophy was scrutinized as feminist philosophers started to systematically assess the gender ideologies of "classical" male authors. In particular, the "dark" sides of Rousseau and Kant provoked a wide range of readings and critiques.

As in the eighteenth century, Rousseau's gender theory has inspired diverse and controversial readings. Lynda Lange, for example, has argued that despite the "very unequal prescriptions he makes for women's and men's lives," Rousseau "nevertheless . . . accords women not-insignificant power and has, after all, claimed that their contributions to family life are of crucial importance to a good civil society" (Lange 2002: 5). Critics such as Susan Moller Okin, on the other hand, have highlighted the fact that equality and freedom, the "two most prevalent values" of Rousseau's social and political philosophy, were only "for men" (Okin 1979: 140). Indeed, for Rousseau, gender difference did not constitute a problem of inequality but on the contrary was introduced as a necessary component of society. Rousseau's account of the education of Sophie that is purely supplementary to that of Emile can thus be understood as paradigmatic of "the exclusion of women from public life and its complement, their relegation to private life," where women are to exercise a moral and cultivating influence on their husbands (Steinbrügge 1995: 6). Within the structure of bourgeois society, Steinbrügge concludes, women "became *the moral sex*" while "humane qualities survived (only) as a female principle" (1995: 6).

Despite the fact that this gender arrangement clearly resonates with a wide range of attempts of the period to naturalize gender hierarchies, other scholars such as Jacques Derrida, Penny Weiss, and Linda Zerilli have pointed to the ambiguity of Rousseau's concept of nature. "Nature," and in particular "woman's nature," is by no means to be understood in a positivistic sense as a set of given data but, for Rousseau, is something that needs to be created and conserved. Accordingly,

> there is a profound sense in his writings that gender boundaries must be carefully fabricated and maintained . . . because what announces "man" or "woman" is not anatomical difference but instead an arbitrary system of signs that stands in permanent danger of collapsing into a frightening ambiguity of meaning and a loss of manly constitution.
>
> (Zerilli 2002: 279)

In contrast to the case of Rousseau, the gendered aspects of Kant's philosophy did not receive much attention in the eighteenth century although they, too, were controversial, as the example of Theodor Gottlieb Hippel shows. Contemporary feminist philosophers, however, have engaged extensively with Kant. His views on women, citizenship, and marriage in the *Metaphysics of Morals*, his distinction between male reason and female emotion in his essay *On the Beautiful and the Sublime*, and his theory of gender complementarity in the *Anthropology from a Pragmatic Point of View* have been heavily researched in the last decades. This research has established that Kant—despite his critical remarks on the tutelage of the "beautiful sex" in his essay *What Is Enlightenment?*—was certainly not an advocate of women's equality.

The controversial question, however, is how far "the basic categories of Kantian moral philosophy contain elements that, irrespective of their author's view on gender differences, admit of a feminist appropriation" (Nagl-Docekal 1997: 102). In particular, the Kantian notions of reason and autonomy have inspired feminist arguments as well as generated wide-ranging critiques. As Geneviève Lloyd put it, Kant's ethical writings introduce "a view of morality as the antithesis of inclinations and feelings—a transcending of the subjectivity and particularity of passion to enter, as free consciousness, the common space of Reason" (Lloyd 1986: 68). The structural omissions that underlie and constitute the Kantian moral philosophy—affect and emotion, collectivity and sociality, the body and non-human nature—have been criticized in different but converging ways by feminist philosophers inspired by psychoanalysis, Marxism, poststructuralism, postcolonial studies, and environmental ethics. It is here that the different branches of feminist critiques of Enlightenment meet.

Indeed, the various feminist critiques of Enlightenment thought have largely focused on the dichotomies that constitute the notions of reason and autonomy. It has been argued that the concepts of freedom, equality, and human rights have proved to be insufficient when it comes to understanding and overcoming gendered forms of domination—or, worse, have even worked to conceal them. The question that has generated the most controversy among feminist philosophers is, then, what theoretical consequences follow from these critiques. Could or should feminist philosophy relate to the egalitarian and rationalist legacy of the Enlightenment and treat it as an unfinished project that has to be further radicalized? Or, on the contrary, could or should feminist philosophy engage in a radical deconstruction of Enlightenment discourse?

Feminist philosophers such as Seyla Benhabib and Nancy Fraser, working in the tradition of Habermasian Critical Theory, have clearly pursued the first path. In particular, Benhabib has formulated a "post-Enlightenment defense of universalism," which rejects the "metaphysical illusions of the Enlightenment," first and foremost that of disembodied reason (Benhabib 1992: 3–4). She therefore replaced the notion of "a disconnected and disembodied subject" with the idea of a "situated self" that is always already engaged in embodied and situated communicative action. Fraser, for her part, has reformulated the notion of the public sphere. In contrast to Habermas' idealization of the liberal public sphere as an institutionalized arena of discursive interaction in which citizens exercise their reason, Fraser has proposed to conceive of public spheres in the plural. She introduced the notion of "subaltern counter-publics . . . where members of subordinated social groups invent and circulate counterdiscourses, which in turn permit them to formulate oppositional interpretations of their identities, interests and needs" (Fraser 1990: 67). Other feminist philosophers have attempted to rethink the *Dialectics of Enlightenment* as formulated by the early Frankfurt School from a feminist perspective. Cornelia Klinger, for example, has explored the "gender dialectics of enlightenment," arguing that the double privatization of family and religion in modernity led to a "sacralization" of the private sphere, so that women and the private came to function as an utopian reservoir that complements the devastations of modern society (Klinger 2003: 200).

If all these readings in one way or the other try to assess and overcome the structural shortcomings of Enlightenment thought while recuperating its critical impulse, an inverse dialectics seems to be at work in the attempts to overcome Enlightenment discourse while nevertheless engaging in radical problematizations of power and subjection. This is most explicit in Judith Butler's writings on "precarious life" and critique, in which the political-ethical horizon of the Enlightenment is re-established. Her question, "Who is normatively human?" critically posed in order to disrupt discursive and practical "dehumanization" (Butler 2004: xv–xvi) and the unequal mourning of deaths, obviously evokes and re-instantiates a political notion of humanity and the claim that everybody should be treated equally. With reference to Kant and Foucault, Butler even states in the essay "Critique, Dissent, Disciplinarity" that "to the degree that we can still ask the question, *what is enlightenment*, we continue . . . to show that critique has not stopped happening, and that in this sense neither has enlightenment stopped happening" (Butler 2009: 787). In light of contemporary complex and intersecting forms of domination and ideology, and in light of our knowledge about the troubles of critique, one might add that the task of scrutinizing and challenging all established authorities has only become more complicated.

Further Reading

Ferguson, Moira (1992) *Subject to Others: British Women Writers and Colonial Slavery, 1670–1834*, New York: Routledge. (A comprehensive account of women writer's positions on slavery and abolitionism.)

O'Brien, Karen (2009) *Women and Enlightenment in Eighteenth-Century Britain*, Cambridge: Cambridge University Press. (Explores the relation of women writers to the British Enlightenment and women as a subject of inquiry by male and female authors.)

Taylor, Barbara (2003) *Mary Wollstonecraft and the Feminist Imagination*, Cambridge: Cambridge University Press. (On Wollstonecraft's utopianism and her relation to the radical-Protestant Enlightenment.)

Trouille, Mary Seidman (1997) *Sexual Politics in the Enlightenment: Women Writers Read Rousseau*, Albany, NY: SUNY Press. (A comprehensive account of interpretations of Rousseau by eighteenth-century women writers.)

Related Topics

Early modern feminism and Cartesian philosophy (Chapter 6); feminist engagements with social contract theory (Chapter 7); feminist engagements with nineteenth-century German philosophy (Chapter 9); rationality and objectivity in feminist philosophy (Chapter 20); the genealogy and viability of the concept of intersectionality (Chapter 28); feminist conceptions of autonomy (Chapter 41); feminist engagements with democratic theory (Chapter 51); feminism and liberalism (Chapter 52); feminism and freedom (Chapter 53); feminism and power (Chapter 54).

References

Benhabib, Seyla (1992) *Situating the Self: Gender, Community, and Postmodernism in Contemporary Ethics*, New York: Routledge.

Butler, Judith (2004) *Precarious Life: The Politics of Mourning and Violence*, London: Verso.

——(2009) "Critique, Dissent, Disciplinarity," *Critical Inquiry* 35(4): 773–795.

Coffee, Alan M. S. J. (2014) "Freedom as Independence: Mary Wollstonecraft and the Grand Blessing of Life," *Hypatia* 29(4): 908–924.

Condorcet, Marquis de (1996) "On the Admission of Women to the Rights of Citizenship," in Lynn Hunt (Ed.) *The French Revolution and Human Rights: A Brief History in Documents*, Boston, MA: Bedford, 119–121.

DeLucia, JoEllen (2015) *A Feminine Enlightenment: British Women Writers and the Philosophy of Progress, 1759–1820*, Edinburgh: Edinburgh University Press.

Deutscher, Penelope (2014) "Analogy of Analogy: Animals and Slaves in Mary Wollstonecraft's Defense of Women's Rights," in Susan Lettow (Ed.) *Reproduction, Race and Gender in Philosophy and the Early Life Sciences*, Albany, NY: SUNY, 187–216.

Ferguson, Moira (1996) "Mary Wollstonecraft and the Problematic of Slavery," in Maria J. Falco (Ed.) *Feminist Interpretations of Mary Wollstonecraft*, University Park, PA: Pennsylvania State University Press, 125–149.

Ferguson, Moira and Todd, Janet (1984) *Mary Wollstonecraft*, Boston, MA: Twayne.

Franklin Lewis, Elizabeth (2004) *Women Writers in the Spanish Enlightenment: The Pursuit of Happiness*, Aldershot: Ashgate.

Fraser, Nancy (1990) "Rethinking the Public Sphere: A Contribution to the Critique of Actually Existing Democracy," *Social Text* 25/26: 56–80.

Goodman, Dena (1994) *The Republic of Letters: A Cultural History of the French Enlightenment*, Ithaca, NY: Cornell University Press.

Goodman, Katherine R. (1999) *Amazons and Apprentices: Women and the German Parnassus in the Early Enlightenment*, Rochester: Camden House.

Gouges, Olympe de (1986a) "Réflexions sur les hommes nègres," in Benoîte Groult (Ed.) *Oeuvres*, Paris: Mercure de France, 83–87.

——(1986b) "Déclaration des droits de la femme et de la citoyenne," in Benoîte Groult (Ed.) *Oeuvres*, Paris: Mercure de France, 101–112.

——(1996) "Declaration of the Rights of Women," in Lynn Hunt (Ed.) *The French Revolution and Human Rights: A Brief History in Documents*, Boston, MA: Bedford, 124–129.

Green, Karen (2014) *A History of Women's Political Thought in Europe, 1700–1800*, Cambridge: Cambridge University Press.

Hunt, Lynne (Ed.) (1996) *The French Revolution and Human Rights: A Brief History in Documents*, Boston, MA: Bedford.

Jones, Vivian (2005) "Advice and Enlightenment: Mary Wollstonecraft and Sex Education," in Sarah Knott and Barbara Taylor (Ed.) *Women, Gender and Enlightenment*, Basingstoke: Palgrave Macmillan, 140–155.

Kaplan, Cora (2002) "Mary Wollstonecraft's reception and legacies," in Claudia L. Johnson (Ed.) *The Cambridge Companion to Mary Wollstonecraft*, Cambridge: Cambridge University Press, 246–270.

Klinger, Cornelia (2003) "Die Dialektik der Aufklärung im Geschlechterverhältnis," in Sonja Asdal and Johannes Rohbeck (Eds.) *Aufklärung und Aufklärungskritik in Frankreich*, Berlin: Berliner Wissenschaftsverlag, 199–229.

Knott, Sarah and Taylor, Barbara (2005) "General Introduction," in Sarah Knott and Barbara Taylor (Eds.) *Women, Gender and Enlightenment*, Basingstoke: Palgrave Macmillan, xv–xxi.

Landes, Joan (1988) *Women and the Public Sphere in the Age of the French Revolution*, Ithaca, NY: Cornell University Press.

Lange, Lynda (2002) "Introduction," in Lynda Lange (Ed.) *Feminist Interpretations of Jean-Jacques Rousseau*, University Park, PA: Pennsylvania State University Press, 1–23.

Lloyd, Geneviève (1986) *The Man of Reason: "Male" and "Female" in Western Philosophy*, New York: Routledge.

Macauley, Catherine (1996) "Letters on Education. Letter XXII: No Characteristic Difference in Sex" and "Letter XXIII: Coquetry," in Janet Todd (Ed.) *Female Education in the Age of Enlightenment*, vol. 3, London: William Pickering, 203–215.

Nagl-Docekal, Herta (1997) "Feminist Ethics: How It Could Benefit from Kant's Moral Philosophy," in Robin May Schott (Ed.) *Feminist Interpretations of Immanuel Kant*, University Park, PA: Pennsylvania State University Press, 101–124.

Okin, Susan Moller (1979) *Women in Western Political Thought*, Princeton, NJ: Princeton University Press.

Scott, Joan (1992) "'A Woman Who Has Only Paradoxes to Offer': Olympe de Gouges Claims Rights for Women," in Sara E. Melzer and Leslie W. Rabine (Eds.) *Rebel Daughters: Women and the French Revolution*, New York: Oxford University Press, 102–120.

Steinbrügge, Liselotte (1995) *The Moral Sex: Woman's Nature in the French Enlightenment*, Oxford: Oxford University Press.

Taylor, Barbara (2002) "The Religious Foundations of Mary Wollstonecraft's Feminism," in Claudia L. Johnson (Ed.) *The Cambridge Companion to Mary Wollstonecraft*, Cambridge: Cambridge University Press, 99–118.

Wollstonecraft, Mary (1989) "A Vindication of the Rights of Women," in Janet Todd and Marilyn Butler (Eds.) *The Works of Mary Wollstonecraft*, vol. 5, London: William Pickering, 79–266.

Zerilli, Linda (2002) "'Une Maitresse Imperieuse': Woman in Rousseau's Semiotic Republic," in Lynda Lange (Ed.) *Feminist Interpretations of Jean-Jacques Rousseau*, University Park, PA: Pennsylvania State University Press, 277–314.

9

FEMINIST ENGAGEMENTS WITH NINETEENTH-CENTURY GERMAN PHILOSOPHY

Elaine P. Miller

Introduction

Immanuel Kant's 1791 *Critique of Judgment* inspired the best of nineteenth-century European philosophy, including German Idealism and Romanticism and the philosophy of Friedrich Nietzsche (Hance 1998; Kreines 2008; Zimmerman 2005). Many feminist scholars have also found the *Critique of Judgment* productive, despite thorough critique of some of Kant's central presuppositions in his other works. Themes of interest to feminists in this work include the turn away from an emphasis on the isolated ego or subject, the value of felt connectedness among humans, the significance of embodiment, and the restoration of narrative complexity (Moen 1997: 214). G. W. F. Hegel's transformation of Kantian morality into a system that unites universal principles with an acknowledgment of the concrete circumstances and self-correcting possibilities of actual historical events and movements is also arguably important for the feminist critique of traditional metaphysics and of moral values that do not take women's concerns into account (Gauthier 1997). A growing recognition of the impossibility of understanding the human being apart from her relation to nature and to a broader political context, and the necessity of attributing a very specific type of purposiveness to natural as well as human phenomena can be added to this list.

The philosophies of both Hegel and Nietzsche have been the target of sustained and intensive feminist critique for decades, in what Paul Patton calls "a battlefield of conflicting interpretations" (1993: xii). Other nineteenth-century thinkers have received less attention, although arguably strands of nineteenth-century German thought, including some readings of Hegel and Nietzsche, opened up new possibilities for thinking about sexual difference and gender equality. In addition, a culture of women's salons in nineteenth-century Europe opened up a new horizon for intellectual contribution by women. In this chapter I will examine the areas of Hegel's and Nietzsche's philosophy that have garnered the most critical attention from feminist thinkers, as well as some lines of thought that also have proved productive but that have received less critical notice. In addition I will consider the intellectual contributions of three of the most celebrated women contributors to nineteenth-century intellectual life: Rahel Varnhagen, Dorothea Veit Schlegel, and Caroline Schelling-Schlegel.

Hegel and German Idealism: Being and Thinking

As early as 1970 the Italian radical feminist manifesto "Let's Spit on Hegel" (Lonzi 1996) attests to the intensity and contentiousness of reaction to the way that traditional views on women have converged onto the figure of Hegel. Even if they do not espouse so passionate a rejection of Hegel's philosophy, many feminist theorists have been wary both of the apparent biases in Hegel's writing and of the explicit content of his philosophical claims. Hegel is famous for comparing women to plants because in his view their actions are guided not by reason but by contingent external conditions, inclinations, and opinions (Hegel 1991: 166Z). Hegel's dialectic, while always taking into account specific historical and material conditions, considers abstraction from every determinacy a necessary condition for spiritual (both legal and symbolic) personhood, leading to the conclusion that any consideration of specific natural difference, including sexual difference, must be left out of a fully articulated account of human development (Nuzzo 2001: 116–121).

Feminist philosophers have extensively analyzed all of Hegel's central concepts, including both their limitations and their further possibilities for development in directions not anticipated by their author but consonant with his philosophical system. Although the majority of feminist work on Hegel has addressed themes in his 1807 work *Phenomenology of Spirit*, in particular the sections "Lordship and Bondage" and "Man and Woman"—on Greek Ethical Life, which draws on Sophocles' *Antigone*—feminist philosophers have engaged with the full spectrum of Hegel's texts, including the *Logic* and the *Philosophy of Nature*.

Early Hegel scholarship by feminists was often configured according to the pros and cons of reading Hegel at all, whereas more recent scholarship uses contemporary insights into sex, gender, and women's roles to illuminate aspects of Hegel's method and central concepts that might be refashioned to ends other than his own (Hutchings and Pulkkinen 2010: 2). Perhaps the most fundamental and important insight that Hegel's philosophy provides develops out of his reading of Kant. Whereas Kant viewed the connection between nature and freedom as a necessary yet indemonstrable postulate of reason, Hegel argued that this connection not only existed but also could be known. Dichotomies, in Hegel's view, were not the result of but rather the catalyst for philosophy. Systems of thought that posit static dualities simultaneously present views that are one-sided and abstract, but also motivate philosophy to find a way of going beyond them. Hegel's dialectical method outlines the movement of a self-positing and self-correcting historically developing system, in which stances that are initially one-sided and mutually opposing overcome themselves and shift to more complex and inclusive positions that preserve the truth of the moments that they supersede even as they destroy their false presuppositions. This movement mirrors the way in which human beings progressively make their home in nature, overcoming obstacles that arise as they proceed in shaping the world to their needs, and making use of their experience and errors to better adapt it to their purposes. Human beings are practically free, according to Hegel, not because they completely conquer a hostile and external world that they view as an antagonist over and against themselves, but rather because they have the capacity to make themselves at home and indeed recognize themselves in and of the world out of which they, like other natural things, have arisen (Hance 1998: 40).

This activity of immanent self-positing and self-overcoming, as well as a continuous transition between nature and spirit, can only be properly conceptualized by understanding the activity and mediation of this process as a living one. This is the legacy Hegel takes from Kant's third *Critique*: purposiveness without a (external, determinate) purpose is the movement of life, which constantly overcomes itself and becomes more complex and inclusive (Lindberg 2010: 180). Purposiveness here does not refer to the finite, external teleological movement that Hegel is sometimes incorrectly accused of according to historical movement—a version of which he himself derided by characterizing those who hold it as believing, for example, that nature created cork in order to give humans something with which to stopper their wine bottles (Hegel 1977: 245Z). Rather, Kant calls purposiveness the infinite capacity, common to all living beings and to nature itself, to attain ends already immanent within a living system. Purposiveness entails self-organization and self-regulation, and is present within living beings and in free action.

Purposiveness without a (determinate, external) purpose is a regulative rather than a constitutive principle. For Kant, this distinction marks the difference between the reason and the understanding. The pure concepts of the understanding constitute, or make possible, any given object of experience, whereas reason has ideas that go beyond any possible experience but that nonetheless play an important role in, or regulate, our philosophizing about the unity of experience. For Kant, although it is indeterminate, purposiveness is the a priori principle upon which reflective aesthetic judgment is based. Its unique quality of pertaining both to judgments of beauty, which are sensory, and supersensible judgments of (indeterminate) purposiveness, makes it suitable to mediate between the realms of nature and freedom. Kant's critique of teleological judgment, in particular the attempt to systematically move beyond a thinking that posited dualistic, static, and hierarchically ordered oppositions, influenced the development of much nineteenth-century philosophy.

This dialectical process of positing and overcoming contradiction has implications for the role of the feminine in Hegel's work. Some scholars have argued that it is precisely the material and the feminine dimension that is lost or that fails to be preserved in this dialectical process, where the "truth" of positions is distilled and the unnecessary is overcome (Efrat-Levkovich 2010; Lindberg 2010). Two central dialectical oppositions in Hegel's work in which the feminine is arguably overcome as a significant category of self-positing have been the focus of the majority of feminist critique of Hegel, as mentioned above. These are the dialectic of master and slave, on the one hand, and the dialectic between natural/divine law and human law divided along gender lines, on the other, which form important nodes of Hegel's *Phenomenology of Spirit*. Spirit, here, refers both to the subject and the object of knowing. Spirit spans individual and collective human experience and achievement, the growing human body of knowledge, works, and institutions, and the unity of the whole as a "world spirit" actualizing itself by coming to know itself.

Hegel's phenomenological description of the progressive development of human consciousness is often figural, depicting constellations of increasingly complex interactions of natural, historical, and symbolic strands of meaning that present the truth of particular moments in history in relation to each other. These nodes are crystallizations, part of a dynamic process and thus incomplete, constantly subject to change, and self-correcting (Lindberg 2010: 178). Hegel uses the figures of master and slave at an early stage of his dialectic in order to illustrate the drama of the most primordial of human intersubjective encounters, what could be called the very emergence of human self-consciousness out of natural human existence.

Simone de Beauvoir famously described the relation of woman to man as analogous to that of slave to master in the Hegelian master–slave dialectic (Beauvoir 1989: 64). In fact, this section of the *Phenomenology of Spirit* is not explicitly gendered, although both antagonists are implicitly male. The scene of master–slave conflict depicts the first encounter between two human consciousnesses (not as yet individuated) who have emerged out of a state of nature characterized by the quest for the immediate satisfaction of desire or the perpetuation of pure life, in which sexual desire and reproduction plays an integral part.

In his description of this initial state of being, Hegel portrays the human being as a fundamentally animal nature, interacting with the natural world around it as something to be consumed. In this world another human is nothing more than either a means or a threat to the preservation and perpetuation of the species, itself an endless cycle of coming into being and passing away. This cyclical natural activity remains fluid and unchecked until one consciousness comes up against another in a desire, not for food or sexual gratification, but rather for recognition from the other. Recognition cannot be acquired from any other non-human living entity and indeed cannot obtain if one of the antagonists consumes the other. The mutual desire for recognition leads to a life-and-death struggle in which each party strives to bend the other's will to its own. When one consciousness necessarily concedes defeat and becomes a "slave" or "bondsman" to the other, it is enjoined to serve the other's needs, transforming both of their existences in the process. The "slave's" existence now comprises nothing more than procuring for the "master" what the other needs to satisfy its desire, thereby deferring the immediacy of its own gratification.

This check in desire has the unanticipated consequence that the slave emerges as the truth of this encounter. The slave becomes a reflective self-consciousness, as opposed to a consumptive animal, by virtue of having controlled the immediacy of its desire and of having worked on the world as a consequence of this task. This "working" on the world, which Hegel characterizes as the creation of a "thing" for the consumption of the master, brings into being a second, humanly crafted nature. The master consciousness, however, by virtue of having neither checked its own desire nor worked on the world, remains a static version of the original animal human nature and eventually simply fades away in this encounter. It never becomes self-conscious, since even in its domination of the other, it cannot be recognized by one who is not of equal stature. True to the form of the Hegelian dialectic—*Aufhebung* or "sublation," denoting both perishing and preserving—one side of the opposition is incorporated into the other, which, here as explicit, reflective, self-consciousness, emerges as the truth of the confrontation.

Feminist commentators have disagreed as to whether or not Beauvoir is correct in aligning woman with the slave in this encounter, and what the implications of reading the dialectic in this way would be. As Tina Chanter notes, Beauvoir not only attributes the woman-as-slave's state of submission to oppression by the dominant consciousness, but also to what she considers her "bad faith" acquiescence in a role closely aligned with nature due to her childbearing (1995: 62). This alignment with life makes woman more likely to concede defeat in the life-and-death struggle that arises when two self-consciousnesses meet and demand recognition from each other. In tension with this view, however, Beauvoir seems to completely disregard the key transformation of the slave at the conclusion of the encounter (Chanter 1995; Oliver 1996; Miller 2000; Mussett 2006).

Arguably, however, Beauvoir's reading of the master–slave dialectic may have a double thrust. If woman actually serves as the catalyst and mediation for man's transcendence, avoiding the life-and-death struggle that characterizes the encounter between the two consciousnesses, she may nonetheless be emancipated through the activity of labor, or "work" on "the thing." Beauvoir herself in *The Second Sex* writes that woman functions as a respite from the constant risking of life that characterizes man's existence (Beauvoir 1989: 141). Mussett argues that we can cull from Beauvoir's reading another kind of "absolute negativity," one that arises not through a life-and-death struggle but precisely through women's historical oppression and their historical position as absolute other. Since women did not choose their historical situation, their passage out of the position of the slave is more precarious than that of men, who demand recognition through confrontation; however, through working on the world women may follow an analogous, albeit a slower, path to subjectivity (Mussett 2006: 288).

In *The Second Sex* Beauvoir also suggests that for women to occupy the transformational position of the "slave" they would need to assert distinctively feminine values in opposition to masculine values (Beauvoir 1989: 141; Miller 2000: 122). Only this kind of creation of values could put women in a position to demand recognition from men in the manner outlined by the master–slave dialectic. This argument implies that there might be two distinct subjectivities differentiated along the lines of sexual difference. In Beauvoir's view the mere demand to "be recognized as existents by the same right as men" has not yet placed women in a position to struggle in the way outlined by the Hegelian master–slave paradigm (Beauvoir 2000: 64–65). This suggests a proximity to the position of Luce Irigaray, who argues that the universal cannot be one, but must be at least two, differentiated along the lines of sexual difference and desire.

Irigaray's famous reading of Hegel, "The Eternal Irony of the Community," opened up a plethora of readings of the second most commented upon section from Hegel's *Phenomenology of Spirit*, "The Ethical World: Human and Divine Law: Man and Woman" (Hegel 1977: 267; Irigaray 1985: 214–226). Hegel chooses to illustrate the tension that potentially arises between man and woman when human law and divine law are assigned according to natural difference, by reading that tension through the central conflict of Sophocles' *Antigone*. Here Hegel initially presents the harmonious first shape of what he calls spirit, the historical stage where human consciousness for the first time explicitly recognizes its world as a product of itself, and the external world begins to appear not as something alien over and against consciousness, but rather as a place in which consciousness is at home. For Hegel, this moment occurs in ancient Greek ethical life, where maintaining allegiance to the law of the family is assigned to women, and the order of the state is assigned to men. Such an historical arrangement presumes that if duties are clearly and distinctly distributed and differentiated, then spheres of human interaction will function seamlessly and harmoniously. The Sophoclean tragedy *Antigone*, by contrast, presents the inevitable conflict that will arise when such prescribed ethical duties clash. Antigone's act of following the dictates of divine law and family allegiance by burying her brother Polynices against King Creon's explicit (human) order leads to the inevitable destruction of the harmonious ethical substance.

As a result of this breakdown, subjectivity becomes an aggregate of lifeless "persons" rather than the unified substance of ethical life. Irigaray's reading emphasizes the "undifferentiated opaqueness" of woman in this paradigm, her role as nothing more than the "store (of) substance for the sublation of self," the historical development of the masculine subject. Woman has no specific historical discourse that would allow her to identify with and return to herself as individuated yet united with a symbolic order; thus her role becomes one of silently facilitating the emergence of the ostensibly neutral but actually masculine individual.

Multiple feminist readings of Hegel's Antigone were inspired by the dissemination of Irigaray's essay (Bernstein 2010; Boer 2003; Butler 2010; Chanter 1995 and 2011; Mills 1986; Oliver 1996). In fact, readings of Antigone have overshadowed any other recent feminist discussion of Hegel, with a few notable exceptions, including Carole Pateman on the *Philosophy of Right*, Alison Stone on the *Philosophy of Nature* (2010; 2013), and Kimberly Hutchings on the *Science of Logic* (2005). In addition, Hannah Arendt and Gillian Rose engage with Hegel's figure of the "beautiful soul" who shrinks from contact with the world and fears to act (Hegel 1977: 383) by reading the role of women intellectuals contemporary with Hegel through this figure from the *Phenomenology of Spirit* (Arendt 1974; Rose 1992).

The most important themes for feminist philosophy arising out of nineteenth-century continental philosophy in general, and Hegel in particular, then, include overcoming the epistemologically and politically isolated subject in favor of an interconnected system that not only links humans with each other individually and socially, but also humans with broader nature; understanding the human being as essentially not only intellectual and moral but also embodied and broadly material; and the relationship between beauty and morality. The overcoming of one-sided antitheses such as the distinctions between nature and culture, the individual and the universal, inclination and duty, body and mind, also constitutes an important part of Hegel's legacy for feminist thought.

Nietzsche, the Eternal Feminine, and Truth as a Woman

Friedrich Nietzsche's philosophy has generated as concentrated a critique from feminists as Hegel's, but a number of commentators, particularly from within contemporary continental philosophy, have also recognized the resources for feminist thinking in Nietzsche's critique of the history of metaphysics and of certain institutions, which, in his words, embody "the will to tradition, to authority, to responsibility for centuries to come" (1990: 105). Feminist philosophy, in other words, shares common enemies with Nietzsche. In addition, Nietzsche's analysis of the ways in which seemingly neutral and universal truths and values develop historically to favor certain groups can contribute to the feminist critique of power relations in patriarchal culture. I will focus here on several particularly productive strains of thought for feminist interpreters of Nietzsche: (1) the idea of truth as a woman; (2) the eternal feminine as a Dionysian affirmation of life; (3) the will to power as an overcoming of philosophical dualisms; and (4) the concept of genealogy. Nietzsche's critique of the philosophical conception of the atomic autonomous subject also provides resources for the feminist critique of traditional conceptions of subjectivity that privilege qualities historically judged to be "masculine" (Oliver and Pearsall 1998: 2).

Probably more than any single phrase of Nietzsche's, the enigmatic beginning of *Beyond Good and Evil*, "Supposing truth were a woman: what then?" (1989: 2) has both intrigued feminist writers and aroused their suspicion. With the publication of two important works treating the subject in France in the 1970s, feminist attention to Nietzsche burgeoned. Jacques Derrida's *Spurs: Nietzsche's Styles* (1979) circles around the above phrase, and is one of the first works to eschew the previous two major attitudes of commentators on Nietzsche's remarks on women in favor of an attention to the polysemic nature of the use of "woman" in his work. One strand of such early commentary rejected Nietzsche's philosophy altogether as misogynistic, while the other simply ignored his inflammatory comments on women as peripheral to his project.

The second important seminal work on Nietzsche and truth as a woman, Sarah Kofman's "Baubo: Theological Perversion and Fetishism," also avoids this double danger by focusing on Nietzsche's critique of metaphysics for its "perverted" perspective, which Nietzsche likens to a rapacious gaze that wants to strip women naked, that claims to be able to see the world as it really is and not as it appears (Kofman 1988: 37; Nietzsche 1989: 21). As "woman," in Kofman's view, Nietzsche's conception of truth makes a claim to be neither appearance nor reality, and thus cannot be expressed metaphysically.

Nietzsche's controversial remarks on women cannot be denied. Among the most infamous, the section "On the Friend" in *Thus Spoke Zarathustra* describes women as cats, birds, or cows, and makes the claim that "Woman is not yet capable of friendship" (1966: 57). The section "On Little Old and Young Women" states that "everything about woman is a riddle, and everything about woman has one solution: that is pregnancy," and has an old woman advise Zarathustra "You are going to women? Do not forget the whip!" (1966: 67). Yet in the same work virtue, truth, and eternity are female figures and virtue is compared to a mother's relationship to her child. Also, Zarathustra's whip is shown to be an ineffective way of approaching life or the feminine (Armstrong, cited in Patton 1993, xiii; Nietzsche 1966: 226). And through Zarathustra's longing to become pregnant with wisdom Nietzsche compares a relationship to the earth—the corrective to a tradition preoccupied with transcending corporeal life—to the capacity to procreate bodily (Nietzsche 1966: 36, 76, 85, 94, 108–109, 124, 224–227, 228–231). Nietzsche also uses pregnancy as a metaphor for self-overcoming and the eternal recurrence of the same in the same work (1966: 16; 115).

Derrida traces the multiple layers of Nietzsche's descriptions of woman as a figure for truth and for distance and as a figure of artifice, veils, and skepticism toward the philosophical idols that have heretofore been set up, in particular toward the metaphysical conception of being as unchanging and transcendent. Truth is a veil that both promises and hides something that seems to lie underneath appearances, but the feminine is that which recognizes both the temptation and the deceptiveness of such an appeal. According to Derrida, the heterogeneity of Nietzsche's text manifests his lack of illusion that he could ever know woman, truth, or the ontological effects of absence and presence (1979: 95). As such, Derrida argues, the figure of woman in Nietzsche performs and unmasks the contingency of every philosophical claim to transcendence and certainty, including those that occlude the claim of women to a specific philosophical role.

Luce Irigaray's *Marine Lover of Friedrich Nietzsche* famously responds to *Spurs* without citing it, insinuating that both Nietzsche and Derrida have appropriated the feminine to their own ends. *Marine Lover* is a conversation with Nietzsche that both responds to figures of the feminine in Nietzsche with love, as the title suggests, but also critically intimates that in addressing or discussing woman Nietzsche speaks into a mirror that ultimately reflects back only himself, or the feminine as it is constituted in the masculine imaginary. For Irigaray, supposing that truth is a woman and figuring woman as veiled, deceptive, or as purely appearance remains, as does its antithesis, within the metaphysical paradigm of truth, where the opposite grounds the economy of sameness (1991: 77). Irigaray writes, addressing Nietzsche directly, that when he finally allows woman to speak for themselves, as in the figures of Truth, Life, and Eternity in *Thus Spoke Zarathustra*, "it is only to bring about—your perspective, your art, your time, your will." This appropriative mimicry takes woman "away from her surfaces, her depths," and allows her to speak only through the ventriloquism of Zarathustra (1991: 36). On this argument, Nietzsche's text remains complicit with the values that it seeks to overturn and does not open up a space for an active feminine subject (Oliver 1995: x–xiii).

Debra Bergoffen negotiates this impasse by suggesting that Nietzsche's task was not to investigate the desire of woman so much as to undo man's desire for transcendence (1989: 82; 1998: 229). Bergoffen relates Nietzsche's attempt to unravel masculine metaphysical desire to his articulation of the temporality of the eternal recurrence of the same, which intertwines masculine and feminine temporalities in a "nonteleological joyful affirmation of life" (1989: 88).

Likewise, Kofman analyzes Nietzsche's appellation of truth as "a woman who has grounds for not showing her grounds," or "Baubo," in *The Gay Science* (Nietzsche 1974: 8), by recounting the story of the witch Baubo who appeared to Demeter during the Eleusinian mysteries. Baubo pulls up her skirts and exposes herself—or, in an alternate version, shows Demeter a picture of Dionysos drawn on her belly—causing Demeter to laugh in the midst of sorrowing for her lost daughter. As Kofman reads it, in the Eleusinian mysteries the female sexual organs are celebratory symbols of fertility and regeneration, and here they represent a return of the fecundity that Hades had stolen away, becoming assurances of the eternal rebirth or return of spring, life, and all life-affirming things. Kofman argues that Nietzsche both identifies and struggles with an ambivalent cultural attitude toward all things feminine, but that, at the end of *Thus Spoke Zarathustra*, his protagonist respects feminine truth, marries feminine eternity, and becomes pregnant with wisdom, himself taking on an androgynous character. Thus, both Baubo and Dionysos are masks for androgynous, protean life (Kofman 1988: 44–46).

Nietzsche's writings, in their Heraclitean emphasis on transitoriness and becoming, also provide resources for a critique of static philosophical dualisms, including the essentialist opposition between male and female. Kofman emphasizes that Dionysos, Nietzsche's privileged metaphorical figure for the principle of will to power and the affirmation of life, lies beyond the metaphysical designations of male and female (1988: 45). Lynne Tirrell juxtaposes Nietzsche's critical remarks on the untenability of hierarchical and often metaphysically loaded dualisms between becoming and being, appearance and reality, and conscious and unconscious psychic activity, with the question as to why he did not direct this same critique toward the opposition between man and woman (1994: 162). She points out that there is much of value for feminists to study in Nietzsche despite this lack, by virtue of his ground-breaking attack on metaphysical dualisms in *Beyond Good and Evil*, his analysis of the power of discourse (in the hands of men) to shape cultural interpretations of what a woman is, and his discussion of the importance of power in shaping identities (Tirrell 1994: 177).

Nietzsche's concept of genealogy interpreted through the mediation of Foucault and Deleuze also informs the feminist philosophy of Judith Butler and Rosi Braidotti. Genealogy, articulated by Nietzsche most forcefully in *On The Genealogy of Morals* (1967), opposes the search for metaphysical origins or essences lying invisibly "behind the world," inquiring instead into the contingencies, piecemeal motivations, and above all values and struggle for mastery that inspire the formation of particular cultural standards (Nietzsche 1967: 17). Genealogy critiques both the causes of the emergence of moral values, but also the values to which they in turn give rise once established. Butler turns the critical gaze of Nietzschean genealogy onto the nature of gender roles, arguing that dualistic and essentialist conceptions of femininity (and masculinity) arise out of a series of interpretations, values, practices, and reinterpretations that in turn engender a compulsion to perform gender norms of behavior and appearance (1990: 5). Such performances of gender render it denaturalized and subject to oppressive reinforcement, but also to reinterpretation and change. Braidotti uses genealogy to argue for a materialist conception of the intersection of bodies and power, rejecting any dualistic separation of nature and culture (2011: 145).

It is in this overcoming of metaphysical dualisms and the description of the will to power as an organic process, a simultaneously creative and destructive force that continually interprets and reinterprets (Nietzsche 1968: 539, 342), that Nietzsche's philosophy reflects the legacy of Kant and German Idealism. However, Nietzsche accords a power to human manipulations of this will to power not found in Kant's conceptualization of the purposiveness of nature, or even in Hegel's articulation of the movement of the historical dialectic of being and thought.

Women's Voices in the Nineteenth Century

Although women's intellectual contributions were increasingly heard in nineteenth-century German culture, the venue for women to express them was primarily restricted to letters, journals, and the conversations of literary salons. Caroline Schlegel-Schelling, married at one time to the literary critic and scholar August-Wilhelm Schlegel and later to the philosopher F. W. J. Schelling, and Dorothea Veit Schlegel, married to A.-W. Schlegel's brother Friedrich, formed part of the important Jena Romantic Circle, where they debated with important intellectual men of their time—including Novalis, Schelling, and Ludwig Tieck—and were acquainted with Goethe, Schiller, and Hegel. The contributions of these two women to the literary journal *Athenäum* edited by the Schlegel brothers cannot be precisely ascertained, since many entries were published anonymously, but it is commonly accepted that their work contributed greatly to early German romanticism. Among themes important to feminist philosophy, these fragments advocated a love relationship characterized by mutual support and respect, envisioned a free society with equal roles for men and women, and critiqued bourgeois marital norms and the notion of forced marriage.

Rahel Varnhagen was a nineteenth-century German intellectual who hosted one of the most prominent Berlin literary salons attended by the likes of the Schlegel brothers, Schelling, the Tieck brothers, the von Humboldt brothers, and even Goethe, as well as being the subject of an early book by the philosopher Hannah Arendt. Arendt reconstructed Varnhagen's life from a series of letters and diaries, proposing to correct the view of her presented after her death by her husband, the bourgeois Prussian civil servant Karl August von Varnhagen, who sought to present his wife in a manner that minimized her Jewishness and presented her as far as possible in line with the conventions of the day. In addition to tracing the evolution of a changing Jewish identity in the Germany of the early twentieth century, Arendt critiques the German Romantic conception of a certain *Innerlichkeit*, a self-professed desire on the part of Varnhagen to "live her life as a work of art," which resulted in a kind of claustrophobic worldlessness, a withdrawal from the world that accords with the appellation that Goethe gave to Varnhagen when he described her as a "beautiful soul." This phrase, which is the subject of a short story "Confessions of a Beautiful Soul" that appears within Goethe's novel *Wilhelm Meister's Apprenticeship*, names one who is isolated from society, who freely follows her own impulse rather than any law imposed from without, and could equally be applied to Caroline Schlegel-Schelling and Dorothea Veit Schlegel.

Dorothea Schlegel was the daughter of Moses Mendelssohn, the Enlightenment philosopher. She left her husband, a respectable Jewish merchant, for Friedrich Schlegel, the philosopher and literary critic. As Arendt describes it, Dorothea Schlegel assimilated completely, but not so much to German society as to Romanticism (2007: 24).

Arendt describes Rahel's *Innerlichkeit* in a negative vision of this seemingly positive appellation, as one who was "exiled . . . all alone to a place where nothing could reach her, where she was cut off from all human things, from everything that men have the right to claim" (1974: xvi). Like the beautiful soul who lacks an actual existence, "entangled in the contradiction between its pure self and the necessity of that self to externalize itself" and dwelling in the immediacy of this antithesis, eventually wasting away in yearning (Hegel 1977: 406–407), Arendt criticizes Varnhagen for the evocation of an endless longing without fruition, concluding that a beautiful soul is not enough.

The philosopher Gillian Rose, however, countered Arendt in proposing that Varnhagen and other nineteenth-century women intellectuals neither accepted exclusion from the universal nor feigned an illusory personal identity outside of the universal, but instead followed a third path beyond clinging to pure-being-for-self, on the one hand, and externalization or actualization in the world, on the other. Instead, Rahel "untangled the contradiction between her pure self and the necessity of that self to actualize itself by refusing to dwell in the immediacy of this antithesis" (Rose 1992: 192). These women intellectuals neither fixed themselves in isolation outside civil society, nor sought solace in an unattainable transcendence, nor reified themselves in one of many available paths through civil society.

Rose argues that by cultivating the life of the salon and the authorship of journals and letters that were eventually published, nineteenth-century women were able to negotiate the limits of civil society and play multiple roles rather than remaining fixed in one of its circumscribed positions (1992: 193). This operation on the borders of civil society allowed nineteenth-century women intellectuals to take on a singular position that eventually worked to effect change in women's education and philosophical authorship.

Further Reading

Although I only referred specifically to some of the essays in the edited collections listed below, all the essays in the collections provide good resources for further reading in these areas.

Bernstein, Richard (2010) "Hegel's Feminism," in Fanny Söderbäck (Ed.) *Feminist Readings of Antigone*, Albany, NY: State University of New York Press. (A defense of Hegel arguing that ethical life ought not to depend on natural distinctions, in particular sexual difference.)

Burgard, Peter (Ed.) (1994) *Nietzsche and the Feminine*, Charlottesville, VA: University Press of Virginia. (Addresses common reactions to Nietzsche's apparently misogynistic comments and suggests new ways of reading Nietzsche on the feminine.)

Hutchings, Kimberly and Pulkkinen, Tuija (Eds.) (2010) *Hegel's Philosophy and Feminist Thought*, New York: Palgrave MacMillan. (A rich collection featuring many European feminists.)

Mills, Patricia Jagentowicz (Ed.) (1996) *Feminist Interpretations of G. W. F. Hegel*, University Park, PA: Penn State Press. (A collection of essays by major commentators addressing the question of the role of the feminine in Hegel's writings.)

Oliver, Kelly and Pearsall, Marilyn (Eds.) (1998) *Feminist Interpretations of Friedrich Nietzsche*, University Park, PA: Penn State Press. (A collection of essays representing a wide range of feminist responses and approaches to Nietzsche.)

Patton, Paul (Ed.) (1993) *Nietzsche, Feminism, and Political Theory*, London: Routledge. (An early collection on Nietzsche's views on women in relation to political theory, featuring many well-known philosophers from England and Australia.)

Schott, Robin (Ed.) (1997) *Feminist Interpretations of Immanuel Kant*, University Park, PA: Penn State Press. (A collection of important essays addressing feminist critiques of and resources in Kant's writings.)

Related Topics

Feminist methods in the history of philosophy (Chapter 1); early modern feminism and Cartesian philosophy (Chapter 6); feminism and the Enlightenment (Chapter 8); historicizing feminist aesthetics (Chapter 37); aesthetics and the politics of gender (Chapter 38); feminist aesthetics and the categories of the beautiful and the sublime (Chapter 39).

References

Arendt, Hannah (1974) *Rahel Varnhagen: The Life of a German Jewish Woman*, trans. Richard and Clara Winston, New York: Harcourt Brace Jovanovich.

——(2007) *The Jewish Writings*, New York: Schocken.

Beauvoir, Simone de (1989) *The Second Sex*, trans. H. M. Parshley, New York: Vintage.

——(2000) *The Ethics of Ambiguity*, trans. Bernard Frechtman, New York: Citadel.

Bergoffen, Debra (1989) "On the Advantage and Disadvantage of Nietzsche for Women," in *The Question of the Other: Essays in Contemporary Continental Philosophy*, Ed. Arleen B. Dallery, Albany: SUNY Press, 77–89.

—— (1998) "Nietzsche Was No Feminist . . . ," in Kelly Oliver and Marilyn Pearsall (Eds.) *Feminist Interpretations of Friedrich Nietzsche*, University Park, PA: Penn State Press, 225–235.

Bernstein, Richard (2010) "Hegel's Feminism," in Fanny Söderbäck (Ed.) *Feminist Readings of Antigone*, Albany, NY: State University of New York Press.

Boer, Karin de (2003) "Hegel's Antigone and the Dialectics of Sexual Difference," *Philosophy Today* 47(5): 140–146.

Braidotti, Rosi (2011) *Nomadic Subjects*, second revised ed., New York: Columbia University Press.

Butler, Judith (1990) *Gender Trouble*, New York: Routledge.

——(2010) *Antigone's Claim: Kinship Between Life and Death*, New York: Columbia University Press.

Chanter, Tina (1995) *Ethics of Eros*, London: Routledge.

——(2011) *Whose Antigone? The Tragic Marginalization of Slavery*, Albany, NY: State University of New York Press.

Derrida, Jacques (1979) *Spurs: Nietzsche's Styles*, trans. Barbara Harlow, Chicago, IL: University of Chicago Press.

Efrat-Levkovitz, Rakefet (2010) "Reading the Same Twice Over: The Place of the Feminine in the Time of Hegelian Spirit," in Kimberly Hutchings and Tuija Pulkkinen (Eds.) *Hegel's Philosophy and Feminist Thought: Beyond Antigone?* New York: Palgrave Macmillan, 153–176.

Gauthier, Jeffrey (1997) *Hegel and Feminist Social Criticism*, Albany, NY: State University of New York Press.

Hance, Allen (1998) "The Art of Nature: Hegel and the *Critique of Judgment*," *International Journal of Philosophical Studies* 6(1): 37–65.

Hegel, G. W. F. (1977) *Phenomenology of Spirit*, trans. A. V. Miller, Oxford: Oxford University Press.

——(1991) *Elements of the Philosophy of Right*, trans. H. B. Nisbet, Cambridge: Cambridge University Press.

Hutchings, Kimberly (2003) *Hegel and Feminist Philosophy*, Cambridge: Polity Press.

Hutchings, Kimberly, and Pulkkinen, Tuija (2010) Introduction in *Hegel's Philosophy and Feminist Thought*, New York: Palgrave Macmillan, 1–18.

Irigaray, Luce (1985) "The Eternal Irony of the Community," in *Speculum: Of the Other Woman*, trans. Gillian C. Gill Ithaca, NY: Cornell University Press, 214–226.

——(1991) *Marine Lover of Friedrich Nietzsche*, trans. Gillian C. Gill, New York: Columbia University Press.

Kant, Immanuel (1987) [1791] *Critique of Judgment*, trans. Werner Pluhar, Indianapolis, IN: Hackett.

Kofman, Sarah (1988) "Baubo: Theological Perversion and Fetishism," in Michael A. Gillespie and Tracy B. Strong (Eds.) *Nietzsche's New Seas*, Chicago, IL: University of Chicago Press, 175–202.

Kreines, Robert (2008) "The Logic of Life: Hegel's Philosophical Defense of Natural Teleology," in Frederick Beiser (Ed.) *Cambridge Companion to Hegel and Nineteenth Century Philosophy*, Cambridge: Cambridge University Press, 344–377.

Lindberg, Susanna (2010) "Woman-Life or Lifework and Psychotechnique," in Kimberly Hutchings and Tuija Pulkkinen (Eds.) *Hegel's Philosophy and Feminist Thought: Beyond Antigone?* New York: Palgrave Macmillan, 177–194.

Lonzi, Carla (1996) "Let's Spit on Hegel," trans. Giovanna Bellesia and Elaine MacLachlan, in Patrica Jagentowicz Mills (Ed.) *Feminist Interpretations of G. W. F. Hegel*, University Park, PA: Penn State Press, 275–298.

Miller, Elaine P. (2000) "The Paradoxical Displacement: Beauvoir and Irigaray on Hegel's Antigone," *Journal of Speculative Philosophy* 14(2): 121–137.

Mills, Patricia Jagentowicz (1986) "Hegel's Antigone," *Owl of Minerva* 17(2): 131–152.

Moen, Marcia (1997) "Feminist Themes in Unlikely Places: Re-Reading Kant's *Critique of Judgment*," in Robin Schott (Ed.) *Feminist Interpretations of Immanuel Kant*, University Park, PA: Penn State Press, 213–256.

Mussett, Shannon (2006) "Conditions of Servitude: The Peculiar Role of the Master-Slave Dialectic in Simone de Beauvoir's *The Second Sex*," in Margaret A. Simons (Ed.) *The Philosophy of Simone de Beauvoir: Critical Essays*, Bloomington, IN: Indiana University Press, 276–294.

Nietzsche, Friedrich (1966) *Thus Spoke Zarathustra*, trans. Walter Kaufmann, New York: Viking Penguin.

——(1967) *On the Genealogy of Morals*, trans. Walter Kaufmann, New York: Vintage.

——(1968) *The Will to Power*, trans. R. J. Hollingdale and Walter Kaufmann, New York: Vintage.

——(1974) *The Gay Science*, trans. Walter Kaufmann, New York: Vintage.

——(1989) *Beyond Good and Evil*, trans. Walter Kaufmann, New York: Vintage.

——(1990) *Twilight of the Idols*, trans. R. J. Hollingdale, London: Penguin.

Nuzzo, Angelica (2001) "Freedom in the Body: The Body as Subject of Rights and Object of Property in Hegel's 'Abstract Right,'" in Robert Williams (Ed.) *Beyond Liberalism and Communitarianism*, Albany, NY: State University of New York Press, 111–123.

Oliver, Kelly (1995) *Womanizing Nietzsche: Philosophy's Relation to the "Feminine,"* New York: Routledge.

——(1996) "Antigone's Ghost: Undoing Hegel's *Phenomenology of Spirit*," *Hypatia* 11(1): 67–90.

Oliver, Kelly and Marilyn Pearsall (1998) "Introduction," in *Feminist Interpretations of Friedrich Nietzsche*, University Park, PA: Penn State Press, 1–17.

Patton, Paul (1993) "Introduction," in *Nietzsche, Feminism, and Political Theory*, London: Routledge, ix–xiii.

Rose, Gillian (1992) *The Broken Middle: Out of Our Ancient Society*, London: Blackwell.

Stone, Alison (2010) "Matter and Form: Hegel, Organicism, and the Difference between Women and Men," in Kimberly Hutchings and Tuija Pulkkinen (Eds.) *Hegel's Philosophy and Feminist Thought: Beyond Antigone?* New York: Palgrave Macmillan, 211–232.

—— (2013) "Hegel on Law, Women and Contract," in Maria Drakopoulou (Ed.) *Feminist Encounters with Legal Philosophy*, London: Routledge, 104–122.

Tirrell, Lynne (1994) "Sexual Dualism and Women's Self-Creation: On the Advantages and Disadvantages of Reading Nietzsche for Feminists," in Peter J. Burgard (Ed.) *Nietzsche and the Feminine*, Charlottesville, VA: The University of Virginia Press, 158–184.

Zimmerman, Robert (2005) *The Kantianism of Hegel and Nietzsche: Reinventions in Nineteenth-Century German Philosophy*, New York: Edwin Mellen Press.

10

INTRODUCING BLACK FEMINIST PHILOSOPHY

Kristie Dotson

Introduction

In her article, "Coalition Politics: Turning the Century," Bernice Johnson Reagon advocates for leaving a legacy of one's liberatory praxis when she writes:

> The thing that must survive you is not just the record of your practice, but the principles that are the basis of your practice. If in the future, somebody is gonna use that song I sang, they're gonna have to strip it or at least shift it. I'm glad the principle is there for others to build upon.
>
> (2000 [1983]: 366)

Reagon articulates not only what people laboring for social change need to leave behind, but also what those who inherit their work should expect to receive. That is to say, those of us who are concerned with social and political change should aim to "throw . . . [ourselves] into the next century," as she suggests, by leaving our practice and our principles (Reagon 2000 [1983]: 365). And those of us who are on the receiving end of messages from previous centuries should, at the very least, work to identify the principles that lay within inherited practices. Accordingly, when exploring Black feminist philosophy this is often what one must do, that is, uncover philosophical positions left for us to discover.

In this chapter, I introduce U.S. Black feminist philosophy by tracing two lessons that can be identified from Black feminist philosophy in that context. They include: (1) oppression as a multistable, social phenomenon; and (2) part of some Black women's experiences of oppression concerns the occupation of negative socio-epistemic space. These two observations gesture to an understanding that liberation agendas require grappling with an ongoing politics of spatiality. These two lessons and their implication can serve as a starting point for the beginner to Black feminist philosophy as they draw on historical and contemporary inquiries in Black feminist thought. Not only do these lessons span over a century of Black women's social theory, including Anna Julia Cooper (1998 [1891–1892]) and Fannie Barrier Williams (2007 [1900]; 1905), but they also remain salient in many Black feminist theoretical positions today. In what follows, I will highlight the above two lessons that can be found in Black feminist philosophy in a US context.

The Multistability of Oppression

There have been and there will continue to be attempts to create metaphors for experiences of oppression where singular analytics fail. Very few feminist and gender scholars are not familiar with critiques from Black feminists on the difficulty of fitting their experience of oppression into categories demarcated by one vector of vulnerability, e.g., gender-based oppression and/or race-based oppression. From Anna Julia Cooper's train station (1998 [1891–1892]), to the Combahee River Collective's idea of interlocking (1995 [1978]), to Frances Beale's double jeopardy (1995 [1969]), to Deborah King's revision of the jeopardy paradigm with her conception of multiple jeopardy (1995 [1988]), to Hortense Spillers' interstices (1984), to Kimberlé Crenshaw's intersection (1989), and beyond, there have been attempts to create metaphors capable of capturing experiences of oppression that seem to twist, turn, twirl, and jump so as to resist being tracked. That Black feminist thought has, and continues to, attempt to track oppression experienced according to multiple aspects of social existence cannot be disputed. However, there seems to be relatively little recognition of what these attempts imply about an overall understanding of oppression as a social phenomenon. That is to say, much of Black feminist philosophy can be said to commit to an underlying assumption that social phenomena, like oppression, are multistable. And the understanding of oppression as multistable puts demands on our theorizing about social phenomena.

The Combahee River Collective's "A Black Feminist Statement," first published in 1978, offers a portrait of the rhetorical landscape within which one can recognize tensions in conceptions of oppression, which one might take as a beginning philosophical problematic about the nature of social phenomenon. The Collective open their famous "Statement" with the call for an:

> *Integrated analysis* and practice based upon the fact that the major *systems* of oppression are interlocking. The *synthesis* of these oppressions creates the conditions of our lives. As Black women we see Black feminism as the logical political movement to combat the manifold and simultaneous oppressions that all women of color face.
>
> (1995 [1978]: 232; emphasis added)

There are two conceptions of oppression conflicting with one another in this passage. There is oppression defined as multiple, interlocking systems and oppression as a holistic, simultaneous experience. These two conceptions of oppression are not wholly compatible. But that the Collective deploy them one after the other indicates a rather sophisticated overall understanding of oppression that has heretofore gone largely unacknowledged. In what follows, I will outline these two clashing conceptions of oppression and the first lesson from US Black women's social theory, i.e. that oppression is a multistable phenomenon.

A System-Based Conception of Oppression

According to the earlier cited passage, oppression can be seen to have several characteristics. It can be seen to be composed of (1) various systems that (2) interlock to create comprehensive wholes. These "wholes" are manifold or varied. This range of descriptors—i.e. systems-based, interlocking, and manifold—can be aligned and realigned in a number of ways to gesture to different overall understandings of oppression. The most common reading is to trace the descriptors—systems-based, interlocking, and manifold—to an additive approach to understanding oppressions. This interpretation can harken to a remnant of critiques of Francis Beale's "Double Jeopardy" (1995 [1969]), which attempts to promote the recognition of the interrelations of race-based and gender-based oppressions, along with a much-overlooked emphasis on class-based oppressions. The jeopardy paradigm would give rise to the use of "triple jeopardy," to indicate race, class, and gender-based oppression and, as some claim, a fourth jeopardy in sexuality-based oppression. Because the jeopardy model grew by "adding-on" other systemic forms of oppression, the jeopardy paradigm is often considered to be an additive approach. This interpretation largely results from placing emphasis on the descriptor, "systems-based." If oppression is composed of diverse systems of jeopardy that interlock and complicate one another, for example, then oppression, itself, can also be functionalized thus.

Oppression, then, can be seen to function according to diverse systems of jeopardy that interlock and complicate one another. The descriptors—systems-based, interlocking, and manifold—seem to fix oppression as a conglomerate of diverse, discrete systems that represent different and complicated sites of jeopardy according to a functionalization by description. Certainly this kind of reading can be supported by the passage "[we] see as our particular task the development of integrated analysis and practice based upon the fact that the major systems of oppression are interlocking," (The Combahee River Collective 1995 [1978]: 232). First, the use of the plural term, "oppressions," and, second, the call for "integrative analysis and practice" imply, for some, that the underlying conception of oppression is one in which discrete systems, which can be analyzed separately (even if only in theory), are locked together in ways that make sites of jeopardy manifold. Varying remarks throughout the text separating sexual oppression from race oppression, for example, further evidence this understanding of how oppression is conceptualized in the Collective's "Statement." That these "oppressions" are, at times, separated from a holistic account of oppression is notable and can be found in the text. This has made many content with the system-based conception of oppression, which most identify with The Combahee River Collective and the jeopardy paradigm.

Although the systems-based conception of oppression is likely the most familiar reading of the Collective's understanding of "interlocking oppression" and, to a certain extent, of the jeopardy paradigm, this is but half of the story of how the term "oppression" is used in the Collective's "Statement." It is also the least defensible, insofar as it lends itself to a *disintegrative* analysis that is done for the sake of an integrative analysis. That may be precisely what the Combahee River Collective, Frances Beale, and many other Black women social theorists in an US context are attempting to compromise due to problematic oversights that such a functionalized model of oppression promotes, e.g. not just race, not just gender (Smith 1998). It is fortunate, then, for Black feminists who inherit this work, that this is not the only way oppression is conceptualized in "A Black Feminist Statement."

An Experiential Conception of Oppression

The second conception of oppression that is present in the Collective's "Statement" can be seen to follow from, first, the following passage, "The synthesis of these oppressions creates the conditions of our lives" (1995 [1978]: 232) and, second, the fact that for the bulk of the essay oppression is invoked *not* as the plural, "oppressions," but as a singular term "oppression." This second conception of oppression, I claim, is experience-based, not systems-based. That is to say, emphasis is put on the simultaneity of one's experience of oppression, which is not easily discernable according to a systems approach. As the Collective write, "we often find it difficult to separate race from class from sex oppression because in our lives they are most often experienced simultaneously" (The Combahee River Collective 1995 [1978]: 234). The term "simultaneity" is used to describe the experience of oppression. And the synthesis of oppression, which harkening to experience can promise, involves another dimension of oppression that cannot be captured by understanding oppression as interlocking systems.

It is the understanding of oppression as a holistic phenomenon, as experience-based and not given to discrete systems that can be analyzed separately, that informs the Collective's call for "identity politics." Identifying oppression as experience-based also required harkening to the reality that addressing oppression will need to track *possible ranges of experiences of oppression*. As one member of The Combahee River Collective recalls:

> I think we came up with the term "identity politics." I never really saw it anywhere else . . . But what we meant by identity politics was a politics that grew out of our objective material experiences as Black women . . . So there were basically politics that worked for us . . . It gave us a way to move, a way to make change. It was not the reductive version that theorists now really criticize. It was not being simplistic in saying I am Black and you are not. That is not what we were doing.
>
> (Harris 2009: 28)

Understanding oppression as outlined by one's range of experiences with oppression changes the formulation of oppression from "discrete systems, which can be analyzed separately, and yet are locked together in ways that make sites of jeopardy manifold" to a range of experiences that can condition one's life according to simultaneous jeopardization. *Jeopardy*, a noun, turns into *jeopardize*, a verb. This latter conception is compatible with Beale's usage of *jeopardize*, as her primary deployment of the term "jeopardy" is the verb "jeopardize." Oppression can be understood, then, according to ranges of jeopardization and the range of one's jeopardization can often be tracked according to one's "read-able" social identities in a given geo-political space. What is important to note is that oppressions (plural) transforms into oppression (singular), for the Collective.

One of the differences between the "integrative analysis" of a system-based conception of oppression and the "synthesis" of an experience-based conception of oppression lies in one's reasons to deploy either conception. A systems-based conception of oppression can be used to find bridges across different experiences of oppression, but it contributes precious little to *comprehending* ranges of jeopardization. In fact, it does much to obscure such ranges. An experience-based conception of oppression can aid in identifying ranges of jeopardization, but often obscures sites of coalition. This is not a simple difference. Those invested in an experience-based conception of oppression often think that sites of coalition are merely illusions, whereas those persuaded by a system-based conception of oppression often find the identification of experiential difference distracting, at best, and irrelevant, at worst. These positions are not easy to reconcile. And it is not clear that reconciliation is a necessary goal. Rather, as is evidenced by the Combahee River Collective's text, each conception can be allowed to exist simultaneously. They can exist side-by-side, clashing horribly at times, but present in a way that calls for a philosophical reading of an operative assumption concerning the nature of oppression, which underwrites the unproblematic deployment of two clashing conceptions of oppression.

The Collective's attempt to examine the "multilayered texture of Black women's lives," takes place among conceptions of oppression that they both utilize and challenge. They complicate the "system or experience" dichotomy that so often plagues reconstructions of Black feminist thought, by refusing to choose one conception over another. They challenge a system-based conception by identifying that their experiences of oppression do not fold nicely into neat analytics, while affirming the necessity of systems-accounts as socialists interested in the articulation of "the real class situation of persons who are not merely raceless, sexless workers, but for whom racial and sexual oppression are significant determinants in their working/economic lives" (The Combahee River Collective 1995 [1978]: 235).

The systems-based theory can work when we are distinctly referring to systems of oppression, and they exist. But such an approach fails miserably to track the range of jeopardization one might face. The Collective affirm an experience-based conception of oppression when they forward that "we know that there is such a thing as racial-sexual oppression that is neither solely racial and solely sexual," even while they proclaim the need to consider system-based analyses (The Combahee River Collective 1995 [1978]: 234, 235). What does this intentional conceptual clashing imply about an overall understanding of oppression? I claim that The Combahee River Collective can be seen to have operated with an understanding that oppression is a multistable social phenomenon.

Lesson 1: *Oppression is a Multistable Phenomenon*

In its simplest formation, an assumption concerning oppression invoked in The Combahee River Collective's "A Black Feminist Statement" is: oppression is complicated. It admits of no privilegeable conceptions that do not also obscure through the privileging. Multistability, here, refers to "an empirically testable hypothesis about how several stable patterns of the same object can be perceived from the first person perspective" (Whyte 2015: 69). Oppression is a multistable social phenomenon. That means that oppression, as it persists, can give rise to numerous different patterns of persistence that can be empirically verified. Taking oppression as a multistable phenomenon is to say that it admits of an open range of "topographic" possibilities (Ihde 1977: 77). Oppression in a given society, on the ground, will have multiple ways one can understand it, and these multiple ways will have a certain "apodicticity" (Ihde 1977: 71). That is to say, one's certitude that oppression simply "is" a certain way or originates from such and such a place, or can be understood according to such and such an orientation, can be experientially fulfilled time and again. This is not simply to say that we see what we want to see, although this is certainly part of it. Rather, oppression admits of a number of interpretations and a number of manifestations and a number of conceptions. How a multistable phenomenon is interpreted *in space* will depend on a variety of factors, not the least of which will be one's "perspectival perception," one's goals (Ihde 2009: 12), including, but not limited to, cultural inheritances, cognitive commitments, and embodied location. The way oppression is perceived will also depend on its social effect and one's relations to it (Frye 1983).

It is no surprise that a middle-class, able-bodied, heterosexual, Christian, English-speaking, Black man who is a long-time citizen in the United States might identify race as "the" primary form of oppression and privilege a systems-based conception of oppression. Accordingly, it is also hardly surprising that I cannot make sense of what it would mean to be oppressed as Black or as a Woman without having a "conceptual" difficulty akin to the difficulty inherent in resolving the mind/body problem. Where do the "raced" parts end and the "woman" parts begin? And how do they interact? When attempting to comprehend the range of jeopardization I face as a Black woman in the United States, I privilege an experiential-based conception, but not in all cases and not consistently. And it should be noted that there are more ways of conceiving of oppression than either system- or experience-based in Black feminist thought. This reality, that oppression holds stable for empirically testable hypotheses across a range of patterns, gestures to an aspect of oppression that is largely overlooked—although not, I would claim, by the Combahee River Collective. There is simply oppression; and it is multistable admitting of a range of conceptualizations, functionalizations, and manifestations.

I believe that this is what many of the theories of oppression in Black women's writings in the US have been aiming to highlight. Anna Julia Cooper's "Woman vs. the Indian" (1983 [1891–1892]), Fannie Barrier Williams' "The Colored Girl" (1905), Frances Beale's, "Double Jeopardy" (1995 [1969]), Pauli Murray's "The Liberation of Black Women" (1995 [1970]), Audre Lorde's "There is No Hierarchy of Oppression" (2009 [1983]), Deborah King's "Multiple Jeopardy" (1985 [1988]), Kimberlé Crenshaw's "Demarginalizing the Intersection of Race and Gender" (1989), Carole Boyce Davies's *Black Women, Writing and Identity* (1994), Carla Peterson's *"Doers of the Word"* (1995), Patricia Hill Collins' *Fighting Words* (1998), Valerie Smith's *Not Just Race Not Just Gender* (1998) and Kimberly Springer's *Living for the Revolution* (2005)—all of these Black women (and many more) have attempted to articulate some metaphor for oppression that can signify the complex ways oppression jeopardizes the lives of Black women, and yet leave room for the realization that oppression is a multistable social phenomenon. Unfortunately, the clashing conceptions of oppression in these texts are often read as a lack of theoretical sophistication, instead of resting on an important insight into the nature of oppression itself. Namely, that oppression holds within its structure the ability to manifest *stably* differently at different times to different people.

Identifying an orientation that oppression is multistable within The Combahee River Collective's clashing conceptions of oppression is not mere conjecture on my part. Identity politics is underwritten by a realization of a real danger in *not* owning one's social identity and how it affects one's understanding of oppression. They write concerning identity politics:

> We believe that the most profound and potentially the most radical politics come directly out of our own identity, as opposed to working to end somebody else's oppression. In the case of Black women this is a particularly repugnant, dangerous, threatening, and therefore revolutionary concept because it is obvious from looking at all the political movements that have preceded us that anyone is more worthy of liberation than ourselves . . . to be recognized as human, levelly human, is enough.
>
> (The Combahee River Collective 1995 [1978]: 234)

This passage draws attention to the often-cited and still under-appreciated statement that "all the women are white, all the Blacks are men" (Hull, Scott, and Smith 1982). This is not a statement of fact. It is a statement of the power to determine dominant narratives of gender-based or race-based oppression. And those narratives are experientially confirmable for certain portions of those populations, but they lead to rendering unintelligible ranges of jeopardization faced by Black women, for example. This is not a surprise: analytics of oppression do work to obscure experiences of oppression complicated by complex social existences. So-called ill-meaning Black men or evil white women are not the sole cause of such misreadings, although there may have been some. Rather, the nature of oppression as multistable encourages such overdetermination, but it also demands more open-ended approaches. This is where I situate the clashing conceptions of oppression in "A Black Feminist Statement." It is a performance of open-endedness required to acknowledge the multistable nature of oppression so as to resist practices of misreading encouraged by the multistability of oppression itself. These performances of openness are common in Black feminist thought, although they are often read as theoretical incontinence.

The next lesson from Black feminist philosophy that I will identify can be posited as a way to understand why the clashing conception of oppression in "The Black Feminist Statement" was largely ignored and, through reductive critiques of identity politics, erased.

Possessing Negative Socio-Epistemic Status

In her book, *Invisibility Blues*, Michele Wallace argues that one of the primary values of Black Women's literature is its ability to render "the negative" presence of Black women substantial (1990: 228). Claiming that Black women are the "other of the other," Wallace (1990) will, I think, appropriately identify a "fear" of a kind of theory in some Black feminist intellectual traditions that is a response to the ways that abstract theorizing about oppression has rendered invisible Black women's experiences of oppression. Black women, in Wallace's estimation, exist in varying states of negation fostered by, in part, the ways Black women's experiences have been overwritten with narratives where they no longer recognize themselves. Wallace, here, is picking up on a common topic in many US Black women's social and political writings that dates back, at least, to Maria Stewart (1832).

The epistemic violence that often hinders one's ability to "make sense" of claims made by and about Black women has been heavily remarked upon. From Fannie Barrier Williams' pronouncement that Black women are "unknowable" (1905) to Paule Murray's understanding of Jane Crow dynamics (1995 [1970]), to Deborah King's articulation of Black women's theoretical invisibility (1995 [1988]: 43–45), to Kimberlé Crenshaw's description of how Black women can be "theoretically erased" (1989: 139). To shed light on Wallace's point and this understanding of Black women's "problematic" occupation of socio-epistemic space in an US context, I will articulate Fannie Barrier Williams' claim that Black women are "unknowable." Williams articulates two fronts on which Black women are unknowable and then turns to offer an account of what is at stake in being unknowable.

At the turn of the twentieth century, Williams explains that Black women were unknowable "qua woman" and "qua race." In her article, "The Woman's Part in the Man's Business," she writes:

The American Negro woman is the most interesting woman in the country . . . She has no history, no traditions, no race ideals, no inherited resources, no established race character. She is the only woman in America who is almost unknown.

(Williams 1907: 544)

To say that Black women, in a US context, were almost "unknown" was not to indicate that there were no stereotypical images of Black women in existence. Williams is well aware of negative portrayals of Black women as she writes numerous articles defending Black women in the face of transient public opinions. However, what provoked Black women's general "unknowability" was a paucity of resources within "fixed public opinion" that one could draw upon when interpreting Black women (Williams 2007 [1900]: 54). I take "fixed public opinion" to be something akin to a "social imaginary." Lorraine Code explains that a social imaginary is a "conceptual analytic resource" that refers to

[i]mplicit but . . . effective systems of images, meanings, metaphors, and interlocking explanations-expectations within which people, in specific time periods and geographical-cultural climates, enact their knowledge and subjectivities and craft their self understandings.

(Code 2006: 29)

The concept of a social imaginary points to the ways that social perceptions are influenced, and the underlying understandings that fashion them. Black women, according to Williams, could not be known via available prevailing social narratives. And though Williams was aware that Black women were subject to social stereotypes, those stereotypes were only one part of the problems Black women faced. She explained that another very real problem for Black women also followed from a lack of available resources within established social imaginaries useful for understanding the lives and plights of Black women.

According to Williams, Black women were situated in a peculiar place. They were not wholly subject to prevailing narratives around race, nor were they wholly subject to prevailing narratives around womanhood. Williams explained, in her article "The Colored Girl," "Man's instinctive homage at the shrine of womankind draws a line of color, which places . . . [the colored girl] forever outside its mystic circle" (1905: 400). She believed that Black women had no male defenders and no prose or literature written to sing the virtues of Black women. It may seem irrelevant to say that there are no poems and literature written in homage to Black women. But what Williams appears to be drawing attention to is a kind of negative socio-epistemic status that is marked by pervasive absence, and not a masked presence. Where Ralph Ellison will express eloquently through the voice of the nameless narrator of *The Invisible Man*, "I am invisible, you understand, simply because people refuse to see me . . . it is as though I have been surrounded by mirrors of hard, distorting glass" (1995 [1947]: 3), Williams expresses a similar edict by indicating that "she is invisible, you understand, because there is no way for her to be seen" (1905: 400).

It is not clear that Williams sees her position as being surrounded by mirrors of any kind. The mirrors are all positioned to reflect other groups, distorting their images, but leaving her image in darkness. So Williams, when speaking of social uplift, expresses the need to address the negative socio-epistemic space Black women exist in within US social imaginaries. Let me suggest that the liminal, outsider-within status that many Black feminists have identified around Black women as a social group within the US parallels Williams' conception of the "unknowability" of Black women (see, for example, Collins 1986; Peterson 1993).

Now there is much about this account that is dated. First, there are and were Black male defenders of Black women. There have also been great strides in cultural production by and about Black women in the US. However, fixating on these clearly dated features misses a larger commonality that Williams shares with more contemporary Black feminist scholars such as Wallace. What survives the cultural production phases of self-determination is an ongoing identification of erasure. What a paucity in fixed public imaginaries harkens to is, at base, a struggle for intelligibility that cannot be satisfied with "controlling images" or "stereotypes," if they are also transient. The problem that Williams and Wallace identify in common is being the "other of an other," which is obviously not a reduction to the same. It is a relegation to a null, *transient space of signification*. A dynamic space, where one can construct Black women as the welfare queen or the mammy; the diseased maid or the emasculating matriarch; or with whatever purpose Black women are introduced into a given narrative.

The effect of being unknowable is hardly limited to an inability to be detected within "fixed" social imaginaries. For Williams, there was a more profound effect of (what Wallace calls) Black women's varying states of negation. Williams writes:

> That the term "colored girl" is almost a term of reproach in the social life of America is all too true; she is not known and hence *not believed* in, she belongs to a race that is best designated by the term "problem" and she lives beneath the shadow of that problem which envelops and obscures her.
>
> (1905: 400; emphasis added)

Again, contrast this quote with a question posed by W. E. B. Du Bois, who opens his book, *The Souls of Black Folks*, with the question, "How does it feel to be a problem?" (1995 [1905]: 43). Williams situates herself, and other Black women, by asking the question, "How does it feel to exist beneath the shadow of a problem?" Du Bois, a Black man subject to semi-permanent race ideas and conceptions of race character, can have the state of embodying "a problem." Williams, on the other hand, as a Black woman is denied that possibility. Williams recognized the ability to positively "embody" an identity, held by both white women and Black men, as a marker of status. What status, you might ask? I want to suggest that deep-seeded "distortions" actually offer a positive socio-epistemic status. Positive, here, simply means social presence or broad detectability. Williams is not alone in making this observation. Kimberlé Crenshaw will make much of anti-discrimination cases where Black women are seen as too special a class to be subject to anti-discrimination correctives either due to the fact that they were not discriminated against because they were Black or because they were women, but because they are Black women, for example (Crenshaw 1989). This kind of erasure, which Deborah King calls "being socialized out of existence," is precisely what Williams is attempting to draw attention to in 1905.

Books such as Melissa Harris-Perry's *Sister Citizen* highlight the problem of being "socialized out of existence" or, as Wallace prescribes, existing in varying states of negation as an ongoing problem for many Black women in the US (Wallace 1990; King 1995 [1988]: 45; Harris-Perry 2011). This is not an accident. There are conditions for the possibility of social presence, i.e. the ability to resist Williams' unknowability, and they concern occupying positive socio-epistemic space. Lesson two, then, is simply that erasures can be affected when one exists in varying states of negation, even if (and, quite possibly, especially if) that negation is theoretically inscribed so as to affect social imaginaries. It is important to note that social imaginaries are by no means uniform and universal. As a result, the occupation of negative socio-epistemic is not itself a uniform or universal state of existence. This is why Wallace identifies it as "varying states of negation." Occupation of negative socio-epistemic space is a dynamic condition that is heightened and lessened depending upon context.

Conclusion: Towards a Politics of Spatiality

If oppression is multistable (given to perspectival perceptions *on the ground*) and if part of Black women's experience of oppression follows from inhabiting a negative socio-epistemic space, then Black women's liberation will need to address far more than material concerns and far more than our own material concerns. One must also address the politics of spatiality that the multistability of oppression and the necessity of positive socio-epistemic space highlight. A politics of spatiality, here, refers to tracking dominant narratives of oppression (and the understandings and pivots on which those dominant forms are tracking or obscuring) and the machinations and composition of negative socio-epistemic space in any given geo-political landscape. Addressing problems that result from the multistability of oppression and the occupation of negative socio-epistemic space would require radical reconceptualizations of how we occupy space as part of a liberation agenda.

The call for this kind of reconceptualization can be seen in Anna Julia Cooper's 1891 article, "Woman vs. the Indian." Cooper offers an anecdote aimed at clarifying her position as a Black woman in the US. She talks of frequenting a train rest stop, with a main foyer area and two clearly labeled rooms. One dingy, lonely room was labeled "FOR LADIES." And another equally depressing room was labeled "FOR COLORED PEOPLE." Cooper briefly describes her confusion. To which room did she belong? The Ladies' room? The "Colored" People's room? What room should she occupy and at what costs? Cooper describes her awareness of the puzzle presented her when she simply stands in place and asks the reader, "What a field for a missionary woman?" (1983 [1891–1892]: 95). The irony of her question should not be lost. One of the points of Cooper's story is that there *is no field* for a Black woman, missionary or otherwise. The marked failure to find "space" where one belongs speaks to many of the concerns raised in Black feminist thought. Let me suggest, then, that the almost rabid focus on "homes" and "home life" as a strategy for social uplift within US Black feminist thought (see, e.g., Smith 1983; hooks 1990; Omolade 1994; Peterson 1995; Tate 2003) is not indicative of an internalization of the "cult of womanhood" ideals, nor is it an outgrowth of some imagined "bourgeois" self-deception.

What Black feminist social theorists such as Williams and Cooper identified was that Black women had no clear spatial placement. This observation has been reaffirmed and extended in the twentieth and, now, twenty-first centuries to also include an absence of theoretical placement (Crenshaw 1989: 139). The spatial nature of the descriptions that Cooper and Williams offer of Black women's situation with respect to oppression should not go unnoticed. For Williams, Black women were "beneath," "beyond," and "outside" of US social imaginaries. For Cooper, Black women simply did not have a "field" or space that lent to interpreting Black women's place in American social landscapes. But, as local as this account has been, this is far from a local problem. Oppression is multistable wherever it occurs. And there are populations all over the world occupying negative socio-epistemic space, which is inherently unstable when one allows this notion to travel. Imagining justice and feminist agendas, then, requires that one harken to the politics of spatiality in a given geo-political context, and this will require open-ended, dynamic theorizing.

Further Reading

Collins, Patricia Hill (2000 [1990]) *Black Feminist Thought: Knowledge, Consciousness, and the Politics of Empowerment*, 2nd ed., New York: Routledge.

Guy-Sheftall, Beverly (Ed.) (1995) *Words of Fire: An Anthology of Black Feminist Thought*, New York: New Press.

Hull, Gloria, Scott, Patricia Bell, and Smith, Barbara (Eds.) (1982) *All the Women Are Whites, and All the Blacks Are Men, but Some of Us Are Brave*, New York: Feminist Press.

James, Stanlie, Foster, Frances Smith, and Guy-Sheftall, Beverley (Eds.) (2009) *Still Brave: The Evolution of Black Women's Studies*, New York: The Feminist Press.

Smith, Barbara (Ed.) (1983) *Home Girls: A Black Feminist Anthology*, New York: Kitchen Table Press.

Related Topics

Feminism and borderlands identities (Chapter 17); epistemic injustice, ignorance, and trans experience (Chapter 22); the genealogy and viability of the concept of intersectionality (Chapter 28); critical race theory, intersectionality, and feminist philosophy (Chapter 29); feminism and power (Chapter 54).

References

Beale, Frances M. (1995 [1969]) "Double Jeopardy: To Be Female and Black," in Beverly Guy-Sheftall (Ed.) *Words of Fire: An Anthology of Black Feminist Thought*, New York: New Press, 146–155.

Code, Lorraine (2006) *Ecological Thinking: The Politics of Epistemic Location*, New York: Oxford University Press.

The Combahee River Collective (1995 [1978]) "A Black Feminist Statement," in Beverly Guy-Sheftall (Ed.) *Words of Fire: An Anthology of Black Feminist Thought*, New York: New Press, 343–355.

Collins, Patricia Hill (1986) "Learning from the Other Within: The Sociological Significance of Black Feminist Thought," *Social Problems* 33(6): 14–32.

——(1998) *Fighting Words: Black Women and the Search for Justice*, St. Paul, MN: University of Minnesota Press.

Cooper, Anna Julia (1983 [1891–1892]) "Woman Versus the Indian," in Charles Lemert and Esme Bhan (Eds.) *The Voice of Anna Julia Cooper: Including a Voice from the South and Other Important Essays, Papers, and Letters*, New York: Rowman & Littlefield, 88–108.

Crenshaw, Kimberlé (1989) "Demarginalizing the Intersection of Race and Sex: A Black Feminist Critique of Antidiscrimination Doctrine, Feminist Theory and Antiracist Politics," *University of Chicago Legal Forum* 1: 139–167.

Davies, Carole Boyce (1994) *Black Women, Writing and Identity: Migrations of the Subject*, New York: Routledge.

Du Bois, W. E. B. (1995 [1905]) *The Souls of Black Folk*, New York: Signet Classic.

Ellison, Ralph (1995 [1947]) *The Invisible Man*, New York: Random House.

Frye, Marilyn (1983) *The Politics of Reality: Essays in Feminist Theory*, Freedom: Crossing Press.

Harris, Duchess (2009) *Black Feminist Politics from Kennedy to Clinton*, New York: Palgrave Macmillan.

Harris-Perry, Melissa (2011) *Sister Citizen: Shame, Stereotypes, and Black Women in America*, New Haven, CT: Yale University Press.

hooks, bell (1990) *Yearning: Race, Gender and Cultural Politics*, Boston, MA: South End Press.

Hull, Gloria, Scott, Patricia Bell, and Smith, Barbara (Eds.) (1982) *All the Women Are Whites, and All the Blacks Are Men, but Some of Us Are Brave*, New York: Feminist Press.

Ihde, Don (1977) *Experimental Phenomenology: An Introduction*, New York: Capricorn Books.

—— (2009) *Postphenomenology and Technoscience: The Peking University Lectures*, Albany, NY: SUNY Press.

King, Deborah R. (1995 [1988]) "Multiple Jeopardy, Multiple Consciousness: The Context of a Black Feminist Ideology," in Beverly Guy-Sheftall (Ed.) *Words of Fire: An Anthology of Black Feminist Thought*, New York: New Press, 294–317.

Lorde, Audre (2009 [1983]) "There Is No Hierarchy of Oppression," in *I Am Your Sister: Collected and Unpublished Writings of Audre Lorde*, Ed. Rudolph P. Byrd, Johnnetta Betsch Cole, and Beverly Guy-Sheftall, Oxford: Oxford University Press, 219–220.

Murray, Pauli (1995 [1970]) "The Liberation of Black Women," in Beverly Guy-Sheftall (Ed.) *Words of Fire: An Anthology of Black Feminist Thought*, New York: New Press, 186–197.

Omolade, Barbara (1994) *The Rising Song of African American Women*, New York: Routledge.

Peterson, Carla L. (1993) "Doers of the Word: Theorizing African American Women Writers in the Antebellum North," in Joyce Warren (Ed.) *The (Other) American Traditions: Nineteenth-Century Women Writers*, New Brunswick, NJ: Rutgers University Press, 183–202.

—— (1995) *"Doers of the Word": African-American Women Speakers and Writers in the North (1830–1880)*, New Brunswick, NJ: Rutgers University Press.

Reagon, Bernice Johnson (2000 [1983]) "Coalition Politics: Turning the Century," in Barbara Smith (Ed.) *Home Girls: A Black Feminist Anthology*, New York: Kitchen Table Press, 343–355.

Smith, Barbara (Ed.) (1983) *Home Girls: A Black Feminist Anthology*, New York: Kitchen Table Press.

Smith, Valerie (1998) *Not Just Race, Not Just Gender: Black Feminist Readings*, New York: Routledge.

Spillers, Hortense (1984) "Interstices: A Small Drama of Words," in Carol Vance (Ed.) *Pleasure and Danger: Exploring Sexuality*, Boston, MA: Routledge, 86–88.

Springer, Kimberley (2005) *Living for the Revolution: Black Feminist Organizations, 1968–1980*, Durham, NC: Duke University Press.

Tate, Gayle T. (2003) *Unknown Tongues: Black Women's Political Activism in the Antebellum Era, 1830–1860*, East Lansing, MI: Michigan State University Press.

Wallace, Michele (1990) *Invisibility Blues: From Pop to Theory*, New York: Verso.

Williams, Fannie Barrier (1905) "The Colored Girl," *The Voice of the Negro* 2(6): 400–403.

—— (1907) "The Woman's Part in a Man's Business," *The Voice of the Negro* 1(7): 543–547.

—— (2007 [1900]) "The Club Movement among Colored Women of America," in Henry Louis Gates Jr. and Gene Andrew Jarrett (Eds.) *The New Negro: Readings on Race, Representation, and African American Culture, 1982–1938*, Princeton, NJ: Princeton University Press, 54–58.

Whyte, Kyle P. (2015) "What Is Multistability? A Theory of the Keystone Concept of Postphenomenological Research," in Jan Kyrre Berg, O. Friis, and Robert P. Crease (Eds.) *Technoscience and Postphenomenology: The Manhattan Papers*, New York: Lexington Books, 69–82.

11

FEMINIST PRAGMATISM

V. Denise James

Classical Pragmatism and Feminist Recovery Projects

In the late nineteenth century, classical pragmatism found its first explicit exponent in the philosopher William James, who credited the epistemological and methodological insights of fellow US philosopher Charles S. Peirce with opening up a new route in philosophical inquiry that was necessarily linked to experience. Although Peirce would later decry the connection between his views and James's interpretation of his epistemology, James went on to develop a theory of truth that he claimed was first articulated by Peirce. Following Peirce's lead, James would call the philosophical orientation associated with this theory of truth and its consequences *pragmatism*. Pragmatism, for James, was a philosophical attitude, "The attitude of turning away from first things, principles, 'categories,' supposed necessities; and of looking towards last things, fruits, consequences, facts" (James 2000: 33). John Dewey took up the banner of James' pragmatism, expanding it to include the associated theories of the social and political world that would be influential not only for academically trained philosophers but also for the growing progressive movements of his day, especially in education policy and democratic theory.

For Dewey, pragmatism was primarily about inquiry and knowing, but what Dewey meant by "to inquire" and "to know" diverged from what he deemed a false dichotomy of knowing versus practice operative in philosophical discourse at the time. Dewey gives a genealogy of pragmatism and an explication of his own views in the essay "The Need for a Recovery of Philosophy" (Dewey 1980: 3–48). He follows James and locates the first use of the term "pragmatism" and the first theoretical commitments to a form of pragmatism in Peirce, with his insistence on the fallibilism and verifiability of knowledge claims. Dewey defends James' notion that ideas must "cash in" to have value, by explaining that verifiability requires existential proof in our lived experience. Dewey deepens James' view and resists the allure of a philosophy that would only deal in concepts. He asserts, "Concepts are so clear; it takes so little time to develop their implications; experiences are so confused, and it requires so much time and energy to lay hold of them" (Dewey 1980: 44). It is this "laying hold" that would characterize Dewey's theoretical production and his work in schools and policy. Intelligence was creative and future oriented on Dewey's view. Inquiry required the use of imagination and vigilance about experience. Philosophy would only prove to be useful if it served to help to articulate, clarify, and ameliorate what Dewey called "human difficulties of a deep seated kind" (Dewey 1980: 46). Attuned to the progressive era in US politics, Deweyan pragmatism was influential both in academic philosophy and wider society.

Even as some of its themes inspired many analytic philosophers such as W.V.O. Quine and Hillary Putnam, pragmatism lost influence as analytic philosophy rose in prominence in US universities. Pragmatist theories of truth, language, and mind, which prioritized consequences and situational thinking over tight, systemic argumentation and linguistic exploration, went out of fashion during what is now sometimes called the "epistemological turn" (Seigfried 2002: 4). However, more recently there has been a revival of interest in pragmatisms old and new, due in no small part to the work of contemporary feminist pragmatists who have undertaken various recovery projects, as well as to those who have begun to use pragmatist methodologies in their work.

It is only in the last few decades that important contributions of women as pragmatists, either as students of the recognized classical male pragmatists or as advocates of their own pragmatic viewpoints, have started to be appreciated by academic philosophers. The list of classical pragmatists is now often updated to include the noted social settlement innovator and contemporary of Dewey, Jane Addams. When the list of early pragmatists is expanded to include other notable figures with Addams, such as Josiah Royce, George Herbert Mead, and George Santayana, increasingly cases have been made for the inclusion of other women who were their contemporaries such as Mary Parker Follett, Charlotte Perkins Gilman, Ella Lyman Cabot, Alice Chippman Dewey, Mary Whiton Caulkins, and Ella Flagg Young. Contemporary feminist pragmatists have recovered the work of these women from the classical era of pragmatism and claimed that there are vital points of connection between feminist philosophical orientations and pragmatism.

Feminist Pragmatism or Pragmatist Feminism?

Contemporary feminist pragmatists have argued that the methodological practices and theoretical claims made by pragmatists and feminists are not only complementary but that a more careful inventory of each would bear fruit for the aims of both. The work of Charlene Haddock Seigfried has been pioneering and pivotal in the emergence of feminist pragmatism as a subfield in pragmatism. In 1993, Seigfried edited a special issue of the feminist philosophy journal, *Hypatia*, about these connections. Seigfried set the stage for the special issue two years earlier, in an edition of the *Transactions of the Charles S. Peirce Society*, when she called feminist pragmatism "the missing perspective" (Seigfried 1991). The *Hypatia* special issue served both to legitimize and galvanize inquiries into feminist pragmatism, as some preferred, or pragmatist feminism, as others preferred. The difference in labels, then and now, seems primarily to reflect priorities in orientation and not deep disagreement. The feminist pragmatist, for the most part, engages with the methods, claims, and conversations of pragmatism from a feminist standpoint. While the pragmatist feminist might use the methods and basic insights of pragmatism, they see their main orientation as feminist, drawing from a wide range of resources in the history of feminist theory and activism. To understand this distinction we only need to look at the difference between the works of two historical women who are often counted as both pragmatists and feminists, Charlotte Perkins Gilman and Jane Addams.

Novelist, essayist, and social reformer Charlotte Perkins Gilman did not work with the early pragmatists to develop her ideas about pluralism and progress, but it could be argued that her understanding of the social formation of the individual and of the possibilities for the amelioration of social problems by human efforts is in line with the overlapping set of ideas that we recognize as characteristic of pragmatism. In works such as her most well-known story, *The Yellow Wallpaper*, Gilman gives a fictionalized account of the life of a housewife confined to a room to protect her delicate nature, only to be driven mad by the control of her husband and the titular wallpaper (Gilman 1997 [1892]). Gilman's attention to the lived experience of white women in her era as sources for social recommendations reflects her deep commitment to the importance of perspective and rejection of the subordination of women. Gilman also wrote about the economic and social repression of women, advocating that women assert new selves to take on new roles in society. Her analyses of class and gender are identifiable as predecessors to more contemporary considerations (Kimmel and Aronson 1998 [1898]). Gilman, virtually overlooked by non-feminist academic pragmatists, is rightly regarded as a key figure in US feminism.

On the other hand, Jane Addams, the renowned writer, peace activist, and social settlement pioneer, worked alongside John Dewey in Chicago, influencing his ideas about democracy. Her place in the history of pragmatism is most often supported through appeals to her ties to Dewey. Dewey did not credit her ideas with citations in his long philosophical works, but he made public and private declarations about the importance of her thinking in speeches and correspondence. While Addams is seen as seminal to the field of social work and is more often considered as part of the canon of classical pragmatists, Addams' feminism was more apparent than explicit, its full expression found in the explication of her work by contemporary feminist pragmatists who have taken up the recovery of her thought with zeal.

The various recovery projects of Addams's work have seeded other feminist investigations into the shared claims, methods, and roots of feminism and pragmatism. Seigfried has argued that despite their similarities, feminists and pragmatists have, for the most part, ignored the fruits of the others' labors (Seigfried 1996: 17–40). Early women pragmatists may have been taken up by feminists, but not explicitly as pragmatists. Pragmatists who had been socially or politically feminist may have pursued studies of Dewey or James or Royce, but little had been done to evaluate their work as good sources for feminism. Seigfried and the contributors to the *Hypatia* special issue in 1993 were the vanguard of a growing group of scholars interested in the connections of feminism and pragmatism. The articles included those that sought to recover women's voices in early pragmatism, those that analyzed the feminist or anti-feminist leaning of the classical male pragmatists, and finally articles that suggested that pragmatism and feminism could be wedded to create better social, epistemological, and political orientations. Yet not all contributors to Seigfried's special issue agreed that pragmatism had something special to offer feminists.

Notably, Richard Rorty claimed that, like postmodernism, which had reached the height of its popularity in the early 1990s, pragmatism was not specially suited for feminist use and could very well be used for cross purposes. He argued,

> Pragmatism—considered as a set of philosophical views about truth, knowledge, objectivity, and language—is neutral between feminism and masculinism . . .
> Neither the pragmatist nor the deconstructionist can do more for feminism

than help rebut attempts to ground these practices on something deeper than a contingent historical fact—the fact that the people with the slightly larger muscles have been bullying the people with the slightly smaller muscles for a very long time.

(Rorty 1993: 101)

Rorty's claim about pragmatism's neutrality met with resistance from feminist pragmatists because it seemed to miss an important set of distinctions that can be made about pragmatism. On the one hand, we can agree with Rorty from a historical perspective if we only count the male pragmatists, such as Peirce, James, or Dewey, as the keepers of the pragmatist tradition. We can follow feminist historian Estelle B. Freedman's claim that "movements cannot be feminist unless they explicitly address justice for women as a primary concern" (Freedman 2002: 8). The most progressive of the big three pragmatists, Dewey, seemed to suggest that the status of women in society ought to be improved but did not take anything close to a decidedly feminist stance in his philosophical writings. There was not, at least if we are only counting the male pragmatists of the end of the nineteenth and early twentieth centuries, a feminist movement in classical pragmatism.

However, Rorty's claim is not primarily historical or about the history of a feminist wave in pragmatism. We can address his claim without appeal even to the women that we have already mentioned as frequently associated with early pragmatism. His claim is that pragmatism's methods and beliefs are neutral. There is good reason to reject neutrality as either the pragmatist's method or attitude. Much of what we recognize as pragmatism comes from Dewey. Dewey extends and deepens the meaning of pragmatism. Whereas Peirce's early pragmatism was a defense of the scientific method and verification through empirical study, and James' pragmatism prioritized practical aims over metaphysical truths, it could be argued that what prevails, especially in conversations about feminism and pragmatism, is not the supposed neutrality of Peirce or James' view, but the pragmatism of Dewey. Dewey's pragmatism, by method, attitude, and in practice required a belief in a democratic way of life that is not value neutral. Perhaps we would not call Dewey a feminist after reading his few sparse lines on women's rights, but he produced a body of work rich for feminist enlargement.

It could be argued that this is what Seigfried had in mind when she countered Rorty's view and argued that

[t]he first-generation pragmatists, like contemporary feminists, refused the false neutrality of the epistemological turn and argued that theory be joined to practice and that practice be held accountable to the values that make life worth living for all members of the varied Communities that make up the larger social order.

(Seigfried 1993: 13)

This perspective is clearly Deweyan. A Deweyan pragmatism is not neutral in the sense that Rorty claims, and lends itself especially to feminist interpretation and uptake. Seigfried's argument relies on the view that Dewey did not live up to the full consequences of his pragmatism in regard to women's issues, but she ably demonstrates that this oversight was that of the man, Dewey, and not of the values or methods of pragmatism. Whereas Rorty claimed that pragmatism was value neutral, Seigfried argues that it is value rich. She even suggests that pragmatism can be understood as a feminine rather than masculine endeavor, arguing that

> [t]he pragmatist goal of philosophical discourse, which is shared understanding and communal problem solving rather than rationally forced conclusions, is more feminine than masculine, as is its valuing of inclusiveness and community over exaggerated claims of autonomy and detachment. The same can be said for its developmental rather than rule-governed ethics.
>
> (Seigfried 1996: 32)

We need not masculinize or feminize pragmatism to take up Seigfried's rebuttal of Rorty's claim. A rightfully pragmatist project would have a difficult time being intentionally masculinist, as the emphasis on shared understanding and pluralism go against that stance. Even if it could be argued that pragmatism had, prior to contemporary feminist intervention, only advanced masculinist projects in the hands of male pragmatists, we need not turn away from the overlapping claims and aims of the two theoretical and practical orientations.

Erin McKenna highlights similar lines of connection in her estimations of pragmatism and feminism. She contends that, "Pragmatism and feminism share philosophical roots in rejecting dualism, taking a perspectival stance, developing values from concrete experience, and giving feeling a role in experience and knowledge" (McKenna 2003: 5). She argues that joining pragmatism—with its emphasis on processes, growth, mutuality, and engaged philosophy—with feminism—which fights against women's subordination—results in a form of flexible feminism. Flexible feminism is found even in the early women pragmatists.

Historical Connections

Jane Addams is the historical woman who is most frequently associated with feminist pragmatism today. It is easy to connect Addams with views readily associated with classical pragmatism, especially those attributed to Dewey. Addams and Dewey each believed that democracy was a way of life that depended on the associational nature of the individual and her or his relationships with others as the source of both social intelligence and progress. Sharing with Dewey as she did a commitment to social reform and melioration, Addams' writings and speeches—most notably *Twenty Years at Hull House*, her book-length reflections about her attempts to support the growing immigrant community in Chicago—can be read as field notes to pragmatism in practice (Addams 1999 [1901]). When contemporary readers have sought to identify Addams' feminist themes, it requires us to use a label "feminist" that Addams did not use herself, so we must proceed with care, making sure not to attribute views to her that she did not hold. Maurice Hammington has argued that Addams' work resists easy labeling because there is a "resistance to ideology inherent in her pragmatism" (Hammington 2009: 30). Yet Hammington, along with others, finds Addams' work ripe for feminist insight.

In her social work and public writings and speeches, Addams supported women's suffrage and worked to garner sympathy as well as social access for prostitutes, immigrant, and other poor, disenfranchised women. In her life and writing about these issues, Hammington identifies several key themes that are easily recognized by contemporary feminists. He argues that Addams employed forms of standpoint epistemology in her writing and care ethics in her practice. As a standpoint epistemologist before the phrase came into use, Hammington asserts, "Addams links social identification, social expression, and democracy together" (Hammington 2009: 55). Addams highlighted the importance of attending to the lived experience of all people in our efforts to address social problems. Of a piece with the attention to standpoint, Addams practiced an ethics of care in her relation to the women at the settlement house, and advocated the importance of deep, reciprocal interactions in her calls for peace at times of war.

Hammington makes a more controversial claim about Addams as a feminist when he contends that we can find a "proto-lesbian ethics" in her life and works (Hammington 2009: 61). Following the biographical explorations of Hull House women produced by Mary Jo Deegan (1996), in spite of Addams making no public assertion of herself as a lesbian, Hammington frames Addams' personal life, deep friendships with women, the formation of an all-female learning and living environment at Hull House, and objections to the prominence of Freudian theories of sexuality, as indicative of an ethos of same-sex love that is hard to pin down as sexual but should not be overlooked (Hammington 2009: 61). Citing Sarah Hoagland's (1988) conceptualization of lesbian ethics, Hammington argues that the all-woman environment at Hull House and Addams' resultant views on social development are in line with Hoagland's claims that a lesbian ethics would emphasize "connection, growth and integrity rather than rules or calculations of straight behavior" (Hammington 2009: 65).

Whether or not one agrees with Hammington's claims about the relevance of Addams' apparent affiliative preferences, his analysis of her work and life along those lines throws into relief one of the (arguably) most distinctive and fruitful parts of the feminist pragmatist historical recovery projects made possible by pragmatism's rejection of traditionalism. Contemporary feminist pragmatists, such as Marilyn Fischer (2013), John Kaag (2008), Erin McKenna (2012), and Judy Whipps (2012) have mined the works of women thinkers from the early twentieth century to offer us not only a glimpse into the past that is more diverse than we once presumed but also to point out new sources for our current feminist and pragmatist projects. The historical consciousness of the feminist pragmatist is most often productive and instructive. The point of recovery projects is not just getting what the classical woman pragmatist said "right" and understanding what she intended in her context. Key to the pragmatist attitude is considering not the eternal veracity of claims but what use they might be to us. Contemporary feminist pragmatists have exemplified what was once considered the distinct attitude of classical pragmatism when they have endeavored to expand and use historical sources for their own purposes.

Contemporary Feminist Pragmatism

The nearly quarter century since the 1993 publication of the special feminist pragmatist issue of *Hypatia* has seen a proliferation of feminist pragmatist academic production. Some of these have been recovery projects, for example Marilyn Fischer and Judy Whipps' book on Jane Addams' peace writing (2003) and John Kaag's exploration of Ella Lymon Cabot as a pragmatist and feminist (2013), while others attempt to use the resources of feminism and pragmatism to articulate new paths for philosophical inquiry. These projects have been wide-ranging and diverse in their methodologies and recommendations. Most of the published work in feminist pragmatism has been in the form of essays and articles. To understand the what and how of feminist pragmatism, it is illustrative to consider two of the few book-length projects in feminist pragmatism (McKenna 2001; Sullivan 2001) and a recent edited collection (Hammington and Bardwell-Jones 2012).

In her 2001 book, *Living Across and Through Skins: Transactional Bodies, Pragmatism, and Feminism*, growing out of what she calls a "cross fertilization" of the ideas and theories of pragmatism and feminism, Shannon Sullivan argues that bodies are transactional (Sullivan 2001: 7). She finds resources for her conception of transactional bodies in Dewey's notion of the organism. In Dewey, Sullivan uncovers the seeds of a deeply phenomenological account of corporeal existence, even as she notes that "the phenomenological side of his pragmatism is not often recognized" (Sullivan 2001: 4). She describes the mutuality of bodies and environments as co-constituting. What results is a self-aware perspectivalism that joins pragmatism and feminism in a project that aims to take the lived experience of gender and race seriously in a standpoint theory of truth that would give "an account of truth as flourishing contact between organic bodies and world" (Sullivan 2001: 10).

In *The Task of Utopia: A Pragmatist Feminist Perspective*, Erin McKenna also advocates a feminist pragmatism that relies on the development of a standpoint theory that would take into account the lived experience of women and others. She sets out to theorize a "process model of utopia" (McKenna 2001: 2). Against those who would argue that utopian thinking and social planning are either too idealistic to be taken seriously or, worse, would only result in a totalitarian society, McKenna asserts that a Deweyan pragmatic method of positing goals and making attempts to reach them while constantly re-assessing both the attempts and the goals would not lead to fascism or escapism. Rather, it would be representative of a dynamic process model of utopia, of which she sees evidence not only in Dewey's philosophy but also in the utopian fiction of feminist writers like Ursula K. Le Guin and Sally Miller Gearhart (McKenna 2001: 3).

Maurice Hammington and Celia Bardwell-Jones' edited volume, *Contemporary Feminist Pragmatism* (2012) is a collection of essays on topics as varied as patriotism, pets, hip-hop, epistemic exclusion, and care ethics. The organizing question of the volume is "What does feminist pragmatism have to offer to reflections on contemporary issues and ideas?" (Hammington and Bardwell-Jones 2012: 1). The editors argue that the framework they present is not a unified answer to the question, rather it shows how the essays hang together. The framework identifies several methodological commitments that the feminist pragmatists all promote in some form throughout the volume. First, they argue that a commitment to "the importance of context and experience" is a binding tie between the texts (Hammington and Bardwell-Jones 2012: 2). Second, joining pragmatism and feminism offers an increased and more nuanced approach to epistemology and value theory. Being a white woman, a Latina, or a Chinese American man are, for the feminist pragmatist, not incidental factors to be bracketed in philosophical explorations. Rather the social and historical occurrence of the use of these identity markers reveals much about the situated, temporal nature of what we value and call knowledge and thus what we mean by objectivity (Hammington and Bardwell-Jones 2012: 3). Third, feminist pragmatism "emphasizes the need for diversity and thus dialogue among differently situated social groups" (Hammington and Bardwell-Jones 2012: 4). Pluralism is valued by both the pragmatist and feminist traditions not only because diverse viewpoints can reveal that our knowledge is contextual, but also because social intelligence offers us different answers to our pressing questions and problems. They contend: "Rather than appealing to abstract conceptions of humanity and ignoring the situated character of experience, feminism and pragmatism conceive of the self engaged in social interactions with others" (Hammington and Bardwell-Jones 2012: 6).

Claudia Gillberg's contribution to the volume, "A Methodological Interpretation of Feminist Pragmatism," serves as a good example both of the methodological commitments that the editors attribute to feminist pragmatists and of what forms the practice of feminist pragmatism can take outside of academic discourse. Gillberg writes, "As an action researcher and educational researcher who embraces feminist pragmatism, I wish to be particularly aware of the role that research can play for social or organizational change towards more inclusive, democratic ways to organize our lives" (Gillberg 2012: 218). Feminist action research, like the practices of pragmatists such as John Dewey and Jane Addams, uses the end goal of a more democratic everyday life to direct collaborative models of social change and problem solving.

Gillberg gives examples of how one might work as a feminist pragmatist action researcher. One of the examples is particularly instructive. She worked with preschool teachers to, first, figure out whether and how the gendered nature of toys and playground equipment was affecting the children in their school. Instead of rushing to de-gender the toys and change the program, the teachers and Gillberg read and discussed research on gender and children, increased their knowledge of associated background theories, visited other schools, and pondered possible parent reactions to any changes. The group considered possible obstacles to their planning and used a collaborative approach to address potential problems. Gillberg played the role of "critical friend" who facilitated the teachers' discussions and actions but did not direct the teachers from on high. From her practices, Gillberg identifies several feminist pragmatist concepts at work that include notions of community, reciprocity, and the use of study to act toward reform and increased democratization (Gillberg 2012: 224–227). While Gillberg makes the connection to pragmatist and feminist academic sources in her practice explicit, the work is reminiscent of work done by other feminist practitioners, such as black feminists, who have long used the label pragmatist and similar methods without an indebted connection to the classical pragmatists or academic feminist philosophy (James 2009).

In the early 1990s, black feminists from a wide range of academic disciplines and areas of activism met several times for a Black Feminist Seminar. These meetings led to the publication of an anthology titled *Theorizing Black Feminisms: The Visionary Pragmatism of Black Women* (James and Busia 1993a). In the introduction, Stanlie M. James articulates a wide-ranging agenda that unites the black feminist work included in the volume.

> Black feminists are simultaneously envisioning incremental changes and radical transformations not only within Black communities but throughout the broader society as well. Ultimately, the humanistic visionary pragmatism of theorizing by Black feminists seeks the establishment of just societies where human rights are implemented with respect and dignity even as the world's resources are equitably distributed in ways that encourage individual autonomy and development.
>
> (James and Busia 1993b: 3)

This "humanistic visionary pragmatism" of black feminists is rooted in a long tradition of black women activists and thinkers, not often included in professional philosophical discourse, as well as black feminist engagement in movements for civil rights and social justice. The pragmatism of the black feminists identified by James has obvious, significant points of overlap with classical and feminist pragmatism in the discipline of philosophy. Many black feminist pragmatists and Dewey agree that having hope or a vision of the future plays a vital role in what we do to promote democracy in writing and in practice today. The emphasis on meliorism, fallibility, and the related view that society and individual are co-constituting are found in both pragmatisms, even as the roots and impetuses for the work diverge. Considering black feminist pragmatism along with contemporary and classical philosophical sources enlarges the available resources for pragmatist social justice and theory projects (James 2009: 93).

Feminist Pragmatist Futures

Pragmatism as an academic discourse arose just as the United States was completing its westward expansion, debating white women's suffrage, codifying Jim Crow laws, and asserting its military power in increasingly global conflicts. America was becoming America. The philosophies of the classical pragmatists came to be and are still often known as American philosophy. Increasingly, just as people have begun to question more frequently the use of the term "American" to signify only the people and products of the United States, there have been calls to rethink the habit of naming only the efforts of the classical US pragmatists "American philosophy." Both these critiques of our naming practices are in line with the methodologies of both pragmatism and feminism. In their myriad expressions, each discourse has sought to question the entrenchment of tradition for tradition's sake and to champion the pluralism of perspectives that is necessary in epistemology and ethics.

Further Reading

Fischer, Marilyn (2004) On Addams, Stanford, CA: Thomson Wadsworth. (An invaluable resource for an introduction to the thinking of Jane Addams as a pragmatist.)

McKenna, Erin and Pratt, Scott L. (2015) American Philosophy: From Wounded Knee to the Present, London: Bloomsbury. (Offers a distinctively thorough and astute introduction for the student or non-specialist seeking to contextualize feminist pragmatism in wider conversations about the history of American philosophy.)

Seigfried, Charlene Haddock (1996) Pragmatism and Feminism: Reweaving the Social Fabric, Chicago, IL: University of Chicago Press. (The seminal text of feminist pragmatism.)

Related Topics

Feminist methods in the history of philosophy (Chapter 1); introducing Black feminist philosophy (Chapter 10); rationality and objectivity in feminist philosophy (Chapter 20); feminist philosophy of social science (Chapter 27).

References

Addams, Jane (1999 [1910]) *Twenty Years at Hull House*, Boston, MA: Bedford/St. Martin's.

Deegan, Mary Jo (1990) *Jane Addams and the Men of the Chicago School, 1892–1918*, New Brunswick, NJ: Transaction Books.

—— (1996) "'Dear Love, Dear Love': Feminist Pragmatism and the Chicago Female World of Love and Ritual," *Gender and Society* 10(5): 590–607.

Dewey, John (1980) "The Need for a Recovery of Philosophy," in Jo Ann Boydston (Ed.) *John Dewey: The Middle Works, 1899–1924, Volume 10: 1916–1917*, Carbondale, IL: Southern Illinois University Press, 3–38.

Fischer, Marilyn (2013) "Reading Addams's Democracy and Social Ethics as a Social Gospel, Evolutionary Idealist Text," *The Pluralist* 8(3): 17–31.

Fischer, Marilyn and Whipps, Judy (Eds.) (2003) *Jane Addams Writings on Peace*, Bristol: Thoemmes.

Freedman, Estelle B. (2002) *No Turning Back: The History of Feminism and the Future of Women*. New York: Ballentine Books.

Gillberg, Claudia (2012) "A Methodological Interpretation of Feminist Pragmatism," in Maurice Hammington and Celia Bardwell-Jones (Eds.) *Contemporary Feminist Pragmatism*, New York: Routledge, 217–237.

Gilman, Charlotte Perkins (1997 [1892]) *The Yellow Wallpaper*, New York: Dover.

Hammington, Maurice (2009) *The Social Philosophy of Jane Addams*, Urbana, IL and Chicago, IL: University of Illinois Press.

Hammington, Maurice and Bardwell-Jones, Celia (Eds.) (2012) *Contemporary Feminist Pragmatism*, New York: Routledge.

Hoagland, Sarah (1988) *Lesbian Ethics: Toward New Value*, Palo Alto, CA: Institute of Lesbian Studies.

James, V. Denise (2009) "Theorizing Black Feminist Pragmatism: Thoughts on The Practice and Purpose of Philosophy as Envisioned by Black Feminists and John Dewey," *Journal of Speculative Philosophy* 23(2): 92–99.

James, Stanlie M. and Busia, Abenia P. A. (Eds.) (1993a) *Theorizing Black Feminisms: The Visionary Pragmatism of Black Women*, London: Routledge.

—— (1993b) "Introduction," in *Theorizing Black Feminisms: The Visionary Pragmatism of Black Women*, London: Routledge, 1–12.

James, William (2000) "What Pragmatism Means," in *Pragmatism and the Meaning of Truth*, Cambridge, MA: Harvard University Press, 27–44.

Kaag, John (2008) "Women and Forgotten Movements in American Philosophy: The Work of Ella Lyman Cabot and Mary Parker Follett," *Transactions Of The Charles S. Peirce Society* 44(1): 134–157.

—— (2013) *Idealism, Pragmatism, and Feminism: The Philosophy of Ella Lymon Cabot*, Lanham, MD: Lexington Books.

Kimmel, Michael and Aronson, Amy (1998 [1898]) "Introduction," in Charlotte Perkins Gilman, *Women and Economics: A Study of the Economic Relation Between Men and Women as a Factor in Social Evolution*, Berkeley, CA: University of California Press, pp. vii–lxx.

McKenna, Erin (2001) *The Task of Utopia: A Pragmatist and Feminist Perspective*, Lanham, MD: Rowman & Littlefield.

—— (2003) "Pragmatism and Feminism: Engaged Philosophy," *American Journal of Theology and Philosophy* 24(1): 3–21.

—— (2012) "Charlotte Perkins Gilman: Women and Pets," in Maurice Hammington and Celia Bardwell-Jones (Eds.) *Contemporary Feminist Pragmatism*, New York: Routledge, 238–254.

Rorty, Richard (1993) "Feminism, Ideology, and Deconstruction: A Pragmatist View," *Hypatia* 8(2): 96–103.

Seigfried, Charlene Haddock (1991) "The Missing Perspective: Feminist Pragmatism," *Transactions of the Charles S. Peirce Society* 27(4): 405–416.

—— (Ed.) (1993) "Special Issue: Feminism and Pragmatism," *Hypatia* 8(2): 1–242.

—— (1996) *Pragmatism and Feminism: Reweaving the Social Fabric*, Chicago, IL: The University of Chicago Press.

—— (2002) "Introduction," in Charlene Haddock Seigfried (Ed.) *Feminist Interpretations of John Dewey*, University Park, PA: Pennsylvania State University Press, 1–24.

Sullivan, Shannon (2001) *Living Across and Through Skins: Transactional Bodies, Pragmatism, and Feminism*, Bloomington, IN: Indiana University Press.

Whipps, Judy (2012) "Feminist-Pragmatist Democratic Practice and Contemporary Sustainability Movements: Mary Parker Follett, Jane Addams, Emily Greene Balch, and Vandana Shiva," in Maurice Hammington and Celia Bardwell-Jones (Eds.) *Contemporary Feminist Pragmatism*, New York: Routledge, 115–127.

12

FEMINIST PHENOMENOLOGY

Alia Al-Saji

To speak of *feminist phenomenology*, or of how feminist philosophers have appropriated phenomenological methods and sources, is to speak in the plural. It is therefore important to begin by noting that I will not offer a survey of what feminist phenomenology has been or a definition of what it should be. Rather, my interest is both in how phenomenology, as a variegated movement, has been useful to feminism and how feminist phenomenologies offer a corrective—or, more precisely, a *critical reconfiguration*—of phenomenology. This reconfiguration sheds light on the social-political possibilities of a movement that might have seemed, on the surface, to be only about description.

There are multiple ways in which one could broach how phenomenology has influenced feminist theory. One could speak of sources, figures, or themes. Feminists have drawn on the works of Edmund Husserl, Emmanuel Levinas, Jean-Paul Sartre, Frantz Fanon and extensively on the works of Simone de Beauvoir and Maurice Merleau-Ponty (and this is only a partial list). And phenomenologists have, arguably from the start, been engaged in feminist questions. One has only to think of Edith Stein (Calcagno 2007) or Simone de Beauvoir (2010 [1949]), to recall that phenomenological approaches to feminist concerns—even when not explicitly labelled "feminist"—are not limited to the current generation of phenomenologists. Moreover, phenomenology addresses dimensions of experience—such as embodiment (see Chapter 15 in this volume), affectivity, perception, temporality, subjectivity, and intersubjectivity—to name but a few thematic threads that have also been of import to feminists.

What feminist phenomenologies add to this list is a sensitivity to how oppression, power, and privilege may form the horizon wherein these dimensions are *differentially* structured—the social-historical context wherein experience is situated and historicized. Feminist phenomenologies provide, then, not simply an additional theme, but a different and arguably deeper way of *thematizing* and contextualizing phenomenology's classical foci—shifting and redefining these foci in the process. Feminist phenomenology shows how the political already structures experience at the lived, "prereflective" level of felt embodiment. And this is not only when experience is self-reflectively or personally ascribed. It points to how the social mediates how I feel and perceive, as well as what I can do—embodied agency—and who I am—identity.

In my view, this means that the richness of phenomenology is best seen when it is understood not simply as tradition, but as method. And this phenomenological method is one that has itself changed over time—that has been revised and reconfigured through multiple appropriations and critiques, including critical race, queer, and feminist ones. To give only a few examples of such appropriations and critiques, I point the reader to: Alcoff (2006); Ahmed (2006); Bartky (1990); Gordon (1995); Heinämaa (2003); Salamon (2010); Weiss (1999); Yancy (2008); and Young (2005). There have also been a number of important special issues and volumes on feminist phenomenology in the last two decades: Fisher and Embree (2000); Heinämaa and Rodemeyer (2010); Schües, Olkowski, and Fielding (2011); Simms and Stawarska (2014); and Zeiler and Käll (2014).

This is to say that phenomenology has the structure of what Husserl and, following him, Merleau-Ponty call *institution* (Husserl 1970 [1954]; Merleau-Ponty 1964b [1960] and 2010 [2003]). It is not a static given, a mere set of texts, or a pre-defined formula. Phenomenological method is a movement that is also tendency and change, a way of being oriented in the world, a style of thinking or way of perceiving. This style should be understood to be dynamic, both weighted by its past and transformed by it, improvising in response to its historical and social situation. Here, I do not mean to divide textual interpretation from "application," but to point to the ways in which phenomenology is a continual taking up and reinvention.

In what follows, I begin with this question of method, as an avenue to elucidating phenomenology's relation to lived experience and to its normative—although not uncontested—assumptions. Because of the introductory nature of this essay, my appeal to sources remains selective. I draw on phenomenology's past, especially on Husserl, Merleau-Ponty, Beauvoir, and Fanon, and on contemporary feminist phenomenologists. But there are many phenomenologists (Binswanger, Minkowski, Patočka, Schutz, Stein, and of course Heidegger) and some entangled intra-phenomenological debates to which I cannot do justice. Because my interest lies in understanding how phenomenology *becomes feminist*, I focus on bringing to light the critical, ethical and political possibilities of what I will call "critical phenomenology."

Phenomenology as Method

It is perhaps commonplace to begin a discussion of phenomenology with an account of the "phenomenological reduction." In its simplest form, the reduction is about "putting into brackets" attitudes to the world, in particular causal-scientist and naturalistic ones. To "bracket" is neither to affirm nor to nullify, but to suspend an attitude, in order to bring into focus its constitutive activity and the web of meaning it has instituted. However, the attitude that most weighs in experience, and that is the most difficult to bracket, is the "natural attitude."

When he introduced the concept of the "natural attitude," Husserl meant to designate not simply a way of conceiving the world, but also a way of living and perceiving the world that takes that world and the objects within it to be "out there," defined apart from consciousness. In other words, this is an attitude of naïve realism toward the world (Husserl 1998 [1976]). This attitude is "natural" both in being the basis upon which other attitudes—theoretical and practical—build, and also in becoming habitual, its operations forgotten, so that it is implicitly and unreflectively lived. To say that this attitude is "natural" is not to endorse it, then, but to indicate that it remains lived-through and is not grasped *as an attitude*, that it is invisible to us since we perceive according to it. This is to say that it has been *naturalized*.

144

More generally, what the phenomenological reduction allows us to see and to interrogate are the naturalizing tendencies within experience. What it reveals are the threads of meaning-making that weave together experience. To paraphrase Merleau-Ponty's *Phenomenology of Perception*, the reduction "loosens" and hence makes visible these intentional threads, but, it should be added, it does not undo them (Merleau-Ponty 2012 [1945]: lxxvii). In its classical Husserlian form, to carry out this kind of "reduction" is to reveal the constituting role of consciousness as the source of sense-giving—as the condition of possibility of there being meaning. It is because it forms the condition of possibility for sense to appear that consciousness—or subjectivity—is revealed to be "transcendental subjectivity." This does not mean that consciousness transcends experience but that it grounds experience—that it makes possible an experience *of something*, which is to say, the appearance of sense to consciousness (or what phenomenology calls "intentionality").

As one reads Husserl more closely, however, transcendental subjectivity is revealed to be not so much a source-point as a *flow* that is paradoxically both constituted through, and constituting of, time (Husserl 1991 [1966]). As one attends to time more concretely, time-consciousness is shown to be more than a formal, linear schema. Rather it is an affectively entangled flow, in which later events make a difference for how earlier ones are retained or fade away (Husserl 2001 [1966]). Moreover, the perceptual field is an *affective relief*; it is a field of contextual contrast, where the relative pull of affections motivates the sensing body to turn toward, and perceive, them (Husserl 2001 [1966]: 216/168). I would add that this affective relief is neither an abstract map that is the same for all bodies, nor is it given once and for all. It is a tissue with variable contours, viscosity and texture, a furrowed terrain in which some bodies move with ease and others get bogged down in ruts. This *differentially* lived and perceived space—sedimented and materialized over time—can be described as a *lifeworld of habitualities*, since it has been shaped through, and in turn shapes, bodily habits. Such habits stem not only from my singular interactions with the world but from my social and historical location and my intersubjective milieu, the others (human or otherwise) with whom I have lived.

Thus the affective map of lived space reflects back to bodies their (differentially socialized) habitualities, the system of their possible actions in the world. The practical significances of things (e.g., a pen to be written with) mirror to my lived body its habitually acquired capacities (in this instance, being-handed, able to write, having acquired a language and literacy in a particular script, etc.). These capacities are felt in my body in terms of possible movement and sensing (by means of the sensory, kinaesthetic and proprioceptive awareness that my body has of itself, a self-awareness that is not yet conceptual or reflective). Husserl calls this bodily feeling of practical possibility the "I can" (Husserl 1989 [1952]: 270/258); for example, the feeling that "I can write" with that pen. Transcendental subjectivity thus appears to be receptive and embodied, affectively embedded in the world and responsive to it (Husserl 1989 [1952]; Welton 2000). As Merleau-Ponty describes it, perception is a dialogue of the lived body with the world (2012 [1945]: 134).

Phenomenology listens in on this dialogue, not simply to record what is said, but to lend an ear to what is not said—the silent relations and differences that structure the meaning of what is said. More specifically, phenomenology is a way of attending to experience, to reveal not only its sense, but also the dimensions that generate sense. Such are the *structuring* and normative dimensions that make meaning, but that do not themselves appear as sense. Drawing on the later Merleau-Ponty, this is not to treat experience as an object—something to be viewed under a microscope or held between forceps—but to accompany experience in its temporal becoming and in the workings of its constitutive dimensions (Merleau-Ponty 1968 [1964]: 101, 128).

In this sense, the phenomenological reduction differs in its scope and depth among phenomenological authors. It differs in what it puts into brackets, what naturalizing tendencies it questions, and what it is thus able to reveal. Here the significance of *feminist, critical race, and queer phenomenologies* comes to view. At stake is not simply a shift in what is being described. Rather, these are critical and creative reconfigurations of phenomenology that deepen and actualize the promise of its method. Before turning to this point in the next two sections, I want to address more explicitly the limitations that feminist critics have found in phenomenology.

With few exceptions (Heinämaa 2003 and Weiss 2008), feminists have historically been wary of the Husserlian line in phenomenology and have more extensively appropriated, in critically careful and innovative ways, that of Merleau-Ponty (for an explanation see Oksala 2006: 231; see also Olkowski and Weiss 2006; cf. Butler 1989 for caution with respect to Merleau-Ponty). I have argued elsewhere that, while feminist readers are right to be hesitant about some aspects of Husserlian phenomenology, his fine-grained analyses of embodiment, temporality, affectivity and sensing offer sites for productive recuperation (Al-Saji 2010). The brief sketch I gave above shows how transcendental subjectivity can be fleshed out temporally, affectively, and in bodily terms. These dimensions are essential to the constitutive work of transcendental subjectivity, not secondary afterthoughts.

While my sketch responds to a long-standing feminist concern that the subject of Husserlian phenomenology is a disembodied pure ego, it does not obviate all worries. For it is one thing to admit an embodied consciousness, quite another to take historicity, habitualities, and social positionality—thus gendering and racialization—to *structure* intentional activity at the transcendental, and not simply empirical level. For instance, Husserl may admit that transcendental subjectivity has a lifeworld of habitualities (as shown above). But the concrete forms that these habits take can still be seen to belong to the empirical ego; this would allow the transcendental ego to be conceived universally, with details filled in locally (see Fisher 2000: 30–31). Categories of "identity" would thus be relegated as characteristics of the "empirical ego." The phenomenological reduction would seem to go both too far—in assuming that we can separate out what is empirical from what is transcendental in the mixture of experience—and yet also not far enough, in ignoring the structuring role of characteristics deemed empirical and contingent. In this vein, the structures of inner time-consciousness might appear as generally founding of experience, yet filled in differently for different gendered and racialized subjects. But what if gendering and racialization make a difference in *how* time is experienced—a difference in the very structure of temporal experience and not simply in its coloration or content (Al-Saji 2013)?

Here we find the knot of the dilemma: this dilemma, I think, is tied up with how phenomenology conceives the commonality of the field of sense. The problem is not simply that phenomenology has often assumed a philosophy of the subject, even when that subject has been an embodied and intercorporeally situated consciousness (cf. Oksala 2006). Phenomenology can arguably account for the meaning-making powers of the world: as sedimented, intersubjective meanings to be re-activated (Husserl 1970 [1954]), as affective relief (Husserl 2001 [1966]), as institution (Merleau-Ponty 2010 [2003]), and as *flesh* (Merleau-Ponty 1968 [1964]).

But what phenomenology presupposes, even when the subject is decentered, is a common horizon of intelligibility—a perceptual world within which "something" appears and can eventually be recognized, that is to say, made sense of. That "there is sense" appears to be the condition of possibility of phenomenology (Merleau-Ponty 2012 [1945]: 309), its primordial "faith" so to speak (2012 [1945]: 359). As Merleau-Ponty says, we are "condemned to sense" (2012 [1945]: lxxxvi, 173). This does not mean that everything makes sense at once: every thematization (i.e., occasion of making determinate sense of something) has as its background an indeterminate horizon that includes the implicit habituality and opacity of one's perceiving and feeling body, as well as the inexhaustible inner and outer horizons of things. While elements of the perceptual field, of which we are a part, can be made explicit, the field as a whole cannot be exhausted nor completely given. And it is this indeterminacy and incompleteness that makes us feel that the perceptual world is real, *always already* there behind our backs.

Perception thus contains an implicit trust, or hope, that through a teleological process of perceptual adjustment and correction, a back-and-forth dialogue with the world, what was experienced as lack can come to expression (Merleau-Ponty 2012 [1945]: 155). There are at least two ways of understanding this teleology of perception. On the one hand, it can be understood to rely on *optimal* bodily attitudes—ways of moving and sensing that allow the practical and perceptual significances of the world to be *better* grasped (a kind of optimal "I can"). Take, for instance, the focusing distance through which a particular object can be better seen, or the weight of touch that allows the textures of a certain surface to be felt (2012 [1945]: 316). On the other hand, this teleology can be understood as an open-ended improvisation or synchronization, through which both sensing and sensible—body and world—take dynamic form, and in which neither preexists their relation (Al-Saji 2008). Since this second option discards the prejudice of an objective in-itself world, multiple "solutions" to the problem of expression may be possible, and different ways in which sense can appear. Here the commonality of the field of sense cannot be assumed, though it can become an epistemic and ethical task.

The first option risks re-naturalizing ways of perceiving—judged optimal—that correspond to certain cultivated capacities and habitualities. These often reside in particular privileged forms of embodiment and are made possible by the colonization of material, social, and economic resources. Forms of behavior that are adapted to, or geared into, current social norms will best succeed on this picture. But the second option is not without its risks. For the improvisation of perception does not take place apart from the normativity of the social world. Indeed, both sensory world and sensing body are already weighted by differential historical and social ways of being. The sensory world is already social and the body is a historical being (Merleau-Ponty 2012 [1945]: 174). What risks being re-naturalized, here, is the radical "alterity" of forms of life. Otherness is de-contextualized and reified into bodies, as if that experience of difference were not also a function of differential positioning on the social map and its constitutive, normative exclusions.

Two examples from critical race and feminist phenomenologies can show what is at stake. In her well-known essay "Throwing Like a Girl," Iris Marion Young shows how "feminine" movements are often restrictive: they are lived in terms of a self-inhibited "I cannot" that is superimposed upon the practical possibilities of a general "human" — but in fact male— "I can" (2005: 37). To leave the analysis there would be to re-naturalize feminine embodiment as inhibited intentionality, as "Other." What needs to be shown, and what Young shows, are the ways in which one learns to move *like a girl* in a social world pervaded by a Western phallocentric gaze and violence that which structure habituation (i.e., what habits one acquires or is dissuaded from acquiring), body image, and affect (Young 2005: 44–45).

A second example can be found in Frantz Fanon's *Black Skin, White Masks* (1967 [1952]), and takes us back to the analysis of temporal experience. Differences in rhythm and sensibility—in bodily, musical and poetic expression—are often taken to belong to blackness and are made into innate bodily forms. This elides how such expressions of "*Négritude*" point to a multiplicity of experiences, situated in a history of slavery, racism and colonization, and formed both in suffering and in resistance to them (Fanon 1967 [1952]: 122–129).

Once the social and the political—once historicity, domination and oppression— are taken to structure perceptual and affective experience all the way down, an incommensurability is introduced into experience that challenges the commonality of the field of sense upon which the recognition of meaning relies. Sociality and historicity differentially structure the very forms of expression that perceptual sense and practical possibility take. Sociality and historicity are not merely added onto meaning-making relations as an extra layer of sense. What does phenomenology need to become in order to do justice to such knotted and entangled experience?

Lived Experience and Pathologies of the Social

The problem of phenomenology as feminist methodology was clearly exposed in a debate between Joan Scott and Linda Martín Alcoff on the status of lived experience for feminist theory (Alcoff 2000 and 2014; Scott 1992). While Scott's critique was levelled at histories of difference, her claim—that "the project of making experience visible precludes analysis of the workings of [the ideological] system and of its historicity; instead it reproduces its terms" (1992: 25)—is an objection often repeated against phenomenology. The claim is that hitherto marginalized and unheard experience is foregrounded in its immediacy at the cost of eliding its social conditions. I would agree with Scott that taking experience as an unproblematized and uncontested foundation for knowledge risks re-naturalizing the oppressive structures that make that experience possible.

However, as Alcoff rightly notes in response to Scott, posing experience and theory, phenomenology and critique, as mutually exclusive terms is a false opposition—one that the practice of feminist phenomenology undercuts (2000: 45–47; 2014: 456). It should be clear from my account thus far that the experience at stake in phenomenological description is neither naïve, nor unproblematized; it is not a "clear datum," as Alcoff points out (2000: 48). Experience is an ambiguous and dense knot of relations, a temporally entangled and non-linear flow that calls for methodological reflection, precisely for phenomenology. The "immediacy" of experience is hence not as straightforward as the term implies. "Immediacy" is a way of describing the "prereflective" self-awareness of experience, the sense in which every experience is *lived-through*, from within, prior to reflection (Zahavi 1999). But "immediacy" also points to the thickness of lived experience— how I cannot detach from it while also living through it, how it cannot be made into an object to be surveyed and grasped—and the ways in which there always remains an excess that has not been made sense of, a core of "non-sense," implicit and opaque. It is in this sense that "the most important lesson of the reduction is the impossibility of a complete reduction," as Merleau-Ponty says (2012 [1945]: lxxvii). This is not to abandon the reduction (Heinämaa 2002), but to take it to be an always renewed effort, questioning and hesitating, without end. Moreover, phenomenological "sense" is not a discrete and static content. Rather it is relational, temporal and processual, more orientation and style than thing (to recall the multiple meanings of the French word "*sens*"; see also Ahmed 2006). I have been careful to discuss "meaning" broadly in this essay, allowing sense to be perceptual, practical and affective—to be kinaesthetically, visually, haptically, aurally and linguistically worked out in the relation between lived body and world, avoiding divisions into preconceptual and conceptual contents.

While giving a "phenomenology of *x*" is sometimes used loosely to mean describing *what it is like* to experience or be *x*, in the first person, this is not all that phenomenology as method must do. Phenomenology both makes experience (partially) explicit and discloses that which is structuring of, which makes a difference in, experience. It gestures toward that which is only indirectly and laterally given in experience—the invisible norms *according to which* meaning appears. Such normativity—of perception, for instance—is historically instituted and socially situated, but it is forgotten as norm and its work remains invisible. Examples of perceptual norms include the dimensionality of depth—which opens up the experience of space as voluminosity and envelopment—and the spatial level that orients and anchors the visual field (Merleau-Ponty 2012 [1945]: 259–279). Merleau-Ponty describes these perceptual norms as invisibles *of* the visible; they *make visible* but are not themselves visible (1964a [1964] and 1968 [1964]). Particularly suggestive is the example of a color, which when it becomes the color of the lighting, is transformed through its own duration to serve as a "neutral" level according to which we see (Merleau-Ponty 2012 [1945]: 322–324). Lighting is invisible, ubiquitous, forgotten in its particularity, but inflects and *differentially* makes visible the rest of the field (Merleau-Ponty 1968 [1964]: 218, 237). As Helen Fielding (2006) has argued, this neutrality of lighting should be questioned. The color and level of lighting cannot be assumed to be perceptual constants. Rather, they point to a social-historical horizon and the racial logics and technologies that take white light to be a neutral and "colourless" hue, optimal for distinguishing bodies, since it optimally distinguishes the features of *white* bodies (Fielding 2006: 87).

Moreover, I would argue that the voluminosity opened up by depth is not a neutral space, a structural invariant that can be configured and encoded differently through the possible actions of different bodies (cf. Fisher 2000: 29–30). Extending a point made by Young, the voluminosity of space is often experienced in "feminine" embodiment as a splitting or "double spatiality," where "here" and "there" are discontinuous (Young 2005: 40–41). "There" does not hold open practical possibilities for *my* body, even while it conjures up a virtual body (not mine) capable of living in it and acting upon it. This closure of the "there" and enclosure in my "here" are felt in my body (hesitantly, as "I cannot"). Understanding this as a limitation of a generalized, seamless, and freely traversed space would be an idealization. This is not merely a question of limited or truncated possibility, but a different sense of possibility that belongs to a *differently structured space*.

To introduce more complexity into this phenomenological account, gender cannot be understood to be the only denominator according to which the spatial world is differentiated, nor is there one single denominator. The spatiality of bodies, racialized as white, is often felt to be "ontologically expansive," to use Shannon Sullivan's term (2006: 10). The space that these bodies project is smooth and open, "available for them to move in and out of as they wish" (Sullivan 2006: 10)—a space where they are free to act, with leeway to improvise and play, and where their actions, moreover, can have traction. In contrast, racialized bodies are policed and hampered in their movements and migrations, internalizing these borders to some degree. Their lived space is permeated by differential viscosities and currents, places where they may get bogged down in stereotypes, atmospheres saturated with bodily suffering, past and present, and fissures weighted by violence and historicity.

Hence, if the first step of phenomenology is to bracket naturalizing tendencies within experience, then the description of *what it is like* must not only be contextualized, but its normative assumptions must also be historicized and its exclusions made visible. This means extending, indeed radicalizing, the scope of the phenomenological reduction to the naturalization of social oppression in experience; and this is what I have called "critical phenomenology." Referring back to the commonality of the field of sense, it might be objected that some omission or forgetting will always accompany the institution of the field and is part of its historically contingent development. It is in this sense that the phenomenological reduction was always incomplete for Merleau-Ponty (2012 [1945]: lxxvii). In the figure-ground structuring of the visual field, that which remains in the background frames, orients and relationally defines what is figured. That the background remains tacit, that it is not explicitly made sense of, precludes neither its affective sway nor its relational power.

But this is not the sense of normative exclusion or elision that I mean. To be precise, there are two forms of exclusion upon which the normativity of the perceptual field might be built, but that I would describe as *pathologies of the social* (to paraphrase Fanon 1967 [1952]: 10). What I mean to point to is not the structure of institution as such, but the pathological recalcitrance of institutions of oppression—racial and colonial formations, as well as sexual and gendering oppressions—in how they manage relationality, in their dependence on, forgetfulness of, and domination of others.

In the first exclusion, what is forgotten is not only one's dependence on a social-historical horizon and on a cultural and linguistic milieu, but also on the materiality, time and bodies of others (e.g., maternal and carer bodies)—on the sociality that has accompanied and supported the development of one's perception. It is this invisible "weight of the past" that institutes a particular way of perceiving as normative (Merleau-Ponty 2010 [2003]). But at the same time, there is a second exclusion: the exclusion of the non-familiar and "alien" other (e.g., the racialized other), whose difference may be represented as exotic or threatening, but whose abjection plays a constitutive role in how one comes to see. This corresponds to the structural elision of other ways of being and perceiving that do not "make sense" within the instituted field of sense. As I have argued elsewhere (Al-Saji 2014), the first exclusion institutes the level according to which I perceive based on the appropriation of the flesh of others to whom my attachment is rendered invisible (Frye 1983; Lugones 1996). The second means that even excluded others are obliquely and structurally inscribed within the perceptual field, as its "constitutive outside" (to use Judith Butler's term, 1993). The "radical difference" of the other cannot be understood to mean absolute separation in this case, as if others were new lands to be discovered. Rather, those defined as "alien" are already relied on and assumed within the workings of perception, even as they are relegated to its intolerable and unrecognized margins.

Institutions of oppression thus manage relational difference by subsuming it into homogeneous identity, into the sphere of the ego, on the one hand, and by abjecting it as inassimilable non-sense, radical alterity, on the other. These two forms of exclusion work together. This means that institutions of oppression suffer from an "affective ankylosis," to use Fanon's diagnosis (1967 [1952]: 121), a rigidity or lack of receptivity to otherness.

In the final section, I argue that phenomenology has generally addressed the first form of exclusion more adequately than the second, and I explore where in phenomenology we might find the means to remedy this.

Critical Phenomenology and Hesitation

My question is, then, how to prevent phenomenology from becoming another "epistemology of ignorance" (Mills 2007), from re-naturalizing oppression to the perceptual and affective realms that it describes. Here the incompleteness of the phenomenological reduction can be redeployed as recommencement and hesitation. While it is possible to read Husserl as searching for a foundationalism that provides certainty, what we learn when we attend to his method is the need to renew, each time, the bracketing operation. I don't think this is a failure on Husserl's part. The phenomenological reduction is not a formula whose outcome can become a stable acquisition; we miss the import of the reduction if we take it to define a teleology. Instead, phenomenology should be understood as an effort of *re-orientation*, a conversion of perception, a way of attending differently (Ahmed 2006; Merleau-Ponty 1964a [1964] and 1968 [1964]; Oliver 2001; Ratcliffe 2012).

As Merleau-Ponty saw, the incompleteness of the phenomenological reduction can also be its virtue. This is not only because the experiences to which phenomenologists attend are singular and multiple, requiring a unique effort each time; nor simply because this effort unwinds in its performance, as naturalizing tendencies seep in. It is also because phenomenology seeks to hold together—and make palpable—both my belonging to the world and my estrangement from it; to dwell in the experience that it is seeking to describe; to keep it alive while excavating its structures. It is hence not simply an epistemological, even ontological, project, but also an affective one. This affect has often been described, following Eugen Fink, as "wonder" in the face of the world (cited in Merleau-Ponty 2012 [1945]: lxxvii), but it can also be anxiety (Sartre 1960 [1936]: 103; see also Carr 1999: 127–128), nausea or despair (Fanon 1967 [1952]: 112, 140).

This discomfort or unease—this hesitation—deepens with critical phenomenologies, where the phenomenological reduction serves not only to reveal one's ties to the social world, but also the exclusions that structure one's positionality and with which one may be complicit (Beauvoir 2010 [1949]; Fanon 1967 [1952]; Al-Saji 2014). The two forms of exclusion that I describe above can hence motivate two different critical orientations. First, a recuperative orientation: a revaluation and disclosure of both the structures of perception and their material, bodily, and temporal grounds. Both Husserl and Merleau-Ponty have addressed the structures of perception, not merely through static but also through genetic phenomenological accounts; that is, they have shown how sense arises within experience and not merely how sense is possible (Husserl 2001 [1966]; Merleau-Ponty 2012 [1945] and 1968 [1964]). But this is not yet to address the generativity or relational dependency of perception (Steinbock 1995). The work of critically uncovering the debt of perception to other bodies, especially maternal and carer bodies, has been largely carried out by feminist theorists (whether or not they would call themselves phenomenologists). Luce Irigaray's critique of Merleau-Ponty's elision of the maternal body is a case in point (1993 [1984] and 2004).

The second exclusion can motivate a different critical orientation, however, one that has not always been easy for phenomenology to negotiate; for the second exclusion calls for a thick intersectional approach. By this, I do not mean simply adding together axes of identity, as attributes in a list, to give an encumbered subject. I mean, rather, analyzing how gendering and racialization, for instance, are interlocking oppressions that may sometimes reinforce, sometimes occlude, and sometimes instrumentalize one another (see Chapters 10, 28, and 29 in this volume). That these cannot be understood as "pure" axes or attributes, and that they need to be known contextually and locally, leads me to suggest that feminist phenomenology might not always be primarily a phenomenology of gender (contra Oksala 2006). Or, less controversially, that if feminist phenomenology comes to experience with a predefined category of "gender," then it risks missing the thick nexus of experience where *gendering* occurs in unrecognizable and entangled ways—where it cannot be thought without an understanding of its coloniality, its reliance on racialization, and its exclusion of other ways of being gendered.

Here we come full circle. For what is required of feminist phenomenology is not only structural analysis but also richly textured and fine-grained description—which listens, checks, and questions (Ortega 2006)—description so attentive that it can become transformative. By dwelling in and mining the affective tissue of intersubjective life, bodily experience can become the source of phenomenological questioning (Fanon 1967 [1952]: 232). Hence the practice of phenomenology as seen in the texts of critical phenomenologists of oppression, such as Beauvoir and Fanon: creating possibility by articulating experience anew, interrupting its naturalizing tendencies and making that experience hesitate. This is not the paralyzing hesitancy of "feminine" habits that Young described, but a hesitation that makes time for experience to be disclosed and re-oriented (Al-Saji 2014). I said, above, that phenomenology listens in on the dialogue of body and world. I should add that it participates in this dialogue, by making it audible and by opening up other ways for bodies to respond, locally and without predetermining what that response may be.

Further Reading

Alcoff, Linda Martín (2000) "Phenomenology, Post-structuralism, and Feminist Theory on the Concept of Experience," in Linda Fisher and Lester Embree (Eds.) *Feminist Phenomenology*, Dordrecht: Kluwer.

Al-Saji, Alia (2010) "Bodies and Sensings: On the Uses of Husserlian Phenomenology for Feminist Theory," *Continental Philosophy Review* 43(1): 13–37.

Heinämaa, Sara (2003) *Toward a Phenomenology of Sexual Difference: Husserl, Merleau-Ponty, Beauvoir*, Lanham, MD: Rowman & Littlefield.

Weiss, Gail (2008) *Refiguring the Ordinary*, Bloomington, IN: Indiana University Press.

Young, Iris Marion (2005) *On Female Body Experience: "Throwing Like a Girl" and Other Essays*, Oxford: Oxford University Press.

Related Topics

Embodiment and feminist philosophy (Chapter 15); materiality: sex, gender, and what lies beneath (Chapter 16); psychoanalysis, subjectivity and feminism (Chapter 19); critical race theory, intersectionality, and feminist philosophy (Chapter 29).

References

Ahmed, Sara (2006) *Queer Phenomenology: Orientations, Objects, Others*, Durham, NC: Duke University Press.

Alcoff, Linda Martín (2000) "Phenomenology, Post-Structuralism, and Feminist Theory on the Concept of Experience," in Linda Fisher and Lester Embree (Eds.) *Feminist Phenomenology*, Dordrecht: Kluwer, 39–56.

—— (2006) *Visible Identities: Race, Gender, and the Self*, Oxford: Oxford University Press.

—— (2014) "Sexual Violations and the Question of Experience," *New Literary History* 45(3): 445–462.

Al-Saji, Alia (2008) "'A Past Which Has Never Been Present': Bergsonian Dimensions in Merleau-Ponty's Theory of the Prepersonal," *Research in Phenomenology* 38(1): 41–71.

—— (2010) "Bodies and Sensings: On the Uses of Husserlian Phenomenology for Feminist Theory," *Continental Philosophy Review* 43(1): 13–37.

—— (2013) "Too Late: Racialized Time and the Closure of the Past," *Insights* 6(5): 1–13.

—— (2014) "A Phenomenology of Hesitation: Interrupting racializing habits of seeing," in Emily Lee (Ed.) *Living Alterities: Phenomenology, Embodiment, and Race*, Albany, NY: SUNY Press, 133–172.

Bartky, Sandra Lee (1990) *Femininity and Domination: Studies in the Phenomenology of Oppression*, New York: Routledge.

Beauvoir, Simone de (2010 [1949]) *The Second Sex*, trans. Constance Borde and Sheila Malovany-Chevallier, New York: Knopf.

Butler, Judith (1989) "Sexual Ideology and Phenomenological Description: A Feminist Critique of Merleau-Ponty's *Phenomenology of Perception*," in Jeffner Allen and Iris Marion Young (Eds.) *The Thinking Muse: Feminism and Modern French Philosophy*, Bloomington, IN: Indiana University Press, 85–100.

—— (1993) *Bodies that Matter: On the Discursive Limits of "Sex,"* New York: Routledge.

Calcagno, Antonio (2007) *The Philosophy of Edith Stein*, Pittsburgh, PA: Duquesne University Press.

Carr, David (1999) *The Paradox of Subjectivity: The Self in the Transcendental Tradition*, Oxford: Oxford University Press.

Fanon, Frantz (1967 [1952]) *Black Skin, White Masks*, trans. Charles Lam Markmann, New York: Grove Press.

Fielding, Helen (2006) "White Logic and the Constancy of Color," in Dorothea Olkowski and Gail Weiss (Eds.) *Feminist Interpretations of Maurice Merleau-Ponty*, University Park, PA: Pennsylvania State University Press, 71–89.

Fisher, Linda (2000) "Phenomenology and Feminism: Perspectives on their Relation," in Linda Fisher and Lester Embree (Eds.) *Feminist Phenomenology*, Dordrecht: Kluwer, 17–38.

Fisher, Linda, and Lester Embree (Eds.) (2000) *Feminist Phenomenology*, Dordrecht: Kluwer.

Frye, Marilyn (1983) *The Politics of Reality: Essays in Feminist Theory*, Freedom, CA: The Crossing Press.

Gordon, Lewis R. (1995) *Bad Faith and Antiblack Racism*, New York: Humanity Books.

Heinämaa, Sara (2002) "From Decisions to Passions: Merleau-Ponty's Interpretation of Husserl's Reduction," in Ted Toadvine and Lester Embree (Eds.) *Merleau-Ponty's Reading of Husserl*, Dordrecht: Kluwer, 129–148.

—— (2003) *Toward a Phenomenology of Sexual Difference: Husserl, Merleau-Ponty, Beauvoir*, Lanham, MD: Rowman & Littlefield.

Heinämaa, Sara, and Lanei Rodemeyer (Eds.) (2010) Special Issue on Phenomenology and Feminism, *Continental Philosophy Review* 43 (1): 1–140.

Husserl, Edmund (1970 [1954]) *The Crisis of European Sciences and Transcendental Phenomenology*, trans. David Carr, Evanston, IL: Northwestern University Press.

—— (1989 [1952]) *Ideas Pertaining to a Pure Phenomenology and to a Phenomenological Philosophy: Second book, Studies in the Phenomenology of Constitution*, trans. Richard Rojcewicz and André Schuwer, Dordrecht: Kluwer.

—— (1991 [1966]) *On the Phenomenology of the Consciousness of Internal Time (1893–1917)*, trans. John Barnett Brough, Dordrecht: Kluwer.

—— (1998 [1976]) *Ideas Pertaining to a Pure Phenomenology and to a Phenomenological Philosophy: First book, General Introduction to a Pure Phenomenology*, trans. Fred Kersten, Dordrecht: Kluwer.

—— (2001 [1966]) *Analyses Concerning Passive and Active Synthesis: Lectures on Transcendental Logic*, trans. Anthony J. Steinbock, Dordrecht: Kluwer.

Irigaray, Luce (1993 [1984]) *An Ethics of Sexual Difference*, trans. Carolyn Burke and Gillian C. Gill, Ithaca, NY: Cornell University Press.

—— (2004) "To Paint the Invisible," trans. Helen Fielding, *Continental Philosophy Review* 37: 389–405.

Lugones, Maria (1996) "Playfulness, 'World'-Traveling, and Loving Perception," in Ann Garry and Marilyn Pearsall (Eds.) *Women, Knowledge and Reality: Explorations in Feminist Philosophy*, New York: Routledge, 419–433.

Merleau-Ponty, Maurice (1964a [1964]) "Eye and Mind," trans. Carleton Dallery, in *The Primacy of Perception and Other Essays on Phenomenological Psychology, the Philosophy of Art, History and Politics*, Evanston, IL: Northwestern University Press, 159–190.

—— (1964b [1960]) *Signs*, trans. R. McCleary, Evanston, IL: Northwestern University Press.

—— (1968 [1964]) *The Visible and the Invisible*, Ed. Claude Lefort, trans. Alfonso Lingis. Evanston, IL: Northwestern University Press.

—— (2010 [2003]) *Institution and Passivity: Course Notes from the Collège de France (1954–1955)*, trans. Leonard Lawlor and Heath Massey, Evanston, IL: Northwestern University Press.

—— (2012 [1945]) *Phenomenology of Perception*, trans. Donald Landes, New York: Routledge.

Mills, Charles W. (2007) "White Ignorance," in Shannon Sullivan and Nancy Tuana (Eds.) *Race and Epistemologies of Ignorance*, Albany, NY: SUNY Press, 11–38.

Oksala, Johanna (2006) "A Phenomenology of Gender," *Continental Philosophy Review* 39: 229–244.

Oliver, Kelly (2001) *Witnessing: Beyond Recognition*, Minneapolis, MN: University of Minnesota Press.

Olkowski, Dorothea and Weiss, Gail (Eds.) (2006) *Feminist Interpretations of Maurice Merleau-Ponty*, University Park, PA: Pennsylvania State University Press.

Ortega, Mariana (2006) "Being Lovingly, Knowingly Ignorant: White Feminism and Women of Color," *Hypatia* 21(3): 56–74.

Ratcliffe, Matthew (2012) "Phenomenology as a Form of Empathy," *Inquiry: An Interdisciplinary Journal of Philosophy* 55(5): 473–495.

Salamon, Gayle (2010) *Assuming a Body: Transgender and Rhetorics of Materiality*, New York: Columbia University Press.

Sartre, Jean-Paul (1960 [1936]) *The Transcendence of the Ego*, trans. Forrest Williams and Robert Kirkpatrick, New York: Noonday Press.

Schües, Christina, Olkowski, Dorothea, and Fielding, Helen (Eds.) (2011) *Time in Feminist Phenomenology*, Bloomington, IN: Indiana University Press.

Scott, Joan W. (1992) "Experience," in Judith Butler and Joan W. Scott (Eds.) *Feminists Theorize the Political*, New York: Routledge, 22–40.

Simms, Eva, and Stawarska, Beata (Eds.) (2014) "Special Issue: Feminist Phenomenology," *Janus Head* 13(1).

Steinbock, Anthony J. (1995) *Home and Beyond: Generative Phenomenology after Husserl*, Evanston, IL: Northwestern University Press.

Sullivan, Shannon (2006) *Revealing Whiteness: The Unconscious Habits of Racial Privilege*, Bloomington, IN: Indiana University Press.

Weiss, Gail (1999) *Body Images: Embodiment as Intercorporeality*, New York: Routledge.

—— (2008) *Refiguring the Ordinary*, Bloomington, IN: Indiana University Press.

Welton, Donn (2000) *The Other Husserl: The Horizons of Transcendental Phenomenology*, Bloomington, IN: Indiana University Press.

Yancy, George (2008) *Black Bodies, White Gazes: The Continuing Significance of Race*, Lanham, MD: Rowman & Littlefield.

Young, Iris Marion (2005) *On Female Body Experience: "Throwing Like a Girl" and Other Essays*, Oxford: Oxford University Press.

Zahavi, Dan (1999) *Self-Awareness and Alterity: A Phenomenological Investigation*, Evanston, IL: Northwestern University Press.

Zeiler, Kristin and Folkmarson Käll, Lisa (Eds.) (2014) *Feminist Phenomenology and Medicine*, Albany, NY: SUNY Press.

Part II

BODY, MIND, AND WORLD

13

THE SEX/GENDER DISTINCTION AND THE SOCIAL CONSTRUCTION OF REALITY

Sally Haslanger

Introduction

The claim that gender (or other categories) is socially constructed is broadly accepted, but what this means is controversial and often unclear. In this chapter, I will sketch some different meanings of the claim that something is socially constructed and why these claims matter. For the purposes of this chapter, my focus will be to consider how the different senses of construction might apply especially in the case of gender.

The Construction of Ideas and Concepts

Ian Hacking urges us to distinguish the construction of ideas and the construction of objects (Hacking 1999: 9–16; Haslanger 2012: ch 3). Let's start with "ideas." What does it mean to say that the concept of gender, or the idea that females should not be sexually attracted to other females, is socially constructed? Plausibly, the claim is simply that they are products of a socio-historical process. However, that would seem to be utterly obvious. Surely at least most ideas and concepts are only possible within and due to a social context (allowing that there are also innate cognitive processes and structures that also play a role). Concepts are taught to us by our parents as we learn language; different cultures have overlapping but also distinct concepts and ideas; and concepts as well as ideas evolve over time as a result of historical changes, science, technological advances, etc. Let's (albeit contentiously) call this the "ordinary view" of concepts and ideas.

Even someone who believes that our scientific concepts perfectly map "nature's joints" can allow that scientists come to have the ideas and concepts they do through social-historical processes. After all, social and cultural forces (including, possibly, the practices and methods of science) may help us develop concepts that are apt or accurate, and beliefs that are true. We may sometimes forget that social forces affect what and how we think because our experiences seem to be caused simply and directly by the world itself. However, it does not take much prompting to recall that our culture is largely responsible for the interpretive tools we bring to the world in order to understand it. Once we've noted that our experience of the world is already an interpretation of it, we can begin to raise questions about the adequacy of our conceptual framework. Concepts help us organize phenomena; different concepts organize it in different ways. It is important, then, to ask: what phenomena does a particular framework highlight and what are eclipsed? What assumptions provide structure for the framework?

For example, our everyday framework for thinking about human beings is structured by the assumption that there are two (and only two) sexes, and that every human is either a male or a female. But in fact a significant percentage of humans have a mix of male and female anatomical features. Intersexed bodies are eclipsed in our everyday framework (Fausto-Sterling 2000; Rubin 2012). Thus, we should ask: why two sexes? Whose interests are served, if anyone's, by the intersexed being ignored in the dominant conceptual framework? (It can't be plausibly argued that sex isn't important enough to us to make fine-grained distinctions between bodies.) Assuming for the moment that sex can be distinguished from gender (more on this later), our everyday framework also assumes that there are only two genders, but this obscures those who are gender queer as well as third sexes found in other cultures (Herdt 1993).

Once we recognize that our everyday framework has eclipsed a kind or category, how should we respond? For example, how should we revise our conceptual framework once we notice the intersexed and gender queer (Butler 1990: ch. 1; Fausto-Sterling 2000)? Should we group humans into more than two sexes or genders, or are there reasons instead to complicate the definitions to include everyone in just two sex/gender categories? Or should we stop classifying by sex and gender altogether? More generally, on what basis should we decide what categories to use? In asking these questions it is important to remember that an idea or conceptual framework may be inadequate without being false, e.g., a claim might be true and yet incomplete, misleading, unjustified, biased, etc. (Anderson 1995; Haslanger 2016).

The point of saying that a concept or idea is socially constructed will vary depending on context. Sometimes it may have little or no point, if everyone is fully aware of the social history of the idea in question or if the social history isn't relevant to the issue at hand. On other occasions, saying that an idea is socially constructed is a reminder of the ordinary view of concepts and, more importantly, an invitation to notice the motivations behind and limitations of our current framework. Every framework will have some limits; the issue is whether the limits eclipse something that, given the legitimate goals of our inquiry, matters.

Often, the claim that a concept or idea is socially constructed is accompanied by genealogical inquiry. The genealogy of a concept or idea explores its history, not because the origin of a concept determines its proper content, but in order to situate the concept within our social practices (Haslanger 2012: ch. 13). Consider, for example, Daston and Galison's recent genealogy of the concept of *objectivity*. They suggest that in the case of complex and historically significant concepts, there is often a "smear of meanings," that cannot be usefully parsed by a priori inquiry alone (Daston and Galison 2007: 52). So their approach is to explore how the ideal of objectivity guided scientific practice in different periods.

If actions are substituted for concepts and practices for meanings, the focus on the nebulous notion of objectivity sharpens. Scientific objectivity resolves into the gestures, techniques, habits, and temperament ingrained by training and daily repetition. It is manifest in images, jottings in lab notebooks, logical notations; objectivity in shirtsleeves, not in a marble chiton . . . . It is by performing certain actions over and over again . . . that objectivity comes into being. To paraphrase Aristotle on ethics, one becomes objective by performing objective acts. Instead of a pre-existing ideal being applied to a workaday world, it is the other way around: the ideal and ethos are gradually built up and bodied out by thousands of concrete actions as a mosaic takes shape from thousands of tiny fragments of colored glass. To study objectivity in shirtsleeves is to watch objectivity in the making.

(Daston and Galison 2007: 52)

They convincingly demonstrate that the notion of objectivity has changed dramatically over time. For example, in Descartes' work, the objective is what is available as the object of consciousness, in contrast to the object in the world. In the eighteenth and early nineteenth centuries, objective inquiry aimed to capture the perfect or ideal exemplar; but soon after, influenced by the development of photography, the goal was to capture the world "untouched by human hands" (Daston and Galison 2007: 43) and to catalogue its detailed specificity and imperfections.

Such genealogies offer two valuable lessons: First, what strikes us as obvious or unquestionable is the result of a complex social and intellectual history; we might have taken very different things for granted, employed very different distinctions, and reasonably so. However, the best genealogies do not leave us with a sense of arbitrariness, but of richness and opportunity. Our conceptual repertoires are at least partly a matter of choice. We can create different and improved tools to accomplish our cognitive ends. Second, our cognitive tools are not just "in the head" but are enacted and embodied in practices that engage the material world. The products of our practices—some of them material, such as lab notebooks and cameras, and others institutional, such as universities and bureaucracies—make a difference to how and what we think.

These two lessons are importantly related. Our practices are shaped by historically contingent assumptions, and the practices, in turn, reinforce those assumptions by materializing them. But genealogy allows us to see that we have choices about the assumptions we make, and material changes—including not only new technologies, but also new institutions and bureaucracies—can render questionable what seemed obvious. A space opens for critique: our ideas and practices are not necessitated by the world, but are the products of history, a history in which we are agents and whose trajectory we can change.

For example, Anne Fausto-Sterling characterizes her book *Sexing the Body* (2000) this way:

The central tenet of this book is that truths about human sexuality created by scholars in general and by biologists in particular are one component of political, social, and moral struggles about our cultures and economies. At the same time, components of our political, social, and moral struggles become, quite literally, embodied, incorporated into our very physiological being. My intent is to show how these mutually dependent claims work, in part by addressing such issues as how—through their daily lives, experiments, and medical practices—scientists create truths about sexuality; how our bodies incorporate and confirm these truths; and how these truths, sculpted by the social milieu in which biologists practice their trade, in turn refashion our cultural environment.

(Fausto-Sterling 2000: 5)

This interdependence between thought and practice is especially evident in feminist work that has documented how the sex/gender binary has not only been assumed, but also *enforced* (Butler 1990; 2004; Fausto-Sterling 2000; Richardson 2012; 2015). For example, intersexed infants have been surgically altered to conform to binary assumptions about the proper size, shape, and function of genitalia (e.g., Kessler 1990, 1998; Dreger and Herndon 2009). However, historical and scientific genealogies of the concepts that guide our enforcement of sex/gender show that our understanding of sex is culturally conditioned; this seems to give us options.

Our bodies are too complex to provide clear-cut answers about sexual difference. The more we look for a simple physical basis for "sex," the more it becomes clear that "sex" is not a pure physical category. What bodily signals and functions we define as male or female come already entangled in our ideas about gender.

(Fausto-Sterling 2000: 4)

Note that Fausto-Sterling's claim here that "sex" *is not a pure physical category* is ambiguous. It could mean that the conditions for being male or female include non-physical properties. This is true according to some definitions of sex (Fausto-Sterling 1997). However, I take her to be making a different point in this quote, namely, that there are a variety of options for defining sex that, *considering the physical facts alone*, are equally good. We have chosen one definition for socio-cultural reasons, but it may be better for us to choose another. So there is an important sense in which how we define the distinction (or whether we do at all) is up to us, but this is consistent with there being physical differences between sexes.

So to claim that our concept of X (or idea concerning X) is socially constructed can be more than to claim that we developed it through a socio-historical process. It adds to this that nature (or whatever foundational source of truth we might be seeking) doesn't necessitate that we opt for one particular understanding, but leaves it at least somewhat open. For example, the fact that nature does not dictate a sex binary—we could identify more than two sexes, or allow some to be without sex—is crucial to the claim that our concept of sex is socially constructed. The fact that we have to surgically create a binary is some evidence that the difference is not "purely natural." But if our particular conception of X is "not inevitable" or required, then we should not only question our thinking, but also the practices that depend on it and enforce it (see also Sveinsdóttir 2011; Haslanger 2016).

Social constructionism is generally offered as an alternative to essentialism; both come in different forms. Drawing on the link between thought and practice, Alison

Stone (2004) explicitly takes up a genealogical approach to the social construction of gender to avoid the pitfalls of an essentialism that assumes there is some feature or features that all women share, by virtue of which they are women. She claims that

> women always become women by reworking pre-established cultural interpretations of femininity, so that they become located—together with all other women—within a history of overlapping chains of interpretation. Although women do not share any common understanding or experience of femininity, they nevertheless belong to a distinctive social group in virtue of being situated within this complex history.
>
> (Stone 2004: 137)

On her account, the group is unified by virtue of the members situating themselves in relation to the lineage of meanings associated with women, i.e., "women only become women, or acquire femininity, by taking up existing interpretations and concepts of femininity . . . . [i.e.] through active appropriation and personalizing of inherited cultural standards" (Stone 2004: 149). By incorporating the historical variability of practices of femininity, Stone aims to identify a unity for gender that is weaker than sharing an essence, but also stronger than family resemblance.

Stone employs the notion of genealogy not only to reconstruct the history of the concept or idea of gender through its practices, but also to identify a source of unity of the group, *women* (2004: 150). Women are a social kind, i.e., the group consists of those who situate themselves within the local practices *as women* (or *as feminine?*). Stone (2004) concludes that this kind has no essence (according to her concept of essence). However, it is arguable that on her account, *women* are a kind with an historical essence, i.e., a kind unified by reference to an historical process of replication and revision (Bach 2012). An historical conception of gender allows for substantial intrinsic diversity, while also providing a basis for political unity through a shared lineage of gender practices. Stone's account gives us important resources to avoid certain forms of essentialism, but because it is focused on the agency and activity involved in "appropriating and personalizing" the norms of femininity, it neglects pre-agentic females and those women whose agency is compromised. Moreover, the account fails to provide a basis for identifying what counts as a *gender* norm or for differentiating *gender* practices from other social practices: if the lineage of relevant practices is not identified by reference to the ideology of bodies that guides them (Alcoff 2005; Haslanger 2012: ch. 6), the content of their identities (Chodorow 1978), or their function (Bach 2012), then by virtue of what are they *gender* practices?

Social Construction and Illusion

It is also possible to find the claim that something or other is "merely" a social construction, with the implication that what we are taking to be real is only a fiction, an idea that fails to capture reality (see also Haslanger 2006). Such eliminativist implications are common in the case of race, i.e., often when someone says that race is socially constructed, they mean that race is an illusion (Glasgow 2008).

Feminists have argued, for example, that certain mental "disorders" that have been used to diagnose battered women are merely social constructions. Andrea Westlund points out how

[b]attered women's "abnormalities" have been described and redescribed within the psychiatric literature of the twentieth century, characterized as everything from hysteria to masochistic or self-defeating personality disorders (SDPD) to codependency . . . Moreover, such pathologies measure, classify, and define battered women's deviance not just from "normal" female behavior but also from universalized male norms of independence and self-interest.

(Westlund 1999: 1050–1051)

Such diagnoses invite us to explain domestic violence by reference to the woman's psychological state rather than the batterer's need for power and control; they also "deflect attention from the social and political aspects of domestic violence to the private neuroses to which women as a group are thought to be prone" (Westlund 1999: 1051). These diagnoses, it could be claimed, are merely social constructions in the sense that they are ideas used to interpret and regulate social phenomena, but do not describe *anything* real. To say, then, that "self-defeating personality disorder" is a social construct is to say that it doesn't exist.

We can gain insight into this eliminativist use of the term "social construction" if we link it to the genealogical approach considered above. Suppose we find through examining the practices in which the concept is used, that the concept we thought was of a certain kind, is not. For example, suppose we think that "self-defeating personality disorder," if it exists at all, must be an individual psychological pathology. If, however, there is no clear psychological phenomenon where we took there to be, and if we take it to be part of the content of the concept that it is a psychological disorder, then it is tempting to conclude that it doesn't exist and we were wrong all along. If, however, we allow that we might have been wrong about the kind of thing we were talking about, then we need not take the eliminativist route. For example, there are family system pathologies and cultural syndromes that are not individual pathologies. One might argue, then, that "self-defeating personality disorder" *really is* a social pathology. In other words, we would offer a very different construal of the target concept. Is this shifting the meaning of the term? Or is it discovering the meaning? Often this is exactly the issue at stake between eliminativist and non-eliminativist social constructionists.

The Social Construction of Objects

Let's now turn to the construction of objects (understanding "objects" in the broadest sense as virtually anything that's not an idea). What are some examples? Beauvoir (1989 [1949]: 267) famously claims, "One is not born, but rather becomes, a woman." But when we say that gender is a social construct, could we possibly mean that individual women and men are social constructions? What could this mean? Aren't women and men human beings, and aren't human beings a kind of animal?

We saw above that our cognitive tools are enacted and embodied in our practices. So at least in social contexts, our classifications may do more than just map pre-existing groups of individuals; rather our attributions have the power to both establish and reinforce groupings that may eventually come to "fit" the classifications. This works in several ways. Ian Hacking (1999) describes the "looping effect" of social kinds. In such cases, forms of description or classification provide for kinds of intention; e.g., given the classification *refugee*, I can set about to become a refugee, or avoid being a refugee (Hacking 1999: 32). And such classifications can function in justifying behavior; e.g., "We cannot send her back to Syria because she is a refugee" (note that there are international laws about the treatment of refugees as opposed to migrants). Such justifications, in turn, can reinforce the distinction between refugees and non-refugees. Social construction in this sense is ubiquitous. Each of us is socially constructed in this sense because we are (to a significant extent) the individuals we are today as a result of what has been attributed (and self-attributed) to us.

To say that an entity is "discursively constructed" in this sense, is not to say that language or discourse brings a material object into existence *de novo* (Haslanger 2012: ch. 2). Rather something in existence comes to have—partly as a result of having been categorized in a certain way—a set of features that qualify it as a member of a certain kind or sort. My having been categorized as a female at birth (and consistently since then) has been a factor in how I've been viewed and treated; these views and treatments have, in turn, played an important causal role in my becoming gendered a woman (see also Haslanger 2012: ch. 1). But discourse didn't bring me into existence.

It would appear that gender (in different senses) is both an idea-construction and an object-construction. Gender is an idea-construction because the classification men/women is the contingent result of historical events and forces. At the same time these classifications are crucial to explaining what Hacking calls "interactive kinds": gender classifications occur within a complex matrix of institutions and practices, and being classified as a woman, or a man, or a different sex/gender, or not, has a profound effect on an individual. Such classification will have a material affect on her social position as well as affect her experience and self-understanding.

Linda Alcoff's (2005) account of gender, or gender identity, provides an excellent example of such looping effects. She suggests, as a start:

> Women and men are differentiated by virtue of their different relationship of possibility to biological reproduction, with biological reproduction referring to conceiving, giving birth, and breast-feeding, involving one's own body . . . . Those classified as women will have a different set of practices, expectations, and feelings in regard to reproduction, no matter how actual [or not] their relationship of possibility is to it.
>
> (Alcoff 2005: 172)

The different relationship of possibility is not, in her terms, an "objective" fact, but is a matter of what socio-cultural resources are available, specifically in constructing horizons of meaning (Alcoff 2005: 125f, 145, 175f):

> [E]ach individual's horizon is significantly incorporative of social dimensions or shared features. The practices and meanings that are intelligible to me are ontologically grounded in group interactions, which are themselves structured by political economies of social structures.
>
> (Alcoff 2005: 121)

> The possibility of pregnancy, childbirth, nursing, and in many societies, rape, are parts of females' horizons that we carry with us throughout childhood and much or all of our adult lives. The way these are figured, imagined, experienced, accepted, and so on, is as variable as culture. But these elements exist in the female horizon, and they exist there because of the ways in which we are embodied.
>
> (Alcoff 2005: 176)

Alcoff's account has an advantage over Stone's insofar as it gives us a basis for distinguishing gender practices and meanings from others via the links to reproductive embodiment. It is somewhat unclear, however, how this account would be developed to accommodate the tensions between the classifications (gender ascriptions), bodies, and identities of transwomen (Connell 2012).

The Social Construction of Kinds

We have considered the social construction of ideas and objects. Yet the most common examples of social construction, it seems, are kinds, e.g., gender, race, disability, family, the nation, meat/food. It is important to distinguish between the social construction of ideas and objects because it is easy to confuse the idea of a kind, i.e., a classificatory tool, from the kind itself. Unless we draw this distinction we won't be able to recognize the interaction between the tool and the reality it purports to track. This looping interaction is crucial to the idea of social construction of all sorts.

Above I argued that we claim that an idea or concept is socially constructed to call attention to the fact that it is a product of a social and intellectual history. I suggested further that, at least in some cases, to attend to the social construction of a concept is to note that it is possible to grasp the relevant phenomena, be it in nature or other form of reality, without employing that exact concept. That is, the framework we have for understanding this bit of the world is "not inevitable" and is in some sense "up to us." This matters because we have a way of making reality conform to our idea of it, and if we are unhappy with the reality, it is useful to know if it is the way it is because we have made it so, or because there is no reasonable or realistic alternative.

How does this bear on kinds? The social constructionist is keen to draw our attention one or another of two mistakes that we are tempted to make about kinds, given how our understanding of them interacts with reality:

i) We may think that the commonality that the members of the kind share is caused by natural facts and forces, but instead, our social arrangements are (in some important way) causally responsible for the commonality. For example, it may be worth pointing out that poverty is socially constructed to make clear that poverty is *not* a result of (alleged) laziness or stupidity of the poor, but due to social/political structures. Or it might be worth pointing out that disability is socially constructed to make clear that disability is *not* the result of impairment, but of the social management of differently abled bodies.

ii) The dominant understanding of the kind might locate the commonality between the members' non-social properties, e.g., natural properties, but what the members of the kind share are really social properties (and relations). For example, it may be worth pointing out that races are *not* constituted by people with a certain "blood," i.e., genetic profile, but by how people with bodily markers associated with relatively recent ancestry in a particular geographical region are viewed and treated (Haslanger 2012: ch. 6). Or it might be worth pointing out that food is *not* what is digestible by humans, but what cultures deem appropriate to eat. To say that food is socially constructed in this sense is not to say that humans cause or create food (though of course we do), but that cultural meanings *constitute what food is.*

The difference between (i) and (ii) is a difference between what *causes* commonality and what *constitutes* commonality. It is important to note that social kinds cannot be equated with things that have social causes. Sociobiologists claim that some social phenomena have biological causes; some feminists claim that some anatomical phenomena have social causes. What is the cause of the average height differences between males and females? Some argue that it is due to the broad preference for males to be the taller in a heterosexual couple. But is that preference a result of social norms or biological imperatives? More generally, it is an error to treat the conditions by virtue of which something counts as a social entity as causing the entity. Something is a house by providing stable shelter to an individual or group of individuals. A builder putting bricks or boards together in a certain way causes the house to exist.

In (ii), the point is to distinguish social kinds from physical or other non-social kinds where what's at issue is the basis of commonality between the members. It is significant that not all social kinds are obviously social. Sometimes it is assumed that the conditions for membership in a kind concern only or primarily biological or physical facts. Pointing out that this is wrong can have important consequences. In the case of gender, the idea would be that gender is not a classification scheme based simply on anatomical or biological differences, but marks social differences between individuals. Gender, as opposed to sex, is not about testicles and ovaries, the penis and the uterus, but about identities or about the location of groups within a system of social relations (MacKinnon 1989; Haslanger 2012: ch. 6). One could allow that the categories of sex and gender interact (so concerns with distinctions between bodies will influence social divisions and vice versa); but even to be clear how they interact, we should differentiate them. Using the terms "male" and "female" to mark the current familiar sex distinction, and "man" and "woman" the gender distinction, one should allow that on this account of gender, it is plausible that some males are women and some females are men. Because one is a female by virtue of some (contextually variable) set of anatomical features, and one is a woman by virtue of one's identity or position within a social and economic system, the sex/gender distinction gives us some (at least preliminary) resources for including trans* persons within our conceptual framework (cf. Jenkins 2016).

Because gender is at least partly a function of one's role in a social framework or identification as one of those who typically (in the local context) occupy that role, if we allow that social phenomena are highly variable across time, cultures, groups, then this also allows us to recognize that the specific details of what it is to be a woman will differ depending on one's race, ethnicity, class, etc. My being a woman occurs in a context in which I am also White and privileged; my actual social position will therefore be affected by multiple factors simultaneously. I learned the norms of WASP womanhood, not Black womanhood. And even if I reject many of those norms, I benefit from the fact that they are broadly accepted. The social constructionist's goal is often to challenge the appearance of inevitability of the category in question. As things are arranged now, there are men and women, and people of different races. But if social conditions changed substantially, there may be no men and women, and no people of different races. To make the category visible as a social as opposed to physical category sometimes requires a rather radical change in our thinking.

Conclusion

In the account of social construction I've sketched, there are several different senses in which gender, race, and the like are socially constructed. First, the conceptual framework that we take as just "common sense" about gender is only one way of understanding the world. There are, and have been, other ways; there are (I believe) better ways. Moreover, there are ideas associated with gender that are "merely" constructions, e.g., fictions about biological essences and genetic determination are used to reinforce belief in the rightness and inevitability of the classifications. This is not to say, however, that gender is not "real." Although some ideas about gender are fictions, these fictional ideas have functioned to create and reinforce gender reality. These categories of people are, I would argue, not just ideas, but social entities. Such entities are socially constructed in the sense that they are caused by social forces, but also because the conditions for membership in a gender group are social (as opposed to, say, merely physical or anatomical) conditions. Finally, individual members of such groups are, in a rather extended sense socially constructed, insofar as they are affected by the social processes that constitute the groups. Human beings are social beings in the sense that we are deeply responsive to our social context and become the physical and psychological beings we are through interaction with others. One feminist hope is that we can become, through the construction of new and different practices, gendered differently and potentially new sorts of beings altogether.

Further Reading

Antony, Louise (2000) "Natures and Norms," *Ethics* 111(1): 8–36. (This title argues that the appeal to nature(s) is compatible with feminism, for the fact that something is natural does not assure its normative status.)

Foucault, Michel (1978) *The History of Sexuality, Volume. I: An Introduction*, New York: Pantheon. (A classic that undertakes a genealogy of sex and sexuality.)

Mallon, Ron (2007) "A Field Guide to Social Construction," *Philosophy Compass* 2(1): 93–108. (Offers a helpful overview of social construction on topics beyond sex/gender.)

Shrage, Laurie (2009) *You've Changed: Sex Reassignment and Personal Identity*, Oxford: Oxford University Press. (A collection of eleven philosophical essays on sex reassignment and its implications for thinking about sex, gender, and identity.)

Witt, Charlotte (2011) *The Metaphysics of Gender*, Oxford: Oxford University Press. (Argues for a social gender essentialism, challenging the idea that essentialism is incompatible with feminism.)

Related Topics

Feminism, philosophy, and culture in Africa (Chapter 4); feminist essentialism and anti-essentialism (Chapter 14); materiality: sex, gender, and what lies beneath (Chapter 16); personal identity and relational selves (Chapter 18); values, practices, and metaphysical assumptions in the biological sciences (Chapter 26); through the looking glass: trans theory meets feminist philosophy (Chapter 32).

References

Alcoff, Linda Martin (2005) *Visible Identities*, Oxford: Oxford University Press.

Anderson, Elizabeth (1995) "Knowledge, Human Interests, and Objectivity in Feminist Epistemology," *Philosophical Topics* 23(2): 27–58.

Bach, Theodore (2012) "Gender Is a Natural Kind with an Historical Essence," *Ethics* 122(2): 231–272

Beauvoir, Simone de (1989 [1949]) *The Second Sex*, trans. H. M. Parshley, New York: Vintage.

Butler, Judith (1990) *Gender Trouble*, New York: Routledge.

_____ (2004) *Undoing Gender*, New York: Routledge.

Chodorow, Nancy (1978) *The Reproduction of Mothering: Psychoanalysis and the Sociology of Gender*, Berkeley, CA: University of California Press.

Connell, Raewyn (2012) "Transsexual Women and Feminist Thought: Toward New Understanding and New Politics," *Signs* (37)4: 857–881.

Daston, Lorraine and Galison, Peter (2007) *Objectivity*, Cambridge, MA: MIT Press.

Dreger, Alice D. and Herndon, April M. (2009) "Progress and Politics in the Intersex Rights Movement: Feminist Theory in Action," *GLQ* 15(2): 199–224.

Fausto-Sterling, Anne (1997) "How to Build a Man," in Roger N. Lancaster and Micaela di Leonardo (Eds.) *The Gender/Sexuality Reader*, New York: Routledge, 244–248.

——(2000) *Sexing the Body: Gender Politics and the Construction of Sexuality*, New York: Basic Books.

Glasgow, Joshua (2008) *A Theory of Race*, New York: Routledge.

Hacking, Ian (1999) *The Social Construction of What?* Cambridge, MA: Harvard University Press.

Haslanger, Sally (2006) "Gender and Social Construction: Who? What? When Where? How?" in Elizabeth Hackett and Sally Haslanger (Eds.) *Theorizing Feminisms*, Oxford: Oxford University Press, 16–23.

——(2012) *Resisting Reality: Social Construction and Social Critique*, Oxford: Oxford University Press.

——(2016) "Theorizing with a Purpose: The Many Kinds of Sex," in Catherine Kendig (Ed.) *Natural Kinds and Classification in Scientific Practice*, New York: Routledge, 129–144.

Herdt, Gilbert (1993) *Third Sex, Third Gender: Beyond Sexual Dimorphism in Culture and History*, New York: Zone Books.

Jenkins, Katharine (2016) "Amelioration and Inclusion: Gender Identity and the Concept of Woman," *Ethics* 126(2): 394–421.

Kessler, Suzanne J. (1990) "The Medical Construction of Gender: Case Management of Intersexed Infants," *Signs* 16(1): 3–26.

——(1998) *Lessons from the Intersexed*, New Brunswick, NJ: Rutgers University Press.

MacKinnon, Catharine (1989) *Towards a Feminist Theory of the State*, Cambridge, MA: Harvard University Press.

Richardson, Sarah S. (2012) "Sexing the X: How the X Became the "Female Chromosome," *Signs* 37(4): 909–933.

——(2015) *Sex Itself: The Search for Male and Female in the Human Genome*. Chicago, IL: University of Chicago Press.

Rubin, David A. (2012) "An Unnamed Blank That Craved a Name: A Genealogy of Intersex as Gender," *Signs* 37(4): 883–908.

Stone, Alison (2004) "Essentialism and Anti-Essentialism in Feminist Philosophy," *Journal of Moral Philosophy* 1:135–153.

Sveinsdóttir, Ásta (2011) "The Metaphysics of Sex and Gender," in Charlotte Witt (Ed.) *Feminist Metaphysics*, Dordrecht: Springer, 47–65.

Westlund, Andrea (1999) "Pre-Modern and Modern Power: Foucault and the Case of Domestic Violence," *Signs* 24(4): 1045–1066.

14

GENDER ESSENTIALISM AND ANTI-ESSENTIALISM

Mari Mikkola

Introduction

It is a widely accepted feminist claim that gender injustice is not incidental and individual, but systematic and structural—it targets women *as women*. Feminism thus seemingly lends itself to identity politics: a form of political mobilization based on membership in women's social kind, where shared experiences or traits delimit kind membership (Heyes 2000; 2012). However, the past few decades have allegedly witnessed a feminist "identity crisis" (Alcoff 1988). Feminist politics presumes the existence of a women's social kind founded on some category-wide common traits or experiences. But as many feminist voices from various disciplines have noted, no such transcultural and transhistorical commonality exists because our axes of identity (for example, gender, race, ability, class) are not discrete and separable. Furthermore, it is misguided to assume that we can simply describe some putatively common gender identity without positing a normative ideal of womanhood. These worries have generated the said crisis: feminist theorists aim to speak and make political demands in the name of women *as a group* at the same time questioning the group's existence.

A dispute about gender essentialism and anti-essentialism theoretically undergirds the crisis. Bluntly put, feminist identity politics seems committed to essentialism, but many feminist theorists have influentially argued for anti-essentialism. Actually, characterizing this as *a* dispute is misleading. Different feminists understand both "essentialism" and "anti-essentialism" differently. They disagree about what is at stake, which side has won (or is winning) and whether the debate is even worth conducting. Cressida Heyes captures the multiplicity of views nicely: "If Wittgenstein is correct that the meaning of a word lies in its use, then feminists will find it hard to know what 'essentialism' means" (2000: 11). This chapter then aims to do two things. First, I will clarify the contours of the gender essentialism/anti-essentialism debate. Second, I will consider the debate's value (if any) for feminist theorizing.

What Is at Stake?

Essentialism may be characterized as the thesis that some of an entity's properties are necessary to it, whereas other properties are merely accidental (Robertson and Atkins 2013). These essential properties fulfill various functions (see Witt 1995).

An entity's essence causes and explains characteristic manifest properties and dispositions. Essences ground our classificatory apparatuses in providing the criteria for classifying entities into kinds. And an entity's essence ensures its identity and persistence through time. The thesis of gender essentialism has been variously formulated relative to these claims. However, gender essentialism is a position that few explicitly endorse. It has become "the prime idiom of intellectual terrorism . . . with the power to reduce to silence, to excommunicate, to consign to oblivion" (Schor 1989: 40). Showing that some account is gender essentialist has often sufficed to reject that position and with good reasons. Positions are usually *deemed* essentialist by critics and one is hard-pressed to find an unequivocal, positive characterization of gender essentialism. I will provide a typology of essentialisms next in order to elucidate what supposedly renders them theoretically untenable. I will also consider why one might find some anti-essentialist critiques insufficient.

First, *biological essentialism* holds that women share some kind of defining biological feature(s), as do men. This position is also known as biological determinism: the view that one's sex determines one's social and cultural traits and roles. Many historical examples demonstrate how social and behavioral differences between men and women were taken to be manifestations of some deeper, underlying physiological differences, which were used to justify a range of oppressive social conditions. Toril Moi characterizes this as a pervasive view of sex (1999: 11). Biological sex traits are thought to pervade every aspect of an individual, down to their social position and intellectual capacities, as well as to provide general frameworks for social and political arrangements. A typical example is that of Geddes and Thompson who, in 1889, argued that social and behavioral traits were caused by metabolic states. Thus, women are passive and uninterested in politics, but men are eager, passionate, and invested in political and social matters. These biological "facts" were used not only to explain behavioral differences, but also to guide socio-political arrangements. They were used to argue for withholding from women political rights accorded to men because "what was decided among the prehistoric Protozoa cannot be annulled by [an] Act of Parliament" (Geddes and Thompson quoted from Moi 1999: 18). It would be both inappropriate and futile to grant women political rights since they are unsuited to hold them and, due to their biology, women are simply uninterested in exercising those rights.

In response, feminists argued that behavioral and psychological differences have social, rather than biological, origins. Simone de Beauvoir famously claimed that one is not born, but rather *becomes* a woman, and that "social discrimination produces in women moral and intellectual effects so profound that they appear to be caused by nature" (1972: 18). In order to distinguish biological differences from social/psychological ones and to talk about the latter, feminists in the 1960s and 1970s appropriated the term "gender" and distinguished it from "sex" (Nicholson 1994; 1998). On standard formulations, "sex" denotes human females and males and depends on *biological* features, like chromosomes, sex organs, hormones, or other physical features. By contrast, "gender" denotes women and men and depends on *social* factors such as social roles, positions, behavior, or self-ascription. Genders (women and men) and gendered traits (being nurturing or ambitious) are socially constructed: they are the "intended or unintended product[s] of a social practice" (Haslanger 1995: 97). This enabled feminists to argue that manifest gender differences are mutable (for more, see Mikkola 2012).

This form of anti-essentialist critique is uncontentious. However, one major sticking point with identity politics is that it presupposes some shared gender-defining experience or trait, which must be socially constructed following the sex/gender distinction. This brings me to the second type of essentialism.

Classificatory gender essentialism is the view that some shared gender-defining social feature(s) exists. Take Beauvoir's claim that one becomes a woman. Gender socialization provides one way to understand this as a *causal* claim: females become women through a process of acquiring feminine traits and behavior—masculinity and femininity are products of nurture. Similarly, Kate Millett took gender differences to be culturally based and to result from differential treatment. For her, gender is "the sum total of the parents', the peers', and the culture's notions of what is appropriate to each gender by way of temperament, character, interests, status, worth, gesture, and expression" (Millett 1971: 31). Catharine MacKinnon's theory of gender as a theory of sexuality provides a *constitutive* understanding of this idea. The social meaning of sex (i.e., gender) is constituted by and created through sexual objectification: women are viewed and treated as objects for the satisfaction of men's desires (MacKinnon 1989). Masculinity is defined as sexual dominance, femininity as sexual submissiveness. And so, genders are "created through the eroticization of dominance and submission. The man/woman difference and the dominance/submission dynamic define each other" (MacKinnon 1989: 113). As a result, genders are *by definition* hierarchical and fundamentally tied to sexualized power relations. This situation is in no sense natural though. Pornography rather constructs a vision of sexuality, where both genders find submissive female sexuality as erotic.

Millett takes gender socialization to be the common experience definitive of womanhood; MacKinnon takes this to be sexual objectification. This form of gender essentialism has come under sustained attack in that it fails to respect women's diversity, and is thus exclusionary. Feminists of color have critiqued the idea that there is some experience that all women as women share (for example, Lorde 1984; Lugones 1991). For instance, bell hooks (1997) has argued that feminism only satisfies white bourgeois women's interests and has left black and working-class women wanting. Take the common feminist view that the family is a major site of gender injustice. This is not, however, shared by all black feminists: "since the family is the site of resistance and solidarity against racism for women of colour, it does not hold the central place in accounting for women's subordination that it does for white women" (Walby 1992: 34). Betty Friedan's (1963) well-known work is another case in point. Friedan saw domesticity as the main vehicle of gender oppression and called upon women in general to find jobs outside the home. But she failed to realize that women from less privileged and poor backgrounds, who were often people of color, already worked outside the home. Friedan's suggestion, then, was largely applicable only to white middle-class American housewives, but was mistakenly taken to apply universally. This mistake results from theorizing gender from the perspective of "white solipsism": the tendency to "think, imagine, and speak as if whiteness describes the world" (Adrienne Rich, quoted in Harris 1993: 356). In so doing, white middle-class Western feminists failed to understand the importance of race and class.

Queer feminist critiques further maintain that traditional feminist theory has endorsed a heteronormative view of gender. This is the tendency to treat heterosexuality as the normative standard and to naturalize heterosexual practices (Butler 1999; see also Wittig 1992). The "generic" woman was conceived as white, middle class, heterosexual, Christian and able-bodied, which privileged some women and marginalized others.

A major point of classificatory anti-essentialism, then, is to highlight women's diverse and dissimilar experiences as women. Consequently, Elizabeth Spelman argues in her classic *Inessential Woman* that there is no single class of women. Rather, there are multiple contextually specific classes. Since gender is socially constructed and social construction differs from one society to the next, womanhood is culturally specific. Females become *particular* kinds of women (Spelman 1990: 113): they become white working-class women, black middle-class women, poor Jewish women, wealthy aristocratic European women and so on.

This highlights a third form of essentialism theoretically underpinning classificatory essentialism: what I here call *divisible-identity essentialism*. This is the view that different facets of identity (gender, race, ability, sexuality, ethnicity, class) are separable and definable independently of one another. As Spelman points out, those who fail to appreciate the difference that race and class make to gender, assume that what makes x a woman is the same as what makes y a woman. By contrast, "gender is constructed and defined in conjunction with [other] elements of identity" (Spelman 1990: 175). This idea is more commonly understood as *intersectionality* (Crenshaw 1989). As individuals, we stand in the intersections of many different constitutively intertwined social categories—structures of privilege and oppression. Not appreciating this prevents an adequate analysis of (say) the structural situation of black women: a focus just on their gendered position leaves out their racialized position and vice versa. An analysis that disregards intersectionality is unsatisfying because it fails to acknowledge that black women's situation cannot be analyzed by focusing just on one identity facet. Rather, critical race theorists have argued that many of the disadvantages black women suffer are due to the intersections of their racialized and gendered social positions (Grillo 2006).

Classificatory anti-essentialism has been extremely influential in feminist philosophy and the failure to think intersectionally about social identities is considered to be a grave intellectual error. For instance, Iris Marion Young holds that Spelman has definitively shown that gender essentialism is untenable (1997: 13; though Haslanger 2000a and Mikkola 2006 disagree). Nevertheless, although these analytical tools highlight important ways in which extant positions have fallen short, they are not without problems. Spelman seems to assume that the categories of race, class, religion, and ethnicity are stable and unified (Young 1997: 20). Independently of Young, Uma Narayan has argued in a similar vein. To assume a commonality among all Western women or all Jewish women (for instance) is just as misguided as the assumption that all women qua women have something in common. After all, particular racial, cultural, and religious groups are themselves internally diverse. This way of attending to women's differences, then, "endorses and replicates problematic and colonialist assumptions . . . Seemingly universal essentialist generalizations about 'all women' are replaced by *culture-specific* essentialist generalizations" (Narayan 1998: 87; see also Fuss 1989).

However, if we take this critique seriously, we end up dissolving groups into individuals. Each individual occupies a unique intersection that constructs their identity and undergirds their social position occupancy. Thus, we can legitimately only address *individual* women's experiences. But for a political project like feminism this looks worrying. In rejecting the existence of a single unified women's social kind, Spelman's view entails that women make up a merely unbound and gerrymandered collection of individuals. This view is in tension with the central feminist claim noted above: that gender injustice targets women in a systematic, group-based fashion. Subsequently, many have found the fragmentation of women's kind problematic for political reasons and have come to question classificatory anti-essentialism (e.g., Alcoff 2006; Bordo 1993; Frye 1996; Haslanger 2000b; Heyes 2000; Martin 1994; Mikkola 2007; Stoljar 1995; Stone 2004; Tanesini 1996; Young 1997; Zack 2005). As Linda Alcoff captures the worry:

> What can we demand in the name of women if "women" do not exist and demands in their name simply reenforce [*sic*] the myth that they do? How can we speak out against sexism as detrimental to the interests of women if the category is a fiction?
>
> (Alcoff 2006: 143)

In response, one might argue for strategic essentialism: despite there being no unifying shared gender-core, we act politically *as if* there were one (Fuss 1989). Anti-essentialism is descriptively true, but essentialism is politically more helpful. However, this view is worrisome due to yet another form of essentialism that I will outline next.

Classificatory anti-essentialism is not alone in challenging the viability of women's social kind. A fourth form of anti-essentialism that does so critiques (what I here call) *prescriptive essentialism*. In her seminal book *Gender Trouble*, Judith Butler takes issue with feminist identity politics (to name but one issue in a rich work). It appears as if the term "woman" has some unitary cross-cultural and transhistorical meaning and that the term picks out some determinate group of people with an identity-defining feature in common. However, this picture is mistaken and "woman" has no stable meaning. Instead, it is "a term in process, a becoming, a constructing that cannot rightfully be said to originate or end. As an ongoing discursive practice, it is open to intervention and resignification" (Butler 1999: 43). (For a similar argument that rejects the position that "woman" has some fixed and invariant meaning, see Cornell 1993.) The feminist picture of gender (for Butler) in no meaningful sense describes reality; rather, it is an unwitting *product* of feminist politics in its effort to represent the interests of certain political subjects (namely, of women). In aiming to represent women's interests, feminism constructs its own political subjects. Hence, any notion of womanhood that is used to capture the class of women unhelpfully masks women's diversity. It "necessarily produce[s] factionalization . . . 'identity' as a point of departure can never hold as the solidifying ground of a feminist political movement. Identity categories are never merely descriptive, but always normative, and as such, exclusionary" (Butler 1991: 160). Gender concepts articulated by feminist theorists turn out to articulate a set of "unspoken normative requirements" (Butler 1999: 9) that those hoping to gain feminist political representation *should* satisfy; thus, they prescribe a supposedly correct picture of womanhood. Butler takes this to be a feature of terms denoting social identity categories. The underlying presumption appears to be that such terms can never be used in a non-ideological way (Moi 1999: 43). They will always prescribe some conditions that ought to be satisfied since all processes of drawing categorical distinctions involve normative commitments that involve the exercise of social power (Witt 1995). Those who do not conform to the normative picture of womanhood risk being alienated and excluded from feminist politics altogether. Nicholson captures this thought nicely: "the idea of 'woman' as unitary operates as a policing force which generates and legitimizes certain practices, experiences, etc., and curtails and delegitimizes others" (1998: 293). Along with other anti-essentialists, Butler thinks that white solipsism and heteronormativity are among the ideological forces that exclude and marginalize some within the feminist movement.

Butler's aim is not, however, merely to critique prevalent ways to understand womanhood. Her argument is stronger than this: *every* definition of "woman" will be insidiously normative and thus politically problematic. The mistake is not that feminists provided the incorrect understanding of womanhood. Rather, their mistake was to attempt to define it at all. Following this line of argument, then, any strategically essentialist position will be politically worrisome. This connects to Butler's view of gender performativity. Gender is not "a stable identity or locus of agency from which various acts follow"; rather, gender comes into being through "a *stylized repetition of* [habitual] *acts*" (Butler 1999: 179). Gender is something that one does in wearing gender-coded clothing, in walking and sitting in gender-coded ways, in styling one's hair in gender-coded manner and in desiring sexually the opposite sex/gender. And repeatedly engaging in "feminizing" and "masculinizing" acts congeals gender, thereby making people falsely think of gender identity as something that they "naturally" possess. This opens up the possibility to undermine gender dualism by subverting the way one "does" one's gender. Subsequently, feminists should actively resist defining womanhood, thereby opening it up for new, more emancipatory conceptions. Butler is not alone in making this anti-essentialist methodological point and it is commonplace in "postmodern" feminism. For instance, Denise Riley (1988) claims that feminists should fight against attempts to classify women since this is always going to be misguided and dangerous. In fact, this is essential to feminism. And Julia Kristeva claims that the notion of womanhood must be deconstructed and cannot be reconstructed: "In [womanhood] I see something that cannot be represented, something that is not said, something above and beyond nomenclatures and ideologies" (1980: 137).

Such postmodern views have been very influential in generating a suspicion of unified gender types. Judith Squires notes that postmodernism "currently sets the tenor of most debates within gender in political theory" (1999: 19). Not everyone finds the upshot of views like Butler's helpful though. For instance, political scientists Nancy Hirschmann and Christine DiStefano ask:

> [I]n making us reluctant to take the risks of offering positive visions, has postmodernism curtailed the usefulness of feminism as a theoretical method? Have we become so afraid of the dangers and pitfalls of totalization, universalism, and absolutism that we shy away from one of the major traditional enterprises of political theory?
>
> (Hirschmann and Stefano 1996: 3)

Many analytic feminist philosophers agree and have endeavored to salvage the social kind of women for feminist purposes (e.g., Haslanger 2000b; Mikkola 2007; Zack 2005). For one thing, the idea that elucidating identity categories is always a normative enterprise may not be so worrisome. Sally Haslanger outlines different ways in which we might elucidate the concept *woman*. A conceptual project aims to articulate our ordinary *woman*-conception by consulting the conditions under which native English speakers think someone satisfies *woman*. Such an analysis probably reveals that women are thought to be human females. By contrast, a descriptive analysis of *woman* would examine our everyday language use and applications of "woman" in order to identify the social kind that the term tracks. However, Haslanger rejects both of these projects as useful for feminist purposes. Instead, she argues for an ameliorative analysis that aims to "elucidate 'our' legitimate purposes and what concept of *F*-ness (if any) would serve them best" (2005: 20). Ameliorative analyses aim to elucidate those concepts that we *should* appropriate given our political goals. And so, feminists should define *woman* in a way that best serves gender justice. Specifically, Haslanger holds that membership in men's/women's types depends on being marked for certain privileged or subordinated treatments (respectively) on the basis of one's observed or assumed reproductive functions. For her, gender captures a multiply realizable relation in a social hierarchy, and there are many ways in which women can be sex-marked for social subordination. This project is not entirely distinct from a descriptive one. An ameliorative analysis of *woman* offers an analysis of the concept that we usually think tracks women's social kind; but it does so in a way that "usefully revise[s] what we mean [by *woman*] for certain theoretical and political purposes" (Haslanger 2000b: 34).

This affords methodological resources to elucidate women's social kind in a normative manner without falling prey to the kinds of worries Butler voices. After all, on Haslanger's picture appropriating particular gender terminology hinges on our political purposes. If they are problematically exclusionary, we have grounds to reject the articulated conception of *woman*. Following Haslanger, though, the conditions definitive of gender are not exclusionary in being multiply realizable. Moreover, we need not abandon gender concepts altogether just because we are unable to articulate some non-normative gender-defining conditions. After all, we can revise gender notions in a meaningful way, which demonstrates that normativity per se is not the problem—misguided and exclusionary normativity is. Thus, we can conceptualize women's social kind for feminist political purposes and avoid the kind's fragmentation, which retains the central claim of feminism and avoids earlier problems that feminist identity politics faced. Haslanger's position might hence be termed (classificatory and prescriptive) "anti-anti-essentialism." Or, as Haslanger (2012) and I (Mikkola 2012) prefer to put it, it is gender realist: there is *something* women by virtue of being women share, which is not intrinsic, innate or necessary to women qua individuals. Women have in common a socially constructed, and yet variously manifested, extrinsic feature. This gender realist view, then, can avoid classificatory anti-essentialism without falling prey to prescriptive essentialism, contra earlier views like Millett and MacKinnon's.

The above hints at a fifth form of essentialism: *individual essentialism*. This is not to be confused with divisible-identity essentialism, although the two are related. Rather, individual essentialism is about individuation: that gender is necessary for women qua individuals. For instance, if being a member of the kind dog is individually essential to Lassie, were Lassie to lose this feature he would not only cease to be a dog, but also Lassie. So, if some property is individually essential to us, we cannot qua individuals survive its loss. This sort of essentialism is sometimes treated as co-dependent with classificatory essentialism (see Stoljar 1995): if some feature is essential for membership in women's kind, then this feature is also essential to individual women qua individuals. Strictly speaking, this does not follow. Being colored red is necessary for membership in the type of red entities but being so colored is not necessarily essential to red entities qua individuals. If a red car were painted blue, the car would no longer be a member of the class of red entities, but the car would not cease to be the very same car. Furthermore, if we were to accept that gender is necessary for individual identity and ensures individuals' persistence through time, transitioning would be impossible: transitioning would mean that the "old" individual ceases to exist and a new one comes into being. But this looks intuitively implausible in that trans individuals persist through time as the very same numerically identical individuals.

Although individual gender essentialism has received much less attention than other essentialisms, Charlotte Witt has prominently argued for such a view. She starts by asking: would you be the same individual if you were gendered differently? According to Witt, most ordinary people take the answer to be easy and obvious: No. She goes on to elucidate such ordinary gender essentialist intuitions by arguing that gender is *uniessential* to us qua social individuals. On this unique Aristotelian-inspired version of individual essentialism, certain functional essences have a unifying role in ensuring that material parts constitute a *new* individual, rather than just a collection of parts. The essential house-functional property (what the entity is for) unifies different material parts so that there is a house, and not just a collection of house-constituting particles. Gender functions in a similar fashion: it provides "the principle of normative unity" that organizes, unifies, and determines the different roles of social individuals (Witt 2011: 73). This requires distinguishing:

- *personhood*: possession of a first-person perspective;
- being a *biologically human organism*;
- being a *social individual*: occupying social positions synchronically and diachronically, where certain social roles are ascribed simply by virtue of one's social position occupancy.

These ontological categories are not equivalent in having different persistence and identity conditions. And importantly, Witt's gender essentialism pertains to *social individuals*, not to persons or human organisms.

Social individuals are those who occupy positions in social reality and have social norms and roles associated with them. Qua social individuals, though, we occupy multiple social positions at ones and over time. However, since a bundle of social position occupancies does not make for an individual, what unifies these positions to constitute a social *individual*? The unifying role is undertaken by gender (being a woman or a man): it is "a pervasive and fundamental social position that unifies and determines all other social positions both synchronically and diachronically. It unifies them not physically, but by providing a principle of normative unity" (Witt 2011: 19–20). By "normative unity," Witt means the following: given our social position occupancies and roles, we are responsive to various "complex patterns of behavior and practices that constitute what one ought to do in a situation given one's social position(s) and one's social context"

(Witt 2011: 82). These patterns can conflict: e.g., the norms of motherhood conflict with the norms of being an academic philosopher. However, in order for this conflict to exist at all, the norms must be binding on a *single* social individual. And what explains the existence and unity of the social individual who is subject to conflicting social patterns is gender (being a woman): a social position that clusters around women's socially mediated reproductive functions to conceive and bear (Witt 2011: 40). Thus, gender is essential to us qua social individuals in unifying our agency.

Worth of the Debate?

Both essentialist and anti-essentialist perspectives have afforded valuable theoretical insights, but they generate a stalemate. If we fail to appreciate women's dissimilar experiences and intersectionality, our accounts of gender will fall prey to exclusionary false universalism. But if we appreciate difference too much and can legitimately only speak of individual women's experiences, we cannot make sense of gender injustice being systematic. How might we overcome this impasse? One might be tempted to find out which perspective captures the way gender *really* is in order to settle the matter. I contend, however, that the stalemate is not to be settled by appealing to the truth or falsity of essentialism, and that nothing much hangs on settling this metaphysical issue. To illustrate, consider three recent views.

First, Alison Stone holds that women have a genealogy, though no essence. Specifically, women become women "by taking over and reinterpreting pre-existing cultural constructions of femininity" (Stone 2004: 153). These interpretations make up an overlapping, complex and multiply branching chain of history within which women are situated. And so, women "are defined as a group by their participation in this history" (Stone 2004: 153). Stone's position is motivated by anti-anti-essentialist political concerns: fighting systematic social injustice demands that we understand women's kind in a way that avoids false universalism and quietism. It would be a mistake, though, to think that her view is essentialist in any of the earlier senses outlined above. Critiquing anti-essentialism does not make one's theory troublingly essentialist and thus, worthy of rejection. Rather, evaluating Stone's view hinges on pragmatic considerations: what do we want a theory of gender to do for us? Genealogy aims to "reject essentialism (and so to deny that women have any necessary or common characteristics), while preserving the idea that women form a distinctive social group" (Stone 2004: 136). So, evaluating Stone's genealogical proposal does not hinge on the truth or falsity of essentialism. Instead, it turns on independent pragmatic and normative considerations: how well does a genealogical theory of gender fulfill these desiderata?

Second, take Theodore Bach's view that gender is a natural kind with a historical essence. For him, women share an essential property that is partaking in a lineage of women: "an individual must be a reproduction of ancestral women, in which case she must have undergone the ontogenetic processes [i.e., gender socialization] through which a historical gender system replicates women" (Bach 2012: 271). Again, evaluating this position does not depend on the truth of essentialism. Rather, we should look at what his theory aims to do and how successful is it. And this, rather than the truth of anti-essentialism, gives us reasons to reject it. For Bach, no one is born a man or a woman; instead, certain ontogenetic processes (most importantly, differential socialization) reproduce members of these kinds out of sexed individuals. In short, female gender socialization fixes gender, but one need not manifest any typical gendered traits: one is a woman because one has "the right history" (Bach 2012: 261). This historical account is allegedly inclusive and non-marginalizing. Only those who have not been socialized as women fail to count as women; but since gender socialization is ubiquitous, Bach takes his account to be genuinely inclusive. There are some individuals, though, who clearly fail to satisfy Bach's criteria for womanhood: trans women. And this is deeply problematic. On Bach's account, they would not count as women, given that the right ontogenetic processes that fix one's gender status as a woman or a man take place "through events that occurred primarily before the age of ten" (Bach 2012: 268). In fact, this suggests that trans women would be gendered men contrary to self-identification, which raises serious questions about how inclusive the historically essentialist account is—it looks instead highly exclusive and thus worthy of rejection. But this rejection does not depend on the truth of anti-essentialism. Rather, it is warranted because Bach's account gives us normatively the wrong results.

Finally, consider Witt's uniessentialism. Witt aims to clarify and understand ordinary gender essentialist claims, while contributing "to ways of thinking [that are] useful to feminism" (2011: xii). This will be achieved by providing a coherent statement of the claim of gender essentialism, a statement that could be true or false (Witt 2011: 66), and Witt's uniessentialism allegedly does so. I am, however, less convinced that gender uniessentialism is important for normative feminist politics. This is not because I find uniessentialism implausible. Rather, I disagree with Witt's claim that "the centrality of the essentialism/anti-essentialism debate within feminist theory is indisputable, and its significance for a wide range of issues in feminist theory is beyond doubt" (2011: 68). Let me clarify: feminist theorists have extensively debated gender essentialism and *descriptively speaking* it is a central feminist issue. But I am less convinced that gender essentialism *ought to* be a central metaphysical concern. Rather, the position we should endorse (again) hinges on our normative commitments, instead of essentialism's truth or falsity.

Much more should be said about this. But take one way in which Witt specifies the centrality of gender essentialism. It trades (at least partly) on questions about agency: individual essentialism, rather than kind essentialism, "intersects with questions of agency, and the issue of agency is central to feminist theory" (Witt 2011: 10). Now, elucidating Witt's feminist account of agency, and its intersection with gender uniessentialism, is not entirely unproblematic since it is not so clear what Witt's picture of agency is meant to do for feminist politics. But a seemingly central claim is the following:

> Gender uniessentialism directs our attention away from individual psychologies, their conscious and unconscious biases, and "deformed" processes of choice, and towards the social world, its available social roles, and the ways in which its available social roles can and cannot be blended into a coherent practical identity.
>
> (Witt 2011: 128)

Since gender uniessentialism demonstrates that our practical, social identities are essentially gendered, Witt suggests, "political and social change for women will require changing existing [disadvantaging and oppressive] social roles" (2011: 128). The politically significant point is that social position occupancies come packaged with problematic social norms; and this should motivate our rejection of those norms, rather than embarking on projects than aim to alter women's individual psychologies.

I agree wholeheartedly that the goal of critiquing and altering oppressive social norms is crucial for feminism. But accepting this is independent of the truth of uniessentialism. I contend that the plausibility of the normative view that "feminist social and political change must include critique of existing, gendered social roles with an eye to changing those that disadvantage and oppress women" (Witt 2011: 129) does not hinge on us accepting the metaphysical thesis of gender uniessentialism—or any metaphysical formulation of essentialism. Although historically a major point of contention, I am unconvinced that feminists need to settle the essentialism/anti-essentialism dispute in order to advance feminist political projects. Much less hangs on finding the metaphysical facts of the matter, and much more depends on what we want gender to do for us in feminist politics. After all, if gender is socially constructed and at least partly dependent on our interests, different metaphysical theories of gender can do different work for us. The issue of what we want gender to do for us, then, strikes me as prior to settling the essentialism/anti-essentialism dispute.

Related Topics

The sex/gender distinction and the social construction of reality (Chapter 13); materiality (Chapter 16); feminism and borderlands identities (Chapter 17); personal identity and relational selves (Chapter 18); values, practices, and metaphysical assumptions in the biological sciences (Chapter 26).

References

Alcoff, Linda (1988) "Cultural Feminism versus Poststructuralism: The Identity Crisis in Feminist Theory," *Signs* 13: 405–436.
—— (2006) *Visible Identities*, New York: Oxford University Press.
Bach, Theodore (2012) "Gender Is a Natural Kind with a Historical Essence," *Ethics* 122: 231–272.
Beauvoir, Simone de (1972) *The Second Sex*, Harmondsworth: Penguin.
Bordo, Susan (1993) *Unbearable Weight: Feminism, Western Culture, and the Body*, Berkeley, CA: University of California Press.
Butler, Judith (1991) "Contingent Foundations: Feminism and the Question of 'Postmodernism,'" *Praxis International* 11: 150–165.
—— (1999) *Gender Trouble: Feminism and the Subversion of Identity*, 2nd ed., New York: Routledge.
Cornell, Drucilla (1993) *Transformations: Recollective Imagination and Sexual Difference*, New York: Routledge.
Crenshaw, Kimberlé (1989) "Demarginalizing the Intersection of Race and Sex: A Black Feminist Critique of Antidiscrimination Doctrine, Feminist Theory and Antiracist Politics," *University of Chicago Legal Forum*: 139–167.
Friedan, Betty (1963) *Feminine Mystique*, Harmondsworth: Penguin Books.
Frye, Marilyn (1996) "The Necessity of Differences: Constructing a Positive Category of Women," *Signs* 21: 991–1010.
Fuss, Diana (1989) *Essentially Speaking: Feminism, Nature and Difference*, New York: Routledge.
Grillo, Trina (2006) "Anti-Essentialism and Intersectionality," in Elizabeth Hackett and Sally Haslanger (Eds.) *Theorizing Feminisms*, New York: Oxford University Press, 30–40.
Harris, Angela (1993) "Race and Essentialism in Feminist Legal Theory," in D. K. Weisberg (Ed.) *Feminist Legal Theory: Foundations*, Philadelphia, PA: Temple University Press.
Haslanger, Sally (1995) "Ontology and Social Construction," *Philosophical Topics* 23: 95–125.
—— (2000a) "Feminism in Metaphysics: Negotiating the Natural," in Miranda Fricker and Jennifer Hornsby (Eds.) *Feminism in Philosophy*, Cambridge: Cambridge University Press, 107–126.
—— (2000b) "Gender and Race: (What) Are They? (What) Do We Want Them To Be?" *Noûs* 34: 31–55.

—— (2005) "What Are We Talking About? The Semantics and Politics of Social Kinds," *Hypatia* 20: 10–26.

—— (2012) *Resisting Reality*, Oxford: Oxford University Press.

Heyes, Cressida (2000) *Line Drawings*, Ithaca, NY and London: Cornell University Press.

—— (2012) "Identity Politics," *The Stanford Encyclopedia of Philosophy* [online] Spring 2012 Edition. Available from: http://plato.stanford.edu/archives/spr2012/entries/identity-politics/.

Hirschmann Nancy and di Stefano, Christine (1996) *Revisioning the Political*, Oxford: Westview Press.

hooks, bell (1997) "Black Women and Feminism," in Judith Squires and Sandra Kemp (Eds.) *Feminisms*, Oxford: Oxford University Press, 227–228.

Kristeva, Julia (1980) "Woman can Never Be Defined," in Elaine Marks and Isabelle de Courtivron (Eds.) *New French Feminisms*, Amherst, MA: University of Massachusetts Press, 137–141.

Lorde, Audre (1984) *Sister/Outsider*, Boston, MA: Crossing Press.

Lugones, Maria (1991) "On the Logic of Pluralist Feminism," in Claudia Card (Ed.) *Feminist Ethics*, Lawrence, KS: University of Kansas Press, 35–44.

MacKinnon, Catharine (1989) *Toward a Feminist Theory of State*, Cambridge, MA: Harvard University Press.

Martin, Jane Roland (1994) "Methodological Essentialism, False Difference, and Other Dangerous Traps," *Signs* 19: 630–655.

Mikkola, Mari (2006) "Elizabeth Spelman, Gender Realism, and Women," *Hypatia* 21: 77–96.

—— (2007) "Gender Sceptics and Feminist Politics," *Res Publica* 13: 361–380.

—— (2012) "Feminist Perspectives on Sex and Gender," *The Stanford Encyclopedia of Philosophy* [online] Fall 2012. Available from: http://plato.stanford.edu/archives/fall2012/entries/feminism-gender/.

Millett, Kate (1971) *Sexual Politics*, London: Granada.

Moi, Toril (1999) *What Is a Woman?* Oxford: Oxford University Press.

Narayan, Uma (1998) "Essence of Culture and A Sense of History: A Feminist Critique of Cultural Essentialism," *Hypatia* 13: 86–106.

Nicholson, Linda (1994) "Interpreting Gender," *Signs* 20: 79–105.

—— (1998) "Gender," in Alison Jaggar and Iris Marion Young (Eds.) *A Companion to Feminist Philosophy*, Malden, MA: Blackwell, 289–297.

Riley, Denise (1988) *Am I that Name?* London: Macmillan.

Robertson, Teresa and Philip Atkins (2013) "Essential vs. Accidental Properties," *The Stanford Encyclopedia of Philosophy* Winter 2013 [online]. Available from: http://plato.stanford.edu/archives/win2013/entries/essential-accidental/.

Schor, Naomi (1989) "The Essentialism which Is Not One: Coming to Grips with Irigaray," *differences* 1: 38–58.

Spelman, Elizabeth (1990) *The Inessential Woman*, Boston, MA: Beacon Press.

Squires, Judith (1999) *Gender in Political Theory*, Oxford: Polity Press.

Stoljar, Natalie (1995) "Essence, Identity and the Concept of Woman," *Philosophical Topics* 23: 261–293.

Stone, Alison (2004) "Essentialism and Anti-Essentialism in Feminist Philosophy," *Journal of Moral Philosophy* 1: 135–153.

Tanesini, Alessandra (1996) "Whose Language?" in Ann Garry and Marilyn Pearsall (Eds.) *Women, Knowledge and Reality*, London: Routledge, 203–216.

Walby, Sylvia (1992) "Post-Post-Modernism? Theorizing Social Complexity," in Michelle Barrett and Anne Phillips (Eds.) *Destabilizing Theory: Contemporary Feminist Debates*, Oxford: Polity Press, 31–52.

Witt, Charlotte (1995) "Anti-Essentialism in Feminist Theory," *Philosophical Topics* 23: 321–344.

—— (2011) *The Metaphysics of Gender*, Oxford: Oxford University Press.

Wittig, Monique (1992) *The Straight Mind and other Essays*, Hemel Hempstead: Harvester Wheatsheaf.

Young, Iris Marion (1997) "Gender as Seriality: Thinking about Women as a Social Collective," in *Intersecting Voices*, Princeton, NJ: Princeton University Press, 12–37.

Zack, Naomi (2005) *Inclusive Feminism*, Lanham, MD: Rowman & Littlefield.

15

EMBODIMENT AND FEMINIST PHILOSOPHY

Sara Heinämaa

Introduction

Questions of embodiment are central in feminist philosophy for several reasons. The sexed body is one of the chief themes of feminist politics, but the body is also a historical-philosophical concept that feminist scholars have problematized and scrutinized, and ultimately it is a metaphysical issue the relevance of which is a feminist philosophical controversy. The thematic, historical-critical, and metaphysical interests often converge in concrete debates, but it is important to distinguish them conceptually and methodologically for the clarity of the goals of our investigations.

First, feminist thinkers have developed philosophical arguments and concepts to tackle problems that are central in women's lives, such as pregnancy, childbirth, abortion, rape, pornography, prostitution, sexual orientation, and the division of labor between the sexes. These classical feminist topics are today expanded by discussions of transsexuality, disability, technology, and animality. All these themes involve problems of bodily integrity and self-determination. In addition, they imply questions concerning physical force and violence, as well as questions concerning sensibility and affectivity and the nature of corporeal life in general. Thus, for strong topical reasons, the concepts of body and embodiment are central to feminist philosophy.

Second, feminist historians of philosophy have questioned the traditional oppositions between soul and body, mind and matter, and reason and sensibility, and critically discussed the adequacy of the concepts of body and embodiment that we inherit from our philosophical forerunners. Feminists have argued that these traditional conceptual oppositions are misleading since they define the two terms in simple contrast, and privilege or valorize one term over the other either epistemologically or ontologically. Moreover, they have demonstrated that our philosophical tradition strongly associates the concept of femininity with the lower terms of these hierarchical oppositions. Thus femininity is conflated with sensibility, body, and matter, while masculinity is coupled with soul, spirit, mind, and reason. With a conceptual repertoire such as this it is hard to argue for the equality of the sexes and for the fruitfulness or productivity of sexual difference. For these critical reasons, feminist philosophy inquires into the genealogies of the concepts of body and embodiment.

Third, the concepts of embodiment and materiality are pressing for any thinker who starts asking political and ethical questions concerning the relations between human beings and human communities. Insofar as one conceives human beings as bodily beings with material environments and concrete histories, one cannot avoid taking a stand on ontological and epistemological questions on embodiment and materiality. Thus there is also a metaphysical motivation for today's feminist philosophy of embodiment.

Historical Starting Points

In the early modern period, with the development of the new natural sciences, the task of rethinking the relation between the body and the soul or mind became acute. The previously dominant Platonic and Aristotelian theories were challenged and abandoned.

The old Platonic similes and metaphors had suggested that the soul, or its highest part, governs the body and its lower appetitive and sensible functions, similar to the manner in which a charioteer or coachman drives his horses and a steersman navigates his ship (Plato 2005: 26–36, 246a–254e). Against this, the Aristotelian concepts of form and matter proposed that the function of the soul is formative rather than governmental. In the Aristotelian understanding, the soul does not control or regulate the body but rather organizes it and gives it a proper form. This implies that disputes about the identity or separateness of soul and body are misguided, since the two phenomena are mutually dependent (Aristotle 1931: ii, 1, 412b6–9).

These ancient conceptions were challenged in the seventeenth century by Descartes. He argued that we fail to account adequately for the relation between mind and matter if we assume that the two relata are both known in a similar manner and order. For Descartes, the mind is neither governmental nor formative but epistemologically fundamental. We know ourselves primarily as ensouled or minded beings, as "thinking things." All our knowledge of other things, including material things and corporeal being as well as ideal entities and the divine being, is grounded on this primary form of knowledge, for Descartes in the *Meditations* of 1641.

Descartes' thesis of the epistemic primacy of the mind implies two different views of the mind–body relation (on Descartes, see also Chapter 6 in this volume). On the one hand, body and mind can be conceived in a general manner as two distinct substances with two different primary attributes: extension and thinking. This implies that they are independently existing things (as Descartes argues in the *Meditations* and in the *Principles of Philosophy* of 1644). Being distinct and completely different in essence, the two substances cannot interact. On the other hand, we know our minds as each being united with one body in particular and as being capable of interacting with other bodies through this one body. In the Fifth Meditation, Descartes draws attention to this unitary notion of the mind–body relation and accordingly questions the adequacy of the ancient similes of navigation and piloting:

> [N]ature . . . teaches me, by these feelings of pain, hunger, thirst, and so on, that I am not merely present in my body as a sailor is present in a ship, but that I am very closely joined, and as it were, intermingled with it, so that I and the body form a unit.
>
> (Descartes 1996: vol. 3, 159)

Descartes develops the idea of soul–body union further in his correspondence with Princess Elisabeth of Bohemia by distinguishing three different objects of knowledge and three different ways of knowing these objects: mind as pure thinking, body as extended matter, and mind–body union. He explains to Elisabeth that mind as pure thinking is known by the intellect alone whereas body as extended matter is known by intellect aided by imagination. So the faculties of intellect and imagination provide us with knowledge of the two substances and their essential attributes. But to know the mind–body union, Descartes argues, we need to interrupt our intellectual studies and suspend our imaginative activities and pay close attention merely to our sensations: "[W]hat belongs to the union of soul and body is known only obscurely by the intellect alone or even by the intellect aided by the imagination, but it is known very clearly by the senses" (Descartes 1996: vol. 3, 691).

This means that the source of the wisdom that concerns the mind–body union is the sensations, perceptions, and emotions that are part of our everyday dealings with the world and with others. Based on this insight Descartes gave Elisabeth the following guidelines:

> Metaphysical thoughts, which exercise the pure intellect, help to familiarize us with the notion of the soul; and the study of mathematics, which exercises mainly imagination in the consideration of shapes and motions, accustoms us to form very distinct notions of body. But it is the ordinary course of life and conversation, and abstention from meditations and from the study of things which exercise imagination, that teaches us how to conceive the union of the soul and the body.
>
> (Descartes 1996: vol. 3, 692)

Elisabeth was intrigued by Descartes' idea of the soul–body union but not satisfied by his dual characterization of the relation between soul and body, so she asked for further explanations. Recent work in feminist history of philosophy has demonstrated that Elisabeth's persistent questions led Descartes to develop his account of the mind–body duality (Alanen 2003; Bos 2010; Shapiro 2013; Tollefsen 1999). Elisabeth challenged Descartes by asking him to explain how his definitions of mind and body as separate substances allow him to form any reasonable notion of mind–body interaction, let alone a theory of intermingling:

> I beseech you tell me how the soul of man (since it is but a thinking substance) can determine the spirits of the body to produce voluntary actions. For it seems every determination of movement happens from an impulsion of the thing moved, according to the manner in which it is pushed by that which moves it, or else, depends on the qualification and figure of the superficies of this latter. Contact is required for the first two conditions, and extension for the third. You entirely exclude extension from your notion of the soul, and contact seems to me incompatible with an immaterial thing.
>
> (Elisabeth to Descartes May 16, 1643 in Descartes 1996: vol. 3, 661)

Descartes answered Elisabeth, but his explanations did not convince her. She required more clarifications, and their philosophical discussion developed further. Eventually the exchange covered metaphysical as well as ethical topics, ranging from mind–body interaction to the passions and to the efficacy of Stoic philosophical therapy in treating emotional distress, sadness, and desperation. Later Descartes dedicated his works, the *Principles of Philosophy* and the *Passions of the Soul* of 1649, to Elisabeth, since her direct questions and ingenious counterarguments helped him to develop his position by theorizing the receptive powers of the human mind: sensation, perception, and emotion.

Contemporary Alternatives

Descartes devised a partial solution to the problem of the mind–body interaction by introducing a theory of the "animal spirits," very small hypothetical movements of matter, "very fine air or wind." According to him these caused images on the surface of the pineal gland, in turn causing experienced sensory perceptions. (The pineal gland is a tiny organ in the brain; Descartes thought it the bodily part in most direct contact with the soul.) Thus extended substance and thinking substance could interact thanks to the mediating operations of the animal spirits.

Since Descartes' time, the psychological and physiological sciences have taken enormous steps and today can explain much of human behavior. Yet the philosophical problem of interaction lingers. We have abandoned the Cartesian notion of animal spirits, but the theoretical task of mediating between the extended and non-extended realms still remains and is undertaken by new candidates. Neurons are the most recent theoretical entities that are supposed to handle the connection between the two realms of being. They are said to "convert" or "interpret" the quantifiable physiological processes of our bodies into the qualitative "form" that is familiar to us from experience. However, philosophically and conceptually the idea of the neuron as converter is no more satisfying than the idea of animal spirits. Both ideas retain the duality of two distinct realms of being, the material and the experiential (or the quantifiable and the qualitative), and only theorize a kind of unit capable of operating in both realms.

Frustrated by such problems, contemporary philosophers have developed metaphysical alternatives to dualism and suggested strategies that do away with problems of interaction altogether. These include reductivism, eliminativism, epiphenomenalism, emergentism, supervenience physicalism, token identity theories, and functionalism. These all build on the modern naturalistic doctrine according to which the natural sciences—or physics as providing the grounds and the methodological model for these sciences—ultimately determine what there is. According to this paradigm, each being is either physical, belonging to the unified totality of physical nature, or a variable dependent on the physical, and thus at best a secondary "parallel accompaniment" (Husserl 1965 [1911]: 169). Most of these approaches allow multiple explanatory concepts but all demand that the explanatory strategies of psychology accord with physicalism. In this paradigm, the human person is conceived as a two-layered reality, in which a material—biological, biochemical, chemical, physical—basis provides the foundation for the emergence of psychical features. So understood, mental features are not properties of any immaterial entities—souls or spirits—but of immensely complex physical systems.

The formation of the higher levels of the psyche is framed as a causal-functional process in these naturalistic theories. Usually it is not assumed to be a monocausal, purely organic process but is understood as involving both internal organic and external environmental causes (see, e.g., Haslanger 2012: 210; Scheman 2000). Environmental factors are seen as influencing the development of psychic features and structures, together with inborn organic factors.

Some feminist philosophers are committed to naturalism or physicalism because of their basic philosophical commitments and interests (e.g., Anthony 2005; 2007; Hankinson Nelson 1990; Hankinson Nelson and Nelson 2003). These philosophers have to find ways of explaining the macro-level phenomena that are crucial to the feminist project without compromising the principles of naturalism or physicalism. This does not demand explanations in terms of physical concepts, but explanations that are in agreement with physicalism or do not conflict with it. The most central of these macro-level phenomena is gender, i.e., the difference between women and men. Sally Haslanger offers a naturalistic analysis of gender, compatible with most physicalist approaches (those articulated by the concepts of supervenience). She argues that the biological categories of female and male are natural kinds, composed of objective things with a physical undercurrent. In contrast, the categories of woman and man are positions of subjection and dominance that female and male entities may occupy in contingent constellations of force and power. If all such constellations were resolved exhaustively, thoroughly and permanently, then there would no longer be women or men (Haslanger 2000a: 11–12; 2000b; 2005: 122–124).

Other feminists have challenged the paradigm of modern naturalism and physicalism and offered alternative analyses of the concepts of gender. Some have developed neo-Aristotelian solutions (e.g., Nussbaum 1999; 2000; Witt 1998; 2003). Others have resorted to Wittgensteinian arguments about the multifunctional character of our mental and experiential concepts (e.g., Scheman 2000).

There is also a growing interest within feminist philosophy in the novel ontological approaches that can be loosely classified under the title "new materialism" (on these approaches, see also Chapter 16 in this volume). These approaches are "new" in the sense that they reject the idea of substance characteristic of classical materialism and build their ontologies on dynamic processes, unpredicted events, and conflicting forces with analogous intensities. They are not naturalistic in the sense discussed above, since they do not relinquish to the natural sciences the ultimate word on what there is but rather argue for materialism or monism on independent metaphysical grounds— Whiteheadian, Bergsonian, Hegelian, or Spinozist (e.g., Braidotti 2002; Dolphijn and van der Tuin 2012; Grosz 2004; Malabou and Johnston 2013).

Phenomenological philosophy diverges from all these approaches in building on the Cartesian insight that it is crucial to keep distinct two different ways of studying human bodies. One proceeds under the guidance of the intellect and imagination and the other is informed by sensations, perceptions, and emotions—and we are not to explain one of these in terms of the other. The French phenomenologist Maurice Merleau-Ponty emphasizes the irreducibility of these epistemic alternatives and argues for a pluralistic understanding of bodily being:

> Thus experience of one's own body runs counter to the reflective procedure which detaches subject and object from each other, and which gives us only the thought about the body, or the body as an idea, and not the experience of the body . . . Descartes was well aware of this, since a famous letter of his to Elizabeth draws the distinction between the body as it is conceived through use in living and the body as it is conceived by the understanding.
>
> (Merleau-Ponty 1995 [1945]: 231)

In the next sections I will introduce some basic concepts of phenomenology, which offers a powerful way of understanding the body, not just as an object of natural scientific knowledge but also as a source of meaning and subject of intending. This alternative has proven fruitful in the study of the multiple differences between women and men as well as the differences between sexed and non-sexed ways of being human.

Phenomenology of Human Embodiment

Phenomenology is a philosophy of experience. It studies human experiences in their qualitative richness, with the aim of clearly distinguishing between different forms of experiencing and identifying their subjective and objective components and the points of correlation between the subjective and the objective. In this context, the term "subjective" does not refer to any inner realm of private states or processes or to the mere qualitative aspects of our immanent lives but refers to the ways in which external (and internal) objects are given to us. (On phenomenology, see also Chapter 12 in this volume.)

The objects experienced come in different sorts: some are material things but others are ideal items, such as numbers and functions; yet others are sources or carriers of meaning, such as novels, theories, and persons. Also, the types of experiences that give us objects are multiple and various. They may be emotional experiences, such as shame, love, and resentment, but they may also be cognitive experiences of believing, knowing, arguing, and criticizing, or practical experiences of projecting goals and determining means. Both individual and collective experiences need to be investigated as well as familiar experiences and historically or culturally distant forms of experiencing.

The aim is not to survey the details of individual experiences or generalize over them to construct a theory of experiencing. Rather, the phenomenologist works on concrete human experiences, and compares and analyzes their features in order to illuminate their necessary structures and forms of change and development. The most important of these structures are temporality and intentionality or directedness. All our experiences flow in time. They pile one upon another and motivate one another, forming complex temporal wholes that can be described and analyzed by the phenomenological concepts of sedimentation and habituation. On the other hand, all experiences are also directed at objects; and the experienced objects characteristic of human lives come in many types. We attend to and focus on not only things but also values and goals; and we are interested in not just states of affairs and facts but also persons, organizations, institutions, and comprehensive histories of such complex objects. All these different types and kinds of objects must be carefully described and their relations of dependency clarified.

Among the pivotal objects of our experience is the human body. We can call the human body a "core object" since it has a central role in our lives both as an experienced object and as an experiencing subject. Most if not all objects of interest relate to human bodies in one way or another, and it is through our sensing, perceiving, and desiring bodies that we relate to things and events in the first place. In *The Second Sex* Simone de Beauvoir formulates this idea by writing that our body is "our grasp upon the world and the outline of our projects" (Beauvoir 1991 [1949]: 66). But she then argues that traditional philosophical discussions of human bodies are dominated by an androcentric bias that leads us to interpret phenomena characteristic of femininity or femaleness as derivative of masculinity or maleness. In Beauvoir's account, this is a fundamental mistake: human embodiment is not a unitary or homogenous phenomenon but involves two main variations—the feminine-female and the masculine-male.

To describe and analyze this duality, Beauvoir resorted to the phenomenology of embodiment developed by Edmund Husserl in the 1920s. While studying the experiential grounds of spatial things and spatiality, Husserl had developed a powerful set of conceptual tools that account for the different ways in which living bodies are given to us in experience (see Husserl 1993 [1952]; 1988 [1954]; see also Heinämaa 2011). Beauvoir and her philosophical colleagues, Emmanuel Lévinas, Jean-Paul Sartre (1956 [1943]), and Maurice Merleau-Ponty (1995 [1945]), applied these concepts to a whole new set of phenomena and complemented Husserl's studies with analyses of affective, sexual, and erotic bodily relations.

Thanks to this groundwork, contemporary phenomenology contains a powerful toolkit for examining human embodiment. In this framework, several different meanings of the human body and embodiment can be distinguished and their relations clearly defined. The human body is not assimilated to an organism or biomechanical system. Rather the human body is conceptualized in a number of different ways depending on the evaluative, practical, and cognitive aspects of the situation in which it is grasped: thing and machine, to be sure, but also tool, expression, sediment, trace, and dwelling (general introductions to feminist phenomenology include Fisher and Embree 2000; Fisher, Stoller, and Vasterling 2005; Heinämaa 2003).

The traditional oppositions of mind/body and culture/nature can be avoided, since all phenomena—mental and bodily, cultural and natural—are studied under their subjective and objective aspects and under the correlation between the subjective and the objective. Instead of two separate realms of reality, the mental and the material, we discover a variety of phenomena with intentional as well as sensible determinants. The human body is not merely grasped as a material thing, a bio-mechanism, or an information-processor, but also as our fundamental way of relating to the material world and worldly objects. The human mind is not a self-enclosed pure spirit or mere epiphenomenon on top of material reality, but a power necessarily expressed in bodily gestures and corporeally related to other "embodied minds" or "minded bodies." Nature is not just an object of the physical sciences but also the common field for all perceiving, moving, and acting bodies, human and animal.

Unlike the traditional concepts of mind and body, the phenomenological concepts of consciousness and intentional objectivity imply one another. Intentional consciousness is always consciousness *of something*, and the intended objectivity is always valid *for someone*. Beauvoir captures this mutual dependency of subjectivity and objectivity: "It is impossible to define an object in cutting it off from the subject through and for which it is object; and the subject reveals itself only through the objects in which it is engaged" (Beauvoir 2004: 159–160).

This means that all bodily experiences and phenomena involve both subjective and objective factors. By differentiating their types and forms, we can disclose several aspects and layers of human embodiment. Most importantly, distinctions between different ways of *being* a body, of *having* a body, and *transforming* as a body allow us to analyze problems central to feminist and post-feminist theory and politics. These include phenomena as diverse as pregnancy, physical work, and artistic expression, cosmetics and body transplants, eating disorders, sexual pleasure and violence, and transsexuality. The next sections discuss more closely some of these phenomena in the framework of contemporary phenomenology.

Bodies as Instruments and Expressions

When human and animal bodies are studied by the experimental and mathematical methods of modern natural sciences—in medicine, physiology, and zoology, for example—they are thematized as complicated mechanisms. They appear as individuals belonging to biological species, as biochemical structures, or as information systems. These causal-functional categories are necessary for natural scientific theorization of bodily relations and behaviors but do not exhaust the senses of human embodiment. Several other senses are essential to and central in our conscious lives.

In everyday practical contexts, our own bodies and those of other humans and animals appear to us primarily as means of perception and manipulation of material things. I roll the ball towards a child who sits on the floor opposite to me, and when the ball comes into her reach, the child catches it with her fingers. I can do this because I see the child's fingers as potential means of controlling environing things and their movements. I do not have to infer or reason that the child's body involves such manipulative means. I immediately see her body as orienting and controlling its environment in a peculiar manner common to all humans (or primates).

The simple example of the child and the ball captures the main idea, but the phenomenon proves more complex in most practical situations involving co-operative, communicative, and historical factors. When a woman in labor is asked to "hold back" and "push," she is asked to use her body as means for the delivery of the child. But her reaction to such instructions depends on the specific condition of her body, on her personal history, and on the social-cultural practices in which she participates. When soldiers are commanded "Left shoulder, ARMS!" they are attended to as functionaries ready to manipulate their weapons with their bodies. But their promptness in obeying the command depends on the situation in which they operate, its social and historical boundaries, and their personal relations to this situation.

The practical framing of the human body involves variations that are crucial to feminist theory and politics. In "Throwing Like a Girl," the American phenomenologist and critical theorist Iris Marion Young draws attention to the fact that women's relations to their own bodies as means of practical governing are delimited and compromised by their training and education (Young 1990). And even before entering such institutional settings, their bodily capacities are shaped and molded by the positive and negative reactions of their elders and their peers (Chisholm 2008). By combining critical-theoretic and phenomenological insights, Young argues that environmental social-historical conditions of experiencing shape us as motor agents and bodily subjects. Further, she suggests that this in turn affects our possibilities of governing our spatial environment. Thus a vicious circle is established in the formation of types of experiences and conditions of experiencing. The concepts of sedimentation and habitation allow a purely phenomenological account of such processes (Heinämaa 2014b; Jacobs 2016).

In addition to operating as our means of manipulating things and governing space our bodies serve other practical purposes. Vitally and symbolically, the most important of these is the function of housing and sheltering another living being attributed to female bodies in pregnancy. The topic of pregnancy is widely discussed in feminist philosophy and its multi-faceted nature is illuminated by bio-ethical, historical, social-scientific, and critical-political inquiries (e.g., Labouvie 1998; Martin 1987). Feminist phenomenologists have contributed by analyzing the experiential structures of pregnancy and childbirth. Their inquiries show how social and practical significances intertwine with deeply emotive, vital, sensory, and subliminal forms of experiencing (Gahlings 2006; Heinämaa 2014a; LaChance Adams 2014; Stone 2012; Young 1990).

It is important to emphasize that the experiential fact that our bodies are given to us as our means of manipulating things also involves the possibility of treating the bodies of all living beings—other bodies as well as our own bodies—as mere material things. In other words, we can "objectify" living experiencing bodies, and we do this for many different purposes. Some of these purposes are violent, alienating, and exclusionary, while others are beneficial, empowering, and consolidating (Haslanger 1993; Morris 1999). Examples range from pornography, torture, and sadism to physical therapy and play.

For political reasons feminist philosophers have mainly discussed the negative senses of objectification (Nussbaum 1995; Papadaki 2014). By combining phenomenological, pragmatic, and critical-theoretical perspectives, Susan Bordo, for example, argues that in modern societies women are urged to treat their bodies primarily as aesthetic and economic objects and to neglect the practical and vital significance of their corporeality. In Bordo's analysis, this inflicts distortions on the body-images of young women and leads to an increase in eating disorders (Bordo 1993). Dorothea Legrand has questioned this explanatory paradigm using the phenomenological theory of bodily intersubjectivity or intercorporeality. Legrand argues that eating disorders should be interpreted not merely in terms of social-historical conditioning but also as special forms of exchange in which the victim is not a passive recipient but a communicating agent. She shows that food, eating, and the body operate in anorexia as means of transmitting emotional desires to others lacking in sensitivity and responsiveness (Legrand and Briend 2015). On this understanding, anorectic starvation is not a neglect of one's own practical-vital body, but rather an attempt at communication in an extreme social-emotional setting.

Legrand's analysis demonstrates that the concepts of objectification do not merely describe situations in which human or animal bodies are subjected to external ends that harm them. Rather, living beings can treat their own bodies as objects of different sorts (e.g., expressive or thingly), and they do so in order to pursue their values and to promote their ends. This means that the concepts of objectification as such are ethically and politically neutral and allow us to analyze several types of corporeal and intercorporeal relations, both harmful and beneficial (Slatman 2014; Weiss 1999; 2009).

A well-known example is provided by Jean-Paul Sartre in *Being and Nothingness* (1956 [1943]). Sartre describes a situation in which a young woman avoids the advances of a male companion by systematically neglecting his words' sexual significance. When the man takes her hand, the woman changes her relation to her own body in order to limit the sexual meanings of this bodily gesture. Instead of identifying with her hand, she distances herself from it and acts as if it were just another thing lying on the table: "the hand rests inert between the warm hands of her companion—neither consenting nor resisting—a thing" (Sartre 1956 [1943]: 97; translation modified).

Sartre studies this example while developing his theory of self-deception ("bad faith") as a structure of human existence. Several feminist commentators have argued that Sartre's choice of examples betrays androcentric or heterosexist bias (Barnes 1999; Hoagland 1999; Le Dœuff 2007 [1989]). Indeed Simone de Beauvoir already argued in *The Second Sex* that Sartre's analysis starts from a simple opposition between attraction and repulsion. She claimed that such concepts could not account for the complex character of feminine desire or the varieties of human sexuality (Beauvoir 1991 [1949]: 81; Heinämaa 2006).

Despite these problems, Sartre's analysis illuminates the experiential fact that we can relate to our bodies in several different ways, and can intend our bodies both as mere things and as our necessary means of having things at the same time. Sartre's case study also allows us to highlight the fact that in many communicative contexts, the practical articulation of human bodies makes way for expressive intentionality, which renders human bodies into expressive vehicles of meaningful gestures. The caressing hand of the lover does not merely appear as a tool for the manipulation of things but is given as an expression of his or her desire.

Erotic situations in general frame human bodies as expressions of desire, passion, and pleasure. The face, the hands, the genitals, and the whole body of the desiring person indicate the presence of his or her passion and express or manifest its particular form. The ecstatic face is not given to us as a goal or a means to a goal, but appears as a manifestation of delight that grows with each turn in the expressive exchange. If we characterize emotional expressions as means that serve predetermined ends, then we subject the phenomenon to inadequate concepts and neglect its specific structure and dynamism. Moreover, in *The Second Sex*, Beauvoir argues that the confusion of erotic intentionality with practical intentionality has lead to a neglect of feminine eroticism and its specific character. Luce Irigaray builds on this insight in *An Ethics of Sexual Difference*, arguing that preoccupation with reproductive goals has blinded us to the true generativity of corporeal love that happens between the sexes:

> [L]ove can be the motor of becoming, allowing both the one and the other to grow. For such love each must keep their bodies autonomous. The one should not be the source of the other nor the other of the one. Two lives should embrace and fertilize each other, without either being a fixed goal for the other.
> (Irigaray 1993: 28)

The Limits of Naturalism

In light of the phenomenological analysis of embodiment, the natural scientific concepts of organism and bio-mechanism prove insufficient for feminist philosophy. They only capture human bodies as components of causal-functional nexuses and thus overlook broad areas of human experience in which bodies appear as motivational, purposeful, and expressive. These latter types of relations are not reducible to causal relations, because their relata—the motivating and the motivated, the intended and the intending, and the expressed and the expressive—are mutually dependent and are not separable parts of a fixed whole. Human bodies are not merely nodes in chains of causal-functional relations but are also expressive units tied to other expressive units by internal relations of sense, motivation, and communication. By definition, the natural scientific concepts of organism and bio-mechanism do not capture such bodily relations.

It is no use to add psychic or psycho-social systems of significance on top of a body defined in purely causal-mechanical terms. Such an addition may present the body as invested with individual and communal significations and meanings, but it does not help us to capture the sense-*forming* aspects of embodiment or the body as a *source* of meaning. More precisely, the idea of cultural and social construction of meaning does not contribute to the philosophical understanding of the experiential foundations of the psycho-physical compound.

Husserl's phenomenology of embodiment offers a philosophical analysis of the grounds and the limits of the psycho-physical articulation of human embodiment. In addition, it includes strong arguments that question the ontological primacy of the bio-mechanical understanding of the living body and demonstrate its dependency on practical and expressive bodies. I have explicated these arguments elsewhere (Heinämaa 2003: 2011). For present purposes it suffices to point out that Husserl's main strategy is to question the internal consistency of the naturalistic project and to argue that, to promote her philosophy, the naturalist has to presuppose in practice what her doctrine denies in theory, i.e. the ideality of sense and reason. That is: to secure the scientific character of her judgments, the naturalist has to submit them to the critical inspection of the scientific community. This demands that she address her fellow scientists as subjects bound by the laws of logic, ethics, and grammar, and not (merely) by the contingencies or probabilities of nature (Husserl 1965 [1911]: 169; Wittgenstein 1997 [1953]: §109, 47e, §531, 145).

Even if one does not accept this argument about the conditions of human reasoning, the conceptual innovations that Husserl and his followers made to distinguish different ways of experiencing living bodies have proven beneficial to feminist philosophy in several areas of study. An adequate account of the relations between women and men must not confuse the alternative ways in which we approach living bodies, or slide from one sense of embodiment to another without an explicit account of their relations. Keeping these senses distinct allows us to discuss critically the co-existence of human beings, not just as female and male animals, but as women and men with divergent histories and prehistories.

Further Reading

Grosz, Elisabeth (1994) *Volatile Bodies: Toward a Corporeal Feminism*, Bloomington, IN: Indiana University Press.

Heinämaa, Sara (2011) "Body," in Sebastian Luft and Søren Overgaard (Eds.) *The Routledge Companion to Phenomenology*, London: Routledge, 222–232.

—— (2012) "Sex, Gender, and Embodiment," in Dan Zahavi (Ed.) *The Oxford Handbook of Contemporary Phenomenology*, Oxford: Oxford University Press, 216–242.

Welton, Donn (Ed.) (1998) *Body and Flesh: A Philosophical Reader*, Malden, MA and Oxford: Blackwell.

—— (Ed.) (1999) *The Body: Classical and Contemporary Readings*, Malden, MA and Oxford: Blackwell.

Related Topics

Early modern feminism and Cartesian philosophy (Chapter 6); feminist phenomenology (Chapter 12); the sex/gender distinction and the social construction of reality (Chapter 13); materiality: sex, gender and what lies beneath (Chapter 16); personal identity and relational selves (Chapter 18).

References

Alanen, Lilli (2003) *Descartes's Concept of Mind*, Cambridge, MA, and London: Harvard University Press.

Antony, Louise M. (2005) "Natures and Norms," in Ann E. Cudd and Robin O. Andreasen (Eds.) *Feminist Theory: A Philosophical Anthology*, Oxford: Blackwell, 127–144.

—— (2007) "Everybody Has Got It: A Defense of Non-Reductive Materialism in the Philosophy of Mind," in Brian McLaughlin and Jonathan Cohen (Eds.) *Contemporary Debates in the Philosophy of Mind*, Oxford: Blackwell, 132–159.

Aristotle (1931) *De Anima*, trans. J. A. Smith, Oxford: Clarendon Press.

Barnes, Hazel E. (1999) "Sartre and Feminism," in Julien S. Murphy (Ed.) *Feminist Interpretations of Jean-Paul Sartre*, University Park, PA: Penn State University Press, 22–44.

Beauvoir, Simone de (1991 [1949]) *The Second Sex*, trans. H. M. Parshley, Harmondsworth: Penguin.

—— (2004) "A Review of *Phenomenology of Perception* by Maurice Merleau-Ponty," trans. Marybeth Timmerman, in Margaret A. Simons (Ed.) *Simone de Beauvoir: Philosophical Writings*, Urbana, IL: University of Illinois Press, 151–164.

Bordo, Susan (1993) *Unbearable Weight: Feminism, Western Culture and the Body*, Berkeley, CA: University of California Press.

Bos, Erik-Jan (2010) "Princess Elizabeth of Bohemia and Descartes," *Historia Mathematica* 37(3): 485–502.

Braidotti, Rosi (2002) *Metamorphoses: Towards a Materialist Theory of Becoming*, Cambridge: Polity.

Chisholm, Dianne (2008) "Climbing Like a Girl: An Exemplary Adventure in Feminist Phenomenology," *Hypatia* 23(1): 9–40.

Descartes, René (1996) *Oeuvres de Descartes*, Eds. Charles Adam and Paul Tannery, Paris: Vrin/C.N.R.S.

Dolphijn, Rick and van der Tuin, Iris (Eds.) (2012) *New Materialism: Interviews and Cartographies*, London: Open Humanities Press.

Fisher, Linda, and Lester Embree (Eds.) (2000) *Feminist Phenomenology*, Dordrecht: Kluwer.

Fisher, Linda, Stoller, Silvia, and Vasterling, Veronica (Eds.) (2005) *Feminist Phenomenology and Hermeneutics*, Würzburg: Köningshausen & Neumann.

Gahlings, Ute (2006) *Phänomenologie der weiblichen Leiberfahrung*, München: Karl Alber.

Grosz, Elizabeth (2004) *The Nick of Time*, Durham, NC: Duke University Press.

Hankinson Nelson, Lynn (1990) *Who Knows: From Quine to Feminist Empiricism*, Philadelphia, PA: Temple University Press.

Hankinson Nelson, Lynn, and Jack Nelson (Eds.)(2003) *Feminist Interpretations of W.V. Quine*, University Park, PA: Penn State University Press.

Haslanger, Sally (1993) "On Being Objective and Being Objectified," in Louise M. Anthony and Charlotte Witt (Eds.) *Mind of One's Own: Feminist Essays on Reason and Objectivity*, Boulder, CO: Westview Press, 209–253.

—— (2000a) "Feminism in Metaphysics: Negotiating the Natural," in Miranda Fricker and Jennifer Hornsby (Eds.) *The Cambridge Companion to Feminism in Philosophy*, Cambridge: Cambridge University Press, 107–126.

—— (2000b) "Gender and Race: (What) are They? (What) do we want them to be?" *Noûs* 34(1): 31–55.

—— (2005) "What Are We Talking About? The Semantics and Politics of Social Kinds," *Hypatia* 20(4): 10–26.

—— (2012) *Resisting Reality: Social Construction and Social Critique*, Oxford: Oxford University Press.

Heinämaa, Sara (2003) *Toward a Phenomenology of Sexual Difference: Husserl, Merleau-Ponty, Beauvoir*, Lanham, MD: Rowman & Littlefield.

—— (2006) "'Through Desire and Love': Simone de Beauvoir on the Possibilities of Sexual Desire," in Ellen Mortensen (Ed.) *Sex, Breath and Force: Sexual Difference in a Post-Feminist Era*, Lanham, MD: Lexington Books, 129–166.

—— (2011) "Body," in Sebastian Luft and Søren Overgaard (Eds.) *The Routledge Companion to Phenomenology*, London: Routledge, 222–232.

—— (2014a) "'An Equivocal Couple Overwhelmed with Life': A Phenomenological Analysis of Pregnancy," *philoSOPHIA* 4(1): 12–49.

—— (2014b) "Anonymity and Personhood: Merleau-Ponty's Account of the Subject of Perception," *Continental Philosophy Review* 48(2): 123–142.

Hoagland, Sarah L. (1999) "Existential Freedom and Political Change," in Julien S. Murphy (Ed.) *Feminist Interpretations of Jean-Paul Sartre*, University Park, PA: Penn State University Press, 149–174.

Husserl, Edmund (1965 [1911]) "Philosophy as Rigorous Science," in Quentin Lauer (trans. and Ed.) *Philosophy as Rigorous Science and The Crisis of Philosophy*, New York: Harper & Row, 71–148.

—— (1993 [1952]) *Ideas Pertaining to a Pure Phenomenology and to a Phenomenological Philosophy, Second Book: Studies in the Phenomenological Constitution*, trans. R. Rojcewicz and A. Schuwer, Dordrecht: Kluwer.

—— (1988 [1954]) *The Crisis of European Sciences and Transcendental Phenomenology: An Introduction to Phenomenological Philosophy*, trans. David Carr, Evanston, IL: Northwestern University Press.

Irigaray, Luce (1993) *An Ethics of Sexual Difference*, trans. Carolym Burke and Gillian C. Gill, Ithaca, NY: Cornell University Press.

Jacobs, Hanne (2016) "Socialization, Reflection, and Personhood," *Analytic and Continental Philosophy: Perspectives of the 37th International Ludwig Wittgenstein Symposium*, Berlin: Walter de Gruyter.

Labouvie, Eva (1998) *Andere Umstände: Eine Kulturgeschichte der Geburt*, Wien: Böhlau.

LaChance Adams, Sarah (2014) *Mad Mothers, Bad Mothers, and What a "Good" Mother Would Do: The Ethics of Ambivalence*, New York: Columbia University Press.

Le Dœuff, Michèle (2007 [1989]) *Hipparchia's Choice: An Essay Concerning Women, Philosophy, etc.*, trans. T. Selous, New York: Fordham University Press.

Legrand, Dorothea and Frédéric Briend (2015) "Anorexia and Bodily Intersubjectivity," in *European Psychologist* 20(1): 52–61.

Malabou, Catherine, and Johnston, Adrian (2013) *Self and Emotional Life: Merging Philosophy, Psychoanalysis, and Neuroscience*, New York: Columbia University Press.

Martin, Emily (1987) *The Woman in the Body: A Cultural Analysis of Reproduction*, Milton Keynes: Open University Press.

Merleau-Ponty, Maurice (1995 [1945]) *Phenomenology of Perception*, trans. C. Smith, New York: Routledge.

Morris, Phyllis Sutton (1999) "Sartre on Objectification," in Julien S. Murphy (Ed.) *Feminist Interpretations of Jean-Paul Sartre*, University Park, PA: Penn State University Press, 64–89.

Nussbaum, Martha (1995) "Objectification," *Philosophy and Public Affairs* 24(4): 249–291.

—— (1999) *Sex and Social Justice*, Oxford: Oxford University Press.

—— (2000) *Women and Human Development: The Capabilities Approach*, Cambridge: Cambridge University Press.

Papadaki, Evangelia (2014) "Feminist Perspectives on Objectification," *Stanford Encyclopedia of Philosophy* [online]. Available from: http://plato.stanford.edu/archives/sum2014/entries/feminism-objectification/.

Plato (2005) *Phaedrus*, trans. Christopher Rowe, Harmondsworth: Penguin.

Sartre, Jean-Paul [1943] (1956) *Being and Nothingness: A Phenomenological Essay on Ontology*, trans. H. E. Barnes, New York: Washington Square Press.

Scheman, Naomi (2000) "Feminism in Philosophy of Mind," in *The Cambridge Companion to Feminism in Philosophy*, Eds. Miranda Fricker and Jennifer Hornsby, Cambridge: Cambridge University Press, 49–67.

Shapiro, Lisa (2013) "Elisabeth, Princess of Bohemia," *The Stanford Encyclopedia of Philosophy* Winter 2014 [online]. Available from: http://plato.stanford.edu/archives/fall2013/entries/elisabeth-bohemia/.

Slatman, Jenny (2014) *Our Strange Body: Philosophical Reflections on Identity and Medical Interventions*, Amsterdam: Amsterdam University Press.

Stone, Alison (2012) *Feminism, Psychoanalysis, and Maternal Subjectivity*, London: Routledge.

Tollefsen, Deborah (1999) "Princess Elisabeth and the Problem of Mind-Body Interaction," *Hypatia* 14(3): 59–77.

Weiss, Gail (1999) *Body Images: Embodiment as Intercorporeality*, London: Routledge.

——(2009) *Refiguring the Ordinary*, Bloomington, IN: Indiana University Press.

Witt, Charlotte (1998) "Form, Normativity and Gender in Aristotle: A Feminist Perspective," in Cynthia Freeland (Ed.) *Feminist Interpretations of Aristotle*, University Park, PA: Penn State University Press, 118–137.

——(2003) *Ways of Being: Potentiality and Actuality in Aristotle's Metaphysics*, Ithaca, NY: Cornell University Press.

Wittgenstein, Ludwig (1997 [1953]) *Philosophische Untersuchungen/ Philosophical Investigations*, second edition, trans. G. E. M. Anscombe, Oxford: Blackwell.

Young, Iris Marion (1990) *Throwing Like a Girl and Other Essays in Feminist Philosophy and Social Theory*, Bloomington, IN: Indiana University Press.

16

MATERIALITY

Sex, Gender, and What Lies Beneath

Claire Colebrook

Matter, Materialism, Materiality

If materialism is a movement, then materiality must be whatever it is that materialism advocates. Or perhaps matter rather than materiality is championed by materialism, and the complicated and more nuanced word "materiality" tries to deconstruct the seeming simplicity of matter. "Matter" is conventionally opposed to "ideality," where matter is real, physical, and grounding, while ideas, culture, or representation are more human, temporal, and malleable. Then one might think of "materiality" as a process that generates or opens the distinction between mind and matter, or ideas and matter.

Sometimes being a materialist or signing up to materialism may have meant having a binary conception of matter. Materialists of this kind range from Marxist historical materialists who contest the notion that thinking occurs in some space of ideas divorced from labor and conditions of need, to philosophical eliminative materialists who are opposed to anything (such as ideas or mental content) that cannot be explained by way of physical material processes. To write, instead, of "materiality" rather than matter is to stake a claim or situate oneself outside older matter/mind or matter/ideality binaries. Yet—like *materialism*—"materiality" or being a "new materialist" makes no sense without some combative notion of just what materiality is *not*.

One thing is perhaps certain: new materialism is well and truly against the notion that it is ideas, language, or texts that construct reality. Here, for example, are four claims about new materialism that rely upon a textualist, linguistic, postmodern, or constructivist past in order for materialism in its new mode to have force.

> Although postmoderns claim to reject all dichotomies, there is one dichotomy that they appear to embrace almost without question: language/reality. . . . [P]ostmodernists argue that the real/material is entirely constituted by language . . . [T]he discursive realm is nearly always constituted so as to foreclose attention to lived material bodies, and evolving material practices. An emerging group of feminist theorists of the body are arguing, however, that we need . . . to talk about the materiality of the body as itself an active, sometimes recalcitrant force.
>
> (Alaimo and Hekman 2008: 3–4)

[W]e are summoning a new materialism in response to a sense that the radicalism of . . . the cultural turn is now more or less exhausted. . . . [T]he dominant constructivist orientation to social analysis is inadequate for thinking about matter, materiality, and politics . . . [A]n allergy to "the real" that is characteristic of its more linguistic or discursive forms . . . has had the consequence of dissuading critical inquirers from the more empirical kinds of investigation that material processes and structures require.

(Coole and Frost 2010: 6)

The emergence of neo-materialism "now" may be understood as the result of the butterfly effect—a confluence of currents across the disciplines . . . Whilst humanist thought placed the human subject firmly at the centre of the social and physical world, discoveries in science, . . . and the emergence of new human-technological relationships have decentred the subject. These movements, in concert with . . . theories that question the privilege given to humans in the human/non-human binary, underpin discourses of new materialism. At the core of the material turn is a concern with agential matter.

(Bolt 2012: 3)

The new materialism is . . . a response to the linguistic turn that . . . , it is claimed, has neglected the materiality of matter. Concerned with rectifying this neglect, the new materialism has developed, in part, in debate with poststructuralism and with Judith Butler's theory of the body, which often serve to exemplify the linguistic turn. Butler's work is criticized for not allowing an adequate role for the materiality of the physical body . . . The new material feminisms attempt to address such an imbalance by returning to the materiality of matter.

(Jagger 2015: 241)

The first three quotations introduce important, definitive essay collections of work on the declared "new materialism." They define themselves against the privileging of mind and subjectivity, and the rendering passive and inert of matter. The fourth is a recent summation of the new materialism movement in feminism. These declarations resonate with a whole series of "turns" that *overturn* the original "linguistic turn." The linguistic turn was primarily a critical movement, insisting that one cannot know or theorize outside the conditions through which the world is given and represented. However, a series of later "turns" sought to speak for reality, materiality, the inhuman, affect, embodiment, and life. In addition to an emphasis on *materiality*, which suggests a dynamic process rather than the simple "matter," there have been new vitalisms, new realisms, and an ongoing rejection of the distance of critique. In its place theorists aim to think about the vibrancy of matter, which has significant consequences for feminist theory and politics.

New Materialism

If one accepts that there has been a binary association between women and their supposedly determining embodiment, biology, and sexuality, and one accepts that one must resist "essentialism" in all its forms, then a turn to matter requires significant theoretical work. It makes sense, then, that new materialisms do not simply take up the other side of the binary, but situate themselves against the mind/matter opposition. They define themselves as distinctly different from supposed older materialisms that regarded matter as a basis, foundation, or substrate.

I suggest, though, that there is a sense in which all materialisms are "new" materialisms, because their notion of materiality must have a gestural or oppositional component. Any intellectual movement must be uncharitable to its previous generation to establish a difference, and intellectual movements come in dialectical response to each other. After years of insisting on social and linguistic construction, then, theorists turn back to materiality and are critical of too immediate an emphasis on matter.

Nonetheless, there is something about the problem of feminist materiality that is more insistent than philosophical squabbles between idealism and realism, or historicism and absolutism (or other conflicts and oppositions). Looking over the debates regarding matter, materialism, and materiality over several decades of feminist scholarship, the problem is not one of ontology—of what really is—that is then applied to feminist politics. Rather, when "matter" is asserted as ontological bedrock, it is already gendered and sexualized. The first possibility is that the assertion of some neutral substrate of matter that then takes on form repeats a passive-matter-versus-active-mind dichotomy that has been aligned with the male-female binary: the concept of matter is gendered, structurally. The second possibility is that resisting the notion of passive matter, or insisting upon mind or language as determining factors, involves a subjectivist and rationalist prejudice against what simply *is*: once again reason and activity are valorized. So one cannot simply assert the side of the binary that was devalued or dismissed, for the binary itself—and even the project of ontology, of finding what really exists—is already sexualized.

This problem is evident in the work of Luce Irigaray—often appealed to in new materialist debates, and also often dismissed as dangerously essentialist. Irigaray argued that the thought of some ultimate, truly existing substance—what really exists and remains present through and beyond mere appearances—possessed an (auto-) erotic structure. If some ultimate substance subtends appearances, and if true knowledge is the grasp of that underlying presence, then one establishes a paradigm for knowledge based on a stable subject intuiting the truth of a world that is also stable and available for representation (Irigaray 1985). What is erased is the coming into being and appearing of the world, and how these supposed subjects of knowledge emerge from relations with other subjects.

Irigaray therefore stressed the materiality of sexual *difference*, meaning not the biological fixity of two sexes but the process and relations through which the complexity of matter generates (at least) two ways of forming oneself in relation to the world. What is significant is Irigaray's attempt to theorize matter as what had been defined as passive substrate but needed to be redefined as a differential relation. Even more significant is the horror with which this project was greeted, as though referring back to matter was essentially essentialist, essentially anti-feminist.

Setting aside whether Irigaray was an essentialist, it is more fruitful to note the *problem* of essentialism. For many, it seemed disastrous to say that there might be something before the discursive and social relation of the sexes. For others, refusing anything that lay outside or before social relations repeated an anti-materialism that was anti-feminist (anti-body, pro-mind, pro-subject, pro-human). So there is no way to decide upon the merits of matter, materialism, or materiality in some politically neutral terrain. To be politically neutral and say that there simply *is* matter is not only metaphysical—positing some ultimate ground—but also sexual. How does one posit neutral pre-sexual matter without saying that there is something prior to the differential, relational processes through which life and being emerge? Of course, matter may exist prior to *human* sexuality—prior to male and female, masculine and feminine—but any being (organic or otherwise) emerges from dynamic relations of existence, in which different forces enter into relation to generate relatively stable entities.

To see "sex" as something that occurs after matter, as the differentiation of matter, is to see matter as a blank, pre-relational, formless base that then takes on form. That notion of formless, pre-relational matter—many feminists have pointed out—has always been sexed. In the history of philosophy, the forming power of light or reason gives shape and identity to a formless matter figured as maternal ground. The notion of blank, formless matter has been dismissed by feminist philosophers because of its long-standing association with *mere matter* brought into life and being by reason and form. But that conception of matter as a neutral and passive building material has also been rejected by physicists and philosophers. Even so, despite a consensus among most twentieth-century theorists that life and the world emerge from matter that is *self*-forming, material*ism* is always a tactic or maneuver that displaces another position deemed insufficiently attentive to what really is.

One of the most-cited volumes on new materialism, Dolphijn and van der Tuin (2012), makes clear this gestural nature of materialism—as always a new materialism. Their volume consists mostly of interviews with a range of thinkers, one of whom—Rosi Braidotti—was writing on sexual difference and materialism well before the appearance of Butler's *Gender Trouble*, against which the new materialism is often defined (Braidotti 1987a; 1987b). Braidotti's "new materialism," then, existed throughout the "cultural turn" and the postmodernism against which materialists react. Indeed, Braidotti's work deploys the very "postmodernists" (Deleuze, Foucault, Irigaray) against whom new materialism is often defined. Acknowledging that the "new" of their materialism is a tactic, rather than a description, the editors of *New Materialism* write:

> It is in the resonances between old and new readings and re-readings that a "new metaphysics" might announce itself. A new metaphysics . . . announces . . . a "new tradition," which simultaneously gives us a past, a present, and a future. Thus, a new metaphysics . . . traverses and thereby rewrites thinking as a whole, leaving nothing untouched.
>
> (Dolphijn and van der Tuin 2012: 13)

In their interview with another key figure of the declared new materialism, Quentin Meillassoux gives an account of matter that is defined against the history of Western philosophy to date, with matter being defined *against* vitality. This is worth noting, because the *only* thing that unites Meillassoux with other materialists is the gesture of positing matter as something beyond the stable identities of experience. What makes his position materialist, and the only thing he shares with Braidotti, Karen Barad, and others, is the reaction against a metaphysics of mind. Meillassoux insists that his position emerges from reason, or what one is able to think:

> [M]aterialism is not a form of animism, spiritualism, vitalism, et cetera. It asserts that non-thinking . . . precede[s] thought, and exists outside of it, following the example of Epicurean atoms, devoid of any subjectivity, and independent of our relationship to the world. . . . [M]aterialism is rationalism . . . in that it is always an enterprise that, through skepticism, opposes . . . knowledge and criticism to religious appeal, to mystery, or to the limitation of our knowledge.
>
> (Dolphijn and van der Tuin 2012: 79)

Materialism is not merely an oppositional gesture; it is always hyper-foundational. Whatever you assert to be at the ground of existence—say Epicurean atoms—I can undermine by saying that there is a matter that precedes even the formation of atoms, and from which atoms are formed. This is Meillassoux's objection to Epicurus, although—in contrast with most proclaimed new materialists—he defends the Epicurean possibility of something existing without life, relation, or vibrancy. Meillassoux's "materialism" is constituted by an objection to others' views of the bedrock of existence. This, indeed, is what materialism *is*; this is why "matter" is rarely matter and more often "materiality," the posited process that accounts for the perceived world of matters (or composed things).

Consider the earliest feminist materialisms, such as Shulamith Firestone's *The Dialectic of Sex*. She contested the Marxist notion that relations among laboring bodies were the underlying process of history, and substituted the biological division of labor:

> I have attempted to take the class analysis one step further to its roots in the biological division of the sexes . . . , granting it an even deeper basis in objective conditions . . . [W]e shall expand Engels's definition of historical materialism . . . now rephrased to include the biological division of the sexes . . . :
> Historical materialism . . . seeks the ultimate cause and the great moving power of all historic events in the dialectic of sex: the division of society into two distinct biological classes for procreative reproduction, and the struggles of these classes with one another; in the changes in the modes of marriage, reproduction and child care created by these struggles.
>
> (Firestone 1970: 29)

Materialism is always a turning back, always part of a materialist *turn*, and therefore always "new" materialism. Karen Barad gets to the heart of this materialist gesture:

> Critique is all too often not a deconstructive practice, . . . but a destructive practice meant to dismiss, to turn aside, to put someone or something down . . . a practice of negativity that I think is about subtraction, distancing and othering.
>
> (Dolphijn and van der Tuin 2012: 49)

By contrast, materialism does not focus on the limitations of opponents' claimed knowledge of the world, but *adds* a dimension that complicates matters. Further, materialism always bears a contrary relation to life. On the one hand it aims to account for life, with matter functioning as that from which life emerges. Yet, on the other hand, the gesture of materialism always aims to think life on its own terms, claiming to make sense of how life really works (without appealing to some external principle such as God, the subject, or logic). Firestone is already directing her feminist materialism against a Marxism that began with labor: by placing labor as the motor of materialism, Marxism occludes the sexual relations and matters that generate bodies who enter into labor relations. Firestone's materialism is, therefore, distinct from any notion of "matter" as a passive or determining cause of human relations, and is not a form of biological essentialism.

We might then ask how and why feminists turned *back* to materialism. Two things need to be taken into account, and they do not marry well. First, materialist feminism of the type that Firestone created came in for severe feminist criticism, with radical feminism (or "difference" feminism that focused on how the sexes could not be considered simply equal) accused of essentialism (Assiter 1996: 113). Second, the supposed era of feminism that came after Firestone and refused materiality was never as simply anti-, counter-, or immaterialist as its later caricature implied (Ahmed 2008: 4). Nevertheless, it became commonplace to think of feminism as having gone through an essentialist phase, so that feminism narrated itself as having overcome a lapse or fall, defining its current sophistication against naïve realisms, materialisms, and biologisms.

The classic example is Toril Moi's 1985 *Sexual/Textual Politics*, the title indicating the view that sexual difference is generated through linguistic/textual narrations. Moi uses "essentialism" as a pejorative, something into which otherwise critical feminists fall. Here she is writing about Hélène Cixous, and then Luce Irigaray, both of whom fall into essentialism:

> So far, then, Cixous's position would seem to constitute a forceful feminist appropriation of Derridean theory. Anti-essentialist and anti-biologistic, her work [advances] . . . towards an analysis of the articulations of sexuality and desire within the literary text itself. Unfortunately this is not the whole story. As we shall see, Cixous's theory is riddled with contradictions: every time a Derridean idea is invoked, it is opposed and undercut by a theory of women's writing steeped in the . . . metaphysics of presence.
>
> (Moi 2002: 108)

> We have seen how Irigaray's attempt to establish a theory of femininity that escapes patriarchal specul(ariz)ation necessarily lapses into a form of essentialism.
>
> (Moi 2002: 142)

Moi's criticism of Cixous and Irigaray in favor of a more properly critical, deconstructive or textualist account of sexual difference offered itself as the definitive narration of late 1980s feminism's refusal of biology (but not of "materiality," which could be attributed to language or signification as the material conditions that generate apparent sexual difference). It became common to see naïve essentialism and biologism as properly displaced by the differential materiality of "signification," the system of signs through which reality, matter, biology, and essence are given. "New materialism" then reacted against this ostensible refusal of a more profound or vital materiality. However, affirming "materiality" is necessarily a gesture that relies on accusing someone else of uncritical essentialism: What you take to be a simple thing or given is *really* the outcome of a process of complex relations, whether those relations are attributed to language (the materiality of the signifier) or vibrant matter, the life from which language emerges.

The very theorists who were charged with unthinking essentialism—especially Irigaray—were not only retrieved by new materialists, they were also crucial to the formation of the supposed movement that new materialism displaced. Elizabeth Grosz and Rosi Braidotti offered readings of Irigaray's work that focused on how "materiality" needs to be seen not as the biological substance from which sexuality is parsed, but rather as a complex differential process that generates an embodied difference that is always relational and can never be grasped as two stable entities (male and female) that then enter into relation. This is Grosz reading Luce Irigaray (one year *prior* to the publication of Butler's *Gender Trouble*, the text that supposedly preceded and prompts new materialism, yet here is Grosz asserting the complexities of matter outside language or subjectivity).

> In utilising the language of ancient alchemy, she reverts to a proto-historical world-view, . . . She uses a logic of interactive forces or combinatory "particles," the "atoms" of all matter in the universe. Taken together, they indicate a logic, not of being, but of perpetual becoming, a world in continuous flux and change. Earth, air, fire and water are the primal ingredients of subjectivity as well as material objects.
>
> (Grosz 1989: 171)

And here is Braidotti, in 1991, delivering a position statement after a decade of defending sexual difference and a corporeal materialist approach:

> The subject is not an abstract entity, but rather a material embodied one. The body is not a natural thing, on the contrary, it is a culturally coded socialized entity; . . . the site of intersection of the biological, the social, and the linguistic . . . Feminist theories of sexual difference have . . . develop[ed] a new form of "corporeal materialism," which defines the body as an interface, a threshold, a field of intersecting forces where multiple codes are inscribed.
>
> (Braidotti 1991: 160)

It would seem that the subsequent "turn" to materialism after the linguisticism of the 1980s and 1990s is turning against an anti-biologism that was the result of a blindspot. That is, as Sara Ahmed has suggested, "'theory' is being constituted as anti-biological by removing from the category of 'theory' work that engages with the biological, . . . [work] which has a long genealogy, especially within feminism" (Ahmed 2008: 26).

Sex, Gender, Mattering

We are already in messy and unclear territory, so let's think about what these concepts of matter, materialism, new materialism, materiality, and then "feminist" materialism *do*. Within recent feminist theory the "clearest" indication of the problem of matter comes in the playful use of the term in Judith Butler's *Bodies That Matter* (1993). Butler uses "matter" as a verb, and as she uses it "mattering" is both what is recognized or taken into account (therefore not physical or natural in any simple sense), and also (because it is *bodies* that matter) she gestures to the fact that seemingly non-physical social processes such as recognition or taking into account rely upon bodies. In short, "to matter" is a verb, but the actions that generate *what matters* occur through bodies. One might ask why Butler makes this basic concept of matter so difficult. Wouldn't it be better if we thought of matter as something like physical substance, the building blocks of the universe, the flesh and blood bodies that then compose social bodies? Some sense of the necessary difficulty of Butler's maneuvers in this text can be given by looking at its place within the history of feminist thought.

When Butler published *Gender Trouble* in 1990 her argument rendered any simple relation between the material and non-material highly problematic. Previously it was standard to distinguish between sex—the physical, biological, material body— and gender—the social meanings and norms through which bodies are lived. The "sex/gender" distinction had been important for warding off the supposed errors of essentialism and biologism. If one distinguishes the physical/material body (the XX chromosome body) from the body as it makes its way in the world as feminine, then one can start to question any "natural" female qualities. Hence those feminists who appealed to the intrinsic difference of the female body were, prior to Butler's *Gender Trouble*, already coming under fire for overlooking how the supposedly basic material body is always constructed through norms of gender.

A sophisticated articulation of sex/gender difference was given by Teresa de Lauretis. Gender, she argued, should *not* be seen as that which makes sense of sex. To assume that there is something stable like sexual difference of which cultural gender codes then make sense maintains the male-female binary that is at the heart of patriarchy, and pays insufficient heed to how technologies of gender create multiple differences that are the effects of representation and not their cause.

> Gender is (a) representation—which is not to say that it does not have concrete or real implications, both social and subjective, for the material life of individuals. . . . On the contrary, . . . The representation of gender *is* its construction—and in the simplest sense it can be said that all of Western art and high culture is the engraving of the history of that construction.
> (Lauretis 1987: 3)

I refer to de Lauretis because any claim for "new materialism" (feminist or otherwise) relies upon reacting against or overturning an undue emphasis on representation. Butler's work in *Bodies That Matter* is crucial because her earlier work in *Gender Trouble* rendered the sex/gender binary even less straightforward. De Lauretis insists that gender has "material implications," but she refuses the notion of real, essential sexual difference being the basis for gender as representation. De Lauretis not only distinguishes the social meaning of gender from the biological "reality" of sex; she also questions whether sexual difference yields anything like a male versus female opposition. Butler's *Gender Trouble* went further. Not only was there no causal or straightforward relation between the sexuality of one's body and the social/cultural norms of gender; also, the very notion that one has a sex that is the ground for gender is actually the effect of gender norms and practices (for Butler).

Here Butler was drawing upon and transforming several poststructuralist strands of thought. Michel Foucault argued that the notion that one has a sexuality that one ought to discover, liberate, and disengage from social control was the effect of practices of self-monitoring and new discourses of sexual knowledge (Foucault 1978). Jacques Derrida had challenged the idea that language or culture imposes itself upon an undifferentiated reality or matter. Rather than see language as that which organizes a prior reality, one should question how the opposition between language/culture/text and reality/nature/matter is itself differentiated (Derrida 1978). For this reason Derrida argued that materialism was a form of metaphysics, privileging a single term—"matter"—that would explain all others.

Butler's *Gender Trouble* had the influence and power it did because it created a specifically feminist form of post-structuralism, but also because it targeted a then almost unquestioned insistence on gender as a cultural or normative overlay upon sexual difference as the preceding material reality. De Lauretis had already begun to criticize this insistence. Butler went even further down the path of anti-essentialism (and possibly anti-materialism) by arguing that one knows one's real biological sex only after the fact, as the supposed cause of which gender is an effect. I do not act a certain way because of my body; it is through acting or performing that my body is then sexed as that which must have been the material ground of gender.

The word "matter" is not used frequently in *Gender Trouble*, but in a key sentence Butler situates matter alongside sex as the supposed ground of gender that is given only through its discursive relations:

> This very concept of sex-as-matter . . . is a discursive formation that acts as a naturalized foundation for the nature/culture distinction and the strategies of domination that that distinction supports. The binary relation between culture and nature promotes a relationship of hierarchy in which culture freely "imposes" meaning on nature, and, hence, renders it into an "Other" to be appropriated to its own limitless uses.
>
> (Butler 1990: 47–48)

Not surprisingly a common criticism of *Gender Trouble* was of its signature move, which shifted so far away from essentialism and biologism that embodiment and matter seemed to be discounted entirely. For Butler, it is not only that we can never know sex as it is in itself, prior to culture, nor only that (as de Lauretis argued) there is no direct causal relation between sex and gender, but also that "sex-as-matter . . . is a discursive foundation" (Butler 1990: 47). Yet Butler was not a social constructivist, and did not see the real world as an effect of language or culture. Rather, her argument was to question any opposition between nature/culture or matter/ideality. But in doing so she did put out of play any straightforward materialism. There could not be anything like matter as ground or basis of relations; rather, it is from relations and differences that oppositions and stable terms are effected.

Even so, when *Gender Trouble* appeared there were already several materialist objections to constructivism and the sex/gender distinction, such as those of Braidotti and Grosz, as we have seen. Perhaps the closest to Butler's critique, but subtly and importantly different, was Moira Gatens's much earlier 1983 objection. For Gatens, seeing gender as the constructing, normative and meaningful term while seeing sex as passive matter awaiting cultural meaning repeated a long-standing rationalist and dualist notion of the body or matter as nothing more than a blank slate awaiting inscription.

Concerning the neutrality of the body, let me be explicit, there is no neutral body, there are at least two kinds of bodies: the male body and the female body. If we locate social practices and behaviours as embedded in the subject . . . then this has the important repercussion that the subject is always a *sexed* subject. If one accepts the notion of the sexually specific subject, that is, the male or female subject, then one must dismiss the notion that patriarchy can be characterized as a system of social organization that valorizes the masculine *gender* over the feminine gender. Gender is not the issue; sexual difference is.

(Gatens 1991: 8)

But Gatens did not simply assert the sexual difference of the body against the constructing power of mind. She insisted that the mind/matter distinction needed to be done away with in favor of something like embodied mind, or a "subject" of perceptions and affections: "Perception can be reduced to neither the body nor consciousness but must be seen as an activity of the subject" (Gatens 1991: 8). Rather than use the term "matter," Gatens and others started writing about a body that was neither a material container and substrate for the mind nor a simple construction or image.

When *Gender Trouble* appeared in 1990 this criticism of constructivism in the name of the body was well under way. Theorists of sexual difference, such as Gatens, Grosz, and Braidotti insisted that one could not reduce sexual difference to biology or essence. Rather than claiming, as Butler was to do in *Bodies That Matter*, that what is given as matter is the outcome of complex discursive formations, social norms, and performances, these feminists—well before Butler's discursive and performative critique of sex—insisted that matter was sexual. Before the non-human turn, before the materialist turn, before Butler's critics asked her "What about the body?" feminists were already insisting that there were different ways of thinking about matter that did not take the form of simple materialism. Rather than treating matter as the ground of culture and meaning, or social formations as based in material processes (such as labor, violence, domination, and need) feminist scholars questioned how "matter" had been situated in a series of binaries. Further, sex itself—sexual difference—was one way to think about matter in a dynamic, inhuman, non-natural manner. Here is Elizabeth Grosz in 1994, giving succinct form to claims about sexual embodiment that she began articulating in the 1980s:

The narrow constraints our culture has imposed on the ways in which our materiality can be thought means that altogether new conceptions of corporeality . . . need to be developed, notions which see human materiality in continuity with organic and inorganic matter but also at odds with other forms of matter, which see animate materiality and the materiality of language in interaction, which make possible a materialism beyond physicalism . . . [C]orporeality must no longer be associated with one sex (or race), which then takes on the burden of the other's corporeality for it. Women can no longer take on the function of being *the* body for men while men are left free to soar to the heights of theoretical reflection and cultural production.

(Grosz 1994: 22)

To give a sense of the force of Grosz's work and the very odd history of "matter," "materiality," and "materialism" in feminist thought, one might look to her earlier *Sexual Subversions*, where she produces highly original and influential readings of Kristeva, Irigaray and Le Doeuff:

> Irigaray has been concerned to explore a mode of women's materiality and corporeality which has been unable to find adequate representation in phal-locentric paradigms. This search for a materialism outside of traditional def-initions is necessary for her project of establishing an identity for women cognisant of women's corporeal specificity. . . . Irigaray thus turns to models and theoretical systems outside of or repressed within mainstream philosoph-ical and religious discourses . . . [such as in] her use of the metaphor of the four elements.
>
> (Grosz 1989: 168)

Butler's *Bodies That Matter* (1993), therefore, should not be seen as an exemplary text from which one can generalize about 1980s and 1990s feminism and its empha-sis on culture and construction. Butler focused on the materiality of signifiers (which could include bodily repetitions of norms and actions), and then argued that mat-ter was not one side of a binary, but something that seemed to generate a binary between mind and matter. Her theorization of matter after *Gender Trouble* was still not a turn back to bodies and materiality, but an ongoing refusal of matter or sex as something prior to normativity. And, yet, if we read her work alongside other feminists writing in the 1980s and 1990s, her focus on performativity and signify-ing materiality is at odds with more avowedly materialist modes of theory, such as those of Gatens, Braidotti and Grosz. Here is Butler responding to the call to think materiality and embodiment:

> It is not enough to argue that there is no prediscursive "sex" that acts as the stable point of reference on which . . . the cultural construction of gender pro-ceeds. To claim that sex is already gendered . . . is not yet to explain in which way the "materiality" of sex is forcibly produced.
>
> (Butler 1993: 11)

> At stake . . . [are] the following: (1) the recasting of the matter of bodies as the effect of a dynamic of power, such that the matter of bodies will be indis-sociable from the regulatory norms that govern their materialization . . . ; (2) the understanding of performativity . . . as that reiterative power of discourse to produce the phenomena that it regulates and constrains; (3) the construal of "sex" no longer as a bodily given on which the construct of gender is artificially imposed, but as a cultural norm which governs the materialization of bodies; (4) a rethinking of the process by which a bodily norm is assumed, appropriated, taken on . . . (5) a linking of this process of "assuming" a sex with the . . . discursive means by which the heterosexual imperative enables certain sexed identifications and forecloses and/or disa-vows other identifications.
>
> (Butler 1993: xiii)

Conclusion

I have suggested that the "new" of "new materialism" should not be seen as a chronological marker (where "new materialists" correct the simplicity of radical feminists like Firestone and then the "cultural turn" of feminists like Butler). But I am not offering my own narrative as giving the proper series of events. Rather, I am suggesting that when we think about materiality the very structure of the concept creates curious before- and after-effects. Materiality is at once the simple "thisness" of all the feminist texts and movements that we have, and to attend to materiality is to read, again, what writers such as Firestone, Irigaray, and Butler actually wrote. This would be an attention to the materiality of the archive of feminist writing. But materiality is also the complex milieu of bodies and habits that surround and generate events of reading. To situate one type of matter—the matter of texts—before another type of matter—the matter of bodies—is to efface the materiality of the world's interactions, and to allow some matters to stand for and speak for others. If feminism has any unity—and it probably doesn't!—one might gesture to all the ways in which any claim about what really matters is precisely what ought to be questioned.

Further Reading

Alaimo, Stacy and Hekman, Susan (Eds.) (2008) *Material Feminisms*, Bloomington, IN: Indiana University Press.
Barad, Karen (2007) *Meeting the Universe Halfway: Quantum Physics and the Entanglement of Matter and Meaning*, Durham, NC: Duke University Press.
Coole, Diana and Frost, Samantha (2010) *New Materialisms: Ontology, Agency, and Politics*, Durham, NC: Duke University Press.

Related Topics

The sex/gender distinction and the social construction of reality (Chapter 13); gender essentialism and anti-essentialism (Chapter 14); embodiment and feminist philosophy (Chapter 15); language, writing, and gender differences (Chapter 24); values, practices, and metaphysical assumptions in the biological sciences (Chapter 26); feminist and queer intersections with disability studies (Chapter 33).

References

Ahmed, Sara (2008) "Some Preliminary Remarks on the Founding Gestures of the 'New Materialism,'" *European Journal of Women's Studies* 15(1): 23–39.
Alaimo, Stacy and Hekman, Susan (Eds.) (2008) *Material Feminisms*, Bloomington, IN: Indiana University Press.
Assiter, Alison (1996) *Enlightened Women: Modernist Feminism in a Postmodern Age*, London: Routledge.
Bolt, Barbara (2012) "Introduction: Toward a 'New Materialism' through the Arts," in Estelle Barrett and Barbara Bolt (Eds.) *Carnal Knowledge: Towards a "New Materialism" Through the Arts*, London: Tauris, 1–14.
Braidotti, Rosi (1987a) "Des Organes Sans Corps," *Les Cahiers du GRIF* 36(1): 7–22.
——(1987b) "Du bio-pouvoir à la bio-éthique," *Le Cahier (Collège international de philosophie)* 3: 123–127.
——(1991) "The Subject in Feminism," *Hypatia* 6(2): 155–172.
Butler, Judith (1990) *Gender Trouble: Feminism and the Subversion of Identity*, New York: Routledge.
——(1993) *Bodies That Matter*, New York: Routledge.

Coole, Diana and Frost, Samantha (2010) *New Materialisms: Ontology, Agency, and Politics*, Durham, NC: Duke University Press.

Derrida, Jacques (1978) *Writing and Difference*, trans. Alan Bass, Chicago, IL: University of Chicago Press.

Dolphijn, Rick and van der Tuin, Iris (2012) *New Materialism: Interviews and Cartographies*, Michigan, MI: Open Humanities Press.

Firestone, Shulamith (1970) *The Dialectic of Sex: The Case for Feminist Revolution*, New York: Morrow.

Foucault, Michel (1978) *The History of Sexuality: Volume One*, trans. Robert Hurley, New York: Pantheon.

Gatens, Moira (1991) "A Critique of the Sex/Gender Distinction," in Sneja Gunew (Ed.) *A Reader in Feminist Knowledge*, New York: Routledge, 139–157.

Grosz, Elizabeth (1989) *Sexual Subversions: Three French Feminists*, Sydney: Allen & Unwin.

——(1994) *Volatile Bodies*, Sydney: Allen & Unwin.

Irigaray, Luce (1985) *Speculum of the Other Woman*, trans. Gillian C. Gill, Ithaca, NY: Cornell University Press.

Jagger, Gill (2015) "The New Materialism and Sexual Difference," *Signs* 40(2): 321–342.

Lauretis, Teresa de (1987) *Technologies of Gender: Essays on Theory, Film, and Fiction*, Bloomington, IN: Indiana University Press.

Moi, Toril (2002) *Sexual/Textual Politics: Feminist Literary Theory*, 2nd ed. London: Routledge.

17

FEMINISM AND BORDERLANDS IDENTITIES

Edwina Barvosa

Scholarly feminist meditations on the inner diversity of the self are many and long-standing. While the inner diversity of the self takes many forms, significant numbers of feminists across disciplines have focused frequently on the empirical phenomenon of the self that is shaped through social life to have an inner configuration of multiple identities that are in tension—a contradictory array of identities that is discussed below has been sometimes referred to as borderlands identities. While feminist considerations have varied widely, they generally share common themes and significant analytic complexity. This complexity arises in part because the very idea of the inner diversity of the self that is socially derived inevitably invokes a wide array of related factors. These factors include issues of agency and autonomy, the imprint on humanity of social constructions of subordination, privilege, and social conflict, including gender hierarchies, the phenomenon of intersectionality, and concepts of the self and subjectivity. In this chapter, I offer a brief review of feminist engagement with the concept of borderlands identities as one form of inner diversity. This account attends to the origins of feminist concern with inner diversity, the social sources of borderland identity formations, and the lasting implications for feminist theory and feminist approaches to envisioning and realizing greater social justice for all.

Feminist Thought on the Inner Diversity of the Self

Feminist engagement with the inner diversity of the self has itself been diverse. It has been informed by various disciplines and undertaken by feminists with an array of subject locations, experiences, and concerns. Some feminist engagement with inner diversity—of which borderlands identities are one kind defined below—critique the long-prevailing Western concept of the unitary self. In that concept, the self is conceived as fully rational, self-transparent, internally consistent, and linguistically immune to the thought distortions of social influence; its subjectivity is defined by its capacity to reason. Ironically feminists have often found socially derived ideological distortions in the depiction of the unitary self, which was debunked as implicitly European, white, masculine, heterosexual, male of means in contrast to the stereotypes of women as reasoning-impaired and prone to flights of emotion and social influence (for feminist arguments against the unified self, see Meyers 1997; Brison 2003).

In her productively critical response, feminist linguist and psychoanalyst Julia Kristeva (1991) argued in the early 1990s that the concept of unitary self was not merely an ideology-biased inheritance—rooted in and perpetuating gender stereotypes— it was also in practice false. Far from self-transparent, internally consistent, and rationally above social influence, *all* human beings are socially shaped in their embodied thoughts and emotions. Human social formation in the disparate discourses and practices of modern life thus heavily influence the shape in a human subjectivity—defined here as *embodied* consciousness. Consciousness is thus often comprised of a hodge-podge of internalized, socially inherited dimensions, many if not all of which are unbidden, and some would be unwanted. In turn, as Kristeva illustrated, unwanted aspects of the self often become the "stranger within"— elements of ourselves that we would cast out were it possible.

Failing that possibility, humans instead often self-deny the presence of unwelcome aspects within ourselves, and then project that element outward as fear and rejection (i.e., "abjection") of others who in our struggling minds represent the attributes of ourselves that we find an anathema. All humans alike are subject to these forms of self-imposed internal blindness, aspects that not only muddle conscious reasoning but also foster conflict (for further detail see Barvosa 2008: 109–139). For Kristeva the feminist project of collective peace required each of us to face and come to peaceful terms with the unwanted diversity within ourselves as a first and necessary step toward peaceful contributions to collective human life. The self that is oriented toward peace and justice must thus see and engage itself as a self "in process."

Other feminist thinkers have also explored diverse aspects of the link between unacknowledged and unaccepted inner diversity of the self and social conflict. Jane Flax (1990), for example, has elaborated the significance of self-fragmentation in social life, including self-fragmentation manifest as contradictions and paradoxes within feminist scholarship itself. Judith Butler (1990, 1993) has elaborated the social construction of gender norms and embodied consciousness and gender identities. Butler's early work focused in part on the formation and stabilization of gender identity through abjection—that is, the casting out or demonizing of unwanted femininity or masculinity as a means to stabilize gender identities based on an alleged gender binary. Such identity-by-abjection aims to deny and—at times violently—tame the otherwise lived diversity and contextual fluidity of human gender expression. In her early analysis Butler at times suggested that identity itself would be best abandoned in order to further the feminist project of peace.

In contrast to the view that identity should be dispensed with in the name of feminist justice, feminist philosopher Linda Martín Alcoff has argued in her book, *Visible Identities*, that although identity politics movements have been problematic in many ways, identity itself cannot plausibly be abandoned, especially in social justice efforts. Alcoff convincingly contends that identities are "in our embodied selves at their deepest level of emotions, perception, imagination, and practical movement" and thus form our "embodied horizons" (Alcoff 2006: 289). Resonant with Alcoff's analysis, many feminists— including feminists of color and feminists working in postcolonial theory—have focused not on the banishing of identity, but on how the inner diversity of the self can take the form of multiple identities that straddle specific social divides. Such borderland identities, many have argued, can have both advantages and hardships in relation to feminist aspirations for peace and justice.

Social Conflict, Borderlands Identities, and Feminism

As just noted, numerous feminist thinkers have explored the formation and implications of borderlands identities. Borderlands identities can be defined as configurations of diversity in the self that include two or more identities that are socially constructed as either uneasily/uncommonly combined, or constructed as entirely mutually exclusive such as the social divided often drawn between Black/white, Jewish/Gentile (for example, see work by feminist writer Rebecca Walker 2001). Borderlands identities are formed through socialization in social contexts domains in which one or more ways of life are in conflict or are at least uneasily co-present in the same location. These uneasy cultural overlapping include areas of settler or neocolonialism, cultural diasporas (Bammer 1994), and sites group displacement and resettlement arising from famines, droughts, wars, migration and other social conflicts (Arana 2001). Tense co-presence of ways of life commonly occur along political borders such as the US–Mexican border. But incidents of group conflict may also occur far away from political borders.

Among many contributions, Chicana poet, activist, and independent feminist scholar Gloria Anzaldúa (1942–2004) has offered one of the most influential accounts of such borderland identities. Raised in and reflecting upon the racial conflict and tension of the South Texas borderlands Anzaldúa used the terms *mestiza consciousness* and *nepantlera* (among others) to refer to those with an embodied consciousness shaped by immersion in multiple cultures that are mutually intolerant of each other: Mexicans against Anglos (white Americans), Anglos against Chicanos (US born/raised of Mexican heritage) and the tortured and adversarial relationships to the indigenous, and the queer in both groups ignored and denied. Chicanas (Mexican Americans) identify across these divides with borderland identities/mestiza consciousness provided immersion in—and identification with—multiple ways of life at war with each other. Anzaldúa holds that such borderland identities offered both personal pain and positive possibility. On the side of hardship, having multiple identities with groups on both sides of a hostile social divide results in inner division—in a consciousness that has absorbed the group conflict into itself where it may either rage on and spill outward, or, with effort, somehow peacefully resolve.

Like Kristeva, Anzaldúa thus meditates on the personal and political effects of the inner war that attend borderlands identities. She writes,

> I have internalized rage and contempt, one part of the self (the accusatory, persecutory, judgmental) using defense strategies against another part of the self (the object of contempt) . . . one does not "see" and awareness does not happen. One remains ignorant of the fact that one is afraid, and that it is fear that holds one petrified.
>
> (Anzaldúa 1987: 45)

In terms of gendered violence, Anzaldúa finds that it is this kind of inner turmoil that produce ongoing forms of gender conflict (1987: 83). At the same time, for Anzaldúa, the person with borderland identities—the *nepantlera* who inhabits the terrain in and between divided groups also has the opportunity to bridge these divided spheres. In so doing, they have the chance to develop within themselves—and then perform for others—the possibility of healing these inner divisions. Anzaldúa writes that the work of the person with borderland identities is to break down the subject-object duality that keeps her a prisoner and to show in the flesh and through the images in her work how duality is transcended. The answer to the problem between the white race and the colored, between males and females, lies in healing the split that originates in . . . our languages and our thoughts.

(1987: 80)

In various ways Anzaldúa's entire corpus is dedicated to elaborating the pain and possibilities arising from living borderland identities (see Anzaldúa and Keating 2000, 2009). The reception of Anzaldúa's work among feminists around the globe indicates that the experience of borderlands identities takes many forms, arises from many global conflicts, and the idea of the life of the *nepantlera* who straddles social divides continues to inspire many who are engaged in feminist practice (Keating and González-López 2011). The qualities of borderlands identities and implications for feminist action have also been taken up by numerous Chicana and Latina thinkers including María Lugones (1990), Mariana Ortega (2016), Deena Gonzales (1997), Norma Alarcon (1994), Cristina Beltrán (2004), Barvosa (2008, 2011) and many others.

Intersectionality within and Borderlands Identities

The concept of intersectionality is an important one in feminist thought. The concept originates in Black feminist thought and can be traced from Sojourner Truth's address "Ain't I a Woman?" in which Truth questions and probes the tendency to see her as either a woman or as Black rather than to address the specificity of her life being and identifying as Black on one hand, a woman on the other *and also her living in the necessity of negotiating both identities in tandem with all the hardships this duality may involve*. Black feminist thinkers Patricia Hill Collins (1998) and Kimberlé Crenshaw (1995) among others have developed and deployed intersectionality as a conceptual framework for understanding the multiple subject locations and identities of Black women in the study of conflicts and patterns of social subordination including in Collins's words: "systems of race, economic class, gender, sexuality, ethnicity, nations and age [that] form mutually constructing features of social organization" (1998: 278).

Building on their work, I have suggested elsewhere (Barvosa 2008: 76–82), that borderlands identities also raise the possibility of seeing intersectionality as not only a factor to be witnessed in the social world, but also as an imprint in embodied consciousness itself. Seen from the perspective of borderlands identities, intersectionality takes the form of internalized or *internal intersectionality* in which the imprint of intersecting complexities in the social world directly shape embodied consciousness. In the case of borderlands identities, for example, this includes both (a) the internalized associations and presumed divisions among identities (group, personal, and intrapersonal) that we inherit from the social world; and (b) any associations among disparate identities that individuals may have created or transformed for themselves. Seeing these intrapsychic interconnections as a form of inner intersectionality is potentially important for feminist practice, because as both Anzaldúa and Kristeva have pointed out, it is the rejecting of associations among diverse aspects of the self that are at the heart of the internal tensions, fears, and turmoil, that—when projected outward—produce and sustain social conflict including conflicts involving race, ethnicity, gender, sexuality, language community, nativity, and so on. In order to fully understand inner intersectionality in relation to borderlands identities, however, it is helpful to recognize in more detail how various identities are produced socially and in the self, and the social and physical formations of borderlands identities.

Types of Identities and Identity Formations

To appreciate the full process of identity formation it is worthwhile to first recall that there are at least three general types of types of identities and that all are in different ways socially constructed either by social groups, the person holding the identity, or both.

In terms of types of identities, sociology and areas of social psychology conventionally recognize at least three types of identity formations: group identities (aka social identities), unique personal identities, and self-identity. Group or *collective identities* are those associated with a social group or category such as ethnic groups, nations, or genders. For our purposes this includes social roles such as mother, teacher, or attorney. A woman's ethnic and gender identities are thus examples of group identities. In this category borderlands identities are those that include a straddling of social groups or domains that are constructed at a given time as socially divided such as hearing/deaf, Black/white, man/woman, and so on.

In addition to group identities, *personal identities* are the unique relationships between pairs of individuals, such as mother of Jamie, brother to Albert, or supervisor to Alex. Collective and personal identities are rarely, if ever, held singularly. Instead human beings—as stressed by Hume and William James—in operating in different social circles and domains, have often gained many different group and individual affiliations and group belongings such that they identify and function differently in different contexts. These multiple identities further combine in the mind with many other internalized elements, e.g., partial identities, isolated encoded beliefs, concepts, experiences, and social scripts. Combined this multiplicity of identities makes up what is referred to philosophically as human *subjectivity*, which can be defined as the totality of a person's embodied consciousness.

The totality of a person's subjectivity leads to the third type of identity, namely *self-identity*. As a term, self-identity is used in many ways, including some usages that refer to an essential pre-linguistic core-self. Here, however, self-identity refers to the unique identification and relationship that a person has with themselves—more specifically with the totality of the many and diverse aspects of themselves as an entire self. As such, self-identity encompasses one's personal self-understanding and relationship with the full collection of identities, partial-identities, fragments and isolated beliefs and concepts that they have gained over the course of their lifetime. It also includes their relationship to the current configuration of their identities, each of which may stand in different—and potentially shifting—relationships to each other. In sum it is a person's overall sense of self, and their view of themselves as a unique configuration of elements. This includes, how, *if at all*, they relate to inherited aspects of themselves internalized from social life. It is not always the case that people identify with inherited identities; for example, someone raised Catholic in childhood may *disidentify* with Catholicism in adulthood and this disidentification becomes part of their self-identity.

Thus self-identities are not static but rather always subject to revision. Self-identity is an evolving sense of self, self-understanding, and self-relatedness, the kind of self "in process" described by Kristeva.

Identity Schemes: The Social Sources and Formation of Borderlands Identities

In their three forms, identities are not static, pre-linguistic forms. They are internalized sets of social meanings, values, and practices that are associated with a given identity as it is socially constructed in a given place and time. As such, identities are in practice formed by the construction of a scheme of interrelated sets of meanings, values, and practices that are constructed to define a given identity. These constructed schemes are produced and circulated socially in and through the media, and major institutions including churches, schools, commercial enterprises, and the state. Informally the constructions of identities—literally what it means socially to have and practice a certain identity—also circulate through social groupings ranging from pairs of friends and nuclear families to large extended families, tribes, and ethnic groups.

These processes of identity formation are not only social and interactive, but they have a material physiological dimension as well. This factor is sometimes overlooked in feminist discussion, but it is significant for understanding both inner intersectionality and the political potential of revising one's borderlands identities as discussed by Anzaldúa (for elaboration of Anzaldúa's "mestiza way" of self craft, see Barvosa 2008: 175–206). Social psychology and neuroscience reveal that the meanings, values, practices, discourses, and other socially constructed aspects of identities are internalized by being physically encoded in the human mind as neural pathways. In turn, interconnects and associations among these neural pathways are formed in the physical brain. Ideas, events, and concepts are linked in social life and become associated and linked in the mind as elated neural pathways that often come to form a kind of web of intersecting ideas, beliefs, and other imprints in the brain. Generally, social psychologists and neuroscientists describe this ongoing process of the linking of encoded meaning in the brain with the catch phrase "what fires together, wires together." The resulting embodiment is a network of associated meanings that exist in the mind as webs intersecting materials socially constructed as related in a given way (Kahneman 2011) such as the dangerous group stereotype "young-black-male-criminal." When this web of interrelated materials is interpreted as relevant to a given context it is "activated" (subconsciously) as the material basis for thought, feeling, and action in a given moment and for as long as that scheme is relevant (Benaji and Greenwald 2013).

Identities can thus be seen within *embodied* consciousness as a socially encoded web of associations in the mind—as a neural web of interconnected meanings, values, and practices associated with what it means to identify in a given way in a given time and place. As such, identities can be conceptualized both theoretically and empirically as *identity schemes* (Barvosa 2008). Identity schemes, however, are not limited to cognitive expression in the mind, but also contain associated ideas, concepts, and practices, that express as feelings, thoughts, and also as material practices and even postures and bodily expressions and experiences. The latter include, for example, identity specific postures and socially constructed physical expressions, such as the postures and practices of a marching soldier or dancing ballerina. The encoding that contains the postures are activated as the frames of reference for thought, feeling, and action in moments when the identities as soldier and ballerina are relevant to the passing moment or "salient."

As social formations, identity schemes in general *are not innate or static aspects of the self*. Rather identity—when considered as a noun—refers to the specific, socially constructed, time, place, and culturally specific content of a given identity scheme, as it is prevails in a given time and place. The specific social constructions of the meanings, values, and practices femininity and feminine identity, for example, have changed over time containing both significant commonalities and extensive variations. Some variations are cross-cultural and admit of variations in expression from one woman or transwoman to the next. As such, identities are complex and socially encoded formations of the mind and body that are formed and may be transformed in and over time. These shifts may include alterations in norms, values, and linguistic and cultural practices. These changes may be brought about by external influence such as war, conflict, or technological change or through collective reimagining that occurs through social movements or other societal transformation or simple changes in fashion.

Moreover in terms of inner intersectionality, different identity schemes may intersect in three different types of associations that may be seen as three different moments of inner intersectionality: additive, overlapping, and crosscutting. First, identity schemes may be associated *additively* in that they come to share identity-related meanings, values, and practices. For example, white male identities and identity as financially affluent may contain separate meanings and practices that combine in the consciousness of wealthy white men to a degree that these elements of their multiple identities reinforce each other, perhaps even to the point that their two identities seem to be nested or converged rather than distinct.

Second, identity schemes may overlap and share common meanings, values or practices even though they are regarded as distinct and generally not overlapping. For example, linguistic diversity among immigrant groups in America is such that some immigrants share an accent with the mainstream Americans and others do not. The overlap in speech patterns may make it easier for some to include linguistically acculturated immigrants over those who have a residual accent on the basis of the overlap in the identity schemes of the person and the mainstream American identity scheme.

Third, socially constructed identity schemes may be *crosscutting* in meaning and influence. For example, Black men have racial and gender identity schemes involving meanings and practices of gender privilege *as men*, but meanings and practices of subordination *as Black*. However, at the time of this writing, youth identity in the US intersects in a crosscutting manner with male privilege and racial subordination, resulting in a disproportionate risk of harm to young Black men at the hands of law enforcement. This is likely attributed to the socially constructed frames of reference that often become constructed as part of law enforcement identities for some officers. When activated by events in context the neural script of "young-black-male-criminal" activates neurologically as part of that lived identity, also trigging neurally linked fear responses *whether or not such fear is warranted by facts of the context*. Likewise, to the extent that young Black men internalize the gendered social relations of hierarchy and risk, they too may have woven into their identities extreme fears related to social contexts involving law enforcement.

In the US, these dynamics have spawned a social movement and debate. Theoretically at least, problematic identity formations admit of being amended and transformed over time. Identity schemes are more fluid than is often thought. Socially, construction of identities and their relationships leaves people with borderlands identities facing unique identity-related challenges and also opportunities. However, to recognize the special opportunities and challenges of borderlands identities, in particular, it is important to first understand how all human identities are fluid and changeable in that they are not ultimately defined by the content of identity schemes, but rather by the daily practices of claiming and negotiating identities in social contexts.

Borderlands Identities and Social Change: Negotiating Identity Claims in Changing Times

Although the socially constructed content of identity schemes is important, it does not ultimately define identities. Instead, as shown in classic anthropology, identities are ultimately defined in and through the ever-ongoing daily processes of casting the boundaries of an identity and having identity claim acknowledged and accepted by others (Barth 1969). As such variation in content—and even role reversals—over time does not dilute or destroy the identity as long as both partners in the connection continue to cast/name and claim the boundary and declare themselves as partaking of that identity in and over time. Ethnic identities, for instance, frequently change over time in the meanings, values, and practices that comprise the specificity of the ethnicity. For example, in the late 1980s and 1990s for instance, in US Chicana/o culture, rap music from hip-hop culture was hybridized by Chicano youth to create Chicano rap. Many Chicana/o youth then claimed their ethnic identities through the new musical form. To the extent that those identity claims were accepted, Chicana/o ethnic identities were maintained but *not* through continuity of ethnic content. Instead Chicana/o ethnic identities endured via the everyday practice of casting identity boundaries and negotiating identity claims even in the face of cultural change. In the case of borderlands identities it is this kind of negotiation of supposedly mutually exclusive identities that is one of the most difficult challenges.

There are many other social cleavages among group identities that also produce contexts in which borderlands identities exist and must be navigated by border crossers (in Anzaldúan terms, *nepantleras*). In some cases, however, social changes over time might alter these cleavages and reduce the need to respond to them as persistent and troublesome divides. For example, María Lugones, a US Latina feminist philosopher who immigrated to the US from Latin America, has written about life as an activist in New Mexico in the 1990s as she negotiated her border identities as a lesbian and a Latina/Hispana. Working with and among poor Hispanos as an activist for social change (idiosyncratically, "Hispanos" was the preferred term among Spanish/Mexican heritage in New Mexico at the time of her writing). Lugones's experience taught her that to identify openly as a lesbian among Hispanos would mean her rejection even as an activist working for social change. Likewise, effective engagement in social activism among the local lesbian community at that time also required Lugones to deemphasize her ethnicity in order to have a voice and accepted presence in the queer community. As I have discussed elsewhere, Lugones negotiated these sets of social foreclosures as part of the border identity as a Latina, lesbian activist working for social change in social contexts that refuse the combination of the identities most meaningful to her (Barvosa 2008). In that refusal of others to acknowledge and accept her identities claims, Lugones is faced with the need to find ways to negotiate the implicit or explicit forms of threatened identity-related rejection, and find a way to integrate her own sense of self as including border identities. Today, however, in a time when strong majorities across the US accept and endorse LGBT equality, it is likely that Lugones might not face the same degree of intolerance as she did in previous decades as a Latina lesbian activist-scholar.

The Special Challenges and Potential of Borderlands Identities

As stressed above, borderlands identities are configurations of multiple identities that include elements socially constructed as mutually exclusive at a given time. Such divided identities are usually cast as an impassable social division such as woman/man, Jewish/Gentile, hearing/deaf. In some cases, however, these constructed divisions are encompassed in the life of a single person. For example, in his book *My Sense of Silence*, Lennard Davis (2000) describes his life as the hearing child of deaf parents. Davis was born and raised in deaf culture, immersed in and identified with that world, practicing its ways. Yet as a hearing person, his identity claims to be a member of the deaf community were at times rejected as a hearing person. His border identities as a hearing person who is also deaf identified require that he endure and negotiate the identity ascriptions that cast him in ways that do not acknowledge his own sense of self. In living across the border between the hearing and deaf worlds, Davis's identity claims and place in each of these social domains is ambiguous, and ever subject to rejection.

Many other social conflicts and cleavages also yield borderland identities of the kind described in this overview. Moreover, borderland identities may appear in any or all of the three major types of identities: group identities, unique personal identities, and self-identity. For example, gay, lesbian or bi-sexual children who are under threat of being disowned by a parent on the basis of their sexual orientation, have a borderland identities regard to their sexual identities (group identities) and their unique personal identities with their parents. This conundrum will certainly also take shape in their unique relationship to themselves or their self-identity. Hence social divides and conflicts that produce borderland identities may take many diverse forms.

In the face of societal, intrafamilial, or interpersonal rejection however, those with borderlands identities as described by Anzaldúa—and actually everyone as stressed by Kristeva—may seek to face and reconcile whatever internalized societal anger, hate, or fear that may exist in themselves. Those social inheritances may appear as patterns of self-disregard, personal blind spots and/or projected anger at others supposedly different from oneself. To consciously encounter and reconcile ourselves to our own diversity in this way can create within ourselves greater comfort, self-acceptance, and inner peace. In turn, becoming a peaceful presence in social life may in time feed back synergistically into social life contributing to greater societal peace with diversity of all kinds. As Anzaldúa stated: "I change myself, I change the world" (1987: 70). This is not an overly idealistic claim. At the time of this writing the increasing visibility of peaceful and self-confident transgender people in the US is fostering increasing recognition and protections for transgender persons in American society. As transgender-related societal meanings, values and practices shift, transgender—once regarded as a borderlands identity that united mutually exclusive aspects of gender—is becoming less contested over

215

time. Transgender-related social change remains incomplete and trans persons may still face refusal of their gender identity claims from one context to the next. Nevertheless the projects of self-remaking that social conflicts, inner diversity, and borderlands identities present *to all of us* are in keeping with longstanding feminist projects of peace and social justice—projects within which everyone may find a role to play.

Further Reading

Alcoff, Linda Martín (2006) *Visible Identities: Race, Gender, and the Self*, New York: Oxford University Press.

Barvosa, Edwina (2008) *Wealth of Selves: Multiple Identities, Mestiza Consciousness, and the Subject of Politics*, College Station, TX: Texas A&M University Press.

Flax, Jane (1990) *Thinking Fragments: Psychoanalysis, Feminism, and Postmodernism in the Contemporary West*, Berkeley, CA: University of California Press.

Kristeva, Julia (1991) *Strangers to Ourselves*, New York: Columbia University Press.

Meyers, Diana T. (1997) *Feminists Rethink the Self*, Boulder, CO: Westview Press.

Ortega, Mariana (2016) *In-Between: Latina Feminist Phenomenology, Multiplicity, and the Self*, Albany: SUNY Press.

Related Topics

Personal identity and relational selves (Chapter 18); psychoanalysis, subjectivity, and feminism (Chapter 19); the genealogy and viability of the concept of intersectionality (Chapter 28); through the looking glass: trans theory meets feminist philosophy (Chapter 32); feminist and queer intersections with disability studies (Chapter 33).

References

Alarcón, Norma (1994) "Conjugating Subjects: Heteroglossia of Essence and Resistance," in Alfred Arteaga (Ed.) *An Other Tongue: Nation and Ethnicity in the Linguistic Borderlands*, Durham, NC: Duke University Press, 125–138.

Alcoff, Linda Martín (2006) *Visible Identities: Race, Gender, and the Self*, New York: Oxford University Press.

Anzaldúa, Gloria (1987) *Borderlands/La Frontera: The New Mestiza*, San Francisco, CA: Aunt Lute Books.

Anzaldúa, Gloria and Keating, Ana Louise (2000) *Interviews/Entrevistas*, New York: Routledge.

_____ (2009) *The Gloria Anzaldúa Reader*, Durham, NC: Duke University Press.

Arana, Marie (2001) *American Chica: Two Worlds, One Childhood*, New York: The Dial Press.

Bammer, Angelika (Ed.) (1994) *Displacements: Cultural Identities in Question*, Indianapolis, IN: Indiana University Press.

Banaji, Mahzarin R. and Greenwald, Anthony G. (2013) *Blind Spot: Hidden Biases of Good People*, New York: Delacorte Press.

Barth, Fredrik (1969), *Ethnic Groups and Boundaries: The Social Organization of Cultural Difference*, New York: Little Brown & Co.

Barvosa, Edwina (2008) *Wealth of Selves: Multiple Identities, Mestiza Consciousness, and the Subject of Politics*, College Station, TX: Texas A&M University Press.

_____ (2011) "Mestiza Consciousness in Relation to Sustained Political Solidarity: A Chicana Feminist Interpretation of the Farmworker Movement," *Aztlán* 36(2): 121–154.

Beltrán, Cristina (2004) "Patrolling Borders: Hybrids, Hierarchies, and the Challenge of *Mestizaje*," *Political Research Quarterly* 57(4): 595–607.

Brison, Susan (2003) *Aftermath: Violence and the Remaking of the Self*, New Haven, CT: Princeton University Press.

Butler, Judith (1990) *Gender Trouble: Feminism and the Subversion of Identity*, New York: Routledge.

_____ (1993) *Bodies That Matter: On the Discursive Limits of "Sex,"* New York: Routledge.

Collins, Patricia Hill (1998) *Fighting Words: Black Women and the Search for Justice*, Minneapolis, MN: University of Minnesota Press.

Crenshaw, Kimberlé (1995) "Mapping the Margins: Intersectionality, Identity Politics, and Violence Against Women of Color," in Dan Danielson and Karen Engle (Eds.) *After Identity: A Reader in Law and Culture*, New York: Routledge, 332–354.

Davis, Lennard J. (2000) *My Sense of Silence: Memoirs of a Childhood with Deafness*, Urbana, IL: University of Illinois Press.

Flax, Jane (1990) *Thinking Fragments: Psychoanalysis, Feminism, and Postmodernism in the Contemporary West*, Berkeley, CA: University of California Press.

González, Deena J. (1997) "Chicana Identity Matters," *Aztlán: A Journal of Chicano Studies* 22(2): 123–38.

Kahneman, Daniel (2011) *Thinking, Fast and Slow*, New York: Straus & Giroux.

Keating, AnaLouise and González-López, Gloria (2011) *Bridging: How Gloria Anzaldúa's Life and Work Transformed Our Own*, Austin, TX: University of Texas Press.

Kristeva, Julia (1991) *Strangers to Ourselves*, New York: Columbia University Press.

Lugones, María (1990) "*Hispaneando y Lesbiando*: On Sarah Hoagland's *Lesbian Ethics*," *Hypatia* 5(3): 138–146.

Meyers, Diana T. (1997) *Feminists Rethink the Self*, Boulder, CO: Westview Press.

Ortega, Mariana (2016) *In-Between: Latina Feminist Phenomenology, Multiplicity, and the Self*, Albany: SUNY Press.

Walker, Rebecca (2001) *Black, White, and Jewish: Autobiography of a Shifting Self*, New York: Riverhead Books.

18

PERSONAL IDENTITY AND RELATIONAL SELVES

Susan J. Brison

It is a truism to say that selves exist in relation to other selves. What is more controversial is the view, defended by many feminist philosophers, that selves exist *only* in relation to other selves, that is, that they are fundamentally relational entities. On this view, persons or selves—I shall be using these terms interchangeably—are what Annette Baier has called "second persons." On her account, "[a] person, perhaps, is best seen as someone who was long enough dependent on other persons to acquire the essential arts of personhood. Persons are essentially second persons who grow up with other persons" (Baier 1985: 84). Another way of putting this is to say that selves are constituted in relationship with other selves.

Precursors to the idea of a relational self may be found in the history of philosophy: Aristotle, for example, held that, in cases of the most genuine friendship, a friend is a second self, and Hegel argued that selves become aware of themselves only though the presence of others. Feminist theorists have articulated, elaborated, and defended the view that the self is essentially relational in a variety of new ways in several philosophical subfields. While much feminist writing about the relational self has come in response to the individualism of the liberal political ideal of autonomy, different theories of the relational self have been developed for different philosophical purposes.

There is no one answer to the question "what is a self?" unless perhaps it is another question: "who wants to know?" The account of the self sought by someone looking for a criterion for personal identity that will enable us to re-identify individuals in changed conditions over time differs from that sought by someone who is interested in the nature of a person's mental states, or in moral personhood, or in how selves are socially constructed. In this chapter, I discuss different approaches to the idea of the relational self that have been taken by feminist philosophers working in ethics, social/political/legal philosophy, philosophy of mind, epistemology, and metaphysics.

In Western philosophical traditions, virtually all of those theorizing about the self were, until recently, white men whose primary preoccupations concerning personal identity were: (1) what makes someone the same unique individual over time—for example, possession of the same body or the same memories or character traits; and (2) what distinguishes human beings from non-human animals—for example, the ability to think or to use language or the possession of an immortal soul. Little attention was paid to the question of how we *become* persons.

Women and people of color have, historically, not been the ones doing the philosophizing and have been either left out or viewed as "other" and devalued to the extent we were seen as deviating from the (white male) norm. That philosophy has traditionally been done primarily by white men is not surprising, given that doing philosophy in the way it's traditionally been done is a luxury, not merely in the obvious material sense that it can be done only if one's basic needs are met, but also in a psychological sense. If one is dealing with racial, sexual, or other group-based harassment or assault, with discrimination, with all-consuming dependency care, or even with a surfeit of empathy that makes the suffering of *others* unbearably vivid and demoralizing, it is virtually impossible to have the sustained concentration needed to solve philosophical problems. Add to this the realities of epistemic and discursive injustice against marginalized groups plus the fact that indifference to real-world concerns is valorized and academically rewarded in the discipline of philosophy—and it is not surprising that certain demographics have been underrepresented in the discipline.

But as more people from underrepresented groups have entered the profession, the discipline has begun to change and new perspectives on the self have emerged. Women philosophers have experienced some form or other of feminine socialization as girls and continue to confront gender-based stereotypes as adults, and so are conscious of the constraints of societal expectations of us. Furthermore, because women have traditionally been the ones caring for children and for others who cannot care for themselves, we have been keenly aware of the extent to which people are dependent on other people for their very survival.

Care Ethics and the Relational Self

In ethics, as well as in social, political, and legal philosophy, the relational self has been defended as an alternative to what Lorraine Code has dubbed "autonomous man" who "is the undoubted hero of philosophical moral and political discourse" (1991: 73).

> Autonomous man is—and should be—self-sufficient, independent, and self-reliant, a self-realizing individual who directs his efforts toward maximizing his personal gains. His independence is under constant threat from other (equally self-serving) individuals: hence he devises rules to protect himself from intrusion.
>
> (1991: 77)

Code acknowledges that "autonomous man" is an abstraction, but one that nonetheless "occupies the position of a character ideal in Western affluent societies" (1991: 78).

Seyla Benhabib criticizes social contract theorists, such as Hobbes and Locke, for regarding the sphere of justice as "the domain wherein independent, male heads of household transact with one another," wheareas

> [a]n entire domain of human activity, namely, nurture, reproduction, love, and care . . . the woman's lot in the course of the development of modern, bourgeois society, is excluded from moral and political considerations, and confined to the realm of "nature."
>
> (Benhabib 1987: 160)

On this view, "in the beginning man was alone," as Benhabib construes Hobbes to be saying in this passage: "'Let us consider men . . . if but even now sprung out of the earth, and suddenly, like mushrooms, come to full maturity, without all kind of engagement to each other.'" Benhabib argues that this "vision of men as mushrooms"—an "ultimate picture of autonomy"—involves "the denial of being born of woman" and thus "frees the male ego from the most natural and basic bond of dependence" (1987: 161). As Christine Di Stefano points out:

> In the state of nature scene being considered here, which we might subtitle the Case of the Missing Mother, the issue is not whether infants would survive untended in the wild. Hobbes . . . never intended self-sufficiency in this sense . . . The issue concerns instead the ways in which early maternal and parental care provide a social, intersubjective context for the development of particular capacities in children—emotive, social and cognitive capacities.
>
> (1983: 638)

Such capacities are required in order for beings in the state of nature to be capable of forming and implementing contracts with one another, but no account is given, by Hobbes or other contract theorists, of how these capacities, which are essential to personhood, are acquired.

The concept of the relational self in feminist ethics has its roots in Carol Gilligan's (1982) psychological research on moral development, Nel Noddings's (1986) account of moral education, Nancy Chodorow's (1978) sociological and psychoanalytic study of children's identity formation, and Sara Ruddick's (1989) account of maternal thinking, drawn from women's lived experience as mothers (see Chapters 19 and 43 in this volume). In their groundbreaking anthology, *Women and Moral Theory*, Eva Feder Kittay and Diana T. Meyers (1987), along with other feminist philosophers, articulate and defend a relational view of the self underlying this distinctively feminist moral theory—the ethics of care.

Although some feminist theorists reject the concept of autonomy because of its perceived commitment to the ideal of the self-sufficient individual and its neglect of the facts—and values—of care and interdependence, others reconceive of autonomy as compatible with the view that persons are constituted by interpersonal relations to others. On this view, autonomy itself is relational, a competency or capacity developed only through interpersonal, societal, and institutional relations of the right sort (Brison 1997; 2000; Friedman 1997; 2003; Mackenzie and Stoljar, 2000; Meyers 1989; 1997; Nedelsky 2011; West 1997; see also Chapter 41 in this volume).

Some theorists have rejected the valorization of maternal thinking in an ethics of care because "participation in nurturing and mothering activities, and the social ideologies and institutions that support them, have been instrumental in maintaining women's subordination, oppression, and economic dependence" (Code 1991: 92). Catharine MacKinnon has argued that "[w]omen value care because men have valued us according to the care we give them" and that "we think in relational terms because our existence is defined in relation to men" (1987: 39).

Lorraine Code has proposed friendship as a preferable model for the relational self since "[f]riendships are created around an implicit recognition that persons are essentially (i.e., essential to their continued sense of self and well-being) 'second persons' throughout their lives." She considers it to be an advantage of the friendship model that it "does not even implicitly exclude women who do not mother or who do not mother well" (1991: 95). In addition, it can more easily acknowledge the value of this kind of relationship for men than can Ruddick's claim that men, too, can be mothers.

Taking friendship between equals as the paradigmatic human relation, however, obscures the fact that we are all, at some point or other in our lives, utterly dependent on others, requiring the care of those Eva Feder Kittay has labeled "dependency workers" (1999). Some of us are dependent on others throughout our lives. The self of a dependency worker, unlike "the self represented as participating as an equal in the social relations of liberal political theory," must be "a self through whom the needs of another are discerned, a self that, when it looks to gauge its own needs, sees first the needs of another" (Kittay 1999: 51). Kittay argues that a just society has an obligation to meet the needs of dependency workers, since "[w]hether or not it is desirable to be a relational, giving self, . . . the moral requirements of dependency work . . . make such a self indispensable" (1999: 51).

Anti-Individualism in Philosophy of Mind

Traditional philosophy of mind has presupposed an individualistic view of the self. As Naomi Scheman defines it, individualism is "the assumption that my pain, anger, beliefs, intuitions, and so on are particular, (in theory) identifiable states that I am in, which enter as particulars into causal relationships" (Scheman, 1983: 226). Scheman argues that individualism in philosophy of mind has been almost universally accepted because apparently it: (1) is demanded by physicalism; (2) follows from our assumed privileged access to our own inner states; and (3) is presupposed by liberal political ideology. In addition, she argues, it accords with male socialization and a male view of the self that is taken to be the norm.

On Scheman's alternative, relational, account of the mind, mental states, or the objects of psychology, are "objects only with respect to socially embodied norms" (1983: 228). As a result, "we are responsible for the meaning of each other's inner lives" (1983: 241).

On this view, referred to as "semantic externalism," meanings aren't in the head; they are not self-contained internal thoughts that get expressed to others via speech. The meanings of words are a function of their use by linguistic communities. So the contents of our thoughts are not in our heads, not introspectible, and not "up to us." Scheman argues that not only are meanings not in the head, but neither are such psychological states as emotions.

Although Scheman draws primarily on the semantic externalism of Tyler Burge (1979) and Hilary Putnam (1975) and a Wittgenstinian use theory of meaning in arguing against individualism in philosophy of mind, she also considers individualism to be "a piece of ideology," one "connected with particular features of the psychosexual development of males mothered by women in a patriarchal society, with the development of the ego and of ego-boundaries" (Scheman 1983: 226).

Scheman's view that such individualism is a piece of patriarchal ideology has its feminist critics. For example, Louise Antony (1995a; 1995b) argues that "[p]sychological individualism is perfectly compatible with and may even be required by feminist political theory" (1995a: 157). Scheman's responses to Antony's objections and those of other critics can be found in 1996a and 1996b.

It is important to note that many of us live, simultaneously, in different linguistic communities and cultural contexts, which, on a relational view of the self, has implications for who we are. For, as María Lugones writes, "[a]s outsiders to the mainstream, women of color in the US practice 'world'-travelling, mostly out of necessity" (1987: 3), having different attributes in different "worlds." On her view, one can inhabit more than one world at a time and, thus, can have and not have an attribute (e.g., playfulness) simultaneously. "In describing my sense of a 'world,'" Lugones writes, "I [am] offering something that is true to experience even if it is ontologically problematic," adding that "any account of identity that could not be true to the experience of outsiders to the mainstream would be faulty even if ontologically unproblematic" (1987: 11).

Another issue in philosophy of mind on which the idea of a relational self bears is that of extended cognition. Clark and Chalmers (1988) have argued for a kind of "active externalism" that goes beyond semantic externalism. On this view, the mind—the locus of cognition—extends beyond an individual's physical boundaries and can include artifacts such as notebooks and iPhones provided certain conditions are met (Clark 2008). As James Lindemann Nelson notes, "externalism allows, at least in principle, that our minds may extend not only into artifacts, but into other people as well" (2010: 235). Clark, Chalmers, and Nelson focus on extended cognition and the question of what beliefs a person can correctly be said to have, but, in addition, a person's emotions and other mental states can be seen to consist, at least in part, in relations to other persons. Sustained by such relations, even someone with advanced Alzheimer's disease can be "held" in personhood by those who know and care for her, in spite of severe mental decline (Lindemann 2010, 2014; Nelson 2010).

Personal Identity and Lived Experience

Philosophers—including those writing about something as personal as the self—have tended to agree with Bertrand Russell that

> the free intellect will value more the abstract and universal knowledge into which the accidents of private history do not enter, than the knowledge brought by the senses, and dependent, as such knowledge must be, upon an exclusive and personal point of view and a body whose sense-organs distort as much as they reveal.
>
> (1969: 160)

In contrast, feminist proponents of relational accounts of the self (including Baier 1985 and Held 1993) agree with critical race theorists, such as Charles Lawrence, Mari Matsuda, Richard Delgado, and Kimberlé Crenshaw (1993) that we all theorize from a positioned perspective—and many of us from multiple perspectives—and that it is important to acknowledge one's own background and experiences. This focus on the actual lives of real people has not only expanded the subject matter considered appropriate for philosophical analysis, but also introduced new methods such as consciousness-raising and the use of first-person narratives into philosophy. As Matsuda writes, "I can take on the cloak of the detached universal, but it is an uncomfortable garment. It is not me, and I do not do my best work wearing it" (1996: 14).

Traditional philosophical discussions of personal identity have tended to rely on either abstract reasoning about the nature of the self or, alternatively, thought experiments to test our intuitions about the criterion or criteria for whether a person continues to exist over time. As I note in "Outliving Oneself: Trauma, Memory, and Personal Identity,"

> Philosophers writing about the self, at least since Locke, have puzzled over such question as whether persons can survive the loss or exchange of their minds, brains, consciousness, memories, characters, and/or bodies. In recent years, increasingly gruesome and high-tech thought experiments involving fusion, fission, freezing, dissolution, reconstitution, and/or teletransportation of an individual have been devised to test our intuitions about who, if anyone, survives which permutations.
>
> (Brison, 1997: 13)

Kathleen Wilkes (1988) was, until recently, one of the few to argue that students of personal identity should eschew thought experiments and, instead, pay attention to scientific research on real people who undergo sometimes stranger-than-fiction transformations of the self. She takes a third-person approach to the self, arguing that we can gain insights into what it is to have a self by studying scientific findings. In contrast, I argue that paying attention to first-person narratives is essential for understanding the self. I pay particular attention to first-person narratives of survivors of trauma who frequently remark that they are not the same people they were before they were traumatized.

Of course, some traditional white male philosophers have purported to use first-person narratives—as did Descartes in his *Meditations*. His argument for his own existence as a thinking thing only works when stated in the first person. But, for Descartes, the *I* was fungible. Any *I* would do, because, qua thinking thing engaged in rational thought, each *I* was the same as every other.

What's different about the *I* in genuine first-person narratives in philosophy is that it is embodied, situated in multiple, ever-shifting contexts, so it *can't* speak for everyone. However, politically significant first person narratives (of discrimination, of oppression, of trauma) involve an *I* speaking *as* a member of a larger, politically significant group.

What led me to a relational view of the self was the experience of having a self shattered by being degraded by just one other person (in a context facilitating and perpetuating that degradation) and then rebuilt only with the help of other persons. In July of 1990, a man assaulted me while I was on a morning walk by myself on a country road in the south of France. He jumped me from behind, threw me into the underbrush, beat me, raped me, strangled me into unconsciousness several times, and then dragged me into a ravine, hit me on the head with a rock, and left me for dead (Brison, 2002).

For a while, it seemed to me that I had failed to survive the assault—that I had somehow managed to outlive myself. This didn't make any sense, but, then, at the time, nothing did. When, a few months after the assault, I sat down at my computer to write about it for the first time, all I could come up with was a list of paradoxes.

> Things had stopped making sense. I thought it was quite possible that I was brain-damaged as a result of the head injuries I had sustained. Or perhaps the heightened lucidity I had experienced during the assault remained, giving me a clearer, although profoundly disorienting, picture of the world.
>
> (Brison 2002: ix)

I wanted—*needed*—to know what a self was in order to figure out what had happened to my old one and whether I could get a new one. I was pretty clear that the old one was in pieces and could not be put back together again. In reading others' first-person accounts of trauma I realized I wasn't alone in feeling this. At the time, there were very few first-person narratives of rape, but there was a whole genre of testimonies by Holocaust survivors as well as third-person narratives by psychotherapists who treated them and other trauma survivors. I came to learn that survivors of trauma frequently remark that they are not the same people they were before they were traumatized.

Philosophers who have written about the self (with some notable exceptions, including Hume and Nietzsche) have tended to be confident that they *had* selves and to feel pretty good about them—good enough, anyway, that their chief concern was "how long can this good thing last?" Plato, in the *Phaedo*, portrays Socrates as taking the hemlock with equanimity, looking forward to his soul's continued existence after his self-administered execution. Descartes comforted himself with the thought that he was, essentially, a thinking thing who would survive the death of his body. More contemporary philosophers writing about the self have wanted to know whether the person one currently clearly is (and is obviously quite attached to) would continue to exist through transformations of various kinds.

My problem was quite the opposite: It seemed I had lost my self and not only was I not sure how to put it back together again or acquire a new one, I wasn't always entirely sure that carrying on—with a new or revamped self—would be a desirable or worthwhile endeavor. It was only after I lost my self that I felt a need to come up with a theory of the self. We so often learn about how things work by studying what happens when they break down, and there's nothing like having a self shattered to make you wonder just what it was you once had.

Following Judith Herman (1992) and others, I defined a traumatic event as one in which a person feels utterly helpless in the face of a force that is perceived to be life-threatening. The immediate psychological responses to such trauma include terror, loss of control, and intense fear of annihilation. Long-term effects include the physiological responses of hypervigilance, heightened startle response, sleep disorders, and the more psychological, yet still involuntary, responses of depression, inability to concentrate, lack of interest in activities that used to give life meaning, and a sense of a foreshortened future. When the trauma is of human origin and is intentionally inflicted, the kind I discussed in *Aftermath*, it not only shatters one's fundamental assumptions about the world and one's safety in it, but also severs sustaining connections between the self and the rest of humanity. Victims of human-inflicted trauma are reduced to mere objects by their tormenters: their subjectivity is rendered useless and viewed as worthless. As Herman observes, "The traumatic event thus destroys the belief that one can *be oneself* in relation to others" (1992: 53). Without this belief one can no longer *be oneself* even to oneself, since the self exists fundamentally in relation to others.

I argued that the undoing of a self in trauma—and the remaking of a self in trauma's aftermath—reveals the fundamentally relational and embodied nature of the self. As Catriona Mackenzie puts it "[t]o be a person is to be a temporally extended embodied subject whose identity is constituted in and through one's lived bodily engagement with the world and with others" (2009: 119). To see this, we need to adopt a first-person perspective on embodiment; our experienced bodies are not just biological entities, things we have or are attached to. Our lived bodies are not just objects for our examination; they are saturated with meaning and they are the grounds and limits of our agency.

Trauma survivors who claim not to be the same persons they once were don't typically lose their memories of their pasts. What they lose is a past that makes sufficient sense cognitively and is bearable enough emotionally to provide a basis for projecting themselves into the future. And yet they often eventually find ways to reconstruct themselves and carry on with reconfigured lives. Working through, or re-mastering, traumatic memory (in the case of *human*-inflicted trauma, anyway), I've argued, involves a shift from being the object or medium of someone else's (the perpetrator's) speech (or other expressive behavior) to being the subject of one's own. The act of bearing witness to the trauma can help to facilitate this shift, not only by reintegrating the survivor into a community, re-establishing connections essential to selfhood, but also by transforming traumatic memory into a narrative that can then be worked into the survivor's sense of self and view of the world.

Being able to carry on after a self-shattering event is facilitated by our being in the right sorts of relations to others. For, as Cheshire Calhoun notes,

> [o]ur having a reason to go on at all—our being "motivationally rooted" in our lives in such a way that we are propelled toward the future—may depend on our being able to sustain deep attachments [among other things].
>
> (2008: 197)

This is why traditional thought experiments analyzed by personal identity theorists may make no sense to those holding a relational view of the self. For what would be there, after arriving, via teletransportation in a distant galaxy? Even if one's intuition is that one would be numerically the same individual, why would one care about that person or look forward to being that person if none of the people one cared about would also be there?

Social Construction and Narrative Self-Constitution

Whereas traditional philosophical discussions of personal identity have focused on what Marya Schechtman (1996) calls the reidentification question—what makes a person numerically the same over time?—Schechtman and others have argued that the account of the self that can helpfully address our ethical and other practical concerns is one that answers the question "Who am I?" One such account, developed by Shechtman and others (Brison 1997; Butler 2003; Cavarero 2000), is that the self is a kind of narrative.

Although calling the self a narrative—or noting that it is constituted by some sort of narrative structure—might seem to suggest that individuals construct themselves *by* themselves in the solitary seclusion of a Cartesian dreamer, this is far from the case. If the self is a narrative, it is made up of social constructs and relations, out of words (whose meanings aren't in the head), tropes, schemas, and narrative trajectories. It is "discursively constructed," to use Sally Haslanger's terminology, which means that "it is (to a significant extent) the way it is because of what is attributed to it or how it is classified" (2012: 123). Although Haslanger's focus is on the discursive construction of social kinds (e.g., gender and race), her account is also relevant to our discussion of relational selves. For, as she notes, "[e]ach of us is socially constructed in this sense because we are (to a significant extent) the individuals we are today as a result of what has been attributed (and self-attributed) to us." She adds, however, that

> to say an entity is "discursively constructed" is not to say that language or dis-course brings a material object into existence de novo. Rather something in existence comes to have—partly as a result of having been categorized in a cer-tain way—a set of features that qualify it as a member of a certain kind or sort.
>
> (Haslanger 2012: 123; see also Chapter 13 in this volume)

To say that selves are socially constructed, however, is not to say that they don't exist. "The socially interconnected nature of human community, however, does not give a sufficient reason for denying the existence of selves," as Marilyn Friedman notes, for "[i]n the midst of social interconnection stands the curious character of embodiment" (2003: 32). Even though I am embodied in a particular body, however, I am a *self* by virtue of my relations to others—and I am the particular self I am by virtue of my relations to particular persons.

On my account, a self is an embodied, socially constructed narrative. On this view, selves are relational in Baier's sense of "second persons," able to be brought into exist-ence as persons only through interactions with a care provider. In addition, others pro-vide the self-in-formation with instruction in language and social norms and skills. Persons do not arise ex nihilo and cannot be generated from human beings—that is, biological entities—in isolation. Given that personhood is a social/legal/moral con-struct, this may be obvious.

I argue for the less obvious view that other persons also *constitute* me as who I am; that is, they participate in the ongoing process of my self-constitution. By "self-constitution," I mean, not the constitution of a self all by itself, but rather the process by which a self is constituted, however that happens. On my view, other selves are essential to this process. More specifically, what others do with words plays a crucial role in my self-constitution.

For example, how others use the term "woman" (and employ the concept *woman*) affects my self-constitution as a woman. If the concept of a woman is, among other things, the concept of someone who is rapeable with impunity, this is an inescapable part of my self-definition, whether I like it or not. I would go so far as to say that even those aspects of others' definition of "woman" of which I am not aware can affect *who I am*. For to the extent that we say (or conceive) anything about ourselves, we are using language to categorize ourselves as members of groups and as bearers of properties.

What I am arguing is that the way we are constructed is both constrained and facilitated by how others use the words (and images) we use to constitute ourselves. For example, it wasn't possible to constitute oneself as a homosexual before the term "homosexuality"—and the category it denoted—came into existence. And even the introductions of new labels *that don't apply to us* can change our identities. The existence of individuals who identify as transgender men and women changes the identity of cisgender men and women by giving rise to a new, cisgender identity (Shotwell and Sangrey 2009).

There are significant constraints on narrative self-construction, and self-reconstruction, and these have been discussed in (among other places) Schechtman (1996) and

Nelson (2001). The main obstacle to self-reconstruction after trauma that I focused on in *Aftermath* was the difficulty of re-establishing bonds of trust with others. But now it is clearer to me that even when one is able to re-establish trust with the help of empathic listeners, there are significant obstacles to overcome, namely the facticity of one's past—the brute facts about what happened, neurological constraints and linguistic constraints, including the fact that there is only a limited stock of tropes and metaphors and other narratives available with which to make sense of one's experience and the fact that the meanings of the words one uses in composing a narrative are socially constructed.

The first two obstacles to self-reconstruction, not only after a discrete traumatic event, but also in the face of ongoing oppression—the givenness of one's past and of one's neurochemistry—might seem to pose the most extreme, unyielding constraints on the narrative reconstruction of a self. But at least sometimes it is the third—the representational constraint imposed by the culturally available means of expression—that actually presents the most difficult obstacles for a trauma survivor to overcome.

Why might this be so? Strangely enough, to the extent that we are stories we tell ourselves, we are *not* in control of our self-definition, because the meanings of the words with which we construct our self-narratives are not in our heads, whereas, to the extent that we are our neurochemistry, we are (at least at times and to some extent) in control of our self-definition, provided we have at least the minimal motivation necessary to follow a therapeutic regimen of, say, taking medications (or meditating or exercising or using some other strategy to alter one's brain chemistry).

But, as noted above, we are not in control of the linguistic means with which we construct our selves narratively. This is another way in which we are fundamentally relational beings. How *other* people use words constrains our self-narratives.

Conclusion

Let me conclude by discussing two of the puzzles that remain for the view that selves are fundamentally relational. First, how are we to reconcile the view of the self as embodied with the view that it is socially constructed and embedded in larger structures? How is it that we are made up of both meanings and molecules (Brison 2002: 77–83)? This is not, however, a problem peculiar to the relational account of the self. It is nothing less than the intractable mind-body problem that vexes any account of the self.

Second, how are we to account for freedom in narrative self-constitution if the self—and the categories that make it up—are social constructs? If our selves are socially constructed, in ways that are, to a significant extent, out of our control, how do we account for our (admittedly constrained) ability to *choose* how to narratively constitute ourselves? How are we able to resist "oppressive self-concepts" (Khader 2011) and how can we narratively repair "damaged identities" (Nelson 2001)?

Nelson (2001) discusses the means by which what she calls "counterstories" can refigure personal identities. And although Serene Khader observes that "oppression marks people as particular types of beings; it shapes people's senses of who they are," she notes that even severely oppressed people are often able to respond with "internal resistance to oppressive self-concepts" (2011: 122). Even in oppressive societies, Khader argues, opportunities for cultivating positive self-images exist in what she calls "resistant social spaces" (2011: 124). This does not relieve others of the responsibility to eradicate oppression. On the contrary, it is, as Scheman urges, up to all of us to pay attention to "how we make each other up, especially across lines of privilege," and to "how we create the possibilities of meaningfulness in each other's lives" (1996a: 234).

Further Reading

Alcoff, Linda (2006) *Visible Identities: Race, Gender, and the Self*, New York: Oxford University Press.
Atkins, Kim and Mackenzie, Catriona (Eds.) (2008) *Practical Identity and Narrative Agency*, New York: Routledge.
Mackenzie, Catriona and Stoljar, Natalie (Eds.) (2000) *Relational Autonomy: Feminist Perspectives on Agency and the Social Self*, Oxford: Oxford University Press.
Meyers, Diana T. (Ed.) (1997) *Feminists Rethink the Self*, Boulder, CO: Westview Press.
Willett, Cynthia, Anderson, Ellie, and Meyers, Diana (2015) "Feminist Perspectives on the Self," *The Stanford Encyclopedia of Philosophy* (Fall 2015 Edition), Edward N. Zalta (Ed.) [online]. Available from: http://plato.stanford.edu/archives/fall2015/entries/feminism-self/.

Related Topics

The sex/gender distinction and the social construction or reality (Chapter 13); embodiment and feminist philosophy (Chapter 15); materiality: sex, gender, and what lies beneath (Chapter 16); feminism and borderlands identities (Chapter 17); psychoanalysis, subjectivity, and feminism (Chapter 19); epistemic injustice, ignorance, and trans experience (Chapter 22); speech and silencing (Chapter 23); through the looking glass: trans theory meets feminist philosophy (Chapter 32); feminist conceptions of autonomy (Chapter 41); feminist ethics of care (Chapter 43).

References

Antony, Louise (1995a) "Is Psychological Individualism a Piece of Ideology?" *Hypatia* 10: 154–174.
——(1995b) "Sisters, Please, I'd Rather Do It Myself: A Defense of Individualism in Feminist Epistemology," *Philosophical Topics* 23(2): 59–94.
Atkins, Kim (2008) "Narrative Identity and Embodied Continuity," in Kim Atkins and Catriona Mackenzie (Eds.) *Practical Identity and Narrative Agency*, New York: Routledge: 78–98.
Baier, Annette (1985) "Cartesian Persons," in *Postures of the Mind: Essays on Mind and Morals*, Minneapolis, MN: University of Minnesota Press: 74–92.
Benhabib, Seyla (1987) "The Generalized and the Concrete Other: The Kohlberg-Gilligan Controversy and Moral Theory," in Eva Feder Kittay and Diana T. Meyers (Eds.), *Women and Moral Theory*, Savage, MD: Rowman & Littlefield: 154–177.
Brison, Susan J. (1997) "Outliving Oneself: Trauma, Memory, and Personal Identity," in Diana T. Meyers (Ed.), *Feminists Rethink the Self*, Boulder, CO: Westview Press: 12–39.
——(2000) "Relational Autonomy and Freedom of Expression," in Catriona Mackenzie and Natalie Stoljar (Eds.), *Relational Autonomy: Feminist Perspectives on Agency and the Social Self*, Oxford: Oxford University Press: 280–299.
——(2002) *Aftermath: Violence and the Remaking of a Self*, Princeton, NJ: Princeton University Press.
Burge, Tyler (1979) "Individualism and the Mental," *Midwest Studies in Philosophy* 4: 73–121.
Butler, Judith (2003) *Giving an Account of Oneself: A Critique of Ethical Violence*, Amsterdam: Koninklijke Van Gorcum.
Calhoun, Cheshire (2008) "Losing One's Self," in Kim Atkins and Catriona Mackenzie (Eds.), *Practical Identity and Narrative Agency*, New York: Routledge: 193–211.

Cavarero, Adriana (2000) *Relating Narratives: Storytelling and Selfhood*, trans. by Paul A. Kottman, New York: Routledge.

Chodorow, Nancy (1978) *The Reproduction of Mothering: Psychoanalysis and the Sociology of Gender*, Berkeley, CA: University of California Press.

Clark, Andy (2008) *Supersizing the Mind: Embodiment, Action, and Cognitive Extension*, New York: Oxford University Press.

Clark, Andy and David Chalmers (1998) "The Extended Mind," *Analysis* 58: 7–19.

Code, Lorraine (1991) "Second Persons," in *What Can She Know? Feminist Theory and the Construction of Knowledge*, Ithaca, NY: Cornell University Press, 71–109.

Di Stefano, Christine (1983) "Masculinity as Ideology in Political Theory: Hobbesian Man Considered," *Women's Studies International Forum* 6: 633–644.

Friedman, Marilyn (1997) "Autonomy and Social Relationships: Rethinking the Feminist Critique," in Diana T. Meyers (Ed.), *Feminists Rethink the Self*, Boulder, CO: Westview Press: 40–61.

—— (2003) *Autonomy, Gender, Politics*, New York: Oxford University Press.

Gilligan, Carol (1982) *In a Different Voice: Psychological Theory and Women's Development*, Cambridge, MA: Harvard University Press.

Haslanger, Sally (2012) *Resisting Reality: Social Construction and Social Critique*, New York: Oxford University Press.

Held, Virginia (1993) *Feminist Morality: Transforming Culture, Society, and Politics*, Chicago, IL: University of Chicago Press.

Herman, Judith Lewis (1992) *Trauma and Recovery*, New York: Basic Books.

Khader, Serene (2011) *Adaptive Preferences and Women's Empowerment*, New York: Oxford University Press.

Kittay, Eva Feder (1999) *Love's Labor: Essays on Women, Equality, and Dependency*, New York: Routledge.

Kittay, Eva Feder and Diana T. Meyers (Eds.) (1987) *Women and Moral Theory*, Savage, MD: Rowman & Littlefield: 154–177.

Lawrence, Charles, Mari Matsuda, Richard Delgado, and Kimberlé Crenshaw (1993) *Words That Wound: Critical Race Theory, Assaultive Speech, and the First Amendment*, Boulder, CO: Westview Press.

Lindemann, Hilde (2010) "Holding One Another (Well, Wrongly, Clumsily) in a Time of Dementia," in Eva Feder Kittay and Licia Carlson (Eds.), *Cognitive Disability and Its Challenge to Moral Philosophy*, Malden, MA: Wiley-Blackwell: 161–169.

—— (2014) *Holding and Letting Go: The Social Practice of Personal Identities*, New York: Oxford University Press.

Lugones, María (1987) "Playfulness, 'World'-Travelling, and Loving Perception," *Hypatia* 2: 3–19.

Mackenzie, Catriona (2009) "Personal Identity, Narrative Integration and Embodiment," in Sue Campbell, Letitia Meynell, and Susan Sherwin (Eds.), *Embodiment and Agency*, University Park, PA: The Pennsylvania State University Press: 100–125.

Mackenzie, Catriona and Stoljar, Natalie (Eds.) (2000) *Relational Autonomy: Feminist Perspectives on Agency and the Social Self*, Oxford: Oxford University Press.

MacKinnon, Catharine A. (1987) *Feminism Unmodified: Discourses on Life and Law*, Cambridge, MA: Harvard University Press.

Matsuda, Mari (1996) *Where Is Your Body? and Other Essays on Race, Gender, and the Law*, Boston, MA: Beacon Press.

Meyers, Diana T. (1989) *Self, Society, and Personal Choice*, New York: Columbia University Press.

—— (1997) "Introduction," in Diana T. Meyers (Ed.), *Feminists Rethink the Self*, Boulder, CO: Westview Press, 1–11.

Nedelsky, Jennifer (2011) *Law's Relations: A Relational Theory of Self, Autonomy, and Law*, New York: Oxford University Press.

Nelson, Hilde Lindemann (2001) *Damaged Identities: Narrative Repair*, Ithaca, NY: Cornell University Press.

Nelson, James Lindemann (2010) "Alzheimer's Disease and Socially Extended Mentation," in Eva Feder Kittay and Licia Carlson (Eds.), *Cognitive Disability and Its Challenge to Moral Philosophy*, Malden, MA: Wiley-Blackwell: 225–236.

Noddings, Nel (1986) *Caring: A Feminine Approach to Ethics*, Berkeley, CA: University of California Press.

Putnam, Hilary (1975) "The Meaning of 'Meaning,'" *Minnesota Studies in the Philosophy of Science* 7: 131–193.

Ruddick, Sara (1989) *Maternal Thinking: Toward a Politics of Peace*, Boston, MA: Beacon Press.

Russell, Bertrand (1969) *The Problems of Philosophy*, New York: Oxford University Press.

Schechtman, Marya (1996) *The Constitution of Selves*, Ithaca, NY: Cornell University Press.

Scheman, Naomi (1983) "Individualism and the Objects of Psychology," in Sandra Harding and Merrill B. Hintikka (Eds.), *Discovering Reality: Feminist Perspectives on Epistemology, Metaphysics, Methodology, and Philosophy of Science*, Dordrecht: Reidel: 225–244.

—— (1996a) "Feeling Our Way toward Moral Objectivity," in Larry May, Marilyn Friedman, and Andy Clark (Eds.), *Mind and Morals: Essays on Cognitive Science and Ethics*, Cambridge, MA: The MIT Press: 221–236.

—— (1996b) "Reply to Louise Antony," *Hypatia* 11: 150–153.

Shotwell, Alexis and Trevor Sangrey (2009) "Resisting Definition: Gendering through Interaction and Relational Selfhood," *Hypatia* 24: 56–76.

West, Robin (1997) *Caring for Justice*, New York: New York University Press.

Wilkes, Kathleen V. (1988) *Real People: Personal Identity without Thought Experiments*, New York: Oxford University Press.

19

PSYCHOANALYSIS, SUBJECTIVITY, AND FEMINISM

Kelly Oliver

Introduction

In this chapter I will argue that traditional psychoanalytic theory has been instructive in formulating a developmental theory of subjectivity—that is, of our senses of ourselves as selves with agency—but it has neglected the social context of subjects and their subject positions—that is their historical and social positions in their culture—which is sometimes off-putting to feminist theorists. Nonetheless, there are various reasons why psychoanalysis can be extremely useful to feminists who are interested in subjectivity and in the relationships of social, historical, and political forces to subject formation. For at least the last twenty years feminist thinkers such as Luce Irigaray, Julia Kristeva, Teresa Brennan, Jane Gallop, Nancy Chodorow, Judith Butler, and Cynthia Willett—among others—have grappled with Freudian psychoanalysis in an attempt to bring its central insights into contemporary feminist contexts.

Certainly subjects, subjectivity, and agency only ever exist in political and social contexts that affect them in their constitution. One's social position and history profoundly influence one's very sense of oneself as an active agent in the world. Yet the contradictions and inconsistencies in historical and social circumstances guarantee that we are never completely determined by our subject position or our social context. It is possible to develop a sense of agency in spite of or in resistance to an oppressive social situation. When the social context provides positive images—figurative and otherwise—with which one can identify, then one's sense of agency and of oneself as a subject are supported within the social sphere. But when the only available images are demeaning, then it can be difficult to sustain a sense of one's active agency and self-worth. Ultimately, our experience of ourselves as subjects is maintained in the tension between our subject positions and our subjectivity.

Subjectivity and Subject Positions

Although Sigmund Freud, the founder of psychoanalysis, acknowledges the effect of social conditions on the psyche, he and his followers rarely consider how those social conditions become the conditions of possibility for psychic life and subject formation outside of the family drama. Like Freud, some contemporary psychoanalytic theorists, including object relations theorists, consider the social to be founded on the relationship between the infant and its caregiver; the social, then, is defined as a relation between two people. But there is another social dimension to consider—the larger socio-historical context and political economy within which that relationship between two develops. Although "object relations" theorists, especially feminists, do consider the ways in which patriarchal culture affects the development of gendered subjects, too often they reduce the psychic dimension to sociological facts about the gender of care-takers and simple imitation of gender roles. For example, this is true of Nancy Chodorow's early work in *The Reproduction of Mothering* (1978) in which, ultimately, she proposes that patriarchal gender roles are perpetuated through women mothering and men being breadwinners. Likewise Carol Gilligan's groundbreaking early work began what is called "care ethics," now so prominent in feminist debates over ethics. Gilligan's thesis that men and women are socialized differently, and therefore develop different moral attitudes, is heavily reliant—like Chodorow's theory—on the fact that most caregivers are women (Gilligan 1982). While these theorists consider subject position, then, they give simplified accounts of subjectivity. It is important to give a more rich and nuanced account of both subject position and subjectivity. Psychoanalysis combined with social theory can help us to do that.

The distinction between subjectivity and subject position is, as I mentioned above, the difference between one's sense of oneself as a self with agency and one's historical and social position in one's culture. Subject positions, although mobile, are constituted in our social interactions, and our positions within cultures and contexts; history and circumstance govern them. Subject positions are our relations to the finite world of human history and relations—the realm of politics. Subjectivity, on the other hand, is experienced as our sense of agency and responsiveness, which is constituted in the encounter with otherness. And although subjectivity is logically prior to any possible subject position, in our experience they are always profoundly interconnected. This is why our experience of our own subjectivity is the result of the productive tension between finite subject position and the infinite response-ability of the structure of subjectivity itself.

By *subjectivity*, then, I mean one's sense of oneself as an "I," as an agent. By *subject position* I mean one's position in society and history as developed through various social relationships. The structure of subjectivity is the structure that makes taking oneself to be an agent (or a self) possible. This structure is a *witnessing* structure because it is founded on the possibility of address and response; it is a fundamentally dialogic struc-ture (in the broadest sense of the term "dialogic"). Subject position, on the other hand, is the particular sense of one's kind of agency, so to speak, that comes through one's social position and historical context. While distinct, subject position and subjectivity are also intimately related. For example, if you are a black woman within a racist and sexist culture, then your subject position as oppressed could undermine your subjectiv-ity, your sense of yourself as an agent. If you are a white man within a racist and sexist culture, then your subject position as privileged could shore up your subjectivity and promote your sense of yourself as an agent. Of course, usually social situations are not so black and white, but rather gray. And, among other things, psychoanalysis teaches us that identity, whatever the situation, is always ambiguous and often ambivalent.

The *subject* is thus a dynamic yet stable structure, which results from the interaction between two sets of forces: finitude, being, and history (subject position) at the one pole and infinity, meaning, and historicity (subjectivity) at the other. Architects and engineers have worked with the principle of tension-loaded structures that use the tension as support. A classic example is the Brooklyn Bridge. We could say that the subject is a tension-loaded structure, but its flexibility makes it more like what architects call a *tensile structure*. The stability of tensile structures is the result of opposing forces pulling in two directions, through which a membrane's double curvature receives its structure and resistance. Subjectivity is analogous to the structure and resistance that result from a membrane or skin being stretched in two directions and held together by tension. The two axes of force whose tension supports the subject are subject position and subjectivity.

One's sense of oneself as a subject with agency is profoundly affected by one's social position. Indeed, we cannot separate subjectivity from subject position; any theory of subjectivity—whether it is psychoanalytic, phenomenological, the result of critical theory, or post-structuralist, etc.—must consider subject position. While Freudian psychoanalytic theory has addressed itself to questions of subjectivity and subject formation, traditionally it has done so without considering subject position, or more significantly the impact of subject position on subject formation. Even some recent applications of psychoanalysis to the social context of subject formation have not reformulated the very concepts of psychoanalysis such that they account for, or explain, how subjects form within particular kinds of social contexts. Instead they apply psychoanalytic concepts in order to diagnose certain kinds of psychic or social formations (see, e.g., Lane 1998). We need more than an application of psychoanalytic concepts to social institutions or psychic formations in order to explain the effects of oppression on the psyche. To explain why so many people suffer at the core of their subjectivity and in their concomitant sense of agency when they are "abjected," excluded, or oppressed by mainstream culture, we need a psychoanalytic social theory that reformulates psychoanalytic concepts *as* social concepts. We need a psychoanalytic social theory that is based on social concepts of subject formation, and that considers how subjectivity is formed and deformed within particular types of social contexts.

Theories that do not consider subject position and the role of social conditions in subjectivity and subject formation not only cover over differential power, but also cover over the differential subjectivities that are produced within those power relations. Without considering subject position, we assume that all subjects are alike, we level differences, or—like traditional psychoanalysis—we develop a normative notion of subject-formation based on a particular group—traditionally, white European men. Instead, a psychoanalytic theory of oppression must consider the role of subject position in subject formation, which is to say the relationships between subject position and subjectivity.

Most psychoanalytic models of subjectivity and subject formation, including both ego psychology and object relations theories, suppose that there is a primary struggle between the individual and the social or others that is constitutive of subjectivity. For example, in *The Bonds of Love* (1988), Jessica Benjamin suggests that the infant develops its individuality and autonomy in a Hegelian master–slave type dialectic with its mother; Axel Honneth (1996), following Benjamin, also imagines relations with others as a constant struggle for recognition; and Judith Butler (1997) describes all subject formation as subjugation. These theorists propose that subjectivity develops through alienation from and/or subjection to the social realm. Likewise most nineteenth- and twentieth-century psychoanalytic theory and continental philosophy (including existentialism, poststructuralism, deconstruction, and critical theory) are based on, or presuppose, an antagonistic relationship between self and other, between subject and object, between individual and society. Contemporary French philosophy (Michel Foucault, Emmanuel Levinas, Gilles Deleuze, Jacques Derrida, Luce Irigaray) has been an attempt to decenter the subject and move away from a subject-centered philosophy toward a relational or other-centered philosophy. These Post-Hegelian theorists—Freudians and post-Freudian psychoanalytic theorists (including object relations theorists), phenomenologists, and critical theorists—recognize the intersubjectivity of subjectivity, but they have not taken the relationality of subjectivity to its limit. To do so would mean going beyond intersubjectivity and admitting that there *is* no subject or individual to engage in a relationship with another subject—to engage in an intersubjective relationship—prior to relationality itself. (For an excellent analysis of how and why primary relationships are not intersubjective, see Willett 1995.)

Relationality is primary. This means that subjectivity is not the result of one autonomous subject in relation with another, or two self-consciousnesses encountering each other and looking for mutual recognition—this can only come later, after the foundation of subjectivity has been established, if only provisionally. Representation, language, and other non-linguistic visceral and more bodily forms of communication and meaning always mediate this relationality—it is always mediated by our attempts to respond. Responsivity is thus both the prerequisite for subjectivity and one of its definitive features. Subjectivity is constituted through response, responsiveness or response-ability and not the other way around (see Oliver 2001). We do not respond because we are subjects; rather, responsiveness and relationality make subjectivity and psychic life possible in the first place. In this sense, response-ability precedes and constitutes subjectivity, which is why the structure of subjectivity is fundamentally ethical. We are by virtue of our ability to respond to others, and therefore we have a primary obligation to our founding possibility, response-ability itself. We have a responsibility to open up rather than close off the possibility of response, both from others and ourselves.

The Unconscious, Sublimation, and Meaning

If Freud normalizes a white male European subject, and we risk perpetuating this normalization by using his concepts without transforming them, then why turn to psychoanalytic theory at all to discuss gender and the effects of sexism on the psyche? Even if we could do away with the prejudice of Freud's nineteenth-century theories and their twentieth-century versions, psychoanalysis still deals with individuals at odds with the social, so what can feminism gain from turning to psychoanalysis? There are at least two primary facets of psychoanalysis that make it crucial for social theory in general, and feminist theory in particular: the centrality of the notion of the unconscious and the importance of sublimation as an alternative to repression. Both of these facets come to bear in important ways on the fact that all of our relationships are mediated by meaning—that we are beings who mean. As beings that mean, our experiences are both bodily and mental. Unconscious drive force or energy operates between *soma* (body) and psyche. We could say that our being is brought into the realm of meaning through unconscious drive energies and their affective representations.

The psychoanalytic concept most appropriate to a discussion of unconscious drive energy making its way into the realm of meaning is sublimation. Although this notion remains underdeveloped in Freud's writings (Freud supposedly burned his only paper on sublimation thus subjecting it to literal sublimation by fire), and it has been used without much further development since, it is central to social theory, especially to a social theory of oppression and sexism. We need a theory that explains how we articulate or otherwise express our bodies, experiences, and affects, all of which are fluid and energetic, in some form of meaningful signification so that we can communicate with others. Oppression and sexism undermine the ability to sublimate by withholding or foreclosing the possibility of articulating and thereby discharging bodily drives and affects. The bodies and affects of those marginalized have already been excluded as "abject" from the realm of proper society.

The colonization of psychic space operates by undermining the ability to sublimate. This is why Freud concludes that women are less able to sublimate than men. But if women are less able to sublimate than men it is not because of their anatomy, psychology, or individual pathologies, but rather because of social repression and the lack of social support required for sublimation. Sublimation is the hallmark of subjectivity, such that an impaired ability to sublimate undermines agency and ultimately leads to depression and melancholy—which, it could be argued, is why within patriarchal cultures women are more likely to be diagnosed as depressed or melancholy than men. The pathologization of women's depression covers over the social and institutional causes for that symptomology. Patriarchal culture continues to devalue and debase women and girls in ways that colonize psychic space by undermining the possibility of sublimation and meaning-making.

Sublimation is necessary for beings to enter the realm of meaning. The first acts of meaning become available through the sublimation of bodily impulses into forms of communication. Moreover, sublimation allows us to connect and communicate with others by making our bodies and experiences meaningful; we become beings who mean by sublimating our bodily drives and affects. Sublimation, then, is necessary for both subjectivity (or individuality) and community (or sociality). Sublimation is the lynchpin of a psychoanalytic social theory, for sublimation makes idealization possible. And without idealization we can neither conceptualize our experience nor set goals or ideals for ourselves. Without the ability to idealize, we cannot imagine our situation otherwise, which is to say, without idealization we cannot resist domination. Sublimation and idealization are necessary not only for psychic life but also for transformative and restorative resistance to racist oppression. Sublimation and idealization are the cornerstones of our mental life, yet they have their source in bodies, bodies interacting with each other. Sublimation is possible through the social relationality of bodies. But in an oppressive culture that abjects, excludes, or marginalizes certain groups, or types, of people by demeaning them, sublimation and idealization can become the privilege of dominant groups. Psychoanalytic notions of sublimation and idealization thus need to be transformed into social concepts.

Subjectivity develops through a process of sublimation, of elevating bodily drives and their affective representations to a new level of meaning and signification. Sublimation is the ongoing process of subjectivity and signification; it is the basis for psychic life insofar as we are beings who mean. In addition, sublimation always and only takes place in relation to others and the Other, which is the meaning into which each individual is born. Sublimation in the constitution of subjectivity is analogous to sublimation in chemistry, which is defined as a chemical action or process of subliming or converting a solid substance by means of heat into a vapor, which resolidifies upon cooling. The process of sublimation transforms bodily drives and affects that seem solid and intractable into a dynamic vapor, which liberates the drives and affects from repression (specifically the repression inherent in oppression) and discharges them into signifying systems, which re-solidify them. This process continues from birth to death without end. Because we can never fully "speak our bodies" or our experiences, we continue to try. We continue to speak and attempt communication precisely because we never succeed, which is not to say that we completely fail. On the contrary, we not only fill our own lives with meaning through sublimation but also make communication with others possible, if always tenuous. The process must continue because the bodily drives and affects are fluid and like vapors dynamic and volatile; therefore they cannot be fixed or re-solidified in signification without a remainder or excess. But this excess is not an alienating lack but is precisely what motivates us to continue to commune. This excess is the unconscious itself, which can never be fully brought to consciousness—that is to say, the singularity of each individual.

Without accounting for the unconscious processes inherent in sublimation and thereby necessary to become beings that mean, we risk falling into the all too popular discourse of autonomous self-governed individuals, which covers over the way in which autonomy, self-governance, and individuality were formed. This discourse erases the unconscious processes by virtue of which we become subjects with a sense of agency. We are not born with feelings of autonomy and self-governance. Rather, these are the effects of unconscious processes of sublimation and idealization. Autonomy, sovereignty and individuality are effects—by-products if you will—and not causes of becoming a being who means, of becoming subjectivity.

If we analyze the social merely in terms of bodies and behaviors without accounting for the unconscious, we cannot fully explain the contradictory effects of oppression. Indeed, in order to explain the bodies and the behaviors of those oppressed, not to mention their oppressors, we need to account for the unconscious effects of oppression. We need to understand how oppression causes depression, shame, and anger. But only a theory that incorporates an account of the unconscious can explain the dynamic operations of the affects of oppression. In order to understand the relationship between oppression or social context and affect, we need to postulate the existence of the unconscious. Without this postulation, we become complicit with those who would blame the victim, so to speak, for her own negative affects. Even if sociological or psychological studies demonstrate a higher incidence of depression, shame, or anger in particular groups, this information cannot be interpreted outside of social context and without consideration of subject position and subject formation. Certainly, affective life is caught up in one's sense of oneself as a subject and an agent. And oppression and the affects of oppression undermine subjectivity and agency such that even those very affects become signs of inferiority or weakness rather than symptoms of oppression.

In other words, it is only by postulating the unconscious that we can explain why many people who are in some way excluded, oppressed, or marginalized at some level blame themselves for their condition. In general, our culture blames individuals rather than social institutions for negative "personality traits" and "flaws." The psychoanalytic notion of the super-ego is useful in diagnosing how and why those who are marginalized internalize the very values that abject and oppress them. Without the psychoanalytic notion of the unconscious, we could not adequately explain the conflicting, and especially the self-destructive, desires of those marginalized. Even the Marxist notion of "false consciousness" implies not only that we are not transparent to ourselves, but also that there are parts of our mental lives that we repress or cannot access without intervention.

There is a complicated relationship between cultural values and an individual's sense of herself as an agent; this relationship goes beyond the internalization of abject images. The internalization of abject images in turn results in ambivalence towards one's own personal and group identity. It also results in ambivalence at the level of one's desires. This is to say, oppression and sexism can lead women and girls to embrace patriarchal traditions and values even as those very values demean them. For example, even some feminists have embraced the notion that women are more caring than men, and that women's nurturing is definitive of women's value. While there is no denying that caring and nurturing are essential values for human existence, it is also true that caring and nurturing are not essential to, or necessarily biologically determined in, women and girls.

Some feminists have argued that women bear the affective or emotional burdens for men in an unequal affective division of labor. As Sandra Bartky (1990) puts it, women feed egos and tend emotional wounds. Like Bartky, Teresa Brennan (1992) describes this emotional labor as feeding the masculine ego and self-esteem by direct-ing attention toward it and away from oneself. And, Gayatri Spivak (1999) claims, the civilizing mission rests on the foreclosure of affects, which are then projected onto the oppressed, who are expected to carry the affective burden for dominant culture. This denial of unwanted affects is not so much a projection as a transfer onto, or injection of, affects into those who are marginalized within dominant society. Philosophers have long associated lack of control over emotions with a lack of reason, and lack of reason with a lack of humanity. Affects are associated with the irrational and barbaric, in a complicated movement through which they are transferred onto the abjected other and at once become signs or symptoms of that abjection. They are further disavowed by the foreclosure of their articulation by those who are forced to carry them. Even main-stream culture's rage over difference—which should be met with anger by those whose difference is abjected—is transferred to those who are marginalized, who are forced to carry it. Their resistance, then, is seen as a symptom of their irrational monstrous rage, while the domination, oppression, and abuse against which that resistance was directed (perhaps misdirected) are normalized and naturalized as rational self-defenses against monstrous evil or disease in order to maintain proper order.

In terms of psychoanalytic theory, those who are marginalized within culture are subject to and interiorize a cruel and punishing super-ego, which excludes them as abject. The super-ego of dominant culture judges them inferior and defective. This harsh super-ego maintains the good upon which dominant values rest by projecting its opposite onto those marginalized and excluded; they become evil. They are expected to carry the burden of evil, sickness, weakness, and dejection for the entire culture. They become the scapegoats of the dominant super-ego. But this super-ego and its good are not only self-contradictory but also self-destructive, and therefore necessarily leave open the possibility of resistance.

Ironically, those who are marginalized seek love and recognition from the very cul-ture that rejects them as inferior. The dominant values with which someone is raised cannot but affect her; she cannot but internalize those values as valuable, even if they devalue her. The contradiction of valuing what devalues oneself can lead to feelings of inferiority, shame, and depression—or it can lead to reflection, resistance, and revolt. Anger and aggression redirected outward or sublimated into creative expression can renew agency and self-esteem. Indeed, feelings of shame and discrimination can become the basis for alternative communities and alternative modes of expression. Eve Sedgwick concludes that because shame is constitutive of identity and not just part of someone's personality, and because shame is performative, it need not be toxic but rather can become transformative (2002: 21). Those who are excluded or abjected because of their race, sex, gender, sexuality, or class have to negotiate shame as an affect that is constitutive of their identities. This negotiation can lead to depression, but it can also lead to transformation, humor, solidarity, or political action.

Without social support and positive self-images available in culture girls, women, and those who are marginalized suffer from the colonization of psychic space, which can result in the inability to sublimate, and ultimately the inability to find or create meaning in their lives. Without this accepting social support, psychic space can become atrophied and impassable. Drives and affects, one's bodily experience itself, devalued in culture, become locked in some unnamable crypt, which either makes of the psyche a prison that confines or immobilizes affects and experience, on the one hand, or flattens psychic space, on the other. In either case, drives and affects—the very passions that give meaning to life and love—become cut off from words and representations. One necessary antidote, if not the cure, for sexism, then, is to have, find, or create the social space within which to articulate women's and girls' drives and affects as positive, lovable, and loved, and thereby supporting of psychic space.

On the other hand, lack of social support can lead to feelings of emptiness, incompleteness, and worthlessness; at the extreme, the lack of social support can lead to the split between words and affects that psychoanalyst Julia Kristeva (1989) identifies with the depressive position. Within patriarchal cultures in which women's affects are not valued, it is no surprise that we lack the social space in which these affects can be sublimated or discharged. Women's experience generally, and women's depression more specifically, remain subterranean within dominant discourses (for information on rates of depression in women, see, for example, Peden *et al.* 2000; Kessler 2003; and Noble 2005). Therefore the depressed woman has given up on finding the words to discharge or manifest her affects. The silence, especially women's silence, which so often accompanies depression, is a socially proscribed silence and its cause. Some, if not all, of women's depression should be diagnosed as social melancholy rather than individual pathology, or merely biological chemical imbalance. The structure of psychic space through which sublimation is possible depends upon the connection between words and affects. It depends upon a primary identification with the meaning of language, which is to say the operation of making meaning one's own through a process of assimilation that allows nourishment for both the body and for the soul or psyche.

Indeed, making meaning for oneself is the seat of subjectivity and agency; and this is what oppression attempts to take away from those oppressed. Exclusion operates most effectively by preventing the assimilation of authority that legitimates the individual and authorizes her agency. This authorization is a prerequisite for the capacity to sublimate, through which an individual makes meaning her own and thereby gains a sense of belonging to the community. Yet in spite of oppression, empowered subjectivity and agency are possible for those marginalized within mainstream culture, by virtue of their own resistance and revolt against oppression. Resistance and revolt reauthorize agency and restore the capacity to sublimate and make meaning one's own. This resistance not only brings people together to create meaning for themselves but also begins to provide the social space that is necessary for empowered psychic space. Creating the social space for resistance to sexism provides the social support that is necessary to reverse and counteract the process of internalization of oppressive values. As we create free and open social spaces, we begin to create free and open psychic spaces. Social revolt and psychic revolt go hand in hand; one is not possible without the other, which is why psychoanalysis is crucial for understanding subject formation within patriarchal cultures.

Further Reading

Benjamin, Jessica (1998) *Shadow of the Other: Intersubjectivity and Gender in Psychoanalysis*, New York: Routledge.

Brennan, Teresa (1992) *The Interpretation of the Flesh: Freud and Femininity*, New York: Routledge.

Chodorow, Nancy J. (1989) *Feminism and Psychoanalytic Theory*, New Haven, CT: Yale University Press.

Khanna, Ranjana (2003) *Dark Continents: Psychoanalysis and Colonialism*, Durham, NC: Duke University Press Books.

Lacan, Jacques (1982) *Feminine Sexuality: Jacques Lacan and the École Freudienne*, Jacqueline Rose and Juliet Mitchell (Eds.), New York: Norton.

Oliver, Kelly (2004) *The Colonization of Psychic Space: Toward a Psychoanalytic Theory of Oppression*, Minneapolis, MN: University of Minnesota Press.

Rose, Jacqueline (2006) *Sexuality in the Field of Vision*, London: Verso.

Seshadri-Crooks, Kalpana (2000) *Desiring Whiteness*, New York: Routledge.

Related Topics

Embodiment and feminist philosophy (Chapter 15); materiality: sex, gender, and what lies beneath (Chapter 16); feminism and borderlands identities (Chapter 17); personal identity and relational selves (Chapter 18); critical race theory, intersectionality, and feminist philosophy (Chapter 29); feminism and power (Chapter 54).

References

Bartky, Sandra (1990) *Femininity and Domination: Studies in the Phenomenology of Oppression*, New York: Routledge.

Benjamin, Jessica (1988) *The Bonds of Love: Psychoanalysis, Feminism, and the Problem of Domination*, New York: Pantheon.

Brennan, Teresa (1992) *The Interpretation of the Flesh: Freud and Femininity*, New York: Routledge.

Butler, Judith (1997) *The Psychic Life of Power: Theories in Subjection*, Stanford, CA: Stanford University Press.

Chodorow, Nancy J. (1978) *The Reproduction of Mothering: Psychoanalysis and the Sociology of Gender*, Berkeley, CA: University of California Press.

Gilligan, Carol (1982) *In a Different Voice: Psychological Theory and Women's Development*, Cambridge, MA: Harvard University Press.

Honneth, Axel (1996) *The Struggle for Recognition: The Moral Grammar of Social Conflicts*, Cambridge, MA: MIT Press.

Kessler, Ronald C. (2003) "Epidemiology of Women and Depression," *Journal of Affective Disorders* 74(1): 5–13.

Kristeva, Julia (1989) *Black Sun: Depression and Melancholia*, New York: Columbia University Press.

Lane, Christopher (Ed.) (1998) *The Psychoanalysis of Race*, New York: Columbia University Press.

Noble, Rudolf E. (2005) "Depression in Women," *Metabolism* 54(5 Supplement): 49–52.

Oliver, Kelly (2001) *Witnessing: Beyond Recognition*, Minneapolis, MN: University of Minnesota Press.

Peden, Ann, Hall, Lynne, Rayens, Mary Kay, and Beebe, Lora L. (2000) "Reducing Negative Thinking and Depressive Symptoms in College Women," *Journal of Nursing Scholarship* 32(2): 145–151.

Sedgwick, Eve Kosofsky (2002) *Touching Feeling: Affect, Pedagogy, Performativity*, Durham, NC: Duke University Press.

Spivak, Gayatri Chakravorty (1999) *A Critique of Postcolonial Reason*, Cambridge, MA: Harvard University Press.

Willett, Cynthia (1995) *Maternal Ethics and Other Slave Moralities*, New York: Psychology Press.

Part III

KNOWLEDGE, LANGUAGE, AND SCIENCE

20

RATIONALITY AND OBJECTIVITY IN FEMINIST PHILOSOPHY

Phyllis Rooney

Starting Places

Although the concept of *knowledge* is usually taken to be the central concept in epistemology (theory of knowledge), the concepts *rationality* and *objectivity* are also very prominent. These three concepts, along with the concept of *truth*, have regularly been understood in terms of each other. "Knowledge" is usually taken to mean "objective knowledge" or "objective truth," and attaining knowledge typically requires the proper exercise of reason or rationality.

Despite such general acknowledgements, philosophers have regularly disagreed about more precise definitions or characterizations of these concepts. In particular, the history of Western philosophy reveals a range of conceptions of rationality and objectivity. In spite of these differences, a particular historical pattern is of special interest to feminist philosophers. Rationality and objectivity as epistemic (knowledge-related) ideals were regularly assumed to be exhibited only or primarily by men and, often too, only by men of "higher" races and classes. This politically problematic history, which regularly reflected and contributed to systems of injustice, marks an important starting place for feminist reflections in epistemology and philosophy of science.

The histories of the "gendering" of rationality and objectivity were clearly linked though not identical. In her influential work, *The Man of Reason: "Male" and "Female" in Western Philosophy*, Genevieve Lloyd documents "the implicit maleness" of ideals of reason in that history—a maleness that, she argues, "is no superficial linguistic bias . . . [but is something that] lies deep in our philosophical tradition" (1993 [1984]: xviii). Women were regularly thought to be less rational than men—a view that still prevails in many places. Hegel's claim has a familiar ring in the history of philosophy:

> [women] are not made for activities which demand a universal faculty [reason] such as the more advanced sciences, philosophy, and certain forms of artistic production. Women may have happy ideas, taste, and elegance, but they cannot attain to the ideal [of reason].
>
> (quoted in Bell 1983: 269)

In addition, gender metaphors were often used to portray the rational faculty in humans as that which requires the exclusion or control of emotion, passion, or instinct which were metaphorically or symbolically cast as "feminine" (Rooney 1991). So, for example, the first-century Alexandrian philosopher Philo stated: "So too with the two ingredients which constitute our life-principle, the rational and the irrational; the rational which belongs to mind and reason is of the masculine gender, the irrational, the province of sense, is of the feminine" (quoted in Lloyd 1993: 27).

The historical association of objectivity with masculinity has played out somewhat differently, in part because that concept has had a more recent history closely linked with the development of modern empirical science since the seventeenth century. Scientific knowledge ideally aims to be objective, the result of careful, unbiased observations of the world. In their detailed history of the concept, Lorraine Daston and Peter Galison argue that our familiar understanding of it ("[t]o be objective is to aspire to knowledge that bears no trace of the knower—knowledge unmarked by prejudice or skill, fantasy or judgment, wishing or striving") only emerged in the mid-nineteenth century (Daston and Galison 2007: 17).

We should note, however, that forerunners of the concept—typically expressed as requirements about proper scientific method or about the proper stance or demeanor of the scientist in relation to the objects of study in scientific inquiry—also had clear gender connotations. Elizabeth Potter observes that prominent seventeenth-century scientist Robert Boyle (of "Boyle's Law of Gases") was quite insistent that only gentlemen of the upper classes had the qualities needed to properly conduct and record scientific experiments—or even to witness and report them. The men who wrote laboratory reports were to be "sober and modest men" who adopted a plain "masculine style" of writing without any flowery "feminine" style of eloquence that would be distracting (Potter 2001: 10–11). In a related vein, Evelyn Fox Keller documents how Francis Bacon (also a prominent theorist of early modern science) celebrated the birth of modern science as a "masculine birth," and metaphorically depicted scientific inquiry in terms of a "chaste and lawful marriage between [male] Mind and [female] Nature" (Keller 1985: 33–42).

In sum, conceptions and valuations of both rationality and objectivity regularly associated both concepts with men, or with "masculine" traits, abilities, or symbols. Familiar philosophical contrasts or dichotomies (reason versus emotion, objectivity versus subjectivity, and mind versus body or nature) thus acquired gender associations that both reflected and reinforced sexist cultural assumptions. In other words, the association of some capacity, element, or symbol with women or "the feminine" was deemed sufficient—typically without any argument—to mark that capacity or element as something that was antithetical to or disruptive of reason, higher intellectual functioning, and proper objective knowledge. Feminist rethinking in epistemology includes critical reassessments of the role of these gender-inflected dichotomies in philosophical and in broader cultural understandings of rationality, objectivity, and knowledge.

Gender, however, was not the only social or cultural differentiation that figured into philosophical associations with epistemic ideals. As Potter notes regarding Boyle's comments about the "sober and modest men" who would be scientists, these men were to have a certain class status. Philosophers also regularly associated "savages" or "primitive people" with inferior intellectual capacities, in statements that often reflected prejudices about racial and ethnic differences. Kant, for instance, asserted, "so fundamental is the difference between [the black and white] races of man . . . it appears to be as great in regard to mental capacities as in color" (quoted in Mills 1997: 70). Thus, it would be a mistake to assume that gender is the only category of social or cultural differentiation that figures into feminist critiques. It is now more accurate to say that a starting point for feminist epistemology is not *gender* per se, but *social injustice* or, more specifically, forms of social injustice that were reinforced by historical assessments of intellectual and epistemic status (Medina 2013). Gender is sometimes a useful category of analysis (especially when philosophers made gender a notable marker of epistemic status), but we should also keep in mind that gender is a social division that intersects with race, class, or other social divisions, and these can mitigate or exacerbate the epistemic fall-out of gender associations.

There is little doubt that the long-term practical and political impact of these cultural associations with rationality and objectivity has been significant. Those deemed intellectually inferior were, for centuries, excluded from educational institutions and other venues of public influence and action. These exclusions have begun to be addressed only relatively recently. What also needs to be addressed, feminist philosophers argue, is the *theoretical* impact of these historical associations, that is, their impact on philosophical theorizing about rationality and objectivity. Following Lloyd's lead, many feminist discussions start with a historical focus, with an examination of the role of problematic cultural associations in the work of particular prominent philosophers. Feminist work on Descartes provides a helpful illustration of what feminist historical reassessments involve.

Lloyd notes that Descartes conceived of reason as involving a precise method of thinking using "rules for the direction of mind," a method that, with sufficient time and energy, anyone could master—"even women" (Lloyd 1993: 44). Yet, she continues, despite his egalitarian intentions, Descartes' reliance on a mind–body split (with reason allied with mind, and the body considered a significant source of deception and illusion) reinforced a distinction that already had a gender history, and "reinforced already existing distinctions between male and female roles" (Lloyd 1993: 39–50). Margaret Atherton, on the other hand, argues specifically for the feminist value of Descartes' conception. She observes that his view of "universal reason" was championed by seventeenth- and eighteenth-century feminists who used it to argue for women's equal access to education (Atherton 2002).

These feminist assessments of Descartes's reason are not necessarily in conflict, of course (and they are not the only such assessments). A given philosopher's view of reason is likely to have various components, some more attuned to progressive political concerns than others. But perhaps more to the point, differing feminist assessments of key conceptions of rationality and objectivity appear to be at odds with one another only if we expect a feminist analysis to take one form. As we will see, feminist work in this area yields a rich variety of approaches, discussions, and insights that help us to think about these central concepts in important new ways.

My emphasis here on historical starting places is designed to counter common misunderstandings of feminist work in epistemology and philosophy of science. First, feminist work is often mistakenly identified with fixed assertions or claims to which all feminists assent. Feminists are certainly in agreement about the importance of particular questions (such as those noted above), but it is the developments generated by *differences and debates* in answering these questions that more accurately define the field. Second, feminists are sometimes characterized as *newly* claiming that reason and objectivity are "male." To the contrary, they are simply pointing out that philosophers often theorized or characterized these concepts as "male" in the ways outlined above. Third (and following on the previous point), feminists are sometimes portrayed as uniformly rejecting reason and objectivity as "male" concepts. While there are differing views about the extent to which these concepts need to be revamped (Alcoff 1995), feminist critiques typically go hand in hand with the understanding that the concepts are important enough to merit better analysis and theorizing, that is, free of limiting historical connotations. Fourth, some have challenged the very idea of "feminist" work in epistemology and philosophy of science, arguing that feminists are introducing "politics" into areas where political "biases" or "agendas" do not properly belong. However, insofar as feminist interventions in these areas are "political" interventions, they are what I call *corrective* political interventions. The original political interventions were the automatic, unreflective sexist, racist, and similarly problematic political assumptions (interventions) that were accepted for centuries, interventions that now warrant focused feminist and social justice critique. Granting that political intrusions into philosophy may sometimes be problematic, it is not clear that feminist interventions are the more problematic ones in this context.

Feminist work on rationality and objectivity goes beyond critiques of traditional conceptions. By highlighting the concrete significance of these concepts across a range of real-world knowledge projects and situations, this work provides new and expanded understandings of these central concepts. We will focus on objectivity in the following section, and on rationality in the third section.

Objectivity Naturalized, Situated

Feminist examinations of what had been forwarded as "objective" scientific knowledge about sex differences (in the biological and social sciences especially) have served to bring the theory and practice of objectivity into productive feminist focus. For example, Anne Fausto-Sterling characterizes as "biological storytelling" the plethora of theories, dating from the late nineteenth century, which purported to explain why women were intellectually inferior to men. When neuroanatomists were convinced that the frontal lobe in the brain was linked with intelligence, they found "that this lobe was visibly larger and more developed in males." However, she continues, "when the parietal lobe rather than the frontal lobe gained precedence as the seat of the intellect," studies began to appear that found that the parietal, not the frontal lobe, was somewhat smaller in women (Fausto-Sterling 1992: 37–38). More recent theories have linked gender differences in cognitive abilities with differences in the functioning of the two hemispheres of the brain. Yet, as Ruth Bleier documents, efforts to find sex differences in specialization between the two hemispheres, have regularly started "with the very questionable assumption that there are true, probably 'innate' sex differences in verbal and spatial abilities" (1984: 92). Other feminist critiques have drawn attention, not just to sexism, but to *androcentrism*, the idea that males and their activities have been the primary agents of biological and cultural change and evolution. In challenging this view (often linked with the "man-the-hunter" hypothesis in anthropological theories), Helen Longino argues that the available fossil data also support an alternative "woman-the-gatherer" hypothesis that locates the pivotal role of the development of tool use with women's activities (1990: 104–111). Background cultural values and assumptions linked to androcentrism, Longino maintains, have long contributed to the acceptance of the "man-the-hunter" hypothesis as the standard hypothesis.

Two important features of feminist philosophical work on objectivity emerge from these and many similar examinations across different sciences. First, this work has been and continues to be notably *naturalized*, that is, it recommends that philosophical accounts of scientific objectivity (and related epistemic concepts) take into account the ways in which scientific projects and theories actually, "naturally" develop. This has also ensured that this area of research continues to be noticeably interdisciplinary: feminist scholars in many sciences and in philosophy have contributed to developments in the field. A second important feature of feminist work is a prominent focus on the social identity or location of scientists—their gender, race, political sensitivities, among other identifying criteria. Many feminist reassessments (such as those noted above) suggest, in Sandra Harding's words, that "women (or feminists, whether men or women) *as a group* are more likely to produce unbiased and objective results than are men (or nonfeminists) as a group" (Harding 1986: 25). In her examination of the sociological significance of Black feminist thought, Patricia Hill Collins similarly documents the anomalies and distortions in knowledge about Black women that had taken root in sociological theory. She argues that (newly admitted) "outsiders" in sociology, like herself, are often able to detect "patterns [in thinking] that may be more difficult for established sociological insiders to see" (Collins 1991: 53).

This attention to the social identity of scientists puts pressure on a central tenet of traditional conceptions of objectivity—that objective knowledge "bears no trace of the knower." Feminists, in general, do not suggest that this attention warrants a rejection of the ideal of objectivity, but they do argue that the concept needs specific refinements. I outline some of these refinements in relation to three (related) topics and developments in feminist epistemology and philosophy of science: *standpoint epistemology*, the significance of *epistemic communities*, and the role of *values in science*.

A recurring idea in work by Harding, Collins, and others, is that those on the margins or in subdominant social locations may have an "epistemic advantage" in certain situations. That is, they may be able to see, understand, or know aspects of reality better than traditional "insiders" do; thus they may be in a position to develop less partial, more objective knowledge in pertinent areas. This is a key idea explored in (feminist) *standpoint epistemology*. There is now general agreement that epistemic advantage does not *automatically* accrue to specific social locations, that is, "that those who occupy particular standpoints (usually subdominant, oppressed, marginal standpoints) automatically know more, or know better, by virtue of their social, political location" (Wylie 2004: 341). Epistemically significant *standpoints* are achieved through critical, conscious reflection on social locations with respect to power structures that play a role in the production of knowledge (Wylie 2004; Intemann 2010). Justice-oriented political sensibilities can often serve to enhance such critical reflection. Harding has drawn from developments in standpoint epistemology to argue for a feminist-inspired conception of "strong objectivity." Drawing on the perspectives and insights of those with marginal "standpoints" contributes, she maintains, to the production of less false or "less partial and distorted" knowledge about human lives (Harding 1993). Alison Wylie also underscores the importance of standpoint theory for "reframing ideals of objectivity," and (stressing a naturalistic focus) she maintains that such ideals cannot be determined in advance of careful study of actual epistemic practices in many areas of knowledge as they unfold in "socially and politically structured fields of engagement" (Wylie 2004: 349).

Some theorists have pursued epistemological issues relating to social identity with an explicit focus on scientific *communities*, their composition and structure. They note that specific assumptions (incorporating limited views of race or gender, for instance) could operate "invisibly" in science for so long because they were shared by all members of the scientific communities in question (Longino 1990; Nelson 1990). Objectivity in science is enhanced by having more diverse communities, but also communities that promote practices of fair and equitable epistemic interaction. Such interaction helps to eliminate individual errors and biases, thus, Longino maintains, the "objectivity of scientific inquiry is a consequence of this inquiry's being a social, and not an individual, enterprise" (Longino 1990: 67). Feminist work in many sciences points to the need for enhanced standards and practices of peer review and critical engagement (including equality of intellectual authority for those who had been marginalized) if objectivity is to be improved or secured (Longino 1996). This attention to social-epistemic interactions among scientists is especially prominent in what is now called *social epistemology* (Solomon 2001: Grasswick 2013).

This emphasis on the epistemic structure of communities upends a view of objectivity as something that is simply a property of individual knowers who can "detach" from their subjective interests and preferences in making judgments. Feminists point out that "objectivity" has, in fact, included a variety of meanings attached to different features or stages of inquiry (Lloyd 1995; Douglas 2004; Anderson 2015). Sometimes "objective" is applied to methods—as in the applications of objective methods. Often "objectivity" has meant "value-freedom," in that objective knowledge does not reflect the moral or political values of a particular culture or community. The role of values in science has also been important in feminist work, particularly since feminists, while being critical of sexist and racist values that have influenced theories of human difference, also argue that values linked to social justice movements, values promoting human equality and respect, can have a positive epistemic impact on scientific development. This work includes analyses of the role of different kinds of values in many stages of scientific inquiry: in the questions and problems that scientists engage, in the design of experiments, in the selection and interpretation of data, in the hypotheses and theories developed to explain the data, and in the dissemination and use of the theoretical and practical products of scientific inquiry (Anderson 1995; Longino 1996; Crasnow 2004; Douglas 2009; Rolin 2015).

Feminist work clearly challenges simplistic conceptions of objectivity rooted in the gender-inflected *objectivity versus subjectivity* dichotomy (and its extension in the *objectivity versus relativism* dichotomy). Lorraine Code challenges this dichotomy by arguing that "often, objectivity requires taking subjectivity into account" (Code 1991: 31). In addition to criteria of evidence and justification, she maintains, an account of objectivity also requires taking into account "the 'nature' of inquirers, their interests in the inquiry, their emotional involvement and background assumptions . . . their material, historical, and cultural circumstances" (Code 1993: 26). Donna Haraway argues that feminist attention to "situated knowledges" challenges the idea of a "disembodied scientific objectivity," and she seeks a "doctrine of embodied objectivity that accommodates paradoxical and critical feminist science projects" (Haraway 1988: 576, 581).

Her account does not recommend relativism, the view that all claims and accounts are equally valuable or true: such an "'equality' of positioning [in relativism] is a denial of responsibility and critical inquiry" (Haraway 1988: 584).

Rationality Situated, Naturalized

Rationality is, at bottom, about reasoning. Different types or forms of reasoning are suitable for different situations. Moral and political situations typically invite forms of *practical reasoning. Arithmetical reasoning* is appropriate when doing arithmetical computations. In logic we distinguish between *deductive reasoning* (when, in arguments, we draw conclusions that aim to follow necessarily from the premises), and *inductive reasoning* (where the conclusion aims to follow, not necessarily, but with good probability from the premises). Different forms of *statistical reasoning* (which includes formalizations of specific forms of inductive reasoning) are appropriate in different areas of inquiry, and different statistical methods applied to a given data set yield different results, depending on the features of the situation that inquirers think are most important. Complex reasoning contexts (in science, for example) incorporate many of these specific forms of reasoning.

This proliferation of forms of reasoning raises questions about the possibility of formulating a single or unitary *concept or theory* of reason or rationality—a point I will return to in the following section. Whether or not we consider such a concept or theory desirable or even possible, we can still value philosophical work that seeks to clarify what specific forms of reasoning or rationality involve, what each purports to accomplish or elucidate. Feminist reflections are very relevant here. I outline what feminist engagement means for three philosophical projects concerning rationality (and these are not the only such projects): moral reasoning, rationality naturalized, and logic and rational argumentation. A feminist critical focus includes assessing whether traditional associations of rationality with masculinity have influenced the selection of situations and practices of reasoning that were thought to best exemplify rationality. A recurring theme in feminist work is the claim that the activities and practices of autonomous, relatively privileged men in public settings have framed many accounts of rationality. Such is the case, some feminists argue, for characterizations of the ideally rational agent in standard accounts of *rational choice theory* (debated by Anderson 2002 and Cudd 2002).

One of the most significant debates about possible gender differences in reasoning resulted from empirical studies that suggested that women are more likely to adopt "care reasoning" in deliberations about moral dilemmas and choices, while men are more likely to exhibit "justice reasoning" (Gilligan 1987: 22). Care reasoners purportedly pay significant attention to relationships and contextual details of moral situations, while justice reasoners appeal more to universal rules and principles concerning fairness and rights among autonomous individuals. Subsequent empirical studies raised doubts about the significance of the gender correlation with the care and justice "voices," and some theorists questioned the role of gender stereotyping in the researchers' assessment and interpretation of differences. The debate, however, has sparked significant discussion among feminist moral philosophers about the "maleness" of much traditional moral philosophy (Kittay and Meyers 1987).

Many feminists note that philosophers' accounts of moral deliberation and action regularly tracked the traditional roles and activities of influential men in public settings. Accounts of moral rationality often represented ideal moral reasoners as autonomous, independent agents acting on principles of impartiality, fairness, and equality. Feminist moral theorists have argued that traditional theories are inadequate when it comes to formulating moral deliberation and action in relationships of dependency and partiality such as the relationships that women have traditionally had in their care of dependent others, or that women and men have in close familial and friendship relationships. Some have also paid particular attention to the role of moral emotions such as compassion and empathy in moral reasoning. In addition, traditional accounts of moral rationality typically presuppose forms of (moral) selfhood and agency that, feminists have argued, give little or no attention to the lives and experiences of those who experience systemic social injustice. In sum, feminists argue, accounts of moral rationality need to be appropriately modified and expanded to take into account the many different moral situations that people inhabit in worlds of social and political complexity (Baier 1986; Jaggar 1989; Held 1990; Walker 2007).

In *naturalized epistemology*, accounts of "rationality naturalized" incorporate cognitive scientific findings about how we humans actually ("naturally") reason when we, for instance, assess evidence to arrive at beliefs and judgements (traditionally captured in understandings of *theoretical reason*), or when we make decisions about how to act (as captured in understandings of *practical reason*). In other words, naturalist epistemologists maintain, normative claims about how we *ought* to reason should take account of descriptive claims about how we *do* reason in various contexts. The many cognitive sciences provide rich ground for (naturalized) epistemological and feminist reflection. Two particular areas of cognitive scientific study—in neuroscience and in the social psychological study of cognition—are of special interest in feminist considerations about rationality.

By the 1990s feminist epistemological critiques contributed to growing interest in the "cognitive role" of emotions, the idea that "appropriate emotions are indispensable to reliable knowledge" (Jaggar 1996: 182). Neuroscientific findings support such moves challenging the *reason versus emotion* dichotomy. In particular, the new "brain science of emotion" led one prominent neuroscientist interested in "the neural underpinnings of reason" to conclude that "certain aspects of the process of emotion and feeling are indispensable for rationality" (Damasio 2005 [1994]: xv, xvii). Yet neuroscientific studies of sex differences in the brain still reveal the lingering effects of the long association of women with emotion and men with rationality and cognitive control. Robyn Bluhm argues that neuroscientists still rely on gender stereotypes in their research, on "the common idea that women are more emotional than men . . . [and that] women are less able to cognitively control their natural emotional responses" (Bluhm 2013: 870, 880). More generally, feminist examinations of neuroscientific work on sex differences in the brain has inspired some scholars to use the term "neurosexism" (Fine 2010: 155–175), a term that inspires its own particular form of feminism, "neurofeminism" (Bluhm et al. 2012).

Findings from social psychology help to uncover some of the lingering cognitive effects of the long historical association of rationality and objectivity with men of particular races and classes. Researchers have documented the operation of "stereotype threat," when subjects perform less well in situations where negative stereotypes about their group have prevailed—for instance, women's stereotypical inferiority in mathematics (Fine 2010; Banaji and Greenwald 2013). Similar research has also uncovered the role of "implicit bias" in the judgments we all make about people's authority, credibility, and competence, based on their group identity—even when we have explicit egalitarian beliefs. For instance, reviewers rate identical CVs somewhat lower when they carry a female instead of a male name. In effect, systematic social injustices have impaired our capacity to make fair (rational) judgements about those who have long been associated with inferior intellectual abilities (Banaji and Greenwald 2013; Saul 2013). This involves what is now called "epistemic injustice . . . [which is] a kind of injustice in which someone is *wronged specifically in her capacity as a knower*" (Fricker 2007: 20). As all of this work advocates, when we take specific steps to counter both explicit and implicit biases we are also taking important steps in improving our reasoning and knowing in situations involving interpersonal interactions and judgments.

As noted above, different forms of rational argumentation are captured in different logical systems; thus, deductive and inductive logic formalize rules of deductive and inductive reasoning respectively. Some feminist critiques have focused on logic as a whole, on the limitations of abstract formal logical systems when we need to reason about the practical realities of different forms of injustice (Nye 1990). Val Plumwood, on the other hand, recognizes "the plurality of logical systems" that correspond to "different forms of rationality," and argues that feminist concerns should be directed to the privileging of some forms of rationality (and logic) over others in the conceptual structures of Western thought (Plumwood 2002). There are many ways in which one might abstract from and reason about particular contexts. Thus, not unlike the situation with moral reasoning discussed above, we need to pay particular attention to which aspects of social and political contexts a given system of logic reveals and articulates, and which aspects are rendered invisible or "illogical" by that same system (Falmagne and Hass 2002).

Many forms of logic present argumentation as a monological process, as something engaged in by individuals making inferences from premises to conclusions. However, argumentation more broadly understood also includes a dialogical model: as in debates, it involves two or more people exchanging arguments and responses to arguments. This form of argumentation is a central focus in "informal logic," which examines "everyday" processes of disagreement and debate and recommends normative procedures for rational resolution. Feminist projects aimed at developing models of reasoning that address social and political change draw productively from developments in this fields (Rooney and Hundleby 2010). Yet feminist examinations are also critical of models of argumentation that limit the possibilities for new insights and understandings across differences, especially across social differences that underwrite specific forms of injustice. I have argued that findings about explicit and implicit biases need to be taken into account in our (normative) accounts of good argumentative exchange (Rooney 2012). In particular, I maintain that some forms of adversarial argumentation can effectively silence or misrepresent the contributions of those who belong to marginalized subgroups, especially when they seek to address concerns that are of special significance for their subgroup.

Wherefore Concepts, Ideals, and Theories?

In the previous sections we have examined how feminist critiques and developments add important new dimensions to our understandings of two central epistemic concepts. So where does that leave us with respect to developing specific feminism-informed unitary definitions and theories of rationality and objectivity? Can we think of these concepts as ideals that lend themselves to precise philosophical characterizations—as many philosophers have traditionally thought?

Toward the end of her work examining the "maleness" of historical conceptions of reason, Lloyd is somewhat optimistic about salvaging something "of the ideal of a Reason which knows no sex . . . ; [though] if there is a Reason genuinely common to all, it is something to be achieved in the future . . ." (Lloyd 1993: 107). Others have questioned the projection of reason or rationality as a singular concept, and on feminist grounds (Le Doeuff 1990). The portrayal of rationality as a specific distinct, measurable trait or ability (rather than as something like an umbrella term covering a range of reasoning capacities, processes, and activities) was, it seems, required in order to readily claim that some people had distinctly more of it than others (Rooney 1995). What if we no longer make such ready assessments? In a related vein, Catharine MacKinnon has questioned the "the stance of 'objectivity'" as a stance that claims an authoritative (objective) knowledge position that resists acknowledgement of social positioning with respect to knowledge assertions. It (as a concept) can thus function politically as a stance that resists or silences challenges to authoritative positions (MacKinnon 1989).

And yet, as we have seen above, the concepts rationality, objectivity, and knowledge do carry significant epistemic, social, and cultural valence, and feminists have drawn on them to advance key new understandings of the importance of better knowledge and better knowing in a variety of contexts. We saw that objectivity has been a central focus in feminist analyses of scientific knowledge: taking the concept seriously as a *regulative ideal* has enabled feminists to develop important insights into the many factors that go into producing good or better science (Harding 2015). Taking account of this work, Naomi Scheman asks what it is about objectivity that makes its preservation so important (Scheman 2001: 23). Despite critics of feminist work who erroneously portray feminists as endangering objectivity, feminist work, she continues, "is better understood as an attempt to save objectivity by understandings why it matters." Objectivity matters as a form of trustworthiness, she contends, since "objective judgments are judgments we can rationally trust" (Scheman 2001: 23, 26).

In a work on "the virtue of feminist rationality," Deborah Heikes argues for "a feminist theory of rationality" that takes account of feminist concerns (2012: 1). She draws attention to central feminist practices of presenting reasons and arguments about the injustices of oppression and the need for change. These practices, she maintains, capture an essential feature of rationality that grounds a feminist theory of rationality. However, as we saw in the previous section, even when we take argumentation as a central practice of human reasoning, we can still critique, from a feminist perspective, the limitations of traditional understandings of rational argumentation. Heikes grants that "reason is not so much a thing or an object as it is an activity," and "[i]ts basic function is to guide our responses to the world around [us] whether that world be material, social, or emotional" (2012: 4).

In taking up questions about what a feminist analysis, concept, or theory of rationality or objectivity might involve, it is helpful to consider Sally Haslanger's (1999) analogous question about what a feminist analysis or theory of knowledge ought to involve. She maintains that an epistemological analysis of *knowledge* as a *normative* concept (as concerned fundamentally with questions about how we *ought* to reason and form beliefs) necessitates examining why we need the concept at all, why the concept is valuable for creatures like us who value certain kinds of moral/autonomous agency. She maintains that when such considerations are in place, "an adequate definition of knowledge will depend on an account of what is cognitively valuable for beings like us, which raises moral and political issues on which feminists have much to contribute" (Haslanger 1999: 473).

To the extent that traditions and conceptions of rationality and objectivity incorporated and reinforced specific forms of injustice, they are concepts that many of us find less than trustworthy, action-guiding, or valuable. When, guided by feminist and other justice-oriented epistemological work, we uncover and uproot these lingering injustices in their many forms, we are taking important steps toward establishing these concepts as normatively significant in improving our many and varied epistemic practices in our many and varied worlds of thought and action.

Acknowledgment

I wish to thank Ann Garry, Ami Harbin, Joyce Havstad, and Mark Navin for helpful comments on an earlier draft of this chapter.

Further Reading

Edited volumes of essays significant for the development of feminist epistemology and philosophy of science include:

Alcoff, Linda and Potter, Elizabeth (Eds.) (1993) *Feminist Epistemologies*, New York: Routledge.

Antony, Louise M. and Charlotte E. Witt (Eds.) (2002) *A Mind of One's Own: Feminist Essays on Reason and Objectivity*, 2nd ed., Boulder, CO: Westview Press.

Garry, Ann and Pearsall, Marilyn (Eds.) (1996) *Women, Knowledge, and Reality: Explorations in Feminist Philosophy*, 2nd ed., New York: Routledge.

Grasswick, Heidi E. (Ed.) (2011) *Feminist Epistemology and Philosophy of Science: Power in Knowledge*, New York: Springer. (The introduction is especially helpful.)

Harding, Sandra (Ed.) (2004) *The Feminist Standpoint Theory Reader: Intellectual and Political Controversies*, New York: Routledge.

Tuana, Nancy (Ed.) (1989) *Feminism and Science*, Bloomington, IN: Indiana University Press.

Another good introductory reading is:

Anderson, Elizabeth (2015) "Feminist Epistemology and Philosophy of Science," *The Stanford Encyclopedia of Philosophy*, Fall [online]. Available from: http://plato.stanford.edu/archives/fall2015/entries/feminism-epistemology.

Related Topics

Early modern feminism and Cartesian philosophy (Chapter 6); testimony, trust, and trustworthiness (Chapter 21); epistemic injustice, ignorance and trans experience (Chapter 22); philosophy of science and the feminist legacy (Chapter 25); values, practices and metaphysical assumptions in the biological sciences (Chapter 26); feminist philosophy of social science (Chapter 27); moral justification in an unjust world (Chapter 40); feminist ethics of care (Chapter 43).

References

Alcoff, Linda Martín (1995) "Is the Feminist Critique of Reason Rational?" *Philosophical Topics* 23(2): 1–26.

Anderson, Elizabeth (1995) "Knowledge, Human Interests, and Objectivity in Feminist Epistemology," *Philosophical Topics* 23(2): 27–58.

—— (2002) "Should Feminists Reject Rational Choice Theory?" in Louise M. Antony and Charlotte E. Witt (Eds.) *A Mind of One's Own*, Boulder, CO: Westview Press, 369–397.

—— (2015) "Feminist Epistemology and Philosophy of Science," *The Stanford Encyclopedia of Philosophy* Fall [online]. Available from: http://plato.stanford.edu/archives/fall2015/entries/feminism-epistemology/.

Atherton, Margaret (2002) "Cartesian Reason and Gendered Reason," in Louise M. Antony and Charlotte E. Witt (Eds.) *A Mind of One's Own*, Boulder, CO: Westview Press, 21–37.

Baier, Annette (1986) "Trust and Anti-Trust," *Ethics* 96(2): 231–260.

Banaji, Mahzarin R. and Greenwald, Anthony G. (2013) *Blindspot: Hidden Biases of Good People*, New York: Delacorte Press.

Bell, Linda (Ed.) (1983) *Visions of Women*, Clifton, NJ: Humana Press.

Bleier, Ruth (1984) *Science and Gender: A Critique of Biology and Its Theories on Women*, New York: Pergamon Press.

Bluhm, Robyn (2013) "Self-Fulfilling Prophecies: The Influence of Gender Stereotypes on Functional Neuroimaging Research on Emotion," *Hypatia* 28(4): 870–886.

Bluhm, Robyn, Jacobson, Anne Jaap and Maibom, Heidi Lene (Eds.) (2012) *Neurofeminism: Issues at the Intersection of Feminist Theory and Cognitive Science*, New York: Palgrave Macmillan.

Code, Lorraine (1991) *What Can She Know? Feminist Theory and the Construction of Knowledge*, Ithaca, NY: Cornell University Press.

—— (1993) "Taking Subjectivity into Account," in Linda Alcoff and Elizabeth Potter (Eds.) *Feminist Epistemologies*, New York: Routledge, 15–48.

Collins, Patricia Hill (1991) "Learning from the Outsider Within: The Sociological Significance of Black Feminist Thought," in Mary Margaret Fonow and Judith A. Cook (Eds.) *Beyond Methodology*, Bloomington, IN: Indiana University Press, 35–59.

Crasnow, Sharon (2004) "Objectivity: Feminism, Values, and Science," *Hypatia* 19(1): 280-291.

Cudd, Ann E. (2002) "Rational Choice Theory and the Lessons of Feminism," in Louise M. Antony and Charlotte E. Witt (Eds.) *A Mind of One's Own*, Boulder, CO: Westview Press, 398–417.

Damasio, Antonio (2005 [1994]) *Descartes' Error: Emotion, Reason, and The Human Brain*, New York: Penguin Books.

Daston, Lorraine and Galison, Peter (2007) *Objectivity*, New York: Zone Books.

Douglas, Heather (2004) "The Irreducible Complexity of Objectivity," *Synthese* 138: 453–473.

—— (2009) *Science, Policy, and the Value-Free Ideal*, Pittsburgh, PA: University of Pittsburgh Press.

Fausto-Sterling, Anne (1992) *Myths of Gender: Biological Theories About Women and Men*, 2nd ed., New York: Basic Books.

Fine, Cordelia (2010) *Delusions of Gender*, New York: W. W. Norton.

Falmagne, Rachel Joffe and Hass, Marjorie (Eds.) (2002) *Representing Reason: Feminist Theory and Formal Logic*, Lanham, MD: Rowman & Littlefield.

Fricker, Miranda (2007) *Epistemic Injustice: Power and the Ethics of Knowing*, New York: Oxford University Press.

Gilligan, Carol (1987) "Moral Orientation and Moral Development," in Eva Feder Kittay and Diana T. Meyers (Eds.) *Women and Moral Theory*, Totowa, NJ: Rowman & Littlefield, 19–33.

Grasswick, Heidi E. (2013) "Feminist Social Epistemology," *The Stanford Encyclopedia of Philosophy* (Spring 2013 Edition), Edward N. Zalta (Ed.) [online]. Available from: http://plato.stanford.edu/archives/spr2013/entries/feminist-social-epistemology/

Haraway, Donna (1988) "Situated Knowledges: The Science Question in Feminism and the Privilege of Partial Perspective," *Feminist Studies* 14(3): 575–599.

Harding, Sandra (1986) *The Science Question in Feminism*, Ithaca, NY: Cornell University Press.

—— (1993) "Rethinking Standpoint Epistemology: 'What Is Strong Objectivity?'" in Linda Alcoff and Elizabeth Potter (Eds.) *Feminist Epistemologies*, New York: Routledge, 49–82.

—— (2015) *Objectivity and Diversity: Another Logic of Scientific Research*, Chicago, IL: The University of Chicago Press.

Haslanger, Sally (1999) "What Knowledge Is and What It Ought to Be: Feminist Values and Normative Epistemology," *Philosophical Perspectives* 13: 459–480.

Heikes, Deborah K. (2012) *The Virtue of Feminist Rationality*, London, New York: Bloomsbury.

Held, Virginia (1990) "Feminist Transformations of Moral Theory," *Philosophy and Phenomenological Research* 50(Supplement): 321–344

Intemann, Kristen (2010) "25 Years of Feminist Empiricism and Standpoint Theory: Where Are We Now?" *Hypatia* 25(4): 778–796.

Jaggar, Alison (1989) "Feminist Ethics: Some Issues for the Nineties," *Journal of Social Philosophy* 20(1–2): 91–107.

—— (1996) "Love and Knowledge: Emotion in Feminist Epistemology," in Ann Garry and Marilyn Pearsall (Eds.) *Women, Knowledge, and Reality: Explorations in Feminist Philosophy*, New York: Routledge, 166–190.

Keller, Evelyn Fox (1985) *Reflections on Gender and Science*, New Haven, CT: Yale University Press.

Kittay, Eva Feder and Meyers, Diana T. (Eds.) (1987) *Women and Moral Theory*, Totowa, NJ: Rowman & Littlefield.

Le Doeuff, Michèle (1990) "Women, Reason, etc." *differences* 2(3): 1–13.

Lloyd, Elisabeth (1995) "Objectivity and the Double Standard for Feminist Epistemologies," *Synthese* 104: 351–381.

Lloyd, Genevieve (1993 [1984]) *The Man of Reason: "Male" and "Female" in Western Philosophy*, 2nd ed., Minneapolis, MN: University of Minnesota Press.

Longino, Helen E. (1990) *Science as Social Knowledge*, Princeton, NJ: Princeton University Press.

—— (1996) "Cognitive and Non-Cognitive Values in Science: Rethinking the Dichotomy," in Lynn Hankinson Nelson and Jack Nelson (Eds.) *Feminism, Science, and the Philosophy of Science*, Dordrecht, Netherlands: Kluwer, 39–58.

MacKinnon, Catharine A. (1989) *Toward a Feminist Theory of the State*, Cambridge, MA: Harvard University Press.

Medina, José (2013) *The Epistemology of Resistance: Gender and Racial Oppression, Epistemic Injustice, and Resistant Imaginations*, New York: Oxford University Press.

Mills, Charles (1997) *The Racial Contract*, Ithaca, NY: Cornell University Press.

Nelson, Lynn Hankinson (1990) *Who Knows: From Quine to a Feminist Empiricism*, Philadelphia, PA: Temple University Press.

Nye, Andrea (1990) *Words of Power: A Feminist Reading of the History of Logic*, New York: Routledge.

Plumwood, Val (2002) "The Politics of Reason: Toward a Feminist Logic," in Rachel Joffe Falmagne and Marjorie Hass (Eds.) *Representing Reason: Feminist Theory and Formal Logic*, Lanham, MD: Rowman & Littlefield, 11–44.

Potter, Elizabeth (2001) *Gender and Boyle's Law of Gases*, Bloomington, IN: Indiana University Press.

Rolin, Kristina (2015) "Values in Science: The Case of Scientific Collaboration," *Philosophy of Science*, 82(April): 157–177.

Rooney, Phyllis (1991) "Gendered Reason: Sex Metaphor and Conceptions of Reason," *Hypatia* 6(2): 77–103.

—— (1995) "Rationality and the Politics of Gender Difference," *Metaphilosophy* 26(1–2): 22–45.

—— (2012) "When Philosophical Argumentation Impedes Social and Political Progress," *Journal of Social Philosophy* 43(3): 317–333.

Rooney, Phyllis and Hundleby, Catherine E. (Eds.) (2010) *Reasoning for Change*, Special Issue of *Informal Logic* 30(3).

Saul, Jennifer (2013) "Implicit Bias, Stereotype Threat, and Women in Philosophy," in Katrina Hutchison and Fiona Jenkins (Eds.) *Women in Philosophy: What Needs to Change?* New York: Oxford University Press, 39–60.

Scheman, Naomi (2001) "Epistemology Resuscitated: Objectivity as Trustworthiness," in Nancy Tuana and Sandra Morgen (Eds.) *Engendering Rationalities*, Albany, NY: SUNY Press, 23–52.

Solomon, Miriam (2001) *Social Empiricism*, Cambridge, MA: MIT Press.

Walker, Margaret Urban (2007) *Moral Understandings: A Feminist Study in Ethics*, 2nd ed., Oxford: Oxford University Press.

Wylie, Alison (2004) "Why Standpoint Matters," in Sandra Harding (Ed.) *The Feminist Standpoint Theory Reader*, New York: Routledge, 339–351.

21

TRUST AND TESTIMONY IN FEMINIST EPISTEMOLOGY

Heidi Grasswick

Feminist Accounts of Trust in Testimony

Trust and its counterpart trustworthiness have played important roles in the development of both feminist ethics and feminist epistemology. This chapter focuses on their role in feminist epistemology, particularly insofar as trust and trustworthiness have been crucial concepts in feminist attempts to draw attention to the ethical dimensions of our epistemic practices (Code 1991; 1995) while coming to terms with the inherently social nature of knowledge-seeking (Grasswick 2013), as seen in part through our deep epistemic interdependence through testimony.

In recent years, epistemologists of various ilks have turned their attention to the role of testimony in knowing, recognizing that individuals are deeply epistemically dependent on one another in everyday mundane epistemic activities such as asking one's housemate what was available at the grocery store that day, or being told when young in what year one was born. They have also recognized the important epistemic role of the testimony of experts, given that our modern world functions by way of a significant cognitive division of labor (Goldman 2001; Kitcher 1990). With this renewed attention to the role of testimony, analyses of how we attribute cognitive authority to others and when we should trust others have proliferated in philosophical literature.

While many epistemological analyses of trust work with a very minimal concept of trust, equating trust with a mere reliance on someone else's word (Goldman 1999), feminist work has tended to work with a much richer sense of trust, examining its relational and interpersonal nature, its potential fragility, the epistemic benefits that can stem from a deep and enduring trust in others, and the epistemic damage that can be done by climates of distrust (Baier 1986; Code 1991, 2006; Jones 1996; Potter 2002). Rather than focusing exclusively (as many testimony theorists do) on identifying the conditions that would justify adopting a specific belief based on testimony, feminists have been more interested in the systems and patterns of knowledge production, seeking to understand the appropriate role of trust in ongoing successful practices of testimonial exchange and inquiry, and pointing out how inappropriate trust relations can harm our epistemic projects. Even more noteworthy, feminist work has focused on the role of social power dynamics in our attributions of epistemic trust and the demands that might reasonably be placed on knowers who wish to be trustworthy in a world permeated by such power dynamics. As Lorraine Code notes, "testimonial exchanges are often tangled negotiations where it matters who the participants are, and where issues of differential credulity and credibility cannot be ignored" (1995: 67).

That feminist analyses of testimony and trust have focused on social power dynamics should be no surprise given that a common theme in feminist epistemologies is that knowing is situated—varying across social locations. The tenet of situated knowing maintains that one's capacity to know is deeply shaped and limited by one's social situation. For example, feminist epistemologists have used the idea of situated knowing to reveal the ways in which the socially privileged position of the dominant classes shapes and limits their range of experiences, experiences that the dominant use as evidence to develop and support particular understandings of the social world. These understandings are then conveyed as objective knowledge, masking their origins in the social position of the dominant, and becoming the established forms of knowledge produced and circulated throughout society (Code 1991; 2006). At the same time, feminists have used the idea of situated knowledge in order to explain how experiences specific to members of oppressed groups can, in the right contexts, serve as the basis of the development of important insights that can counter the dominant understandings of social relations, providing richer understandings of the workings of oppression (Harding 1991; Hartsock 1983).

If, as feminists suggest, one's social location shapes and limits one's knowing possibilities, then testimony as a way of knowing takes on an even greater importance in epistemology; we will be dependent on others for accessing that knowledge which we are not in a position to obtain on our own, and the limitations of independent knowing may be quite significant when it comes to knowledge of social relations, a full understanding of which will require consideration of the experiences of those situated differently from oneself.

At the same time, the idea of situated knowing complicates one's analysis of testimony. While it is one thing to suppose, as most testimony theorists do, that knowing beyond one's experience requires that we rely on the experiences of others who can then offer testimony to us, if one's social location runs deep enough that it helps shape one's epistemic perspective, it may be challenging to take the testimony of another who is differently situated from oneself as seriously as one needs in order to know well. Testimony from those differently situated from oneself may not easily fit in with the body of one's beliefs, experiences, and epistemic frameworks, sometimes leading one to reject another's testimony "not out of prejudice but out of sheer incomprehension" (Anderson 2012: 170). Differences in social position and corresponding differences in epistemic frameworks between speakers and hearers make a simple model of testimony as a one-way transmission of knowledge implausible (Bergin 2002). Feminist accounts of trust and testimony grapple with the challenges of negotiating through epistemic differences across agents who are at the same time deeply dependent on each other.

Trust Relations and the Ethical Dimension of Testimony Practices

Even within feminist work, sometimes "trust" in testimony is simply used as a synonym for relying on someone else's word, and being trustworthy amounts to merely being a reliable source of the knowledge claim in question in that particular circumstance.

But once we start investigating testimonial exchanges beyond the mundane, examining cases where we are potentially seriously harmed by failures in testimony and where we develop long-term relationships with other knowers, it becomes clear that in many contexts epistemic trust involves more than mere reliance. Trust relations between inquirers—that is patterns of relative trust/distrust and trustworthiness/untrustworthiness—run thick through our cooperative epistemic practices, and their specifics crucially contribute to epistemic success or failure. Several feminists have drawn attention to both the cognitive and affective dimensions of trust in their explanations of how our epistemic practices function, and how well-placed trust, or "responsible trust" (Grasswick 2014) can foster successful epistemic endeavors (Code 1991; Jones 1996; Townley 2011).

Just as prominent trust theorist Annette Baier has argued for the case of moral theory (Baier 1985; 1986), in epistemology trust has historically received insufficient attention, and yet remains a concept with rich potential for feminists. An epistemology that focuses on trust directly confronts epistemic interactions where power differentials make exploitation a real possibility. Trust in other knowers is not always a good thing; feminists require an analysis of trust relations that explains not only when and how people tend to trust or distrust others epistemically, but when and why such trust is or is not well placed, or epistemically responsible.

When we trust, we make ourselves vulnerable. Trust is dangerous (McLeod 2015). We depend on another's good will and competence for something that we care about, placing ourselves in a position where if we bump up against the limits of that person's good will or competence, we may be harmed (Baier 1986). In trusting another, we take up a certain attitude towards the trusted. Karen Jones describes trust as involving an attitude of optimism in the goodwill and competence of another, and adds the expectation that the trusted one "will be directly and favorably moved by the thought that we are counting on her" (Jones 1996). We develop expectations of how the trusted will (and should) behave in the long run. Furthermore, by adopting an affective attitude towards another through epistemic trust, one implicitly recognizes them as an agent rather than as a mere instrument of information conveyance (Townley 2011). There is then, an ethical dimension to relationships of epistemic trust.

The affective component of trust helps identify one of the major differences between relying on someone and trusting someone. When we trust, we are subject to betrayal if we are let down, whereas if we rely on someone, we are merely disappointed in their failure (Baier 1986). The difference between trust and reliance then is significant when we move beyond an analysis of a singular testimonial exchange and consider the importance of building healthy climates and networks of trust that contribute to cooperative and successful epistemic practices in the long term. Climates of trust and their benefits can be destroyed quickly in the face of trust betrayals, and this feature of trust is not captured in a description of disappointed reliance.

The building of such climates of trust in order to generate knowledge of the forces and dynamics of oppression has been key to epistemic methods adopted by feminist theorists and activists. The early feminist idea of consciousness-raising groups, in which women come together in women-only spaces to share their gender-specific experiences, is a case in point. Such groups provide climates of trust where very personal experiences can be shared, allowing the common dimensions and structural elements of these experiences to be revealed and then identified as connected to the forces of oppression.

Furthermore, feminist theorists have recognized that even within feminist communities themselves, trust relations across differently situated women cannot be taken for granted, but require both ethical and epistemic work to generate relationships that are strong enough to sustain the difficulties of working together across positions of relative privilege and marginalization to come to understand oppression. Pressed most prominently by the demands of women of color—but also by the demands of women marginalized through their sexual orientation, economic status, or disabilities—white, heterosexual, middle-class, and able-bodied women have had to come to terms with their relative privilege and the dominance of their voices in constructing feminist knowledge. It has become clear that feminists with relative privilege need to learn to listen hard to differently situated women in order to incorporate, and allow others to incorporate, the multiplicity of marginalized gendered experiences, and need to decenter their own experiences in the development of a robust understanding of oppression. This is taxing work, both cognitively and emotionally, and some have argued that it is difficult enough that only a relationship of friendship between differently situated women could sustain the challenges that it brings (Lugones and Spelman 1983). The common motivation and commitment that comes through friendship offers the possibility of strong trust relations through which each party can take risks with each other in the pursuit of feminist knowledge.

Though discussions of trust often focus on the expectations the truster places on the trusted in the relationship, Cynthia Townley (2011) also points out that the demands of a trust relationship are not just one-sided, setting up expectations of the one trusted. She argues that when one trusts another epistemically, the truster makes an implicit commitment *not* to check up on the one trusted, but to take their word instead. At least some forms of checking up on another's testimony would violate the trust relationship. Determining where the limits are of one's employment of critical and evidence-seeking capacities that are compatible with a trust relationship is a highly contextual matter, but Townley's point is that there is a limit, and "ignorance is embedded in the structure of trust" (2011: 27), even as we use trust to widen our capacities to gain knowledge. Townley understands this to mark a significant shift in the framing of epistemology: it describes a way in which the acceptance of ignorance plays a central role in epistemic practices, and demonstrates that epistemic practices are misconstrued if they are conceptualized as always and only focused on the goal of attaining knowledge.

If certain forms of ignorance are a necessary part of social epistemic practices, then the idea of epistemic responsibility cannot simply be about what kind of dispositions and behavior leads one to *more* knowledge, but rather what kind of dispositions and behavior leads one to the *right kind* of knowledge, alongside an acceptance of appropriate forms of ignorance—that is, forms of ignorance that are not harmful to others or oneself. For an epistemology that sees trust relations as central and takes situated knowledge seriously, accountability issues in inquiry loom large (Code 1991; 2006).

Testimonial Exchanges: Social Identity as a Credibility Marker

In examining social practices of testimonial exchange, feminists are well aware that not everyone is treated equally as a reliable testifier. As we engage with each other in epistemic matters we implicitly assign varying degrees of credibility to our fellow testifiers.

We participate in economies of credibility (Fricker 2007). In making credibility assignments, we use a variety of heuristics and cognitive strategies (Origgi 2012), some of which may be good indicators of the reliability of the testifier, others less so.

A crucial question for testimony theorists is of course, to distinguish what kind of *indicator-properties* (Fricker 1998) reasonably create credibility and trust in a speaker and in what contexts. What serves as good evidence for the trustworthiness of a testifier, and what kind of indicators do epistemic damage and lead to poorly grounded trust that does not properly match a speaker's trustworthiness? In sharp distinction from traditional epistemological approaches that have emphasized the interchangeability of knowers and the irrelevance of social identity as an independent credibility-marker (as noted by Code 1991), feminists have investigated extensively the complex role social identity plays in the economies of credibility and the grounding of trust.

On the one hand, feminists have argued that in some contexts, social identity can serve as an important marker of epistemic trustworthiness, especially in cases where the socially underprivileged may have experiences of oppression that shed light on a particular issue or when the perspective of the marginalized might be required to correct for a bias in the dominant perspective. For example, a woman of color who has experienced racism and sexism in the classroom (and in other environments) might be better able than her white male colleagues to recognize cases of other professors experiencing racism and sexism (Alcoff 2001). On the other hand, when social identities do not line up with specific epistemic resources that can be brought to the table, their use as credibility markers is both unfair and epistemically unsound.

Of particular concern for feminists are the ways in which social power dynamics and cultural forces result in gendered and racialized stereotypes and identity prejudices that affect the patterns and norms of credibility assignments. For example, the fact that women have often been conceptualized as less rational and less measured in their judgments than men leads their testimony in many contexts to be taken less seriously than that of similarly positioned men. In such cases, a woman may suffer a credibility deficit, as she is attributed less credibility than she deserves because of her gender and its cultural associations. Similarly, Patricia Hill Collins (2000) argues that prevailing stereotypes of black women make it more difficult for them to be seen as epistemically competent. Such credibility deficits can be characterized as a misplaced withholding of epistemic trust on the part of the hearer, where prejudices are getting in the way of sound cooperative epistemic endeavors. Though this misguided distrust surely results in an epistemic loss for the hearer, several feminists have focused their attention on the epistemic wrongs done to the speaker in such cases, seeing these epistemic wrongs as part of the dynamics of oppression.

Miranda Fricker has argued that when a speaker is attributed a credibility deficit due to an identity prejudice (that is, a prejudice connected to their social identity), they suffer a form of epistemic injustice that she calls *testimonial injustice*. According to Fricker, testimonial injustice is both an ethical and an epistemic wrong; at its core, testimonial injustice wrongs one as a giver of knowledge (2007: 45), which she takes to be a central feature of our epistemic agency in a social world of cooperative knowledge production and circulation. Fricker argues that testimonial injustice "excludes the subject from trustful conversation" (2007: 53). Kristie Dotson (2011) characterizes such failures to recognize someone as a knower as an epistemic violence perpetrated on the speaker—a particular kind of silencing that she refers to as *testimonial quieting*. Importantly, when regularly subjected to such silencing and epistemic injustices, a speaker can also suffer long-term damage to their self-trust that transpires by way of a loss of confidence in their own epistemic abilities through the experience of others regularly doubting them (Jones 2012). But even without any erosion of self-trust, Dotson points out that epistemic violence and a coerced silencing of speakers can occur through the phenomenon of *testimonial smothering*, in which speakers restrict their testimony to hearers because they know their testimony will not be understood and given proper uptake by perniciously ignorant hearers (Dotson 2011).

José Medina also notes that we must consider the epistemic harms of credibility excesses as well as credibility deficits, arguing that credibility judgments are "implicitly comparative and contrastive" (2013: 63). For example, gender biases often simultaneously result in credibility excesses attributed to men and credibility deficits attributed to women, especially (but not exclusively) when the content of the testimonies conflict with each other. At the same time, these relative excesses and deficits will be further complicated by cultural biases associated with additional social groupings such as race and class. Medina seeks a broad analysis of the epistemic harms that follow from maladapted practices of credibility assignments, including medium and long range harms that affect an agent's continued engagement in the practices, and harms that involve not just the speaker, but also the hearer, other interlocutors, and members of the relevant social groups who are affected in the network of ongoing testimonial exchanges. Medina notes that credibility "never applies to subjects individually and in isolation from others, but always affects clusters of subjects in particular social networks and environments" (2013: 61).

Correcting for Maladapted Norms of Credibility

Recognizing the ways in which identity prejudices and their accompanying stereotypes differentially affect speakers in the economies of credibility, feminists have sought to articulate remedies that would right these epistemic and ethical wrongs, and improve the soundness of our epistemic practices. Looking at individuals engaged in testimonial exchanges, Fricker develops the idea of the virtue of *testimonial justice*, by which hearers can correct for testimonial injustices by developing appropriate testimonial sensibilities that contain an anti-prejudicial current (Fricker 2007: 86). Testimonial justice involves a *reflexive* critical social awareness through which a hearer considers and corrects for how prejudices might be influencing her perception of the credibility of the testifier (Fricker 2007: 91).

Relatedly, Nancy Daukas offers a broad interpretation of the virtue of *epistemic trustworthiness*, understanding it as a social virtue that incorporates our abilities to make sound credibility assignments of others. Epistemic trustworthiness amounts to a disposition to behave (in a given context and for a given domain of knowledge) in accordance with one's actual epistemic status (Daukas 2006: 112). An epistemically trustworthy person does not over inflate the certainty of a claim when sharing it with others due to excessive self-confidence, and does not under sell a claim out of undue diffidence. Initially then, epistemic trustworthiness concerns each of us as speakers. But because we are engaged in cooperative epistemic pursuits within a network of knowers, one's virtue of epistemic trustworthiness depends not only on one's awareness of the strength of one's own abilities to know, but also on one's attitudes to other knowers and corresponding ability to assess *their* trustworthiness. Trustworthiness is possible "only when an agent is attuned to her own, and particular others', epistemic strengths and weaknesses relative to particular context and projects" (Daukas 2011: 52). When prejudices and stereotypes adversely affect the relative level of credibility I assign to others, with these credibility judgments helping to shape my beliefs, then so long as I am unaware of this weakness in my epistemic work and do not account for it, my own trustworthiness as a contributor to shared inquiry will be damaged. Similar to Fricker, Daukas recommends that agents who wish to be epistemically trustworthy exercise a kind of "oppositional agency" that resists the social norms of credibility assignments where social prejudices play a problematic role (Daukas 2011: 64), such that: "the epistemic agent works from dispositions which enable her to unmask and transform epistemically unsound (and socially unjust) practices of epistemic exclusions (i.e., testimonial injustice)" (Daukas 2011: 52).

The virtues suggested by Fricker and Daukas can be interpreted in two different ways. First, they can be understood as neutralizing the effects of social identity as a credibility marker by counteracting social identity prejudices. But they can also be interpreted as incorporating social identity into testimonial judgments. These virtues do not assign credibility directly from a marginalized social identity, but they do attend to social identity and encourage epistemic agents to seek out marginalized voices when working within practices of maladapted credibility norms.

Though neither Fricker nor Daukas are oblivious to the structural components of these problems, they do focus on the transactional aspect of testimonial exchanges and remedies that reside in individual agents, and many argue that such a focus is inadequate. One reason for this is that remedies requiring individual reflection to correct for bias are quite cognitively taxing (Anderson 2012: 168). What Fricker and Daukas propose as individual reflective correctives is far from easy to pull off. Another reason is that by focusing on individual exchanges the remedies may well be insufficient for change by failing to challenge the overall structures of the practices of credibility attributions (Dotson 2012). Understanding the significance of unequal credibility deficits across groups and the depth of the challenges of remedying them requires that we look to the full range of contributing factors that go well beyond identity prejudices held by individuals.

For example, among the variety of heuristics and credibility markers that hearers use to identify trustworthy speakers, some may work less well in socially unjust contexts. Elizabeth Anderson argues that education levels might be reasonably used as credibility markers in certain contexts, but in socially unjust systems where there is unequal access to education, they can contribute to group-based credibility deficits for socially marginalized members of society (Anderson 2012). Additionally, she notes that psychological tendencies to give higher levels of credibility to in-group members, and the "shared reality bias" through which people who interact frequently tend to converge in their perspectives on the world can create unfair patterns of credibility assignments in socially unjust contexts where certain groups are underrepresented in recognized epistemic communities (Anderson 2012: 169–170). Jones makes the related point that because social identity makes a difference to one's experiential base, a report of an event or experience (or, an interpretation these) may seem astonishing to members of some groups, while seeming quite likely to others who share a different experiential base (Jones 2002: 157). This makes it challenging for the marginalized to be heard by the dominant, especially if there are patterns of isolation or segregation between stratified groups in society. As Anderson makes the point, it is only through creating epistemic democracies, in which there is "universal participation on terms of equality of all inquirers" that sufficient remedies can be found to these structural problems (Anderson 2012: 172).

One source of these problems concerns the generation of the very conceptual resources required for knowledge, and correspondingly, the need for those conceptual resources need to be shared across knowers for one's testimony to be at all intelligible. An important feature of social marginalization is "hermeneutical marginalization"— being unable to participate fully in the development of the community's conceptual resources. In cases where groups experience hermeneutical marginalization, society as a whole (including the marginalized) will likely lack the hermeneutical resources required to make the experiences of the marginalized intelligible, and without intelligibility, they cannot be heard or given uptake. Fricker (2007) calls this *hermeneutical injustice*, and offers the example of the evolution of the concept of sexual harassment: before the concept was developed, women (and society as a whole) lacked the conceptual resources to be able to adequately interpret and describe what was happening to them, and so their concerns about their experiences of harassment could not be heard.

Importantly, Medina has argued that hermeneutical and testimonial injustices are deeply interconnected; they are maintained and passed on through the dynamics of each other as those without adequate hermeneutical resources struggle to be granted credibility, while low credibility assigned to a speaker due to prejudice makes it less likely that a hearer will be able to attend to any hermeneutical kernels provided by the speaker that could be developed into an insightful interpretation (Medina 2013: 96). Dotson also makes the point that hermeneutical resources are actually much more dispersed than Fricker's original idea of hermeneutical injustice makes out. She argues that there often are conceptual resources available within marginalized communities through which they can understand their experiences (Dotson 2012). But these resources are not recognized or taken up by the dominant due to what Gaile Pohlhaus (2012) has termed a "willful hermeneutical ignorance" that transpires when dominantly situated knowers refuse to learn to use the epistemic resources that marginally situated knowers have developed to understand their experiences. For Dotson, such refusals to look for and employ such epistemic resources of the marginalized constitutes another kind of epistemic injustice: *contributory injustice* (Dotson 2012).

As feminist analyses begin to integrate the structural and individual dimensions of practices of testimony, interesting implications emerge concerning accounts of the epistemic virtues. For example, Medina's work emphasizes the need for a variety of epistemic virtues and argues that some (such as epistemic humility and open-mindedness) are more difficult for the socially privileged to develop (alongside a preponderance of epistemic vices such as epistemic laziness and closed-mindedness), with other virtues being more of a challenge for the marginalized (such as epistemic confidence or self-trust) (Medina 2013). Karen Frost-Arnold argues that even trustworthiness itself is not always virtuous. She finds value in tricksters, and points out that for the marginalized, there can at times be epistemic value in betraying the trust of the privileged when it results in the expansion of networks of trust across the oppressed (Frost-Arnold 2014).

Trust in Knowledge-Producing Institutions and Communities: The Case of Science

Beyond epistemic trust relations between individuals, feminists are also interested in the fact that we regularly depend upon and place our trust in communities and institutions themselves as testifiers and bearers of knowledge. This is especially true in the case of specialized knowledge, in which individuals undertake education and training to become experts in particular fields, and then participate in specific practices of knowledge-producing communities and institutions. Whether through individual spokespersons or consensus statements from research communities, members of the public look to these communities and institutions to fulfill the role of providing specialized knowledge and informed judgments on topics relevant to their lives.

Most trust theorists agree that interpersonal trust remains the paradigmatic form of trust, with institutional trust being modeled after it (McLeod 2015). Trust in institutions and communities shares core features of interpersonal trust: vulnerability, an attitude of optimism toward the institution with certain expectations developing concerning its ability to provide me with reliable knowledge, the possibility of being betrayed, and the possibility of trust being more or less well grounded.

What is different about epistemic trust in institutions and communities compared with trust in persons, however, is that evidence of the trustworthiness of the specific *practices* of the institution (Frost-Arnold 2014) play a more significant role in determining well-placed trust than in the case of individual testifiers. It may be less important that every participant in the institution be perfectly trustworthy if an institution operates with robustly trustworthy practices that help protect against the undue influence untrustworthy individual members.

For example, many cite the objectivity of the scientific method (as a recognized central piece of scientific practice) as justification for the trust they place in the testimony of scientific research communities. While feminists tend to agree that the objectivity of a practice grounds trust (Scheman 2001), they argue that focusing on the scientific method is too narrow a characterization of the practices of science; to understand how objectivity can ground trust in the testimony of scientific institutions (or any knowledge-producing institution), we must also investigate the many social dimensions of the communal practices, scrutinizing the social arrangements under which science is done (Addelson 1983; Longino 1990; Scheman 2001). Because scientific knowledge has such an overwhelming influence on the conditions of contemporary life, it has received significant attention from feminists interested in trust relations with communities and institutions and serves as an excellent example of the issues at stake.

The highly specialized and in many cases complex and resource-intensive nature of scientific research means that a large proportion of it needs to take place within organized research communities and institutions of knowledge production. Trust relations operate internally among members of these communities (and among multiple scientific sub-communities), as well as among these same knowledge-producing communities and those who fall outside of the scope of the knowledge production, that is, layperson communities and/or the general public. Internal trust relations must be relatively healthy if scientific institutions are to function well in producing reliable knowledge, and trust relations with those external to institutions must in turn be relatively healthy if these institutions are to successfully provide the right kind of knowledge to lay communities.

Within scientific research communities there is a strong division of cognitive labor, with scientists lacking both the time and money to fully replicate the results of others, and the necessary background to understand very highly specialized work of others that might serve as important evidence for their own research (Hardwig 1991; Kitcher 1990). For many, the main concern of this large role of trust in the production of scientific knowledge lies in the potential for fraudulent results from unscrupulous scientists. But feminists have argued that trust relations within scientific communities depend on not just the character and work of the individual scientists, but also the structure and practices of these institutions themselves. As Kristina Rolin explains, trust in scientific testimony depends in part on "trust in the community's ability to facilitate inclusive and responsive dialogue based on shared standards of argumentation" (Rolin 2002: 106). Inclusive dialogue not only offers a deterrent to unscrupulous individual scientists, but increases the chances of detecting error and bias in the science itself. Focusing on gender, Rolin cites evidence suggesting our current scientific institutions are not as trustworthy as we might hope. For example, empirical evidence suggests a gender bias within the established evaluation processes of scientific institutions, processes that are the very means through which scientists decide who within their community is trustworthy and competent (Rolin 2002: 105). Additionally, micro inequities exist within scientific communities that can "limit women's opportunities to participate in scientific dialogue" (Rolin 2002: 109), again threatening to skew the relative credibility assignments upon which the generation of scientific knowledge depends.

Scientific institutions also have histories of interactions with lay communities that are relevant to ascertaining their epistemic trustworthiness. Here, feminists have applied the insights of situated knowing to cases where knowledge depends on trust, arguing that it is possible for a scientific institution to fail to be trustworthy for a particularly situated lay community, especially a marginalized community, given certain histories of interactions (Grasswick 2014; Scheman 2001). Most prominently, Naomi Scheman argues that when there has been a poor history of scientific communities generating knowledge that addresses serious concerns of the marginalized, and when instead there has been a history of exclusion from scientific communities, poor quality research on questions relevant to the lives of the marginalized, and abuse of the marginalized as research subjects, the marginalized have good reason not to trust the practices and results of science. As she notes: "It is, in short, irrational to expect people to place their trust in the results of practices about which they know little and that emerge from institutions—universities, corporations, government agencies—which they know to be inequitable" (Scheman 2001: 43).

Additionally, the epistemic tasks scientific institutions are entrusted with include making judgments concerning what areas of knowledge are important enough to be researched, what results need to be shared with laypersons, and what results need to be filtered out (Grasswick 2010; 2011). Yet differently situated laypersons have different epistemic needs and determinations of what knowledge is relevant for them. In the case of marginalized groups for which scientific institutions have done a historically poor job of producing and sharing knowledge of most importance to them, such a history can contribute to good reasons for a marginalized group to distrust a particular scientific institution.

Implications of Feminist Analyses of Testimony

As feminist analyses of the role of trust in testimony have developed, they have increasingly shown an awareness of the need to account for ways in which individual epistemic dispositions are deeply interdependent with structural features of the social practices of inquiry. They also clearly draw the connection between social conditions generally and our specific epistemic practices. According to feminist accounts of testimony, working toward the larger goal of social justice will simultaneously move us toward more reliable and responsible epistemic practices. But these accounts also imply that responsible interventions into our epistemic practices can help move society in the direction of increased social justice overall.

Further Reading

Code, Lorraine (1991) *What Can She Know?: Feminist Theory and the Construction of Knowledge*, Ithaca, NY: Cornell University Press. (Code's landmark work critiquing standard epistemological inquiry and setting out her feminist approach to epistemology, with a focus on interpersonal relations between interdependent knowers.)
——— (1995) *Rhetorical Spaces: Essays on Gendered Locations*, New York: Routledge. (A collection of Code's essays, many of which take up the nuances of gendered credibility attributions.)
Fricker, Miranda (2007) *Epistemic Injustice: Power and the Ethics of Knowing*, Oxford: Oxford University Press. (Provides the first extensive handling of the ideas of epistemic injustice and its combined epistemic and ethical dimensions.)
Medina, José (2013) *The Epistemology of Resistance: Gender and Racial Oppression, Epistemic Injustice, and Resistant Imaginations*, Oxford: Oxford University Press. (Provides both extensive critique and further development of Fricker's original idea of epistemic injustice, using virtue theory to understand the challenges of knowing from one's particular social location.)

Related Topics

Epistemic injustice, ignorance, and trans experience (Chapter 22); speech and silencing (Chapter 23); philosophy of science and the feminist legacy (Chapter 25); feminist philosophy of social science (Chapter 27); feminist virtue ethics (Chapter 45).

References

Addelson, Kathryn Pyne (1983) "The Man of Professional Wisdom," in Sandra Harding and Merrill Hintikka (Eds.) *Discovering Reality: Feminist Perspectives on Epistemology, Metaphysics, Methodology, and Philosophy of Science*, Dordrecht: D. Reidel, 165–186.
Alcoff, Linda Martín (2001) "On Judging Epistemic Credibility: Is Social Identity Relevant?" in Nancy Tuana and Sandra Morgen (Eds.) *Engendering Rationalities*, Albany: SUNY, 53–80.
Anderson, Elizabeth (2012) "Epistemic Justice as a Virtue of Social Institutions," *Social Epistemology* 26: 163–173.
Baier, Annette (1985) "What Do Women Want in a Moral Theory?" *Noûs* 19: 53–63.
——— (1986) "Trust and Antitrust," *Ethics* 96: 231–260.
Bergin, Lisa (2002) "Testimony, Epistemic Difference, and Privilege: How Feminist Epistemology Can Improve Our Understanding of the Communication of Knowledge," *Social Epistemology* 16: 197–213.
Code, Lorraine (1991) *What Can She Know?: Feminist Theory and the Construction of Knowledge*, Ithaca, NY: Cornell University Press.
——— (1995) *Rhetorical Spaces: Essays on Gendered Locations*, New York: Routledge.
——— (2006) *Ecological Thinking: The Politics of Epistemic Location*, Oxford: Oxford University Press.
Collins, Patricia Hill (2000) *Black Feminist Thought: Knowledge, Consciousness, and the Politics of Empowerment*, New York: Routledge.
Daukas, Nancy (2006) "Epistemic Trust and Social Location," *Episteme* 3: 109–124.
——— (2011) "Altogether Now: A Virtue-Theoretic Approach to Pluralism in Feminist Epistemology," in Heidi Grasswick (Ed.) *Feminist Epistemology and Philosophy of Science: Power in Knowledge*, Dordrecht: Springer, 45–67.
Dotson, Kristie (2011) "Tracking Epistemic Violence, Tracking Practices of Silencing," *Hypatia* 26: 236–257.
——— (2012) "A Cautionary Tale: On Limiting Epistemic Oppression," *Frontiers* 33: 24–47.
Fricker, Miranda (1998) "Rational Authority and Social Power: Towards A Truly Social Epistemology," *Proceedings of the Aristotelean Society* 98: 156–177.
——— (2007) *Epistemic Injustice: Power and the Ethics of Knowing*, Oxford: Oxford University Press.
Frost-Arnold, Karen (2014) "Imposters, Tricksters, and Trustworthiness as an Epistemic Virtue," *Hypatia* 29: 790–807.

Goldman, Alvin (1999) *Knowledge in a Social World*, Oxford: Clarendon Press.

——(2001) "Experts: Which Ones Should You Trust?" *Philosophy and Phenomenological Research* 63: 85–110.

Grasswick, Heidi (2010) "Scientific and Lay Communities: Earning Epistemic Trust through Knowledge Sharing," *Synthese* 177: 387–409.

—— (2011) "Liberatory Epistemology and the Sharing of Knowledge: Querying the Norms," in Heidi Grasswick (Ed.) *Feminist Epistemology and Philosophy of Science*. Dordrecht: Springer, 241–262.

——(2013) "Feminist Social Epistemology," in Edward Zalta (Ed.) *Stanford Encyclopedia of Philosophy*, Spring 2013 edition [online]. Available from: http://plato.stanford.edu/archives/spr2013/entries/feminist-social-epistemology/

——(2014) "Climate Change Science and Responsible Trust: A Situated Approach," *Hypatia* 29: 541–557.

Harding, Sandra (1991) *Whose Science? Whose Knowledge?: Thinking from Women's Lives*, Ithaca, NY: Cornell University Press.

Hardwig, John (1991) "The Role of Trust in Knowledge," *Journal of Philosophy* 88: 693–708.

Hartsock, Nancy (1983) "The Feminist Standpoint: Developing the Ground for a Specifically Feminist Historical Materialism," in Sandra Harding and Merrill Hintikka (Eds.) *Discovering Reality: Feminist Perspectives on Epistemology, Metaphysics, Methodology, and Philosophy of Science*, Dordrecht: D. Reidel, 283–310.

Jones, Karen (1996) "Trust as an Affective Attitude," *Ethics* 107: 4–25.

——(2002) "The Politics of Credibility," in Louise M. Antony and Charlotte E. Witt (Eds.) *A Mind of One's Own: Feminist Essays on Reason and Objectivity*, Boulder, CO: Westview Press, 154–176.

——(2012) "The Politics of Intellectual Self-Trust," *Social Epistemology* 26: 237–251.

Kitcher, Philip (1990) "The Division of Cognitive Labor," *Journal of Philosophy* 87: 5–22.

Longino, Helen (1990) *Science as Social Knowledge: Values and Objectivity in Scientific Inquiry*, Princeton NJ: Princeton University Press.

Lugones, María, and Spelman, Elizabeth (1983) "Have We Got a Theory for You! Feminist Theory, Cultural Imperialism, and the Demand for 'The Woman's Voice,'" *Women's Studies. International Forum* 6: 573–581.

McLeod, Carolyn (2015) "Trust," in Edward Zalta (Ed.) *Stanford Encyclopedia of Philosophy*, Fall 2015 edition [online]. Available from: http://plato.stanford.edu/archives/fall2015/entriesrust/

Medina, José (2013) *The Epistemology of Resistance: Gender and Racial Oppression, Epistemic Injustice, and Resistant Imaginations*, Oxford: Oxford University Press.

Origgi, Gloria (2012) "Epistemic Injustice and Epistemic Trust," *Social Epistemology* 26: 221–235.

Pohlhaus Jr., Gaile (2012) "Relational Knowing and Epistemic Injustice: Toward a Theory of Willful Hermeneutical Ignorance," *Hypatia* 27: 715–735.

Potter, Nancy Nyquist (2002) *How Can I Be Trusted?: A Virtue Theory of Trustworthiness*, Lanham, MD: Rowman & Littlefield.

Rolin, Kristina (2002) "Gender and Trust in Science," *Hypatia* 17: 95–120.

Scheman, Naomi (2001) "Epistemology Resuscitated: Objectivity as Trustworthiness," in Nancy Tuana and Sandra Morgen (Eds.) *Engendering Rationalities*, Albany: SUNY, 23–52.

Townley, Cynthia (2011) *A Defense of Ignorance: Its Value for Knowers and Roles in Feminist and Social Epistemologies*, Lanham MD: Lexington Books.

22

EPISTEMIC INJUSTICE, IGNORANCE, AND TRANS EXPERIENCES

Miranda Fricker and Katharine Jenkins

What is the relation between ignorance and one or another kind of epistemic injustice? First, let us set out the core concepts of epistemic injustice that we shall be using: "testimonial injustice," "hermeneutical injustice," and its precondition "hermeneutical marginalization" (Fricker 2007). Testimonial injustice is the injustice of receiving a degree of credibility that has been reduced by some kind of prejudice. This kind of epistemic injustice consists in *an unjust deficit of credibility*. If a female politician's policy proposal receives a reduced level of credibility from the electorate owing to gender prejudice, for instance, then she has been subject to a testimonial injustice. (Testimonial injustices need not strictly be in respect of *testimonial* speech acts, but rather any speech act whose acceptance depends on its receiving sufficient credibility; see Fricker 2007: 60.)

Hermeneutical injustice is the injustice of being frustrated in an attempt to render a significant social experience intelligible (to oneself and/or to others) where hermeneutical marginalization is a significant causal factor in that failure. Someone counts as hermeneutically marginalized insofar as they belong to a social group that under-contributes to the common pool of concepts and social meanings. And where this under-contribution results in an experience being less than fully intelligible, either to oneself or to another in a failed attempt to communicate it, a hermeneutical injustice thereby occurs. Hermeneutical injustice therefore consists in *an unjust deficit of intelligibility*. Imagine, for example, someone with a disability the experience of which is well understood by him, by his family and friends, and also by some other social groups to which he belongs (perhaps, for instance, those who have themselves had relevantly similar life experiences) but not by members of other groups to whom he may on occasion need to communicate his distinctive experience, such as his employer or his neighbor. Such a person is frustrated in his attempts to render his experiences intelligible to those significant others owing to the requisite concepts not being sufficiently widely shared, and where a significant part of the explanation why they are not sufficiently widely shared is his hermeneutical marginalization. When this happens, his communicative frustration exemplifies hermeneutical injustice.

In the original elaboration of these concepts (Fricker 2007) testimonial injustices always have a perpetrator (a hearer, individual, or collective, who makes a credibility judgment that is negatively affected by prejudice); but hermeneutical injustices do not—they are purely structural. Hermeneutical injustices are moments of unmet needs of understanding where the explanation is an underlying poverty of intelligibility for which (on Fricker's definition) no individual agent is at fault. But it is instructive to see how far testimonial injustice might be developed into a purely structural phenomenon, and conversely how far hermeneutical injustice might be augmented to become a kind of injustice that can sometimes involve individual culpability.

Taking testimonial injustice first, Elizabeth Anderson has offered the helpful distinction *within* testimonial injustice between "transactional" and "structural," which helps us imagine cases of testimonial injustice where there is no particular perpetrator but, owing to a purely structural mechanism, some voice or voices fail to be heard, and in a context that renders their silencing unjust (Anderson 2012). Perhaps a real-life example of such a structural testimonial injustice might be the infamous all-white Oscar nominations in 2016, inasmuch as this was the direct result of the Academy's being overwhelmingly composed of white voters. The white-majority Academy structurally silenced the voices of potential black Academy members, who can therefore be considered the subject of a structural testimonial injustice. (And, as is typical, this epistemic injustice then causes a secondary injustice: the reasonable presumption in this case being that some black actors missed out on nominations they would have received were it not for the structural epistemic injustice in the Academy.)

From the other direction, and now considering the augmentation of hermeneutical injustice, José Medina has challenged Fricker's characterization of it as "purely structural," arguing that we should see hermeneutical injustices as having *perpetrators* (at least sometimes) inasmuch as members of the epistemic community may have colluded in the structural ignorances that sustain the hermeneutical marginalization fueling the injustice (Medina 2012 and 2013). Individuals may be colluding in this way any time they fail to be sufficiently open to the unfamiliar or alien concepts being used by others, whether this is due to sheer laziness or to forms of motivated resistance— such as when a socially privileged person resists social meanings that state or imply unsettling challenges to their social standing. Both Fricker and Medina regard this as a failure of epistemic virtue (specifically the virtue of hermeneutical justice), but Medina presses the idea that such failure of virtue reveals an important sense in which hermeneutical injustices can have perpetrators, and so are not always purely structural.

Epistemic Injustice and Ignorance

Let us, then, try to explore the relation of the phenomena of epistemic injustice as described above to ignorance. It might be tempting to say that all prejudice is a kind of ignorance, but that would be a stretch. Prejudice is better conceived as a determinant of what one knows and ignores; and if we take prejudice always to involve some motivated maladjustment to the evidence (see Fricker 2007 and 2016; Maitra 2010: 206–207), then its tendency will be to produce ignorance, for maladjustment to the evidence tends to produce epistemic error and distorted social perception. Someone who perceives social others according to an array of prejudicial stereotypes will get many things wrong, thereby ignoring at least as many potential items of knowledge. In a case of testimonial injustice the hearer whose judgment of credibility is affected by a prejudice that consists, for instance, in a jingoistic mistrust of foreigners may well fail to acquire knowledge from a foreigner-interlocutor, and that failure—that blockage in the interpersonal flow of knowledge—*preserves* ignorance. The hearer had something to learn from the speaker, but prejudice got in the way, and so the ignorance remains. Moreover, any further epistemic import that the missed item of propositional knowledge might have had, for instance its inferential, justifying or defeating significance for other beliefs in the hearer's psychology, are blocked along with the primary content of the testimony. So the preservation of ignorance that p, where p is the propositional content of what was said, may often entail further missed epistemic opportunity to better shape or inferentially enrich one's belief system (see Fricker 2016). We might express this by saying that testimonial injustice tends to preserve not only immediate ignorance but also inferentially ramified ignorance. Imagine, for instance, a patient who has a jingoistic mistrust of foreigners being told by his doctor of Pakistani origin that he needs to lose weight or risk cardiovascular disease. Now if the patient's jingoistic mistrust of foreigners depresses the level of credibility given to the doctor, then the patient may not only miss out on this knowledge of the health risk he is running (already a significant epistemic loss) but moreover when he later experiences chest pain combined with shortness of breath he is likely to be in a worse position to infer that he is experiencing symptoms of cardiac arrest. This latter, life-threatening, epistemic disadvantage is a secondary one, occurring further down the inferential chain from the original testimonial injustice.

The relationship between epistemic injustice and ignorance is not only a matter of *preservation*, however. Prejudice that blocks the flow of knowledge in the epistemic system also *produces* ignorance—not propositional ignorance this time but rather what we might usefully think of as a special sort of practical ignorance: *lack of conceptual know-how*. Some social patterns of testimonial injustice will produce similar patterns of hermeneutical marginalization. This is because a sustained susceptibility to testimonial injustice in one's attempts to put one's point across concerning social phenomena will tend to contribute to, and ultimately constitute some sphere of, hermeneutical marginalization: persistent testimonial injustice prevents the subject from achieving normal levels of participation in the generation of commonly held concepts and social meanings. Thus there is a causal and, at the limit, constitutive relation between persistent testimonial injustice and hermeneutical marginalization. If a social group is hermeneutically marginalized in this way, then their would-be contributions to the common store of social meanings (the collective hermeneutical resource) will remain private. Such local or in-group meanings might be actively corralled or kettled by resistant out-groups who are resistant to knowing; or again they may be more passively ignored by out-groups' simply not making the effort to step outside their default ways of viewing the world and their place in it. (Sometimes this will be a dereliction of epistemic and ethical duty; though it need not be. There is no standing epistemic obligation to make efforts to know how the world looks from absolutely all social points of view—an impossible task—but there *is* such an obligation to make relevant efforts to do so in relation to many social groups other than one's own.)

Where an in-group's concepts and social meanings are actively kettled by resistant out-groups, the result in the out-group is what Gaile Pohlhaus has labeled "willful ignorance," and José Medina "active ignorance" (Pohlhaus 2012; Medina 2013; see also Mason 2011; Mills 2007 and 2015; and Dotson 2012). Whether willful or inadvertent, active or passive, the upshot from the point of view of ignorance is that members of out-groups do not gain the conceptual know-how embodied in the in-group's would-be hermeneutical contributions. And, in turn, nor do they gain the social understanding those concepts would have furnished. Thus sustained testimonial injustice regarding some patch of the social world and the sphere of hermeneutical marginalization to which it leads, can *produce* a patch of ignorance—namely, an area of *practical conceptual ignorance* or lack of conceptual know-how. When this happens, members of the relevant out-groups fail to acquire a range of conceptual competences requisite for understanding a sphere of social experience had by the in-group. Furthermore, when this happens, the conditions are in place for members of the in-group to experience hermeneutical injustice as regards the intelligibility of their experiences to out-groups— the speakers who possess the requisite conceptual competencies suffer an unjust deficit of communicative intelligibility at the hands of those who lack such competencies (see Medina 2013: 108).

As an illustration, imagine once again the man who has a disability that is not properly understood by certain people to whom he needs to render it intelligible. Let's imagine he has a specific post-traumatic stress disorder (PTSD) for which there is a specific trigger that tends to come up in his work context. If his boss is unversed in issues of PTSD, and/or resistant to their significance for her as an employer, then our employee may suffer a hermeneutical injustice when he requests exemption from the work-related activity that contains the trigger. Insofar as his boss continues to resist, remaining closed to the new meanings being used by the employee (notions of specific triggers, for instance), then not only does she actively facilitate the hermeneutical injustice experienced by the employee, but she herself misses out on new conceptual competences she might otherwise have gained, and so a certain lack of conceptual know-how on her part is maintained. This scenario exemplifies what Medina has termed "active ignorance" that is motivated (perhaps unconsciously) by interests, or other biases on the part of the resisting hearer (Medina 2013: ch. 1). Similarly, Kristie Dotson has identified a phenomenon she names "contributory injustice," where a hearer is willfully insensible to what a (conceptually well-resourced) speaker is attempting to get her resistant interlocutor to understand (Dotson 2012).

Such hermeneutical injustices preserve the out-group's ignorance, just as straightforward cases of testimonial injustice do. And so we see that hermeneutical marginalization produces *practical conceptual ignorance*; and testimonial and hermeneutical injustice both preserve *propositional ignorance* on the part of the interlocutor. Despite the fact that, in general, knowledge is an enabling asset in life and ignorance a liability, in cases of epistemic injustice, where the unwholesome catalyst is either prejudice or hermeneutical marginalization, it is overwhelmingly likely that the reverse is true: in such cases it is rather the *knower* who will suffer from the effects of the various ignorances that are produced or preserved in their interlocutors. (This generalization is compatible with the point, emphasized by both Mills and Medina, that sometimes oppressed groups can successfully exploit their oppressors' ignorance of them, turning it in strategic ways to their own advantage (Mills 2007: 18; Medina 2013: 116).)

Trans Experiences and Testimonial Injustice

We now have a characterization in place that presents us with a rough and ready causal flow chart of broadly categorized moments of epistemic injustice: (1) socially patterned testimonial injustice tends to produce (2) hermeneutical marginalization in relation to one or more areas of social experience; which in turn tends to produce (3) hermeneutical injustice in relation to the intelligibility of those areas of experience. We would like to explore and illustrate these phenomena of epistemic injustice and their relation to ignorance by reference to the current and fast-changing issue of trans experience and identity. By "trans" we mean to refer, without distinction, to all people who identify as transgender, as transsexual, as trans*, or as trans (*simpliciter*). The movement for trans rights is not only a particularly pressing strand of social and legislative change, it is also one with special relevance to questions of ignorance, for there has long been (and continues to be—ourselves being no exception) widespread ignorance of trans perspectives, experiences, and the shared social meanings they call for. We believe the overcoming of ignorances that attend epistemic injustice in the manner set out above is an important part of the wider social project of overcoming ignorance in relation to trans experiences and identities. For our conception of trans experiences we shall rely almost entirely on the written testimony of people who are trans. It goes without saying that our bringing these experiences under this or that category of epistemic injustice is done tentatively, and in an exploratory spirit that welcomes multiple corrective responses on these complex and fast-evolving issues.

Trans people report experiences that are surely ones of testimonial injustice. One context in which this can occur is the clinical setting. Historically, at gender clinics in the sixties, seventies, and eighties, trans people who presented with requests for hormones and surgery to facilitate gender transition were required to fit a very narrow set of criteria in order to access these things. Trans people were expected to have a gender presentation and a sexual orientation that were normative for their identified gender—so a trans woman, for example, would need to present a traditionally feminine appearance and to report sexual attraction to men. Trans people were also required to report a strong sense of loathing towards their bodies and to say that these experiences dated from their early childhood (Green 2004: 46; Serano 2007: ch. 7). A trans person who did not meet these criteria would often be judged not to really need to transition, and would be denied access to transition-related medical procedures. Such a person would suffer a testimonial injustice: their testimony concerning their conviction that they were trans and had a genuine need to access transition-related medical procedures was subject to an unjustified credibility deficit stemming from identity prejudice concerning trans identities. This kind of testimonial injustice was supported by the interaction of anti-trans prejudice with mental health stigma: the positioning of trans people as by definition experiencing a psychiatric disorder—"gender identity disorder"—made them vulnerable to having their reports of their own experience dismissed on the spurious grounds that mental health problems made them unreliable or even deceptive (Green 2004: 93; Serano 2007: ch. 7). The immediate upshot as regards ignorance is that the healthcare worker learned very little of trans experience from the "patient," because the prejudicial pathologization blocked crucial aspects of the informational flow. Jamison Green relates a particularly pronounced expression of such ignorance: "As recently as 1999," he writes, "I heard a physician declare, 'All *my* FTMs [i.e., trans men] want tattoos,' as if this proved 'his' FTMs were typical men, or that FTMs who didn't want tattoos were somehow less authentic than 'his' FTMs" (Green 2004: 46).

Moreover, trans people are also susceptible to the specifically "pre-emptive" form of testimonial injustice (Fricker 2007: 130–131 and *passim*). Pre-emptive testimonial injustice is effectively an advance credibility deficit sufficient to ensure that your word is not even solicited. All too often for trans authors this kind of epistemic injustice threatens when attempts are made to address a wider audience. The media, including publishing and the film industry, has for some time seemed most willing to publish work by trans people that is autobiographical, and that focuses on the process of transition, often in a sensationalizing way (Serano 2007: 2). For example, in some cases, trans people report being invited to participate in news articles or documentaries only to be dropped when it becomes clear that they will not pander to a preconceived narrative, often one that includes normative gender presentation and detailed discussion of genital surgery (Serano 2007: 44–45). Such pre-emptive testimonial injustice functions to maintain ignorance regarding trans experiences and identities by ensuring that only a narrow subset of those experiences and identities reach a wider audience.

In some cases, an author may compromise in order to at least get some version of her message across: recognizing that the media industries simply do not want to hear about a certain range of trans life experiences, she may decide to curtail and adjust her message in order at least to succeed in conveying some approximation of what she originally intended. Such cases constitute what Dotson has identified as "testimonial smothering" (Dotson 2011)—a partial kind of silencing. Juliet Jacques, a writer and journalist, reports an experience of testimonial smothering in relation to her autobiography, *Trans: A Memoir*: "Initially, I wanted to write a wider history of trans people in Britain, as well as short stories, but all I could get publishers to consider was a personal story" (Jacques 2015: 299).

Testimonial smothering also contributes to ignorance, because the audience receives only the compromised (and in some cases possibly even misleading) version, and so learns less than they might have done had the speaker been able to communicate in accordance with their original intentions.

Trans Experiences, Hermeneutical Marginalization, and Hermeneutical Injustice

The testimonial injustices of various kinds suffered by trans people offer a particularly stark illustration of the connection between testimonial injustice and hermeneutical marginalization. Discourses surrounding trans experiences and identities have tended to develop out of clinical settings within which trans people held the status of patients or research subjects, and cis (that is, non-trans) clinicians wielded considerable institutional power, including the power to control access to transition-related medical services. Since trans people were not able to contribute to this discourse on a footing of equality, rather than being seen as experts on their own lives their voices were effectively overridden by those of cis people with medical training but no first-hand experience of being a trans person. Not only did trans people in these contexts suffer testimonial injustice, as described above, but the pattern of silencing and dismissal has also constituted a serious case of hermeneutical marginalization.

Hermeneutical marginalization, in turn, is the key condition for hermeneutical injustice, which will occur with any failed or frustrated attempt at intelligibility that is significantly due to the marginalization. This may involve an attempt to communicate with another person, or it may simply involve the subject's attempt to understand their own situation. In the case under consideration, the concepts and terms that arose from medicalized discourses were not shaped by trans people themselves, and so were often ill-suited to describing the experiences of trans people. Moreover, testimonial injustice in other contexts, such as the media, has hindered the development and circulation of better concepts and terms. For example, the mistaken idea that the desire for genital surgery is a necessary condition of being trans is a product of the problematic medicalized discourse just described, and is also maintained and reinforced by the mainstream media's often prurient emphasis on genital surgery in depictions of trans experiences (Serano 2007: 44–45). Hermeneutical injustice may also take more specific forms in particular contexts. For example, B. Lee Aultman (2016) argues that trans people suffer hermeneutical injustice in the US legal system because their claims of discrimination are handled according to a model that takes cis people with non-normative gender expression as the paradigm, rather than engaging with trans people on their own terms.

The various ways in which hermeneutical resources can fall short of what is required to accurately describe trans experiences are illustrated in Jacques' description of the dissatisfaction she felt regarding the concepts and terms that, as a teenager, she took to be available to describe her experience of gender:

> I wasn't sure if [wearing women's clothing] made me a "cross-dresser," which seemed the least loaded term, or "transvestite," or "transsexual." I didn't much like any of those labels . . . . The word [transvestite] . . . felt sexual in a seedy, lonely way—the kind of thing featured on *Suburbia Uncovered* shows on late-night television. It was not a word I wanted to apply to myself. "Transsexual" wasn't accurate either. You needed to be someone who'd been through some medical process to alter your body, right? I hadn't, and didn't plan to: *they're not like me either*, I thought.
>
> (Jacques 2015: 14)

Jacques is looking for the social meanings she needs in order to render her experience fully intelligible, both to herself and to others. There are many misfit concepts in the vicinity, but that merely exacerbates the problem. In the case of "transvestite," the word is loaded with negative connotations that do not fit with her understanding of herself, while in the case of "transsexual," the word implies criteria that are too narrow to include her, at least at that point in time (Jacques 2015: see also Mock 2014: chs. 6 and 8).

The primary harm of hermeneutical injustice is the intrinsic one—the unjust deficit of intelligibility. But such injustices also have practical consequences that constitute secondary harms. For example, difficulty in rendering their identities intelligible to medical practitioners has meant that trans people have found it hard to access medical care related to transition. More generally, the fact that trans people have faced an uphill struggle merely to explain how they identify and what that means has facilitated the stigmatization of trans people, resulting in worsened access to basic social goods such as employment and housing, and in their being victims of physical violence (Levitt and Ippolito 2014).

Besides these negative practical consequences of hermeneutical injustice, there can be further, and perhaps deeper, harm caused by the intrinsic injustice—identity related harm (Fricker 2007: ch. 7, esp. 163–166). Trans people can all too often experience such identity-related harm, either in relation to what they socially "count" as, and/or in relation to how they thereby even come to see themselves. Although the stigmatization of trans identities is surely diminishing in some contexts, trans people in many other contexts may still come to "count socially" as a particular "type" in a way that is objectionable. Most notably, trans people are often misgendered, being socially counted as members of the gender to which they were assigned at birth. Such misgendering can become a matter of life and death, as it did in the tragic case of Vicky Thompson, a trans woman sent to a men's prison who killed herself in custody, just as she had publicly declared she would if sent to the prison (see www.bbc.co.uk/news/uk-england-leeds-34869620). Trans people may also be interpreted through negative interpretive tropes or stereotypes, such as the "deceptive transsexual" who tries to trick people into sexual relations under false pretences, or the "pathetic transsexual," whose gender presentation is tragi-comically unsuccessful (Bettcher 2007). In such cases they would "count" as deceptive/pathetic even if this is not how they see themselves.

Trans people may also suffer the second kind of identity-related harm, in which a person's very sense of their own identity comes to be shaped by the negative meanings structuring the social space. Serano eloquently describes such an experience:

> And maybe I was born transgender—my brain preprogrammed to see myself as female despite the male body I was given at birth—but like every child, I turned to the rest of the world to figure out who I was and what I was worth. And like a good little boy, I picked up on all of the not-so-subliminal messages that surrounded me. TV shows where Father knows best and a woman's place is in the home; fairy tales where helpless girls await their handsome princes; cartoon supermen who always save the damsel in distress; plus schoolyard taunts like "sissy" and "fairy" and "pussy" all taught me to see "feminine" as a synonym for "weakness." And nobody needed to tell me that I should hate myself for wanting to be what was so obviously the lesser sex.
>
> (Serano 2007: 273–274)

Serano describes this self-directed hatred in relation to gender as having a deep impact on the development of her identity, resulting in a sexual "submissive streak," which she describes as a "scar" left by an abusive culture (2007: 273–277). Serano's experience seems to us like a clear case of the second type of identity-related harm that can result from hermeneutical injustice. Other cases that fall under this category of harm include cases where a person experiences a delay in coming to realize that they are trans, a delay that could have been avoided had relevant concepts been more readily to hand. As Green puts it, "It is so easy to dismiss what we know to be true about ourselves because the only words we have can so easily sound preposterous" (2004: 64).

It seems, then, that trans people may suffer the full range of harms associated with hermeneutical injustice: unjust intelligibility deficit (the intrinsic, primary harm), its negative practical consequences (secondary harms), and moreover those extended and specifically identity-related secondary harms concerning both social perceptions (what one "counts" as) and one's actual self-identity. In such cases of hermeneutical injustice, ignorance is preserved not only on the part of out-groups, but in some cases on the part of the subject, too, for she is hindered in the process of gaining self-knowledge. Moreover, ignorance on the part of out-groups, in this case cis people, is a key component in the kind of negative identity prejudices that lead in turn to further cases of testimonial injustice. Thus, here we see a complex interweaving of testimonial injustice, hermeneutical marginalization and hermeneutical injustice that functions to produce and maintain ignorance with regard to trans experiences.

Combatting Epistemic Injustice by Overcoming Conceptual Practical Ignorance

These reflections on the various epistemic injustices suffered by trans people also serve to highlight some of the complexities involved in combatting epistemic injustice. We propose that part of an effort to combat epistemic injustice can usefully be conceived in terms of overcoming ignorance in conceptual know-how. We turn to Sally Haslanger's invaluable distinction between "manifest concepts" and "operative concepts" to help us substantiate this idea (Haslanger 2012). She illustrates this distinction by reference to the concept of being "tardy," or late to school. Tardiness might be officially defined by the school rules as "arriving after 8.50 am"; but if no one is ever marked "tardy" unless they miss the ten-minute registration period entirely, then in practice students will only count as being tardy if they arrive after 9.00 am. If different teachers have different practices for taking the register, with some marking a student as tardy if she is not present when her name is called and others taking a more lenient approach, then what counts as tardy will vary from classroom to classroom. The manifest concept of tardiness in this case would be the one given the by the school rules, and the practice followed by each teacher would constitute a distinct operative concept.

Remedying hermeneutical injustice often begins by developing an operative concept that is used by a particular community (an in-group, as we have been putting it) to fill the hermeneutical lacuna. This means remedying a particular kind of ignorance: practical ignorance in relation to a certain set of concepts. What must be learned or acquired is not any body of propositional knowledge in the first instance, but rather a patch of conceptual know-how. In the Carmita Wood case discussed in Fricker 2007 (ch. 7), it takes her participation in a consciousness-raising group to generate the concept she needs to make proper sense of her experience—an experience we would now easily identify as one of sexual harassment. In the case of trans people, this might mean that a trans community adopts a practice of relating to everyone as members of their identified gender, using the word "woman," for example, to mean anyone who identifies as a woman, regardless of birth-assigned gender or genital status (see, for example, Bettcher 2009). Often, then, operative concepts are more progressive than manifest concepts. Consequently, a common focus of activism is trying to encourage people to use the operative concept instead of the existing manifest concept: lobbying for laws and policies on sexual harassment to be drawn up, or for legal recognition of trans people as members of their identified genders. Insofar as the activist effort is successful, practical ignorance of how to use the operative concept will have been overcome. That concept will have started out as local to the in-group, but spread outwards to other groups, perhaps ultimately forming part of the universally shared collective hermeneutical resource, so that anyone could use the concept and expect to be understood by just about anyone else.

We should, however, be alert to the fact that where activism is successful, we may end up with a situation in which the manifest or official concept is better than the operative concept actually used by most people (Jenkins 2017). In such circumstances, what is needed is to make good the practical ignorance in the other direction by acquiring more know-how vis-à-vis our manifest concept and its cognates. It seems that we may be in such a situation in the UK at present. The Gender Recognition Act of 2004 allows for trans people to have their identified gender legally recognized without requiring them to have undergone genital surgery. However, many people wrongly understand transition as being defined by genital surgery, and will not consider trans people to be members of their identified gender unless they have had genital surgery. This shows that although fixing manifest concepts is a crucial part of combatting hermeneutical injustice, it is not the end of the story. Besides continued work to improve manifest concepts, ongoing efforts are needed to make sure that operative concepts are brought into line with the improved manifest concepts.

Quite how we might learn a new concept and its cognates in any given case is far from straightforward. It may not be possible to simply *add* a given operative concept and make it manifest in a conceptual practice into which it does not easily fit. Sometimes we need stepping-stone concepts, which might ultimately be found seriously wanting by the community whose intelligibility they are meant to assist. Take the idea of being a "woman trapped in the body of a man":

> [This] has become so popular and widespread that it's safe to say these days that it's far more often parodied by cissexuals than used by transsexuals to describe their own experiences. In fact, the regularity with which cissexuals use this saying to mock trans women has always struck me as rather odd, since it was so clearly coined not to encapsulate all of the intricacies and nuances of the trans female experience, but rather as a way of dumbing down our experiences into a sound bite that cissexuals might be better able to comprehend.
>
> (Serano 2007, 215; see also Bettcher 2014)

The use of this phrase to belittle trans people does not, however, indicate that it was always without value. Sometimes, as Serano suggests, a concept or interpretive trope plays a useful transitional or stepping-stone role for those outside the core community (and perhaps sometimes for those inside it too), and it can be thought of as destined to be discarded after it has served its enabling purpose (see also Green 2004: 83). Perhaps the final point to be made here, then, is that when it comes to the social evolution of our shared hermeneutical resource (principally by way of an increasing contribution from more localized hermeneutical resources) our collective hermeneutical progress may sometimes be two steps forward, one step back; but it will be no less progress for that.

Further Reading

Bettcher, Talia (2014) "Trapped in the Wrong Theory: Rethinking Trans Oppression and Resistance," *Signs* 39(2): 383–406. (A good entry point to philosophical work on trans experiences.)

Fricker, Miranda (2007) *Epistemic Injustice: Power and the Ethics of Knowing*, Oxford: Oxford University Press. (The primary source for the notion of "epistemic injustice.")

Kidd, Ian James, Medina, Jose, and Pohlhaus Jr., Gaile (Eds.) (2017) *The Routledge Handbook of Epistemic Injustice*, London: Routledge. (Offers a wide-ranging collection of new essays.)

Medina, José (2013) *Epistemologies of Resistance: Gender and Racial Oppression, Epistemic Injustice, and Resistant Imaginations*, Oxford: Oxford University Press. (Develops interweaving themes of epistemic injustice, "white ignorance," and associated epistemic vices and virtues.)

Sullivan, Shannon and Tuana, Nancy (Eds.) (2007) *Race and Epistemologies of Ignorance*, Albany, NY: SUNY University Press. (A good reference for more on the epistemology of ignorance.)

Related Topics

Testimony, trust, and trustworthiness (Chapter 21); speech and silencing (Chapter 23); feminist philosophy of social science (Chapter 27); through the looking glass: trans theory meets feminist philosophy (Chapter 32); moral justification in an unjust world (Chapter 40).

References

Anderson, Elizabeth (2012) "Epistemic Justice as a Virtue of Social Institutions," *Social Epistemology* 26(2): 163–173.

Aultman, B. Lee (2016) "Epistemic Injustice and the Construction of Transgender Legal Subjects," *Wagadu: A Journal of Transnational Women's and Gender Studies* 15(Summer): 11–34.

Bettcher, Talia Mae (2007) "Evil Deceivers and Make-Believers: On Transphobic Violence and the Politics of Illusion," *Hypatia* 22(3): 43–65.

——(2009) "Trans Identities and First-Person Authority," in Laurie J. Shrage (Ed.) *"You've Changed": Sex Reassignment and Personal Identity*, New York: Oxford University Press, 98–120.

—— (2014) "Trapped in the Wrong Theory: Rethinking Trans Oppression and Resistance," *Signs* 39(2): 383–406.

Dotson, Kristie (2011) "Tracking Epistemic Violence, Tracking Practices of Silencing," *Hypatia* 26(2): 236–257.

——(2012) "A Cautionary Tale: On Limiting Epistemic Oppression," *Frontiers* 33(1): 24–47.

Fricker, Miranda (2007) *Epistemic Injustice: Power and the Ethics of Knowing*, Oxford: Oxford University Press.

——(2016) "Epistemic Injustice and the Preservation of Ignorance," in Martijn Blaauw and Rik Peels (Eds.) *The Epistemic Dimensions of Ignorance*, Cambridge: Cambridge University Press.

Green, Jamison (2004) *Becoming a Visible Man*, Nashville, TN: Vanderbilt University Press.

Haslanger, Sally (2012) *Resisting Reality: Social Construction and Social Critique*, New York: Oxford University Press.

Jacques, Juliet (2015) *Trans: A Memoir*, London: Verso.

Jenkins, Katharine (2017) "Rape Myths and Domestic Abuse Myths as Hermeneutical Injustices," *Journal of Applied Philosophy* 34(2): 191–206.

Levitt, Heidi M. and Ippolito, Maria R. (2014) "Being Transgender: Navigating Minority Stressors and Developing Authentic Self-Presentation," *Psychology of Women Quarterly* 38(2): 46–64.

Maitra, Ishani (2010) "The Nature of Epistemic Injustice," *Philosophical Books* 51: 195–211.

Mason, Rebecca (2011) "Two Kinds of Unknowing," *Hypatia* 26(2): 294–307.

Medina, José (2012) "Hermeneutical Injustice and Polyphonic Contextualism: Social Silences and Shared Hermeneutical Responsibilities," *Social Epistemology* 26(2): 201–220.

—— (2013) *Epistemologies of Resistance: Gender and Racial Oppression, Epistemic Injustice, and Resistant Imaginations*, Oxford: Oxford University Press.

Mills, Charles (2007) "White Ignorance," in Shannon Sullivan and Nancy Tuana (Eds.) *Race and Epistemologies of Ignorance*, Albany, NY: SUNY Press, 11–38.

——(2015) "Global White Ignorance," in Matthias Gross and Linsey McGoey (Eds.) *Routledge International Handbook of Ignorance Studies*, London/New York: Routledge, 217–227.

Mock, Janet (2014) *Redefining Realness*, New York: Atria Books.

Pohlhaus Jr., Gaile (2012) "Relational Knowing and Epistemic Injustice: Toward a Theory of Willful Hermeneutical Ignorance," *Hypatia* 27(4): 715–735.

Serano, Julia (2007) *Whipping Girl: A Transsexual Woman on Feminism and the Scapegoating of Femininity*, Emeryville, CA: Seal Press.

23
SPEECH AND SILENCING
Ishani Maitra

Introduction

A recurring concern within feminist philosophy of language has been with the ways in which women (and others) are systematically disadvantaged qua language users. There are several dimensions to this kind of disadvantage, but one that has particularly interested theorists is *silencing*. It is clear that a speaker can be silenced by being prevented from uttering words. But what about a speaker who is able to say something? In recent years, several theorists have argued that such a speaker may also be silenced, if they are prevented from *doing* certain things with their words. Call this "silencing in the broad sense." This chapter explores several different conceptions of silencing in this sense. It also asks when some related phenomena should be regarded as further kinds of silencing.

Much of the recent literature on silencing gets its start from the work of Catharine MacKinnon (MacKinnon 1987; 1993). In her 1993 monograph *Only Words*, MacKinnon argues that we have failed to take seriously enough women's testimony about sexual abuse in the making and use of pornography. She writes:

> Protecting pornography means protecting sexual abuse *as* speech, at the same time that both pornography and its protection have deprived women *of* speech, especially speech against sexual abuse. There is a connection between the silence enforced on women, in which we are seen to love and choose our chains because they have been sexualized, and the noise of pornography that surrounds us, passing for discourse (ours, even) and parading under constitutional protection.
>
> (MacKinnon 1993: 9–10, original emphasis)

MacKinnon thus points to two harms of pornography in this passage: first, that it deprives women of speech, specifically speech about sexual abuse; and second, that it passes for women's speech. She also points to a tension between protecting pornography "*as* speech" while it functions to deprive women of speech. I'll return to each of these points in the discussion below.

This chapter proceeds as follows. In the next section, I introduce several distinct conceptions of silencing in the broad sense, focusing particularly on the work of Rae Langton and Jennifer Hornsby. After that, I sketch what has come to be called "the Silencing Argument," which connects silencing in some of the senses distinguished in the previous section with infringement of a right to free speech. In this section I also describe what I take to be the most significant objections to that argument, and some avenues of response to those objections. In the final section of this chapter, I consider some further phenomena that are related to the conceptions of silencing introduced earlier, and ask whether those phenomena should also count as kinds of silencing. I offer two distinct approaches to this question, and compare them. In this section I also discuss further wrongs, beyond infringement of a speech right, that may be associated with one or another conception of silencing.

Though I will say more about MacKinnon's influence in what follows, my focus in this chapter is not on pornography per se (as opposed to other potential contributors to silencing). There is at this point a vast literature on pornography and its functioning, which I will not attempt to summarize here. Rather, my focus in this chapter is more narrowly on silencing itself. That is to say, I will mostly be interested here in what silencing in the broad sense amounts to, and following MacKinnon, in what harms—and wrongs—it perpetrates against women, and others.

Conceptions of Silencing

In her 1993 paper, "Speech Acts and Unspeakable Acts," Rae Langton uses J. L. Austin's theory of speech acts to unpack MacKinnon's claim that pornography silences women. Austin (1975 [1962]) famously emphasized that speech is action, that words can do things and not just say things. Extending this thought, Langton argues that silence can consist in a *failure* to act, that a speaker can be silenced if she is prevented from doing things she wants to do with her words.

Langton distinguishes three importantly distinct kinds of silence, each corresponding to the failure of one of the parts of Austin's tripartite distinction between locutionary, perlocutionary, and illocutionary acts (Langton 1993: 314–315). Simple silence happens when a speaker is prevented from uttering words at all, as might be the case if she is threatened or intimidated. Perlocutionary frustration takes place when the speaker utters words, but is prevented from achieving the (perlocutionary) effects she intends via those words; this might be the case, for instance, if what she says fails to *persuade* others to see things her way. And finally, illocutionary disablement happens when the speaker is prevented from (fully successfully) performing the illocutionary act she intends.

Following Austin, Langton takes illocutionary acts—e.g., warning, telling, promising, christening, voting, and so on—to require uptake. Without that uptake, the utterance in question is deprived of its intended illocutionary force (Langton 1993: 316). To illustrate, consider Donald Davidson's example of an actor on stage trying to warn their audience about an actual, not fictional, fire (Davidson 1984: 269–270). The audience takes the actor to still be performing; their lack of uptake prevents the actor's utterance from being a warning. What precisely is necessary for uptake in this sense is an interesting question on its own, but one that I'll leave aside here. (For discussion of whether uptake is genuinely necessary for illocutionary success, see Jacobson 1995; Hornsby and Langton 1998; Bird 2002; McGowan et al. 2010; Mikkola 2011; Tumulty 2012.)

Further, Langton also takes illocutionary acts to have felicity conditions—roughly, conditions that have to be satisfied for such acts to be fully successful—that are fixed by convention (Langton 1993: 319). When those conditions are not satisfied, the attempted illocutionary act will go wrong in some way, perhaps by failing to secure uptake. (For discussion of the role that conventions play in silencing, see Wieland 2007; Wyatt 2009.)

Failure of uptake, Langton argues, is precisely what happens when a woman attempts to refuse a sexual overture or protest sexual abuse in a context in which the felicity conditions of those acts are "set" by pornography (Langton 1993: 324). She writes:

> Pornography might legitimate rape, and thus silence refusal, by doing something other than eroticizing refusal itself. It may simply leave no space for the refusal move in its depictions of sex. In pornography of this kind there would be all kinds of locutions the women depicted could use to make the consent move. "Yes" is one such locution. "No" is just another. Here the refusal move is not itself eroticized [as in other pornography]: it is absent altogether.
>
> (Langton 1993: 324)

Pornography might do this by, for example, setting the felicity conditions for refusal in such a way that a woman's "No" in a sexual encounter is just a way in which she plays along in a sexual game, rather than a genuine refusal. When this happens, that "No" will not secure the necessary uptake, and so, will fail to count as a refusal. Note that Langton's account here picks up on both of MacKinnon's claims about the harms of pornography mentioned in the Introduction: pornography can deprive women of speech (by disabling our refusals), and pass for women's speech (by making it appear as though we are consenting). (For further discussion of how pornography might do these things, see Langton and West 1999; McGowan 2003.)

(It is worth noting at this point that Langton's project is to show that pornography *could* silence women, i.e., that that claim is not incoherent. Whether pornography *does* silence is a further question, and a partly empirical one; she does not purport to have settled that further question.)

Besides possibly contributing to illocutionary disablement, Langton argues that pornography may also contribute to simple silence and perlocutionary frustration as well. Indeed, when a speaker's intended illocutionary acts are disabled in the manner just described, her intended perlocutionary acts are also likely to fail. Nevertheless, silencing understood as illocutionary disablement occupies a special place in Langton's discussion, in large part because of its connection to free speech; I'll return to that connection in the next section.

Langton's way of unpacking MacKinnon's view is closely related to Jennifer Hornsby's (Hornsby 1993; 1995). Hornsby distinguishes two kinds of silencing, namely, inaudibility and ineffability. Inaudibility is similar to Langton's illocutionary disablement: a speaker's attempt to refuse by saying "No" becomes inaudible when her audience fails to recognize it *as* an attempt to refuse. In such a case, writes Hornsby, the speaker "through no fault of her own, is deprived of her illocutionary potential" (Hornsby 1995: 137). She is thus deprived of the power to do as she wishes with her words.

Despite these similarities, there are also some interesting differences between Hornsby's account and Langton's. For example, where Langton emphasizes the conventional aspects of illocutionary acts, Hornsby draws attention to their role in communication ("When we uncover a concept of illocution, we reveal the use of words to be *communicative* action" (Hornsby 1995: 133, original emphasis). (For more on

Hornsby's view of illocution, see Hornsby (1994).) Further, where Langton talks about pornography illocutionarily disabling women by *setting*—i.e., constituting—felicity conditions, Hornsby argues that pornography can contribute to inaudibility by *causing* a breakdown in the reciprocity between speaker and audience that is needed for successful communication (Hornsby 1995: 133–134).

Ineffability—Hornsby's other notion of silencing—is importantly different. Whereas inaudibility involves a speaker failing to get across what she means, ineffability has to do with the speaker being unable to express that meaning in the first place. More carefully, a content becomes ineffable in a given language when any way of expressing it in that language carries with it other contents that the speaker does *not* wish to convey. Hornsby illustrates this phenomenon with the word "quota": in the aftermath of right-leaning criticisms of affirmative action and related controversies, the word has come to be associated in the US with practices that are unfair or unreasonable. Accordingly, writes Hornsby, it is difficult to speak favorably of, e.g., a school having a quota without "representing yourself as a dangerous liberal (or perhaps by engaging in such circumlocution as is bound to detract from the main message)" (Hornsby 1995: 135).

Unlike illocutionary disablement/inaudibility, ineffability has not received much attention in the philosophical literature. The notion is arguably related to several others that have been discussed in recent years, such as Miranda Fricker's conception of hermeneutical injustice, Kristie Dotson's conception of testimonial smothering, and Jason Stanley's account of propaganda operating via not-at-issue content (Fricker 2007; Dotson 2011; Stanley 2015; see also Chapter 22 in this volume). Further discussion of ineffability, its harms/wrongs, and its connection to the other notions just mentioned would, in my view, be a welcome addition to the literature.

The Silencing Argument

Not every speaker who is silenced in one of the senses just distinguished is thereby harmed, or wronged. If I'm trying to make an argument, and you raise a devastating objection to one of its premises, you may frustrate my intended perlocutionary act (namely, persuasion); but at least if the stakes are low enough, you haven't harmed me. Nevertheless, it's also clear that many speakers who are silenced *are* harmed—and wronged—as a result of being silenced. Thus, the following questions should be crucial to discussions of silencing: Given any particular conception of silencing, when does silencing in that sense harm/wrong the silenced speaker? When does it harm/wrong others? And what is the nature of those harms/wrongs?

Much of the literature on silencing has focused on one particular (moral and legal) wrong, namely, infringement of the silenced speaker's right to free speech. I'll present that argument below; but in the next section, I'll emphasize that there are reasons to be morally and politically concerned with silencing that go well beyond its relation to free speech.

Let's begin with Langton's threefold distinction between simple silence, perlocutionary frustration, and illocutionary disablement. A speaker who is prevented from uttering words at all—and so has simple silence enforced upon her—may well suffer an infringement of her right to free speech. By contrast, a speaker who is perlocutionarily frustrated need not have her speech right violated. Consider again the example in the opening paragraph of this section, in which I am perlocutionarily frustrated by having my argument undermined. My speech right is surely not infringed in that case.

(Of course, this leaves open the possibility that *some* kinds of perlocutionary frustration—e.g., frustration of certain perlocutionary acts, or frustration that's systematic in certain special ways—could qualify as infringements of a right to free speech. That possibility has not been discussed much in the literature.)

What about a speaker who is illocutionarily disabled? Both Langton and Hornsby argue that at least some illocutionary disablement should qualify as an infringement of the silenced speaker's right to free speech (Langton 1993: 327–328; Hornsby 1995: 140; Hornsby and Langton 1998: 35–37). For both, free speech is valuable not only because it allows us to utter words, but because it enables us to do other things—such as refusing and protesting and questioning and warning—*in* uttering those words. If we couldn't do those things, speech would not be nearly as valuable. Thus, Langton and Hornsby both argue, our reasons for protecting speech extend beyond locution to illocution as well. And insofar as pornography contributes to women's illocutionary disablement, i.e., insofar as pornography *prevents* us from refusing, protesting, and so on, it infringes women's right to free speech.

This argument is often dubbed "the Silencing Argument." Note that the argument focuses on silencing (i.e., illocutionary disablement) that is connected to an aspect of the speaker's social identity, namely, their gender. As such, that silencing is not incidental, but systematic in a certain way. Not all illocutionary disablement is systematic in this way: for example, a speaker's intended illocutionary act may fail because her audience is being particularly obtuse, for example. But it is systematic illocutionary disablement that is most plausibly an infringement of the speech right.

The Silencing Argument offers a response to those who would acknowledge that pornography systematically harms women, but still argue that, as speech, it must be protected under any reasonable principle of free speech. On this latter line of thinking, pornography's harms create a tension between pornographers' (and consumers') right to free speech, and women's right to equality and respect. But in that conflict, free speech has the greater priority (see, for example, Dworkin 1993 for an argument along these lines). So the tension must be resolved in favor of pornography.

The Silencing Argument offers a re-framing of this debate. It suggests that there is more at stake here than a conflict between two distinct rights (speech, equality). There is also a conflict within the speech right itself, between pornographers' (and consumers') exercise of that right, and women's exercise of the same right. The argument doesn't purport to settle what ought to be *done* about this conflict. In particular, it doesn't establish that pornography should be censored on these grounds. But if successful, the argument does make pressing a question about how these competing claims should be balanced against each other.

This argument has been widely discussed—and criticized—over the last several years. In what follows, I'll focus on three criticisms that are particularly noteworthy in my view, in part because they have inspired philosophically interesting responses. I'll briefly sketch some of those responses as well, though I won't be able to do them justice here.

The Scope of the Right to Free Speech

The first, and perhaps most obvious, response to the Silencing Argument takes issue with its interpretation of the right to free speech, arguing that that interpretation makes the right out to be implausibly broad and overly demanding. A particularly trenchant example of this sort of criticism is offered by Ronald Dworkin (Dworkin 1993). Dworkin argues that the Silencing Argument is committed to an understanding of the right to free speech that "includes a right to circumstances that encourage one to speak, and a right that others grasp and respect what one means to say" (Dworkin 1993: 38). But this understanding is just "unacceptable" (Dworkin 1993: 38).

Daniel Jacobson also criticizes the understanding of free speech at play in the Silencing Argument, drawing upon John Stuart Mill's influential defense of free speech for his critique (Jacobson 1995). Mill, on Jacobson's construal, held that "no speech should be restricted on grounds of its content" (Jacobson 1995: 68). But this prohibition on content-restriction was married with a recognition that not every speech act should be protected: "even opinions lose their immunity, when the circumstances in which they are expressed are such as to constitute their expression a positive instigation to some mischievous act" (Mill 2008: 62, quoted in Jacobson 1995: 68). Mill is thus committed, Jacobson thinks, to something like a freedom of locutionary acts, but not to a more general freedom of illocutionary acts (Jacobson 1995: 71–72). In fact, there are plenty of instances of illocutionary disablement—e.g., convicted felons being unable to vote, and would-be-bigamists and twelve-year-olds being unable to marry—where that disablement constitutes no infringement of the right to free speech at all. Even in cases where the disablement does contribute to an injustice, as when women's sexual refusals are disabled, Jacobson argues that we can capture the injustice by appealing to the attendant disablement of autonomy (Jacobson 1995: 75–76). (For a related but distinct Millian argument against the invocation of free speech in the Silencing Argument, see Bird 2002: 4–6.)

In a joint response to Jacobson, Hornsby and Langton contest his interpretation of Mill (Hornsby and Langton 1998: 32–35). They argue, for example, that in the passage quoted, Mill intended to exclude *perlocutionary* acts, not illocutionary ones, from the realm of free speech. Though they agree that the right to free speech cannot extend to all illocutionary acts, they also stress the importance of communication, and so of illocutionary acts that are distinctively communicative, to free speech. (For more on this latter line of thought, see Maitra 2009.)

Hornsby and Langton also argue that an illocutionarily disabled speaker suffers more than a disablement of autonomy. They point to "a distinctively human capacity that one has as a member of a speech community," possession of which is crucial for an individual "to flourish as a knowledgeable being," for the spread of knowledge across individuals, and for nonviolent decision-making, among other things (Hornsby and Langton 1998: 37). It's this human capacity that is undermined by illocutionary disablement.

More recently, Caroline West has sketched an understanding of free speech that also requires something more than the mere liberty to utter words (West 2003). She asks us to imagine speakers whose words are systematically misheard because their government has secretly implanted "voice scramblers" in their hearers; these speakers are able to produce utterances, but still suffer infringements of their right to free speech. West takes this case to suggest that the right to free speech comes with a "minimal comprehension requirement," but one that stops well short of Dworkin's "right that others . . . respect what one means to say" (West 2003: 409–410). And this interpretation of the speech right, West argues, may be enough to vindicate the Silencing Argument. (For more on this interpretation of the right to free speech, see also West 2012.)

Authority to Silence

A second line of criticism focuses on how pornography can contribute to silencing. Recall here Langton's suggestion that pornography *sets* the felicity conditions for women's speech, at least in some contexts. Some speech can clearly set felicity conditions for other speech: Langton's example of lawmakers in apartheid-era South Africa enacting, via voice vote, voting restrictions that disenfranchise black voters is a particularly vivid example (Langton 1993: 317). But in the clearest cases, this sort of enactment of felicity conditions happens via speakers' exercise of authority over some relevant domain. Lawmakers clearly have the authority to enact voting restrictions. Pornographers, by contrast, don't seem to have the authority to enact norms about sexual (or other) interactions. So pornography cannot set felicity conditions for women's speech in the relevant contexts. Or so the objection goes.

This objection is one aspect of a more general concern about how pornography has the authority to subordinate women, by silencing them or in other ways. I've elsewhere dubbed this "the Authority Problem" (for pornography) (Maitra 2012: 95). Versions of this problem have been raised by several commentators (Butler 1997; Green 1998; Sumner 2004; Bauer 2006, among others). Leslie Green, for example, argues that pornography is, for us, "low-status speech," speech that is "permitted although disapproved" (Green 1998: 297). That means that even if it can articulate norms about sexual behavior, it cannot enact those norms on others. That's especially so given that pornography must compete with other sources, such as "the state, the family, and the church," that do possess authority, and that prescribe countervailing norms (Green 1998: 296).

The Authority Problem has inspired several distinct kinds of responses. Some have argued that, contrary to first appearances, pornography *does* have the authority to subordinate women, at least in some contexts (Langton 1993; 1998; Wieland 2007; Maitra 2012). Langton, for example, argues that for certain consumers, pornography "has all the authority of a monopoly" (Langton 1993: 312); while Nellie Wieland compares the authority of pornographers to a kind of linguistic authority over what certain words mean in sexual discourse (Wieland 2007: 441–445).

On other views, however, the Authority Problem is not so pressing. Recall, for example, Hornsby's view that pornography contributes to silencing by *causing* a breakdown in reciprocity between speakers and hearers (Hornsby 1995). Speech can erode the sort of minimal receptiveness needed for reciprocity by, e.g., relentlessly vilifying members of a particular group, even if those doing the vilifying don't possess any particular authority. If that's right, then authority may not be necessary for silencing (or subordination).

Mary Kate McGowan has also defended this last claim, though along very different lines. McGowan suggests that we can think of sexual interactions as cooperative, rule-governed activity, at least in a thin sense (McGowan 2003). In other cooperative, rule-governed activities—including ordinary conversations—participants can set felicity conditions for the speech of other participants. One way that this can happen is via the operation of rules of accommodation. And this kind of accommodation can occur even when the participants being accommodated have no particular authority. If pornography can set felicity conditions for women's speech via accommodation on the part of consumers and others, then perhaps no authority on the part of pornographers is required for silencing. The Authority Problem is then dissolved.

Silencing, Consent, and Responsibility

The final response to the Silencing Argument that I will consider focuses on the question of responsibility, both for silencing and for its aftermath. Consider again disablement of women's sexual refusals. One major reason to be concerned with this kind of silencing is that it is likely to result in rape. But—according to this final response—we cannot coherently say this. For if women's sexual refusals are disabled, that means that women are prevented from refusing sex. But if there is no refusal, then we cannot say that there is rape (Jacobson 1995: 77).

Hornsby and Langton forcefully rebut this version of the objection (Hornsby and Langton 1998: 31). They point out that absence of refusal is not the same as consent: even if a woman is prevented from refusing, it does not follow she has consented. In fact, even if her interlocutor takes her to be consenting, it still does not follow that she has consented. And it's the absence of consent that matters for whether there is rape.

Some more recent commentators have granted this as a reply to the initial objection, but argued that the reply raises a further issue. That issue has to do with whether silencing in some way *mitigates* the rapist's responsibility for the rape (Bird 2002; Wieland 2007). Wieland, for example, argues that if pornography contributes to silencing in the way suggested by the Silencing Argument, then it must also deprive its consumers—including those who go on to force sex on women—of the interpretive resources necessary for recognizing women's sexual refusals as such. That is to say, on this picture, "whereas women are illocutionarily disabled, rapists are *interpretively* disabled" (Wieland 2007: 452). And this in turn means that rapists could reasonably interpret their victims as consenting. That's enough to diminish rapists' responsibility for their actions, even if it doesn't remove that responsibility altogether.

Again, there is more to say here. In particular, even if it's true that pornography contributes to interpretive mistakes, as the Silencing Argument suggests, it doesn't immediately follow that those mistakes are *reasonable*. For example, if we're prone to mistakes of certain kinds, it might fall upon us to take extra steps to avoid them; then, when we fail to take those steps, we fail to behave reasonably. So, at the very least, more needs to be said to establish that the interpretive mistakes at issue here are reasonable, and so, responsibility-mitigating. (For related discussion, see Maitra and McGowan 2010; McGowan et al. 2010; Tumulty 2012.)

Summing up: I began this section by emphasizing questions about how silencing (in any sense) harms/wrongs the silenced speakers, and others. I've focused in this section on one particular wrong that has been connected to silencing, namely, infringement of the right to free speech. I'll discuss some further wrongs in the next section.

Before leaving the Silencing Argument, though, let me emphasize again that my survey of the literature related to that argument has not been exhaustive. I'll close this discussion by briefly mentioning one final question, namely, whether Austinian speech act theory (and its successors) are well suited to capturing MacKinnon's insights about pornography, and its contribution to silencing. Applying speech act theory in this way involves regarding pornography as speech, produced by certain individuals (pornographers) and consumed by other individuals. But it has been argued that this way of framing things gives rise to worries—e.g., about whether pornography genuinely is speech, about variation in pornography's illocutionary force across contexts, about the difference between illocution and perlocution, about whether pornographers have speaker authority, and so on—that end up detracting from the plausibility of MacKinnon's claims. (For related discussion, see Saul 2006; Antony 2011; Hornsby 2011; MacKinnon 2012; Finlayson 2014.) This in turn raises an interesting question about whether some alternate framing would be better, or whether any framing is needed at all.

Related Phenomena

In an earlier section, I presented several conceptions of silencing due to Hornsby and Langton: simple silence, perlocutionary frustration, illocutionary disablement/inaudibility, and ineffability. As I mentioned then, these notions are importantly different from each other. That raises two questions. First, what makes all of these quite distinct phenomena kinds of *silencing*? And second, what other related phenomena should also count as kinds of silencing?

The second question is made pressing by recent discussions that present further phenomena that resemble, at least superficially, those listed above. These discussions fall into three (not mutually exclusive) categories. First, there are accounts that take as paradigmatic the same examples that motivate one of the conceptions above—usually, illocutionary disablement/inaudibility—but argue that those examples should be theorized differently. (See Wieland 2007 on meaning switches and Maitra 2009 on communicative disablement for examples of this kind.) Second, there are accounts that introduce further conceptions of silencing, understood as such. (See McGowan 2013 on sincerity silencing for an instance of this kind.) And finally, there are accounts that introduce phenomena involving some kind of linguistic incapacitation, very broadly speaking, where that is *not* described as a further kind of silencing. (See Fricker 2007 on hermeneutical injustice, Kukla 2014 on discursive injustice, and Stanley 2015 on not-at-issue content for examples of this kind.)

Here's the most straightforward way to approach questions about what should count as silencing: we can say that a speaker is silenced just in case she is prevented from doing something she intends to do with her words. Call this the "silencing-as-linguistic-frustration" approach. This approach has the twin virtues of simplicity and coverage: unlike the alternate approach I'll discuss below, silencing as linguistic frustration can explain, in a relatively simple fashion, why all the distinct phenomena discussed by Hornsby and Langton should qualify as kinds of silencing. And it arguably counts much of the additional phenomena described in the previous paragraph as kinds of silencing as well.

The capaciousness of this first approach is, however, also a drawback. On this approach, silencing turns out to be a *hugely* varied phenomenon, because there are so many different kinds of things that we intend to do with our words in various circumstances. Thus, on this approach, being prevented from doing any of the following can count as an instance of silencing: scaring someone by yelling "boo"; amusing someone by telling them a joke; marrying someone (because one is already married to someone else); and persuading someone (because one's credibility is unfairly deflated by racist/sexist prejudice). But these instances are all very different from each other. And if silencing includes all of them, then it becomes hard to say what is philosophically interesting about the category as a whole.

A different approach to what should count as silencing might tie silencing more closely to a particular kind of wrong. Just as some theorists have talked about injustices that are distinctively *epistemic* in nature (compare Fricker 2007 and others), we might also talk about injustices that are distinctively speech-related, or linguistic, in nature. We could then say that a speaker is silenced just in case they suffer such a speech-related, or linguistic, injustice. (For further discussion of speech-related/linguistic injustices in connection with silencing, see Hornsby and Langton 1998; Maitra 2009; McGowan 2013.) Henceforth, I'll use the phrase "linguistic injustice" for wrongs in this category.

But what *is* a linguistic injustice? There are several options here. On one view, a linguistic injustice is related to unfairness in the distribution of *linguistic* goods, such as the opportunity to speak, or to be heard. (Compare here epistemic goods, such as credibility or information. Some goods may be both linguistic and epistemic.) On a second view, a linguistic injustice may be an injustice committed against someone in their capacity as a linguistic agent, e.g., a speaker or hearer. (Again, compare here injustices committed against someone in their capacity as an epistemic agent, e.g., a knower.) And on yet another view, a linguistic injustice may be unfair exclusion from a linguistic community. (Compare here unfair exclusion from an epistemic community.) And there may be further options as well.

These understandings of linguistic injustice are not equivalent; but I won't try to decide between them here, or to flesh them out further. Rather, I'll note that given any of these understandings, the silencing-as-linguistic-injustice approach gives us a much narrower category than the earlier silencing-as-linguistic-frustration approach. To see this, recall the four examples I used above to illustrate the capaciousness of the earlier approach. Neither being prevented from scaring someone nor being prevented from amusing someone counts as silencing on the second approach, since neither is an injustice. Being prevented from marrying someone (because one is already married) may be an injustice; but it is not a *linguistic* injustice, on any of the available understandings. Being prevented from persuading someone (because of credibility unfairly deflated by racist/sexist prejudice) is most clearly an injustice; but most usually, it will be an *epistemic* injustice, not a linguistic one. More specifically, it is something like a testimonial injustice, in Fricker's sense (Fricker 2007). The fact that the current approach doesn't regard all testimonial injustice as silencing is, in my view, a point in its favor.

The considerations raised above also show that the current approach counts only some instances of the phenomena discussed by Hornsby and Langton to be silencing. However, because silencing on this approach is tied to a particular kind of injustice, it is easier to see why it is a philosophically interesting category. Further, if—as I think is plausible—gender is systematically connected to injustices of this kind, it is also easy to see why the category should be of interest to feminists.

To close my discussion of this second approach, I'll briefly apply it to some of the related phenomena mentioned near the beginning of this section. First, consider discursive injustice, in Rebecca Kukla's sense. Roughly, a speaker suffers such an injustice when they are entitled to perform a speech act of a given type, they use the "conventionally appropriate words, tones, and gestures to produce it," but nevertheless, due to their disadvantaged social identity, end up producing a speech act of some other type that further disadvantages them (Kukla 2014: 445). To illustrate, Kukla gives the example of a woman manager in a nearly all-male factory giving what she intends to be orders, but having her speech acts constituted as requests by the response of her subordinates (Kukla 2014: 445–448).

Being able to perform speech act types that one is entitled to perform—and that other speakers would be able to perform in the same circumstances, using the same words—is plausibly a linguistic good. Being prevented from performing such acts by one's gender is also plausibly an injustice, and one committed against an agent in their capacity as a speaker. If so, discursive injustice in Kukla's sense is a *linguistic* injustice (on multiple understandings of the latter notion). As such, it would count as a further kind of silencing on the current approach.

By contrast, consider hermeneutical injustice, in Fricker's sense. Again roughly, an agent suffers such an injustice when they are prevented—by "hermeneutical marginalization," a kind of structural prejudice—from understanding some significant part of their social experience (Fricker 2007: 154–155). Targets of sexual harassment prior to the coinage of the expression can be said to have suffered this injustice (Fricker 2007: 149–152).

Fricker considers hermeneutical injustice to be a species of epistemic injustice. But it's at least arguable that the injustice here is in fact *primarily* linguistic. The agent suffering this wrong is prevented from accurately *describing* their own experience, and as a result, from communicating the nature of that experience to others. But these look like linguistic capacities that are undermined; so it seems plausible to say that this is an injustice committed against someone in their capacity as a linguistic agent. If all of that's right—and of course, there is more to be said here—there is a *prima facie* case for regarding hermeneutical injustice as a kind of silencing, rather than as an epistemic injustice, on the current approach.

As I hope is clear at this point, discussions of silencing in the philosophical literature intersect with a wide range of interesting philosophical questions, including questions about how gender systematically disadvantages women, about the scope of the right to free speech, about the nature of speaker authority, about the assignment of (moral and legal) responsibility, and about the difference between linguistic and other injustices. Further clarifying each of these intersections will help us better understand what is at stake when a speaker is silenced in any of the senses I've discussed in this chapter.

Acknowledgment

Many thanks to Ann Garry and Mary Kate McGowan for helpful comments on a draft of this chapter.

Further Reading

Langton, Rae (2012) "Beyond Belief: Pragmatics in Hate Speech and Philosophy," in Ishani Maitra and Mary Kate McGowan (Eds.) *Speech and Harm: Controversies over Free Speech*, Oxford: Oxford University Press, 72–93.

Saul, Jennifer and Diaz-Leon, Esa (2017) "Feminist Philosophy of Language," in Edward N. Zalta (Ed.) *The Stanford Encyclopedia of Philosophy* [online]. Available from: http://plato.stanford.edu/entries/feminism-language/.

Tanesini, Alessandra (1996) "Whose Language?" in Ann Garry and Marilyn Pearsall (Eds.) *Women, Knowledge, and Reality: Explorations in Feminist Philosophy*, 2nd ed., New York: Routledge, 353–365.

Related Topics

Testimony, trust and trustworthiness (Chapter 21): epistemic injustice, ignorance, and trans experience (Chapter 22); language, writing, and gender differences (Chapter 24).

References

Antony, Louise (2011) "Against Langton's Illocutionary Treatment of Pornography," *Jurisprudence* 2(2): 387–401.

Austin, J. L. (1975 [1962]) *How to Do Things with Words*, 2nd ed., Eds. J. O. Urmson and Marina Sbisà, Cambridge, MA: Harvard University Press.

Bauer, Nancy (2006) "How to Do Things with Pornography," in Sanford Shieh and Alice Crary (Eds.) *Reading Cavell*, London: Routledge, 68–97.

Bird, Alexander (2002) "Illocutionary Silencing," *Pacific Philosophical Quarterly* 83(1): 1–15.

Butler, Judith (1997) *Excitable Speech: A Politics of the Performative*, New York: Routledge.

Davidson, Donald (1984) "Communication and Convention," in *Inquiries into Truth and Interpretation*, Oxford: Oxford University Press, 265–280.

Dotson, Kristie (2011) "Tracking Epistemic Violence, Tracking Practices of Silencing," *Hypatia* 26(2): 236–257.

Dworkin, Ronald (1993) "Women and Pornography," *The New York Review of Books* 40(17): 36–42.

Finlayson, Lorna (2014) "How to Screw Things with Words," *Hypatia* 29(4): 774–789.

Fricker, Miranda (2007) *Epistemic Injustice: Ethics and the Power of Knowing*, Oxford: Oxford University Press.

Green, Leslie (1998) "Pornographizing, Subordinating, and Silencing," in Robert C. Post (Ed.) *Censorship and Silencing: Practices of Cultural Regulation*, Los Angeles, CA: Getty Research Institute for the History of Art and the Humanities, 285–311.

Hornsby, Jennifer (1993) "Speech Acts and Pornography," *Women's Philosophy Review* 10: 38–45.

——(1994) "Illocution and Its Significance," in Savas L. Tsohatzidis (Ed.) *Foundations of Speech Act Theory: Philosophical and Linguistic Perspectives*, London: Routledge, 187–207.

——(1995) "Disempowered Speech," *Philosophical Topics* 23(2): 127–147.

——(2011) "Subordination, Silencing, and Two Ideas of Illocution," *Jurisprudence* 2(2): 379–385.

Hornsby, Jennifer and Langton, Rae (1998) "Free Speech and Illocution," *Legal Theory* 4(1): 21–37.

Jacobson, Daniel (1995) "Freedom of Speech Acts?: A Response to Langton," *Philosophy & Public Affairs* 24(1): 64–79.

Kukla, Rebecca (2014) "Performative Force, Convention, and Discursive Injustice," *Hypatia* 29(2): 440–457.

Langton, Rae (1993) "Speech Acts and Unspeakable Acts," *Philosophy & Public Affairs* 22(4): 293–330.

——(1998) "Subordination, Silence, and Pornography's Authority," in Robert C. Post (Ed.) *Censorship and Silencing: Practices of Cultural Regulation*, Los Angeles, CA: Getty Research Institute for the History of Art and the Humanities, 261–283.

Langton, Rae and West, Caroline (1999) "Scorekeeping in a Pornographic Language Game," *Australasian Journal of Philosophy* 77(3): 303–319.

McGowan, Mary Kate (2003) "Conversational Exercitives and the Force of Pornography," *Philosophy & Public Affairs* 31(2): 155–189.

——(2013) "Sincerity Silencing," *Hypatia* 29(2): 458–473.

McGowan, Mary Kate, Adelman, Alex, Helmers, Sara, and Stolzenberg, Jacqueline (2011) "A Partial Defense of Illocutionary Silencing," *Hypatia* 26(1): 132–149.

MacKinnon, Catharine A. (1987) "Frances Biddle's Sister: Pornography, Civil Rights, and Speech," in *Feminism Unmodified: Discourses on Life and Law*, Cambridge, MA: Harvard University Press, 163–197.

——(1993) *Only Words*, Cambridge, MA: Harvard University Press.

——(2012) "Foreword," in Ishani Maitra and Mary Kate McGowan (Eds.) *Speech and Harm: Controversies over Free Speech*, Oxford: Oxford University Press, vi–xviii.

Maitra, Ishani (2009) "Silencing Speech," *Canadian Journal of Philosophy* 39(2): 309–338.

—— (2012) "Subordinating Speech," in Ishani Maitra and Mary Kate McGowan (Eds.) *Speech and Harm: Controversies Over Free Speech*, Oxford: Oxford University Press, 94–120.

Maitra, Ishani and McGowan, Mary Kate (2010) "On Silencing, Rape, and Responsibility," *Australasian Journal of Philosophy* 88(1): 167–172.

Mikkola, Mari (2011) "Illocution, Silencing, and the Act of Refusal," *Pacific Philosophical Quarterly* 92(3): 415–437.

Mill, John Stuart (2008) *On Liberty and Other Essays*, Ed. John Gray, Oxford: Oxford University Press.

Saul, Jennifer (2006) "Pornography, Speech Acts, and Context," *Proceedings of the Aristotelian Society* 106(1): 229–248.

Stanley, Jason (2015) *How Propaganda Works*, Princeton, NJ: Princeton University Press.

Sumner, L.W. (2004) *The Hateful and the Obscene: Studies in the Limits of Free Expression*, Toronto, ON: University of Toronto Press.

Tumulty, Maura (2012) "Illocution and Expectations of Being Heard," in Sharon L. Crasnow and Anita M. Superson (Eds.) *Out from the Shadows: Analytical Feminist Contributions to Traditional Philosophy*, Oxford: Oxford University Press, 217–244.

West, Caroline (2003) "The Free Speech Argument Against Pornography," *Canadian Journal of Philosophy* 33(3): 391–422.

—— (2012) "Words That Silence? Freedom of Expression and Racist Hate Speech," in Ishani Maitra and Mary Kate McGowan (Eds.) *Speech and Harm: Controversies over Free Speech*, Oxford: Oxford University Press, 222–248.

Wieland, Nellie (2007) "Linguistic Authority and Convention in a Speech Act Analysis of Pornography," *Australasian Journal of Philosophy* 85(3): 435–456.

Wyatt, Nicole (2009) "Failing to Do Things with Words," *Southwest Philosophy Review* 25(1): 135–142.

24
LANGUAGE, WRITING, AND GENDER DIFFERENCES

Gertrude Postl

Introduction

Concern with language has not been limited to feminist philosophy, but already emerged in the early debates of the second wave of the Women's Movement during the late 1960s and 1970s in the US and in Europe. The underlying assumption was that a patriarchal world produces a patriarchal language, which in turn means that women and men are not on the same playing field with respect to linguistic expression, either in speech or writing. The most prominent themes of these early days—outside of philosophy—were the issue of sexist language (e.g., the generic use of male pronouns and male job titles, derogatory reference terms for women), the discovery that there were no linguistic expressions to refer to certain gender-related phenomena (e.g., sexual harassment, date rape), and different speech behaviors between the genders (e.g., an allegedly more assertive speech style for men versus a more timid, hesitant style for women).

Thus, language was understood from the beginning as a matter of power relations between women and men, and language was commonly viewed by feminists as one of the main means of women's oppression. Contrary to the long held assumption that language is gender-neutral, feminists considered the world we live in to be named by men and thus to some extent created by men. While the view that language is actually constitutive of reality was not shared by feminists across the board, the idea that language is more than a mere reflection of reality—more than just a set of words referring to non-linguistic entities—was already implied in some of the early debates. The emphasis was on the effects that this male gesture of naming the world had on women. Most feminists agreed that the language that we all speak disadvantages, alienates, excludes, or even annihilates women.

A Language of the Body

The feminist approach to language within philosophy—especially within the so-called continental tradition—is closely tied to authors such as Luce Irigaray, Hélène Cixous, and Julia Kristeva. Grouped together (with others) under the labels of "French Feminists" or "Difference Feminists," these authors claimed that woman, or "the feminine," has never been adequately represented within the signifying economies of the Western cultural and philosophical tradition.

While these philosophers were influenced by a number of male thinkers (e.g., Merleau-Ponty's concept of the lived body, Foucault's analysis of power, and Derrida's deconstructive reading strategies and his notion of *différance*, to just mention a few), their common, most influential theoretical framework was psychoanalysis. Although critical of some fundamental psychoanalytic premises (e.g., Freud's notion of penis envy or Lacan's notion of the phallus as transcendental signifier), notions such as the unconscious, the drive (desire), the repressed, sublimation, and also the distinction between primary and secondary processes, all served as helpful analytic tools for continental feminists' work on language.

Freud's notion of the unconscious and Lacan's reworking of it on the level of language, in particular his reading of Freud's concepts of condensation and displacement (the functioning of the primary processes of the dream work) as metaphor and metonymy, set the stage for a feminist psychoanalytic approach to understanding women's oppression through language. Lacan's claim that the unconscious is structured like a language, and his privileging of the signifier over the signified, were to become highly influential for a feminist dismantling of the dominance of consciousness and reason within Western metaphysics. The particular target of feminist critique was the hierarchically organized dualisms characteristic of most of Western thought, such as body/mind, body/language, nature/culture, matter/form, emotion/reason, dark/light, etc., all of which were gender-marked by associating the feminine with the less-valued element of the two. Accordingly, the disappearance of woman was already written into the very structure of Western thought and language. As Hélène Cixous and Catherine Clément put it: "Always the same metaphor . . . wherever discourse is organized . . . throughout literature, philosophy, criticism, centuries of representation and reflection. Thought has always worked through opposition" (Cixous and Clément 1986: 63). The psychoanalytic notion of the drive as being physiological as well as psychic served to unhinge the much despised oppositional thinking of the past, most importantly the opposition between material body and immaterial thought/language.

Feminists pointed out the exploitative relationship, which had never been admitted, between the complementary elements of the respective pairs: "Language, however formal it may be, feeds on blood, on flesh, on material elements. Who and what has nourished language? How is this debt to be repaid?" (Irigaray 1993: 127). Given the cultural association of the feminine with matter, nature, and the body (its blood and flesh), woman was excluded from any form of representation. The female body, female desire, and female sexuality were considered to be as repressed as the unconscious—accordingly, a freeing of the body was synonymous with freeing the unconscious. Defined in terms of a lack, a hole, a castrated being with invisible sexual organs, woman was forever left out of systems of signification that represented only that which was visible and that fitted an economy of calculable exchange and intelligibility. Summarized in Lacan's dictum that the phallus is the transcendental signifier, woman as castrated body-being never had a voice of her own. The only way of expressing herself was to mime the masculine codes, to participate in a language that she never contributed to creating. In a situation in which a bodiless language encounters a voiceless body, her actual experiences cannot be expressed. "What she 'suffers,' what she 'lusts for,' even what she 'takes pleasure in,' all take place upon another stage, in relation to already codified representations" (Irigaray 1985a: 140).

In order to liberate this voiceless, castrated mime or mirror-woman (Irigaray 1985a) and to bring about a "new woman" (Cixous 2000 [1975]) a new language had to be created, a language that gives woman a voice and frees her from a situation of cultural repression, a language capable of expressing woman's experience—her desire, her lust, her suffering. "Write your self. Your body must be heard" (Cixous 2000 [1975]: 262). Or, in the words of Irigaray: "We have to discover a language . . . which does not replace the bodily encounter, as paternal language . . . attempts to do, but which can go along with it, words which do not bar the corporeal, but which speak corporeal" (Irigaray 1991: 43). Disregarding the logical order of philosophical argumentation or the established grammatical rules of a patriarchal linguistic economy, this language escapes any prede-termined regulations and categories; instead, it aims for nearness, proximity, for sound and touch. "How can we speak so as to escape from their compartments, their schemas, their distinctions and oppositions . . . How can we . . . free ourselves from their catego-ries, rid ourselves of their names?" (Irigaray 1985b: 212).

Interested in the role of language for a theory of subjectivity, Julia Kristeva found this bodily-charged form of signification in the individual development of any subject. She called it the "semiotic"—a form of expressivity that precedes the representational modes of the symbolic or phallic order and that will later, from the Oedipal period on, exist alongside them. Modelled on Freud's pre-Oedipal primary processes (the mecha-nisms of condensation and displacement), Kristeva uses the term "semiotic" to refer to the rhythmic waves of energy that regulate the drives in their relation to the body of the mother. Appropriating Plato's notion of the *chora*—a formless receptive space, in its original meaning also associated with the womb—Kristeva views the semiotic as being structured and unstructured at once, a continuous movement of energy flows that are bound and released time and again. Not yet signifying in the sense of the sym-bolic order, this minimally structured totality already contains rudimentary forms of expression—the immediate expressions of bodily functions and demands of the drives. "Analogous only to vocal kinetic rhythm," the semiotic *chora* is neither a sign nor a signifier but precedes and prepares the stage for the symbolic to eventually take hold of the system: "a modality of signifiance in which the linguistic sign is not yet articulated as the absence of an object" (Kristeva 1984: 26).

However, although the semiotic is pre-linguistic, its movements dictated primarily through auditory and tactile stimulation, it is nevertheless exposed to cultural influ-ences or "socio-historical constraints such as the biological difference between the sexes or family structure" (Kristeva 1984: 27). The semiotic continues its presence in the symbolic by undermining or disrupting the latter's *thetic* activities: i.e., the ability to make statements as a result of identification and differentiation, which is learned—in Lacanian terms—by passing through the mirror stage and the threat of castration. These two heterogeneous forms of expressivity, semiotic and symbolic, continue to coexist, albeit in an ongoing tension, since each functions according to a different sig-nifying mechanism. Although this might sound like a gender-neutral theory of language acquisition, the psychoanalytic foundation of Kristeva's account suggests that those two signifying systems are, in fact, gender marked—the semiotic in its directedness towards the body of the mother associated with the feminine, the symbolic as manifestation of the law of the father.

Kristeva's own attitude to the gender-designation of the semiotic and the symbolic was ambiguous. On the one hand, she viewed them as two distinct modes of expres-sion and was interested in the connection between the semiotic and experimental forms of modernist poetry (e.g., those of Mallarmé and Lautréamont). On the other hand, she suggested that the feminine position, in its incarnation as mother, shifts or mediates between those two modes of expression, thus considering the possibility of a feminine voice within the symbolic: "A mother is a continuous separation, a division of the very flesh. And consequently a division of language—and it has always been so" (Kristeva 1986: 178).

The Politics of Writing

The idea of a distinct feminine style has been considered by feminist philosophers in relation to speech as well as writing. Irigaray, for example, talks about *parler femme* or "speaking (as) woman" and mentions a particular speaking style that might develop in places of "women-among-themselves" (Irigaray 1985b: 135). And Cixous discusses, for instance, the problems that women face when trying to speak in public (2000 [1975]: 262).

However, it was probably the idea of a distinct feminine style of writing that popularized the language debate and made it known far beyond philosophical circles. The concept of *écriture féminine* became the best-known shorthand reference for the claim that women use language differently from men. Associated predominantly with the work of Hélène Cixous, *écriture féminine* was considered either as a practice to follow in the pursuit of women's liberation or as something to be ridiculed and ignored for its allegedly inherent misconception of women.

If we take Cixous's "The Laugh of the Medusa" as a key text for understanding *écriture féminine*, the first sentence already reveals that this feminine writing style is a genuine political project: "I shall speak about women's writing: about *what it will do*. Woman must write her self: must write about women and bring women to writing" (Cixous 2000 [1975]: 257). Thus, the aforementioned speaking or writing of the body and the unconscious is never to be understood in a self-referential fashion but always as an attempt to build a connection among women. "I write woman: woman must write woman" (Cixous 2000 [1975]: 259). Cixous's view of writing does not presuppose a text to be the product of an individualized author creating an unchangeable written manifestation. Rather, writing is to generate other writings, texts producing other texts—a continuous writing-reading practice whose main goal is not to produce a text in terms of a final product, but to initiate a textual chain that allows women to put themselves onto the map of cultural history. "Woman must put herself into the text—as into the world and into history" (Cixous 2000 [1975]: 257).

And while this writing process is crucial for women's liberation, Cixous refuses to offer any stylistic characteristics of these women-generated texts (comparable to Kristeva's refusal to define *woman*): "It is impossible to *define* a feminine practice of writing . . . for this practice can never be theorized, enclosed, coded" (Cixous 2000 [1975]: 264). Or, in the words of Irigaray: "This 'style,' or 'writing,' of women tends to put the torch to fetish words, proper terms, well-constructed forms . . . It is always fluid . . . [it] resists and explodes every firmly established form, figure, idea or concept" (Irigaray 1985b: 79). This style is as manifold and endless in its possibilities as woman herself—a point frequently misunderstood by critics of *écriture féminine* who tended to conceive of the entire project as an attempt to reduce the feminine to the irrational stammering of a hysteric, and as an allegedly incomprehensible play with words, closer to poetry than philosophy. The stylistic linguistic innovations and creative impulses that resulted from this concept of a feminine writing style went unnoticed by critics.

This view of writing, particularly in the version of Hélène Cixous, owes a lot to Jacques Derrida. Like Derrida, Cixous privileges writing over speech, she employs several layers of meaning at once, and she argues for a writing style that through the very process of writing deconstructs the already mentioned traditional dualisms, including those between writing/speech, literature/philosophy, unconscious/conscious, and poetry/politics. And, like Derrida, she does not suggest a shift to the lower position in the hierarchy but rather aims to open up a space between the two elements for something new, something yet unknown, to appear—in short, Derrida's notion of *différance*. Cixous goes beyond Derrida, though, in the way that she explores the signifying capacities of the body in all its poetic, audible, and theoretical facets.

The Derridian roots of Cixous's thinking reveal that this project is not about a simple reversal, about making the body more important than language or thought. Rather, it means that body and language can no longer be separated from each other— bodies speak (so to speak) and in turn, linguistic signification has a materiality that is anchored in the body. In the words of Rosi Braidotti: "it is crucial to see that the 'body' in question in the *écriture féminine* movement is not a natural, biologically determined body, but rather a cultural artifact that carries a whole history, a memory of coding and conditioning" (Braidotti 1991: 243). This body, and the experiences that are inscribed onto it, has to be put into writing (comparable to Irigaray's "corporeal speaking") so as to make visible what had to be left out in traditional kinds of texts. On the other hand, language—especially in its written form—has to be conceived of as the conveyer of bodily occurrences, such as rhythm, touch, flows of energy, musicality (comparable to Kristeva's semiotic). This view of writing is political in so far as it responds to prohibitions, exclusions, and the workings of mechanisms of power with respect to texts.

These political implications of *écriture féminine* are also relevant to a feminist response to the history of philosophy. According to continental feminist thinkers, existing texts as the manifestation of established systems of representation are to be analyzed with respect to an unconscious undercurrent that reveals what was left out, excluded, or repressed, for these texts to materialize. The actual meaning of texts is exactly that which is not explicitly said. In short, authors such as Irigaray, Cixous, or Kristeva treat texts similarly to the analysand in the clinical psychoanalytic situation— using the explicit words of a text as a springboard to reach those layers of meaning that are hidden, prohibited, or repressed. The most famous example of this type of reading/ writing strategy is Irigaray's reading of the philosophical canon, which is central to a feminist criticism of the philosophical discourse "as this discourse sets forth the law for all others, inasmuch as it constitutes the discourse on discourse" (Irigaray 1985b: 74). Rather than critically interpreting texts by neatly arranging argument and counter-argument, Irigaray inserts herself into those texts and re-writes them from within, in a way deconstructing and subverting them with their own words. Given the male hegemony over philosophical discourse as well as its dominance and influence on the history of Western thought, strategies to challenge these conditions certainly contribute to a reconfiguration of given power arrangements.

This new "corporeal" language can be brought about only through radical linguistic experimentation in writing. Cixous's texts as well as the early texts of Irigaray offer an overabundance of stylistic innovations, unheard-of metaphors, multiple layers of meaning, and instances of irony and playfulness, and they certainly mark a cross-over between philosophy and literature. Work on language itself became a political act. Be it Cixous's utopian vision of the daring, stormy, laughing "new woman" who refuses to be cast in terms of a lack, or Irigaray's reading/re-writing of Plato's Cave allegory and Freud's notion of penis envy (and many others)—these texts offered stylistic options, previously unknown, that other feminist philosophers could employ, adapt, play with, or simply use as stimulating inspirations for their own writing and reading. "She lets the other language speak—the language of 1,000 tongues which knows neither enclosure nor death . . . Her language . . . does not hold back, it makes possible" (Cixous 2000 [1975]: 270). And it is this "making possible," the opening up of new (linguistic) spaces and forms, of an entirely different economy of producing texts—writing as an open-ended, not author-oriented process, in which anybody can participate at any time, where previous texts are not enshrined and untouchable—that gives the concept of a feminine reading/writing style its political significance.

Sexual Difference and Many Languages

Shared among all the authors presented so far is the assumption of a radical sexual difference and accordingly, of two types of language or two modes of signification: one is associated with the masculine, the language we speak, the language used for all the grandiose manifestations of Western philosophical and cultural history. The other is a language still to come, a language of the repressed unconscious, a language of the body, a language associated with woman and the feminine. Irigaray literally talks about "two syntaxes": "a double syntax, without claiming to regulate the second by the standard of representation, of re-presentation, of the first" (Irigaray 1985a: 138).

Neither the assumption of a sexual difference nor that of two distinct languages was uncontroversial. Difference feminism with its discourse of two forms of desire, two types of sexuality, two modes of thinking, two distinct representational economies, even two distinct ontologies or ways of being (as to some extent is suggested by Irigaray), challenged a fundamental premise of the women's movement: the notion of equality. This is not to say that difference feminists were opposed to women's equal access to economic, legal, or cultural resources. But their focus was on making visible sexual difference on the level of representation, so as to escape the dominant standards of the masculine.

And according to difference feminists, those standards of the masculine were everywhere. Seeming cultural differences between women and men in terms of behavior, looks, profession, language use, etc., were taken to be just pseudo-differences, still operating according to the order of the same, with woman being assigned the complementary part respective to the original masculine one. Talking about Freud, Irigaray asks: "Why make the little girl, the woman, fear, envy, hope, hate, reject, etc. in more or less the *same terms* as the little boy, the man?" (Irigaray 1985a: 59). Difference feminists criticized this misleading construction of difference—in their eyes no difference at all—and aimed to make woman as the real other appear through radically new forms of linguistic expression.

But since these new forms of expression or the "other" language of the feminine were closely tied to the body, to materiality, to desire, and sexuality, critics quickly accused difference feminists—in particular Irigaray and Cixous—of essentialism, more specifically biological essentialism—the belief that certain "characteristics defined as women's essence are shared in common by all women at all times" and that "the existence of fixed characteristics, given attributes, and ahistorical functions . . . limit the possibilities of change and thus of social reorganization" (Grosz 1994: 84). The preferred target of critics was Irigaray's extensive metaphorical use of the morphology of the female body (e.g., her image of the "two lips"), which was taken as ultimate proof of the looming danger of a biological determinism of gender under the disguise of an alleg-edly new language, a language that actually only re-affirmed women's lack of rational ability and reduced (political) reality to texts.

What critics overlooked, though, was—first—the insistence on the part of differ-ence feminists that this new language of the feminine is a linguistic position, that it can be spoken/written by either gender. Thus, for example, Cixous's and Kristeva's ref-erences to and analyses of male writers and poets (Genet, Kleist, Kafka, Joyce, among many others) who, in their view, employed a version of this "other" language already, long before the onset of the women's movement. And second, there was a refusal to define woman or a feminine style of writing—as stated already, Cixous talks about "the language of 1,000 tongues" (2000 [1975]: 270). And Irigaray muses: "Neither one nor two. I've never known to count" (1985b: 207). Thus this other, feminine language is open-ended with respect to its possible forms of stylistic realization—it is exactly not one language but opens up many languages. And we should not forget Irigaray's claim that woman is different in herself and that her language is "fluid": "Woman never speaks the same way. What she emits is flowing, fluctuating. *Blurring*" (Irigaray 1985b: 111, 112). If the feminine and the language it speaks are different in themselves, constantly changing, "fluid," then the notion of unchangeable essences becomes meaningless. The very idea of essentialism rests on a concept of identity—but it is exactly the notion of identity that the "new woman" with her fluctuating, blurring, fluid language is supposed to undermine.

This controversy over the alleged essentialism of *écriture féminine* or "speaking (as) woman" could never really be solved and marked the feminist debate for many years (see Schor and Weed 1994). The alleged assumption of two genders and two languages was evoked again within the more recent contexts of queer theory and the transgender debate. Here, too, it was overlooked that difference feminism did favor a multiplicity of genders (and not the overused two) and, furthermore, that Irigaray, Cixous, and Kristeva all addressed issues of bisexuality and of lesbianism by discussing the (sexual) relation among women.

Less well-known in the Anglo-American academic scene is a group of women philos-ophers from Italy, particularly Verona and Milan, who called themselves the Diotima group, and included authors such as Adriana Cavarero, Luisa Muraro, Diana Sartori, and Chiara Zamboni. Their contributions to the question of gender and language reso-nate with some of the ideas of the French authors, in particular those of Irigaray. But their position is overall rather unique in that they aimed at political and institutional interventions and a new form of women-centered authority, based on the superiority of knowledge or experience, free from any exercise of power. This was called *affidamento*—literally "trust," "confidence," or "assurance"—indicating a relationship among women based on respect, trust, and acceptance of other women's authority, thereby recognizing differences in knowledge and experience.

Insisting on a theory of sexual difference and analyzing the impact that language has on the immediate level of experience, these Italian authors understood their philosoph-ical work to be in continuous interaction with the creation of new forms of life and dif-ferent social institutions, e.g., experimentation with publishing or pedagogy. However, while their texts are highly popular (outside of Italy) among feminist philosophers in the German language context, hardly any—apart from Cavarero—have been translated into English. Thus, this brief remark on the Diotima group shall suffice here.

Mary Daly's *Wickedary Dictionary*

Among US feminist philosophers a dominant figure in the discussion of language is, of course, Mary Daly. While Daly does not share the psychoanalytic influence typical of the authors discussed so far, she too assumes a radical gender difference and treats the issue of language accordingly. Immensely popular among US feminists during the 1970s and 1980s (even outside of strictly philosophical circles) and still quite influential for feminist theology, her work on language is no longer very much present in contemporary feminist debates. Nevertheless, her position on issues of representation is unique and may serve to clarify difference feminism further by way of comparison.

While many of the themes that are relevant for difference feminists can also be found in Daly's texts—women's commodification and exploitation within a patriarchal culture, their closeness to nature, the importance of women's connectedness, the role of language in women's oppression and liberation—Daly's contributions to the language debate differ significantly from those of the authors discussed so far. Although also working within the continental tradition, most importantly phenomenology and existentialism, Daly's explicit critique of psychoanalysis prevents any interest in the unconscious or the (female) body as the foundation of woman's experience. Daly approaches the distortions and destructions of patriarchy that make the "real" woman disappear—resonating with Heidegger—via an interplay of forgetting and memory, as a journey into the future through the past. Language is viewed as one of the prime means for these distortions and destructions and has thus to be carefully analyzed—in all its popular forms, not just focusing on philosophical discourse—and changed. Contrary to the authors already discussed, Daly's sources for linguistic transformation are the etymology of the English language, orthographical experimentation, and, time and again, a re-definition of the meaning of certain words. Women's language, for Daly, is not so much something that has to be newly created but rather results from a process of re-appropriation: "For it is, after all, our 'mother-tongue' that has been turned against us by the tongue-twisters. Learning to speak our Mothers' Tongue is exorcising the male 'mothers'" (Daly 1978: 330).

Daly's theoretical world is somehow split in two: patriarchy, characterized by misogyny, necrophilia and destruction, and a utopian, future world of women, brought about by women embarking on a so-called metapatriarchal journey in order to reach a forgotten background, a time/space where women were together and one with nature, and that needs to be re-evoked through "deep memory." According to Daly, this journey will succeed only if women learn to speak a different language, if they manage to escape the lies and distortions of patriarchal naming, in particular the derogatory and misleading naming of women: "This means going beyond the imposed definitions of 'bad woman' and 'good woman,' beyond the categories of prostitute and wife" (Daly 1985 [1974]: 65–66).

This quote indicates already that Daly's focus is on the vocabulary of the English language, and she is the only feminist philosopher who actually published a dictionary, her *Websters' First New Intergalactic Wickedary of the English Language* (1987, together with Jane Caputi). There we find, in neatly separated categories or "word-webs," lists of familiar words with Daly's redefinition as well as newly created words. To just give a few examples: patriarchy is—among other definitions—a "cockocracy: the state of supranational, supernatural erections," or "Godfather, Son & Company: the church, the state, the family, and all other firms dedicated to the propagation of the male line" (Daly and Caputi 1987: 191, 203). Philosophy is turned into "foolosophy" or "phallosophy" (Daly and Caputi 1987: 200, 217). Reference terms for women are endless, partly drawing upon a revival of old meanings and partly redefining commonly known derogatory terms: e.g., "Witch . . . : an Elemental Soothsayer; one who is in harmony with the rhythms of the universe: Wise Woman, Healer," or "Bitchy adj.: . . . a woman who is active, direct, blunt, obnoxious, competent, loud-mouthed, independent, stubborn, demanding, achieving . . . strong-minded, scary, ambitious" (Daly and Caputi 1987: 180, 108–109).

Daly's approach to language is a theory of naming; concerns about syntax or speech behavior are as absent as suggestions for a different style of writing. Absent, furthermore, is—in spite of her constant reiteration of an elemental togetherness of women—any indication as to what women are supposed to do with her dictionary entries. Appropriate them for themselves and employ them as they are? Create similar words or modified meanings? Continue to use the old words with the altered meanings suggested by Daly?

Daly too believes in a radical gender difference and in two languages. Contrary to the French feminist authors, though, her two languages turn out to be two sets of words, with the second set lacking the openness and ongoing transformative potential that we found in *écriture féminine*. Without a doubt, introducing new meanings to already established words could be viewed as a deconstructive gesture (comparable to Derrida's notion of *paleonymics*). But in spite of Daly's creative and often funny suggestions for linguistic renewal, she seems to be stuck in a black and white account of language, of the world, of women. There is a bad world (patriarchy) and a good world (the future), there are bad women (those manipulated into serving patriarchal demands, called "fembots" or "painted birds"), and good women ("Hags," "Crones," "Amazones," the "wild race of raging women"), there are wrong words (the English language as it is) and there are correct words (Mary Daly's dictionary entries). Contrary to, for example, Cixous' many layers of meaning of a text and the open-ended writer/reader exchange that this is supposed to generate, or Irigaray's linguistic interventions in male-authored philosophical texts, Daly's work on language seems like a closed system. She revolutionized the vocabulary of the English language, but it is far from obvious how women readers of her texts can enter the process and continue the project on their own terms. Furthermore, it is not fully convincing that turning to the etymology of words, to the meaning they had in past periods of patriarchy, should serve as source for a post-patriarchal semantics.

Furthermore, Daly's account of sexual difference focuses not so much on making sexual difference visible but on women. In Daly's vision of a feminist future, men disappear from the scene; her utopia is literally a world of women only—difference does not have to be negotiated any longer. For comparison, here is Irigaray: "what I want . . . is not to create a theory of woman, but to secure a place for the feminine within sexual difference" (Irigaray 1985b: 159). In short, Daly's work, including her work on language, is about women and not about the feminine.

After Sexual Difference and *Écriture Féminine*: Judith Butler's Performative

Judith Butler, with the publication of *Gender Trouble* (1990) and the subsequent *Bodies That Matter* (1993), moved the feminist discussion of language to an altogether new level, thus establishing a link between the earlier debates over sexual difference and a feminine writing style and contemporary concerns regarding gender identity, the multiplicity of genders, and transgender identities. Most importantly, for Butler as well, language is crucial for the construction of gender.

Drawing upon J. L. Austin's speech act theory, Butler claimed that sex is "a performatively enacted signification" (Butler 1990: 33) and thus is always already part of gender. In that gender is produced by a repetition of normative discursive acts, it becomes a "doing" and not something "to be." This "doing"—as in speech act theory—is always also a doing through words. However, these words are not limited to either speech ("speaking (as) woman") or writing (*écriture féminine*) but are conceived of within the totality of a performative enactment, an assumed interplay of language and the postures and gestures of the body. "Gender identity . . . is performatively constituted by the very 'expressions' that are said to be its results" (Butler 1990: 25). Butler's notion of the performative added a dimension to the feminist discussion of language that freed it from the confinements of the actual linguistic sign: the performative presupposes a context (social, historical, artistic, etc.), an interaction between bodies, and a dimension of meaning that cuts across the old divide between physicality and immateriality.

According to Butler, the discursive construction of gender can be conducted either in an affirmative or a deviant fashion. Contrary to repeating the given gender norms, a parodic re-signification of them has the potential to undermine established gender arrangements. Thus Butler's position is clearly political as well, and it opened the theoretical doors for what is now called gender identity. Challenging a seeming "natural" alignment between a particular sexed body, gender roles, and sexual preference (or desire) allowed for a (performative) disruption of the so-called heterosexual matrix and thus for "abject" bodies to transgress the normativity of given gender arrangements.

Butler was also concerned with exclusions and with making the excluded visible through language or discursive acts; in her case, though, it was not the exclusion of the feminine but of those abject bodies that did not submit to the heterosexual norm. Butler's constructivist position was therefore soon posited against Irigaray's alleged essentialism of the female body. While Irigaray's account of a radical sexual difference, enacted in language, probably has little to offer for questions concerning queer or transgender identity, what does connect her with Butler (in spite of all the arguments to the contrary, too numerous to retrace within the given context) is a view that the body is not just a naturally given entity outside of culture or language. The following statement by Butler underscores this: "Every time I try to write about the body, the writing ends up being about language . . . The body is that upon which language falters, and the body carries its own signs, in ways that remain largely unconscious" (Butler 2004: 198). Thus, in spite of all the differences of positions, styles, political interventions, what connects the various debates on gender and language within the continental tradition of philosophy is a view of the body as a signifying entity.

Further Reading

Fuss, Diana (1989) *Essentially Speaking: Feminism, Nature, and Difference*, New York: Routledge. (Discusses various positions on the issue of essentialism and language.)

Minh-ha, Trinh T. (1989) *Woman, Native, Other: Writing Postcoloniality and Feminism*, Bloomington, IN: Indiana University Press. (Explores issues of women's writing from the non-Western perspective of the other.)

Moraga, Cherríe and Anzaldúa, Gloria (Eds.) (2015) *This Bridge Called My Back: Writings by Radical Women of Color*, 4th ed., Albany, NY: State University of New York Press. Originally published (1981), Boston, MA: Women of Color Press. (Women and writing from the perspective of women of color, includes Audre Lorde's critique of Mary Daly and her essay on the "Master's Tools.")

Spivak, Gayatri Chakravorty (1987) "French Feminism in an International Frame," in *In Other Worlds: Essays in Cultural Politics*, New York: Routledge. (Critique of French Feminism from a post-colonial perspective. Volume includes also other essays on the relationship between women, language, and culture.)

Stone, Alison (2006) *Luce Irigaray and the Philosophy of Sexual Difference*, Cambridge: Cambridge University Press. (Discusses question of Irigaray's essentialism by comparing her position to Butler, in particular with respect to the body.)

Related Topics

Embodiment and feminist philosophy (Chapter 15); materiality: sex, gender and what lies beneath (Chapter 16); psychoanalysis, subjectivity, and feminism (Chapter 19); speech and silencing (Chapter 23); feminist theory, lesbian theory, and queer theory (Chapter 31); aesthetics and the politics of gender (Chapter 38).

References

Braidotti, Rosi (1991) *Patterns of Dissonance*, New York: Routledge.

Butler, Judith (1990) *Gender Trouble: Feminism and the Subversion of Identity*, New York: Routledge.

——(2004) *Undoing Gender*, New York: Routledge.

Cixous, Hélène (2000 [1975]) "The Laugh of the Medusa," in Kelly Oliver (Ed.) *French Feminism Reader*, Lanham, MD: Rowman & Littlefield.

Cixous, Hélène and Clément, Catherine (1986) *The Newly Born Woman*, trans. Betsy Wing, Minneapolis, MN: University of Minnesota Press.

Daly, Mary (1978) *Gyn/Ecology. The Metaethics of Radical Feminism*, Boston, MA: Beacon Press.

——(1985 [1974]) *Beyond God the Father. Toward a Philosophy of Women's Liberation*, Boston, MA: Beacon Press.

Daly, Mary, and Jane Caputi (1987) *Websters' First New Intergalactic Wickedary of the English Language*, Boston, MA: Beacon Press.

Grosz, Elizabeth (1994) "Sexual Difference and the Problem of Essentialism," in Naomi Schor and Elizabeth Weed (Eds.) *The Essential Difference*, Bloomington, IN: Indiana University Press, 82–97.

Irigaray, Luce (1985a) *Speculum of the Other Woman*, trans. Gillian Gill, Ithaca, NY: Cornell University Press.

——(1985b) *This Sex Which Is Not One*, trans. Catherine Porter and Carolyn Burke, Ithaca, NY: Cornell University Press.

——(1991) "The Bodily Encounter with the Mother," in Margaret Whitford (Ed.) *The Irigaray Reader*, Oxford: Blackwell, 34–46.

——(1993) *An Ethics of Sexual Difference*, trans. Carolyn Burke and Gillian Gill, Ithaca, NY: Cornell University Press.

Kristeva, Julia (1984) *Revolution in Poetic Language*, trans. Margaret Waller, New York: Columbia University Press.

——(1986) "Stabat Mater," in Toril Moi (Ed.) *The Kristeva Reader*, New York: Columbia University Press, 160–186.

Schor, Naomi, and Elizabeth Weed (Eds.) (1994) *The Essential Difference*, Bloomington, IN: Indiana University Press.

25

PHILOSOPHY OF SCIENCE AND THE FEMINIST LEGACY

Janet A. Kourany

Philosophy of science is concerned with the nature of science, its practices and results. But unlike other fields concerned with science, such as history of science and sociology of science, philosophy of science aims not simply to describe science but to articulate and even improve upon what lies at the very heart of its success, scientific rationality itself. Feminist philosophy of science has furthered this enterprise in a variety of ways. One way, for example, concerns the scope of the enterprise. Traditional philosophy of science failed to consider women whether as scientific researchers, as subjects of scientific research, or as individuals affected by such research, and feminist philosophers of science have done much to rectify that failure. Many of these philosophers have even suggested that women *must* be included in philosophy of science in at least some of these capacities if scientific rationality is to be captured at all. But there are also other contributions feminist philosophers have made to philosophy of science. In what follows we shall consider some of the most important of these contributions and their impact on science and society as well as philosophy.

Pre-Feminist Philosophy of Science

Start with the way philosophy of science was before the advent of feminism. Most scholars locate its roots in the "Vienna Circle," that group of scientists, mathematicians, and scientists-turned-philosophers who regularly met in Vienna at the beginning of the twentieth century. What distinguished the group—aside from the illustriousness of many of its members (such as Moritz Schlick, Rudolf Carnap, Otto Neurath, and Kurt Gödel) and followers (such as A. J. Ayer, Carl Hempel, and Alfred Tarski)—was the ambitious task it had set for itself: the development of a "scientific world-conception." What this meant was a worldview based not on a priori speculation, as the metaphysical system-building of the past had been, but instead on the results of empirical science. The plan was to build into a unified whole the individual contributions of scientists from all the various fields of study. And the method adopted to do this was two-fold: both active encouragement of collaboration among scientists from different fields and countries to gear their research toward such a unified result, and logical and epistemological analysis of their contributions using a neutral system of symbols to make explicit the connections among these contributions and thereby their overall unity.

The most impressive feature of the Vienna Circle's activities, however, was the over-arching goal that motivated them: not only progress in science, but also progress in social life.

> One cannot begin to give an account of the Vienna Circle without seeing it not only as a movement for a scientific world conception in terms of its logical, epistemological and methodological content, but also as a movement which conceived of its theoretical contributions as being in the service of social reform, and as, in significant measure, allied with the left social movements of its time.
>
> (Wartofsky 1996: 60)

And one of the important accomplishments of the Vienna Circle, as its 1929 "manifesto" proclaimed, was just such social reform:

> We witness the spirit of the scientific world-conception penetrating in grow-ing measure the forms of personal and public life, in education, upbringing, architecture and the shaping of economic and social life according to rational principles. *The scientific world-conception serves life, and life receives it.*
>
> (Carnap, Hahn, and Neurath 1973 [1929]: 317–318)

By the time "logical empiricism," as the movement begun by the Vienna Circle came to be called, had been transplanted to the United States after the war, however, this concern with social life and social reform had disappeared. Philosophy of science was still committed to unified science. But the commitment had degenerated from an active movement—seeking to regularize collaboration among scientists from different coun-tries and different academic fields for the improvement of both science and human life—to an academic thesis—a hypothesis concerning the future internal development of science "viewed, so to speak, from across the quadrangle as an independent intel-lectual project neither requiring nor requesting input from philosophy" (Reisch 2005: 375). And, as time went on, even this very truncated connection with science fell away. By the early 1960s logical empiricism was accused of having become little more than the investigation of abstract logical and epistemological puzzles. What had happened?

According to recent scholarship, a variety of things (see, for various accounts, Giere 1999; McCumber 2001; Howard 2003; and Reisch 2005). For one, the North American social/political context in which the surviving members of the Vienna Circle and their followers found themselves after the war was much more stable, democratic, and liberal than that of pre-war central Europe, much less evocative of the reformist zeal of the Vienna Circle. Conceptualizing science and the philosophy of science within this new context as sources of social transformation must have seemed increasingly out of place.

Second was the McCarthyism of 1950s America and its antipathy to anything that even smacked of socialism. That certainly would have squelched the kind of politically engaged philosophy of science championed by the Vienna Circle. The public record, after all, "clearly indicates that philosophy was the most heavily attacked of all the academic disciplines" (McCumber 2001: 37). Philosophers of science who hoped to retain their jobs and flourish in the field would have gotten the message to pursue safe, politically neutral, socially disengaged research.

Third, the conception of science as a politically detached search for truth had been institutionalized in the United States, thanks largely to Vannevar Bush and his 1945 *Science—The Endless Frontier: Report to the President on a Program for Postwar Scientific Research*. It was this conception, in fact, that set science policy for much of the rest of the century. Not surprisingly, therefore, philosophy of science, engaged as it was with science and also modeling itself on science, embarked on its own similarly detached intellectual enterprise.

Doubtless there were also other factors in play in mid-century America besides the above three that moved philosophy of science away from the kind of social engagement exemplified by the Vienna Circle, and doubtless many of these factors (such as the impact of McCarthyism) changed over time. Yet, philosophy of science largely continued its social disengagement right up to the end of the twentieth century. The main exception to this was feminist philosophy of science.

The Birth of Feminist Philosophy of Science

Feminist philosophy of science emerged in the 1980s, and from the start it was a very different sort of enterprise from its parent discipline. True, its proponents were trained in the same ways as other philosophers of science of the time, and their academic employment and advancement largely depended on their pursuing the same kinds of projects as these other philosophers. Yet, by the 1980s other conditions were operating to move them in a different direction.

First, the women's movement was exposing the inequalities that characterized even liberal, democratic societies like the United States—the inequalities of job opportunities and pay and advancement; the "second shift" of housework, child care, and elder care expected of women even when they worked full-time outside the home; the ever-present threats of rape and domestic violence, sexual harassment, and other forms of violence directed at women; the constrictions of feminine gender socialization; and so on.

Second, feminist scientists and historians of science were exposing the role that science had played in perpetuating and even adding to these problems. Of course, the hope had always been that science would help solve these problems—that it would replace prevailing ignorance and prejudice and misinformation about women with more adequate perspectives. But now feminists were showing that science all too frequently had done just the opposite. Indeed, in fields such as anthropology, sociology, political science, medical research, psychology, biology, and archaeology feminist scientists and historians of science were documenting how extensively sexism had infected research. And they documented, as well, the obstacles women scientists faced in such fields.

These events evoked in feminist philosophers of science a kind of reformist zeal very like that previously exemplified by the Vienna Circle: a commitment to work with scientists to reform science in order to reform society. But how? Feminist scientists were not only exposing sexism in their fields, they were also correcting it. Sometimes the corrections were quite straightforward. A great deal of sexist science was, by the lights of traditional scientific methodology, simply bad science—science that failed to satisfy accepted standards of concept formation, experimental design, data analysis, or the like (see, for example, Hubbard 1979; Bleier 1984; Fausto-Sterling 1985). Correcting such sexism was simply a matter of enforcing accepted standards. At other times, however, the accepted standards themselves had to be reformed, and feminist scientists proposed and put into effect appropriate revisions to rid their fields of sexism. For example, feminist sociologist Margrit Eichler (1988) proposed a set of general "guidelines for non-sexist research" to supplement what science students and researchers were already expected to live up to. Her guidelines distinguished, illustrated, and offered recipes for eliminating seven different types of sexism in their most frequently occurring forms, and they covered all aspects of the research process, from the title right down to the policy recommendations that might follow from the results. Other scientists proposed more specialized revisions designed specifically for their own areas of research.

The problem, however—the problem many feminist scientists were loath to acknowledge—was that all these revisions were just as feminist as what they replaced was sexist, and yet they resulted in, not new examples of biased science (though biased in a different way from before), but *less biased* science (more accurate, more thorough, more comprehensive, and better justified than what had gone before). And how was that possible if science was, or at least was supposed to be, the politically detached search for truth that Vannevar Bush had applauded? It was here that feminist philosophers of science could and did make an important contribution—a very traditionally philosophical contribution that attempted anew to articulate and even improve upon scientific rationality, and yet one whose content in many ways broke with the philosophical tradition as it was thus far formed. Actually, feminist philosophers of science provided a number of such reconceptualizations of scientific rationality, each conflicting with the others (what else would you have expected from philosophers?), and yet each also supplying new insights complementing those of the others.

Scientific Rationality through Feminist Eyes

Consider just four of these reconceptualizations of scientific rationality offered by feminist philosophers of science. Probably the most sophisticated is "critical contextual empiricism" put forward by Helen Longino (see especially Longino 1990; 1993; 2002). According to this approach, the scientific search for truth need not be politically detached (that is, value-free). What it needs to be is rational. For it is rationality that will get scientists to the truth, if anything will. But contrary to what feminist scientists assumed, rationality is to be understood in social terms, as a characteristic of scientific communities, not in individual terms, as a characteristic of the methods or attitudes or behavior of individual scientists. Why is that?

According to Longino, scientists are "situated" in particular social/cultural (gender, racial/ethnic, class, sexual-orientation, political, etc.) as well as spatial-temporal locations (these are the "contextual" factors Longino wants to emphasize). As a result, scientists conduct their research from particular—and different—spatial-temporal-social/cultural vantage points, and these can have a decided effect on the nature of that research. Though scientists might be trained in comparable ways and might use comparable research methods, neither the training nor the methods, however rigorous and however rigorously applied, can be guaranteed to screen out the difference in vantage points from which scientists approach their research. Indeed, such vantage points, and the histories, interests, values, and sensitivities they incorporate, can and do affect which questions scientists investigate and which they ignore, which background assumptions they accept and which they reject, which observational or experimental data they select to study and the way they interpret those data, and so on.

Now rationality, the effective search for truth, depends on limiting the intrusion of these individual scientists' subjective inputs into the scientific community's shared beliefs, its "knowledge," and, hence, depends on the scientific community's critical scrutiny of each scientist's particular vantage point and resulting scientific work. But rationality in this sense is a matter of degree. More specifically, it depends on the degree to which a scientific community satisfies four conditions. First, the community must have public venues for criticism, such as journals and conferences. Second, it must have publicly recognized standards—shared values as well as substantive principles—by reference to which the criticism can be made. Third, it must be responsive to the criticism. That is, the beliefs of the community as a whole and over time—as measured by such public phenomena as the content of textbooks, the distribution of grants and awards, and the flexibility of dominant worldviews—must change in response to the critical discussion taking place within it ("uptake"). And fourth, the community must recognize the equal intellectual authority of all the parties qualified to engage in the debate ("tempered equality"), among whom all relevant points of view that can serve as sources of criticism must be represented.

A science will, then, be rational to the degree that it satisfies these four conditions— to the degree that it permits what Longino calls "transformative criticism." And the output of such a science will constitute *knowledge*, even if that output is inspired and informed by social/political values, if the community that practices it meets these conditions and the output conforms sufficiently to its objects to enable the members of the community to carry out their projects with respect to those objects.

Since feminist scientists starting in the 1970s were frequently new additions to their fields, and since they approached their fields from vantage points different from those of their colleagues (among other things, they were women whereas their colleagues were men, and they shared feminist commitments not frequently shared by the men), they provided new points of view from which to criticize the scientific contributions of the men and, hence, they increased the rationality of the resulting science. Small wonder what resulted was less biased than before.

Sandra Harding and other "standpoint theorists" offer a different analysis (see, e.g., Harding 1986; 1991). According to this analysis, just as the various spatial-temporal-social/cultural vantage points of scientists can have a decided effect on what they understand and can contribute, the various vantage points of everyone else can have a decided effect on what they understand and can contribute. But these various vantage points are not always equally valuable, epistemologically. Individuals who are in the socially disadvantaged positions in society are often able to recognize more readily than those in the more advantaged positions the structures that keep in place the hierarchy of advantage and disadvantage. "They have less to lose by distancing themselves from the social order; thus, the perspective from their lives can more easily generate fresh and critical analyses" (Harding 1991: 126). As a result, the wheelchair-bound person is painfully aware of the architectural choices and conventions (stairs and escalators rather than elevators, for instance) that disenable her mobility while they enable the mobility of the abled; the abled are likely oblivious to all this. Gays and lesbians are aware of the heterosexual expectations and customs that deny their sexuality while straights comfortably take them for granted; women continue to be amazed by the sexism that men fail to see; and so on.

This epistemological advantage especially holds if the wheelchair-bound, the gays and lesbians, and the women have been engaged in the kinds of consciousness-raising group activities and political activism that have characterized recent movements for social equality, such as the civil rights, gay rights, and disability rights movements and the women's movement. "Only through such struggles can we begin to see beneath the appearances created by an unjust social order to the reality of how this social order is in fact constructed and maintained" (Harding 1991: 127). Such struggles help to create a more collective vantage point, which Harding calls a "standpoint." Thus, we can speak of a women's standpoint or a gay and lesbian standpoint or a disability standpoint. Of course, men, straight persons, and abled persons can learn—have learned—to see things from these less partial, less distorted, collective vantage points, these *standpoints*, but the ones whose standpoints they are will typically have to be their teachers and will still tend to be the epistemological path-breakers.

So some vantage points—those associated with social disadvantage—can bring with them epistemological advantage. But this holds in science as well as out of it. Women scientists, for example, though they may enjoy the class-related and other social advantages associated with being scientists, still struggle both in and out of science with the gender-related disadvantages associated with being women. And this can provide them with vantage points on gender-related issues in their fields less distorted than the ones available to their male colleagues. Small wonder it was the women scientists whose consciousness had been raised by feminism, not the men, who uncovered and helped to rectify the gender-related shortcomings in the sciences.

"Feminist naturalists" such as Elizabeth Anderson, Louise Antony, and Miriam Solomon provide a still different analysis (see, e.g., Anderson 1995; 2004; Antony 1993; 1995; Solomon 2001). Indeed, their approach rejects a priori prescriptions regarding the proper composition of scientific communities or the proper conduct of inquiry. It rejects, as well, the single-minded focus of the other approaches on scientific practice to the exclusion of scientific outcome. What the naturalist approach advocates instead is a close look at *successful* scientific practice in order to identify those of its features that contribute to and explain its success. For the naturalist approach, in fact, scientific rationality just *is* whatever contributes to and explains scientific success.

When we take a close look at successful scientific practice during the last three decades, however, we find that a great deal of that part of it that is gender-relevant has been produced by feminists. We find, that is to say, that the contributions of feminists—the wide-ranging critiques of traditional science in such fields as psychology, sociology, economics, political science, archaeology, anthropology, biology, and medical research, and the new research directions and research results forged in the wake of those critiques—those contributions have been not only free of sexism but also more empirically successful than the sexist science that went before (see, e.g., Schiebinger 1999, and Creager, Lunbeck, and Schiebinger 2001 for the kinds of wide-ranging changes in science that have occurred due to feminism).

Advocates of the naturalist approach hypothesize that those successes are a function of feminists' political values, where political values, like any other apparently non-epistemic feature of scientific practice (such as competitiveness or the desire for credit for one's accomplishments) need not function as hindrances but might actually function as aids in the acquisition of objective knowledge. Indeed, supporters of the naturalist approach point out that cases in which feminist values have clearly influenced science (for example, by motivating particular lines of research or the maintenance of particular social structures) have been cases in which the science produced is not only free of sexism but also more developed and more empirically adequate than before (see, e.g., Antony 1993; 1995; Campbell 2001; Anderson 1995; 2004; and Wylie and Nelson 2007). And since feminist values produce greater scientific success than sexist values we have reason to rid science of the latter.

The "political" approach put forward by Janet Kourany (2010) moves in a somewhat different direction. Like the naturalist approach, it advocates a close look at successful scientific practice and what contributes to and explains its success. But it advocates this close look in the context of the wider society in which science takes place. Indeed, it emphasizes that society ultimately pays for science—through taxes and through consumer spending. And it emphasizes that society is deeply affected by science. Science shapes our lives, and perhaps most important, science shapes our conception of ourselves. As philosopher and theologian A. J. Heschel explained half a century ago:

> A theory about the stars never becomes a part of the being of the stars. A theory about man enters his consciousness, determines his self-understanding, and modifies his very existence. The image of a man affects the nature of man . . . We become what we think of ourselves.
>
> (Heschel 1965: 7)

As a result, science, so much a shaper of society and so much a beneficiary of society, should be deeply responsive to the needs of society.

The political approach thus suggests that scientific success should be defined in terms of social success—human flourishing, what makes for a good society—as well as epistemic success. But it also suggests, like the naturalist approach, that scientific rationality should be defined in terms of whatever contributes to and explains scientific success. Hence, scientific rationality should be defined in terms of those features of science that contribute to and explain the social as well as epistemic success of science. Regarding gender-related research in particular, since one of the needs of society—of both women and men—is justice, and equality for women is one aspect of that justice, those features should include, in addition to ones that relate to epistemic goals, ones that relate to feminist goals.

Returning, then, to the feminist scientists who, starting in the 1970s, did innovative critical and constructive work in fields such as anthropology, sociology, political science, medical research, psychology, biology, and archaeology, we can easily explain why their work was superior to the sexist work that preceded it, and we can do this without invoking any speculative hypotheses regarding the causes of the improvements. The explanation is simply that they were scientists trying to do epistemically responsible research, that at the same time they were feminist scientists trying to root sexism out of that research, and that rooting sexism out of that research was tantamount to implanting egalitarian social values in it. Thus, their research, unlike that of their colleagues, ended up satisfying both epistemic criteria and criteria related to feminist goals and, thus, fulfilled more stringent standards of scientific rationality than their colleagues' research.

The Legacy

Feminist philosophy of science has thus contributed new understandings of scientific rationality that are especially helpful to feminist scientists. For, in each case, these new understandings show that feminism is not antithetical to the requirements of good science. Indeed, in each case they show that feminism is *partially constitutive* of the requirements of good science.

But these new understandings of scientific rationality are especially helpful to philosophers of science as well. For one thing, they take into account the complex roles of social values in science, and thereby, the complex ways in which science both shapes and is shaped by society. And this answers a need pervasive in philosophy of science since it came into its own as a professional discipline in the middle of the twentieth century. Indeed, even after the demise of logical empiricism, and even after the historicizing and naturalizing and socializing of philosophy of science that occurred thereafter, science was still treated in twentieth century philosophy of science as detached from its social (political/cultural/economic) surround—as science in a vacuum. The roles of social values in science either failed to enter philosophical discussion at all or they were limited to the choice of research questions in the "context of discovery" and the choice of research applications in the "context of application." And now, in the twenty-first century, science is still largely treated in the same way—even though questions regarding the social relevance of science and the social responsibilities of scientists have become particularly pressing in the world beyond philosophy of science, and funding from sources such as the US National Science Foundation and the US National Institutes of Health now requires detailed analysis and assessment of the social values that operate in research. In short, the contributions of feminist rationality studies regarding the roles of social values in science continue to be of prime importance to philosophy of science.

Feminist rationality studies provide other important benefits to philosophy of science as well. As we have seen, they deal with socially important problems—the problems of gender inequality women still contend with and the roles that science has played and is still playing in perpetuating these problems—problems that most non-feminist philosophers of science completely ignore. Moreover, feminist rationality studies suggest well-reasoned responses to these problems. For example, both Longino and Harding argue that the distinctive vantage points from which women scientists pursue their research are crucial to achieving objective results in at least all the fields in which gender is relevant to the subject matter of the field. For Longino these objective results are achieved through the increased critical dialogue to which women's vantage points contribute. For Harding they are achieved through the decreased distortion potentially present in the women's vantage points themselves. Either way, the contributions of women scientists are necessary if scientific rationality is to be maximized and genuine scientific knowledge produced, the kind of knowledge needed to correct the prejudice and misinformation about women that still prevails.

Longino goes even further. She suggests that the world may be so complex that a multiplicity of approaches may be required to capture all its various aspects. That is to say, a pluralism in the conduct of inquiry, the pluralism that Longino holds to be methodologically necessary, may also yield as its final outcome an irreducible pluralism of representations, a pluralism that includes women's distinctive contributions. But, of course, even if the final outcome of inquiry is a single unified representation of the world rather than a pluralism of representations, that single representation may still include women's distinctive contributions. Either outcome would furnish an additional reason women's contributions are crucial to science.

Thus, both Longino and Harding provide reasons to develop affirmative action programs for women in the sciences, affirmative action programs that ultimately will help deal with the problems that women in society still face thanks in significant part to science. Other feminist philosophers of science suggest other policy initiatives to the same end (see, e.g., Kourany 2010 and 2016, regarding the need for change in the professional values and associated research programs of the sciences and some of the ways to bring that about). All this is especially important to philosophy of science right now. For philosophers of science—at least many of them—are now trying to be socially relevant. Thus, organizations such as the Joint Caucus for Socially Engaged Philosophers and Historians of Science (JCSEPHS), the Consortium for Socially Relevant Philosophy of/in Science and Engineering (SRPoiSE), and the Society for Philosophy of Science in Practice (SPSP) have been formed, and their meetings and other activities are designed to develop and/or communicate information about socially relevant projects for philosophers of science to pursue. They are also designed to encourage philosophers of science to pursue these projects. Feminist philosophy of science, however, can offer more than three decades of work on such projects. So, at the very least, it can serve as a source for generating the more impressive sorts of philosophy of science programs that many in the field now desire.

A third benefit feminist rationality studies provide to philosophy of science is attention to the work of women scientists. At a time when women are still not being fully welcomed into the sciences (see, e.g., Hill, Corbett, and Rose 2010; Pollack 2013), and much biological and psychological research is still devoted to finding out whether women are as analytically able to do science as men (see, e.g., Caplan and Caplan 2005; Ceci and Williams 2007, 2010)—that is, whether women really belong in the sciences, or at least the upper reaches of the sciences—it is especially important not to ignore the scientific achievements of women. This is particularly true regarding the scientific achievements of feminists, almost all of whom have been women. For here, the relevant take-home message is not that women were able to do the same kinds of scientific work as even the most distinguished men, but rather that women did importantly different work from these men—work that was more accurate, more thorough, more comprehensive, and better justified than the men's work that preceded it, and yet at the same time was also more egalitarian, more fair-minded and more helpful to more people than the men's work. It is valuable, then, to have the case studies and theorizing about women's research that is provided by feminist philosophers to add to the non-feminist philosophy of science corpus, almost all of which is devoted exclusively to the scientific research of men.

There are, of course, still other benefits feminist philosophy of science provides to philosophy of science: long-overdue attention to the social and biomedical sciences to supplement all the attention that, traditionally, the physical sciences and, more recently, certain parts of the biological sciences have received in philosophy of science; contributions to important work in race studies of science, sexuality studies, disability studies, and a number of other socially important areas whose development is also long overdue; case studies and analyses informed by cutting-edge work in the sciences as well as the social studies of science, and frequently the product of close interdisciplinary collaborations; and so on. But the most important benefit that feminist philosophy of science provides to philosophy of science is an array of fascinating questions on a host of very challenging new topics that philosophers of science are especially well equipped to handle. All in all, an impressive legacy to philosophy of science from one of its own offspring!

Related Topics

Rationality and objectivity in feminist philosophy (Chapter 20); testimony, trust, and trustworthiness (Chapter 21); values, practices, and metaphysical assumptions in the biological sciences (Chapter 26); feminist philosophy of social sciences (Chapter 27).

References

Anderson, Elizabeth (1995) "Knowledge, Human Interests, and Objectivity in Feminist Epistemology," *Philosophical Topics* 23(2): 27–58.
——(2004) "Uses of Value Judgments in Science: A General Argument, with Lessons from a Case Study of Feminist Research on Divorce," *Hypatia* 19(1): 1–24.
Antony, Louise (1993) "Quine as Feminist: The Radical Import of Naturalized Epistemology," in Louise Antony and Charlotte Witt (Eds.) *A Mind of One's Own: Feminist Essays on Reason and Objectivity*, Boulder, CO: Westview, 110–153.
——(1995) "Sisters, Please, I'd Rather Do It Myself: A Defense of Individualism in Feminist Epistemology," *Philosophical Topics* 23(2): 59–94.
Bleier, Ruth (1984) *Sex and Gender*, New York: Pergamon Press.
Bush, Vannevar (1945) *Science—The Endless Frontier: Report to the President on a Program for Postwar Scientific Research*, United States Office of Scientific Research and Development, Washington, DC: United States Government Printing Office.
Campbell, Richmond (2001) "The Bias Paradox in Feminist Epistemology," in Nancy Tuana and Sandra Morgen (Eds.) *Engendering Rationalities*, Albany, NY: State University of New York Press, 195–217.
Caplan, Jeremy B. and Caplan, Paula J. (2005) "The Perseverative Search for Sex Differences in Mathematics Ability," in Ann M. Gallagher and James C. Kaufman (Eds.) *Gender Differences in Mathematics: An Integrative Psychological Approach*, Cambridge: Cambridge University Press, 25–47.
Carnap, Rudolf, Hahn, Hans, and Neurath, Otto (1973 [1929]) "The Scientific Conception of the World: The Vienna Circle [trans. of *Wissenschaftliche Weltauffassung: Der Wiener Kreis*]," in Marie Neurath and Robert S. Cohen (Eds.) *Empiricism and Sociology*, Dordrecht: Reidel, 298–318.
Ceci, Stephen J. and Williams, Wendy M. (Eds.) (2007) *Why Aren't More Women in Science? Top Researchers Debate the Evidence*, Washington, DC: American Psychological Association.
—— (2010) *The Mathematics of Sex: How Biology and Society Conspire to Limit Talented Women and Girls*, New York: Oxford University Press.
Creager, Angela N., Lunbeck, Elizabeth, and Schiebinger, Londa (Eds.) (2001) *Feminism in Twentieth-Century Science, Technology, and Medicine*, Chicago, IL: Chicago University Press.
Eichler, Margrit (1988) *Nonsexist Research Methods: A Practical Guide*, Boston, MA: Allen & Unwin.
Fausto-Sterling, Anne (1985) *Myths of Gender*, New York: Basic Books.
Giere, Ronald N. (1999) *Science without Laws*, Chicago, IL: University of Chicago Press.
Harding, Sandra (1986) *The Science Question in Feminism*, Ithaca, NY: Cornell University Press.
——(1991) *Whose Science? Whose Knowledge?: Thinking from Women's Lives*, Ithaca, NY: Cornell University Press.
Heschel, Abraham J. (1965) *Who Is Man?*, Stanford, CA: Stanford University Press.
Hill, Catherine, Corbett, Christianne, and St. Rose, Andresse (2010) *Why So Few? Women in Science, Technology, Engineering, and Mathematics*, Washington, DC: AAUW [online]. Available from: www.aauw.org/files/2013/02/Why-So-Few-Women-in-Science-Technology-Engineering-and-Mathematics.pdf.

Howard, Don (2003) "Two Left Turns Make a Right: On the Curious Political Career of North-American Philosophy of Science at Mid-Century," in Alan Richardson and Gary Hardcastle (Eds.) *Logical Empiricism in North America*, Minneapolis, MN: University of Minnesota Press, 25–93.

Hubbard, Ruth (1979) "Have Only Men Evolved?" in Ruth Hubbard, Mary Sue Henifin, and Barbara Fried (Eds.) *Women Look at Biology Looking at Women: A Collection of Feminist Critiques*, Cambridge, MA: Schenkman, 7–36.

Kourany, Janet A. (2010) *Philosophy of Science after Feminism*, New York: Oxford University Press.

—— (2016) "Should Some Knowledge Be Forbidden? The Case of Cognitive Difference," *Philosophy of Science* 83(5): 779–790.

Longino, Helen (1990) *Science as Social Knowledge: Values and Objectivity in Scientific Inquiry*, Princeton, NJ: Princeton University Press.

—— (1993) "Subjects, Power, and Knowledge: Description and Prescription in Feminist Philosophies of Science," in Linda Alcoff and Elizabeth Potter (Eds.) *Feminist Epistemologies*, New York: Routledge, 101–120.

—— (2002) *The Fate of Knowledge*, Princeton, NJ and Oxford: Princeton University Press.

McCumber, John (2001) *Time in the Ditch: American Philosophy and the McCarthy Era*, Evanston, IL: Northwestern University Press.

Pollack, Eileen (2013) "Why Are There Still So Few Women in Science?" The *New York Times*, 3 October [online]. Available from: www.nytimes.com/2013/10/06/magazine/why-are-there-still-so-few-women-in-science.html?pagewanted=all&_r=0.

Reisch, George (2005) *How the Cold War Transformed Philosophy of Science: To the Icy Slopes of Logic*, New York: Cambridge University Press.

Schiebinger, Londa (1999) *Has Feminism Changed Science?* Cambridge, MA: Harvard University Press.

Solomon, Miriam (2001) *Social Empiricism*, Cambridge, MA: MIT Press.

Wartofsky, Marx W. (1996) "Positivism and Politics: The Vienna Circle as a Social Movement," in Sahotra Sarkar (Ed.) *The Legacy of the Vienna Circle: Modern Reappraisals*, New York and London: Garland, 53–75.

Wylie, Alison and Nelson, Lynn Hankinson (2007) "Coming to Terms with the Values of Science: Insights from Feminist Science Studies Scholarship," in Harold Kincaid, John Dupre, and Alison Wylie (Eds.) *Value-Free Science? Ideals and Illusions*, New York: Oxford University Press, 58–86.

VALUES, PRACTICES, AND METAPHYSICAL ASSUMPTIONS IN THE BIOLOGICAL SCIENCES

Sara Weaver and Carla Fehr

Introduction

The biological sciences provide ample opportunity and motivation for feminist interventions. Today, some claims such as Dr. Clark's nineteenth-century warning that education placed women at risk of "hysteria, and other derangements of the nervous system" seem ludicrous (Clark 2006 [1874]: 18). However, harmful biological accounts of sex/gender continue to be produced and reproduced in scientific and public spheres. Only forty years ago, E. O. Wilson argued that, for humans and non-humans alike, "It pays for males to be aggressive, hasty, fickle and undiscriminating," but that "it is more profitable for females to be coy, to hold back until they can identify males with the best genes" (1978: 125). This sort of biological claim is still echoed in a range of contexts. Twenty-first century evolutionary psychology developed similar harmful accounts of human sex differences. For instance, Randy Thornhill and Craig Palmer (2001) suggest that human sexual assault is a facultative evolutionary reproductive strategy, and a primary way to prevent it is to educate men about their evolutionary drives. Harmful theories about inherent sex differences also continue to make their way to the center of public attention. In 2005, Harvard President Lawrence Summers argued that "issues of intrinsic aptitude" provide an important explanation of the dearth of women in high-powered science careers (*Harvard Crimson* 2005). Regarding the serious problem of sexual harassment in the Canadian military, the Canadian Chief of Defense General Tom Lawson explained in 2015 that, "it's because we're biologically wired in a certain way and there will be those who believe it is a reasonable thing to press themselves and their desires on others" (CBC News 2015).

Feminist philosophy of biology focuses on the ethical and epistemic adequacy and responsibility of biological claims about sex/gender. This work is critical in the sense of identifying epistemically and ethically irresponsible knowledge claims, research practices, and dissemination of biological research regarding sex/gender, including ways that sex/gender interacts with other social categories. This critical work involves investigations of sciences ranging from evolutionary psychology (e.g., Lloyd 1993; 1999; 2003; Fausto-Sterling 2000a; Dupré 2001; 2012; Travis 2003; Meynell 2012), to neuroscience (Bluhm et al. 2012; Jacobson 2012; DesAutels 2015a; 2015b), to genetics and genomics (Keller 1992; Richardson 2008; 2013). Feminist philosophy of biology is also constructive in the sense of developing accounts of the role of values and of epistemic frameworks in scientific practice (Longino 1990; 1997; 2002), metaphysical approaches (Fehr 2004), and methods (Lloyd 2005). While some earlier work tended to focus on identifying and eradicating sexist and androcentric bias, it is now more common to focus on identifying values in knowledge production and determining whether the deployment of particular values is responsible.

It is exciting to see new feminist scholarship keep pace with and engage with emerging areas of biological research. However, feminists have found that this emerging biological research remains vulnerable to what have become classic feminist critiques. In the rest of this chapter we describe classic themes in feminist philosophy of biology, with particular regard to research practices and metaphysical assumptions. We then go on to argue that these classic themes remain salient in contemporary neuroscientific investigations of human emotion and in feminist research on the evolution of human behavior.

Values and Research Practices

Feminist philosophers of biology have demonstrated ways in which harmful values can negatively affect the choice and structure of research questions, evidence, and arguments in the biological sciences. Values influence a scientist's choice of research question. This seems obvious when we think of questions about how we can cure cancer or make our drinking water safe. In these cases the role of values is obvious and unproblematic. However, research questions can be value-laden in ways that are less obvious (to many) and that have a significant and problematic impact on knowledge production. They can direct our attention away from potentially important questions, lead us to believe that our claims have a broader scope than they actually do, or give us confidence that our claims are accurate representations of the world when they are not. Of particular interest to feminist philosophers of biology are research questions that are loaded with sexist gender stereotypes, and with heterosexist and androcentric assumptions. For instance, investigating questions about romantic relationships between men and women is loaded with the assumption that romantic relationships are heterosexual and hence obscure LGBTQ relationships.

Paving the way for considerations of androcentrism in the production of biological knowledge, feminists such as Donna Haraway, Evelyn Fox Keller, Ruth Hubbard, and Sarah Hrdy drew attention to how the biological sciences were dominated both by male researchers and an interest in males as the primary research subject. Striking examples of this can be found in evolutionary biology, early primatology, and sociobiology whose research questions assumed that natural selection acted primarily on males. This gendered assumption led to the production of biological research that confirmed the importance of males for evolution. This sort of critique is evident in Donna Haraway's analysis of Zuckerman's (1933) theory of non-human primate society. Zuckerman sought to explain the origins of human society by studying the foundations of non-human primate social order. He theorized that the advent of continuous female sexual receptivity created the impetus for the development of social order. Because female primates are continuously receptive, he reasoned that social order required cooperation among males in order to control female sexuality. He postulated that the "harem" was a fundamental feature of human evolution. Supporting this, he argued that through the "harem" such structures as grooming, feeding order, vocal and gestural expression, and allotment of social space were able to take shape in primate societies (Haraway 1978: 45). Commenting on how Zuckerman's theory not only embodies androcentric ideology but also contributes to a continuing androcentric knowledge framework, Haraway says the following:

> Zuckerman set questions for workers to follow that even in their asking reinforced scientific beliefs about natural male competition and dangerous female sexuality. His tie of sexuality to dominance in ways acceptable to the physiological and behavioral sciences of the 1930s helped establish the status of dominance as a trait or fact rather than a concept.
>
> (1978: 47)

As Haraway demonstrates, the value laden beliefs that scientists like Zuckerman had about males and females have the power to influence research questions and in turn the kinds of knowledge produced about the natures of males and females and dominance relations between them.

Connecting the preponderance of male researchers to a hyper-focus on male primates, Haraway (1989) also drew attention to how the influx of women in primatology led to critiques of existing androcentric theory and methods. Additionally, she pointed out how this demographic shift lead to new theoretical and methodological approaches that facilitated investigations of a wider range of phenomena including the study of female primates.

Feminist philosophy of biology has also drawn attention to ways that evidence and arguments can be problematically laden with implicit values that are both epistemically and ethically harmful. This can take the form of scientists overlooking or discounting evidence that was inconsistent with traditional gender values. Birke (1986) and Bleier (1988), for instance, discussed how guiding paradigms in neuroscientific and psychological research prevented scientists from seeing or making sense of data that challenged prevailing views about the cognitive differences between men and women. Bleier (1988) puzzled over why research on sex differences in visuospatial cognition often promoted the idea that robust differences exist both in terms of the types of hemispheric structure underlying visuospatial processing and in men's and women's visuospatial abilities (men were reported to have superior visuospatial skills). However, looking more closely at the literature as a whole revealed that neither of these findings were in any sense robust. The number of studies that confirmed the differences were matched by the number of studies that turned up negative results. Variability within the sexes was often matched or exceeded variability across the sexes. What differences that were found were often weak and attributable to a variety of factors that had nothing to do with sex per se, such as age, test procedures, task difficulty, information-processing strategies of the individual, practice, attention, motivation, memory, and aptitude.

Another way implicit values influenced data was evidenced in the tendency of some scientists to go beyond their data in order to confirm hypotheses that supported gender stereotypes. Emily Martin (1991) and Ruth Hubbard (1990) provide examples of cultural beliefs about gender that are so powerful that they can influence interpretations of observations of plants and cells. Hubbard (1990) cites Wolfgang Wickler, an ethologist in the 1970s, who read Victorian gender stereotypes into his observations of algae:

> Even among very simple organisms such as algae, which have threadlike rows of cells one behind the other, one can observe that during copulation the cells of one thread act as males with regard to the cells of a second thread, but as females with regard to the cells of a third thread. The mark of male behavior is that the cell actively crawls or swims over to the other; the female cell remains passive.
>
> (cited in Hubbard 1990: 98)

The problem is that algae do not actually have sexes in the way that many other organisms do. The "males" that he is describing do not have sperm, testes, or XY chromosomes. They are only male insofar as Wickler has decided that that which is active is male and that which is passive is female.

The examples in this section exemplify research practices in which: (1) research questions are limited by gender values such as androcentrism; (2) data contrary to gender stereotypes are discounted; and (3) conclusions that are consistent with gender stereotypes are drawn but are not warranted by the available evidence.

Values and Metaphysics

> People aren't malleable enough to create a society of perfect behavioral symmetry between men and women. Some changes simply can't be made, and others will come only at some cost.
>
> (Robert Wright 1994, cited in Fausto-Sterling et al. 1997: 414)

The relationship between values and metaphysical assumptions about the biology of sex/gender is important because these assumptions facilitate the production and reproduction of biological knowledge claims that are implicitly laden with stereotypical gender values. Classic and contemporary feminist philosophy of biology critically engages the commonplace view that gender differences are the inevitable result of biological sex differences. According to this essentialist/determinist model, "male" and "female" are distinct categories, and sex differences in individual temperament and behavior, as well as gendered patterns of social organization are natural and fixed. This is because they are thought to be caused by low-level, putatively fixed biological facts about things like genes, hormones, and brain structures. Feminist interventions regarding this model address both essentialist assumptions of distinct sex/gender categories and the determinist assumptions regarding causal relations and fixity.

To be essentialist about sex/gender is to assume that males and females belong to natural categories much like gold and silver do. And that to be a male or female is to have a set of defining characteristics that assigns you to one or the other category. Essentialist views about sex/gender have been problematized in feminist theory (e.g., Beauvoir 1953 [1949]; Frieden 2001 [1963]; for reviews see Grosz 1994; Weaver 2011). Essentialism has been criticized on metaphysical grounds since human categories like sex/gender are not kinds like gold and silver. The variation within most human categories and the similarities across them do not allow for robust sets of defining characteristics. Feminists have also argued on ethical grounds that essentialism about human categories reifies these categories in harmful ways. For example, claiming that competitiveness and nurturance are essential male and female traits respectively creates norms that associate gender with those traits and that can marginalize nurturing men and competitive women.

Biological determinism is the view that higher-level phenomena, such as gendered characteristics of people, institutions, and social organization, are only or primarily caused by fixed and often low-level biological entities such as genes or hormones. There are two metaphysical assumptions constitutive of biological determinism. The first is a *reductionist account of causation* such that the only, or primary, relevant causes act at relatively low levels of biological organization and are internal to the organism in question. The second is the assumption that the *causally efficacious bits of biological nature are static and fixed.* These two metaphysical aspects of biological determinism work together to support the view that sex/gender differences are inevitable because they are caused by genes, hormones, or brain structures.

Feminist concerns with causal reductionism are generally not with the investigation of low-level or internal causes, such as genetic and neurobiological causes of traits and behavior, per se. Rather feminist concerns involve the failure to respect, or engage in research that investigates social and environmental causes, as well as interactions among causes acting at multiple levels (Fehr 2004). Focusing exclusively on low-level and internal causes blocks consideration of a wider range of causal factors. Once researchers in biology are willing to consider social and environmental causes it becomes possible to explore ways that sex/gender differences can be the effect of culture. If we find that cultural causes are efficacious and culture is changeable, then sex/gender differences can be changeable as well.

This also has bearing on assumptions of fixity of low-level phenomena. It may not only be the case that culture could impact gendered behavior, but it also becomes possible to explore the possibility that these higher level causes can have an impact on low-level biological processes like gene expression, hormone action, and brain development and activity. Consistent with this, feminists have offered salient critiques of the notion that processes such as gene expression (Keller 2000), hormone activity (Longino and Doell 1983; Birke 1986; Longino 1990), and neurodevelopment (Bleier 1984) are static in the face of higher level causal influences.

These metaphysical critiques are evident in feminist analyses of the linear-hormonal model for the development of behavioral sex differences. Rats are a common model system for this type of research. The model is based on essentialist, determinist assumptions that male and female sexual behaviors are the result of a causal chain moving up through levels of biological organization from genes, to hormones, to brain structures, to behavior. According to this model, a gene on the Y chromosome triggers testes development, and then these testes release hormones that cause male brains to develop such that males perform stereotypical male sexual behavior. For females the absence of a Y chromosome, testes, and the relevant hormones results in the development of a brain that causes the female to perform stereotypical female behavior. Feminist concerns with this model were not that chromosomes, hormones and brain structures are not causally relevant. Their concerns had to do with near exclusive focus on these low-level causes (Birke 1986: 96). Longino points out that in this explanatory model it is assumed that there is a "unidirectional and irreversible sequence of (biochemical) events" (Longino 1990: 135).

Birke (1986) advocated an *interactionist model* instead of the linear-hormonal model. She argued that biological research actually provided a much more complex understanding of the causes of sexual behavior. This new model includes interactions among the mother, the fetus, the environment as well as the genes, the internal anatomy and the brain structure of the developing fetus. Prenatal factors such as the sex of other members of the litter, the mother's environment, and the mother's hormonal states have also been shown to influence pup development. Birke also argued that there is a wide range of postnatal influences on adult sexual behavior. In addition to the hormones that the pup produces, postnatal influences such as maternal care, sibling interactions, and the physical environment have an impact. This causal complexity extends into adulthood when an individual's behavior and hormonal states as well as its physical and social environment influence its sexual behavior. Environmental factors can cause males to perform stereotypical female behavior and vice versa. The interactionist model does not ignore low-level causes, such as genes or hormones; it simply refuses to privilege them over what may be thought of as higher level environmental and social causes of behavior (Birke 1986).

This example demonstrates the critical and the constructive elements of feminist philosophy of biology and the fruitfulness of questioning commonplace metaphysical assumptions about the development of sex/gender differences.

Values, Practices, and Metaphysical Assumptions in Neuroscience

Two influential themes running throughout feminist philosophy of biology are critical and constructive investigations of the role of gender values in both (1) research practices and (2) underlying metaphysical assumptions in the biological sciences. Recently, there has been significant feminist analysis of contemporary neuroscience (Fine 2010; Bluhm et al. 2012; DesAutels 2015b). Although this feminist work investigates new and in some cases technologically sophisticated areas of scientific research, the science has many of the same problematic practices and assumptions, and has sparked similar kinds of critical and constructive feminist responses, as much earlier research.

Robyn Bluhm offers incisive critique of contemporary research practices in neuroimaging work on human emotion. According to Bluhm this research produces results that are consistent with what Stephanie Shields calls a "master stereotype" linking women with emotion (Bluhm 2013a). She analyses studies that conclude that women are more emotional and have less emotional control than men do, even though these studies did not find gender differences in emotional experience or in the activity of relevant areas of the brain. Bluhm also found that this research suffers from methodological and statistical weaknesses, and in many cases "its conclusions owe more to gender stereotypes than to evidence" (Bluhm 2013b: 870). These problems with methods, data, and evidential inferences include cases in which experimental results are ignored in favor of what researchers should have observed were the stereotypes true, and cases in which gender stereotypes are used to bridge the gap between data and theory (Bluhm 2013b: 870).

Feminist philosophers of biology are also raising familiar metaphysical concerns about this neuroscience research. While none of the scientists frame their work in terms of necessary and sufficient conditions for membership in sex/gender categories, much of this research is based on assumptions of distinct, binary gender categories. It often starts from the position of looking for sex/gender differences rather than looking for similarities or simply investigating these phenomena from a sex/gender neutral perspective.

Assumptions of causal reductionism and the fixity of low-level causes are also targets of this contemporary feminist critique of neuroscience. Rebecca Jordan-Young (2010) demonstrates that models of development, very similar to the linear hormonal model discussed above, in which there is a linear and unidirectional causal pathway from hormones to brain structures to gendered behavior, remain very much in vogue in spite of empirical evidence that is contrary to the model and weak evidence in favor of it. Discussions of sex differences being "hardwired" in the brain are similarly a target of contemporary, yet familiar, feminist critique. The critique points out the significance of neuroplasticity and of social and environmental factors influencing both the developmental and ongoing changes in neurological structures as well as human experience and behavior. We see similar research problems, and correspondingly similar critiques in the 2010s as were raised in the 1980s (see also Bluhm 2013a on these similarities).

At first glance, it might seem as though neurobiology is inherently oriented toward reductive explanations because it investigates things such as brain structure and physiology. However, Peggy DesAutels's research in feminist neuroethics provides an example of how metaphysical assumptions interact with the choice of research questions and methods in a way that unnecessarily limits our research perspectives on sex/gender. DesAutels argues that the differences we see between men's and women's brains with respect to broadly ethical traits are more consistent with differences between those who are members of oppressing and of oppressed groups, rather than sex/gender differences (DesAutels 2015a). DesAutels's research makes obvious the importance of attending to social categories in addition to sex/gender.

Values, Practices, and Metaphysical Assumptions in Feminist Evolutionary Psychology

Over the last five years there has been an increase in scholarship attempting to integrate feminism with evolutionary psychology (EP). Noteworthy work here includes a collection of essays from a 2011 issue (no. 64) of *Sex Roles* and an anthology (Fisher et al. 2013) arising from the Feminist Evolutionary Psychology Society (see Sokol-Chang and Fisher 2013). Scholars from both of these sources label their work as feminist since the aim of their research is to promote female-centered research. Here, female-centered research refers to the study of females as relevant objects of evolutionary study, and considers how they contribute to evolutionary change. This kind of focus on females is meant to respond to androcentric bias in evolutionary studies, where competition among males was assumed to be the main driver of evolutionary change. Feminist evolutionary psychologists are also interested in how an understanding of the evolutionary causes of human behavior can inform feminist social issues. In this section we offer analysis and critique of this feminist evolutionary psychology (FEP). In particular we find that FEP includes research practices and metaphysical assumptions laden with the same kinds of implicit and harmful gender values that feminists have criticized more traditional brands of EP and sociobiology for.

Gender stereotypes are integrated into FEP research questions and methods. While FEP researchers have made substantial strides to direct evolutionary psychology research to focus on women and their significance for evolution, just how they focus on women and which women they study remain influenced by cultural assumptions about sex/gender. For example, because FEP researchers already assume women are primarily caregivers, social supporters, and preoccupied with finding a long-term pro-visioning mate, FEP research reflects a hyper-focus on women in domestic contexts. In general there is a dearth of discussions or studies of women in professional, political, technical, or competitive contexts (except for discussions of women's competition for men). This is particularly alarming in cases where FEP research is *focused* on women's aggression or competition (e.g., Fisher 2013; Liesen 2013). Even in these studies, dis-cussions are limited to ways that women aggress or compete at home or among their close friends. The lack of research questions about women's competitive performances and strategies outside of the home is surprising, especially when we consider how many women compete (even aggressively) in professional contexts every day. It is important to ask why women's competitive performances and strategies outside of the home are not relevant to FEP scholars.

Gender values also influence how FEP researchers construct and present their own and secondary source data. On many occasions, FEP scholars cite contentious and con-troversial research on sex differences, but do not draw any attention to the controver-sies. Instead, findings of sex differences are presented as robust and widely agreed upon (see especially presentations of controversial sex differences in cognitive research in Ellis 2011; Oberzaucher 2013). This elision of controversies in putatively supporting bodies of literature results in spurious support of gender stereotypes.

There are also cases in which FEP scholars make claims that are stronger than war-ranted by their data. For example, referring to women as the "empresses of the kitchen," Coe and Palmer (2013) claim that selection on women's cooking activities in the Stone Age set the stage for the development of the human capacity to create traditions. The evidence they provide for this view that Stone Age women's cooking has evolutionary import is that women are the primary cooks in all of the thirty-nine African cultures recorded in the *Human Relations Area Files* (HRAF 2016). There are several significant and unjustified assumptions that need to be made in order for this evidentiary relation-ship to hold. In particular, no justification is provided for the troubling assumption that African cultures offer insight into prehistoric human practices. Indeed, Coe and Palmer need to do far more work to demonstrate that the division of labor in these cultures is not the result of political factors—factors that are impermanent and could have cer-tainly been different hundreds of thousands of years ago.

FEP also makes familiar assumptions regarding essentialism and causation. According to some FEP research, because men and women experienced very particular selection pressures in our prehistoric past, we can expect men and women in general to have spe-cific sets of defining characteristics. In particular, this research is often based on familiar accounts of the evolution of sex/gender differences: caring work was selected in women, resulting in the evolution of nurturing, empathetic, and emotionally supportive women focused on finding a good mate (e.g., Oberzaucher 2013). FEP scholars do maintain that we should expect variation within the sexes and perhaps much overlap between them (Buss and Schmitt 2011; Ellis 2011). Despite this, FEP scholars are primarily interested in what makes the sexes robust, separate categories with characteristics that we can measure and make predictions about. The consequence is that evolutionary psychologists and FEP scholars reflect back to their readership a poorly justified yet rhetorically powerful set of generalizations about and comparisons between men and women.

Like other evolutionary psychologists, many FEP researchers assign primacy to biological causes of behavior, often ignoring or only gesturing toward possible sociocultural causes. For example, often when FEP researchers "find" differences between men and women, they tend to attribute these differences to inherent biological causes (e.g., Betzig 2013; Wilbur and Campbell 2013). Sociocultural causes are frequently not considered, even to rule those causes out.

There is also current work that sends highly reductionist messages regarding genetic causes of behavior. Consider Frederick et al. (2013: 304): "Reproduction is the engine that drives evolution. Genes that produce traits, tactics, and behaviors that promote reproduction . . . can carry forward to future generations." The idea that behaviors can be influenced by heritable genetic processes is not controversial; however, there is controversy regarding *how* behaviors are influenced by genes and *the extent to which* genes play a role in producing human behavior. FEP, like non-feminist evolutionary psychology, is very dependent on the idea that many contemporary behaviors are relics from the past that have carried forward because they have been conserved in our genome. However, evolutionary psychologists have yet to offer an acceptable genetic account of behavior that explains how this is possible (Plaisance et al. 2012). The pathway from genotype to phenotype is a very complex process and often involves a myriad of other factors (developmental, epigenetic, environmental), many of which prevent reliable phenotypical replication across individuals, generations, environments, and circumstances (Plaisance et al. 2012). Behavior is a special sort of phenotype in that it is variable and flexible. It is quite possible that the genetics underlying behavior are similar to those underlying the immune system (Buller 2005). The immune system is specialized to fight diseases, but the particular diseases it can fight will depend on environmental input and other physiological conditions of the individual. So it likely is with behavior: because behaviors must be extremely variable and flexible, the genetics that underlie them have to be domain general (Buller 2005; Plaisance et al. 2012). This, combined with the complexity of phenotype expression, complicates the extent to which highly specific behavioral phenotypes can be conserved in our genome.

Either explicitly or implicitly, FEP research often sends the message that because behaviors have biological causes they are fixed and unchanging. Evolutionary psychology has been criticized so often for its messages of fixity that many researchers now preface their discussions of biological causes of behavior with promises of plasticity (e.g., Buss and Schmitt 2011; Johow et al. 2013). That is, they say, just because behaviors have biological causes, it does not follow that we shouldn't work toward social change or assume that humans are destined to be one way or another. Nevertheless, much FEP research is lined with assumptions about fixity that come out in subtle (and in some cases not-so-subtle) ways. The most general way in which fixity is implicated in FEP goes something like this: putative sex differences and gender roles are the way they are because they were once adaptive in a distant past. That we still see these behavioral and psychological relics despite thousands of years of evolution and cultural and environmental change and variability suggests (with or without evolutionary psychologists explicitly saying so) that these traits are very hard to change. Adding to this, some FEP scholars have proposed that FEP research be used to inform social policy (e.g., see especially Buss and Schmitt 2011; Fisher et al. 2013; and Reiber 2013). This notion of shaping policy to conform to our evolutionary biological nature is consistent with the view of a static and unchanging biological nature. Altogether, this brief analysis of FEP scholarship shows it to echo problematic research practices and metaphysical assumptions that have been the target of feminist criticism for decades.

Conclusion

In this chapter, we demonstrate the continued relevance of classic feminist critiques of biology. We focused on two categories of critique. The first reveals how gender stereotypes and cultural expectations influenced research questions, methods, and inferences in biology. The second reveals how reliance on an essentialist/deterministic model of sex/gender illegitimately prioritizes explanations of sex/gender that promote ideas of inherent and fixed differences between men and women. Both contemporary, technically sophisticated neuroscience research on gender and emotion, and current research on human evolution that is intended by its practitioners to be feminist, are vulnerable to feminist criticisms that have been available for nearly forty years.

It is reassuring that there are some feminist critiques of biology that have had an impact on the science by contributing to improvements in biological research. Consider Jeanne Altman. As a result of her concerns about androcentrism in primatology, she significantly improved the methodology of animal behavior research (Haraway 1989; Fehr 2011). Joan Roughgarden (2012) has also received much attention for her development of social selection, an alternative to sexual selection, which is so closely associated with male competition and promiscuity, and female nurturing and coyness. Nevertheless, as the troubling research coming out of neuroscience and feminist evolutionary psychology shows, scientists are still embedded in social and institutional structures that promote, enable, and reward sexist research. As we have demonstrated, scientists still choose to study sex differences, look for evidence of the naturalness of putative gender roles and norms, then to jump through hoops in order to present that evidence as corroborating mainstream assumptions about sex/gender. As a result, many classic feminist critiques of the biological sciences remain salient.

There are many opportunities for further research in feminist philosophy of biology. First, the need for continued iterations of classic critiques demonstrates the importance of research on the scientific, policy, and public uptake of this feminist work (Fehr and Plaisance 2010; Fehr 2012). This includes philosophical research on how the culture and structure of scientific communities and institutions allows them to avoid engaging critical responses to their ongoing research. Second, there is an opportunity for more research that engages axes of oppression in addition to sex/gender and takes an intersectional approach to analyses of the biological sciences. Much feminist philosophy of biology engages with science that investigates sex/gender per se, and the critical response mirrors this focus on sex/gender; however, feminist philosophy of biology is constructive as well as critical. This sort of constructive feminist work is exemplified in recent neurofemninist scholarship that facilitates and advocates biological research that is attentive to social categories such as race and sexuality that interact with sex/gender (e.g., Dussauge and Kaiser 2012; Kraus 2012; Roy 2012; Jacobson and Langley 2015). For example, Jacobson and Langley (2015) look at interactions among critical race theory, cognitive neuroscience, and moral theory in order to develop an interdisciplinary understanding of some kinds of racial bias. Finally, much feminist philosophy of biology is critical of the essentialist/determinist model of sex/gender. Some feminists have provided alternative approaches to thinking about sex/gender. Consider Anne Fausto-Sterling's metaphysical argument that because of the multiplicity of ways in which sex and gender identity are realized in people's lives and on their bodies, sex and gender should not be understood as binary. She argues instead that "sex and gender are best conceptualized as points in a multidimensional space" (Fausto-Sterling 2000b: 22). Opportunities remain for more engagement with feminist metaphysics on this topic (for a review, see Mikkola 2016). The biological sciences are seen by many as an authority on human nature and are highly relevant to many issues of social justice and public policy. Feminist philosophy of biology has tools to determine if this science is being produced and used in an epistemically and ethically responsible manner.

Related Topics

The sex/gender distinction and the social construction of reality (Chapter 13); gender essentialism and anti-essentialism (Chapter 14); materiality (Chapter 16); rationality and objectivity (Chapter 20); philosophy of science and the feminist legacy (Chapter 25); feminist philosophy of social science (Chapter 27); the genealogy and viability of the concept of intersectionality (Chapter 28).

References

Beauvoir, Simone de (1953 [1949]) *The Second Sex*, Howard Parshley trans. and Ed., New York: Knopf.

Betzig, Laura (2013) "Fathers Versus Sons: Why Jocasta Matters," in Maryanne Fisher, Justin R. Garcia, and Rosemarie Sokol-Chang (Eds.) *Evolution's Empress: Darwinian Perspectives on the Nature of Women*, New York: Oxford University Press, 187–204.

Birke, Lynda (1986) *Women, Feminism, and Biology: The Feminist Challenge*, New York: Methuen.

Bleier, Ruth (1984) *Science and Gender: A Critique of Biology and Its Theories on Women*, Elmsford: Pergamon Press.

—— (1988) "Sex Differences Research: Science or Belief?" in Ruth Bleier (Ed.) *Feminist Approaches to Science*, Elmsford: Pergamon Press, 147–164.

Bluhm Robyn (2013a) "New Research, Old Problems: Methodological and Ethical Issues in fMRI Research Examining Sex/Gender Differences in Emotion Processing," *Neuroethics* 6: 319–330.

——(2013b) "Self-Fulfilling Prophecies: The Influence of Gender Stereotypes on Functional Neuroimaging Research on Emotion," *Hypatia* 28: 870–886.

Bluhm, Robyn, Jacobson, Anne Jaap, and Maibom, Heidi Lene (Eds.) (2012) *Neurofeminism: Issues at the Intersection of Feminist Theory and Cognitive Science*, New York: Palgrave Macmillan.

Buller, David J. (2005) *Adapting Minds: Evolutionary Psychology and the Persistent Quest for Human Nature*, Cambridge: MIT Press.

Buss, David Michael and Schmitt, David P. (2011) "Evolutionary Psychology and Feminism," *Sex Roles* 64: 768–787.

CBC News (2015) *Military Sexual Misconduct Due to "Biological Wiring," Gen. Tom Lawson Tells CBC News*, June 16 [online]. Available from: www.cbc.ca/news/politics/military-sexual-misconduct-due-to-biological-wiring-gen-tom-lawson-tells-cbc-news-1.3115993.

Clark, Edward (2006[1874]) *Sex in Education: Or a Fair Chance for Girls*, [online] Boston, MA: James R. Osgood and Co. Project Guttenburg. Available from: www.gutenberg.org/files/18504/18504-h/18504-h.htm.

Coe, Kathryn and Palmer, Craig (2013) "Mothers, Traditions, and the Human Strategy to Leave Descendants," in Maryanne Fisher, Justin R. Garcia, and Rosemarie Sokol-Chang (Eds.) *Evolution's Empress: Darwinian Perspectives on the Nature of Women*, New York: Oxford University Press, 115–132.

DesAutels, Peggy (2015a) "Feminist Ethics and Neuroethics," in Jens Clausen and Neil Levy (Eds.) *Handbook of Neuroethics*, Dordrecht: Springer, 1421–1434.

—— (2015b) "Feminist Neuroethics: Introduction," in Jens Clausen and Neil Levy (Eds.) *Handbook of Neuroethics*, Dordrecht: Springer, 1401–1404.

Dupré, John (2001) *Human Nature and the Limits of Science*, Oxford: Clarendon Press.

—— (2012) *Processes of Life*, New York: Oxford University Press.

Dussauge, Isabella and Kaiser, Anelis (2012) "Re-Queering the Brain," in Robyn Bluhm, Anne Jaap Jacobson, and Heidi Lene Maibom (Eds.) *Neurofeminism: Issues at the Intersection of Feminist Theory and Cognitive Science*, New York: Palgrave Macmillan, 121–144.

Ellis, Lee (2011) "Evolutionary Neuroandrogenic Theory and Universal Gender Differences in Cognition and Behavior," *Sex Roles* 64: 707–722.

Fausto-Sterling, Anne (2000a) *Sexing the Body: Gender Politics and the Construction of Sexuality*, New York: Basic Books.

—— (2000b) "The Five Sexes, Revisited," *The Sciences* 40: 18–23.

Fausto-Sterling, Anne, Gowaty, Patricia Adair, and Zuk, Marlene (1997) "Evolutionary Psychology and Darwinian Feminism," *Feminist Studies* 14: 402–417.

Fehr, Carla (2004) "Feminism and Science: Mechanism without Reductionism," *National Women's Studies Association Journal* 16: 136–156.

—— (2011) "What Is in It for Me? The Benefits of Diversity in Scientific Communities," in Heidi Grasswick (Ed.) *Feminist Epistemology and Philosophy of Science: Power in Knowledge*, Dordrecht: Springer, 133–155.

—— (2012) "Feminist Engagement with Evolutionary Psychology," *Hypatia* 27: 50–72.

Fehr, Carla, and Plaisance, Kathryn S. (2010) "Socially Relevant Philosophy of Science: An Introduction," *Synthese* 177: 301–316.

Friedan, Betty (2001 [1963]) *The Feminine Mystique*, New York: W. W. Norton & Company.

Fine, Cordelia (2010) *Delusions of Gender: How our Minds, Society, and Neurosexism Create Difference*, New York: W. W Norton & Company.

Fisher, Maryanne (2013) "Women's Intrasexual Competition for Mates," in Maryanne Fisher, Justin R. Garcia, and Rosemarie Sokol-Chang (Eds.) *Evolution's Empress: Darwinian Perspectives on the Nature of Women*, New York: Oxford University Press, 19–42.

Fisher, Maryanne, Justin R. Garcia, and Rosemarie Sokol-Chang (Eds.) (2013) *Evolution's Empress: Darwinian Perspectives on the Nature of Women*, New York: Oxford University Press.

Frederick, David. A., Reynolds, Tania. A., and Fisher, Maryanne. L. (2013) "The Importance of Female Choice: Evolutionary Perspectives on Constraints, Expressions, and Variations in Female Mating Strategies," in Maryanne Fisher, Justin R. Garcia, and Rosemarie Sokol-Chang (Eds.) *Evolution's Empress: Darwinian Perspectives on the Nature of Women*, New York: Oxford University Press.

Grosz, Elizabeth (1994) "Sexual Difference and the Problem of Essentialism," in Naomi Schor and Elizabeth Weed (Eds.) *The Essential Difference*, Indianapolis, IN: Indiana University Press, 82–97.

Haraway, Donna (1978) "Animal Sociology and a Natural Economy of the Body Politic, Part II: The Past is the Contested Zone: Human Nature and Theories of Production and Reproduction in Primate Behavior Studies," *Signs* 4: 37–60.

—— (1989) *Primate Visions: Gender, Race, and Nature in the World of Modern Science*, New York: Routledge.

Harvard Crimson (2005) President Summers' Remarks at the National Bureau of Economic Research, January 14 [online]. Available from: www.thecrimson.com/article/2005/2/18/full-transcript-president-summers-remarks-at/.

Hubbard, Ruth (1990) *The Politics of Women's Biology*, New Brunswick, NJ: Rutgers University Press.

HRAF (2016) *Human Relations Area Files*, New Haven, CT: HRAF [online]. Available from: http://hraf.yale.edu.

Jacobson, Anne (2012) "Seeing as a Social Phenomenon: Feminist Theory and the Cognitive Sciences," in Robyn Bluhm, Anne Jaap Jacobson, and Heidi Lene Maibom (Eds.) *Neurofeminism: Issues at the Intersection of Feminist Theory and Cognitive Science*, New York: Palgrave Macmillan, 216–229.

Jacobson, Anne J. and Langley, William (2015) "A Curious Coincidence: Critical Race Theory and Cognitive Neuroscience," in Jens Clausen and Neil Levy (Eds.) *Handbook of Neuroethics*, Dordrecht: Springer, 1435–1446.

Johow, Johannes, Voland, Eckart, and Willfür, Kai P. (2013) "Reproductive Strategies in Female Postgenerative Life," in Maryanne Fisher, Justin R. Garcia, and Rosemarie Sokol-Chang (Eds.) *Evolution's Empress: Darwinian Perspectives on the Nature of Women*, New York: Oxford University Press, 243–259.

Jordan-Young, Rebecca M. (2010) *Brain Storm: The Flaws in the Science of Sex Differences*, Boston, MA: Harvard University Press.

Keller, Evelyn Fox (1992) *Secrets of Life Secrets of Death: Essays on Language, Gender and Science*, New York: Routledge.

——(2000) *The Century of the Gene*, Cambridge, MA: Harvard University Press.

Kraus, Cynthia (2012) "Linking Neuroscience, Medicine, Gender and Society through Controversy and Conflict Analysis: A 'Dissensus Framework' for Feminist/Queer Brain Science Studies," in Robyn Bluhm, Anne Jaap Jacobson, and Heidi Lene Maibom (Eds.) *Neurofeminism: Issues at the Intersection of Feminist Theory and Cognitive Science*. New York: Palgrave Macmillan, 193–215.

Liesen, Lauretta (2013) "The Tangled Web She Weaves: The Evolution of Female–Female Aggression and Status Seeking," in Maryanne Fisher, Justin R. Garcia, and Rosemarie Sokol-Chang (Eds.) *Evolution's Empress: Darwinian Perspectives on the Nature of Women*, New York: Oxford University Press, 43–62.

Lloyd, Elisabeth (1993) "Pre-Theoretical Assumptions in Evolutionary Explanations of Female Sexuality," *Philosophical Studies* 69: 139–153.

——(1999) "Evolutionary Psychology: The Burdens of Proof," *Biology and Philosophy* 14: 211–233.

——(2003) "Violence against Science: Rape and Evolution," in Cheryl Travis (Ed.) *Evolution, Gender, and Rape*, Cambridge, MA: MIT Press, 235–262.

——(2005) *The Case of the Female Orgasm: Bias in the Science of Evolution*, Boston, MA: Harvard University Press.

Longino, Helen (1990) *Science as Social Knowledge: Values and Objectivity in Scientific Inquiry*, Princeton, NJ: Princeton University Press.

—— (1997) "Feminist Epistemology as a Local Epistemology," *Proceedings of the Aristotelian Society Supplementary Volume* 71: 19–35.

——(2002) *The Fate of Knowledge*, Princeton, NJ: Princeton University Press.

Longino, Helen and Doell, Ruth (1983) "Body, Bias and Behavior: A Comparative Analysis of Reasoning in Two Areas of Biological Science," *Signs* 9: 206–227.

Martin, Emil (1991) "The Egg and the Sperm: How Science Has Constructed a Romance Based on Stereotypical Male-Female Roles," *Signs* 16: 485–501.

Meynell, Letitia (2012) "Evolutionary Psychology, Ethology, and Essentialism (Because What They Don't Know Can Hurt Us)," *Hypatia* 27: 3–27.

Mikkola, Mari (2016) "Feminist Perspectives on Sex and Gender," in Edward N. Zalta (Ed.) *The Stanford Encyclopedia of Philosophy*, Spring 2016 Edition [online]. Available from: http://plato.stanford.edu/archives/spr2016/entries/feminism-gender/.

Oberzaucher, Elisabeth (2013) "Sex and Gender Differences in Communication Strategies," in Maryanne Fisher, Justin L. Garcia, and Rosemarie Sokol-Chang (Eds.) *Evolution's Empress: Darwinian Perspectives on the Nature of Women*, New York: Oxford University Press, 345–360.

Plaisance, Kathryn S., Reydon, Thomas A. C. and Elgin, Mehmet (2012) "Why the (Gene) Counting Argument Fails in the Massive Modularity Debate: The Need for Understanding Gene Concepts and Genotype-Phenotype Relationships," *Philosophical Psychology* 25: 873–892.

Reiber, Chris (2013) "Women's Health at the Crossroads of Evolution and Epidemiology," in Maryanne. L. Fisher, Justin L. Garcia, and Rosemarie Sokol-Chang (Eds.) *Evolution's Empress: Darwinian Perspectives on the Nature of Women*, New York: Oxford University Press.

Richardson, Sarah (2008) "When Gender Criticism Becomes Standard Scientific Practice: The Case of Sex Determination Genetics," in Londa Schiebinger (Ed.) *Gendered Innovations in Science and Engineering*, Palo Alto, CA: Stanford University Press, 22–42.

—— (2013) *Sex Itself: The Search for Male and Female in the Human Genome*, Chicago, IL: University of Chicago Press.

Roughgarden, Joan (2012) "The Social Selection Alternative to Sexual Selection," *Philosophical Transactions of the Royal Society of London B Biological Sciences* 367(1600): 2294–303.

Roy, Deboleena (2012) "Cosmopolitics and the Brain: The Co-Becoming of Practices in Feminism and Neuroscience," in Robyn Bluhm, Anne Jaap Jacobson, and Heidi Lene Maibom (Eds.) *Neurofeminism: Issues at the Intersection of Feminist Theory and Cognitive Science*, New York: Palgrave Macmillan, 175–192.

Sokol-Chang, Rosemarie and Maryanne L. Fisher (2013) "Letter of Purpose of the Feminist Evolutionary Psychology Society," *Journal of Social, Evolutionary, and Cultural Psychology* 7(4): 286.

Thornhill, Randy and Craig T. Palmer (2001) *A Natural History of Rape: Biological Bases of Sexual Coercion*, Cambridge: MIT Press.

Travis, Cheryl Brown (Ed.) (2003) *Evolution, Gender, and Rape*, Cambridge, MA: MIT Press.

Weaver, Sara (2011) *A Crossdisciplinary Exploration of Essentialism about Kinds: Philosophical Perspectives in Feminism and the Philosophy of Biology*, MA thesis. University of Alberta.

Wilbur, Christopher and Campbell, Lorne (2013) "Swept off Their Feet? Females' Strategic Mating Behavior as Means of Supplying the Broom," in Maryanne Fisher, Justin L. Garcia, and Rosemarie Sokol Chang (Eds.) *Evolution's Empress: Darwinian Perspectives on the Nature of Women*, New York: Oxford University Press, 330–344.

Wilson, Edward O. (1978) *On Human Nature*, Boston, MA: Harvard University Press.

Zuckerman, Solly (1933) *Functional Affinities of Man, Monkeys and Apes: A Study of the Bearings of Physiology and Behavior on the Taxonomy and Phylogeny of Lemurs, Monkeys, Apes, and Men*, New York: Harcourt Brace.

27

FEMINIST PHILOSOPHY OF SOCIAL SCIENCE

Alison Wylie

Defining "feminist philosophy of social science" is a tricky business, not least because philosophy of social science is itself such a sprawling, heterogeneous field. I begin with a brief account of these field-defining difficulties as a way of situating the focus of this chapter: the work analytic feminist philosophers of science have done, often in dialog with practitioners, on a set of epistemic and methodological questions raised by explicitly *feminist* research programs in the social sciences. Most fundamentally the issue here is how to make sense of the fact that feminists, who bring to bear an explicitly situated, political angle of vision, have made significant, often transformative contributions across the social sciences. Their critical and constructive interventions pose a significant philosophical challenge to dominant "value free" ideals of epistemic integrity and objectivity. I consider two points of feminist engagement with this challenge. One is the "feminist method" debate of the 1970s and 1980s in which feminist social scientists, joined by feminist philosophers, wrestled with the question of what it means to do social science as a feminist. The second is feminist standpoint theory, as developed since the early 1980s by feminist social scientists and philosophers who take on directly the question of why it is that, contra dominant wisdom, situated interests and values not only play an ineliminable role in inquiry but, time and again, prove to be a crucial resource in improving the reach and credibility of social research. This analytic, epistemic engagement with feminist social science is just one area in which feminist philosophers have addressed issues central to philosophy of social science, anticipating by several decades a number of themes that are now coming to prominence in philosophy of social science.

The Broader Context

The social sciences are themselves enormously diverse in subject and method, and they raise issues that have been taken up by philosophers working in virtually all the major subfields and traditions of philosophy. These include just the kinds of issues that interest feminist philosophers given a commitment to rethink the conceptions of moral, political, and epistemic agency that underpin mainstream philosophy, bringing into focus features of the social, relational contexts of action that "ideal philosophy" (Mills 2005) has systematically read out of account. Most obviously, feminist philosophers address questions of social ontology and action theory that are the conceptual core of philosophy of social science; they ask how individual agency is enacted in social contexts, and whether social institutions and collectives reduce to the intentions and behaviors of their members, as individualists would claim, or have standing as entities in their own right, as holists have argued. Feminist ethicists and political theorists also address questions that fall within the ambit of philosophy of social science when they investigate the scope of moral responsibility when social conditions that constrain or enable agency. In contesting conventional ideals of rationality and asking how understanding is possible across differences in worldview, feminist epistemologists engage many of the issues central to the "rationality and relativism" debate of the 1970s and 1980s that set the framework for contemporary analytic philosophy of social science.

There is, then, a case to be made that feminist philosophers have contributed to philosophy of social science on many different fronts—contributions that are well represented in this volume. But despite these points of connection, little explicitly feminist work figures in the various anthologies, handbooks, and companion volumes on philosophy of social science that have appeared in recent decades. Indeed, with one exception, the representation of women authors in these collections is low: closer on average to the 15 percent reported for women in philosophy of science (Solomon and Clarke 2010) than the 20 percent to 30 percent reported for women in Anglophone philosophy generally (Hutchinson and Jenkins 2013). Take as a baseline for comparison the influential collection, *Readings in the Philosophy of the Social Sciences*, edited by May Brodbeck in 1968. She and one other woman contributed 4 of the 41 entries. They account for 5 percent of contributing authors and 10 percent of the entries; not surprisingly, there was no feminist content. Since the mid-1990s when the first of the contemporary anthologies appeared (Martin and MacIntyre 1994), a pattern emerges that is remarkably stable whether these collections are made up of new work by currently active scholars or, as in the case of Brodbeck's *Readings*, they include reprints of classic articles that date to periods when the field was more heavily male dominated and feminist philosophy was yet to take shape. The representation of feminist work in these anthologies ranges from 4 percent to 8 percent of contributions, and 8 percent to 18 percent of authors are women. The one exception is the 2015 collection, *Philosophy of Social Science: A New Introduction*, for which Nancy Cartwright and Eleanora Montuschi assembled sixteen contributions, all by women, many of whom directly engage or are clearly cognizant of relevant work by feminist philosophers.

More work is needed to fully understand the feminist and gender profile of philosophy of social science, but this snapshot, based on field-defining anthologies, does raise the question of why more feminist philosophers have not made philosophy of social science their disciplinary home. They have taken up philosophical issues raised by and about the social sciences in other contexts: in feminist philosophy journals and collections, and in publications on feminist social science.

The Feminist Method Debate

This debate took shape in the 1980s in response to feminist critiques of mainstream social science, which, by that time, had exposed some remarkable gaps and distortions in the treatment of women and gender. Particularly sharp criticism was directed at research programs that had traditionally pinned their authority on claims to scientific status, emphasizing their reliance on rigorously "objective" research tools and methodologies modeled on those of the natural sciences. These include, for example, hypothesis testing strategies designed to approximate experimental protocols, standardized interview and survey research, quantitative sampling strategies and statistical analysis. Despite their precision and analytic rigor, feminists found the results of these research programs rife with androcentric and, in some cases, manifestly sexist bias. Experimental and longitudinal studies of sex difference in cognitive function are an especially notorious example. Several recent retrospective studies document how gender-normative assumptions about sex/gender difference pervade not just the articulation of hypotheses, but also the definition of analytic categories and the choice of empirical measures used to evaluate them. This, feminist critics argue, has ensured that, for decades, these research programs have generated results that confirm bio-essentialist claims about sex differences. When confronted with evidence that does not fit these expectations a typical response had been to shift the terms of reference (Jordan-Young 2010), a pattern of insulating favored hypotheses from challenge that has been reinforced by ignoring the implications of a growing body of research which shows that even sex-gender differences that prove to be robust can often be explained in terms of patterns of gender socialization (Fine 2010). The issue is not (or, not necessarily) that this work is fraudulent, but that conventional assumptions about gender difference are so deeply embedded in the conceptual framing of these research programs they are simply taken for granted. Rigorously applied analytic and quantitative research methods can discriminate between hypotheses formulated within this framework but, on their own, they cannot be counted on to expose problematic assumptions that they all share (Okruhlik 1994); they reproduce gender-normative bias built into the research framework.

Similar critiques had been leveled against the design of census surveys and indices of national economic productivity based on these census data (GDP, GNP), to name just two such examples. In the late 1970s feminist economists, sociologists and political scientists drew attention to class-specific and ethnocentric as well as androcentric assumptions that predetermine, for example, what will count as economically productive "work" and which domestic arrangements constitute a "household." In many jurisdictions, the data underlying official labor statistics had been gathered using survey tools that explicitly exclude the unpaid work women were doing "at home for their families" and on a volunteer basis in other contexts (Armstrong and Armstrong 1987: 56; Oakley and Oakley 1979: 180); those engaged in even the most casual and temporary work were counted as "economically productive" so long they were paid, but those doing unpaid domestic labor were considered "economically inactive" no matter how essential it might be. Questions about household structure likewise assumed that every household must have a "head" and that the "head of household" or "household maintainer" must be a man, regardless of who brings in the primary income or pays the expenses. These gender-normative background assumptions determine, for example, "the areas chosen for analysis, the data that are collected and the way in which the statistics are both processed and presented" so that, "far from being a superstructure imposed on raw unbiased data," the data themselves and the statistics based on them are constituted by this underlying "conceptual scheme" (Oakley and Oakley 1979: 174). Although objections to this literal erasure of women's labor resulted in changes to census questionnaires in many contexts, as Marilyn Waring argues in *If Women Counted* (1988) the proxies standardly used to measure economic wealth and productivity—GDP and GNP—still equate economically valuable work with cash (or profit) generating activity, excluding the reproductive and care work largely carried out by women that is required to maintain an employable workforce.

As critiques of these kinds proliferated, feminist social scientists came to question the conviction that the gaps and distortions they were identifying could be corrected by applying existing methodologies more systematically. Even the most rigorously "objective" methods—those it was hoped would establish the bona fides of social research as scientific—had failed to protect against the influence of gender normative assumptions which, when made explicit, were unsustainable on empirical and conceptual as much as on political grounds. Worse, the conviction that these methods are self-correcting had insulated the research programs that rely on them from critique. One response was to reject them as inherently patriarchal and incapable of recuperation. Dorothy Smith (1978) argued that, by enforcing a hierarchical dissociation of researcher from research subject and attributing epistemic authority exclusively to professional researchers, the social sciences had become "ruling practices" (1974: 8) that systematically "eclipse" the lives, activities, interests, and expertise of women (1987: 17–36). Others objected that the positivist rhetoric of objectivity and value neutrality compounded these problems, masking the context-specific interests that animate the social sciences (Mies 1983; Stanley and Wise 1983).

At this juncture some argued that what was needed as an antidote were precisely the qualitative, engaged, interpretive methods that had been rejected by the advocates of self-consciously "scientific" approaches to social inquiry. These would allow women's voices to be heard, bringing into focus the experience, knowledge, and critical perspectives of insiders to the social worlds that social scientists had ignored. Smith advocated a program of ethnomethodological research designed to understand how the "everyday world" looks to those who operate off-stage, in gender-normative roles that put them in the position of maintaining social relationships and collective physical well being (Smith 1974). She studied the ways in which school-day routines and the work organization of women's lives amplify rigidly gendered parenting responsibilities (Smith 1987: 181–187), documenting women's own understanding of "mothering as work" and the "concrete actualities" (Howard 1988: 21) that are ignored or caricatured when "work" is equated with wage labor. Rather than impose categories that reflect the situated experience and assumptions of privileged outsiders, she urged feminist researchers to take as their point of departure the experience, perspectives, and categories of those who had been "eclipsed." This would bring into focus oppressive institutions and norms that are often not visible to those who operate "center stage," and whose privilege put them in a position to define the agenda of social sciences.

These research strategies are by no means unique to feminist social research. They are stock in trade in fields like social anthropology, qualitative sociology, and oral history, and they had been put to good use for just the purposes Smith cites in a number of well-established traditions of collaborative and participatory action research (Hickey and Mohan 2004: 3–10). In many contexts they provided the empirical and conceptual resources feminists needed to grasp what it was that dominant modes of practice had left out of account or misrecognized, and they continue to be a crucial resource for feminist research (Hesse-Biber 2012). But as Smith herself had argued, it is not the methods themselves that countered the "objectifying" effects of traditional social science; what has given feminist research its distinctive critical edge and opened up new lines of inquiry is the use of these methods in the context of research that "starts from the margins." Moreover, it was quickly pointed out that, as powerful and useful as they are, "face-to-face," interpretive modes of practice are no methodological panacea; androcentric and sexist partiality was as ubiquitous in the areas of social research that had traditionally relied on them as in those that staked their reputation as scientific on quantitative, "objectifying" methods.

For example, feminist critiques in anthropology of the 1960s documented a strik-ing lack of attention to women's roles and relationships, subcultures and activities in many of the most highly regarded ethnographic accounts; despite being deeply immersed in the lives and cultures of their subjects, anthropologists had routinely brought to bear "dominant male [androcentric] systems of perception" (Ardener 1975: xiii). This could sometimes be attributed to issues of access, but often the preoccupa-tion with male-associated roles and activities reflected an entrenched assumption that these are what matter: men are the primary locus of authority; what they value defines what counts as cultural identity and accomplishment; masculine roles and activities determine the dynamics characteristic of society as a whole. A classic example is the research on "hunter-gatherers" that had largely ignored the "gathering" activities of women even though, on reanalysis, these proved to account for as much as 70 percent of the dietary intake in all but the most extreme arctic and subarctic environ-ments. Recognizing the critical role of women not only reshaped the ethnography of "foragers," as they came to be known, but also called into question "man the hunter" theories of human evolution that had assumed the activities of male hunters to be the primary determinant of group success and reproductive fitness in foraging societies (e.g., Dahlberg 1981; Slocum 1975).

In practice, few feminist social scientists advocated wholesale abandonment of any of the tools of social research—scientistic or otherwise. Why limit feminist initiatives to one particular set of methods or research strategy, they asked (Jayaratne, 1983)? By the mid-1990s feminist practitioners had made a decisive "move from [methodological] singularity to plurality" (Gottfried 1996: 12); the contributors to an influential collec-tion, *Feminist Methods in the Social Sciences* (Reinharz 1992) make use of virtually every research method available to social scientists. The pressing question was how to do better, more inclusive research using these tools: How might feminists best address the questions that had been left out of account and are especially relevant for understand-ing and changing oppressive sex/gender systems? More generally, what research strate-gies could ensure that feminists would recognize and hold accountable assumptions of privilege that configure research and its results, including their own?

These issues were also a matter of active interest for feminist philosophers. They fig-ure prominently in *Discovering Reality* (Harding and Hintikka 1983) and were the focus of two essays that appeared in a special issue of *Hypatia* on "Feminism and Science": "Can There Be a Feminist Science?" by Helen Longino (1987), and "The Method Question," by Sandra Harding (1987a). Longino and Harding rejected the idea that there might be a distinctive "feminist science" (or method, or "way of knowing") for reasons like those given by feminist social scientists; such claims simply reaffirm the faith in method that practitioners had called into question in mainstream social science, and they presuppose the very essentialism about gender difference that feminists were intent on challenging more generally. That said, they recognized that feminist research programs pose a distinctive challenge to conventional ideals of objectivity. As Harding put it in her 1983 essay, "Why Has the Sex/Gender System Become Visible Only Now?" there was little indication that business-as-usual in the social and biological sciences would ever have exposed the pervasive errors and distortions to which feminists drew attention (Harding 1983: 26); the "infusion of [feminist] politics into scientific inquiry" had improved research in these fields by many standard measures, including "empirical quality," comprehensiveness and explanatory breadth, among other core epistemic virtues associated with "objectivity." She further argued that none of the epistemologies then on offer—especially not "received view" empiricism (Suppe 1977)—had the resources to make sense of how research programs rooted in a political movement could have generated "transformative criticism" (as Longino (1990) describes it), destabilizing entrenched assumptions and bringing sex/gender systems into focus as a "newly visible object . . . of scientific scrutiny" (Harding 1983: 312–313). What was needed, she argued, is a "revolution in epistemology" (1983: 311). In their different ways, Harding and Longino both took up this challenge, addressing two issues that arise directly out of the method debate. One is the question of what methodological and epistemic norms of practice characterize feminist research; I focus here on Longino's account. The other is the question of why these norms are epistemically salient, in connection with which I consider the formulations of feminist standpoint theory associated with by Harding.

Feminist "Community Values"

Longino's response to the method debate was to reframe its motivating question: the issue is not whether there is a distinctive "feminist science," but what it means to "do science *as a feminist*" (1987: 53). A robust methodological pluralism, like that endorsed by feminist social scientists, follows directly; feminist research will be as diverse as the feminism(s) that inspire it, and as situationally specific as the challenges posed by research traditions they critique and the questions they take up. Longino does, however, locate common ground in a set of "community values" that inform feminist research across the sciences.

Longino's point of departure was a suite of well-established philosophical arguments for recognizing that social, contextual values and interests pervade scientific inquiry of all kinds. These presuppose a distinction between these "non-cognitive" values—considerations that, on standard accounts, should never intrude into the practice of science—and the "cognitive," epistemic values, like truth-seeking and empirical adequacy, that were widely assumed to be the only factors that can legitimately play a role in scientific "contexts of justification" (Longino 1990: 4–7). Longino has since called into question this "cognitive/social" divide. But even if you accept it, she argued, "underdetermination" arguments establish that purely epistemic, cognitive considerations rarely, if ever, determine theory choice.

The underdetermination arguments Longino drew on arise from an appreciation that the evidence we rely on to judge the empirical adequacy of a claim is inevitably "theory laden" (Hanson 1958: 19). Empirical observations stand as evidence only under interpretation given an array of "auxiliary hypotheses" that link observational data to the phenomena under investigation. These include, for example, the normative, evaluative assumptions that justify treating data on paid employment as a proxy for economic productivity described above. This means that a requirement of empirical adequacy—the central "cognitive" value invoked as a guide for scientific practice—cannot, on its own, determine whether a given body of evidence "confirms" (or disconfirms) a hypothesis. Longino draws the conclusion that "whatever grounds for knowledge we have, they are not sufficient to warrant the assertion of claims beyond doubt" (Longino 1994: 472); scientists must inevitably take an inferential leap that is guided by other considerations. For a "critical contextual empiricist" (2002: 208) like Longino, what follows from these "inferential gap" arguments (Intemann 2005) is a recognition that social, contextual factors must take up the slack; they are essential to scientific reasoning, not a regrettable intrusion that compromises its integrity. Whatever counts as epistemic integrity and credibility, it cannot plausibly be equated with "value free" ideals of objectivity that require the elimination of non-cognitive values. Longino's response to the epistemic challenge posed by the successes of explicitly feminist research programs is to argue that any viable philosophical theory of science must take into account the irreducibly situated nature of social scientific inquiry and inquirers. On this view, doing (social) science as a feminist is a matter of insisting that researchers be accountable for the values and interests that inevitably play a role in all aspects of scientific inquiry.

In this spirit Longino's contribution to the "method debate" was to make explicit and provide a justification for six "community values" that she finds cited by feminist researchers. These, she argues, are justified both on general epistemic grounds and in terms of an explicitly feminist "bottom line" principle: they *"prevent gender from being disappeared"* (1994: 481; 1995: 391). I organize them around four focal themes (Longino 1994: 476–478; 1995: 386–389):

1. *Epistemic values*: Doing science as a feminist requires, first and foremost, a commitment to empirical adequacy.
2. *Ontological pluralism*: Feminist researchers should give preference to hypotheses that are novel and to those that take full account of the causal complexity and ontological diversity of their objects of study.
3. *Pragmatic values*: Feminists should use the tools of scientific inquiry to produce knowledge that is "applicab[le] to current human needs."
4. *Diffusion of power*: Feminists should "democratize" knowledge production in ways that foster an "equality of intellectual authority."

Each of these "community values" is subject to a further principle of epistemic provisionalism; they must be held open to revision (Longino 1994: 483).

Although Longino was not specifically concerned with social science, there is a striking resonance between this roster of orienting commitments and the guidelines that feminist social scientists developed, from the ground up, as they pursued an increasingly diverse array of research initiatives (Wylie 1995; 2012a). The cornerstone of these guidelines for practice is a specification of Longino's third value; the "human needs" that should be addressed by feminist researchers are defined by the interests of women or, more generally, of those who are oppressed by sex/gender systems of inequality. There was much debate about whether this required all feminist researchers to do intervention-oriented research, and whether research counts as "feminist" if, as intersectional analysis suggests it must, it focuses on factors other than gender. The wisdom of Longino's "bottom line" commitment is that it requires an attentiveness to gender but does not assume that this will prove to be the only or the primary dimension of difference in a given context of inquiry or intervention.

Although the requirement of empirical adequacy seems generic to empirical inquiry, feminist social scientists often make the point that it has an ethical, political justification as well. Far from being a license to project expectations and gerrymander wished-for outcomes, a commitment to produce knowledge relevant to feminist political goals raises the epistemic stakes. If feminist research is to produce a robust understanding of sex/gender systems that can inform effective action it is especially important that it be empirically accurate and explanatorily probative. Even strengthened in this way, however, arguments from underdetermination establish that this guideline is never adequate on its own.

The arguments Longino gives for the second and fourth community values are also both ethical/political and epistemic and have wide relevance. A preference for novelty—a willingness to think outside the box—has been crucial for counteracting the gender-disappearing effects of conventional wisdom, and it has often led feminist social scientists to emphasize ontological and causal complexity that had been treated as irrelevant "noise." Although Longino originally argued that this is a value that feminist researchers should embrace so long as "feminism has oppositional status" (1994: 477), she has since made the case that a pragmatic pluralism—a commitment to support diverse lines of inquiry—is important for all of science (Kellert et al. 2006; Longino 2012).

Where the principle of "democratizing" research practice is concerned, Longino's argument for giving priority to accessible, widely distributed, non-hierarchical forms of practice converges on a recurrent theme in the guidelines for feminist social science: that feminist research practice must not, itself, be exploitative or oppressive, consistent with feminist ethical commitments. She argues that such "diffusion of power is a key means of ensuring that gender will be recognized as "a relevant axis of investigation" wherever it is salient (Longino 1994: 481). Patricia Hill Collins powerfully illustrates the epistemic value of fostering an "equality of intellectual authority" among researchers when she describes the "mismatch" between her own working-class Black experience and the "taken-for-granted assumptions" of her discipline—sociology—about family structures, "human capital," and the causes and effects of poverty (1991: 47–54). It was this dissonance that put her in a position to identify ways in which core sociological concepts reflect the dominantly white, middle-class, male-gendered experience of its practitioners, and to reframe them in terms adequate to the social and economic realities navigated by black women.

A commitment to counteract "testimonial" and "hermeneutical" injustice (Fricker 2007; Chapter 22 in this volume) as it affects research practice is a reason for *feminists* to embrace the "democratizing" principle, and in guidelines for feminist social research this is often articulated as a demand for reflexivity. As Uma Narayan puts it, "one of the most attractive features of feminist thinking is its commitment to contextualizing [and critically scrutinizing] its claims" (1988: 32). Longino argues, however, that the justification for a norm of "tempered equality of epistemic authority" (2002: 131–133) extends well beyond research animated by social justice concerns. It is one of four social/cognitive norms central to her influential "proceduralist" account of objectivity, in connection with which she argues that the beliefs we ratify as knowledge should be those that arise from processes of critical scrutiny designed to ensure that contending beliefs are subject to "criticism from multiple points of view" (Longino 2002, 129): "not only must potentially dissenting voices not be discounted, they must be cultivated"; to fail to do this is "not only a social injustice but a cognitive failing" (2002: 132). Given that there is no self-warranting foundation or transcendent "view from nowhere" that can serve as a standard for assessing epistemic credibility, Longino argues that our evolving practices of vigilant empirical and conceptual critique are the only basis we have for determining which beliefs warrant acceptance (1994: 483; 2002: 128–133). And in identifying norms of inclusiveness as pivotal for ensuring that these practices will be accountable, she draws inspiration from the role of feminist community values in successful research programs across the sciences.

Standpoint Theory

In the hands of feminist standpoint theorists, this commitment to democratize research is interpreted as requiring that "intellectual authority" be attributed, not just to all members of a research community, but to research subjects and a diversity of external stakeholders as well. Smith (1997) characterizes this as a methodological directive to "start from the margins," while for Harding it was the centerpiece of a broader epistemic stance. Integrating and extending the insights of feminist social scientists, Harding elaborated standpoint theory as an alternative to empiricist and postmodern epistemologies that has the resources, she argues, to explain the (counter-intuitive) successes of explicitly political feminist research programs (1986: 136–162). What is distinctive about feminist research practice she argued, in response to the "method debate," is a commitment to "locate the researcher in the same critical plane" as those they study (Harding 1987b: 8), so that the epistemic resources of the excluded "standpoint" of women—their experience, understanding, critical angle of vision—can be brought to bear on all aspects of research, from agenda setting and research design to the interpretation of results. In its most radical formulations, the rationale for democratizing research practice is a conviction that those who suffer systematic oppression have an experience-grounded understanding of dimensions of the world we live in that those who benefit from social and political-economic privilege typically do not have, and of the ways in which these are obscured or misrecognized by dominant knowledge systems. They are, in this sense, *epistemically* privileged (Petras and Porpora 1993: 107), and for this reason researchers should deliberately subvert the conditions of epistemic injustice that systematically marginalize what they know and the critical insights about dominant social and epistemic norms that arise from their "bifurcated consciousness" as subjugated social agents.

The theoretical underpinnings of a distinctively feminist standpoint theory had been developed by political scientist Nancy Hartsock (1983). She reframed class-based, Marxist formulations of standpoint theory showing how, in a society structured by hierarchical sex-gender norms and institutions, our material conditions of life and social relations can result in systematic differences in what we experience and what we know that runs along gender as well as class lines (Hartsock 1983). Harding (2006) expanded the scope of this analysis to a wider range of dissident standpoints rooted, for example, in social divisions entrenched by systems of colonial and race-based oppression. Her influential argument for "strong objectivity" likewise reinforces and generalizes arguments for reflexivity that were central to feminist guidelines for social research (Harding 1991: 138–163; 1993). Rather than adjudicate knowledge claims strictly in terms of established conventions of "good method," credible attributions of objectivity require, as well, systematic investigation of the conditions under which these conventions have arisen. If all knowledge production and all knowledge claims are situated—if there is no possibility of "purifying" research of contextual influences (Harding 1993: 56)—it is incumbent upon researchers to make "the relation[s] between knowledge and politics" an explicit subject of critical appraisal. An integral part of all inquiry must be the use of the tools of scientific inquiry to understand how particular research programs have been shaped by, and reflect the interests of elites in inegalitarian societies that are structured by racism and global imperialism, as well as gender and class divisions. This is, in effect, a matter of calibrating the claims made for accepting (or rejecting) research results in light of an appraisal of the ways in which these contexts of research practice "enable and set limits on what one can know" (Harding 1993: 55).

Feminist standpoint theory has faced a number of critical challenges since its initial formulation in the 1970s and 1980s. Chief among them are two concerns raised by Longino in the context of the method debate when she cautioned against appeals to a generic women's standpoint as the basis for positing a distinctive feminist method or "women's way of knowing": that women's experience is too diverse to underwrite an epistemically robust "standpoint" and, even construed as "critically self-conscious female experience," it cannot sustain any but the most limited claims of epistemic "privilege" (1994: 474–475). Although Harding, Hartsock, and Smith, among other prominent advocates of standpoint theory, share Longino's mistrust of essentializing appeals to a "women's" standpoint and do not invoke the resources of standpoint theory to support the claim that women, or feminists, have a distinctive "way of knowing," objections of the kind she sketches were prominent in the 1990s and led many to reject standpoint theory as a crude form of epistemic identity politics (Hekman 1997): a counsel of relativist despair at best or, at worst, a capitulation to cynical arguments that science is just politics (Haack 2003 [1993]; Wylie 1995). In fact, standpoint theory is much more subtle and complex than this; its advocates give it a variety of formulations and Harding's own account has evolved over time. Considered as a purpose-specific epistemic stance rather than an all-purpose epistemology, I argue that it is characterized by three central tenets that can be formulated in terms that do not assume or entail commitment to an untenable epistemic essentialism of the "girls-know-best-because-they're-girls" variety (Wylie 2012b).

1. A *structural "situated knowledge" thesis*: Standpoint theorizing takes as its point of departure a recognition that all knowers and all research programs are shaped by their histories and social contexts, but focuses specifically on the epistemic effects of hierarchical systems of power relations.

2. An *"inversion" thesis*: Formulated in terms of contingent advantage rather than automatic privilege, this is the claim that those who occupy subdominant or marginal social positions often have epistemic resources that the comparatively privileged lack. These epistemic advantages can take a number of different forms: access to evidence, interpretive heuristics, explanatory resources and, crucially, critical dissociation from the taken-for-granteds of a dominant worldview (Wylie 2003).

3. An *"accomplishment" thesis*: Situated experience is a crucial resource, but articulating an epistemically salient standpoint requires, as well, "critical practice": the articulation of a "disidentifying collective subject of critique" through systemic analysis of the social production of difference and the ways this configures the production and authorization of knowledge (Hennessy 1993).

337

Formulated in these terms, standpoint theorists need not invoke an "essential" gender, race, or class identity as the ground for an epistemically distinctive "standpoint on" the claims of a dominant worldview and the social/cognitive norms that legitimate them. Historical materialists like Hartsock (1983) emphasized the contingency of the lines of social differentiation that underpin systemic inequality, and Linda Alcoff (2006, 2010) has developed compelling arguments for recognizing that historically and culturally contingent collective identities can be a robust basis for mobilizing political and epistemic critique. Standpoint theorists certainly recognize the ways systems of oppression perpetuate epistemic disadvantages, but their emphasis is on bringing into focus the flip side of epistemic injustice in order to understand how it is that explicitly political research programs, like feminist social science, have repeatedly generated transformative criticism of dominant systems of knowledge. As such, standpoint theory is an innovative contribution to philosophical thinking about the social sciences that crystallizes three decades of close analysis by feminist philosophers and social scientists of the role these values play in social inquiry, questions that have always been central to philosophy of social science, and are especially relevant now. It also offers lessons that apply reflexively to philosophy social science.

Further Reading

Anderson, Elizabeth (2004) "How Not to Criticize Feminist Epistemology: A Review of *Scrutinizing Feminist Epistemology*," *Metascience* 13(3): 395–399. (A longer version is available online from: www-personal. umich.edu/%7Eeandersn/hownotreview.html.)

Haraway, Donna (1991) "Situated Knowledges," *Feminist Studies* 14(3): 575–599.

Intemann, Kristen (2010) "25 Years of Feminist Empiricism and Standpoint Theory: Where Are We Now?" *Hypatia* 25(4): 778–796.

Potter, Elizabeth (2006) *Feminism and Philosophy of Science: An Introduction*, London: Routledge.

Wylie, Alison (1997) "Good Science, Bad Science, or Science as Usual?: Feminist Critiques of Science," in Lori D. Hager (Ed.) *Women in Human Evolution*, New York: Routledge, 29–55.

Related Topics

Rationality and objectivity in feminist philosophy (Chapter 20); epistemic injustice, ignorance, and trans experience (Chapter 22); philosophy of science and the feminist legacy (Chapter 25); values, practices, and metaphysical assumptions in the biological sciences (Chapter 26).

References

Alcoff, Linda Martin (2006) "Real Identities," in *Visible Identities: Race, Gender, and the Self*, Oxford: Oxford University Press, 84–126.

—— (2010) "Sotomayor's Reasoning," *Southern Journal of Philosophy* 48(1): 122–138.

Ardener, Shirley (Ed.) (1975) *Perceiving Women*, London: J. M. Dent & Sons.

Armstrong, Pat and Armstrong, Hugh (1987) "Beyond Numbers: Problems with Quantitative Data," in Greta Hofmann Nemiroff (Ed.) *Women and Men: Interdisciplinary Readings on Gender*, Montreal: Fitzhenry & Whiteside, 54–79.

Brodbeck, May (Ed.) (1968) *Readings in the Philosophy of the Social Sciences*, New York: Macmillan.

Cartwright, Nancy and Montuschi, Eleanora (Eds.) (2015) *Philosophy of Social Science: A New Introduction*, Oxford: Oxford University Press.

Collins, Patricia Hill (1991) "Learning from the Outsider Within," in Mary Margaret Fonow and Judith A. Cook (Eds.) *Beyond Methodology: Feminist Scholarship as Lived Research*, Bloomington IN: Indiana University Press, 35–39.

Dahlberg, Frances (Ed.) (1981) *Woman the Gatherer*, New Haven, CT: Yale University Press.

Fine, Cordelia (2010) *Delusions of Gender: How Our Minds, Society, and Neurosexism Create Difference*, New York: W. W. Norton.

Fricker, Miranda (2007) *Epistemic Injustice: Power and the Ethics of Knowing*, Oxford: Oxford University Press.

Gottfried, Heidi (Ed.) (1996) *Feminism and Social Change: Bridging Theory and Practice*, Urbana, IL: University of Illinois Press.

Haack, Susan (2003) [1993] "Knowledge and Propaganda: Reflections of an Old Feminist," in Cassandra L. Pinnick, Noretta Koertge, and Robert F. Almeder (Eds.) *Scrutinizing Feminist Epistemology: An Examination of Gender in Science*, Rutgers, NJ: Rutgers University Press, 7–19.

Hanson, Norwood Russell (1958) *Patterns of Discovery*, Cambridge: Cambridge University Press.

Harding, Sandra (1983) "Why Has the Sex/Gender System Become Visible Only Now?" in Sandra Harding and Merrill B. Hintikka (Eds.) *Discovering Reality: Feminist Perspectives on Epistemology, Metaphysics, Methodology, and Philosophy of Science*, Boston, MA: D. Reidel, 311–325.

—— (1986) *The Science Question in Feminism*, Ithaca, NY: Cornell University Press.

—— (1987a) "The Method Question," *Hypatia* 2(3): 19–36.

—— (1987b) "Is There a Feminist Method?" in Sandra Harding (Ed.) *Feminism and Methodology*, Bloomington, IN: Indiana University Press, 1–14.

—— (1991) *Whose Science? Whose Knowledge? Thinking From Women's Lives*, Ithaca, NY: Cornell University Press.

—— (1993) "Rethinking Standpoint Epistemology: What Is 'Strong Objectivity'?" in Linda Alcoff and Elizabeth Potter (Eds.) *Feminist Epistemologies*, New York: Routledge, 49–82.

—— (2006) *Science and Social Inequality: Feminist and Postcolonial Issues*, Chicago, IL: University of Illinois Press.

Harding, Sandra and Hintikka, Merrill B. (Eds.) (1983) *Discovering Reality: Feminist Perspectives on Epistemology, Metaphysics, Methodology, and Philosophy of Science*, Boston, MA: D. Reidel.

Hartsock, Nancy C. M. (1983) "The Feminist Standpoint: Developing the Ground for a Specifically Feminist Historical Materialism," in Sandra Harding and Merrill B. Hintikka (Eds.) *Discovering Reality: Feminist Perspectives On Epistemology, Metaphysics, Methodology and Philosophy of Science*, Boston, MA: D. Reidel, 283–310.

Hekman, Susan (1997) "Truth and Method: Feminist Standpoint Theory Revisited," *Signs* 22(2): 341–365.

Hennessy, Rosemary (1993) "Women's Lives/Feminist Knowledge: Feminist Standpoint as Ideology Critique," *Hypatia* 8(1): 14–34.

Hesse-Biber, Sharlene Nagy (Ed.) (2012) *Handbook of Feminist Research: Theory and Praxis*, 2nd ed., Los Angeles, CA: Sage.

Hickey, Samuel and Mohan, Giles (Eds.) (2004) *Participation: From Tyranny to Transformation? Exploring New Approaches to Participation in Development*, New York: Zed Books.

Howard, Judith (1988) "Sociology With a Difference," *The Women's Review of Books* 6(3): 20–21.

Hutchinson, Katrina and Jenkins, Fiona (Eds.) (2013) *Women in Philosophy: What Needs to Change?* Oxford: Oxford University Press.

Intemann, Kristen (2005) "Feminism, Underdetermination, and Values in Science," *Philosophy of Science* 72: 1001–1012.

Jayaratne, Toby Epstein (1983) "The Value of Quantitative Methodology in Feminist Research," in Gloria Bowles and Renate D. Klein (Eds.) *Theories of Women's Studies*, London: Routledge & Kegan Paul, 140–162.

Jordan-Young, Rebecca M. (2010) *Brainstorm: The Flaws in the Science of Sex Differences*, Cambridge, MA: Harvard University Press.

Kellert, Stephen H., Longino, Helen E., and Waters, C. Kenneth (2006) "The Pluralist Stance," in Stephen H. Kellert, Helen E. Longino, and C. Kenneth Waters (Eds.) *Scientific Pluralism*, Minneapolis, MN: University of Minnesota Press, vii–xxix.

Longino, Helen E. (1987) "Can There Be a Feminist Science?" *Hypatia* 2(3): 51–64.

—— (1990) *Science as Social Knowledge: Values and Objectivity in Scientific Inquiry*, Princeton, NJ: Princeton University Press.

—— (1994) "In Search of Feminist Epistemology," *The Monist* 77(4): 472–485.

—— (1995) "Gender, Politics, and the Theoretical Virtues," *Synthese* 104: 383–397.

—— (2002) *The Fate of Knowledge*, Princeton, NJ: Princeton University Press.

—— (2012) *Studying Human Behavior: How Scientists Investigate Aggression and Sexuality*, Chicago, IL: University of Chicago Press.

Martin, Michael and McIntyre, Lee C. (Eds.) (1994) *Readings in the Philosophy of Social Science*, Cambridge, MA: MIT Press.

Mies, Maria (1983) "Towards a Methodology for Feminist Research," in Gloria Bowles and Renate D. Klein (Eds.) *Theories of Women's Studies*, London: Routledge and Kegan Paul, 117–139.

Mills, Charles W. (2005) "'Ideal Theory' as Ideology," *Hypatia* 20(3): 165–183.

Narayan, Uma (1988) "Working Together Across Difference," *Hypatia* 32: 31–48.

Oakley, Ann and Oakley, Robin (1979) "Sexism in Official Statistics," in John Irvine, Ian Miles and Jeff Evans (Eds.) *Demystifying Social Statistics*, London: Pluto Press, 172–189.

Okruhlik, Kathleen (1994) "Gender and the Biological Sciences," in Mohan Matthen and R. X. Ware (Eds.) *Biology and Society: Reflections on Methodology*, *Canadian Journal of Philosophy*, Supplementary Volume 20, Calgary: University of Calgary, 21–42.

Petras, Elizabeth McLean and Porpora, Douglas V. (1993) "Participatory Research: Three Models and an Analysis," *The American Sociologist* 23(1): 107–126.

Reinharz, Shulamit (1992) *Feminist Methods in Social Research*, New York: Oxford University Press.

Slocum, Sally (1975) "Woman the Gatherer: Male Bias in Anthropology," in Rayna Reiter (Ed.) *Toward an Anthropology of Women*, New York: Monthly Review Press, 36–50.

Smith, Dorothy E. (1974) "Women's Perspective as a Radical Critique of Sociology," *Sociological Inquiry* 44(1): 7–13.

—— (1978) "A Peculiar Eclipsing: Women's Exclusion from Man's Culture," *Women's Studies International Quarterly* 1: 281–295.

—— (1987) *The Everyday World as Problematic: A Feminist Sociology*, Toronto, ON: University of Toronto Press.

—— (1997) "Comment on Hekman: Whose Standpoint Needs the Regimes of Truth and Reality?" *Signs* 22(2): 392–398.

Solomon, Miriam and Clarke, John (2010) "Demographics of the Philosophy of Science Association 2010," Report to the PSA (Philosophy of Science Association) Women's Caucus.

Stanley, Liz and Wise, Sue (1983) *Breaking Out: Feminist Consciousness and Feminist Research*, London: Routledge and Kegan Paul.

Suppe, Frederick (1977) "The Search for Philosophical Understanding of Scientific Theories," in Frederick Suppe (Ed.) *The Structure of Scientific Theories*, 2nd ed., Urbana, IL: University of Illinois Press, 32–33.

Waring, Marilyn (1988) *If Women Counted: A New Feminist Economics*, San Francisco, CA: Harper and Row.

Wylie, Alison (1995) "Doing Philosophy as a Feminist: Longino on the Search for a Feminist Epistemology," *Philosophical Topics* 23(2): 345–358.

—— (2003) "Why Standpoint Theory Matters: Feminist Standpoint Theory," in Robert Figueroa and Sandra Harding (Eds.) *Philosophical Explorations of Science, Technology, and Diversity*, New York: Routledge, 26–48.

—— (2012a) "The Feminism Question in Science: What Does It Mean to 'Do Social Science as a Feminist?'" in Sharlene Nagy Hesse-Biber (Ed.) *Handbook of Feminist Research: Theory and Praxis*, Thousand Oaks, CA: Sage, 544–556.

—— (2012b) "Feminist Philosophy of Science: Standpoint Matters," *Proceedings and Addresses of the American Philosophical Association* 86(2): 47–76.

Part IV

INTERSECTIONS

28

THE GENEALOGY AND VIABILITY OF THE CONCEPT OF INTERSECTIONALITY

Tina Fernandes Botts

The focus of this chapter is the concept of intersectionality, primarily in the North American context. By turns a research program, a description of personal identity, a theory of oppression, a counter-hegemonic political agenda, a symbolic antidote to mainstream (liberal) legal theory, and a critique of the methods and practices of mainstream philosophy, the concept of intersectionality (or simply "intersectionality") wears many hats. The concept is at the center of much contemporary research in the social sciences and humanities, is the fulcrum around which contemporary feminist theory and practice rotates, and is at the same time systematically ignored by mainstream philosophy.

As a research program, the concept of intersectionality is pervasively deployed in the social sciences and the humanities, and stands for the proposition that no phenomenon is adequately researched or understood without factoring in the ways in which socialized identity markers like race, gender, sexuality, ability status, and class interact and affect the phenomenon being researched (McCall 2005). As a description of personal identity, intersectionality disrupts the idea that personal identity can be described in terms of neat, mono-linear, timeless categories (see, e.g., Shrage 2009; Garry 2011; Levine-Rasky 2013; Botts 2016). As a theory of oppression, intersectionality represents the idea that forms, modes, or "axes" of oppression (such as race, gender, class, sexuality, and ability status) overlap and fuse in the lives of the oppressed, resulting in an account of oppression that highlights its complexity and its resistance to being addressed through means that focus exclusively on one form, mode, or "axis" of oppression or another (see Crenshaw 1989; 1991).

As a counter-hegemonic political agenda, intersectionality is a call to remember the oppositionality that originally motivated intersectional analysis (Bilge 2013) as well as the concept's roots in radical women of color feminism (Gines 2014; Waters 2014). As a symbolic antidote to mainstream (liberal) legal theory, intersectionality is a practical call to the complex legal and social needs of the oppressed, including a suspicion that mainstream jurisprudence cannot meet those needs adequately (Cho, Crenshaw, and McCall 2013). And finally, as a critique of the methods and practices of mainstream philosophy, intersectionality calls the discipline of philosophy to take account of its European, androcentric, and white biases as a rudimentary first step toward opening its curricular and conceptual vista to the myriad ways of knowing and being the discipline currently systematically excludes from the realm of legitimate knowledge and reality claims (Goswami, O'Donovan, and Yount 2014).

The aim of this chapter is to examine the evolutionary trajectory of the concept of intersectionality, with the goal of shedding light on both its centrality to contemporary feminist work and its anomalous absence from mainstream philosophizing. To accomplish this aim, I will first develop a genealogy of the concept, after which I will consider contemporary articulations of the concept. After that, I will explore critiques and controversies surrounding the concept, and then end with an inquiry into the future of the concept. Despite being mired in controversy, the prospects for the survival of the concept of intersectionality look good, especially as a reminder to those who study and work to combat oppression to remain self-reflexive and attendant to the unique and multivariate experiences of the particular oppressed person(s) involved in a given set of circumstances.

Genealogy

While it is difficult to pinpoint the exact starting point for any concept, the concept of intersectionality can be traced back at least as far as nineteenth-century black feminist thought (Gines 2014). For nineteenth-century black feminists, race, gender, and class oppression operated in tandem to oppress black American women in the post-Civil War era in unique ways. For example, Maria Stewart was concerned with the exploitation of young black women in the labor force, noting that many white women's hands had not been soiled, nor their muscles strained in similar ways; Sojourner Truth "interrupted representations of 'woman' as exclusively white and of 'black' as only male"; and Anna Julia Cooper identified that black women were simultaneously impacted by racism and sexism, while at the same time unacknowledged as agents in the examination or elimination of these forms of oppression (Gines 2014: 14–17). By focusing on the ways in which race, gender, and class overlapped to generate a distinctive form of oppression experienced by black women, nineteenth-century black feminists set the stage for the concept of intersectionality

First formally theorized in the 1950s, the social science research method known as multivariate analysis (or multilinear regression analysis) has also contributed to what we now call intersectionality. Multivariate analysis is a way of analyzing social problems that utilizes multivariate statistical methods (Randolph and Myers 2013). Multivariate analysis involves the examination of several interrelated statistical variables at the same time, including the causal effects of some variables on other variables (Anderson 2003). Based on the idea that social problems are more complex than traditional statistical methods are able to accommodate, multivariate analysis stresses the interrelatedness between variables and within sets of variables. Historically, most applications of multivariate research methods were in the behavioral and biological sciences, but recently interest in multivariate methods has spread into many other fields (Rencher and Christensen 2012). At least to the extent that the concept of intersectionality acknowledges the interrelatedness of seemingly disparate variables that affect research outcomes, multivariate analysis is at work in the concept.

The critical legal studies movement also influenced the evolution of the concept of intersectionality. An intellectual movement in the late 1970s and early 1980s that stood for the proposition that there is radical indeterminacy in the law, and conceptually based in the critical theory of the Frankfurt School, critical legal studies stood for the idea that legal doctrine is an empty shell. There is no such thing as the law, on this view (Binder 1999: 282). For the advocates of critical legal studies, "the Crits," the liberal ideal of the rule of law devoid of influence from power differentials was an illusion. The disconnect the Crits saw between the law and its efficacy arguably laid the groundwork for what later became known as "critical race theory" and, after that, "outsider jurisprudence," although part of early critical race theory was certainly the view that the Crits had failed to take adequate account of the fact that antidiscrimination law had proven effective for change for persons of color (see Crenshaw 1988).

In the late 1980s, legal scholars of color began explicitly interrogating the ways in which the law and mainstream legal theory (including that of the Crits) appeared to ignore and disregard the lived experiences of African Americans, particularly the ways in which African Americans were uniquely affected or ignored by the law. The main question for these scholars, was how to achieve racial justice in a society teeming with systemic racism. The starting point for all of these theorists was that a given culture constructs its social reality in ways that promote its own self-interest. This means denying the rights and realities of those whose very existence challenges that self-interest, for example, persons of color. One goal of these scholars was to confront the presuppositions upon which the racist institutional structures of American society have been built. The ultimate goal was to create new realities, new structures, and new laws in which the rights of African Americans could be satisfactorily addressed. The work of Derrick Bell, Richard Delgado, Kimberlé Crenshaw, Randall Kennedy, and Patricia J. Williams were early examples of this movement in legal scholarship (Bell 1987; Williams 1992; Crenshaw et al. 1996; Kennedy 1998; Delgado and Stefancic 2012).

Within this context, legal theorist Kimberlé Crenshaw first used the term "intersectionality" to highlight the experiences of black *women* in particular with the American legal system (Crenshaw 1989). For Crenshaw, race and gender discrimination combined on the bodies of black women in a way that neither race discrimination nor gender discrimination alone captured or addressed. Crenshaw's point was that ignoring race when taking up gender reinforces the oppression of people of color, and anti-racist perspectives that ignore patriarchy reinforce the oppression of women (Crenshaw 1991: 1252). But, more specifically, taking up any form of oppression in a vacuum ignores the way that oppression actually works in the lives of the oppressed. For the law to help combat oppression, it must grapple with the complexities and nuances of the lived experience of oppression. Intersectionality is alive and well in critical race theory today, operating as the key theoretical fulcrum around which it rotates (see, e.g., Walby 2007; Walby, Armstrong, and Strid 2012; Cho et al. 2013; MacKinnon 2013). To the extent that the intersectional frameworks central to critical race theory have been expanded to avenues of oppression beyond race, gender, and class—including sexuality, ability status, and other marginalized identity markers—these ideas have come to be subsumed under the title "outsider jurisprudence," the key idea of which is that the law does not well accommodate the complexities of human difference (Delgado 1993).

Queer theory is another area of inquiry that has had significant impact on the concept of intersectionality. An interdisciplinary way of thinking about personal identity, the human experience, sexuality, knowledge, and politics that is rooted in work of Michel Foucault, Judith Butler, and Eve Sedgwick, among others, queer theory's focus is inquiry into the perceived difference between natural and unnatural (sexual) identities and acts (Foucault 1978; Butler 1990; Sedgwick 1994; Jagose 1996; Turner 2000). Motivating queer theory is the debunking of stable (sexual) identities in favor of understanding identity as a conglomeration of unstable identities. Queer theory, like intersectionality theory, is "world-making" (Duong 2012: 378), that is, it has the power "to wrench frames" (Duong 2012: 371). It is capable of producing schemas of reality that are beyond preconceived (metaphysical and epistemological) sense-making mechanisms. Queer worlds, thus defined, transcend conventional notions of personal identity and politics to create room for countercultural (sexual) practices, ways of being in the world, and alternative accounts of phenomenological experience (Halperin 1990; Ahmed 2006). Such a vision of personal identity is central to the concept of intersectionality.

Postmodern theory, another key influence on the concept of intersectionality, focuses on skepticism regarding modernity's narratives of universalism. Having its start in the 1970s and gaining prominence in the 1990s, postmodern theory denies the existence of one, universal, objective truth or reality in favor of a multiplicity of realities and ways of knowing. Postmodernism holds that there are no "grand narratives" or metanarratives that accurately describe the world, only micronarratives. In other words, there is only the particular for the postmodernist, not the universal. And there are only stories about the world, no objective world itself (Lyotard 1984; Hassan 1987; Benhabib 1995; Butler 1995). At the core of postmodern theory is a profound anti-realism that implicitly posits a world (or anti-world) beyond categorical description.

Hermeneutic ontology can also be said to foreshadow intersectional themes. Contained in the hermeneutical concepts of "being-in-the-world" and "being-with-others," a core idea of hermeneutic ontology is that things are what they are as a result of how they pragmatically operate in the world (Heidegger 1962 and 1999). This characterization of the nature of reality is at odds with traditional presumptions about a separation between mind and body that allows, for example, a subject to stand back from an object and make an assessment about what it is. From a hermeneutical point of view, such a process is nonsensical. Instead, to navigate the terrain of that which is, it is necessary to understand that the persons and things within what we call "reality," are world disclosing. In other words, what things are and what they mean (or in the case of human beings, who they are) tell tales about the varied and complex ways in which persons and things act on, and are acted upon by, each other and the world. This is particularly the case with regard to phenomena such as race and gender, mired as they are in the messy realities of our corporeal world (Botts 2014). Such an interpretation of (human) identity lies at the core of the concept of intersectionality, calling the researcher to take sober account of the wide array of factors affecting the lived experience of a given social agent.

Standpoint epistemology has arguably had one of the strongest influences on the concept of intersectionality. While mainstream epistemology understands its objective as the pursuit of "justified true belief" (code for so-called objective knowledge), standpoint epistemology begins with the idea that all social knowledge claims are not only gendered but also

> drawn from, bear the marks of, and perpetuate structures of power and privilege that are sustained as much by racial, class, religious, ethnic, age, and physical ability differentials as they are by a sex/gender system that could be discretely and univocally characterized.
>
> (Code 2000: 174)

For the standpoint epistemologist, in other words, the business of knowledge production is necessarily political. Within this context, standpoint theories take as their starting point "the material-historical circumstances of female lives" (Code 2000: 180). According to standpoint theorists,

> the minute, detailed, strategic knowledge that the oppressed have had to acquire of the workings of the social order just so as to be able to function within it can be brought to serve as a resource for undermining that very order.
>
> (Code 2000: 180)

The concept of intersectionality can be understood to have taken from this framework its focus on the experience of oppression of the marginalized knower.

Within the realm of continental ethics, the work of Emmanuel Levinas in the twentieth century in many ways presaged the concern for the "radical alterity of the other" inherent in the concept of intersectionality. For Levinas, our encounter with the alterity of others (that which makes them different from ourselves) is an ethical call to acknowledge the complexity of the human experience (Levinas 1969). For Levinas, the Enlightenment focus on identity, sameness, and the individual subject reflects an extreme neglect for the other that is indicative of a deep neglect of the ethical. For Levinas, then, the traditional focus on the importance of epistemology and metaphysics in Western philosophy must accordingly be abandoned in favor of an ethics of alterity that places epistemology and metaphysics at the bottom of the priority list, rather than at the top (Levinas 1987). In practice, this would seem to mean focusing on the ethical needs of others *qua others*, which, in the case of the oppressed, means understanding their oppression *as it is experienced by them*, and taking whatever steps are morally necessary based on that understanding.

Finally, there are themes in moral particularism and care ethics that have had clear impact on the concept of intersectionality. According to moral particularism, there are no moral principles that can be applied broadly across all cases and the legitimacy of moral decisions is limited to particular situations (see, e.g., Hooker and Little 2001; Dancy 2004). Care ethics, in its appreciation for context and its insistence that others should be taken on their own terms, challenges mainstream ethical inquiry, which blindly applies rules or principles to facts without regard to the unique particularity of those facts, and without regard for the alterity of the others affected by the ethical decision. From the vantage point of care, the utilitarian focus on the greatest good for the greatest number and the Kantian focus on duty, just to name two examples, both miss a key aspect of a satisfactory approach to morality: care, or a concern for the welfare of the specific moral patient before one rather than an appeal to abstract principle (see, e.g., Jaggar 1992; Held 1995; Noddings 2003).

Contemporary Articulations

Whatever its origins, the concept of intersectionality is at the center of an ever-growing field known as "intersectional studies" that some scholars characterize as an "analytic disposition," that is, a "way of thinking about and conducting analyses" (Cho et al. 2013: 795). For these scholars, what makes an analysis intersectional is "its adoption of a particular way of thinking about the problem of sameness and difference and its relation to power" (2013: 795). Keeping the focus on the permeability of categories and emphasizing what intersectionality *does* instead of what it *is*, say these thinkers, is the core of intersectional studies. Also important is continuing to expand our conception of intersectional methods to include interdisciplinary projects that bring critical theoretical, methodological, and substantive resources to the table. There is much scholarship on the scene that self-consciously adopts the concept of intersectionality as its "analytic disposition."

For example, Priscilla Ocen has suggested that applying intersectional analysis to black women in prison could have a liberatory effect as yet unexplored (Ocen 2013). Focusing on legal scholarship, Ocen has pointed out that although black women are the fastest growing segment of the prison population, they are largely invisible in mass-incarceration discourse. She cites the handling of prison rape, medical services, and reproduction concerns in prison as examples of this intersectional fissure. In the case of prison rape, mainstream feminist legal scholarship, according to Ocen, fails to account for the ways in which the construction of black women as sexually available influences the forms of violence imposed upon black women in prisons. In terms of medical services, the same feminist legal scholarship focuses on access to abortion rather than the ways in which black women have been historically punished for exercising their reproductive capacities.

Similarly, Tricia Rose uses the concept of intersectionality to confront head-on what she calls the "invisible intersections of colorblind racism" (Rose 2013). Through deconstructing the case of Kelly Williams-Bolar, an African American single mother from Akron, Ohio who in 2011 was arrested, charged with a felony, and jailed for sending her two daughters to a predominantly white suburban public school in Copley Township without meeting the town's residency requirements, Rose self-consciously deploys the classical critical race theory method of storytelling. Rose's goal is to generate outrage and concern over a clear and unambiguous example showing that the concept of intersectionality is uniquely suited to explain and address the oppression experienced by black women in the United States of America in the twenty-first century. The retelling of the real details of a real story about a real experience of a real woman who underwent a ludicrously racist and sexist experience reminds the reader that these sorts of things *actually occur*, not just in theory but in life; which simultaneously reminds the reader that simplistic, mono-linear, theoretical solutions to the lived experience of oppression cannot and do not exist. One must begin with the complex reality, grounded in facts.

The concept of intersectionality is frequently deployed in contemporary inquiries into the transgender experience. Julie Nagoshi, Stephan/ie Brzuzy, and Heather K. Terrell recently used the concept, for example, to interview eleven self-identified transgender individuals about their definitions of, understanding of the relationships between, and perceptions of their own gender roles, gender identity, and sexual orientation (Nagoshi, Brzuzy, and Terrell 2012), and what they perceive to be the intersectional relationships between gender roles, gender identity, and sexual orientation. What was revealed was that all of the participants viewed gender roles to be social constructs, viewed gender identity as fluid, and viewed gender itself in a way that transcended both essentialist, traditional ideas, and the social constructionist views of feminist and queer theories. Citing transgender theorists like Katrina Roen (2002) and Surya Monro (2000), Nagoshi et al. (2012) highlight that through an intersectional lens, transgenderism can be understood more as transgressing the gender binary than as a story about physically transitioning from one gender category to another. The concept of intersectionality is at work in this analysis through the focus on the perceptions of transgender people themselves as the starting point for the research, rather than, say, available data on the relevant topics derived from other sources. The authors explain,

> While previous qualitative research with female-to-male transsexuals by Devor (1997) and Rubin (2003) has attempted to discuss [the issues of gender roles, gender identity, sexual orientation and the intersections between these], the present research advances this knowledge by interviewing a more diverse sample of trans individuals using a comprehensive interview *that explicitly gave participants a chance to compare and contrast concepts of gender identity, gender roles, and sexual orientation.*
>
> (Nagoshi et al. 2012: 406; emphasis added)

In other words, explicitly asking study participants not only to provide testimony, but also *analysis* provided new (intersectionally generated) and important insights into the relevant topics. Moreover, deductive qualitative analysis of the data was done based on verbatim transcripts of the responses to interview questions rather than characterizations of the data by the researchers. Some of the results were surprising. For example, when asked about whether they considered themselves masculine or feminine, all eleven participants responded that they expressed both masculine and feminine behaviors and physical characteristics. This is in contrast to the popular idea that a transgender person feels like "a man trapped in a woman's body" or "a woman trapped in a man's body." Instead, at least according to the study, transgender persons feel "trapped" somewhere in between, finding the entire notion of having to choose out of step with their experience.

The field of disability studies is heavily infused with intersectional inflections. For example, Alfredo J. Artiles has recently approached racial inequities in special education with analysis of the problem through an intersectional lens (Artiles 2013). Noting that within the educational system, both racial minorities and disabled learners have "complicated and politically charged histories linked to assumptions of deficit often used to justify inequities" (Artiles 2013: 329), Artiles highlights that remedies for one group can have deleterious consequences for the other, "thus muddling the effects of well-intentioned justice projects" (2013: 329). Artiles provides the example of a "double bind" that is created when disabled students of color seek to obtain benefits under the Individuals with Disabilities Education Act. Although a disability diagnosis is often beneficial to covered students, in practice there is a disproportionate diagnosis of disability in students of color, further compounding the structural disadvantages that each group has historically endured.

Feminist philosophy engages with the concept of intersectionality primarily at the meta level; that is, with notable exceptions, feminist philosophers tend to engage in defenses and critiques of the concept, rather than taking a more hands-on approach (see, e.g., Lugones 2007; Zack 2005; Garry 2011; Dotson 2014). Feminist philosophers who see a window through which to theorize a new socialized difference tend to defend the concept; while those who see it more as an ideological plaything that accomplishes little to combat oppression tend to critique it. The most popular defense of the concept is that it can operate as a vehicle through which differences among and between women, and groups of women, can finally be theorized and addressed satisfactorily. Some popular critiques of the concept are that: (1) it contains no clear theory; (2) it contains no clear method; (3) it is too focused on black women; (4) it has been disturbingly appropriated by white feminism to the detriment of black feminism; (5) it is vacuous; (6) it is a disturbing form of identity politics; and (7) the concept has an ontological problem that cannot be surmounted (see Gimenez 2001; Razack 2005; Srivastava 2005; Zack 2005; Ludvig 2006; Sengupta 2006; Russell 2007; Cole 2008; Yuval-Davis 2011; Bilge 2013; and Carastathis 2014).

In addition, within feminist philosophy, intersectionality has recently developed a metaphilosophical strain that operates as a statement on the ineffectiveness of traditional ways of doing philosophy. Notorious for excluding information coming in from the lived realities of members of marginalized, oppressed, and subjugated groups from the systems and structures of philosophical knowledge production on the grounds that these realities are insufficiently "universal" to count as philosophically relevant, intersectionality theory has recently been deployed in an attempt to disrupt the business-as-usual dismissiveness of mainstream philosophy. The claims to knowledge access and production of persons other than white, cis-gendered, heterosexual, able-bodied, males, insist thinkers who use intersectionality theory in this way, are legitimate claims; and if philosophy is to truly seek wisdom, it should open itself up to include the knowledge production of those historically excluded from the philosophical canon (Dotson 2011; Goswami et al. 2014: 1; Botts 2016).

For example, Kristin Waters is concerned with mainstream philosophy's summary dismissal of intersectionality as a topic worthy of consideration (Waters 2014). Given that research guidelines, codes of ethics, and institutional review boards place restrictions on studies that do not include representative populations, as well as the fact that both private and public funding agencies in the United States (such as the National Science Foundation and the National Institutes for Health) are hesitant to finance research restricted to select populations, particularly those that occupy dominant positions of power, Waters argues, philosophy's rejection of the call to implement intersectional research methods is self-deception at best and bad faith at worst. Waters paints a picture of philosophy, borrowed from critical philosopher of race Charles Mills, in which whiteness is central to philosophy's self-conception (Mills 2013; Waters 2014: 28). The result, for Waters, is that "common topics often assumed not to be raced or gendered may reveal themselves to be so under close scrutiny" (Waters 2014: 33).

Critiques and Controversies

In recent years, along with immense popularity within the social sciences, the humanities, and feminist scholarship more broadly, the concept of intersectionality has elicited much criticism.

The charge has been levied, for example, that intersectionality's claim that the social world is beyond categorization inherently entails that combatting oppression is an exercise in futility (Ludvig 2006; Sengupta 2006; Russell 2007). These thinkers raise the question of how exactly the responsible intersectional researcher can or should go about addressing oppression if not through each axis of oppression, one at a time.

The concept of intersectionality has also been charged with lacking clarity as to the scale of its applicability (Gimenez 2001; Razack 2005). Does the concept apply to structural and institutionalized oppression or does it apply to the lived experience of oppression of individuals or both? (see Collins 2000; Davis 2008). If both, then just exactly how would the responsible intersectional researcher go about addressing that fact?

Similarly, to the extent that intersectionality grapples with intergroup, and not intragroup, oppression, some charge the concept with being necessarily reduced to additivity (Cole 2008; Yuval-Davis 2011). Moreover, some are concerned that the concept simply cannot deliver on its promise of inclusion, generating, as it does, a seemingly infinite number of micro-groups leading to a fragmentation among women that undermines the achievement of common goals (Zack 2005).

Still others are concerned that intersectionality has been systematically depoliticized by mainstream academic feminism through the calibration of intersectionality with neoliberal knowledge production (Bilge 2013). For these thinkers, restricting feminist engagement with intersectionality to "metatheoretical contemplation" or understanding intersectionality as the product of mainstream feminism is counterproductive for intersectionality's original purposes. Sirma Bilge uses the examples of SlutWalks and the Occupy Movement to develop this concern. Bilge reports that during an October 2011 NYC SlutWalk, at least two young white women carried placards reading: "Woman is the N* of the world" (referencing a John Lennon and Yoko Ono song and using the complete racial slur). Similarly, the Occupy Movement's motto ("occupy") "re-enacts colonial violence and disregards the fact that, from the indigenous standpoint, those spaces and places it calls for occupation are *already* occupied" (Bilge 2013: 406). On this view, to the extent that intersectionality is deployed within the context of neoliberal political agendas, it is robbed of its power due to the inability of neoliberalism to speak a "*complex*" language of diversity (emphasis in original) (Bilge 2013: 408). In order to get back to the root aims of intersectionality, on this view, the task at hand for feminist work is to counteract this trend by "encouraging methods of debate that reconnect intersectionality with its initial vision of generating counter-hegemonic and transformative knowledge production, activism, pedagogy, and non-oppressive coalitions" (Bilge 2013: 408).

Finally are those who are concerned about what they see as the flippant and non-substantive way that intersectionality has been brought into mainstream feminist theorizing. For these thinkers, mass appropriation of the concept has brought into the light of day the fact that intersectional identity and intersectional oppression are not side issues in feminist work but rather lie at the very core of it (Carastathis 2014). Problematically, according to Anna Carastathis, intersectionality has "come to play a role in the historical construction of white feminist moral identity," which has been "historically focused on the benevolence and innocence" of white women (2014: 68). Citing Sarita Srivastava, Carastathis points out that some of the deadlocks of anti-racist efforts are linked to white feminist preoccupations with morality and self (Carastathis 2014: 68; Srivastava 2005). The observation is that often when white feminists are challenged on their stance of non-racism, they reply defensively and with emotional resistance. Anger, tears, indignation, and disbelief are common reactions that can be summed up in the defensive question, "You're calling me a racist?" (Srivastava 2005). Carastathis' point is that such defensive posturing often serves to impede personal and organizational change:

> [T]he problem is that discussions about personnel, decision-making, or programming become derailed by emotional protestations that one is not a racist and by efforts to take care of colleagues upset by antiracist agendas . . . . Intersectionality is often used, in these contexts . . . to diffuse moral anxieties about racism, and to project an ethical white feminist self.
> (Carastathis 2014: 68)

Carastathis concludes that "intersectionality reassures white feminists that they have not become obsolete or superfluous in what is heralded as a new feminist paradigm that decenters them and centers women of color" (2014: 68). Meanwhile, white, liberal feminists motivated by the internalization of egalitarian values to appear non-racist "have also internalized a systemic racism, which influences their implicit, unconscious and automatic attitudes, of which they are typically unaware or unreflective" (Carastathis 2014: 69). One result is that the reification of the concept of intersectionality as the guarantor of inclusion and diversity may actually impede meaningful engagement with the lived experience of oppression itself, and with women of color feminisms. In this way, to the extent that mainstream feminism purports to speak for women of color feminisms, the ethical and epistemological issues raised by the concept of intersectionality can remain unresolved. Here, Carastathis cites Linda Martín Alcoff, "[T]he impetus to always be the speaker . . . must be seen for what it is: a desire for mastery and domination" (Alcoff 1991–1992: 7; Carastathis 2014: 69).

Future of the Concept

Here, early in the twenty-first century, a lot is demanded of the concept of intersectionality. The concept lies at the core of contemporary feminist theory and practice, and stands for many different things at once. The concept is by turns a research program, a description of personal identity, a theory of oppression, a counter-hegemonic political agenda, and a symbolic antidote to mainstream (liberal) legal theory. In feminist philosophy, the concept operates primarily as a vehicle through which to critique mainstream philosophy, charging it with a Eurocentric, gendered, heteronormative, cis-gendered, classist bias that is both out of step with standards for scholarly research programs in most other related disciplines, but also undermines meaningful knowledge production in a disturbing and pervasive way. At the same time, however, mainstream feminist philosophy itself has been subject to intersectional critique on charges of a Eurocentric, bias that operates to exclude from received feminist discourse the voices of women of color feminist thinkers (see, e.g., Botts and Tong 2014).

Moreover, for many, the concept of intersectionality is so vague and amorphous that attempts at pinning down a methodology or modus operandi for it have proven almost impossible. While the concept calls on scholars, thinkers, and seekers of social justice to proactively include considerations of race, gender, sexuality, ability status, class, and other socialized identity markers into their programs, the concept provides little or no guidance on just how that process should take place.

Nonetheless, when one digs into specific examples of intersectional analysis at work, the lesson of intersectionality is clear: As regards the lived experience of oppression, the responsible approach to addressing that oppression is through attendance to the multiple modes of oppression that may be at work in the given oppressed person before one, particularly as regards the ways in which the various modes of oppression may operate in tandem so as to overshadow each other.

So, it seems that if the concept of intersectionality is to have longevity, it may be most productive to keep the focus on specific applications; that is, it may be best to avoid abstract discussions about whether intersectionality can work conceptually and focus on attending to the particular needs of the specific oppressed person(s) at hand. If the concept of intersectionality has any lasting lesson, in other words, it may be that the key to combatting oppression is a radical openness to the other. In practice, this would mean, at a minimum, consultation with the particular victim of oppression herself for clues as to what exactly the problem is and what she thinks should be done about it.

In keeping with this train of thought, Tina Chanter has suggested that if we are to achieve the ostensible goals of intersectional analysis (for example, combating the essentializing and otherwise limiting epistemological frameworks for analyzing oppression rooted in Enlightenment thought), it may be necessary to "get beyond" intersectionality *as an abstract ideal* and back into the specific particularities of the individual lives of the oppressed (Chanter 2014). As the history of anti-racism within feminist struggles has shown, in other words, the master's tools—in this case abstraction—will likely never dismantle the master's house (Lorde 1984).

Accordingly, since a radical openness to the other seems to be at the heart of the concept of intersectionality, it should be no surprise that the concept has not found a home in mainstream philosophy. With mainstream philosophy's focus on abstraction, the making of distinctions, universal principles, endless categorization, and the fetishization of the "objective," in a sense mainstream philosophy *cannot hold* a concept as amorphous, fluid, and subjectively grounded as intersectionality within its tightly held grasp, a grasp forever attempting to impose order and structure on a world (including multivariate personal identity and oppression forms) that is arguably far more complex and unstable than the boundaries of the discipline can accommodate.

However, intersectionality's necessary incompatibility with mainstream philosophy need not bode intersectionality's imminent demise. On the contrary, mainstream philosophy's failure to acknowledge its Eurocentric, androcentric, homophobic biases arguably says more about *mainstream philosophy*'s prospects for survival than about the survival prospects of intersectionality. For intersectionality is not a theory, nor an epistemological paradigm, nor a fantastical metaphysical fantasy designed to reinforce its own privileged status in the Western intellectual hierarchy. Instead, it is a sober acknowledgment of the epistemological, metaphysical, ethical, and political value of the lived experiences of the vast majority of human beings on the planet (who are not white, male, heterosexual, "able-bodied," or wealthy). Posterity will decide which is more valuable and has more endurance.

Further Reading

Collins, Patricia Hill and Bilge, Sirma (2016) *Intersectionality (Key Concepts)*, Cambridge, UK and Malden, MA: Polity Press.

Grzanka, Patrick R. (2014) *Intersectionality: A Foundations and Frontiers Reader*, Boulder, CO: Westview Press.

Hancock, Ange-Marie (2016) *Intersectionality: An Intellectual History*, Oxford: Oxford University Press.

Lorde, Audre (2016) "There Is No Hierarchy of Oppressions," UC San Diego LGBT Resource Center [online]. Available from: https://lgbt.ucsd.edu/education/oppressions.html.

Mohanty, Chandra (1991) "Under Western Eyes: Feminist Scholarship and Colonial Discourses," in Chandra Mohanty, Ann Russo, and Lourdes Torres (Eds.) *Third World Women and the Politics of Feminism*, Bloomington, IN: Indiana University Press, 51–80.

Related Topics

Feminism, philosophy, and culture in Africa (Chapter 4); feminist engagements with social contract theory (Chapter 7); Black women's intellectual traditions (Chapter 10); feminist phenomenology (Chapter 12); the sex/gender distinction and the social construction of reality (Chapter 13); essentialism and anti-essentialism (Chapter 14); feminism and borderlands identities (Chapter 17); epistemic ignorance, injustice, and trans experience (Chapter 22); intersectional themes (Chapters 29–33); feminist ethics of care (Chapter 43); multicultural and postcolonial feminisms (Chapter 47); neoliberalism, global justice, and transnational feminisms (Chapter 48); feminism, structural injustice, and responsibility (Chapter 49); feminist philosophy of law, legal positivism, and non-ideal theory (Chapter 56).

References

Ahmed, Sara (2006) *Queer Phenomenology: Orientations, Objects, Others*, Durham, NC: Duke University Press.

Alcoff, Linda Martín (1991–1992) "The Problem of Speaking for Others," *Cultural Critique* 20: 5–32.

Anderson, Theodore Wilbur (2003) *An Introduction to Multivariate Statistical Analysis*, New York: John Wiley & Sons.

Artiles, Alfredo J. (2013) "Untangling the Racialization of Disabilities: An Intersectionality Critique across Disability Models," *Du Bois Review: Social Science Research on Race* 10: 329–347.

Bell, Derrick (1987) *And We Are Not Saved: The Elusive Quest for Racial Justice*, New York: Basic Books.

Benhabib, Seyla (1995) "Feminism and Postmodernism," in *Feminist Contentions: A Philosophical Exchange*, New York: Routledge, 17–34.

Bilge, Sirma (2013) "Intersectionality Undone: Saving Intersectionality from Feminist Intersectionality Studies," *Du Bois Review: Social Science Research on Race* 10: 405–424.

Binder, Guyora (1999) "Critical Legal Studies," in Dennis Patterson (Ed.) *A Companion to Philosophy of Law and Legal Theory*, Malden, MA: Blackwell, 280–290.

Botts, Tina Fernandes (2014) "Hermeneutics, Race, and Gender," in Jeff Malpas and Hans-Helmuth Gander (Eds.) *The Routledge Companion to Hermeneutics*, London: Taylor & Francis, 498–518.

—— (Ed.) (2016) *Philosophy and the Mixed Race Experience*, Lanham, MD: Lexington Books.

Botts, Tina Fernandes and Tong, Rosemarie (2014) "Women of Color Feminisms," in Rosemarie Tong, *Feminist Thought: A More Comprehensive Introduction*, Boulder, CO: Westview Press, 211–254.

Butler, Judith (1990) *Gender Trouble: Feminism and the Subversion of Identity*, New York: Routledge.

—— (1995) "Contingent Foundations," in *Feminist Contentions: A Philosophical Exchange*, New York: Routledge, 35–58.

Carastathis, Anna (2014) "Reinvigorating Intersectionality as a Provisional Concept," in Namita Goswami, Maeve O'Donovan and Lisa Yount (Eds.) *Why Race and Gender Still Matter*, London and Brookfield, VT: Pickering & Chatto, 59–70.

Chanter, Tina (2014) "'Big Red Sun Blues': Intersectionality, Temporality and the Police Order of Identity Politics," in Namita Goswami, Maeve O'Donovan, and Lisa Yount (Eds.) *Why Race and Gender Still Matter*, London and Brookfield, VT: Pickering & Chatto, 71–85.

Cho, Sumi, Crenshaw, Kimberlé W., and McCall, Leslie (2013) "Toward a Field of Intersectionality Studies: Theory, Applications, and Praxis," *Signs* 38: 785–810.

Code, Lorraine (2000) "Epistemology," in Alison M. Jaggar and Iris Marion Young (Eds.) *A Companion to Feminist Philosophy*, Malden, MA: Blackwell, 173–184.

Cole, Elizabeth R. (2008) "Coalitions as a Model for Intersectionality: From Practice to Theory," *Sex Roles* 59: 443–453.

Collins, Patricia Hill (2000) *Black Feminist Thought: Knowledge, Consciousness, and the Politics of Empowerment*, New York: Routledge.

Crenshaw, Kimberlé W. (1988) "Race, Reform, and Retrenchment: Transformation and Legitimation in Antidiscrimination Law," *Harvard Law Review* 101(7): 1331–1387.

—— (1989) "Demarginalizing the Intersection of Race and Sex: A Black Feminist Critique of Antidiscrimination Doctrine, Feminist Theory, and Antiracist Politics," *University of Chicago Legal Forum* 140: 139–167.

—— (1991) "Mapping the Margins: Intersectionality, Identity Politics, and Violence against Women of Color," *Stanford Law Review* 43: 1241–12499.

Crenshaw, Kimberlé, Gotanda, Neil, Peller, Gary, and Thomas, Kendall (Eds.) (1996) *Critical Race Theory: The Key Writings that Formed the Movement*, New York: The New Press

Dancy, Jonathan (2004) *Ethics Without Principles*, Oxford: Clarendon Press.

Davis, Kathy (2008) "Intersectionality as Buzzword: A Sociology of Science Perspective on What Makes a Feminist Theory Successful," *Feminist Theory* 9: 67–85.

Delgado, Richard (1993) "The Inward Turn in Outsider Jurisprudence," *William and Mary Law Review* 34: 741.

Delgado, Richard and Stefancic, Jean (2012) *Critical Race Theory: An Introduction*, 2nd edition, New York: New York University Press.

Devor, Holly (1997) *FTM: Female-to-Male Transsexuals in Society*, Bloomington, IN: Indiana University Press.

Dotson, Kristie (2011) "Concrete Flowers: Contemplating the Profession of Philosophy," *Hypatia* 26: 403–409.

—— (2014) "Making Sense: The Multistability of Oppression and the Importance of Intersectionality," in Namita Goswami, Maeve O'Donovan and Lisa Yount (Eds.) *Why Race and Gender Still Matter*, London and Brookfield, VT: Pickering & Chatto, 43–57.

Duong, Kevin (2012) "What Does Queer Theory Teach Us about Intersectionality?" *Politics and Gender* 8: 370–386.

Foucault, Michel (1978) *The History of Sexuality, Volume 1: La Volonté de Savoir*, New York: Vintage Books.

Garry, Ann (2011) "Intersectionality, Metaphors, and the Multiplicity of Gender," *Hypatia* 26: 826–850.

Gimenez, Martha (2001) "Marxism, and Class, Gender, and Race: Rethinking the Trilogy," in *Race, Gender, and Class* 8.2: 23–33.

Gines, Kathryn T. (2014) "Race Women, Race Men and Early Expressions of Proto-Intersectionality, 1830s–1930s," in Namita Goswami, Maeve O'Donovan, and Lisa Yount (Eds.) *Why Race and Gender Still Matter*, London and Brookfield, VT: Pickering & Chatto, 13–25.

Goswami, Namita, O'Donovan, Maeve, and Yount, Lisa (Eds.) (2014) *Why Race and Gender Still Matter: An Intersectional Approach*, London and Brookfield, VT: Pickering & Chatto.

Halperin, David M. (1990) *One Hundred Years of Homosexuality: And Other Essays on Greek Love*, New York: Routledge.

Hassan, Ihab (1987) *The Postmodern Turn: Essays in Postmodern Theory and Culture*, Columbus, OH: Ohio State University Press.

Heidegger, Martin (1962) *Being and Time*, trans. J. Macquarrie and E. Robinson, New York: Harper & Row.

—— (1999) *Ontology: Hermeneutics of Facticity*, trans. John van Buren, Bloomington, IN: Indiana University Press.

Held, Virginia (1995) *Justice and Care: Essential Readings in Feminist Ethics*, Boulder, CO: Westview Press.

Hooker, Brad and Little, Margaret (2001) *Moral Particularism*, Oxford: Oxford University Press.

Jaggar, Alison M. (1992) "Feminist Ethics," in Lawrence C. Becker and Charlotte B. Becker (Eds.) *Encyclopedia of Ethics*, New York: Garland Press, 363–364.

Jagose, Annamarie (1996) *Queer Theory: An Introduction*, New York: New York University Press.

Kennedy, Randall (1998) *Race, Crime, and the Law*, New York: Vintage Books.

Levinas, Emmanuel (1969) *Totality and Infinity*, Pittsburgh, PA: Duquesne University Press.

—— (1987) *Time and the Other, and Additional Essays*, trans. R. A. Cohen, Pittsburgh, PA: Duquesne University Press.

Levine-Rasky, Cynthia (2013) *Whiteness Fractured*, Surrey, England and Burlington, VT: Ashgate.

Lorde, Audre (1984) "The Master's Tools Will Never Dismantle the Master's House," in Cherríe Moraga and Gloria Anzaldúa (Eds.) *This Bridge Called My Back: Writings by Radical Women of Color*, Albany, NY: SUNY Press, 94–103.

Ludvig, Alice (2006) "Differences Between Women? Intersecting Voices in a Female Narrative," *European Journal of Women's Studies* 13: 245–258.

Lugones, María (2007) "Heterosexualism and the Colonial/Modern Gender System," *Hypatia* 22: 186–209.

Lyotard, Jean-François (1984) *The Postmodern Condition: A Report on Knowledge*, Minneapolis, MN: University of Minnesota Press.

McCall, Leslie (2005) "The Complexity of Intersectionality," *Signs* 30: 1771–1800.

MacKinnon, Catharine (2013) "Intersectionality as Method: A Note," *Signs* 38: 1019–1030.

Mills, Charles W. (2013) "Philosophy Raced/Philosophy Erased," in George Yancy (Ed.) *Reframing the Practice of Philosophy: Bodies of Color, Bodies of Knowledge*, Albany, NY: SUNY Press, 45–70.

Monro, Surya (2000) "Theorizing Transgender Diversity: Towards a Social Model of Health," *Sexual and Relationship Therapy* 15: 33–45.

Nagoshi, Julie L., Brzuzy, Stephanie, and Terrell, Heather K. (2012) "Deconstructing the Complex Perceptions of Gender Roles, Gender Identity, and Sexual Orientation Among Transgender Individuals," *Feminism and Psychology* 22: 405–322.

Noddings, Nel (2003) *Caring: A Feminine Approach to Ethics and Moral Education*, 2nd edition, Berkeley, CA: University of California Press.

Ocen, Priscilla A. (2013) "Unshackling Intersectionality," *Du Bois Review: Social Science Research on Race* 10: 471–483.

Randolph, Karen and Myers, Laura (2013) *Basic Statistics in Multivariate Analysis*, New York: Oxford University Press.

Razack, Narda (2005) "'Bodies on the Move': Spatialized Locations, Identities, and Nationality in International Work," *Social Justice: A Journal of Crime, Conflict, and World Order* 32: 87–104.

Rencher, Alvin C. and Christensen, William F. (2012) *Methods of Multivariate Analysis*, 3rd edition, Hoboken, NJ: John Wiley & Sons.

Roen, Katrina (2002) "'Either/Or' and 'Both/Neither': Discursive Tensions in Transgender Politics," *Signs* 27: 501–522.

Rose, Tricia (2013) "Public Tales Wag the Dog: Telling Stories about Structural Racism in the Post-Civil Rights Era," *Du Bois Review: Social Science Research on Race* 10: 447–469.

Rubin, Henry (2003) *Self-Made Men: Identity and Embodiment among Transsexual Men*, Nashville, TN: Vanderbilt University Press.

Russell, Kathryn (2007) "Feminist Dialectics and Marxist Theory," *Radical Philosophy Review* 10: 33–54.

Sedgwick, Eve Kosofsky (1994) *Epistemology of the Closet*, London: Penguin.

Sengupta, Shuddhabrata (2006) "I/Me/Mine: Intersectional Identities as Negotiated Minefields," *Signs* 31: 629–639.

Shrage, Laurie (Ed.) (2009) *You've Changed: Sex Reassignment and Personal Identity*, New York: Oxford University Press.

Srivastava, Sarita (2005) "You're Calling Me a Racist? The Moral and Emotional Regulation of Antiracism and Feminism," *Signs* 31: 29–62.

Turner, William B. (2000) *A Genealogy of Queer Theory*, Philadelphia, PA: Temple University Press.

Walby, Sylvia (2007) "Complexity Theory, Systems Theory, and Multiple Intersecting Social Inequalities," *Philosophy of the Social Sciences* 37: 449–470.

Walby, Sylvia, Armstrong, Jo, and Strid, Sofia (2012) "Intersectionality: Multiple Inequalities in Social Theory," *Sociology* 46: 224–240.

Waters, Kristin (2014) "Past as Prologue: Intersectional Analysis from the Nineteenth Century to the Twenty-First," in Namita Goswami, Maeve O'Donovan, and Lisa Yount (Eds.) *Why Race and Gender Still Matter*, London & Brookfield, VT: Pickering & Chatto, 27–41.

Williams, Patricia (1992) *The Alchemy of Race and Rights*, Cambridge, MA: Harvard University Press.

Yuval-Davis, Nira (2011) *The Politics of Belonging: Intersectional Contestations*, London: Sage.

Zack, Naomi (2005) *Inclusive Feminism: A Third Wave Theory of Women's Commonality*, Lanham, MD: Rowman & Littlefield.

29

CRITICAL RACE THEORY, INTERSECTIONALITY, AND FEMINIST PHILOSOPHY

Falguni A. Sheth

Introduction

Critical Race Theory (CRT) arose as a legal approach to address racial invisibility, exploitation, and injustice in the early 1980s and 1990s. It emerged in dissension with the Critical Legal Studies (CLS) movement. CLS, which came into existence alongside the Civil Rights movements of the 1960s and 1970s, took issue with the notion that law was marked by historical progress. CLS emerged from the tradition of Legal Realism of Justice Oliver Wendell Holmes, as well as from Marxian notions of "the radical contingency of law" (Belliotti 1995: 23). Critical Legal scholars argued that rather than being marked by historical progress, law was a form of political legitimation and ideology and was radically indeterminate rather than objective (Belliotti 1995: 27). Correspondingly, justice was elusive and should be sought by any and all means at one's disposal. For Critical Legal scholars, law and politics were the same.

Critical Race Theorists challenged the anti-teleological stance that was the hallmark of CLS, even as they agreed with CLS scholars that law favored the side of the powerful. CRT initially emerged in response to several events: (1) a challenge to the liberal discourse that framed intellectual merit as color blind and rising above the particularities of race; and (2) a challenge to the Critical Legal Studies school of thought, which defined rights and justice as tools to advantage those who already had power, and that considered itself radical, but also did not acknowledge the influence of race in shaping legal outcomes. Critical Race Theorists challenged this definition by arguing that a number of legal concepts, such as rights, were in fact of use to those who were politically and legally vulnerable, especially African Americans (Williams 1991).

One of the more prominent members of CRT to critique the CLS movement was Kimberlé Crenshaw, a feminist legal scholar. Crenshaw, along with other feminists of color such as Angela Harris, Mari Matsuda, and Dorothy Roberts, were active participants in CRT. Crenshaw describes Critical Race Theorists as having two interests in common, regardless of the approaches taken and the specific arguments made by any given scholar: (1) An interest in the way white supremacy, as a political framework, enabled the maintenance of "the subordination of people of color . . . in America"; and (2) The "desire not merely to understand the vexed bond between law and racial power but to *change* it" (Crenshaw et al. 1995: xiii; author's emphasis).

Critical Race Theory

Methodologically, Critical Race Theory emerges as a framework to challenge several problems that have long held in politics and law. First, it challenges the abstract model of universal inclusion, which assumes that general principles apply equally and relevantly to individuals regardless of their particular characteristics or situations. Second, it challenges set assumptions about what kinds of situations and traits subsets of the population embody.

The first problem that the framework of Critical Race Theory was addressing was that of a deceptive universality, which assumes that justice can be extended equally to all individuals through the assertion of universal principles. The framework of universality has systematically ignored gender and racial differences, in many ways that have been illustrated by many feminist and race theorists, on the grounds that these differences are as inconsequential as the color of one's eyes. As such, the argument continues, even though the original foundation of US society, namely the US Constitution, was limited to able-bodied, property-owning white men, today the protections of the US Constitution are easily extended to all who live within its purview. There is a question about the veracity of this position: for example, why does the right to free speech, that is, speech free from interference of the US government, apply to all people equally? Does the abolition of slavery immediately put Blacks and whites on an equal footing in terms of justice? Intersectionality, to be explained below, addresses such questions by taking up the historical, economic, political—as well as the gender, race, and social— ramifications of such changes.

Critical Race Theory challenges the ideas that: (1) discrimination can be adequately addressed through single-concept analytical perspectives; and (2) differences can be productively neglected or ignored. Patricia Williams, another Critical Race Theorist, argues that Critical Race Theory addresses the absence of protections for minorities in a way that other frameworks such as Critical Legal Studies do not. Telling a story in which she and Peter Gabel, a white law professor and proponent of Critical Legal Studies, simultaneously began a search for apartments in New York City, she highlights the different attitudes each took. Gabel approached the search by showing how informal, flexible, and trusting he was, handing over a deposit for an apartment without having a signed a contract, received keys, or obtained a receipt. Williams, who found an apartment in a building owned by friends, was eager to illustrate her "good faith and trustworthiness" by signing a finely detailed and lengthily negotiated contract (Williams 1991: 147). She points to this anecdote, among many other examples, to show that rights—a concept dismissed or devalued by Critical Legal Studies scholars—is in fact a crucial institution for populations who are much less powerful, indeed who are often powerless to challenge their legal or political exploitation, abuse, or oppression. She argues as well that often rights are important to challenge the perception that lack on the part of minorities is not merely a question of need or want. Rather, these needs are often the target of legislation "against the self-described needs of black people" (Williams 1991: 151). This legislation exemplifies a structural exploitation that is often camouflaged as a rhetoric of cultural inadequacy or inferiority of reason or rational thinking, often implied by beliefs such as "Blacks are lazy," etc. (Williams 1991: 151). As she argues:

> For blacks, then, the battle is not deconstructing rights, in a world of no rights; nor of constructing statements of need, in a world of abundantly apparent need. Rather the goal is to find a political mechanism that can confront the *denial* of need.
>
> (Williams 1991: 152; emphasis in original)

Rights, then, in Williams' analysis, is also a concept that affects different populations differently. As such, it can be understood more vividly through an approach that illustrates the different consequences of the same concept for disparate populations.

As importantly, the assumption that race or gender as identity categories could simply represent all members of a particular group emerges from a liberal framework that does not assign much significance or complexity to either race or gender. In part, this is because liberal political frameworks posit that the ontological status of any given person can abstract away identity features such as race, ethnicity, nationality, gender as extraneous to one's basic existence (Rawls 1971). Feminist and race theorists have shown that in fact that such features are not only crucial to understanding the basic ontological status and/or social/political location of an individual, but must be part of an analysis of discrimination, exploitation, or oppression (Collins 2000; Lorde 1984; Mills 1997).

Some may object that if race and gender are socially constructed, as has been claimed by many theorists over the last few decades, then shouldn't such differences indeed be seen as incidental? (see Sally Haslanger, Chapter 13 in this volume). Technically, this might seem a proper response; however, the missing dimension from that analysis is the issue of power: the concept of universality is often shaped by those who have the power to make and shape the dominant political conversation, whether through media, community mores, or law.

Thus, consider the following questions as more specific instances that betray the promise of equal and universal protection of all individuals who fall under the purview of the US Constitution: Why does the right to free speech, free from the interference of the US government, apply to white men who make social media comments about raping Black women (Latimer 2016), but not to Black women who make social media comments about killing white police officers in retaliation for brutality against Black men (*Atlanta Journal Constitution* 2016)? Another question: Does abolishing slavery, whereby Black men, women and children were legally exploited for their labor and sexuality by white slave owners, immediately put the free descendants of slaves on an equal footing with the descendants of slave-owning families or the descendants of free people generally? If this is true, then why are whites wealthier than Blacks? If we rule out the "character" explanation, namely that whites are smarter, more productive and more able than Blacks (which would contradict the need for slavery), then we must turn to other sources for our answer, such as racism, power, or structural bias.

The editors of one of the first Critical Race Theory anthologies speak to this point in their introduction:

[W]e began to think of our project as uncovering how law was a constitutive element of race itself: in other words, how law constructed race. Racial power, in our view, was not simply—or even primarily—a product of biased decision-making on the part of judges, but instead the sum total of the pervasive ways in which law shapes and is shaped by "race relations" across the social plane. Laws produced racial power not simply through narrowing the scope of, say, anti-discrimination remedies, nor through racially-biased decision-making, but instead, through myriad legal rules, many of them having nothing to do with rules against discrimination, that continued to reproduce the structures and practices of racial domination. In short, we accepted the crit [CLS] emphasis on how law produces and is the product of social power and we cross-cut this theme with an effort to understand this dynamic in the context of race and racism. With such an analysis in hand, critical race theory allows us to better understand how racial power can be produced even from within a liberal discourse.

(Crenshaw et al. 1995: xxv)

Intersectionality as a Feminist Response to Race and Racism

Crenshaw offered a feminist framework, which would be called "intersectionality," that responded directly to these worldviews. The initial concern that Crenshaw had was with the way that antidiscrimination law attempted to assess discrimination through whole categories such as "woman" or "race," which often had the tendency of excluding numerous populations. She centered Black women as the focal point and example of her analysis so as to offer a vivid illustration of how this exclusion occurs. She pointed to the limitations of the single-axis framework (considering discrimination from the perspective solely of race or solely from gender), such that anti-discrimination law was not very effective in identifying and addressing the injustices of groups who weren't evoked or didn't fit easily into such wholesale categories.

Crenshaw first popularized the term "intersectionality" in two important articles (Crenshaw 1989; 1991). In her 1989 article, she illustrated the difficulty of rectifying race and gender discrimination through the US legal system due to the overly abstract categories of race and gender that mark those subsets of the population who have more symbolic resonance (thus, race marks Black men and gender signifies white women), which has the effect of rendering Black women invisible. As Crenshaw says there, discrimination was assumed to be linked across singular widespread concepts such as race or gender. "I want to suggest further that this single-axis framework erases Black women in the conceptualization, identification, and remediation of race and sex discrimination by limiting inquiry to the otherwise-privileged members of the group" (Crenshaw 1989: 140).

In her 1991 article, Crenshaw illustrates that the overly general nature of domestic violence laws again are more effective for those groups who fall squarely within the focus of the law (i.e., white women who are US citizens) than poor US or migrant women of color. As such, Crenshaw argues for an intersectional approach by which multiple analytic axes (race *and* gender *and* class) can better attend to populations who exist on the margins of society and law (Crenshaw 1991). She argues that "[t]he concept of political intersectionality highlights the fact that women of color are situated within at least two subordinated groups that frequently pursue conflicting political agendas," something that the more visible, powerful members of racial or gendered groups did not have to address very often (Crenshaw 1991: 1251–1252). As such, intersectionality draws on a multiple-axis approach to attend more aptly to the multiple structural sources of oppression that produce the marginalized subject or population.

What's Critical about Intersectionality?

Crenshaw's approach to intersectionality fits well with a CRT approach to oppression and discrimination, since, like CRT, intersectional approaches assume that hierarchies of power influence how we cognize and identify marginalized populations, whether through the production of their identity or through the racialized, gendered focus of the legal structures that either recognize or render certain subgroups invisible.

In this sense, the conceptual link between CRT and intersectionality is an intimate one. Both explore the role that power has in constructing our ideas of race, gender, and how social and political (and legal) institutions shape those categories to reflect certain facets or populations more visibly than others. Intersectionality, then, illustrates the way that power shapes abstract categories such as race and gender and class, such that the intersections of these factors will reveal different political standings, different (more or less) just outcomes, and different legal protections (or lack of such protections) for various populations. In this way, intersectional frameworks challenge the idea that racial, gender, and class differences are incidental or additive features of individuals who are assumed to have identical interests or concerns but for these features. Intersectionality shows instead that understanding subjects through their racial, gendered, and class identities reveals qualitatively (and quantitatively) different outcomes in terms of exploitation, discrimination and justice.

Other feminist Critical Race Theorists draw on intersectionality in their approaches in order to combat such essentialisms or conflations. For example, legal scholar Angela Harris argues that even feminist theorist Catharine MacKinnon, whose pointed arguments that patriarchal and heterosexist culture is oppressive to women, is engaging in essentialisms. MacKinnon conflates the situations of white women and Black women, such that Black women become white women except more so. As Harris explains, MacKinnon points to heterosexual sex as a form of rape, whereby women have no ability truly to engage in consent as long as they are dominated by men. MacKinnon, as Harris points out, adds Black women to this analysis, but does not see that rape for Black women does not exist in the same form as it does for white women. For Black women, rape is complicated by race, by political institutions such as slavery, and by being forced to labor for white men who have both economic and racial/cultural advantages over them. These are conflations that cannot be disarticulated merely by distinguishing between white and Black women, but rather must be accounted for by understanding the differences in their situations historically, politically, and, indeed, through gender as well. Rape was considered an act of terrorism against white women, most often assumed to have been committed by Black men, regardless of facts to the contrary or of white women's participation in interracial sexual relationships. For Black women, the notion of rape was thought to have been irrelevant, since there was neither acknowledgment that such an act could occur nor were there legal protections against such acts for Black women. As Harris states, "[t]he rift between white and black women over the issue of rape is highlighted by the contemporary feminist analyses of rape that have explicitly relied on racist ideology to minimize white women's complicity in racial terrorism" (Harris 1995: 263). In contrast, an intersectional analysis of the historical, political, legal, and cultural differences would illustrate that different acts, practices, and protections have distinct consequences for subjects in terms of race, gender, and class.

Feminist theorist Patricia Hill Collins develops another perspective on intersectionality as a framework that reveals how race and gender are shaped by power. She argues that race, class and gender should be thought of as "interlocking systems of oppression," rather than as axes of identity or simple categories. The second version of intersectionality allows for these axes to be understood as "interlocking," which implies that our analysis must take into account these axes as necessarily linked and intersecting in order to truly understand how oppression works. Collins's position emerges from the view that historical, political, social situations, along with other institutions—such as marriage, heterosexuality, slavery, immigration, national boundaries—must be considered as producing both categories/axes such as race and gender and also constructing identities. These institutions connect with each other to form common but also unique situations for any given subject (Collins 1990: 222).

Collins looks to geopolitical history, among other factors, in implementing an intersectional analysis. For example, in a 2000 article, she points to a racial hierarchy that emerges from the unique history of colonialism, slavery, and geographical annexation that locates white men and women at the top of a "familial" racial hierarchy, with American Indians, Latinos, and Black Americans arranged below them. Her racial hierarchy can be seen as a critical analysis of the history of the United States, in which

> [n]otions of US national identity that take both family and race into account result in a view of the United States as a large national family with racial families hierarchically arranged within it. Representing the epitome of racial purity that is also associated with US national interests, Whites constitute the most valuable citizens. In this racialized nation-state, Native Americans, African-Americans, Mexican-Americans, and Puerto Ricans become second-class citizens, whereas people of color from the Caribbean, Asia, Latin America, and Africa encounter more difficulty becoming naturalized citizens than immigrants from European nations. Because all of these groups are not White and thereby lack appropriate blood ties, they are deemed to be less worthy actual and potential US citizens.
>
> (Collins 1998: 70)

Collins's version of intersectionality brings a range of structural features to the issue of how to make less visible, or more marginal (and more marginalized), populations more prominent in the landscape of political and legal justice.

What's Intersectional about Critical Race Theory?

How do we understand intersectionality within the context of Critical Race Theory? Critical Race Theory not only challenges the universal categories of liberalism, but also endorses the idea that multiple axes of analysis facilitate a better understanding of different subjects and populations, to borrow Michel Foucault's terms (Foucault 1982; 2003). Since Critical Race Theory's debut among US legal scholars, CRT's worldview has expanded to attract scholars in numerous fields, including English, Comparative Literature, Ethnic Studies, and Philosophy. Understandably, the contours of the field have also changed in relation to the fields in which scholars have approached CRT. One prominent example of this uptake would be the work of Charles Mills, whose book, *The Racial Contract*, not only adhered to some of the same basic tenets as those articulated by Crenshaw, but also explored and developed a strong theoretical framework that theorized white supremacy in intrinsic relation to the tenets of liberal political philosophy (Mills 1997).

Mills' analysis of the trope of the Social Contract in the tradition of liberal political theory draws on an intersectional framework, at least partially, to dissect its racial and economic underpinnings. He points to the inherent contradiction in the claim of the universality of the Social Contract, namely that The Social Contract enfranchises white men in the same breath that it accommodates, perhaps even requires, the enslavement of black men and women—a pact that he calls the Racial Contract. In his book, Mills argues that the Racial Contract is the counterpart and foundation of the Social Contract. By insisting that the universal claims of the Social Contract cannot possibly hold given the facts of colonialism and imperialism, he requires us to consider race and class in order to understand which populations are entitled to political and legal enfranchisement and recognition. However, he does not explicitly include gender in this analysis, a fact that has been criticized by feminist theorists. (In later work Mills attends more directly to gender and intersectionality, e.g., in Pateman and Mills 2007.) Mills' interpretation of the Social Contract as a fundamental Racial Contract has expanded the space by which to discuss race as a philosophical concept in the twenty-first century, as have the writings of other philosophers of race. (See also Richardson, Chapter 7 in this volume.)

Similarly, for many scholars who work in Critical Race Theory—from Kevin Johnson, Devon Carbado, Keith Aoki, Angela Harris, Richard Delgado, to Leti Volpp, and many others—their analyses are fundamentally informed by intersectionality. For example, Keith Aoki's article, "No Right to Own?: The Early Twentieth-Century 'Alien Land Law' as a Prelude to Internment" (1998) illustrates how the disenfranchising of Asian populations (mostly Japanese-American or migrants of Japanese descent, but also other Asian populations), was but one important stage in the stripping of economic and legal protections that paved the way to facilitating the incarceration of Japanese-Americans at the onset of World War II. Such an analysis would not have been possible had Aoki not taken as his fundamental question: What were the historical, institutional, racial, and economic factors that led to the internment of Japanese Americans—full US citizens—despite the ostensible promise of the universal protections of the US Constitution?

Intersectionality across Time and Multiple Fields

It is important to note that the conceptual framework known as intersectionality names a number of different phenomena that span a broad range of thinkers and historical epochs. Others have mapped it thoroughly (e.g., see Botts, Chapter 28 in this volume). This section explores a more specific question about the breadth of intersectionality.

As feminist philosophers Kathryn Gines and Kristie Dotson have noted, intersectional frameworks are not new to our contemporary moment; they have been articulated in different ways for centuries (see Dotson, Chapter 10 in this volume). Gines points to Maria Stewart who, in 1831, criticized paternalism and racism while "calling on all Black women—'the fair daughters of Africa' to unite in support for one another"; as well as ex-slave and activist Sojourner Truth, whose famous question, "Ain't I a woman?" challenged the idea that white women or Black men were more deserving of rights than Black women; and numerous other Black feminist thinkers and activists who raise the importance of thinking race and gender together intersectionally (Gines 2014: 15–16).

Truth is reputed to have responded as follows:

> That man over there says that women need to be helped into carriages, and lifted over ditches, and to have the best place everywhere. Nobody ever helps me into carriages, or over mud-puddles, or gives me any best place! And ain't I a woman? Look at me! Look at my arm! I have ploughed and planted, and gathered into barns, and no man could head me! And ain't I a woman? I could work as much and eat as much as a man—when I could get it—and bear the lash as well! And ain't I a woman? I have borne thirteen children, and seen most all sold off to slavery, and when I cried out with my mother's grief, none but Jesus heard me! And ain't I a woman?
>
> Then they talk about this thing in the head; what's this they call it? [member of audience whispers, "intellect"] That's it, honey. What's that got to do with women's rights or negroes' rights? If my cup won't hold but a pint, and yours holds a quart, wouldn't you be mean not to let me have my little half measure full?
>
> Then that little man in black there, he says women can't have as much rights as men, 'cause Christ wasn't a woman! Where did your Christ come from? Where did your Christ come from? From God and a woman! Man had nothing to do with Him.
>
> (Truth 1851)

[Note that this speech may not have been delivered exactly in these words; see Gines 2014: 16.]

As can be seen in Truth's response, she challenged the notion that women were inferior intellectually or physically to men; she challenged as well the embedded, implicit assumption that Black women were inferior to white men or women. She pointed to her capacity to labor and to endure suffering—whether grief or cruelty—as being inferior to none. Her response regarding the assumed inferiority of intellect was that it had little bearing on the entitlement to rights. In her comments, we begin to glimpse the urgency of an intersectional framework: it enables the separation of multiple social features of groups—race, gender, class (and political caste) that converge into a myopic picture of which subset of the population deserves political rights. White men? White women? Where do Black women and women of color fit into this picture? Wealthy and poor women?

Today intersectionality, as a method, has become so widespread and prominent as to be an institutional anchor of many Women's/Gender/Sexuality Studies programs. It is for example, part of the National Women's Studies Association mission statement ("National Women's Studies Association" 2016). As Leslie McCall noted in 2005,

"One could say that intersectionality is the most important theoretical contribution made to women's studies, in conjunction with related fields, so far" (McCall 2005: 1771). In part, this may be because intersectionality has been so useful in reformulating identity-based knowledge fields, due to the approach of using multiple axes to understand both individual subjects and groups. I make this point not to valorize intersectionality, but to point to its entrenched status in many areas.

In addition to Crenshaw, Williams, and other Critical Race Theorists' writing on intersectionality, many other scholars—especially feminist scholars of color—have engaged in similar considerations. These include Patricia Hill Collins (as discussed above), Angela Davis (2003), bell hooks (1990), Cherríe Moraga and Gloria Anzaldúa (2002), Barbara Smith (1978), Chela Sandoval (2000), Chandra Mohanty (1991), and María Lugones and Elizabeth Spelman (1983), among others.

As intersectionality has become better known across a variety of disciplines and fields, there have been a number of rejoinders and discussions about intersectionality. In particular, questions have arisen about whether the "multiple axis" model of intersectionality could adequately address the problem of occlusion or the eclipse of different kinds of populations. For example, Nira Yuval-Davis offers a challenge to one reading of intersectionality by asking whether multiple overlapping oppressions is really useful to seeing invisible populations. She argues that there is no such thing as suffering merely "'as Black,' 'as a woman,' 'as a working-class person'" because these identities are too complex to be treated as essential, simple concepts. Thus, being Black does not necessarily entail that all subjects who fit this category necessarily experience oppression in the same way. The contrary assumption, for Yuval-Davis, reflects "hegemonic discourses of identity politics that render invisible experiences of the more marginal members of that specific social category and construct an homogenized 'right way' to be its member" (Yuval-Davis 2006: 195). Yet, as Yuval-Davis points out, it was this very problem—of not being seen or always having to be seen in the "right way"— that led scholars of color to try to theorize frameworks such as intersectionality.

Some scholars, such as Jennifer Nash, have argued that intersectionality is a framework that, in becoming institutionalized, has also become a stand-in for situations pertaining primarily to women of color, and even more specifically to Black women, rather than for a range of vulnerable populations. Further, she suggests that intersectionality initially emerged as the product of black feminism, and expanded across disciplinary boundaries and populations. However, while it has the potential to expand across numerous populations, axes, and issues, it has morphed into a narrower form of intersectionality that attends to race and gender but not the other possible analytical axes, such as class, nationality, sexuality, etc. As she suggests,

> [M]arginalization has emerged as the principal analytic used to study this intersection. Because intersectionality has come to equate black women's lived experiences with marginalization, black feminism has neglected to rigorously study the heterogeneity of "black woman" as a category. Second, because black feminism attends to race/gender almost exclusively, black feminism has effectively subcontracted out explorations of other intersections to a range of related intellectual projects. Third, and most importantly, because intersectionality has become the preeminent black feminist lens for studying black women's experiences, intersectionality itself is never subjected to critical scrutiny.
>
> (Nash 2011: 446)

Nash's concern is that the equation between Black women's experiences and marginalization renders intersectionality the primary, if not the sole, framework into which to force black women's experiences, and conversely, that Black women's experiences cannot be understood in more expansive, complex ways. Her diagnosis is that this narrowness is the result of understanding intersectionality as an ahistorical construct, rather than a framework that is both continually altered and whose terrain has been and should remain to be continually contested (Nash 2011: 449).

Another critical response to intersectionality in relation to Critical Race Theory is one that I have addressed in previous writing (Sheth 2014). There I suggest that intersectionality could usefully be augmented by a larger-scale analysis in which historical, institutional, legal, and migratory factors also be taken into consideration in order to help understand: (1) invisible or less obvious populations; (2) nuances of interests and features pertaining to subjects of the same perceived populations; (3) why certain members of the same perceived populations might understand themselves to be distinct in key ways from others in "their own group"; and (4) why certain members of different populations might understand themselves to have more in common with each other than with other members of "their own group."

Thus, I suggest that historical factors such as the 1948 Partition between India and Pakistan might help to explain why South Asian Hindu women and Muslim women of a certain generation in the United States might not necessarily see themselves as part of a group with similar interests, whereas their daughters might very well see themselves as part of group with similar concerns. This approach takes into consideration history, migration law, visa statuses, geopolitical concerns, property laws, and foreign and domestic policies designed to scrutinize certain populations as being threats to the safety of a nation or other populations (as in the case of the "War on Terror").

This view is an augmentation to intersectionality and Critical Race Theory, building on Crenshaw's metaphor of road intersections to consider their interstices, which would include building codes, regulations, policies, and other structural factors as a way of recognizing the particular features of a variety of populations who may not be otherwise visible.

Conclusion

Critical Race Theory can be used to highlight multiple populations that might have heretofore been invisible, as well as to illustrate the contingent details and situation of a given population. CRT can also show how a richer and more adequate understanding of a population can enable us to see a population in its own singular light without necessarily conflating its experiences with those of other populations. Also, an important version of intersectionality arose in tandem with the field of (legal) Critical Race Theory, which then quickly gained popularity across a range of disciplines over the last several decades. Kimberlé Crenshaw, a Critical Race Theory legal scholar, had an important role in popularizing one of the predominant forms of intersectionality that is still drawn on by feminist theorists and race theorists. However, intersectionality has existed for decades, if not centuries, prior to Crenshaw's important articles. It is important to note that Crenshaw herself makes no claims about being the original proponent of intersectionality; rather, she challenges those who attribute the original framework to her (Crenshaw 2011).

There are multiple viewpoints on the usefulness or the confusing aspects of intersectionality, as manifested through the critical responses of, for example, Nira Yuval-Davis, Jennifer Nash, and myself. However, these critical responses are an important element of enabling and enlivening intersectionality and Critical Race Theory as useful analytic tools. Intersectionality, combined with a Critical Race Theory perspective, can help us to understand historical institutions—such as the Social Contract and its counterpart, the Racial Contract—and the consequences of such institutions— slavery, subpersonhood, vulnerability, precarity, etc.—as they manifest themselves in unique ways for different groups.

Related Topics

Feminist engagements with social contract theory (Chapter 7); introducing Black feminist philosophy (Chapter 10); the sex/gender distinction and the social construction of reality (Chapter 13); gender essentialism and anti-essentialism (Chapter 14); the genealogy and viability of the concept of intersectionality (Chapter 28); feminist philosophy of law, legal positivism, and non-ideal theory (Chapter 56).

References

Aoki, Keith (1998) "No Right to Own?: The Early Twentieth-Century 'Alien Land Law' as a Prelude to Internment," *Boston College Law Review* 40: 37–72.

Atlanta Journal Constitution (2016) "East Point Woman Who Threatened to Kill Police Makes Public Apology," May 6 [online]. Available from: www.ajc.com/news/news/local/woman-who-threatened-kill-police-makes-public-apol/nrJKS/

Belliotti, Raymond (1995) "Introduction," in *Radical Philosophy of Law: Contemporary Challenges to Mainstream Legal Theory and Practice*, Atlantic Highlands, NJ: Humanities Press.

Collins, Patricia (1990) "Black Feminist Thought in the Matrix of Domination," in *Black Feminist Thought: Knowledge, Consciousness, and the Politics of Empowerment* Boston, MA: Unwin Hyman [online]. Available from: www.hartford-hwp.com/archives/45a/252.html

—— (1998) "It's All in the Family: Intersections of Gender, Race, and Nation," *Hypatia* 13(3): 62–82.

—— (2000) *Black Feminist Thought: Knowledge, Consciousness, and the Politics of Empowerment*, London: Routledge.

Crenshaw, Kimberlé (1989) "Demarginalizing the Intersection of Race and Sex: A Black Feminist Critique of Antidiscrimination Doctrine, Feminist Theory, and Antiracist Politics," *University of Chicago Law Review* 1: 139–167.

—— (1991) "Mapping the Margins: Intersectionality, Identity Politics, and Violence against Women of Color," *Stanford Law Review* 43(6): 1241–1299.

—— (2011) "Postscript," in Helma Lutz, Maria Teresa Herrera, and Linda Supik (Eds.) *Framing Intersectionality: Debates on a Multi-Faceted Concept in Gender Studies*, Burlington, VT: Ashgate.

Crenshaw, Kimberlé, Gotanda, Neil, Peller, Gary and Thomas, Kendall (Eds.) (1995) *Critical Race Theory: The Key Writings That Formed the Movement*, New York: New Press.

Davis, Angela (2003) "Racialized Punishment and Prison Abolition," in Tommy Lott and John P. Pittman (Eds.) *A Companion to African-American Philosophy*, Malden, MA: Blackwell, 360–368.

Foucault, Michel (1982) "Subject and Power," *Critical Inquiry* 8(4): 777–795.

—— (2003) *Society Must Be Defended: Lectures at the Collège de France 1975–1976*. trans. David Macey, New York: Picador Press.

Gines, Kathryn T. (2014) "Race Women, Race Men and Early Expressions of Proto-Intersectionality," in Maeve M. O'Donovan, Namita Goswami, and Lisa Yount (Eds.) *Why Race and Gender Still Matter: An Intersectional Approach*, London and Brookfield, VT: Pickering & Chatto, 13–26.

Harris, Angela (1995) "Race and Essentialism in Feminist Legal Theory," in Richard Delgado (Ed.) *Critical Race Theory: The Cutting Edge*, Philadelphia, PA: Temple University Press, 253–266.

Latimer, Sydney (2016) "Online Activists Question Facebook's Anti-Racism Stance after One Woman's Terrifying Death Threat Goes Viral," *Huffington Post*, March 3 [online]. Available from: www.huffingtonpost. com/sydney-latimer/online-activists-question_b_9372588.html

Lorde, Audre (1984) "Age, Race, Class and Sex: Women Redefining Difference," in *Sister Outsider: Essays and Speeches*, Berkeley, CA: Crossing Press, 114–123.

Lugones, Maria, and Elizabeth Spelman (1983) "Have We Got a Theory for You! Feminist Theory, Cultural Imperialism and the Demand for 'The Woman's Voice'," *Women's Studies International Forum* 6(6): 573–581.

McCall, Leslie (2005) "The Complexity of Intersectionality," *Signs* 30(3): 1771–1800.

Mills, Charles (1997) *The Racial Contract*, Ithaca, NY: Cornell University Press.

Mohanty, Chandra Talpade (1991) "Under Western Eyes: Feminist Scholarship and Colonial Discourses," in *Third World Women and the Politics of Feminism*, Bloomington and Indianapolis: Indiana University Press.

Moraga, Cherríe, and Gloria Anzaldúa (Eds.) (2002) *This Bridge Called My Back: Writings by Radical Women of Color*, New York: Third Woman Press.

Nash, Jennifer (2011) "'Home Truths' on Intersectionality," *Yale Journal of Law and Feminism* 23: 445–470.

National Women's Studies Association (2016) *National Women's Studies Association: About*, Baltimore, MD: National Women's Studies Association [online]. Available from: www.nwsa.org/content.asp?pl= 19&contentid=19

Pateman, Carol and Charles Mills (2007) *Contract and Domination*, Cambridge and Malden, MA: Polity Press.

Rawls, John (1971) *A Theory of Justice*, Cambridge, MA: Harvard University Press.

Sandoval, Chela (2000) *Methodology of the Oppressed*, Minneapolis: University of Minnesota Press.

Sheth, Falguni A (2014) "Interstitiality: Making Space for Migration, Diaspora, and Racial Complexity," *Hypatia* 29 (1): 75–93.

Smith, Barbara (1978) "Towards a Black Feminist Criticism" *The Radical Teacher* 7 (March): 20–27.

Truth, Sojourner (1851) *Ain't I a Woman* [speech] Women's Convention, Akron, Ohio, May 29. Available from: http://legacy.fordham.edu/halsall/mod/sojtruth-woman.asp

Williams, Patricia J. (1991) "The Pain of Word Bondage," in *The Alchemy of Race and Rights: Diary of a Law Professor*, Cambridge, MA: Harvard University Press, 146–165.

Yuval-Davis, Nira (2006) "Intersectionality and Feminist Politics," *European Journal of Women's Studies* 13(3): 193–209.

30
NATIVE AMERICAN CHAOS THEORY AND THE POLITICS OF DIFFERENCE

Shay Welch

Introduction

Native American philosophy raises feminist philosophical questions and offers a new perspective for rethinking longstanding feminist disputes. I focus in this chapter on ways Native American metaphysics can contribute to a question in feminist political philosophy. I choose this approach over a focus on Native American feminisms for three reasons. First, what Western women call "feminist" is just the core set of Native American philosophical values. I see feminism as a construct invented to redress atrocities committed by and through the Western worldview. Second, Native American women would prefer that Western feminists live up to their own values; the failure of Western feminists to put their money where their mouth is, is the reason why many Native women, like many other women of color, do not identify as feminist (Anderson 2010; Mayer 2007). Third, the more Western feminism interacts with Native American philosophy, the better chance Native American philosophers have to revive, substantiate, and legitimate their worldview in the discipline and in the world.

I argue here that Native metaphysics can help Western philosophy imagine socio-political communities in ways that do not regard difference as a threat. Native chaos theory is useful for imagining an inclusive non-oppressive, normative democratic harmony. Native metaphysics portrays creativity vis-à-vis difference as, not only inherently valuable as an individual and social attribute, but also as vital to an inclusive, democratic political structure. To demonstrate both how this is possible and why this is desirable, I resituate Iris Marion Young's conceptions of a politics of difference and democratic inclusion in the Native American metaphysical system of chaos theory. A Native American metaphysical foundation includes chaos, creativity, and difference, and so escapes the trappings of liberalism against which feminist politics of difference continues to hammer.

Within diverse communities, individuals' and groups' motley modes of political participation produce friction. Feminist philosophers have criticized liberal political philosophy for aiming to eliminate or conceal differences. Many feminists rightly argue that the traditional liberal aim of achieving and enforcing cooperation via the values of universality and impartiality excludes, marginalizes, and silences diverse perspectives that fall outside of the arbitrarily conceived universal norm. The politics of difference is one approach through which feminist political philosophers have attempted to alleviate this problem. A central claim of the politics of difference is that traditional liberal objectives of universality, individualism, and impartiality are inapt conditions for democratic mechanisms, such as inclusion and representation. Feminist models of politics of difference strive to eliminate the lived consequences of liberal political theory by demonstrating the inclusive capabilities of the acceptance, normalization, and valuation of diversity in social and political interaction. Liberal universality is predisposed towards, and so ultimately produces, sameness for the purpose of manageable unity. It hinges on an assimilation ideal. A politics of difference rejects universality, and so sameness, insofar as the end of sameness marks distinction as deviance and yields hostile competition rather than presumed cooperation. Liberal values, and not the differences themselves, are inadvertently the source of antagonism between community members. A politics of difference opens space for agonism but does so purposefully for the sake of democracy. Difference generates tension but the struggle of negotiation results in a form of cooperation that is not a feigned, obedient, conformity to what is signified as "normal."

The reductive tendency of universality in politics of difference not only stifles, but also intentionally controls, creativity. It smothers communities' motivation for agonistic public participation. Yet it is for the sake of democratic cooperation, one might purport; otherwise, agonism would revert to antagonism and society would quickly collapse into chaos. The irony, or rather the ignorance, of preventing agonistic chaos to promote cooperation is that chaos is a creative and harmonizing energy. The discipline of quantum mechanics is just now learning what Native Americans have known all along—chaos is a natural ordering process through which the balancing and self-organization of collectives emerges. The liberal operation of stultifying a natural ordering process in fact generates massive breakdowns in social harmony by over-determining an unnatural state of stagnate sameness. Through chaos, balance is short-lived yet is forever renewing through intervals of varied interaction and the introduction of new elements into the ordering schema. Through chaos, rich forms of organization and cooperation can be achieved through unpredictable, creative activity rather than enforced through formalized procedures of suppression. From a Native American perspective, the socio-political differences that agonism thrives on are forces through which inclusive and representative democratic arrangements can flourish, since these arrangements are incessantly rearranged in the direction of cooperative harmony through the ongoing stabilizing of perpetually new contributions. Even if the liberal ideals of universality and impartiality could give rise to strict equality among community members, the requisite conformity underlying sameness would preclude innovative ways of producing, and living in, multifarious arrangements for interaction required for an explorative and expressive society. Exploration and expressiveness qua creativity are central to a properly democratic society; without inclusive and diverse participation, democratic practices turn subsumptive and reduce individual contributions into a singularity, contrary to normatively ideal democratic mechanisms. Chaos, creativity, and difference are the life forces of difficult yet non-oppressive democratic structures grounded in agonism, since they can simultaneously integrate community members in explorative dispute and attune them to the advantages of complicated but malleable and expressive collaboration. A true politics of difference must regard these metaphysical life forces as legitimate and justifiable. Native American metaphysics is a resource for conceiving difference as inherently liberatory and cooperative.

A Brief Overview of the Native American Worldview

The Native American philosophical worldview does not demarcate different ethical, social, metaphysical, and epistemological domains. Native logic is a non-hierarchical logic that informs knowledge and living vis-à-vis a complementary, non-oppositional, non-dualistic, fluid system that acknowledges and accounts for the connections between phenomena and their relationships to entities both similar and distinct (Cajete 2000, 2004; Fixico 2003; Peat 2002; Waters 2004) Brian Burkhart terms this worldview as the moral universe principle: "The idea is simply that the universe is moral. Facts, truth, meaning, even our existence are normative. In this way, there is no difference between what is true and what is right" (Burkhart 2004: 17). In simplistic terms, from the Native perspective, what ought to be is and so what is ought to be.

Given the integration of facets of philosophical inquiry, the values of interrelatedness, relationality, and equality are primary. The framing commitment of the Native worldview is that of respectful coexistence, which, as I will show shortly, grounds the epistemological conception of truth as respectful success. In Navajo thought, this concept is called hózhó, but it is a common value throughout the Native framework. Hóz signifies a life path, which should always flow towards wellness, happiness, and sustainability. Lloyd Lee explains that life is comprised of energies, both positive and negative, and one must live a life that strives towards equilibrium between them. Balance and harmony, particularly concerning social arrangements, are taken as the norm and it is the responsibility of both individuals and communities to sustain them (Lee 2014: 56). Similarly, Viola Cordova uses the notion of kinship to explain the relationship between and responsibility to balancing and sustaining harmony between all of the world's occupants: "The Native American recognizes his dependence on the Earth and the Universe. It recognizes no hierarchy of 'higher' or 'lower' or 'simple' or 'complex,' and certainly not of 'primitive' and 'modern.' Instead of hierarchies he sees differences, which exist among equal 'beings' (mountains, as well as water and air and plants and animals would be included here). The equality is based on the notion, often unstated, that everything that is, is of one process" (Cordova 2004: 177).

Taiaiake Alfred sees respectful coexistence as a universal value affecting all elements of creation and he posits it specifically as the goal of justice (Alfred 2009a: 14). All persons are co-creators of and with the world, so every action we engage in or commitment we affirm affects and substantiates nature and other persons (Cajete 2000: 76). Justice, he says, requires the restoration of harmony to social relations and a perpetually renewing commitment to the integrity of all individuals and communities (Alfred 2009a: 66); the process of justice, he states, is the healing of relations to ensure individuals can fulfill their responsibilities to one another (Alfred 2009a: 67).

Narrative is the heart and soul of both knowledge and ethical relations in the Native tradition, particularly because narrative is born through an oral tradition that relies on the sharing of individual experiences for knowledge construction. Narrative serves many complementary functions. First, narrative bonds members of the community (Fixico 2003: 29). This is possible because, second, narrative helps individuals apprehend and handle the complexity of the world through a storied picture through which to see particular instantiations of more general occurrences (Deloria 1999: 67; McPherson and Rabb 2011: 110). An audience is imbued with a "reactionary power waiting to be acted upon" (Fixico 2003: 27) by speakers and the stories told by others provide a medium through which to share experiences and generate meaning and connection. As a result, community members can better engage in public forms of moral deliberation because stories feed collective knowledge and imagination and reveal potential trajectories for individuals to determine and converge on the right path of respectful coexistence. Put another way, narrative effects respectful coexistence through deliberative engagements, because experiential knowledge is the fundamental source of moral education, and thus identity formation, within communities (McPherson and Rabb 2011: 104).

From within a Native American paradigm knowledge functions as a conduit between community members and allows them to converge on the right path to respectful coexistence. This understanding of knowledge as an active and interactive means through which to discover the right path requires a shift in how we understand the conception of truth itself. Because individuals co-create the world, their creative participation in construction processes is a meaning-shaping principle of action (Burkhart 2004: 16–17). Truth, which emanates from narrative sharing aimed at harmonious collective living, is determined by successful respect. Narrative does not emerge from knowledge; rather, knowledge emerges from narrative. It cannot exist apart from persons or communities. Knowledge is relational. The centrality of narrative to knowledge construction presents knowledge as lived and embodied (Norton-Smith 2010: 60), active—procedural. One cannot "know P" without "knowing how to P." Because knowledge is ethical and relational, the procurement of knowledge imposes stringent constraints on the way knowers go about acting in, and thus knowing about, the world.

Since science is the product of information that is gifted to us from and through nature, the domain of Native scientific inquiry intertwines with epistemology so tightly that knowledge and science are used interchangeably (Cajete 2000: 21). Ultimately, the objective of Native science is to integrate the heart and being with rational perception to surpass superficial understanding of what is toward a deeper understanding of one's relationship to that thing (Cajete 2000: 72). Thus, Native science is procedural. Its truth is not fixed but rather evolves and renews with all new interactions with nature. Gregory Cajete explains: "Native science reflects the unfolding story of a creative universe in which human beings are active, creative participants. When viewed from this perspective, science is evolutionary—its expression unfolds through the general scheme of the creative process of first insight, immersion, creation, and reflection. Native science is a reflection of the metaphoric mind and is embedded in creative participation with nature. It reflects the sensual capacities of humans" (Cajete 2000: 14).

Because the world is in constant flux, codifying knowledge is unnecessary. Flux and flexibility involve substantial creativity by both individual actors and the universe. A deep understanding of creativity as a foundation of action and, thus, knowledge makes the notion of animism within Native ontology intelligible. The universe, and all of its inhabitants—human and non-human—possess, act on, and contribute their own unique energies to the creative, collaborative function of natural organization; they are all regarded and respected as alive (Cajete 2000: 21). Without creativity and flux, the world can be nothing other than static—dead.

According to both Native American science and Western quantum mechanics, chaos is non-linear movement and evolution. It is itself the generative force and thus the process of becoming for the universe. Cajete describes chaos as flux, as ebb and flow, that is in everything at all times and in all places (Cajete 2004: 48). Chaos theory is predominantly characterized by the butterfly effect; it is not a massive wave of influence that hurls about radical change. Contrary to many folk conceptions, chaos, as a process, is subtle; it nudges the natural world through small-scale adjustments and connections that are imperceptible in a time slice, but are, cumulatively and over time, momentously dynamic. The chaos driving these tiny connections and reconnections and progressions progresses from the synergism of unpredictability, flux, and socio-ecological participation. All aspects of the universe interact in a sort of cosmic dance where all participants interact but only some, by sheer chance of attraction, emerge as temporary partners in the grand scheme of things. Chance or, rather, spontaneity, is a core signifier of chaos, which indicates an inherent indeterminism within the universe (Sheldrake, McKenna, and Abraham 1992: 26). Given these traits, chaos theory elucidates social life qua human creativity, which Cajete terms our "butterfly power." Chaos is embodied in persons and it is this that allows us to respond creatively to constant change. He explains: "The basic presupposition of chaos theory is that predictability and control over nature, persons, and society is therefore impossible and their creative participation cannot be trapped or stamped out without inevitable systemic collapses at the individual and collective levels" (Cajete 2000: 19).

The product of cycles of indeterminate but creative chaos is, unexpectedly, order. According to quantum mechanics, there is an underlying relationship between order and chaos such that order cannot exist without chaos and each follows from the other (Peat 2002: 176). The chaotic interactions between natural phenomena actualize new forms and structures from potentiality and then re-organizes them as they continue to interact. Though chaos is uncontrolled and unpredictable, like all highly complex systems, the magnitude of chance causes the relations of the universe to be probabilistic (Sheldrake, et al. 1992: 26). Order, in this sense, is better thought of as an equilibrium or bifurcation point in the midst of the chaos, which Cajete refers to as an eye of a hurricane (Cajete 2004: 48). He posits order as the point when a connection is made to a natural principle manifesting itself in the unfolding of the greater natural process (Cajete 2004: 48); the equilibrium occurs just as the system begins to transform itself (Cajete 2000: 18). But order in this sense, reflects not a convergence on or in conformity but rather convergence in diversity—in this paradigm, there is no such thing as an anomaly. In generating organized structures, the universe does not discard any participatory activity or phenomena, which means that apprehension of the workings of the world requires us not to dismiss any of our experiences.

Chaos imparts a particularly meaningful prescription about how individuals should interpellate social life. All information and experiences must be conceived of in relation to the framework of moral interpretation in the community. For stable organization, differing experiences among individuals cannot be pushed to the margins of respectability (Cajete 2000: 44). That chaos drives change and movement in nature reveals the senselessness of externally imposed mechanisms of control. The presumption of control demonstrates Western intellectual chauvinism (Deloria 1999: 6). Western metaphysics discards anomalous occurrences because, as Deloria apprehends, these facts are discerned through their own measuring devices that disrupt the security of the "universal" laws (Deloria 1999: 12). Deloria expounds: "Any damn fool can treat a living thing as if it were a machine and establish conditions under which it is required to perform certain functions—all that is required is a sufficient application of brute force" (Deloria 1999: 6). Chaos theory asserts that predictability and control over nature, persons, and society is impossible. Their creative participation cannot be trapped or stamped out without systemic collapses at the individual and collective levels.

The Politics of Difference and Native American Chaos Theory

Though the politics of difference is a socio-political framework, the questions of difference and creative chaos boil down to ontology. The functioning of difference and its relationships to creativity and chaos require a particular metaphysical system that recognizes both phenomena as inherent. To be workable and sustainable, a politics of difference must replace its Western colonizing worldview with one that centers creativity and chaos. The Native American worldview is the apposite theoretical home for a politics of difference.

Native chaos theory illuminates a strong correlation between organizational practices at the ontological level and ethico-political relations. The universe aims at a cooperative harmony that sustains the interdependence of all participants. Nature and all of its infrastructures demonstrate a tendency to self-organize and generate balance. This balance is achieved when there is no interference or attempt to control its organizing capacities—the only restriction on equilibriums is that organization follows ethically from diversity. The notion of respectful success as the foundation of truth in the Native schema mirrors the efficacy of this ethical restraint. Whereas the Western paradigm marks stark differentiations between nature and humans, the Native framework understands humans as just one among different kinds of persons and phenomena that must flourish. If the entirety of the universe must, does, and can self-organize in ways that respect difference and interrelatedness, then so too can humans and/with all other persons. The Native worldview conceives of this global interrelation and cooperation within nature as a communal soul that operates according to a natural democracy (Cajete 2000, 2004). Native chaos theory evidences how creativity and spontaneity among wildly divergent community members gives rise to order and permits continual renewal and reorganization, which, politically, manifests as freedom in and through revolving social consent and participation in social arrangements (Welch 2012). Liberation is only possible when different selves recognize and respond to their radical relationality with all others (Alfred 2009a; 2009b; Cordova 2007; Deloria 1999; Norton-Smith 2010).

Young grounds a politics of difference in a diachronic conception of equality that emanates from a cultural democratic pluralism. Cultural democratic pluralism is a communicative mode of democracy predicated on a heterogeneous public that exacts mutual respect among socially and culturally differentiated groups and affirms as valuable the differences between them (Young 1990: 163). Recognition of cultural and individual difference is crucial to equality; a homogenous society is not only undesirable but it is impossible (Young 1990, 163). Cultural democratic pluralism fosters equality through individual and social group participation in democratic practices (Young 1990: 158). When community members value group differences as positive social goods they are then positioned to communicate with others through relations of perspectival difference rather than deviance from a normative perspective (Young 1990: 166). Narrative is essential to democratic communication under a politics of difference (Young 1996: 120). By refusing that shared understandings are given, Young unknowingly aligns her political theory with the Native scientific commitment to anomalies as enlightening and instructive.

Through her emphasis on narrative, Young positions recognition as a starting point rather than the end of equality (Young 2000: 61). Substantive recognition is inextricable from processes of listening. What must accompany the listener's recognition, is an ongoing openness to hear the speaker (Young 2000: 112). The dismissal or discounting of others' perspectives post-recognition often occurs because of community members' ignorance of their unique experiences and differing shared histories. When community members are unfamiliar with others' trajectories, they bring to the table empty generalities and/or false assumptions about those with whom they interact, which habitually triggers the othering of those perspectives as insignificant anomalies (Young 2000: 74). Recognition without listening is merely a glorified form of tolerance.

Narrative does its democratic work by transmuting anomaly into collective knowledge contribution. It conveys one's subjective particularity through the uniqueness of one's story and the cultural specificity of social group membership by unveiling systemic patterns of shared histories and social locations between group members. And while narrative proves central to demonstrating the particularity of "others," it also illuminates one's own particularity and difference. In light of multifarious expositions about differing lived experiences and preferences, individuals can see that their perspective regarding subjective being, social life, and political organization is just one of many, rather than wrongly presuming their standpoint aligns with some presumed majority view from which divergent experiences can or should be othered.

The process of distinction reveals how entrenched community members are in relations of mutual effect. Stories, rather than claims, reflect how they are shaped by and through one another as a result of their intersecting social relations. Narrative makes it possible for community members to discern at least some shared premises from which to build and sculpt dialogical understanding because narratives target underlying false assumptions for correction (Young 2000: 53, 74). When values and priorities are shared through experiences and histories in narrative form, listeners can grasp more meaning behind the values invoked than they would if the values had been presented as uncontextualized, impartial claims. Public narratives of plural perspectives are essential for understanding individuals' needs for inclusion, the consequences of being excluded, and the significance of differing values, since stories impart affective illocutionary force. This affective force resonates and can motivate listeners to hear and attempt to apprehend others' narratives to effect individual and social group participatory parity, which positions community members in relations of mutual respect.

According to Young, shared understandings inadvertently force assimilation because any narrative that is "anomalous" is marked as deviant. Therefore, the success of this narrative-based sculpting process depends on the ability of community members to navigate the chaos of infinite perspectives creatively through agonistic negotiation of what is, can, and should be shared as knowledge, Native philosophy presumes a shared epistemology by virtue of far-reaching interaction and the fact that language constructs a shared cognitive orientation among community members without also presuming shared understandings (Overholt and Callicott 1982: 11). Native philosophers hold that a right understanding of the world, requires communities to synthesize diverse experience through interpretive practices to reflect evolving knowledge that emanates from and builds on the communal narrative (Overholt and Callicott 1982: 73). Because Native philosophy sees knowledge as procedural, it cannot be acquired independently. For individuals or social groups to have shared understandings, they must be co-creative through active praxes of learning. Narrative as a performative practice fosters the creation of the same thin shared understandings that Young posits as central to deliberation, because unique interpretations are excavated through ethical discursive relations.

In a Native American worldview, dictates for the community are modeled after an ethically interdependent nature. In nature, all participants and contributions are useful and so beneficially interact either directly or tangentially. This implies, rather than invites, mutual reciprocity as respect for what participants bring to the wholeness of the systemic structure. Will Roscoe avows that you don't waste people because every person has a gift (Roscoe 2000: 4). All beings must in principle be respectfully recognized for the reciprocity inherent in their unique talents without which there would be no system and no organizational arrangements (Fixico 2003: 52). This interdependence between, and reliance on, all of nature's and humanity's contributions to sociality exists in the Western schema but goes unnoticed because the foundational metaphysical conditions of Western philosophy encourage marginalization and fragmentation. Fragmentation comes from the impolitic splitting of domains: the personal from the political, the public from the private, the metaphysical from the ethical. Relatedly, the binary logic that motivates such boundaries is hierarchical, which parses domains of activity and contributions within them so that some are worthy of recognition and others are not. Human efforts are more valuable than natural efforts and one of the objectives of personhood involves controlling and dominating nature to the point of its extermination through imbalance. The partitioning between the valuable and not-valuable continues to bracket down between the normative and the deviant, the regular and the anomalous, and the desirable and detestable until the vast majority of individual and social group contributions that differ from those of the dominant groups no longer have any recognizable value.

One example of the relationship between Native logic and practices of inclusive and intersectional reciprocity is that Native communities often have third and fourth genders. The spectrum contains sharp instantiations only on each of its ends but the spectrum itself is constituted by multifarious versions of ambiguity, amalgamation, and complexity. Native North America is believed to have been the queerest continent on the planet (Roscoe 2000: 4). Individuals who are multigendered are deemed as having pivotal roles in the community by virtue of the specificity of their intersectional gender expressions. Third and fourth genders participate in creative contributions in community praxes such as crafting, warring, advising, and healing or ethical relations such as non-procreative sex and romantic love (Roscoe 2000; Waters 2004). Other times, gender is wholly contextually and relationally dependent.

In the Native framework, difference is neither as a site of competition nor conflict. Differences, much as feminists like Young attempt to advocate, are unproblematically sites of inherent intersectionality by virtue of systemic interdependence; difference is required for balance and cooperative harmony. At its metaphysical foundation, the Native framework is inclusive and designates difference as crucial strata rather than as anomalous glitches. The "Native mind" operates from "a symbolic kinship based on the ethos of totality and inclusions" (Fixico 2003: 48) because no system can be regarded as complete. All that can be known are patterns in arrangements, but difference stimulates our ability to see patterns and interactions change. Bohm and Peat (1987) assert that fundamental ideas must always be subjected to differences to ensure that society does not become rigidly committed to normative assumptions and conformist arrangements. Individuals must engage in free and creative play to test the legitimacy of their conditions because it is only through free play vis-à-vis difference that the true creative potential of society can emerge (Bohm and Peat 1987: 59, 111). But Western philosophy repudiates difference and creativity for specifically this reason; it is committed to stasis and control that resists the liberatory practices of a politics of difference.

Even as Young encourages inclusive deliberation, inclusive forms of deliberation are not without their own melees. Young notes that inclusion can make deliberative exchanges more difficult and less efficient (Young 2000: 119). A justice framework imbued by a politics of difference fosters conditions for agonism. This is because relations of mutual effect are relations of togetherness, which means that disagreements and conflicts arise simply as a result of inevitable relationality. As Honig argues, taking differences seriously requires communities to "affirm the inescapability of conflict and the ineradicability of resistance to the political and moral projects of ordering subjects, institutions, and values" (Honig 1996: 258). Additionally, the shift in focus from the atomistic individual to individuals as members of social groups doubles the acceptable number of justice claims for equality (Honig 1996; 2001). Discord and dispute in deliberation must be met head on if equality and justice can ensue. Without the acknowledgement of difference and the profound importance of negotiating difference through assorted modes of public participation, an inclusive and equal—harmonious and balanced—social configuration will be impossible.

What Young overlooks due to her Western metaphysical assumptions—and that a Native philosophical metaphysics can make sense of—is that agonism inherent in a politics of difference thrives on and evokes the creative force of chaos. Agonistic, creative chaos manifests in the clash of different narratives, preferences, and lived experiences, in individuals' attempts to reconcile and adapt to varying modes of communication, in the deliberative negotiation process, and in the commotion of packed out participatory activities. When resituating a politics of difference into a Native worldview, chaos is less about conflict than creative participation. It is a mere fact about the universe that if we desire order, there must be moments of disorder, but disorder does not lead to the Leviathan.

In the Native American worldview, equality is not a state but is achieved through participatory activity. Chaos is not one of the flaws in inclusive practices but is merely the Archimedean point of participation. Equality through inclusion is a wildly eventful endeavor. Deliberative practices must proceed hither and thither through convoluted channels of interpellation, interpretation, and collaboration instead of down the linear, sterile method undergirding liberalism. Chaos and disorder mark the moments of participation and negotiation prior to the settling of justice claims and the realization of intermittent relations of equality. Because community members incessantly and creatively co-construct one another via their individuality and the social group memberships, justice claims will never be fully settled and a state of equality will never be permanent. Even though narrative and other creative communicative devices aim at familiarizing others with the distinctive experiences of social groups, there will always be a gap in the understanding between those who have particular experiences and those who do not—at least until they have engaged in extensive public exchanges to construct bridges. And because gaps exist, states of equality between individuals and between social groups will never be for once and all achieved. Though the processes of a politics of difference cultivate equality through equalizing practices, differences that need attending to, whether innocuous or oppressive will always cause an undulation of power relations. Between the valleys of the chaos of discursive play and disconnect exist peaks of balance through which cooperation and harmony can emanate. The Native American view expands on a politics of difference's acceptance of flux in social location in participation, by taking flux to be given as a fact of collective existence.

Young argues that community members should interact in respectful wonder (Young 1996), which directly connects to Native American metaphysics. Respectful wonder calls on community members to engage imaginatively to try to understand the needs of others. Imagination is a creative and chaotic place. This wonder must be respectful, since chaotic imaginative capacities unconstrained by normative dictates sometimes trend toward exoticization rather than empathizing. The employment but management of imaginative perceptions involves creatively piecing together pictures of lived experience that are both similar to and different from one's own. Respectful wonder facilitates deliberation and negotiation, which are themselves creative in three ways. First, individuals must employ creativity to determine how to communicate their perspectives in pointed but rhetorical ways to ensure uptake. Second, individuals' suggestions and input require the excavation of experience and the shaping of contributions that speak to their own and others' justice claims and social arrangements. Third, praxes of negotiation are raucous as much as they are intentional and end-directed. Negotiation fashions itself much like the process of a group trying to work together to construct a jigsaw puzzle with too many pieces.

Young is well aware that many liberatory impediments reduce to problems with liberal social ontology (Young 1990: 228). Yet knowing how to get outside of one's own worldview is nearly inconceivable if other reasonable worldview perspectives have themselves been all but vanquished by the worldview in question. If the perspective is there but foreign, the possibility of traversing a foreign worldview is, well, chaotic. This is why I think Western feminists must see the power and liberatory potential inherent in Native American metaphysics. For it just is the case that we live in Western society, and feminists need to see that their values are not utopian goals but have been the norm for successful, healthy democratic societies. Unfortunately, the perspective that shares feminist goals has been subject to genocide, which ultimately reveals how dangerous—and so liberatory—metaphysical assumptions of given interrelatedness and harmony can truly be.

Further Reading

DuFour, John (2004) "Ethics and Understanding," in Anne Waters (Ed.) *American Indian Thought*. Oxford: Blackwell, 34–41.

Hester, Thomas Lee (2004) "Choctaw Conceptions of the Excellence of the Self, with Implication for Education," in Anne Waters (Ed.) *American Indian Thought*, Oxford: Blackwell, 182–187.

Napoleon, Val (2005) "Aboriginal Self-Determination: Individual Self and Collective Selves," *Atlantis* 29(2): 1–21.

Nichols, Robert and Singh, Jakeet (Eds.) (2014) *Freedom and Democracy in an Imperial Context: Dialogues with James Tully*, New York: Routledge Press.

Simpson, Audra and Smith, Andrea (Eds.) (2014) *Theorizing Native Studies*, Durham, NC: Duke University Press.

Tsosie, Rebecca (2010) "Native Women and Leadership: An Ethic of Culture and Relationship," in Cheryl Suzack, Shari M. Huhndorf, Jeanne Perreault, and Jean Barman (Eds.) *Indigenous Women and Feminism: Politics, Activism, and Culture*, Vancouver, BC: The University of British Columbia Press, 29–52.

Vandenabeele, Bart (2012) "No Need for Essences. On Non-Verbal Communication in First Inter-Cultural Contacts," *South African Journal of Philosophy* 21(2): 85–96.

Related Topics

Dao becomes female (Chapter 3); feminism and borderlands identities (Chapter 17); personal identity and relational selves (Chapter 18); moral justification in an unjust world (Chapter 40); feminist engagements with democratic theory (Chapter 51); feminism and freedom (Chapter 53).

References

Alfred, Taiaiake (2009a) *Wasáse: Indigenous Pathways of Action and Freedom*, Toronto, ON: University of Toronto Press.

—— (2009b) *Peace, Power, and Righteousness: An Indigenous Manifesto*, Oxford: Oxford University Press.

Anderson, Kim (2010) "Affirmations of an Indigenous Feminist," in Cheryl Suzack, Shari M. Huhndorf, Jeanne Perreault, and Jean Barman (Eds.) *Indigenous Women and Feminism: Politics, Activism, and Culture*, Vancouver, BC: The University of British Columbia Press, 81–91.

Bohm, David and Peat, F. David (1987) *Science, Order, and Creativity*, New York: Routledge Press.

Burkhart, Brian (2004) "What Coyote and Thales Can Teach Us: An Outline of American Indian Epistemology," in Anne Waters (Ed.) *American Indian Thought*, Oxford: Blackwell, 15–26.

Cajete, Gregory (2000) *Native Science: Natural Laws of Interdependence*, Santa Fe, NM: Clear Light.

—— (2004) "Philosophy of Native Science," in Anne Waters (Ed.) *American Indian Thought*, Oxford: Blackwell, 45–56.

Cordova, V. F. (2004) "Ethics: The We and the I," in Anne Waters (Ed.) *American Indian Thought*, Oxford: Blackwell, 173–181.

—— (2007) *How It Is: The Native American Philosophy of V. F. Cordova*, Kathleen Dean Moore, Kurt Peters, Ted Jojola, and Amber Lacy (Eds.) Tucson, AZ: University of Arizona Press.

Deloria, Vine Jr. (1999) *Spirit and Reason: The Vine Deloria, Jr. Reader*, Sam Scinta and Kristen Foehner (Eds.) Golden, CO: Fulcrum.

Fixico, Donald (2003) *The American Indian Mind in a Linear World*, New York: Routledge.

Honig, Bonnie (1996) "Difference, Dilemmas, and the Politics of Home," in Seyla Benhabib (Ed.) *Democracy and Difference: Contesting the Boundaries of the Political*, Princeton, NJ: Princeton University Press, 120–135.

Lee, Lloyd L. (Ed.) (2014) *Diné Perspectives: Revitalizing and Reclaiming Navajo Thought*, Tucson, AZ: University of Arizona Press.

McPherson, Dennis and Rabb, J. Douglas (2011) *Indian from the Inside: Native American Philosophy and Cultural Renewal*, Jefferson, NC: McFarland & Company.

Mayer, Lorraine (2007) "A Return to Reciprocity," *Hypatia* 22(3): 22–42.

Norton-Smith, Thomas (2010) *The Dance of Person and Place: One Interpretation of American Indian Philosophy*, Albany, NY: SUNY Press.

Overholt, Thomas and Callicott, J. Baird (1982) *Clothed-in-Fur and Other Tales: An Introduction to an Ojibwa Worldview*, Lanham, MD: University Press of America.

Peat, F. David (2002) *Blackfoot Physics*, Boston, MA: Weiser Books.

Roscoe, Will (2000) *Changing Ones: Third and Fourth Genders in Native North America*, London: Palgrave Macmillan.

Sheldrake, Rupert, McKenna, Terence, and Abraham, Ralph (1992) *Chaos, Creativity, and Cosmic Consciousness*, Rochester, VT: Park Street Press.

Waters, Anne (2004) "Language Matters: Nondiscrete Nonbinary Dualism," in Anne Waters (Ed.) *American Indian Thought*, Oxford: Blackwell, 97–115.

Welch, Shay (2012) *A Theory of Freedom: Feminism and the Social Contract*, London: Palgrave Macmillan.

—— (2014) "Radical-cum-Relational: Bridging Feminist Ethics and Native Individual Autonomy," *Philosophical Topics* 41(2): 203–223.

Young, Iris Marion (1990) *Justice and the Politics of Difference*, Princeton, NJ: Princeton University Press.

—— (1996) "Communication and the Other: Beyond Deliberative Democracy," in Seyla Benhabib (Ed.) *Democracy and Difference: Contesting the Boundaries of the Political*, Princeton, NJ: Princeton University Press, 120–136.

—— (2000) *Inclusion and Democracy*, Oxford: Oxford University Press.

31

FEMINIST THEORY, LESBIAN THEORY, AND QUEER THEORY

Mimi Marinucci

Introduction

Feminist theory intersects with theories of sexuality in rather complicated ways. There are many different forms of feminism, but the most widely represented (and misrepresented) include what is usually referred to as liberal feminism and what is usually referred to as radical feminism. Liberal feminism is often presented as the definitive version of feminism. Rachel Fudge, for example, characterizes liberal feminism as "just plain feminism" (Fudge 2006) and the definition of feminism found in most general use dictionaries is best characterized as a liberal feminist position. Liberal feminism focuses on the cornerstone Western democratic ideal of equality, which is probably why it is the form of feminism that people often refer to when they are motivated to make feminism seem uncontroversial. Feminist analyses focused on equality have also been referred to as libertarian feminism, equality feminism, and equity feminism.

To the extent that liberal feminism is the example offered in order to make feminism seem as accessible and acceptable as possible, radical feminism is the example offered in order to make it seem as extreme and objectionable as possible. Unlike liberal feminism, which is focused on establishing equality within existing social structures, radical feminism regards the oppression of women by men as the inevitable product of patriarchy, which is believed to be a system of power that is built into existing social institutions. Radical feminism therefore seeks a more thorough (that is to say, more radical) restructuring of the social order than liberal feminism. Some radical feminists find oppression of women by men in virtually all contexts where women and men interact and, for this reason, advocate a completely separatist agenda. When critics of feminism, particularly those associated with the emerging men's rights movement, characterize feminism as anti-male, radical feminism is the position to which they are usually referring. An online men's rights movement frequently asked questions (FAQ) page, for example, identifies "vilification" of men as the first of several "focal topics" within the men's rights movement, and claims, "Men are regularly vilified and demeaned, both in the media and by feminist and government groups" (MensRights FAQ 2015).

From the somewhat superficial point that feminism takes an interest in women, and at least some women identify as lesbian or queer, to the more substantive point that feminism is invested in expanding the social roles to which women have access, and women who identify as lesbian or queer typically disrupt at least some of the expectations associated with traditional women's roles, feminist theory is closely connected with theories of sexuality. This connection notwithstanding, however, these fields also have areas of disconnection and disagreement, particularly regarding the question of essentialism. Briefly, essentialism is the idea that there are specific properties that are intrinsic to and definitive of any particular thing or type of thing.

Born This Way

The prevailing position among many contemporary lesbian and gay rights advocates is that sexuality is fixed from birth. Those who adhere to this account often regard the suggestion that sexual identity is a matter of personal choice or the product of socialization as a threat to the campaign for legal and social equality. This concern is likely fueled by critics of lesbian and gay acceptance who have been quick to attribute lesbian and gay identity to personal and social causal factors. Lesbian and gay rights advocates, however, often maintain that sexuality is something that we simply are, and not something that we do or become. The reasoning that accompanies this position is that it makes sense to hold people accountable, be it individually or collectively, only for what can be attributed to human agency, and not for what is beyond our individual or collective control.

Whereas many lesbian and gay rights advocates deny that sexuality is something for which we can be held personally or socially responsible, radical feminism has a history of enthusiastically and unapologetically attributing lesbian identity to personal choice and even upholding lesbian identity as something that can be adopted, and indeed should be adopted, as a voluntary alternative to what is sometimes referred to as compulsory heterosexuality, or heteronormativity. This branch of radical feminism, which is less prevalent today than it was in the late 1960s and early 1970s, is usually referred to as radical lesbian feminism, though it is sometimes also referred to simply as lesbian feminism, or as separatist feminism, lesbian separatism, radical lesbian separatist feminism, and so forth. Regardless of the label used, it is important to note that the pairing of "lesbian" and "feminist" is not simply a reference to lesbians who just happen to be feminists (nor to feminists who just happen to be lesbians). Nor does this pairing indicate an automatic connection between being a lesbian and being a feminist; there are certainly lesbians who do not identify as feminists (as well as feminists who do not identify as lesbians). According to the ideology of radical lesbian feminism, however, such a connection *ought* to exist between feminist identity and lesbian identity, because, on this account, lesbian existence is the ultimate expression of feminist ideals. According to many, including Charlotte Bunch (1975), Sheila Jeffreys (1991), Monique Wittig (1992), and Adrienne Rich (1993), and others, heterosexuality supports the oppression of women by men. Monique Wittig, for example, indicates that heterosexuality allows men to "appropriate for themselves the reproduction and production of women and also their physical persons by means of a contract called the marriage contract" (1992: 7). Adrienne Rich refers to lesbian existence as "an act of resistance" against this arrangement, "a direct or indirect attack on male right of access to women." (1993: 239). Similarly, Sheila Jeffreys (1991) suggests that women who experience sexual pleasure with men do so by only by eroticizing their own subordination, while lesbian existence offers women the possibility of experiencing sexual pleasure between equal partners.

Just what is meant by lesbian existence is neither clear nor consistent, even among those who seem united through their shared interest in promoting it as an expression of feminism. It might be tempting to assume that it refers unproblematically to women whose preferred object of sexual intimacy is other women, but Audre Lorde resists this definition, along with the notion that lesbian consciousness arises from specific sexual experiences (Hammond 1980).

For Lorde, lesbian sexuality is a potential component of lesbian existence, and hence of lesbian feminism, but it is not a necessary component of either. On this understanding, being a lesbian has at least as much to do with being aligned emotionally, politically, and symbolically with other women as it has with being aligned sexually with other women. Even so, words are not chosen at random. "Lesbian" has unmistakably sexual connotations, and the decision to characterize lesbian identity as a voluntary form of feminist expression is simultaneously a decision to characterize lesbian sexuality in a manner that runs counter to the rhetoric of contemporary lesbian and gay rights advocacy. Contemporary lesbian and gay rights advocacy centers on the assumption that, whatever our sexuality, we were, in the words of pop icon Lady Gaga, "born this way."

Not Born a Woman

Gender is a familiar concept today, but it did not come into widespread popular use until the 1970s. Feminist theorists introduced the distinction between sex and gender in order to provide the necessary terminology to differentiate the characteristics of women and men that are thought to be the direct result of biological sex, such as different genital and hormonal patterns, from the characteristics of women and men that are thought to be the result of socialization and learning, such as differences in clothing and grooming patterns. There is a great deal of disagreement in scholarly as well as popular discussions regarding the boundary between sex and gender, both in general and in regard to particular characteristics. Some have little use for the concept of gender because they attribute virtually everything—from how likely we are to seek multiple sexual partners to whether we are good at multitasking—to biological sex. Others, however, particularly some feminists, attribute the vast majority of what makes us who we are as women and men to gender socialization.

To add an element of confusion to the public discourse on gender, its popular use seems to have drifted away from what feminists had in mind when they began using it in the 1970s as a strategy for expressing the belief that, in the words of Simone de Beauvoir, "One is not born, but rather becomes, a woman" (1974 [1949]: 295). Increasingly, references to gender within mainstream popular culture use it as a straightforward synonym for biological sex. Consider, for instance, the use of the expression "gender testing" to refer both to the controversial practice of performing DNA tests on athletes to ensure that those competing as women are indeed biologically female (Kolata 1992; Saner 2008), as well as the somewhat less controversial practice of using ultrasound imaging of unborn fetuses to help expectant parents select names, clothing, and toys in accordance with cultural norms about raising girls and boys. What a DNA test can actually identify is one set of biological criteria (in this case, chromosome patterns) used for categorizing people as female, as male or, less frequently, as intersex. What an ultrasound can actually identify is another set of biological criteria (in this case, genital structures) used for categorizing people as female, as male or, less frequently, as intersex. In the case of the athletes, the *gender* is already known. The question that underlies the testing is not an effort to determine the gender of the athletes, but rather to determine whether their gender matches the sex categories to which they are believed to belong. In the case of unborn fetuses, their gender socialization begins when, perhaps as a result of an ultrasound, they are assigned the names, clothing, toys, and various other artifacts that will begin to identify them, not merely as newborn infants, but as newborn girls and boys.

To add yet another element of confusion to an increasingly complicated conversation, while many feminist theorists, particularly most liberal feminists, are critical of the process of gender socialization, there are also some feminist theorists, particularly some radical feminists, who reject the very concept of gender and therefore identify as gender critical feminists. What makes this situation confusing, of course, is that, to the uninitiated, it would be impossible to determine whether the label "gender critical feminism" denotes the belief that gender exists, accompanied by a critical perspective on how gender impacts our existence, or whether it denotes the belief that gender does not exist, accompanied by a critical perspective, not on gender as a phenomenon, but rather on the existence of the concept of gender.

Not all radical feminists label themselves as gender critical. Among those who do, this label was developed as an alternative to "trans exclusionary," which has been applied to them by others, particularly transgender theorists, who reject their position regarding transgender identity (Williams 2014). According to trans exclusionary radical feminism, the separation of the sexes, and the subsequent oppression of women by men, is an innate feature of human existence. On this account, transgender women are, in virtue of their assignment at birth as male, inevitably still men, and this is not something that can be changed by act of will, nor even as the result of medical intervention.

Whereas contemporary lesbian and gay rights theory maintains that, regardless of how we identify our sexuality, we were "born this way," liberal feminism claims that "one is not born, but rather becomes a woman" through the process of gender socialization. In other words, lesbian and gay rights theory claims that important identity features (namely, sexuality) are innate, and therefore are beyond the scope of what we change, while liberal feminism claims that important identity features (namely, gender) are socially constructed and therefore fall within the scope of what we can change. Both positions are present within radical feminism. Gender critical radical feminism maintains that some identity features (namely, sex) are innate and thus beyond the scope of change, while radical lesbian feminism maintains that some identity features (namely, sexuality) are within the scope of change. It might seem as if these two forms of radical feminism have nothing in common because of their different ideas about what is innate and what is open to change. However, when we shift to examine the motivations and consequences attached to each of these positions, different connections are revealed.

We Are the Same

Unlike lesbian and gay rights advocates who defend biological determinism in order to deny personal or social accountability for the production of lesbian and gay identities, liberal feminists use the distinction between sex and gender to deny biological determinism. Despite their mutual interest in securing legal and social equality, lesbian and gay rights theorists and liberal feminists adopt what initially might appear to be antithetical strategies. Ironically, however, closer inspection reveals that the reasoning that goes into these two strategies is actually quite similar. In either case, the twofold message to the dominant group is, first, that we are all fundamentally the same and, second, that the absence of a principled basis for unequal treatment constitutes a case in favor of equal treatment. In the case of sexuality, the claim that we are all fundamentally the same refers, not to our sexual inclinations themselves, but rather to the manner in which those inclinations are experienced. While lesbian women and gay men are not the same as heterosexual women and men when it comes to partner choice, we are all the same insofar as we experience our sexual attractions as spontaneous and natural, rather than as the product of conscious choice. People who disrupt this line of thought—be it the conservative Christian who touts the alleged success of sexual reorientation therapy or the radical feminist who claims to have chosen lesbian sexuality as an alternative to sleeping with the enemy—pose a threat to the prevailing position within contemporary lesbian and gay rights theory.

The liberal feminist claim that we are all fundamentally the same is in apparent conflict with the countless ways in which women and men are believed to differ. This is where the concept of gender is especially useful, as it attributes many of the differences that might otherwise be enlisted in order to justify different treatment for women and men to that different treatment itself. Early examples of this reasoning (which predate the term "feminism," but may nevertheless be regarded as proto-feminist, or pre-feminist) can be found in Mary Wollstonecraft's 1792 essay, "A Vindication of the Rights of Woman" (1967 [1792]), and John Stuart Mill's 1869 essay, "The Subjection of Women" (1970 [1896]), both of which raise the possibility that, given the same education and opportunities as men, women might be capable of far more than they were known to achieve at that time. Instead of using the apparent differences between women and men to justify different education and opportunities, which was an even more prevalent practice then than it is today (refer, for example, to Jean-Jacques Rousseau's 1762 book, *Emile* (2003 [1762])), Wollstonecraft and Mill identified the differences in education and opportunities as the potential source of those apparent differences.

In more recent years, liberal feminists have successfully used this same basic line of reasoning when advocating to increase the opportunities available to girls and women. One such example is Title IX of the 1972 Education Amendment to the United States Constitution. Although Title IX mandates gender equality in all educational programs that receive federal funding, it is known primarily for its impact on athletic programs. Prior to the implementation of Title IX, those who even bothered trying to defend the disproportionate investment in athletic programs for boys and men often did so by highlighting the inclination toward and aptitude for physical activity that seemed to come so naturally for boys but not for girls. In 1972, when Title IX was first enacted, only 7.4 percent of all athletes in US high schools were girls. After almost 30 years under Title IX, however, that number had risen to 41.5 percent. In 1972, there were only 32,000 women who participated in college athletics, but by 2007 there were more than 166,000 (ACLU 2015). These are just a few of the many statistics, from various surveys and reports, that all seem to indicate that it simply is not the case that girls are naturally disinclined to participate in athletics when given the opportunity to do so. It would seem to be the case, instead, that the apparent lack of athleticism among girls prior to Title IX was not an innate characteristic, but rather the consequence of limited opportunity.

Ever mindful of equality—even when it comes to establishing the value of equality— liberal feminists are often quick to acknowledge that gender socialization prevents men, as well as women, from achieving their full human potential. In a more recent example of liberal feminist thinking, United Nations Goodwill Ambassador Emma Watson made the following remarks in a 2014 speech to the United Nations entitled "Gender Equality is Your Issue Too."

> We don't often talk about men being imprisoned by gender stereotypes but I can see that that they are and that when they are free, things will change for women as a natural consequence.
>
> If men don't have to be aggressive in order to be accepted women won't feel compelled to be submissive. If men don't have to control, women won't have to be controlled.
>
> Both men and women should feel free to be sensitive. Both men and women should feel free to be strong . . . It is time that we all perceive gender on a spectrum not as two opposing sets of ideals.
>
> (Watson 2014)

According to this line of reasoning, women and men are fundamentally the same, but gender socialization creates the appearance that we are different. Furthermore, because women and men are fundamentally the same, we deserve to be treated the same. Finally, both women and men are in a position to benefit from eliminating the inequality that sexism has produced. If we could eliminate gender socialization, we could thereby create the opportunity, for example, not just for women to become better negotiators thus enabled to enjoy more rewarding careers, but we could likewise create the opportunity for men to become better nurturers thus enabled to enjoy more rewarding family lives.

For liberal feminists, the justification for social reform is an unwavering commitment to the belief that people are basically the same, regardless of their gender. Similarly, for lesbian and gay rights advocates, it is the belief that people are basically the same, regardless of their sexuality. The difference between the liberal feminist perspective and the lesbian and gay rights perspective is not so much what they say, but rather who they make the effort to say it about. Liberal feminist theory focuses on the oppression of women, but nothing inherent within liberal feminist theory precludes extending the same framework to an analysis of oppression based on sexuality. Likewise, nothing inherent within lesbian and gay rights theory precludes extending the same framework to an analysis of oppression based on gender. Indeed, there is nothing inherent within either theory that precludes extending the same framework to oppression based on transgender identity, racial identity, disability status, and various other dimensions of identity for which people are systematically oppressed.

It's Complicated

Unlike both liberal feminist theory and lesbian and gay rights theory, which presuppose that people are fundamentally the same, radical feminism in general, as well as radical lesbian feminism and gender critical radical feminism in particular, presupposes fundamental differences among people. For this reason, radical feminism does not generalize as a framework for addressing other forms of oppression. According to radical feminism, we divide naturally into two sex categories—in this regard they are in agreement with those who make the same claim as the foundation for deeply sexist ideas. For radical feminism, the sex-based system of categorization is an inherent feature of human existence, and the sex-based system of oppression is likewise an inherent feature of human existence. Because it takes sexism to be the primary form of oppression, radical feminism is not directly concerned with, and is occasionally even dismissive of, other forms of oppression.

While radical feminism is supportive of lesbian women, it is not similarly supportive of gay men. This is not to imply that it is actively hostile toward gay men, but rather that it is simply unconcerned with working to improve social conditions for men. For gender critical radical feminists, however, the notion that men are the natural enemy of women is so powerful that it extends even to transgender women simply in virtue of their biological history. Radical feminism is similarly critical when those who are biologically female express their identity in ways typically reserved for men. As Judith Roof explains, radical lesbian feminism is critical of the butch–femme dichotomy, which is assumed to constitute "an imitation of heterosexuality as *the* central form of sex/gender oppression" (1999: 29). On this line of reasoning, all other forms of oppression, including racism, are secondary to sexism. Dismissing racism is itself a form of racism, although it is certainly less blatant than the overtly hostile attitude displayed within radical feminism toward all men, including transgender and gay men, as well as some women, including transgender and butch women. As Barbara Crow explains, "While radical feminists attempted to work against racism with the tools that were available to them at the time, white women had yet to learn how central racism was to the struggle for social change" (2000: 4). White radical feminists eventually began to take seriously the experiences of Black radical feminists, and the movement has overcome much of the carelessly racist perspective of some of its early proponents (Crow 2000: 4–5).

Centered on the basic assumption of human equality, liberal feminist theory and lesbian and gay rights theory are consistent with other movements that emphasize equality, such as the movement to secure transgender acceptance and the movement to end racism. Even so, however, neither liberal feminism nor lesbian and gay rights theory has an unproblematic history of solidarity with other oppressed groups. Consider, for example, that when the National Organization for Women was first formed, its founder, Betty Friedan, sought to distance the organization from the concerns of lesbian women, and focused the 1966 NOW Statement of Purpose on the concerns of mainstream, white, straight women (National Organization for Women 2015a). Today, however, NOW clearly identifies "opposing bigotry against lesbians and gays" among the organization's official priorities (National Organization for Women 2015b).

The desire to avoid associating NOW with lesbian women is reminiscent of the desire, several decades earlier, among many suffragettes to avoid any affiliation between their movement and the abolitionist movement. In both cases, the underlying concern was strategic rather than principled. The strategy was not particularly effective, given that the Fifteenth Amendment to the US Constitution extended elective franchise to Black men fifty years before the Nineteenth Amendment did the same for women. What at least some suffragettes believed, however, was that it would be easier to gain support for the rights of just one group (namely, white women) than it would to gain support for the rights of two groups (namely, all women and all Blacks). Meanwhile, many abolitionists shared this belief and focused their attention on just one group (namely, Black men).

Similar negotiations are ongoing in contemporary discussions about the rights of gay men and lesbian women in connection with transgender rights. The Human Rights Campaign, for example, has been accused of devoting insufficient resources to supporting transgender people and issues.

> The point is that this has been a pattern with HRC over the years: proactively taking steps to publicly promote the idea that they're trans-inclusive and supportive, but then quickly throwing those ideals and the promises they represent out the window the moment they become a little inconvenient, the very moment when being a true trans ally would mean that HRC would have to be willing to step aside, just a little, and share the spotlight with the trans people that they say they want to represent and support.
>
> (Juro 2013)

Like so many other movements in the past, the contemporary lesbian and gay rights movement has been known to sacrifice the interests of other oppressed groups when they are in competition for limited resources. A common response to this concern is that it is sometimes necessary to focus on one group at a time because it is simply not possible to attend to the needs of all groups at the same time. Sometimes we just have to wait for our turn. Although Black men got there first, US women eventually got the opportunity to go to the polls as well. If we inadvertently (or perhaps strategically) draft non-discrimination legislation that does not specifically include transgender identity as a protected category, we can remedy that omission later.

Sometimes the concern is not so much which group of people is first to gain access to a particular goal (such as elective franchise, educational opportunities, marriage equality, quality healthcare, etc.), but rather who gets to decide which goals the movement should even pursue. Now that same sex marriage is legal in all fifty US States, transgender people are not therefore seeking legislation regarding transgender marriage. Although many transgender people supported the campaign for marriage equality, it was never really their issue. Transgender people were, and still are, more personally invested in issues related to healthcare, for example. This is where the notion, central to both liberal feminist theory and lesbian and gay rights theory, that we are all the same and deserve, therefore, to be treated the same, begins to lose relevance. Whatever rhetorical strength is gained by assuming that we all share a common human essence is lost with the realization that sometimes we are not the same, that sometimes we do not want the same things. Ignoring relevant differences in who we are and what we desire amounts to erasure. Far too often, the suggestion to ignore our differences and focus on our common humanity, is really code for doing whatever it is that the most privileged (or least oppressed) person or group involved in the conversation wants to do.

Queering It Up

Queer theory offers an alternative to the rhetoric of an underlying human essence that renders everyone equal. "Broadly speaking," according to Annamarie Jagose, "queer describes those gestures or analytical models which dramatize incoherencies in the allegedly stable relations between chromosomal sex, gender and sexual desire" (1996: 3). To put it another way, much of what we think we know about how sex, gender, and sexuality are interconnected is confused as well as confusing; queer theory makes a project out of coming up with ways to demonstrate this confusion. Queer theory tends to employ the concept of social construction, thus regarding sex, gender, and sexuality, not as innate natural properties, but rather as categories created under particular social conditions, historical conditions, political conditions, economic conditions, and so on.

Queer theory takes the liberal feminist idea that gender is not something we inherently are, but something we become, and extends it to both sex and sexuality. Indeed, queer theory tends to be suspicious of essentialist claims, certainly about sex, gender, and sexuality, but about virtually all other concepts as well:

> Queer theory disrupts lesbian and gay studies, as well as women's studies, by avoiding binary contrasts between female and male, feminine and masculine, homosexual and heterosexual, and so on. Nevertheless, queer theory is compatible with the existence of female and male identities, butch and femme identities, homosexual and heterosexual identities, transgender identities, and various other identities that exist, be it comfortably or uncomfortably, within the binary system. Quite simply, queer theory does not dictate the eradication of existing categories of gender, sex, and sexuality, though many people assume that it must. Within queer theory, what is sometimes described as a rejection of binary contrasts is perhaps better described as social constructionism with respect to those contrasts. Recall that essentialism is the belief that various identity categories, such as female and male, feminine and masculine, homosexual and heterosexual, reflect innate characteristics that comprise the fundamental nature of the members of those categories, whereas social constructionism is the belief that such identity categories are historical and cultural developments.
>
> (Marinucci 2010: 34)

Liberal feminism implies that stripping away the socialization by which our gender identities are constructed, were it possible to do so, would expose our essential human nature underneath. Given the more thoroughgoing social construction associated with queer theory, however, there is no underlying human essence.

Abandoning the notion of a common human essence means abandoning the notion that our common human essence provides the foundation for human equality. It means abandoning the problematic assumption that we are all basically the same, and along with it, the equally problematic tendency to ignore our differences. It means recognizing our differences, but without thereby attributing them to differences in our essential nature in the way that radical lesbian feminism attributes the differences between women and men to differences between the essential nature of women and the essential nature of men. It means extending the liberal feminist project of interrogating the mechanisms involved in the social construction of gender to an interrogation into the mechanisms involved in the social construction of other identity features as well. It means interrogating the mechanisms involved in the social construction, for example, of sex categories, by examining the enforcement of rigid bodily norms. It means interrogating dramatic examples of this, like the practice of subjecting intersex infants to surgical alteration of otherwise healthy genitals, and it also means interrogating more subtle examples, like the widespread practice of pretending to be utterly baffled about which gender pronouns to apply in conversations with or about transgender people. Moreover, it means interrogating these practices as mechanisms that produce and reproduce the categories that structure our existence, and not merely interrogating them as possible human rights violations or examples of unequal treatment—though it does not necessarily mean abandoning the rhetoric of rights and equality insofar as this rhetoric continues to be a useful tool for resisting existing forms of power and control. Indeed, a queer theoretical framework can be meaningfully understood as an extension of the liberal feminist project, the lesbian and gay rights project, and even the radical feminist project, insofar as each of these projects, in one form or another, make it a priority to resist structures of power and control.

Further Reading

Calhoun, Cheshire (1994) "Separating Lesbian Theory from Feminist Theory," *Ethics*, 104(3): 558–581. (Addresses the complicated relationship between lesbian and feminist theory.)
Fudge, Rachel (2006) "Everything You Always Wanted to Know About Feminism but Were Afraid to Ask," *Bitch Magazine* 31: 58–67. (Summarizes various positions within contemporary feminism.)
Jagose, Annamarie (1996) *Queer Theory: An Introduction*, New York: New York University Press. (Discusses queer theory in some depth and detail.)
Marinucci, Mimi (2010) *Feminism Is Queer: The Intimate Connection between Queer and Feminist Theory*, London: Zed Books. (Discusses queer theory in some depth and detail.)

Related Topics

The sex/gender distinction and the social construction of reality (Chapter 13); gender essentialism and anti-essentialism (Chapter 14); through the looking glass: trans theory meets feminist philosophy (Chapter 32); feminist and queer intersections with disability studies (Chapter 33); feminism and liberalism (Chapter 52).

References

American Civil Liberties Union (2015) *Title IX Fact Sheet*, New York: American Civil Liberties Union [online]. Available from: www.aclu.org/title-ix-facts-glance?redirect=womens-rights/title-ix-facts-glance.
Beauvoir, Simone de (1974 [1949]) *The Second Sex*, trans. H. M. Parshley, New York: Vintage Books.
Bunch, Charlotte (1975) "Not for Lesbians Only," *Quest: A Feminist Quarterly* 2: 50–56.
Crow, Barbara (2000) "Introduction: Radical Feminism," in Barbara Crow (Ed.) *Radical Feminism: A Documentary Reader*, New York: New York University Press, 1–9.
Fudge, Rachel (2006) "Everything You Always Wanted to Know About Feminism but Were Afraid to Ask," *Bitch Magazine* 31: 58–67.
Hammond, Karla (1980) "An Interview with Audre Lorde," *American Poetry Review* March/April: 18–21.
Jagose, Annamarie (1996) *Queer Theory: An Introduction*, New York: New York University Press.
Jeffreys, Sheila (1991) *Anticlimax: Feminist Perspective on the Sexual Revolution*, New York: New York University Press.
Rebecca Juro (2013) "Even After All These Years, HRC Still Doesn't Get It," *Huffington Post* (April 1, 2013) [online]. Available from: www.huffingtonpost.com/rebecca-juro/even-after-all-these-years-hrc-still-doesnt-get-it_b_2989826.html
Kolata, Gina (1992) "Who Is Female? Science Can't Say," *The New York Times*, February 16.
Marinucci, Mimi (2010) *Feminism Is Queer: The Intimate Connection between Queer and Feminist Theory*, London: Zed Books.

MensRights FAQ (2015) *MensRights Subreddit* [online]. Available from: www.reddit.com/r/MensRights/wiki/faq

Mill, John Stuart (1970 [1869]) "The Subjection of Women," in Alice S. Rossi (Ed.) *Essays on Sex Equality: John Stuart Mill and Harriet Taylor Mill*, Chicago: University of Chicago Press, 125–156.

National Organization for Women (2015a) *The National Organization for Women 1966 Statement of Purpose* [online]. Available from: http://now.org/about/history/statement-of-purpose

National Organization for Women (2015b) *What Are NOW's Official Priorities?* [online]. Available from: http://now.org/faq/what-are-nows-official-priorities

Rich, Adrienne Rich (1993) "Compulsory Heterosexuality and Lesbian Existence," in Henry Abelove, Michele Barale, and David Halperin (Eds.) *The Lesbian and Gay Studies Reader*, New York: Routledge, 227–254.

Roof, Judith (1999) "1970s Lesbian Feminism Meets 1990s Butch-Femme," in Sally Munt and Cherry Smyth (Eds.) *Butch/Femme: Inside Lesbian Gender*, London: Cassell, 27–36.

Rousseau, Jean-Jacques (2003 [1762]) *Emile: Or Treatise on Education*, trans. William H. Payne, Amherst, NY: Prometheus Books.

Saner, Emine (2008) "The Gender Trap," *The Guardian*, July 30.

United States Department of Justice (2015) *Overview of Title IX of the Education Amendment of 1972* [online]. Available from: www.justice.gov/crt/about/cor/coord/titleix.php

Williams, Cristan (2014) "Gender Critical Feminism, the Roots of Radical Feminism and Trans Oppression," *The TransAdvocate*, December 8 [online]. Available from: www.transadvocate.com/gender-critical-feminism-the-roots-of-radical-feminism-and-trans-oppression_n_14766.htm

Watson, Emma (2014) *Gender Equality Is Your Issue Too*, [speech] HeforShe Campaign, United Nations Headquarters, September 20. Available from: www.unwomen.org/en/news/stories/2014/9/emma-watson-gender-equality-is-your-issue-too

Wittig, Monique (1992) *The Straight Mind and Other Essays*, Boston, MA: Beacon Press.

Wollstonecraft, Mary (1967 [1792]) *A Vindication of the Rights of Woman*, New York: Norton.

THROUGH THE LOOKING GLASS

Trans Theory Meets Feminist Philosophy

Talia Mae Bettcher

Judith Butler argues that professional philosophy has, in a kind of Hegelian dialectic, created its own mirror image by seeking to police its boundaries: There is much exciting theoretical work in *other* disciplines in the humanities and elsewhere, Butler says, that draws on philosophical traditions. As mainstream Anglo-American philosophy becomes increasingly rarified, this work outside of the boundaries of professional philosophy flourishes. Indeed, suggests Butler (2004), this work of the Other more properly captures the meaning of "philosophy."

This matters when it comes to trans theory since most of it has blossomed from outside the bounds of professional philosophy, which itself has demonstrated little interest in trans issues. Yet, while there is something right about Butler's view about the dialectical rise of Philosophy's Other, it also carves too sharp a binary. There is work being done *inside* the profession of philosophy that interfaces with the other philosophical work being done beyond its confines. Butler seems to suggest incorrectly that all of the feminist philosophers have left the profession of philosophy. And when one works at the boundaries of philosophy, in feminist philosophy, the line between philosophy and its Other becomes somewhat blurred.

This chapter considers some of the most important philosophical questions that have been explored by trans and non-trans feminist philosophers in the liminal space between philosophy and its Other: What is a woman? How should we understand trans experiences of dissatisfaction with their assigned gender, their bodies, and their desires to transition (I use the expression "gender dissatisfaction" in light of the pathologizing character of "gender dysphoria")? Finally, how might we understand sexist and transphobic oppression as both distinct and yet intersecting? And what light can an answer to this question shed on the first two questions?

Preliminaries

While trans people have been theorized by sexologists since the late 1800s, trans theory proper didn't emerge until the early to mid-1990s. Part of the nascence of US transgender politics in the nineties, trans theory was characterized by the coming to authorship of (at least some) trans people. Standard medicalized accounts of transsexuality came under fire and trans theory began to make explicit the oppression of trans and gender variant people as a distinctive form of gender oppression, one that wasn't reducible to sexist oppression (Stone 1991). Indeed, trans studies emerged *in response* to feminist politics and theory that had been expressly skeptical, even outright hostile, to trans people since the early seventies, best exemplified by the work of Mary Daly (1978) and Janice Raymond (1994 [1979]).

Instead, trans theory developed in tense, but close symbiotic relation to the queer theory that was then being pioneered by Judith Butler (1991, 1993). Indeed, it often drew on Butler's theory, which destabilized the notion of gender oppression by showing how queer gender (e.g., butch, femme, trans) subverted heteronormative gender in ways that traditional feminist theory foreclosed (Stone 1991). There were tensions, however, since some trans theorists strongly objected to the assimilation of trans theory into a queer paradigm. They worried that while Butler harnessed the trope of trans to make her points, she obscured the real violence that trans people faced (Namaste 2000 [1996]; Prosser 1998); they worried that Butler's theories required trans subversion to be understood in such a way that trans people who attempted to conform to heteronormative gender relations, could only be viewed as politically complicit (Namaste 2000 [1996]; Prosser 1998; Rubin 2003). Despite such opposition, trans theory has remained closely linked to queer theory. Yet with queer theory now finding an institutional home in academia, Susan Stryker argues, it has come to privilege the theorization of gender through the lens of sexuality and even left trans as the site of all gender trouble. As a consequence, she suggests, trans theory has become queer theory's "evil twin" (Stryker 2004).

Trans feminist theory and politics have now come into increasing prominence, promising an integrative analysis of sexist, trans, racial, and other forms of oppression. Consider a few examples. Intersex activist Emi Koyama pioneered an expressly intersectional analysis that highlights the importance of race and class (2003, 2006). Julia Serano (2007), the "Kate Bornstein" of a new generation, introduced and popularized concepts such "trans-misogyny." In Spanish and some Latin American contexts where "queer" has little semantic or political resonance, *transfeminismo* may now seem to replace or supersede it (Espineira and Bourcier 2016: 90; Stryker and Bettcher 2016). This is hopeful because it suggests a locus for shifting the center of gravity away from a universalizing tendency of Anglo, First-World-centered, trans studies towards something more genuinely transnational and trans-lingual.

Finally, "trans*" is increasingly being used as a replacement for "transgender" and "trans." The asterisk was introduced largely because those who saw themselves as gender fluid or genderqueer, neither man nor woman, had been left out of the "trans" of "transgender." This is ironic since at the inception of transgender politics, Virginia Prince's "transgenderist" (people who live in their gender of preference without undergoing medical interventions) was expanded into a broad umbrella term that was supposed to capture a host of gender variant people (Stryker 2008). Indeed, the theories of trans oppression largely identified a hostile gender binary as the source of transgender oppression. No doubt owing to the de facto dominance of binary-identified trans people (itself a dissonance between theory and practice), it appeared necessary adjust to the terminology. Whether "trans*" or "trans" ought to be used remains a controversial matter: some worry that it erases the specificity of violence against trans women, and others worry that it does no real work combating the erasure of non-binary identified people. Because most of the issues I discuss centralize trans people who are binary-identified, at any rate, I will use the term "trans" in part to avoid duplicating the problem that led to introduction of "trans*" in the first place.

Conceptual Analysis of Gender Categories

Philosophers have a long history of asking questions of the form "What is an x?" (I'll treat the analysis of the concept of x, the analysis of the category of x, and the analysis of the meaning of the term "x" as equivalent answers to the question "What is an x?"). And one can pose such questions about *man* and *woman*. Insofar as these are contested political concepts, however, they raise important political questions as well as methodological issues about the nature of analysis.

Consider the traditional analysis of *woman* as "adult, female human being." This Socratic-style definition specifies necessarily and sufficient conditions for membership. Such a standard definition can appear problematic from a feminist perspective in suggesting *woman* isn't a cultural category through which women are oppressed, but rather, a biological one. Moreover, it appears to invalidate the identities of many trans people who live as men and women but who may be regarded (by some) as female and male respectively. So it's also important from a trans political stance.

Jennifer Saul (2012) argues that the political intuition that trans women are women may lead one to rightfully reject certain analyses of gender terms excluding them or trivializing their identity claims. In effect, she argues, politics may be relevant to one's philosophy of language. Katharine Jenkins (2016) has pursued this insight by critiquing Sally Haslanger's (2012) feminist account of gender concepts.

Haslanger distinguishes between conceptual analysis, which yields the ordinary or manifest concept, descriptive analysis, which yields the operative concept (the concept as it is actually deployed), and ameliorative analysis, which yields "the target concept" that we should use for "our" legitimate purposes (2012: 376). She proposes the target concept of *woman* as, roughly, someone systematically subordinated on "the basis of actual or imagined bodily features presumed to be evidence of a female's role in biological reproduction" and *man* as, roughly, someone systematically privileged on "the basis of actual or imagined bodily features presumed to be evidence of a male's role in biological reproduction" (Haslanger 2012: 230). As Jenkins (2016) argues, trans women who don't pass as female or who aren't validated as women on the basis of presumptions about their bodily sex won't be viewed as women in this account.

Jenkins proposes another target concept in addition to the concept of gender as social class, namely, gender as gender identity (as a woman, say), where this is understood as an internal "map" that is "formed to guide someone classed as a woman through the social and/or material realities that are, in that context, characteristic of women as a class" (Jenkins 2016: 410).

She concludes that gender as class and gender identity ought to have equal weight in the ameliorative project which may take a branching route—two target concepts emerging from the same preliminary commitments.

Providing an account of gender identity is a messy business, however. Consider that in some ways, many trans women don't, when they first transition, have much of a map to guide them through the social and material realities of being classed as a woman. Sadly, this can leave some ill-prepared to deal with sexist threats about to befall them. Admittedly, in Jenkins' account, one need only take the social and material realities of womanhood as relevant to oneself in some way (2016: 412). One might worry, however, that in this account it will turn out that some trans women have gender identities of *both* men and women. Raised as males, some trans woman may have acquired a decent internalized map of the social and material realities for men taken as a class. The cleanest move may well involve avoiding the issues altogether through an appeal to sincere self-identification. Admittedly, this means trans women who don't yet self-identify as women aren't yet women (in this sense). That said, once she does self-identify as a woman, she may well re-assess her entire life by saying she's always been a woman (something we should respect, too).

Just as there are conceptual analyses proceeding from *a feminist vantage point*, however, there can be analyses of the gender concepts that proceed from *a trans political vantage point*. While ultimately *a trans feminist* analysis may be preferable, let's not insist on this for the moment in order to make explicit the possibility of such a politico-conceptual project. Instead let's note that an analysis shaped by a trans political perspective ought to accomplish at least two things: (1) provide an analysis that validates trans identities; and (2) provide an explanation of the invalidation of trans identities as a form of transphobic oppression.

Haslanger's analysis can be critiqued from a trans political vantage point as failing to aim for, let alone achieve, the second desideratum. The account does little work illuminating why claims that trans women aren't women and trans men aren't men, are in fact, instances of transphobic invalidation. The analysis of *woman* as "subordinated on the basis of presumed female sex" cannot accommodate trans-specific oppression. While such an account could explain how a trans man, presumed to be of the female sex, may be oppressed as a woman, it doesn't elucidate the mechanisms of his identity invalidation. The oppression involves not merely being placed in a subordinated class, but *in being categorized at odds with his gender identity*. While a class-based analysis may be useful from a feminist perspective, an interpretation-based analysis may be more useful from a trans political perspective. Methodologically, such an approach requires particular attention to ordinary concepts that are given in socio-linguistic practices insofar as they're often used to categorize/interpret trans people in hostile ways. For the rest of this section, I'll consider such a strategy.

In one of the earliest papers in trans philosophy of language, C. Jacob Hale (1996) argues that *woman* can be analyzed as what Wittgenstein called a family-resemblance concept. Such an analysis rejects the Socratic demand for the specification of necessary and sufficient conditions. One merely lists several overlapping features that some, not all, of the members have in common. While several of the features Hale lists are biological, many are explicitly cultural, such as leisure pursuits, occupation, and gender presentation.

The analysis has a benefit, from a feminist perspective, in elucidating how *woman* contains at least some cultural content. And it may also appear to support a trans political project by broadening the analysis of gender concepts in moving away from traditional definitions. For example, at least some trans women will count as women since they'll possess enough of the features. Moreover, the invalidation of their identities can be understood as the wrongful insistence on a Socratic-style definition that, in centralizing sex characteristics such as genitalia, leaves out the cultural content that is in fact relevant to the concept.

Yet, it appears the analysis is actually problematic from a trans political vantage point in implying many trans people are still wrong about their self-identities. Consider that in Corvino's (2000) family resemblance account, individuals who possess some of the features (gender identity, gender expression, sexual orientation, gender presentation) but not all (biological sex) ought to be considered "intergendered." This leads to the result that such individuals who identify as men and women are wrong. Moreover, in *any* family-resemblance analysis, even in those cases in which a trans person's identity *is* validated, they'll nonetheless count as members of the relevant category only to a marginal extent, unlike many non-trans women who fall centrally within the category (Bettcher 2013).

To validate the identities of trans people, it seems to me, we must turn instead to the socio-linguistic practices that exist in trans subcultures (Bettcher 2013, 2014). In many of these subcultures, being a trans woman is a sufficient condition for being a woman and being a trans man is a sufficient condition for being a man. Thus, I've argued, there must be at least two sets of concepts in play—the ones that are given in dominant socio-linguistic practices, and the ones that are given in resistant socio-linguistic practices. From the "logic" of trans subcultures, which says trans women are paradigmatic women, it follows possession of XY chromosomes, a penis, etc., goes no distance in detracting from the womanhood of a trans woman. This inarguably departs significantly from dominant socio-linguistic practice. Indeed, it's *such* a significant departure that we must surely speak of two sets of concepts/meanings rather than one (Bettcher 2013, 2014).

With trans identities validated, it is possible to elucidate transphobic invalidation. Since trans identities are validated through trans subcultural linguistic practices, it can be useful to understand the ways in which the dominant socio-linguistic practices function to *invalidate* trans identities. The invalidation of trans identities can be understood in terms of a conflict between mainstream socio-linguistic practices and trans subcultural socio-linguistic practices (Bettcher 2014). This, in turn can be framed in terms of Lugones's notion of "worlds"—sufficiently coherent instances of the social that exist in semantical/ontological tension with other sufficiently coherent instances of the social where these relations are shot through with relations of power, that is to say, oppression and resistance (Lugones 2003). For instance, one might argue the standard definitions of gender terms that deploy the genus human being and the differentia of sex and maturity are actually close to the best analysis of dominant gender concepts/meanings.

This raises fascinating politico-methodological questions about analysis. Typically philosophers draw on their own linguistic intuitions in developing an analysis of ordinary concepts. However, there can be radically different intuitions depending upon whether one is familiar with only dominant socio-linguistic practices, or resistant subcultural ones as well. Which intuitions are of more philosophical value in performing the analysis? Why? This also raises important methodological considerations with regard to any ameliorative analysis of gender concepts. Can a target concept be given first by an ordinary concept arising in resistant subcultures? Indeed, *must* an ameliorative analysis be grounded in a pre-existing resistant concept if it is to have reach outside the narrow bounds of professional philosophy? And if so, has not the ameliorative analysis simply collapsed into a conceptual/descriptive analysis of resistant concepts?

Trans Embodiment

Trans gender dissatisfaction and the motivation to transition out of one's assigned gender category to another has traditionally been explained by appeal to a Wrong Body Account, which postulates an innate gender identity or body scheme incongruent with what is materially given. While that type of account certainly came under attack with the rise of the queer-inflected transgender politics of the 1990s, Jay Prosser (1998) theoretically and politically reinvigorated the view, bringing it into conversation with a social constructionist queer theory, and, in particular the early work of Judith Butler (1991, 1993), with the aim of carving out a space for trans politics that doesn't reduce to queer politics. Appealing to Didier Anzieu's psychoanalytic notion of the "skin ego" as well as Oliver Sacks' discussions of proprioceptive awareness, Prosser argues that the Wrong Body trope is a phenomenologically apt description of trans body dysphoria (1998: 68–69): For the pre-transition transsexual there is a contrast between internal felt self and external, material body. Crucially, Prosser proposes that the bodily sense of oneself arises fundamentally *from* the body, undercutting social constructionist theories of sex of the type posited in queer theory (1998: 7, 65).

There are, however, serious difficulties with this view. Once the categories *female* and *male* are viewed as every bit as socially constituted as the categories *man* and *woman*, the claim that there is an innate experience of oneself as male or female can't get off the ground. Moreover, the account forces a sharp theoretical distinction between trans people who desire technological alterations of the body and those who desire only a change in gender presentation and social recognition. But the differences between binary-identified trans people (trans men and trans women) who seek various types of bodily alterations and those who do not appear to be merely idiosyncratic.

In response to Prosser's view, Gayle Salamon (2010) has highlighted the implausibility of viewing proprioceptive awareness of the body as somehow culturally-transcendent. She argues that the body postulated in such a view is ultimately unrecognizable as human (Salamon 2010: 88). Indeed, she argues that "Prosser asks the wrong question" and suggests "that the usefulness of the body image for theorizing gendered embodiment is precisely not that the body image is material, but that it allows for a resignification of materiality itself" (Salamon 2010: 38)

While Salamon draws from many psychoanalytic thinkers, Schilder's (1950) account of body image plays an important role in her understanding of how it works (Salamon 2010: 29–34). In this view, the postural body image rather than arising innately is built up over time through experiential contact with the world (including interactions with other people) (Schilder 1950: 30). Crucially, this body image is much dependent upon one's history of experience, unintelligible without memory: The body image is historically-layered, and "encrusted" as an accumulation over time. Consequently, the body image may well be at odds with one's material body, allowing for a lack of complete fit between body image and the material body. Schilder thereby de-pathologizes phantom limb experiences, pointing to the normality of a disjunction between internal body image and the material body. This is important for Salamon, who wishes to argue that since an incongruence between body image and body is an ordinary affair, trans people who experience this incongruence cannot be viewed as aberrant (2010: 2).

It is doubtful, however, that this can adequately explain the origin of trans experiences of incongruence. Consider a trans person who is raised to see themselves as male and to follow male-assigned gender norms. While the body image may be layered, saturated and encrusted through historical accumulation, it is difficult to see why there would be a significant gendered incongruence between body image and the material body. What are the worldly experiences that this trans woman might have had that could have given her the body image of a woman, given her constant subjection to the norms that determine and gender such interactions in advance?

To be sure, both Schilder and Salamon allow for more than mere environmental engagement—affective investment in one's body is paramount. Salmon writes that "without that investment, our relationship to our bodies is one of depersonalized estrangement: my sense of the 'mine-ness' of my own body—and, crucially, even my sense of its coherence—depends on this narcissistic investment" (2010: 42). And certainly such investments allow for much less tethering to environmental engagement, thereby offering at least the possibility of an affect-saturated body image arising at odds with the environmental engagements proscribed in advance by gender norms. What remains unexplained, however, are just what these affective investments are and how they arise in the first place. Far from an account of the origins of trans gender dissatisfaction, it appears to be the virtual absence of one.

In this respect, nativist and constructionist accounts may be operating at different theoretical levels. While the broad sweep of the constructionist argument appears convincing enough, by itself it provides insufficient detail in explaining how trans gender dissatisfaction arises. By contrast, while the nativist account purports to provide such detail, thereby answering the question how one's sense of embodiment could arise in incongruence with not only one's material body but also the environmental engagements that have been normatively laid out, it is rendered ineligible by these general constructionist insights.

To be sure, the very question which demands a causal explanation for trans gender dissatisfaction may be rightfully viewed with suspicion: Does it not proceed with the assumption that trans lives are anomalous, in need of targeted explanation for their deviance from the norm? In this respect, Salamon's generalizing account does work disabling the marginalizing character of such a question. Yet a version of the question exists not for intrigued theorists aiming to explaining a curious phenomenon, but for trans people themselves who may very well wonder about the why's and the how's. Viewed in such a light, the question is not theoretical so much as existential, bearing on one's understanding one's own life. In this respect, Salamon may leave those trans theorists who point to the question how their gender dissatisfaction could have possibly arisen at odds with the norm-determined environmental engagements, still searching for answers.

It is also notable that Salamon's account, like the nativist account, centralizes internal awareness as an *awareness of one's body*. As such, the social phenomenon of public gender presentation seems somewhat marginalized. To be sure, in her account gender presentation *can* be incorporated into one's internal bodily awareness. For example, in engaging with one's environment through use of walking stick, a person without sight could incorporate the stick into her experience of her body as it served as a means of sensory, navigational engagement with the world (Salamon 2006). But what would it be to take the role of public gender presentation more seriously?

In Prosser's view, a transsexual's change in embodiment is deep, while a mere change in gender presentation is superficial. In my view, by contrast, what I call "proper" and "intimate" appearances are on par, equally morally laden, equally culturally constituted appearances. Consider that human nakedness as a cultural possibility is socially constituted through the subjection of bodies to moral boundaries governing sensory access within a system of interpersonal spatiality (Bettcher 2014, 2016). Indeed, because these boundaries are sex-differentiated, we may speak of two boundary structures, two forms, of moral nakedness, male and female. For example, female nakedness has two tiers (topless, fully naked) while male nakedness doesn't. When viewed this way, differentiated forms of nakedness (intimate appearances) couldn't exist without the presumption of clothedness—their possibility depends upon differential forms of public gender presentation (proper appearances). A change in one's proper appearance must surely be viewed as just as weighty as a change in one's intimate appearance; therefore, both are essential in the constitution of one's physical person as morally bounded. So what would it be to understand one's bodily experience as necessarily including normative boundaries, as bifurcated between the experience of the proper and intimate appearance of one's physical person? Such a view is certainly suggestive of particularly moral affective investments such as gendered dignity, indignity, vulnerability, and so forth. While this line of thought cannot be pursued in depth here, at the end of this chapter I briefly suggest one way these investments might arise in opposition to societal expectations.

Trans Feminism Conversations

Trans/feminist engagements can be distinguished into intersectional and interactive variations (Scott-Dixon 2006). Presupposing the concept of intersectionality, the former proceeds with the insight that trans and sexist oppressions can be blended with each other in complex ways. For example, Rachel McKinnon (2014) argues that trans women face "dual layer" stereotype threats. While a non-trans woman may avoid being "assertive or firm in argumentation" due to the threat of being perceived as manly, a trans woman may avoid it due to the threat of being perceived as manly, and hence a man.

An interactional approach, by contrast, proceeds by viewing feminist and trans theory/politics as distinct and asks questions about their possibilities for solidary. At first blush, this approach seems to arise from a mere failure to take seriously intersections of sexist and transphobic oppressions: The alleged contrast between feminism and trans theory/politics turns out to be nothing more than a contrast between (non-trans) feminist and trans theory/politics. Yet the historical facts are that US trans theory/politics arose in partial response to forms of feminism that were outright hostile to trans people. We can therefore raise questions about the underlying theoretical basis of those forms of feminism as well as the trans politics that emerged in response.

Cressida Heyes (2003) critiques the radical feminism of Janice Raymond (1994 [1979]), while raising worries about the particular vision of transgender liberation espoused by Leslie Feinberg (1998). Heyes argues that while Raymond erases the agency of trans people altogether, Feinberg endorses an agency unfettered by a feminist ethics of self-transformation. To say that one should be free to express gender however one pleases is to treat gender as a property of an atomic self, rather than as relational (i.e., expressing one's gender involves interacting with others in particular ways). When viewed as relational, it is clear certain gender enactments (e.g., misogynistic forms of masculinity) *ought* to be subject to both feminist and trans political critique. While rhetorically useful, the appeal to unfettered gender expression isn't a viable political move.

Beyond such concerns, however, there is an argument to be found in the work of Raymond (and others) that had hitherto remained unanswered—one concerning the semantics and politics of resistant terms such as "lesbian," "womon," and "woman" (when taken up for feminist purposes) (Bettcher 2016). Raymond's own version of the argument is obscured by an appeal to chromosomal essentialism as well as virulent transphobia (1994 [1979]). Because there is no space for detailed exegesis, I'll simply reconstruct what I take to be the best version of the argument.

The idea is that the self-identifying use of a term in resistance to oppression is both morally/politically and semantically constrained. It would be morally/politically inappropriate for a white person to claim to be "a person of color" because the resistant self-identification emerges from a specific history of oppression to which this white person has not been subjected. In effect, it would be appropriative. Moreover, the very meaning of the resistant term is given by a history of oppression *to which it is a response*. When a white person who hasn't experienced racial oppression claims the label "person of color" it cannot possibly have resistant meaning, and it's unclear what meaning it does have.

Heyes takes up some of Raymond's racial analogies. She points to Raymond's rhetorical question, "Does a Black person who wants to be white suffer from the 'disease' of being a 'transracial'?" and her reply, "there is no demand for transracial medical intervention precisely *because* most Blacks recognize that it is their society, not their skin, that needs changing" (Raymond 1994 [1979]: xvi). She points out, first, Raymond's claim is false insofar as there exists a veritable industry for cosmetic technologies designed to lessen the ethnically and racially marked features of the body. More deeply, she argues, the historical conditions of the construction of race and gender are importantly different, preventing easy analogies. She points to the historical role played by heredity in determining race, which helps undermine the possibility of "transracialism" (Heyes 2006: 271). By contrast, insofar as sex has been constituted as a core ontological fact in a strict binary scheme (unlike race), the conditions are ironically in place for the possibility of sex change as well as medicalized discourse, which reinscribes the binary (Heyes 2003: 1102; 2006: 277).

However, Heyes doesn't appear to address the radical feminist argument. While she points to the way that "changing race" has a history of being associated with "racial passing," leaving a nonwhite-to-white transitioner subject to accusations of "passing" (2006: 272), Heyes underdescribes cases in which white people pass as people of color. It's not clear why the argument that white people are both semantically and morally ruled out from using racially resistant terms doesn't apply in the case of gender terms as well.

Consider an individual, assigned male at birth, who lives part of their life "as a man," who then goes on to transition, now self-identifying as a woman. Since they may not have yet experienced sexist oppression, how can "woman" be claimed in any resistant sense? To be sure, one might allow that at some point down the road they may experience enough sexist oppression for the term to take on that resistant sense (Raymond wouldn't agree, of course). But this doesn't help secure a trans political vision that she's a woman as soon as she self-identifies and possibly earlier, so that the denial of her self-identity is a form of transphobic invalidation. It won't do any good to claim that she counts as a woman in the dominant sense. At best she might count marginally. But if the legitimacy of her claim arises as a resistant sense, we'll need to know the oppression from which that claim derives its resistant import (Bettcher 2016).

I begin by noting that trans people are regularly harassed, assaulted, raped, and murdered *because* they're trans. They have trouble finding employment, have difficulties with appropriate healthcare. The list goes on. And I would argue that identity invalidation can only be understood as oppressive when it's situated within such a broader context of violence and harassment. Consider a particular kind of trans identity invalidation—"reality enforcement." In such cases trans women are not merely viewed as men, but as "*really* men, *appearances* to the contrary." This appearance/reality contrast is the basis for regarding trans people as either deceivers and pretenders. Such representations are not mere stereotypes, but arise as a consequence of gendered sartorial practices of bodily concealment. Because public gender presentation (proper appearance) communicates the form of one's intimate appearance, trans people taken to "misalign" public gender presentation with private body are situated within an appearance/reality contrast and consequently viewed as either deceivers or pretenders. The reason for this is that within dominant practices, public gender presentation *communicates* genital status. Importantly, this system of communication is an abusive practice of mandatory disclosure of private information about genitalia, revealed by genital verification practices and, less severely, euphemistic but invasive questions ("Have you had the surgery?") that attend reality enforcement (Bettcher 2014, 2016).

This view lays the ground for an intersectional trans feminist analysis as the communication of genital status is part of a more general system that constitutes and provides the resources for negotiating, closeness and distance between people ("interpersonal spatiality") (Bettcher 2014, 2016). It lays down the possibilities of standard manipulative (hetero) sexual engagements (for example, a woman's gender presentation, or her accepting a drink, may be taken to euphemistically communicate sexual interest, regardless of her intentions). While distinct, transphobic, and sexist violence are therefore blended together in a unitary system that leaves trans women vulnerable to both forms of oppression in interblended ways (Bettcher 2014).

And it also affords an answer to the radical feminist argument by linking the change in meaning of gender terms to a more fundamental resistance to an inherently abusive gender system relevant to trans-specific oppression (Bettcher 2016). In trans subcultures such abusive practices are not in play—public gender presentation does *not* communicate genital status, and the nature of one's intimate appearance is left entirely open. It's not merely that the meanings of "man" and "woman" have changed in trans resistant cultures, rather, the extra-linguistic (primarily sartorial) practices that provide the social context for the linguistic practices have themselves necessarily changed (Bettcher 2014, 2016).

This points to the resistant force of trans identities *prior* to transitioning, even though much of the violence bound-up with reality enforcement occurs afterwards. For example, the struggle to come out to oneself and to others as a woman or a man is invariably informed by the appearance/reality contrast and the deceiver/pretender bind (e.g., the fear that one might be engaging in deception, that one can only pretend). That is, reality enforcement as a condition of violence against trans people typically saturates the entire process of transition, leading to the conclusion that the work of transition is, of necessity, resistant. Indeed, it's not implausible to suppose that very trans affective investments in both public and intimate manifestations of their bodies that help motivate transition (discussed in the previous section) might themselves be seen as arising at odds with their original assignments, providing the foundation for trans gender dissatisfaction and the desire to transition. That is, trans affective investments at the root of gender dissatisfaction may be inherently resistant in character—a reaction to an inherently abusive system. If so, the problematic nature of the question why trans people are motivated to transition might be turned inside out by asking, instead, why non-trans people aren't similarly motivated.

Further Reading

Diaz-Leon, Esa (2016) "'Woman' as a Politically Significant Term: A Solution to the Puzzle," *Hypatia* 31(2): 245–258.

Heyes, Cressida (2003) "Feminist Solidarity after Queer Theory: The Case of Transgender," *Signs: Journal of Women in Culture and Society* 28(4): 1093–1120.

Kapusta, Stephanie (2016) "Misgendering and Its Moral Contestability," *Hypatia* 31(3): 502–519.

McKinnon, Rachel (forthcoming) "The Epistemology of Propaganda," *Philosophy and Phenomenological Research*.

Overall, Christine (2004) "Transsexualism and 'Transracialism,'" *Social Philosophy Today* 20(3): 183–193.

Watson, Lori (2016) "The Woman Question," *Transgender Studies Quarterly* 3(1–2): 248–255.

Related Topics

The sex/gender distinction and the social construction of reality (Chapter 13); gender essentialism and anti-essentialism (Chapter 14); materialism: sex, gender, and what lies beneath (Chapter 16); personal identity and relational selves (Chapter 18); epistemic injustice, ignorance, and trans experience (Chapter 22); the genealogy and viability of the concept of intersectionality (Chapter 28); feminist theory, lesbian theory, and queer theory (Chapter 31); feminist and queer intersections with disability studies (Chapter 33).

References

Bettcher, Talia (2013) "Trans Women and the Meaning of 'Woman,'" in Alan Soble, Nicholas Power, Raja Halwani (Eds.) *Philosophy of Sex: Contemporary Readings* 6th ed., Lanham, MD: Rowman & Littlefield, 233–250.

—— (2014) "Trapped in the Wrong Theory: Rethinking Trans Oppression and Resistance," *Signs: Journal of Women in Culture and Society* 39(2): 43–65.

—— (2016) "Intersexuality, Transsexuality, Transgender," in Lisa Jane Disch and Mary Hawkesworth (Eds.) *Oxford Handbook of Feminist Theory*, Oxford: Oxford University Press, 407–427.

Butler, Judith (1990) *Gender Trouble: Feminism and the Subversion of Identity*, New York: Routledge.

—— (1993) *Bodies that Matter: On the Discursive Limits of Sex*, New York: Routledge.

—— (2004) "Can the 'Other' of Philosophy Speak?" in *Undoing Gender*, New York: Routledge, 232–250.

Corvino, John (2000) "Analyzing Gender," *Southwest Philosophy Review* 17(1): 173–180.

Daly, Mary (1978) *Gyn/Ecology: The Metaethics of Radical Feminism*, Boston, MA: Beacon Press.

Espineira, Karine and Bourcier, Marie-Hélène/Sam (2016)"Transfeminism: Something Else, Somewhere Else," *Transgender Studies Quarterly* 3(1–2): 86–96.

Feinberg, Leslie (1998) *Trans Liberation: Beyond Pink or Blue*, Boston, MA: Beacon Press.

Hale, C. Jacob (1996) "Are Lesbians Women?" *Hypatia: A Journal of Feminist Philosophy* 11(2): 94–121.

Haslanger, Sally (2012) *Resisting Reality: Social Construction and Social Critique*, Oxford: Oxford University Press.

Heyes, Cressida (2003) "Feminist Solidarity after Queer Theory: The Case of Transgender," *Signs: Journal of Women in Culture and Society* 28(4): 1093–1120.

——(2006) "Changing Race, Changing Sex: The Ethics of Self-Transformation," *Journal of Social Philosophy* 37(2): 266–282.

Jenkins, Katharine (2016) "Amelioration and Inclusion: Gender Identity and the Concept of Woman," *Ethics* 126(2): 394–421.

Lugones, María (2003) *Pilgrimages/Peregrinajes: Theorizing Coalition against Multiple Oppressions*, Lanham, MD: Rowman & Littlefield.

Koyama, Emi (2003) "The Transfeminist Manifesto," in Rory Dicker and Alison Piepmeier (Eds.) *Catching a Wave: Reclaiming Feminism for the 21st Century*, Boston, MA: Northeastern University Press, 244–259.

—— (2006) "Whose Feminism Is It Anyway? The Unspoken Racism of the Trans Inclusion Debate," in S. Stryker and S. Whittle (Eds.) *The Transgender Studies Reader*, New York: Routledge, 698–705.

McKinnon, Rachel (2014) "Stereotype Threat and Attributional Ambiguity for Trans Women," *Hypatia* 29(4): 857–872.

Namaste, Viviane (2000 [1996]) "'Tragic Misreadings': Queer Theory's Erasure of Transgender Subjectivity," in *Invisible Lives: The Erasure of Transsexual and Transgendered People*, Chicago, IL: University of Chicago Press, 9–23.

Prosser, Jay (1998) *Second Skins: The Body Narratives of Transsexuality*, New York: Columbia University Press.

Raymond, Janice (1994 [1979]) *The Transsexual Empire: The Making of the She-Male*, New York: Teachers College Press.

Rubin, Henry (2003) *Self-Made Men: Identity and Embodiment among Transsexual Men*, Nashville, TN: Vanderbilt University Press.

Salamon, Gayle (2006) "'The Place Where Life Hides Away': Merleau-Ponty, Fanon, and the Place of Bodily Being," *differences: A Journal of Feminist Cultural Studies* 17(2): 96–112.

——(2010) *Assuming a Body: Transgender and Rhetorics of Materiality*, New York: Columbia University Press.

Saul, Jennifer (2012) "Politically Significant Terms and the Philosophy of Language: Methodological Issues," in Sharon L. Crasnow and Anita M. Superson (Eds.) *Out from the Shadows: Analytical Feminist Contributions to Traditional Philosophy*, Oxford: Oxford University Press, 195–216.

Schilder, Paul (1950) *The Image and Appearance of the Human Body*, New York: John Wiley and Sons.

Scott-Dixon, Krista (2006) *Trans/forming Feminisms: Trans/Feminist Voices Speak Out*, Toronto, ON: Sumach Press.

Serano, Julia (2007) *Whipping Girl: A Transsexual Woman on Sexism and the Scapegoating of Femininity*, Emeryville, CA: Seal Press.

Stone, Sandy (1991) "The *Empire* Strikes Back: A Posttransexual Manifesto," in Julia Epstein and Kristina Straub (Eds.) *Body Guards: The Cultural Politics of Gender Ambiguity*, New York: Routledge, 280–304.

Stryker, Susan (2004) "Transgender Studies: Queer Theory's Evil Twin," *GLQ: A Journal of Lesbian and Gay Studies* 10(2): 212–215.

——(2008) *Transgender History*, Berkeley, CA: Seal Press.

——and Talia M. Bettcher (2016) "Editors' Introduction," *Transgender Studies Quarterly* 3(1–2): 1–4.

33

FEMINIST AND QUEER INTERSECTIONS WITH DISABILITY STUDIES

Kim Q. Hall

The meanings of disability and gender are taken for granted in dominant Western contexts. Both are presumed to be the inevitable consequence of "bodymind" characteristics. However, just as feminist theory questions the taken-for-grantedness of gender, disability studies advance a critical approach to disability that denaturalizes and politicizes it. Within disability studies, the meaning of the concept and lived experience of disability is not understood to be an inevitable, unmediated result of bodymind impairment. Instead, disability studies theorizes disability as an important social category whose contingent meanings are forged, negotiated, and transformed within a cauldron of lived experience and relationships, conceptual and built architectures, normalizing ideologies, and the globalized uneven distribution of life chances. Disability studies scholars posit disability as a critical concept with which to imagine and create a theory and politics aimed at social, political, and economic justice.

Like all dynamic, vibrant fields, disability studies is itself contested terrain, and differences within the field have generated feminist, queer, transnational, and decolonial approaches. In what follows, I lay out some important discussions in the field, focusing specifically on intersections with feminist philosophy in disability theorizing about feminist, queer, transnational, and decolonial approaches; the models and meanings of disability and its relation to impairment; sex, gender, and disability; minds, bodies, and mental disability; disability epistemology; dependency, vulnerability, and justice; and the nature of philosophy itself.

Feminist, Queer, Crip: Theorizing Disability and Debility

Feminist disability studies is an interdisciplinary field that draws upon both disability studies' critique of disability and feminist theory's critique of sex and gender, along with their co-constitutive interrelationship with other axes of difference such as race, class, and sexuality in an effort to forge new understanding of power and difference. Despite various areas of contestation, feminist disability theorists share a concern that the co-constitutive relationship between gender and disability has been undertheorized in both feminist theory and disability studies. Feminist disability studies calls for more than an additive approach to gender and disability, aiming instead for a transformation of both fields (Garland-Thomson 2011).

Queer disability studies, or crip theory, shares feminist disability studies' interest in understanding the mutually reinforcing relationship between gender, sexuality, and disability. In addition, crip theory is influenced by queer theory's critique of normalization and identity, as well as the queer of color critique of whiteness as the unexamined identity that orients queer theory (see Muñoz 1999; Johnson 2001). Thus, crip theory builds on queer theory's critique of identity by questioning normalizing conceptions of disability in disability theory, politics, and communities, while acknowledging the crucial role of identity in disability activism (Sandahl 2003: 27; McRuer 2006: 35). While pointing to areas of generative intersection between queer theory and disability studies, crip theorists also caution against conflation of the two fields, turning their critical attention to exclusions within queer theory. Carrie Sandahl writes,

> My project of extricating disability studies from queer theory echoes the work of other scholars who have criticized queer theory's tendency to absorb and flatten internal differences, in particular to neutralize its constituents' material and cultural differences and to elevate the concerns of gay white men above all others.
>
> (2003: 27)

Crip theory interrogates the interdependence of systems of compulsory heterosexuality, compulsory ablebodiedness, and compulsory ablemindedness that deploys queerness and disability in the service of normalizing and naturalizing heterosexuality, ablebodiedness, and ablemindedness (McRuer 2006: 89). Building on Judith Butler's (1993) concept of critically queer, Alison Kafer and Robert McRuer argue for a disability theory and politics that is "critically crip" (Kafer 2013: 15–18; McRuer 2006: 40–41). A critically crip position understands the meaning of disability as open to revision and possible replacement (McRuer 2006; Kafer 2013).

Crip theorists critique the neoliberalism of a rights-based, inclusion-centered approach to disability justice (McRuer 2006: 2). Thus, rather than assume the common ground of disability identity, crip theory questions the normalizing boundaries that define membership in the category of disability. In so doing, crip theorists point to exclusions within disability theories and politics that also, paradoxically, reinforce one of the main targets of disability studies critique: namely, that the distinction between disability and ability is self-evident. The emphasis on inclusion of disabled people often relies on claims of similarity between disabled and abled people. Most often, the inclusion-centered argument focuses on disability as a shared human characteristic, something all human beings experience in infancy, when injured or ill, or in our elder years. Such arguments, according to McRuer, reflect a liberal disability rights politics that fails to pay sufficient critical attention to the fact that celebration and recognition of different identities is consistent with neoliberalism (2006: 2). One problematic consequence of a neoliberal, rights-based, inclusion-centered politics is that it enables the incorporation of privileged members of a minority group at the expense of its more marginalized members.

David Mitchell and Sharon Snyder use the term "able-nationalism" for disability politics centered on quests for access to the full benefits of US citizenship. Able-nationalism, according to Mitchell and Snyder, is a tactic of interpreting a privileged minority at the expense of the further abjection of the many . . . Ablenationalist inclusion models involve treating [disabled people] as exceptional bodies in ways that further valorize able-bodied norms as universally desirable and as the naturalized qualifications of fully capacitated citizenship to which others inevitably aspire.

(2015: 44–45)

Mitchell's and Snyder's concept of able-nationalism is informed by Jasbir Puar's (2007) notion of homonationalism. Both homonationalism and ablenationalism promote US exceptionalism by portraying the US as a beacon of a just and inclusive society that recognizes the rights of minority groups (in this case, LGBTQ and disabled people) and then uses this purported evidence of social justice to justify its violent practices in other countries characterized as more oppressive. As Nirmala Erevelles points out, globalized neoliberal capitalism and war produce disability in third world contexts, thus producing a situation in which Western countries like the United States point to anti-disability discrimination policies in order to portray themselves as promoters of disability rights while producing disability in non-Western countries (Erevelles 2011, 2014b). Additionally, a disability identity politics of inclusion obscures the neoliberal elimination of social services that support disabled people (Mitchell and Synder 2015: 38).

Puar questions the distinction between abled and disabled at the heart of Western disability studies' preoccupation with a representational, identity politics conception of disability. Reflecting on the assertion that we will all be disabled if we live long enough, a claim that has played a pivotal role in depathologizing and destigmatizing disability, Puar (2009) asserts that this claim normalizes a conception of ordinary life that is available only to the global elite. Locating disability at the end of "ordinary life," Puar contends, assumes that all bodies share a common temporal horizon characterized by general bodymind stability and health (barring congenital impairment, illness, or injury), a conception that relies on a universalized Western distinction between normal and abnormal to define disability (2009: 165–166). Instead, Puar proposes to place in question globalized assumptions about able-bodied capacity (2009: 166). Influenced by Julie Livingston's analysis of how the meanings of disability and impairment in Botswana challenge Western assumptions about distinctions between disability and ability, Puar uses Livingston's term debility to develop a critique of globalized neoliberalism's production of precarity (Livingston 2006: 112–113; Puar 2009). Puar argues that, within a context of neoliberalism, all bodies are debilitated or incapacitated in some way, but only the bodies of global elites are able to be recapacitated while other bodies are expendable (2009: 167–168).

Investigations into the history of disability as an exclusionary rather than unifying category reveal the white and Western-centeredness of disability studies. Accordingly, Chris Bell (2006) argues that the field remains ignorant of its white-centeredness. In his critique of the field Bell points out that most examples of disability discrimination and experience focus on white disabled people and that citational practices in disability studies privilege white scholars in the field (277–278). Given this, Bell contends that white disability studies is a more accurate name for the field. Erevelles (2011) critiques both the white and Western-centeredness of US feminist disability studies and the ableism of third world feminism. In addition, Erevelles (2014b) questions queer and feminist conceptions of disability's desirability as possibly constitutive of another version of disability as universal human condition. Erevelles asks, "How is disability celebrated if its very existence is inextricably linked to the violence of social/economic conditions of capitalism?" (2011: 17). As Erevelles points out, the social, political, and economic conditions that produce disability (e.g., poverty, lack of access to healthcare, war, epidemics, and racism) are not equally shared by all bodies; therefore, in order to avoid false universalization of the experiences of globally privileged bodyminds, disability studies must contextualize its analysis (2011: 17–18). In order to address these concerns, Erevelles calls for a transnational materialist critical disability studies (Erevelles 2014b).

Clare Barker and Stuart Murray (2010) also challenge the assumption of the universal applicability of Western disability studies' framework. They observe that while disability may be deemed abnormal in the economic north, the violence of colonialism, neocolonialism, and neoliberal globalization have normalized disability in the economic south. Barker and Murray argue for a situated approach to disability that resists universalizing Western ontological and epistemological assumptions about disability (2010: 228–229). In pointing toward indigenous communal conceptions of health, they challenge Western individualist definitions of normalcy that are embedded in Western disability studies' critiques and suggest possible future directions for a decolonial disability studies (Barker and Murray 2010: 229).

Kafer names her approach "feminist queer crip" in order to acknowledge the importance of feminist and queer theories, activism, and communities, as well as affirm crip resistance to normalization and commitment to radical politics of disability (2013: 15). Rather than present a more unifying, inclusive approach, Kafer aims to keep in productive tension areas of contestation and achieved provisional common ground that characterize coalitional possibilities between feminist, queer, and crip politics. Within a feminist queer crip approach, Kafer contends, disability is best understood as a set of questions rather than fixed definitions (2013: 11). To understand disability as a site of questions maintains a critically self-reflexive perspective on the use of disability as a unifying term, to situate its political potential, and acknowledge "the exclusions enacted in the desire for a unified disability community" (Kafer 2013: 17).

Impairment and Disability

Kafer offers a coalitional method that places in question distinctions between impairment and disability and the medical and social models that have been foundational in disability studies. Its critique of the medical model distinguishes disability studies from clinical and rehabilitative approaches to disability. The medical model conceives of disability as the inevitable result of bodymind impairment and is informed by what Rosemarie Garland-Thomson (2012) calls a "eugenic logic" that aims to eradicate or prevent disability. Thus the medical model conceives of disability as an individual's problem characterized by disruption of norms of bodymind function and/or bodily appearance.

By contrast, the social model distinguishes between impairment and disability and conceives of disability as produced by norms that characterize the built and attitudinal environment. Not all impairments count as disabilities. For instance, high blood pressure and nearsightedness are not considered disabilities in Western cultural contexts. While the medical model conceives of disability as a problem rooted in the abnormality of an individual's bodymind, the social model conceives of disability as a social justice problem (Clare 1999: 105–106).

While the distinction between the medical and social models of disability has been politically useful in the fight against disability discrimination, a critique of the social model has emerged within disability studies. Some contend that by overemphasizing the social model, disability theory and activism ignores rather than de-pathologizes real disabled bodies (Siebers 2001; Wendell 2001; Siebers 2008a). For example, Tobin Siebers and Susan Wendell assert that while disability is certainly a social formation, it is also an embodied experience of limitation that is not solely a result of ableist ideology. Siebers writes,

> I am not claiming that the body exists apart from social forces or that it rep-resents something more *real*, *natural*, or *authentic* than things of culture. I am claiming that the body has its own forces and that we need to recognize them if we are to get a less than one-sided picture of how bodies and their represen-tations affect each other for good and bad. The body is, first and foremost, a biological agent teeming with vital and chaotic forces. It is not inert matter subject to easy manipulation by social representations.
>
> (2001: 749)

In his efforts to develop a disability studies analysis of the body's agency, Siebers situates his approach within new materialist emphasis on the interaction between matter and meaning, nature and culture (Siebers 2008b). Similarly, Garland-Thomson proposes the concept of "misfit" as a feminist new materialist understand-ing of disability as "a dynamic encounter between flesh and world" (2011: 592). Such an account strives to be attuned to both the embodied experiences of disability and the social world that influences but does not wholly determine that experience. Conceived as a "material-discursive site of becoming," disability from a feminist new materialist perspective is neither individual pathology nor social construction (Garland-Thompson 2011: 592).

Pain figures centrally in both Siebers's and Wendell's critique of the social model. In their accounts, pain marks a boundary of the real bodymind that pushes back against the social model. Wendell (2001) argues that the centrality of the social model in dis-ability studies reflects the privileged experiences of the "healthy disabled." According to Wendell, the healthy disabled are people whose impairments have permanent and predictable effects on their lives (2001: 19). Conversely, the "unhealthy disabled" are people whose impairments affect their lives in unpredictable and inconsistent ways (2001: 19). Simply put, healthy disabled people are not ill, and unhealthy disabled people have disabling illnesses. Wendell argues that the distinction between the social model and the medical model has produced a distinction between disability and illness within disability studies and activism that fails to accommodate those who are chronically ill, many of whom are disabled women (2001: 19). Wendell asserts disability studies can

> pay more attention to impairment while supporting a social constructionist analysis of disability, especially if we focus our attention on the phenomenology of impairment, rather than accepting a medical approach to it. Knowing more about how people experience, live with, and think about their own impair-ments could contribute to an appreciation of disability as a valuable difference from the medical norms of body and mind.
>
> (2001: 23)

In other words, refusing to be silent about experiences of impairment need not involve a re-medicalization of disability (Wendell 2001: 23).

Other critics of the social model express concern about how distinctions between impairment and disability, like feminist distinctions between sex and gender, tend to naturalize impairment (Clare 1999: 6–7). According to Kafer, the assumption that disability is social and impairment is a physical fact ignores the extent to which impairment is also social (2013: 7). While some critics often invoke pain as evidence of impairment's non-socially constructed reality, other disability theorists discuss the impossibility of extracting pain's physiological features from social and cultural dimensions in lived experience (Pastavas 2014). For example, as Alyson Pastavas notes, the experience of pain is also significantly gendered and shaped by gender, medical and popular discourse, and the pharmaceutical industry, as well as biology (2014: 212). Understanding "pain as a cultural event" allows Pastavas to critically intervene in dominant cultural narratives that assume an intrinsic connection between pain and suffering (2014: 203).

Questioning the social model's distinction between impairment and disability leads Kafer (2013) to propose a third model that she calls the political relational model. The political relational model situates impairment and disability within social, cultural, political, and economic structures. It offers a provisional account of impairment and disability in the service of coalitional, transformative disability politics (Kafer 2013). A political relational model is critically and reflexively attuned to both ableist exclusions and exclusions within disability communities, and it emerges from provisional, coalitional ground between disability activism and other political movements that are not typically perceived as connected to disability, such as transgender activism (Kafer 2013: 12–13, 150–151).

Sex, Gender, and Disability

Feminist and queer disability studies challenges ableist and heteronormative conceptions of sex and gender. For instance, Eli Clare points out that gender norms are ableist (1999: 112). Being disabled places one outside the categories of "real man" and "real woman." As a result of failure to successfully embody dominant gender norms, the sexuality of disabled people has been rendered invisible in dominant contexts (Garland-Thomson 2011; Wilkerson 2011; McRuer and Mollow 2012). Thus, while feminist theory critiques the sexual objectification of women, many feminist disability theorists argue for the importance of sexual visibility and sexual agency of disabled women (Garland-Thomson 2011; Wilkerson 2011). Many queer crip feminist theorists advance a disability sexual politics that both makes visible disabled people's sexual desire and experience and offers resistant alternatives to compulsory able-bodiedness and compulsory heterosexuality (Finkelstein 2003; McRuer and Mollow 2012).

Rethinking sex and gender through the lens of critical disability studies suggests possible connections between transgender studies and disability studies (Clare 1999; Hall 2009; Kafer 2013; Baril 2015). Like lesbian, gay, bisexual, and transgender people share with disabled people a history of pathologization. For example, both homosexuality and gender identity disorder (GID) were categories in the *Diagnostic and Statistical Manual of Medical Disorders*, and many people diagnosed with homosexuality or GID were incarcerated in mental institutions and subjected to various treatments designed to cure them. Homosexuality was removed from the *DSM* in 1973, and in 2013 Gender Dysphoria (GD) replaced GID in the *DSM-V*. The intention behind changing GID to

GD was to destigmatize gender nonconformity by emphasizing the feeling of dysphoria with one's assigned sex and gender rather than gender nonconformity itself (American Psychiatric Association 2013).

Despite a shared history of pathologization, some transgender people reject the notion that there are similarities between transgender and disability. While he is concerned about the need to rely on disability anti-discrimination law to advocate for transgender rights, Dean Spade cautions against a transgender politics that aims to de-stigmatize transgender by re-stigmatizing disability (2003: 34). Spade resists the ableism that refuses to make connections between disability and transgender and instead focuses his critique on the medicalization of transgender that follows from the need to rely on a GID (or now GD) diagnosis in legal arguments for trans rights (2003: 34–35). While many transgender people desire diagnosis, Spade is concerned about the coercive and regulatory effects that seem to reinforce rather than challenge binary gender and the misuse of diagnosis (2003: 34–35).

There are important critical resonances between Spade's concerns about the medicalization of transgender and Kafer's critique of unintended implications of distinctions between the medical and social models in disability studies. Kafer stresses that criticism of the medical model is not a rejection of medicine or healthcare; rather, to critique the medical model is to critique the depoliticization of disability (2013: 5). Similarly, Spade's critique of the medicalization of transgender is not directed at the desire for access to hormones, surgical procedures, or psychiatric treatment. Instead, Spade critiques the gatekeeping function of diagnosis that determines access to health care and legal recognition of identity for transgender people. Spade argues for access to healthcare and legal protections that do not require proof of "desire for gender conformity" (2003: 26), and Kafer argues for conceptions of disability identity and forms of disability solidarity that do not rely on a diagnosis as proof of belonging in disability community (2013: 12–13).

Alexandre Baril makes a case for commonalities, not absolute identity, between transsexuality and transability (an able-bodied person's desire for body modification to acquire an impairment), arguing that both challenge cis and abled assumptions about "real" bodies (2015: 31, 39). Baril is concerned about a cisgender bias in disability studies and an ableist bias in trans studies that informs resistance to the development of intersectional approaches between these two fields. While both transability and transsexuality involve voluntary body modifications, Baril contends that the majority of work in trans and disability studies seems to assume that body modifications involving primary and secondary sex characteristics belong to gender and trans studies and all other body modifications belong to disability studies (2015: 37–38). Baril critiques "the ableist gendering and sexualization of specific parts of the body" (2015: 35). Against feminist and disability studies arguments against body modification premised on the value of real bodies, Baril contends that the assumption of a real body that is transformed by body modification relies on a distinction between "real" and "artificial" bodies that pathologizes and erases trans embodied experience (2015: 40–41).

Minds, Bodies, and Knowledge

Disability studies' prevailing emphasis on the body has tended to ignore mental disability and compulsory able-mindedness, resulting in a reinforcement of the notion that mental disability is innate and biologically real in ways that physical disability is not

(Price 2011; Kafer 2013). Furthermore, as Margaret Price argues, the marginalization of mentally disabled people within disability studies reinforces the Western assumption of a mind/body binary, an assumption whose gendered and racialized dimensions have been the subject of much discussion within feminist and critical race theories (2015: 268–269).

Feminist and queer disability studies approaches to mental disability suggest that philosophy's ableism may be rooted in assumptions about the relationship between personhood and rationality that are normalized in the field. In her critique of "conceptual exploitation" in philosophical writing about disability, Licia Carlson clarifies the connection between how disability is conceptualized in case studies and how disabled people are treated in the world (2010: 199). Her analysis reveals disability's ghostly presence in philosophical arguments about human nature, personhood, and justice. While disabled people serve as fodder for marginal cases in philosophy, their perspectives on their own lives remain largely absent (Carlson 2010; Garland Thomson 2015). According to Carlson, intellectually disabled people circulate in philosophical texts as silent, passive others against which philosophy defines what it means to be rational and thus a person. Working against philosophy's ableism requires understanding that the perspectives of disabled people along with critical inquiry into the social, cultural, and historical meanings of disability must be recognized as central to philosophical concerns about disability (Carlson 2010: 12, 17).

A note about terminology is important here since the words used to characterize mentally disabled people are part of historical and contemporary discrimination against them (Clare 1999). As Price puts it,

> the problem of naming has always preoccupied DS scholars, but acquires a particular urgency when considered in the context of disabilities of the mind, for often the very terms used to name persons with mental disabilities have explicitly foreclosed our status *as* persons. Aristotle's famous declaration that man is a rational animal . . . gave rise to centuries of insistence that to be named mad was to lose one's personhood.
>
> (2011: 9)

Carlson (2010) uses the term intellectual disability for conditions that have been included under the more pejorative category "mental retardation." Other disability studies scholars use the term mental disability to refer more broadly to the myriad ways in which one may fail to conform to "the normal mind" (Price 2011). The identity categories used by people with mental disabilities reflects how they choose to situate themselves in relation to the history of conceiving and treating mental disability, a history that has denied their personhood and agency (2011: 11–12).

Reason is a prized, defining ability in philosophy, and its conception as white and male has worked against perceiving white women, women of color, and men of color as "real" philosophers (Haslanger 2008; 2013; Hutchison and Jenkins 2013; Jenkins 2013). Dominant conceptions of rationality also circulate at the expense of disabled people. According to Price (2011), assumptions about rationality, truth, and coherence can function as unacknowledged modes of social purification in academia. As a mode of social purification, assumptions about rationality de-authorize members of marginalized groups as legitimate producers of knowledge.

Critics of mainstream philosophy's conception of rationality are often accused of advocating for the elimination of all standards. However, Price (2011) argues for the creation of greater access for mentally disabled students and faculty who have the potential to make important contributions to academia but who are unjustifiably excluded by institutions that are unwilling to think creatively about access. As both Carlson (2010) and Genevieve Lloyd (1993) assert, one can critique conceptions of rationality or reason without advocating for irrationality or relativism. After all, part of what philosophers do is unearth and question underlying assumptions, including assumptions about reason, rationality, and knowledge (Lloyd 1993).

In their 2014 special issue of *The Journal of Literary and Cultural Disability Studies* McRuer and Lisa Johnson use the term "cripistemology" to invite reflection on the meaning of disability as an epistemic space, a space from which one can know and a space from which knowledge might be reconceived (2014: 149). Cripistemology is informed by feminist, queer, and disability epistemologies (2014: 214). In his contribution to McRuer and Johnson's virtual roundtable that serves as an introduction to the special issue, Jack Halberstam suggests that cripistemology should focus only on limitations and failure at the heart of claims to know (2014: 152). However, some feminist queer crip theorists contest the use of disability as a metaphor for failure in queer theory (Johnson 2015). For example, Johnson critiques the romanticization of bodymind failure as a form of queer resistance, asserting that such appropriations ignore what mentally disabled people know about the embodied, lived experience of failure (2015: 251). Rather than a failure of knowledge, a feminist queer crip epistemology seeks to know truth and identity differently and reconceives what one thought one knew (Hall 2015; 2017, forthcoming).

Dependency, Vulnerability, and Justice

Ableist assumptions about personhood have informed Western philosophical theories of justice. Eva Kittay and Anita Silvers have offered major contributions to rethinking justice from the perspective of disability experience and what Kittay (1999) calls "dependency workers," people who care for those who are dependent. Kittay points out that dependency characterizes the beginning and the end of human life and that the majority of dependency workers are women (1999: xii). She argues that the exclusion of dependency from social and political concerns supports the pretense that all humans are independent and that any interdependence is simply voluntary, reciprocal cooperation between persons (1999: xii).

Disability theorists affirm the importance of critiquing the myth of human independency but nonetheless point to the reality that dependency workers do not always act in the best interests of disabled people. In fact, disabled people are often abused by family members and other dependency workers (Clare 1999; Silvers 2015). Accordingly, Silvers argues for the importance of acknowledging the violence that can be perpetrated by care workers and for a conception of disability justice that places the interests of disabled people at its center. As Silvers (2015) points out, improving conditions for dependency workers does not necessarily translate into ending discrimination against disabled people.

The term "severely disabled" is often used to distinguish between disabled people who are dependent from those who are able to live independently; however, feminist and queer theorists attempt to reframe and crip the meaning associated with it. Such efforts reconceive severe as "fierce critique" in order to "reverse the able-bodied understanding of severely disabled bodies as the most marginalized, the most excluded from a privileged and always elusive normalcy, and would instead suggest that it is precisely those bodies that are best positioned to refuse 'mere toleration' and to call out the inadequacies of compulsory able-bodiedness [and I would add compulsory able-mindedness]" (McRuer 2006: 30–31). Queer crip feminist reframing of the meaning of severely disabled fosters critique of the various ways compulsory able-mindedness and compulsory able-bodiedness "contain" disabled people (McRuer 2006: 31).

Disability justice also attends to the literal containment of disabled people in prisons, nursing homes, and mental institutions, and a number of disability scholars argue that prisons and carceral power are disability issues (Ben-Moshe et al. 2014). In particular, they investigate how assumptions about disability inform the historical and contemporary manifestations of carceral power in Western contexts (Ben-Moshe et al. 2014). Sue Schweik traces the history of "unsightly beggar ordinances" in the US in the 1880s and 1890s and demonstrates how discourses of disability, poverty, gender, and race produced the "unsightly beggar" as an unbearable "street obstruction" in need of removal and containment (2009: 1–2). Such laws appeared in cities all over the United States and targeted poor people who were forced to beg due to impairments, including impairments resulting from work or war-related injuries, that made it impossible for them to find employment. Schweik demonstrates how the ideology of individualism informed the ugly laws by casting the dependency as an individual problem rather than a problem of justice (2009: 5).

The "unsightliness" of disability and poverty in public is perceived as even more threatening when embodied by people of color. Erevelles explains how disability informs the school-to-prison pipeline that results in the disproportionate incarceration of Latinos and black men (2014a: 91). For example, students of color are disproportionately perceived as behavioral problems, a perception that leads to their segregation in school or their removal from school (Erevelles 2014a: 91–92). While bodies of white class-privileged disabled people may be objects of pity in an abled society, bodies of black disabled disabled people are targets for violence. As Michelle Jarman notes, there is an understanding in black communities that "acting crazy" in public can get you killed (2011: 21). In revealing and analyzing connections between disability and carceral power, disability studies theorists focus on state sanctioned violence against disabled people in public spaces and the violence of institutionalization, as well as forms of state punishment, like solitary confinement, that produce disability (Guenther 2013, Ben-Moshe et al. 2014).

Cripping Philosophy

Butler characterizes the contemporary situation of philosophy as one in which "the other" that has been excluded from institutionalized philosophy has become the site of philosophy (2004: 233). As she points out, it is precisely this so-called "non-philosophical" other that most people in other disciplines now recognize as philosophy. Thus, the question for Butler is not whether philosophy's other should count as philosophy; the question is whether institutionalized philosophy is itself philosophy (2004: 242). As Butler's discussion of the other of philosophy indicates, critical engagement with the disciplinary borders of philosophy itself is philosophical, and some contend that thinking philosophically from the perspective of disability occasions critical engagement with the disciplinary borders of philosophy (Hall 2015).

Cripping philosophy invites critical attention to how the philosophical is distinguished from the non-philosophical and to the consequences of that distinction, as well as the underlying "culture of philosophy" that informs it (Dotson 2012). It also enables, as Garland-Thomson puts it, a practice of recruitment that claims as relevant for disability studies work that may not be explicitly situated within the field (2005: 1561).

Philosophers who work in feminist and disability studies have discussed philosophy's ableism in two ways: (1) the field's demographics; and (2) the culture and borders of philosophy. In looking at the low numbers of self-identified disabled people in philosophy, some speculate that stigma and implicit bias against disabled people may prevent some philosophers from identifying as disabled (Tremain 2013). While acknowledging the importance of strengthening the inclusiveness of the field, others suggest that demographics alone cannot resolve philosophy's ableism for at least two reasons: (1) the question of who counts as disabled is itself a subject of much debate (Kafer 2013); and (2) members of targeted groups can harbor biases against their own group (Valian 1998; Fine 2010). Thus, addressing philosophy's inclusiveness also requires attention to the culture and self-definition of the field (Parker 2014: 223; Hall 2015).

Cripping philosophy claims disability as constitutive of philosophy itself. In their discussion of what philosophy is, Deleuze and Guattari state that the time for the question of the meaning of philosophy is the time of old age (1994: 1). It is, as they put it, a question that if asked correctly cannot be controlled. It is a question that opens its subject to transformation, to the possibility of becoming something other than it has been (Deleuze and Guattari 1994: 1). By locating the time of the question of philosophy in the time of old age, Deleuze and Guattari locate it in the time of disability, in crip time. Crip time resists normalizing, linear progressions of ableist time (Kafer 2013; Hall 2015). As Wendell (1997) contends, ableism is fueled by the illusion of control over our bodyminds, a control that denies the ever-changing, interactive emergent nature of material reality (Barad 2007; Alaimo 2010). These denials include, for Wendell, a denial of aging—the fact that no matter how strong the illusion of bodymind control, aging reminds us that our bodyminds constantly change. Perhaps one way to understand the significance of the claim that the time of philosophy is the time of old age is that it understands the desire for control as an illusion, control here conceived as desire for control over what philosophy is, can be, or will become. Cripping philosophy opens philosophy to transformation by the perspectives of underrepresented groups, and it posits disability and disabled experience as subjects, rather than only objects or case studies, of philosophy.

Further Reading

Barker, Clare and Murray, Stuart (Eds.) (2010) *Disabling Postcolonialism: Global Disability Cultures and Democratic Criticism*, a special issue of *Journal of Cultural and Literary Disability Studies* 4(3). (A collection of essays that analyze the meaning of disability in non-Western contexts and critique ableism in postcolonial theories and the presumed universality of the foundational distinction between impairment and disability in Western disability studies.)

Bell, Christopher M. (Ed.) (2011) *Blackness and Disability: Critical Examinations and Cultural Interventions*, Berlin: LIT Verlag and East Lansing. MI: Michigan State University Press. (A collection of essays that analyze the meanings of blackness and disability and critically intervene in the able body centeredness of African American Studies and the white body centeredness of Disability Studies.)

Davis, Lennard J. (Ed.) (1997) *The Disability Studies Reader*, New York: Routledge. (The first of five editions and a good introduction to early work in Disability Studies. It is worth looking at later editions of this text because each edition contains new essays.)

Hall, Kim Q. (Ed.) (2015) *New Conversations in Feminist Disability Studies*, Special Issue of *Hypatia* 30(1). (A collection of essays that offers a critical feminist disability studies perspective on how assumptions about disability inform feminist philosophy, feminist theory more generally, queer theory, and disability studies.)

Kittay, Eva, Schriempf, Alex, Silvers, Anita, and Wendell, Susan (Eds.) (2001) *Feminism and Disability*, Part 2, Special Issue of *Hypatia* 17(3). (A collection of essays that analyze concepts and issues of feminist philosophy and feminist organizing from the perspective of disabled women's experiences, as well as critically examine the meaning and significance of disabled women's experiences in political, professional, and personal contexts. See also Part 1 of this special issue of *Hypatia* 16(4) for essays that analyze the intersections of gender and disability and the meaning of disabled women's identity.)

McRuer, Robert and Wilkerson, Abby (Eds.) (2003) *Desiring Disability*, a special issue of *GLQ: Journal of Lesbian and Gay Studies* 9(1–2). (A collection of essays that seek to queer disability studies and consider how critical disability analysis might transform queer theory.)

Snyder, Sharon L. and Mitchell, David T. (2006) *Cultural Politics of Disability*, Chicago, IL: University of Chicago Press. (Examines the history of eugenics as a site for the emergence of the idea of disabled people as biologically abnormal. Suggests alternative ways to know disability.)

Related Topics

Embodiment and feminist philosophy (Chapter 15); materiality: sex, gender, and what lies beneath (Chapter 16); rationality and objectivity in feminist philosophy (Chapter 20); the genealogy and viability of the concept of intersectionality (Chapter 28); feminist theory, lesbian theory, and queer theory (Chapter 31); through the looking glass: trans theory meets feminist philosophy (Chapter 32); feminist ethics of care (Chapter 43); feminist bioethics (Chapter 46).

References

Alaimo, Stacy (2010) *Bodily Natures: Science, Environment, and the Material Self*, Bloomington, IN: Indiana University Press.

American Psychiatric Association (2013) "Gender Dysphoria" [online]. Available from: www.dsm5.org/documents/gender%20dysphoria%20fact%20sheet.pdf.

Barad, Karen (2007) *Meeting the Universe Halfway: Quantum Physics and the Entanglement of Matter and Meaning*, Durham, NC: Duke University Press.

Baril, Alexandre (2015) "Needing to Acquire a Physical Impairment/Disability: (Re)thinking the Connections Between Trans and Disability Studies through Transability," *Hypatia: Journal of Feminist Philosophy* 31(1): 30–48.

Barker, Clare and Murray, Stuart (2010) "Disabling Postcolonialism: Global Disability Cultures and Democratic Criticism," *Journal of Literary and Cultural Disability Studies* 4(3): 219–236.

Bell, Chris (2006) "Introducing White Disability Studies: A Modest Proposal," in Lennard J. Davis (Ed.) *The Disability Studies Reader*, 2nd ed., New York: Routledge, 275–282.

Ben-Moshe, Liat, Chapman, Chris, and Carey, Allison C. (Eds.) (2014) *Disability Incarcerated: Imprisonment and Disability in the United States and Canada*, New York: Palgrave Macmillan.

Butler, Judith (1993) *Bodies That Matter: On the Discursive Limits of "Sex,"* New York: Routledge.

——(2004) *Undoing Gender*, New York: Routledge.

Carlson, Licia (2010) *The Faces of Intellectual Disability*, Bloomington, IN: Indiana University Press.

Deleuze, Gilles and Guattari, Félix (1994) *What Is Philosophy?* New York: Columbia University Press.

Clare, Eli (1999) *Exile and Pride: Disability, Queerness, and Liberation*, Boston, MA: South End Press.

Dotson, Kristie (2012) "How Is This Philosophy?" *Comparative Philosophy* 3(1): 3–29.

Erevelles, Nirmala (2011) *Disability and Difference in Global Contexts: Enabling a Transformative Body Politics*, New York: Palgrave Macmillan.

——(2014a) "Crippin' Jim Crow: Disability, Dis-location, and the School-to-Prison-Pipeline," in Liat Ben-Moshe et al. (Eds.) *Disability Incarcerated: Imprisonment and Disability in the United States and Canada*, New York: Palgrave Macmillan, 81–99.

——(2014b) "Thinking with Disability Studies," *Disability Studies Quarterly* 34(2) [online]. Available from: dsq-sds.org/article/view/4248/3587.

Fine, Cordelia (2010) *Delusions of Gender: How Our Minds, Society, and Neurosexism Create Differences*, New York: W. W. Norton and Co.

Finkelstein, S. Naomi (2003) "The Only Thing You Have To Do Is Live," *GLQ* 9(1–2): 307–319.

Garland-Thomson, Rosemarie (2005) "Feminist Disability Studies," *Signs: Journal of Women in Culture and Society* 30(2): 1557–1587.

——(2011) "Misfits: A Feminist Materialist Concept," *Hypatia: Journal of Feminist Philosophy* 26(3): 591–609.

——(2012) "The Case for Conserving Disability," *Journal of Bioethical Inquiry* 9(3): 339–355.

——(2015) "A Habitable World: Harriet McBryde Johnson's 'Case for My Life,'" *Hypatia: Journal of Feminist Philosophy* 30(1): 300–306.

Guenther, Lisa (2013) *Solitary Confinement: Social Death and Its Afterlives*, Minneapolis, MN: University of Minnesota Press.

Hall, Kim Q. (2009) "Queer Breasted Experience," in Laurie J. Shrage (Ed.) *You've Changed: Sex Reassignment and Personal Identity*, New York: Oxford University Press, 121–134.

—— (2015) "New Conversations in Feminist Disability Studies: Feminism, Philosophy, and Borders," *Hypatia: Journal of Feminist Philosophy* 30(1): 1–12.

—— (2017) "Queer Epistemologies," in Gaile Pohlhaus, Ian James Kidd, and Jose Medina (Eds.) *The Routledge Handbook on Epistemic Injustice*, New York: Routledge.

Haslanger, Sally (2008) "Changing the Ideology and Culture of Philosophy: Not By Reason (Alone)," *Hypatia: Journal of Feminist Philosophy* 23(2): 210–223.

——(2013) "Women in Philosophy? Do the Math," *The New York Times*, Sept. 2 [online]. Available from: http://opinionator.blogs.nytimes.com/2013/09/02/women-in-philosophy-do-the-math/?_r=0.

Hutchison, Katrina and Jenkins, Fiona (2013) "Searching for Sophia: Gender and Philosophy in the 21st Century," in Katrina Hutchison and Fiona Jenkins (Eds.) *Women in Philosophy: What Needs to Change?* New York: Oxford University Press, 1–20.

Jarman, Michelle (2011) "Coming Up from Underground: Uneasy Dialogues at the Intersections of Race, Mental Illness, and Disability Studies," in Christopher M. Bell (Ed.) *Blackness and Disability: Critical Examinations, Cultural Interventions*, Berlin: LIT Verlag and East Lansing, MI: Michigan State University Press, 9–29.

Jenkins, Fiona (2013) "Singing the Post-Discrimination Blues: Notes for a Critique of Academic Meritocracy," in Katrina Hutchison and Fiona Jenkins (Eds.) *Women in Philosophy: What Needs to Change?* New York: Oxford University Press, 81–102.

Johnson, E. Patrick (2001) "'Quare' Studies or (Almost) Everything I Know about Queer Studies I Learned from My Grandmother," *Social Text* 21(1): 1–25.

Johnson, Merri Lisa (2015) "Bad Romance: A Crip Feminist Critique of Queer Failure," *Hypatia: Journal of Feminist Philosophy* 30(1): 251–267.

Kafer, Alison (2013) *Feminist Queer Crip*, Bloomington, IN: Indiana University Press.

Livingston, Julie (2006) "Insights from an African History of Disability," *Radical History Review* 94: 111–126.

Kittay, Eva (1999) *Love's Labor: Essays on Women, Equality, and Dependency*, New York: Routledge.

Lloyd, Genevieve (1993) *The Man of Reason*, 2nd ed., London: Routledge.

McGruer, Robert (2006) *Crip Theory: Cultural Signs of Queerness and Disability*, New York: New York University Press.

McGruer, Robert and Mollow, Anna (Eds.) (2012) *Sex and Disability*, Durham, NC: Duke University Press.

McGruer, Robert and Johnson, Merri Lisa (2014) "Proliferating Cripistemologies: A Virtual Roundtable," *Journal of Literary and Cultural Disability Studies* 8(2): 149–169.

Mitchell, David T. and Snyder, Sharon L. (2015) *The Biopolitics of Disability*, Ann Arbor, MI: University of Michigan Press.

Muñoz, José (1999) *Disidentifications: Queers of Color and the Performance of Politics*, Minneapolis, MN: University of Minnesota Press.

Parker, Emily Anne (2014) "Beyond Discipline: On the Status of Bodily Difference in Philosophy," *philoSOPHIA* 4(2): 222–228.

Pastavas, Alyson (2014) "Recovering a Cripistemology of Pain: Leaky Bodies, Connective Tissue, and Feeling Discourse," *Journal of Literary and Cultural Disability Studies* 8(2): 203–218.

Price, Margaret (2015) "The Bodymind Problem and the Possibilities of Pain," *Hypatia: Journal of Feminist Philosophy* 30(1): 268–284.

—— (2011) *Mad at School: Rhetorics of Mental Disability and Academic Life*, Ann Arbor, MI: University of Michigan Press.

Puar, Jasbir (2009) "Prognosis Time: Towards a Geopolitics of Affect, Debility, and Capacity," *Women and Performance* 19(2): 161–173.

—— (2007) *Terrorist Assemblages: Homonationalism in Queer Times*, Durham, NC: Duke University Press.

Sandahl, Carrie (2003) "Queering the Crip or Cripping the Queer? Intersections of Queer and Crip Identities in Solo Autobiographical Performance," *GLQ: A Journal of Lesbian and Gay Studies* 9(1–2): 25–56.

Schweik, Susan M. (2009) *The Ugly Laws: Disability in Public*, New York: New York University Press.

Siebers, Tobin (2001) "Disability in Theory: From Social Constructiveness to the New Realism of the Body," *American Literary History* 13(4): 737–754.

—— (2008a) *Disability Theory*, Ann Arbor, MI: University of Michigan Press.

—— (2008b) "Disability Experience on Trial," in Stacy Alaimo and Susan Hekman (Eds.) *Material Feminisms*, Bloomington, IN: Indiana University Press, 291–307.

Silvers, Anita (2015) "Becoming Mrs. Mayberry: Dependency and the Right to be Free," *Hypatia: Journal of Feminist Philosophy* 30(1): 292–299.

Spade, Dean (2003) "Resisting Medicine, Re/modeling Gender," *Berkeley Women's Law Journal* 18: 15–37.

Tremain, Shelley (2013) "Introducing Feminist Philosophy of Disability," *DSQ* 33(3) [online]. Available from: http://dsq-sds.org/article/view/3877/3402.

Valian, Virginia (1998) *Why So Slow? The Advancement of Women*, Boston: MIT Press.

Wendell, Susan (1997) *The Rejected Body: Feminist Philosophical Reflections on Disability*, New York: Routledge.

—— (2001) "Unhealthy Disabled: Treating Chronic Illnesses as Disabilities," *Hypatia: Journal of Feminist Philosophy* 16(4): 17–33.

Wilkerson, Abby (2011) "Disability, Sex Radicalism, and Political Agency," in Kim Q. Hall (Ed.) *Feminist Disability Studies*, Bloomington, IN: Indiana University Press, 193–217.

34

WOMEN, GENDER, AND PHILOSOPHIES OF GLOBAL DEVELOPMENT

Sandra Harding and Anna Malavisi

Introduction

In his 1949 second inaugural speech, President Harry Truman introduced a narrative about the need for well-off societies around the globe to help poor societies improve their standard of living.

> More than half the people of the world are living in conditions approaching misery. Their food is inadequate, they are victims of disease. Their economic life is primitive and stagnant. Their poverty is a handicap and a threat both to them and to more prosperous areas. For the first time in history humanity possesses the knowledge and the skill to relieve the suffering of these people . . . I believe that we should make available to peace-loving peoples the benefits of our store of technical knowledge in order to help them realize their aspirations for a better life . . . Greater production is the key to prosperity and peace. And the key to greater production is a wider and more vigorous application of modern scientific and technical knowledge.
>
> (Truman 1964)

Only the introduction of market economies into the underdeveloped societies could eliminate their poverty, he claimed. Poverty should be perceived as "a threat both to them and to more prosperous areas" because it had caused the social disorders that had enabled the rise of fascism in Europe and military expansionism in Japan. Moreover, the consequences of social disorder were even more terrifying to imagine after Hiroshima and Nagasaki. The availability of nuclear weapons increased the urgency of addressing how to eradicate poverty around the globe.

This narrative has now directed development projects for over six decades. Much that today is regarded as wrong with development theory, policies and practices has its origins in the narrative's assumptions. As critics have pointed out for decades, development policies and practices have succeeded primarily in de-developing and mal-developing most of the globe's already existing poor, and in further "developing" mostly the investing classes of the North and what have become middle-class allies around the world (Escobar 1995; Sachs 1992; Third World Network 1993). The gap between rich and poor both within and between societies around the globe has vastly increased during the development decades.

With the emergence of women's movements around the globe beginning in the late 1960s, feminists began to raise critical questions about how development policies usually not only failed to improve poor women's conditions but, worse, tended to remove even more resources from their control. The Danish economist Ester Boserup's (1970) influential account of how women were being left out of development was just the first of an illuminating series of analyses that came out of the new women's movements. Yet today leading feminist development theorists hold that women and their dependents have never been left out of development planning. Rather, women's labor and rights to land (along with those of poor men) were always intended to subsidize—to make possible—both continued capitalist expansion and the legitimacy of state policies that oppress the poor (Agarwal 1994; Jaggar 2009). In these accounts, "millions of men are missing" (to riff on a phrase from Amartya Sen 1990) from taking responsibility for the persistent impoverishment of women and their dependents through sexist, racist, and profiteering development theory, policy, and practice (Chant 2011). Of course one should expect the gap between rich and poor to expand under such conditions! Of course one should expect women's conditions to worsen!

Though philosophers have tended to focus on the ethics of development, a small number of analyses by feminist philosophers have recently begun to take up political philosophy and structural economic issues about development as well as revisions in epistemology and ontology of development that such work requires (e.g., Jaggar 2014; Jaggar and Wisor 2013; Khader 2011; Koggel 2013). These have learned from accounts by feminist economists especially (e.g., Benaria, Berik and Floro 2015; Visvanathan et al. 2011).

The first section of this chapter briefly sketches out the history since 1970 of how feminist economists and political scientists have changed how they think about the causes of women's poverty in development contexts. The second section focuses on the failures of mainstream development theory and policies to engage with just who is poor, what counts as women's work, and consequently how to reduce poverty effectively. The third section takes up mainstream philosophy's ethical issues about development and its failure to address both issues of social justice in general and of feminist social science and political theory in particular. The fourth section then goes on to highlight some of the recently emerging feminist approaches to social justice issues in development theory, policies and practices. In the final section of the chapter, questions are raised about how to improve the performances of the development professionals who design, manage and evaluate projects around the globe, but usually have little knowledge of either critical political philosophy in general or of feminist findings beyond the early liberal work on how women were left out of development projects.

Were Women Left Out of Development?

Ester Boserup's (1970) influential study argued that women had been left out of development policies and practices. Their brothers were given the technical education necessary to work in the new export economies created by the corporations and financial institutions that directed international development projects. Such jobs entailed rural men having to move to the new, often distant, agricultural plantations or manufacturing industries. The formerly communally held land, on which they and their women kin had worked to supply the daily subsistence needs of households and communities, had been appropriated as "unowned" by the newly empowered Northern development corporations and their local allies. Rural women were left as the primary providers of the everyday resources needed for their own survival and that of their families and communities. Yet they lacked the labor that their menfolk had provided as well as the traditional rights to the land on which they had farmed and herded cattle, and that had provided also water and the raw materials for clothing and shelter. The solution, Boserup argued, was to educate girls and women so that they, too, could earn wages in the new cash economies of these societies.

Of course there is much to be said for such efforts to increase girls' and women's literacy and their access to cash resources. Yet providing literacy for girls is not as simple a matter as development professionals have assumed. In poor families, girls' labor is needed in their households for child care, elder care, water fetching, cooking, gardening, and cleaning, as well as for work on household manufacturing for both household use and for sale or exchange: this is one reason why poor families need many children (Hartmann 1995). Moreover, poor families lack resources to pay school fees for daughters. Additionally, the absence of private toilets in public places such as schools leaves girls and women vulnerable to shaming, harassment, and worse.

The assumptions of 1970s socialist feminisms contrasted with Boserup's liberal assumptions. These feminists focused on how men's control of women's lives in households all too often meant that women could not get permission to work outside or often even to leave the household. When they were permitted to do so, their household duties siphoned off energy and time that limited their abilities to be as productive as their brothers in wage labor. Moreover, the sexist assumptions of their bosses and co-workers invariably led to their being underpaid and under-valued. This weak position in wage labor in turn deprived them of the financial resources needed to gain power in, or to leave, their often abusive households. This interlocking of women's disempowerment in households and in wage labor, and its accompanying violence, must end, feminists argued. Recently Alison Jaggar (2009) has pointed out how this interlocking of patriarchy and capitalism has insured women's inequality in globalization processes just as it does in local contexts.

Meanwhile, German sociologist Maria Mies (1986) argued that in fact women had never been left out of development planning. Their further immiseration, along with that of male peasants, had been envisioned from the beginning. Appropriation of rural women's and men's labor and land rights was *planned* as the source of the "primitive capital accumulation" that would enable development projects to succeed. Thus development was planned as a violent project from its origins. Yes, the "transfer" of scientific rationality and technical expertise from North to South did contribute to creating effective market economies. But the huge wealth that development delivered to already privileged groups around the globe required much more land and labor on which capitalism could exercise its exploitative magic. The kind of feminist analysis exemplified by Mies undermined conventional liberal assumptions of Boserup's account as well as Marxian assumptions.

Though the history of feminist approaches to development recounted above emphasizes its relations to Northern feminist theoretical traditions, attention to development issues has been one of the most important contexts in which alliances and collaborations with Southern grass-roots activists and theorists have influenced Northern feminist theory in general and especially its postcolonial theory. We return to important epistemological and methodological issues here.

More Unrecognized Facts about Women's Poverty

Mainstream development theory has consistently misunderstood and/or ignored additional gender facts (Benaria et al. 2015; Visvanathan et al. 2011). Failure to recognize these realities of development contexts accounts for a great deal of the persistent increase in gaps between the rich and the poor during the development era. Note how ontological, epistemological, methodological, and philosophy of science assumptions characteristic of research disciplines, including philosophy, are explicitly or implicitly contested in these analyses, as are the ethics and political philosophies of development to be addressed further in later sections.

First women's labor is consistently undercounted. Feminists have insisted on the importance of counting women's work not just as what they do when they are employed full-time, year-round, for wages, in child-free, outside the household, and formal labor contexts. These are the conditions that characterize the idealized male workers of modernization and its development theory. Women's labor, which also delivers socially necessary benefits, has not been recognized as real work by international agencies, social science data collectors, or labor unions (with the exception of the International Labor Organization) (Benaria 2011; Waring 1988).

What kinds of undercounted work do women perform? Domestic work in households: shopping, cooking, and cleaning. They work in informal markets, both street markets and paid or exchange work done in their own or others' households, such as cooking, child care, washing, cleaning, and managing household activities. They do "caring labor" with children, the sick and elderly, both in their own households and in their communities (Folbre 2001). In the context of globalization, this caring labor has become an international issue. Elites in the North are "care deficient," as middle-class women have increasingly entered wage labor outside their households. Consequently the North needs huge supplies of foreign service workers to do child care, cleaning, cooking and healthcare in households and public institutions. Women also voluntarily organize and do domestic, caring and advocacy work for each other in their own impoverished communities, both on an everyday basis and especially in times of economic crises. The latter situation has been especially visible in poor communities' responses to "structural adjustment" policies of the 1980s and recently again in response to the 2008 global financial crises (Elson 2011; Harcourt 1994).

This kind of analysis begins to reveal a second underappreciated issue in the mainstream development theory, policy, and practice: women and their dependents constitute the vast majority of the world's poor. Women, and especially mothers, still earn less than men in virtually all wage-labor contexts in the developing world. Moreover, men tend to distribute their "family wages" unequally in households, depriving women and children of kinds of resources that men reserve for themselves. So women would be the majority of the poor on these measures alone. But when one adds to the count the huge number of children, sick, elderly, and others who depend on women's labor to stay functioning and even alive on an everyday basis, especially in the constantly increasing number of female-headed households around the globe, it is clear that women and their dependents constitute a vast majority of the poor everywhere around the globe. Of course poor men's needs also should be met. But lack of attention to the particular needs of poor women guarantees that the gap between the rich and the poor will continue to grow both locally and globally.

The underappreciation of these two facts draws attention to a third: eliminating the impoverishment of women and their dependents requires direct attention to the needs of these groups. The typical "trickle-down" strategy of development theory, in which it is assumed that men who head households are the appropriate recipients of development aid, does little to improve the conditions of women and their dependents, and thus does little to lower poverty levels in general (Khader 2015). Yet to address women's needs directly requires transformations of social and political theory and of the policies and practices of dominant economic, political, and social institutions. This means direct attention to creating equitable gender relations in households as well as in public life, and thereby to changing prevailing conceptions of desirable masculinity. These two projects have always been taboo for public policy, and few development projects have designed programs to address such challenges. Moreover, to get these issues addressed in public policy, requires addressing similar gender relations also among the professional men who theorize, design, fund, administer, and carry out development projects, including male philosophers (Agarwal 1997; Elson 1995; Khader 2015). How can these taboo projects be addressed? But how can poverty be eliminated if they are not addressed?

To summarize, development theory, including the work of male philosophers, has not much been touched by the most innovative feminist work on development, which has focused on the kinds of facts and new directions produced by economists and political theorists. At issue are ontological, epistemological and methodological assumptions and principles that are embedded in mainstream development theory, policy, and practices. For example, women's domestic, child care, and caring activities have been reconceptualized as *labor*, as "real work" no less socially necessary than men's paid labor. "The poor" have been expanded to explicitly include women and their dependents. Gender has been re-conceptualized not just as an identity of individuals, but also of structural *relations* between men and women as well as between men such as fathers and sons, and between women such as wives and daughters-in law. One challenge here is that this feminist work clearly defies conventional standards for objective research that demand the exclusion of emotions and politics from research processes. Yet feminist work begins with anger at mainstream toleration of women's exploitation and impoverishment, and then continues with specifically feminist political frameworks for research projects (Jaggar 1989). Thus feminist research is overtly value- and interest-rich, instead of adopting a "weakly objectivist" posture that invariably obscures those widely shared exploitative values and interests that shape mainstream Northern research processes (Harding 2004; 2015).

Moreover, feminist work assumes that poor women themselves can identify many of the ontological realities and appropriate methodological and epistemological approaches required to improve the conditions of their lives. And researchers, whatever their gender or class, can learn to start off their research and analyses from the daily lives of such oppressed groups and from their testimony in order to "study up" and identify just which dominant concepts, theories, policies and practices are responsible for such immiseration. Thus feminist development theory and analyses stay close to a diverse set of global social justice movements through which the daily lives of women and other oppressed and exploited groups are made visible. In doing so, these produce "rear guard" theory and analyses, in contrast to the "avant garde" theory typical of mainstream philosophic and social theory approaches to such real-life situations.

The Rise of Development Ethics

It is time to focus on mainstream development ethics. As indicated earlier, by the 1970s development theory, policy and practices were widely perceived to have failed to reduce poverty. Philosophers began to notice that there could be an important role for them in development theory. They began to ask how should the ethical and practical effects of development be conceptualized and measured, and even how development should be redefined. These analyses have successively expanded the criteria for what should count as valuable forms of development.

Yet in 2010, philosopher Thomas Pogge could still say that

> world poverty has overtaken war as the greatest source of avoidable human misery. Many more people—some 360 million—have died from hunger and remediable diseases in peacetime in the 20 years since the end of the Cold War than perished from wars, civil wars, and government repression over the entire twentieth century.

(Pogge 2010: 11)

In the context of a globally affluent world, Pogge charged that these huge death rates from poverty signified a continued moral failing on the part of citizens of rich countries. Yet Pogge, like other mainstream development theorists and policy-makers, ignores powerful feminist economic analyses. One can wonder if a focus on the moral failings of citizens is an adequate response to this horror. Just what were the contributions of philosophers to development thinking since the 1970s?

In the 1970s Denis Goulet (1997), who can be considered the pioneer of development ethics, strongly contested the lack of a normative framework with which to evaluate the means and goals of development policies and practices. Goulet's thinking was heavily influenced by three notable precursors whose analyses of development were value oriented: Mahatma Gandhi, French economist L.-J. Lebret, and Swedish economist Gunnar Myrdal. Goulet argued that development policies and programs espoused by the United Nations and other multilateral agencies should be guided by such normative goals as reduced suffering, the attainment of a better life, and enhanced freedoms. The concept of development was in need of redefinition within an ethical framework.

As Goulet saw, development theory and practice must be linked; yet theorists have tended to give little attention to practice. Consequently, they lack resources to analyze how development projects have succeeded primarily in "developing" the investing classes in the North, while de-developing and mal-developing the world's poor, as indicated earlier. Thus development requires a type of philosophy that is both critical and practical: one that thus moves away from the Western philosophical tradition of ideal theory, consisting of abstract principles, and focused on the moral obligations of individuals. It has taken philosophers some time to recognize and begin to address the several components of this challenge.

Another influential philosophical analysis of the 1970s was Peter Singer's "Famine, Affluence and Morality." Singer's utilitarian argument is focused on individuals and their moral obligations. He argued, "If it is in our power to do or prevent something bad from happening without thereby sacrificing anything of moral importance, we ought morally to do it" (Singer 1972: 231). Although this argument was not directly focused on development, it did provoke much discussion about people in vulnerable conditions, the moral obligations of those living in affluent countries, and the work of charities. Singer's argument has been criticized by many for being too morally demanding, but it also elicited the charge that his focus was too narrow. Poverty and famine are structural problems that require different kinds of strategies than are possible for the moral actions of individuals. They require a political philosophy (Kuper 2002).

Meanwhile, by the early 1990s the concept of development started to shift from measures of only economic growth, such as of a country's gross domestic product (GDP), to ones that included "human values." This new conception soon influenced how development was carried out. In the 1990s the United Nations Development Program (UNDP) announced a new definition of development: "Development embraces not only access to goods and services, but also the opportunity to choose a fully satisfying, valuable and valued way of living together, the flourishing of human existence in all its forms and as a whole" (Gasper 2004: 37).

This human development conception was made popular by Nobel Prize winning economist and philosopher, Amartya Sen. For Sen (1999), the absence of individual freedoms is one of the main obstacles today to the ability of individuals to flourish. Development must therefore be the expansion of freedom. He focused on how increasing people's capabilities would lead to an enhanced quality of life. As a practical approach, this theory is widely regarded as a more reasonable attempt to address global poverty and inequities. Especially valuable has been his insistence on the normative meanings of development. Yet, in itself, this approach is not sufficient for addressing the structural causes of poverty since it still retains a focus only on individuals, and is silent on the responsibilities to address these structural causes..

Meanwhile, the "basic needs" approach was yet one more theory in the 1970s that was committed to shifting the focus of development away from economic growth (Rai 2011). The argument here was that basic needs must be satisfied in order to reach a morally acceptable standard of living. Basic needs were conceptualized as physical ones, such as water, nutrition, shelter, and access to healthcare, but also less tangible ones such as participation, empowerment and agency. Although the basic needs approach was lauded as a step in the right direction, it was still embedded within a paradigm that neglected the dimensions of power and oppression within the social structures of society, such as in families, communities, and other social institutions. Thus it failed to address the main causes of gender inequity. Yet this approach provided the groundwork for the transformation of Sen's human development model into the capability approach. Here, finally, gender inequalities begin to be addressed in more than demographic contexts. Martha Nussbaum (2000) later provided further insights from a feminist theoretical perspective.

There is widespread agreement within a conventional ethics framework that the capabilities approach is the most desirable counter to the traditional conception of development as only economic growth. Nussbaum's renaming it as a capabilities approach is a post-humanist move that allows for the inclusion of non-human animals as ethical subjects. This shift away from anthropocentric assumptions aligns the theory with a progressive environmental ethic (Nussbaum 2011).

One of the most important contributions of the capabilities approach is that it is not an ideal theory. It is not a "theory from above," but rather starts off from considering the injustices and inequalities experienced by people in their everyday lives, which is consistent with feminist methodologies. It gestures toward social structures, such as institutionalized preferences for male children as a cause of such inequalities. This marks a major shift in development ethics. Yet, critics point out that in both Sen's and Nussbaum's accounts, this approach still retains the focus on what individual agents are morally obligated to do. It still doesn't address social structural issues, or, consequently, a wider array of political philosophy issues that feminist philosophers have identified (Malavisi 2014).

Feminist Philosophic Issues about Development

Philosophical work on global gender justice has begun to appear only over the last ten years. It is not that it was completely ignored in the work of pioneers such as Pogge (2010), Miller (2010), Singer (1972), and others, but it was never their focus, and failed to engage with the scope of feminist economic analyses. Feminist philosophic accounts bring the powerful history of forty-five years of debate between feminist theorists and activists representing many different groups of women from around the globe to bear on women's diverse family and public life situations in development contexts (Jaggar 2014). (Note that this feminist work has not limited its focus to such issues as female genital mutilation, sex trafficking, and violence against women, important as these are.)

Feminist philosophy provides useful resources for analyses of development theory, policies and practices for the obvious reason that it addresses a crucial but missing topic, namely poor women's issues. But it also does so because it had never assumed that economic issues were the only important ones in women's lives, crucial as they are, or that they can be effectively addressed without attention to men's control of women's lives in households and in the public sphere. It understood that the immiseration of women could not be effectively addressed by a focus only on individual women, either on those immiserated or on the development professionals trying to eliminate such misery. Rather it required attention to the macro social structures that both enabled and limited every single person's life both in households and in the public sphere, though in different ways for different groups. Moreover feminist philosophy had already gone through decades of vigorous and often painful critical discussions of the problems with relying on elite white women's conceptions of the important feminist approaches to guide policies—ones that inevitably turned out to be disastrous for other groups of women. Central tendencies of feminist thinking had long rejected ideal theory as a guide to policies and to research designs and, instead, achieved startling empirical and theoretical revelations in biology and the social sciences by starting off research and planning from women's daily lives. And feminist criticism of familiar sexist practices of associating women with nature and with animals had produced rich post-humanist feminist accounts.

Here there is space only to gesture toward a few examples of this recent work. Uma Narayan (2002) challenges the objectionable assumptions that Other women (not white, well-off, of European ancestry, heterosexual, abled) are either "just like us" relatively privileged women, or else that they are totally different from us. Rather, women in every culture always "bargain with patriarchy," giving up some freedoms to obtain others (Kandiyoti 1988). Thus it is a mistake to assume that Other women whose life-choices are different from ours, are dupes of their patriarchal cultures. As Narayan puts the point, they have "a mind of their own." And it is a mistake to assume that Other cultures cannot be sources of both theory frameworks and practical information about what constitutes women's empowerment. Westerners, including feminists, tend to lack the kinds of critical perspectives on themselves that they insist mark women in other cultures as immiserated and backward.

Serene Khader (2011) focuses such insights on the central Northern value of autonomy. She argues that Western thinking about autonomy fails to grasp how women's "adaptive preferences" do not invariably express some kind of deficit in autonomy. That is, a woman's choice to veil or for an arranged marriage, for example, does not necessarily indicate that she is a dupe of her particular patriarchy and has not really been free to form her own values. Rather, adherence to cultural norms need not be regarded as manifesting a lack of autonomy; cultural belonging is not necessarily a constraint on autonomy.

Christine Koggel (2013) argues for a relational approach, which draws from feminist care ethics. It puts relationships instead of individuals at the center of analysis. Its focus is on how concepts such as agency and autonomy, which are central to Sen's and Nussbaum's capability approach, must be understood within a complex network of power relationships that are constantly changing. Such an account expands agency in ways that challenge mainstream policies for removing gender inequalities. At the same time, a relational approach can capture an account of empowerment with valuable implications for undermining power and empowering women.

Alison M. Jaggar (2014) points to the consequences of feminist assessments of how what are presumed to be gender-neutral institutions and policies, such as those that deliver global development, nevertheless "have had systematically disparate and often burdensome consequences for specific groups of women in both the global North and the global South" (2014: 10). They then began to produce charges that "go beyond recent recognition that the domain of justice includes the sphere of global politics and trade and that states as well as individuals may be subjects of justice claims" (2014: 13). They argued that "the *domain* of justice includes households and families . . . the *subjects* of justice in the global sphere include gendered and sometimes transnational collectivities, . . . the *objects* of global justice include the transnational organization of caretaking contributions and responsibilities" (2014: 13). In these respects feminists are challenging fundamental assumptions of political philosophy more generally.

A Fourth Fact: Inadequate Resources and Competence Requirements for Development Designers, Funders, Managers, and Other Professionals

There is a fourth fact that has been ignored by all too many sponsors, funders, and development professionals. This is that in two respects the current competence requirements for development professionals are insufficient to enable them effectively to contribute to eliminating global poverty. First, women should be considered highly desirable leaders and managers of progressive social change. They should be recruited and resourced at the very highest levels of development design and funding to shape the selection of the development policies and practices that will have such huge effects on women and their dependents around the globe. And top-level designers and funders of any gender should also come from the groups so affected, not just from elite strata.

Second, both men and women development professionals should have a solid grasp of the best of critical theoretical shifts during the development era—and, we argue, especially of the critical feminist insights—in order to understand and interpret the nature, implications, and constraints of existing development interventions (Hanna and Kleinman 2013). Unfortunately, women and men at higher and lower levels usually lack such backgrounds, and their work schedules do not offer the space or time to gain them.

One situation where this problem shows up is in the prevalence of cultural paternalism among development practitioners (and, of course, among scholars also). This kind of thinking "from above" disables them from fully understanding the context of others, and especially their suffering. Extreme poverty, hunger, squalor, and endemic disease are difficult situations for outside observers to understand or even empathize with. For those living under these conditions, feelings of helplessness and hopelessness can prevail (Goulet 1997; Malavisi 2010). Martha Nussbaum's work has often been criticized as only theorizing "from above" (Ackerly 2000; Charusheela 2009; Jaggar 2006; Nzegwu 1995; and Tobin 2007).

Another challenge is the ongoing one of pushing "gender mainstreaming" to more competent projects. It took huge global political struggles to get such a perspective into development agencies at all. At least it does put women's concerns on the development agenda. Yet the gender assumptions inherent to these projects often seem little advanced from Ester Boserup's in 1970. Although practitioners tend to be well aware of cultural differences, development plans and strategies tend to see such differences only as obstacles to achieving Western goals, rather than as resources for rethinking them (Saunders 2002: 14). Moreover, gender mainstreaming, too, is often grounded in anthropocentric assumptions (Apffel-Marglin and Sanchez 2002). It only focuses on the human and does not consider the inter-relationality and interdependence between humans and the non-human world. Thus it fails to engage with issues of human relations to land and of ecology.

A further problem with gender mainstreaming projects is that they add a third burden to demands on women's time and energy in wage labor and domestic responsibilities, namely attendance at meetings and workshops. This is a version of a familiar challenge for participatory democracy more generally. Additionally, enthusiasm for small-scale projects tends to obscure the need for attention to issues that require long-term solutions. The feminist criticisms of micro-credit schemes target one example of this tendency (Khader 2014). Finally, Chant (2011) has argued against the "feminization of responsibility" that all too often characterizes gender mainstreaming.

Underlying many of these issues about development professionals is the fact that both development research and policy structurally tend to replicate colonial relations to the objects of their attention—an old issue since the 1960s for social scientists committed to social justice. Alison M. Jaggar and Scott Wisor (2013) have designed a feminist research methodology that can effectively counter the tendency for development agencies' Western assumptions and practices to dominate the expertise of vulnerable groups. This requires collaboration with a "partner organization" of "Southern feminist scholars and Southern-based feminist organizations that are driven by citizens rather than by donors" (Jaggar and Wisor 2013: 512). Then there are several steps that must be taken to block domination:

> Making decision-making formal and transparent (even if discussions leading to decisions are informal); providing avenues for dissent, with regard to both individual decisions or evaluations and the overarching structure of the project; tracking such dissent over time; committing to producing a minority report of disagreements; . . . and explicitly recognizing the differential social locations of official team members and other project participants and explaining in official publications how this may have affected research results.
>
> (Jaggar and Wisor 2013: 512)

Thus feminist philosophical attention to the fieldwork situations that development professionals encounter is also producing valuable guides to more desirable outcomes for women (see also Wylie 2015).

Conclusion

Issues about women and gender in global development projects provide a fine opportunity to link feminist philosophy to progressive real life contexts. Moreover, feminist philosophers' struggles to get the voices and everyday needs of poor women heard in development theory, policy and in practice are leading them to make significant contributions not only to ethics or only to development theory, but also to political philosophy, epistemology, ontology, philosophy of science, and research methodology more generally. This feminist philosophic work can benefit development institutions, agencies and, most importantly, the huge numbers of poor women and their dependents around the globe who are the targets of development policies and practices. It also makes important contributions to decentering problematic Eurocentric assumptions from feminist theory more generally.

Related Topics

Epistemic injustice, ignorance, and trans experience (Chapter 22); feminist philosophy of social science (Chapter 27); feminist intersections with environmentalism and ecological thought (Chapter 35); feminist conceptions of autonomy (Chapter 41); feminist ethics of care (Chapter 43); multiculturalism and postcolonial feminisms (Chapter 47); neoliberalism, global justice, and transnational feminisms (Chapter 48); feminism, structural injustice, and responsibility (Chapter 49).

References

Ackerly, Brooke A. (2000) *Political Theory and Social Criticism*, Cambridge: Cambridge University Press.
Agarwal, Bina (1994) *A Field of One's Own: Gender and Land Rights in South Asia*, Cambridge: Cambridge University Press.
Apffel-Marglin, Frederique and Sanchez, Loyda (2002) "Developmentalist Feminism and Neocolonialism," in Kriemild Saunders (Ed.) *Feminist Post-Development Thought*, London: Zed Books, 159–179.

Benaria, Lourdes (2011) "Accounting for Women's Work: The Progress of Two Decades," in Nalini Visvanathan, Lynn Duggan, Nan Wiegersma, and Laurie Nisonoff (Eds.) *The Women, Gender and Development Reader*, New York: Zed Books, 114–120.

Benaria, Lourdes Berik, Gunseli and Floro, Maria (Eds.) (2015) *Gender, Development and Globalization*, New York: Routledge.

Boserup, Ester (1970) *Women's Role in Economic Development*, London: Earthscan.

Chant, Sylvia (2011) "The 'Feminization of Poverty' and the 'Feminization' of Anti-Poverty Programs: Room for Revision," in Nalini Visvanathan, Lynn Duggan, Nan Wiegersma, and Laurie Nisonoff (Eds.) *The Women, Gender and Development Reader*, New York: Zed Books, 174–196.

Charusheela, S (2009) "Social Analysis and the Capability Approach: A Limit to Martha Nussbaum's Universalist Ethics," *Cambridge Journal of Economics* 33(6): 1135–1152.

Elson, Diane (1995) *Male Bias in the Development Process*, Manchester: Manchester University Press.

——(2011) "International Financial Architecture: A View From the Kitchen," in Nalini Visvanathan et al. (Eds.) *The Women, Gender, and Development Reader*, New York: Zed Books, 295–305.

Escobar, Arturo (1995) *Encountering Development: The Making and Unmaking of the Third World*, Princeton, NJ: Princeton University Press.

Folbre, Nancy (2001) *The Invisible Heart: Economics and Family Values*, New York: New Press.

Gasper, Des (2004) *The Ethics of Development: From Economism to Human Development*, Edinburgh: Edinburgh University Press.

Goulet, Denis (1997) "A New Discipline: Development Ethics," *International Journal of Social Economics*, 24(11): 1160–1171.

Hanna, Bridget and Kleinman, Arthur (2013) "Unpacking Global Health," in Paul Farmer, Jim Yong Kim, Arthur Kleinman, Matthew Basilico (Eds.) *Reimagining Global Health*, Berkeley, CA: University of California Press, 15–32.

Harcourt, Wendy (Ed.) (1994) *Feminist Perspectives on Sustainable Development*, London: Zed Books.

Harding, Sandra (Ed.) (2004) *The Feminist Standpoint Theory Reader*, New York: Routledge.

—— (2015) *Objectivity and Diversity: Another Logic of Scientific Research*, Chicago, IL: University of Chicago Press.

Hartmann, Betsy (1995) *Reproductive Rights and Wrongs: The Global Politics of Population Control*, Boston, MA: South End Press.

Jaggar, Alison M. (1989) "Love and Knowledge: Emotion in Feminist Epistemology," in Susan Bordo and Alison Jaggar (Eds.) *Gender/Body/Knowledge*, New Brunswick, NJ: Rutgers University Press, 154–171.

—— (2006) "Reasoning about Well-being: Nussbaum's Methods of Justifying the Capabilities," *Journal of Political Philosophy* 4(3): 301–322.

—— (2009) "Transnational Cycles of Gendered Vulnerability: A Prologue to a Theory of Global Gender Justice," *Philosophical Topics* 37(2): 33–52.

—— (Ed.) (2014) *Gender and Global Justice*, Cambridge: Polity Press.

Jaggar, Alison M. and Scott Wisor (2013) "Feminist Methodology in Practice: Learning From a Research Project," in Alison M. Jaggar (Ed.) *Just Methods: An Interdisciplinary Feminist Reader*, 2nd ed, Boulder, CO: Paradigm Press, 498–518.

Kandiyoti, Deniz (1988) "Bargaining with Patriarchy," *Gender and Society* 2(3): 274–90.

Khader, Serene (2011) *Adaptive Preferences and Women's Empowerment*, Oxford: Oxford University Press.

—— (2014) "Empowerment Through Self-Subordination? Microcredit and Women's Agency," in Diana Tietjens Meyers (Ed.) *Poverty, Agency, and Human Rights*, Oxford: Oxford University Press, 223–248.

—— (2015) "Development Ethics, Gender Complementarianism and Intrahousehold Inequality," *Hypatia* 30(2): 352–369.

Koggel, Christine (2013) "Is the Capability Approach a Sufficient Challenge to Distributive Accounts of Global Justice?" *Journal of Global Ethics* 9(2): 145–157.

Kuper, Andrew (2002) "More than Charity: Cosmopolitan Alternatives to the 'Singer Solution,'" *Ethics and International Affairs* 16(1): 107–120.

Malavisi, Anna (2010) "A Critical Analysis of the Relationship between Southern Non-Government Organizations and Northern Non-Government Organizations in Bolivia," *Journal of Global Ethics* 6(1): 45–56.

—— (2014) "The Need for an Effective Development Ethics," *Journal of Global Ethics* 10(3): 297–303.

Mies, Maria (1986) *Patriarchy and Accumulation on a World Scale: Women in the International Division of Labor*, Atlantic Highlands, NJ: Zed Books.

Miller, Richard W. (2010) *Globalizing Justice: The Ethics of Poverty and Power*, Oxford: Oxford University Press.

Narayan, Uma (2002) "Minds of Their Own: Choices, Autonomy, Cultural Practices and Other Women," in Louise M. Antony and Charlotte E. Witt (Eds.) *A Mind of One's Own: Feminist Essays on Reason and Objectivity*, 2nd edition, Denver, CO: Westview Press, 418–432.

Nussbaum, Martha (2000) *Women and Human Development: The Capabilities Approach*, Cambridge: Cambridge University Press.

—— (2011) *Creating Capabilities: The Human Development Approach*, Cambridge, MA: Harvard University Press.

Nzegwu, Nkiru (1995) "Recovering Igbo Women's Traditions for Development: The Case of Ikporo Onitsha," in Martha Nussbaum and Jonathan Glover (Eds.) *Women, Culture and Development*, Oxford: Oxford University Press, 444–465.

Pogge, Thomas (2010) *Politics as Usual*, Cambridge: Polity Press.

Rai, Shirin M. (2011) "The History of International Development: Concepts and Contexts," in Nalini Visvanathan, Lynn Duggan, Nan Wiegersma, and Laurie Nisonoff (Eds.) *The Women, Gender and Development Reader*, New York: Zed Books, 14–21.

Sachs, Wolfgang (Ed.) (1992) *The Development Dictionary: A Guide to Knowledge as Power*, Atlantic Highlands, NJ: Zed Books.

Saunders, Kriemild (2002) *Feminist Post-Development Thought: Rethinking Modernity, Post-Colonialism and Representation*, London: Zed Books.

Sen, Amartya (1990) "More than 100 Million Women Are Missing," *New York Review of Books*, December 20, 61–66.

—— (1999) *Development as Freedom*, New York: Anchor Books.

Singer, Peter (1972) "Famine, Affluence, and Morality," *Philosophy and Public Affairs* 1(3): 229–243.

Third World Network (1993) "Modern Science in Crisis: A Third World Response," in Sandra Harding (Ed.), *The Racial Economy of Science*, Bloomington, IN: Indiana University Press, 484–518.

Tobin, Theresa (2007) "On Their Own Ground: Strategies of Resistance for Sunni Muslim Women," *Hypatia* 22(3): 152–174.

Truman, Harry (1964) "Inaugural Address," *Public Papers of the Presidents of the United States: Harry S. Truman*, Washington, DC: US Government Printing Office.

Visvanathan, Nalini, Lynn Duggan, Nan Wiegersma, and Laurie Nisonoff (Eds.) (2011) *The Women, Gender, and Development Reader*, 2nd ed., New York: Zed Books.

Waring, Marilyn (1988) *If Women Counted: A New Feminist Economics*, San Francisco, CA: Harper & Row.

Wylie, Alison (2015) "A Plurality of Pluralisms: Collaborative Practice in Archaeology," in Flavia Padovani, Alan Richardson, and Jonathan Y. Tsou (Eds.) *Objectivity in Science: New Perspectives from Science and Technology Studies*, Dordrecht: Springer, 189–210.

35

FEMINIST INTERSECTIONS WITH ENVIRONMENTALISM AND ECOLOGICAL THOUGHT

Trish Glazebrook

Feminism has intersected with environmentalism and ecological thinking since the 1970s. Concerning method, both feminists and ecofeminists recognize the value of empirical data, and re-conceive epistemic authority in terms of narrative voice. Ecofeminism deploys feminist conclusions in environmental philosophy where justice-based analysis shows that women suffer disproportionate economic and other harms in consequence of environmental degradation. As a standpoint issue, women bring unique perspectives to environmental issues, and their women's cultural location situates them well to critique prevailing norms. Ecofeminism draws insights from feminist policy analysis: functional policy cannot address environmental problems without challenging women's marginalization and incorporating information on their daily living conditions. Ecofeminism brings novel research to growing bodies of literature that assess strategies for gender-sensitive policy and recognize women's resilience, as well as the remedial potential of their approaches.

In the 1970s, the earth goddess was a focal symbol in women's reclamation and celebration of the female creative principle. Feminist spirituality offered an alternative to the modernist, patriarchal ideology of science and technology that defines rationality in terms of objectivity. Because "objectivity" universalizes the Cartesian subject, it is androcentric. At the same time, the ideology of science and technology dismisses other knowledge systems as "old wives' tales," and women's embodied knowledge as "intuition." Because natural sciences aim to understand nature, ecofeminism is extremely amenable to such feminist critiques of science. It diagnoses science as a logic of domination that treats both women and nature as "object," and seeks to validate alternative knowledge systems, e.g. traditional ecological knowledge. Such knowledge systems are built over generations as cultures develop expertise in survival and thriving in their particular ecological context. Globally speaking, ecofeminism is therefore not just a theory, but a praxical examination of women's experience of their environment and the livelihoods it affords.

Ecofeminism arose in the United States out of non-violent, direct action against nuclear weaponry. Ynestra King, Anna Gyorgy, Grace Paley, and other activists in anti-nuclear, lesbian feminist, and environmental movements organized a conference at Amherst College in 1980 that led to demonstrations and other actions. The Women's Pentagon Actions of 1980 and 1981 connected sexism, racism and classism with militarism and environmental destruction. Irene Diamond and Gloria Orenstein organized a second conference in 1987 that connected these activists with a developing group of ecofeminist academics.

Throughout the last four decades, massive environmental catastrophes and threats have emerged from the practices of technoscientific-empowered global capital. At the intersection of feminism with environmentalism and ecological thinking, critiques of science, technology and global capital, coupled with articulation of ways of thinking and praxes of care that are alternate to modernity's assault upon nature, have led to a productive thinking of gender difference that is at present emerging. Crucial to this genesis and development of ecofeminism has been the presence since the 1980s of voices from the global South that have led ecofeminists away from the "feminist" label and deep into world-changing, gender-conscious interventions into policy and practice. This chapter traces that story.

Nature, Culture, Feminism

Ecofeminism began conceptually with a deep entanglement of woman and nature. In 1952, Simone de Beauvoir argued that "One is not born, but rather becomes, a woman," (Beauvoir 1952: 267) in a revolutionary move to free woman from biological reductionism. Yet she also aligned woman with nature by arguing that they both appear as other to man in the logic of patriarchy (1952: 144). She later criticized the merging of feminism with ecology because appeal to "traditional feminine values, such as woman and her rapport with nature, . . . [is a] renewed attempt to pin women down to their traditional role" (Beauvoir 1984: 103). Ecofeminism's early theoretical challenge was accordingly how to critique the politics of patriarchy without re-inscribing biological essentialism.

Challenging assumptions at the heart of this question, Sherry Ortner asked in 1974, "Is woman to nature as man is to culture?" She answered that though woman is not closer to nature than man, she is culturally constructed to appear so; thus genuine change concerning women's secondary societal status can only come about through simultaneous change to social institutions and cultural assumptions. Catherine Roach argued further that the phrases "Mother nature" and "Mother Earth,"

> given the meaning and function traditionally assigned to "mother" and "motherhood" in patriarchal culture, will not achieve the desired aim of making our behavior more environmentally sound, but will instead help to maintain the mutually supportive, exploitative stances we take toward our mothers and our environment.
>
> (Roach 1991: 46)

That is, the association of women with nature reciprocally reinforces the denigration of each. The initial encounter of feminism with environment and ecology is, on one hand, an attempt to retrieve women's relationship to nature by re-appropriating the creative, reproductive function in women's embodied experience, and on the other, a struggle not to "other" woman into an alterity shared with nature that reduces her to her body and universalizes women as mothers.

While Ortner was writing in the United States, Francoise d'Eaubonne was coining the term 'l'écofeminism' in France. Her book *Feminism or Death* (*Le féminisme ou la mort*) aligned, as de Beauvoir had, the oppression of women with the exploitation of nature. Her title was not a battle cry so much as a warning. She argued that just as the exploitation of nature in an excess of production was creating resource scarcity, so exploitation of women's bodies in an excess of reproduction was causing overpopulation. She warned that these factors in tandem were a threat to the human species. This was the first shot across the bow of not just patriarchy, but capitalist patriarchy. The history of ecofeminism is the history of its movement from metaphysics of gender to a critical, global, political critique of capital.

Ecofeminism in the Global North: The Goddess, Science, and Deep Ecology

Feminists in the late 1960s and early 1970s were typically North American, white, married, college educated and middle class. They found themselves still entrenched in a public/private split that consigned them to labor in the home, while the public realm remained a "man's world." Post-1950s conceptions of the nuclear family measured middle-class success by a male "breadwinner's" ability to support the family. Feminists accordingly focused on equal rights in the workplace, and thereby won more access to middle-class jobs. Yet traditional divisions of labor did not change substantially. The "supermom" emerged, working hard both at the office and at home. This woman is thoroughly vulnerable to internalizing feminist backlash—she has no spare time and is exhausted, while her "exceptional" status in exceeding gender expectations alienates her from traditional female gender identity. The stay-at-home mom can be just as alienated from feminism, perhaps projecting that her choices let feminism down. Women in the societal mainstream are accordingly not likely to identify as feminist. The "second wave" of feminism that began with de Beauvoir thus washed over North America, and dissipated from the mainstream.

Yet in the 1970s and 1980s, interest in gender difference remained among activist and academic feminists. Doulas and midwives re-appropriated women's reproductive capacity from the male-dominated medical industry. A concurrent symbolic of the earth mother informed women's self-conception and self-definition in contrast to patriarchal conceptions. A retrieval of goddess mythologies, whether or not historically or anthropologically accurate, reclaimed woman from patriarchy by exploring their connections to nature and the earth. In 1978, Mary Daly's radical feminist *Gyn/ecology* was published, and Susan Griffin's *Woman and Nature: The Roaring Inside Her*. Each argued that philosophy and religion have bolstered patriarchal power over women and nature. The journal *Heresies* also published "The Great Goddess" that reclaimed religion from patriarchy through the "Goddess as symbol of life and death powers and waxing and waning energies in the universe and in themselves" (Christ 1978). Ecofeminists were developing a spiritual alternative of nourishing, love, and life in contrast to patriarchal religions, while critiquing modernity's materialist, scientific worldview. Judith Plant (1989) writes of "healing the wounds." Karen

Warren (1993; 2000) assesses ecofeminsm's healing power for women, men, and the planet. Rosemary Radford Reuther (1994) provides an ecofeminist theology of earth-healing, and Reuther (1996) recounts how environmental degradation exacerbates global poverty by increasing women's labor and suffering. The goddess's promise of healing became a liberation theology, i.e., more a prayer for a promised future than the Dionysian celebration of 1978 to reclaim the power of creation and life.

Native American voices work in knowledge systems that do not separate science from religion. Starhawk (1979), Paula Gunn Allen (1990), and Winona LaDuke (2005) write fiction and non-fiction, and it makes little sense to speak of how their work is at the intersection of gender, indigenous rights and environment as if these things can be easily separated out. They have academic affiliations, but also are activists. Discourse in North America concerning indigenous knowledge systems has moved from the language of "spirituality" to "traditional ecological knowledge" in order in large part to avoid landing on the wrong side of the modernist distinction that identifies science with knowledge and religion with superstition and myth. This transition has made indigenous knowledge systems more compatible with academic practices of science, and easier to integrate into equally male-dominated science-driven environmental policy contexts; but it has also cut out gender. LaDuke, who has a strong voice in environmental policy critique, does not identify as an ecofeminist, Nonetheless, she wrote the introduction to Baumgardner and Richards's field guide for feminist activists (2005). No one has to be an ecofeminist to be working toward ecofeminist goals. But anyone with gender consciousness and commitment can contribute to the ecofeminist struggle to overcome logics of domination.

Concerning science, feminists have strongly critiqued gender bias in the ideology and practice of science (Harding 1986; 1991; Tuana 1989). Merchant (1980) offers a much stronger critique, and moreover connects gender issues with ecology. She identifies misogyny at the roots of modern science in Bacon's writings. He used language from witch trials to describe how nature's secrets could be extracted "out of the very bowels of nature" (Bacon 1980 [1620]: 23) when "she" is "under constraint and vexed; that is to say, when by art and the hand of man she is forced out of her natural state, and squeezed and moulded" (Bacon 1980 [1620]: 27). Merchant argues moreover that the mechanistic model of the universe, epitomized in Cartesian metaphysics that reduce nature to inert matter standing by for appropriation to man's needs, sanctions the domination of both women and nature. As nature is a machine at man's disposal, so woman can likewise be reduced to a body that can be used instrumentally for reproduction and pleasure. Val Plumwood lays out the Western intellectual history of domination over women and nature from the Greeks to its culmination in modern science. She assesses also how "dominant trends in environmental philosophy . . . embed themselves within rationalist philosophical frameworks which are not only biased from a gender perspective, but . . . inimical to nature as well" (Plumwood 1993: 165). Deep ecology in particular remains sexist because it fails to acknowledge gender difference, and retains dualisms that support logics of mastery (Plumwood 1993: 174).

The ecofeminism/deep ecology debate is significant not just as a debate about environmental issues, but about gender bias and exclusion in environmental philosophy. It began when Ariel Salleh argued that from the ecofeminist standpoint, deep ecology is just another self-congratulatory, reformist move that "fails to face up to the uncomfortable psychosexual origins of our culture and its crisis" in motives of control (Salleh 1984: 344). In 1987, Jim Cheney (1987) accused deep ecology of being androcentric, and Janet Biehl (1987) argued that deep ecologists implicate women in the male project of domination over nature. Salleh returned to the debate to argue that deep ecologists underestimate both the ecofeminist challenge to epistemology, and how much work is necessary to bring about social change (Salleh 1992: 195). Deep ecology is incapable of social critique because its political attitudes are meaningful only to "white-male, middle-class professionals whose thought is not grounded in the labor of daily maintenance and survival" (Salleh 1993: 225). Slicer argued that unless deep ecologists read feminist analyses, genuine debate would not be possible (Slicer 1995: 151). In continuing failure to engage ecofeminism, deep ecologists reproduce the very logic of domination they want to overcome.

Ecofeminism: Discipline and Praxis

One of the first times the word "ecofeminism" appeared in print in North America was in Diamond and Orenstein's edited volume *Reweaving the World: The Emergence of Ecofeminism* (1990) from the 1987 conference noted in the introduction above. Contributions from poets, artists, novelists, scholars, scientists, ecological activists, and spiritual teachers captured how ecofeminism began as a social movement and philosophy, initiated a critique of science and technology, and sought healing in the face of contemporary destructive, life-denying practices. The diversity of genres and perspectives show that ecofeminism in the 1980s was much more than an academic enterprise. Karen Warren nonetheless planted a solid ecofeminist foot in the Academy over the next few years.

Warren's influential 1990 essay argued that the power of ecological feminism is its promise to re-conceive feminism and develop an environmental ethic founded in the idea that the domination of women and the domination of nature, in fact, all the "-isms" of domination, are connected insofar as they arise from the oppressive conceptual framework of patriarchy. Oppressive frameworks generate a logic of domination based on dualisms, e.g., man/nature, man/woman, reason/emotion, that privilege one term over the other, and thereby justify domination of the latter by the former. She also described and defended narrative voice as a research method, in contrast to the dismissal of experience-based arguments as anecdotal and unscientific. In 1991, she edited a special issue of *Hypatia* that was the first philosophical collection on ecological feminism, later revising and expanding it into a book (Warren 1991, 1996). These essays assess what is unique about ecofeminist ethics and philosophy, but they also address the grassroots origins of ecofeminism, revisit the debate with deep ecology, and present ecofeminist perspectives on concrete issues of animal rights, abortion, and nuclear deterrence.

Feminist philosophy had been coming to terms with its own logic of domination since bell hooks's 1984 critique that it marginalized black voices. Drawing on "emergent Afrocentric eco-womanism" Riley (1992) argues, however, against thinking of environmentalism as a "white issue." She connects ecofeminism to African activism—not just its direct-action protests but its remedial activity, e.g., Wangari Maathai's Green Belt program in Kenya, and other women's work in Kenya and Niger. Riley argues against dualism; in these African women's perspectives, people are part of nature, nature and humans are interdependent, and the life force that permeates all nature is sacred. This Africanist account shares what Salleh (1984) also noted distinguishes ecofeminism from other environmental philosophies. Women's experience of embodiment does not readily generate a dualism against nature that must be overcome. Environmental ethicists have been at great pains to argue that human being is part of the natural order rather than superior to it. The feminist problem has been, rather that woman is relegated to the nature side of the man/nature dichotomy. Ecofeminism turns this feminist problem into a solution, and can get on addressing actual issues in the world rather than remaining caught up in providing theoretical argument for what is already the case.

The turn to real-world issues, to "taking empirical data seriously," as Warren (1997; 2000) puts it, immediately uncovers urgent global issues in women's daily lived experience as food providers and primary caregivers tasked with meeting the daily living needs of their family. Marilyn Waring's groundbreaking work exposed the global invisibility of women's livelihoods (1988; 1999). The invisibility of women's agricultural labor in developing countries has in particular been documented (Dixon-Mueller 1991), despite the fact that their traditional agricultural expertise has been successful in feeding populations over long historical periods (Curtin 1999). In 1991, Cheryl Johnson-Odim argued that feminists in the global North need to do more than include women from the global South on their conference agenda. The Third World feminist agenda is different because feminists in the global South are "connected as much to the struggle of their communities for liberation and autonomy as to the work against gender discrimination" (Johnson-Odim 1991: 317). They cannot depoliticize feminism to issues of equality and women's rights because the men of their community also suffer from and share their struggle against racism, imperialism and economic exploitation. Rather than just including women from the global South in discussion, Northern feminists should include them in agenda-setting.

From an ecofeminist perspective, "letting" anyone set the agenda re-inscribes a logic of domination—as if the agenda belonged to ecofeminists anywhere who might magnanimously share it. In its earliest beginnings, ecofeminism connected sexism with exploitation and destruction of the environment. When Warren (1990) made explicit that all the "-isms" of domination (including but not limited to colonialism, imperialism, racism, heterosexism, ableism, ageism, classism) are connected by logics of domination, it was clear that the agenda was already shared. The ecofeminist agenda connects women everywhere, not because of biology, but through shared (which does not mean undifferentiated) oppression.

Ecofeminism is accordingly far too of-this-world to be only theoretical. When feminism meets environmentalism and ecological thinking, not only are connections between the South and North shown already to exist, but also connections between theory and practice are revealed as always already in play. Ecofeminism arose out of women's lived experience in a world of gender discrimination, heterosexism, environmental devastation and threat, increasing militarism, and nuclear proliferation. Changing this world means understanding it through historical and other analyses that uncover the role of science and technology in supporting and enabling the degradation of ecosystems, labor conditions, and lived experience. It means uncovering alternative logics—ways of thinking—in gynocentric practices of livelihood, labor and care. That is, it means praxis—the inseparability of thoughtful, intentional activity and experience-generated reflection.

Changing the World: Food, Care, and Climate

Contemporary ecofeminism takes environmental philosophy beyond traditional debates in deep ecology, anthropocentrism, and the land ethic to real-world impacts in daily, lived experience. In the United States, ecofeminism has moved into political ecology. Chaone Mallory (2009; 2010) argues, for example, that ecofeminist activism opens spaces for subaltern others. She includes non-humans in these others, and argues that non-human species have sufficient agency and subjectivity to warrant ethico-political consideration. Her 2013 analysis of locavorism, i.e., eating only locally produced foods, assesses how gender, race, and class affect food access and food choices. Is such discussion of privileged food choices appropriate or irresponsible in a world where others face pressing issues of food insecurity? As Salleh notes, "we in the North are the biggest problem for the South" (2006: 56–57). The question of responsibility serves as a reminder that everybody's choices are much more connected with people's experiences elsewhere than it may seem. Food transport generates greenhouse gases that contribute to climate change that is already causing droughts and subsequent starvation in Ethiopia (Lott, Christidis, and Stott 2013). Everyone is deeply entangled in the web of global capital and its impacts.

The intersection of feminism with environmentalism and ecological thought increasingly engages global issues of environmental justice that are socio-political and economic. For example, industry generates profits; but the environmental costs of toxins also generated are "externalities" typically not borne by the polluter. Though sperm can also be damaged by environmental toxins, women's reproductive systems are uniquely vulnerable. Carcinogens collect in fatty tissue, e.g., the breasts. The womb is every person's first environment; developing organisms are drastically impacted by exposure to toxins in utero, with results that often have lifelong consequences. Sperm survive for a few days, so risk of exposure to toxins is short-lived in comparison with the nine months of human gestation. Women's role in housing the fetus accordingly entails relational duties of care that environmental toxins deny her the capacity to meet. Ecofeminists connect this gendered health issue to the environmental issue. Gender disparity in corporate ownership and reproductive health impacts means that principles of distributive justice are doubly breached by the costs and benefits of environmental toxins.

Women also bear a significant disproportion of harms when environmental degradation affects their labor and livelihood. Since women in developing countries work closely with nature to reproduce the material conditions of daily living through agriculture, foraging, and water and fuel collection, environmental degradation can have an immediate, potentially catastrophic impact on their livelihoods and food security. In response to challenges women face everywhere in bearing the costs of environmental degradation, ecofeminism aims at world-changing praxis. As d'Eaubonne knew when she coined the word l'écoféminisme, it's a question of survival.

From 1986 to 1989, physicist turned ecofeminist turned environmental, gender, and development policy critic Vandana Shiva led a major project on resource conflicts over forests and water in the Punjab region of India. This project led to three books. Shiva (1988) made a plea for recovery of the feminine principle as the living force of nature, in contrast to modern science that drives economies from the goal of sustenance toward profit. This happened in India through intensive Green Revolution agricultural practices that deforested much of India and left the land either waterlogged or desertified. Shiva thus argued that ecology is a politics of survival (1991a) and showed the extent of what science-based agriculture threatens through analysis of the violence of the Green Revolution toward nature, soil, seeds, biodiversity and farmers (1991b).

Given her background in physics and philosophy of science, Shiva is well placed to critique science. Her 1988 analysis characterizes the "destruction of ecologies and knowledge systems . . . as the violence of reductionism." Reductionist ecology is at the root of growing ecological crisis, she argues, because reductionism transforms nature into passive, inert, manipulable matter—"its organic processes and regularities and regenerative capacities are destroyed" (1988: 24). By denying the validity of other knowledge systems, contemporary science reduces knowledge in three ways: (i) ontologically (other properties, e.g., regenerative capacity, are excluded from the account); (ii) epistemologically (alternative ways of perceiving and knowing can no longer be recognized); and (iii) sociologically (the non-expert is deprived of the right to access knowledge and judge its claims) (Shiva 1988: 30). In contradiction of its own epistemological standards, contemporary scientific knowledge "declares organic systems of knowledge irrational, and rejects the belief systems of others . . . without full rational evaluation" (Shiva 1988: 26). Violence is thus done not just to nature and to people, but to knowledge itself.

In 1993, Maria Mies and Shiva published *Ecofeminism* as a North-South collaboration in which they argued that women bear the burden of responding to life-threatening industrial disasters and ecological devastation. Drawing on analyses of women's experience of poverty globally, the impact of GATT on women in the global South, reproductive technologies in the global North, and the Chipko movement in India, Mies and Shiva condemn the destructive, homogenizing and fragmenting ideology and practices of science-enabled global capital. They offer instead women's subsistence practices as functional, liberating alternatives that meet human needs by working within the limits of nature. By denying nature's reproductive function, the modern scientific worldview instead privileges production. The logic of industrial science accordingly enables the patriarchal, capital economy to feminize global poverty and exploit the labor and resources of the global South while profiting from environmental destruction.

Salleh, noted above for her part in the ecofeminism/deep ecology debate, is long familiar with critiques of global capital and wrote a Preface for Shiva and Mies (1993). Salleh's "embodied materialism" accepts neither that woman is closer to nature, nor that gender is a purely cultural phenomenon (1997). She negotiates the nature/nurture dichotomy as I do by accepting neither that nature reduces women to her body, nor that her social construction as female has no grounding in the material conditions of her lived reality (Glazebrook 2010b). She envisions ecofeminism that can ground, unify and empower socialism, ecology, feminism and postcolonial struggle. Salleh (1997: 190) argues that women's work, their "mothering or organic cultivation," for example, demonstrates that "mastery is not the only model for agency." Women's daily chores "are not just 'running around in circles' . . . but exercises in balancing internal relations with decentered foresight." This work generates "an estrangement of consciousness that provides reflexivity and the possibility of new insights" (Salleh 1997: 190). This labor-based analysis of embodied materialism provides Salleh with a conceptual framework that can be brought to bear on a variety of cross-disciplinary topics. Over the next two decades, her work focuses on the problematic impacts of the global North on the South while ranging across climate change, global justice and political economy, ecological economics, and the politics of reproduction. What ties her work together is a critique of global capital, and attention to the economic realities of women's everyday life as they bear the costs of ecodegradation and the exploitation of their labor.

Shiva's work subsequent to the 1993 volume is also materialist and economic, and focused on the everyday realities of women's experience. She provides gendered analysis of ecological issues in health and development and argues against the destructive force of globalization on women's agriculture-based livelihoods and food security (Shiva 1994a; 1996, 2000). Further work—for example, on hijacking of the global food supply, water privatization, justice and sustainability, the impacts of globalization on seeds, water and life, and climate justice—engages women's experiences and needs, but aims more generally at critique of the politics that submit both men and women to food insecurity, livelihood threat and loss, increased poverty, and deteriorating ecosystem and labor conditions. Her point is to work in the complex constellation of globalization, patriarchy, capitalism, and technoscience-enabled environmental devastation where struggles affect not only women. Shiva goes beyond ecofeminist theory to expose policies and practices that cause suffering by destroying environments and damaging human health, food security, and well-being.

When theorizing solutions, Shiva proposes women's agricultural practices as sustainable knowledge systems that work within the cyclical limits of nature. When assessing the violence of the Green Revolution, Shiva argued for organic-based agricultural strategies aimed at "preserving and building on nature's process and nature's patterns" (Shiva 1991b: 26), and traditional practices "built up over generations on the basis of knowledge generated over centuries" (Shiva 1991b: 44–45). She quotes Dr. John Augustus Voelker reporting on Indian agriculture to the Royal Agricultural Society of England: "I, at least, have never seen a more perfect picture of careful cultivation" (Shiva 1991b: 26). The "cultivation" he is describing is subsistence agriculture, which is overwhelmingly practiced by women. Shiva is soon arguing that women's "experience of interdependence and integrity is the basis for creating a science and knowledge that nurtures, rather than violates, nature's sustainable systems" (Mies and Shiva 1993: 34). She promotes reinstatement of "organic metaphors, in which concepts of order and power were based on interdependence and reciprocity" (Mies and Shiva 1993: 23).

Shiva's 1994 article, "Empowering Women," is a heart-wrenching reflection written on a train after working all day with rural Punjabi women, but also an argument for a return to women's knowledge systems and technologies. The Punjab was the "home of the green revolution," so heavily criticized by Shiva while working in the Punjab several years earlier. Now its consequences are fully evident. Rather than deliver on the promise to eliminate a threat of a mass starvation, the Green Revolution put farmers in debt in order to commercialize their farming. When these debts could not be paid because practices of commercialization, e.g., eucalyptus plantation, sucked down the water table and caused widespread drought that created poverty and starvation, farmers resorted to suicide. Their debts grew alongside an ecological burden that the earth also could no longer carry—traditional biodiversity was displaced by monoculture, disease and pest explosions led to large-scale pesticide use, and overuse of water caused desertification. Shiva argues that women pay the highest price for this so-called development: while adult women are displaced from their traditional agriculture, disempowered, and faced with food insecurity as mothers, girls are murdered in prenatal femicide through sex-selective abortion as gender discrimination and dowry practices make women disposable in "'development' which excludes and devalues women" (Shiva 1994b). In the face of these realities, Shiva argues against the "patriarchal logic of exclusion" informing industrial agriculture on the grounds that women's traditional agriculture is more productive. Women's "knowledge systems and technologies produce more while using less." But also, in women's value system, "it is unacceptable that in 2015, 500 million should continue to go hungry," she wrote, anticipating the Millennium Development Goals target date for hunger alleviation (Shiva 1994b).

That date has now past. A multi-agency, international report (FAO, IFAD, and WFP 2015) indicates that "hunger remains an everyday challenge" for almost 795 million people worldwide in 2014–2016 (FAO et al. 2015: 4). Over 98 percent of the hungry are in the global South, almost a quarter in India, and some 220 million in sub-Saharan Africa (FAO et al. 2015: 46, 12). This is the current, pressing challenge in ecofeminism: a humanitarian crisis in hunger in which women are globally responsible for meeting their family's daily needs, but are unable to do so.

But if women's knowledge systems and activities—farming to feed their family, cooking, cleaning, provision of primary medical care, and all the other things a woman might do in a day to met the needs of others—are care practices rather than logics of domination, why do women care? I argue that woman's body is a political site that situates her in society, culture, and the family by establishing her labor role (Glazebrook 2010b). In this neo-Marxist, materialist perspective, women are not inherently or inevitably caring. Yet they exercise (more or less) a capacity to care in their work that provides new logics contrary to the destructive logic of capitalist patriarchy that is incapable of ethical decision-making even when corporate leaders want to do the right thing (Glazebrook and Story 2012).

Looking at Ogoni women's resistance to oil development in the Niger Delta, women's labor can be seen not as actualization of a biological essence or destiny, but as care that arises relationally in their work (Glazebrook and Olusanya 2009; 2011). Ten years of field data collected in Ghana working with women subsistence farmers has shown how vulnerable these women are to impacts of climate change, but also how resilient they are in adapting, and what potential their knowledge systems have to contribute to adaptation in similarly changing ecosystems elsewhere, including the global North (Glazebrook 2010b; 2011; Glazebrook and Tiessen 2011; Glazebrook 2016a; 2016b). Women's care practices promote cooperation because many women are already so over-worked that sharing responsibilities is a benefit, while valuing well-being above profit safeguards precious, limited resources (Glazebrook 2016c). Women's agriculture and knowledge systems offer a new beginning for understanding nature and human possibilities of dwelling. These possibilities are alternative economics aimed not at the individual accumulation of private wealth. Rather, capital can appears in an alternative economics as a sociocultural system aimed at opening the public space to promote the thriving of people, non-human others, ecosystems and future generations (Glazebrook and Story 2015).

Patriarchal logics of domination, environmental degradation and its impacts on women's lives, global South–North relations, and the role of technoscience in enabling global conquest of the earth by capital come together in the perfect storm of climate change. Buckingham (2004) outlined impacts of ecofeminism-influenced groups on European environmental and equalities policy, and national forestry policy impacts of Chipko women's interventions in India have been well documented. The women's caucus of the United Nations Framework Convention on Climate Change hoped that the stalled process for an international climate agreement would be pushed forward by the increasing intervention of women's voices and growing awareness of women's situations. As early as 1987, Michael Zimmerman was arguing for "the global awakening of the quest for the feminine voice" to counter-balance the one-sidedness of the masculine voice (1987: 44). The Paris Agreement indeed achieved more than seemed possible, though still not enough, and possibly nothing if the Agreement remains unsigned by UN member states. It is impossible to know if ecofeminism influenced the discussions to break the deadlock. The most recent UNFCCC Gender Decision was taken in 2012 under the executive leadership of Christiana Figueres and with the strong and extremely active support of Mary Robinson, former President of Ireland. The presence of women's leadership with deep gender consciousness and strong commitment to women's needs advanced ecofeminist goals while making the explicit discourse of ecofeminism redundant.

Before we all hang up our ecofeminist hats and call it a day, however, it is important to remember how fragile gender gains can be. Gender difference is easily forgotten in patriarchy's logic that totalizes the human experience in the absence of explicitly gendered discourse. A post-ecofeminist world in which real change is being made toward the ecofeminist vision of alternative logics of human practice, policy and experience risks loss of momentum if academic, activist, spiritual and other ecofeminists do not keep theorizing, poetizing, acting, and intervening in policy. Insofar as feminism intersects with environmental and ecological thinking, it is clear that when it comes to logics of domination and the struggle to end oppression, we are all in it together. None of us are free, if one of us is chained.

Related Topics

Native American chaos theory and the politics of difference (Chapter 30); women, gender, and philosophies of global development (Chapter 34); feminist ethics of care (Chapter 43); neoliberalism, transnational feminisms, and global justice (Chapter 48); feminism, structural injustice, and responsibility (Chapter 49).

References

Allen, Paula Gunn (1990) "The Woman I Love Is a Planet; The Planet I Love Is a Tree," in Irene Diamond and Gloria Feman Orenstein (Eds.) *Reweaving the World: The Emergence of Ecofeminism*, San Francisco, CA: Sierra Club Books, 52–57.

Bacon, Francis (1980 [1620]) *The Great Instauration and New Atlantis*, J. Weinberger (Ed.) Arlington Heights, IL: Harlan Davidson.

Beauvoir, Simone de (1952) *The Second Sex*, H. M. Parshley (trans.), New York: Vintage Books.

—— (1984) *After the Second Sex: Interviews with Simone de Beauvoir*, Alice Schwarzer (Ed.) New York: Pantheon Books.

Biehl, Janet (1987) "It's Deep, but Is It Broad? An Ecofeminist Looks at Deep Ecology," *Kick It Over* (Special Supplement)(Winter), 3A.

Buckingham, Susan (2004) "Ecofeminism in the Twenty-First Century," *The Geographical Journal* 170: 146–154.

Cheney, Jim (1987) "Ecofeminism and Deep Ecology," *Environmental Ethics* 9: 115–149.

Christ, Carol P. (1978) "Why Women Need the Goddess: Phenomenological, Psychological, and Political Reflections," *Heresies: A Feminist Publication on Art and Politics* 5: 8–13.

Curtin, Deane (1999) *Chinnagrounder's Challenge: The Question of Ecological Citizenship*, Bloomington, IN: Indiana University Press.

Daly, Mary (1978) *Gyn/Ecology: The Metaethics of Radical Feminism*, Boston, MA: Beacon Press.

Diamond, Irene and Orenstein, G. F. (Eds.) (1990) *Reweaving the World: The Emergence of Ecofeminism*, San Francisco, CA: Sierra Club Books.

Dixon-Mueller, Ruth (1991) "Women in Agriculture: Counting the Labor Force in Developing Countries," in Mary Margaret Fonow and Judith A. Cook (Eds.) *Beyond Methodology: Feminist Scholarship as Lived Research*, Bloomington, IN: Indiana University Press, 226–247.

d'Eaubonne, Francoise (1974) *Le Féminisme ou la mort*, Paris: Pierre Horay.

FAO, IFAD and WFP (2015) *The State of Food Insecurity in the World 2015. Meeting the 2015 International Hunger Targets: Taking Stock of Uneven Progress* [online], Rome: FAO. Available from: www.fao.org/3/a-i4646e.pdf.

Glazebrook, Trish (2010a) "Gender and Climate Change: An Environmental Justice Perspective," in Ruth Irwin (Ed.) *Heidegger and Climate Change*, London: Continuum, 162–182.

——(2010b) "What Women Want: An (Eco)feminist in Dialogue with John D. Caputo," in Mark Zlomislić and Neal Deroo (Eds.) *Cross and Khôra: Deconstruction and Christianity in the Work of John D. Caputo*, Eugene, OR: Pickwick Publications, 230–258.

——(2011) "Women and Climate Change: A Case-Study from Northeast Ghana," *Hypatia* 26: 762–782.

——(2016a) "An Ecofeminist Analysis of Climate Change Adaptation in sub-Saharan Africa," in Mary Phillips and Nick Rumens (Eds.) *Reinvigorating Eco-Feminism: New Themes and Directions*, London: Routledge, 111–131.

——(2016b) "Anthropocenic Abjectification and Alternative Knowledge Traditions: A Geology of Method," in Richard Polt and John Wittrock (Eds.) *The Task of Philosophy in the Anthropocene: Axial Echoes in Global Space*, New York: Rowman & Littlefield, 164–171.

——(2016c) "Ecofeminism Without Borders: The Power of Method," in Byron Williston (Ed.) *Environmental Ethics for Canadians*, 2nd ed., Oxford: Oxford University Press, 61–82.

Glazebrook, Trish and Kola-Olusanya, Anthony (2009) "Role of Niger Delta Women in Ecological Justice Struggles," *Proceedings of the North American Association for Environmental Education*, [online] Oregon Convention Center, Portland OR. Available from: www.allacademic.com//meta/p_mla_apa_research_citation/3/1/9/7/9/pages319794/p319794-1.php.

——(2011) "Justice, Conflict, Capital, and Care: Oil in the Niger Delta," *Environmental Ethics* 33: 163–184.

Glazebrook, Trish and Story, Matt (2012) "The Community Obligations of Canadian Oil Companies: A Case Study of Talisman in the Sudan," in Ralph Tench, William Sun, and Brian Jones (Eds.) *Corporate Social Irresponsibility: A Challenging Concept*, Bingley, UK: Emerald Group, 231–261.

——(2015) "Heidegger and International Development," in Tziovanis Georgakis and Paul J. Ennis (Eds.) *Heidegger in the Twenty-First Century. Contributions to Phenomenology* 80, Dordrecht: Springer Science + Business Media, 121–139.

Glazebrook, Trish and Tiessen, Rebecca (2011) "Women, the Environment and Justice: Climate Change in North-East Ghana," in Anthony Kola-Olusanya, Ayo Omotayo, and Olanrewaju Fagbohun (Eds.) *Environment and Sustainability: Issues, Policies and Contentions*, Ibadan, Nigeria: University Press, 249–265.

Griffin, Susan (1978) *Woman and Nature: The Roaring Inside Her*, New York: HarperCollins.

Harding, Sandra (1986) *The Science Question in Feminism*, Ithaca, NY: Cornell University Press.

——(1991) *Whose Science? Whose Knowledge?* Ithaca, NY: Cornell University Press.

hooks, bell (1984) *Feminist Theory: From Margin to Center*, Brooklyn, NY: South End Press.

Johnson-Odim, Cheryl (1991) "Common Themes, Different Contexts: Third World Women and Feminism," in Chandra Talpade Mohanty, Ann Russo, and Lourdes Torres (Eds.) *Third World Women and the Politics of Feminism*, Bloomington, IN: Indiana University Press, 314–327.

LaDuke, Winona (2005) *Recovering the Sacred: The Power of Naming and Claiming*, Brooklyn, NY: South End Press.

Lott, Fraser C., Christidis, Nikolaos and Stott, Peter A. (2013) "Can the 2011 East African Drought Be Attributed to Human-Induced Climate Change?" *Geophysical Research Letters* 40(6): 1177–1181.

Mallory, Chaone (2009) "Ecofeminism and the Green Public Sphere," in Liam Leonard and John Q. Barry (Eds.) *Advances in Ecopolitics: The Transition to Sustainable Living and Practice*, London: Emerald Group, 139–154.

—— (2010) "What Is Ecofeminist Political Philosophy? Gender, Nature and the Political," *Environmental Ethics* 32: 305–322.

—— (2013) "Locating Ecofeminism in Encounters with Food and Place," *Journal of Agricultural and Environmental Ethics* 26: 171–189

Merchant, Carolyn (1980) *The Death of Nature: Women, Ecology, and the Scientific Revolution*, San Francisco, CA: Harper and Row.

Mies, Maria and Shiva, Vandana (1993) *Ecofeminism*, London: Zed Books.

Ortner, Sherry B. (1974) "Is Female to Male as Nature is to Culture?" in Michelle Zimbalist Rosaldo and Louise Lamphere (Eds.) *Woman, Culture, and Society*, Stanford, CA: Stanford University Press, 68–87.

Plant, Judith (Ed.) (1989) *Healing the Wounds: The Promise of Ecofeminism*, Santa Cruz, CA: New Society Publishers.

Plumwood, Val (1993) *Feminism and the Mastery of Nature*, London: Routledge.

Reuther, Rosemary Radford (1994) *Gaia and God: An Ecofeminist Theology of Earth Healing*, New York: HarperCollins.

—— (1996) *Women Healing Earth: Third World Women on Ecology, Feminism and Religion*, Maryknoll, NY: Orbis.

Riley, Shamara Shantu (1992) "Ecology Is a Sistah's Issue Too: The Politics of Emergent Afrocentric Ecowomanism," in Carol J. Adams (Ed.) *Ecofeminsim and the Sacred*, New York: Continuum, 191–203.

Roach, Catherine (1991) "Loving Your Mother: On the Woman-Nature Relation," *Hypatia* 6: 46–59.

Salleh, Ariel (1984) "Deeper Than Deep Ecology: The Eco-Feminist Connection," *Environmental Ethics* 6: 339–345.

—— (1992) "The Ecofeminist/Deep Ecology Debate: A Reply to Patriarchal Reason," *Environmental Ethics* 14: 195–216.

—— (1993) "Class, Race, and Gender Discourse in the Ecofeminism/Deep Ecology Debate," *Environmental Ethics* 15: 225–244.

—— (1997) *Ecofeminism as Politics: Nature, Marx and the Postmodern*, London: Zed Books.

—— (2006) "We in the North are the Biggest Problem for the South: A Conversation with Hilkka Pietila," *Capitalism Nature Socialism* 17: 44–61.

Shiva, Vandana (1988) *Staying Alive: Women, Ecology, and Development*, London: Zed Books.

—— (1991a) *Ecology and the Politics of Survival: Conflicts over Natural Resources in India*, London: Sage.

—— (1991b) *The Violence of the Green Revolution*, London: Zed Books.

—— (1993) "The Impoverishment of the Environment: Women and Children Last," in Maria Mies and Vandana Shiva (Eds.) *Ecofeminism*, Atlantic Highlands, NJ: Zed Books, 70–90.

—— (Ed.) (1994a) *Close to Home: Women Reconnect Ecology, Health, and Development Worldwide*, Gabriola Island, BC: New Society Publishers.

—— (1994b) "Empowering Women" [online]. Available from: https://likeawhisper.files.wordpress.com/2009/03/empoweringwomen.pdf.

—— (1996) *Caliber of Destruction: Globalization, Food Security and Women's Livelihoods*, Manila: Isis International.

—— (2000) *Stolen Harvest: The Hijacking of the Global Food Supply*, Cambridge, MA: South End Press.

Slicer, Deborah (1995) "Is There an Ecofeminism/Deep Ecology Debate?" *Environmental Ethics* 17: 151–169.

Tuana, Nancy, Ed. (1989) *Feminism and Science*, Bloomington, IN: Indiana University Press.

Starhawk (1979) *The Spiral Dance: A Rebirth of the Ancient Religion of the Great Goddess*, New York: Harper & Row.

Waring, Marilyn (1988) *If Women Counted: A New Feminist Economics*, New York: Harper & Row.

—— (1999) *Counting for Nothing: What Men Value and What Women Are Worth*, Toronto, ON: University of Toronto Press.

Warren, Karen (1990) "The Power and Promise of Ecofeminism," *Environmental Ethics* 12: 125–46.

——(Ed.) (1991) *Hypatia* 6(1): Special Issue on Ecological Feminism.

——(1993) "A Feminist Philosophical Perspective on Ecofeminist Spiritualities," in Carol J. Adams (Ed.) *Ecofeminism and the Sacred*, New York: Continuum, 119–132.

——(Ed.) (1996) *Ecological Feminist Philosophies*, Bloomington, IN: Indiana University Press.

—— (1997) "Taking Empirical Data Seriously: An Ecofeminist Philosophical Perspective," in Karen J. Warren (Ed.) *Ecofeminism: Women, Culture, Nature*, Bloomington, IN: Indiana University Press, 3–20.

——(2000) *Ecofeminist Philosophy: A Western Perspective on What It Is and Why It Matters*, Oxford: Rowman & Littlefield.

Zimmerman, Michael (1987) "Feminism, Deep Ecology, and Environmental Ethics," *Environmental Ethics* 9: 21–44.

36
ENCOUNTERING RELIGIOUS DIVERSITY
Perspectives from Feminist Philosophy of Religion
Patrice Haynes

Introduction

While feminist theology has flourished since the 1970s, it is something of a marginalized enclave in feminist theory, which is largely secular, if not thoroughly anti-religious, in outlook. However, the late 1990s saw the publication of two monographs expounding a feminist philosophy of religion (Anderson 1998; Jantzen 1998). Since then the field continues to reconfigure "malestream" philosophical reflection on religion in cogent and novel ways (on some of these, see Chapter 5 in this volume). Nevertheless, feminist philosophy of religion remains curiously mute on the topic of religious diversity (but see Anderson 2011). This is an oversight, not least because recent post-secular debates are often cashed out in terms of the "Muslim issue" (Braidotti 2008: 4), thus fuelling a toxic climate of "gendered Islamophobia" (see Perry 2014; Zine 2006).

In this chapter I consider how feminist philosophy of religion might address the so-called "problem" of religious diversity (see Gross 2005 for a critique of the treatment of religious diversity as a problem). While appreciating the overlapping terrain that brings feminist philosophy of religion and feminist theology into creative proximity, I highlight the epistemological issues raised by religious diversity as an area in which the feminist philosophy of religion can offer analyses distinct from feminist theology. I then suggest that dialectical materialism offers resources for avoiding the modern, secular reduction of religion to pure thought—i.e., to consciously held beliefs. Dialectical materialism endorses the feminist insistence on contextualizing truth claims, such that feminist philosophy of religion must seek to make explicit the socio-cultural and historical milieu in which religious beliefs gain their valence. But when women's religious subjectivity is contextualized the emancipatory impulse driving feminist critique is thrown into a disorienting spin. For the encounter with religiously diverse women reveals forms of religious subjectivity that conserve rather than confront the patriarchal gender hierarchy of their religious tradition. Insofar as this chapter ends with a provocation, it testifies to the richness and vitality promised by feminist philosophy of religion as we move through the twenty-first century.

Gendering Religious Diversity

The 1893 World Parliament of Religions, a feature of the Chicago World Fair held to celebrate the 400th anniversary of Christopher Columbus' "discovery" of the "New World," marks the first trial of modern interreligious dialogue. This watershed event saw religious leaders from around the world convene to promote mutual understanding between different religious traditions and a spirit of "brotherhood." Jeannine Hill Fletcher suggests that the Parliament is a useful point of departure for discussion on women in interreligious dialogue. She cites a newspaper account of the event, which noted: "The fair sex were there, too, and they were not neglected. But sisterhood in such a gathering was superfluous. The air was full of brotherhood, and it was of the generic kind, such as fits both sexes" (Fletcher 2013: 169). As feminists routinely explain, however, the notion of generic man is mistaken: supposedly universally applicable to both men and women, it implicitly presupposes the perspectives and experiences of men, which are held to be normative.

As it turns out, Fletcher explains, women were very much present at the Parliament— no doubt spurred by the growing global women's movement in the late nineteenth century. That said, women's involvement in the Parliament was downplayed in John Barrow's official editorship of the Parliament's proceedings (he failed to record that a distinct Women's Committee had even taken place). Nevertheless, after the 1893 Parliament, women from different religious traditions would increasingly foster interreligious encounters and relations with each other, seeking solidarity across religious borders in the face of shared patriarchal oppression, and desiring to share stories of their faith *as lived*. However, at official and formal levels women remained overlooked in the work of interreligious dialogue. As late as 1998, feminist theologian Ursula King remarked that "feminism remains a missing dimension in interreligious dialogue" (King 1998: 42).

While feminist theology gained serious traction in the academy from the 1970s on, the standard preoccupation revolved around questioning and reconfiguring Christian doctrines. At the turn of the twenty-first century, feminist theologian Rita Gross (who was raised in the Judeo-Christian tradition but became a Western Tibetan Buddhist as an adult) would rightly complain that whenever feminist theology addressed religious diversity it would principally be in the Christian context—intra-Christian, not inter-religious, diversity (Gross 2000: 73). With the twenty-first century well underway the picture has begun to change: Gross' plea for feminist theology to engage seriously with religious diversity is being heeded in various ways.

Feminist theologians promise distinctive contributions to debates on religious diversity (Egnell 2009; Fletcher 2013). These include: (1) a hermeneutics of suspicion sensitive to ways religions uncritically justify and propagate gendered norms; (2) an emphasis on sharing personal experiences and life stories, placing the accent on religion as lived rather than grounded in doctrine; (3) a stress on relationality and recognition of multiple or "hybrid" identities; (4) orienting interreligious dialogue so that it is life-enhancing; and (5) probing the category "religions" in ways that resist reifying traditions and effacing their dynamic and internally diverse character.

Indeed, regarding (5), the very terms "religion" and "the religions"—the former a generic notion and the latter particular expressions of religious beliefs and practices—are decidedly modern, Western (Christian) categories. They emerge in theological and philosophical discourses grappling with Enlightenment disputes on faith and reason, and with a colonial project bringing Europeans into contact with people and cultures around the world. Feminist perspectives on religious diversity must, therefore, engage with postcolonial critiques of the Eurocentrism prevailing in theoretical reflection on religious diversity (Daggers 2012; Kwok 2005).

It is by addressing the epistemic implications of religious diversity that feminist philosophy of religion can bring a perspective distinct from feminist theology to debates on religious diversity. Both feminist theology and feminist philosophy of religion share a common dedication to a feminist project that is at once theoretical, seeking to disclose the multiple causes of women's subordination, and practical, aiming to bring about equitable relations between women and men. Feminist theology and feminist philosophy of religion diverge, though, insofar as the former can legitimately appeal to scriptural texts and religious doctrines informed by scripture, while the latter admits no confessional authorities. However, if feminist philosophy of religion restricts itself to reason alone, it does *not* assume the universal reason of much analytic philosophy of religion but takes seriously the feminist contention that there is no impossible God's eye view, because thought is always situated in embodied life and socio-historical context.

Feminist Epistemology and Religious Beliefs

By complicating notions of truth and rationality, feminist philosophy of religion can create illuminating pathways through the issues generated by religious diversity. Indeed, incorporating developments in feminist epistemology into philosophy of religion is an important way in which this sphere may be transformed by feminist perspectives. Admittedly, not all feminist philosophers of religion would foreground epistemology in this way, suspecting that epistemology remains invested in a "masculinist" symbolic (see Jantzen 1998: 77–99). However, religious diversity raises the question of truth in a stark way: How to make sense of varying religious propositions, regarding ultimate sacred reality and human salvation (or fulfilment), when these often appear to conflict with each other? Is, for example, ultimate sacred reality to be identified with a personal God as in the Abrahamic traditions (Judaism, Christianity, and Islam), or with an impersonal Oneness (as in certain forms of Hinduism) or emptiness (as in Buddhism)? Is human salvation to be attained through faith in Christ and the gift of God's grace (Christianity), or by abolishing all desires and cravings (Buddhism)? Typically, analytic philosophers of religion hold to the realist tenet that there is "a truth to the matter" (Basinger 2014). But rather than sidelining questions of truth, feminist philosophy of religion can contest religious truth claims from a feminist perspective without abandoning the notion of truth altogether (see Anderson 2011: 406).

In keeping with a standard move in feminist epistemology, Pamela Sue Anderson maintains that feminist philosophical reflection on religious diversity should uncover points of gender-blindness that create sites of "epistemic inertia" (Anderson 2011: 409). Such inertia not only impedes efforts to ascertain the truth of religious beliefs but also leaves unchallenged the ethical implications of certain religious beliefs for women (and, similarly, some groups of men).

To elaborate, for the feminist philosopher of religion it is not simply a matter of disputing, say, the nature of ultimate sacred reality—God, Oneness, emptiness—but of recognizing how beliefs about ultimate sacred reality inform our understanding of sexual difference. For instance, Jewish and Christian feminists have noted that the prevalence of male imagery for God in Judeo-Christian religious language reinforces a gender hierarchy whereby men are considered more God-like than women—as Mary Daly once claimed, "If God is male, then the male is God" (Daly 1973: 19). Rita Gross points out that Buddhist women do not face the issue of the maleness of God since Buddhism is a non-theistic religion. Nevertheless the Buddhist tradition devalues women in different ways. One is the contention that to be born a woman is the result of bad karma (see Anālayo 2014). As to accounts of human salvation, the major world religions tend to view women as more prone to err from the righteous path, often leading men astray in the process. In the Abrahamic religions, Eve disobeys God by eating the forbidden fruit of the tree of knowledge, tempting Adam to do the same. Consequently, Jewish, Christian, and Muslim women are viewed to be the gateway to sinfulness, guilt and immorality. It then becomes the role of men to ensure that women uphold "female" virtues: chastity, fidelity, and modesty. Indian religions also contain sacred writings (e.g., *The Laws of Manu* in Hinduism) that stress the need for women to defer to men to ensure a well-functioning society.

These examples only touch on some ways in which a range of religious traditions often produce claims that denigrate women. However, when analytic philosophy of religion considers the implications of religious diversity for religious truth it rarely considers how religious beliefs depict women in controversial, often sexist, ways. In seeking to glean the truth of religious beliefs, feminist theologians might bring a hermeneutical lens, reinterpreting tradition in ways that disclose insights congruent with feminist thought that have been suppressed by patriarchal society. A Muslim feminist might point out that unlike the Genesis story in Judeo-Christian scripture, the Qur'an holds Adam and Eve equally responsible for defying God. She could argue that those hadiths—the sayings and actions of the Prophet Mohammed recorded by others after his death—that proclaim Eve to be the first transgressor are most likely influenced by Jewish and Christian thought (for a critique of such a reading see Hidayatullah 2013). By contrast, feminist philosophers of religion can interrogate religious claims to truth by examining epistemological problems arising from the repeated failure to consider religions' assumptions around sex and gender.

The following illustrates this gender-blindness. In *Religious Ambiguity and Religious Diversity*, Robert McKim explains why religious diversity may be viewed as problematic:

> It is not just the fact that there are diverse [religious] beliefs that is striking: it is the fact that wise people who think carefully and judiciously, who are intelligent, clever, honest, reflective and serious, . . . who admit ignorance when appropriate and who have relied on what has seemed to them to be the relevant considerations in . . . acquiring their beliefs, hold these diverse beliefs.
> (McKim 2001: 129)

For McKim, the philosophical task is to reflect critically on the fact of disagreement about religious beliefs among "people of integrity." The contentious point, for McKim, is how far one must hold one's religious beliefs (or rejection of such beliefs) tentatively given conflict among one's "epistemic peers" (Basinger 2014). However, no consideration is given to how norms and values regarding rationality and belief formation are imbricated in a context of relations of power that downgrades women's epistemic status so that they cannot be regarded as epistemic peers. Here is a case of epistemic inertia that feminists can overcome by raising questions about epistemic norms and who counts as a knowing subject (Fricker 2000; Langton 2000).

Furthermore, the attempt to resolve (or minimize) conflict among religious epistemic peers presumes that there are "experts" capable of grasping the whole of a religious tradition and representing it in interreligious dialogue (McKim 2001: 134–135). Indeed, the very term "dialogue" is moot because it overemphasizes intellectual argument at the expense of creative, affective encounters. However, as Fletcher notes, what counts as representing a religious tradition is problematic (2013: 173). Insofar as women in interreligious settings often draw attention to religion as lived and embodied in everyday life (not reducible to propositions and doctrinal orthodoxy), philosophy of religion, mindful of women's voices, may be reminded that "'religions' are ultimately unrepresentable in any totalizing or comprehensive sense" (Fletcher 2013: 173).

Anxiety about truth in the face of religious diversity has since the 1980s seen philosophical and theological discussions circulate around three main positions (Race 1983). The first is exclusivism: the claims of one's own religious tradition are true while all others are false. The second is inclusivism, which grants that other religions may recognise *some* truths while upholding one's own tradition as possessing the most complete and significant religious truths. Finally, religious pluralism (at least the sort inspired by John Hick) asserts that many of the world's religions are different yet equally veridical manifestations of, and responses to, one ultimate sacred reality.

At first glance, religious pluralism seems the most promising option for a feminist perspective on religious diversity. This is certainly Gross's view. For her it is inconceivable that a feminist, committed to affirming diversity, would emphasize the superiority of one religious tradition over others—particularly since all religions historically enshrine patriarchal beliefs and practices that harm women (Gross 2001: 89). For Gross, religion's proper job is "transforming humans into gentler, kinder, more compassionate beings" (2001: 90). Accordingly, she gives primacy to ethics rather than doctrinal truth, and so holds that exclusivist and inclusivist positions can only ever invite discord and, at worse, conflict.

However, feminist theologian Jenny Daggers is wary of the sort of transreligious theology of religions proposed by Gross because it excludes women committed to the truth and integrity of their religious tradition—even as these demand critical scrutiny with respect to their engrained patriarchy (Daggers 2012). Moreover, the pluralist position viewed through a postcolonial lens could be charged with reinstating Eurocentric universalism in a new guise, as it downplays differences in favor of highlighting commonalities between religious traditions. Seeking to preserve the incommensurable differences between religious traditions without homogenizing them, while also encouraging creative interreligious relations, Daggers turns from pluralism to particularism. She does so with the aim of articulating a *Christian* (white) feminist theology of religions (2012: 159–184). Presumably feminist theologians from other religious traditions and socio-cultural locations could adopt the sort of particularism elaborated by Daggers so that they too may engage in interreligious relations using terms drawn from their particular religion.

By contrast, a feminist philosopher of religion concerned with making visible the gender-blindness of epistemological models, could examine the theories of truth and error, epistemic norms around disagreement, and values (both constitutive and contextual) that guide exclusivist, inclusivist, pluralist, and even particularist positions. For example, Anderson (2011: 408–409) targets the epistemic framework espoused by Christian exclusivists such as Alvin Plantinga. For Plantinga there are central Christian tenets that are "properly basic." That the world was created by God, an almighty, all-knowing and perfectly good personal being, and that human salvation is by way of the life and sacrificial death of God's son, are two such beliefs (Plantinga 2008 [1995]: 41). Aside from his failing to address the gendered conception of the divine, Anderson indicts Plantinga for exempting core religious beliefs from questioning and revision. The trouble is, Anderson argues, upholding such exemption leads to an epistemic inertia at odds with the pursuit of truth. For Anderson, it is only by pursuing truth that we can discern how religious beliefs contribute to women's subjugation.

This suggests that commitment to a particular religious tradition risks producing epistemic inertia insofar as such commitment demands treating certain doctrinal claims as unquestionable. Does this mean that Daggers' particularism is at odds with the effort to surmount epistemic inertia endorsed by Anderson? Seeking to show how her revised particularism, with its stress on the incommensurability of religious traditions, does not preclude interreligious exchange, Daggers indirectly responds to Anderson's concerns. Drawing on theologian Catherine Cornille, Daggers maintains that commitment to a religious tradition must be tempered by openness to other traditions. This encourages a level of "'doctrinal humility' and 'doctrinal hospitality'" (Daggers citing Cornille 2012: 173) that can provoke the transformation of—in Daggers' case—Christian tradition. Yet if the *integrity* of a religious tradition is to hold then the transformation occasioned by encountering religious others can only go so far. There is, therefore, a tension between the desire for openness and transformation (countering epistemic inertia) and upholding the particularity of religious traditions. However, it is my contention that feminist theorists must question all religious beliefs and practices that enhance men's lives at the expense of women's. Such questioning need not be antipathetic to tradition—feminist theology shows how critique is possible while remaining rooted within a religious tradition.

A further intervention that a feminist philosopher might make in debates about exclusivism, inclusivism and pluralism is to question the demand for neutral or common ground from which to assess the truth of competing claims objectively. That neutral ground must be sought is a claim that most feminist thinkers would contest (Jantzen 2001). Such ground presupposes a disinterested subject detached from any socio-cultural location: an ideal observer able to achieve a "view from nowhere." This conception of the subject is the centerpiece of an androcentric philosophy that refuses to admit the relevance of socio-cultural location to epistemic practitioners. Without abandoning rationality, feminist philosophers of religion can draw on feminist epistemology to tackle the difficult aim of establishing ways to adjudicate competing religious beliefs without presupposing an impossible view from nowhere.

I have suggested that epistemology offers a fertile site for bringing feminist philosophical perspectives to bear on the "problem" of religious diversity. A key strategy for feminist philosophy of religion, then, is to expose how epistemological models used by "malestream" philosophy of religion entrench the discipline in gender-blindness. In taking a constructive turn, feminist philosophy of religion could seek to articulate an epistemology that is both attentive to epistemic locatedness and, given an adequately revised conception of rationality, emboldened to tackle thorny questions on how truth should be figured in discussions on religious diversity. Could a feminist philosopher of religion defend some form of exclusivism? Or, approaching the question of truth from another angle, how might the feminist philosopher of religion facilitate learning the truths, however disputed, of other religious traditions? This could be an exercise in cross-cultural understanding that dovetails with the ethical intent to promote open and hospitable relations with religious others. I am sympathetic to Gross' criticisms of religious exclusivism and inclusivism noted earlier. Nevertheless, I do not think that commitment to the truth claims of a particular religious tradition is necessarily hostile to the feminist endeavour to overcome women's subjugation by patriarchal orders. Daggers' revised particularism points to the idea of "critical commitment" to one's religious tradition, which values both its integrity and its receptiveness to critique from those internal and external to that tradition.

Materialist Interventions: Religion as Real Abstraction

Insofar as feminist philosophy of religion is *feminist* it is at once a form of social criticism—its theoretical reasoning strives to connect with collective efforts to overcome the devaluing of women by patriarchal socio-cultural orders. It may be feared that this practical orientation of feminist philosophy of religion evades questions regarding the epistemic truth of religious beliefs and the rationality of maintaining an exclusivist, inclusivist or pluralist response to religious diversity. For sure, feminist philosophy of religion directed towards the "problem" of religious diversity will seek to examine how traditional epistemic norms implicitly support false and damaging beliefs about women. However, I have advocated a more rigorously self-reflexive philosophical method that refuses to excise contextual socio-cultural values and interests as irrelevant to philosophical inquiry. Such a method can enhance our ability to rationally assess religious truth claims.

That said, fixation on the epistemic status of religious belief may be queried by post-secular discourse informed by Marx's dialectical materialism. Seeking to develop a critical philosophy of religion, Daniel Whistler draws on Marxist social theorist Alberto Toscano and feminist philosopher Gillian Howie to rethink religions in terms of "real abstraction" (Whistler 2014). For all his antipathy towards religion, along with his Feuerbachian contention that "man makes religion," Marx "provides us with a potent *critique* of the [Enlightenment] critique of religion" (Toscano 2010: 10). Boldly put, for Marx, religion is a form of real abstraction because it is both true and false. It is true because it bears witness to an antagonistic social reality (namely, social relations that produce economic inequality); false because it invokes an autonomous, spiritual reality independent of humanity. For Marx, "the crucial error is to treat real abstractions as mere 'arbitrary product[s] of human reflection'" (Marx cited in Toscano 2010: 12)—for they are *necessary* illusions. Theistic beliefs, therefore, are not founded on a mistaken understanding of reality that can be corrected by pointing out the lack of evidence for the existence of God. Rather such beliefs are a rational way of making sense of, and living in, a world characterized by social injustice—a world that fails to deliver genuine freedom, equality, and happiness. The emancipatory task, for Marx, is not to correct religious beliefs as illusory but to "give up a [social] condition that requires illusion" (Marx cited in McLellan 2000: 72).

Religious realists (myself included) who maintain that ultimate sacred reality is objectively real may worry that Marx undermines religious truths by anthropologizing or naturalizing them. However, I leave this concern in suspense so that we do not miss the key point that, for Marx, religion as real abstraction has material efficacy. Religion concretely articulates the complex and contradictory lived experience of alienated social relations produced by the capitalist system. The notion of religion as real abstraction shifts attention away from its conceptual representation (i.e., religious beliefs) to its extra-conceptual social actuality.

Given these insights, Marx criticizes anti-religious critique for focusing on the truth content of religious belief when a materialist, emancipatory critique requires scrutiny of the social relations constitutive of such beliefs. Whistler suggests that philosophy of religion in accord with dialectical materialism continually oscillates between critique and the critique of critique (Whistler 2014: 184). Citing Toscano, Whistler explains that the principal task for a critical philosophy of religion is "to confront the social logic into which they [religious abstractions] are inscribed, and the dependence of these abstractions on given modes of production and social intercourse" (2014: 191).

This materialist re-orienting of critique is, as Whistler notes, paralleled in Howie's important work *Between Feminism and Materialism*. Whistler's focus on real abstraction in Howie's work reveals that the feminist critique of reason, identity and universality must also be critiqued. For feminist theory to begin at all, according to Howie, it must use theoretical abstractions as tools that afford the "critical distance" needed to turn real abstractions (e.g., epistemic norms such as identity and objectivity) against themselves by tracing their imbrication in contingent socio-cultural conditions (Howie 2010: 58).

Taking its lead from dialectical materialism, critical theory reminds us that critique must not be limited to theoretical disputes. There must also be a dialectical critique of critique. Thus, the critique of religion will remain myopic so long as it remains gripped by arguments about the truth of religious beliefs and epistemic justifications for upholding exclusivism, inclusivism or pluralism. With this in mind, feminist philosophy of religion in a dialectical materialist register would not repeat the Enlightenment reduction of religion to mere thought. Rather it would challenge "both the universalising and ahistoricising tendencies of contemporary philosophy of religion" (Whistler 2014: 192) by conceiving religions as real abstractions, thus attending to the concrete ways in which religious beliefs are efficacious in women's lives.

One area in which feminist philosophers of religion would do well to view religion in terms of real abstraction, i.e., as socially located, is regarding the practice of veiling by some Muslim women. Islam has long been criticized by Western societies for being oppressive towards women, the veil serving as the most potent symbol of (purported) Islamic misogyny. The scriptural basis for veiling can be found in certain verses of the Qur'an and some hadiths. For example, the Qur'an states: "And say to the believing women that they should avert their gaze and guard their modesty . . . and they should throw their veils over their bosoms, and not display their adornment except to their husbands or fathers" (Holy Qur'an 33: 59 cited in Zine 2006: 243). Islamic scholars dispute how to interpret scripture, particularly the hadiths, with respect to women's veiling. However, of interest here is the set of beliefs concerning ideals of Islamic womanhood that support the practice of veiling: modesty, obedience, humility, and similar qualities. It might be tempting for liberal-minded feminists—whether secular or religious—to discredit such beliefs by pointing out their erroneous sexist assumptions, lack of adequate justification and harsh disciplining of women's bodies. But this reduces the issue of veiling to a matter of Muslim patriarchal ideology, that is, a set of beliefs to be debunked by liberal feminist theory. Such an approach overlooks the specific socio-historical, cultural and political matrix in which Muslim women veil.

In her work on Islamic women's organizations in Cairo, Egypt, Sherine Hafez explains that efforts to understand the situation of pious, veil-wearing Muslim women in contemporary Egypt are thwarted if the focus is solely on how Islamic beliefs shape these women's lives. Rather, the status of such women must be "contextualized within the historical development of anti-colonial nationalism, state building projects, and nationalism" (Hafez cited in Kassam 2013: 145). In the particular locale of Egypt's Islamic revival over the last two decades or so, the increasing number of women wearing the veil cannot be entirely attributed to the imposition of androcentric Islamic ideals. Geopolitical and socio-historical factors also affect the practice of veiling and the religious comportment of contemporary Egyptian women. The significance of the veil shifts according to the specific contexts within which it is worn. The veil worn in Taliban-ruled Afghanistan cannot be understood in the same way as the veil worn by, for example, converted (or reverted, to use the preferred Muslim term) African American Sunni Muslim women in twenty-first-century South Central Los Angeles (Rouse 2004). By taking heed of how women's religiosity is distinctively contextualized, feminist philosophers of religion can avoid the simplistic identification of religion with religious beliefs.

Contextualizing Women's Religious Subjectivity

I now wish to return to the issue of religious diversity to highlight how feminist philosophy of religion is faced with a frankly alarming challenge when it reflects on certain models of women's religious subjectivities evident in a range of religious traditions—namely, those subjectivities that appear to be fundamentally at odds with feminist emancipatory aspirations.

In recent years anthropologists (e.g., Saba Mahmood) and historians of religion (e.g., Mary L. Keller and Phyllis Mack) have provided rich empirical details on how women in particular socio-historical situations construct their religious subjectivity and with this establish distinctive forms of agency. All too briefly: Mahmood's *Politics of Piety* examines the women's mosque movement in 1990s Cairo, Egypt, which saw participants endeavoring to cultivate a pious subjectivity by fostering "those bodily aptitudes, virtues, habits and desires that serve to ground Islamic principles" (2012 [2005]: 45); Keller's work has explored the religious subjectivity of spirit-possessed women in Shona (Zimbabwean) history (Keller 2003); and Mack's research on Quaker women in eighteenth-century England highlights their efforts to do "what is right" as this is determined by God, rather than personal desires (Mack 2003: 156).

These studies elucidate notions of religious subjectivity that do not centre on an individual's assenting to a set of consciously held beliefs, in the manner of the autonomous, rational subject of Western modernity. Rather, the religious subjectivities described are constituted by a woman embodying practices that endeavour to accomplish a way of life, an ethos, delineated by the norms and ideals of her tradition.

Scholars such as Mahmood, Keller, and Mack concentrate on the local conditions in which women live their lives: the specific social relations, institutions, discursive traditions, embodied practices and networks of power. They identify notions of (religious) subjectivity that challenge what Keller calls the "hypervaluation of autonomy" (Keller 2003: 78) in secular, Western thought, including feminist theory. Liberal, humanist subjects act according to their *own* will or conscious intention. In contrast the religious subjectivity of the women described above is characterized less by self-expression and more by self-transcendence (Mack 2003: 153). However, to interpret such women as exhibiting no more than a "deplorable passivity and docility" (Mahmood 2012 [2005]: 15) would be to presume a Western, secular conception of agency. It would miss how religious subjectivity may be understood as achieving agency and selfhood *through* embodied, normative relations (e.g., obedience, duty, responsibility, etc.) with otherness (e.g., the will of God, tradition, the needs of others), relations that constrain as well as empower.

Of course, the liberal account of agency premised on an autonomous, fully rational subject unencumbered by social relations has been criticized by feminist philosophers (Stoljar 2013). However, despite the various theories of agency and autonomy developed in feminist thought, Mahmood contends that they rarely problematize "the universality of the desire—central for liberal and progressive thought, and presupposed by the concept of resistance it authorizes—to be free from relations of subordination, and for women, from structures of male domination" (Mahmood 2012 [2005]: 10).

While feminism is far from uniform, it is fair to say that the basic axiom shared by all feminists is that the patriarchal subordination of women by men is unjust and must be overcome. In that feminist philosophy of religion is committed to opposing gender inequality could it be viewed as eulogizing a Eurocentric, secular idea of subjectivity at odds with socially conservative models of religious subjectivity and agency? The danger is twofold. Either feminist philosophy of religion risks finding itself deaf to those voices that sound out a different story to that of the supposedly universal liberal subject. Or it takes seriously the historicization of religious subjectivity but, unable to adopt a critical position, finds itself swept off by the currents of cultural relativism.

These are grave difficulties that I cannot address here. Certainly the dialectical materialist approach to feminist philosophy of religion developed in this chapter would press for fine-grained, localized conceptions of religious subjectivity and agency. But as a form of social criticism, feminist philosophy of religion would also seek to identify unjust relations between men and women so that these may be overcome. Howie suggests that a focus on interests offers a way to make sense of the patriarchal relation as one of domination: "the systematic subordination of the interests of women to those of men" (2010: 200). However, problems arise when feminist theory takes into consideration women whose religious subjectivity pursues fulfilling the interests of God or their community rather than their own personal interests.

We need to avoid treating conservative religious subjectivities as merely instances of false consciousness (the internalization of oppressive norms). Instead, a key task for feminist philosophy of religion is to theorize how concepts such as interest, constraint, power and patriarchy may do explanatory work while being appreciative of "what agency means in relation to specifically *religious* grammars" (Bracke 2008: 63). Because I believe it is overly simplistic to ossify a distinction between liberal "agency as autonomy" and religious "agency as submission," I am drawn to Tanya Zion-Waldok's concept of "devoted resistance." She seeks to articulate the possibility of social critique and political resistance for women who, nevertheless, are deeply committed to their religious tradition (Zion-Waldok 2015).

The dialectical materialist insight to be added is that social transformation is unlikely to result simply by changing consciousness (Mahmood 2012 [2005]: 188). Rather concrete transformation will be prompted by, and organized around, local problems. To the extent that these problems concern women's interests or flourishing the response may be considered feminist in character. The forming of alliances between (differently) religious and secular women, between socially conservative and progressive women need not appeal to a priori, universal principles but to relations of solidarity that emerge as similarities are discerned "between one woman's situation and another's, between this local group of women and other groups" (Howie 2010: 204).

Conclusion

According to Basinger, among the issues philosophers discuss that have practical bearings "none is more relevant today than the question of religious diversity" (Basinger 2014). Given this, it is incumbent on feminist philosophers of religion to address the gendered implications of debates on religious diversity and interreligious encounters. Challenging gender-blind concepts of truth and rationality is one way feminist philosophers of religion can agitate this field. The notion of religion as "real abstraction" helps us circumvent interminable debates about the epistemic status of religious belief, focusing instead on religion as a lived experience, enmeshed in specific socio-historical relations. However, contextualized accounts of women's religious subjectivities tug at the secular, Eurocentric values woven into progressive feminism. Feminist philosophy of religion is thus provoked to think afresh the nature of its emancipatory aims in light of women who prioritise their religious commitments over resisting the patriarchal structure of their tradition. The way forward for feminist philosophy of religion is far from obvious. The dialectical materialist point is that feminist philosophy of religion must remain alert to the concrete actualities of women's religious lives, including any local problems such women seek to address, such as the problem of piety. The wider point for feminist theory is that it must engage with the experiences of religiously diverse women if it wishes to expose its entanglement with assumptions regarding subjectivity, agency and even the nature of critique that could only ever blunt its emancipatory force.

Further Reading

Cady, Linell E. and Tracy Fessenden (2013) *Religion, The Secular and the Politics of Sexual Difference*, New York: Columbia University Press. (A timely, interdisciplinary collection of essays questioning whether secularism is good for women as often presumed.)

Cheetham, David, Pratt, Douglas, and Thomas, David (2013) *Understanding Interreligious Relations*, Oxford: Oxford University Press. (A comprehensive volume on engaging with religious others; Part One offers perspectives from a range of world religions.)

Griffiths, Paul J. (2001) *Problems of Religious Diversity*, Oxford and Malden, MA: Blackwell. (A clear overview of philosophical approaches to debates on religious diversity.)

King, Ursula and Beattie, Tina (Eds.) (2005) *Gender, Religion and Diversity: Cross-Cultural Perspectives*. (A useful volume of essays on women and contemporary religious studies.)

Related Topics

Feminist engagement with Judeo-Christian religious traditions (Chapter 5); rationality and objectivity in feminist philosophy (Chapter 20); testimony, trust, and trustworthiness (Chapter 21); epistemic injustice, ignorance, and trans experience (Chapter 22); the genealogy and viability of the concept of intersectionality (Chapter 28); feminist conceptions of autonomy (Chapter 41); multicultural and postcolonial feminisms (Chapter 47); feminism and freedom (Chapter 53); feminism and power (Chapter 54); feminist approaches to violence and vulnerability (Chapter 55).

References

Anālayo, Bhikkhu (2014) "Bad Karma and Female Birth," *Journal of Buddhist Ethics* 21: 109–153.

Anderson, Pamela Sue (1998) *A Feminist Philosophy of Religion: The Rationality and Myths of Religious Belief*, Oxford: Blackwell.

—— (2011) "A Feminist Perspective," in Chad Meister (Ed.) *The Oxford Handbook of Religious Diversity*, Oxford: Oxford University Press, 405–420.

Basinger, David (2014) "Religious Diversity (Pluralism)," *Stanford Encyclopedia of Philosophy* [online] Fall 2015 edition. Available from: http://plato.stanford.edu/entries/religious-pluralism/.

Bracke, Sarah (2008) "Conjugating the Modern/Religious, Conceptualizing Female Religious Agency: Contours of a 'Post-secular' Conjuncture," *Theory Culture & Society* 25(6): 51–67.

Braidotti, Rosi (2008) "In Spite of the Times: The Postsecular Turn in Feminism," *Theory, Culture and Society* 25(6): 1–24.

Daggers, Jenny (2012) "Gendering Interreligious Dialogue: Ethical Considerations," in Jenny Daggers (Ed.) *Gendering Christian Ethics*, Newcastle-upon-Tyne: Cambridge Scholars, 51–74.

Daly, Mary (1973) *Beyond God the Father: Towards a Women's Liberation*, London: The Women's Press.

Egnell, Helene (2009) "The Messiness of Actual Existence: Feminist Contributions to Theology of Religions," in Annette Esser et al. (Eds.) *Journal of the European Society of Women in Theological Research* 17: 13–27.

Fletcher, Jeannine Hill (2013) "Women in Inter-Religious Dialogue," in Catherine Cornille (Ed.) *The Wiley-Blackwell Companion to Inter-Religious Dialogue*, Oxford and Malden, MA: Wiley-Blackwell, 168–183.

Fricker, Miranda (2000) "Feminism in Epistemology: Pluralism Without Postmodernism" in Miranda Fricker and Jennifer Hornsby (Eds.) *The Cambridge Companion to Feminism in Philosophy*, Cambridge: Cambridge University Press: 146–165.

Gross, Rita M. (2000) "Feminist Theology: Religiously Diverse Neighborhood or Christian Ghetto? Roundtable Lead-In," *Feminist Studies in Religion* 16(2): 73–78.

—— (2001) "Feminist Theology as Theology of Religions," *Feminist Theology* 26: 83–101.

—— (2005) "Excuse Me, But What's the Question? Isn't Religious Diversity Normal?" in Paul F. Knitter (Ed.) *The Myth of Religious Superiority: Multifaith Explorations of Religious Diversity*, Mary Knoll, NY: Orbis, 75–87.

Hidayatullah, Aysha (2013) "The Qur'anic Rib-ectomy: Scriptural Purity, Imperial Dangers, and Other Obstacles to the Interfaith Engagement of Feminist Qur'anic Interpretation," in Catherine Cornille and Jillian Maxey (Eds.) *Women and Interreligious Dialogue*, Eugene OR: Wipf & Stock, 150–167.

Howie, Gillian (2010) *Between Feminism and Materialism: A Question of Method*, Basingstoke: Palgrave Macmillan.

Jantzen, Grace M. (1998) *Becoming Divine: Towards a Feminist Philosophy of Religion*, Manchester: Manchester University Press.

Kassam, Zayn (2013) "Constructive Interreligious Dialogue Concerning Muslim Women," in Catherine Cornille and Jillian Maxey (Eds.) *Women and Interreligious Dialogue*, Eugene, OR: Cascade Books, 127–149.

—— (2001) "What Price Neutrality? A Reply to Paul Helm," *Religious Studies* 37(1): 87–92.

Keller, Mary (2003) "Divine Women and the Nehanda Mhondoro: Strengths and Limitations of the Sensible Transcendental in a Post-Colonial World of Religious Women," in Morny Joy, Kathleen O'Grady, and Judith L. Poxon (Eds.) *Religion in French Feminist Thought*, London: Routledge, 68–82.

King, Ursula (1998) "Feminism: The Missing Dimension in the Dialogue of Religions," in John May (Ed.) *Pluralism and the Religions: The Theological and Political Dimensions*, London: Cassell, 40–55.

Kwok, Pui-Lan (2005) *Postcolonial Imagination and Feminist Theology*, Louisville, KY: Westminister John Knox Press.

Langton, Rae (2000) "Feminism in Epistemology: Exclusion and Objectification" in Miranda Fricker and Jennifer Hornsby (Eds.) *The Cambridge Companion to Feminism in Philosophy*, Cambridge: Cambridge University Press, 127–145.

Mack, Phyllis (2003) "Religion, Feminism, and the Problem of Agency: Reflections on Eighteenth-Century Quakerism," *Signs: Journal of Women in Culture and Society* 29(1): 149–177.

McKim, Robert (2001) *Religious Ambiguity and Religious Diversity*, Oxford: Oxford University Press.

McLellan, David (2000) *Karl Marx: Selected Writings*, Oxford: Oxford University Press.

Mahmood, Saba (2012 [2005]) *Politics of Piety: The Islamic Revival and the Feminist Subject*, Princeton, NJ: Princeton University Press.

Perry, Barbara (2014) "Gendered Islamophobia: Hate Crime Against Muslim Women," *Social Identities: Journal of Race, Nation and Culture* 20(1): 74–89.

Plantinga, Alvin ([2008] 1995) "Pluralism: A Defense of Religious Exclusivism," in Chad Meister (Ed.) *The Philosophy of Religion Reader*, London and New York: Routledge, 40–59.

Race, Alan (1983) *Christian and Religious Pluralism: Patterns in the Christian Theology of Religions*, London: SCM Press.

Rouse, Carolyn Moxley (2004) *Engaged Surrender: African American Women and Islam*, Berkley, CA and Los Angeles, CA: California University Press.

Stoljar, Natalie (2013) "Feminist Perspectives on Autonomy," *Stanford Encyclopedia of Philosophy* [online]. Available from: https://plato.stanford.edu/entries/feminism-autonomy.

Toscano, Alberto (2010) "Beyond Abstraction: Marx and the Critique of the Critique of Religion," *Historical Materialism* 18: 3–29.

Whistler, Daniel (2014) "Howie's *Between Feminism and Materialism* and the Critical History of Religions," *SOPHIA* 53(2): 183–192.

Zine, Jasmin (2006) "Unveiled Sentiments: Gendered Islamophobia and Experiences of Veiling among Muslim Girls in a Canadian Islamic School," *Equity and Excellence in Education* 39: 239–252.

Zion-Waldoks, Tanya (2015) "Politics of Devoted Resistance: Agency, Feminism, and Religion among Orthodox Agunah Activists in Israel," *Gender & Society* 29(1): 73–97.

Part V

ETHICS, POLITICS, AND AESTHETICS

Aesthetics

37

HISTORICIZING FEMINIST AESTHETICS

Tina Chanter

This chapter is organized around two central questions. First, if art is political, in what ways is it political? Most theorists who identify themselves in some way with feminist aesthetics agree that art is political, but differ in how they think it is political. The second question is, if we assert that art is political in some way—although we need to clarify in exactly what ways it is political—is there anything to be learned from those philosophers such as Immanuel Kant who have argued for the universality of aesthetics?

Feminists have produced a variety of answers to this question. In order to appreciate why and how the question has been answered so variously, we will need to understand something about the arguments that Kant put forward for the universality of aesthetics, and the relation between his view of aesthetic judgment and the other two domains of his critical philosophy, i.e. the metaphysical and the practical. We will also need to understand how and why, despite the severely problematic sexist, classist, and racist claims that Kant makes, his philosophy—in particular his aesthetics—remains a source of inspiration for some feminists and social-political philosophers.

In the first section I expand on the sense in which art is political; in the second section I expand further on exactly how this is so; and in the remaining sections I play this out in relation to Kant. The third section explores the paradoxes that structure Kant's philosophy of aesthetics, embedded in which are both progressive and regressive elements. The fourth section situates Kant's aesthetics in his philosophy as a whole. Finally, in the fifth section I explore some ways in which feminists have responded to Kant's aesthetics and reworked it.

Art as Political

The very architecture of aesthetics—its conceptual vocabulary—has unfolded and developed in ways that cannot be divorced from social and political assumptions, which are local and contingent rather than universal and necessary. What counts as art is itself a matter of judgment that is subject to political, cultural, and historical shifts. If the history of aesthetics shows itself open to challenge, and capable of reworking, this includes the history of feminist aesthetics.

Not only are aesthetic criteria open to challenge, and capable of undergoing redefinition, but so too what counts as political is open to challenge. Insofar as some versions of feminist aesthetics have been blind to the dynamic of race, for example, those versions of feminist aesthetics have tended to represent the traditions or conventions against which they define themselves, and which they attempt to reshape, as masculinist, but not as white. We might say then that to the extent that the politics of feminism has played out in ways that are not racially inclusive, the very shape of both feminist aesthetics and the masculinist aesthetic traditions that it has reflected have been infused with a political inability of their practitioners to think through their racial implications.

This inability has much to do with the race of those who have taken it upon themselves to define the terms of feminism, and those to whom it has fallen—or who have arrogated to themselves—the prerogative to define the terms of aesthetics. If white, masculinist theories predominate in aesthetics as traditionally defined, this is in no small part due to the parameters that have defined the communities of practitioners who have set the terms of aesthetic enquiry. So too the communities of those who have come to represent feminist aesthetics, those whose voices have been defined as its credible representatives and spokespersons, have been constituted in terms of racial parameters. In turn, the very differentiation between ostensibly formal and universal features of both art works and aesthetics, and the ways in which these features organize, specify, and define the material content of works of art are laden with historical and sociopolitical assumptions. What counts as art is open to question, so that, for example, some might grant that a quilt has the status of a work of art, while others would discount it. The dividing line between art and non-art is unstable. This opens up questions about aesthetic judgment itself, as something that is applicable beyond any specific domain of aesthetic objects, establishing the relevance of aesthetic judgment to that which as a rule might be cordoned off from aesthetics: reason, morality, and concepts, for example.

How Is Art Political?

If there is general agreement in the field of feminist aesthetics that art is political, it remains to clarify exactly what this means. At issue is whether there is a complete collapse of the boundaries between aesthetics and politics, or whether some kind of boundary remains, even if it is fungible and fuzzy rather than rigid and static.

Rita Felski (1989) sets up two extremes that she argues must be avoided in aesthetics. On the one hand, she wants to avoid positing a rigid, dualistic dichotomy between art and politics, and on the other hand, she is wary of identifying art and politics so that they become indistinguishable. To endorse a rigidly dichotomous view of art and politics suggests that art can exist as a pure, transcendent realm, uncontaminated by the political sphere. To equate art and political ideology would be to reduce art to an unambiguous political content, where its use value prevails, such that it immediately and directly reflects a political message. Distancing herself from both these positions, Felski defends the "relative autonomy" of art, in order to avoid construing art as mere ideology, as if art were merely a reflection of politics, while also rejecting the other extreme, the idea that art is impervious to all political influence (Felski 1989: 176).

Felski identifies feminist aesthetics with the reduction of art to political ideology. Consequently she argues that the very attempt to formulate what might be regarded as feminist aesthetics is fundamentally misguided. While I think that Felski is right to avoid reducing art to politics or maintaining the purity of art, her identification of feminist aesthetics with the equation of art and political ideology needs to be rethought.

At the same time, Felski's understanding of politics needs to be complicated, insofar as she assumes that the politics of feminist aesthetics is unidimensional—it is a politics opposed to patriarchy. The demands of thinking through intersectionality mean that things are not so simple.

To characterize the entire field of feminist aesthetics as rendering art equivalent to ideology is to misrepresent what is in fact a much more variegated set of views. I suggest not that we should abandon feminist aesthetics, but that we take its development, history, and differentiations seriously. My effort here is intended to contribute to that project. It is true that some feminists—although certainly not all—have claimed that feminist art is an instrument of feminist politics. Hilde Hein states, for example, "Feminist art is . . . a means to consciousness raising" (1995: 452). In defending such a position Hein makes the point that those who object that politics has "no place in art" fail to "grasp that 'conventional' art is equally political," but its politics is "cast as 'neutral' or masculinist" in a way that "appears invisible" (1995: 451). The suggestion is that art in general has been inadvertently political: that is, even if it has presented itself and has been regarded as art that occupies an autonomous realm purified of politics, in fact it has been thoroughly imbued with political assumptions.

By contrast, feminist art has cast itself as self-consciously political, overtly advocating a particular ideological stance. In doing so, it uncovers and reworks masculinist procedures and assumptions embedded in the tradition of art. These include the fact that women have often been the objects of art, rather than its creators, and that the conventions of artistic representation have tended to confirm, rather than interrogate, women's subservient socio-political roles—painterly representations of women performing tasks and duties typically coded as feminine in domestic interiors, for example (Gallop 1986). Feminist reworking of more conventional approaches to art also include the use of new materials, the introduction of new subject matter, and the interrogation and rethinking of the boundaries distinguishing women as objects of the male gaze from artists as creators. Feminist painters, photographers, and film directors, for example, have orchestrated the gaze in new ways that subvert, remake, and intervene in artistic conventions.

Two issues demand attention. The first is that the claim that "conventional" art is political, but is so in a way that disavows its political character, tends to play itself out by reducing art's politics to white patriarchy. Although Hein nods toward the diversity of women, this diversity plays no substantial role in her analysis, in which the two major examples that she develops—Laura Mulvey (1988) and Susan Stanford Friedman (1987)—occupy mainstream positions that do not challenge the default whiteness and heteronormativity of feminist theory. Mulvey's article on the male gaze, though making some important conceptual breakthroughs, has been rightly criticized for ignoring the question of race, and Friedman's argument, which focuses upon birthing metaphors, tends to reinscribe the normative identification of women with maternity. The demands of an intersectional approach to feminist aesthetics require that we take into account and challenge the ways in which art and aesthetics have not merely perpetuated and recreated gender hierarchies, but have also participated in and confirmed racial and other disparities. The second issue is that in contesting artistic conventions that have previously passed as neutral, while in fact being implicated in classist, gendered, and racist assumptions, there is a need to confront how the history of aesthetics has condoned, produced, and articulated standards and values that are complicit with such assumptions.

It becomes clear that the very terms in which art has been defined as art are infused with political assumptions and moral judgments about the relative worth of artworks based on their provenance. So, for example, the effort to specify art as pure has typically proceeded in ways that privilege certain types of art over others precisely by drawing upon pre-existing cultural and political stereotypes. These stereotypes are informed by prejudices, which have resulted in various hierarchies such that some art genres have been valued above others, and such that distinctions have been erected in the name of distinguishing high art from low or popular art, or art from craft. These very distinctions are informed by assumptions about the relative worth of the originators and creators of artworks, such that, for example, gendered and raced assumptions play into aesthetic decisions about which objects come to accrue value in certain contexts, and which do not. The articulation of the relationship between concepts such as form and matter, which has been central to aesthetics, is itself infused with assumptions that are not immune from cultural bias.

Aesthetic judgments occur within cultural contexts that accord to privileged voices the authority to define the boundaries of art, and those definitions will inevitably influence both consumers of art and creators of art. Consequently the communities that cohere around these judgments and definitions in the hope of legitimation will in turn shape and circumscribe aesthetic taste and the possibilities, aspirations and legitimacy of artists. Members of such communities, both artists and consumers of art, will be acculturated by the aesthetic standards and values that circulate between artists and aestheticians. The transformation of aesthetics then is bound up with challenging which voices are counted as definitively authoritative when it comes to defining what qualifies as art.

In the remainder of this chapter, I turn to Kant. I do so not only in order to play out the political imperative to contest the biases built into his aesthetic philosophy, which has accumulated such authority as to have become almost synonymous with the field of aesthetics, at least in some circles. I turn to Kant also because his aesthetic philosophy is rife with paradoxes that have proven to be productive for some feminist and political philosophers, even as they have alienated others. In the very same contexts in which he denigrates the humanity of women, certain races, and certain classes, Kant also offers insights as to how such judgments might be contested.

Kant's Aesthetics: Regressive or Progressive?

Kant confronts us with a contradictory state of affairs on several levels. He makes universal communicability a requirement of aesthetic judgments in a way that is belied by his own raced and gendered denigrations of those whose inclusion in the community of rational and moral subjects Kant imagines is thereby put in doubt. On the one hand, Kant demonstrates by his own subjective judgments concerning race and gender, art and craft, the beautiful and the sublime, the partiality to which our judgments can incline. On the other hand, he acknowledges the importance of opening up the particularity of taste to the influence of others, appealing to a universal community in which everyone is enjoined to assent to subjective judgments of the beautiful, but in which assent cannot be mandated. For Kant, sociability is built into his account of aesthetic judgment such that to make an aesthetic judgment is both to demand that others see the beauty that I see, and to open myself up to the possibility of challenge. It is to invite the views of others, to open up a conversation, and in doing so to position oneself in such a way as potentially to revise one's own aesthetic sensibility.

Kant's articulation of aesthetic judgment suggests a significant reworking of his earlier claims for the operative conditions for knowing the world and acting morally. Therefore, we might say that Kant's aesthetics offers the resources for rendering his transcendental approach to philosophy as a whole more open-ended and provisional than his presentation of it in its earlier formulations. Given this, Kant's insistence upon the purity not only of aesthetic judgment but also of cognition and morality is potentially undercut by the claims that he makes in articulating how judgment functions. Going beyond the letter of Kant, his work has been enlisted in philosophical projects that acknowledge the radical potential that art has to reconfigure that which previously passed as impervious to interrogation. There is something powerful and unsettling about aesthetic judgment, something that renders it capable of refiguring that which had established itself in the sedimented grooves of accumulated knowledge. That knowledge turns out to be capable of reconfiguration, so that concepts such as universality no longer seem tenable—or at least the parameters of what counts as universal are shown to be riven with contingency, such that what counts as universal itself undergoes constant rethinking. What seemed to be indispensable conditions of possibility, not only for aesthetics but also for knowledge in general, thereby present themselves for interrogation.

Situating Kant's Aesthetics in the Context of His Philosophical Project

Kant articulates aesthetic judgment in such a way as to provide tools that bring into question his own earlier stipulations regarding transcendental philosophy. It can be argued that his discussion of aesthetics in *The Critique of the Power of Judgment* (2000 [1790])—which has come to be known as Kant's third *Critique*—significantly revitalizes the parameters of his philosophical project. It does so to the point that even the meaning of terms that played a vital and decisively determining role in his earlier philosophy undergo significant transformation. How key terms such as "universality," "necessity," and "a priori" function, for example—and therefore the very meaning of a transcendental approach to philosophy as the search for the conditions of the possibility of experience—appear to be thought in a way that departs from how these terms operate in the first two *Critiques*. The very conditions that Kant stipulates as a priori, universal, and necessary for knowledge and morality are thus cast in a new light by Kant's discussion of aesthetics, which has been seen by some readers as not merely bridging a divide between nature and freedom created by his two earlier *Critiques*, but as potentially renegotiating the terrain of knowledge and morality. To put the point more forcefully, some have claimed that Kant's discussion of aesthetics effects a radical disruption of and reworking of Kant's transcendental philosophy.

To explain: Kant wrote three *Critiques*, the first of which deals with the legislative function of the understanding for the domain of nature, and the second of which deals with the legislative function of reason for freedom. These two philosophical investigations concern respectively the necessary conditions for how we can have objective knowledge of the world and for the moral law that determines how we should act. In both cases, Kant articulates rules that he takes to be universally applicable for all subjects of cognition, or for all moral agents.

The first *Critique* asks about the universal, necessary, a priori conditions according to which we have knowledge of nature, the way in which we cognize objects. Kant describes the process of understanding in terms of subsumption of particulars under universals. The universals under which we subsume particulars are given to us. We do not have to seek after them. The understanding provides the general form according to which our experience must proceed in order for us to represent objects. The second *Critique* asks after the universal moral law, according to which all our actions should conform. In both the case of theoretical cognition of nature and that of practical reason that guides moral actions, Kant asserts the objective necessity of the law (Kant 2000 [1790]: 121). The form that this argument takes in the case of cognition is that objects conform to our understanding in such a way that we bring sensible intuitions of the empirical world under concepts of nature. These concepts constitute universal rules for understanding. With regard to morality, it is in accordance with the concept of a pure will that moral actions must be determined.

A tension arises between the epistemological account that Kant provides in the *Critique of Pure Reason*, in which he articulates how the understanding provides rules that organize intuitions according to concepts of nature that hold universally, and the moral account he provides in the *Critique of Practical Reason*, where he argues that reason provides the concept of the pure will that holds universally. For, in the former, Kant treats humans as if they were subject to the mechanical laws of nature. In the latter, however, he considers humans from the perspective of our capacity to be moral agents, that is, to act in the world in such a way as to affect it with the purpose that consists of intervening in a morally meaningful way, based on our freedom to act in conformity with the moral law. The third *Critique* is then invested with a transitional or mediating role, which creates a bridge that can span the chasm between the mechanical causality of the natural world and the moral will of human agents capable of affecting change in the world on account of their freedom (Kant 2000 [1790]: 81).

Feminist Philosophers Rework Kant

In her essay "Crystallisation: Artful Matter and the Productive Imagination," Rachel Jones (2000) takes up and exploits a tension that structures how Kant construes the reflective judgments of aesthetics. By taking seriously, and pushing to its limits, the analogical relationship that Kant posits between nature and art, Jones focuses on the instance of crystallization, which presents an anomaly to the rule-governed explanatory models on which Kant usually relies to account for natural processes. On the one hand Kant suggests that nature must be thought as if it were art, yet on the other hand he proposes to think art as nature.

Exploring the complex analogical relationship between nature and art that Kant sustains throughout his discussion of aesthetic judgment, Jones suggests that in the third *Critique* Kant revises the mechanical concept of nature operative in the first *Critique*. In the third *Critique*, says Jones, we can no longer construe nature as a "blind mechanism"; rather "we must see nature as if it were intentionally designed, as if it were art" (Jones 2000: 20–21). On the basis of this, she argues that Kant formulates a productive, rather than a legislative, role for imagination, emphasizing creativity and unpredictability rather than a rule-bound approach.

Jones shows that there are moments in which the distinction between form and matter can be seen to break down and is reworked within Kant's philosophy, for example, in relation to his account of crystallization, which Jones takes up and invokes as a metaphor for the productive imagination of artistic genius. Jones suggests that the process of crystallization breaks with the governing model of active form as the organizing principle of passive matter. This parallels the sense in which the originality of the genius, in Kant's philosophy, consists not in following pre-existing rules, but rather in inventing new rules. The natural process of crystallization, Jones argues, can be read as an image for the productive imagination, whereby unexpected formations occur, which do not follow any rule, but are accomplished, rather, by a leap. The notion of unpredictability embedded in the formation of crystals is disruptive of the model that otherwise governs Kant's understanding of the relation of form to matter in the natural world, whereby form is endowed with an active power of organization over passive or inert matter. As Jones says, then, "Kant's text itself can be made to leap and move in unpredictable ways, allowing new possibilities to emerge, new insights, and crystallisations" (2000: 33).

Kant's third *Critique* revises his previous accounts of understanding and reason in a variety of ways. As suggested by Jones, not only does the concept of nature undergo a shift, but Kant also reserves a more creative and pervasive role for imagination than previously, and suggests that the judgment operative in the aesthetic realm has implications for judgment in the realms of knowledge and morality too. Furthermore, the account of aesthetic judgment stipulates a decisive role for the feeling of pleasure in which aesthetic judgment is said to consist, thus highlighting the significance of feeling in a way that Kant had not done before. At the same time, by building into his account of aesthetic judgment a reference to the judgment of others, Kant can be said to bring to the fore the communal aspect of judging in a way that goes beyond his previous claims.

Unlike the realms of theoretical cognition and knowledge or that of practical reason and morality, whatever necessity might be attributed to aesthetic judgment cannot be conferred by the universality of rules. In cognition and morality there are rules that determine their object, which Kant asserts are objectively valid and universal—the concepts of nature and of pure will. In the case of aesthetic judgment there are no such rules. In the matter of taste, judgments are singular, indeterminate, and subjective. Yet Kant still maintains that aesthetic judgments have a priori validity. The question remains as to the sense in which aesthetic judgments can have a priori universality that is subjective.

As we have said, Kant's aesthetics reworks his earlier philosophy by building into his account of the specific feeling of pleasure, in which he understands subjective aesthetic judgment to consist, a reference to community. In his analysis, the subjective judgment that something is beautiful is at the same time an appeal to the assent of the universal community of judging subjects. It is a call to humanity in general also to find the object in question beautiful. Even if, as a matter of empirical fact, others do not share the judgment that a given object is beautiful, Kant maintains that to pronounce something beautiful is at the same time to propose that others should agree. The trouble is that the claim that some subjects have on humanity, on Kant's account, is distinctly tenuous, such that whether they qualify as part of the ostensibly universal community of judging subjects is dubious at best. This presents a problem for feminist and race theorists, namely how to respond to Kant's prejudicial account of women and of subjects whom Kant regards as racially differentiated from white, European men. Before developing this point further, we need first to say more about the specific feeling of pleasure in which aesthetic pleasure consists.

Kant specifies the peculiarity of aesthetic judgment in terms of what he identifies, on the one hand, as conceptual indeterminacy and on the other hand as subjective universality (Rehberg 2015). Cognitive judgment, which produces knowledge, proceeds by subsuming particular instances under universal concepts, such that the concept is given, and the particular has to be recognized as conforming to it, and is thus subsumed under it. In aesthetic judgment, however, there is no determinate concept. The concept is not provided in advance but has to be discovered, or rather "generated" through imaginative reflection (Moen 1997: 237). Kant specifies the type of judgment that is peculiar to aesthetic judgment—as distinct from cognitive judgment—as "reflective" judgment. In reflective judgment, the form of a particular object is apprehended by the imagination. Whereas in cognitive judgment, knowledge is produced through the subsumption of particulars under universal concepts, in the case of aesthetic judgments, no such concept is available as pregiven. There is no subsumption of the particular under a concept; there is "no definite concept" and thus there is "no knowledge" as John Sallis says (1987: 90).

In reflection, there is a comparison between how the imagination apprehends forms and how they *would be* taken up by the understanding through the referral of intuitions to concepts (Kant 2000 [1790]: 26). Yet there is no such referral, as Sallis emphasizes, since there are no determinate concepts in aesthetic judgment, and since aesthetic judgment is not a matter of knowledge, but rather a feeling of pleasure. If there is agreement between the imagination and understanding, this harmony produces a feeling of pleasure. It is the free play between imagination and understanding in which the feeling of pleasure of aesthetic judgment consists. There is an "interplay" between the understanding and imagination, one in which the understanding does not govern the imagination, but in which they are "mutually conducive" for one another (Sallis 1987: 94). As we have seen, Kant proposes an analogical relationship between nature and art, on the basis of which we presuppose nature's purposiveness. In so far as the purposiveness is presupposed as an aim, it is provisional and indeterminate. As Jones puts it,

> all human subjects must be able to see the world as harmonising with the potential of their own ordering faculties [and] this singular feeling of pleasure reflects a universal *a priori* principle, which is nothing other than the indeterminate principle of judgment itself.
>
> (2000: 21)

The relation between the understanding and imagination becomes a site of free play, which Kant describes in terms of spontaneity. That which produces aesthetic pleasure cannot be anticipated in advance nor determined by intent. It arises unsolicited. Neither can it be subordinated to a higher end. It is not a mere means to an end. Aesthetic judgment, Kant argues, is disinterested. The argument that aesthetic judgment is disinterested suggests that there are strict boundaries between art and politics. Yet as we have begun to see, Kant's own argument is freighted with difficulty in that the very texts in which he puts forward his arguments themselves betray consistent racist and sexist biases and prejudice, which suggest that the purity of aesthetic judgment is not easily achieved. So too we have seen that in specifying the role of reflective judgment, Kant admits unpredictability into his system of thought, in such a way as to undercut the purity of both the transcendental and the separation of his thought into hermetically sealed domains of cognition, morality, and aesthetics. While Kant captures something vital about aesthetic judgment when he insists that it arises spontaneously, rather than being something we intend or will, even this insight must be surrounded by qualifications if we are to take seriously other features of his account.

In keeping with the earlier suggestion that the conceptual vocabulary of aesthetics is infused with normative assumptions, Christine Battersby suggests that Kant does not manage to sustain his attempt to treat "aesthetic philosophy in purely formal terms (in terms of the 'universal')" (2007: 46). And, Battersby says, his

> very way of marking out the "truly universal" and distinguishing it from the "merely particular" and the "detailed" relies on racial and cultural norms that privilege the non-sensuous, the conceptual, the abstract and the logical as viewed from the perspective of "old Europe."
>
> (2007: 83)

If there is a normative framing of universal claims, then this suggests that Kant's claims for a transcendental approach to philosophy need to be interrogated. This is not only from a standpoint interior to the lexicon of Kant's own philosophy, with respect to the hermeneutical relationship between the three *Critiques*, but also from a critical standpoint that raises questions about and puts pressure on the integrity of the distinction between the empirical and the transcendental as it functions in his texts.

As we have seen, Kant's aesthetics appeals to the notion of community as definitive of the dynamic at stake in aesthetic judgment. Feminist theorists have argued that the formal requirements that Kant builds into his account of aesthetic judgments, which includes their universal communicability, are undercut by his raced and gendered disparagement of some subjects. Both Kim Hall and Battersby focus on the fact that Kant specifies that aesthetic judgment must be universally communicable (Battersby 2007: 31; Hall 1997: 258). Yet at the same time he disqualifies "whole classes" of people from counting properly human or as enjoying full personhood, placing them "outside the imagined community of rational beings" (Battersby 2007: 46). In doing so, he differentiates between white or European women and ostensibly "primitive" or "uncivilized" women. As Hall puts it, "While European women occupy a secondary place in the community of judging subjects in the third *Critique*, Carib and Iroquois women have no place" (1997: 265). Thus "Kant's ideal of universal communicability is encoded through cultural and sexual difference" (Battersby 2007: 42).

Respecting and attending to the singularity of the gestures by which various others are written out of full humanity in Kant, Gayatri Chakravorty Spivak emphasizes the discontinuity between rhetorical gestures of exclusion. Spivak understands the occlusion of the native informant as constituting the "condition of possibility" of Kant's investigation (1999: 9). She reminds us to bear in mind that the disciplining mechanisms of gendered subjects and "geo-politically differentiated" subjects are not figured in the same way (1999: 31). While the former are "argued into" dismissal, the latter are "foreclosed" (1999: 30). We need to resist efforts to reduce all difference to the same model, as if they all followed the same dynamic, as if all differences were equivalent to one another, as if it were merely a question of slotting in the relevant grounds of oppression, marginalization, discrimination, or domination into a preconceived mold, as if gender and race and class could somehow be thought according to the same logic.

At the same time as attending to the specificity of the rhetoric according to which certain subjects are barred from full access to subjectivity in Kant's texts, I would argue that we also need to resist the impulse to structure feminist aesthetics by appealing to transcendental grounds, as if such grounds were themselves free of political imperatives. We should therefore avoid making any kind of oppression the ground of another, as if one were more foundational than another. For example, we should be wary of feminism that foregrounds whiteness as the condition of possibility of discourses of sexual difference or feminism.

Concluding Remarks

In Kant's aesthetics there is an appeal to the similarity of how judgment occurs in all those who, as Kant puts it, "lay claim to the name of a human being" (2000 [1790]: 173), and it is on the basis of our common potential to order our faculties that Kant claims that aesthetic judgments can have universal a priori status. Yet as we have seen there is a tension between the argument for the a priori status of aesthetic judgment and the disparaging remarks that Kant makes about women and certain racial groups. One way of responding to this is to argue that the barriers Kant erects between aesthetics on the one hand and ethics and politics on the other hand need to be broken down. As Battersby puts it, "feminist philosophers should refuse Kantian markers for the boundary between the aesthetic, the ethical, and the political" (2007: 46). In the preceding discussion I have suggested that Kant's own aesthetic philosophy begins to dismantle the barriers that his earlier systematic philosophy erected. If, as I have also suggested, aesthetics is embedded in discourses that accord legitimacy to some voices over others, any transformation of aesthetics will at the same time intervene in the politics that accord some voices legitimacy over others. The development and transformation of aesthetics goes hand in hand with negotiations that determine whose claims to humanity are heard, and whose are discounted. If the relative autonomy of politics and aesthetics needs to be respected, it also needs to be appreciated that the very distinction between aesthetics and politics is one whose articulation is a matter of political negotiation. The politics of feminist aesthetics constitutes one such area of negotiation.

Further Reading

Freeman, Barbara Claire (1995) *The Feminine Sublime: Gender and Excess in Women's Fiction*, Berkeley, CA: University of California Press.
Hughes, Fiona (2010) *Kant's Critique of Aesthetic Judgement: A Reader's Guide*, London: Continuum.
Jones, Rachel, and Rehberg, Andrea (Eds.) (2000) *The Matter of Critique: Readings in Kant's Philosophy*, Manchester: Clinamen Press.
Lyotard, Jean-François (1991) *Lessons on the Analytic of the Sublime*, trans. Elizabeth Rottenberg, Stanford, CA: Stanford University Press.
Schott, Robin May (Ed.) (1997) *Feminist Interpretations of Immanuel Kant*, University Park, PA: Pennsylvania State University Press.

Related Topics

Feminist engagements with nineteenth-century German philosophy (Chapter 9); critical race theory, intersectionality, and feminist philosophy (Chapter 29); aesthetics and the politics of gender (Chapter 38); feminist aesthetics and the categories of the beautiful and the sublime (Chapter 39).

References

Battersby, Christine (2007) *The Sublime, Terror and Human Difference*, New York: Routledge.

Felski, Rita (1989) *Beyond Feminist Aesthetics: Feminist Literature and Social Change*, Cambridge, MA: Harvard University Press.

Gallop, Jane (1986) "Annie Leclerc Writing a Letter, with Vermeer," in Nancy K. Miller (Ed.) *The Poetics of Gender*, New York: Columbia University Press, 137–156.

Hall, Kim (1997) "*Sensus Communis* and Violence: A Feminist Reading of Kant's *Critique of Judgement*," in Robin May Schott (Ed.) *Feminist Interpretations of Immanuel Kant*, University Park, PA: Pennsylvania State University Press, 257–272.

Hein, Hilde (1995) "The Role of Feminist Aesthetics in Feminist Theory," in Peggy Zeglin Brand and Carolyn Korsmeyer (Eds.) *Feminism and Tradition in Aesthetics*, University Park, PA: Pennsylvania State University Press, 446–463.

Jones, Rachel (2000) "Crystallisation: Artful Matter and Productive Imagination in Kant's Account of Genius," in Andrea Rehberg and Rachel Jones (Eds.) *The Matter of Critique: Readings in Kant's Philosophy*, Manchester: Clinamen Press, 19–36.

Kant, Immanuel (2000 [1790]) *Critique of the Power of Judgement*, trans. Paul Guyer and Eric Matthews, Cambridge: Cambridge University Press.

Moen, Marcia (1997) "Feminist Themes in Unlikely Places: Re-Reading Kant's *Critique of Judgment*," in Robin May Schott (Ed.) *Feminist Interpretations of Immanuel Kant*, University Park, PA: Pennsylvania State University Press, 213–256.

Mulvey, Laura (1988) "Visual Pleasure and Narrative Cinema," in Constance Penley (Ed.) *Feminism and Film Theory*, New York: Routledge, 57–68.

Rehberg, Andrea (2015) "On Affective Universality: Kant and Lyotard on *sensus communis*," Paper presented at the Society for European Philosophy Conference, Dundee.

Sallis, John (1987) *Spacings—of Reason and Imagination in Texts of Kant, Fichte, Hegel*, Chicago, IL: University of Chicago Press.

Spivak, Gayatri Chakravorty (2000) *A Critique of Postcolonial Reason: Toward a History of the Vanishing Present*, Cambridge, MA: Harvard University Press.

Stanford Friedman, Susan (1987) "Creativity and the Childbirth Metaphor: Gender Difference in Literary Discourse," *Feminist Studies* 13: 49–82.

38

AESTHETICS AND THE POLITICS OF GENDER

On Arendt's Theory of Narrative and Action

Ewa Plonowska Ziarek

Dilemmas of Feminist Aesthetics

The relation between gender and aesthetics is central to any formulation of feminist aesthetics, and yet the meanings of these terms are continually contested and revised. Both gender and aesthetics carry diverse, interdisciplinary significations, which are shaped by complex histories of disagreements. When the term "aesthetic" was first introduced in the eighteenth century by the German philosopher Alexander Baumgarten, it did not refer to artistic production but rather to the mode of knowledge gained through the senses. Aesthetics today can have at least three different meanings: (1) a general theory of artistic practices; (2) a theory of reception, focused upon how we appreciate or judge natural beauty and artworks; and (3) a theory of sensibility shaping our experience, practice, and knowledge. In this last sense aesthetics does not have to refer to art at all, but is rather concerned with the role of different senses, such as touch, sight, taste, smell, or with different affects: pleasure, pain, or disgust (Korsmeyer 2012). One could make an argument that the affective turn in feminist and queer theory today is also implicitly informed by this third historical meaning of aesthetics, even if theorists themselves do not engage aesthetics directly (Ahmed 2004; Berlant 2011). Gender is also a contested category in feminist philosophy and theory (Chanter 2007); in general it refers to social and political determinations and regulations of biological sex and sexual practices, but there is no consensus on the relationship of gender to power, the body, sexuality, or sensibility. Following feminist theories of intersectionality, introduced by black feminists (Crenshaw 1991), I assume in this chapter that the category of gender is relational, political, and historical; that is, that its significance and its relation to embodiment are shaped by desire and power relations, which also determine the meaning of class, race, labor, environment, and other political phenomena.

As Korsmeyer argues, different traditions of aesthetics and different methodologies of gender lend different meanings to feminist aesthetics (Korsmeyer 2012). Although in this chapter I will primarily focus on aesthetics as a feminist theory of artistic practice, I also want to stress that one of the most significant feminist interventions is a critique of the gendered and racialized lexicon of aesthetics, such as genius, taste, form/matter distinctions, originality, and the disinterestedness of aesthetic judgment (Battersby 1989; Felski 1989; Korsmeyer 2004, 2012; Ziarek 2013). Equally important is the contestation of the gendered and racialized divisions between high art, on the one hand, and decorative arts, fashion, and popular art, on the other (Hanson 1993; Korsmeyer 2012; Worth 2001). Feminist theorists of aesthetic sensibility have contested what counts as the aesthetic cultivation of the senses and have expanded the field to include eroticism, bodily feelings, and such non-aesthetic phenomena as appreciation of food (Korsmeyer 2004: 84–103). For example, Elizabeth Grosz (2012) sees art as an enhancement of bodily sensations, intensities, and sexual attractions.

Despite the fact that art and aesthetics, implicitly or explicitly, have been a rich resource for feminist thinking about gender, sexuality, and politics, the project of feminist aesthetics has also suffered from a double marginalization. Feminist aesthetics is marginalized not only in continental philosophy, included in various collections at the very end as a gesture of tokenism, but also within feminist philosophy and cultural theory where it is subordinated to the more urgent issues of feminist politics (Musgrave 2014). Although Luce Irigaray (1993) has argued that the new politics and ethics of sexual difference are inseparable from a new feminist poetics, this argument has received more attention from feminist artists than from feminist philosophers or theorists. The effects of this subordination of aesthetics to the more pressing issues of gender politics are insufficient attention to the liberating potential of aesthetics in feminist antiracist struggles (hooks 1995) and skepticism about the feasibility of gendered aesthetics (Felski 1989).

However, the fact that gender is an eminently political category can also invite feminist re-articulations of the long-standing philosophical debate about aesthetics and politics (Adorno 1997; Benjamin 1968; and Rancière 2006). What has been most frequently and rigorously criticized by numerous feminist theorists in this respect is the idea of art's autonomy, that is, its independence from politics. This critique of autonomy often leads to formulations of the political function of art. However, the autonomy of art can have different meanings: it can mean art for art's sake or, on the contrary, it can emphasize the capacity of art to resist market ideology and its instrumentality (Adorno 1997). If most feminist critics reject the first meaning of autonomy, understood as the aesthetic transcendence of politics, desires, and market driven instrumentality, the second meaning of autonomy as the contestation of the status quo is presupposed by any argument about the transformative effects of feminist artistic practices, which can resist gender, racist, and imperialist domination. Without the assumption that art can intervene in dominant power relations, the artistic practices of such diverse women writers and artists as Lyn Hejinian, Kara Walker, Mary Kelly, Adrian Piper—to name only a few—would simply be limited to the reproduction of the status quo, and the role of feminist criticism would be reduced to the critique of power shaping these artists' work, or to what Eve Kosofsky Sedgwick (2003) calls paranoid reading.

Another way to approach the relationship between feminist art and the politics of gender is to recognize the mutual interdependence and difference between artistic and political practices (Ziarek 2012). This position rejects both the anti-aesthetic determination of women's artistic practices by political power and the apparent separation (autonomy) of women's art from politics. However, this approach also contests the autonomy of politics, that is, its separation from all aspects of aesthetics. Such a feminist analysis of the interdependence between art and gender politics is partially indebted to Adorno's theory of the heteronomous autonomy of modern art. Heteronomous autonomy means that art is both determined by and independent of its socio-political material conditions. This contradictory and ambivalent relation of art to its material conditions calls for both a feminist analysis of the emancipatory possibilities of women's art and for a critique of art's complicity with power.

The greatest limitation of Adorno's aesthetic theory is his failure not only to analyze different forms of racist and gender oppression but also, more importantly, to provide a theory of transformative political action. In contrast to Adorno, I argue that both feminist artworks and gender politics can be forms of transformative practice (Ziarek 2012: 1–15). Furthermore, their relative inter-dependence means that there are enabling aesthetic elements in politics, such as creativity, experimentation, sensible experience, and novelty, just as there are political aspects of artistic practices—such as contestations of gendered modes of being and language, or experimentation with alternative possibilities of living and signification. This interaction between aesthetics and politics does not mean that feminism aspires to some imaginary aesthetic unity of the political collectivity modeled on the harmonious structure of a great artwork, as Walter Benjamin worries. Nor does it mean that art is merely a means for women to accumulate more cultural capital and gain social status (Bourdieu 2013), though of course it can partially serve this purpose as well; or that women's artworks should help to achieve feminist political goals. Rather the interaction means that both aesthetic and political practices lose their complete separation from each other and from other aspects of our collective lives, without losing their relative specificity. For example, we can tell apart political manifestations and protests—which can incorporate many creative elements—from theatrical performances, poetry readings, or public artistic installations.

Between Politics and Aesthetics: Action, Narrative, and Gender Intersectionality

To explore the interdependence between political and aesthetic practices in the context of gender intersectionality, I want to focus on the mutual relation between political action and narrative in Arendt's work and to reinterpret this relation in the context of feminist aesthetics. In contrast to Adorno's political pessimism, Arendt defends the possibilities of transformative political action as the only weapon we have against totalitarianism, biopolitics, and the destruction of the planet, even though she recognizes the fragility and limitations of action. Although she is not consistent, Arendt reflects on the similarities and differences between aesthetics and politics. On the one hand, she famously bases political judgments of action on Kant's judgments of beauty and she argues that what both political and aesthetic judgments share is the evaluation of the particular—this event, this work of art—without subordinating them to general concepts (Arendt 1982). She also stresses the crucial role of imagination not only in art but also in politics and testimony. On the other hand, she argues that there is a difference between political action and artistic practice in so far as the latter does not always require direct involvement of other people, and especially not of non-artists (although contemporary artists and numerous artistic practices would contest this claim).

Although Arendt's own reflections on artistic practice are limited, several of her critics have debated the aesthetic elements of Arendt's theory of political action (Curtis 1999; Kateb 1983: 30–35; Sjöholm 2015; Villa 1995: 81–92). Curtis even goes so far as to argue that Arendt's philosophy as a whole takes "an aesthetic turn" (1999: 10–13). We have to stress that these aesthetic elements are irreducible to what Benjamin calls an aesthetic unity of politics because Arendt rejects any notion of action and narrative based on the model of fabrication, understood as the realization of one central idea, and she argues instead that politics requires a plurality of participants, conflicting perspectives, and acknowledgment of unpredictability. What her critics identify as "aesthetic" elements of politics is, therefore, not the aesthetic unity of the people, but, on the contrary, multiplicity of the sensible appearances of actors and artworks in the public space (Sjöholm 2015), the expression of the uniqueness of political agents (Curtis 1999: 23–66), and the creation of a new beginning in political life (Ziarek 2012: 10–26).

The most explicit intersection between Arendt's theories of political and artistic practices is a mutually constitutive relationship between action and narrative. Arendt famously argues that action "'produces' stories" the way other activities, such as work, produce objects (Arendt 1958: 184). Why is this relationship important for feminist aesthetics? First of all, both political acts and narrative acts have transformative potential even though they occur in the midst of historical domination. That is why Adriana Cavarero and Shari Stone-Mediatore deploy Arendt's concept of narrative for a feminist analysis of storytelling as a means of the political expression of marginalized subjectivities. Second, in Arendt's work both political and aesthetic acts are mutually related: transformative political practice produces stories while narrative supplements action by making it memorable (Kristeva 2001), by retrospectively shaping its meaning. Focusing on this intersection between action and narrative allows us, therefore, to analyze both the political elements of women's art and the aesthetic elements of intersectional gender politics. And finally, the consideration of feminist aesthetics through the prism of narrative reveals not only the necessary aesthetic supplement of the political act but also the heterogeneity of aesthetic practices (or in Adorno's terms—theirs heteronomous autonomy). Narrative not only pertains to multiple arts—there are narrative elements in fiction, poetry, paintings, songs, film, theater, installations—but storytelling is irreducible to artistic practice alone. It is also a ubiquitous practice of everyday life and an established methodology of the human sciences (Mitchell 1981: ix–x), including history, anthropology, sociology, critical race studies, law, disability studies, and queer transgender studies. Consequently, although narrative alone cannot express the specificity of diverse artistic practices, it is an important example as it subverts numerous distinctions that are contested by feminist critiques of aesthetics, such as the hierarchies between high and low art or artistic practices and everyday life.

Since narrative is both produced by and supplements action, let us begin with Arendt's theory of action, which, though not explicitly connected with gender, is useful for feminist politics because it does not presuppose a common collective identity or shared experience of oppression, presuppositions that have been contested by feminists since the 1980s, and yet Arendt provides a robust theory of agency, based on the mutual commitment to act together. Second, Arendt's model reverses the agent/action relation: it is not subjective agency—identity, initiative, capacity to act—that explains action, but rather acting together that creates inter-subjective agency. The urgency of action is especially acute in response to political and economic injustices, such as the resurgence of anti-black racism and police brutality in the US. It is this political urgency that has led to the new wave of activism—from rallies and die-ins, to the formation of the #BlackLifeMatters and #SayHerName movements.

In the context of feminist debates about aesthetics and politics, the main intervention that Arendt allows us to make is that political action is irreducible to means-ends rationality. This claim subverts the usual opposition between a narrow view of politics driven by pragmatic interests and goals and the creative artistic practice that exceeds such instrumentalism. According to Arendt, not only artistic practice but also political action has to be considered in non-instrumental terms. Action is an end in itself because what is at stake in every political act is the struggle for freedom. Of course, every action is mobilized by specific goals and strategies, but these are not determined in advance by existing power/knowledge relations because they are also generated by conflicting alliances among actors. That is why the material objective "interests" of action, such as struggles against gender discrimination, poverty, and racism, disclose not only patterns of domination, but also an objective "inter-esse" (Arendt 1958: 182), or in-betweenness, by which the participants of action are inter-related, separated, or excluded from each other. More importantly, in the course of the struggle with these objective patterns of domination, political actors perform among themselves the second level of in-betweenness. In so far as they act together, the participants of action create together mutual equality and intersubjective freedom, if only for the duration of the event. Acting together for the sake of intersubjective freedom is an end in itself, and this is ultimately what distinguishes political action from what feminist sociologist Margaret Somers criticizes as the instrumental category of "behavior . . . [measured by] rational preferences" (1994: 615).

By rejecting the instrumentality of politics, Arendt also contests any ideological uses of the aesthetic to suggest the fictitious unity of the people. On the contrary, if we can speak of the aesthetic dimensions of political action in Arendt's work, these would include: (a) the creation of a new beginning, and thus the initiation of unpredictable difference in public lives; and (b) the negotiation between the plurality and uniqueness of political actors. The new beginning in public lives and the singularity of actors can be called the aesthetic dimensions of the political because their particularities exceed the available general political, philosophical, and linguistic meanings. Evocative of the modernist artistic slogan, "make it new," the new beginning in action, whether it occurs on a miniscule local or a revolutionary collective scale, initiates something unexpected, "infinitely improbable" (Arendt 1958: 178): it interrupts historical continuity and the re-production of the relations of power/knowledge in which it is situated. Action can initiate a new beginning precisely because it creates intersubjective agency and new forms of political power. Arendt distinguishes power generated through action, which depends upon human plurality and alliances, from the violence that destroys such plurality, and from the already constituted, systemic, or structural relations of power/knowledge—the complex patterns of racism, capital, anti-Semitism, homophobia, gender discrimination, and biopolitics—in the context of which action occurs. We can point to many contemporary examples of such unpredictable new beginnings, for instance, political protests in Istanbul's Gezi Park in 2013, which began as a protest against the destruction of the park and grew into the demand to change the government. Although this unpredictable novelty is what action shares with experimental artistic practice, at the same time it contests the traditional aesthetic notion of the originality of the isolated artist or genius. And since the new beginning in politics is intertwined with a transformation of both inter-human relations and human relations to the world, such transformation is fundamentally different from the production and consumption of the ever-same "novelty" of commodities.

The second aesthetic element of action consists in the disclosure of the uniqueness of political agents in the context of human plurality. Being unique means being unrepeatable, unreplaceable, but it is not the same as having individual identity in isolation from other people. On the contrary, from birth we appear first to others then to ourselves; our singularity depends, therefore, on being with others. Since there is no speaker without the speech act, no agent without the act, uniqueness can be glimpsed only retrospectively, in the aftermath of speaking and acting with others. Why is this relation between human plurality and uniqueness an aesthetic as well as a political problem? In the history of aesthetics, it was Kant in the *Critique of Aesthetic Judgment* who first posed the question about the communication of the particular—in his case, the communication of judgments about the beautiful and the sublime—and the idea of community. In *The Human Condition*, Arendt reformulates the Kantian aesthetic problematic as the political relation between the uniqueness and the plurality of political actors. At the end of her life she directly returns to Kant and rereads the *Critique of Judgment* as his most political work (Arendt 1982: 14–22).

Arendt calls the unrepeatable singularity of the agent "who" and distinguishes it from "what," or the general meaning of individual or collective identities. The *whatness* of identity is composed of the attributes and qualities that we share with others and of the differences that set us apart. In feminist interpretation (although not in Arendt's) these differences and attributes include race, gender, class, profession, ethnicity, age, nationality, occupation, religion, as well as all kinds of affiliations, and so forth. Only the *whatness* of racialized gendered subjects can be defined—and, as feminist scholars have argued, this definition occurs in the context of the political relations of power/knowledge and therefore is intertwined with discipline, normalization, and domination. However, what a feminist interpretation of Arendt's work can add to feminist theory is the claim that political struggles not only transform the power relations of race, gender, and class, but also disclose the uniqueness of every participant. In the world increasingly defined by big data and statistical analysis, in which we figure as exchangeable numbers, both uniqueness and action are threatened by being converted into predictable, calculable behavior.

The final disclosure of a who in the web of relations of gender, class, and race occurs in the form of a life story. This narrative disclosure of uniqueness is most debated among feminist theorists (Butler 2005; Cavarero 2000; Kristeva 2001), though not always in the context of feminist aesthetics. In her response to Cavarero's interpretation of Arendt's conception of narrative, Butler (2005: 15) argues that uniqueness emerging from the address to the other provides an alternative to Nietzsche's punitive account of morality and to Hegel's reciprocity of recognition. However, according to Butler (2005: 36), any narrative account of singularity is interrupted by the indifference of discursive norms, which make us recognizable to others but also "substitutable" (2005: 37–39). Second, narrative fails to account for those relations to others that precede our memory. Ultimately, norms, relations to others, and disconnection of narrative from lived bodily experience reveal not only uniqueness but my "opacity to myself."

However, these tensions between uniqueness and generality of norms, or what Arendt calls "who" and "what," do not undermine irreplaceable singularity but precisely characterize its political/aesthetic mode of disclosure in language and narrative.

According to Kristeva, such disclosure is characterized by the uncanny interplay between disalienation and estrangement (2001: 86, 83). Arendt stresses the constitutive relationship between the disclosure of uniqueness and the obscurity of agents to themselves (Arendt 1958: 179). Since the uniqueness of a "who" exceeds any political category of classification and normalization as well as the philosophical or cultural attributes of identity, it cannot be defined but only posed in the form of a question, "who are you?" Any answer to such a question in the form of self-definition—I am an immigrant white feminist—is necessarily general, shared by other white feminist immigrants, and therefore slides into a "what." As Arendt underscores, "The moment we want to say *who* somebody is, our very vocabulary leads us astray into saying *what* he is" (1958: 181). That is why uniqueness seems to push the generality of language to the limits of expression: "The manifestation of who the speaker and doer unexchangeably is . . . retains a curious intangibility that confounds all efforts toward unequivocal verbal expression" (Arendt 1958: 181). Could we say that this challenge posed to political, ordinary, and philosophical languages calls for their expansion towards the literary or the aesthetic manner of expression, which, in the post-Kantian tradition, seems to be better suited toward the negotiation between generality and singularity?

In the context of narrative, whether it is a fictional or a true story, what maintains this tension between singularity and exposure to otherness, between irreplaceable uniqueness and the shared generality of language, is a specific interplay between narrators, characters, and open-ended plot. Despite obscurity, the exposure of agents to others through speech and action prior to their relation to themselves also positions those others—whether they are actors or spectators—as potential narrators. Because of the multiplicity of inter-human relations in which these potential narrators are situated, such a narrative point of view, invariably gendered and racialized, can never aspire to the impersonal or omniscient narrator, because it always represents a partial, contingent perspective. Since life is narratable thanks to others in their role as potential narrators, the crucial implication of this indebtedness of narration to others does not lie in my dispossession from my own story as Butler argues. More fundamentally, it lies in the reframing of any autobiography as always already a biography: "*Who* somebody . . . was we can know only by knowing . . . his biography" (Arendt 1958: 186). The reason why the primary genre of any life story is biography rather than autobiography is because every auto/biography takes place within the parameters of stories told or withheld by others. It is especially the case with the beginning and the end of life—birth and death—which, if narratable at all, are always told by others.

The second narrative element that makes the disclosure of uniqueness possible is the construction of a plot. In Aristotle's *Poetics*, plot or *mythos* constitutes the primary feature of narratives imitating, or more precisely, re-enacting, action (Aristotle 1989: 13–14). For Aristotle as for Arendt action enables stories because the events it initiates create the possibility of a plot; however, by re-enacting action, narrative becomes a new performative act in its own right. For both Arendt and Aristotle, plot, which establishes a temporal sequence among the selected events, cannot be explained by the psychological or moral makeup of the characters. Despite these similarities, Arendt's and Aristotle's understandings of the plot or *mythos* differ. In contrast to the Aristotelian definition of *mythos*, the Arendtian notions of action and plot do not have a clear sense of an ending, or narrative closure, because Arendt focuses primarily on the way action creates a new beginning, which in turn calls for a new story. Without a new beginning, there is neither need nor desire for a new story. Paradoxically, it is this open-endedness of action, its lack of a predictable *telos*, which generates storytelling, which reveals the meaning of action retrospectively through the act of narrative recollection. Furthermore, such a retrospective disclosure of the meaning of action through the narrative act is itself incomplete; it engenders further, often conflicting, plots and the interpretations of these narratives.

It is thanks to the contingent plot and partial, plural narrative points of view that the uniqueness and plurality of agents can be expressed in narrative. As Arendt suggests, the disclosure of uniqueness in the web of conflicting relationships "eventually emerges as the unique life story of the newcomer, affecting uniquely the life stories of all those with whom he comes into contact" (Arendt 1958: 184). What political action discloses as the uniqueness of agents in relation to others, the narrative act transforms into a distinct character in a life story. However, this transformation is by no means self-evident or based on realist assumptions. In addition to the construction of plot and multiple points of view, it involves, as Kristeva suggests, the complex negotiations among individual and public memories, contestations of the available narrative norms, modes of storytelling, discourses (Kristeva 2001: 75–76), as well as a confrontation with the politics of culture. One of the effects of these multiple negotiations is Arendt's rejection of authorship, before such rejection became a hallmark of postmodernism. As she puts it, "Nobody is the author or producer of his own life story" (Arendt 1958: 184). If there is an "author" of a life story at all then perhaps it is an interplay of political and narrative acts, which, according to Arendt, create stories the way other activities produce objects. My emphasis on the performativity of the narrative act contests not only the autonomy of the political subject but also the originality of the author, so frequently criticized by postmodern as well as feminist theorists and artists.

Despite Arendt's, Butler's, and Cavarero's disregard of textuality, consideration of the political and aesthetic aspects of the narrative act brings back the question of form, or the manner of storytelling. We can recall at this point Adorno's claim that formal aspects of literary works, and in fact all artworks, are implicated in political antagonisms, which the artworks both reproduce and contest (Adorno 1997: 6). Although Arendt does not develop the politics and aesthetics of form, it is clear that not every story performs a disclosure of uniqueness or safeguards a new beginning. In fact, quite the opposite is the case. The politics of narration has both normalizing and subversive functions, which manifest themselves on the level of narrative form. For example, the familiar gender, class, and race master plots in Western culture—the Oedipal plot, the Orpheus plot, the Medusa plot, the terrorist plot, the from rags to riches plot, the alien invasion plots (ranging from science fiction to immigration policy), the war and marriage plot—all perform disciplinary and normalizing functions. It is the relationship between narrative and power that determines the choice of the actors as characters (for example, the rulers and generals rather than workers) or the selection of significant events (Barthes 1989; White 1981). These "master plots," selected from the vast repertoire of possible stories, become foundational for a given society, a political group, or a state. Consequently, for a story to disclose uniqueness and to open a new beginning, it has to contest these recurrent plots in the public imaginary and invent new ways of storytelling. And vice versa, feminist storytelling has to be attentive to many marks of erasure, silencing, and invisibility in the politics of narration. By acknowledging these erasures, feminist politics and the aesthetic of experimental narrative form challenge the way storytelling is entangled in the network of gendered power/knowledge, which makes some narrative forms more readily disseminated and others more easily silenced. What I call here briefly a political function of narrative form, and of aesthetic experimentation more generally, is an ongoing formal struggle against normalization and exclusion in order to keep the possibility of a new beginning viable within language and culture.

Life and Narrative

A different politics of narration is suggested by Kristeva, according to whom narrative produces political forms of life, understood as *bios* (that is, as politically significant) rather than *zōē* (biological). The interpretation of political *bios* in terms of narratability is also suggested by Arendt's own claim that life without action and speech is dead to the world, that is, it stops being *bios* and becomes superfluous, or to use Agamben's term (1998), is reduced to bare life. This interpretation of the political *bios* in terms of narrativity is a crucial supplement to citizenship and human rights. And, vice versa, the notion of narrative *bios* effects a shift in narrative studies, away from structural analysis or epistemic problems (focused on the relation between narrative and knowledge). The shift is instead to narrative's ontological functions—to the way narratives change the political status of collective and singular lives. In particular, the narrative formation of the political *bios* undermines the sovereign power of the state to devalue the symbolic significance of dominated groups—refugees, racial minorities, or immigrants—by suspending or limiting their rights. Although the rights of citizens can be curtailed by sovereign power in a state of emergency (Agamben 1998), sovereignty alone cannot altogether destroy inter-human relations and narratives, which constitute the political meanings of *bios*. One could even claim that sovereign decision alone cannot silence storytelling, which continues to circulate, protest against justice, and thus preserve the web of human relations.

Although narratives cannot be suspended by sovereign decision, the paradox of the narrative *bios* lies in the simultaneous ubiquity and fragility of life stories. The narratability of life, its status as a *bios*, does not guarantee that every life will have a narrated story, because the telling or writing of such a story depends not only on the recollections of others and their willingness to narrate a story, but also on multiple, often invisible, power relations determining whose life stories are "worthy" of narration and memorialization in the public sphere. In the context of the ever-growing circles of superfluous humanity, value judgments about whose stories are told are eminently political, implicated in the race, gender, capitalist, and imperialist institutions and networks of power. It is precisely because of the ontological status of narrative, of its capacity to constitute *bios*, that subjugated groups deprived of narration are even further denigrated and dispossessed (Somers 1994: 63). According to Cavarero, "what is intolerable" is not only the life of poverty and exclusion but also the fact "that the life-story that results from it remains without narration" (2000: 57). By contrast, as Stone-Mediatore argues, narration and counter histories, which challenge the dominant assumptions, values, and boundaries of the political, become powerful political weapons of dispossessed groups (2003: 5–10).

Conclusion

In this chapter I have argued that the most productive way to approach the relation between feminist aesthetics and gender politics is to treat both of them as hybrid and mutually dependent areas of human activity. This means that we should explore not only the political, gendered elements of artistic practices but also the enabling aesthetic elements of political activism. One possible model of such mutual interdependence can be found in Arendt's theory of action and narrative. By reinterpreting her work in the context of gender intersectionality, I have argued that both narrative—which at first glance belongs to literature—and action—which is preeminently political—are in fact heterogeneous practices, through which gender politics and aesthetics ceaselessly confront each other in order to expand or to shrink their limits.

Further Reading

Chanter, Tina (2008) *The Picture of Abjection: Film, Fetish, and the Nature of Difference*, Bloomington, IN: Indiana University Press.

Davis, Whitney (2010) *Queer Beauty: Sexuality and Aesthetics from Winckelmann to Freud and Beyond*, New York: Columbia University Press.

Moten, Fred (2003) *In the Break: The Aesthetics of the Black Radical Tradition*, Minneapolis, MN: University of Minnesota Press.

Ziarek, Ewa (2014) "The Stakes of Feminist Aesthetics: Transformative Practice, Neoliberalism, and the Violence of Formalism," *differences* 25: 101–115.

Related Topics

Language, writing and gender differences (Chapter 24); the genealogy and viability of the concept of intersectionality (Chapter 28); historicizing feminist aesthetics (Chapter 37); feminist aesthetics and the categories of the beautiful and the sublime (Chapter 39); feminism and freedom (Chapter 53); feminism and power (Chapter 54).

References

Adorno, Theodor W. (1997) *Aesthetic Theory*, Gretel Adorno and Rolf Tiedemann (Eds.), trans. Robert Hullot-Kentor, Minneapolis, MN: University of Minnesota Press.

Agamben, Georgio (1998) *Homo Sacer: Sovereign Power and Bare Life*, trans. Daniel Heller-Roazen, Stanford, CA: Stanford University Press.

Ahmed, Sara (2004) *The Cultural Politics of Emotion*, 1st edition, New York: Routledge.

Arendt, Hannah (1958) *The Human Condition*, 2nd edition, Chicago, IL: University of Chicago Press.

—— (1982) *Lectures on Kant's Political Philosophy*, Ronald Beiner (Ed.) Chicago, IL: University of Chicago Press.

Aristotle (1989), *On Poetry and Style*, trans. G. M. A. Grube, Indianapolis, IN: Hackett.

Barthes, Roland (1989) "The Discourse of History," in *The Rustle of Language*, trans. Richard Howard, Berkeley, CA: University of California Press, 127–140.

Battersby, Christine (1989) *Gender and Genius: Towards a Feminist Aesthetics*, Bloomington, IN: Indiana University Press.

Benjamin, Walter (1968) "The Work of Art in the Age of Mechanical Reproduction," in Hannah Arendt (Ed.) *Illuminations: Essays and Reflections*, trans. Harry Zohn, New York: Schocken Books, 217–252.

Berlant, Lauren (2011) *Cruel Optimism*, Durham, NC: Duke University Press.

Bourdieu, Pierre (2013) *Distinction: A Social Critique of the Judgement of Taste*, London: Routledge.

Butler, Judith (2005) *Giving an Account of Oneself*, New York: Fordham University Press.

Cavarero, Adrianna (2000) *Relating Narratives: Storytelling and Selfhood*, trans. Paul A. Kottman, London: Routledge.

Chanter, Tina (2007) *Gender: Key Concepts in Philosophy*, New York: Continuum.

Crenshaw, Kimberlé (1991) "Mapping the Margins: Intersectionality, Identity Politics, and Violence against Women of Color," *Stanford Law Review* 43: 1241–1299.

Curtis, Kimberley (1999) *Our Sense of the Real: Aesthetic Experience and Arendtian Politics*, Ithaca, NY: Cornell University Press.

Felski, Rita (1989) *Beyond Feminist Aesthetics: Feminist Literature and Social Change*, Cambridge, MA: Harvard University Press.

Grosz, Elizabeth (2012) *Chaos, Territory, Art: Deleuze and the Framing of the Earth*, New York: Columbia University Press.

Hanson, Karen (1993) "Dressing Down Dressing Up: the Philosophic Fear of Fashion," in Hilde Hein and Carolyn C. Korsmeyer (Eds.) *Aesthetics in Feminist Perspective*, Bloomington, IN: Indiana University Press, 229–240.

hooks, bell (1995) *Art on My Mind: Visual Politics*, New York: The New Press.

Irigaray, Luce (1993) *An Ethics of Sexual Difference*, trans. Carolyn Burke and Gillian C. Gill, Ithaca, NY: Cornell University Press.

Kant, Immanuel (1951) *Critique of Judgment*, trans. J. H. Bernard, New York: Hafner Press.

Kateb, George (1983) *Hannah Arendt: Politics, Conscience, Evil*, New Jersey, NJ: Rowman & Allanheld.

Korsmeyer, Carolyn (2004) *Gender and Aesthetics: An Introduction*, New York: Routledge.

—— (2012) "Feminist Aesthetics," in Edward N. Zalta (Ed.) *Stanford Encyclopedia of Philosophy*, Winter [online]. Available from: http://plato.stanford.edu/archives/win2012/entries/feminism-aesthetics/.

Kristeva, Julia (2001) *Hannah Arendt*, trans. Ross Guberman, New York: Columbia University Press.

Mitchell, W. J. T. (Ed.) (1981) *On Narrative*, Chicago, IL: University of Chicago Press.

Musgrave, Lisa Ryan (2014) "Introduction," in *Feminist Aesthetics and Philosophy of Art: The Power of Critical Visions and Creative Engagement*, New York: Springer.

Rancière, Jacques (2006) *The Politics of Aesthetics: The Distribution of the Sensible*, trans. Gabriel Rockhill, London: Continuum.

Sedgwick, Eve Kosofsky (2003) "Paranoid Reading and Reparative Reading," in *Touching Feeling: Affect, Pedagogy, Performativity*, Durham, NC: Duke University Press, 123–152.

Sjöholm, Cecilia (2015) *Doing Aesthetics with Arendt*, New York: Columbia University Press.

Somers, Margaret (1994) "The Narrative Constitution of Identity," *Theory and Society* 23: 605–649.

Stone-Mediatore, Shari (2003) "Hannah Arendt and the Revaluing of Storytelling," in *Reading Across Borders: Storytelling and Knowledges of Resistance*, New York: Macmillan, 17–96.

Villa, Dana R. (1995) *Arendt and Heidegger: The Fate of the Political*, Princeton, NJ: Princeton University Press.

White, Hayden (1981) "The Value of Narrativity in the Representation of Reality," in W. J. T. Mitchell (Ed.) *On Narrative*, Chicago, IL: University of Chicago Press, 1–23.

Worth, Sarah (2001) "Feminist Aesthetics," in Berys Gaut and Dominic McIver Lopes (Eds.) *The Routledge Companion to Aesthetics*, London: Routledge, 436–446.

Ziarek, Ewa (2012) *Feminist Aesthetics and the Politics of Modernism*, New York: Columbia University Press.

—— (2013) "From Parody to the Event, From Affect to Freedom: Observations on the Feminine Sublime in Modernism," in Jean-Michel Rabaté (Ed.) *A Handbook of Modernism Studies*, Oxford: Blackwell, 399–414.

39
FEMINIST AESTHETICS AND THE CATEGORIES OF THE BEAUTIFUL AND THE SUBLIME

Christine Battersby

Introduction

Feminist explorations of the sublime and the beautiful have developed in markedly different directions. This is not surprising given the different histories of the two terms. Whereas the nature of the beautiful had been of key importance to Plato, Aristotle, and other ancient Greek and Roman philosophers, it was only during the Enlightenment period that a strong contrast was established between the beautiful and the sublime. But this was also the time when there was a decisive shift away from regarding the well-honed male body as best exemplifying the ideal of the beautiful, and beauty itself was domesticated and downgraded. As Mary Wollstonecraft registered in *A Vindication of the Rights of Woman* (Wollstonecraft 1996 [1792])—one of the earliest European feminist texts—to associate women with the duties of being beautiful in this newly demoted mode was, in effect, to give them the status of subordinate beings. Instead, Wollstonecraft aspired to the newly emergent category of the sublime, which was all too frequently being denied to ideally "feminine" women.

Beauty

In the case of beauty, philosophers generally maintained that what is involved is a response to an object or entity which is universal, disinterested, with all questions of desire, use-value, and personal taste set to one side. By contrast, in the case of the sublime, philosophers claimed that the pleasure in the sublime is not universal and also not simply formalist. Disinterestedness and embodiment were also given an entirely different role, in that physiological affect was registered as a significant element in the response to the sublime, even when the bodily response was also "transcended" or subsequently brought back under control. As a consequence, feminists have required different strategies when analyzing and countering two very different models of aesthetic judgement.

Feminist philosophers who write about the beautiful have primarily concentrated on showing the inadequacy of claims that peoples across all cultures, periods of history, and ethnicities agree on the qualities, properties, or descriptors of beauty. This is evident in such significant anthologies as Peg Zeglin Brand's *Beauty Matters* (Brand 2000) and her later collection, *Beauty Unlimited* (Brand 2013). These two books include essays on beauty in the early modern era, in contemporary non-Western cultures, and also distinct modes of beauty in particular genres of art, such as ballet, Bollywood cinema, and Balinese dance. Alongside these pieces, there are also articles on two related topics that frequently crop up in other major feminist texts on beauty and taste, for example, in Carolyn Korsmeyer's *Gender and Aesthetics* (2004) and *Savoring Disgust* (2011). The first topic involves challenging the traditional linking of aesthetics, beauty, and disinterestedness. The second, related issue concerns the role of the body—and more specifically the female body—in the making of and appreciation of beautiful art. These emphases mean that relatively little attention has been paid to the beauty of natural landscape by those working in the field of feminist aesthetics, as Sheila Lintott (2010) somewhat despairingly observes.

Much of the most popular work by feminists on beauty has been by non-philosophers. A recent example is Natasha Walter's *Living Dolls: The Return of Sexism* (2010), which focuses on the socialization of women, and the role that the ideal of beauty plays in our hypersexualized society. Walters can be read as updating the argument of Naomi Wolf in her bestselling book, *The Beauty Myth* (1990), who argued that contemporary women imbibe from patriarchal society an ideal of beauty that is as psychologically disabling as the medieval torture apparatus of the "iron maiden." During the middle ages, Wolf claims, transgressive women were on occasions enclosed within "a body-shaped casket painted with the limbs and features of a lovely, smiling young woman" (1990: 493). Within these wooden caskets, women's bodies were pierced by protruding iron spikes, or if these missed the mark, the women lost consciousness as they slowly suffocated and died. It turns out, however, that in repeating this story Wolf has herself been taken in by a different kind of male myth. The machinery of these "iron maidens" does not date back to the twelfth century, but was devised in the late eighteenth century at the earliest. Featuring in nineteenth-century "cabinets of curiosities" we find various authentic medieval artefacts, but displayed in a way that is entirely inauthentic, giving rise to the myth of the "iron maidens" which figure so often in later fictions and films, as well as in sensationalist museum displays. In this, males projected back onto the past their fears of female sexuality and of the newly emergent claims for female equality. Philosophically speaking, the male philosophers linked with this "invented history" also aimed to keep unruly matter within the constraints of form as they struggled to secure male dominance (Tanner 2006). Since beauty has been so frequently linked with the pleasures of "form," and since women have been historically linked to a materiality that is uncontrollable, chaotic and hence also formless (Battersby 1989), these fantasy "iron maidens" are more philosophically interesting, and more closely linked to an ideal of beauty, than Wolf's account initially suggests.

Much more careful, and also more philosophically sophisticated, is Sandra Lee Bartky's *Femininity and Domination* (1990). Although not primarily a series of essays on aesthetics, Bartky's text explores what she terms "the fashion-beauty complex," which "produces in woman an estrangement from her bodily being" through the projection of an image of her own body as somehow lacking, of being "*what I am not*" (1990: 40).

Bartky situates herself in a phenomenological tradition, and is expanding on Simone de Beauvoir's analysis of the condition of woman, as "made, not born," in *The Second Sex* (Beauvoir 1952 [1949]). Beauvoir engaged extensively with the ways in which "beauty" and "woman" align to produce alienation between the lived body and the body as object of the gaze—not only of the other, but also the gaze of one's own self, which internalizes the viewpoint of the other. Susan Bordo's *Unbearable Weight* (2005 [1993]) is another important philosophical exploration of twentieth-century beauty ideals, especially that of the ideal of the well-honed, slim and athletic body. Bordo's highly influential analysis of female beauty was groundbreaking in its use of feminist and empirical research, but nevertheless it fits awkwardly within the category of feminist aesthetics, especially since it challenges analyses that remain at the level of "the merely aesthetic" (2005 [1993]: 46).

The Sublime: Early Developments

The fuzzy boundaries of the category of the "aesthetic" are particularly clear in the case of the sublime, as the history of the term makes clear. The craze for the sublime can be traced back to Nicolas Boileau's 1674 translation of a fragmentary Greek text on rhetoric by Longinus, *Peri Hypsous* (*On the Sublime*) (2005 [c.100–c.200]), written sometime between the first and third centuries CE. The Greek author—whose true identity is not known—set out to analyze an apparently simple style of communication, which has such "irresistible power and mastery" that it produces "wonder" and transports the hearer (2005 [c.100–c.200]: 163). Longinus put down the effects to the "divine frenzy" of the speaker (2005 [c.100–c.200]: 258) and to a simple style that "casts a spell" on the audience (2005 [c.100–c.200]: 287). In Boileau's version of the text, the power of the sublime is ascribed to an obscure quality, a "*je-ne-sais-quoi*" ("I-know-not-what"), leading others to focus on Longinus' examples, including the love poetry of Sappho and also the account of creation in the Old Testament, as they attempted to understand the audience response.

By the middle of the eighteenth century, British writers on theatre, landscape, literature, and the visual arts could not get enough of the sublime; but now the focus had shifted to the nature of the sublime object, rather than questions of style. The sublime was said to involve an encounter with that which seems infinite, indefinitely large or microscopically small, uncanny, mysterious, obscure, dark, or sudden. What was essential was a feeling of terror, astonishment, or awe in the face of that which exceeds man's cognitive, visual, auditory, or imaginative grasp, leading to a sense of the ineffable: something that language, music, or the visual arts can only point towards, and that remains suggestively half-hidden. Breaking with conscious control and individual personality or preferences, the pleasure-in-pain that was integral to the sublime seemed to take man temporarily beyond the human; but the pleasure was generated by the object—not by a god or by the divine—and opened up a kind of split within the subject before consciousness and reason re-established control.

When Wollstonecraft protests angrily about the way in which women are educated to render themselves beautiful and also shun the sublime, she was responding to Jean-Jacques Rousseau, but also to Edmund Burke's enormously influential A *Philosophical Enquiry into the Origin of our Ideas of the Sublime and Beautiful* (1987 [1757/1759]). Wollstonecraft took on Burke's ideal of the sublime, but argued that, in the case of women, "artificial notions of beauty and false descriptions of sensibility" distort the educational and moral development of girls, making "genteel" women "slaves to their bodies" so that they come to "glory in their subjection" (Wollstonecraft 1996 [1792]: 42–43). Wollstonecraft argues vehemently against those writers who try to make women "more pleasing" by giving "a sex to morals" (1996 [1792]: 35); and in so doing she also offers a critique of those who—like Burke—either implicitly or explicitly gender the categories of the beautiful and the sublime. Women, she maintains, should be allowed to "cultivate their minds," including with "the salutary, sublime curb of principle" (1996 [1792]: 35), since it is only through cultivating a sense of moral duty and obligation that women can free themselves from their slave-like state. (On Wollstonecraft, see also Chapter 8 in this volume.)

Burke had divided the passions into two broad types: those that are "social" and linked to sexual reproduction and care for others; and those which are linked with "self-preservation" and the protection of the individual's body or mind (Burke 1987 [1757/1759]: 38–42). Burke saw beauty as bound up with the social passions; by contrast, the enjoyment in the sublime is generated when the ego operates in a defensive mode. In particular, Burke links the sublime to "astonishment," "horror," "fear," and "terror," but also to "delight": a term that is given a narrow and technical definition involving the "removal of pain or danger" (1987 [1757/1759]: 57, 37). Burke's examples of the sublime include terrifying kings and commanders; incomprehensible darkness and depths; looming towers and awe-inspiring mountains; and a range of other experiences that engender mental and also physiological (muscular and nervous) tension. Although the sublime is only *implicitly* linked to the male body (by means of Burke's chosen examples), its polar opposite—beauty—is quite explicitly linked to the bodies of women which are described as (ideally) small, smooth, delicate and graceful, to match women's "weak" temperament and social disposition (1987 [1757/1759]: 116, 117).

Burke describes beauty as being intimately bound up with the need to propagate the species:

> The object, therefore, of this mixed passion which we call love is the *beauty* of the *sex*. Men are carried to the sex in general, as it is the sex, and by the common law of nature; but they are attached to particulars by personal *beauty*.
> (1987 [1757/1759]: 42)

The "we" that Burke uses here is sexually specific, and "men" means "males." According to Burke, it is the beautiful that operates on the (male) observer by a form of flattery, the sublime that threatens to overwhelm the ego through a form of mental rape that renders him (temporarily) passive:

> There is a wide difference between admiration and love. The sublime, which is the cause of the former, always dwells on great objects, and terrible; the latter on small ones, and pleasing; we submit to what we admire, but we love what submits to us; in one case we are forced, in the other we are flattered into compliance.
> (1987 [1757/1759]: 113)

Beauty, Burke claims, involves properties that "operate by nature," and our responses are unaffected by "caprice" or by "a diversity of tastes" (1987 [1757/1759]: 117). But he never made the adjustments to his vocabulary that would have been necessary had he thought at all about the sexual, or aesthetic, pleasures of *women*. He also failed to consider the question of racial and cultural differences, insisting that "darkness and blackness" are always psychologically and physiologically "painful," and hence excluded from the beautiful (1987 [1757/1759]: 144). As evidence, Burke cites the example of a (white) boy who was blind from birth who feels "great horror" when he first sees "a negro woman" after regaining his sight (1987 [1757/1759]: 144–145). In failing to explore how the world might seem to black or dark-skinned persons, Burke does, in effect, place non-white humanity outside the confines of those idealized human beings—not only male, but also belonging to the white and Northern races—whose responses serve as the aesthetic norm. In so doing, Burke prefigures a tendency in later literature and philosophy, which not only genders sublimity in complex fashions, but also links it to specific races and ethnicities (Battersby 2007).

Thus, in the historical discourse of the sublime, the (male) subject who is celebrated as mastering terror is generally of European stock and white. The sublime became linked with the exploration of oceans, deserts and wildernesses, insofar as the potential extent or features of these territories remained excessive to the "human" (European/white) imagination. Certain indigenous peoples—most notably Arabs and North American Indians—who inhabited the wildernesses were allowed sublimity (Kant 2011 [1764]: 2/252–253; 58–59). However, once the landscape was tamed by the colonists, its perceived sublimity—and those of its inhabitants—tended to decline. Indeed, towards the end of the eighteenth century, we see the emergence of a third aesthetic category—the picturesque—which was treated as intermediate between the beautiful and the sublime, and that set out to frame, map, block, or otherwise contain the potential disturbance to the observer which was presented by the more raw experience of the sublime. We also find a fourth aesthetic category—the grotesque—increasingly deployed to separate European high arts, religions, and physiognomic features from those of Asia, Africa, and other so-called "primitive" cultures (Mitter 1992 [1977]; Cassuto 1996).

Kant's Aesthetics

Strictly speaking, Burke and his contemporaries do not offer an aesthetics of the sublime and the beautiful, but what might instead be termed a philosophy of taste. Although some philosophers and historians trace the notion of aesthetics back to Alexander Gottlieb Baumgarten (1714–1762), it is Immanuel Kant's development of the concept of aesthetic judgment in his critical writings that is important in terms of the distinction between aesthetics and a philosophy of taste. Kant's writings are generally divided into two distinct periods: the pre-critical writings (1746–1770) and the critical writings (1781–1804), and the distinctive emergence of the notion of aesthetic judgment did not occur until late in the critical period, with *The Critique of the Power of Judgment* (1790), also sometimes referred as Kant's Third *Critique*. (On Kant's aesthetics, see also Chapters 37 and 38 in this volume.)

At the start of Kant's critical project, he outlined two primary philosophical enquiries: into pure reason (concerning what we can know) and pure practical reason (concerning how we should act). The power of judgment that Kant explores in his Third *Critique* is hollowed out in the space between these two enterprises. Judgment is concerned with aesthetic experience—and the beautiful and the sublime in particular—but also with the way in which we treat nature as an ordered whole. It is the task of judgment to determine what everyone *ought* to judge on the basis of the data that is available to them. It is in this context that Kant develops the argument that aesthetic judgment is not just a response to external stimuli, but a response that is simultaneously immediate and also compelling. Pleasure (or displeasure) is an integral part of the experience, but the pleasure is such that we have to suppose that *all* human subjects would respond in exactly the same kind of way if they were in a similar position and faced with the same type of sensory input. In other words, Kant insists that in the case of a pure aesthetic judgment—and, for Kant, it is *only* judgments of *beauty* that count as pure—there is always a *normative* element.

For Kant, the pleasure in beauty comes not from a particular sense or taste, but through the mode in which all the different faculties of the mind operate harmoniously. Beauty, he argues, is so pleasing to mankind that it seems *as if* the world had been created for man's delight, and that means, he maintains, that we have to assume subjective universalizability. Aesthetics is more than simply a report on what the individual does or does not like. This is, however, where problems of sexual and racial difference intrude, and in very different ways insofar as the beautiful and the sublime are involved. In the case of beauty, the judgment that the "I" makes is so abstract that cultural differences are made to seem irrelevant; but Kant also fails to question his own (Northern European) standards of what is "harmonious" to the various faculties of the mind. By contrast, in the case of the sublime—which is not a *pure* aesthetic judgment, but a "mixed" judgment straddling the aesthetic and the moral—Kant differentiates between the two sexes and also between specific racial groupings. Women, "Orientals," and Africans are debarred from the sublime, but males of Arab and North American Indian descent are credited with the noble character necessary for its enjoyment (Kant 2011 [1764]: 2/252–253, 58–59, and see Battersby 2007).

For Kant, the pleasures of the sublime are linked to mental turmoil. And this is because what is enjoyed in the first place is not, as with the beautiful, the sense of a perfect "fit" between the self and its surroundings. Instead, what is striking about the sublime is precisely the impression of something ineffable, indefinite, infinitely great (or small), and the incapacity of the mind to grasp what it is that is being observed or otherwise sensed or contemplated. Instead of the pleasure coming from the feeling that the world or the object had been created for my delight, the pleasure now comes from an initial sense of horror, terror, or astonishment, which is then overcome as the mind moves up a level—to that of the supersensible—and registers that at this level there is, after all, an order that was initially obscured. The sublime allows us a glimpse of something that we simply cannot know: a supersensible power (infinite nature or a God) in relation to which man can only feel humble and weak. In giving us some sense of what might lie beyond the knowable space–time world, the sublime is thus not a purely aesthetic pleasure, but one intermediate between the aesthetic and the moral. Crucially it involves an attitude of respect (*Achtung*) for that which could conceivably annihilate the "I" that Kant positions as being at the center of the knowable world.

For Kant, "true sublimity must be sought only in the mind of the one who judges, not in the object in nature, the judging of which occasions this disposition in it" (2000 [1790]: 5/256, 139). Thus, whereas for Burke, the enjoyment of the sublime was a matter of *taste* and of *affect*, for Kant what is involved is *judgment*: the mind responds to the data or "intuitions" that come in through the senses and, in so doing, the "I" discovers **a faculty of the mind that surpasses every measure of the senses** (2000 [1790]: 5/250, p. 134; bold in original). The enjoyment of the sublime is produced by the "I" as it responds to—and masters—the initial fear, disharmony, or discomfort that is produced as it encounters those vast, infinite, and indefinite entities that seem to threaten its very survival. Kant's claim is that only those who have undergone an appropriate "moral" education and also have a suitable, non-timorous, and also non-sensuous character have the capacity to rise above the initial response of fear or bafflement, and to respond to the sublime with the appropriate feelings of enjoyment, respect, and "awe."

Kant makes it clear in a series of minor texts that bridge the critical and pre-critical periods that he does not think that women should be educated to transcend fear. In his *Lectures on Anthropology* (2012 [1782–1789]), for example, he claims that "preservation of the species" is an "aim" of nature, "which is entrusted to the woman's womb," limiting women's education to care for "three items, kitchen, children, and sick room." It is the "tenderness" of nature that makes women more "fearful" than men, and this is a "universal" quality of women—even those who are "savages" (2012 [1782–1789]: 25/706–707, 236–238). Woman's timidity is a social and biological necessity, since *"nature has entrusted to woman her dearest pledge, the child."* "Feminine qualities," such as fearfulness, which are regarded as weaknesses in males, are thus entirely appropriate for women since, in them, "masculine qualities are always unseemly" (2012 [1782–1789]: 25/1189, 322, emphasis in original).

In his *Lectures on Anthropology*, Kant maintains that women *should* never transcend fear and take delight in the sublime. However, in his early essay, *Observations on the Feeling of the Beautiful and Sublime* (2011 [1764])—which is clearly influenced by both Burke and by Rousseau—Kant makes the more empirical claim that women are *incapable* of acting on the basis of true moral "principle" and enjoying the sublime:

> The virtue of the woman is a **beautiful virtue**. The virtue of the male ought to be a **noble virtue**. Women will avoid evil not because it is unjust, but because it is ugly, and for them virtuous actions mean those that are ethically beautiful. Nothing of ought, nothing of must, nothing of obligation. . . . It is difficult for me to believe that the fair sex is capable of principles, and I hope not to give offense by this, for these are also extremely rare amongst the male sex.
> (2011 [1764]: 2/231–232, 39; bold in original)

In other words, Kant adopts in this early work exactly the type of view to which Wollstonecraft objected so vehemently in 1792: he sexes morality and reserves for males "the salutary, sublime curb of principle" (Wollstonecraft 1996 [1792]: 35).

The "Feminine" Sublime

There is by now a large body of feminist literature analysing the significance of sexual difference in Kant's aesthetics—including texts by Cornelia Klinger (1997 [1995]), Timothy Gould (1995), Battersby (1995; 2007)—or charting female writers' responses to Kant (Jones 2000). However, it's only very recently that a reliable English translation has been offered of Kant's *Lectures on Anthropology* (2012 [1782–1789]) and his misogynistic marginal "Remarks" (1764–1765) to the *Observations* (2011 [1764]), meaning that more work remains to be done. As well as these feminist approaches, a number of extremely influential theorists of the "feminine" have also drawn on Kant's writings—and often in rather surprising ways.

For Kant, as well as for many of the post-Kantian philosophers, the sublime is barred to *women*, but is associated with a *feminine* object, and with a (terrifying and awe-inspiring) female figure, who is concealed behind a veil. The key passage in Kant is to be found in the Third *Critique* (2000 [1790]):

> Perhaps nothing more sublime has ever been said, or any thought more sub-limely expressed, than in the inscription over the Temple of **Isis** (Mother Nature): "I am all that is, that was, and that will be, and my veil no mortal has removed."
>
> (2000 [1790]: 5/316 n., 194 n., bold in original)

For many post-Kantian writers—including the influential philosopher, poet and dramatist Friedrich von Schiller (1759–1805), and the widely-read German novelist, poet, and philosopher Novalis (1772–1801)—the sublime became associated with an "unveiling" of this infinite "other," but, as I have argued in detail elsewhere (Battersby 2007), it remains a male agent who encounters the "feminine" other and, as such, the sexual biases of the sublime are not deeply disturbed.

Kant himself (2002 [1796]) was deeply scornful of those philosophers who thought that they could lift the veil of Isis, and access the sublime "truth" concealed beneath it. More recently, Jacques Derrida (1993 [1981]) has responded to Kant's ban on access to Isis, emphasizing that Kant requires this unknowable and feminine "other" to secure the boundaries of what can be known and what can be expressed. In the wake of Derrida, a school of literary and cultural criticism has developed which looks to deconstruction to develop a positive account of a "feminine" sublime. Some of these critics engage productively with women writers, and also with questions of race (Freeman 1995). However, the link between "the feminine" and women is not straightforward. As Joanna Zylinska explains,

> The feminine sublime . . . is born from the excess that the earlier theorists of the sublime attempted to tame or annul. I am not interested . . . in determining whether or not there *is* a sublime which is specific to women. Instead, I use this term to explore instances in which absolute and incalculable alterity can no longer be housed by the discursive restraints of traditional aesthetics, leading, as a consequence, to the eruption of affect and the weakening of the idea of the universal subject.
>
> (2001: 8, emphasis in original)

Zylinska then goes on to equate "death" with "the ultimate source of fear in the experience of the sublime," and to interpret "the feminine sublime" as a "recogni-tion" of "mortality and finitude to which the self is exposed in its encounter with absolute difference" (2001: 8). We thus find a curious contrast between two strands of gendered critique. Whereas most feminist theorists of the beautiful have been concerned to argue that aesthetic qualities cannot be universalized, in critical theory a distinctive mode of analysis has emerged that emphasizes the *feminine* whilst, at the same time, downplaying sexual, racial, and ethnic differences in face of the universal experience and fear of death.

Arguably there are analogous difficulties with Jean-François Lyotard's extensive engagement with the Kantian sublime, which has also been extremely important for some feminist critics (Klinger 1997 [1995]; Zylinska 2007). In *Peregrinations* (1988) Lyotard argues that Kant's account of the sublime dissolves the subject into a "stream of sensitive clouds," through which "no 'I' swims or sails; only mere affections float. Feelings felt by no one, attached to no identity, but making one cloud 'affected' by another" (1988: 34). Lyotard himself floats happily along with this notion of the dissolution of the subject; but for women who have historically been denied full personhood, and whose subject position has yet to be adequately theorized from a philosophical point of view, this embrace of disembodied affect is premature. By treating difference in an extremely abstract way, Lyotard makes specific bodily, cultural, and historical differences disappear. By contrast, Lyotard's emphasis on the role of dissensus and inaudibility in the Kantian account of the sublime is politically useful for feminists (Ziarek 2001; Grebowicz 2007).

Thus in his *Lessons on the Analytic of the Sublime* (1994 [1991]), Lyotard argues that what is distinctive about the Kantian sublime is that it involves a "differend," which entails "neither moral universality nor aesthetic universalization, but is, rather, the destruction of the one by the other" (1994 [1991]: 239). This differend involves irresolvable tension and "cannot demand, even subjectively, to be communicated to all thought" (1994 [1991]: 239). In political terms, the differend involves a conflict or dispute that is irresolvable because it brings into play at least two language games that would describe what is at stake in incommensurable terms. Any resort to "solving" the dispute by appeal to one of the language games simply covers up the difference and rests on something that is, from the perspective of the language game adopted, "unpresentable." I find Lyotard's emphasis on differences concealed within languages, and also within history, enabling. What is also important is the way in which he puts gender issues at the center of philosophical debate. However, gender for Lyotard does not mean sexual difference, but rather the feminine/masculine distinction. And since the sublime is so often linked to a "feminine" object or a passive—"feminine"—spectator who is nevertheless allocated the body of a male, Lyotard's position is promising but also ultimately disappointing for those who are concerned to develop an aesthetics that is feminist, and who are not simply concerned with a concealed Otherness which is coded as "feminine."

Also important to these developments has been the psychoanalytic theory of Jacques Lacan who draws on Hegel—as well as Kant—as he positions "woman" as a kind of unrepresentable "Other" that cannot be spoken or, indeed, represented, but that also forever haunts the boundaries of language and also of vision. In his 1959–1960 *Seminar* Lacan turns to Kant's account of the beautiful and the sublime in the *Critique of the Power of Judgment* as a means of understanding the character of Sophocles' Antigone who, for Hegel, represented "woman" in her purest form (Hegel 1977 [1807]: §456–475, 273–289; Battersby 1998: 109–116). Lacan's Antigone/woman is constructed as beautiful (as the object of desire), in order to cover over that which threatens the ego (death and the sublime). Antigone "pushes to the limit the realization of something that might be called the pure and simple desire of death as such. She incarnates that desire" (Lacan 1992 [1959–1960]: 282).

Lacan's Antigone/woman represents the threat of the dissolution of the self into the Otherness that bounds it; but, for Lacan, "woman" and "women" are two quite different things. He argues that women only attain identity by separating from the Other/the Mother, and taking on a masculine subject-position. *Women* can speak; but they can't speak as "*woman*": that inexpressible and unrepresentable Otherness, which constitutes a *feminine*—not *female*—sublime. Given this framework, it is not surprising that several of the most important French theorists of the *féminin*, including Julia Kristeva, Hélène Cixous, Catherine Clément, and Luce Irigaray, engage with the question of the sublime as they explore how the *féminin* functions in language in ways that give it more power than Lacan allowed. In none of their writings, however, can the *féminin* be equated with the female. It is Irigaray who comes closest to promoting a *female* sublime, especially in *Speculum of the Other Woman* (1985 [1972]); but her approach to the sublime is always mediated by Lacan and her wish to "jam" the machinery of psychoanalysis and philosophy (Irigaray 1985 [1977]: 78).

Reimagining the Sublime

Bonnie Mann's *Women's Liberation and the Sublime* (2006) engages with both Irigaray and Lyotard. And whereas I have argued that Lyotard pays insufficient attention to bodily differences, Mann shows how Lyotard gets "entangled" in the complex temporalities of the sublime while neglecting spatiality and locatedness (2006: 69). She "talks back" to theorists of the postmodern sublime, and argues that "certain kinds of sublime experience are both rooted in and disclosive of our relations of dependency on other persons and on places, of our vulnerability and injurability" (2006: 145). Drawing on the "fickle feeling" (2006: 131) of the sublime and also feminist theory and practice, she develops a powerful argument for the need to develop an ethics and aesthetics of place and of environmentalism (2006: 159ff).

Less influential than Irigaray in terms of English-language feminism, but more consistently engaged with the question of the sublime, was Sarah Kofman (1934–1994). Opposed to the stylistic obfuscation of both Lacanianism and *l'écriture féminine*, she was nevertheless always interested in showing how philosophy has been driven not solely by reason and rationality, but also by male libido and sexual desire. Thus, for example, she reads the Kantian sublime through Freudian psychoanalysis, linking respect for women to a horror of their bodies (Kofman 2007 [1982]). Writing as a Jew whose rabbi father had been deported from Paris and killed in Auschwitz, she is also painfully aware of the links between "the sublime," the "smothered words," and the "infinite, untransmissible knowledge" of the detainees in the Camps (Kofman 1998 [1987]: 40–41, 37) As well as engaging extensively with Freud, she was also a close reader of Nietzsche, who was profoundly influenced by—and ultimately an opponent of—Arthur Schopenhauer and his aesthetics of the sublime. Like Nietzsche, Kofman developed an ideal of counter-sublime "laughter," in the face of the profound despair at living which Schopenhauer linked to the sublime in *The World as Will and Representation* of 1818–1859. Haunted, however, by "the inexpressible affliction" of Auschwitz, and the demand to express "that which cannot be said and yet *must* be said" (Kofman 1998 [1987]: 31), Kofman's life ended not in laughter, but in suicide—on Nietzsche's birthday, in an apparently symbolic act.

The sublime is an elusive category, and one that stretches the boundaries of aesthetics. Responses to the Lisbon earthquake of 1755, the genocide at Auschwitz, the ground zeroes of Hiroshima and 9/11, the Middle Passage endured by those transported on the slave ships, and the tortured bodies of slaves, have all been linked to the thematics of the sublime (Gilroy 1993: 187–223; Fulford 2005; Ray 2005; Battersby 2007). Elsewhere I have argued that what is needed is an aesthetics that pays attention to embodiment. I have also emphasized (Battersby 1998; 2007) the need to treat pregnancy as normal to the human subject position: the sublime is transformed if we stop treating the "I"/"other" boundary in a way that normalizes the body of males. From such a *female* perspective, the sublime object is not simply an excess, pushed beyond the limits of language, but is instead more like an "other within," concealed within diverse histories and cultures—or rather one of a number of "smothered others" whom we need to learn to hear and also to see.

Further Reading

Ashfield, Andrew and De Bolla, Peter (Eds.) (1996) *The Sublime: A Reader in British Eighteenth Aesthetic Theory*, Cambridge: Cambridge University Press.

Brady, Emily (2013) *The Sublime in Modern Philosophy*, Cambridge: Cambridge University Press.

Brand, Peg Zeglin and Devereaux, Mary (Eds.) (2003) *Women, Art and Aesthetics*, Special Issue of *Hypatia* 18(4).

Korsmeyer, Carolyn (2012) "Feminist Aesthetics," in Edward N. Zalta (Ed.) *Stanford Encyclopedia of Philosophy*, Winter 2012 Edition [online]. Available from: http://plato.stanford.edu/archives/win2012/entries/feminism-aesthetics/.

Llewellyn, Nigel and Riding, Christine (Eds.) *The Art of the Sublime*, [online] London: Tate Gallery. Available from www.tate.org.uk/art/research-publications/the-sublime.

Related Topics

Feminist methods in the history of philosophy (Chapter 1); feminism and the Enlightenment (Chapter 8); feminist engagements with nineteenth-century German philosophy (Chapter 9); language, writing and gender differences (Chapter 24); historicizing feminist aesthetics (Chapter 37); aesthetics and the politics of gender (Chapter 38).

References

Bartky, Sandra Lee (1990) *Femininity and Domination: Studies in the Phenomenology of Oppression*, New York: Routledge.

Battersby, Christine (1989) *Gender and Genius: Towards a Feminist Aesthetics*, London: The Women's Press.

——(1995) "Stages on Kant's Way: Aesthetics, Morality and the Gendered Sublime," in Peggy Zeglin Brand and Carolyn Korsmeyer (Eds.) *Feminism and Tradition in Aesthetics*, University Park, PA: Pennsylvania University Press, 88–114.

——(1998) *The Phenomenal Woman: Feminist Metaphysics and the Patterns of Identity*, New York: Routledge.

——(2007) *The Sublime, Terror and Human Difference*, New York: Routledge.

Beauvoir, Simone de (1952 [1949]) *The Second Sex*, trans. Howard M. Parshley, New York: Knopf.

Bordo, Susan (2005 [1993]) *Unbearable Weight: Feminism, Western Culture, and the Body: Tenth Anniversary Edition*, Berkeley, CA: University of California Press.

Brand, Peg Zeglin (Ed.) (2000) *Beauty Matters*, Bloomington, IN and Indianapolis, IN: Indiana University Press.

——(Ed.) (2013) *Beauty Unlimited*, Bloomington, IN and Indianapolis, IN: Indiana University Press.

Burke, Edmund. (1987 [1757/59]) *A Philosophical Enquiry into the Origin of our Ideas of the Sublime and Beautiful*, James T. Boulton (Ed.) Oxford: Blackwell.

Cassuto, Leonard (1996) *The Inhuman Race: The Racial Grotesque in American Literature and Culture*, New York: Columbia University Press.

Derrida, Jacques (1993 [1981]) "Of an Apocalyptic Tone Recently Adopted in Philosophy," in Peter Fenves (Ed.) *Raising the Tone of Philosophy: Late Essays by Immanuel Kant, Transformative Critique by Jacques Derrida*, Baltimore, MD: Johns Hopkins University Press, 117–171.

Freeman, Barbara Claire (1995) *The Feminine Sublime: Gender and Excess in Women's Fiction*, Berkeley, CA and London: University of California Press.

Fulford, Sarah (2005) "David Dabydeen and Turner's Sublime Aesthetic," *Anthurium: A Caribbean Studies Journal* [online] 3(1). Available from: http://scholarlyrepository.miami.edu/anthurium/vol3/iss1/4.

Gilroy, Paul (1993) *The Black Atlantic: Modernity and Double Consciousness*, London: Verso.

Gould, Timothy (1995) "Intensity and Its Audiences: Toward a Feminist Perspective on the Kantian Sublime," in Peggy Zeglin Brand and Carolyn Korsmeyer (Eds.) *Feminism and Tradition in Aesthetics*, University Park, PA: Pennsylvania University Press, 66–87.

Grebowicz, Margret (Ed.) (2007) *Gender after Lyotard*, Albany, NY: State University of New York Press.

Hegel, G. W. F. (1977 [1807]) *Phenomenology of Spirit*, trans. A. V. Miller, Oxford: Oxford University Press.

Irigaray, Luce (1985 [1974]) *Speculum of the Other Woman*, trans. Gillian C. Gill, Ithaca, NY: Cornell University Press.

—— (1985 [1977]) *This Sex Which Is Not One*, trans. Catherine Porter and Carolyn Burke, Ithaca, NY: Cornell University Press.

Jones, Rachel (2000) "Aesthetics in the Gaps: Subverting the Sublime for a Female Subject," in Penny Florence and Nicola Foster (Eds.) *Differential Aesthetics: Art Practices, Philosophy and Feminist Understandings*, Farnham: Ashgate, 119–140.

Kant, Immanuel (1902–) *Gesammelte Schriften*, Ed. der Deutschen [formerly Königlich Preussischen] Akademie der Wissenschaften, Berlin: Walter de Gruyter.

—— (2000 [1790]) *The Critique of the Power of Judgment*, trans. and Ed. Paul Guyer, Cambridge: Cambridge University Press. Marginal references to Kant (1902) are provided in the text.

—— (2002 [1796]) "On a Recently Prominent Tone of Superiority in Philosophy," in *Kant, Theoretical Philosophy after 1781*, Ed. and trans. Henry Allison and Peter Heath, trans. Gary Hatfield and Michael Friedman, Cambridge: Cambridge University Press, 425–446. Marginal references to Kant (1902) are provided in the text.

—— (2011 [1764 and 1764–1765]) *Observations on the Feeling of the Beautiful and Sublime and Other Writings*, "Remarks on the Observations on the Feeling of the Beautiful and Sublime (1764–65)," Ed. and trans. Patrick Frierson and Paul Guyer, Cambridge: Cambridge University Press. Marginal references to Kant (1902) are provided in the text.

—— (2012 [1782–1789]) *Lectures on Anthropology*, Eds. Allen W. Wood and Robert B. Louden, trans. Robert B. Louden, Allen W. Wood, Robert R. Clewis, and G. Felicitas Munzel, Cambridge: Cambridge University Press. Marginal references to Kant (1902) are provided in the text.

Klinger, Cornelia (1997 [1995]) "The Concepts of the Sublime and the Beautiful in Kant and Lyotard," in Robin May Schott (Ed.) *Feminist Interpretations of Immanuel Kant*, University Park, PA: Pennsylvania State University Press, 191–211.

Kofman, Sarah (1998 [1987]) *Smothered Words*, trans. Madeleine Dobie, Evanston, IL: Northwestern University Press.

—— (2007 [1982]) "The Economy of Respect: Kant and Respect for Women," in Thomas Albrecht, Georgia Albert, and Elizabeth G. Rottenberg (Eds.) *Selected Writings*, Redwood City, CA: Stanford University Press, 187–204.

Korsmeyer, Carolyn (2004) *Gender and Aesthetics: An Introduction*, London: Routledge.

—— (2011) *Savoring Disgust: The Foul and the Fair in Aesthetics*, Oxford: Oxford University Press.

Lacan, Jacques (1992 [1959–60]) *The Ethics of Psychoanalysis: The Seminar of Jacques Lacan, Book 7*, Jacques-Alain Miller (Ed.), trans. Dennis Porter, London: Routledge.

Lintott, Sheila (2010) "Feminist Aesthetics and the Neglect of Natural Beauty," *Environmental Values* 19: 315–333.

Longinus (2005 [c.100–c.200]) "On the Sublime," trans. W. H. Fyfe, rev. Donald Russell, in Loeb Classical Library *Aristotle Volume XXIII*, Cambridge, MA: Harvard University Press, 157–308.

Lyotard, Jean-François (1988) *Peregrinations: Law, Form, Event*, New York: Columbia University Press.

——(1994 [1991]) *Lessons on the Analytic of the Sublime*, trans. Elizabeth Rottenberg, Stanford, CA: Stanford University Press.

Mann, Bonnie (2006) *Women's Liberation and the Sublime: Feminism, Postmodernism, Environment*, Oxford: Oxford University Press.

Mitter, Partha (1992 [1977]) *Much Maligned Monsters: History of European Reactions to Indian Art*, Oxford: Clarendon Press.

Ray, Gene (2005) *Terror and the Sublime in Art and Critical Theory: From Auschwitz to Hiroshima to September 11*, New York: Palgrave Press.

Schopenhauer, Arthur (1966 [1818–1859]) *The World as Will and Representation*, trans. E. F. J. Payne, New York: Dover Publications.

Tanner, Jakob (2006) "Stoff und Form: Menschliche Selbsthervorbringung, Geschlechterdualismus und die Widerständigkeit der Materie," in Barbara Naumann, Thomas Strässle, and Caroline Torra-Mattenklott (Eds.) *Stoffe. Zur Geschichte der Materialität in Künsten und Wissenschaften*, Zürich: Hochschulverlag, 83–108.

Walter, Natasha (2010) *Living Dolls: The Return of Sexism*, London: Virago.

Wolf, Naomi (1990) *The Beauty Myth: How Images of Beauty Are Used against Women*, London: Chatto & Windus.

Wollstonecraft, Mary (1996 [1792]) *A Vindication of the Rights of Woman*, 2nd edition, Candace Ward (Ed.), Mineola, NY: Dover Publications.

Ziarek, Ewa Plonowska (2001) *An Ethics of Dissensus: Postmodernity, Feminism, and the Politics of Radical Democracy*, Stanford, CA: Stanford University Press.

Zylinska, Joanna (2001) *On Spiders, Cyborgs and Being Scared: The Feminine and the Sublime*, Manchester University Press.

—— (2007) "'Nourished . . . on the Irremediable Differend of Gender': Lyotard's Sublime," in Margret Grebowicz (Ed.) *Gender After Lyotard*, Albany, NY: State University of New York Press, 155–170.

Ethics

40

MORAL JUSTIFICATION IN AN UNJUST WORLD

Alison M. Jaggar and Theresa W. Tobin

Diversity, Inequality, and Moral Justification

Social inequality and cultural diversity are inescapable features of our world. Their conceptual richness and variety of perspectives provide valuable resources for moral thinking but they also complicate moral reasoning, especially reasoning among members of differently situated social groups. When cultural values are diverse, different groups may prioritize similar values differently, the values of one culture may not have obvious correlates in another, and different forms of reasoning may be taken as authoritative. Inequality may allow members of powerful social groups to repress the moral views of the less powerful by ignoring, dismissing, or silencing them.

Many inter-group disputes concern gender norms. Examples include: female genital cutting, abortion, marriage equality, and legislation that requires or bans women's veiling. In order to address such disputes equitably, Western philosophers have proposed a variety of methodological models. Feminist philosophers have criticized many of these models because they are too easily used to justify the oppression of women or render invisible moral issues that are especially significant in the lives of women. In the longer work from which this article is drawn, we build on these criticisms. We examine several popular models of moral justification and find that, in contexts of diversity and inequality, they often facilitate epistemic and moral injustice, allowing members of more powerful groups to rationalize proposals that favor their own partial interests. We, along with many other feminist philosophers, tried initially to fix or tweak existing models to make them less gender biased and more likely to yield warranted moral outcomes (Okin 1989; Benhabib 1992; Jaggar 1995; Mills 1994). Yet the revised models failed to escape the problems of their originals, remaining insufficiently responsive to the ways in which differences in situation and social identity markers such as race, ethnicity, class, and global positioning influence credibility judgments about who and what may count as reasonable. This chapter offers one illustration of how this can happen and uses it to motivate our proposal for an alternative mission and method for moral epistemology.

Our alternative proposal rejects the epistemological assumption that there exists a single, one-size-fits-all model of moral justification capable of reliably yielding warranted moral conclusions in all contexts. The approach we advocate is inspired by previous feminist work and suggests one direction for pushing that work further toward realizing the goals of epistemic justice in the practice of moral justification.

Epistemic Injustice and Moral Justification

Epistemic injustice occurs when processes of knowledge production are influenced by social power in ways unfair to some inquirers. Philosophers, including many feminists, have long reflected on the relations between power and knowledge but the term "epistemic injustice" recently gained currency in Western analytic philosophy with the publication of Miranda Fricker's influential book, *Epistemic Injustice: Power and the Ethics of Knowing* (2007; Collins 2000; Mills 1994).

Fricker identifies two main forms of epistemic injustice, testimonial and hermeneutic. Testimonial injustice occurs when hearers assess knowledge claims wrongly because they hold unjust prejudices, either positive or negative, about the credibility of those putting forward the claims. Negatively prejudiced listeners often hold some wrongful stereotype or "identity prejudice" about the epistemic capacity of a group to which the individual belongs. Positive epistemic prejudice allows the claims of some speakers to be accorded more weight than the speakers' credentials deserve. Not all prejudices are overt or explicit; some stereotypes affect people's perceptions without their conscious awareness and they are called implicit biases. Implicit biases may not be easily accessible through introspection and sometimes are outside people's intentional control.

Hermeneutic injustice occurs when the available linguistic resources are inadequate for communicating what a speaker wishes to convey. Feminists of the 1960s and 1970s famously used the practice of consciousness-raising to develop a new vocabulary for expressing previously unarticulated wrongs, such as date rape, sexual harassment, and hostile work environments. Canadian aboriginal people have contended that "A distinct category of Aboriginal property rights demands the willingness and capacity to comprehend and evaluate an altogether different (alterior) concept of property" (Means 2003: 224). They have argued in Canada's Supreme Court "for the right to present various sacred 'texts'; oral history, totems, and other 'expressive discourses'" (Means 2003: 223).

The harms resulting from epistemic injustice fall disproportionately, though not exclusively, on those with less power. When testimonial or hermeneutical injustice hinder people in voicing or even articulating their moral perspectives, those people are wronged in their distinctively human capacities as givers of knowledge, reasoners, or subjects of social understanding. They are epistemically marginalized, excluded from trustful conversation, and may lose faith in their own epistemic capacities (Fricker 2007).

As well as harming particular individuals, epistemic injustice tends to produce untrustworthy outcomes. Knowledge claims produced via unjust processes are more likely to be biased, incomplete, misleading, or distorting. Epistemic injustice in moral discourse typically results in moral conclusions that obscure social injustice, sometimes by promoting systematic ignorance. For instance, those who are more powerful may

502

dismiss reports of wrongs committed against those less powerful or they may frame moral wrongs in misleading ways that blame bad luck or individual perpetrators while ignoring systemic factors.

We wish to develop an approach to moral reasoning that is less susceptible to epistemic injustice than many familiar philosophical approaches. Our approach invokes the ideal of epistemic democracy, which has gained considerable traction in feminist philosophy since 1990 (Longino 1990; 2002; Anderson 1995; 2010: 89–111). We think that this can provide valuable guidance for moral epistemology but we regard it as a thin and contestable ideal that must be specified differently in different contexts. In particular, we think that the frequent formulation of "universal participation on terms of equality of inquirers" (Anderson 2012: 172) may not always ensure epistemic justice among people reasoning together in contexts of diversity and inequality.

One way in which "formal" epistemic democracy may be less than just is by refusing to take account of legitimate differences in people's moral competence or expertise. For instance, some cultural or religious communities regard the words of particular community members as having extra moral weight, perhaps in virtue of their having privileged access to divine meaning or the wisdom of the ancestors. In other contexts, some individuals have specialized or deeper knowledge of salient hermeneutical resources, such as sacred texts or cultural traditions. Some individuals have firsthand experience of various kinds of oppression (Thomas 1992–1993). Because moral expertise is typically limited to specific domains, epistemic justice requires that moral experts receive due deference when they speak about the areas in which they are experts. We advocate a version of epistemic democracy that we call "inclusive." Although it requires universal participation, it is nonetheless open to the possibilities of differing moral expertise in some domains and consequent legitimate differences in epistemic authority for some individuals in some contexts.

Four Necessary Conditions of Inclusive Epistemic Democracy

Our conception of inclusive epistemic democracy is specified in terms of four conditions. In contexts of diversity and inequality, we think that the best chance of reaching reliable and authoritative moral conclusions is gained by relying on models and practices of moral reasoning that are able to meet the following conditions:

- *Plausibility.* To justify a normative conclusion is to explain convincingly why it has moral authority. All disputants must recognize the reasoning practice as capable of conferring moral authority on the conclusions reached.
- *Usability.* Everyone involved in a particular dispute must be able to utilize the justificatory practices employed. This does not mean that everyone must be able to participate as a formal equal; instead, people must be able to participate in a way that accords with whatever strategies of moral justification their communities regard as authoritative. Our interpretation of "usability" may seem to open the door to injustice, but our first and third conditions are designed to block this door.
- *Non-abuse of power and vulnerability.* No reasoning practice is epistemically inclusive if it relies on abusing power or vulnerability. In contexts of moral reasoning,

there are innumerable ways short of overt physical coercion in which some disputants make their own views appear unduly credible while taking advantage of others' vulnerability to discredit them. Abuse can include misrepresentation or selective presentation of evidence, distortion, intimidation, logical trickery, mystification, ridicule, disregard, and refusal to understand. It also occurs when some disputants insist on a particular style of argumentation in which others are unskilled or uncomfortable or on using a vocabulary that does not fit well with the moral concepts of some disputants or is inadequate to express their perspectives.

- *Practical feasibility*. Finally, no model or practice of moral justification is inclusive in a given context if it prescribes a course of action that is not feasible or realistically possible for some people in the situation. As Onora O'Neill writes, "Proposals for action will . . . not be reasoned unless they are not only intelligible, but real possibilities for those who are to be offered reasons for certain recommendations or prescriptions, warnings or proscriptions" (1996: 57–58).

Even when our four conditions are accepted in principle, it is always possible for people to disagree about how to apply them in specific contexts. None of our conditions can be deployed mechanically, and, as we invoke them to assess the use of particular reasoning strategies, we offer arguments about what should count in particular contexts as plausibility, usability, power abuse, and practical feasibility.

Moral and Political Universalism

Our larger work examines several methodological models of moral justification, such as intuitionism, original position thinking, discourse ethics, and communitarianism. Here we sketch two examples of the method of appealing to universal principles.

Moral universalism is the idea that there exist substantive moral values, norms or principles valid in all times and places. Universal values and norms seem especially promising as courts of appeal for disputes among different communities or among diverse members of one community. One example of a principle asserted to be universally valid is the "moral law" or Categorical Imperative proposed by Immanuel Kant (1785). Moral agents checking whether a particular action they contemplate accords with the Categorical Imperative should ask themselves whether or not their maxim, or reason for action in that case, could be universalized or whether it would produce any contradictions or irrationalities if everyone acted on the same maxim in similar cases. The Principle of Utility is another example of a moral principle claimed to hold universally. Proposed by British utilitarians in the nineteenth century, the principle states that an action or practice is morally right when it leads to the greatest possible balance of good over bad consequences. Different utilitarian philosophers characterize good and bad consequences differently but, regardless of how they define the good, all utilitarians regard the Principle of Utility as morally supreme.

Although these two supposedly universal principles present famously sharp contrasts to each other, they also resemble each other in significant ways. Both insist that all persons have equal moral weight and that moral reasoning should be impartial; both focus on assessing specific actions or practices, as opposed to qualities of character; and both purport to provide a single standard of morality that enables moral agents to determine objectively what is right and wrong. Both assume that practical moral reasoning has a deductive structure, in which general moral principles are applied to specific situations.

Adjudicating cross-cultural disputes by invoking supposedly universal moral principles raises several problems. One concerns the justification of the principles themselves. The moral core of each principle is controversial in Western societies, let alone beyond them, in part because each principle appears to mandate some actions that are morally wrong. One famous problem for Kantian theory is posed by the hypothetical murderer at the door who is seeking someone hidden in the house. According to Kant's exposition of the Categorical Imperative, lying is never permissible even though telling the truth to the potential killer is likely to enable murder. The Principle of Utility also justifies many morally problematic actions, such as killing one person to save others or torturing someone in hope of extracting information about a ticking time bomb.

A second cluster of problems concerns the formulation, interpretation and application of the principles. Formulating them can be controversial. For instance, as Henry Sidgwick noticed (1962 [1907]) and as Derek Parfit among others has elaborated (1984), increasing the numbers of human (or sentient) beings might maximize the total utility in the world but at the cost of decreasing each individual's utility. Moreover, even when their formulation is agreed, the principles are extremely general and vague, so that appealing to them in particular situations leaves enormous scope for further dispute.

Partly because of these difficulties, recent efforts to address intercultural disputes often appeal to principles that are political rather than moral. Political principles may appear more plausible than moral principles, in part because they are taken to be universal in a sense that is more constrained. Rather than being considered timeless or holding in all possible moral worlds, most contemporary political principles are designed for the existing world at the present time. Although they have far-reaching implications for individual conduct, they are designed to apply in the first instance to legislation and social practices. Their justifications are more explicit than the rationales for supposedly ultimate moral principles and they are open in theory to revision or amendment. Finally, these political principles promise to reduce indeterminacy because they do not attempt to define moral rightness and wrongness in terms of a single broad principle but instead offer longer and more specific lists.

The most familiar example of political universalism is the 1948 Universal Declaration of Human Rights (UDHR). This is the basis not only of a cosmopolitan or global morality but an international law above national law. A second example of political universalism is the idea of capabilities, developed originally by Amartya Sen (1984). Sen intended the capabilities as a global standard of human well-being and he defined them as socially available opportunities for valuable functioning. Sen has resisted offering a comprehensive list of capabilities, but Martha Nussbaum has developed an explicit list that purports to provide a universal standard for assessing local ways of life and thus offers a concrete alternative to cultural relativism (Nussbaum 2000: 13).

Unfortunately for those hoping to adjudicate inter-group disputes by reference to universal political principles, such principles are assailed by the same problems of justification and interpretation that beset universal moral principles. Neither moral nor political universalism is able to meet our adequacy conditions.

Plausibility. First, problems with justification. The human rights accepted across the world are justified by explicit political consensus but real world consensus is always shaped by the context in which it occurs. Some countries have ratified human rights with many reservations and many countries that have ratified them are not democratic, so that their governments may not reflect the views of their citizenry. Moreover, many civil society groups believe that currently recognized rights need to be supplemented and there is constant political pressure to reinterpret and expand them. For instance, lively controversy currently exists over whether the right to sex equality should include sexuality and abortion. Whether or not revisions to rights are accepted depends on the outcome of political contests in which the views of small groups may well go unheard. Attempting to resolve cross-cultural disputes by appealing to human rights that are themselves contested begs crucial questions at issue.

Nussbaum uses four methods to legitimate her list of capabilities but all have been subjected to various criticisms. The methods that Nussbaum invokes are: (1) The Aristotelian approach of critically refining *eudoxa* or reputable beliefs; (2) the narrative method; (3) morally constrained proceduralism; (4) the non-platonic substantive good method. All these methods have been challenged by, respectively (Ackerly 2000; Okin 2003; Robeyns 2005; Jaggar 2006). Underlying many particular criticisms of Nussbaum's methods is the larger thought that no political ideals are legitimate or authoritative if they are not justified through processes of public reason, which is not the case for the capabilities (Robeyns 2005; Jaggar 2006).

Usability. As we noted earlier, general ideals and principles are inevitably indeterminate and although indeterminacy can be reduced by producing relatively specific lists of human rights and capabilities, it cannot be eliminated. Neither of the two lists we have given as examples offers a priority ranking among its items; human rights are said to be indivisible and Nussbaum denies that capabilities can be traded off against each other. Furthermore, even quite specific items on any list must be interpreted in particular situations and increasing specificity to reduce indeterminacy heightens the risk of tendentiousness. The method of invoking universal principles as guides to action always struggles with a dilemma between appealing to principles that are, on the one hand, so broad or general that they are too vague to provide specific guidance or, on the other hand, so narrow that they are applicable only to a limited range of situations and may even appear arbitrary or ad hoc.

Non-Abusiveness. Universal principles always require interpretation in particular contexts, which often provide opportunities for the abuse of power and vulnerability. For instance, items on the lists may be spelled out in ways that repress the moral views of less powerful groups. In the following section, we illustrate how this can occur by showing how the principle of women's human rights has been deployed in oppressive and disrespectful ways against some communities, particularly in Africa (Nnaemeka 2005).

Practical Feasibility. Whether or not the use of a model or practice of moral justification prescribes a course of action that is feasible or realistically possible for everyone in that situation can be determined only in particular contexts. In the next section, we describe one case study where the use of this model failed to meet our condition of practical feasibility.

Case Study: Is Female Genital Cutting (FGC) as Practiced by the Maasai a Violation of Women's Human Rights?

Over the past three decades, eradicating a cluster of practices known as female genital cutting (FGC) has been a high priority on the moral agenda of many women's human rights and development organizations. These organizations argue that FGC is morally wrong and that the international community has a moral responsibility to support eradication efforts or even spearhead them. We call this influential line of thinking the Women's Human Rights Approach (WHR). WHR has come under criticism from some scholars and activists who study or work in communities where FGC is practiced. Their shared line of critique is that WHR generates misleading, and even morally mistaken, conclusions about why these practices are wrong, who is responsible for the harm, and how to address the harm. The critics offer an alternative moral evaluation of FGC that relies on a different method of justification. Both "sides" of this dispute use human rights as moral standards to evaluate FGC and both find moral fault with FGC. However, each uses a distinct practice of moral justification in which human rights function very differently, generating divergent grounds for their respective assessments.

WHR asserts that what it calls female genital mutilation is an act of violence against women, which violates their human rights (United Nations 2015). It also states that this violence is rooted in historically unjust power relations between men and women, which derive essentially from certain traditional or customary practices (United Nations 2015). The method of moral justification WHR uses deductively applies a very specific interpretation of women's rights women's human rights which is assumed to apply in all global contexts to concrete cases in order to demonstrate to doubters that particular instantiations of FGC violate women's human rights.

The specific interpretation of the WHR standard already defines which social practices are morally wrong and provides an account of why they are wrong, so that anyone using the standard starts her moral evaluation with a prefabricated moral frame that foregrounds gender and culture. When the standard is applied in particular cases, it is assumed that other contextual information has no moral salience. For example, FGC as practiced among the Maasai in Kenya is very different from FGC as practiced among Muslims in Indonesia but, when using the WHR approach, a person enters both contexts already knowing that these practices are wrong, and knowing why they are wrong (i.e., all instances of FGC reflect and reinforce culturally specific gender relations premised on male domination and female subordination). Contextual details are used to recruit evidence showing how a particular practice is indeed an instance of FGC, but not to revise the standard or determine its meaning.

The critics of WHR whose approach we favor do not deny that many practices of FGC are in some sense harmful nor do they reject women's human rights as important moral tools. Rather, they object to the moral reasoning used by WHR advocates and the way that WHR advocates frame the issue and characterize moral agency. Taken collectively, the work of these critics offers a sustained argument that WHR systematically conceals features of the social and historical contexts in which FGC occurs that are highly relevant for an adequate moral evaluation of these practices. It offers an alternative moral analysis of FGC as practiced in spe-cific communities through the frame of colonial history. We call this a postcolonial analysis approach (PCA).

PCA begins by looking at a specific practice of FGC among a particular group of people within a specified historical time frame. The scholars whose work we highlight focus on understanding the evolving cultural and moral significance of FGC among Maasai communities of Tanzania and Kenya from the pre-colonial period of the late nineteenth century through the period of formal colonization by the British from 1920–1961. For the Maasai, FGC initiates the social transition of a girl into womanhood. In the period prior to formal colonization, social responsi-bilities associated with Maasai womanhood included a significant amount of eco-nomic and political authority. For example, Maasai wives had authority to initiate and testify at judicial proceedings and they participated in dispute resolution both within and between homesteads. They were also the primary economic agents in a barter economy trading surplus milk and hides in exchange for other important goods. During and after formal colonization by the British, however, Maasai gender relations shifted dramatically.

At least three colonial policies significantly altered Maasai gender relations. First, the policy of indirect rule required identifying a central Maasai authority to act as an intermediary between the Maasai and the British. In implementing this policy, British authorities assumed that male elders were already "the" political lead-ers, thereby extending the authority of select male elders over both women and junior men, strengthening and consolidating their power. Second, needing to cre-ate a cash economy in order to produce tax revenue for the crown, the British also transformed a previously female-based barter economy into a newly male-dominated cash economy. Livestock was now to be bought and sold on the market for cash and colonial authorities *assumed* that males were the "owners" of cattle. So Maasai men were integrated into the new economy as buyers and sellers of livestock, while Maasai women were dispossessed from their previously shared cattle rights and now struggled to gain access to cash "indirectly through gifts from men or the sale of cattle by their sons or husbands (Hodgson 1999: 57)." The third policy, which followed directly from the second, was to implement a new system of taxation. This system designated male elders as "tax payers" and "heads of household," who were now required to pay a "plural wives" tax for "dependent" women living on their homestead (Hodgson 1999: 58).

These policies reflected a British gender ideology that was deeply patriarchal. Their combined effect was severe political and economic disempowerment and symbolic devaluation of Maasai women. Foregrounding colonial history reveals that contempo-rary Maasai gender relations, which today are identified as "authentically" and deeply embedded in Maasai culture, are really a "co-invention" by British colonial authorities and opportunistic Maasai in a fairly recent struggle for power.

Where WHR concludes that the harmful gender relations supporting Maasai FGC derive from cultural patterns that belong *essentially* to the Maasai (see IRIN 2005), PCA argues that this claim is false. Physical harms or risks associated with Maasai FGC likely have always been present, but PCA suggests that the practice becomes a tool of male domination only in the context of the colonial encounter. The harm-ful gender relations that today give symbolic meaning to Maasai FGC derive from cultural patterns, but these resulted from a forced blend of British gender ideology with pre-existing Maasai social categories.

PCA relies on an alternative practice of moral justification, although advocates of this approach do not make it explicit. PCA uses women's human rights as one important moral tool in an empirically informed reflective equilibrium which takes human rights as moral standards that need interpreting in light of particular cases rather than just being implemented in a deductive manner. Contextual details have salience in shaping the moral assessment of the situation and the interpretation of women's human rights and not just in persuading doubters or tailoring eradication efforts. In this case, PCA uses historical details to generate a more transparent moral analysis of contemporary practices of FGC among the Maasai based on a more comprehensive account of the human rights abuses Maasai women have suffered, which includes the abuse of colonial experience (see Walker 2002 on transparency in moral life).

We use our four conditions for inclusive epistemic democracy—plausibility, usability, non-abuse of social power or vulnerability, and feasibility—to argue that PCA is more likely than WHR to yield authoritative moral conclusions about FGC in this situation.

Plausibility. WHR and PCA both appeal to human rights, but in this case we think that, PCA enables a more plausible way of using human rights as tools of moral assessment than WHR does. WHR assumes that "the" answer to "the" problem exists already in the form of a universal principle of women's human rights that is already formulated at the appropriate level of abstraction for application in all contexts; it is not too thin and not too thick. By contrast, PCA assumes that the relevant standard or principle and the appropriate level of interpretation for it, will emerge as the "wrong" comes into clearer focus. Using PCA does not preclude questioning the universal validity of the human rights framework, but opens the possibility that more than one human rights principle may be morally relevant here and assumes that human rights principles always need interpreting in a way appropriate to the facts and the context. Interpreting human rights in light of the details of a particular practice of FGC in a specific place is more likely to be able to link the moral authority of the conclusion with the reasoning that generates that conclusion, to tell a more plausible story about the variety of rights violations involved in this case, and to offer a more plausible interpretation of those violations that is likely to seem less arbitrary or baffling to those most directly impacted.

Usability. This condition requires that all those affected be able to participate in moral reasoning; this may require, for example, that participants utilize particular rituals or forms of speech. In this case, most Maasai people who are directly affected are not actually using either reasoning strategy, which is a significant weakness of both approaches. However, in our view, PCA has greater potential than WHR to better satisfy the usability condition in situations like this one. The WHR strategy does not make room for cultural standards or contextual details to interpret or reinterpret the meaning of rights, but only to tailor eradication efforts. Moreover, Maasai opposition to moral arguments supported by WHR reasoning suggests that the reasoning being offered is not plausible to many Maasai. One reason for this may be that the

WHR reasoning strategy is not usable by them in the sense of broadly conforming to internal cultural standards. PCA leaves open the possibility for Maasai standards of justification to be used because the reasoning strategy of PCA encourages its users to continually seek out new information from the particular social context under scrutiny, and so it can incorporate Maasai moral perspectives in order to interpret, revise, or broaden human rights principles.

Non-Abuse of Power or Vulnerability. In this case, we think that WHR is lends itself more readily to abusing power and vulnerability than does PCA. WHR as used in this case brings under moral scrutiny the least powerful while shielding the most powerful from scrutiny. WHR also makes its own moral framework appear incontrovertible while too easily lending itself to discrediting anyone who uses an alternative framework. In our assessment, WHR is more susceptible to power abuse in this context for at least three reasons. First, it relies on a static and oversimplified notion of culture in a context in which cultural interventions are not innocent but track global power relations both historically and at present. Second, it also tends to assign "culture" to those with the least global power while simultaneously making dominant global perspectives appear cultureless, which they are not. Finally, WHR foregrounds gender but places gender relations in a historical vacuum, and so obscures the complex web of historical interactions among nations and cultures that have produced the specific gender relations within Maasai communities that are today the object of global moral criticism. The epistemic stance enabled by WHR is eerily similar to the perspective of British colonizers who perceived gender and culture in the Maasai practices that were exotic or foreign to them, but failed to see their own policies as gendered and instead regarded them as natural. Although PCA is certainly not immune from being used in abusive ways, it enables corrigibility and discourages dogmatism. PCA's insistence on seeking out empirical information relevant to understanding the contemporary social meaning of Maasai FGC and the conditions that enable its continuance, as well as PCA's ability to incorporate Maasai perspectives, make this reasoning strategy less apt to be used abusively than WHR in this situation.

Feasibility. Maasai are reported as very resistant to eradication efforts justified using WHR reasoning. These efforts include state prohibition of FGC coupled with NGO and religious organization interventions that advocate cultural change. In our view, this resistance provides prima facie evidence that the moral conclusions defended by WHR are not feasible to many Maasai. The conclusions may seem arbitrary, baffling, or suspicious given previously devastating interventions premised on cultural change. The interventions might also be materially or existentially devastating for many Maasai given the real limitations of their situation and the complicated links between Maasai FGC and social life. In our view, PCA is likely more capable of delivering more feasible recommendations than WHR because people using PCA are less rigidly committed to prejudging cases, and instead try to seek out all morally salient information including alternative moral perspectives. This means that PCA-derived solutions are likely to be premised on more nuanced assessments of the risks and benefits of eradication efforts in particular situations and to find solutions that are more likely to be real possibilities for people in the contexts they actually live in.

Changing the Mission and Method of
Moral Epistemology

Many philosophers have assumed that moral justification can be pared down to a single reasoning practice or set of practices, which can be used to justify moral claims in any context. They therefore take the mission of moral epistemology to be discovering or constructing a single, multi-purpose model of moral justification (Walker 2002: ch. 1–2). Philosophers have typically pursued this mission using "armchair" philosophical methods. They imagine what moral reasoning should be like either by constructing fictitious models of justification or by conceptualizing the logical constraints of moral reasoning under ideal conditions. In our view, the fruits of this philosophical labor as well as this way of laboring—i.e., of doing moral epistemology—are inadequate for understanding how justified moral claims can be established in situations of cultural diversity and power inequality. We have come to believe that no single method or model of moral rationality can yield substantive and authoritative normative conclusions in all circumstances. On our view, reasoning strategies must fit the context in which they are used.

A model of moral justification developed under the controlled conditions of the philosopher's imagination and relying on his or her acknowledged or unacknowledged assumptions may or may not be capable of justifying moral claims under the conditions of real life. This may not be because the model has been applied incorrectly or unfairly, but because it has been developed assuming a context with one set of features and then prescribed for all contexts, are very unlike that assumed in the philosopher's imagination. For example, the controlled conditions of philosophical imagination have tended to assume conditions in which interlocutors exchanging reasons have equal social power, and so philosophers have developed models of moral justification based on this assumption. Yet a model of moral justification designed for conditions of social equality may be ineffective in situations where people have unequal social power, and may even be harmful if the model obscures or makes it easy to rationalize power abuse.

These considerations suggest two points about moral epistemology. First, moral epistemology should adopt a more modest mission. A single, multi-purpose model of reasoning might be suitable for a world in which diversity and inequality were not ubiquitous. However, in our world, to prescribe for all contexts a single practice of justification that has been developed under the controlled conditions of the philosopher's imagination may at best be ineffective and at worst epistemically unjust in situations that do not match these conditions. Certain features of the context partially determine which reasoning practices are capable of justifying moral claims in that context.

Second, the study of moral justification needs to be much more empirically grounded (Walker 2002). In order to understand which reasoning practices are capable of justifying moral claims in different types of contexts, we need to study empirically the relationships between reasoning practices and the contexts in which they work well. Features of a context that influence the adequacy of a method of moral justification include social relations of power and vulnerability among interlocutors as well as particular moral vocabularies and styles of reasoning that are available, meaningful, and usable to and by various parties. Many areas of contemporary philosophy have recently seen a methodological turn toward more empirically informed research. This turn is often called a move toward naturalizing methodology because philosophers are attempting to make their research more continuous with results from empirical science. Our proposal shares in the naturalizing spirit of these developments, but suggests a new and distinct method for doing empirically grounded—naturalized—moral epistemology.

Specifically, we propose that philosophers investigate case studies of real world moral disputes in which people lack shared cultural assumptions and/or are unequal in social power rather than relying exclusively or too heavily on thought experiments about what philosophers imagine these situations to be like. Case studies always focus on what is being studied in relation to its environment, which makes this a promising method for investigating relationships between reasoning practices and their contexts of use (Flyvbjerg 2011: 301). Working through case studies may enable philosophers to understand better how various features of the context operate either to support or undermine reasoning that is plausible, usable, power sensitive, and capable of delivering feasible conclusions.

Our main point is not the uncontroversial claim that empirical information is required at the stage of applying philosophical models of moral and political justification; instead, we propose that the development of the models be empirically informed. This means that those developing models of moral justification must incorporate multidisciplinary scholarship at all stages. Identifying case studies of successful reasoning practices requires collaborating with scholars from many disciplines, and with moral reasoners who are not academics.

Finally, philosophers working collaboratively to develop new philosophical models of justification must reflect continually on our specific identities and situations. Who are we? For whom are we philosophizing? What are our credentials and authority? This kind of reflexivity will help us stay modest and humble, to remember that, if our conceptions of justification are useful at all, they are useful only for particular contexts, not for all times and places. Moral justification, like justice, cannot be viewed *sub specie aeternitatis*.

Note

This paper draws on a book project tentatively titled, *Undisciplining Moral Epistemology*. Our work on this project has been supported over several years by the Research Council of Norway through its Centres of Excellence funding scheme, project number 179566/V20. Parts of this work are published in Jaggar and Tobin 2013 and Tobin and Jaggar 2013.

Related Topics

Feminism, philosophy, and culture in Africa (Chapter 4); epistemic injustice, ignorance, and trans experience (Chapter 22); women, gender, and philosophies of global development (Chapter 34); feminist metaethics (Chapter 42); feminist ethics of care (Chapter 43); Confucianism and care ethics (Chapter 44); multicultural and postcolonial feminisms (Chapter 47); neoliberalism, global justice, and transnational feminisms (Chapter 48).

References

Ackerly, Brooke A. (2000) *Political Theory and Feminist Social Criticism*, Cambridge: Cambridge University Press.

Anderson, Elizabeth (1995) "The Democratic University: The Role of Justice in the Production of Knowledge," *Social Philosophy and Policy* 12: 186–219.

——(2010) *Imperative of Integration*, Princeton, NJ: Princeton University Press.

——(2012) "Epistemic Justice as a Virtue of Social Institutions," *Social Epistemology* 26(2): 163–173.

Benhabib, Seyla (1992) *Situating the Self: Gender, Community, and Postmodernism in Contemporary Ethics*, New York: Routledge.

Collins, Patricia Hill (2000) *Black Feminist Thought: Knowledge, Consciousness, and the Politics of Empowerment*, New York: Routledge.

Flyvbjerg, Bent (2011) "Case Study," in Norman Denzin and Yvonna Lincoln (Eds.) *Sage Handbook of Qualitative Research*, 4th ed., Thousand Oaks, CA: Sage, 301–316.

Fricker, Miranda (2007) *Epistemic Injustice: Power and the Ethics of Knowing*, Oxford: Oxford University Press.

Hodgson, Dorothy L. (1999) "Pastoralism, Patriarchy, and History: Changing Gender Relations Among Maasai in Tanganyika, 1890–1940," *The Journal of African History* 40: 41–65.

IRIN (2005) *In Depth: Razor's Edge—The Controversy of Female Genital Mutilation/Kenya: FGM among the Maasai Community of Kenya* [online]. Available from: www.irinnews.org/InDepthMain.aspx?InDepthId =15&ReportId=62470.

Jaggar, Alison M. (1995) "Toward a Feminist Conception of Moral Reasoning," *Morality and Social Justice*, Lanham, MD: Roman & Littlefield, 115–146.

——(2006) "Reasoning about Well-Being: Nussbaum's Methods of Justifying the Capabilities," *Journal of Political Philosophy* 14(4): 301–322.

Jaggar, Alison M. and Tobin, Theresa W. (2013) "Situating Moral Justification: Rethinking the Mission of Moral Epistemology," *Metaphilosophy* 44(4): 383–408.

Kant, Immanuel (1785) *Groundwork of the Metaphysic of Morals*, Cambridge: Cambridge University Press.

Longino, Helen E. (1990) *Science as Social Knowledge: Values and Objectivity in Scientific Inquiry*, Princeton, NJ: Princeton University Press.

——(2002) *The Fate of Knowledge*, Princeton, NJ: Princeton University Press.

Means, Angelia K. (2003) "Narrative Argumentation: Arguing with Natives," *Constellations* 9(2): 221–245.

Mills, Charles W. (1994) "Ideal Theory as Ideology," in Peggy DesAutels and Margaret Urban Walker (Eds.) *Moral Psychology: Feminist Ethics and Social Theory*, Lanham, MD: Roman & Littlefield, 163–182.

Nnaemeka, Obioma (2005) *Female Circumcision and the Politics of Knowledge: African Women in Imperialist Discourses*, Westport, CT: Praeger.

Nussbaum, Martha C. (2000) *Women and Human Development: The Capabilities Approach*, Cambridge: Cambridge University Press.

Okin, Susan Moller (1989) *Justice, Gender, and the Family*, New York: Basic Books.

——(2003) "Poverty, Well-Being, and Gender: What Counts, Who's Heard?" *Philosophy and Public Affairs* 31(3): 280–316.

O'Neill, Onora (1996) *Towards Justice and Virtue: A Constructive Account of Practical Reasoning*, Cambridge: Cambridge University Press, 57–58.

Parfit, Derek (1984) *Reasons and Persons*, Oxford: Oxford University Press.

Robeyns, Ingrid (2005) "Selecting Capabilities for Quality of Life Measurement," *Social Indicators Research* 7: 191–215.

Sen, Amartya (1984) *Resources, Values and Development*, Oxford: Blackwell.

Sidgwick, Henry (1962 [1907]) *The Methods of Ethics*, 7th ed., London: Macmillan.

Thomas, Laurence (1992–1993) "Moral Deference," *Philosophical Forum* 14(1–3): 233–250.

Tobin, Theresa W. and Jaggar, Alison M. (2013) "Naturalizing Moral Justification: Rethinking the Method of Moral Epistemology," *Metaphilosophy* 44(4): 409–439.

UN General Assembly (1948) *Universal Declaration of Human Rights* [online]. Available from: www.refworld. org/docid/3ae6b3712c.html.

United Nations (2015) "Beijing Declaration and Platform for Action," adopted at the *Fourth World Conference on Women* (September 15, 1995) [online]. Available from: www.un.org/womenwatch/daw/ beijing/platform/.

Walker, Margaret Urban (2002) *Moral Understandings: A Feminist Study in Ethics*, Oxford: Oxford University Press.

41

FEMINIST CONCEPTIONS OF AUTONOMY

Catriona Mackenzie

Introduction

Autonomy is both a status and a capacity concept. As a status concept, it refers to the idea that individuals are entitled to exercise self-determining authority over their own lives. A foundational principle of liberal democratic societies is that each individual should be respected as having this authority. As a capacity concept, autonomy refers to the capacity to be self-defining and self-governing; that is, to make decisions and act on the basis of preferences, values or commitments that are authentically "one's own." Debates about autonomy in the mainstream philosophical literature seek to analyze the characteristics of self-governing agency and to explain how it can be undermined by external threats, such as coercion, manipulation or paternalistic interference, and impaired by internal threats, such as compulsion, addiction and failures of self-control, including weakness of will.

Feminist relational theories of autonomy are motivated by the intuition that gender oppression can threaten women's abilities to lead self-determining, self-governing lives—to different degrees and in different ways. Gender oppression includes overt forms of domination, such as gender-based violence, sexual harassment and sexual exploitation, as well as gender-based discrimination and inequalities of opportunity. It also includes more subtle manifestations such as implicit bias, for example in hiring practices; silencing, or the discrediting of women's testimony and epistemic authority (see e.g., Roessler 2015); and gender-based stereotyping schemas, the internalization of which can undermine women's sense of themselves as competent and autonomous agents (see e.g., Benson 2015). Relational autonomy theorists charge that the mainstream literature fails to recognize or account for the autonomy-undermining effects of oppression. One of the central aims of relational theories is to address this deficit in the literature, and to explain how the internalization of gender and other kinds of social oppression, such as racial oppression, can threaten the autonomy of persons who are subject to such oppression.

Some feminist theorists have criticized autonomy on grounds that it reinforces hyper-individualism and is inimical to social relationships of care and interdependence (e.g., Code 1991). This criticism is misplaced insofar as it conflates autonomy with a carica-ture of self-sufficient independence (Friedman 1997). Nevertheless, relational autonomy theorists are sensitive to the feminist critique of hyperindividualism. A further aim of relational theories is therefore to counter the overly individualistic assumptions about agency and identity that are prevalent in much of the mainstream literature. Relational theories remain committed to a form of normative individualism, that is, to the view that the rights, welfare, dignity, freedom, and autonomy of individuals matter and impose normative constraints on the claims of social groups or collectives. However, these theories are relational in at least two senses. First, they are committed to a socio-relational ontology of persons; that is, to the view that we develop our individual identities only in and through interpersonal, familial and social relationships, and through processes of enculturation into specific linguistic, cultural, political and historical communities. Second, they hold that autonomous agency involves a complex suite of competences, which can only be developed and exercised with extensive interpersonal, social, and institutional scaffolding.

Relational autonomy theorists thus seek to explicate both the social constitution of autonomy and the ways in which the internalization of oppressive social relationships can impair its development and exercise. Relational autonomy is, however, an "umbrella term" (Mackenzie and Stoljar 2000), and over the last decade there has been substantial debate about the adequacy of rival relational theories to explain how oppressive socialization can threaten personal autonomy. This debate centers on the question of whether a procedural account of autonomy is sufficient to explain the autonomy-impairing effects of oppression or whether autonomy needs to be understood more substantively, and, if so, what kind of substantive theory is most plausible. The next section provides an overview of the main positions in this debate. In the course of outlining these positions, it will also briefly address two further questions: Is autonomy social in a causal or constitutive sense? and should autonomy be understood globally, as a characteristic of a person's life overall, or locally, as a characteristic of particular actions or decisions? The final section sketches out a positive proposal for moving the debate beyond the current impasse in the literature concerning procedural versus substantive theories, suggesting that autonomy should be understood as a multidimensional concept involving three distinct but causally interdependent axes: self-determination, self-governance, and self-authorization.

Relational Autonomy and Social Oppression

One challenge facing relational autonomy theorists is to explicate the sense in which individual autonomy is social and to explain how the internalization of oppression can undermine autonomy. Responses to this challenge fall into two broad categories: procedural and substantive theories.

Procedural Theories

Procedural theories explain the necessary and sufficient conditions for a particular preference, motive, commitment, or value to count as autonomous by appealing to a critical reflection procedure of some kind. The focus of these theories is predominantly on local, rather than global, autonomy. Further, according to procedural theories, the specific content of a person's preferences, commitments or values is immaterial; what matters for autonomy is whether these pass the test of the relevant critical reflection procedure.

John Christman (2009) distinguishes two broad kinds of procedural conditions for autonomy: authenticity and competence. Authenticity conditions explicate what it means for a person's preferences, motives, commitments or values to count as one's own. Competence conditions explicate the range of cognitive, volitional, emotional and other competences a person must possess in order to be self-governing.

Authenticity

There is substantial debate in the literature concerning the meaning of authenticity and the necessary and sufficient conditions for authentic critical reflection. The influential *hierarchical* theories of Gerald Dworkin (1988) and Harry Frankfurt (1988) characterize critical reflection as the capacity for second-order reflection on one's first-order preferences, commitments or values. These elements of a person's motivational structure count as authentically her own if she identifies with them or endorses them in light of such reflection. However, if upon reflection she feels alienated from these elements of her motivational structure, she is not autonomous with respect to them. Hierarchical reflective endorsement procedures therefore explain autonomy in terms of structural features of the agent's will at the time of reflection and action, specifically internal psychic coherence between second-order reflection and first-order elements of the agent's motivational structure.

Relational autonomy theorists argue, however, that, this analysis is not sufficient to distinguish autonomous from non-autonomous reflection. First, it overlooks the historical processes of identity formation, the way a person acquired her preferences, commitments, values and so on (Christman 1991; 2009). Attention to these historical processes is crucial, however, for understanding how the psychologies of persons who are subject to oppression may have been shaped by the internalization of autonomy-impairing oppressive norms and stereotypes. Second-order reflection is insufficient to address this problem, because a thoroughly socialized agent is likely to endorse oppressive preferences and norms as her own when engaging in such reflection.

This problem is particularly salient to the phenomenon of adaptive preference formation—the phenomenon whereby persons who are subject to social domination, oppression or deprivation adapt their preferences (or goals) to their circumstances, eliminating or failing to form preferences (or goals) that cannot be satisfied, and even failing to conceive how their preferences might differ in different circumstances (for further discussion of adaptive preferences and autonomy see e.g., Stoljar (2014), Cudd (2015), Mackenzie (2015); for a critique of the view that adaptive preferences should be defined in terms of autonomy impairment see Khader (2011). The upshot of the argument is that hierarchical reflective endorsement procedures are insufficient to distinguish authentic from inauthentic critical reflection.

Second, the requirement of internal coherence between second-order reflection and first-order elements of the agent's motivational structure seems to rule out any kind of ambivalence or internal psychic conflict or fragmentation as inconsistent with self-governance. Frankfurt, for example, regards ambivalence as a "disease of the will" (1999: 100). But this view seems to set the bar for self-integration unrealistically high and to equate autonomous agency with psychological rigidity. Ambivalence and some degree of inner psychic conflict or fragmentation are not only inescapable aspects of individual identity formation but also may be necessary for psychological health (Velleman 2002; Christman 2009), even if too much ambivalence and psychic fragmentation can impair autonomy.

Procedural relational autonomy theorists have responded to these two problems in different ways. Marilyn Friedman recognizes that the internalization of oppression is not typically global but rather partial, and may give rise to internal conflict, struggle, and resistance to some degree. One of her examples is of a conflicted 1950s housewife who has internalized prevailing social norms that a good wife and mother should stay at home and put her own needs secondary to those of her husband and children (Friedman 1986). At the second-order level, the housewife endorses these norms. However, she is frustrated and unhappy and frequently experiences what she regards as wayward first-order preferences and emotions in conflict with these norms. Friedman proposes that in situations such as these, second-order reflection may simply reinforce oppressive social conditioning, whereas the woman's apparently wayward first-order desires and emotions may be more expressive of her authentic wants and values. Friedman thus proposes an *integration* reflective endorsement test, such that reflective endorsement is autonomous when lower order preferences and higher-order normative commitments are integrated in a person's motivational structure as a result of two-way processes of bottom up and top down reflection.

John Christman's response to these two problems is to propose a historical, counterfactual, *non-alienation* test for authentic critical reflection (see e.g., Christman 1991, 2009). Christman recognizes that a person may be autonomous with respect to elements of her motivational set even if she has not consciously and critically reflected on whether she endorses them. He also recognizes that as agents we are often not motivationally transparent to ourselves. His counterfactual test therefore specifies that an element of a person's motivational set is authentically her own if, were she counterfactually to engage in reflection on the historical processes of its formation, she would not repudiate or feel alienated from that element. Christman defines authenticity as "non-alienation upon (historically sensitive, adequate) self-reflection, given one's diachronic practical identity and one's position in the world" or as reflective self-acceptance (2009: 155). The non-alienation test is weaker than endorsement tests in acknowledging that there are elements of our motivational set that we may not endorse but nevertheless accept as our own.

Like hierarchical procedural theories, both Friedman's integration test and Christman's non-alienation test understand authentic critical reflection and autonomy as requiring some degree of coherence within the agent's psyche. Unlike standard hierarchical views, however, their versions of procedural theory are premised on a thick, socio-historical conception of the person, and Christman's historical analysis of authenticity is dynamic, rather than static and structural. Both theories are relational in a causal sense, insofar as they regard interpersonal relationships and background social conditions as crucial causal conditions for the development and exercise of autonomy. Substantive theorists, in contrast, hold that autonomy is social not just causally but also constitutively. They also argue that despite being relational, procedural theories such as those of Christman and Friedman are insufficient to account for the autonomy-impairing effects of internalized oppression.

Competence

Competence conditions specify the range of competences or skills a person must possess, to some degree at least, in order to be self-governing. Relational autonomy theorists, such as Diana Meyers (1989), argue that conceptions of competence in the mainstream literature over-emphasize the importance for autonomy of cognitive skills and of volitional skills, such as self-control, while neglecting a broad array of emotional, imaginative and reflective competences. Meyers proposes that autonomy competence requires a complex repertoire or suite of reflective skills, which may be developed and exercised to varying degrees and in different domains. These include emotional skills, such as the capacity to interpret and regulate one's own emotions; imaginative skills, required for understanding the implications of one's decisions and envisaging alternative possible courses of action; and capacities to reflect critically on social norms and values. According to Meyers, a person is autonomous, and her choices are authentically her own, to the degree that she has developed these skills and can exercise them in understanding herself (self-discovery), defining her values and commitments (self-definition), and directing her life (self-direction).

Meyers' response to the problem of how to distinguish authentic from non-authentic forms of critical reflection appeals to this notion of autonomy competence. Reflection is authentic, in her view, if a person possesses and can exercise the full repertoire of cognitive, volitional, emotional, and imaginative competences required to direct her life and make choices that express her authentic self-conception. Oppressive socialization can impair autonomy by truncating the development or stunting the exercise of these skills. For example, gender socialization tends to encourage in girls the development of emotional skills that are important for self-discovery, but thwarts the development and exercise of some of the skills required for self-definition and self-direction.

Meyers' account of autonomy competence is procedural or content-neutral, because she thinks judgments about autonomy do not turn on the specific content of the person's preferences, values and commitments, but rather on whether or not she exercises the necessary reflective skills to express her authentic self-conception. Meyers' theory is also causally relational insofar as it emphasizes the crucial role of social relationships and institutions in scaffolding the development and exercise of autonomy competences. An important feature of Meyers' account is that she regards autonomy as a matter of degree and domain rather than an all or nothing matter. Meyers distinguishes several different levels at which a person can exercise autonomy: episodic, narrowly programmatic, and programmatic. Episodic autonomy refers to the capacity to exercise autonomy with respect to a particular action or decision. Narrowly programmatic autonomy refers to the capacity to exercise autonomy with respect to a series of actions and decisions. Programmatic autonomy refers to the capacity to exercise autonomy with respect to a range of long-term life plans and goals. For example, while Friedman's 1950s housewife might exercise episodic and narrowly programmatic autonomy with respect to matters of household organization and mothering responsibilities, she does not exercise programmatic autonomy with respect to her life overall since she places her own needs secondary to those of her husband and children and is unlikely to have developed the skills and competences needed to have a successful career, or organize her financial affairs.

Substantive Theories

Procedural relational theorists are committed to developing theories of autonomy that are maximally socially and politically inclusive and that respect agents' first-person perspectives on their values and commitments, whatever their content (Friedman 2003). For these theorists, this is a strong reason to favor content-neutrality. Substantive theorists charge, however, that procedural theories such as Friedman's, are either overly inclusive and set the bar for autonomy too low, thus failing to explain how oppressive socialization impairs autonomy, or implicitly appeal to more substantive constraints. It is sometimes claimed that Meyers' and Christman's theories, for example, are more substantive than they acknowledge (see e.g., Benson 2005b; Mackenzie 2008).

In the literature, a distinction is often drawn between strong and weak substantive theories (see e.g., Mackenzie and Stoljar 2000; Benson 2005a; Stoljar 2013). Strong substantive theories are typically characterized as being committed to the view that, to count as autonomous, a person's preferences, values or commitments must meet specific normative, rational, or other constraints. While this characterization is true of some strong substantive theories, it is misleading when applied to Marina Oshana's (2006; 2015) socio-relational theory of autonomy.

Oshana is primarily concerned with autonomy as a status concept and with global, rather than local autonomy. Her theory is substantive in the sense that she thinks a person's socio-relational status is the crucial determinant of her autonomy. Oshana argues that to be autonomous is to have both *de jure* and *de facto* authority and power to exercise effective practical control over important aspects of one's life. For this reason, certain structural, socio-relational conditions must be in place for an agent to be genuinely autonomous. Agents who stand in relations of subordination, subservience, deference, or economic or psychological dependence, such as Friedman's housewife for example, cannot be autonomous because they do not enjoy effective practical control over significant domains of their life. This is the case even if the agents in question endorse (or are not alienated from) their subordinate, subservient or dependent position, and even if they seem to satisfy the authenticity and competence requirements for self-governance. This is why Oshana thinks that neither Friedman's nor Christman's procedural theories can explain the autonomy-impairing effects of oppression. Oshana uses an array of examples—voluntary slaves, prisoners, women subject to extreme forms of gender oppression, members of restrictive religious orders—to support the guiding intuition behind her account; namely, that a person cannot lead an autonomous life if her options are severely restricted and she is effectively under the control of others, whether financially, legally, or psychologically. Oshana understands autonomy as constitutively social, because autonomy, in her view, is a function of a person's socio-relational status.

Critics of Oshana's view argue that it expects the concept of autonomy to do too much work in explaining the ills of social and political domination and injustice (Benson 2014); that it conflates autonomy with substantive independence; that it is overly prescriptive in dictating to people the kind of lives they should lead; and that it disrespects the autonomy of agents who have managed to lead self-governing lives despite being subject to crushing forms of oppression (Christman 2004). Such critics point to people like Martin Luther King as counter-examples to Oshana's view. In response, Oshana acknowledges that King, and others like him who struggled against racial oppression and injustice, managed to exercise some degree of autonomy despite the oppression and domination to which they were subject. However, rather than demonstrating the implausibility of the socio-relational account, she suggests that such heroism "should rather serve as an example of an *exception* to the socio-relational account" (Oshana 2015: 11). In my view, the guiding intuition behind Oshana's analysis, that social relationships involving domination and subordination compromise autonomy, is correct. However, Oshana and her critics may be talking past each other because their debate has focused on the conditions for self-governance. Oshana's concern, however, is to explain how social and political domination and oppression can impair not only self-governance, but also self-determination and self-authorization. The distinction between these different dimensions of autonomy will be discussed in the following section.

Other strong substantive theorists, such as Paul Benson in his earlier work (1991) and Natalie Stoljar (2000), object to procedural theories on different grounds. Their strong substantive theories hold that only preferences, values or commitments that meet specific normative constraints count as autonomous. Benson proposes a *normative competence* constraint such that, to be autonomous a person must be able to critically discern the difference between true and false norms and her choices and actions must be guided by true norms. He uses the example of a college student who, despite being intelligent and capable, lacks a sense of self-worth because she has internalized the false norm that a woman's worth is bound up with conventional ideals of feminine beauty. Stoljar (2000) takes up Benson's notion of normative competence in discussing a study of women who repeatedly fail to take contraceptive precautions and end up seeking multiple abortions. Stoljar appeals to what she terms the "feminist intuition" in arguing that these women fail to act autonomously with respect to their own sexual activity because they have internalized oppressive sexual double standards, and do not want to think of themselves as the kind of women who have sex outside of marriage. Benson and Stoljar thus characterize the agents in their examples as non-autonomous insofar as their choices and actions are guided by false social norms, which they have internalized without critically reflecting on them.

It is important to note that in characterizing the agents in their examples as non-autonomous, neither Benson nor Stoljar are making global claims about these agents' autonomy. Their claim is rather that these agents' autonomy is impaired with respect to the specific norms in question and the choices and actions that flow from them. Despite this caveat, the normative competence view has been criticized for failing to recognize the range of reasons that people might have for complying with oppressive norms (Narayan 2002; Khader 2011; Sperry 2013), thereby encouraging condescending attitudes towards persons who are subject to oppression, impugning their agency, and opening the door to objectionably paternalistic and coercive forms of intervention in their lives. Khader, for example, argues that it might be instrumentally rational for a woman to comply with oppressive norms in one domain of life, for example, with respect to cultural norms of feminine beauty or sexuality, in order to achieve her goals in another domain. Although this argument conflates autonomy with instrumental rationality (Stoljar 2014; Cudd 2015; Mackenzie 2015), critics such as Khader are correct to point to the importance of recognizing the diversity of autonomous responses to oppression.

Benson (2014) has also recently rejected the normative competence account on similar grounds. He further claims that it conflates autonomy (or self-rule) with "orthonomy" (or right rule, that is the ability to discern the true and the good). Benson nevertheless remains committed to the view that competence and authentic critical reflection are insufficient to secure autonomy. The weak substantive view he has proposed in recent work seeks to reconcile procedural theorists' concern with respecting agents' first-person perspectives, or what he refers to as agential "voice," with substantive theorists' focus on agential authority (Benson 2005a; 2014). According to this view, autonomous agency is characterized by a sense of ownership of one's choices and actions. It involves regarding oneself as positioned, and as having the appropriate authority, to speak for oneself and to answer others' critical perspectives. One of the effects of internalized oppression on this account is that it impairs autonomy by impairing an agent's sense of herself as having a legitimate voice, and as competent and authorized to speak or answer for her values and commitments. Andrea Westlund (2009) proposes a similar view of autonomy as the capacity for interpersonal accountability and answerability. Being accountable does not require being accountable to certain specific others. Nor does it mean being held to account for each and every belief, value, commitment or action. What it requires is what Westlund refers to as a disposition for "dialogical answerability" or "the disposition to hold oneself answerable to external critical perspectives" (2009: 28).

Other weak substantive theorists propose a related view, according to which a condition for autonomous agency is that a person holds certain self-regarding attitudes, in particular attitudes of appropriate self-respect, self-trust, and self-esteem or self-worth. To have appropriate self-respect is to regard oneself as the moral equal of others and hence entitled to call them into account. To have appropriate self-trust is to have a sense of basic self-confidence in one's judgment. To have appropriate self-esteem or self-worth is to regard one's life and one's commitments as meaningful and worthwhile (see especially Anderson and Honneth 2005; see also Benson 1994; 2000; 2005a; Govier 2003; Mackenzie 2008). According to this view, internalized oppression can impair autonomy by undermining these self-regarding attitudes.

Weak substantive views are both causally and constitutively relational. They are causally relational because psychologically our self-regarding attitudes are typically dependent on the character of our social relationships. It is difficult to develop a sense of self-respect, for example, if by virtue of one's social group membership one is systematically treated as an inferior. Likewise, it is difficult to develop a sense of trust in one's judgment if by virtue of one's social group membership one is susceptible to stereotype threat (the fear that one will conform to negative stereotypes about the social group to which one belongs, for example, that women are irrational and overly emotional). Weak substantive views are constitutively relational because self-regarding attitudes of self-respect, self-trust and self-esteem, and the sense of oneself as authorized to answer for one's conduct, require participating in social relationships in which one is recognized by others as a respect-worthy, self-authorizing agent. In other words, these attitudes are constituted within normative structures and practices of *social recognition*. In oppressive social contexts, for example of institutionalized racism or sexism, the prevailing normative structures and practices do not afford to members of oppressed social groups the kind of recognition required to regard oneself as positioned to speak for oneself or to answer to others for one's conduct.

Jennifer Warriner (2015) argues, however, that weak substantive theories such as Benson's are as vulnerable as procedural theories to the problem of oppressive socialization. She discusses the example of women who belong to Christian Evangelical churches, who have thoroughly internalized oppressive gender norms according to which women's subordination to male authority is normatively required by their religious commitments. These women are likely to satisfy the weak substantive constraints on autonomy because, despite willingly accepting their subordinated status, within their community they are nevertheless still "expected to regard themselves as having agential authority and are expected to authorize their agency" (Warriner 2015: 37). However, it seems counter-intuitive to say these women are autonomous, because their agential authority can only be exercised within the constraints of a social script of male dominance and female subordination, the reasons for which they are not permitted to question or challenge.

The debates between procedural and substantive relational theorists have yielded important insights into the autonomy-impairing effects of oppression. However, the trading back and forth of examples and counterexamples designed to challenge the necessity and sufficiency of rival views has also led to something of an impasse, since different examples pull our philosophical intuitions in different directions. The multidimensional analysis of autonomy outlined in the following section aims to help in diagnosing, and hopefully suggesting a route beyond this impasse. It also helps to respond to the concerns raised by critics of strong substantive theories. By identifying different dimensions or axes of autonomy, this analysis can explain how oppression might impair an agent's autonomy in one domain but not in others.

Beyond the Procedural/Substantive Debate: A Multidimensional Theory of Autonomy

Autonomy is a complex concept. As the discussion in the preceding sections has shown, it refers to both status and capacity, and is conceptually allied to a range of other concepts, such as freedom, authenticity, responsibility for self, and self-respect. This conceptual complexity may explain why our philosophical intuitions are pulled in different directions by examples that highlight different aspects of the concept. For example, returning to the example of Martin Luther King, if autonomy is understood as a status concept allied to the concept of freedom, Oshana seems correct in pointing out that King's ability to lead a self-determining life was highly restricted, since as an African American in the Jim Crow era he did not enjoy the socio-relational status of a free and equal citizen entitled to be treated with respect by others. However, if autonomy is understood in terms of taking responsibility for self, or having an authentic voice and a sense of agential authority, and if we focus on King's heroic defense of the rights of African Americans to equal treatment and his persistence in the face of brutal oppression, he seems an exemplar of self-governing, self-authorizing agency. A multidimensional analysis of autonomy seeks to do justice to these conflicting intuitions, drawing on the important insights developed by relational autonomy theorists over the last two decades.

My proposal is that the concept of autonomy refers to three distinct but causally interconnected axes: self-determination, self-governance and self-authorization (Mackenzie 2014). Each of these dimensions can and should be understood as a matter of degree and domain. A person can be self-determining, self-governing and self-authorizing to differing degrees, both at a time and over the course of her life. This explains how it is possible for a person such as King, whose freedom and opportunities have been severely curtailed, nevertheless to exhibit high degrees of self-governance and have a strong sense of himself as a self-authorizing agent.

Self-Determination

The *self-determination* axis is conceptually allied to the notion of freedom. To be self-determining is to be able to exercise control over important domains of one's life and to make and enact decisions of practical import, concerning what matters, who to be, and what to do. This requires being free from domination and undue interference by others as well as having the freedom and opportunities required to exercise this kind of control. The notion of *self-determination* thus identifies the kind of external, structural conditions for personal autonomy to which Oshana draws attention, specifically *freedom* and *opportunity*.

Freedom is necessary for autonomy because, as Oshana insists, people's abilities to lead self-determining lives are severely curtailed if they lack political and personal liberty, and if they are subject to social and political domination. Opportunity is important for autonomy because opportunities translate formal liberties into substantive freedom. A person who has formal access to political and personal liberty but lacks access to an adequate array of genuine opportunities will find it difficult to lead a self-determining life (Raz 1986). Poor education, limited employment opportunities, poverty, and social marginalization, can all undermine a person's ability to exercise control over important domains of her life.

Self-determination is therefore both causally and constitutively social because individual freedom and opportunity are both constituted and enabled (or hindered) by social relationships and by social, political, legal, economic, and educational structures.

Self-Governance

Whereas the self-determination axis identifies external, structural conditions for autonomy, the self-governance axis identifies internal conditions for autonomy, specifically authenticity and competence, as explicated by procedural theorists, such as Christman, Friedman, and Meyers. To be self-governing is to have the skills and capacities necessary to make and enact decisions that express or cohere with one's deeply held values and commitments. However, the distinction between internal and external conditions is complicated. For if, as relational autonomy theorists claim, persons are socially constituted, then external conditions (social relationships, political, legal, and economic structures, available opportunities) shape the historical processes of individual identity formation—both who a person is, or the authentic *self* of self-governance, and the development and exercise of the skills and competences required for *governing* the self. This is why, in oppressive social contexts, the internalization of limited freedom and opportunity, and of social relationships structured by relations of domination and subordination, can manifest in adaptive preference formation (Stoljar 2014; Cudd 2015), restricted imaginative horizons (Mackenzie 2000) and constricted psychological freedom (Stoljar 2015).

Self-governance is therefore both causally and constitutively social, because our individual identities are constituted in and through social relationships, and the competences required for being self-governing agents can only be developed and exercised with extensive interpersonal, social, and institutional scaffolding.

Self-Authorization

To be self-authorizing is to regard oneself as normatively authorized to take responsibility for one's life, one's values and one's decisions, and as able to account for oneself to others. Self-authorization is a central concern of Oshana's socio-relational view, which holds that autonomous persons have a "characteristic type of social standing"

(2014: 159). It is also central to the concerns of weak substantive theorists who hold that to be autonomous an agent must hold certain self-regarding attitudes. Rather than understanding these attitudes as conditions of self-governance, however, the multidimensional analysis proposed here suggests that they should be understood as a separate axis of autonomy. This axis signals the importance to autonomy of *accountability*, or regarding oneself as a responsible agent who is able to stand in relations of reciprocal accountability with others; of having appropriate *self-regarding attitudes*, in particular of self-respect, self-trust, and self-esteem; and of *social recognition*, or being regarded by others as having the social standing of an autonomous agent. The self-authorization axis provides a further explication of autonomy as a status concept and of the sense in which autonomy is constitutively relational.

A virtue of my multidimensional analysis is that it can diagnose multiple pathways via which internalized oppression can damage autonomy. Social relations of domination, restrictions on political and personal freedom, and limited opportunities are structural constraints on autonomy that make it difficult to lead a self-determining life. Internalized oppression shapes the very self of self-governance, as well as the skills and competences needed to govern that self. Social relations of misrecognition can erode agents' self-regarding attitudes and their sense of themselves as self-authorizing agents.

Conclusion

Relational autonomy theory seeks to explain the sense in which autonomy is social and to analyze the ways that internalized oppression can impair autonomy. In providing an overview of recent debates within the literature, this chapter has explicated a variety of views among relational theorists concerning whether autonomy is social in a causal or constitutive sense, whether procedural or substantive theories provide more plausible analyses of the autonomy-impairing effects of internalized oppression, and whether autonomy should be understood as a local characteristic of specific choices and actions, or more globally, as a characteristic of a person's life overall. The multidimensional analysis of autonomy proposed in the final section has sought to do justice to the important insights of relational autonomy theorists while suggesting a way of moving beyond some of the impasses in the current debate.

Related Topics

Feminism and borderlands identities (Chapter 17); personal identity and relational selves (Chapter 18); feminist ethics of care (Chapter 43); feminist bioethics (Chapter 46).

References

Anderson, Joel and Honneth, Axel (2005) "Autonomy, Vulnerability, Recognition and Justice," in John Christman and Joel Anderson (Eds.) *Autonomy and the Challenges to Liberalism*, Cambridge: Cambridge University Press, 127–149.

Benson, Paul (1991) "Autonomy and Oppressive Socialization," *Social Theory and Practice* 17: 385–408.

——(1994) "Free Agency and Self-Worth," *Journal of Philosophy* 91: 650–668.

——(2000) "Feeling Crazy: Self-Worth and the Social Character of Responsibility," in Catriona Mackenzie and Natalie Stoljar (Eds.) *Relational Autonomy: Feminist Perspectives on Autonomy, Agency and the Social Self*, New York: Oxford University Press, 72–93.

—— (2005a) "Taking Ownership: Authority and Voice in Autonomous Agency," in John Christman and Joel Anderson (Eds.) *Autonomy and the Challenges to Liberalism*, Cambridge: Cambridge University Press, 101–126.

—— (2005b) "Feminist Intuitions and the Normative Substance of Autonomy," in James Stacey Taylor (Ed.) *Personal Autonomy: New Essays on Personal Autonomy and Its Role in Contemporary Moral Philosophy*, Cambridge: Cambridge University Press, 124–142.

—— (2014) "Feminist Commitments and Relational Autonomy," in Andrea Veltman and Mark Piper (Eds.) *Autonomy, Oppression, and Gender*, New York: Oxford University Press, 87–113.

—— (2015) "Stereotype Threat, Social Belonging, and Relational Autonomy," in Marina Oshana (Ed.) *Personal Autonomy and Social Oppression: Philosophical Perspectives*, New York: Routledge, 124–141.

Code, Lorraine (1991) "Second Persons," in *What Can She Know? Feminist Theory and the Construction of Knowledge*, Ithaca, NY: Cornell University Press, 71–109.

Christman, John (1991) "Autonomy and Personal History," *Canadian Journal of Philosophy* 21: 1–24.

—— (2004) "Relational Autonomy, Liberal Individualism and the Social Constitution of Selves," *Philosophical Studies* 117: 143–164.

—— (2009) *The Politics of Persons: Individual Autonomy and Socio-Historical Selves*, Cambridge: Cambridge University Press.

Cudd, Ann (2015) "Adaptations to Oppression: Preference, Autonomy and Resistance," in Marina Oshana (Ed.) *Personal Autonomy and Social Oppression: Philosophical Perspectives*, New York: Routledge, 142–160.

Dworkin, Gerald (1988) *The Theory and Practice of Autonomy*, New York: Cambridge University Press.

Frankfurt, Harry (1988) "Freedom of the Will and the Concept of a Person," in *The Importance of What We Care About*, Cambridge: Cambridge University Press, 11–25.

—— (1999) "The Faintest Passion," in *Necessity, Volition, and Love*, Cambridge: Cambridge University Press, 95–107.

Friedman, Marilyn (1986) "Autonomy and the Split-Level Self," *Southern Journal of Philosophy* 24(1): 19–35.

—— (1997) "Autonomy and Social Relationships: Rethinking the Feminist Critique," in Diana Meyers (Ed.) *Feminists Rethink the Self*, Boulder, CO: Westview Press, 40–61.

—— (2003) *Autonomy, Gender, Politics*, New York: Oxford University Press.

Govier, Trudy (2003) "Self-Trust, Autonomy, and Self-Esteem," *Hypatia* 8: 99–120.

Khader, Serene (2011) *Adaptive Preferences and Women's Empowerment*, New York: Oxford University Press.

Mackenzie, Catriona (2000) "Imagining Oneself Otherwise," in Catriona Mackenzie and Natalie Stoljar (Eds.) *Relational Autonomy: Feminist Perspectives on Autonomy, Agency and the Social Self*, New York: Oxford University Press, 124–150.

—— (2008) "Relational Autonomy, Normative Authority and Perfectionism," *Journal of Social Philosophy* 39: 512–33.

—— (2014) "Three Dimensions of Autonomy: A Relational Analysis," in Andrea Veltman and Mark Piper (Eds.) *Autonomy, Oppression, and Gender*, New York: Oxford University Press, 15–41.

—— (2015) "Responding to the Agency Dilemma: Autonomy, Adaptive Preferences and Internalized Oppression," in Marina Oshana (Ed.) *Personal Autonomy and Internalized Oppression*, New York: Routledge, 48–67.

Mackenzie, Catriona and Stoljar, Natalie (2000) "Introduction: Autonomy Refigured," in Catriona Mackenzie and Natalie Stoljar (Eds.) *Relational Autonomy: Feminist Perspectives on Autonomy, Agency and the Social Self*, New York: Oxford University Press, 3–31.

Meyers, Diana (1989) *Self, Society and Personal Choice*, New York: Columbia University Press.

Narayan, Uma (2002) "Minds of Their Own: Choices, Autonomy, Cultural Practices, and Other Women," in Louise Antony and Charlotte Witt (Eds.) *A Mind of One's Own: Feminist Essays on Reason and Objectivity*, 2nd ed., Boulder, CO: Westview Press, 418–432.

Oshana, Marina (2006) *Personal Autonomy in Society*, Aldershot, UK: Ashgate.

—— (2014) "A Commitment to Autonomy Is a Commitment to Feminism," in Andrea Veltman and Mark Piper (Eds.) *Autonomy, Oppression and Gender*, New York: Oxford University Press, 141–160.

—— (2015) "Is Socio-Relational Autonomy a Plausible Ideal?" in Marina Oshana (Ed.) *Personal Autonomy and Social Oppression: Philosophical Perspectives*, New York: Routledge, 3–24.

Raz, Joseph (1986) *The Morality of Freedom*, Oxford: Clarendon Press.

Roessler, Beate (2015) "Autonomy, Self-Knowledge, and Oppression," in Marina Oshana (Ed.) *Personal Autonomy and Social Oppression: Philosophical Perspectives*, New York: Routledge, 68–84.

Sperry, Elizabeth (2013) "Dupes of Patriarchy: Feminist Strong Substantive Autonomy's Epistemological Weakness," *Hypatia* 28(4): 887–904.

Stoljar, Natalie (2000) "Autonomy and the Feminist Intuition," in Catriona Mackenzie and Natalie Stoljar (Eds.) *Relational Autonomy: Feminist Perspectives on Autonomy, Agency and the Social Self*, New York: Oxford University Press, 94–111.

—— (2013) "Feminist Perspectives on Autonomy," *Stanford Encyclopedia of Philosophy* [online]. Available from: http://plato.stanford.edu/entries/feminism-autonomy/.

—— (2014) "Autonomy and Adaptive Preference Formation," in Andrea Veltman and Mark Piper (Eds.) *Autonomy, Oppression and Gender*, New York: Oxford University Press, 227–252.

—— (2015) "'Living Constantly at Tiptoe Stance': Social Scripts, Psychological Freedom, and Autonomy," in Marina Oshana (Ed.) *Personal Autonomy and Social Oppression: Philosophical Perspectives*, New York: Routledge, 105–123.

Velleman, J. David (2002) "Identification and Identity," in Sarah Buss and Lee Overton (Eds.) *Contours of Agency: Essays on Themes from Harry Frankfurt*, Cambridge, MA: MIT Press, 91–123.

Warriner, Jennifer (2015) "Gender Oppression and Weak Substantive Theories of Autonomy" in Marina Oshana (Ed.) *Personal Autonomy and Social Oppression: Philosophical Perspectives*, New York: Routledge, 25–47.

Westlund, Andrea (2009) "Rethinking Relational Autonomy," *Hypatia* 24(4): 26–49.

42

FEMINIST METAETHICS

Anita Superson

Introduction

Ethics is the study of moral behavior, specifically, how we ought to act or what kind of persons we ought to be. Metaethics literally means "about" or "beyond" ethics. It has been described as the attempt to understand the metaphysical, epistemological, semantic, and psychological presuppositions and commitments of moral thought, talk, and practice (Sayre-McCord 2015 [2012]: 1). It presupposes no commitments to particular normative moral theories but goes beyond them or talks about them and their underlying assumptions. One major topic in metaethics concerns moral ontology. This issue covers the question of whether there are moral facts, and if there are, what their nature is. Are moral facts like scientific facts? Does wrongness exist in the world the way the water in your glass does? Suppose moral facts exist in some sense. Is the truth they yield relative to societies or even to individuals, or is it absolute, holding for all persons at all times? A second major topic in metaethics concerns the interconnection between moral action, reasons, and motivation. How can we rationally justify morally required action? Which theory of practical reason is best for grounding moral reasons? Does having a moral obligation to act necessarily entail having a motive to act? A third major topic in metaethics is that of moral epistemology: how do we come to know our moral duties? Is reason sufficient for knowing them, or do emotions play a role? These topics, which feminist philosophers have only recently begun to explore from a feminist angle, will be the focus of this chapter.

But there are other issues in traditional metaethics—e.g., the meaning of moral terms, the nature of moral disagreement, whether moral reasons are binding on us, and whether morality is just a fiction—that feminists have not yet directly explored. I suspect that this is largely because metaethics in general is done at a highly abstract level, allegedly completely independent of gender. Perhaps much of the work can be done at the level of normative ethics, modifying traditional theories in ways that address the main aim of feminism, which is to end women's oppression (Dillon 2012; Hampton 2002; Kittay 1999; Tessman 2001), and then the answers to traditional metaethical questions will fall out in ways informed by feminist aims. Alternatively, feminists might challenge some of the assumptions made in traditional metaethics (Anderson 2002; Cudd 2002; Driver 2012; Superson 2009). More radically, feminists might question whether the entire framework of metaethics is askew by demonstrating that there is something sexist, or at least antithetical to the aim of ending women's oppression, about the methodology or questions asked in metaethics (Noddings 1984: 50;

Tessman 2011). Such groundbreaking work that would effect a wholesale change in the nature of the discussion in metaethics has not yet been robustly taken on. It might entail a shift away from issues such as the nature of moral disagreement or the meaning of moral terms to issues such as questioning the point of morality if actual persons do not follow it especially in oppressive contexts, or how best to bring about moral progress. This shift highlights the disconnection between theory and practice in much of traditional ethics that feminists have complained about, but it is just one direction feminists might go in a field that is largely untapped. Meanwhile, let us turn to areas where there has been feminist progress.

Truth in Ethics

Moral realism is the view that moral claims such as "Rape is morally wrong" report facts and are true if they get the facts right, and that at least some moral claims are actually true (Sayre-McCord 2015 [2012]: 1). Some philosophers believe that on moral realism, moral facts have to be independent of humans, that they are somehow "out there" in the real world like natural properties, or occupy their own world like Platonic facts, while others believe that moral facts need not be real in these senses. For instance, Thomas Hobbes and Immanuel Kant believe that human reason gives us moral truths, so truth is not "out there" in the world awaiting human discovery. Feminists have said very little about this contentious metaphysical issue.

One worry that Julia Driver raises is that feminism is transformative, that is, that it creates new "realities" in the context of social change (Driver 2012: 175), which seems to be at odds with moral realism, especially the view that moral facts exist independent of humans. In light of this concern, Driver offers a complex version of feminist moral realism that construes moral facts to be dependent on humans. Driver's theory is constructivist. Constructivism is the view that insofar as there is truth in ethics, it is determined by an idealized or hypothetical process of rational deliberation, choice, or agreement (Bagnoli 2015 [2011]). Hobbes is a classic example of a constructivist who believes that in order to arrive at the true moral code, we should presuppose hypothetically that persons are equal in strength and intent to satisfy their own desires, have as their strongest desire a desire for self-preservation, are self-interested in the sense that they want to maximize the satisfaction of their own desires whatever these are, have a right or privilege to everything including use of another's body, and that goods are scarce. Hobbes argues that under these conditions, which he called a hypothetical State of Nature, rational beings would agree to give up some of their liberties in order to avoid a state of all-out war and to achieve the benefits of cooperation. When persons give up these liberties, they incur corresponding obligations. For example, if a person had a desire to harm others, she would be rational to give up the pursuit of satisfaction of this desire and incur an obligation not to harm others—provided that others do so as well, Hobbes believes, since otherwise she would jeopardize her self-preservation, which would never be rational to do. Hobbes believes that any rational person would agree to give up the same rights or liberties. The list of corresponding obligations constitutes the true moral code. Hobbes's account is constructivist since morality is constructed by human reason, not "out there" waiting to be discovered.

Driver's feminist constructivism also purports to avoid a feminist worry about moral relativism—the view that truth in ethics is relative to cultures—which is that culturally relative truth might entrench oppressive norms. Her theory builds on Hume's sentimentalism, the view that morality is grounded in emotion. It is in line with the ethic of care, a moral theory proposed by a number of feminists in the 1980s in response to Carol Gilligan's book on moral psychology that argued that females' responses to moral dilemmas were generally different from those of males in that they focused on caring, maintaining relationships, and fulfilling needs, while the "justice" perspective largely followed by male subjects in her experiments focused on rule-following (Gilligan 1982). Care ethicists argued that moral theories need to import emotions, particularly care, more than they do. Hume, however, did import emotion in his version of sentimentalism, arguing that our feeling of approval or disapproval of a number of instances of acts of a certain kind, such as honest acts, determines whether the act is a virtue or a vice. Hume's theory has won the favor of some feminists because of its emphasis on virtues, particularly those concerning our relations with others. These involve the heart's response to particular persons rather than universal principles of justice (Baier 1987: 41). His theory is also constructivist in that an impartial observer, one removed from the particular act in question, determines the moral status of an act. An act is deemed a virtue when an impartial observer has a feeling of approval of acts of this kind. The feeling of approval stems from this kind of act being pleasant or useful. An act is deemed a vice when acts of this kind generate a feeling of disapproval. Hume's theory does not generate such idiosyncratic results as first meets the eye, not only because it invokes an impartial observer, but also because the feeling of approval is generated by a universal sentiment of benevolence that causes us all to make the same pronouncements about an act's moral status. These assumptions, though controversial, attempt to remove the relativism in his theory that concerns some feminists.

Yet many feminists worry that if rape is morally wrong, it is morally wrong regardless of how anyone feels about it. Hume's theory seems to make wrongness contingent on emotional responses, albeit those of an impartial observer under the right conditions. But Driver's Humean feminist constructivist theory has it that moral norms are both mind-dependent, because the property of being a virtue rests on the feeling of approval in an observer, and mind-independent in the sense that they are independent of any individual and cultural beliefs. This addresses the feminist worry that were moral norms mind-dependent in virtue of an observer's approval, it could not be the case that rape is universally wrong. The notion of truth that emerges from Driver's feminist constructivism is that there is no possible world exactly descriptively like our own but different normatively (Driver 2012: 189). This is not to endorse relativism; rather, the view is that wherever certain acts turn out to be morally wrong, in any society with the same conditions they will be wrong. Furthermore, Driver's theory adds to Hume's by requiring that caring agents, in order to be caring agents, endorse certain features of acts. Driver believes that this makes the view of moral truth almost universal. Almost, because non-caring agents will likely not endorse these features, but Driver dismisses these agents as not moral agents. Hers is a complex view, no doubt, but it demonstrates how feminists can be moral realists, incorporate care in their moral theory, and avoid a problematic relativism.

Most of the feminist debate about truth in ethics has not been about the nature of moral facts, but about whether feminists should endorse moral absolutism or moral relativism. While moral relativists believe that truth in ethics is relative to cultures or even individuals, moral absolutists believe that there is one true moral code. For the moral absolutist, if rape is wrong, it is wrong full stop, while for the relativist, rape can be morally wrong in one society but morally permissible in another. Why would feminists endorse moral relativism? If rape, or more generally, oppression is morally wrong, it would seem that it is wrong universally, and that there is some fact about it that explains its wrongness. Indeed, for any feminist claims about oppression to have any bite, it would seem that moral absolutism must be true.

One of the main reasons why some feminists have hesitations about moral absolutism is the worry about judging other cultures and tolerance. Since women have been judged throughout history according to patriarchal standards (e.g., "A good woman is not aggressive"; "A good woman serves her family first"; "A childless woman is selfish"), some feminists believe that we should refrain from judging women any further. A common belief is that if we are moral relativists, the only judgments we can legitimately make are ones about persons in our own culture who fail to live up to the culture's moral code. Additionally, Western feminists have been accused of unfairly judging women in other cultures while not pointing the finger at women in their own culture for participating in patriarchal practices. Uma Narayan accuses Western feminists of unfairly judging Sufi Pirzada women in Old Delhi who veil for having a compromised agency because they see these women as either the "dupes of patriarchy," who have only desires deformed by patriarchy, or the "prisoners of patriarchy," who have extreme restrictions on their liberty (Narayan 2002). Narayan believes that the situation is much more complex. She portrays these women as "bargainers with patriarchy" who have both external constraints on their liberty as well as internal constraints in the form of deformed desires, but who also have non-deformed desires and can make autonomous choices about veiling. They both want to veil because of the message it sends about their sexuality, and do not want to veil because veiling is uncomfortable and restrictive, but not veiling flies in the face of deeply held religious convictions. Narayan compares them to Western women who do not go out in public without makeup or with their hairy legs uncovered and argues that Western women are wrong to judge veiling women as constrained while viewing Western women as having choices and full agency (Narayan 2002: 421). Narayan herself does not explicitly endorse moral relativism, but her concerns about unfairly judging women from other cultures make moral relativism appealing to some feminists.

Having said all of this, however, it is false that moral relativism necessarily endorses tolerance, since it is an open question whether any particular moral code endorses tolerance. Thus this is not a good reason for feminists to favor relativism over absolutism. Additionally, Margaret Urban Walker argues that it is possible to criticize prevailing moral standards while recognizing that morality is culturally and socially situated (Walker 2008). Walker believes that we justify and critique morality from the standpoint of our own society's moral perspective, rather than from the standpoint of an objective, universal standard, in a way that is sensitive to the standpoint of the non-privileged in our society. We ask how we fare under our morality, what we get from it, and what we pay for it, moving back and forth and making changes as needed (Walker 2008: 247–249).

Another reason feminists might shy away from moral absolutism is their belief that it can lead to moral imperialism, having moral standards, particularly ones grounded in patriarchy, dictated for all. To avoid moral imperialism, some feminists endorse multiculturalism, the view that minority cultures should be protected by special group rights or privileges. But other feminists such as Susan Moller Okin, urge that feminists should be skeptical about multiculturalism because it is often at odds with the basic tenets of feminism—that women should not be disadvantaged by their sex, that they have human dignity equal to that of men, and that they should have the same opportunity as men to live fulfilling and freely chosen lives (Okin 2004: 192). Okin cites the French government's tolerance of men bringing multiple wives into the country in the 1970s despite the fact that these arrangements were detrimental to the women involved because they lived in overcrowded apartments and had immense hostility and resentment and were even violent against the other wives and each other's children (Okin 2004: 192). Lurking behind the tolerance of this practice is the belief that moral truth is relative to cultures: it is true that polygamy is morally permissible for these men, while it is true that it is morally wrong for others. Okin endorses an objective, universal standard of value consistent with the feminist aims listed above, using it to critique such practices. She rejects multiculturalism because it is at odds with a universal standard of value that protects the dignity, rights, and opportunities of women as well as men, and in doing so she rejects the moral relativism that lurks behind it. Similarly, Martha Nussbaum criticizes female genital mutilation on the grounds that it is objectively bad for women: it causes repeated infections, painful intercourse, obstructed labor and delivery, involves force against usually very young girls who have no chance to refuse it, is irreversible, and is practiced on females who are illiterate or poor or intimidated and so have compromised autonomy (Nussbaum 1999). These and other feminists who identify certain objective values that should apply universally are moral absolutists.

But this raises a third concern that feminists have about moral absolutism, namely, how do we defend universal values in a non-patriarchal way? How do we show, non-paternalistically, that some practices are objectively bad for women? Nussbaum is one feminist who offers a detailed account, what she calls the "capabilities theory," an absolutist moral view according to which we should pursue the fulfilment of central human capabilities that are common to all, thereby treating each person as an end rather than as a tool of the ends of others (Nussbaum 2000: 5). Nussbaum dismisses the worries about imperialism and paternalism about women's good as being unfounded. While she acknowledges that many existing value systems are paternalistic toward women, she believes that we should endorse a universalistic one that respects the universal value of having the opportunity to think and choose for oneself (Nussbaum 2000: 51). The capabilities that Nussbaum believes all humans have that, when fulfilled, lead to a good life include: being able to live to the end of a human life of normal length, to have good health, to have one's bodily boundaries treated as sovereign, to use one's senses, imagination, thought, and reason especially in ways that produce self-expression, to form a conception of the good and plan one's life critically, and to engage in social interaction and to play (Nussbaum 2000: 78–80). Feminists could use the objective value of having a good life, and the capabilities that go into it, as a standard by which to measure and judge the practices in which women engage in any society. Using our example, the practice of rape would be condemned universally because it violates a person's bodily boundaries and disrespects her own choice about having sex. Whether they endorse the capabilities theory, most feminists are moral absolutists because they believe there are objectively wrong acts and practices. This does not mean that feminists have not found Nussbaum's approach unproblematic. Alison Jaggar critiques the methodology—but not the notion of universal value—used to obtain the list of capabilities (Jaggar 2006). She argues that it is a combination of a substantive-good approach that appeals to an independent standard of value and an informed-desire approach that relies on reflective equilibrium to eliminate preferences corrupted by patriarchy and misinformation. At base, however, Jaggar says that the method is a kind of intuitionism because we test out the list against our intuitions (Jaggar 2006: 307–308). Jaggar's objections include the following: there is no guarantee that our desires are free from corruption or error; the procedure may be exclusionary because it fails to mandate that everyone participate; and the procedure is non-egalitarian because some unidentified "we" has the authority to determine whether people's desires are "informed," "corrupt," or "mistaken" (Jaggar 2006: 307–308, 318). Thus, the approach might not avoid paternalism and imperialism after all.

Most feminists also believe that we have made feminist progress, politically, socially, and economically, though we still have a way to go. Were moral relativism true, there could be no feminist moral progress, since progress implies a standard by which we measure improvement. Some feminists suggest that feminists make advances in moral knowledge faster than the general public because they engage in sophisticated analysis of oppression and come up with new terminology (e.g., "marginalize") and categories that others do not have, at least not until this knowledge gets disseminated into the general public (Calhoun 1989). Once it does, there is room for blaming and holding responsible those who fall short, judging them according to the newly acquired knowledge about a universally true moral code.

Moral Skepticism

Suppose that moral realism and moral absolutism are true. Do we have reason to follow the true moral code? The skeptic about acting morally—the practical skeptic—denies that we do. The challenge for the moral philosopher is to show that every morally required action is rationally required.

On the traditional view, the practical skeptic adopts a theory of practical reason according to which rational action is action that maximizes the agent's expected utility, or, the satisfaction of the agent's interests, desires, or preferences. This is the expected theory of utility. In order to defeat the skeptic, the moral philosopher must show that practical reason dictates acting in morally required ways, even when doing so is against the agent's self-interest, defined as maximal desire or preference satisfaction.

Feminists have raised a number of challenges to the project of defeating the practical skeptic. One objection is whether the expected theory of utility, or rational choice theory, is compatible with feminism, since if it is not, it is a poor starting point for attempting to defeat skepticism. Rational choice theory is put forth as a theory that explains and predicts behavior, which seems to be a purely empirical matter. But Elizabeth Anderson argues that it has normative import, and for this reason feminist values are relevant in determining rational action (Anderson 2002). Anderson recognizes different dimensions of rational choice theory. One is its formal version according to which people tend to maximize their utility. Anderson argues that this dimension is not nuanced enough to relate to feminist concerns for at least the reason that it is oblivious to how the formation of people's preferences is socially influenced. Anderson favors, but still finds problematic, the rhetorical version of the theory, which is supposed to explain how people actually behave. According to this version, the rational agent, who is deemed to be male, is described as follows: he is self-transparent in that he knows what he wants and has no unconscious drives that interfere with his conscious desires; is opportunistic in that he takes every opportunity to advance his goals; is resourceful and enterprising; is self-reliant and expects others to be so too; is coolly calculating and not impeded by irrational thinking; and is autonomous and self-confident, in that he knows his own preferences and orders them as he sees fit, and sees himself as their source and feels entitled to be such (Anderson 2002: 375–378).

Some feminists take issue with this view of rational agency because it is at odds with the caring and emotional engagement that are common in intimate interactions associated with women, such as mothering. However, other feminists welcome the same view because it counteracts stereotypically feminine vices of self-effacement, passivity, servility, and niceness (Anderson 2002: 378). Anderson suggests that this view of rational agency is a good model for all, so we could use it as a standard by which to measure how women fall short and to try to overcome the obstacles in their way. Moreover, this view of rational agency can account for the fact that women do not always act on their own preferences but are sometimes under the sway of oppressive social norms. But it wrongly assumes that we develop our autonomy in a vacuum without the support of others, particularly mothers who enable their children in this way (Anderson 2002: 392–393).

Some feminists see rational choice theory as a useful tool for feminism because it requires self-interested or "non-tuistic" action, which is action that is not motivated by the preferences of others. Self-interested action is distinguished from selfish action, which is to prefer one's own well-being to that of others. Since women have tended to be caregivers, even to the point of losing their selves or not having or asserting their own interests, rational choice theory can show that it is not rational for them to give care unless doing so is reciprocated (Cudd 2002: 412–413). Alternatively, suppose we supplement the Hobbesian model of the State of Nature discussed earlier with Kant's notion that every rational agent has intrinsic value. This would make it the case that all the bargainers in an interaction could assert their interests equally rather than [having] counting only the interests of the strong [count]. Rational action would not require servility on behalf of the weak, who have less to offer (Hampton 2002).

Rational choice theory can also be used for feminist ends by revealing that social structures need to be changed in order to promote feminist ends such as equality. Consider Ann Cudd's analysis of the gendered wage gap (Cudd 1988: 36–40). Suppose Larry and Lisa believe that it is best for their family if one stays home with their children while the other enters the paid labor force, and neither subscribes to gendered social norms. They are rational in that they act self-interestedly by maximizing the amount of money their family obtains so that they can provide for their children as best they can. Since women make much less than men for equal work, they reason that it would be best for the family were Lisa to raise the children while Larry becomes the wage earner. One problem, however, is that if enough women make Lisa's choice, this reinforces the stereotype that women are unreliable wage workers who put domestic work ahead of wage work, which was the cause of the gendered wage gap in the first place. A vicious cycle is set up where women make voluntary, rational choices that contribute to their own oppression if enough others do so as well. Rational choice theory reveals how this happens, and shows how women have bad or unfair options that need to be rectified.

So far, we have questioned the skeptic's starting point of rational choice theory and its implications for feminism. Other feminists question specifically how the skeptic's position bears on demonstrating the rationality of morally required action. One issue is whether the traditional account of the skeptic is too narrow because a defeat of the skeptic would demonstrate that acting morally was rationally required only when moral action conflicts with self-interested action. The traditional picture of the skeptic is, among other things, supposed to leave open no further skeptical challenge by representing the worst-case scenario in opposition to morally required action. Defeating skepticism is a huge challenge because the skeptic accepts only self-interested reasons, and it might be the case that we have set up too big of a challenge, much like Descartes's attempt to defeat the epistemological skeptic by doubting all of his beliefs. I argue that, nevertheless, we need to broaden the skeptic's position so that it is more politically sensitive than the traditional one (Superson 2009). A complete defeat of skepticism would demonstrate that actions that discount, ignore, or even set back the status of women as full and equal persons would be irrational. Thus feminists should challenge the view that self-interested action provides the biggest challenge to morality because it is most in opposition to moral action. Other immoral actions that take sexist forms, such as doing evil for its own sake, displaying moral indifference, moral negligence, conscientious wickedness, and weakness of will, and acts that are performed as part of harmful social practices that may not directly be in the agent's self-interest but only indirectly benefit the group of which he is a member, should also be represented in the skeptic's challenge to morality. I argue for changing the skeptic's position to one according to which the skeptic endorses reasons relating to privilege rather than self-interest so as to capture many immoral acts other than self-interested ones, particularly ones that take sexist forms.

I also endorse the Kantian view that each person has intrinsic value, which gives each equal standing to make claims on anyone else or to put forward reasons relating to her ends. These reasons are sufficient for making her a being we ought to respect. Failure to respect another is to privilege oneself, by not recognizing another's worth, disregarding it, seeking to set it back, failing to focus on it, or not caring about it, all of which are captured in the various forms of immoral action. On my view, feminists might re-construe the skeptic's position as the view that rationality requires acting in ways that privilege oneself and one's reasons. A successful and comprehensive defeat of skepticism will demonstrate that these kinds of disrespect for others are irrational. We might apply my account to the issue of rape: a common feminist view is that rapists rape because it gives them a sense of power over their victim and over all members of her group (Hampton 1999), not because they are self-interested and seek to satisfy a preference. Rape attempts to lower the victim's worth along with the worth of all women. My account of the skeptic in terms of privilege rather than self-interest can make better sense of the irrationality of rape, were skepticism defeated.

Yet other feminists believe that the project of defeating the practical skeptic ought to be jettisoned or at least reframed. Some are suspicious that reason, though put forward as universal, is a male-biased concept since women have been associated only with emotions and men with reason throughout the history of philosophy (Lloyd 1984; Tong 1993; Tuana 1992). Some believe that the notion of reason could never be neutral, but that it has gender built into it in such a way that it would have to be a different concept were gender eradicated from it (Held 1990: 323). Feminists must be careful, however, in jettisoning reason and the project of justification lest they reinforce the stereotype that women are more emotional than rational.

A more recent suggestion in the realm of action theory is to expand the scope of philosophy to include psychology and other empirical sciences to help critique actual moral practices with an eye toward making them not support oppression. Lisa Tessman argues that the project of defeating skepticism needs to speak to actual persons, not the skeptic, since real people are not skeptical in the sense that they refuse morality only if they are given justifying reasons for following it, but only in the sense that they question or reject pieces of morality or ground morality in something other than merely their rationality (Tessman 2011: 884). But Tessman misses the point about the traditional skeptic's position, which is defined broadly to cover all possible cases of immoral action, and thus assumes that any rationally required act is self-interested. Describing the skeptic's position this way does not mean that actual people reject moral action wholesale; rather, it means that were the skeptic defeated, there would be no immoral action about which the skeptic can claim that it may be rationally required or at least permissible to act that way. The description is strategic, not intended to represent reality. Tessman's suggestion that the project of defeating skepticism tap into other disciplines in order to change oppressive practices is addressed by my expansion of the skeptic's position to include behaviors that are performed as part of harmful social practices that indirectly benefit an agent who is a member of a privileged group. Both Tessman and I want changes in oppressive social structures, but I insist on the project of justification because demonstrating the rationality of acting morally would strengthen morality by backing it with reason, whether or not the reasons take on real people. When they do take, a successful defeat of the skeptic promises to make head-way in achieving the desired effect of people's acting morally.

Suppose we defeat the skeptic. How do we motivate persons who recognize moral reasons to act on them? Internalists about reasons and motivations believe that reasons necessarily motivate a rational agent who recognizes them, while externalists deny that they necessarily do so (Smith 2007). Some feminists question internalism and its conse-quences. Some challenge the view that part of the concept of a reason is that it motivates, arguing that unrecognized psychological habits such as stereotyping, or social pressure to conform to the attitudes of others, can make a person who is somewhat aware of her moral demands fail to attend fully to them and be motivated to act (DesAutels 2004). Other feminists question whether if a rational agent acts immorally because he is not motivated, he could not possibly have believed the relevant moral judgment. Lacking the motivation need not mean that he completely lacks an authentic belief about what morality demands. He might truly believe that his society takes something to be morally required, but not be fully motivated by these requirements because they dictate sexist behavior (Nelson 2004). Still other feminists question the view that if an agent fails to be motivated by her moral judgment, she must be irrational. Some people who are vic-tims of oppressive socialization are confused about their worth as persons and so fail to be moved by the moral judgment that one ought to be self-respecting. For instance, the deferential wife puts her husband's and family's interests ahead of her own when she even recognizes the latter because she believes that women ought to serve their families (Hill 1995). Since she does not see herself as having the same worth as a person as others, she is unlikely to be motivated by the moral judgment that one ought to be self-respecting rather than servile. Judging such persons to be irrational when they fail to be motivated is to blame the victim for her bad circumstances (Superson 2009). Some feminists suggest that we ought not to blame persons for harboring implicit bias, the unconscious bias that affects how we perceive, evaluate, and interact with people who are members of groups at which our biases are directed, for at least the reason that they may be completely unaware of having the bias which is the product of living in, for instance, a sexist society (Saul 2013: 40, 55). Thus invoking internalism does not solve the motivation issue about acting morally, even if the skeptic is defeated.

Moral Epistemology

How do we know that rape is morally wrong? According to traditional moral philosophy, reason gives us this information, and our will or motivational capacity responds or not. Reason and motivation are completely separate on this model; a person can know what is morally called for yet fail to be moved in the right way. Margaret Little objects to this model of obtaining moral knowledge. Borrowing from the ethic of care, which showed the significance of emotion to morality, Little argues that the possession of various emotions and desires is a necessary condition for seeing the moral landscape (2007: 421). Little attributes the separation of reason from affect to the historical association with and subsequent devaluation of emotion along with women. Contrary to the traditional model, Little argues that moral deliberation begins with being aware of the salient features of a moral situation, which involves emotion. In particular, if one cares about something, one is ready to respond on its behalf in a way that is receptive to the particularities of one's situation, including one's hopes, fears, and worries, as is a mother who notices that her child needs help (Little 2007: 423, 245). Someone who is truly morally aware has a certain attentiveness, a gestalt view of a situation that allows her to see things a certain way rather than to approach a moral situation with a conscious grocery list of moral features to check for (Little 2007: 423). She sees an action that causes pain not just in this way but also as a cruel action. Furthermore, she sees it as meriting a response, such as calling for some action or responding appropriately emotionally. Most importantly, she sees the morally salient features of the situation as constituting a reason for the response, as when a person sees the evil of torture as constituting a reason not to torture because of the revulsion of torture (Little 2007: 426). If a person lacks the appropriate response, she does not see clearly the moral status of a situation. Only when she has the response and lets it inform her moral judgment of the situation can she acquire moral knowledge. Little gives the following example to illustrate the gestalt switch and appropriate emotionality involved in seeing the moral landscape. Suppose that a woman gives to a homeless person only because she wants to avoid guilt, but one day has a change in perspective and identifies with the person's loneliness, and helps him because he is a fellow human in need. (Little 2007: 426).

Applying Little's view to our example, a person who has the right perspective on morality comes to know that rape is wrong not just in virtue of its meeting certain objective criteria of wrongness, but also because he has the right affect about it in that he sees it as cruel, disgusting, and degrading of a person's worth, sees how it affects a particular victim, and sees that this response yields a reason to avoid rape. The insight from feminism is that traditional moral theory has ignored affect because of its association with women, when it turns out that affect is necessary to knowing the moral landscape, making correct moral judgments, and acquiring moral truths.

Conclusion

We have seen that feminists have weighed in on some timeless, intractable issues in metaethics. They have offered accounts of moral realism that incorporate the sentiment of caring rather than being grounded strictly in reason. They have debated whether it is better for feminism for us to be relativists or absolutists about moral truth, and have offered ways of justifying objective, universal values. They have challenged many of the assumptions associated with the project of defeating the skeptic about moral action, including the notion of rationality and whether traditional philosophers have described the project broadly enough to cover all sexist behaviors. Finally, they have expanded traditional philosophy's view of how we acquire moral knowledge to a more poignant account that is grounded in both reason and emotions so that we can better respond to our moral world. The area of metaethics is ripe for further feminist challenges.

Related Topics

Moral justification in an unjust world (Chapter 40); feminist conceptions of autonomy (Chapter 41); multicultural and postcolonial feminisms (Chapter 47).

References

Anderson, Elizabeth (2002) "Should Feminists Reject Rational Choice Theory?" in Louise M. Antony and Charlotte E. Witt (Eds.) *A Mind of One's Own: Feminist Essays on Reason and Objectivity*, 2nd ed., Boulder, CO: Westview Press, 369–397.

Bagnoli, Carla (2015) [2011] "Constructivism in Metaethics," in Edward Zalta (Ed.) *The Stanford Encyclopedia of Philosophy* (Spring) [online]. Available from: http://plato.stanford.edu/archives/spr2015/entries/constructivism-metaethics/.

Baier, Annette C. (1987) "Hume, the Women's Moral Theorist?" in Eva Feder Kittay and Diana T. Meyers (Ed.) *Women and Moral Theory*, Totowa, NJ: Rowman & Littlefield, 37–55.

Calhoun, Cheshire (1989) "Responsibility and Reproach," *Ethics* 99(2): 389–406.

Cudd, Ann E. (1988) "Oppression by Choice," *Journal of Social Philosophy* 25: 22–44.

—— (2002) "Rational Choice Theory and the Lessons of Feminism," in Louise M. Antony and Charlotte E. Witt (Ed.) *A Mind of One's Own: Feminist Essays on Reason and Objectivity*, 2nd edition, Boulder, CO: Westview Press, 398–417.

DesAutels, Peggy (2004) "Moral Mindfulness," in Peggy DesAutels and Margaret Urban Walker (Eds.) *Moral Psychology: Feminist Ethics and Social Theory*, Lanham, MD: Rowman & Littlefield, 69–81.

Dillon, Robin S. (2012) "Critical Character Theory: Toward a Feminist Perspective on 'Vice' (and 'Virtue')," in Sharon L. Crasnow and Anita M. Superson (Eds.) *Out from the Shadows: Analytical Feminist Contributions to Traditional Philosophy*, New York: Oxford University Press, 83–114.

Driver, Julia (2012) "Constructivism and Feminism," in Sharon L. Crasnow and Anita M. Superson (Eds.) *Out from the Shadows: Analytical Feminist Contributions to Traditional Philosophy*, New York: Oxford University Press, 175–94.

Gilligan, Carol (1982) *In a Different Voice: Psychological Theory and Women's Development*, Cambridge, MA: Harvard University Press.

Hampton, Jean (1999) "Defining Wrong and Defining Rape," in Keith Burgess-Jackson (Ed.) *A Most Detestable Crime*, New York: Oxford University Press, 118–156.

—— (2002) "Feminist Contractarianism," in Louise M. Antony and Charlotte E. Witt (Eds.) *A Mind of One's Own: Feminist Essays on Reason and Objectivity*, Boulder, CO: Westview Press, 337–368.

Held, Virginia (1990) "Feminist Transformations of Moral Theory," *Philosophy and Phenomenological Research* 1: 321–344.

Hill, Thomas E., Jr. (1995) "Servility and Self-Respect," in Robin S. Dillon (Ed.) *Dignity, Character, and Self-Respect*, New York: Routledge, 76–92. Reprinted from *Monist* (1973), 87–104.

Jaggar, Alison (2006) "Reasoning about Well-Being: Nussbaum's Methods of Justifying," *Journal of Political Philosophy* 14(3): 301–322.

Kittay, Eva (1999) *Love's Labor: Essays on Women, Equality, and Dependency*, New York: Routledge.

Little, Margaret (2007) "Seeing and Caring: The Role of Affect in Feminist Moral Epistemology," in Russ Shafer-Landau and Terence Cuneo (Eds.) *Foundations of Ethics: An Anthology*, Malden, MA: Blackwell, 420–432. Reprinted from *Hypatia* (1995), pp. 117–137.

Lloyd, Genevieve (1984) *The Man of Reason: "Male" and "Female" in Western Philosophy*, Minneapolis, MN: University of Minnesota Press.

Narayan, Uma (2002) "Minds of Their Own: Choices, Autonomy, Cultural Practices, and Other Women," in Louise M. Antony and Charlotte E. Witt (Eds.) *A Mind of One's Own: Feminist Essays on Reason and Objectivity*, Boulder, CO: Westview Press, 418–432.

Nelson, James L. (2004) "The Social Situation of Sincerity: Austen's *Emma* and Lovibond's *Ethical Formation*," in Peggy DesAutels and Margaret Urban Walker (Eds.) *Moral Psychology: Feminist Ethics and Social Theory*, Lanham, MD: Rowman & Littlefield, 83–98.

Noddings, Nel (1984) *Caring: A Feminine Approach to Ethics and Moral Education*, Berkeley, CA: University of California Press.

Nussbaum, Martha C. (1999) "Judging Other Cultures: The Case of Genital Mutilation," in *Sex and Social Justice*, New York: Oxford University Press, 118–129.

—— (2000) *Women and Human Development: The Capabilities Approach*, New York: Cambridge University Press.

Okin, Susan Moller (2004) "Is Multiculturalism Bad for Women?" in Amy Baehr (Ed.) *Varieties of Feminist Liberalism*, Lanham, MD: Rowman & Littlefield, 191–205.

Saul, Jennifer (2013) "Implicit Bias, Stereotype Threat, and Women in Philosophy," in Katrina Hutchison and Fiona Jenkins (Eds.) *Women in Philosophy: What Needs to Change*, New York: Oxford University Press, 39–60.

Sayre-McCord, Geoff (2015) [2012] "Moral Realism," in Edward Zalta (Ed.) *The Stanford Encyclopedia of Philosophy*, Spring Edition. Available from: http://plato.stanford.edu/archives/spr2015/entries/moral-realism/.

Smith, Michael (2007) "The Externalist Challenge," in Russ Shafer-Landau and Terence Cuneo (Eds.) *Foundations of Ethics: An Anthology*, Malden, MA: Blackwell, 231–242. Reprinted from *The Moral Problem* (Oxford: Blackwell, 1994).

Superson, Anita M. (2009) *The Moral Skeptic*, New York: Oxford University Press.

—— (2010) "The Deferential Wife Revisited: Agency and Moral Responsibility," *Hypatia: A Journal of Feminist Philosophy* 25(2): 253–275.

Tessman, Lisa (2001) "Critical Virtue Ethics: Understanding Oppression as Morally Damaging," in Peggy DesAutels and Joanne Waugh (Eds.) *Feminists Doing Ethics*, Lanham, MD: Rowman & Littlefield, 79–99.

—— (2011) "Book review of *The Moral Skeptic*, by Anita Superson," *Hypatia* 26 (4): 883–887.

Tong, Rosemarie (1984) *Feminine and Feminist Ethics*, Belmont, CA: Wadsworth.

—— (1993) *Feminine and Feminist Ethics*, Belmont, CA: Wadsworth.

Tuana, Nancy (1992) *Women and the History of Philosophy*, New York: Paragon House.

Walker, Margaret Urban (2008) *Moral Understandings: A Feminist Study in Ethics*, New York: Routledge.

43

FEMINIST ETHICS OF CARE

Jean Keller and Eva Feder Kittay

Care ethics has changed dramatically over the decades. Initially articulated by moral psychologist, Carol Gilligan, the key concepts of care ethics have not only been further developed by feminist philosophers; care has become a key concept for political science, economics, sociology, history, nursing and biomedical ethics, and theology. This article will focus on philosophical conceptions of care, yet given the interdisciplinary investigation and development of this concept, our analysis cannot be limited to philosophical conceptions of care alone.

While often initially depicted as an ethic of interpersonal relations, in the past two decades, the political and global dimensions of care, which were pointed to early on by Sara Ruddick in *Maternal Thinking*, have taken on ever greater importance in the theory.

Early Articulations of Care Ethics

Articulated nearly simultaneously, but in somewhat different forms, by Carol Gilligan (*In a Different Voice*, 1982), Nel Noddings (*Caring*, 1986), and Sara Ruddick ("Maternal Thinking," article in 1980 and book in 1989), care ethics was initially conceived as providing an alternate frame to the justice-oriented moral theories of utilitarianism, deontology, and rights theory that then predominated in Western philosophy. Focusing on domains of life in which women were the major ethical actors, these early care theorists addressed topics such as mothering; abortion decisions; caring for the sick, elderly, disabled; and caring within intimate relations. These topics had been largely neglected by dominant moral theories, because they were viewed as "private" concerns most naturally dealt with by women, rather than as moral concerns per se. Care ethicists challenged this implicit public/private divide in moral theory (Tronto 1993; Clement 1996), contending that the moral domain, as traditionally conceived, was too narrow; it cut off from theoretical consideration important dimensions of human life, particularly those aspects associated with human dependency and reproduction. Thus, needs that arise from inevitable human dependencies became a central concern of care ethics. Care ethicists demonstrated that the sorts of moral considerations operative within caring relations involved different sets of moral questions than those addressed in justice-oriented moral theories, as well as distinctive moral capacities and forms of deliberation. Furthermore, they believed that these moral considerations proffered resources that could inform other spheres such as education, politics, and peace politics.

By affirming care and caregiving as morally significant, care ethics both reflected and gave shape and form to the feminist concern that moral theories written by men do not adequately address the range of women's life experiences. It also provided affirmation and validation for a set of activities that, for most women, takes up much of their energy and attention. This feminist reappropriation of some aspects of "femininity," as opposed to the feminist critique of women's roles as tout court oppressive, was appealing to many and helps account for the wide-ranging discussion and debate that emerged.

From the beginning, care ethicists had to address concerns raised by both moral-philosophical and feminist-philosophical skeptics. These debates took place as moral philosophers attempted to articulate, evaluate, and situate within the broader tradition of moral theory the new concepts presented by early care theorists, and as feminist philosophers attempted to evaluate care ethics against the background of enduring feminist insights and commitments. Some of these debates continue to preoccupy care ethicists while others are viewed as more or less settled.

Moral-Philosophical Debates Regarding Care Ethics

Since care ethics was first articulated as providing an alternative to justice theories, early philosophical debates, reviewed below, centered on whether or not central components of care theory truly provided a theoretically and morally defensible alternative approach.

The Relational Self vs. the Independent and Autonomous Self

Western philosophy has overwhelmingly depicted the moral and political agent as an independent and autonomous adult. Yet, as Seyla Benhabib (1992) points out, humans don't just pop up out of the earth like mushrooms. Care ethicists see this dependence and interdependence of persons as a central aspect of human experience that requires a new model of moral agency. Thus care ethicists not only conceive the self as constituted through and situated in relationships with others, but they also insist that the full range of human experience, from dependence and vulnerability at birth to frail old age, be considered when conceiving human agency and interactions.

This relational conception of moral agency has implications for how autonomy is conceived. On the relational view of self, others play a constitutive role in moral deliberation, both because of the way we, and hence our thinking, have been shaped through our relationships to others, and because we often make moral decisions by deliberating with others (Keller 1997). In the moral tradition, particularly stemming from Kant, others were seen as heteronomous influences that impeded autonomy, but the understanding of the self as relational requires that autonomy itself must be conceived relationally. (For a detailed discussion of how the relational self reconfigured philosophy's conception of agency and autonomy see Chapters 18 and 41 in this volume.)

The Role of Emotion vs. Reason in Moral Deliberation

Although care ethicists are not the only moral theorists who have questioned the exclusion of emotions as morally important (Williams 1973; Rorty 1980; Nussbaum 2001; see also sentimentalist moral theorists, such as Slote 2010), care as a phenomenon presents a serious problem for purely rationalistic theories. Care done without the right affect, such as love and empathy, is often not experienced as care at all. Similarly, when care is not offered through an intuitive and immediate response but mediated by reasoning, care can be experienced as insincere and calculated. But reason and principled thinking still play a role in care thinking. We care and because we care we ask—what are our responsibilities for this situation? When the feeling of care is absent or is insufficient to motivate action despite the very real need or vulnerability before us, care guides us to ask about why care broke down. Has the caregiver received inadequate care herself, is she overburdened, has care been insufficiently supported by social norms and social systems? Thus, for care ethicists, morality focuses on how reason and emotion, together, inform and motivate moral deliberation and moral action.

The Role of Partiality vs. Impartiality in Moral Judgment

Impartiality has been considered the hallmark of moral thinking in the modern era. Care ethicists, by contrast, think partiality in one's moral thinking can be a moral good. Our relationships with others come with privileged access to the other's thoughts, feelings, cares, and concerns—and with such knowledge comes special responsibilities to respond to the other in a caring way. This special consideration is part of what it means to care for another; it confirms the special status of the relationship. Thus, partiality is a mark of care that enhances the sense of intimacy and closeness within the relationship and helps ensure that a person's particular needs will be met.

Care ethics was swept up in what became known as the partiality/impartiality debates within moral theory (See Friedman 1991). While care and justice theory clearly have very different starting points for describing moral deliberation, few impartialists claim that special relationships with others should never receive special consideration (Friedman 1991: 174). For its part, care ethics recognizes the need to critically engage partialist moral judgments, as some forms of partiality, such as whites giving preference to members of their racial group, are clearly morally suspect. Thus the apparent gulf between impartialist and partialist moral may not be as large as it at first appeared.

Moral Deliberation as Entailing Context, Narrativity, and Particularity vs. Deduction from Universal Pre-Established Principles

Nel Noddings described care ethics as eschewing universal principles, a view that later care ethicists distanced themselves from (see for example, Kittay and Meyers 1987, Held 1995 and 2007, Clement 1996). Maintaining caring relations and responding to those in need, two central tenets of care ethics, are themselves moral principles. Rather than being derived from a rationalistic ideal theory, however, they emerge from philosophical observations of caring relations themselves. This highlights a key difference between care and other dominant moral theories. Care ethics doesn't see a particular "moral dilemma" as one discrete event, but as unfolding in time and involving multiple sets of relationships. To understand what went wrong in a particular situation and how one might go about addressing the moral problem, care ethics emphasizes that one needs to know more about the story. Thus, care ethics emphasizes that moral deliberation itself is contextual and narrative in approach. It must attend to the particular features of the situation, as these often make a difference for what actions are considered right or wrong. Thus care ethics tends to be a "bottom up" moral theory rather than one relying on a top-down application of universal principles.

Even while care ethicists have come to acknowledge that care incorporates moral principles, some justice theorists have acknowledged the importance of context and narrativity in moral deliberation but limit their role to the application of principles—a limitation that care ethicists resist (see, for example, Habermas 1993).

Care and Justice as Contrasting vs. Complementary Perspectives

Carol Gilligan (1987) depicted care and justice as contrasting moral frames: one either sees a duck or a rabbit, care or justice. As can be seen from the discussion thus far, as the care/justice debates evolved, this conception of the relation between the two theories was increasingly called into question. Care ethics' insights influenced philosophers' understanding of fundamental moral categories and conception of the moral domain. At the same time, care ethics integrated within its theory key components of justice theory that were seen as too valuable for feminists to give up, such as, moral principles and the notion of autonomy. Thus, as a result of these debates, care and justice no longer seemed to be the polar opposite moral perspectives that they at first appeared to be, and the door was opened for rich and varied analyses of how the two theories might fit together. Questions regarding the relation of these two perspectives are ongoing and will be discussed further in the next section.

Early Feminist Misgivings Regarding Care Ethics

Even as care ethicists addressed the moral-philosophical concerns just elucidated, feminist skeptics raised a number of objections to early versions of the theory. The most trenchant concerns have informed the subsequent development of the ethic.

Feminine or Feminist Ethic?

Gilligan's initial finding were based largely on girls and women, thus opening her to the charge that she merely described a "feminine" ethic expected of women by the patriarchal culture. And Noddings (2002) initially called care ethics a "feminine" (rather than feminist) ethics, although she later abandoned the claim that this was a gendered ethic. Ruddick, by contrast, theorized a putatively feminine practice, "mothering," but maintained that the practice could be carried on by men no less than women, and she explicitly addressed inequalities of power between genders. However, because few early care theorists systematically addressed inequalities of power, the question of whether care is a feminine or feminist ethic has endured. (See, for example, Houston's critique of Noddings 1989 and 1990; Hoagland 1991; see also Card 1990; Scaltsas 1992; Tong 1993).

Intersectionality and Postcolonial Concerns

Concerns that the gender claims associated with care ethics are oversimplified and don't do justice to the complexity of women's lived experiences emerged early on (Stack 1986; Harding 1987; Moody Adams 1991; Lugones 2003 [1991]; Nicholson 1993). Patricia Hill Collins's ground-breaking work, *Black Feminist Thought* (1990), gave proof to these concerns with her analysis of racially specific controlling images (such as the matri-arch or welfare queen) that contribute to the oppression of black mothers, as well as her rich account of extended kin networks and "other-mothering" practices in African American communities. Her work inspired and informed both the development of womanist theological ethics and further research into black motherhood studies, two cognate traditions to philosophical accounts of care ethics. (See, for example Bailey 1995; Townes 1998; Story 2014; Craddock 2015). Taking this concern in a somewhat different direction, Narayan (1995: 134) cautioned care theorists to attend to the ways in which the value of care has been invoked to support and justify colonial practices and thus, has been used to justify practices of imperialism, domination, and control.

Care: A Parochial Ethic?

Early feminist critics insisted that fulfilling our obligations to care for proximate others can obscure the ways in which such actions negatively impact distant others (Card 1990; Hoagland 1991). For example, consumption habits of persons in developed coun-tries, to satisfy individual desires or meet the needs of dependent others, may rest on the exploitation of people around the globe. Moreover, obligations to care for proximate others may be so demanding as to eclipse obligations to distant others. Despite the fact that Ruddick explicitly saw (maternal) care as offering resources for global peace poli-tics, in its early years care ethics as a whole did not have sufficient conceptual resources to address global care concerns systematically and well. Contemporary care ethicists, as we will see, have gone into the breach and tried to develop care ethics in a way that allows it to challenge systems of global inequality and domination.

Subsequent Developments

From the mid 1990s onward, care theorists apply and further refine the care concepts introduced above. They address why we ought to care and what is meant by care, raise epistemic questions revealed through practices of care, and draw attention to the politics of care. Theorists begin to analyze care as labor and with this develop-ment they necessarily draw more explicit and sustained attention to the larger social, political, and economic contexts in which care practices are embedded and that con-strain how care labor will be carried out. Care theorists, from multiple disciplines, draw attention to the fact that our social and political life is dependent both on the labor of care and the ethics that accompanies such labor, and that therefore the ethics and labor of care should inform our social and political life. These develop-ments belie the concern that care is limited to an ethic of interpersonal relationships and even call into question whether care and care ethics ought to be understood as gendered. Examination of the social context in which care labor is carried out requires that issues of power are given a more prominent focus. Ultimately we are required to rethink the relation between care and justice.

Re(de)fining the Concept of Care

In the 1990s Tronto and Fisher moved to define care so that it accommodated a broader swath of our lives than relationships among intimates. They define care as all the ways in which we "maintain, continue, and repair our 'world' so that we can live in it as well as possible" (Fisher and Tronto 1990: 40). They define four "moments" of care. Care begins by a concern for the other, "caring about." Such concern prompts a move to take on responsibility for care: "taking care of." The actual meeting of the needs is the "caregiving." The final moment occurs when the other takes up the caregiver's actions as care, "care receiving." The last of these phases is one that Nel Noddings calls "the completion of care" in the other. It is the least developed, but according to Kittay is the aspect of care that dictates many of the terms of the preceding phases. Kittay (2014) asks, is care that is not taken up as care by the cared for, normatively speaking, care at all?

Parsing the concept differently, we can define care as a virtue (or moral value), an attitude or disposition to act (wherein the motivation comes not from one's own needs and wants, but rather from those who require care), and as a labor. Each emphasis gives rise to different, though related, sets of concerns.

Care as a Virtue (or Moral Value) and as Disposition (or Attitude)

When we ask about care as a virtue, the following foundational questions arise: from whence comes an ethic of care, why ought we to care, is care a distinctive ethic, and what is its moral epistemology? Kittay gives a naturalist answer to the question of why we ought to care. We care because humans, with their extended periods of dependency, require care to survive. In order to survive as a species, we had to evolve physiologically as well as emotionally and morally, such that we would value care and develop the socio-emotional means of responding (Hrdy 1999; Kittay 2012; see also Engster 2015). Miller (2005) gives a Kantian response, deriving a duty to care from the Kantian duty of beneficence. Walker (1998) speaks of care as being part of an expressive collaborative model that utilizes expressive means such as narrative, along with collaborative efforts at living together well, to help us come to shared moral understandings. Walker thereby distinguishes her model from the regnant ones that are judicial and deduce moral prescriptions from full blown theoretical constructs. In the process, she develops a moral epistemology for an ethics of care. Michael Slote makes care central to virtue theory and develops virtue theory as an ethics of care (2001; 2007; 2010). We care because care emerges out of the development of a natural disposition, empathy, one that he argues is basic to all moral concepts.

Virginia Held, Joan Tronto, Fiona Robinson and many others explore how care as a moral value and a virtue can be expanded to areas far from the intimate domain that tended to occupy the earliest period. The possibilities of using the values of care to govern domains such as social welfare (Tronto 2013), healthcare and biomedicine (Sherwin 1989 and 1992; Nelson, Verkerk, and Walker 2008), culture (Held 2003 and 2007), economic structures (Folbre 2002 and 2012), environmental policies (Moosa 2015), citizenship (Sevenhuisen 1998), animal welfare (Donovan and Adams 2000 and 2007; Gruen 2011; Crary 2016), international relations (Robinson 1999 and 2011a), LGBTQ relationships (Hoagland 1989), and disability (Kittay 2011; Rogers 2016) are added to the peace politics Sarah Ruddick advocated and the educational reform called for by Nel Noddings (1986 and 2005).

From an Ethic of Care to a Politics of Care

The neglect of care as an important concept in moral and political philosophy derives in part from a perception that care is merely a "natural sentiment" largely exhibited by women. An ethic built on care, however, allows us to understand care as more than a natural sentiment. Rather, it is a moral concept and its significance extends beyond the gender of the moral agent. An ethic of care requires cultivation and the resources to align the normative demands of care with other morally important values, and its demands are no less binding for men than for women. When care is viewed as labor, not just the natural response born of affection for someone, another important moment in de-naturalizing and de-gendering care is reached. We ask about how to "socialize care" (Hamington and Miller 2006). Once we ask, "who cares for whom?" what comes into view is the way in which power relations structure and are implicated in the labor of care. Just as important are the questions of the adequacy of support and just organization offered by social, political and economic institutions—both to those who are carers and those who are cared for (Hamington and Engster 2015). The questions of caring are no longer set in opposition to questions of justice. Instead we ask how can caring be just, and justice be caring.

Care as Labor

Care theorists have demonstrated that the social organization of care work today continues to impede the full political and economic participation of those who have traditionally, and continue to be, charged with the task of caring labor. For instance, Selma Sevenhuisjen (1998) looks at the implications of care work for citizenship; Diemut Bubeck (1995), using the Marxian concept of "necessary labor," explores the economic implications for women; Nancy Folbre (2002; 2012) investigates the economic value of women's caring labor; Eva Kittay (1999) demonstrates that the contractualist foundations of liberal democratic society have failed adequately to include women who serve as "dependency workers," thus disadvantaging them with respect to political and economic participation.

Furthermore care theorists have asked: Which persons' social realities are illuminated and obscured by how one defines and delineates care? What are the gender, cultural, racial, and colonial histories and politics behind this? Have more privileged women achieved their success in male-dominated fields, in part, by relying on less privileged women to replace the caring labor they would otherwise be expected to do? And what are the implications of the answers to these questions for the ongoing project of women's liberation? (Tronto 1993; Bubeck 1995; Roberts 1997; Sevenhuisjen 1998; Kittay 1999; Folbre 2002 and 2012; Duffy 2005 and 2011; Nakano Glenn 2012).

Reconceiving the Connection of Care and Gender in Light of Intersectional Concerns

As the definition of care and examples of care are broadened, the connection of care to gender is altered and attenuated in a number of interesting ways. Developing an intersectional analysis, Evelyn Nakano Glenn, Mignon Duffy, and Joan Tronto point out that it is not only white women who have been assigned a disproportionate responsibility to engage in care work but also, and perhaps primarily, men and women of color, especially when they are also from the working class. Intersectional concerns have also challenged the definition of care, prompting a distinction between nurturant and non-nurturant care. Duffy describes nurturant work as having a significant relational dimension; it is more visible and public, and white and privileged women continue to carry on this sort of care work even as they delegate to women of color the less visible, "backroom work" of non-nurturant care (Nakano Glenn 2012)—cleaning, food preparation and service, laundry (Duffy 2007; see also Roberts' distinction between "spiritual" and "menial" work, 1997).

In a different vein, Tronto (2013) expands the virtue of care beyond what have traditionally been women's domains, by pointing out that police work and firefighting are two ways in which men have traditionally satisfied a social imperative to care. Care, surprisingly, is a value that is sometimes fostered even in the military—although the attitude is confined to those who are not the designated enemy. Against this background, perhaps it should not be surprising when Hankivsky (2014) recommends that care theorists abandon the association of gender and care in the interest of developing a truly intersectional understanding of care ethics.

At the same time, research into similarities between African moralities and care ethics and between Confucian ethics and care ethics indicate that care has not always been conceived and carried out as a distinctively feminine practice (see Harding 1987; Gouws and Zyl 2015; Chapter 44 in this volume). Even though in non-Western societies care work often remains the domain of women, care is not construed as a feminine virtue, as it has been in the West. Rather, in the concepts of *ren* for Confucians (see also Chapter 44 in this volume) and *ubuntu* in some African cultures care is recognized as a universal feature of morality. In a related vein, Vrinda Dalmiya (2016) develops a care-based epistemology by drawing on classic texts in Indian philosophy, thereby demonstrating how these two traditions can strengthen each other.

This decoupling of care and gender is, from a feminist perspective, both troubling and promising. Troubling in that women still do most of the care work around the globe. Furthermore, care became an important concept by examining and taking seriously women's lives. Thus, a de-gendered conception of care risks losing the political importance of the place of care in actual women's lives. At the same time, this development is promising—in that care is, after all, an important (albeit frequently marginalized) human value. De-gendering the concept facilitates the recognition of care as a universal moral value and can spur us to insist that the work be shared equitably between men and women.

Inequalities of Power and the Reconception of the Care/Justice Relations

As the discussion thus far indicates, from the 1990s on analyses of power are more explicitly and more frequently developed as part of care ethics, thereby securing its position as a feminist rather than a feminine ethic. Theorists address not only inequalities of power among women, but also the power of those outside the care relation and how their actions or lack thereof impact caregivers' ability to provide care. Thus the concept of care and development of a public ethic of care prove useful for criticizing the system of welfare targeting poor families in the United States today and provide theoretical grounds for envisioning the social welfare policies that ought to be in place to support poor families and families caring for frail elderly relatives and disabled people.

Attention to the influence of power in structuring relations of care calls attention to the need for an ethics of care that insists that care work be non-exploitative and so brings concerns traditionally conceived as matters of justice into care ethics. Once care theorists start discussing the distribution of care work and the institutional structures necessary to carry out care well, we move to a public ethic of care and the question of justice. At the same time we see that caring relations are a necessary precondition for a just society—in order to have citizens at all, children need adequate care to survive childhood; to have citizens who are prepared to engage in the responsibilities of citizenship and who have a developed sense of justice, they need to be raised such that their basic emotional and physical needs are met and they receive adequate support/stimulation necessary to develop their basic capabilities. Once we no longer posit an opposition between care and justice, we also recognize that citizens need a well-developed sense of caring for citizens and distant others. Care, as Engster (2007) puts it, is at the heart of justice, even as justice is needed for a true ethics of care.

Care in a Global Context

While Ruddick (1989), Narayan (1995), Harding (1987), and Robinson (1999) conceived care ethics in global terms from its inception, it wasn't until the 2000s that care theorists as a whole began systematically to address what it might mean to consider care a global ethic (Ehrenreich and Hochschild 2002; Kittay 2005; 2008; 2009; Weir 2005; Miller 2006; 2011; Held 2007; Eckenweiler 2009; and Eckenweiler and Meghani 2009). At the same time, feminist theorists from the Global South have found care ethics to be a useful framework for analyzing the failure of states with more minimal welfare provisions and a traditional sexual division of labor firmly entrenched. In South Korea, for example, several feminists have used a framework of care ethics to address the pressing issue of long-term care (Cheon 2010; Kim and Kang 2010).

Central concerns addressed in this period include using care theory to diagnose a crisis of care on a global scale; utilizing care premises to provide alternate moral approaches to international concerns, such as development ethics and military conflict; and a more systematic examination of similarities between care ethics and non-Western ethical traditions, such as Confucianism, African, and Indian philosophies.

The Crisis of Care on a Global Level

Developed countries have implemented the comprehensive policies necessary to meet the care and caregiving needs of their populace to a greater or lesser extent. The United States remains an outlier among wealthy industrial societies in so poorly meeting these needs. Neoliberal structural adjustment programs promoted by the World Bank and International Monetary Fund have required that developing countries in need of loans sharply curtail their investments in social programs (Schutte 2002). As large numbers of women entered the paid workforce, as care needs have increased with the aging of the population globally, as pandemics such as AIDS and ebola eviscerated local populations of care workers, and as armed conflicts have resulted in widespread displacements and disruption, these policy failures have contributed to a global care deficit. With faltering economies and shredded safety nets at home, and with gendered expectations of who engages in care work firmly entrenched in countries around the globe, large numbers of women from economically stressed families, especially from the global south, are "pushed" to migrate to the Global North to provide for their loved ones. At the same time, the relatively generous social welfare system of Western Europe and the higher salaries in wealthy nations have exerted a "pull." Given the global care deficit, most of the available jobs entail doing care work, both in the domestic sphere and in the public sector. Ironically, the aspirational models for care in Western Europe that feminists and care theorists from the US extoll are often staffed by doctors, nurses, educators, and childcare workers hired from third world countries, a situation that exerts a greater strain on care resources in the poorer nations. (Ehrenreich and Arlie Hochschild 2002; Kittay 2008; Eckenwiler 2009; and Robinson 2011b). As migrant women leave their home countries for extended periods of time, they "pass on" their own care obligations, often to even poorer women with the result that, on a global scale, care work is typically done by the least advantaged. For feminist care theory, which is not only premised upon rendering care work visible and valuing/supporting it, but is also committed to ending systematic exploitation and oppression, such an outcome violates its core values.

The transfer of care from developing to developed countries becomes still more problematic when we consider how privileged women have appropriated the reproductive labor of third world women through the practices of global surrogacy (Parks 2010; Bailey 2011; Panitch 2013; Banerjee 2014) and, some might argue, international adoption. Viewed together, these practices ensure that first world women will be able to carry out the nurturant work associated with raising children and will receive the emotional and status enhancing benefits associated with this practice at the same time they outsource the non-nurturant aspects of care—domestic work, childbearing, and some aspects of childrearing. While privileged women have long relegated non-nurturant care work to less privileged women, the global scale of this transfer, the transfer of the task of reproduction itself, and the creation of what some have called a permanent servant class based on race, nationality, gender, and social class (Tronto 2013) bring this practice to a new and troubling low. The global sex trade and procurement of "mail order brides" are distinctive but related practices that likewise exploit the bodies of vulnerable women and children (Brennan 2002; Hankivsky 2011).

In the wake of such empirical considerations, care theorists have posed the following theoretical questions and asked if care ethics can address them: What is the nature of the moral harm that is inflicted by the practice of hiring immigrant women to do care work, especially when these women must leave their children behind? Is there a right to provide care for one's loved ones, and can a care ethics issue in rights as well as responsibilities (West 2002; Weir 2005; Engster 2007; Kittay 2009; Gheaus 2013)? Can a care ethics or a related "social-connection model" articulated by Iris Young (2011) address the responsibilities and duties we have to persons around the globe, particularly with regard to ensuring that the right to give and receive care is upheld? In particular, does the ethic of care give us a different way to think of the nature of harms suffered by women globally (such as genocide by rape) (Miller 2009)? As we draw this discussion to a close, it is noteworthy that we are deploying notions such as "rights" and "duties," language more readily associated with justice rather than care. When care is examined on a global scale, the interrelatedness of care and justice, noted earlier, becomes even more evident and the necessity of conceptualizing the two theories together becomes more urgent.

Care Ethics Provides an Alternative Moral
Approach to Global Concerns

Global care theorists have not only analyzed the breakdown of care relations on a global scale, they have also utilized the concepts of care ethics to propose new and innovative theoretical approaches and solutions to issues of global concern. Serene Khader (2011) argues that if care virtues, specifically those of loving attention, the transparent self, and narrative understanding, were used in the practice of international development, they would help correct the tendency of development practitioners to paternalistically (and often unconsciously) substitute their judgment for that of their intended beneficiaries. Daniel Levine (2010) argues that successful counter-insurgency efforts require use of the care virtues of attentiveness, restraint, and creativity to win over the "hearts and minds" of citizens alienated from their government and to re-establish relationships of trust.

Virginia Held (2008), Jess Kyle (2013), Sigal Ben Porath (2008), Joan Tronto (2007), and Fiona Robinson (1999, 2011a, and 2011b) explore what an ethic of care brings to international relations, specifically with regard to the ethics of military intervention. An emphasis on prevention versus intervention, on attending to the long-term relationships between countries and peoples, and on the responsibility to protect promises that a care-based approach to international relations would be dramatically different from the current one. For example, Fiona Robinson argues that a feminist care ethic cannot conceive of security solely in militaristic terms. She insists that "efforts to enhance human security must recognize the importance of relations and networks of responsibility and care in determining people's everyday experiences of security and insecurity" (2011a: 10). Human security is not only threatened by violent conflict, but also by environmental degradation, food insecurity, economic insecurity, tyrannical governments, and violation of religious rights. Each of these has contributed to the violent confrontations and refugee crises with which we are faced in the mid-2010s. Thus, we need a broader understanding of human security than military intervention if we are to have a caring system of international relations. Such an approach would give center stage to ensuring that people from around the globe can meet their responsibilities to care for themselves, their families, their communities, and the natural world around them. Such a world would be more caring, more just, and more secure than the one in which we currently live.

In this section we have suggested that as care "goes global" it proposes a new moral grounding on the basis of which we reprioritize and reorganize international policies, from migration, to development, to our approach to human security. Against this backdrop, the theoretical project noted previously, of drawing attention to similarities between the ethics of care and similar values in the Confucian tradition, Buddhism, and among some African philosophies, takes on added import. Namely, by demonstrating that care is not only a Western or a women's value but a fundamental human value already acknowledged by peoples around the globe, care theorists could help facilitate this larger practical project of international cooperation on fundamental issues of human well-being and security.

Conclusion

Care ethics has come a long way since its near-simultaneous inception in the work of Gilligan, Noddings, and Ruddick and has also come full circle in demonstrating how care ethics can illuminate our global connections and responsibilities that Ruddick first foresaw in trying to use maternal thinking for a peace politics.

Rather than being limited to an ethics of interpersonal relationships, care ethics has shown that it can help illuminate not only important moral dimensions of these relations but of domestic policies and international relations as well. Moreover, care ethics has made a major contribution to moral theory by introducing a new ethical vocabulary, bringing renewed moral attention to human relationships, and new moral attention to the role of dependency in human life. Along with the development of care ethics, there has been a resurgence of interest in virtue ethics, in friendship and interpersonal ethics, new approaches to autonomy (see Chapter 41 in this volume), explorations of the moral dimensions of dependency relations and the emergence of particularism in moral theory (Friedman 1993; Blum 1994; Little and Hooker 2000; MacIntyre 2001; Nussbaum 2007). Thus, care ethics has significantly influenced the field of ethics in developing an ethic of care, by acknowledging and developing the role of emotion and empathy in moral deliberation and action, as well as by calling attention to the partialist, particularist, and contextual features of our ethical life with both intimates and distant others.

Examination of care as labor, both within the US and internationally, has brought to the foreground of care ethics the intersectional and power analyses that were seen as missing by early feminist critics of the theory. At the same time, examination of the political, social, and economic context of care has laid the groundwork for a rethinking of the relationship between care and justice.

Related Topics

Personal identity and relational selves (Chapter 18); the genealogy and viability of the concept of intersectionality (Chapter 28); feminist and queer intersections with disability studies (Chapter 33); feminist approaches to autonomy (Chapter 41); Confucianism and care ethics (Chapter 44); neoliberalism, global justice, and transnational feminisms (Chapter 48).

References

Bailey, Alison (1995) "Mothering, Diversity, and Peace: Comments on Sara Ruddick's Feminist Maternal Peace Politics," *Journal of Social Philosophy* 25(1): 162–182.

—— (2011) "Reconceiving Surrogacy: Toward a Reproductive Justice Account of Indian Surrogacy," *Hypatia* 26(4): 715–741.

Banerjee, Amrita (2014) "Race and a Transnational Reproductive Caste System: Indian Transnational Surrogacy," *Hypatia* 29(1): 113–128.

Ben-Porath, Sigal (2008) "Care Ethics and Dependence: Rethinking Jus Post Bellum," *Hypatia* 23(2): 61–71.

Benhabib, Seyla (1992) "The Generalized and the Concrete Other," in *Situating the Self*, New York: Routledge, 148–177.

Blum, Lawrence (1994) *Moral Perception and Particularity*, New York: Cambridge University Press.

Brennan, Denise (2002) "Selling Sex for Visas: Sex Tourism as a Stepping-Stone to International Migration," in Barbara Ehrenreich and Arlie Russell Hochschild (Eds.) *Global Woman: Nannies, Maids, and Sex Workers in the New Economy*, New York: Metropolitan Books, 154–168.

Bubeck, Diemut (1995) *Care, Gender, and Justice*, New York: Oxford University Press.

Card, Claudia (1990) "Caring and Evil," *Hypatia* 5(1): 101–108.

Cheon, Byung-You (2010) "Problems of Long-term Care Worker for the Elderly and Search for Alternative Model and Policy Improvements in Korea," *Korea Social Policy Review* 17(3): 67–91 [In Korean].

Clement, Grace (1996) *Care, Autonomy, and Justice: Feminism and the Ethic of Care*, Boulder, CO: Westview Press.

Collins, Patricia (1990) *Black Feminist Thought*, New York: Routledge Press.

Craddock, Karen (2015) *Black Motherhoods: Contours, Contexts and Considerations*, Toronto, ON: Demeter Press.

Crary, Alice (2016) *Inside Ethics: On the Demands of Moral Thought*, Cambridge, MA: Harvard University Press.

Dalmiya, Vrinda (2016) *Caring to Know: Comparative Care Ethics, Feminist Epistemology and the Mahābhārata*, India: Oxford University Press.

Donovan, Josephine and Adams, Carol (2000) *Beyond Animal Rights: A Feminist Caring Ethic for the Treatment of Animals*, New York: Continuum Press.

——(2007) *The Feminist Care Tradition in Animal Ethics*, New York: Columbia University Press.

Duffy, Mignon (2005) "Reproducing Labor Inequalities: Challenges for Feminists Conceptualizing Care at the Intersections of Gender, Race, and Class," *Gender and Society* 19(1): 66–82.

——(2007) "Doing the Dirty Work: Gender, Race and Reproductive Labor in Historical Perspective," *Gender and Society* 21(3): 316–319.

——(2011) *Making Care Count: A Century of Gender, Race, and Paid Care Work*, Piscataway, NJ: Rutgers University Press.

Eckenwiler, Lisa (2009) "Care Worker Migration and Transnational Justice," *Journal of Public Health Ethics* 2(2): 171–183.

Eckenwiler, Julie and Meghani, Zahra (2009) "Care for the Caregivers: Transnational Justice and Undocumented Non-Citizen Care Workers," *International Journal of Feminist Approaches to Bioethics* 2(1): 77–101.

Ehrenreich, Barbara and Hochschild, Arlie (Eds.) (2002) *Global Woman: Nannies, Maids, and Sex Workers in the New Economy*, New York: Harry Holt & Co.

Engster, Daniel (2007) *The Heart of Justice: Care Ethics and Political Theory*, New York: Oxford University Press.

——(2015) "Care in the State of Nature: The Biological and Evolutionary Roots of the Disposition to Care in Human Beings," in Daniel Engster and Maurice Hamington (Eds.) *Care Ethics and Political Theory*, Oxford: Oxford University Press, 227–251.

Fisher, Berenice and Tronto, Joan (1991) "Toward a Feminist Theory of Care," in Emily Abel and Margaret Nelson (Eds.) *Circles of Care: Work and Identity in Women's Lives*, Albany, NY: SUNY Press.

Folbre, Nancy (2002) *The Invisible Heart: Economics and Family Values*, New York: The New Press.

——(2012) *For Love and Money: Care Provision in the United States*, New York: Russell Sage Foundation.

Friedman, Marilyn (1991) "The Social Self and the Partiality Debates," in Claudia Card (Ed.) *Feminist Ethics*, Wichita, KS: University of Kansas Press, 161–179.

——(1993) *What Are Friends for? Feminist Perspectives on Personal Relationships and Moral Theory*, New York: Cornell University Press.

Gheaus, Anca (2013) "Care Drain: Who Should Provide for the Children Left Behind?" *Critical Review of International Social and Political Philosophy* 16(1): 1–23.

Gilligan, Carol (1982) *In a Different Voice*, Cambridge, MA: Harvard University Press.

——(1987) "Moral Orientation and Moral Development," in Eva Kittay and Diana Meyers (Eds.) *Women and Moral Theory*, New York: Rowman & Littlefield, 19–23.

Gouws, Amanda and van Zyl, Mikki (2015) "Towards a Feminist Ethics of *Ubuntu*: Bridging Rights and *Ubuntu*," in Daniel Engster and Maurice Hamington (Eds.) *Care Ethics and Political Theory*, New York: Oxford University Press, 165–186.

Gruen, Lori (2011) *Ethics and Animals*, New York: Cambridge University Press.

Habermas, Jürgen (1993) *Justification and Application: Remarks on Discourse Ethics*, trans. Ciaran P. Cronin, Cambridge, MA: MIT Press.

Hamington, Maurice and Miller, Dorothy C. (Eds.) (2006) *Socializing Care: Feminist Ethics and Public Issues*, Lanham, MD: Rowman & Littlefield.

Hamington, Maurice and Engster, Daniel (Eds.) (2015) *Care Ethics and Political Theory*, New York: Oxford University Press.

Hankivsky, Olena (2011) "The Dark Side of Care: The Push Factors of Human Trafficking," in Riane Mahon and Fiona Robinson (Eds.) *Feminist Ethics and Social Policy: Towards a New Global Political Economy of Care*, Vancouver: University of British Columbia Press, 145–161.

——(2014) "Rethinking Care Ethics: On the Promise and Potential of an Intersectional Analysis," *American Political Science Association*: 1–13.

Harding, Sandra (1987) "The Curious Coincidence of Feminine and African Moralities: Challenges for Feminist Theory," in Eva Feder Kittay and Diana T. Meyers (Eds.) *Women and Moral Theory*, New York: Rowman & Littlefield, 296–315.

Held, Virginia (1995) *Justice and Care: Essential Readings in Feminist Ethics*, Boulder, CO: Westview Press.

——(2003) *Feminist Morality*, Chicago, IL: University of Chicago Press.

——(2007) *The Ethics of Care: Personal, Political, Global*, New York: Oxford University Press.

——(2008) "Military Intervention and the Ethics of Care," *Southern Journal of Philosophy* 46: 1–20.

Hoagland, Sarah Lucia (1989) *Lesbian Ethics: Toward New Values*, Palo Alto, CA: Institute of Lesbian Studies.

—— (1991) "Some Thoughts about 'Caring,'" in Claudia Card (Ed.) *Feminist Ethics*, Lawrence, KS: University of Kansas Press, 78–104.

Houston, Barbara (1989) "Prolegomena to Future Caring," in Mary Brabeck (Ed.) *Who Cares? Theory, Research, and Educational Implications of the Ethic of Care*, Westport, CN: Praeger Press, 90–91.

——(1990) "Caring and Exploitation," *Hypatia* 5(1): 115–119.

Hrdy, Sarah Blaffer (1999) *Mother Nature: Maternal Instincts and How They Shape the Human Species*, New York: Ballantine Books.

Kant, Immanuel (1981) *Grounding for a Metaphysics of Morals*, trans. James W. Ellington, Indianapolis, IN: Hackett.

Keller, Jean (1997) "Autonomy, Relationality, and Feminist Ethics," *Hypatia* 12(2): 152–164.

Khader, Serene (2011) "Beyond Inadvertent Ventriloquism: Caring Virtues for Anti-Paternalist Development Practice," *Hypatia* 26(4): 742–761.

Kim, Hee-Kang and Kang, Moon Sun (2010) "A Public Ethics of Care: Eva Kittay and the 'Care Aid Program to Families with Disabled Children' in South Korea," *Korean Political Science Review* 44(4): 45–72 [In Korean].

Kittay, Eva (1999) *Love's Labor: Essays on Women, Equality, and Dependency*, New York: Routledge Press.

——(2005) "Dependency, Difference and the Global Ethic of Longterm Care," *Journal of Political Philosophy* 13(4): 443–469.

—— (2008) "The Global Heart Transplant and Caring Across National Boundaries," *Southern Journal of Philosophy* 46: 138–165.

——(2009) "The Moral Harm of Migrant Care Work: Realizing a Global Right to Care," *Philosophical Topics* 37(2): 53–73.

——(2011) "The Ethics of Care, Dependence and Disability," *Ratio Juris* 24(1): 49–58.

——(2012) "Getting from Here to There: Claiming Justice for People with Severe Cognitive Disabilities," in Rosamund Rhodes, Margaret Battin, and Anita Silvers (Eds.) *Medicine and Social Justice: Essays on the Distribution of Health Care*, 2nd ed., New York: Oxford University Press, 313–324.

——(2014) "The Completion of Care—with Implications for a Duty to Receive Care Graciously," in Ana Marta Gonzalez and Craig Iffman (Eds.) *Care Professionals and Globalization: Theoretical and Practical Perspectives*, New York: Palgrave MacMillan Press, 33–42.

Kittay, Eva and Meyers, Diana (Eds.) (1987) *Women and Moral Theory*, New York: Rowman & Littlefield.

Kyle, Jess (2013) "Protecting the World: Military Humanitarian Intervention and the Ethics of Care," *Hypatia* 28(2): 257–273.

Levine, Daniel (2010) "Care and Counterinsurgency," *Journal of Military Ethics* 9(2): 139–159.

Lindemann, Hilde, Verkerk, Marian, and Walker, Margaret Urban (2008) *Naturalized Bioethics: Toward Responsible Knowing and Practice*, New York: Cambridge University Press.

Little, Margaret and Hooker, Brad (Eds.) (2000) *Moral Particularism*, Oxford: Clarendon Press.

Lugones, Maria (2003[1991]) "On the Logic of Pluralist Feminism," in *Pilgrimages/Peregrinajes: Theorizing Coalition against Multiple Oppressions*, New York: Rowman & Littlefield, 65–76.

MacIntyre, Alisdair (2001) *Dependent Rational Animals: Why Human Beings Need the Virtues*, Peru, IL: Carus.

Miller, Sarah Clark (2005) "A Kantian Ethic of Care?" In Barbara Andrew, Jean Keller, and Lisa H. Schwartzman (Eds.) *Feminist Interventions in Ethics and Politics*, New York: Rowman & Littlefield, 111–130.

—— (2006) "The Global Duty to Care and the Politics of Peace," *International Studies in Philosophy* 38(2): 107–121.

—— (2009) "Moral Injury and Relational Harm: Analyzing Rape in Darfur," *Journal of Social Philosophy* 40(4): 504–523.

—— (2011) "A Feminist Account of Global Responsibility," *Social Theory and Practice* 37(3): 391–412.

Moody Adams, Michelle (1991) "Gender and the Complexity of Moral Voices," in Claudia Card (Ed.) *Feminist Ethics*, Lawrence, KS: University of Kansas Press, 195–212.

Moosa, C. Shaheen (2015) "Causation, Connection, and Care: Three Ways of Understanding Responsibility for Climate Change," presented paper, *Feminist Ethics and Social Theory*, Clearwater Beach, Florida.

Nakano Glenn, Evelyn (2012) *Forced to Care: Coercion and Caregiving in America*, Cambridge, MA: Harvard University Press.

Narayan, Uma (1995) "Colonialism and Its Others: Considerations on Rights and Care Discourses," *Hypatia* 10(2): 133–140.

Nicholson, Linda (1993) "Women, Morality, and History" in Mary Jeanne Larrabee (Ed.) *An Ethic of Care: Feminist and Interdisciplinary Perspectives*, New York: Routledge Press, 87–101.

Noddings, Nel (1986) *Caring: A Feminine Approach to Ethics*, Berkeley, CA: University of California Press.

—— (2002) *Starting at Home: Caring and Social Policy*, Berkeley, CA: University of California Press.

—— (2005) *The Challenge to Care in Schools*, New York: Teacher's College, Columbia University.

Nussbaum, Martha (2001) *Upheavals of Thought: The Intelligence of Emotions*, New York: Cambridge University Press.

—— (2007) *Frontiers of Justice, Disability, Nationality, Species Membership*, Cambridge, MA: Harvard University Press.

Panitch, Vida (2013) "Global Surrogacy: Exploitation to Empowerment," *Journal of Global Ethics* 9(3): 329–343.

Parks, Jennifer (2010) "Care Ethics and the Global Practice of Commercial Surrogacy," *Bioethics* 24(7): 330–340.

Roberts, Dorothy (1997) "Spiritual and Menial Housework," *Yale Journal of Law and Feminism* 9(51): 51–80.

Robinson, Fiona (1999) *Globalizing Care: Ethics, Feminist Theory, and International Relations*, New York: Westview Press.

—— (2011a) *The Ethics of Care: A Feminist Approach to Human Security*, Philadelphia, PA: Temple University Press.

—— (2011b) "Towards a Transnational Analysis of the Political Economy of Care," in Rianne Mahon and Fiona Robinson (Eds.) *Feminist Ethics and Social Policy: Towards a New Global Political Economy of Care*, Vancouver, BC: The University of British Columbia Press.

Rogers, Chrissie (2016) *Intellectual Disability and Being Human: A Care Ethics Model*, New York: Routledge Press.

Rorty, Amelie Oksenberg (1980) *Explaining Emotions*, Berkeley, CA: University of California Press.

Ruddick, Sara (1980) "Maternal Thinking," *Feminist Studies* 1: 342–367.

—— (1989) *Maternal Thinking*, Boston, MA: Beacon Press.

Scaltsas, Patricia Ward (1992) "Do Feminist Ethics Counter Feminist Aims?" in Eve Browning Cole and Susan Coultrap-McQuin (Eds.) *Explorations in Feminist Ethics*, Bloomington, IN: Indiana University Press, 15–26.

Schutte, Ofelia (2002) "Dependency Work, Women, and the Global Economy" in Eva Kittay and Ellen Feder (Eds.) *The Subject of Care*, Lanham, MD: Rowman & Littlefield, 138–158.

554

Sevenhuijsen, Selma (1998) *Citizenship and the Ethics of Care: Feminist Considerations on Justice Morality and Politics*, New York: Routledge.

Sherwin, Susan (1989) "Feminist and Medical Ethics: Two Different Approaches to Contextual Ethics," *Hypatia* 4(2): 57–72.

——(1992) *No Longer Patient: Feminist Ethics and Health Care*, Philadelphia, PA: Temple University Press.

Slote, Michael (2001) *Morals from Motives*, New York: Oxford University Press.

——(2007) *The Ethics of Care and Empathy*, New York: Routledge Press.

——(2010) *Moral Sentimentalism*, Oxford: Oxford University Press.

Stack, Carol B (1986) "The Culture of Gender: Women and Men of Color," *Signs* 11(2): 321–324.

Story, Kaila Adia (2014) *Patricia Hill Collins: Reconceiving Motherhood*, Toronto, ON: Demeter Press.

Tong, Rosemarie (1993) *Feminine and Feminist Ethics*, Belmont, CA: Wadsworth.

Townes, Emily (1998) *Breaking the Fine Rain of Death*, Eugene, OR: Wipf & Stock.

Tronto, Joan (1993) *Moral Boundaries: A Political Argument for an Ethic of Care*, New York: Routledge.

——(2007) "Is Peace Keeping Care Work?" in Rebecca Whisnant ad Peggy DesAutels (Eds.) *Feminist Global Ethics: Feminist Ethics and Social Theory*, Lanham, MD: Rowman & Littlefield, 179–200.

——(2013) *Caring Democracy: Markets, Equality, and Justice*, New York: New York University Press.

Walker, Margaret Urban (1998) *Moral Understandings: A Feminist Study in Ethics*, New York: Routledge Press.

Weir, Allison (2005) "The Global Universal Caregiver: Imagining Women's Liberation in the New Millennium," *Constellations: An International Journal of Critical and Democratic Theory* 12(3): 308–330.

West, Robin (2002) "The Right to Care," in Eva Kittay and Ellen Feder (Eds.) *The Subject of Care*, Lanham, MD: Rowman & Littlefield, 88–114.

Williams, Bernard (1973) *Problems of the Self*, New York: Cambridge University Press.

Young, Iris (2011) "A Social Connection Model," in *Responsibility for Justice*, New York: Oxford University Press, 95–122.

44

CONFUCIANISM AND CARE ETHICS

Sin Yee Chan

As a critical response to the prevailing ethical theories of Utilitarianism and Kantianism that emphasize individual judgment, rational thinking, and reliance on impartial, universalistic and general principles, care ethics breaks significant new ground. Drawing heavily from women's experience of caring for dependents, care ethics focuses on relations, contextual thinking, emotions, partiality, and particularity. Interestingly, Confucianism, developed more than two centuries ago, shares many of these foci. Consequently, many scholars consider Confucianism a kind of care ethics. In what follows, I shall first explain briefly the main ideas of Confucianism and care ethics, provide an overview of the debate of whether Confucianism is a kind of care ethics, and reflect on one major question raised from the debate, namely what constitutes a generic account of care ethics. Finally, I suggest that Confucian scholars and care ethicists should collaborate, especially on the issue of how to extend from partial caring (caring for close relations) to general caring (caring for people outside one's close circle). In explaining Confucianism, I shall reference to the Confucian canons the *Analects*, the *Mencius*, the *Xunzi* and the *Liji* (*Book of Rites*). I shall rely mostly on Noddings's account when outlining care ethics.

Confucianism

The cardinal concept in Confucianism is *ren* (仁)which is often translated as love, goodness, benevolence, or humaneness. The Chinese character of "*ren*" is a combination of the two characters, "person" (人) and "two" (二). *Ren* pertains to human relatedness (Tu 1985), especially about their embedment in relationships. In the *Analects*, the term has two meanings (Shun 1993). The first refers to a perfect virtue that includes various specific virtues such as loyalty, purity, diligence, wisdom, respectfulness, courage, etc. (*Analects* 4: 15, 5: 18, 7: 24, 12: 1, 20, 13: 4, 19, 14: 5, 12, 17: 6). The second refers to love or benevolence and includes both familial sentiments and general benevolent sentiments towards anyone in the world. A *junzi* (gentleman) is someone who is committed to moral cultivation to acquire the virtue of *ren* and has attained a certain level of accomplishment in doing so. Since *ren* includes benevolence/love, which implies a motivation to benefit others for their own sake, personal moral cultivation is connected to worldly obligations. The ideal of "inner sage, outer king" ascribes to a *junzi* the moral obligation to bring benefits and peace to the world through political participation, either as a ruler or as an official, unless political participation involves immorality due to a corrupted government.

Let us examine the meaning of *ren* as love/benevolence more closely. The text clearly connects *ren* to love/benevolence: "The man of *ren* loves people" (*Analects* 12: 22),

> Zigong asked, "If a person can shower benefits widely among people, and provide relief to them, will you call him a person of *ren*?" Confucius replied, "It would no longer be a matter of *ren*. He would no doubt be a sage."
>
> (*Analects* 6: 30)

The above passages relate *ren* to loving people in general and bringing benefit to them. In addition, *ren* is constituted by familial sentiments: "Loving one's parents is *ren*," (*Mencius* 7A: 15) "The way of (the sages) Yao and Shun is simply to be filial to one's parents and respectful to one's elder brother" (*Mencius* 6B: 2). Moreover, familial sentiments such as loving one's father and elder brother are seen as innate (*Mencius* 7A: 15). These two meanings of *ren*—as familial love and as general benevolence—are not isolated from each other. Familial love is fundamental to, as well as instrumental in developing general benevolence: "Youzi said, 'few of those who are filial sons and respectful brothers will show disrespect to superiors . . . Filial piety and brotherly respect are the root of *ren*'" (*Analects* 1: 2),

> Treat the aged of your own family in a manner befitting their venerable age and extend the treatment to the aged of other families; treat your own young in a manner befitting their tender age and extend this to the young of other families.
>
> (*Mencius* 1A: 7)

In this way, the family is viewed as an essential training ground for both familial and general love. *Ren* is not merely about sentiments; it also requires altruistic actions: "The actuality of *ren* is the serving of one's parents" (*Mencius* 4A: 27), showering benefits widely among people is also *ren* (*Analects* 6: 30).

Ren is also seen as stemming from innate compassion besides the familial sentiments. The innateness of compassion is presumably illustrated in the following famous anecdote:

> Suppose a man were, all of a sudden, to see a young child on the verge of falling into a well. He would certainly be moved to compassion, not because he wanted to get in the good graces of the parents . . . The mind of compassion is the germ of *ren*.
>
> (*Mencius* 2A: 6)

Compassion serves as the basis of a government of *ren*—a compassionate government (*Mencius* 1A: 7). The role of compassion and love in *ren* underpins the importance of emotions in Confucian ethics.

Since familial sentiments constitute the core of *ren*, Confucian social order consists in a nexus of personal relationships modeling after the family. It is epitomized by the Five Relationships: ruler–minister, father–son, older–younger brother, husband–wife, friend–friend relationships. In this social order, each person is an occupant of various relationship roles and incurs the related role duties. For example,

What makes a person a father? I reply: To be generous, kind, and to possess ritual principles . . . What makes a person a wife? I reply: if the husband possesses ritual principles, then meekly follow after him and docilely attend him; if he lacks them, then be fearful, anxious, and apprehensive about herself.

(Xunzi 12: 3)

All of these relationships are governed by reciprocity and, with the exception of friends, are hierarchical. For example, father and son are urged to reciprocate love (*Mencius* 7B: 24) and rulers and ministers respect. (*Mencius* 2B: 2). Thus Confucianism can be understood as a kind of relationship-role ethics (Chan 2000b; Ames 2011). One implication of taking family as the microcosm of the social/political order is that the private (domestic) and the public (social/political) are not sharply divided and familial virtues presumably can be applicable in the public sphere as well: filial piety towards parents can be extended to serve the ruler.

In addition to familial sentiments and compassion, following *li* (禮 rites) is another important way to develop the virtue of *ren*. *Li*, which originally refers to ritual rules but then expands to include rules of varied nature such moral, conventional, religious, ceremonial and etiquette rules. To support one's parents, to mourn in accordance with certain rites, to bow before ascending to a hall, all are examples of rules of *li*. *Li* is seen by Confucius as the expression of *ren*: "What can a man do with *li* who does not have *ren*?" (*Analects* 3: 3). Following *li* presumably makes one act in a civil, refined and aesthetically pleasing manner. More importantly, following *li* helps one acquire *ren* and brings about social harmony: "To return to the observance of *li* through overcoming the self constitutes *ren*" (*Analects* 12: 1); "Of the things brought about by *li*, harmony is the most valuable" (*Analects* 1: 12). *Li*, however, is not normative principles or standards like utilitarianism or the Categorical Imperatives that define morally rightness and presume universal applicability. *Li* pertains to specific rules of conduct. Exceptions to and changes in *li* are often allowed to ensure adaptation to particular circumstances and changing times (*Analects* 9: 3) in order to attain social harmony. Above all, it is *ren* rather than strict rule-following that enables one to make the most sagacious responses to a situation: "A gentleman needs not keep his word nor does he necessarily see his action through to the end. He aims only at what is right" (*Mencius* 4B: 11). Confucius claims, "I have no preconceptions about the permissible and the impermissible" (*Analects* 18: 8). Besides practicing *li*, learning, thinking, music, and dancing also contribute to develop *ren*. When one has *ren* and follows *li*, often one does what is morally proper or *yi* (義 moral rightness).

Care Ethics

In *In a Different Voice* (Gilligan 1982), Carol Gilligan argues that women have "a different voice" in ethical thinking, which she calls the "care perspective." This perspective emphasizes responsibility, relationships, interconnectedness, response, contextual judgments, and using emotions and intuitions. The care perspective is juxtaposed against the traditional "justice perspective" often embraced by men. This latter perspective assumes independent, autonomous agency, and approaches ethical problems by rational application of impartial, general and universal principles.

Nel Noddings in her groundbreaking work, *Caring: A Feminine Approach to Ethics and Moral Education* (Noddings 2003 [1984]) develops a comprehensive and distinct ethical perspective and eschews the justice perspective altogether. And since her account is the one most referenced by philosophers comparing Confucianism and care ethics I shall focus on her account when expounding care ethics below.

This new ethical vision articulated by Noddings comprises several elements. First, it assumes a relational ontology: "Relations, not individuals, are ontologically basic" (Noddings 2003 [1984]: xiii). Humans are born into relationships, and they depend on relationships for their survival as infants and flourishing as adults. Of special importance are close personal relationships, with the mother–child as the paradigm of relationship.

Second, this new ethics revolves around caring rather than morally right action. Caring refers to many things. It is a form of relationship: "caring is a relationship that contains another." It is also an activity or practice that often takes place in the context of close personal relationships. It can also be an attitude and a motive con-stituting a virtue (Noddings 2003 [1984]). A caring relationship includes the caring person/the one-caring (who gives caring) and the cared-for (who receives caring). There are three components of caring: (1) engrossment (which she changes to recep-tive attention and then attention in her later works); (2) motivational displacement, on the part of the caring person; and (3) reception or reciprocity on the part of the cared-for (Noddings 2003 [1984]: 69). To be engrossed is to be in a receptive state: "I receive the other into myself, and I see and feel with the other. I become duality" (Noddings 2003 [1984]: 30). "Apprehending the other's reality, feeling what he feels as nearly as possible" (Noddings 2003 [1984]: 16). Engrossment requires abstaining from evaluation of the cared-for. Motivational displacement means rendering the caring person's motivational energy and resources at the service of the cared-for and adopting his/her goal as the caring person's goal (Noddings 2003 [1984]: 17). To reciprocate, the cared-for responds, for example, in the form of being happy, or sharing his/her aspirations and worries, or vigorously pursuing his/her own projects (Noddings 2003 [1984]:72). More basically, merely receiving the caring is counted as reciprocity. Reciprocity completes the caring.

The third element of the ethical vision is valuing particularity and rejecting any appeal to impartial, general, and universal principles. Valuing particularity means appreciating a relationship and persons in a relationship as unique and irreplace-able and the embedding situation of an action as concrete and particular. "To act as one-caring, then, is to act with special regard for the particular person in a concrete situation." Rules and principles are only held "loosely, tentatively, as economies of a sort" (Noddings 2003 [1984]: 24, 55). Appreciation of particularity calls forth contextual judgment, use of emotions, intuitions and engrossment.

In addition to particularistic caring within relationships, which Noddings calls natural caring, we also need to develop an ethical ideal of caring to ensure our car-ing about people outside our close circles from whom we cannot receive reciprocity. To Noddings, natural caring has ethical priority because it is the root and the goal of the ethical ideal of caring.

Other philosophers continue to develop versions of care ethics, distinct from those of Noddings and Gilligan, and extending it to social, political, and global contexts, and out of the sphere of intimate family relationships on which Noddings focuses (Tronto 1993; Kittay 2001; Slote 2001; Held 2006). It should also be noted that most of the later versions are feminist, i.e. stressing more the identification as well as the elimina-tion of the injustice associated with caring work assigned to women, as contrasted to the feminine approach of Gilligan and Noddings who focus on articulately a distinctive perspective of women. Nonetheless, for purposes of comparison with Confucianism I shall continue to focus on Noddings's version.

Is Confucianism a Kind of Care Ethics?

Confucianism shares significant commonalities with care ethics. Both accounts assign utmost ethical importance to some kind of affective concern for others—caring or love/benevolence. Both consider close personal relationships as the optimal context in which this kind of concern is nurtured and expressed. Engagement in close personal relationships are also seen as instrumental to the development of an ethical ideal that requires partiality towards one's close relationships as well as general caring for people not related to oneself. In addition, both assume a relational ontology and conceive of close personal relationships as the primary form in which humans relate to each other.

Thus it is not surprising that scholarship relating Confucianism to care ethics in the past two decades has evolved around the question of whether Confucianism is a kind of care ethics. Chenyang Li initiated this dialogue by arguing that Confucianism can be seen as a kind of care-ethics (Li 1994) because (1) the Confucian ethical ideal, *ren*, is about love; (2) Confucian ethics, like care ethics, is not based on general, universal principles; and (3) Confucianism values close personal relationships and allows partiality.

Julia Tao describes Confucianism as Confucian care ethics because of its basic orientation towards caring. Yet she also observes important differences between Confucianism and care ethics (Tao 2000). Tao points out that care ethics resists impartial ethical reasoning, i.e. reasoning done from an impartial perspective, which treats everyone alike and does not accord anyone more or less ethical consideration, regardless of the person's relationship to the agent. In contrast, even though Confucianism does not discuss the issue, one could imagine it accepting principles endorsed from an impartial perspective (Chan 1993: 69). For example, particularistic principles such as "To care for one's family more than a stranger" or impartial principles like "Everyone should be treated equally before the law." Tao believes that a Confucian agent is indeed required to develop both particularistic and impartial perspectives, though the two perspectives may sometimes generate conflicting duties.

Another difference noted by Tao concerns virtue. *Ren* is a virtue and Confucianism can be seen as a form of virtue ethics (Sim 2015). Noddings, however, is skeptical of virtue ethics and rejects understanding caring as a virtue (Noddings 2003 [1984]: 96) though she sometimes does describe caring as a virtue (Noddings 2003 [1984]: xiii).

Concurring that Confucianism is a care ethics, Ann Pang notes a further similarity between Confucianism and care ethics in that neither postulates a sharp division between the private and the public, and both use domestic relationship as a model for relationship in the public sphere (Pang-White 2011).

There are dissenters. One type of opposition is based on noting the close connection between care ethics and gender. Gilligan's "In a Different Voice" is often seen as marking a distinct voice of women in ethical reasoning. The word "feminine" occurs in the title of Noddings's groundbreaking book. By now, care ethics is generally accepted as a feminist ethics. Bundling Confucianism with the feminine or feminism, however, is seen by some as too restrictive: *ren* applies to both genders. For example, Karyn Lai objects, "the Confucian notion of interdependence of relationship reaches beyond the confines of gender-determined construction of relationality and ethics" (Lai 2013: 128). Lijun Yuan argues that since the Confucian texts contain so many sexist assumptions and claims, Confucianism is not feminist ethics (Yuan 2002).

Another set of objections focus on the issue of particularity. Ranjoo Seodu Herr observes that Noddings's engrossment enables the capturing of the particularity of the cared-for as it eradicates the emotional boundaries separating the caring person and the cared-for. Engrossment, however, is impossible in Confucianism. Confucianism requires people in relationships to follow *li* in their interaction. The attitude of respect embodied in *li*, however, emphasizes vigilance about one's duties and deferential distance from others. In this way, respect checks one's spontaneous emotional expression and prohibits engrossment (Herr 2012). This concern about particularity is shared by Daniel Star. Star worries that cardinal relationship roles in Confucianism such as mother, husband, friend are "communally based categories, through which others are approached primarily (although not necessarily only) via general types, rather than as unique concrete individuals" (Star 2002: 90). Particularity is lost when one is perceived merely as an instance of a general category. Star concludes that Confucianism is "a care-originating or care-interested virtue ethics," but not a care ethics (2002: 86).

Some care ethicists raise similar concerns. Believing that Confucianism emphasizes too much on rules and prioritizes the development of virtues over relationship caring, Noddings objects to seeing Confucianism as a care ethics (Noddings 2010: 137–138). Held judges that the inclusion of a non-feminist version of relational ethics such as Confucianism into care ethics is to "unduly disregard the history of how this ethics has developed and come to be a candidate for serious consideration among contemporary moral theory" (Held 2006: 22).

Beyond the Question of Whether Confucianism Is a Care Ethics

The discussions outlined above certainly shed interesting and helpful light on the question of whether Confucianism is a care ethics. To strive for a definitive answer at this point, however, seems futile. Given that Confucianism was developed more than two centuries earlier than care ethics, and hence there are drastic differences between the two accounts with respect to their embedding ways of life and their social, cultural, political, and economic backgrounds, it is obvious that the two are not exact counterparts. A straightforward approach to map Confucianism onto the account of care ethics developed by Noddings and others might yield the answer that Confucianism is not a care ethics. But to do so is like rejecting Confucianism as a virtue ethics merely because it differs from Aristotle's account of virtue ethics. This does not make sense! The straightforward approach is ill-advised also because it treats the account of care ethics put forward by Noddings and others—a young, evolving moral theory—as a well-established, paradigmatic account to which other theories need to conform. To do so seems chauvinistic, not paying due respect to other kindred theories. It also thwarts the various potential ways in which this young account of care ethics can usefully develop. Whether the decision concerning what constitutes a generic account of care ethics is a political—in the sense that it is about who has the power to decide (Li 2015), or a philosophical matter, it seems premature at this point to claim that we already have a yardstick to determine which care-based account is a care ethics and which is not. (For clarity's sake, I shall henceforth call the account developed by Noddings and others as Care Ethics without implying that it is the paradigmatic or generic account of care ethics.)

To continue to explore and contest the nature of Care Ethics so as to arrive at a generic account of care ethics therefore is imperative. The Confucianism-Care Ethics discussions outlined above are extremely useful in this regard as they highlight certain "core elements" based on which Confucianism is rejected as a care ethics. These elements include the priority of relationships over virtues, particularity, and the tie to gender. Should they be the core elements of a generic account of care ethics?

Let us look at the priority of relationship first. Whether Care Ethics should be incorporated under virtue ethics is much debated among care ethicists. Raja Halwani (2003) and Michael Slote (2001), for example, believe that doing so will make Care Ethics become a comprehensive theory and help it address criticisms such as its neglect of our responsibility for people not closely related to us (Card 1990), and of the interests and integrity of the caring person (Davion 1993). Virtue ethics can help because it requires the cultivation of virtues besides caring such as justice, wisdom, etc., which enable a caring person to critically evaluate her caring. Held (2006) responds that Care Ethics can also attend to these other virtues as they contribute to the success of caring.

More important, however, is the worry, shared by Noddings, Held, and others, that virtue ethics misses out a distinctive insight of Care Ethics—ethics is about relationships. "It is the relatedness of human beings, built and rebuilt, that the ethics of care is being developed to try to understand, evaluate, and guide" (Held 2006: 30). Noddings similarly emphasizes caring as a relationship (2003 [1984]: xiii). Held criticizes virtue ethics for assuming an individualistic perspective because it often takes caring as benevolence. Benevolence is problematic because it is an altruistic attitude. Since an altruistic act is done by one person for the sake of a separate person, an altruistic attitude assumes a "radical separation between self and others" (Blum 1994: 195). In contrast, "to be concerned for a friend . . . is to reach out not to someone or something wholly other than oneself but to what shares a part of one's own self and is implicated in one's sense of one's own identity" (Blum 1994: 195). The interests of people in relationships are inevitably and deeply interconnected.

Furthermore, like Noddings (2003 [1984]: xiii), Held believes that virtue ethics assumes an individualistic perspective because of its focus on the dispositions of an individual rather than relationships. Virtue ethics does not prioritize or require participation in caring relations, the cultivation of mutuality in the contexts of interdependencies or evaluations of relations between persons (Held 2006: 52). Consequently, virtue ethics may help to nurture effective caring agents but not good, fulfilling relationships (Held 2006: 53). Besides Held, Sara Ruddick also emphasizes relationship in caring. She comments, "Caring labor is intrinsically relational. The work is constituted in and through the relation of those who give and receive care" (Ruddick 1998: 13–14).

Does virtue ethics fail to capture the priority of relationship? We do not need to settle the issue here, but some points are worth pondering. If virtue ethics cares about a flourishing life and a flourishing life must include having deep, affectionate, and close personal relationships, as care ethicists so firmly insist, why would virtue ethics ignore them? As a matter of fact, both Aristotle's and Confucius's account require cultivation of relationships: Aristotle values friendship and takes relationship among citizens as basing on friendship like sentiments; Confucianism can be understood as a relationship-role ethics. And both discuss and provide normative guides on how to sustain good relationships, hence promoting mutuality and interconnectedness.

And focusing on the dispositions of an agent need not assume an individualistic framework, if the dispositions are about caring and engaging in personal relationships. Above all, if focusing on disposition is problematic, it would mean that Care Ethics can never render a developmental account of caring agency. And that will be a serious weakness for caring to be a workable practice! Or does priority of relationship mean that caring is confined to relationship caring as Ruddick's comment seem to suggest? Since virtue ethics allows caring to go beyond relationship it fails to capture the priority of relationship? This cannot be right, however, because even Noddings allows for caring for anonymous strangers.

The second element we should examine is particularity. Particularity in Care Ethics involves seeing a situation as unique and perceiving a person as irreplaceable and having distinctive traits and preferences. Particularity of situations calls forth the use of contextual judgments and does not invoke much dispute (especially if it is seen as accepting general rule following as expedient measures). Particularity of individual persons, on the other hand, is more controversial. Diemut Elisabet Bubeck (1995) puts meeting needs ahead of particularity. She worries that requiring particularity would limit caring only to close personal relationships and disallow us to care for others who may have strong and urgent needs. In reply, many care ethicists agree with Noddings's prioritization of personal relationships though they also advocate extending particularistic caring attitude to the public settings.

Whether particularistic caring is viable in non-personal settings, however, is dubitable. Absent the support of strong emotional attachments and sustained interactions inherent in close personal relationships, it requires tremendous conscious efforts and determination to capture the particularity of a stranger, if it can ever be done. Even if the practice is feasible, it remains unclear whether public/social policy should require such practice. Take the example of healthcare. It will be ideal if each patient's particular needs are met in a way that is attuned to her personality and circumstances. Such quality care, however, must be prohibitively expensive. A more caring goal is to provide basic, generic, but affordable, healthcare to more people who would otherwise be in poor or even inhumane conditions. It is more realistic to accept that relations are inevitably more "extended and thinner" in the public settings and that "considerations of care will not deal well with all issues" (Held 2006: 136). Shouldn't Care Ethics allow some form of impersonal ethics?

Particularity in the context of close personal relationships is also problematic. For it is an unambiguous expression of individualism. It is ironic that many care ethicists who so vehemently argue against, rightly or wrongly, liberalism's stark individualism and blindness to the relational nature of humans are themselves unconscious subscribers to individualism. Admittedly, for (good) close personal relationships anywhere, there must be some degree of recognition between the individuals of each other's personal traits, specific emotional contours, particular dreams and aversions. Each must also value the other as a distinct and irreplaceable person. One does not love and will not feel loved if particularistic recognition, given or taken, is totally absent. However, it is another question whether this kind of particularity is constantly sought, emphasized, and celebrated in close personal relationships globally, especially for societies that are more communitarian or collectivistic oriented. Yet it would be arrogant, unfair and mistaken to judge personal relationships in those societies as less fulfilling, deep or valuable. Focusing on the connectedness between herself as a mother and her child as a daughter, and seeing both as part of a cherished family, a Chinese woman, for example, can be appreciated and loved dearly as a wonderful mother by her children. Her identity can be constituted by her relationships with her children to an equal, if not higher, degree as an ideal mother in Noddings's account without her practicing Noddings's notions of engrossment or motivational displacement. Instead of busily tending to the individual needs and traits of her children, she may be preoccupied with creating common goods for the whole family: cooking a delicious dinner, planning a family vacation, fixing up the bathroom and working for an income. She endeavors tirelessly to forge and maintain a powerful bond binding everyone in the family together, including herself and her daughter.

The third issue concerns the connection between Care Ethics and gender. As a historical fact, Care Ethics was associated with feminism. Care Ethics was meant to articulate women's distinctive moral vision, a vision that was presumed to source from and be grounded in the moral experience of women as carers. For a long time in history women have been assigned that role and often they discharge their caring duties at the expense of their own interests and opportunities, sometimes voluntarily, sometimes not. Developing Care Ethics as a moral theory therefore can be understood as a way in which women are empowered to find their own voice and perspective in the ethical realm. A wide acceptance and practice of the theory evidences and further enhances women's power to shape the world in accordance with their vision and values. Moreover, Care Ethics' recognition of the ethical, social, cultural and political significance of caring work will contribute to advance women's status. In these ways, Care Ethics constitutes a move towards attaining gender equality. And, as caring is still mostly done by women, their experience and insights will continue to be a major resource fueling the development of Care Ethics.

On the other hand, the content of Care Ethics has no inherent connection with gender. Noddings stresses that both males and females can be carers (2003 [1984]: 4). If we examine care ethics as ethicists and not as historians of ethics, we should not focus on gender. Perhaps, as widely recognized by care ethicists such as Kittay, Ruddick, and Held, the feminist goal will be served better if we exhort everyone, male and female, to adopt the caring perspective, knowing that its wide acceptance will improve everyone's well-being, including, and, especially, that of women.

The Path of Comradeship in Caring

Confucians and care ethicists can definitely be comrades with the shared goal of promoting caring and close personal relationships as ethical priorities. As comrades, they should share experiences, insights, and raise friendly challenges to each other. Attempts have indeed been made to use resources from Confucianism to inform Care Ethics (Chan 2000a; Epley 2015). From the other end, the idea of family in Care Ethics is considered when developing the model of modern Confucian family (Herr 2012).

One topic that Confucianism and care ethics should collaborate is: how to extend from partial caring to general caring. The topic can be broken down into two parts: (1) how to grow general caring from partial caring; and (2) how to promote and institute caring in the public settings.

Let us examine the second part first. Traditionally, Confucianism adopts a top-down approach in instituting caring in the public setting. The ideal of "inner sage, outer king" entails that it is the responsibility of a few elites—the "sage" or the "*junzi*"—who have acquired the virtue of *ren* and the privileged access to government, to enact policies of *ren*. Unfortunately, the mass is excluded from sharing the task of general caring. Perhaps, this approach was pragmatic in traditional China where authoritarian governments allowed no mass political participation. Citizens' political participation makes this exclusion unacceptable today. Care Ethics as a newly developed theory rooted in democratic societies should be able to demonstrate how to involve and mobilize people to navigate caring in a public setting. Kittay's work, for example, will be a useful reference for the Confucians (Kittay 2001). On the other hand, if care ethicists believe that the role of a government should not be limited to the protection of rights or promotion of preference satisfaction but should include fostering the value and practice of caring (Held 2006), then they should look at Confucianism with its strong perfectionistic commitment.

Let us now turn to the issue of developing general caring from partial caring. Due to its focus on promoting close personal relationships, Confucianism has sometimes been criticized as breeding nepotism, cronyism, narrow familism, and various kinds of unethical networking (Liu 2003). The practice of Confucianism in history therefore provides good lessons, for better or for worse, for Care Ethicists when they ponder the practical implications of their theories. The voluminous scholarship on the Confucian developmental process would certainly shed light on the issue of bridging partial and general caring. Moreover, Confucianism credits general caring to multiple sources (e.g. compassion, following *li*) besides partial caring. If care ethicists take general caring seriously, then perhaps they need to re-examine Noddings's idea that general caring stems merely from the memories of being cared for or caring.

On the other hand, unlike Care Ethics, the development of Confucianism received little input from women—the experts on the subject of caring due to their role as primary carers and the gender that has often been placed in a subordinate, dominated position. Consequently, it is reasonable to speculate that Confucianism might be missing important insights about caring and power dynamic in relationships that might be captured in Care Ethics. The importance of garnering input from one's child, the object of one's caring, is an excellent example of such insight.

One thing that does not require speculation, however, is that when these two accounts care more about each other, we will develop better caring!

Further Reading

Chan, Alan and Tan, Sor-hoon (Ed.) (2006) *Filial Piety in Chinese Thought and History*, London: Routledge. (Contains many interesting discussions on the prized relationship-role virtue of filial piety.)

Chan, Joseph (2004) *Confucian Perfectionism: A Political Philosophy for Modern Times*, Princeton, NJ: Princeton University Press. (Provides an in depth defense of perfectionism by appealing to Confucianism conceptions.)

Dalmiya, Vrinda (2009) "Caring Comparisons: Thoughts on Comparative Care Ethics," *Journal of Chinese Philosophy* 36(2): 192–209. (An insightful piece comparing care ethics with Confucianism and Indian philosophy.)

Sander-Staudt, Maureen (2006) "The Unhappy Marriage of Care Ethics and Virtue Ethics," *Hypatia* 21(4): 21–39. (Examines various attempts to subsume care ethics under virtue ethics and recommends the two accounts should collaborate but remain separate.)

Related Topics

Dao becomes female (Chapter 3); feminist engagements with social contract theory (Chapter 7); rationality and objectivity in feminist philosophy (Chapter 20); feminist and queer intersections with disability studies (Chapter 33); feminist intersections with environmentalism and ecological thoughts (Chapter 35); moral justification in an unjust world (Chapter 40); feminist conceptions of autonomy (Chapter 41); feminist metaethics (Chapter 42); feminist ethics of care (Chapter 43); feminist virtue ethics (Chapter 45); feminist bioethics (Chapter 46); neoliberalism, global justice, and transnational feminisms (Chapter 48); feminism, structural injustice, and responsibility (Chapter 49); Latin American feminist ethics and politics (Chapter 50); feminism and liberalism (Chapter 52).

References

Ames, Roger (2011) *Confucian Role Ethics: A Vocabulary*, Honolulu, HI: University of Hawaii Press.

Blum, Lawrence (1994) *Moral Perception and Particularity*, London: Routledge.

Bubeck, Diemut Elisabet (1995) *Care, Gender and Justice*, Oxford: Clarendon Press.

Card, Claudia (1990) "Caring and Evil," *Hypatia* 5(1): 101–108.

Chan, Sin Yee (1993) *An Ethic of Loving: Ethical Particularism and the Engaged Perspective*, Dissertation, Ann Arbor, MI: University of Michigan.

—— (2000a) "Can 'Shu' Be the One World that Serves as the Guiding Principle of Caring Actions?" *Philosophy East and West* 50(4): 507–524.

—— (2000b) "Gender and Relationship Roles in the 'Analects' and the 'Mencius,'" *Asian Philosophy* 10(2): 115–132.

Davion, Victoria (1993) "Autonomy, Integrity, and Care," *Social Theory and Practice* 19(2): 161–182.

Epley, Kelly (2015) "Care Ethics and Confucianism: Caring through *Li*," *Hypatia* 30(4): 881–896.

Gilligan, Carol (1982) *In a Different Voice*, Cambridge, MA: Harvard University Press.

Halwani, Raja (2003) "Care Ethics and Virtue Ethics," *Hypatia* 18(3): 161–192.

Held, Virginia (2006) The *Ethics of Care: Personal, Political, and Global*, New York: Oxford University Press.

Herr, Ranjoo (2012) "Confucian Family for a Feminist Future," *Asian Philosophy* 22(4): 327–346.

Kittay, Eva (2001) "A Feminist Public Ethic of Care Meets the New Communitarian Family Policy," *Ethics* 111: 523–547

Lai, Karyn (2013) *Learning from Chinese Philosophies: Ethics of Interdependent and Contextualised Self*, Burlington, VT: Ashgate.

Li, Chenyang (1994) "The Concept of Jen and the Feminist Ethic of Care," *Hypatia* 9(1): 70–89.

—— (2015) "Confucian Ethics and Care Ethics: The Political Dimension of a Scholarly Debate," *Hypatia* 30(4): 897–903.

Liu, Qingping (2003) "Filiality versus Sociality and Individuality: On Confucianism as 'Consanguinitism,'" *Philosophy East and West* 53(2): 234–250.

Noddings, Nell (2003 [1984]) *Caring: A Feminine Approach to Ethics and Moral Education*, 2nd ed., Berkeley, CA: University of California Press.

—— (2010) *The Maternal Factor: Two Paths to Morality*, Berkeley, CA and Los Angeles, CA: University of California Press.

Pang-White, Ann (2011) "Caring in Confucian Philosophy," *Philosophy Compass* 6(6): 374–384.

Ruddick, Sara (1998) "Care as Labor and Relationship," in Mark Halfon and Joram Haber (Eds.) *Norms and Values: Essays on the Work of Virginia Held*, Lanham, MD: Rowman & Littlefield, 3–25.

Shun, Kwong-loi (1993) "Jen and Li, in the 'Analects,'" *Philosophy East and West* 43(3): 457–479.

Sim, May (2015) "Why Confucian Ethics Is a Virtue Ethics," in Lorraine Besser-Jones and Michael Slote (Eds.) *The Routledge Companion to Virtue Ethics*, New York: Routledge, 63–76.

Star, Daniel (2002) "Do Confucians Really Care? A Defense of the Distinctiveness of Care Ethics: A Reply to Chenyang Li," *Hypatia* 17(1): 77–106.

—— (1997) *Mencius and Early Chinese Thought*, Stanford, CA: Stanford University Press.

Slote, Michael (2001) *Morals from Motives*, New York: Oxford University Press.

Tao, Julia (2000) "Two Perspectives of Care: Confucian *Ren* and Feminist *Care*," *Journal of Chinese Philosophy* 27(2): 215–240.

Tronto, Joan C. (1993) *Moral Boundaries: A Political Argument for an Ethic of Care*, New York: Routledge.

Tu, Wei-ming (1985) *Confucian Thought*, Albany, NY: SUNY Press.

Yuan, Lijuan (2002) "Ethics of Care and Concept of *Jen*: A Reply to Chenyang Li," *Hypatia* 17(1): 107–129.

45

FEMINIST VIRTUE ETHICS

Robin S. Dillon

Feminist virtue ethics is an approach to issues in moral philosophy that draws from both one of the oldest approaches, virtue ethics, and one of the more recent developments in ethical theorizing, feminist ethics. It brings to the concerns that animate feminist ethics a particular orientation to the moral life, a set of questions, and an array of concepts that have long been of importance in virtue ethics, and to the concerns that animate virtue ethics, a certain perspective, a set of questions, and tools and methods that are distinctively feminist. Thus, an understanding of feminist virtue ethics requires understanding something of both traditional virtue ethics and feminist ethics.

Virtue Ethics, Feminist Ethics, and Feminist Virtue Ethics

Virtue Ethics

Traditional normative ethics can be understood to address four interrelated moral questions: How should we act and how can we determine what actions are right? What should we value and how should we value it? What kind of person(s) is it good to be and how should such a person live? How would it be best for all of us to live together? An ethical theory may address all four questions and issues related to them, but different kinds of theories can be distinguished by which question they prioritize or focus on. Traditional virtue ethics focuses on the third question. Rather than centering actions and the principles that should guide them, as is the case with deontological and consequentialist theories, virtue ethical theories address the whole trajectory of human lives and ways that it would be best to live; and rather than taking the kind of persons we should be to be wholly determined by, e.g., our duties to act rightly, virtue ethics works with rich conceptions of admirable qualities of character, or virtues, which compose the kinds of lives that it is good for human beings to live but that are not reducible to following moral rules. On this approach, the moral task facing a person is that of striving to develop and exercise the moral virtues that will enable her to live well. Virtue ethics is the oldest form of moral philosophy, tracing its origins to ancient Greek philosophy. It was eclipsed in the eighteenth and nineteenth centuries by the development of Kantian deontology and utilitarianism, but was revived in the late 1950s and 1960s and is now regarded as one of the chief contemporary approaches to ethics. (The approach has also been taken up in epistemology by theorists who examine intellectual virtues, traits that contribute to doing well as a cognizer. While there are interesting connections between intellectual virtues and moral virtues, this essay will focus just on the latter.)

There are a variety of theories that can be classified as virtue ethics, but they all share an emphasis on virtues of character as an organizing concept for philosophical inquiry. A person's character is the kind of person she is, morally speaking—a kind or inconsiderate one, a brave or cowardly one, a trustworthy or unreliable one, overall a good person or a despicable one. Typically, "character" refers not to what makes someone a unique individual, but, rather, to a person's overall ethical structure and so to the combination of qualities that make someone, on the whole, a morally admirable person or an unworthy one. A moral virtue is a specific trait of character that makes a person to that extent morally admirable, while a vice is a character trait that makes a person to that extent unworthy of admiration, despicable or shameful, or even wicked. Virtues and vices are what Rosalind Hursthouse (1999) calls "complex mindsets" that involve relatively settled patterns of sensibility, perception, attention, reasoning, value, interest, desire, attitude, emotion, commitment, expectation, motive, choice, and action.

Two approaches to virtue ethics have been of particular interest to feminist theorists. The first, and traditionally dominant, approach is eudaimonism. The Greek term "eudaimonia" refers to the good life for a human, which is a life of long-term well-being, happiness, or flourishing. According to Aristotle, whose ethics is the paradigm eudaimonistic theory, the flourishing life is the greatest good and the ultimate aim of all human activity. To flourish as a human is to live a rich and fulfilling life in which one engages well or excellently in the activities that are distinctively human. Chief among these is rational activity, which includes not only thinking and reasoning but also acting, desiring, and experiencing emotions in ways that are guided by practical wisdom. The virtues, as dispositions to engage in excellent rational activity in this broad sense, are necessary for or partially constitutive of human flourishing. Thus, on this view, nothing counts as a virtue that is not beneficial in this way to its possessor, and the possession of (enough or particular) vices precludes living a good life. While the virtues are necessary for flourishing, they are not sufficient; as Aristotle recognizes, external goods, especially an appropriate social context and proper education, are also necessary. Attention to social context gives eudaimonism a potentially critical orientation that has made it attractive to many feminist theorists.

The other approach includes a variety of non-eudaimonistic virtue theories that take virtue and morality to depend on feelings and feeling-based motivations rather than on reason or rationality and that regard the virtuousness of a character trait as not dependent on its contribution to the possessor's long-term welfare. Because this kind of approach emphasizes emotional aspects of our nature, which have been marginalized by the male-dominant rationalistic theories of Enlightenment philosophy, it has been appealing to other feminist theorists.

Feminist Ethics

By contrast with the long tradition of virtue ethics, this is a relatively new approach in normative ethics, developing only since the 1980s as increasing numbers of women philosophers who self-identify as feminists have entered the profession. It is distinguished from other ethical approaches by its concern with the moral status of women and its critical examination of the cultural devaluation of women and everything feminine. It cuts across all of the central questions of normative ethics, asking each in a way that centers the subordination in society of women and women's interests to men and men's interests. A defining tenet of feminist ethics is that the systematic subordination of any group of humans is wrong, and so feminist ethics seeks to develop practical approaches to subverting the subordination of all peoples but especially women. Feminist ethics is also concerned with the depreciation or exclusion in moral philosophy of women's perspectives. It takes the experiences of women to be as worthy of respect and concern as men's, and so it seeks to revise or rethink aspects of ethical concepts, methods, and theories that ignore or denigrate women's experiences.

The concepts of gender and power are focal for feminist ethics. Margaret Walker, for example, holds that "feminist ethics is inevitably and fundamentally about morality and power and the moral meaning of relations of unequal power" (Walker 2001: 4); indeed, as Susan Sherwin says, "feminist ethics asks about power, about domination and subordination, even before it asks about good and evil" (Sherwin 1992: 54). Feminist ethics begins with the recognition that in human societies that are organized along lines of gendered hierarchies of power and so in which women are subordinated and men are privileged (which is to say, all known societies), gender makes a great deal of difference to how human lives go and to how social institutions and practices, including the practices of mainstream moral philosophy, are structured, function, and shape our lives individually and collectively. The questions feminist ethics asks about action, values, character, thought, emotion, motivation, responsibility, and individual and collective lives take seriously the contexts of unequal power, opportunities, and possibilities into which we are born, in which we develop, from which we absorb values that affirm some kinds of us and devalue others kinds of us, and in which we live together, some kinds of us privileged because other kinds of us are constrained, marginalized, exploited, or harmed.

Feminist Virtue Ethics

Feminist virtue ethics can be understood, then, as an approach to moral theorizing that examines issues of character critically in light of gender and power, and highlights character dimensions of gendered subordination and dominance. As feminist, it is critical of traditional virtue ethics insofar as the latter's lack of explicit, prioritized attention to the effects of systemic forces of unjust power hierarchies on the constitutions of selves makes it liable to define virtue and vice in general, and specific virtues and vices, in ways that reinforce domination values, and liable also to distort what would count as flourishing of both those who are subordinated and those who are privileged in various power hierarchies. As virtue-theoretic, it holds that examinations of character are important for understanding the nature, mechanisms, and harms of oppression and for envisioning possibilities for genuinely free and fully human lives.

Susan Moller Okin once asked, "How does virtue ethics look from a feminist point of view—that is to say, from a perspective that expects women and men to be treated as equally human and due equal concern and respect?" (Okin 1996: 211). We can now identify a number of features characteristic of feminist virtue ethics (hereafter, FVE) that distinguish it from both traditional virtue ethics (TVE) and feminist ethics more generally (FE). I will highlight three.

First, as feminist, FVE has an explicitly political orientation and aim: it shares with FE the goal of theorizing women's subordination in order to help end it, but does so by focusing on character and lives and on philosophical theories about character and lives. In particular, FVE theorists address distortions of character that are engendered under conditions of subordination and privilege and that contribute to the maintenance of oppression; they identify virtues that might enable their possessors to resist or struggle against oppression in morally justifiable and non-self-corrupting ways; they bring to the foreground virtues and vices that have been neglected by TVE or that take on a new significance, even a different valence, when viewed from a feminist perspective; and they envision possibilities for all human beings of developing genuinely good characters and living humane, free, and mutually respectful lives in just societies.

Feminist theorists have also been concerned to identify ways in which traditional Western philosophical approaches to virtue, such as the accounts of Aristotle, Hume, Rousseau, Kant, Schopenhauer, and Nietzsche, reinforce the devaluation and subordination of women. Accounts like these, Nancy Snow says,

> either expound different lists of virtues that apply separately to men and women and privilege men's virtues over women's; apply the same virtues, such as chastity, unequally to men and women; or elaborate social roles with accompanying virtues—such as wife and mother—that require women to subordinate themselves to men.
>
> (1992: 34–35)

More troubling is the way such accounts

> set identity conditions for women by making descriptive claims about women's nature that have normative implications for the kinds of virtues women can hope to achieve . . . [and so] limit who they can and should be. At their worst, these claims deny women's full and equal humanity.
>
> (Snow 1992: 34–35)

Thus an important task for FVE is to develop accounts of virtue and vice that express right valuing of women. This involves rethinking traditional virtues and vices, as well as identifying heretofore unacknowledged virtues and vices. More interestingly, it has proved to involve the transvaluation of traditional virtues and vice. Traits that have traditionally been regarded as virtues, particular those thought to be distinctive of "good women," such as patience, obedience, and humility, have been reconceptualized as vices that contribute to women's continued subordination, while other traits traditionally regarded as vices, or vices of women, such as defiance, distrustfulness, unreliability, and arrogance, have been reclaimed as liberatory virtues.

A second feature of FVE is its emphasis on the great significance for character and life possibilities of social contexts and social institutions as shaped by hierarchies of power. This focus makes FVE, unlike most TVE, both non-universalizing and more likely to hold that the characters of individuals cannot be understood or evaluated in isolation from social context. TVE is a universalizing approach: it typically assumes that character psychology is universally human, that virtues and vices are linked to human goodness and human flourishing, and that all humans are liable to the same deficiencies of character for which the same virtues are universally corrective. But FVE holds social contexts shape psychologies differently, depending on the social location of individuals, that social context matters to the development of various character traits and to possibilities for flourishing, and that differently situated people may be subject to different kinds of character problems calling for different forms of character transformation, or may have opportunities or the need to develop different, context-specific virtues. FVE

571

also recognizes that social and theoretical conceptions of virtues, vices, and flourishing are linked in important ways to conceptions of gender: traits have long been differentially identified as virtues or vices depending on whether it is women or men who possess and exercise them.

TVE also has an individualist focus: it evaluates character based on facts about individuals' psychologies, such as individuals' motivations, values, and cognitive, affective, and desiderative dispositions, and it regards individuals as having primary responsibility for the development of their characters and sole responsibility for maintaining or changing them. FVE, by contrast, takes the more realistic view that character dispositions are inculcated, nurtured, directed, shaped, and given significance and value by social interactions, institutions, cultural understandings, and traditions. Thus, certain character traits may not be well understood or even visible apart from particular social contexts; some FVE theories, such as Nancy Potter's (2002) account of trustworthiness, maintain that some virtues and vices are not dispositions of individuals at all but are constituted by relations among individuals. Moreover, FVE recognizes that individuals are never the sole architects of their own characters, that it may take interpersonal interaction or social change to make character transformation possible, and that social circumstances can damage people's characters in ways that are not reparable.

In emphasizing issues of character development and transformation, FVE has also, as TVE has not, called attention to which groups are assigned what kinds of responsibility, and with what kind of acknowledgement (or lack thereof), for what dimensions of character development and transformation; and it asks how relationships and institutions would have to be reconfigured so that no group of humans is excluded from the possibility of becoming and staying good and living flourishing lives. As Okin has argued, even when TVE accounts, such as Aristotle's, attend to character development and point to the importance of proper moral education, they typically covertly rely on women, who are subordinated in the family and the larger society, to do the important work of guiding character development in early childhood, while simultaneously regarding women as inherently defective beings who are incapable of full human virtue, without facing the question of how children could develop good moral characters within a "defective," not to mention unjust, environment.

A third feature of FVE is one essential to FE generally, according to Alison Jaggar (1991): FVE takes women's experiences seriously, but not uncritically. Because some FE theories give special emphasis to women's experiences in relationships, particularly mothering and caring for dependent elderly, disabled, and infirm persons, which have long been neglected in mainstream philosophy, some FVE theories attend especially to virtues that are important for good mothering and caring. Insofar as FVE views women's experiences critically, it takes them as likely to reflect in manifold ways the interplay of subordinating and privileging contexts of diverse women's lives. In particular, it is alive to the possibility that in contexts of oppression, the characters of both subordinated and privileged people can have been distorted in ways that makes it difficult if not impossible for them to live flourishing lives.

Care Ethics and Virtue Ethics

One prominent branch of feminist ethics with virtue theoretic dimensions is care ethics. Drawing on the work of psychologist Carol Gilligan (1982), who identified a distinctive moral voice speaking a language of care that emphasizes relationships and responsibilities, in contrast to the dominant voice in moral philosophy whose language of justice stresses rights and principles, feminist theorists such as Nel Noddings (1984), Sara Ruddick (1989), Eva Kittay (1999), and Virginia Held (2006) have developed theories that commend virtues and values traditionally linked to women and activities for which women have traditionally born the primary responsibility. These theories emphasize the kinds of human relationships that hold between unequal and interdependent persons, including mothers and children, those Kittay refers to as "dependency workers" and dependents, and in general caregivers and those cared for. While the initial focus of care ethics was on personal relationships in the private realm, these theorists and others have argued that values central to care ethics can and should be extended to the public realm, relations among strangers, and even global contexts (e.g., Khader 2011).

Although some care theorists maintain that care should be understood primarily as a practice rather than as a virtue, others have developed accounts in a non-eudaimonistic vein that focus on emotion-based care as a virtue or on virtues that develop or are needed in care-taking or relational contexts. For example, in *Maternal Thinking* Ruddick analyses what she calls "maternal practice," identifying several virtues, such as the ability to see things in perspective, humility, cheerfulness, and conscientiousness, that equip mothers to engage in activities necessary both to realize the maternal goals of preserving the lives and fostering the growth of their children and also to negotiate tensions between training children to conform to society's needs and expectations and encouraging them to challenge morally objectionable social norms.

Early versions of care ethics drew criticisms from many feminists who identified problems facing the project of what Barbara Houston (1987) called "rescuing womanly virtues." While virtues such as care, compassion, sympathy, and altruism have long been assigned to women, not only have these traits been valued less than virtues traditionally assigned to men, such as justice, rationality, and self-sufficiency, but the gendering of caring virtues bolsters the subordinating view that women are well-suited to domestic duties but unsuited to public life. An uncritical valorization of care, critics fear, may promote gender essentialism by implying that the virtues of caring are ones that only women can have or that all women have—so that caring is something that all and only women should do—or it may reinforce the view that women's other-directed care is virtuous no matter the cost to the carer; and in either case it would buttress rather than undermine women's continued subordination. Nevertheless, many feminist theorists regard care as the *sine qua non* of genuinely good human relations, and so they have engaged in rethinking virtues of care to avoid reinforcing subordinating implications.

While the task of retrieving virtues of care from distortions wrought by women's subordination is one with which many FVE theorists may agree, there is a debate about how to understand the general relation between care ethics and virtue ethics. Some theorists such as Michael Slote (2007) and Margaret McLaren (2001) situate care ethics within virtue ethics. Slote, for example, takes the morality of caring to be best understood as a form of non-eudaimonistic, "agent-based" virtue ethics, in which caring motivation is the most basic feature of morality. McLaren highlight similarities between virtue ethics and care ethics, such as that both emphasize relationality, partiality, and emotions, both hold that intentions and actions are important, and both take the concrete, particular aspects of moral situations to be morally salient. She argues that embedding care ethics in virtue ethics allows the dissociation of care from gender and so from subordinating feminine stereotypes. Other theorists, such as Maureen Sanders-Staudt (2006), resist the "marriage" of care ethics and virtue ethics. Sanders-Staudt highlights differences between care ethics and virtue ethics, opposes subsuming care ethics under virtue ethics, and argues for, at most, a collaborative relationship that preserves the distinctively feminist dimensions of care ethics. We could also see in the appropriation of care ethics by virtue ethicists a theoretical recapitulation of the social subordination of women's work, both domestic and philosophical. In my view, any connection between care ethics and virtue ethics must not only preserve but also give priority in moral theorizing to the feminist goal of examining the subordination of women and seeking to end it. But given that some virtue theorists define "virtue ethics" as giving priority to virtue concepts in theorizing morality, it is not at all clear whether a care-virtue ethics that prioritizes a feminist orientation, rather than merely valorizing traditionally feminine virtue or treating care as a non-gendered virtue, is even possible.

Critical Feminist Eudaimonism

Care ethics was for some time the dominant approach in feminist ethics and so feminist discussions of virtue. More recently, however, as feminist ethics has broadened, so feminist work on virtues has embraced other approaches, especially eudaimonism. Despite the sexism inherent in his writings, Aristotle's virtue ethics has been of particular importance. For example, some of Martha Nussbaum's work on the capability approach to justice and development ethics, especially as it affects women, draws on an Aristotelian view of human flourishing (Nussbaum 1992; 2000). According to this view, because humans have certain inherent capabilities the development and exercise of which is essential for living a life that is both recognizably human and flourishing, justice requires that societies be organized so as to enable every human to flourish by developing and exercising the distinctively human capabilities. Marcia Homiak has argued that Aristotle's ideal of the flourishing for a rational being provides valuable resources for feminist theory and has defended his account against charges of elitism that, if applicable, would make it uncongenial for feminist theorizing (Homiak 1993; 2010). Among the most interesting work in feminist eudaimonism is that of Lisa Tessman. In a series of essays and her book, *Burdened Virtues: Virtue Ethics for Liberatory Struggles* (2005), Tessman draws on a reconstructed Aristotelian eudaimonism to focus on ways that oppression can damage character and so interfere with flourishing.

Aristotelian eudaimonism takes the flourishing life to be the ultimate aim of all human activity. Tessman holds further that flourishing is the implicit aim of liberatory struggles and an ideal that guides feminist activism, and that flourishing provides a framework for analyzing the badness of oppression. Instead of focusing, as does traditional Aristotelian eudaimonism, on the goodness of the virtuous and flourishing life, Tessman employs eudaimonism to focus on ways that oppression seriously harms people. She identifies three kinds of character-related harm. First, oppression can impede the development or exercise of certain virtues or encourage the development of certain vices, such as dishonesty, cunning, or manipulativeness. Since the possession of virtue and the absence of vice are required for flourishing, oppression thus interferes with individuals living good lives. And if the virtues that can't be developed are precisely those that would enable people to resist their oppression, character damage can help sustain subordination. Second, surviving or resisting oppression can require the cultivation of traits, which Tessman calls "burdened virtues," that are virtues only under non-ideal conditions, that do not contribute to the possessor's well-being, and that one has good reason to regret having to cultivate. So, whereas Aristotle held that virtues necessarily contribute to or constitute the possessor's flourishing, Tessman argues that oppression disrupts the connection between virtue and flourishing. Third, while Aristotelian eudaimonism emphasizes that virtues contribute to the possessor's well-being, Tessman holds that a trait cannot count as a virtue if it does not also contribute to the general flourishing of the members of an inclusive community.

Several criticisms have been raised against feminist eudaimonism. One is a version of a question as old as Plato: is it indeed the case that the wicked cannot flourish? Marilyn Friedman (2009) has argued that it is not obvious that, e.g., men who live lives of privilege and are socially supported in their view of themselves as good persons living good lives aren't happy or living well. Yet such a claim has to be made for feminist eudaimonism to have any motivational power for ending domination. This leads to a second criticism. The justification that eudaimonistic theories provide for ending domination and subordination points primarily to the consequences for the possessors of virtue or vice (and, on Tessman's view, for other members of the community). Since most of those putatively experiencing the character harms from oppression don't perceive their lives as unhappy and defective, the virtue-consequentialist justification strikes some theorists as a less strong moral argument against oppression than, say, a Kantian one that centers the inherent injustice of not respecting all persons as equals. A third criticism addresses the conceptual relation between flourishing and virtues. Feminist eudaimonism needs liberatory accounts of both. But the history of accounts of virtues that rationalize the subordination of women makes the project of developing an account of flourishing from a list of virtues problematic. It would seem, then, that a specific account of flourishing is required in order to determine which traits of character are really virtues and which are vices. But, as Macalester Bell (2006) has noted, different theorists and groups engaged in liberatory struggle, such as liberal feminists and lesbian separatists, have quite different conceptions of flourishing; which one should be the basis for FVE? Fully resolving these problems requires further work on flourishing, virtues, and vices.

Feminist Accounts of Specific Virtues and Vices

An alternative TVE approach that avoids many of the problems associated with both care virtue ethics and feminist eudaimonism is Christine Swanton's (2003) target account of virtue. On this account, a virtue is disposition to respond in an excellent way to objects, people, actions, situations, etc., that are in the field, or sphere of concern, of the virtue. For example, the traditional virtue of courage is the disposition to respond excellently to dangerous situations. Although it has not received much explicit attention from feminist theorists, Swanton's approach has several features that recommend it for feminist theorizing: it is pluralistic, allowing that different kinds of virtues and vices might be analyzed in quite different ways, so it doesn't require, e.g., privileging one among the many accounts of flourishing; it is non-idealizing, so it doesn't require reconstruction to be able to address the non-ideal circumstances of oppression; and its call for analyses of contexts, targets, and responses gives room for distinctively feminist analyses that center issues of gender and power. In not being tied to a particular kind of virtue theory, such as eudaimonism, the target approach also fits with an interesting feature of feminist virtue theorizing: most of the work in this area has not been concerned to develop full-blown ethical theories but has focused on analyses of specific virtues or vices. Although there are, of course, problems with Swanton's account, I think feminist work on virtues and vices might be helped by drawing explicitly on such an approach.

Feminist theorists have addressed specific virtues and vices in three ways. First, some have identified new virtues or vices or brought forward neglected ones. For example, care virtue theorists have moved caring virtues to the center of ethics; Ruddick analyzed maternal humility; Tessman has identified the burdened virtues of sensitivity and attentiveness to others' unjust suffering and of hard resolve against oppressors; Margaret Walker (1991) has drawn attention to grace and lucidity as "virtues of impure agency" in contexts of moral bad luck, such as oppression; Rebecca Whisnant (2004) analyzed self-centering as a virtue for resisting sexist exploitation and for maintaining oneself as a fully responsible person. Second, theorists have analyzed traditional virtues and vices in new ways. For example, Cheshire Calhoun (1995) and Victoria Davion (1991) developed accounts of integrity that take seriously the experiences of people facing multiple and conflicting oppressions; Anne Barnhill (2012) has developed an account of modesty as a female sexual virtue that promotes feminist change; Macalester Bell's (2009) examination of the Aristotelian virtue of appropriate anger in the non-ideal conditions of life under oppression leads her to argue that its justification as a virtue should not appeal to considerations of flourishing; Marilyn Frye (1983) has argued that arrogance is at the heart of male domination; I have developed feminist accounts of self-respect (Dillon 2004). Other traditional virtues and vices explored by FVE theorists include justice, inattention, honesty, submissiveness, generosity, chastity, shame, self-trust, trustworthiness, responsibility, hospitality, and decency.

Finally, some theorists have engaged in transvaluation of character traits, arguing that some traits traditionally viewed as virtues are actually vices that keep women subordinated, or advocating other traits, traditionally viewed as vices, as feminist virtues. For example, Claudia Card (1996) argued that women's gratitude to men who don't abuse them or who protect them in quid pro quo arrangements is a vice, and that politeness is not a feminist virtue but feisty insubordination is (Card 1991); in contrast to the dominant view that trust is unqualifiedly a virtue, Annette Baier (1994) took a more cautious approach, advocating women's cultivation of appropriate distrust in exploitative conditions; Lisa Heldke has praised unreliability (1997) and being a responsible traitor (1998); Bell (2006) and I (Dillon 2012) have suggested that arrogance might be a virtue that enables subordinated people to demand respect and develop self-respect. Among other traits that have been seen in different lights by FVE theorists are forgiveness, defiance, altruism, bitterness, obedience, resentfulness, self-coherence, envy, selflessness, selfishness, vulnerability, and deference.

One valuable aspect of feminist work in this area has been an increased emphasis on vice. VE has assumed that people are mostly good and so has emphasized virtues (hence, the name of the approach). But it is implausible that mostly good people could create and maintain oppressive structures, or participate in them in ignorance of the manifest injustice of their societies, or actively resist emancipatory efforts; and yet innumerably many of us do just these things. Tessman (2005) and Anita Superson (2004) identify a number of traits that Tessman calls "ordinary vices of domination," which enable members of dominant groups to maintain their dominance without thinking themselves unjust. The widespread possession of these vices entails that dominants as well as subordinates, and hence most people, do not live flourishing lives. Continued work on vices of domination, as well as vices of the oppressed that reinforce continued subordination, would be of great value to feminist ethics for understanding the nature and mechanisms of oppression and what needs to be done towards emancipation. In highlighting the character issues connected with

576

unjust hierarchies of power, uncovering heretofore ignored admirable dimensions of women's lives, and identifying virtues needed for resisting oppression and living fully human lives, feminist virtue ethics has already made a tremendous contribution to moral philosophy.

Related Topics

Feminism and ancient Greek philosophy (Chapter 2); personal identity and relational selves (Chapter 18); feminist ethics of care (Chapter 43); Confucianism and care ethics (Chapter 44); feminist bioethics (Chapter 46); feminism and freedom (Chapter 53); feminism and power (Chapter 54).

References

Baier, Annette (1994) *Moral Prejudices: Essays on Ethics*, Cambridge, MA: Harvard University Press.

Barnhill, Anne (2012) "Modesty as a Feminist Sexual Virtue," in Sharon L. Crasnow and Anita M. Superson (Eds.) *Out From the Shadows: Analytical Feminist Contributions to Traditional Philosophy*, New York: Oxford University Press, 115–137.

Bell, Macalester (2006) "*Burdened Virtues: Virtue Ethics for Liberatory Struggle* by Lisa Tessman," in *Notre Dame Philosophical Review* [online]. Available from: https://ndpr.nd.edu/news/25046-burdened-virtues-virtue-ethics-for-liberatory-struggles/.

—— (2009) "Anger, Virtue, and Oppression," in Lisa Tessman (Ed.) *Feminist Ethics and Social and Political Philosophy: Theorizing the Non-Ideal*, Dordrecht: Springer, 165–183.

Calhoun, Cheshire (1995) "Standing For Something," *The Journal of Philosophy* 92: 235–260.

Card, Claudia (Ed.) (1991) *Feminist Ethics*, Lawrence, KS: University Press of Kansas.

—— (1996) *The Unnatural Lottery: Character and Moral Luck*, Philadelphia, PA: Temple University Press.

Davion, Victoria M. (1991) "Integrity and Radical Change," in Claudia Card (Ed.) *Feminist Ethics*, Lawrence, KS: University Press of Kansas, 180–192.

Dillon, Robin S. (2004) "'What's a Woman Worth? What's Life Worth? Without Self-Respect?': On the Value of Evaluative Self-Respect," in Peggy DesAutels and Margaret Urban Walker (Eds.) *Moral Psychology: Feminist Ethics and Social Theory*, Lanham, MD: Rowman & Littlefield, 47–66.

—— (2012) "Kant on Arrogance and Self-Respect," in Cheshire Calhoun (Ed.) *Setting the Moral Compass: Essays by Women Philosophers*, New York: Oxford University Press, 191–216.

Friedman, Marilyn (2009) "Feminist Virtue Ethics, Happiness, and Moral Luck," *Hypatia* 24: 29–40.

Frye, Marilyn (1983) *The Politics of Reality: Essays in Feminist Theory*, Freedom, CA: The Crossing Press.

Gilligan, Carol (1982) *In a Different Voice: Psychological Theory and Women's Development*, Cambridge, MA: Harvard University Press.

Held, Virginia (2006) *The Ethics of Care: Personal, Political, and Global*, Oxford: Oxford University Press.

Heldke, Lisa (1997) "In Praise of Unreliability," *Hypatia* 12: 174–182.

—— (1998) "On Being a Responsible Traitor: A Primer," in Bat-Ami Bar On and Ann Ferguson (Eds.) *Daring to Be Good: Essays in Feminist Ethico-Politics*, London: Routledge, 41–54.

Homiak, Marcia (1993) "Feminism and Aristotle's Rational Ideal," in Louise M. Antony and Charlotte E. Witt (Eds.) *A Mind of One's Own: Feminist Essays in Reason and Objectivity*, Boulder, CO: Westview, 1–17.

—— (2010) "Virtue and the Skills of Ordinary Life," in Cheshire Calhoun (Ed.) *Setting the Moral Compass: Essays by Women Philosophers*, New York: Oxford University Press, 23–42.

Houston, Barbara (1987) "Rescuing Womanly Virtues: Some Dangers of Moral Reclamation," in Marsha Hanen and Kai Nielsen (Eds.) *Canadian Journal of Philosophy*, 13 (Supplementary): 237–262.

Hursthouse, Rosalind (1999) *On Virtue Ethics*, Oxford: Oxford University Press.

Jaggar, Alison M. (1991) "Feminist Ethics: Projects, Problems, Prospects," in Claudia Card (Ed.) *Feminist Ethics*, Lawrence, KS: University Press of Kansas, 78–104.

Khader, Serene (2011) "Beyond Inadvertent Ventriloquism: Caring Virtues for Anti-Paternalist Development Practices," *Hypatia* 26: 742–761.

Kittay, Eva F. (1999) *Love's Labor: Essays on Women, Equality, and Dependency*, New York: Routledge.

McLaren, Margaret (2001) "Feminist Ethics: Care as a Virtue," in Peggy DesAutels and Joanne Waugh (Eds.) *Feminist Doing Ethics*, Lanham, MD: Rowman & Littlefield, 101–117.

Noddings, Nel (1984) *Caring: A Feminine Approach to Ethics and Moral Education*, Berkeley, CA: University of California Press.

Nussbaum, Martha (1992) "Human Functioning and Social Justice: In Defense of Aristotelian Essentialism," *Political Theory* 20: 202–246.

——(2000) *Women and Human Development: The Capabilities Approach*, Cambridge: Cambridge University Press.

Okin, Susan Moller (1996) "Feminism, Moral Development, and the Virtues," in Roger Crisp (Ed.) *How Should One Live?: Essays on the Virtues*, Oxford: Oxford University Press, 211–229.

Potter, Nancy (2002) *How Can I Be Trusted? A Virtue Theory of Trustworthiness*, Lanham, MD: Rowman & Littlefield.

Ruddick, Sara (1989) *Maternal Thinking: Toward a Politics of Peace*, New York: Ballantine Books.

Sanders-Staudt, Maureen (2006) "The Unhappy Marriage of Care Ethics and Virtue Ethics," *Hypatia* 21: 21–39.

Sherwin, Susan (1992) *No Longer Patient: Feminist Ethics and Health Care*, Philadelphia, PA: Temple University Press.

Slote, Michael (2007) *The Ethics of Care and Empathy*, London: Routledge.

Snow, Nancy (1992) "Virtue and the Oppression of Women," *Canadian Journal of Philosophy*, 32: 33–61.

Superson, Anita M. (2004) "Privilege, Immorality, and Responsibility for Attending to the 'Facts about Humanity,'" *Journal of Social Philosophy* 35: 34–55.

Swanton, Christine (2003) *Virtue Ethics: A Pluralistic View*, Oxford: Oxford University Press.

Tessman, Lisa (2005) *Burdened Virtues: Virtue Ethics for Liberatory Struggles*, New York: Oxford University Press.

Walker, Margaret Urban (1991) "Moral Luck and the Virtues of Impure Agency," *Metaphilosophy* 22: 14–27.

——(2001) "Seeing Power in Morality: A Proposal for Feminist Naturalism in Ethics," in Peggy DesAutels and Joanne Waugh (Eds.) *Feminist Doing Ethics*, Lanham, MD: Rowman & Littlefield, 3–14.

Whisnant, Rebecca (2004) "Woman Centered: A Feminist Ethic of Responsibility," in Peggy DesAutels and Margaret Urban Walker (Eds.) *Moral Psychology: Feminist Ethics and Social Theory*, Lanham, MD: Rowman & Littlefield, 201–217.

46

FEMINIST BIOETHICS

Wendy A. Rogers

Introduction

Bioethics emerged as an academic discipline in the 1960s and 1970s, largely in response to social and technological changes that challenged established attitudes and practices. Questions arose concerning the rights of patients and research participants, while the use of emerging medical technologies raised moral questions about the nature of life, decision-making and the legitimate boundaries of medicine. Bioethics as a discipline sought to foster ethical debate about challenging cases; provide ethical guidance to physicians and researchers about practice; and advise governmental authorities regarding relevant policy. However, the nascent discipline seemed oblivious to many of the gendered aspects of healthcare and the ways that healthcare practices reinforced oppressive gender norms. Entrenched gender biases in the foundational disciplines of bioethics such as philosophy, law, medicine, and theology were transplanted largely intact into the new discipline. By the late 1980s, feminist bioethicists, drawing upon feminist ethics and epistemology, started to challenge the gendered norms and assumptions of bioethics. While early feminist attention focused on reproductive practices, a sustained critique of the assumptions and theoretical approaches of traditional bioethics emerged during the 1990s. Since then, contributions of feminist bioethics have shaped the way that central bioethical notions, such as autonomy, are conceptualized; provoked methodological diversity; and extended the agenda of bioethics to include global and social issues far beyond the initially narrow concerns of medical care and biomedical research.

Alison Jaggar acknowledges the challenge of characterizing feminist approaches to ethics, but nonetheless, identifies three "minimum conditions of adequacy for any approach to ethics that purports to be feminist" (1989: 910). These are: to offer action guides aimed at subverting the subordination of women; to span both the public and the private realms; and, to take seriously, but not uncritically, the experiences of all women. Following Jaggar, the term "feminist bioethics" is used here to describe an approach to bioethics that takes gender to be a central analytic category, and that is concerned with identifying and seeking to change relations of oppression and domination (Sherwin 1992). Within this broad definition, there are many differences among feminist bioethicists in terms of methodology, theoretical foundations, focus, and so forth.

In what follows, I describe some of the broad concerns motivating feminist bioethics before describing substantive and methodological contributions made by feminist bioethics to the field. The chapter ends with a survey of future directions and emerging topics attracting feminist analysis.

Bioethics and Gender

Feminist bioethics is premised upon the notion that both the focus of traditional bioethics, and its very concepts, are imbued with unacknowledged androcentric bias, thereby marginalising gender as a significant category when considering the ethical issues that arise in the biological and life sciences. Yet gender permeates the subject matter of bioethics in multiple ways. Hierarchies and power relations are ubiquitous within the institutions and practices of healthcare, often to the disadvantage of women. Gender bias exists in research, and in the definition of various conditions that track gender. There are gendered aspects to many medical interventions; while gendered patterns associated with social inequities and the distribution of resources perpetuate women's poverty and oppression. While women are marginalized as a group in male dominated societies, nonetheless there are also hierarchies and inequities among women themselves due to race, ethnicity, class, sexuality and so forth, which intersect in various ways with explicitly gendered hierarchies.

Gender-based hierarchies are widespread within healthcare. Men continue to dominate high-prestige and high-income medical specialties, while the nursing workforce remains largely feminized, creating an inter-professional knowledge and power hierarchy. Those providing personal care are further disenfranchised. In healthcare consultations, women are more likely to be patients than men for reasons including higher rates of morbidity, gendered patterns of help-seeking behavior, and the medicalization of normal female reproductive functions. These factors replicate wider societal patterns in which men are seen as experts, well suited to rational decision-making based upon privileged knowledge, while women are associated with the irrationalities of the flesh and a lack of knowledge and expertise, especially where this is based upon personal experience.

Implicit hierarchies of knowledge and power contribute to both gender essentialism and insensibility to gender in healthcare. The former manifests in viewing women largely in terms of their reproductive capacities, leading to a focus on the medical management of various aspects of reproductive functions ranging from menstruation to menopause; and the associated skewing of research on women towards disorders affecting the female reproductive tract (Rogers and Ballantyne 2008). Gender essentialism also underlies the historic (and in some areas) continuing exclusion of women from research due to concerns that they may be, or become, pregnant thus risking harm to the fetus, or that the menstrual cycle will unduly interfere with research results.

Gender insensibility exerts the opposite effect by denying any significant difference between men and women such that the results of research performed with exclusively male cohorts are deemed to be equally applicable to women. This approach takes no account of relevant physiological or anatomical differences between men and women that can affect both manifestations of disease and responses to treatment (Adshead 2011; Bluhm 2011; Mosca et al. 2011). In addition, it fails to apprehend the wide-reaching impact of entrenched gender norms on all aspects of health and healthcare. Taken together, gender insensibility and gender essentialism result in a skewing of medical attention towards the female reproductive tract and its functions, and away from other health problems that affect women just as much as men.

Gender bias, evident in the ways that diseases are defined, diagnosed and treated, illustrates another way in which gender and bioethics intersect. There is a long history of associating femaleness with madness, reflected in gendering within psychiatric diagnostic categories (Chesler 2005; Bluhm 2011; Gould 2011). In diseases that affect both men and women, there are gendered patterns in medical responses to presentations of the same disorders. Cardiovascular disease, for example, has been under recognized and under treated in women, with men more likely than women to receive appropriate interventions; and women are under treated for pain compared with men (Hoffman and Tarzian 2001). There may be many reasons for these gender-based disparities. They may, for example, reflect stereotypical views about women's behavior or propensity to complain, but at the very least, findings such as these indicate that gender equity in healthcare is an ongoing challenge.

Next, some of the signature technological advances that ignited interest in bioethics relate to reproduction, and are mediated in and through the bodies of women. Assisted reproductive technologies, from artificial insemination and in vitro fertilization through to surrogacy and uterus transplantations, take place exclusively in female bodies. Likewise the creation of embryos for donation or research is a gendered activity, with different consequences for those donating ova rather than sperm (Dickenson 2006). Abortion is a perennially contentious topic in bioethics, where mainstream discussions tended to focus on the status of the fetus while failing to take account of the unavoidable impact of continuing or terminating a pregnancy on the woman involved (Tooley 1972; Marquis 1989).

Finally, in what is by no means an exhaustive list of the ways that gender is central to its subject matter, bioethics is concerned with issues of justice, ranging from local resource allocation decisions through to global inequities. Around the globe, women are over-represented among the socio-economically disadvantaged, have access to fewer material resources than men, and form the vast majority of those providing personal care to others. These are clearly matters of social injustice in their own right, but these social inequities are amplified through the effects of social disadvantage on health, leading to inequitable burdens of morbidity on women.

All of the factors discussed briefly above support the view that the central concerns of bioethics are deeply gendered, and that gender is a morally relevant category when discussing and analyzing the ethical issues associated with healthcare and the life sciences. Yet, as Susan Wolf notes (1996), bioethics was relatively oblivious to gender and slow to adopt relevant developments in feminist ethics and epistemology. Wolf attributes this tardiness to a number of causes. First, from its earliest inception, bioethics was concerned with the rights of patients and research participants. This led to a focus on decision-making in the clinical/research encounter, understood in terms of individual autonomy. Drawing upon the resources of liberal individualism, the autonomous individual was conceptualized in terms of isolated and self-serving decision-making; a being bereft of morally significant relationships and with no identifiable group characteristics, such as race or gender.

Second, bioethics was dominated by principles, understood as universal moral rules for generic and substitutable individual persons. In the interests of impartiality, gender and other potentially relevant contextual features were stripped from the generic individuals subject to these abstract principles. Third, bioethics emerged in response to the concerns of physicians and policy makers, thus the viewpoint and interests of those male-dominated groups dictated the subject matter under investigation. Once again, women, especially women as patients and carers, were not among those setting the agenda for the new discipline. Finally, Wolf argues that bioethics developed in relative isolation from areas of scholarship where feminist concerns were firmly on the agenda, such as critical theory and postmodernism.

These reasons help to explain both the androcentric bias of bioethics, and why there was little engagement with feminism despite the highly gendered nature of much of the substance of bioethics. Starting in the 1980s, a series of feminist critiques sought to remedy this situation.

Feminist Critiques of Bioethics

In a comprehensive history of feminist bioethics, Anne Donchin and Jackie Leach Scully (2015) identify a number of key publications from the early 1980s onwards. These include work by Helen B. Holmes (with Betty Hoskins and Michael Gross 1980; 1981; with Laura Purdy 1982), Gena Corea (1985), Susan Sherwin (1992), and Wolf (1996). Much of this initial work focused on critiques of healthcare practices affecting women, largely to do with reproduction. These concerns broadened to include the experiences of women as patients (Sherwin 1992); the politics of women's health (Sherwin et al. 1998); disability standpoint (Wendell 1996); and broader cultural critiques of attitudes towards women's bodies (Bordo 1993; Mahowald 1993). Wolf (1996) explicitly expanded the horizons of feminist bioethics beyond reproduction to an overt critique of both the subject matter and the methodological approaches of bioethics, drawing attention to androcentric biases affecting the structure and nature of the field. Further critiques drew on key thinking in feminist ethics by scholars such as Carol Gilligan (1982), Nel Noddings (1984), Eva Kittay and Diana Meyers (1987), Jaggar (1989), Sarah Ruddick (1989), Rosemary Tong (1993), Margrit Shildrick (1997), Kittay (1999), and Catriona Mackenzie and Natalie Stoljar (2000).

Despite considerable diversity in approaches among the authors mentioned above, they are all identified as feminist by their commitment to identifying and correcting male bias in theory and in practice. And while these critiques of male-dominated bioethics are by no means univocal, I discuss them here in terms of two overarching concerns: to do with conceptions of agency, and to do with equality.

The identity of the individual agent in early bioethics discourse can be traced back to two sources: that of the neo-Cartesian ideal moral self; and the independent rational decision maker of liberal individualism (Jaggar 1989; Wolf 1996). Jaggar describes the neo-Cartesian ideal moral self as "a disembodied, separate, autonomous, unified, rational being, essentially similar to all other moral selves" (1989: 99), while Wolf (1996) characterizes the liberal individual as serving only his own atomistic interests. Feminists found much to criticise in this conception of the agent.

First, this account of agency strips away the body in order to valorize the independent and rational decision-making capacities of the agent. But of course, the decision maker does not exist independent of her body. An individual's body is central to, or constitutive of her identity, and inexorably shapes the choices and options open to that individual (Young 1980). Being a human agent is a lived experience, such that an individual's subjectivity and desires stem from her experiences with this rather than that kind of body, while her options for choice and action are likewise shaped by physical characteristics such as age, shape, gender, race, ability or disability. To many feminists, it makes no sense to consider the agent as disembodied; agents are always this particular person with these specific bodily characteristics. Further, it seems that the agent of bioethical theory does in fact have a bodily identity, but the body in question is male rather than female, thereby building in a bias towards male experience and male values at the centre of the notionally universal agent of bioethical theory. The disembodied agent of bioethical theory just happens to have characteristics (such as rationality and objectivity) that are traditionally associated with being male, and that are frequently described in opposition to characteristics attributed to women (such as irrationality, partiality).

This covert male gendering of the bioethical subject disenfranchises the experiences of women and disregards the effects of embodiment on subjectivity. Such an approach discounts the central role of the (gendered) body in constituting identity, ignores the lasting effects of interventions in the body, and overlooks the role of the body in mediating perception, consciousness and action. In addition, adopting an implicitly male universal agent thereby excludes consideration of the bodily experiences of women, such as pregnancy and childbirth, physical vulnerability, or providing personal care to others. These experiences are thereby stripped of their moral import and deemed irrelevant to bioethics. Where the body does intrude, it is largely construed as property, as something owned by the agent and therefore something that may be disposed of as the agent sees fit. This view is reflected in arguments for free markets in organs or in surrogacy, on the grounds that the individual owns her body and can therefore sell its parts or services as one would sell other property (Radcliffe-Richards 2007).

Questions about control over one's body lead directly to the conception of autonomy associated with the universal moral agent of early bioethics. Feminists were concerned about the largely individualistic view of autonomy attributed to such agents, especially in its more libertarian manifestations (e.g., Englehardt 1986). This view was characterized by a focus on state neutrality regarding values; freedom from interference; and satisfaction of preferences through the exercise of choice. On this account, the prevention of harm to others is the only justification for interfering in an autonomous individual's uncoerced choices. However, there are concerns regarding libertarian accounts of autonomy (Mackenzie 2015). First, freedom from interference or negative liberty is insufficient for guaranteeing autonomy, because autonomy requires both freedom and access to genuine opportunities. Second, the notion of freely exercised choice fails to take account of the social context of, and constraints on, individual choice. Many individuals have a limited palette of opportunities from which to choose (circumscribed not only by their gender, but also by their class, ethnicity, sexuality, etc.), significantly constraining their autonomy. These kinds of limits cannot be remedied by non-interference alone. Third, by discounting the need for opportunities as well as freedom, and the inequalities that exist in access to opportunities, libertarian approaches to autonomy ignore questions of social justice, overlook exploitation, and may exacerbate existing inequalities (Sherwin 1992). For example, on libertarian accounts, a person may be deemed to be exercising her autonomy if she enters into a surrogacy arrangement, so long as her choice is not coerced (narrowly understood). But this approach fails to take account of the person's context; her lack of other opportunities; the nature of her relationships and the responsibilities these entail; her sense of herself as an agent in the world; the corrosive and patterned effects of poverty; hierarchies in the commissioning process, and so forth, all of which undermine claims about the freedom of her choice. Feminist methodologies draw attention to these concerns through a focus on embodiment, personal identity, relationships and opportunities, and through interrogation of the context within which individuals have more or less power to imagine or realize their chosen ends.

Feminists are particularly concerned about the asocial and self-interested nature attributed to the universal agent. This approach takes social relationships to be contingent rather than necessary in any way to the development or exercise of individual autonomy. To the extent that an individual does have social relationships, these are understood to be voluntary, as for example, a friendship between colleagues at work. Any responsibilities engendered by relationships are understood as voluntarily assumed constraints on autonomy. Wolf argues that this notion that autonomous agents are self-sufficient and independent is impoverished, harmful, and inaccurate. In particular, it takes no account of the dependency and interdependency that characterizes human relationships, and by focusing on the individual, it excludes consideration of the moral dimensions of relationships. Claiming that relationships are voluntary and largely between equals takes no account of the dependency of children and frail adults. Furthermore, this gender-insensible approach ignores the fact that the responsibilities of caring for dependent others fall largely to women, whether or not those relationships are undertaken voluntarily. Many relationships, biological or otherwise, are non-voluntary, creating networks of unavoidable rather than assumed responsibilities that constrain and shape the autonomy of those involved.

A second group of feminist concerns about traditional bioethics focuses on equality. These concerns overlap to some extent with issues emerging from the critiques of agency and autonomy noted above, such as lack of opportunities, exploitation, and disadvantage. Jaggar (1989) tracks the history of feminist debate about sexual equality, initially premised on the belief that equality before the law for men and women would lead to an end to gender-based inequalities. By the late 1970s, it became clear that legal equality did not always lead to substantive equality. For example, "no-fault" divorce settlements in which men and women received equal shares of household assets left women in substantially weaker economic positions than men, exacerbating existing inequalities (Weitzman 1985). Feminist philosophers wrestled with how to resolve this problem, acutely aware both of the shortcomings of gender-insensible approaches and of the danger that initiatives intended to recognize sexual difference and redress inequalities might equally be used to disadvantage women, reinforce notions of gender essentialism and entrench gender-based hierarchies. Gilligan's key work (1982) supporting the view that there are gendered differences in moral reasoning lead to vigorous debates about the value of this line of reasoning (see for example Kittay and Meyers 1987).

Despite differences between theorists, feminist ethics and bioethics generally assumes that gender is a morally salient feature of individuals. Rather than accepting that individuals are identical and substitutable, feminist approaches argue that, unless proven otherwise, men and women are not equally situated and that equality requires taking account of gendered (and other) differences. These views challenge liberal notions of justice that focus on equality as procedural fairness or freedom to pursue opportunities, accounts that fail to consider either the patterning of inequalities or the actual outcomes of "fair" procedures.

Feminist critiques of equality are linked to concerns about impartiality. Central to liberal notions of justice is the requirement that individuals be treated impartially by weighing the interests of each person equally. Jaggar identifies two feminist critiques of this view. First, Noddings' 1984 account of the ethics of care is premised upon the claim that care is the natural basis of morality, in which case impartiality would require us to care equally for all humankind. But, Noddings argues, given that we cannot care equally for all, but only for those with whom we are in specific relationships, it is impossible and hypocritical to make claims about impartiality understood as a universal moral duty. Many feminist bioethicists treat Noddings' ethics of care warily as it is premised on ostensibly essentialist claims about women being better at caring than men. Nonetheless, she has been highly influential in establishing the moral relevance and gendered nature of caring and care work, and the significance of the context within which care is offered. In addition, her work has contributed to debates about the respective roles of justice and care as foundations of morality.

Sherwin (1989) and Code (1988) provide an alternative critique of impartiality, claiming that impartiality paradoxically undermines respect for individuals and fairness, as without knowledge of context it is not possible to distinguish appropriately between individuals and thus treat them accordingly. On these accounts individuals are not substitutable; rather it is imperative to understand and take account of context, as individual circumstances are morally relevant in assessing claims and weighing interests. In feminist bioethics, this has led to a focus on thick descriptions and detailed narratives in ethical analysis. Sherwin (1992) makes the related point that an impartial individualistic approach to morality ignores socially patterned inequalities that track membership of groups, and is thus unable to tackle inequalities that are distributed differentially among identifiable social groups.

This brief summary focused on feminist critiques of the abstract and individualistic notions of agency, autonomy, and equality seen to be implicit or explicit within early and dominant bioethical theory. Feminists built on these critiques by developing competing accounts of key concepts and new methodological approaches, and countering male bias by extending the scope of bioethical concern to wider social and global issues.

Shaping the Field: Feminist Contributions to Bioethics

Feminist bioethics is now a recognized academic sub-discipline, with its own specialist journal (*International Journal of Feminist Approaches to Bioethics* [IJFAB]), and national and international organizations and conferences. Given the disciplinary and methodological diversity within the field, it is challenging to single out a few key contributions. Here I focus on relational autonomy and feminist accounts of care, dependency and vulnerability; and identify features of feminist methodological approaches.

Relational autonomy is the term used to describe feminist approaches to understanding and analyzing autonomy. As discussed above, feminists were critical of the notion of autonomy implicit within bioethics, understood as the free and rational exercise of will by atomistic and self sufficient agents (Stoljar 2013). The qualifier "relational" refers to the claim that any plausible theory of autonomy must concede that exercising autonomy is compatible with agents being part of and valuing social relationships (Mackenzie and Stoljar 2000). In addition, "relational" emphasizes the nature of agents as socially and historically embedded and shaped by their circumstances.

There are four key features of relational theory (Mackenzie 2015). The first concerns the socially scaffolded nature of the skills that are required to exercise autonomy, known as autonomy competencies. Autonomous decisions require the individual to understand information, imagine the effects of different options, reflect on her values, make a decision taking a range of relevant information into account, and so forth. These skills do not arise fully formed; rather they are developed in and through interactions with others in socially significant relationships. No one is born with autonomy competency; rather we are born vulnerable, dependent, and requiring care. Relational autonomy recognizes that achieving autonomy competencies relies upon the relationships through which care and support are provided to the initially vulnerable.

The second feature of relational theory concerns the identity of the autonomous agent. Rather than taking identity to be given, isolated and self-sufficient, relational theorists argue that identity is constituted in and through social relationships that take place in specific historical contexts and that are subject to prevailing social norms regarding race, gender, ability, and so forth. This view of socially constituted identity has implications for how we think about authenticity, and about the sources and meaning of our preferences. The view of the self as socially constituted recognizes that values and preferences may change as identity evolves over time.

The third and fourth features of relational accounts concern internal and external constraints on autonomy. Exercising autonomy requires the individual to hold a set of self-evaluative attitudes that allow her to see herself, and be seen as autonomous—attitudes such as self-trust, self-respect and self-esteem. And just as supportive relationships can scaffold and build autonomy competency, hostile, abusive or oppressive relationships can undermine or destroy the self-regarding attitudes that enable individuals to exercise autonomy. This feature of relational theory helps to explain why a person may hold autonomy competencies, but be unable to act autonomously if she lacks the requisite self-attitudes. Finally, relational theorists identify external barriers to exercising autonomy in the form of access to meaningful opportunities. This feature of relational theory clearly links autonomy and justice by identifying that freedom to make choices is not sufficient to guarantee autonomy as individuals require resources to put their preferences into action.

Relational theory has been hugely influential in feminist bioethics. Feminist scholars have drawn upon insights from relational theory to develop accounts of self-trust (McLeod 2002), informed consent (Stoljar 2011), conscientious autonomy (Kukla 2005), public health ethics (Baylis et al. 2008) and healthcare ethics more broadly (Sherwin et al. 1998); as well as to investigate related concepts.

The moral salience of relationships figures prominently in feminist contributions to our understanding of care, dependency, and vulnerability. Regarding care, Gilligan (1982) argues for a form of moral reasoning specific to women that prioritizes care and relationships of care, in contrast to the justice orientation attributed to male moral reasoning. On her account, the highest level of female moral reasoning is characterized by an individual considering what is best for herself and others, taken as a relational unit. Noddings (1984), who identifies her work as feminine rather than feminist, takes care to be the fundamental moral virtue of women, expressed in and through the relationship of the "one-caring" and the "cared-for." For Noddings, care is specific, occurring between identifiable individuals, and providing the cared-for with a model for future relationships (Tong 2009). The ethics of care has been highly influential in nursing ethics as this approach provides a theoretical framework for the practical work of providing patient care (Kuhse 1997; Groenhout 2004).

While many disagree with the specifics of Gilligan and Noddings, the recognition that relationships are not between equals, and often if not always involve some degree of dependency, has been highly influential on thinkers such as Sara Ruddick (1989) and Eva Kittay (1999). Kittay uses the language of dependency and dependency work, thereby avoiding concerns about stereotyping women as natural carers. On Kittay's account, it is relationships rather than rights that ground the care of dependents, where relationships morally demand meeting the needs of dependents. Dependency relations are socially constructed, but often not voluntarily chosen as they arise in the context of existing relationships and responsibilities. Kittay bases her account of equality in the notion that we are totally dependent as infants and children, and that our very survival is premised upon the labors of some mother (or dependency worker), making dependency a universally shared experience grounding our common humanity. In turn, this universal experience gives rise to a responsibility on the part of society to recognize and support dependency workers.

Like care and dependency, vulnerability is a third concept taken up by feminist theorists interested in relational theory. The concept of vulnerability is foundational in bioethics, grounding protections for patients and research participants. Yet for some time the concept was little theorized, leading at times to a labeling approach associated with stereotyping and discrimination (Rogers 2014). Florencia Luna (2009) proposes an account of vulnerability understood as separate layers rather than a general attribute, requiring careful examination of context-sensitive features to inform responses. In their account, Mackenzie et al. (2014) propose a typology of vulnerability that draws particular attention to vulnerability arising as the result of oppressive social relations. They argue that responses to the vulnerable must be directed by the obligation to foster autonomy, in order to counter objectionable paternalism and mitigate the threats to agency that often accompany vulnerability.

Questions of social justice permeate feminist discussions of autonomy, dependency and vulnerability (Mackenzie 2014). Social justice is crucial to the development and exercise of autonomy, understood relationally. Achieving this requires recognition of inequalities, including those that are gendered, in ways that explicitly address their causes. On feminist accounts, social justice requires attention to the distribution of power as much as of material resources (Young 1990). Sherwin (2008) develops this line of reasoning in her work, arguing for a focus on the social and institutional constitution of agency and the need to understand how patterns of power and privilege, which shape the opportunities and choices available to citizens, are reinforced or challenged by public practices, policies and institutions. Feminist accounts of public health ethics are likewise premised on the demand for social justice (Rogers 2006; Baylis et al. 2008), partly in recognition of the connections between disadvantage, discrimination and ill health. Baylis et al. argue that a relational account of public health illuminates the ways in which health policy decisions shape opportunities, and exert different effects on different social groups.

In addition to substantive contributions to theory, feminist approaches have had a lasting impact upon methodology in bioethics. There is no single feminist methodological approach to bioethics. Nonetheless, it is reasonable to claim that feminist bioethics is characterized by an interest in rich empiricism, attention to lived experiences and explicit recognition of one's own perspective or standpoint (Wolf 1996). Feminists favor an expanded understanding of the dimensions of moral reasoning, in contrast to the abstract principlism of at least some mainstream bioethics (Rawlinson 2008). One response to abstraction lies in the use of narrative, placing great emphasis upon hearing and understanding the specific details of a bioethical issue from the perspective of the main protagonists (Lindemann 1997). Mary Rawlinson (2001) draws on resources from European philosophy to argue for greater attention to lived experience and proposes the pregnant body as a metaphor for relations of moral decision-making in bioethics. Postmodern approaches provide another avenue for critiquing claims about universalism to build a more particularist feminist framework (Shildrick 1997; Shildrick and Mykitiuk, 2005; see also the work of Margaret Little 2001). Philosophy of the body has proved to be a useful tool in investigating the moral dimensions of lived experience, the integrity of the body, and the boundaries between life and death (Young 1980; Shildrick 2008), while insights from disability theorists have illustrated the complex interplay of power, discrimination and limited choice affecting people living with disability (Leach Scully 2010).

This section has briefly surveyed some of the main contributions of feminist bioethics to the field, of which relational theory is the most influential. Relational autonomy is now a widespread, although not always accurately employed concept in bioethics, while thick descriptions of cases and attention to context have become commonplace. In the final section, I consider future directions for feminist bioethics.

Future Directions for Feminist Bioethics

Feminist bioethics has moved far beyond an early focus on reproduction, although aspects of reproduction such as surrogacy, uterus transplantation, gender selection and genetic technologies continue to attract attention. A scan of issues of *IJFAB* (for example, 6.2, 7.2 and 8.2) reveals growing interest in globalism, and attention to the way that national domestic issues reverberate on a global scale. Investigations into the long-term care needs of ageing populations in wealthy countries, treatment of migrant health workers, the effects of health tourism, transnational reproduction, and inter-country disparities reflect the concerns and methods identified above while extending the scope of bioethics beyond the clinical encounter. Transnational interest encompasses a critique of Western-centric perspectives in bioethics, with attempts to engage feminist bioethics scholars from around the globe (Narayan and Hardy 2000; Tong et al. 2001; Ryan 2004). There is developing interest in environmental bioethics, drawing upon resources from environmental ethics and ecofeminism (Mies and Shiva 1993; Mellor 1997). Environmental concerns link to those about sustainability and food ethics (Rawlinson 2016), both of which lend themselves to feminist analysis, as does the topic of animal ethics. Technological innovations continue to drive debate, with a new investigation of sexism sparked by developments in neural imaging (Fine 2010), while old inequities recur in new clinical contexts such as surgery (Biller-Andorno 2002).

Anne Donchin describes feminist bioethics as a response to the "tepid agenda and exclusionary practices of the burgeoning field of bioethics" (2008, 146). The scholars who first identified themselves as feminist bioethicists, as well as those joining the field subsequently, have challenged theoretical foundations, demanded justice, opposed oppression and discrimination and developed new avenues of enquiry. Nonetheless, there remains much to do.

Related Topics

Feminist methods in the history of philosophy (Chapter 1); the sex/gender distinction and the social construction of reality (Chapter 13); embodiment and feminist philosophy (Chapter 15); personal identity and relational selves (Chapter 18); rationality and objectivity in feminist philosophy (Chapter 20); feminist and queer intersections with disability studies (Chapter 30); feminist conceptions of autonomy (Chapter 41); feminist ethics of care (Chapter 43); neoliberalism, global justice, and transnational feminisms (Chapter 48).

References

Adshead, Gwen (2011) "Same but Different: Constructions of Female Violence in Forensic Mental Health," *International Journal of Feminist Approaches to Bioethics* 4(1): 41–68.

Baylis, Françoise, Kenny, Nuala P., and Sherwin, Susan (2008) "A Relational Account of Public Health Ethics," *Public Health Ethics* 1(3): 196–209.

Biller-Andorno, Nikola (2002) "Gender Imbalance in Living Organ Donation," *Medicine, Health Care and Philosophy* 5: 199–204.

Bordo, Susan (1993) *Unbearable Weight: Feminism, Western Culture, and the Body*, Berkeley, CA: University of California Press.

Bluhm, Robyn (2011) "Gender Differences in Depression: Explanations from Feminist Ethics," *International Journal of Feminist Approaches to Bioethics* 4(1): 69–88.

Chesler, Phyllis (2005) *Women and Madness: Revised and Updated*, New York: Palgrave Macmillan.

Code, Lorraine (1988) "Experience, Knowledge and Responsibility," in Morwenna Griffiths and Margaret Whitford (Eds.) *Feminist Perspectives in Philosophy*, Bloomington, IN and Indianapolis, IN: Indiana University Press, 187–204.

Corea, Gena (1985) *The Mother Machine: Reproductive Technologies from Artificial Insemination to Artificial Wombs*, New York: Harper & Row.

Dickenson, Donna (2006) "The Lady Vanishes: What's Missing from the Stem Cell Debate," *Journal of Bioethical Inquiry* 3(1–2): 43–54.

Donchin, Anne (2008) "Remembering FAB's Past, Anticipating Our Future," *International Journal of Feminist Approaches to Bioethics* 1(1): 145–160.

Donchin, Anne and Scully, Jackie Leach (2015) "Feminist Bioethics," *The Stanford Encyclopaedia of Philosophy* [online]. Available from: http://plato.stanford.edu/entries/feminist-bioethics/.

Engelhardt, Hugo T. (1986) *The Foundations of Bioethics*, New York: Oxford University Press.

Fine, Cordelia (2010) *Delusions of Gender*, London: Icon Books.

Gilligan, Carol (1982) *In a Different Voice: Psychological Theory and Women's Development*, Cambridge, MA: Harvard University Press.

Gould, Carol Steinberg (2011) "Why the Histrionic Personality Disorder Should Not Be in the DSM: A New Taxonomic and Moral Analysis," *International Journal of Feminist Approaches to Bioethics* 4(1): 26–40.

Groenhout, Ruth E. (2004) *Connected Lives: Human Nature and the Ethics of Care*, Lanham, MD: Rowman & Littlefield.

Hoffmann, Diane E. and Tarzian, Anita J. (2001) "The Girl Who Cried Pain: A Bias against Women in the Treatment of Pain," *Journal of Law and Medical Ethics* 29: 13–27.

Holmes, Helen B. and Purdy, Laura M. (Eds.) (1992) *Feminist Perspectives in Medical Ethics*, Bloomington, IN: Indiana University Press.

Holmes, Helen B., Hoskins, Betty B. and Gross, Michael (Eds.) (1980) *Birth Control and Controlling Birth: Women-Centered Perspectives*, Clifton, NJ: Humana Press.

Holmes, Helen B., Hoskins, Betty B., and Gross, Michael (Eds.) (1981) *The Custom-Made Child? Women-Centered Perspectives*, Clifton, NJ: Humana Press.

Jaggar, Allison (1989) "Feminist Ethics: Some Issues for the Nineties," *Journal of Social Philosophy* 20(1–2): 91–107.

Kittay, Eva Feder (1999) *Love's Labor: Essays on Women, Equality, and Dependency*, New York: Routledge.

Kittay, Eva Feder and Meyers, Diana T. (1987) *Women and Moral Theory*, Totowa, NJ: Rowman & Littlefield.

Kuhse, Helga (1997) *Caring, Nurses, Women and Ethics*, Oxford: Blackwell.

Kukla, Rebecca (2005) "Conscientious Autonomy: Displacing Decisions in Health Care," *Hastings Center Report* 35(2): 34–44.

Leach Scully, Jackie (2010) "Hidden Labor: Disabled/Nondisabled Encounters, Agency, and Autonomy," *International Journal of Feminist Approaches to Bioethics* 3(2): 25–42.

Lindemann, Hilde (Ed.) (1997) *Stories and Their Limits: Narrative Approaches to Bioethics*, New York: Routledge.

Little, Margaret O. (2001) "On Knowing the 'Why': Particularism and Moral Theory," *Hastings Center Report* 31(4): 32–40.

Luna, Florencia (2009) "Elucidating the Concept of Vulnerability: Layers not Labels," *International Journal of Feminist Approaches to Bioethics* 2(1): 121–139.

Mackenzie, Catriona (2014) "The Importance of Relational Autonomy and Capabilities for an Ethics of Vulnerability," in Catriona Mackenzie, Wendy A. Rogers, and Susan Dodds (Eds.) *Vulnerability: New Essays in Ethics and Feminist Philosophy*, New York: Oxford University Press, 33–59.

—— (2015) "Autonomy," in John Arras, Elizabeth Fenton and Rebecca Kukla (Eds.) *Routledge Companion to Bioethics*, New York and London: Routledge, 277–290.

Mackenzie, Catriona and Stoljar, Natalie (Eds.) (2000) *Relational Autonomy: Feminist Perspectives on Autonomy, Agency and the Social Self*, New York: Oxford University Press.

Mackenzie, Catriona, Rogers, Wendy A., and Dodds, Susan (2014) "Introduction: What Is Vulnerability and Why Does It Matter for Moral Theory," in Catriona Mackenzie, Wendy A. Rogers, and Susan Dodds (Eds.) *Vulnerability: New Essays in Ethics and Feminist Philosophy*, New York: Oxford University Press, 1–29.

McLeod, Carolyn (2002) *Self-Trust and Reproductive Autonomy*, Cambridge, MA: MIT Press.

Mahowald, Mary B. (1993) *Women and Children in Health Care: An Unequal Majority*, New York: Oxford University Press.

Marquis, Don (1989) "Why Abortion Is Immoral," *The Journal of Philosophy* 86(4): 183–202.

Mellor, Mary (1997) *Feminism and Ecology*, New York: New York University Press.

Mies, Maria and Shiva, Vandana (1993) *Ecofeminism*, North Melbourne: Spinifex Press.

Mosca, Lori, Barrett-Connor, Elizabeth, Wenger, and Kass, Nanette (2011) "Sex/Gender Differences in Cardiovascular Disease Prevention: What a Difference a Decade Makes," *Circulation* 124(19): 2145–2154.

Narayan, Uma and Harding, Sandra (Eds.) (2000) *Decentering the Center: Philosophy for a Multicultural, Postcolonial, and Feminist World*, Bloomington, IN: Indiana University Press.

Noddings, Nel (1984) *Caring: A Feminine Approach to Ethics and Moral Education*, Berkeley, CA: University of California Press.

Radcliffe-Richards, Janet (2007) "Selling Organs, Gametes and Surrogacy Services," in Rosamond Rhodes, Leslie P. Francis, and Anita Silver (Eds.) *The Blackwell Guide to Medical Ethics*, Malden MA: Wiley Blackwell, 254–268.

Rawlinson, Mary C. (2001) "The Concept of a Feminist Bioethics," *The Journal of Medicine and Philosophy* 26(4): 405–416.

—— (2008) "Introduction," *International Journal of Feminist Approaches to Bioethics* 1(1): 1–6.

—— (2016) *Just Life: Bioethics and the Future of Sexual Difference*, New York: Columbia University Press.

Rogers, Wendy. A. (2006) "Feminism and Public Health Ethics," *Journal of Medical Ethics* 32: 351–354.

—— (2014) "Vulnerability and Bioethics," in Catriona Mackenzie, Wendy A. Rogers and Susan Dodds (Eds.) *Vulnerability: New Essays in Ethics and Feminist Philosophy*, New York: Oxford University Press, 60–87.

Rogers, Wendy. A. and Ballantyne, Angela J. (2008) "Exclusion of Women from Clinical Research: Myth or Reality?" *Mayo Clinic Proceedings* 83(5): 536–542.

Ruddick, Sara (1989) *Maternal Thinking: Toward a Politics of Peace*, Boston, MA: Beacon Press.

Ryan, Maura A. (2004) "Beyond a Western Bioethics?" *Theological Studies* 65(1): 158–177.

Sherwin, Susan (1989) "Feminist and Medical Ethics: Two Different Approaches to Contextual Ethics," *Hypatia*, 4(2): 57–72.

—— (1992) *No Longer Patient: Feminist Ethics and Health Care*, Cambridge: Cambridge University Press.

—— (2008) "Whither Bioethics? How Feminism Can Help Reorient Bioethics," *International Journal of Feminist Approaches to Bioethics* 1(1): 7–27.

Sherwin, Susan et al. (1998) *The Politics of Women's Health: Exploring Agency and Autonomy*, Philadelphia, PA: Temple University Press.

Shildrick, Margrit (1997) *Leaky Bodies and Boundaries: Feminism, Postmodernism and Bioethics*, London: Routledge.

—— (2008) "The Critical Turn in Feminist Bioethics: The Case of Heart Transplantation," *International Journal of Feminist Approaches to Bioethics* 1(1): 28–47.

Shildrick, Margrit and Mykitiuk, Roxanne (Eds.) (2005) *Ethics of the Body: Postconventional Challenges*, Cambridge, MA: MIT Press.

Stoljar, Natalie (2011) "Informed Consent and Relational Conceptions of Autonomy," *Journal of Medicine and Philosophy* 36: 375–384.

—— (2013) "Feminist Perspectives on Autonomy," *The Stanford Encyclopedia of Philosophy* [online]. Available from: http://plato.stanford.edu/entries/feminism-autonomy/.

Tong, Rosemarie (1993) *Feminine and Feminist Ethics*, Belmont, CA: Wadsworth.

Tong, Rosemarie and Williams, Nancy (2009) "Feminist Ethics," *The Stanford Encyclopedia of Philosophy* [online]. Available from: http://plato.stanford.edu/archives/fall2014/entries/feminism-ethics/.

Tong, Rosemarie, Anderson, Gwen, and Santos-Maranan, Aida (Eds.) (2001) *Globalizing Feminist Bioethics: Crosscultural Perspectives*, Boulder, CO: Westview.

Tooley, Michael (1972) "Abortion and Infanticide," *Philosophy and Public Affairs* 2: 37–65.

Wendell, Susan (1996) *The Rejected Body: Feminist Philosophical Reflections on Disability*, New York: Routledge.

Weitzman, Lenore J. (1985) *The Divorce Revolution*, New York: The Free Press.

Wolf, Susan (Ed.) (1996) *Feminism and Bioethics: Beyond Reproduction*, New York: Oxford University Press.

Young, Iris M. (1980) "Throwing Like a Girl: A Phenomenology of Feminine Body Comportment, Morality, and Spatiality," *Human Studies* 3: 137–156.

—— (1990) *Justice and the Politics of Difference*, Princeton, NJ: Princeton University Press.

Social and Political Philosophy

47

MULTICULTURAL AND POSTCOLONIAL FEMINISMS

Monica Mookherjee

The growth of writings on multiculturalism and postcolonialism over the past decades has produced new approaches to feminist philosophy associated with the "third wave." These approaches have heightened appreciation of differences among women, such as class, geopolitical region, religion, and culture. This chapter examines and contrasts postcolonial and multicultural feminist approaches, and suggests that the main controversy between them lies in the multicultural feminists' acceptance of the Enlightenment humanist subject, in relation to which the rights and interests of women are presented. Fraught debates around the world over practices like genital cutting and sexist cultural membership rules have heightened the relevance of these critical projects. Multicultural and postcolonial feminisms are increasingly crucial in a globalizing, diverse world. Though supporting the multicultural feminist agenda of pluralizing the rights of the humanist subject, this chapter also recommends engagement with postcolonial critics, who problematize the very notion of a unified subject of rights. Briefly, postcolonial feminists raise important moral-epistemological questions about knowledge of women's interests, and reject a framing of their entitlements in terms of "culture" in any simple sense. However, common to both feminisms is the task of unsettling some universalist certainties of earlier liberal feminists. The approaches also share a desire to avoid the relativism of postmodern positions, which question the possibility of certain knowledge about human beings generally, and, in this context, of diverse women who are differently located in structures of power.

Multiculturalism Feminism: Rethinking Liberal Humanism

The term "multiculturalism" is deeply contested, and bears different sociological and philosophical meanings. In one sense, the word is descriptive, and denotes the reality of many states in the world today, namely the fact that most countries are composed of different cultural and ethnic groups. The term may also be understood, in the normative sense of many liberal theorists, as suggesting that cultural diversity is valuable and requires institutional and social support. Liberals, concerned to equalize minorities' access to the opportunities that members of the dominant culture enjoy, usually hold that the social bases of minority peoples' dignity should be ensured by respecting their cherished traditions. In spite of deep controversies following heightened post-9/11 scrutiny of Muslims in the West in particular, multiculturalism informs distinct approaches in contemporary liberal and republican political theories (e.g., Laborde 2008; Levey 2010).

Furthermore, following controversies surrounding gendered issues like female genital mutilation and the Muslim veil, "multicultural feminism" has itself emerged as a specific area of research. The early years of the new millennium witnessed innovative negotiations of conflicts of gender and culture (e.g., Deveaux 2006; Dhamoon 2006; Baumeister 2009). The questions that motivated these approaches included: Which interests and needs are shared across cultural boundaries? Which risk being hidden if cultural diversity is not recognized?

Going beyond earlier second-wave debates about a biological or affective essence of womanhood (e.g., Firestone 1970), the new multicultural feminists are wary of universal theories that confine women to particular roles. They seek to pluralize feminism, without renouncing some universal claims. Taking up and extending the liberal humanist faith in a society of free and equal autonomous subjects, moreover, they follow the general multicultural demand for inclusion in the social contracts of much political theory. Historically, feminist political theorists took their male counterparts to task for focusing on masculine interests, and for disregarding reproductive and other gender rights (Pateman and Shanley 1991). Multicultural feminists extend this challenge. While supporting the values of bodily integrity and autonomy, they add that the good of cultural belonging sometimes necessitates different rights. Instead of rejecting the rational liberal subject of classical political thought, they pluralize it and orient it to "communitarian" concerns.

There is, however, much debate between multicultural feminists, and Eisenberg (2010) distinguishes two emerging approaches. The first focuses on the value of autonomy; and the second on political inclusion and humanist democracy. Anne Phillips's idea of "multiculturalism without culture" (2007) could be taken to illustrate the first approach. It recommends that feminist theories conscious of disparities of social power focus on the value of personal autonomy across cultures (Narayan 1997; Meyers 2014). While Phillips does not disregard the importance of democratic deliberation, she focuses on how sensitivity to culture yields different understandings of the pressures that undermine women's abilities to choose. In doing so, she relies on a conception of "culture" as fluid and contested, and avoids an exaggerated "clash-of-civilizations" narrative that takes the ideal of the autonomous, humanist subject to be Eurocentric and inapplicable to cultures that diverge from a Western norm (cf. Saharso 2006). However, confronted with the need to say how, without a stable concept of culture, there would be anything for multicultural policy to do, Phillips explains that minority membership can still affect life-chances. This is so, just as denying the concept of "race" does not rule out considering the impact of racial discrimination on people's lives (Phillips 2007: 21).

Therefore, although Phillips accepts the liberal feminist ideals of autonomy and equality, she asks: "Who is to say what gender equality is? And by what right does someone with one set of cultural experiences have the right to comment on and judge the practices and beliefs of someone from a different background?" (Phillips 2007: 38). While values may be interpreted differently across cultures, agreement may be taken to exist on basic norms, she believes, at least in North American and European immigrant societies (2007: 41). On this reading, autonomy-based theories like Phillips's help to pluralize a feminist understanding of human interests, without falling prey to "cultural essentialism."

However, a number of challenges confront this approach, including defining the emotional and cognitive threshold of self-determination across cultures. How much control over one's life should a person have to be regarded as autonomous? Moreover, the approach faces the task of specifying a distinction between the "core" meaning of a value and its interpretation. What is the limit to the different cultural interpretations of autonomy that human beings might endorse? In addition, even accepting that most conflicts over gender and culture tend not to raise questions of fundamental value-conflict, one might question the seemingly controversial assumption that the autonomous life has more value than a mode of life that emphasizes, say, communal harmony.

A possible response to this question would be to suggest that non-domination does not require a "thick" theory of autonomy of the kind associated, say, with Nussbaum's (1999) capabilities approach. However, partly because of the difficulties of defining a "thinner" concept of autonomy, some theorists turn instead to democratic deliberation as a resource for resolving conflicts over gendered practices (Deveaux 2006; Baumeister 2009). Eisenberg (2010) identifies Seyla Benhabib's (2002) approach as a key example. Drawing from Habermas' discourse theory, Benhabib supports Phillips's conception of cultural groups as fluid and internally contested. But she focuses on inclusive deliberation to encourage understanding between different perspectives. However, conscious that the conduct of democracy itself requires normative guidelines, she specifies three conditions: (a) egalitarian reciprocity; (b) voluntary self-ascription; and (c) freedom of exit and assimilation (Benhabib 2002: 132). These considerations infer that participants in democratic dialogue must enjoy at least some independence to voice an undominated view. Yet, while appearing modest and realistic, ambiguities could arise in practice over which forms of deliberation should count as "democratic." In addition, such efforts to constrain democratic deliberation may ultimately involve prioritizing humanist ideals like individual agency and sex equality (Eisenberg 2010: 132). On this reading, there may be not so great a distance between the two multicultural feminist approaches, and both may ultimately confront similar challenges.

This is to say, if multicultural humanist feminists join other third-wave feminists in celebrating differences between women (Gillis, Howie, and Munford 2007) and aim to foster unity within this diversity, they seem to bring both advantages and drawbacks. Positively, their concern for social equality absolves them from criticisms of certain forms of multiculturalism, which presuppose cultural essences, and have been faulted for creating divisions and for failing to attend to economic inequalities or structural power (Barry 2001). They avoid what has been called an "ossificatory imperative"—i.e., the tendency to freeze cultural groups into preconceived definitions (Bannerji 2000). The multicultural feminist agenda unsettles the assumption that multicultural theory need be merely decorative, or exclusionary in paradoxical ways (Chanady 1995: 426).

However, perhaps the real cost of bringing a humanist framework into the third wave—whether based on autonomy or democracy—is that of ultimately relying on the contestable normative assumption that women share generalizable interests in autonomy and market-based equality. While it could be thought that feminism cannot do without some conception of autonomy or agency (Saharso 2006; Madhok 2013), multicultural feminists might risk assuming static distinctions between acceptable and unacceptable diversity (Chanady 1995: 421). Although the focus on inequalities arising from minority membership seems informative and valuable, multicultural feminists risk failing to offer a realistic account of how "culture" and "cultural differences" are materially, socially, and geopolitically constructed.

We will turn to these problems; but, for now, it is worth emphasizing that the new multicultural feminisms seem particularly helpful and insightful in societies characterized by immigration, with long traditions of human rights and civil liberties. Addressing issues that had not been considered fully by "First World" liberal feminists, they pluralize an understanding of women's interests, and encourage deeper reflection on issues that might otherwise be regarded as simple instances of patriarchy, such as the *hijab*, polygamy, or gender-differentiated membership rules. Their approaches offer, therefore, a diversity-centered third-wave approach, at once sensitive to culture *and* strongly humanist and anti-relativist.

Postcolonial Feminists Unsettle the Humanist Subject

While the concept of multiculturalism is variously interpreted, "postcolonialism" may appear still more complex. Rather than referring to the historical period after the end of colonialism, the term signals awareness of the persistence of colonial structures of thought after decolonization, or what has been termed "re-colonization" (Schutte 2007). The idea of the "postcolonial" also overlaps with the related concepts of the "transnational" and the "de-colonial." Transnational feminism is related to "postcolonial" counterpart, but its focus could be thought to differ. Although transnational feminists are concerned about the effects of colonialism, and particularly of "neo-colonialism," on gendered subjects, they view the issues confronting women, say in relation to human rights and humanitarian interventions, through a reading of how "race," gender, and sexuality are constructed by the ongoing imperialism that certain nations exert in relation to others. The general idea of transnational feminism is that, as "nations" with distinct identities and values are constructed through the neo-imperialism of global capitalist relations, any gendered analysis should remain cognizant of this in considering the disadvantages that women experience in distinct parts of the world (Mohanty 2003, 2013; Razack 2004; Alexander and Mohanty 2013). Thus, transnational feminists have located the debate about the assumed subjection of women in Islam within an understanding of the US invasion of Iraq, for instance, to show that women are further subjugated when humanitarian groups represent the "Muslim woman" solely as victims and portray those who assist them as paternal saviors (Hesford and Kozol 2005; Conway 2012). Briefly, then, transnational feminism unsettles the concept of the nation to better understand and intervene in gender disadvantages. While their approach is consistent with postcolonial feminism, the latter, as we will see, concentrates on the distinct ways that women in postcolonial contexts may reclaim a distinctive "voice," agency or identity.

Turning to another similar term, decolonial feminists (e.g., Alcoff 2007; Lugones 2010) focus on Latin American and Caribbean modernities, and, specifically, on the oppositional strategies that challenged colonialist representations of abjectness, dehumanization, and slavery that began in sixteenth-century occupations of these territories, and coexisted with colonial power. Decolonial feminism, therefore, re-reads the histories of such early colonial encounters to theorize what Lugones calls "the coloniality of gender." This term refers to the fact that, owing to the hierarchical dichotomies constructed by colonization, the idea of the "colonized female" could not emerge. As the hierarchical relation between male and female was contingent on the human/non-human distinction created by colonization, on account of which the colonized were not deemed fully human, it was impossible to conceive of a "colonized woman" subject within normative gender codes. Against this background, decolonial feminism depicts a process by which the identities of women under colonialism become subject to racialized, capitalist, and gender oppressions (Lugones 2010: 747). Thus, while the terms are linked, decolonialism focuses on subjection and resistance that precedes the oppositional strategies on which postcolonial writers focus.

Postcolonial feminists, for their part, are influenced by figures as diverse as Gramsci, Said, and Fanon. In spite of this theoretical diversity, an integrated perspective has emerged in cultural studies by, among others, Gayatri Spivak (1987), Anne McClintock (1995), Sara Suleri (1992), and Chandra Mohanty (2003). Their perspective goes deeper than the new multicultural feminists in rethinking the conceptual basis for gender interests in a more nuanced and challenging approach. As we shall see, however, questions arise as to whether postcolonial feminists succeed in unsettling the unified humanist Enlightenment subject, and, if they do, a question arises as to the basis on which they may challenge patriarchy, which survives after colonialism's formal end.

By way of a working definition, postcolonial feminism provides "an exploration of, at the intersections of, colonialism and neo-colonialism with gender, nation, class, race and sexualities in the different contexts of women's lives" (Rajan and Park 2005: 53; see also Kapur 2002). The postcolonial desire to unsettle the unified subjectivity of liberal humanist thought is linked to an understanding of gender interests as continually produced and re-produced by the webs of power relations that persist after colonization and that form the subject's identity. A stable individual should not be presupposed, according to this view, because notions of "gender" and "culture" that produce individuality are themselves products of power. Postcolonial feminists focus on the potential arising from this instability, drawing attention to the significance of what is excluded by dominant interpretations of individual interests.

Gayatri Spivak, in particular, follows Derrida in suggesting that these gaps signal the "quite other" (tout-autre) (1987: 573; Derrida 1967), or an other who is not the counter-image of the self. She encourages those writing in and about postcolonial contexts to see that the representation of others often involves a certain "epistemic violence," in the sense of presenting others through colonial dualities—e.g., oppressor/oppressed; powerful/vulnerable—and, thus, failing to portray them accurately. Such representations fail critically to engage and question colonial relations. More critical engagement would enable a "third space" of articulation, to use Homi Bhabha's (1994) term, neither purely modern nor an expression of authentic, traditional culture.

Spivak understands this third space to be productive in theorizing gender, because awareness of the potential for resistance that it contains allows the theorist to learn from women whose experiences differ considerably from her own (1986: 287). Furthermore, if the subaltern female cannot speak or be spoken for, in the sense of fully represented, then Spivak argues that one must learn not to speak in her place. This imperative challenges feminists of more dominant positions to attempt to "unlearn female privilege" (1986: 294), by considering the history of her relation to other women in regards to the production of social meanings. Spivak (1993) and

Rajan (1993) later clarify that the different subject-positions that emerge through this critical awareness bring to light a conception of agency, which relates strongly to indigenous females (Mills 1988). Such an insight also suggests that the multiculturalist focus on "culture" or "cultural practices" could constitute a form of epistemic violence that repeats colonialism (Jaggar 2005).

These insights are extremely important because, historically, practices like veiling and polygamy constituted significant areas of conflict and negotiation between colonizers and colonized (Narayan 1997: 16). By locating their analysis in global economic relations, postcolonial feminists clear space to theorize new forms of subjectivity. Awareness of the possibility of agency even in the most constraining social circumstances entails recognition that conventional assumptions of colonial subjection often conceal resistance (Khader 2009; 2011). Thus, postcolonial writers do not reject concepts of justice and human rights as bourgeois ideology in a Marxist sense. Rather, combining Marxist and poststructuralist insights, they work within the problematic of Western Enlightenment thought as it operates after the formal end of colonialism (Spivak 2004; Sa'ar 2005). In doing so, they recognize the possibility of what Spivak calls subaltern "catachresis," or in Homi Bhabha's (1984) phrase, "in-betweenness." This is the creativity that arises from re-presenting the colonizer's language in ways that are, to cite Bhabha again, "almost the same, but not quite." The hybrid ways that women in postcolonial situations use classic Enlightenment notions generates new meanings. These concepts should not be rejected for being the "master's tools," in Audré Lorde's phrase.

Postcolonial feminists therefore go beyond the focus in the new multicultural feminisms on inequalities arising from cultural membership, straightforwardly understood. A wider study of history and geopolitics is needed, because, as Jaggar (2005: 67) observes, when multinational corporations exploit women in export-processing zones in poor countries, for instance, it is impossible to say that this practice reflects "Western" or "non-Western" culture. Yet, although postcolonial feminists destabilize the terms on which transcultural gender interests are formulated, by suggesting the provisionality of all human interests articulated in the context of power, they value the possibility of creating new meaning through this problematic. As we have seen, the new multicultural feminists pluralize the liberal agenda, by deepening debate about the rights of women in Enlightenment arising from values of autonomy and equality. In contrast, postcolonial feminists characterize these expressions of humanist universalism as the products of power relations. Yet, because they have a political project too, they concede the need at times to rely on a stable concept of women's interests, in what Spivak (1990) calls "strategic essentialism." Without assuming, she suggests, that women in any culture or tradition *are* particular kinds of subjects with interests that may be revealed through interpretation, it should be conceded that women will find it necessary at times to take up a subject position out of political necessity. Here, Spivak considers the remobilization of women during the Algerian liberation struggle, based upon their stereotyped image as bomb carriers or messengers. Although it served a goal, Spivak concedes that invoking such fixed images of "Algerian womanhood" was unlikely to be empowering. As she concludes, a "strategy is a situation; it is not a theory" (1993: 104; Morton 2007). The issue of mobilizing upon a "cultural" or "nationalist" concept of women's interests, in the absence of a firm grounding, is therefore a controversial issue arising from postcolonial feminism.

Although multicultural feminists might be advised to take seriously postcolonial feminist insights concerning the geopolitical specificities that configure "gender" and "culture," questions do remain. If women's interests may be fixed for strategic purposes only, one might ask about the normative basis of feminism under the postcolonial approach, and its capacity to theorize the frequently extreme material disadvantages experienced by women globally. Furthermore, Mukherjee (1991) is concerned that in spite of their attention to diversity, postcolonial theorists perhaps re-create a fixed subject, one defined by the experience of marginality. Similarly, Suleri (1992) asks whether the celebration of hybridity can amount to an orthodoxy, which assumes that individual experiences of resisting power inevitably amount to a capacity to overturn it. Such difficulties can lead to wariness of some writing in postcolonial situations to call themselves feminists (Kishwar 1990). At an extreme, some have even found post-colonial feminist writings to be "self-indulgent, polemic and self-righteous" (cited in Rajan and Park 2005: 54).

Although these criticisms may go too far, given the progressive motivations of post-colonial feminists, a difficult question remains as to whether they ultimately rely on the universalist gender images they aim to transcend. Is the figure of the "female subaltern" another subject position with humanist interests in autonomy and equality? This is a difficult question; and without having space in this chapter fully to address it we turn to the issue of how valuable postcolonial insights have been taken up in feminist philo-sophical debates concerning the person, the body and the mind.

Bringing Postcolonial Insights to Philosophy: Selves and Others, Reasons and Emotions

Feminists outside cultural and literary studies have brought postcolonial insights productively into current philosophical debate. Uma Narayan (1997; 2002), for instance, questions the colonialist presuppositions that affect an understanding of the relationship between self and other. Kanchana Mahadevan (2014) furthers the debate about rational individualism and care ethics in culturally diverse, postcolonial conditions. Their contributions demonstrate that, while feminism may be sensitive to diversity and critical of structures of power, these commitments need not rule out defining some universal gender interests too.

Narayan, for her part, concentrates on the fact that those writing from the diaspora or from within decolonized countries often encounter unexpected reactions to their feminist ideas. In their dialogue with others, they are often assigned particular roles, which risk forestalling an understanding between self and the other. The first role, the "emissary," involves placing on the critic of third world origin a responsibility to convey her culture in wholly celebratory terms. Referring to Ananda Coomaraswamy's *The Dance of Shiva* (1957), Narayan explains that this text utilizes clichéd oppositions between "materialist" Western and "spiritual" Indian culture; and that those who question these dichotomies, such as feminists critical of gender disparities, are met with anxiety and defensiveness (Narayan 1997: 131). In contrast, the second role, the "mirror," suggests that the post-colonial writer's representation of gender issues within their culture is often treated as an opportunity to reflect on the limitations, or "orientalism," of Western, Enlightenment values (Narayan 1997: 138). The risk is that discussions about gender issues within "other" cultures become a foil through which the dominant reflect upon their norms.

While Narayan's depiction of these roles might seem controversial from some feminist perspectives, she alerts attention to the important ways in which knowledge of "the other" can be foreclosed. The problem is deepened by a third role, the "authentic insider." Narayan explains that the insider, though licenced to raise certain cultural criticisms, is deemed representative of the whole society that she discusses. Narayan worries that this tendency makes it easy to reject, when convenient to do so, her views as being "too Westernized" or "not really different enough." The role therefore works to silence or de-legitimize differences (Narayan 1997: 148). Narayan later connects these issues to the difficulties that feminists confront of comprehending the agency of diverse women more broadly (Narayan 2002). The tendency to generalize the view of certain women within the culture regarding autonomy or human rights makes it hard to appreciate that others within the tradition rationally accept different trade-offs between goods and interests, without false consciousness and without being "dupes of culture" (Saharso 2006). Although the three roles may function more complexly than Narayan depicts, her focus emphasizes the challenges involved in understanding the self–other relation in such a way that sensibly recognizes differences and commonalities both within cultural traditions and outside them.

Meanwhile, other feminists draw on postcolonial insights to rethink feminist debates about the mind and the body and between individualism and relationality. This seems important because of the controversial historical association of the ethic of care with female bodily and psychological difference. It is significant, too, owing to the association of the care ethic with non-Western, formerly colonized cultures (Narayan 2009).

Rather than accept what she views as an unrealistic distinction between individualism and relationality, in *Between Femininity and Feminism* (2014) Kanchana Mahadevan turns to debates about rationalism and embodiment in depth. She defends a notion of embodied and relational freedom relevant to postcolonial theories of gender. For Mahadevan, the historical writings of Indian thinker, Pandita Ramabai, and British political philosopher, Mary Wollstonecraft—women on different sides of a colonial relationship—equally reveal the need to integrate these concepts. Mahadevan re-reads the history of feminist thought in a way that unsettles the association of "women" or "other" cultures exclusively with the body or with care. Wollstonecraft and Ramabai were both committed, Mahadevan observes, to the equal rationality of the sexes, and the co-dependence of reason and emotion in all humanity.

For Mahadevan, moreover, postcolonial hybridity and syncretism are not new ideas, but were implicit in the twentieth-century Western feminisms of Simone de Beauvoir (1949) and Carole Gilligan (1982). Associated with the second wave, Gilligan's account of the "different voice" in which women express their ethical natures has been criticized for its seeming gender essentialism. Beauvoir, for her part, is often interpreted to defend the "masculine" requirement that women reclaim a disembodied form of freedom. As all notions of the Eternal Feminine are socially constructed, according to Beauvoir, she believed that women may only assert their humanity by practicing freedom (1949: 41). Although wary that global feminists like Maria Mies (1996) have taken issue with both care ethics and Western existentialist philosophies for failing to respond to the structural gender equalities in postcolonial conditions, Mahadevan's reading compellingly demonstrates that these approaches need not oppose care to freedom; and that appreciating their integration may prove useful to theorizing gender in multicultural and postcolonial conditions.

More specifically, Mahadevan interprets Beauvoir not to defend disembodied freedom so much as an embodied conception relevant not only to women but to historically dominated cultural traditions, too. Locating in Beauvoir's thought an opposition to all manifestations of colonial power (Murphy 2010), she invokes existentialist thought to contest the assumed incapacity of certain individuals for freedom, by unsettling the association of subaltern cultures or women with the body—an idea that was invoked historically to deny their self-determination. While Beauvoir acknowledged the difficulties of representing a universal "women's experience," particularly in the context of colonial relations between France and Algeria, she acknowledges individual subjectivity as dependent on others' (Beauvoir 1949: 14; Vintges 2006). Many questions remain as to how multicultural and postcolonial feminists might build further on Beauvoir's existentialism to form a theory that fully responds to the multiple, cross-cutting axes of power through which postcolonial subjectivities are formed. However, recent feminists not only suggest this possibility. Moreover, they do so by deepening debate about universal gender interests, without silencing the others for whom they cannot speak.

Conclusion

I have contended in this chapter that the development of multicultural and postcolonial approaches has challenged earlier feminist certainties about the priority of universal political rights. In doing so, these discourses contribute significantly to contemporary feminist thought. Both approaches destabilize, without discrediting, the idea of universal gender interests that concern feminism as a critical movement. We also found, more specifically, that both multicultural and postcolonial feminist thinkers assist feminism to surpass the problems with assuming a uniform set of rights arising from a "common humanity," unproblematically understood. Given the forms of dehumanization that colonialism involved, not least through the construction of "cultural" and "ethnic" differences, feminists in this field draw significant critical attention to cross-cutting lenses of gender, culture, class, and geopolitical location without losing feminism's normative potential. As the perspectives considered in this chapter demonstrate, the project of formulating interests in multicultural and postcolonial times might involve continual rethinking, in light of one's embodied nature and location in different structures of power.

Further Reading

Fatima, Saba (2013) "Muslim-American Scripts," *Hypatia* 28(2): 341–349.

Harding, Sandra (2009) "Postcolonial Feminist Philosophies of Science and Technology," *Postcolonial Studies* 12(4): 401–421.

Mendoza, Breny (2002) "Transnational Feminisms in Question," *Feminist Theory* December 3(3): 295–314.

Mookherjee, Monica (2005) "Affective Citizenship," *Critical Review of International Social and Political Philosophy* 8(1): 31–50.

Puar, Jasbir (2008) "'The Turban is not a Hat': Queer Diaspora and Practices of Profiling," *Sikh Formations* 4(1): 47–91.

Reitman, Oonagh (2005) "Multiculturalism and Feminism: Incompatibility, Compatibility or Synonymity," *Ethnicities* 5(2): 216–248.

Volpp, Leti (2011) "Framing Cultural Difference: Immigrant Women and Discourses of Tradition," *differences* 22(1): 90–110.

Related Topics

Dao becomes female (Chapter 3); feminism, philosophy, and culture in Africa (Chapter 4); introducing Black feminist philosophy (Chapter 10); gender essentialism and anti-essentialism (Chapter 14); feminist borderlands identities (Chapter 17); critical race theory, intersectionality, and feminist philosophy (Chapter 29); Native American chaos theory and politics of difference (Chapter 30); women, gender, and philosophies of global development (Chapter 34); moral justification in an unjust world (Chapter 40); Confucianism and feminist ethics of care (Chapter 41); neoliberalism, global justice, and transnational feminisms (Chapter 48); feminism, structural injustice, and responsibility (Chapter 49); Latin American feminist ethics and politics (Chapter 50); feminism and liberalism (Chapter 52).

References

Alcoff, Linda Martin (2007) "Mignolo's Epistemology of Coloniality," *Centennial Review* 7(3): 79–101.

Alexander, M. Jacqui and Mohanty, Chandra Talpade (Eds.) (2013) *Feminist Genealogies, Colonial Legacies and Democratic Futures*, London: Routledge.

Bannerji, Himani (2000) *The Dark Side of the Nation*, Toronto, ON: Canadian Scholars Press.

Barry, Brian (2001) *Culture and* Equality, London: Polity Press.

Baumeister, Andrea (2009) "Gender, Culture and the Politics of Identity in the Public Realm," *Critical Review of International Social and Political Philosophy* 12(2): 259–277.

Beauvoir, Simone de (1949) *The Second Sex*, Harmondsworth: Penguin Classics.

Benhabib, Seyla (2002) *The Claims of Culture*, Princeton, NJ: Princeton University Press.

Bhabha, Homi K. (1994) *The Location of Culture*, London: Routledge.

Chanady, Amaryll (1995) "From Difference to Exclusion: Multiculturalism and Postcolonialism," *International Journal of Politics, Culture and Society* 8(3): 419–437.

Conway, Janet (2012) "Transnational Feminisms Building Anti-Globalization Solidarities," *Globalisations* 9(3): 379–393.

Coomaraswamy, Ananda (1957) *The Dance of Shiva*, New York: The Noonday Press.

Deveaux, Monique (2006) *Justice and Gender in Multicultural Liberal States*, Oxford: Oxford University Press.

Derrida, Jacques (1967) *Of Grammatology*, Baltimore, MD: Johns Hopkins.

Dhamoon, Rita (2007) "The Politics of Cultural Contestation," in Barbara Arneil, Monique Deveaux, Rita Dhamoon and Avigail Eisenberg (Eds.) *Sexual Justice/Cultural Justice*, London: Routledge, 30–49.

Eisenberg, Avigail (2010) "Multiculturalism, Gender and Justice," in Duncan Ivison (Ed.) *The Ashgate Research Companion to Multiculturalism*, London: Ashgate, 119–139.

Firestone, Shulamith (1970) *The Dialectic of Sex*, New York: Morrow.

Gilligan, Carol (1982) *In a Different Voice*, Cambridge, MA: Harvard University Press.

Gillis, Stacy, Howie, Gillian and Munford, Rebecca (Eds.) (2007) *Third Wave Feminism: A Critical Exploration*, London: Palgrave Macmillan.

Hesford, Wendy S. and Kozol, Wendy (2005) *Just Advocacy: Women's Human Rights, Transnational Feminisms and the Politics of Representation*, New Brunswick, NJ: Rutgers University Press.

Jaggar, Alison M. (2005) "'Saving Amina': Global Justice for Women and Intercultural Dialogue," *Ethics and International Affairs* 19(3): 55–75.

Kapur, Ratna (2002) "Tragedy of Victimization Rhetoric: Resurrecting the 'Native' Subject in International/Postcolonial Feminist Legal Politics," *Harvard Human Rights Journal* 15(1): 1–38.

Khader, Serene (2009) "Adaptive Preferences and Procedural Autonomy," *Journal of Human Development and Capabilities* 10(2): 169–187.

——(2011) *Adaptive Preferences and Women's Empowerment*, Oxford: Oxford University Press.

Kishwar, Madhu (1990) "Why I Do Not Call Myself a Feminist," *Manushi* 61: 2–8.

Laborde, Cécile (2008) *Critical Republicanism*, Oxford: Oxford University Press.

Levey, Geoffrey Brahm (2010) "Liberal Multiculturalism," in Duncan Ivison (Ed.) *The Ashgate Research Companion to Multiculturalism*, London: Ashgate, 19–37.

Lorde, Audre (1984) *Sister Outsider*, California: Crossing Press.

Lugones, Maria (2010) "Toward a Decolonial Feminism," *Hypatia* 25(4): 743–759.

McClintock, Anne (1995) *Imperial Leather: Race, Gender and Sexuality in the Colonial Contest*, London: Routledge.

Madhok, Sumi (2013) "Action, Agency and Coercion," in Sumi Madhok, Anne Phillips and Kalpana Wilson (Eds.) *Gender, Agency and Coercion*, London: Palgrave Macmillan, 102–121.

Mahadevan, Kanchan (2014) *Between Femininity and Feminism: Colonial and Postcolonial Perspectives on Care*, New Delhi: Indian Council of Philosophical Research & D. K. Printworld.

Meyers, Diana Tietjens (2014) "The Feminist Debate over Values in Autonomy Theory," in Mark Piper and Andrea Veltman (Eds.) *Autonomy, Oppression and Gender*, Oxford: Oxford University Press, 114–140.

Mies, Maria (1986) *Patriarchy and Accumulation on a World Scale*, London: Zed Books.

Mills, Sara (1998) "Postcolonial Feminist Theory," in Stevi Jackson and Jackie Jones (Eds.) *Contemporary Feminist Theories*, Edinburgh: Edinburgh University Press: 98–112.

Mohanty, Chandra Talpade (2003) *Feminism without Borders*, Durham, NC: Duke University Press.

—— (2013) "Under Western Eyes Revisited: Feminist Solidarity through Anti-Capitalist Struggles," *Signs* 28(2): 499–535.

Morton, Stephen (2007) *Gayatri Spivak: Ethics, Subalternity and the Critique of Postcolonial Reason*, London: Polity.

Mukherjee, Arun P. (1991) "The Exclusions of Postcolonial Theory and Mulk Raj Anand's *Untouchable*," *Ariel* 22(3): 27–48.

Murphy, Julien (2010) "Beauvoir and the Algerian War: Towards a Postcolonial Ethics," in Margaret A. Simons (Ed.) *Feminist Interpretations of Simone de Beauvoir*, University Park, PA: Penn State University Press, 263–298.

Narayan, Uma (1997) *Dislocating Cultures*, London: Routledge.

—— (2002) "Minds of Their Own," in Louise Antony and Charlotte Witt (Ed.) *A Mind of One's Own: Feminist Essays in Reason and Objectivity*, 2nd ed., Boulder, CO: Westview, 418–432.

—— (2009) "Colonialism and Its Others: Considerations on Rights and Care Discourses," *Hypatia* 10(2): 133–140.

Nussbaum, Martha. (1999) "Women and Equality: The Capabilities Approach," *International Labour Review* 138(3): 227–245.

Pateman, Carole and Shanley, Mary Lyndon (Eds.) (1991) *Feminist Interpretations of Political Theory*, Oxford: Polity Press.

Phillips, Anne (2007) *Multiculturalism without Culture*, Princeton, NJ: Princeton University Press.

Rajan, Rajeswari Sunder (1993) *Real and Imagined Women*, London: Routledge.

Rajan, Rajeswari Sunder and Park, You-me (2005) "Postcolonial Feminism/Postcolonialism and Feminism," in Henry Schwarz and Sangeeta Ray (Eds.) *A Companion to Postcolonial Studies*, Oxford: Blackwell, 53–72.

Razack, Sherene (2004) "Imperilled Muslim Women, Dangerous Muslim Men and Civilized Europeans," *Feminist Legal Studies* 12: 129–174.

Sa'ar, Amalia (2005) "Postcolonial Feminism: The Politics of Identification and the Liberal Bargain," *Gender and Society* 19(5): 680–700.

Saharso, Sawitri (2006) "Is Freedom of the Will but a Western Illusion? Individual Autonomy, Gender, and Multicultural Judgement," in Barbara Arneil, Monique Deveaux, and Rita Dhamoon (Eds.) *Sexual Justice/Cultural Justice*, London: Routledge, 122–138.

Schutte, Ofelia (2007). "Postcolonial Feminisms: Genealogies and Recent Directions," in Linda Martin Alcoff and Eva Feder Kittay (Eds.) *The Blackwell Guide to Feminist Philosophy*. Oxford: Blackwell, 165–176.

Spivak, Gayatri Chakravorty (1987) "Can the Subaltern Speak?" in Cary Nelson and Lawrence Grossberg (Eds.) *Marxism and the Interpretation of Culture*, Chicago, IL: University of Illinois Press, 271–316.

—— (1988) "Can the Subaltern Speak?" in C. Nelson and L.Grossberg (Eds.) *Marxism and the Interpretation of Culture*, Basingstoke: MacMillan Education, 271–313.

—— (1990) *The Postcolonial Critic: Interviews, Strategies*, Dialogues, London: Psychology Press.

—— (1993) *Outside, in the Teaching Machine*, London: Routledge.

—— (2004) "Righting Wrongs," *South Atlantic Quarterly* 103(2/3): 523–581.

Suleri, Sara (1992) "Woman Skin Deep: Feminism and the Postcolonial Condition," *Critical Inquiry*: 756–764.

Vintges, Karen (2006) "Simone de Beauvoir: A Feminist Thinker for the Twenty-First Century," in Margaret A. Simons (Ed.) *The Philosophy of Simone de Beauvoir: Critical Essays*, Bloomington, IN: Indiana University Press, 214–227.

48

NEOLIBERALISM, GLOBAL JUSTICE, AND TRANSNATIONAL FEMINISMS

Serene J. Khader

The processes collectively referred to as "globalization" have shifted our moral and political landscape. The transnational flow of ideas, people, and capital that began during the colonial period continues at an unprecedented speed. Neoliberalism, a school of economic thought that favors deregulation of markets and privatization of social services, drives international trade and development agendas. This has produced new vulnerabilities and contributed to existing ones. According to the World Bank, 700 million people live in extreme poverty (earning less than $1.90 a day) (Cruz, et al. 2015). In the last five years, the wealth of the poorer half of the world's population has fallen by almost 40 percent (Oxfam 2016). Almost a quarter of the GDP of poor countries is owed as external debt (MDG Task Force 2015).

Many contemporary forms of deprivation are poorly understood without attention to gender and race. Women are especially vulnerable to poverty because environmental degradation and economic liberalization increase their unpaid work burdens (Jaggar 2013b), they are less likely to own assets, and they are more likely to engage in precarious employment with no cash returns (United Nations Statistics Division 2010). New cross-border markets place specific labor demands on women of color. Women constitute the vast majority of the garment labor force (International Labor Organization 2014). They are often targeted for gendered reasons—such as that they will accept lesser pay. Sex trafficking is increasing, especially in outsourcing and processing zones created by "free trade" (O'Brien 2008/2009). Transnational labor flows have also altered the distribution of care and domestic work, creating what Rhacel Salazar Parrenas calls a "three-tier" transfer wherein the public sphere labor of women in rich countries is sustained by immigrant women who leave their own children behind with women who are too poor to migrate (Salazar Parrenas 2000).

Feminist philosophies of global justice, like all philosophies of global justice, develop normative frameworks for evaluating and responding to practices that cross national borders. Characteristic of feminist approaches is an insistence that evaluating the effects of globalization requires attention to social and structural hierarchies. These social and structural hierarchies include, but are not limited to, sexist and racist oppression, colonialism, and cultural domination. It is striking that, in a world where women's susceptibility to poverty is far greater than men's, that the vast majority of the philosophical literature on global justice makes no mention of women or gender.

I focus in this chapter on another characteristic feature of feminist philosophies of global justice—their emphasis on questions that arise out of practices, especially practices of transnational movement building. In their orientation toward political praxis, many feminist philosophies of global justice belong to the realm of what Charles Mills refers to as non-ideal theory. Non-ideal theory attempts to "cope with injustices in our current world and move to something better" (Anderson 2010: 3) rather than develop a vision of a just world. Feminist philosophies of global justice respond to the needs of a world that is, in Chandra Mohanty's words,

> only definable in relational terms, a world traversed with intersecting lines of power and resistance, a world that can only be understood in terms of its destructive divisions of gender, color, class, sexuality, and nation, a world that must be transformed through a necessary process of "pivoting the center."
> (Mohanty 2003: 43)

Feminist philosophers expand the set of questions raised by prevailing liberal theories of global justice. The latter have focused on identifying duties to the global poor and developing principles of justice for the global order. Feminist philosophers add questions that arise out of real-world difficulties recognizing and rectifying cross-border injustices, such as: What types of processes are appropriate to developing normative goals across differences of culture and power? What kinds of representations of "others" prevent Northerners from perceiving their own responsibilities? and What can we learn about justice from social movements? In what follows, I describe three concerns of feminist philosophies of global justice that demonstrate a commitment to analyzing political practices under non-ideal conditions. I use the term "feminist philosophies" broadly and include normative insights from interdisciplinary feminist theory.

Relational Understandings of Harm and Responsibility

Many feminist philosophers criticize individualistic approaches to diagnosing and rectifying harm. Rather than denying that individual humans can be loci of harm and reparation, they argue that we cannot see many injustices without looking at patterns of relationship. Following Iris Young, feminist philosophers argue that many emerging practices are harmful insofar as they establish certain relational patterns—not merely insofar as they cause suffering to individuals or distribute goods unfairly (Young 1990). According to Ofelia Schutte, for instance, neoliberal economic policies that pressure women to migrate to the United States have caused a "care deficit" in Latin America (Schutte 2003). As I will discuss in more depth in the last section of this chapter, the unpaid labor of women in the global South is effectively subsidizing the lifestyle of those in the affluent North (see Jaggar 2013b). I argue elsewhere that a transnational surrogacy industry wherein South Asian women gestate babies for Northerners, promotes recognition harms to women of a color as a group. It perpetuates a global view of women of color as unentitled to have their own children, capable of producing only inferior, commodified forms of affect (Khader 2013). A distinctive moral epistemological shift underlies this focus on unjust patterns of relationship. Recognizing these patterns requires looking at multiple interactions and how actors are reconfigured relative to one another through these interactions—or what Fiona Robinson call "the permanent background of interaction." Robinson suggests that a feminist moral epistemology would recommend a distinctive approach to poverty alleviation, one that focused on long-term connections between people in the global North and South rather than isolated charity. Such an approach would lead, in the long term, not only to ending poverty, but ending domination (Robinson 1999: 153).

Institutional Rather than Individualist Approaches

When feminists ask us to turn our moral attention to relations and contexts, they often mean *institutional* contexts—not just relations among private actors like citizens of the North and the "global poor." Many of the earliest feminist interventions in the global justice literature rejected what might be called the "moral methodological individualism" of mainstream philosophical approaches. By "moral methodological individualism," I mean the view that rectifying injustice is primarily the responsibility of individual actors. The watershed article in Anglo-American global ethics, Peter Singer's "Famine, Affluence, and Morality" (1972) analogized the relationship between people in the North and the global poor to the relationship between a passerby and a drowning child. Uma Narayan argues that the methodologically individualist emphasis ignores the role Northern corporations, states, and development actors actually play in promoting poverty in the global South (Narayan 2005). According to Hye-Ryoung Kang, even state-focused understandings of transnational justice are insufficiently institutional. International institutional practices, such as International Monetary Fund-imposed Structural Adjustment Programs (SAPs), have required Southern states to decrease spending on health and education. According to Kang, we cannot morally evaluate these effects on women by looking at the actions of states alone (Kang 2014: 42).

According to feminist philosophers, existing patterns of domination matter in determining who owes what to whom and why. Alison Jaggar, Diana Meyers, Shelley Wilcox, and Iris Marion Young independently argue that Northerners incur special obligations to women in the global South because of existing institutional relationships. Among the institutional harms Jaggar mentions are SAPs, unfair trade agreements (wherein, for example, Southern countries must weaken labor regulations), and militarism (Jaggar 2001; 2002; 2005a; 2005b; 2009). These cause gender-based harms beyond poverty. For example, military bases increase the demand for sex work. Jaggar argues that Northern feminists should make reforming these institutional relationships a high priority goal, both because Northern countries cause harm through them, and because international institutions are more likely to listen to the voices of Northerners than poor women in the global South (Jaggar 2005b). Similarly, Wilcox develops a Global Harm Principle, according to which agents who harm others must stop harming them immediately and provide reparation. Using the example of Agent Orange in the Vietnam War, Wilcox argues that Northern-caused human rights deficits in the global South that can trigger a reparative duty to admit immigrants (Wilcox 2007: 277). Where Jaggar and Wilcox argue that institutionally caused harms trigger reparative duties, other feminists develop institutional understandings of obligation that do not rely on historical claims about harm. Meyers argues that Northerners have special moral obligations to trafficked women because Northern governments "provide strong markets for sex work and little deterrent to sex traffickers" (Meyers 2016). Young argues against a "liability model" of responsibility in general (Young 2006). According to Young, it is difficult to isolate an agent—even a collective agent—that is causally responsible for global poverty, and inequalities within Northern counties dictate that not all Northern agents are equally responsible. However, because of existing social and institutional connections, Northerners bear forward-looking responsibilities to engage in collective action.

Relational Notions of Duty, Harm, and Repair

Other feminists take more metaphysical forms of social embeddedness to be morally significant. Sarah Clark Miller argues for a "global duty to care." This duty differs from Kantian duties, because it takes human interdependence, rather than the ability of each human person to reason, as foundational (Miller 2011: 41). Some feminists, especially care ethicists, argue that obligation itself—and not merely obligations to rectify global injustice—arise from relationships. Virginia Held (2005) argues that, even if individual human beings are loci of moral worth, we should think of caring relationships as "normatively prior" to individual rights. According to her, respect for individuals can only be actualized in contexts where caring relations are sustained.

Feminist philosophers also envision the types of relationships that would prevail under a more just global order. Part of this task is, of course, envisioning more just institutional structures. For instance, Gillian Brock (2014) advocates reforming the international tax regime in ways that promote gender equality. However, many argue that sustaining just institutions requires more; in Ann Ferguson's words, fostering "felt senses of community or publics when they don't initially exist" (Ferguson 2011: 232; Held 2005: 102). In this vein, Held argues that creating and sustaining caring relations across borders is more important for ending human rights abuses than enforcing international law. Her point is not that international law lacks value, but rather that proclamations do little in the absence of relationships that ground genuine concern for specific distant others (Held 2005: 166). Kang argues that cross-border women's movements, such as the Central American Network of Women in Solidarity with Maquila Workers, play a crucial role in moving toward a more just global order; they allow women to theorize and act against new forms of vulnerability in ways that national-level associations do not (Kang 2014: 54–56). Breny Mendoza, however, argues that the focus on transnational-level associations privileges the concerns of elite women in the global South (Mendoza 2002). Feminists have also envisioned new forms of relationship for international development practice that take seriously power differences between practitioners and intended beneficiaries (Ferguson 1998; Cudd 2005; Jaggar 2006; Tobin 2009; Khader 2010; Khader 2011; Rivera 2011; Tobin and Jaggar forthcoming).

Feminists have also developed relational conceptions of harm and repair. Drawing on narratives from victims and activists responding to the Darfur genocide, Miller argues that the genocidal rape causes a distinctive type of harm. It impairs the victim's community standing, impairs her relationships with others, and harms her community as well as her (Miller 2009). Using Margaret Urban Walker's work on moral repair (Walker 2006), Alisa Carse and Lynne Tirrell (2010) argue that forgiving very grave wrongs, such as the wrongs of genocide, requires extended processes of reclaiming moral authority and resituating one's self understanding in relation to both the perpetrator(s) and one's community. Eva Feder Kittay argues that what she calls the "global heart transplant" wherein women from the global South migrate to care for children in the North must be understood as a harm to a relationship between caregivers and their children. Filipina domestic workers in the United States see their migration to the United States as undermining forms of care they wish they could offer their own children (Kittay 2008: 156).

Naturalized Approaches to Normative Frameworks

In addition to beginning from existing unjust practices, many feminists demonstrate non-ideal theoretical commitments by taking a naturalized moral epistemological approach. In her groundbreaking *Moral Understandings*, Walker argues that morality itself should be understood as a set of social practices (Walker 2007). Developing Walker's argument, Jaggar describes feminist ethics as naturalized in the same sense that certain approaches to epistemology are naturalized; rather than positing that inquiry occurs in a "pure" form uncontaminated by social practices, inquiries themselves are subject to analysis as social phenomena (Jaggar 2000: 457). Naturalists see empirical knowledge as relevant to normative inquiry. An important upshot is that the normative frameworks can be assessed in terms of their practical effects. Contemporary feminist approaches to global justice take into account the way theoretical approaches to global justice continue gender, colonial, racist, and class domination. The point of naturalized approaches is not to do away with normativity; feminists cannot do without concepts like justice and harm. Instead, moral and political philosophy should not ignore the effects of concepts and discourses on the world.

The Moral Graphics of Global Justice

Feminist philosophers argue that what Walker calls the "moral graphics" of discussions of global justice affect our perceptions of what we owe to one another. For example, Scott Wisor rejects Singer's aforementioned analogy of the global poor to children drowning in a pond on the grounds that it encourages harmful interventions. Singer's analogy, and the utilitarian reasoning behind it, suggest that people should intervene in whatever way is most likely to be efficacious. According to Wisor, this in turn suggests that it is easy to know whether aid is harming or helping and promotes a focus away from long-term solutions and institutional reform (Wisor 2011: 24; see also Kuper 2002).

Another moral graphical frame challenged by feminists depicts "other" women as victims of brutal cultures. This frame interweaves normative and non-normative assumptions. In her classic *Dislocating Cultures*, Narayan argues that the idea that injustices toward "other" women are culturally caused prevents Westerners from perceiving their role in these injustices. The practice of sati (ritualized widow immolation) in India, widely perceived as an "indigenous" practice, became more prominent because of the British colonial fascination with it. The colonial construction of new gender roles and/or heightening of sexist oppression did not only occur in India (Nzegwu 1995, 2006; Narayan 1997; Lugones 2010; Whyte 2013). This culture-focused moral graphical frame misassigns moral responsibility, first by preventing Westerners from perceiving remedial responsibility they incur because of their causal roles in sexist oppression of "other" women. Second, as Jaggar argues, it causes Westerners to weight their moral responsibilities inappropriately—a preoccupation with burqas or female genital mutila-tion conveniently distracts from other very severe harms they cause, such as militarism and poverty (Jaggar 2005a, 2005b). Third, it may lead to development interventions that villainize "other" men, do not rectify colonial and economic injustices to men and burden "other" women with sole responsibility to improve their societies (Chant 2006; Narayan 2010; Khader 2016).

Fourth, the view of "other" women's oppression as culturally caused may suggest that eradicating their cultures is a solution. This has been a common criticism of Susan Moller Okin's influential work on feminism and multiculturalism. Though Okin explicitly argues for cultural reform over destruction, she also writes that some women might be better off if "their cultures became extinct" (Okin 1999: 22). Two distinct worries have stemmed from the potential recommendation that other cul-tures should be eradicated. One is that it promotes marginalization of immigrant com-munities living in the West (Spinner-Halev 2001; Deveaux 2007; Phillips 2009). Another is that it makes Western militarism appear morally necessary. The idea that "other" cultures needed to be eradicated because of how they treat their women was widespread during the (colonial) Victorian period and revived with the so-called war on terror (Grewal 1996).

Recent feminist work on Muslim women is an important locus of feminist theoretical attention to the moral graphics of global justice. Images of Muslim women as oppressed by a backward, medieval culture are ubiquitous in the post-September 11 West (Razack 2008). Rhetorical justifications of the wars in Afghanistan and Iraq portrayed freedom from culture as necessary for women's liberation. In Europe and Canada, the values of both freedom and secularism are routinely evoked to justify policies that marginalize Muslims, such as the banning of Mosques and Muslim women's forms of modest dress. Though many liberals would reject these policies, many justifications of such policies involve plausible interpretations of liberal values. For instance, some justify bans on veiling by portraying public exposition of one's body as an enactment of freedom (Abu-Lughod 2002; Mahmood 2005) or by claiming that religion threatens the democratic public sphere (Oliver 2010; Scott 2010). Responding to such political effects of cer-tain forms of liberalism has led feminist philosophers to argue against certain osten-sibly liberal commitments (Hirschkind and Mahmood 2002; Laborde 2008; Razack 2008; Khader 2016). For instance, Sherene Razack argues that religion became a racial dog-whistle in Canadian debates about faith-based arbitration (Razack 2008). I argue elsewhere that this work on the moral graphics surrounding Muslim women should be viewed as an invitation to question the normative importance of freedom from tradition to feminism (Khader 2016; see also Weir 2013). I suggest that feminism as a normative doctrine does not require the view that traditional dictates are inherently oppressive.

Connection to Cross-Border Movements and Practices

Feminist philosophers also demonstrate a naturalized and non-ideal approach to ethics by approaching transnational movements as sites of normative inquiry. Ofelia Schutte uses Latin American social movements to argue that the ideal of women's independ-ence promoted by neoliberalism is deeply self-contradictory. It purports to increase women's ability to pursue education, participation in public life, yet at the same time makes them dependent by cutting social supports for care work. For Schutte, this con-tradiction suggests a need to recognize that what neoliberalism calls "freedom" may not be freedom at all. Jaggar (2001) argues that the women's human rights movement is a site of the creation of new norms. According to Jaggar, feminist human rights arguments have brought forward important questions regarding the relationships between first-generation (so-called "liberty") rights and second-generation ("social") rights. They show how women cannot attain the objects of first-generation rights unless their societies secure second-generation ones.

Feminist philosophers, often responding to the needs of activists, also work to correct theoretical gaps in human rights discourse. Meyers responds to advocacy discourses about sex trafficking in her work on victim narratives and human rights. According to Meyers, many difficulties in victim advocacy arise partly from a legal and cultural association of victimhood with the lack of agency. As she puts it, "an undocumented transnational migrant's fate hangs on whether that individual is deemed an agent or a victim of the transport process" (Meyers 2014: 10). Women who collaborate with their traffickers (a large number of those trafficked) have difficulty making legal claims, because they lack the passivity associated with victimhood—even though many experience "slavery-like conditions" and severe physical and psychological trauma. Serena Parekh notices a different theoretical gap in human rights practice. The absence of an understanding of the relationship between gender and injustice has made it difficult to win asylum cases on grounds of gender-based persecution. In cases of domestic violence and rape, it is often argued that the state can protect women. According to Parekh, the idea of structural injustice both makes sense of why states often do not protect women when they can and explains why this failure is an issue for justice (Parekh 2012: 277).

A second element of the feminist view of social movements and practices as sites of normative inquiry is a methodological commitment to seeing women in the global South as theorizers. Many feminist philosophers argue that theorizing *about* "other" women treats them as "raw data" (Nnaemeka 2004), and this produces normative and non-normative distortions. This point has been particularly important in discussions of how to measure and respond to poverty. Feminists have long been attentive to the ways in which concepts of deprivation can further marginalize the deprived— particularly when those concepts are formulated without their input. For example, the idea that dependency work is inherently mindless and degrading has perpetuated stereotypes of women as irrational. Though there is disagreement about the role and extent of involvement, there is broad agreement among feminist philosophers on the idea that the perspectives of women in the global South are key to developing measures of deprivation and implementing them (Nzegwu 1995; Ferguson 1998; Ackerly 2000; Nussbaum 2001; Nnaemeka 2004; Jaggar 2006; Charusheela 2008; Khader 2011; 2012; Jaggar 2013a; Khader 2015). One reason for the insistence on what are often called "pro-poor methodologies" is prudential. People's lives get worse when they are subject to misguided attempts to "develop them," and as Jaggar puts it, "poverty is a stigmatizing term" (2013a: 6). To call someone "poor" in our current global order is to make them a legitimate target of certain social policies—policies that may worsen their lives and/or that they themselves may find objectionable. Consider one of the most controversial feminist philosophical claims about poverty, Martha Nussbaum's claim that literacy is a basic capability to which everyone should have access (Nussbaum 2001). Nussbaum's basis for this claim is that literacy is important for political participation and access to income. As Brooke Ackerly (2000), Nkiru Nzegwu (1995), and S. Charusheela (2008) have all argued, Nussbaum's claim about the instrumental value of literacy varies in truth from context to context. That is, whether literacy secures these other functionings depends on certain context-variant facts about how income and power can be accessed (Nzegwu 1995; Ackerly 2000; Charusheela 2008). Ackerly argues that, in rural Bangladesh, literacy just is not that important to the types of jobs that women need to gain a basic income. Nzegwu argues that focusing on literacy in certain sub-Saharan African contexts is likely to further the marginalization of women who are not from the upper classes. Charusheela interprets Nzegwu as claiming that the assumption that literacy is a requirement for power facilitates upper-class women's exclusion of lower-class women from leadership positions in Igbo society. She also argues that it causes illiterate women to see themselves as lesser and accept domination by women from the other classes (Charusheela 2008: 8–9).

Though it might be argued that expanding literacy would reduce domination of non-elite women, Charusheela's point is that policies that advance literacy are not neutral among ways of life. Literacy is more important to securing other goods within certain class and cultural contexts, and taking literacy promotion supports making cultural contexts of poor rural women more like those contexts—and not vice versa. Some arguments against methodologies for diagnosing deprivation that originate from "above" also point to deeper metaethical issues making judgments across difference. For instance, it is a consequence of the view of morality as a social practice that values may not always be translatable from context to context. See Jaggar and Tobin (Chapter 40 in this volume) for further discussion of the relationship of the non-modularity of moral knowledge to global justice.

Feminized Labor as a Justice Concern

Feminist philosophers also demonstrate a non-ideal theoretical orientation to global justice by calling for renewed moral and political attention to labor. On one hand, attention to what counts as labor and its distribution among social groups is a classic feminist concern, especially in socialist feminism. Feminists argue that dependency/care work, housework, and sex work maintain unjust power relations. On the other hand, the renewed emphasis on labor directly reflects the embeddedness of feminist theory in contemporary social movements and practices. Chandra Mohanty argues that changes in the material conditions of women's lives in recent years justify a shift in philosophical attention. Her 1988 "Under Western Eyes," perhaps the most influential essay in third-world feminist theory, concentrated on cultural imperialism. In the intervening years, according to Mohanty, neoliberalism created new forms of gender and racial oppression and has fomented the view that unregulated capitalism is both "natural" and normatively justified. In the words of Mohanty's 2008 essay, "Under Western Eyes Revisited," "global political and economic processes have become more brutal, exacerbating economic, racial, and gender inequalities, and thus they need to be demystified, re-examined, and theorized" (Mohanty 2008: 230; see also Schutte 2000; Weir 2008; Ruiz-Aho 2011).

New Forms of Gendered, Racialized Labor

Feminist philosophers analyze the resultant forms of gendered, racialized vulnerability. For instance, Vandana Shiva argues that the spread of genetically modified organisms has marginalized poor farmers, who are often women, all over the world (Mohanty 2008: 230). Neoliberal globalization has also made women, and especially women of color, the preferred workforce in "'flexible, temporary'" labor markets (Mohanty 2008: 232). Some of the gendered and racialized occupations in this new disposable economy are sweatshop labor (women are more "docile" and can be paid less (Ong 1987; Mohanty 2008: 246), the international "maid [and nanny] trade," and reproductive and sex tourism. Further, the international economic policies initially adopted as part of SAPs continue to increase women's unpaid labor burdens. SAPs were a package of conditions poor countries must meet to receive IMF loans. These conditions included privatization, currency devaluation, and cuts in social expenditures. Such policies have forced women to perform unpaid labor to fill in the gaps in care for children, the elderly, and the disabled. The environmental effects of such policies have also increased women's unpaid labor, since women are traditionally tasked with collecting firewood and water (Desai 2002). Moral and political questions about feminized and racialized forms of labor under neoliberalism align with an analytical paradigm recently developed in interdisciplinary Women's Studies, transnational feminisms. Transnational feminist theorists emphasize the ways in which globalization, in its economic, military, and political forms, creates both impediments and opportunities for transnational feminist solidarity.

Feminists have also engaged in constructing philosophical frameworks for assessing injustices enacted through labor. Jaggar (2009) offers the notion of "transnational cycles of gendered vulnerability" to criticize the effects of the global economy on women in the global South. Jaggar states that interlocked global and local cultural processes make some people especially vulnerable to abuse, violence, and exploitation. The targeting of certain people for such heightened vulnerability is a distinct moral and political problem. According to Jaggar, recognizing this requires going beyond Rawlsian approaches to distributive justice that insist we must be able to identify the "least well-off." In another constructive approach to labor, Wisor (2014) extends arguments about what has come to be known as "the resource curse" to include gender impacts. The term "resource curse" describes a difficulty facing many resource-rich countries. The presence of desirable resources creates incentives for other nations to plunder them, and/or make deals with authoritarian political actors to access the resources. Wisor argues that we must take gender impacts into account to morally evaluate the resource curse. The labor impacts of the resource curse can adversely affect gender equality; for instance, oil production prevents the establishment of a highly developed service sector and thus reduces the likelihood that women will participate in the workforce (Jaggar 2009). In addition to offering gender-sensitive frameworks for normatively evaluating the impacts of gendered labor, Jaggar (2005a, 2005b) and Wisor (2014) offset the tendency to assume that "other" women's oppression is simply "culturally caused" and/or that changing local cultural norms is the highest moral priority.

Renewed Interest in Exploitation

Feminist philosophical discussions of gendered labor have also led to a revival of interest in the concept of exploitation. Where discussions of exploitation in Anglo-American philosophy in the last thirty years have been largely restricted to "taking unfair advantage of a situation" over "taking advantage of an unfair situation," feminist philosophers increasingly recognize a need to describe unfair situations as themselves exploitative. Jaggar argues that gendered time-use disparities can only be morally understood within an exploitation framework. We need to understand poor Southern women's nearly endless and increasing work burdens as both coerced and benefitting not only men, but private employers and state institutions (Jaggar 2013a, 2013b). Sylvia Chant argues that international development policy has created a "feminization of responsibility" in which women's unpaid labor is a vehicle for the development of their countries (Chant 2006). I draw on Chant's work to argue that the feminization of responsibility constitutes exploitation, because it shifts an obligation of people in the global North onto women in the global South (Khader 2017). Agomoni Ganguli (Ganguli 2016, 2017) and Monique Deveaux (2016) argue that cross-border markets in reproductive labor require an analysis of structural injustice as producing exploitation. Understanding the moral dimensions of transnational surrogacy requires attention to the ways in which legal structures protecting surrogates have been responsive to international financial pressures (Ganguli 2016, 2017). According to Deveaux (2016), brokers in markets for ova who pay women less than is required to meet their needs take advantage of the economically vulnerable in ways that constitute exploitation. The notion of exploitation as mere extraction of an unfair price fails to capture the ways in which women who "donate" eggs are being used because of their economic need.

Though she does not explicitly use an exploitation framework, Narayan (2010; see also Khader 2014) argues that microcredit conscripts women into reproducing a colonial economic system that is ultimately bad for them and their states. Though celebratory development discourses paint microcredit as "entrepreneurship" that empowers women, most microcredit initiatives encourage women to operate in the informal economy. Not only does the informal economy provide women with few workplace protections or opportunities for advancement, the informal economy is, by definition, not taxed. External encouragement of untaxable forms of labor encourages continued poor country dependence on rich countries and makes it difficult for poor countries to provide social services to their citizens.

Conclusion

Feminist philosophical approaches to globalization often begin from non-ideal theoretical commitments. They start with an analysis of the real-world problems wrought by neoliberalism and maintain an active dialogue with social movements attempting to respond to those problems. This continued dialogue with political practices has produced heightened attention to the political effects of academic and advocacy discourses, as well as attention to the processes by which deprivation and oppression are generated and diagnosed. It has offered reasons to change intellectual priorities as real world political realities shift as the shift from the focus on "cultural" oppression of women to transnational flows of feminized labor suggests. Feminist approaches have also highlighted the multidimensional character of oppression and deprivation; political responses to our current transnational landscape must take into account disparities besides poverty, such as gendered and racialized vulnerabilities.

Related Topics

Critical race theory, intersectionality, and feminist philosophy (Chapter 29); women, gender, and philosophies of global development (Chapter 34); feminist intersections with environmental and ecological thought (Chapter 35); moral justification in an unjust world (Chapter 40); feminist ethics of care (Chapter 43); multicultural and postcolonial feminisms (Chapter 47); feminism, structural injustice, and responsibility (Chapter 49); Latin American feminist ethics and politics (Chapter 50).

References

Abu-Lughod, Lila (2002) "Do Muslim Women Really Need Saving?" *American Anthropologist* 104(3): 783–790.

Ackerly, Brooke A. (2000) *Political Theory and Feminist Social Criticism*, Cambridge: Cambridge University Press.

Anderson, Elizabeth (2010) *The Imperative of Integration*, Princeton, NJ: Princeton University Press.

Brock, Gillian (2014) "Reforming Our Global Taxation Arrangements to Promote Gender Justice," in Alison Jaggar (Ed.) *Gender and Global Justice*, 147–167.

Carse, Alisa and Tirrell, Lynne (2010) "Forgiving Grave Wrongs," in Christopher Allers and Marieke Smit (Eds.) *Forgiveness in Perspective*, Amsterdam: Rodopi, 43–65.

Chant, Sylvia (2006) "Re-Thinking the Feminization of Poverty in Relation to Aggregate Gender Indices," *Journal of Human Development* 7(2): 201–220.

Charusheela, S. (2008) "Social Analysis and the Capabilities Approach," *Cambridge Journal of Economics* 33(6): 1–18.

Cruz, Marcio, Foster, James, Quillin, Bryce, and Schellekens, Philip (2015) "Ending Extreme Poverty and Sharing Prosperity," *Policy Research Notes*, The World Bank Group [online]. Available from: http://documents.worldbank.org/curated/en/801561468198533428/Ending-extreme-poverty-and-sharing-prosperity-progress-and-policies.

Cudd, Ann (2005) "Missionary Positions," *Hypatia* 20(4): 164–182.

Desai, Manisha (2002) "Transnational Solidarity: Women's Agency, Structural Adjustment, and Globalization," in Nancy A. Naples and Manisha Desai (Eds.) *Women's Activism and Globalization*, New York: Routledge, 15–34.

Deveaux, Monique (2007) *Gender and Justice in Multicultural States*, New York: Oxford University Press.

—— (2016) "Exploitation, Structural Injustice, and the Cross-Border Trade in Human Ova," *Journal of Global Ethics* 12(1): 48–68.

Ferguson, Ann (1998) "Resisting the Veil of Privilege: Building Bridge Identities as an Ethico-Politics of Global Feminisms," *Hypatia* 13(3): 95–113.

——(2011) "The Global Reach of Our Political Responsibilities," *Radical Philosophy Review* 14(2): 227–233.

Ganguli, Agomoni (2017) "Exploitation Through the Lens of Structural Injustice," in Monique Deveaux and Vida Panitch (Eds.) *Exploitation: From Practice to Theory*, London: Rowman & Littlefield, 139–156.

Grewal, Inderpal (1996) *Home and Harem: Nation, Gender, Empires, and the Cultures of Travel*, Durham, NC: Duke University Press.

Held, Virginia (2005) *The Ethics of Care: Personal, Political, and Global*, New York: Oxford University Press.

Hirschkind, Charles and Mahmood, Saba (2002) "Feminism, The Taliban, and the Politics of Counterinsurgency," *Anthropological Quarterly* 25(2): 339–354.

International Labor Organization (2014) *Wages and Working Hours in the Textiles, Clothing, Leather, and Footwear Industries*, Geneva: ILO [online]. Available from: www.ilo.org/wcmsp5/groups/public/@ed_dialogue/@sector/documents/publication/wcms_300463.pdf.

Jaggar, Alison (2000) "Ethics Naturalized," *Metaphilosophy* 31(5): 452–468.

——(2001) "Is Globalization Good for Women?" *Comparative Literature* 53(4): 298–314.

——(2002) "A Feminist Critique of the Alleged Southern Debt," *Hypatia* 17(4): 119–142.

——(2005a) "'Saving Amina': Global Justice for Women and Intercultural Dialogue," *Ethics and International Affairs* 19(3): 55–75.

—— (2005b) "Western Feminism and Global Responsibility," in Barbara Andrew, Jean Keller, and Lisa H. Schwartzman (Eds.) *Feminist Interventions in Ethics and Politics*, Lanham, MD: Rowman & Littlefield, 185–200.

—— (2006) "Reasoning about Well Being: Nussbaum's Methods of Justifying the Capabilities Approach," *The Journal of Political Philosophy* 14(3): 301–322.

——(2009) "Transnational Cycles of Gendered Vulnerability," *Philosophical Topics* 37(2): 33–52.

——(2013a) "Does Poverty Wear a Woman's Face," *Hypatia* 28(2): 240–256.

——(2013b) "We Fight for Roses, Too: Time Use and Global Gender Justice," *Journal of Global Ethics* 37(2): 115–129.

Kang, Hye-Ryoung (2014) "Transnational Women's Collectives and Global Justice," in Alison Jaggar (Ed.) *Gender and Global Justice*, Cambridge: Polity, 40–62.

Khader, Serene J. (2010) "Beyond Inadvertent Ventriloquism: Caring Virtues for Participatory Development," *Hypatia* 25(1): 742–761.

——(2011) *Adaptive Preferences and Women's Empowerment*, Oxford: Oxford University Press.

—— (2012) "Must Theorizing about Adaptive Preferences Deny Women's Agency," *Journal of Applied Philosophy* 29(4): 302–317.

——(2013) "Intersectionality and the Ethics of Transnational Commercial Surrogacy," *International Journal for Feminist Approaches to Bioethics* 6(1): 68–90.

—— (2014) "Empowerment Through Self-Subordination? Microcredit and Women's Agency," in Diana Meyers (Ed.) *Poverty, Agency, and Human Rights*, New York: Oxford University Press, 223–248.

—— (2015) "Development Ethics, Gender Complementarianism, and Intrahousehold Inequality," *Hypatia* 30(2): 352–369.

——(2016) "Do Muslim Women Need Freedom?" *Politics and Gender* 12(4): 727–753.

—— (2017) "Women's Labor, Global Gender Justice, and the Feminization of Responsibility," in Kory Schaff (Ed.) *Fair Work*, Lanham, MD: Rowman & Littlefield.

Kittay, Eva Feder (2008) "The Global Heart Transplant and Caring Across National Boundaries," *Southern Journal of Philosophy* 46(S1): 138–165.

Kuper, A. (2001) "More than Charity: Cosmopolitan Alternatives to the 'Singer Solution,'" *Ethics & International Affairs* 16(1): 107–128.

Laborde, Cecile (2008) *Critical Republicanism*, Oxford: Oxford University Press.

Lugones, Maria (2010) "Toward A Decolonial Feminism," *Hypatia* 25(4): 742–759.

Mahmood, Saba (2005) *Politics of Piety*, Princeton, NJ: Princeton University Press.

MDG Gap Task Force (2015) *The State of the Global Partnership for Development*, New York: The United Nations.

Mendoza, Breny (2002) "Transnational Feminisms in Question," *Feminist Theory* 3(3): 313–322.

Meyers, Diana Tietjens (2014) "Recovering the Human in Human Rights," *Law, Culture, and the Humanities*: 1–11.

—— (2016) "Victims of Trafficking, Reproductive Rights, and Asylum," in Leslie Francis (Ed.) *Oxford Handbook on Reproductive Ethics*, New York: Oxford University Press.

Miller, Sarah Clark (2009) "Moral Injury and Relational Harm: Analyzing Rape in Darfur," *Journal of Social Philosophy* 40(4): 504–523.

——(2011) "A Feminist Account of Moral Responsibility," *Social Theory and Practice* 37(3): 391–412.

Mills, Charles (2005) "Ideal Theory as Ideology," *Hypatia* 20(3): 165–184.

Mohanty, Chandra (1988) "Under Western Eyes," *Feminist Review* 30: 61–88.

——(2008) *Feminism without Borders*, Durham, NC: Duke University Press.

Narayan, Uma (1997) *Dislocating Cultures: Identities, Traditions, and Third-World Feminism*, New York: Routledge.

—— (2005) "Informal Sector Work, Microcredit, and Women's Empowerment: A Critical Overview," unpublished work on file with the author.

—— (2010) "Symposium: Global Gender Inequality and the Empowerment of Women," *Perspectives on Politics* 8(1): 280–284.

Nnaemeka, Obioma (2004) "Nego-Feminism: Theorizing, Practicing, and Pruning Africa's Way," *Signs* 29(2): 357–385.

Nussbaum, Martha C. (2001) *Women and Human Development: The Capabilities Approach*, Cambridge: Cambridge University Press.

Nzegwu, Nkiru (1995) "Recovering Igbo Traditions," in Martha C. Nussbaum and Jonathan Glover (Eds.) *Women, Culture, and Development*, New York: Oxford University Press, 332–360.

——(2006) *Family Matters: Feminist Concepts in African Philosophy of Culture*, Albany, NY: SUNY Press.

O'Brien, Cheryl (2008/9) "An Analysis of Global Sex Trafficking," *Indiana Journal of Political Science* 11: 7–19.

Okin, Susan Moller (1999) "Is Multiculturalism Bad for Women?" in Joshua Cohen, Matthew Howard, and Martha Nussbaum (Eds.) *Is Multiculturalism Bad for Women?* Princeton, NJ: Princeton University Press, 9–24.

Oliver, Kelly (2010) *Women as Weapons of War: Iraq, Sex, and the Media*, New York: Columbia University Press.

Ong, Aihwa (1987) *Spirits of Resistance and Capitalist Discipline: Factory Women in Malaysia*, Albany, NY: SUNY.

Oxfam (2016) "An Economy for the 1%," *Oxfam Briefing Papers*, Cowley: Oxfam.

Parekh, Serena (2012) "Does Ordinary Injustice Make Extraordinary Injustice Possible," *Journal of Global Ethics* 8(2): 269–281.

Phillips, Anne (2009) *Multiculturalism without Culture*, Princeton, NJ: Princeton University Press.

Razack, Sherene (2008) *Casting Out: The Eviction of Muslims from Western Law and Politics*, Toronto, ON: University of Toronto Press.

Rivera, Lisa (2011) "Harmful Beneficence," *Journal of Moral Philosophy* 8(2): 197–222.

Robinson, Fiona (1999) *Globalizing Care: Ethics, Feminist Theory, and International Relations*, Boulder, CO: Westview.

Ruiz-Aho, Elena (2011) "Feminist Border Thought," in Gerard Delanty and Stephen P. Turner (Eds.) *Routledge International Handbook of Contemporary Social and Political Philosophy*, New York: Routledge, 350–357.

Salazar Parrenas, Rhacel (2000) "Migrant Filipina Domestic Workers and the International Division of Reproductive Labor," *Gender and Society* 14(4): 560–580.

Schutte, Ofelia (2000) "Cultural Alterity: Cross-Cultural Communication and Feminist Theory in North-South Praxis," in Uma Narayan and Sandra Harding (Eds.) *Decentering the Center*, Bloomington, IN: Indiana University Press, 47–66.

——(2003) "Dependency Work, Women, and the Global Economy," in Ellen K. Feder and Eva Feder Kittay (Eds.) *The Subject of Care*, Lanham, MD: Rowman & Littlefield, 138–159.

Scott, Joan Wallach (2010) *The Politics of the Veil*, Princeton, NJ: Princeton University Press.

Singer, Peter (1972) "Famine, Affluence, and Morality," *Philosophy and Public Affairs* 1(3): 229–243.

Spinner-Halev, Jeff (2001) "Feminism, Multiculturalism, Oppression, and the State," *Ethics* 112(1): 84–113.

Tobin, Theresa W. and Jaggar, Alison (forthcoming) *Undisciplining Philosophy*.

Tobin, Theresa W. (2009) "Globalizing Feminist Methodology," *Hypatia* 24(4): 145–164.

United Nations Statistics Division (2010) *The World's Women 2010: Trends and Statistics*, New York: United Nations.

Walker, Margaret Urban (2006) *Moral Repair*, New York: Cambridge University Press.

——(2007) *Moral Understandings*, New York: Oxford University Press.

Weir, Allison (2008) "Global Feminism and Transformative Identity Politics," *Hypatia* 23(4): 110–133.

——(2013) "Freedom and the Islamic Revival," *Identities and Freedom*, New York: Oxford University Press.

Whyte, Kyle (2013) "Indigenous Women, Climate Change Impacts, and Collective Action," *Hypatia* 29(3): 599–616.

Wilcox, Shelley (2007) "Immigrant Admissions and Global Relations of Harm," *Journal of Social Philosophy* 38(2): 274–291.

Wisor, Scott (2011) "Against Shallow Ponds," *Journal of Global Ethics* 7(1): 19–32.

——(2014) "Gender Injustice and the Resource Curse," in Alison Jaggar (Ed.) *Gender and Global Justice*, Cambridge: Polity, 168–193.

Young, Iris Marion (1990) *Justice and the Politics of Difference*, Princeton, NJ: Princeton University Press.

——(2006) "Responsibility for Justice," *Social Philosophy and Policy* 23(1): 365–388.

49

FEMINISM, STRUCTURAL INJUSTICE, AND RESPONSIBILITY

Serena Parekh

One of the enduring questions of feminist philosophy is how to conceptualize the injustices that women experience. The term most often used to express this unjust treatment is *oppression*, defined by Ann Cudd as "a harm through which groups of persons are systematically and unfairly or unjustly constrained, burdened, or reduced by any of several forces" (Cudd 2006: 23). However, driven largely by the work of Iris Young, some recent feminist scholarship has moved toward a particular understanding of oppression as a *structural injustice* as a better way to account for many, if not all, of the particular kinds of injustices women around the world experience today and to explain why oppression persists despite changes in laws and policies aimed at reducing inequality and discrimination. Structural injustice refers to unjust structural limitations that unfairly constrain the opportunities of some while granting privileges to others. However, understanding women's oppression as structural presents a challenge around *responsibility*. One feature of structural injustice is that it is often unintentional, that is, it is often grounded in "unquestioned norms, habits, and symbols, in the assumptions underlying institutional rules" (Young 1990: 41) rather than in the malicious intent of an individual or intentionally discriminatory policies or practices. How then do we determine who is responsible for this and how do we hold people responsible for remedying it? If oppression results for interpersonal interactions, then we can ascribe responsibility to the individual doing the oppressive actions; if oppression is rooted in unjust and discriminatory laws, policies, and institutions, then responsibility entails changing these so that they eliminate their unjust elements. However neither the source of the injustice nor what needs to be done to change it is so clear when oppression is understood as structural. Yet nonetheless, contemporary philosophers have argued for changing our notion of responsibility to better address this. Though some feminist analyses of injustice have focused on how it is possible for collectives to be responsible (see Isaacs 2011 and May and Strikwerda 1994), I focus here on the concept of structural injustice. In the entry below, I will give a deeper explanation of the concept of structural injustice and show why many thinkers hold that it is a better way to account for contemporary forms of oppression. I will then outline ways thinkers have tried to overcome the problem of responsibility and note some of the lingering problems.

My approach to this issue is representative of a feminist method of theorizing injustice. It is representative of a feminist approach to injustice not merely because its primary focus is the injustice experienced on the basis of gender; the structural injustice approach can be brought to bear on a variety of persistent injustices such as those connected to race, religion, and economic status, among others. Rather, what makes it a feminist analysis is that it is in the long line of feminist scholarship that seeks to go beyond traditional concepts and categories and articulate new ways of understanding many of the persistent and deep injustices and inequalities in the world today. For example, in more traditional methodologies, either an individual is responsible or she is not, either a law is non-discriminatory and therefore just, or it is not; the structural injustice approach challenges both of these assumptions. In Susan Sherwin's view, the feminist methodology has been helpful in pointing out that the danger "within traditional methodologies is that of accepting dichotomies. Dichotomous thinking forces ideas, persons, roles, and disciplines into rigid polarities. It reduces richness and complexity in the interest of logical neatness, and in doing so, it distorts truth" (Sherwin 1998: 25). In this chapter, I demonstrate how feminist methodology can help us to expand our dichotomous thinking around concepts of injustice, oppression, and responsibility by showing that often these concepts—and the problems they are intended to reveal—are much more complex than usually understood.

What Is Structural Injustice?

The most influential account of structural injustice originates in the work of Iris Young. In her early and very influential book, *Justice and the Politics of Difference*, Young writes that that oppression is best conceptualized as the structural and systemic constraints that arise from the everyday practices of ordinary people, rather than intentional harm or discrimination on the part of individuals or the state. Oppression is structural in the sense that it is based on, "unquestioned norms, habits, and symbols, in the assumptions underlying institutional rules and the collective consequences of following those rules," and further, in "unconscious assumptions and reactions of well-meaning people in ordinary interactions, media and cultural stereotypes, and structural features of bureaucratic hierarchies and market mechanisms—in short, the normal processes of everyday life" (Young 1990: 41).

In her posthumously published book, *Responsibility for Justice*, Young develops this understanding of oppression in more detail and applies the concept to the global level (Young 2011). She notes that individuals vulnerable to structural injustice differ from other people in terms of the range of options available to them and the kind of constraints on their actions. The kind and degree of harm experienced by people in a particular structural position will vary and depend on numerous other factors (including their own choices, luck, the actions of others), but the injustice is simply that some are made vulnerable to harms because of the social structural position they are in, while others are not and may even benefit. This position of vulnerability occurs on the global, as well as domestic, levels.

Two features of structural injustice are worth highlighting for the way that they complicate the question of responsibility. First, though a form of severe injustice, it is often not *intentionally* caused. Structural injustice arises from the actions of many people acting according to normal rules and accepted, morally justifiable practices

(Young 2011: 48). In other words, structural injustice arises from people living their everyday lives and pursuing their own interests uncoordinated with each other. Like gridlock traffic, the outcome is not intended and may even run counter to the intentions of the individuals who contribute to it. This lack of direct causal agency is also why people often fail to recognize oppression as structural. The results, however, are social-structural processes that create channels for action, channels that guide people to act in certain ways and constrain them in others. These structures, Young notes, appear as objective, given, and constraining. Institutional and social rules, implicit and explicit, function to limit the kinds and range of options open to people in various structural positions, but this is rarely experienced as a limitation. Freedom is not eliminated, but individuals are channeled towards some possibilities and blocked from others. Even Claudia Card, who had previously argued that evils such as oppression were the result of culpable wrongdoing, agrees with Young's position that oppression does not necessarily presuppose culpability (Card 2005; 2009). "Evil," Card writes,

> in institutions or practices can, of course, take the form of inexcusably culpable deeds by individuals. But it can also, or instead, take the form of norms that are utterly indefensible, from a moral point of view, whether those who are guided by those norms are aware of it or not.
>
> (Card 2009: 158)

Second, structural injustice differs from other forms of oppression because of its focus on background conditions. "When we judge that structural injustice exists," Young writes, "we are saying precisely that at least some of the normal and accepted background conditions of action are not morally acceptable" (Young 2004: 378). Because structural injustice is embedded in background conditions, norms, habits, and everyday interactions most people remain unaware of it. In fact, Young notes that we often only become aware of structural injustice when we determine something is morally wrong but can find no other clear causal explanation, that is, the harm cannot be attributed to the victim's poor choices, bad luck, the wrongful actions of some persons, or overtly discriminatory laws and policies, or other powerful institutions. This feature of structural injustice, as we'll see below, complicates the question of responsibility since, as Cudd notes, most moral theories agree that you cannot hold a person responsible to end a situation that one does not see; to put it in terms of a well-known example, you cannot have a responsibility to pull a child out of a shallow pond if you do not see the child struggling in the pond (Cudd 2006). Coming to critically evaluate the justice of the status quo and the background conditions against which we act and live is one of the challenges of thinking of oppression as structural.

We can understand gender oppression as a form of structural injustice because it constrains and shapes individual choices and circumstances, not through intentional, conscious actions but rather through largely unconscious and implicit norms, habits, and institutions. For example, the range of careers that young women aspire to are not limited because of explicit rules or policies, but often because of the implicit understanding of the roles a woman ought and ought not to play in society. It may seem natural and normal for women to aspire to jobs that center around care taking, but unnatural, and perhaps even inconceivable, to aspire to leadership roles, either in government or the corporate world. When an individual decides to pursue a career as an elementary school teacher, for example, rather than something with higher pay or prestige, the individual herself does not experience this as a limitation or constraint, nor does she experience herself as being channeled in one direction rather than another. Social structures seem objectified and not controllable by human agency. This is what Young means by saying that social structures appear as objective, given and constraining, and why they are so important in understanding gender injustice.

Understanding why such patterns may constitute an injustice requires taking a broad view of the *systematic* relations that provide the context for individual action to occur. This means confronting the structural categories that are largely grounded on inequality—class, race, gender, ability, sexual orientation, and gender presentation—that shape and constrain individuals. Young insists that focusing too much on individual actions and intentions takes away the focus from systematic relations in the context of which structural injustice may arise. As Elizabeth Anderson has shown, it is impossible to understand the persistence of racism without seeing how it is embodied in structural relations and sustained through social practices such as segregation. In her view, counteracting racial inequality requires more than celebrating cultural diversity or focusing on distributive justice; it requires attention to the structural processes such as housing and work integration that sustain and often even cause inequality (Anderson 2010). "To capture the race-based injuries we need a theory that begins from a structural account of the systematic disadvantages imposed on people because of their race in society" (Anderson 2013: 6).

Sally Haslanger has recently situated the concept of implicit bias within the account of oppression as structural injustice. She agrees that the best way to understand social injustices like sexism or racism is not through focusing on action and attitudes of individuals, but in terms of unjust and interlocking social structures. "The *normative core* of what is wrong with racism/sexism lies not in the 'bad attitudes' of individuals but in the asymmetrical burdens and benefits and inegalitarian relationships that societies impose on such groups" (Haslanger 2015: 2). Without seeing injustice as structural it is hard to explain the persistence of racism and sexism despite changing legal and social norms. In addition to social structures, structural injustice must be understood to include *schemas* or social meanings, "clusters of culturally shared (public) concepts, propositions, and norms that enable us, collectively, to interpret and organize information and coordinate action, thought, and affect," as well as the presence or absence of resources for certain social groups (Haslanger 2015: 4). Taken together, these three factors—interacting structures, schemas, resources—go a long way in explaining the persistence of social injustices like sexism and racism.

Yet for many reasons, much recent feminist scholarship has focused on implicit bias as a source of oppression and explanation for the persistence of racism and sexism, rather than structural conditions. An individual can be said to harbor an implicit bias against a stigmatized group when "she has automatic cognitive or affective associations between (her concept of) G and some negative property (P) or stereotypic trait (T), which are accessible and can be operative in influencing judgment and behavior *without the conscious awareness of the agent*" (Holroyd 2012: 275, italics added; also see Crouch 2012 and Saul 2013). If many agents hold implicit bias without realizing it, they can perpetuate norms around gender and race that are oppressive. Even though individuals may wish to avoid racist or sexist actions, they may find themselves still acting according to negative implicit biases. Though Haslanger acknowledges that implicit bias is appealing as an explanation for the persistence of sexism and racism and understanding it may play a role in achieving justice, this role is tangential to what are really needed, namely structural change, cultural contestation, and a more just distribution of resources. The focus on implicit bias makes it appear, erroneously, that if we merely change how we think, we can end injustice without attending to the material and structural roots of the problem.

Haslanger demonstrates this clearly with the example of Lisa and Larry's parental leave. In this scenario, Lisa and Larry are married, work at the same company and earn the same income. Once they have a baby, Lisa ends up taking maternity leave (the company does not offer paid parental leave and so Larry cannot stay home to take care of the infant), and having spent more time early on with the baby, ends up becoming the primary care giver. When she returns to work, she asks for more flexibility in her schedule. Ten years later, Larry's salary is significantly higher than Lisa's and this gives him more power both at home and in the workplace. The point of Haslanger's example is that the interacting structures of work and family life, and the norms and practices around them, are what explain Larry's ability to accumulate power and wealth, not implicit bias. In other words, the way sexism manifests itself in this scenario is through structural processes, social schemas (the assumption, for example, that maternity leave is necessary but paternity leave is not), and the distribution of resources (care work does not earn economic rewards) and not implicit biases on the part of Lisa, Larry, or their employer.

To summarize, structural injustice refers to harms that arise from the accumulated outcomes of millions of people pursuing their own morally acceptable ends but who are unintentionally producing outcomes that constrain some based on their social position and benefit others. The outcomes are often reified and experienced as natural and unchangeable. Alison Jaggar has shown how structural injustice may be applied in a more global context. Jaggar has argued that global gender inequalities ought to be understood as arising not merely from harmful domestic laws or practices, but as linked with transnational arrangements (Jaggar 2014: 171). These arrangements, while not intending to contribute to gender injustice, play a role in the structural injustice that gives rise to gender specific harms. For example, on the global level, feminized labor has come to be associated with informal work, low pay, and a lack of labor protections. Feminized labor can be understood as a gendered exploitation insofar as it takes advantage of people who have been made vulnerable due to structural injustice (in this case, specific gender norms about women's labor capacities). Without seeing exploitation at a systematic level, it is impossible to account for why women are often in positions of vulnerability. Jaggar argues that the most important aspect for understanding the root of gender injustice is social institutions that make various menus of options socially available and assign costs and benefits to various decisions (Jaggar 2014). In this sense, particular gendered harms must be understood in the context of the structural injustices that support and inculcate them.

For Jaggar, it is "interlocking transnational cycles of gendered vulnerability" that place women in systematically weaker bargaining situations and enable gender rights violations and exploitation (Jaggar 2014). An adequate understanding of structural injustice requires the inclusion of transnational actors and institutions. Her example is the maid trade. Annually, thousands of women choose to leave their home countries to become domestic workers in foreign lands, making themselves vulnerable to exploitation and other harms. That so many choose to place themselves in this vulnerable situation is often the result of a rational response to gendered institutional constraints. For example, women are often unable to get good paying jobs in their home countries and this might be a push factor for women to leave. On the other hand, in Western countries because of the decline in real wages, two income families often need child and other domestic help; because care work is gendered female, there is a demand for female care workers. In addition, there are transnational factors that contribute to the situation of vulnerability as well. In this case, global inequality makes it appealing for people from poor countries to want to migrate to wealthier ones (one of the major sources of income in the Philippines, for example, is remittances from workers abroad, especially domestic workers). In short, labor migration is gendered and is in part grounded on globally shared views of how labor should be distributed among different genders so that we must understand that systematic gender vulnerabilities are produced by interactions among both national and transnational factors. Importantly, structural injustice produced by transnational factors can undermine the effectiveness of national policies that aim to eradicate gender injustices.

Young, Haslanger, and Jaggar show that understanding gender injustice as structural leads to a different way of addressing the problem. If sexism were a matter of interpersonal interaction or unjust laws, we could address it directly. But as Young notes, addressing structural injustice requires collective action to address unjust social norms and practices, on the level of individuals, not the state. For Haslanger, addressing enduring inequalities like sexism or racism requires that we challenge social structures, schemas, and the distribution of resources. For Jaggar, if we are going to address gender injustice at the global level, we must also address transnational cycles of gendered vulnerability that are part of global political and economic arrangements that function as a kind of structural injustice that make women vulnerable to and permit many forms of gender injustice. Recommendations for institutional reform to end gender disparities should address not only situations in particular countries but also transnational arrangements that perpetuate structural injustice. But before any of these changes can be implemented a more fundamental question must be answered: who is *responsible* for changing social structures and transnational arrangements?

Responsibility for Structural Injustice

Young acknowledges that the question, "How shall moral agents think about our responsibility in relation to social injustice?" is a particularly challenging one when discussing structural injustice (Young 2011: 75). The fact that we recognize something as an injustice implies that someone ought to be held responsible (we don't, for example, talk about the wind that blew my hat off my head as being unjust because there would be no one to hold responsible). Yet structural injustice is produced and reproduced through the actions of many people acting within accepted norms and rules. As a result, there is no clear wrongdoer as is often the case with interpersonal injustice. Because of this, our usual methods of assigning responsibility are not applicable. To respond to this dilemma, Young proposes her own account of *political* responsibility grounded in the social connection model. Political responsibility is "a duty for individuals to take public stands about actions and events that affect broad masses of people, and to try to organize collective action to prevent massive harm or foster institutional change for the better" (Young 2011: 76).

Young begins her defense of this kind of responsibility by explaining why other attempts have failed. Traditionally, individuals can be held responsible for an unjust outcome if they are causally connected to the harm, acted voluntarily and with sufficient knowledge. Yet these conditions do not apply to structural injustice, which, as noted above, is often the result of good intentions and ordinary actions on the part of many individuals who may not even be aware of the effects of their action. Further, traditional responsibility is backwards looking—it aims to remedy a past injustice without thinking about how to alter conditions so that future harms do not arise. For Young, the goal of responsibility is to change unjust structures so that they do not reproduce injustice going forward. On the global level, both dominant schools of thought—cosmopolitans and nationalists—also fail to provide a ground for responsibility for structural injustice. Cosmopolitans, who hold that we are responsible to all people equally, have an account of responsibility that is implausibly demanding in Young's view. Nationalists, on the other hand, seem to root their account in something morally arbitrary, namely, our social location in particular nations that have arisen contingently. Neither traditional conceptions of responsibility nor contemporary global reformulations seem adequate to address responsibility for structural injustice according to Young.

Young refers to her alternative as "political responsibility," a term she takes from an essay by Hannah Arendt (Young 2004; 2011; Arendt 2003). Political responsibility is a form of collective responsibility that holds individuals responsible for contributing to injustice, regardless of their intentions. It says that individuals bear responsibility for structural injustice because they contribute by their actions to the processes that produce unjust outcomes (Young 2011: 105). In other words, though individuals are not *guilty* of a crime, they nonetheless bear responsibility because of their connection to unjust social processes. Responsibility is grounded not in a shared nation-state or in the universal category of humanity, but rather it arises from our belonging together in a system of interdependent processes of cooperation and competition, through which we try to realize our aims. "Responsibility in relation to injustice thus derives not from living under a common constitution, but rather from participating in the diverse institutional processes that produce structural injustice" (Young 2011: 105).

Political responsibility is the appropriate form of responsibility for structural injustice because it includes the following features: it is not isolating (it does not seek to pick out an individual responsible for a harm and find them guilty of wrongful action); it judges background conditions (it does not merely evaluate the harm, but brings into question the background conditions that may themselves not be morally acceptable); it is forward, not backward looking (the aim is not to ascribe guilt but to improve conditions in the future); it is fundamentally a shared responsibility (though an individual personally bears responsibility, she does not bear it alone; there is a tacit acknowledgment of the collective that together produces injustice); and it can only be discharged through collective action (political responsibility cannot be born alone but requires that we work together with others to discharge our duty). Though Young makes clear that it is individuals who bear political responsibility, states too can play important roles in helping individuals discharge their political responsibility (Parekh 2011).

What Young means by "political" must be understood through her reading of Hannah Arendt. For Arendt, to be political means to *act* in concert with other people, not merely to participate in elected office or to pass laws (Arendt 1998). Reflecting this understanding of politics, Young writes that politics is the activity in which people organize collectively to regulate or transform some aspect of their shared social conditions, along with the communicative activities in which they try to persuade one another to join such collective action or decide what direction they wish to take it.

(Young 2004: 377)

To say that we have a political responsibility for Young is to say that we have a responsibility not just to change discriminatory laws or unjust practices, but also to work with others to transform the world through speech and action and to challenge the status quo.

This is an extremely tall order. Young acknowledges that many will resist the idea that they are responsible for large-scale social processes, the injustice of which they do not directly bring about or intend. To use Samuel Scheffler's phrase, Young's conception of responsibility goes against our ordinary "phenomenology of agency," where we are responsible only for what we experience ourselves as causing (Scheffler 2008). Even if we were willing to embrace responsibility, it may simply be too overwhelming for us to bear. Young fully acknowledges the challenge of political responsibility but rather than dwell on its seemingly overwhelming character, we ought to seek to understand what is possible and reasonable to expect of our selves and of others. To achieve this, Young proposes some *parameters of reasoning* that individuals can refer to in order to workout how they can discharge their responsibility for structural injustice.

There are four "parameters" that we can use to reason through how to discharge our political responsibility: power, privilege, interest, and collective agency. Different agents have different kinds and degrees of responsibility depending on first, how much power they have over or influence on the processes that produce structural injustice. For example, the anti-sweatshop movement focused on those with most power to change conditions for the workers producing their garments, namely multinational designers and retailers. Second, we are responsible to the extent that we are the beneficiaries of the processes that produce structural injustice. For example, middle-class clothing consumers while not necessarily powerful in regards to the injustice of sweatshops, are nonetheless privileged vis-à-vis the sweatshop workers. Third, responsibility maps onto the extent of our interest in the structural injustice. For example, victims of structural injustice have a unique interest in remedying it, and thus share responsibility for changing the structures (along with others, to be sure). Finally, we are responsible to the extent that we have a "collective ability," that is, we are in positions where we can draw on the resources of already organized entities and use them in new ways to promote change (Young 2011: 147). In this sense, unions, churches, student groups, etc., have a particular kind and degree of responsibility because they can help to coordinate action.

One of the unique features of Young's account is that individuals can be held responsible for structural injustice even though they are not *guilty* for producing it, in the sense of being isolated for a culpable wrongdoing. Further, individuals have a *responsibility* and not a strict *duty* to rectify injustice. For Young, duties specify moral rules of what we must and must not do, while responsibility, though no less obligatory, does not specify precisely which actions one must do or refrain from doing. There is more discretion for individual agents to decide how to discharge responsibility and ultimately it is up to each individual to do what she thinks is best. This claim has opened Young up to criticism. For example, Jeffrey Reiman (2012) has argued that Young's account of political responsibility requires a stronger conception of *guilt*. He argues that there is a logically reciprocal relationship between prospective responsibility and retrospective guilt. For Reiman, it does not make sense to say that someone is responsible to fix something in the future if they did nothing wrong in the past and were guilty of nothing. Further, if an individual is responsible for doing something, then, logically speaking, she must be guilty for not doing it. Using Young's example, if people are responsible to join with others to making sure that conditions are more just in the future, then individuals would be guilty by omission is they failed to do this. Reiman insists that we can only hold people politically responsible for their contribution to structural injustice if they are retrospectively responsible as well.

If Reiman is right, then we are left without a satisfying account of responsibility. Reiman is not so pessimistic; he thinks that it is possible to supplement political responsibility with a form of guilt and draws on the law to demonstrate this. He points out that legally, there are crimes where individual actions are hard to disentangle from the totality—much like structural injustice—but nonetheless individuals are held legally responsible, such as conspiracy, racketeering and felony murder. In these examples, the crimes are so multifaceted that it is difficult to pick out who did what and caused which harm, yet nonetheless, prosecutors are able to charge individuals for particular crimes. The difference, however, between these crimes and structural injustice is that in the former, the individuals held guilty are in some way connected to the crimes, even if not directly. This is not the case for structural injustice. If Young is right that structural injustice is sustained by the actions of ordinary people, which indirectly contributes to and sustains the injustice, then it is much harder to pick out a guilty party than, for example, in the case of felony murder (where any individual who participated in a felony that ended in murder can be held guilty for the murder even if they did not participate in the murder itself). It is not at all clear that individuals can be held guilty for structural injustice in the way that Reiman suggests.

David Miller, working in the context of global justice, provides another plausible route to think about responsibility for injustice that is structural. For Miller, responsibility for global justice must be divided into two different kinds of responsibility. The first, outcome responsibility, is the responsibility that we bare for the results of our actions and decisions. The second, remedial responsibility, is the responsibility that we have to help others, even when we may not have caused the problem. Outcome responsibility is not applicable to structural injustice because as we have noted, structural injustice by definition does not have a single causal agent who can be held responsible for the outcome. Remedial responsibility, however, is particularly appropriate for assessing responsibility for structural injustice since it starts with the injustice or harm and asks who is best positioned to help; the source of the harm is not relevant and we do not need to assign guilt before determining responsibility. In assigning remedial responsibility we may be justified or unjustified, but we cannot be wrong (unlike the case for outcome responsibility).

What justifies an assignment of remedial responsibility for Miller? One is remedially responsible for an outcome if one is connected to the outcome in one of the following six ways. He refers to this as his "connection theory" of remedial responsibility (Miller 2007: 99). The first three ways have to do with being *causally* connected to the harm through being morally responsible, outcome responsible, or causally responsible. That is, if our actions can be shown to be in some way connected to the harm in question, remedial responsibilities also follow. Even if not directly connected to the harm, we may be connected through benefitting from the harm, having the capacity to fix the harm (by both being able to bear the cost of redressing the harm and being able to do so effectively), and finally by simply sharing community (through family, nationality, or religious ties). Miller notes that there may be many cases where people are connected to a harm in different ways and most deprivation involves numerous people who are connected in varying ways and to varying extents. Thus the precise way to locate remedial responsibility remains a matter of some debate. Nonetheless, its clear that for Miller at least, prospective responsibility does not require retrospective guilt, and to deal with the most pressing structural and global problems requires this broader conception of responsibility.

Conclusion

Is political responsibility, even supplemented with Miller's conception of remedial responsibility, adequate to say who is responsible for changing structural injustice? Even if it is the best way to think about responsibility, is it so different from our everyday intuitive sense of responsibility and agency as to be meaningless to the vast majority of people? Perhaps. Nonetheless, structural injustice, like all injustice, demands that we address it, and Young has at the very least given us a platform from which to begin.

In taking up this challenge it is helpful to return to the work of Hannah Arendt, on whom Young draws for many of her concepts. Arendt argued that when we are acting politically, we ought to be concerned, not with ourselves, but with the *world*. To act politically for Arendt is to transcend individual interests and particularities and focus instead on that which we hold in common, the common world. Such an understanding of politics while not completely idiosyncratic (Aristotle held a similar view of politics, for example) is certainly very different from how we think about politics today. To be politically active today is to work on election campaigns, attend rallies, or try to influence elected officials in some other capacity, to encourage them to reflect our interests and concern for particular groups or set of issues. Political responsibility as Young presents it asks us to return to a more Arendtian conception of politics, premised on the determination to make the common world more just. Rather than focusing on whether I myself am acting unjustly, it asks that we take the larger perspective of the world and think about the ways in which the common world can be made less unjust in the future. Moving beyond private morality to a more robust sense of politics does require a shift in perspective, but it is one that for Arendt at least, is rooted in our experience of living together with others. Understood in this way, political responsibility for structural injustice, while still quite different than our traditional conception of responsibility, can be seen as grounded in the uniquely human experience of living and acting with others who, though unlike ourselves, share the same common world.

Related Topics

Feminism, philosophy, and culture in Africa (Chapter 4); feminist engagements with social contract theory (Chapter 7); Native American chaos theory and the politics of difference (Chapter 30); women, gender, and philosophies of global development (Chapter 34); feminist bioethics (Chapter 46); neoliberalism, global justice, and transnational feminisms (Chapter 48); feminism and liberalism (Chapter 52); Feminism and power (Chapter 54); feminist approaches to violence and vulnerability (Chapter 55); feminist philosophy of law, legal positivism, and non-ideal theory (Chapter 56).

References

Anderson, Elizabeth (2013) *The Imperative of Integration*, Princeton, NJ: Princeton University Press.

Arendt, Hannah (1998) *The Human Condition*, Chicago, IL: University of Chicago Press.

—— (2003) "Collective Responsibility," in Jerome Kohn (Ed.) *Responsibility and Judgment*, New York: Schocken Books, 147–158.

Card, Claudia (2005) *The Atrocity Paradigm: A Theory of Evil*, Oxford: Oxford University Press.

—— (2009) "Injustice, Evil, and Oppression," in Ann Ferguson and Mechthild Nagel (Eds.) *Dancing with Iris: The Philosophy of Iris Marion Young*, Oxford: Oxford University Press, 147–160.

Crouch, Margaret A. (2012) "Implicit Bias and Gender (and Other Sorts of) Diversity in Philosophy and the Academy in the Context of the Corporatized University," *Journal of Social Philosophy* 43(3): 212–226.

Cudd, Ann (2006) *Analyzing Oppression*, Oxford: Oxford University Press.

Haslanger, Sally (2015) "Distinguished Lecture: Social Structure, Narrative and Explanation," *Canadian Journal of Philosophy* 45(1): 1–15.

Holroyd, Jules (2012) "Responsibility for Implicit Bias," *Journal of Social Philosophy* 43(3): 274–306.

Isaacs, Tracy (2011) *Moral Responsibility in Collective Contexts*, Oxford: Oxford University Press.

Jaggar, Alison (2014) "'Are My Hands Clean?' Responsibility for Global Gender Disparities," in Diana Meyers (Ed.) *Poverty, Agency, and Human Rights*, Oxford: Oxford University Press, 170–196.

May, Larry and Strikwerda, Robert (1994) "Men in Groups: Collective Responsibility for Rape," *Hypatia* 9(2): 134–151.

Miller, David (2007) *National Responsibility and Global Justice*, Oxford: Oxford University Press.

Parekh, Serena (2011) "Getting to the Root of Gender Inequality: Structural Injustice and Political Responsibility," *Hypatia* 26(4): 672–689.

Reiman, Jeffrey (2012) "The Structure of Structural Injustice: Thoughts on Iris Marion Young's *Responsibility for Justice*," *Social Theory and Practice* 38(4): 738–751.

Saul, Jennifer (2013) "Implicit Bias, Stereotype Threat and Women in Philosophy," in Fiona Jenkins and Katrina Hutchison (Eds.) *Women in Philosophy: What Needs to Change?* Oxford: Oxford University Press, 39–60.

Scheffler, Samuel (2008) *Boundaries and Allegiances: Problems of Justice and Responsibility in Liberal Thought*, Oxford: Oxford University Press.

Sherwin, Susan (1998) "Philosophical Methodology and Feminist Methodology: Are They Compatible?" in Lorraine Code, Sheila Mullett, and Christine Overall (Eds.) *Feminist Perspectives: Philosophical Essays on Method and Morals*, Toronto, ON: University of Toronto Press, 13–28.

Young, Iris Marion (1990) *Justice and the Politics of Difference*, Princeton, NJ: Princeton University Press.

—— (2004) "Responsibility and Global Labor Justice," *The Journal of Political Philosophy* 12(4): 365–388.

—— (2011) *Responsibility for Justice*, Oxford: Oxford University Press.

50

LATIN AMERICAN FEMINIST ETHICS AND POLITICS

Amy A. Oliver

Examining feminist ethics in Latin America is necessarily an interdisciplinary endeavor. While the number of feminists in professional philosophy in Latin America continues to increase, historians and social scientists such as the Mexican anthropologist Lourdes Arizpe, of the Universidad Nacional Autónoma de México, and Elizabeth Jelin, an Argentine sociologist who earned her doctorate at the University of Texas, have been important forerunners in engaging in feminist ethical discussions. Human rights and relatively new academic fields such as memory studies also intersect with feminist ethics. Writers, artists, and filmmakers additionally contribute to shaping the contours of feminist ethics. This chapter addresses common practices in women's expression, ethical perspectives on women's historical struggles, late twentieth-century consciousness-raising, and contemporary feminist ethics.

Testimonio and Public Protest

An especially effective means of conveying women's situations is the genre known as *testimonio*:

> an *authentic* narrative, told by a *witness* who is *moved* to *narrate* by the *urgency* of a situation (e.g., war, oppression, revolution, etc.) Emphasizing *popular oral discourse*, the witness portrays his or her own *experience* as a *representative* of a *collective memory* and *identity*. *Truth* is summoned in the cause of denouncing a present situation of exploitation and oppression or exorcising and setting aright official history.
>
> (Yúdice 1991: 17; original emphasis)

For example, *Let Me Speak!* is an account by a woman married to a Bolivian tin miner of her efforts to organize women in the mining community and confront class struggle, exploitation, and repression (Barrios de Chúngara et al. 1978). Similarly, the 1992 Nobel Peace Prize Winner, Rigoberta Menchú, details the plight of indigenous Guatemalans in one of the most violent contexts in the Americas (Menchú 1987).

In *Massacre in Mexico* (Poniatowska 1991), a collection of cleverly imbricated, eyewitness accounts of the massacre of 325 students who had peacefully protested police repression the week before the 1968 Olympics in Mexico City combine to portray an assault that went far beyond the Kent State and Jackson State shootings and the incident of the eleven people who were bayoneted by National Guardsmen at the University of New Mexico. The military repression of Mexican students continues to resonate, particularly in the context of the 2014 kidnapping of forty-three student teachers of the Raúl Isidro Burgos Teachers College in Ayotzinapa, Mexico.

In the above *testimonios*, more educated, literate women facilitate the transmission of other women's accounts of their lives. This practice in itself generates ethical issues as some accounts stem from responses to a series of guided questions and others are more free-flowing transcriptions with few prompts (Patai 1993 [1988]). Documentary films incorporate *testimonio* in various ways. Rigoberta Menchu's fight for existence and political voice during troubled United States-Guatemala relations is featured in *Cuando tiemblan las montañas* (1983, *When the Mountains Tremble*). *Que bom te ver viva* (1989, *How Nice to See You Alive Again*) graphically explores the brutal challenges women face decades after they were tortured during Brazil's military dictatorship.

Beyond the academy, Chilean women who created *arpilleras*, colorful patchwork scenes on burlap that depict the abuses of General Augusto Pinochet's regime, powerfully express their ethical indignation. The Mothers of the Plaza de Mayo, the human rights group formed in 1977 by women whose children were disappeared by the military regime in Argentina, had to witness the pardons of military leaders in the early 1990s, but now many of these women may live to see their children's torturers and murderers sentenced to prison terms. Ongoing trials represent an overwhelming achievement after long years of struggle. In most Latin American countries, women have had occasion to participate in the *caceroleada*, the simple act of taking to the streets as a group and banging on pots and pans to draw attention to their ethical indignation over events or policies.

Theorizing Women's Ethical Challenges in History

Throughout Latin American history women have faced ethical challenges, and some have been able to report on how they handled them. More than five centuries ago, the woman known alternately as Malinal, Malintzin, Malinche, or Doña Marina was assigned to Hernán Cortés as a slave. La Malinche (the Traitor) became one of the most reviled figures in Mexican history because she was believed to have opened the door to the European invaders and enabled the conquest. La Malinche and a Spanish priest, Gerónimo Aguilar, worked in tandem to interpret for Cortés by transferring Nahuatl (the Aztec language) first to the Chontal Mayan language and then to Spanish. They continued this practice until La Malinche learned Spanish and could herself interpret directly from Nahuatl to Spanish for Cortés. La Malinche also had a child by Cortés. Sandra Cypess interprets Malinche as "Protector of the foreigner, she was also the Great Mother; the child she bore Cortés, Don Martín, was considered the first mestizo, origin of the Mexican nation, the union of the Amerindian and European" (Cypess 2010: 9). Gloria Anzaldúa portrays Malinche as one of three Chicana mother figures, the others being the Virgin of Guadalupe and La Llorona, the weeping woman featured in a well-known Mexican legend (Anzaldúa 2012: 54). Used as an adjective, Malinche's name is synonymous with "traitorous," but what if La Malinche had been a man? While he would not have had a child with Cortés, he would presumably still have been his interpreter. Rather than becoming known as El Malinche, he instead might be viewed today as a brilliant entrepreneur who secured privilege and status for himself, cleverly working his way out of slavery. Gerónimo Aguilar, the Spanish priest who co-interpreted with La Malinche, appears to share none of the blame for the betrayal. He has been de-emphasized almost to the point of invisibility, as if La Malinche had single-handedly interpreted for Cortés and must, therefore, assume all of the blame for the conquest.

Another noteworthy woman who experienced ethical dilemmas was Sor Juana Inés de la Cruz, a nun, Mexican baroque poet and philosopher who has become a powerful symbol for independent and socially exploratory thought in the Americas (Oliver 2014). Octavio Paz, Nobel Prize Winner and Mexican poet and essayist, wrote a sensitive biography of Sor Juana in which he did not fully develop her feminist dimensions though he did compellingly reveal her to be a poet of equal standing in the Americas with Walt Whitman and Emily Dickinson (Paz 1990). A decade after Paz's biography, Stephanie Merrim published *Feminist Perspectives on Sor Juana Inés de la Cruz* (Merrim 1999), in which key feminist essays explore Sor Juana's ethical dilemmas. In the world of seventeenth-century Mexico in which women had only two lifestyle options, marriage or the convent, Sor Juana chose the one she perceived as the lesser of evils, and the one that would give her the greatest independence.

A passage in her poem, "Foolish Men," questions the hypocrisy of men regarding sexual behavior, especially prostitution, and the Eve-Mary dichotomy many such men seek to perpetuate:

Or which is more to be blamed--
though both will have cause for chagrin:
the woman who sins for money
or the man who pays money to sin?

So why are you men all so stunned
at the thought you're all guilty alike?
Either like them for what you've made them
or make of them what you can like.
(Trueblood 1988: 113)

Sor Juana, battling the "primitive instincts" of men during the colonial period, was certainly a thinker ahead of her time, and it took considerable courage to express her views, perspectives that revealed hypocritical stereotypes that trapped women into spaces that stunted their intellectual and moral growth. Indeed, Sor Juana's writings put her at great risk for censure and punishment. Sor Juana's most famous essay, "Reply to Sister Philothea de la Cruz," has been translated into English five times, which gives a measure of its perceived importance. This essay resulted from a discussion with Sor Juana's long-time friend, the Bishop of Puebla, Manuel Fernández de Santa Cruz, in which she expressed criticism of a well-known sermon given forty years earlier by an eminent Portuguese Jesuit, Antonio de Vieyra. The bishop was impressed with Sor Juana's argument and requested that she put it in writing. Without Sor Juana's permission or knowledge, the bishop then paid for her critique to be published and titled it "Missive Worthy of Athena." However, in an apparent contradiction, he simultaneously sent a letter to Sor Juana admonishing her for her intellectualism and suggesting that she comport herself more like other nuns by devoting her time to religious rather than secular matters. He signed his letter with a feminine pen name, Sor Philothea de la Cruz.

The bishop was evidently not the friend Sor Juana thought him to be, since his letter left her open to attack from a rather misogynist establishment in the Mexico City of her day. The bishop benefited from the public circulation of Sor Juana's critique because it coincided with his own negative assessment of Vieyra's sermon and because it helped him advance in his rivalry with the Archbishop of Mexico, Francisco Aguiar y Seijas, who was an admirer of Vieyra in addition to being well known for his misogyny. That a woman wrote a brilliant critique of Vieyra's sermon was heresy enough, but that Sor Juana was a nun also raised issues of religious authority and hierarchy. Sor Juana found herself entangled in the contentious relationship between two powerful figures in the Church. Thus, it comes as no surprise that she was pressured to conform to traditional expectations for nuns by accepting the punishment of selling her substantial library and musical and scientific instruments.

Among the many techniques analyzed in *How to Suppress Women's Writing* (Russ 1983), the one that most closely corresponds to the suppression of Sor Juana's expression is, "She wrote it, but she shouldn't have." In an extraordinary twist on how to perpetrate this particular form of suppression, the bishop asked Sor Juana to put in writing an oral analysis he thought brilliant, then without her permission paid for her written analysis to be published, and finally admonished her in writing for having written it. Sor Juana's case, then, requires an unusual addition to the suppression technique described by Russ, and becomes "She wrote it, but she shouldn't have (*even though she was asked to*)." Sor Juana's response to this treatment by the bishop came to be a famously defining moment in her life.

After maintaining a silence of several months following the surprise publication of the "Missive Worthy of Athena" and receipt of the bishop's letter of admonition, and no doubt acutely aware of the greatly circumscribed space available to women in colonial times, Sor Juana wrote her now famous "Reply to Sister Philothea de la Cruz." In *Talking Back: Toward a Latin American Feminist Literary Criticism*, Debra A. Castillo distinguishes between choosing to remain silent and simply remaining silent: "One reaction to the pressures of the dominant social force is silence. Initially, however, silence is not a response but a condition imposed from outside: silencing, rather than silence freely chosen" (Castillo 1992: 37). Sor Juana announces her silence in her *Reply*; that is, she explains that she is not going to remain silent, but that talking back, or breaking her silence, is her choice. Castillo rightly argues that "*no decir*" (not speaking) and "*callar*" (remaining silent) are actions of different orders. After months of not commenting, Sor Juana chose to break her silence by voicing through the *Reply* at least a partial version of her objections. In view of the sad politics of her context, she most likely could not have gotten away with more than what she writes explicitly and implies indirectly in her *Reply*.

The *Reply* is largely autobiographical and what little we know of Sor Juana's life comes primarily from this crucial letter. Sor Juana seeks through her own example, and the example of classical and biblical women, to defend a woman's right to education, knowledge, and reflection. She also manages to extract from St. Paul and St. Jerome passages that she uses to support a woman's right to be educated. The *Reply* showcases Sor Juana's mastery of theology, but she devotes much of the letter to explaining how the study of the secular world enhances and is necessary for the understanding of theology. Thus, she indirectly challenges the bishop's contention that she should devote herself solely to religious matters by proving her erudition in theology and church history at the same time as she demonstrates her mastery of many secular intellectual domains. Following St. Theresa of Avila, Sor Juana explains to "Sor Philothea" how she philosophizes even while cooking. She writes, "If Aristotle had been a cook, he would have written much more" (Trueblood 1988: 226). Ultimately, Sor Juana proves that devoting herself solely to religious matters would not serve to enhance her unparalleled knowledge or practice of them, but would only diminish her knowledge of the secular subjects that she had also mastered. In this sense, Sor Juana demonstrates that the bishop's "suggestion" that she limit her pursuits to the religious could only be interpreted as arbitrary and punitive.

A few years after sending the *Reply* to the bishop, and after having been forced to give up her books and instruments for having written this missive, Sor Juana succumbed to a plague while ministering to her sisters. Her last years were undoubtedly marked by frustration, fear, and repression, but the *Reply* serves as an inspiring defense of her earlier participation in public life, her studies, and her poetry and prose writings. The ways in which she defends intellectual autonomy, particularly for women, and indirectly questions authority that seeks to repress such an endeavor, have led many to champion her as a symbol of independent thought.

Suffrage and Women's Rights

With the stirrings of suffrage in the beginning of the twentieth century, a wide swath of women in Latin America engaged in discussion of women's rights and possibilities. Perhaps unexpected was that a man was the first philosopher to write a book on feminism. Carlos Vaz Ferreira (1872–1958) was Uruguay's leading twentieth-century philosopher. He was exceptionally dedicated to public education at all levels and was arguably the most famous and public professor at the University of Montevideo. Almost all of his published work stemmed from lectures he gave at the university. Among the best known of his many works are *Lógica viva* (*Living Logic*) and *Moral para intelectuales* (*Ethics for Intellectuals*). To the surprise of many male colleagues, who did not see a particular need to think seriously about feminism, Vaz Ferreira delivered a series of public lectures on feminism between 1914 and 1917.

Vaz Ferreira, in the context of a progressive political climate in Montevideo, later published *Sobre feminismo* (1945 [1933]). During the two presidencies of José Batlle y Ordóñez (1903–1907 and 1911–1915), Uruguay became the first country to legislate the eight-hour workday, the first to guarantee healthcare to the poor, and the home of a social security system that served as a model for the rest of the continent. Changes in the law also made it easier for women to divorce and gain access to higher education and social services, and in 1932 Uruguay became the second Latin American nation to grant women the vote in national elections (after Ecuador in 1929). Vaz Ferreira's feminist thought was supported by the progressive political climate established by politicians such as Batlle y Ordóñez and Baltasar Brum, but Vaz was himself an agent of change. Concerned with the civil and political rights of women and the social participation of women, Vaz Ferreira, working with many others, had a decisive impact in favor of women in the Uruguayan legislature. Vaz Ferreira proposed a bill that passed into law exactly as he had conceived it: the law of "unilateral divorce," which gave "women the power to obtain a divorce at will, without giving cause, while men have to show just cause" (Vaz Ferreira 1945 [1933]: 83). This law is consistent with his theory that the situations of men and women are fundamentally different.

In confronting the problem of the social situation of women, Vaz Ferreira's philosophical strategy had two steps: (1) examining questions of fact, the possible questions about the similarities and differences between the two sexes; (2) examining normative problems. Vaz distinguished factual questions from normative ones in his *Lógica viva* (1910). Factual questions were those of knowledge and verification. Among the questions of fact, of similarities and differences between the sexes, Vaz Ferreira maintained that debatable data and undebatable data existed. The undebatable detail that was most crucial to him and most radical for his time was: "From the union between a man and a woman, the woman can become pregnant; nothing happens to the man." He argued further, "Finding this fact to be satisfactory is to be 'antifeminist'" (Vaz Ferreira 1958: 25). Normative questions were those of action, preference, and choice. For Vaz Ferreira, the normative issues were most relevant to the condition of women. The normative feminist problems for Vaz Ferreira were: (1) a woman's political rights; (2) a woman's activity in society, her access to public office, her access to careers, professions, and education; (3) civil rights; and (4) the relations between the sexes and the organization of the family. He addressed such structural issues sometimes before suffragist feminists did, and made significant contributions to theorizing about women in relation to the family. Two Uruguayan scholars argue, "Vaz Ferreira's ideas about the family and the role of women in it constitute, even today, a kind of paradigm in Uruguayan society" (Rodríguez and Sapriza 1984: 12).

A central idea in his analysis of the above issues was to maintain the difference between feminism of equality and affirmative or corrective feminism. Feminism of equality was based on the idea that

> jobs and careers should be open to women as they are to men; that women should have the same civil capacity as men, the same level of education; that, in general, the sexes should be equalized by diminishing the difference between them and by placing women in the same situation as men, making them more like men.
>
> (Vaz Ferreira 1933: 16)

For Vaz Ferreira, "feminism of equality" did not merit much attention because of the fact that women were biologically mistreated by the likelihood of pregnancy in their unions with men and, therefore, to speak of "equalization" was not pragmatic. The only acceptable feminism, for Vaz Ferreira, was corrective, based on the idea that society must compensate physiological injustice given that it will never be possible to equalize it and that it would be counter-productive to attempt to do so. For Vaz Ferreira, "Antifeminism takes as its guide that fact [women's biological disadvantage]. Bad feminism does not even take it into account. Good feminism strives to correct it and compensate for it" (Vaz Ferreira 1933: 38).

Vaz Ferreira examined a wide range of additional issues affecting women as he formulated theories about what would be necessary to correct their disadvantaged status. Contemporary readers may be made uncomfortable by some of his assertions, which seem antiquated or lodged in Uruguayan social conditions now nearly a century old, but at other moments, his ideas seem contemporary and insightful. The occasional presence in the text of its author being in the patriarchal mode of helping women does not, in the end, taint the surprisingly early advances that men and women together achieved in early twentieth-century Uruguay. Maximizing freedom for women and men was a prominent theme in much of Vaz Ferreira's work:

> His thought was fragmentary and spontaneous and germinal; he opposed systematizing; he sought to open windows, not to build walls; he describes "two types of souls: liberal souls and tutorial souls—souls whose instinctive ideal is freedom (for themselves and for others) and souls which have an ideal of tutelage and consequently of authority," identifying the former position as his own.
>
> (Haddox 1966: 596)

Shortly after Uruguay enacted suffrage, women in other South American countries gained the vote, and it extended throughout most of Latin America by the late 1950s, with Paraguay being the last in 1961.

Modern Women's Movements and Consciousness-Raising

The International Year of the Woman in 1975 was a catalyst for the women's movement in much of Latin America. In 1973, Mexican author and feminist Rosario Castellanos published *Mujer que sabe latín* (the title is an abbreviated version of the expression "A woman who knows Latin has no husband and does not come to a good end"), a collection of essays on nineteenth- and twentieth-century women and feminist topics, which was widely read and appreciated as women prepared for the 1975 events. Her short story collection *Album de familia* (1971) features "Lección de cocina" (Cooking lesson) in which a recently married woman contemplates the requirements brought about by her new civil status such as cooking, remaining silent, obeying her husband, and being a perfect housekeeper. While reflecting on the double standards present in Mexican society, the protagonist comes to identify with a piece of meat she is cooking, and eventually overcooks, a metaphor for the state in which she finds herself.

After 1975, films about the plight of women in Latin America were made more frequently and involved a wider range of themes. *Retrato de Teresa* (*Portrait of Teresa*, 1979) examines gender relations, double standards, *la doble jornada* (the double workday of working for pay and then doing all the household tasks once home), and domestic violence. This film powerfully raised awareness of male privilege and the need for gender equality in Cuba. Although day care centers were established to free women to do paid work, and although Cuban law demanded gender equality, stereotypes endure. "Camila" is based on a true story of nineteenth-century Argentina about Camila O'Gorman, and is a reflection on strategies women use to try to cope with patriarchy and authoritarian governments. It was no accident that this film was made in 1984 and served as a thinly veiled call for resistance to the "dirty war" that was ravaging the country. In Brazil, *A hora da estrela* (*Hour of the Star*, 1986) highlights the marginality of the poor, and the phenomenon of rural women who are forced to move to urban centers to find work. This naturalist film portrays work as underemployment that stems from lack of access to education, leading finally to mental underdevelopment of the poor. Lastly, the Mexican film *Danzón* (1991) shows how a single, middle-class woman, while initially trapped in the typically female occupation of telephone operator, can exercise the right to self-discovery in a man's world with the result of gaining substantial autonomy and relative empowerment. These films and many others were an effective way for women to reflect on the women's movement and social change on various levels.

Contemporary Feminist Ethics

Consciousness-raising about feminism through literature, *testimonio*, art and film, and studies and publications by social scientists have been followed by more philosophical treatments of feminist ethics. Most Latin American feminist ethicists have no quarrel with the contention by Western feminists that women have not been granted equal value with men in traditional Western ethical theory. There is substantial interest among Latin American feminist philosophers in reading translations of key works by colleagues outside Latin America. Among the thinkers who have been translated into Spanish are Carol Gilligan, Marilyn Frye, Adrienne Rich, Simone de Beauvoir, Juliet Mitchell, Kate Millett, Alison M. Jaggar, and Arleen L. F. Salles. Far fewer works by Latin American women have been translated into English and there is a great need to remedy this discrepancy.

María Pía Lara Zavala is a Mexican moral and political philosopher at the Universidad Autónoma Metropolitana Iztapalapa, several of whose works have been translated into English, which has allowed her to engage fruitfully with American and British ethicists. In *Moral Textures: Feminist Narratives in the Public Sphere* (1999), Lara employs Hannah Arendt's notion of storytelling to establish feminist narratives as critical sources of identity production, which have impact in quests for justice. Lara explores human cruelty in history, moral memory, and reflective judgments in *Narrating Evil: A Post-Metaphysical Theory of Reflective Judgment* (2007). While Lara does not work exclusively on feminist topics, her work has much to suggest in this area.

An alternative understanding exists across borders that different epistemologies and ontologies can undergird feminist ethics. Francesca Gargallo studied philosophy in Rome before moving to Mexico, where she earned a doctorate in Latin American Studies at the Universidad Nacional Autónoma de México, specializing in the history of feminist thought, especially indigenous feminisms. Gargallo observes, "Noting that criticism of European and North American feminist concepts and categories has been present throughout the history of Latin American thought is imperative because recovering universals to interpret societies where no underlying political unity exists is impossible" (Femenías and Oliver 2007: 75).

Accordingly, the differences that obtain between Northern and Southern feminist ethics are perhaps more worthy of study than the points of common discourse. In Latin American feminist philosophy, greater concerns with violence, development, and domestic work are three distinctive traits (Schutte 1989). Violence against women includes domestic violence, which is not uncommon, rape, and torture, but these categories should be updated and extended to include hostility and violence toward lesbians, human trafficking, sex trafficking, forced exile, and forced residency of women who would prefer to flee their countries as refugees. Mexico, Guatemala, and El Salvador are the three countries with the highest levels of community violence against women, or violence committed by organized crime as distinguished from domestic violence. "Pleasure kidnappings" are quite common in which a member of organized crime decides he wants a certain girl or woman. She is then abducted and sexually abused, and, if she is lucky, she is not killed.

Femicide is a pandemic in Mexico partly because of social acceptance of violence against women, but also because murders of women have been caught up in the phenomena of other murders stemming from increasing drug violence and lack of reliable law enforcement. After twenty years of denouncing femicides, activists and experts see the same pattern that was observed in Ciudad Juarez at the beginning of the 1990s throughout Mexico; that is, disappearance, followed by sexual torture, murder, and later the dumping of bodies or body parts in public spaces. Feminist and human rights groups are much more proactive about collecting data and finding solutions than are local, regional, or national governments. Still, rape, torture, and femicide are increasing problems in several countries, so it makes a good deal of sense for feminist ethicists to think and write urgently about ways to ameliorate the systemic violence. Philosopher Urania Ungo of Panama believes that femicide is "a concept that synthesizes and comprises the extreme form of violence founded on gender inequalities" (Ungo 2008: 13). Violence against feminists is a problem of long standing as well. One of the founders of the celebrated journal *fem*, which was published in Mexico from 1976 to 2005, Alaíde Foppa, was abducted in Guatemala in 1980 and later killed. Some Latin American feminists, journalists, and other women who fear for their lives have been forced into exile (Agosín and Sepúlveda 2001).

These kinds of extreme conditions have made theory a luxury for many, but a necessary luxury. Philosopher and writer Francesca Gargallo provides compelling reasons for putting feminist ethics into practice:

> Feminist ethics acts against male social and moral privilege, recognized universally in culture, and discovers that this constitutes a fundamental injustice upon which a political system has been constructed that has led humanity down a path of destruction and made it incapable of peace.
>
> (Bedregal 1994: 24)

Gargallo's work makes clear that women must participate in change. The current challenge resides in continuing to find how and where women can best access solidarity and participatory democracy.

Mexican philosopher Graciela Hierro (1928–2003) maintained that liberation of pleasure for women is a necessary condition for them to exercise power. Her philosophy contributed to women reflecting on their having a body under their control, and deriving pleasure from it. These topics were generally taboo in Mexican society prior to Hierro writing explicitly about them. She identified women's oppression as the ethical problem of our time (Hierro 2014 [1985]: 8). Much of her work explores the masculine slant found throughout the history of Western ethics. She believed that respect for human rights is the point on which women and men most coincide. More bridges between scholarly and political work still need to be constructed to continue dialogue between the feminist movement and supporters of human rights.

Further Reading

Bellatin, Mario, Poniatowska, Elena and Itúrbide, Graciela (2010) *Graciela Itúrbide: Juchitán de las Mujeres 1979–1989*, Mexico City: RM/Editorial Calamus. (Iconic photographs taken in a matriarchal society in southern Oaxaca.)

Debate feminista (1990– present) Mexico City. (These journal issues contain a wealth of reflection on women's issues in Latin America.)

De la Cruz, Sor Juana Inés, and Arenal, Electa (1994) *The Answer/La Repuesta, Including a Selection of Poems*, New York: The Feminist Press at the City University of New York. (One of five translations of Sor Juana's letter, this edition provides a facing translation.)

Gargallo, Francesca (2012) *Feminismos desde Abya Yala: 607 Pueblos en Nuestra América*, Colombia: Editorial Desde Abajo. (Exploration and analysis of indigenous feminisms throughout Latin America.)

Lavrín, Asunción (1995) *Women, Feminism, and Social Change in Argentina, Chile, and Uruguay, 1890–1940*, Lincoln, NE: University of Nebraska Press. (A half-century of Women's history during a period of rapid modernization.)

Meyer, Doris (1995) *Rereading the Spanish American Essay: Translations of 19th and 20th Century Women's Essays*, Austin, TX: University of Texas Press. (Makes available excellent essays by writers and thinkers.)

Partnoy, Alicia (1998 [1986]) *The Little School: Tales of Disappearance and Survival*, Berkeley, CA: Cleis Press. (Memoir of abduction and torture during Argentina's "dirty war.")

Related Topics

Feminism and borderlands identities (Chapter 17); testimony, trust, and trustworthiness (Chapter 21); women, gender, and philosophies of global development (Chapter 34); feminist ethics of care (Chapter 43); multicultural and postcolonial feminisms (Chapter 47).

References

Agosín, Marjorie and Sepúlveda, Emma (2001) *Amigas: Letters of Friendship and Exile*, trans. Bridget M. Morgan, Austin, TX: University of Texas Press.

Anzaldúa, Gloria (2012) *Borderlands/La frontera*, San Francisco, CA: Aunt Lute Books.

Barrios de Chungara, Domitila, Ortiz, Victoria and Viezzer, Moema (1978) *Let Me Speak! Testimony of Domitila, a Woman of the Bolivian Mines*, New York: Monthly Review Press.

Bedregal, Ximena (Ed.) (1994) *Ética y feminismo*, Mexico City: Fem-e-libros.

Castellanos, Rosario (1971) *Album de familia*, Mexico City: Joaquin Mortiz.

——(1973) *Mujer que sabe latín*, Mexico City: SepSetentas.

Castillo, Debra (1992) *Talking Back: Toward a Latin American Feminist Literary Criticism*, Ithaca, NY and London: Cornell University Press.

Cypess, Sandra Messinger (2010) *La Malinche in Mexican Literature: From History to Myth*, Austin, TX: University of Texas Press.

Femenías, María Luisa and Oliver, Amy A. (Eds.) (2007) *Feminist Philosophy in Latin America and Spain*, Amsterdam, New York: Rodopi.

Haddox, John H. (1966) "Carlos Vaz Ferreira: Uruguayan Philosopher," *Journal of Inter-American Studies*, Special Issue 8(4): 595–600.

Hierro, Graciela (2014 [1985]) *Ética y feminismo*, Mexico City: Universidad Nacional Autónoma de México.

Lara Zavala, María Pía (1999) *Moral Textures: Feminist Narratives in the Public Sphere*, Berkeley, CA: University of California Press.

——(2007) *Narrating Evil: A Post-Metaphysical Theory of Reflective Judgment*, New York: Columbia University Press.

Menchu, Rigoberta (1987) *I, Rigoberta Menchu: An Indian Woman in Guatemala*, Ed. Elisabeth Burgos-Debray trans. Ann Wright, Brooklyn, NY: Verso.

Merrim, Stephanie (1999) *Feminist Perspectives on Sor Juana Inés de la Cruz*, Detroit: Wayne State University Press.

Oliver, Amy A. (2014) "Seeking Latina Origins: The Philosophical Context of Identity," *Inter-American Journal of Philosophy* 5(1): 65–80.

Patai, Daphne (1993 [1988]) *Brazilian Women Speak: Contemporary Life Stories*, New Brunswick, NJ: Rutgers University Press.

Paz, Octavio (1990) *Sor Juana: Or, The Traps of Faith*, Cambridge, MA: Belknap Press.

Poniatowska, Elena (1991) *Massacre in Mexico*, Columbia, MO: University of Missouri Press.

Rodríguez, Villamil and Sapriza, Gabriela (1984) *El voto femenino en el Uruguay ¿conquista o concesión?* Montevideo, Uruguay: Grupo de Estudios sobre la Condición de la Mujer en el Uruguay.

Russ, Joanna (1983) *How to Suppress Women's Writing*, Austin, TX: University of Texas Press.

Schutte, Ofelia (1989) "Philosophy and Feminism in Latin America: Perspectives on Gender Identity and Culture," *The Philosophical Forum* 20: 62–84.

Trueblood, Alan S. (1988) *A Sor Juana Anthology*, Cambridge, MA: Harvard University Press.

Ungo, Urania (2008) *Femicidio en Panamá 2000–2006*, San José, Costa Rica: Asociación Feminista de Información y Acción.

Vaz Ferreira, Carlos (1945) [1933] *Sobre feminismo* [On Feminism], Buenos Aires: Editorial Losada.

—— (1958) *Obras: Homenaje de la Cámara de Representantes de la República Oriental del Uruguay*, volumes 3, 4, and 9, Uruguay: Montevideo.

Yúdice, George (1991) "*Testimonio* and Postmodernism," *Latin American Perspectives* 18(3): 15–31.

51

FEMINIST ENGAGEMENTS WITH DEMOCRATIC THEORY

Noëlle McAfee

Introduction

Democratic theory is manifold; there are those who think of democracy as a representative form of government and those who think of it as direct self-rule. There are those who think of it in empirical terms—for example, charting out the rise and fall of successful democratic regimes (Diamond 2015)—and those who prefer to inquire about the norms that ought to be followed for democracy to work. An empirical focus on democracy zeroes in on the facts on the ground, including people's actual interests, levels of participation and representation, that is, the actual workings of democratic communities. The normative approach focuses not on what is, but on what ought to be, that is, the proper principles and methods that would be most democratic, and what the ideals of democracy ought to be.

This chapter focuses on the normative rather than solely empirical dimensions of democratic theory and practice. It does so by explaining the normative turn in democratic theory, about forty years ago, which began with John Rawls' work and continued through Jürgen Habermas's development of discourse ethics and subsequent work in what came to be known as deliberative democratic theory. Throughout these four decades, feminist theorists have raised key objections and made important interventions that have led to what is today a more robust and inclusive democratic theory.

Democratic Theory in the Twentieth Century

Through most of the twentieth century, political thought took as self-evident that modern day democracies must be representative and that the role of the citizen was to elect its leaders and, if those leaders did a poor job, elect someone else. It also approached democracy with the tools of behaviorism, statistics, and science (hence the rise of "political science" programs). Parting ways with idealistic notions of democracy as self-governance, political thought was taken up by the empirical, the scientific, and the descriptive. What they found did not bode terribly well for ancient models of democracy where each citizen (however delimited that class) had a large role in deciding matters of common concern. Leading political thinkers such as Walter Lippmann and Joseph Schumpeter pointed to the ignorance and apathy of the typical voter and the need for better governance structures and elite rule. Some noted that it would in fact be *irrational* for people to squander their valuable time on investigating how to vote when the typical person's vote did not matter anyway (Buchanan and Tullock 1962). Instead of the ideals of democratic self-governance, these thinkers focused on interests, power, and expediency. They were hard-headed realists.

In that milieu, the philosopher John Rawls' 1971 book, the unabashedly normative *Theory of Justice*, caused quite a stir. Instead of reporting on how politics worked in the real world, it provided a justification for how it *ought* to work and of what kind of principles of justice would square with what a thoughtful public would support as legitimate. Where earlier normative theories rested on supposed universal truths or natural law, foundations that had become untenable in a "post-metaphysical" world, Rawls developed a way to derive principles of justice that were rooted in human reason, not metaphysical absolutes. The key device was a notion of an "original position" where one could imagine oneself behind a "veil of ignorance" as to what one's fortunes and skills might be in a possible political society. "The idea of the original position," Rawls writes, "is to set up a fair procedure so that any principles [of justice] agreed to will be just" and this is best achieved by nullifying the "effects of specific contingencies" that some might exploit at the expense of others (Rawls 1971: 136). By imagining themselves behind a veil of ignorance, they disregard their own circumstances in order to arrive at principles of justice that would be best for everyone, no matter their particular circumstances (Rawls 1971: 137). Rawls argued that through such a procedure, any participant would arrive at two principles of justice: one that would guarantee equal rights to basic liberties and another that would set limits to the degree of social and economic inequality, only allowing that which also benefits those at the bottom. After decades of hard-headed (and hard-hearted) empirical theorizing, Rawls provided a theory of justice that was normative and rooted in what would be agreed to by people when they deliberate rationally.

Just two years later, Jürgen Habermas coined the term "legitimation crisis" to point to the ways in which, in liberal capitalist societies, economic systems have become decoupled from public will; and then governmental systems, which act to ease the way for economic systems, and also aim toward independence from the public, trying to maintain public support but with as little public input as possible (Habermas 1975). Thus arises a conflict between the imperatives of systems and the imperatives of society, or between functionalist reason and what Habermas would later call communicative reason. With Rawls, Habermas shares a view dating back to Locke, Rousseau, and Kant, that governmental legitimacy can only be grounded in public will and consent. In this view, only a public can decide political legitimacy and any governmental institutions that disregard the public will hence lack legitimacy. These twentieth-century theories of legitimacy emerged, perhaps not coincidentally, as the Watergate crisis led to large-scale disenchantment with the workings of modern-day political parties and bureaucratic governments. Between the works of Rawls and Habermas and those who worked in the space their works created, the seemingly passé notion that governmental systems were legitimate only to the extent that they could have been authored by a democratic public was rejuvenated. And so the door opened to thinking about the role that citizens themselves could play in democracy.

While Rawls' theory rejuvenated normative political philosophy, it also opened itself to charges from two distinct but interconnected realms: communitarians and feminist care ethicists. Drawing on Aristotle, Hegel, and the civic republican tradition, communitarian thinkers (such as Amitai Etzioni, Alasdair MacIntyre, Michael Sandel, Charles Taylor, and Michael Walzer) worried that the classical liberalism resurrected in Rawls' *Theory of Justice* glorified the individual over community and rights over responsibilities (Daly 1994). With some leaning left (e.g., Walzer) and others leaning right (namely MacIntyre), they shared an understanding of human beings as social creatures who do not originate prior to their social conditions. In many ways they echo, and some like MacIntyre (1999) draw explicitly, on feminist criticisms of liberal theory. (Habermas, to whom I will return below, shares the communitarians' view of individuation being a social process.) Hence they criticized Rawls's central device of the original position from which deliberators decide what the principles of justice should be.

Likewise, feminist ethics of care theorists worried about liberalism's tendency to value the universal over the particular and justice over care. (See Chapter 43 in this volume on ethics of care feminism.) Beginning with Carol Gilligan's criticism of the Kantian bias in mainstream developmental psychology (Gilligan 1982), a bias that saw principled universalist reason as superior to context-sensitive reason and care, ethics of care theorists have sought to show the importance of the role of care in the development of individuals and society (Gilligan 1982; Ruddick 1989; Kittay 1999; Held 2006). Where liberal theory would relegate care to the private realm as a private matter unfit for politics, ethics of care theorists argue that care has a place in the public realm. Moreover, they argue, many of the qualities that are cultivated in the home are much needed in public life.

It was not just the communitarians and ethics of care theorists who took on liberal democratic theory. As Alison Jaggar explained in her 1983 book, *Feminist Politics and Human Nature*, approaches as different as liberal, radical, Marxist, and socialist feminism were all concerned with liberal democratic theory. Liberal feminists did much to call into question some of the underlying misogynist elements of liberal democratic theory, including the very idea of the "man of reason" (Lloyd 1979) as well as the social contract (Pateman 1988). Liberal feminist critics of mainstream political philosophy called into question the supposed gender-neutrality of terms like "man" as well as the sequestering of the household from political scrutiny, which allowed men heads of households free rein in the household along with supposedly being able to represent the interests of their dependents in public life. But most importantly, they questioned the supposed objectivity and neutrality of leading political notions of justice, freedom, and autonomy, ideals that emerged most clearly during the Enlightenment era of eighteenth-century Europe.

For the past century, philosophers, including feminist theorists, have vigorously debated the status of such ideals as reason, principle, truth, freedom, justice, and autonomy. Are they metaphysical truths about human nature? Or, more modestly, are they ideals we hold as measures by which to judge existing conditions, virtues that might be achieved through historical progress? Or, as some argue, are they hopelessly patriarchal notions founded on a binary dichotomy of male reason and its feminine other, marginalizing and denigrating important features that allow communities to flourish, such as emotion, relatedness, particularity, and care?

Radical feminists for the most part turned away from all "male-stream" political philosophy and identified the violence and domination at the root of patriarchal systems. MacKinnon (2005), for example, argues that feminists' focus on where it is and isn't appropriate to treat women differently (e.g., with maternity leave) completely overlook the fact that the social system was set up to oppress and exploit women. From a radical feminist perspective, governments are tools of a patriarchal ruling class and should be dismantled or rejected altogether.

Socialist and Marxist feminists focused on issues of class and the economic reproduction of labor, e.g., the role of housewives as unpaid tools of capitalism. Capitalism, they note, is founded on the "primitive accumulation" of resources through exploitation and the unpaid labor of the household. Along with other leftist critics going back a century, they generally saw the state as a "superstructural" outgrowth of capitalism. Any notion that democracy itself could lead to freedom and equality, or vice versa, was simply naïve given that capitalistic governmental structures would never tolerate full and equal participation.

Looking back now from the vantage point of the second decade of the twenty-first century, it is easy to see that through much of the twentieth century, especially through the Cold War, political philosophy had its eyes trained on forms of governance and on economic systems. Moreover, these were seen as thoroughly entwined, so much that it seemed to be a truism that capitalist economies accompanied liberal democracies, welfare state systems went with more socialist politics, and planned economies went with communist party led governments. If an anomaly arose, such as the democratically elected socialist government of Salvador Allende in Chile, a coup d'état quietly orchestrated by the United States Central Intelligence Agency quickly and conveniently restored the world order (Prados 1986: 315–322). Whether liberal or Marxist, socialist or anarchist, political philosophers, feminists included, theorized largely about forms of governance and the kinds of economies they fostered.

Almost entirely absent was any attention to the practices of the people themselves or to the networks of associations and civil society they moved within. Few theorists recognized the political power of associational life. In fact, while theorists were ruminating about the state and states were engaged in their machinations, many people within oppressive regimes were organizing themselves in ways that created nascent but very real political power. In Poland during the 1980s, the Solidarity labor movement defied the oppressive state to take to the streets. In Czechoslovakia of Eastern Europe, firmly on the other side of the Iron Curtain, people were defying laws against meeting outside Party sanctioned meetings to form literary societies, to read books, put on plays, to "act as if they were free until they became so" (Goldfarb 2006). One of the very few theorists to recognize this kind of power was Hannah Arendt who, in her 1958 masterpiece, *The Human Condition*, described the power that springs up in the space of appearance when people come together to speak and act on matters of common concern. This is a power potential—a power with, not a power over—that emerges in their coming together and dissipates when they move apart. Arendt's work remained largely idiosyncratic to her, though a certain young Jürgen Habermas did pay attention.

The Sea Change in Democratic Theory

Up through the 1980s, Soviet-backed communist parties ruled the countries of the Eastern Europe, claiming to be "the People's" parties. But in at least two of these countries, Poland and Czechoslovakia, the people themselves were quietly organizing (Goldfarb 2006). So when opportunities arose as the Soviet Union began to crumble and pulled its tanks out of Eastern Europe, the real people's civic organizations began to call the lie of the faux People's parties. During a few heady weeks in November 1989 the

Czechoslovakian citizen group, Civic Forum, protested, brought down the government, and from its membership produced the first democratically elected president of Czechoslovakia since 1946, Vaclav Havel. Poland had a longer history of a self-organized public apart from the state apparatus, thanks to the labor movement Solidarity and the somewhat less repressive state. Finally recognized by the government in February 1989, Solidarity negotiated a process for open and democratic elections, leading to the end of authoritarian rule. The most memorable part of the end of the Cold War was the opening and then the fall of the Berlin Wall, precipitated by a hapless bureaucrat who on November 9, 1989, announced that the wall was open for passage and then thousands of East Germans seizing the opportunity. But it was the work of regular citizens in their associations in civil society that paved the way for peaceful transition. (The best counterexample is Romania, which had neither a memory nor a practice of civil society and in December 1989 summarily executed the dictator and his wife, hardly a peaceful transition nor a good omen for any future democracy.)

The fall of the Berlin Wall not only ended the Cold War, it also ended political theorists' exclusive focus on the state. Previously, debates between liberals, socialists, and Western Marxists (who had long eschewed Soviet-style communism), had all revolved around matters of state governance and economic systems. With the supposed triumph of capitalism and liberal democracy, liberal theorists' positions stayed mostly the same, but those on the radical left were rather unmoored since their old categories no longer seemed to matter. In fact, when the Cold War ended, all the Marxists seemed to disappear. As Douglas Kellner explains it,

> With the collapse of communism in Eastern Europe and then the Soviet Union in the late 1980s and early 1990s, . . . there was a turn against many versions of Marxism and toward newer forms of postmodern and poststructural theory and multicultural approaches of a variety of forms, often based on identity politics, as well as a turn by many former leftists to liberal theory and politics. Ernest Laclau and Chantal Mouffe's *Hegemony and Socialist Strategy* helped shape an influential version of post-Marxism that criticized the orthodox model and developed a model of "radical democracy" based on "new social movements." A later dialogue between Laclau, Judith Butler, and Slavoj Zizek continued to reconstruct the Western Marxist project on poststructuralist and multicultural lines.
>
> (Kellner 2005)

For many theorists post-1989, what became really interesting were civil society and the public sphere, namely the *non-governmental* arenas of public life, the very spaces from which eastern-European challenges to communism emerged. Propitiously, Jürgen Habermas's book of the 1960s, *Strukturwandel der Öffenticheit*, was translated into English just after the wall fell as *The Structural Transformation of the Public Sphere*. While the reviews were mixed, the book added a new dimension to the word, *public*, from a mass of people with little power to a network of people capable of creating sound public opinion and will on matters of public concern. Now seen as a potent political actor, the public, along with its space, the public sphere, drew the attention of political theorists from many orientations. Politics suddenly seemed to be about much more than state and economy, it was also about civil society and the public sphere, about inclusion and identity, about new social movements, and, increasingly over the next decade, about public deliberation.

While this all looked good for progressive politics, the feminist philosopher Nancy Fraser quickly raised a key concern: Was Habermas's conception of the public sphere empowering for women, or was it another patriarchal construction? Fraser pointed out that a notion of a unitary public sphere could easily become masculinist and exclusionary; and so she called for notions of multiple publics, some strong and some weak, including counterpublics that would allow for the development of public voices from those who have been excluded, including women's groups, from the mainstream of society (Fraser 1992). This piece seems to have had an effect on Habermas's thinking as he later developed a theory of a more decentered and pluralized the public sphere (Habermas 1996).

Discourse Ethics

With the turn from state to society, much political theory of the 1990s took up the question of how to make the political system—understood broadly to include the public sphere—more democratic, not just with electoral politics but with the ways in which society overall deliberates and chooses (see Barker et al. 2012). This "deliberative turn" in politics was aided by Habermas' new discourse ethics, which built upon his two-volume work, the *Theory of Communicative Action* (TCA), and paved the way for his subsequent work on deliberative democracy. Previous thinkers in the history of philosophy, especially Kant and Hegel, had identified reason as an inherent faculty of the subject, a kernel of hope for the eventual development of a more rational and just society. Contrary to this philosophical thinking, Habermas argues against the old idea of a presocial being with a monological or purely individual capacity for reason. Following G. H. Mead's pragmatic account of socialization, Habermas argues that we are individuated through a social process of role taking, being called to and responding. If our individuation and development as rational beings is socially constituted, then we can hardly appeal to an Enlightenment notion that reason would lead to freedom and justice.

So in many respects, Habermas is just as skeptical as many contemporary feminist theorists about there being any antecedent metaphysical truths. At the same time, though, Habermas refused to dispense with the ideal of reason itself. Instead of residing in the subject as some kind of faculty, he located it pragmatically in the social realm as a set of presuppositions that made communication possible. "I call interactions *communicative*," Habermas writes, "when the participants coordinate their plans of action consensually, with the agreement reached at any point being evaluated in terms of the intersubjective recognition of validity claims" (Habermas 1990 [1983]: 58).

Habermas identifies three validity claims that people are making as they reach agreement through speech acts: "claims to truth, claims to rightness, and claims to truthfulness, according to whether the speaker refers to something in the objective world . . . , to something in the shared social world . . . , or to something in his own subjective world" (Habermas 1990 [1983]: 58). These validity claims are pragmatic presuppositions that make discourse possible. If we did not hold them, we would not bother to talk with each other. But at the same time, that we do tend to hold them means that we are easily preyed upon, for example in celebrity endorsements of products that may not be as good as the celebrity says. When the validity claims are warranted, speech can go well; when exploited, the result can be systematically distorted communication, that is, manipulation. Habermas calls the first communicative action and the second strategic action. That others will prey upon our expectations is not reason to abandon hope; rather, those validity expectations are the source for identifying and calling out manipulation.

From this theory of communicative action it was a short step to discourse ethics, a theory of how moral agreement can be reached communicatively. Unlike non-cognitivists who think there is no truth of the matter on moral claims, Habermas argues that there is a truth. But unlike emotivists who think these truths are simple empirical observations of likes and dislikes, moral "truths" are not empirical but linked to a *social* reality of interpersonal relationships in which people are trying to decide together what to do (Habermas 1990 [1983]: 60–61). Any "truth" of such matters arises through agreement. Discourse ethics is based on a principle of universalization (U), which holds that "[a]ll affected can accept the consequences and the side effects its *general* observance can be anticipated to have for the satisfaction of *everyone's* interests (and these consequences are preferred to those of known alternative possibilities for regulation" (Habermas 1990 [1983]: 65; emphasis in original).

But the trouble with something like U, Habermas realized, is that it is impossible to know abstractly whether any given norm could pass this test, hence the need for another principle, D, for the Discourse Principle. D holds that a norm for action—that is, a decision about what ought to be done—is valid if all those affected by it could accept it in a reasonable discourse. So where U posits the more general claim of universalization, D brings it down to earth by testing whether people would actually agree to it in their discussions with others. In a post-metaphysical era only actual agreements that people are willing to make with each other can provide justification, certainly not abstract appeals to truth or validity.

The upshot of Habermas's discourse principle is a conception of legitimacy that does not rely on metaphysical or objective truths. What is valid is only what withstands the tribunal of public judgment. This shows how radical democracy really is—and always has been—to those who want truth to be independent of the vagaries of public opinion. This is what makes democracy's "truths," which are always contingent and up for revision, so threatening to philosophers like Plato and his heirs who wanted truth to be timeless and constant. The radical side of Habermas's theory is that it is non-foundational in very deep way. But the rub for Habermas's position is that it is also hard for it to be cógnitivist, even though Habermas wants his theory to be cognitivist. What is the cognition, that is, what is the truth that discourse ethics tries to get a hold of? Is there a truth waiting to be discovered by discourse ethics? Habermas seems to think there is, though not in any straightforward way. It is to be found through a rational, procedural form of deliberation.

First, moral-practical judgments will be based not on subjective opinions, emotions, and opinions but on reasons that participants offer in their discourse (Habermas 1990 [1983]: 120). These reasons have cognitive content that others can accept or deny, unlike statements of preference that have no hold over anyone else. In principle if someone agrees with a reason then that person is compelled to go along with what follows from it. (If I agree with reasons against the death penalty then I ought to agree that the death penalty is wrong.) The upshot is that all who agree with a set of reasons for some moral judgment should share the same moral judgments. Unlike preferences, reasons compel agreement. And to the extent that all agree, then the judgment is universal. Second, the U principle "works like a rule that eliminates as nongeneralizable content all those concrete value orientations with which particular biographies or forms of life are permeated" (Habermas 1990 [1983]: 121). So, reminiscent of Rawls' original position with its veil of ignorance, any particular contingencies or particularities should be stripped away. They are not only irrelevant to deliberations about normative issues, they also distort these deliberations. The goal is for deliberations to be as impartial as possible. This is the only way people might possibly get hold of any truth of the matter.

Many poststructuralist theorists and feminist theorists are deeply suspicious of there being any truths waiting to be discovered by rational discourse or otherwise. Moreover, many worry that the focus on rationality, universality, and objectivity in effect sidelines the concerns and perspectives of those on the margins and ends up maintaining systems of domination and exclusion.

Feminist Responses to Discourse Ethics

Of the overlapping worries, first is the worry that the model of the self is too atomistic, shorn of any social roots or attachments. Rawls' deliberator behind the veil of ignorance is a prime example of this error. As Virginia Held has noted, such a view, going back to Hobbes, presumes that the self emerges as a full-grown adult with no assistance of a mother or community (Held 1993, 2006). Habermas, as noted above, eschews the philosophy of a monological subject in favor of a view of individuation occurring through socialization. Still, his insistence that, when it comes to discourse on normative matters people should set aside their particularities, subjects his theory to this criticism. As care ethicists, communitarians, and some pragmatists have long pointed out, it is our particular solidarities and attachments that both make us who we are and dispose us to look after the welfare of others.

To address these concerns, especially the challenge that Carol Gilligan poses to one of his heroes, Lawrence Kohlberg, Habermas has sharpened his Hegelian distinction between ethics and morality, that is, between *Sittlichkeit* and *Moralität*, or between the good and the right (Habermas 1990 [1983]: 175–182). It is true, he grants, that in our actual communities, particularity matters; but when we are trying to ascertain universal moral principles, particularities and solidarity have to be set aside. But this "response" to feminist criticisms only served to sharpen the divide.

Another worry is that Habermas's discourse ethics valorizes some forms of speech over others, especially in how it came to be used in deliberative democratic theory. In her essay, "Communication and the Other: Beyond Deliberative Democracy," Iris Marion Young criticizes the ideal of deliberative speech for the way that it valorizes the kinds of speech practiced by those in power and sidelines the modes of speaking engaged by those on the margins, such as greeting, rhetoric, and storytelling. Young's criticism got a lot of traction, leading many on the left, especially those concerned about multiculturalism and identity, to write off deliberative democratic theory as antithetical to a more multicultural politics. (As noted below, Habermas' later work addressed Young's real-world concerns, offering a "de-centered" account of deliberation that she came to champion.)

Some feminist theorists, who have more sympathy to Habermas's project, argue that there is a conflict between those committed to, on the one side, a critical theory of social change, and on the other, postmodern feminists and other feminists who criticize reason itself (e.g., Benhabib et al. 1995; Meehan 2000). They claim that postmodern philosophers (a) eschew reason altogether and (b) engage in reason to debunk reason. Hence, they argue, critics fall into a "performative contradiction." This argument reprises a claim that Habermas made repeatedly in his *Philosophical Discourse of*

Modernity, arguing that Derrida and other postmodernists had fallen into this trap. The problem with his criticism and like ones of his followers is that postmodern theorists do not eschew the ability to make claims and offer reasons; rather, they are worried about claims that stretch too far and try to say too much, often at the expense of other voices and concerns. A more accurate claim is that feminist theorists more broadly have questioned the primacy of reason as an attribute for being human. Stretching back to Aristotle, philosophers have made this claim broadly, saying that what distinguishes us from other animals is our ability to reason and speak, and also noting that men seem to be better able than women to reason. The feminist response to this claim has been twofold: (1) give women enough education and they can reason like men do (Wollstonecraft 1792); and/or (2) that the strict delineation between reason and other attributes, such as feeling, is overdrawn and masculinist (Lloyd 1983).

The most trenchant critics of discourse ethics and deliberative theory are those who follow the agonistic model of radical democracy where the very search for consensus is seen as anti-democratic (e.g., Mouffe 1999). Many feminists who draw on Hannah Arendt's political theory find this agonistic critique of deliberative theory to be persuasive. But Arendt can also be used to support a deliberative model of politics. In Arendt's "space of appearance," it is true that there is debate and disagreement, but there is also a search for deciding together what ought to be done (Lederman 2014).

Conclusion: Deliberation in a Decentralized Public Sphere

Feminist calls for a less idealized and more inclusive politics seem to have made their way into Habermas's work following his writings on discourse ethics, namely in *Between Facts and Norms* (1996) where instead of pure rational proceduralism we get an account of how democracy can operate in complex modern societies. Here deliberation occurs throughout society from the informal decentered public spheres of public life to more formal bodies that are able to translate publicly generated public will into law.

Iris Young, whose 1996 article did so much to disparage deliberative theory, found Habermas' new account to be much richer and more promising (Young 2012). Other feminist theorists also found this decentered approach promising (Jaggar 1998; Mansbridge 2012). Its virtues include the possibility of more diversity and inclusion, the recognition of alternative venues for political action, and the linking up of informal spaces otherwise unrecognized as political. While it would be a stretch to say that Habermas became a feminist, it is no stretch at all to say that feminist engagements with discourse ethics made this theory as inclusive and robust as it is today.

Related Topics

Epistemic injustice, ignorance, and trans experience (Chapter 22); multicultural and postcolonial feminisms (Chapter 47); feminism and liberalism (Chapter 52); feminism and freedom (Chapter 53).

References

Arendt, Hannah (1958) *The Human Condition*, Chicago, IL: University of Chicago Press.
Barker, Derek W. M., McAfee, Noëlle, and McIvor, David W. (Eds.) (2012) *Democratizing Deliberation: A Political Theory Anthology*, Dayton, OH: Kettering Foundation Press.

Benhabib, Seyla, Butler, Judith, Cornell, Drucilla, and Fraser, Nancy (1995) *Feminist Contentions: A Philosophical Exchange*, London: Routledge.

Buchanan, James M. and Tullock, Gordon (1962) *The Calculus of Consent: Logical Foundations of Constitutional Democracy*, Ann Arbor, MI: University of Michigan Press.

Daly, Markate (1994) *Communitarianism: A New Public Ethics*, Belmont, CA: Wadsworth.

Diamond, Larry (2015) "Facing up to Democratic Recession," *Journal of Democracy* 26(1): 141–155.

Fraser, Nancy (1992) "Rethinking the Public Sphere," in Craig Calhoun (Ed.) *Habermas and the Public Sphere*, Cambridge, MA: MIT Press, 109–142.

Gilligan, Carol (1982) *In a Different Voice: Psychological Theory and Women's Development*, Cambridge, MA: Harvard University Press.

Goldfarb, Jeffrey C. (2006) *The Politics of Small Things: The Power of the Powerless in Dark Times*, Chicago, IL: University of Chicago Press.

Habermas, Jürgen (1996) *Between Facts and Norms*, trans. William Rehg, Cambridge, MA: MIT Press.

—— (1975) *Legitimation Crisis*, trans. Thomas McCarthy, Boston, MA: Beacon.

—— (1990 [1983]) *Moral Consciousness and Communicative Action*, trans. Christian Lenhardt and Shierry Weber Nicholsen, Cambridge: MIT Press.

—— (1991) *The Structural Transformation of the Public Sphere: An Inquiry into a Category of Bourgeois Society*, trans. Thomas Burger, Cambridge, MA: MIT Press.

Held, Virginia (1993) *Feminist Morality: Transforming Culture, Society, and Politics*, Chicago, IL: The University of Chicago Press.

—— (2006) *The Ethics of Care: Personal, Political, and Global*, Oxford: Oxford University Press.

Jaggar, Alison (1983) *Feminist Politics and Human Nature*, Lanham, MD: Rowman & Littlefield.

—— (1998) "Globalizing Feminist Ethics," *Hypatia* 13(2): 7–31.

Kellner, Douglas (2005) "Western Marxism," in Austin Harrington (Ed.) *Modern Social Theory: An Introduction*, Oxford: Oxford University Press, 154–174.

Kittay, Eva Feder (1999) *Love's Labor: Essays on Women, Equality, and Dependency*, New York: Routledge.

Lederman, Schmuel (2014) "Agonism and Deliberation in Arendt," *Constellations* 21(3): 327–337.

Lloyd, Genevieve (1979) "The Man of Reason," *Metaphilosophy* 10(1): 18–37.

—— (1983) "Reason, Gender, and Morality in the History of Philosophy," *Social Research* 50(3): 490–513.

MacIntyre, Alasdair (2007 [1981]) *After Virtue*, 3rd ed., Notre Dame, IN: University of Notre Dame Press.

—— (1999) *Dependent Rational Creatures: Why Human Beings Need the Virtues*, Chicago, IL: Open Court.

MacKinnon, Catherine (2005) "Difference and Dominance: on Sex Discrimination," in Ann E. Cudd and Robin O. Andreasen (Eds.) *Feminist Theory: A Philosophical Anthology*, Oxford/Malden, MA: Blackwell, 392–402.

Mansbridge, Jane (2012) "Everyday Talk in the Deliberative System," in Derek Barker, Noëlle McAfee, and David McIvor (Eds.) *Democratizing Deliberation*, Dayton, OH: Kettering Foundation Press, 85–112.

Meehan, Johanna (2000) "Feminism and Habermas's Discourse Ethics," *Philosophy & Social Criticism* 26(3): 39–52.

Mouffe, Chantal (1999) "Deliberative Democracy or Agonistic Pluralism," *Social Research* 66(3): 745–758.

Pateman, Carole (1988) *The Sexual Contract*, London: Polity Press.

Prados, John (1986) *Presidents' Secret Wars*, New York: Quill.

Rawls, John (1971) *A Theory of Justice*, Cambridge, MA: Harvard University Press.

Ruddick, Sara (1989) *Maternal Thinking: Toward a Politics of Peace*, New York: Ballantine Books.

Wollstonecraft, Mary (1792) *A Vindication of the Rights of Woman* [online]. Available from: www.marxists.org/reference/archive/wollstonecraft-mary/1792/vindication-rights-woman/.

Young, Iris M. (1996) "Communication and the Other: Beyond Deliberative Democracy," in Seyla Benhabib (Ed.) *Democracy and Difference. Contesting the Boundaries of the Political*, Princeton, NJ: Princeton University Press, 120–136.

—— (2012) "De-Centering Deliberative Democracy," in Derek Barker, Noëlle McAfee, David McIvor (Eds.) *Democratizing Deliberation*, Dayton, OH: Kettering Foundation Press, 113–125.

52

FEMINISM AND LIBERALISM

Clare Chambers

For some feminists, liberalism is little more than patriarchy in disguise; for others, it is the framework for securing justice. Feminism, like all other positions in political philosophy, is a range of views rather than a single determinate viewpoint. One aspect of this range is that feminism includes both academics and activists, for whom the term "liberalism" can signify rather different things; after all, liberalism is not one single thing either.

In this chapter I start by considering feminist criticisms of liberalism. I discuss two aspects of feminist critique: first, academic feminist critiques of non-feminist liberal philosophy; second, activist feminist critiques of what is variously called "choice feminism," "third-wave feminism," or simply "liberal feminism."

I then move to those feminists who endorse liberalism and argue that a suitably modified liberalism offers the best path to gender equality. This position, "feminist liberalism," is mostly found in contemporary Anglo-American political philosophy. Feminist liberals understand liberalism as a commitment to substantive, demanding principles of justice based on freedom and equality. Included in this section are those feminist approaches that combine radical feminism's insights about the limitations of individual choice with feminist liberalism's commitment to autonomy, equality, and justice.

Feminist Critiques of Liberalism

To get a handle on feminist critiques of liberalism, we first need an account of what liberalism is. Landmark twentieth-century liberal John Rawls defines liberal accounts of justice as having "three main elements: a list of equal basic rights and liberties, a priority for these freedoms, and an assurance that all members of society have adequate all-purpose means to make use of these rights and liberties" (Rawls 2007: 12). A simplified version of Rawls's account would describe contemporary liberalism as combining two key values: freedom and equality. Liberals want individuals to have a significant and protected domain of freedom, they believe that individuals are equally eligible for this freedom, and they believe that this freedom requires a certain amount of, and possibly even equal, economic resources.

Beyond these basic liberal premises there is much variation. For example, some but not all liberals base their understanding of justice and obligation on a contractarian view of relationships between individuals, and between individuals and the state. Liberals also differ in how they understand freedom—is it constituted by the mere absence of coercion, or does it require the presence of rationality? All liberals utilize some sort of distinction between the public or political sphere, considered to be the appropriate place for politics and power, and the private or non-political sphere, considered to be the appropriate place for non-interference. But, once again, there is significant variation in the detail.

A detailed, critical account of liberalism is offered by radical feminist Catharine MacKinnon in her major work *Toward A Feminist Theory of The State* (1989). MacKinnon identifies five aspects of liberal theory: individualism, naturalism, voluntarism, idealism, and moralism (1989: 45). For MacKinnon, each of these is problematic and must be rejected. Feminism, she argues, must necessarily be radical rather than liberal.

Individualism means that liberalism sees people as individuals first and foremost, and assesses the political position of each individual separately. John Stuart Mill, for example, devotes much of his *On Liberty* to defending the rights and interests of the individual and the need for individuality in living; Rawls criticizes utilitarian theory for failing to respect the separateness of persons (Mill 1993 [1859]; Rawls 1971). Radical feminism, in contrast, sees people as necessarily socially constructed and analyses their freedom and equality as a structural aspect of the social group to which they belong (MacKinnon 1989; see also Jaggar 1983).

Naturalism means that liberalism assumes that there is such a thing as human nature. For classical liberals, accounts of human nature are often substantive and gendered. For example, John Locke connects political power and freedom to a rationality that is denied to women (Hirschmann 2008: 48), and Immanuel Kant "constructs women as unfree subjects" (Hirschmann 2008: 62). Some later liberals reject crude versions of essentialist gender roles: Mill argues at length that most differences between men and women are wrongly attributed to nature rather than culture (Mill 1996 [1868]). Nonetheless, liberals generally assume that there is some biological truth to sex difference, and may employ a sex/gender distinction to separate biological from cultural roles. So liberals might critically assess masculinity and femininity, but they tend to retain faith in male and female as natural, biological categories. For MacKinnon, feminism shows that even biological sex difference is social, since it is a social act to identify particular biological features as politically relevant and to create social hierarchy around them (MacKinnon 1989).

Voluntarism occurs when liberalism conceptualizes people as autonomous, choosing, intentional individuals. According to voluntarism people have freedom before and unless they are constrained by others. This way of thinking about freedom is often referred to as negative liberty, and is a central tenet of much liberal thought. Negative liberty means the absence of coercion, understood as intentional interference by other humans (Hayek 1960; Berlin 1969). Liberals focus on minimizing coercion: a person is free just so long as there is no other human being deliberately interfering in her actions, and the way to maximize liberty is to minimize wrongful interference (Mill 1993 [1859]). MacKinnon argues that feminists reject voluntarism in favor of "a complex political determinism" (MacKinnon 1989: 46). Our actions and our identities are socially constructed: they respond to the social conditions in which we find ourselves. But our actions also act as conditions for other people: we both react to, and create, the social conditions in which we must all operate MacKinnon recognizes and praises Mill's recognition that liberty is restricted by private oppression and social norms as well as formal coercive law, but for her his fundamentally voluntaristic instinct remains problematic (MacKinnon 1989: 41).

Idealism means that liberalism tends to "treat thinking as a sphere unto itself and as the prime mover of social life" (MacKinnon 1989: 46). Rationality, on this view, exists independently of action and of social context. This tendency can be seen in the core tenets of Enlightenment liberalism, in contemporary liberal theories that focus on idealized accounts of justice, and indeed in early feminists such as Mary Wollstonecraft and Mill (Wollstonecraft 2003 [1792]; Mill 1993 [1859], 1996 [1868]). Radical feminism requires the rejection of idealism in favor of an account that sees consciousness as inseparable from the social conditions in which it is situated, and sees consciousness-raising as the method by which change can be effected (MacKinnon 1989).

Finally, *moralism* means that liberalism proceeds in terms of principles of behaviour that are right or wrong in themselves, viewed in the abstract. Contemporary liberal theory provides many examples of this approach, with Rawls's principles of justice being the most prominent (Rawls 1971). Rawls also distinguishes political and comprehensive liberalism. Comprehensive liberalism is a controversial commitment to autonomy and equality as essential parts of a good or valuable life, but Rawls argues that political liberalism is neutral between conceptions of the good and thus acceptable to all reasonable people (Rawls 1993). Many feminists find political liberalism appealing as it offers a way of protecting equality while respecting diversity (Nussbaum 1999b; Hartley and Watson 2010), but others criticize it for failing to protect women adequately from cultural oppression (Okin 1999; Chambers 2008). A more general problem with moralism is that claims to neutrality and objectivity often conceal partiality and bias, specifically the bias of the dominant group (MacKinnon 1989; see also Young 1990). Radical feminism proceeds in terms of an analysis of power and powerlessness, and aims for a redistribution of power as a precondition of a theory of justice.

A recurring theme in MacKinnon's account of liberal theory is thus liberalism's failure to understand the existence and significance of *power*. A number of contemporary feminists take up that theme, often using the work of non-liberal theories of power such as those of Michel Foucault to explore the ways that power exists in all social interactions, and is thus both the cause and the effect of gender hierarchy (Butler 1989; McNay 1992; Ramazanoğlu 1993).

A failure to recognize the significance of power is one of the five feminist critiques of liberalism identified by Ruth Abbey. The others are: a critique of *contract thinking*, a critique of the *public/private distinction*, a critique of the *gendered* nature of liberalism as a tradition, and the significance of *care* (Abbey 2011).

Feminism's critique of liberal *contract theory* is most significantly stated in Carole Pateman's classic text *The Sexual Contract* (1988). Pateman argues that liberalism bases its ideas of freedom and equality on contract thinking, most prominently in liberal social contract theory. Social contract theory is the approach exemplified by philosophers such as Thomas Hobbes, John Locke, and Jean-Jacques Rousseau, who justify political obligation (the obligation we have to obey the law) by reference to some sort of contractual agreement between people, or between citizens and the state (Hobbes 1994 [1651]; Locke 1994 [1689]; Rousseau 1987 [1762]). This contract may be explicit or tacit, actual or hypothetical. Social contract theorists argue that contract is a mechanism for preserving equality and freedom while justifying authority and constraint, solving the puzzle of how a liberal state could ever be legitimate. But Pateman asks how a social contract, supposedly based on free consent between equals, can justify the existing social order in which men and women are unequal. She concludes that women are excluded from the social contract both implicitly and explicitly. Instead of a social contract women are the subjects of a sexual contract, one that subordinates them to men in marriage and private life. Liberals continue to use contract thinking as a mechanism for securing freedom in areas such as economics, employment, and marriage. But, for Pateman, the sexual contract shows that contract thinking does not always secure freedom. If the parties are unequal, the contract entrenches inequality.

Pateman's account leads to the feminist criticism of liberalism's *public/private distinction*. This distinction takes different forms in different versions of liberalism. In some versions of liberalism the public/private distinction separates a public sphere of government, law, economics, and civil society from a private sphere of family and intimate relationships. The public sphere, on this account, is the proper concern of politics and also of men, whereas the private sphere lies outside the purview of justice and is the proper location for women (Elshtain 1981). More recent versions of this idea include the Rawlsian notion that justice should apply only to the basic structure of society (Rawls 1971; for discussion see Okin 1989; Abbey 2011; Chambers 2013). In other versions of liberalism, the distinction concerns the appropriate scope of interference from others: interference may be legitimate in the public sphere but not in the private sphere. For Hayek the private sphere is an area of state non-interference, a necessary protection from coercion (Hayek 1960); for Mill the public/private distinction is best understood as the distinction between other-regarding and self-regarding actions and should not be understood as corresponding to the distinction between public life and family life (Mill 1993 [1859]). But many feminists point out that the public/private distinction, in whatever form, generally serves to exclude women's lives and activities from consideration as matters of politics, as relevant for justice, as areas of freedom or unfreedom, power and subordination, when in fact they are all of these things (Hochschild 1989; Okin 1989; Fineman 1995; Card 1996; Kittay 1999; Williams 2000). "The personal is political" is a feminist slogan that insists that the distinction is untenable.

Much liberal theory pays no special attention to sex. Feminists argue that liberalism is a *gendered tradition*, sometimes explicitly and sometimes not. Susan Moller Okin identifies what she calls "false gender neutrality" in philosophers of all kinds, from Aristotle to the present day. Even if they abandon the use of "man" and "he" as generics in favor of gender-neutral terms, liberals and other non-feminists err by "ignoring the irreducible biological differences between the sexes, and/or by ignoring their different assigned social roles and consequent power differentials, and the ideologies that have supported them" (Okin 1989: 11). A prominent example of false gender neutrality is the fourteenth Amendment to the US Constitution (1868), which declares "No state shall . . . deny to any person within its jurisdiction the equal protection of the laws" but goes on to guarantee the vote only to "male citizens." It seems that, at the time of writing, the only "persons" were men. As MacKinnon puts it:

> Men's physiology defines most sports, their health needs largely define insurance coverage, their socially designed biographies define workplace expectations and successful career patterns, their perspectives and concerns define quality in scholarship, their experiences and obsessions define merit,

> their military service defines citizenship, their presence defines family, their
> inability to get along with each other—their wars and rulerships—defines
> history, their image defines god, and their genitals define sex. These are the
> standards that are presented as gender neutral.
>
> (MacKinnon 1989: 229)

Finally, a strand of feminist philosophy known as the *ethics of care* criticizes liberalism
for focusing on justice and abstract reasoning at the expense of care and relationships.
Many feminists argue that liberalism fetishizes abstract principles of impartial justice
between isolated independent individuals (Gilligan 1982; Jaggar 1983; Tronto 1993;
Kittay 1999; Held 2007; Nedelsky 2012). This fetish is problematic for several reasons. First, it is based on distortion: all human beings are dependent on others. No
human being reaches adulthood without extensive care from parents or guardians, and
we all need care throughout our lives when ill or frail. Moreover, the sort of care that
is required for human flourishing and even basic well-being goes beyond the provision
of basic survival needs: we are fundamentally social beings who cannot do well without
intimate, reciprocal relationships. It follows, according to advocates of the ethics of
care, that a liberal approach to morality and justice that relies on abstract principles of
impartial rights and obligations misses the most salient and valuable forms of human
interaction and normative thinking.

The criticisms of liberalism discussed so far come from academic feminism.
Contemporary radical feminist activists extend this critique to include what they sometimes call "liberal feminism." In the activist context, and sometimes elsewhere, "liberal
feminism" refers to a version of feminism that prioritizes the individual above the social,
and choice above social construction. Liberal feminism of this kind is mostly located in
popular culture and media, associated with terms like "girl power," "choice feminism,"
and "third-wave feminism." It involves the claim that feminism means allowing individual women to make their own choices free from judgment, even if those choices
involve participating in activities that other feminists criticize, such as pornography,
prostitution, or cosmetic surgery (Wolf 1993; Walker 1995; Walter 1998; Baumgardner
and Richards 2000; Snyder-Hall 2010; for discussion see Levy 2006; Snyder 2008;
Ferguson 2010; Hirschmann 2010; Kirkpatrick 2010).

Radical feminists criticize this focus on choice. Miranda Kiraly and Meagan Tyler argue:

> Individualism lies at the heart of liberal feminism, championing the ben-
> efits of "choice" and the possibility that freedom is within reach . . . Liberal
> feminism has helped recast women's liberation as an individual and private
> struggle, rather than one which acknowledges the systemic shortcomings of
> existing systems of power and privilege that continue to hold women back,
> as a class.
>
> (Kiraly and Tyler 2015: xi; see also Jeffreys 1997
> and 2005; MacKinnon 2001)

For radical feminists, gender inequality is explained by structural patterns of male dominance, particularly centered around sex. Women are a sex class, subordinated by virtue
of their sex and by the eroticization of male dominance and female submission. Practices
such as pornography, prostitution, BDSM, and beauty practices are thus not neutral
choices but structural *requirements*, part and parcel of women's subordination.

Feminist Liberalism

In this section I discuss those feminists who recognize or even endorse the strong critiques of liberalism just described, yet who still think that liberalism is the best path towards women's equality. The feminists discussed in this section do not support the simplistic choice-based liberal feminism that has just been considered. I refer to them as "feminist liberals" to distinguish them from that approach. This section also discusses how feminist liberals respond to some of the critiques of liberalism raised earlier in this chapter.

For feminist liberals writing within contemporary political philosophy, "liberalism" signals the strongly egalitarian school of thought that is exemplified, in its non-feminist form, by the work of theorists such as John Rawls (1971) and Ronald Dworkin (2000). Feminist liberalism focuses on the implications of that work for women, and on the question of whether the extremely demanding egalitarianism of this sort of liberalism is, or can be, enough to satisfy the feminist demand for gender equality. For feminist liberals a version of contemporary liberal egalitarianism is the correct approach, perhaps after modification in response to the criticisms described earlier.

Martha Nussbaum is a feminist liberal who argues that three liberal insights are crucial to women. These are that all humans are "of equal dignity and worth," that "the primary source of this worth is a power of moral choice within them," and that "the moral equality of persons gives them a fair claim to certain types of treatment at the hands of society and politics" (Nussbaum 1999a: 57). Nussbaum endorses some of the feminist critiques of liberalism that have been discussed so far: she rejects the *public/private distinction* in favor of paying close attention to inequality within families and relationships; she rejects simple *voluntarism* and *idealism* in favor of recognizing the social construction of choices, emotions, and desires—although choice retains a prominent role in her account (see Chambers 2008 for discussion). In these respects, then, Nussbaum endorses the general feminist critique of liberalism. But she argues that liberalism should not be abandoned. On the contrary, she argues that the liberal values of *individualism* and *moralism* both require liberalism to become more feminist, and provide reasons for feminism to be liberal.

For Nussbaum, the individualism of liberalism is not a problematic egoism or a denial of the significance of groups. Instead

> it just asks us to concern ourselves with the distribution of resources and opportunities in a certain way, namely, with concern to see how well *each and every one of them* is doing, seeing each and every one as an end, worthy of concern.
> (Nussbaum 1999a: 63; emphasis in original)

This concern is vital for feminism, Nussbaum argues, since "women have too rarely been treated as ends in themselves, and too frequently been treated as means to the ends of others . . . where women and the family are concerned, liberal political thought has not been nearly individualist enough" (Nussbaum 1999a: 63). In making this claim Nussbaum endorses the feminist critique of the liberal *public/private distinction*. It is necessary to apply liberal principles within the family, and to the care work that is an essential part of human life, because both care and family have been a source of gender injustice. Liberals have largely failed to take that into account (Nussbaum 2004). But Nussbaum believes that liberalism is up to the challenge: its commitment to individualism provides the conceptual tools and the conceptual necessity to do so, particularly if complemented by a focus on capabilities (Nussbaum 1999a; 2004).

Nussbaum also sees *moralism* and one version of *idealism* as strengths rather than weaknesses of liberalism. Moralism, recall, is the idea that there can be abstract principles of right and wrong or, as contemporary liberals would put it, principles of justice. Idealism is the related idea that reason is at least some of the way to get there. While it is true that reason and justice are historically associated with men, and tradition and emotion are associated with women, Nussbaum argues that reason and justice actually serve women's interests. As she puts it,

> wherever you most mistrust habit, there you have the most need for reason. Women have lots of grounds to mistrust most habits people have had through the centuries, just as poor people have had reasons to distrust the moral emotions of kings. This means that women have an especially great need for reason.
> (Nussbaum 1999a: 79; see also Laden 2013)

In a similar vein, Jean Hampton argues that *contractarianism* can actually help the feminist concern to secure justice in all relationships, including intimate ones (Hampton 2004: 172; for discussion see Richardson 2013). Hampton's idea is that relationships can be subjected to a "contractarian test" that asks:

> Given the fact that we are in this relationship, could both of us reasonably accept the distribution of costs and benefits (that is, the costs and benefits that are not themselves side effects of any affective or duty-based tie between us) if it were the subject of an informed, unforced agreement in which we think of ourselves as motivated solely by self-interest?
> (Hampton 2004: 173)

For Hampton, this test enables us to take full account of a person's human worth and legitimate interests, and avoids making women into martyrs to others as the ethics of care threatens to do.

More specifically, various feminists find the work of paradigmatic contemporary liberal Rawls useful for feminism. Prominent among them is Okin, who criticizes Rawls for failing adequately to take gender inequality to account in his actual writing, while at the same time praising his theory for having the potential to be profoundly feminist. Okin joins the chorus of feminists who have no time for liberalism's *public/private distinction*: justice must apply to the family, she argues, since the personal is political in four different ways. First, the private sphere is a sphere of power: "what happens in domestic and personal life is not immune from the dynamics of power, which has typically been seen as the distinguishing feature of the political" (Okin 1989: 128). Second, the private sphere is a political creation: it is law that defines what counts as a family or a marriage or a legitimate sexual relationship. Third, the private sphere creates psychological conditions that govern public life: it is an important school of justice and injustice (see also Mill 1996 [1868]). Fourth, the gendered division of labor within the family affects women everywhere: it creates barriers in public life, as women are not represented in positions of power or when their words are not taken seriously in the workplace, in civil society, or in personal relationships.

Justice must apply within the family, then, and Okin is highly critical of Rawls's *A Theory of Justice* for considering only heads of households and for failing adequately to consider whether sex should be concealed behind the veil of ignorance (Okin 1989; Rawls 1971). "On the other hand," she argues,

> the feminist *potential* of Rawls's method of thinking and his conclusions is considerable. The original position, with the veil of ignorance hiding from its participants their sex as well as their other particular characteristics, talents, circumstances, and aims, is a powerful concept for challenging the gender structure.
>
> (Okin 1989: 109)

Justice, including as Rawls conceives it, is incompatible with gender difference and requires significant changes to all aspects of society. In his later work, Rawls directly addresses Okin's critique and concludes "I should like to think that Okin is right" (Rawls 2001: 176; for discussion see Baehr 1996; Abbey 2011; Chambers 2013). Moreover, whereas Okin sees feminist potential mainly in Rawls's earlier work, other feminists argue that his later political liberalism best meets women's interests (Cornell 1995; Nussbaum 1999b; Lloyd 2004; Hartley and Watson 2010; Brake 2012; Baehr 2013; Laden 2013).

Some feminist liberals argue that liberalism can—and should—take proper account of *care*. Eva Kittay argues that care and caring relationships count as primary goods in the Rawlsian sense, even though Rawls himself fails to recognize this, so that care is a crucial part of liberal justice (Kittay 1999; see also Brake 2012). Jennifer Nedelsky develops an account of relational autonomy that, she argues, speaks to both feminist and liberal concerns (Nedelsky 2012). And Elizabeth Anderson develops a version of democratic equality that is both fundamentally relational and appeals to liberal egalitarianism (Anderson 1999).

Finally, a number of contemporary feminists argue that it is possible to develop feminist approaches that combine a deep understanding of *power* of the sort that is found in radical feminism, critical theory, or postmodern/poststructural theory with a commitment to liberal values such as autonomy, equality, democracy, and universalism. For Nancy Hirschmann feminism requires both a detailed understanding of the processes of social construction and a liberal-like commitment to freedom as a fundamentally important political value (Hirschmann 2003). The problem with liberalism, Hirschmann argues, is that its conception of freedom is inadequate. What is needed is a "feminist freedom" with a "*political* analysis of patriarchal power" (Hirschmann 2003, 217) and an understanding of how the very subject of freedom is shaped. Marilyn Friedman (2003) argues that the liberal conception of autonomy is vital for women, and that understanding it requires deep analysis of the limiting conditions of systematic injustice, subordination, and oppression; oppression is also the focus of the work of feminist liberal Ann Cudd (2006).

Seyla Benhabib argues that there is a "powerful kernel of truth" in many feminist criticisms of liberalism. Nonetheless, she argues in favor of what she calls a "post-Enlightenment defence of universalism," one that is "interactive not legislative, cognizant of gender difference not gender-blind, contextually sensitive and not situation indifferent" (Benhabib 1992: 3). In later work Benhabib develops "discourse ethics," a version of deliberative democracy that draws on both liberal principles of freedom and equality and feminist/postmodern theories of power (Benhabib 2002; see also Benhabib et al. 1995).

Nancy Fraser argues in favor of a feminism that combines both an awareness of inequalities of power and recognition with a commitment to egalitarian redistribution (Fraser 1997; 2013). Fraser identifies redistribution and recognition as "two analytically distinct paradigms of justice" (Fraser 1997: 13), the former allied with liberalism and the latter with communitarianism and postmodernism. But women, she argues, face both distributive and recognitional injustice, requiring "socialism in the economy plus deconstruction in the culture" (Fraser 1997, 31). Realising this sort of justice requires the sort of universal standpoint that liberals advocate: "all people [must] be weaned from their attachment to current cultural constructions of their interests and identities" (Fraser 1997: 31).

Finally, in my own work I argue that the liberal reliance on choice is deeply problematic since it makes it difficult for liberalism to explain or criticize what is going on when people make choices that harm them (Chambers 2008). For liberals, choices that harm only the choosing individual are normatively unproblematic; and yet social norms mean that many such choices are gendered. That is, women are strongly encouraged to choose or accept many harmful practices ranging from gendered appearance norms and sexual objectification to the gendered division of labor and explicit political and legal inequality. Liberals tend to argue that these inequalities are unproblematic if they are chosen, as in this example from Brian Barry:

> Suppose . . . that women were as highly qualified as men but disproportionately chose to devote their lives to activities incompatible with reaching the top of a large corporation. An egalitarian liberal could not then complain of injustice if, as a result, women were underrepresented in "top corporate jobs."
>
> (Barry 2001: 95)

In this example Barry is using choice as what I call a "normative transformer," something that transforms an inequality from unjust to just by its mere presence. This is a common move in liberalism just as it was in liberal or choice feminism. But it is deeply problematic to consider choice as a normative transformer.

The reason that choice is problematic is that we choose in a context of social construction. There are two main aspects of social construction: the construction of options and the construction of preferences. The social construction of options means that our social context affects which options are available to us and which options are cast as appropriate for us. The choice to be a rocket scientist, for example, is only available in a society that contains rocket science; and it will be available to women only if it is not set up an exclusively male role. The social construction of preferences means that we often want precisely those things that our society presents as appropriate for us. Extensive gendered socialisation means that women are more likely to want careers, activities, and products that are gendered as female and men are more likely to want things that are gendered as male.

But if our options and our preferences are socially constructed, it does not make sense to use those choices to legitimate the social context on which they depend. We choose things because our society makes those things available to us and, in large part, because it casts them as appropriate for us. Women are more likely than men are to choose family over career because gendered societies construct working life around the assumption that someone else will be looking after children, and social norms dictate that that person should almost always be a woman.

Liberal values still have a place, though. If social construction is not to lead to relativism (a situation in which we may as well rely on choice since we have no standards of judgement) then we need normative standards and a commitment to at least some universal values. Liberalism offers both. It offers the twin values of freedom and equality, so crucial to women's liberation, and it offers a variety of philosophical mechanisms for theorizing those values as universal, crucial to ensuring that liberation is not the preserve of the privileged. What we need is an uncompromisingly feminist liberalism that takes social construction seriously.

Conclusion

It is possible, then, to combine feminist and liberal insights, and many contemporary feminist liberals do just that. But why should feminists want to be liberals? As MacKinnon points out, liberalism has

> yet to face either the facts or implications of women's material inequality as a group, has not controlled male violence societywide, and has not equalized the status of women relative to men. . . . if liberalism "inherently" can meet feminism's challenges, having had the chance for some time, why hasn't it?
>
> (MacKinnon 2001: 709)

Some feminists thus abandon the language and traditions of liberalism, arguing for, as MacKinnon puts it in the title of one of her books, *Feminism Unmodified*.

For other feminists, the language and "radical vision" of liberalism still resonate (Nussbaum 1999a: 79). Liberalism has certainly failed fully to realise its commitments to universal freedom and equality, both philosophically and politically, but few if any liberals claim that the project is complete. The political and philosophical dominance of liberalism makes constructive engagement with it essential. Feminists cannot ignore liberalism, and liberalism certainly cannot ignore feminism. The question is how to realise both liberal and feminist commitments to genuine equality and liberation for all.

Further Reading

Abbey, Ruth (2011) *The Return of Feminist Liberalism*, Durham: Acumen. (An in-depth discussion of the work of contemporary feminist liberalism, with particular focus on Susan Moller Okin, Martha Nussbaum, and Jean Hampton.)

—— (2013) *Feminist Interpretations of John Rawls*, University Park, PA: Pennsylvania State University Press. (An edited collection in which theorists consider feminist implications for, and criticisms of, Rawls's work.)

Baehr, Amy R., Ed. (2004) *Varieties of Feminist Liberalism*, Oxford: Rowman & Littlefield. (An edited collection of leading feminist and liberal philosophers, exploring the ways that the two traditions can work together.)

Zerilli, Linda M. G. (2015) "Feminist critiques of liberalism," in Steven Wall (Ed.) *The Cambridge Companion to Liberalism*, Cambridge: Cambridge University Press, 355–380. (A discussion of feminist criticisms of liberalism, with a focus on contemporary political philosophy.)

Related Topics

Feminism and enlightenment (Chapter 8); feminist engagements with social contract theory (Chapter 7); feminist conceptions of autonomy (Chapter 41); feminist care ethics (Chapter 43); multicultural and postcolonial feminisms (Chapter 47); neoliberalism, global justice, and transnational feminisms (Chapter 48); feminism and freedom (Chapter 53); feminism and power (Chapter 54).

References

Abbey, Ruth (2011) *The Return of Feminist Liberalism*, Durham: Acumen.

Anderson, Elizabeth (1999) "What is the Point of Equality?" *Ethics* 109: 287–337.

Baehr, Amy R. (1996) "Toward a New Feminist Liberalism: Okin, Rawls, and Habermas," *Hypatia* 11(1): 49–66.

—— (2013) "Liberal Feminism: Comprehensive and Political," in Ruth Abbey (Ed.) *Feminist Responses to John Rawls*, University Park, PA: The Pennsylvania State University Press.

Barry, Brian (2001) *Culture and Equality: An Egalitarian Critique of Multiculturalism*, Cambridge: Polity Press.

Baumgardner, Jennifer and Richards, Amy (2000) *Manifesta: Young Women, Feminism and the Future*, New York: Farrar, Straus, & Giroux.

Benhabib, Seyla (1992) *Situating the Self: Gender, Community and Postmodernism in Contemporary Ethics*, Cambridge: Polity Press.

—— (2002) *The Claims of Culture: Equality and Diversity in the Global Era*, Princeton, NJ: Princeton University Press.

Benhabib, Seyla, Butler, Judith, Cornell, Drucilla, and Fraser, Nancy (1995) *Feminist Contentions*, London: Routledge.

Berlin, Isaiah (1969) "Two Concepts of Liberty," in *Four Essays on Liberty*, Oxford: Oxford University Press.

Brake, Elizabeth (2012) *Minimizing Marriage: Marriage, Morality, and the Law*, Oxford: Oxford University Press.

Butler, Judith (1989) *Gender Trouble*, London: Routledge.

Card, Claudia (1996) "Against Marriage and Motherhood" *Hypatia* 11(3): 1–23.

Chambers, Clare (2008) *Sex, Culture, and Justice: The Limits of Choice*, University Park, PA: The Pennsylvania State University Press.

—— (2013) "'The Family as a Basic Institution': A Feminist Analysis of the Basic Structure as Subject," in Ruth Abbey (Ed.) *Feminist Responses to John Rawls*, University Park, PA: The Pennsylvania State University Press, 75–95.

Cornell, Drucilla (1995) *The Imaginary Domain: Abortion, Pornography, and Sexual Harassment*, London: Routledge.

Cudd, Ann E. (2006) *Analyzing Oppression*, Oxford: Oxford University Press.

Dworkin, Ronald (2000) *Sovereign Virtue: The Theory and Practice of Equality*, Cambridge, MA: Harvard University Press.

Elshtain, Jean Bethke (1981) *Public Man, Private Woman*, Princeton, NJ: Princeton University Press.

Ferguson, Michaele L. (2010) "Choice Feminism and the Fear of Politics," *Perspectives on Politics* 8(1): 247–253.

Fineman, Martha (1995) *The Neutered Mother, The Sexual Family, and Other Twentieth Century Tragedies*, New York: Routledge.

Fraser, Nancy (1997) *Justice Interruptus: Critical Reflections on the "Postsocialist" Condition*, London: Routledge.

—— (2013) *Fortunes of Feminism: From State-Managed Capitalism to Neoliberal Crisis*, London: Verso.

Friedman, Marilyn (2003) *Autonomy, Gender, Politics*, Oxford: Oxford University Press.

Gilligan, Carol (1982) *In a Different Voice*, Cambridge, MA: Harvard University Press.

Hampton, Jean (2004) "Feminist Contractarianism," in Amy R. Baehr (Ed.) *Varieties of Feminist Liberalism*, Oxford: Rowman & Littlefield, 246–274.

Hartley, Christie and Watson, Lori (2010) "Is a Feminist Political Liberalism Possible?" *Journal of Ethics and Social Philosophy* 5(1): 1–21.

Hayek, Friedrich von (1960) *The Constitution of Liberty*, London: Routledge and Kegan Paul.

Held, Virginia (2007) *The Ethics of Care: Personal, Political, Global*, Oxford: Oxford University Press.

Hirschmann, Nancy (2003) *The Subject of Liberty: Toward a Feminist Theory of Freedom*, Princeton, NJ: Princeton University Press.

—— (2008) *Gender, Class, and Freedom in Modern Political Theory*. Princeton, NJ: Princeton University Press.

—— (2010) "Choosing Betrayal," *Perspectives on Politics* 8(1): 271–278.

Hobbes, Thomas (1994 [1651]) *Leviathan*, Edwin Curley (Ed.) Indianapolis, IN: Hackett.

Hochschild, Arlie Russell (1989) *The Second Shift: Working Parents and the Revolution at Home*, New York: Viking Press.

Jaggar, Alison (1983) *Feminist Politics and Human Nature*, Totowa, NJ: Rowman & Allanheld.

Jeffreys, Sheila (1997) *The Idea of Prostitution*, Melbourne: Spinifex Press.

—— (2005) *Beauty and Misogyny: Harmful Cultural Practices in the West*, London: Routledge.

Kiraly, Miranda and Tyler, Meagan (2015) *Freedom Fallacy: The Limits of Liberal Feminism*, Brisbane, QLD: Connor Court.

Kirkpatrick, Jennet (2010) "'Selling Out': Solidarity and Choice in the American Feminist Movement," *Perspectives on Politics* 8(1): 241–245.

Kittay, Eva (1999) *Love's Labor*, New York: Routledge.

Laden, Anthony Simon (2013) "Radical Liberals, Reasonable Feminists: Reason, Power, and Objectivity in MacKinnon and Rawls," in Ruth Abbey (Ed.) *Feminist Responses to John Rawls*, University Park, PA: The Pennsylvania State University Press, 24–39.

Levy, Ariel (2006) *Female Chauvinist Pigs: Women and the Rise of Raunch Culture*, New York: Free Press.

Lloyd, S. A. (2004) "Toward a Liberal Theory of Sexual Equality," in Amy R. Baehr (Ed.) *Varieties of Feminist Liberalism*, Oxford: Rowman & Littlefield, 99- 119.

Locke, John (1994 [1689]) "Second Treatise of Government," in *Two Treatises of Government*, Peter Laslett (Ed.) Cambridge: Cambridge University Press.

MacKinnon, Catharine (1988) *Feminism Unmodified: Discourses on Life and Law*, Cambridge, MA: Harvard University Press.

—— (1989) *Toward a Feminist Theory of the State*, Cambridge, MA: Harvard University Press.

—— (2001) "'The Case' Responds," *American Political Science Review* 95(3), 709–711.

McNay, Lois (1992) *Foucault and Feminism*, Cambridge: Polity Press.

Mill, John Stuart (1993 [1859]) "On Liberty," in *Utilitarianism, On Liberty, Considerations on Representative Government*. London: Everyman.

—— (1996 [1868]) "The Subjection of Women," in *On Liberty and The Subjection of Women*. Ware: Wordsworth, 89–150.

Nedelsky, Jennifer (2012) *Law's Relations: A Relational Theory of Self, Autonomy, and Law*, Oxford: Oxford University Press.

Nussbaum, Martha C. (1999a) *Sex and Social Justice*, Oxford: Oxford University Press.

—— (1999b) "A Plea for Difficulty," in Susan Moller Okin, Joshua Cohen, Matthew Howard, and Martha Nussbaum (Eds.) *Is Multiculturalism Bad for Women?* Princeton, NJ: Princeton University Press, 105–114.

—— (2004) "The Future of Feminist Liberalism," in Amy R. Baehr (Ed.) *Varieties of Feminist Liberalism*, Oxford: Rowman & Littlefield, 149–198.

Okin, Susan Moller (1989) *Justice, Gender, and the Family*, New York: Basic Books.

—— (1999) "Is Multiculturalism Bad for Women?" in Susan Moller Okin, Joshua Cohen, Matthew Howard, and Martha Nussbaum (Eds.) *Is Multiculturalism Bad for Women?* Princeton, NJ: Princeton University Press, 8–24.

Pateman, Carole (1988) *The Sexual Contract*, Cambridge: Polity Press.

Ramazanoğlu, Caroline (1993) *Up against Foucault: Explorations of Some Tensions between Foucault and Feminism*, London: Routledge.

Rawls, John (1971) *A Theory of Justice*, Oxford: Oxford University Press.

—— (1993) *Political Liberalism*, New York: Columbia University Press.

—— (2001) *Justice as Fairness: A Restatement*, Cambridge, MA: Harvard University Press.

—— (2007) *Lectures on the History of Political Philosophy*, Cambridge, MA: Harvard University Press.

Richardson, Janice (2013) "Jean Hampton's Reworking of Rawls: Is 'Feminist Contractarianism' Useful for Feminism?" in Ruth Abbey (Ed.) *Feminist Responses to John Rawls*, University Park, PA: The Pennsylvania State University Press, 133–149.

Rousseau, Jean-Jacques (1987 [1762]) "On the Social Contract," in Donald A. Cress (Ed. and trans.) *The Basic Political Writings*, Indianapolis, IN: Hackett, 141–227.

Snyder, R. Claire (2008) "What Is Third-Wave Feminism? A New Directions Essay," *Signs* 34(1): 175–196.

—— (2010) "Third-Wave Feminism and the Defense of 'Choice,'" *Perspectives on Politics* 8(1): 255–261.

Tronto, Joan C. (1993) *Moral Boundaries: A Political Argument for an Ethic of Care*, London: Routledge.

Walker, Rebecca (Ed.) (1995) *To Be Real: Telling the Truth and Changing the Face of Feminism*, New York: Anchor.

Walter, Natasha (1998) *The New Feminism*, London: Little, Brown & Company.

Williams, Joan (2000) *Unbending Gender: Why Family and Work Conflict and What To Do about It*, Oxford: Oxford University Press.

Wolf, Naomi (1993) *Fire With Fire: The New Female Power and How It Will Change the 21st Century*, London: Chatto & Windus.

Wollstonecraft, Mary (2003 [1792]) "A Vindication of the Rights of Woman," in Janet Todd (Ed.) *A Vindication of the Rights of Woman and A Vindication of the Rights of Man*, Oxford: Oxford University Press, 63–284.

Young, Iris Marion (1990) *Justice and the Politics of Difference*, Princeton, NJ: Princeton University Press.

53

FEMINISM AND FREEDOM

Allison Weir

In New York harbor, at the entrance to the United States of America, stands the Statue of Liberty: *Liberty Enlightening the World*. Liberty stands as a beacon welcoming all to the land of the free, holding a torch and a tablet inscribed with the date of American Declaration of Independence. At her feet lies a broken chain. The Statue of Liberty, like the statue of *Freedom* on top of the Capitol in Washington, is modeled on the Roman goddess *Libertas*, who was also a symbol of the French Revolution: Delacroix's painting of the 1830 July Revolution, *Liberty Leading the People*, shows her holding the French flag and a bayonet. Through the history of Western civilization, freedom, like other abstract ideals, has been personified as a woman. This is ironic, given the status of actual women in these societies. Though women in Rome who were "freeborn" were classed as citizens, they could not vote or hold public office. Neither the Declaration of the Rights of Man in France nor the Declaration of Independence and Bill of Rights in America granted full citizenship or equal rights to women. Today the Equal Rights Amendment to the American Constitution, which would accord equal rights to women, still has not been ratified. Many are excluded from the ideal of freedom: the American Declaration of Independence was signed by slave owners, and the land that was declared independent was stolen from indigenous peoples; America has one of the highest rates of incarceration in the world, and more than 60 percent of the prison population is Black or Hispanic; Indigenous peoples around the world struggle for freedom from colonization; and the land of the free, like other "developed" nations, polices its borders to keep out unwanted foreigners. Worldwide, the freedom of some depends on the exploitation and oppression of most of the world's people.

None of this should be surprising: throughout the history of Western civilization and Western philosophy, freedom has been defined through opposition to the unfreedom of slaves, barbarians, foreigners, and women. The concept of freedom in ancient Greek and Roman societies was defined in opposition to slavery. The fathers of modern Western philosophy—Hobbes, Locke, Rousseau, Kant, Mill—all defined human freedom through explicit opposition to the "savage peoples" of the Americas and Africa, thus legitimizing colonization and slavery by constructing raced others as not fully human (Gordon 1995; Tully 1995; Mills 1997). And as many feminist theorists have pointed out, the freedom of men in the public realm has been enabled by the imprisonment of women, as housewives, and as servants and slaves, in the private realm: women have done the work of caring for children and households so that free men could be free (Pateman 1988; Okin 1989; Folbre 1994). Thus, as Nancy Hirschmann writes, there is a tension in modern theories of freedom between "the theoretical need to define freedom as a universal concept and the political need to exclude most people, including laborers and women, from its expression and enactment" (Hirschmann 2003: 70).

These are arguably constitutive exclusions: in other words, these exclusions are not contingent or secondary to a prior concept of freedom, but have shaped the ways in which we define what freedom is. If our modern Western conception of freedom has been produced through the explicit exclusion of women and raced others, then it will not be enough to just add those who have been excluded. Feminist philosophers and activists thus face a challenge: when we struggle for freedom, we need to reimagine what freedom might be. To do this we can draw critically on the history of philosophies of freedom, but we also need to draw on histories of local and global struggles for and practices of freedom.

In her provocative 1986 essay, "Who Is Your Mother? Red Roots of White Feminism," Paula Gunn Allen argued that the power and agency of Indigenous women in Indigenous communities served as a model of freedom for the white suffragist feminist movement in America. She also argues that Indigenous practices of freedom, and in particular the role of women in Indigenous communities, served as a model for American and European ideals of freedom, and influenced the work of philosophers including Michel de Montaigne and Frederick Engels (Allen 1986). While many of her claims are unsubstantiated, some are supported by scholars who argue that American ideals of freedom, and the American constitution, were influenced by the settlers' encounter with Indigenous peoples, who were seen as exemplars of freedom (Grinde and Johansen 1991). This is just one example of the ways in which concepts and philosophies of freedom are influenced by struggles for and practices of freedom.

Struggles for freedom have historically been central to feminist movements and activism. The "second wave" of the feminist movement in Europe and North America was referred to as the "women's liberation movement," and while the ideal and possibility of liberty are subjects of controversy, feminist activists continue to struggle for individual and collective freedoms, including freedom from male domination and violence and from many forms of oppression, including heterosexism, racism, capitalism, colonization, and imperialism.

Feminists struggle for freedom of choice and autonomy, freedom of movement, freedom of expression and assembly, and freedom of participation in the public realm and in political governance. The ideal of freedom is central to feminism. But what is freedom?

Freedom in Theory and Practice: Rights and Privacy, Interdependence and Solidarity

The ancient Greeks and Romans understood freedom as the capacity to participate in the public realm, in collective self-government. The Roman conception of republicanism—freedom as popular sovereignty, or freedom of collective self-government—strongly influenced modern European and North American conceptions of freedom as collective resistance to tyranny, in particular the tyranny of monarchies, through the establishment of democratic governments. But in modern Western philosophies, the ideal of freedom took on a new emphasis: individual freedom, understood as freedom from constraint, not only by tyrannical governments but by other individuals.

In the social contract theories of Hobbes and Locke, freedom was understood to be an individual's capacity to act without constraint, to own private property, to own oneself as property, and to exercise rational self-interest, through freely entering into contracts with other men. Hobbes imagined a state of nature in which every individual lived in fear of attack. To alleviate this fear, men agree to submit to government and laws to protect themselves: thus society is born of the rational self-interest of individuals, men who freely enter into social contracts to avoid being killed. (Though whether any action taken to avoid being killed is an act of freedom is an interesting question.) The image of the state of nature driving men to form society, understood as a set of legal contracts among individuals, proved to be an enduring fantasy. Thus the social contract theories of the early modern Anglo-European philosophers conceptualized modern society through an explicit contrast with an imagined state of nature populated by savages and barbarians who lived either in a condition of abject unfreedom or in a state of primitive natural freedom, which is in turn either feared as lawless and chaotic, as in Hobbes, or romanticized as idyllic, as in Rousseau. As Charles Mills has argued, these images were not just imagined but were inspired by perceptions of what Hobbes termed "the savage people in many places in America" and in Africa (Mills 1997).

The civilized freedom of the modern Western world was thus understood to be founded on rational agreements to respect individual rights, and the imagined freedom as absolute lack of constraint was traded for freedom within the security of law, as a contracting bearer of rights. Thus in the tradition of liberal individual freedom, freedom is often privatized as a circumscribed area within which a man can be free from interference by others. While the public freedom of participation in democracy is highly valued, it is also treated with suspicion: J. S. Mill criticized democracy as the tyranny of the majority over the individual; Isaiah Berlin argued that what he called "positive freedoms" in the tradition of Rousseau, Kant, Hegel, and Marx—freedom to align one's will with an ideal, and with the general will—supported totalitarian rule. Berlin held that the only freedom worthy of the name was "negative freedom"—an individual's freedom to act without constraint (Berlin 2008). Mill, on the other hand, argued for the importance of the "positive freedoms" of the individual to engage in a project of self-realization and self-determination, through exploring the world, and through freedom of expression and debate. Neither had much interest in what has been called a third form of freedom: freedom in solidarity (the French *fraternité*), and in collective resistance to colonization. (Note that the term "positive freedom" is used to refer to many different kinds of freedom; I discuss some of these below. While some theorists distinguish between individual liberty and a broader conception of freedom, many use the terms interchangeably to refer to individual freedom.)

As critics of liberal individualism since Hegel have pointed out, the social contract theories are based on a strange conception of history: society is born of freely contracting individuals, who are fundamentally atomistic, independent, and competitive. Drawing on ancient philosophy, and especially Aristotle, Hegel and Marx argued that human beings are essentially social beings, and that individuals develop through social relations. Marx argued that the liberal conception of the self as private property, and of freedom as the right of individuals to compete with each other in the marketplace, is produced through the capitalist system: thus this ideal of freedom is founded on class exploitation and inequality. Because capitalism values individuals only insofar as they produce commodities for the private profit of the owners of factories and corporations, individuals are themselves reduced to commodities. Individuals come to define their very selves as private property (as in Locke) rather than as humans—as social beings. True individual freedom, for both Hegel and Marx, could only be found in self-realization in social relations. For Marx, freedom would be possible only through solidarity to resist class exploitation and alienated labour (Marx 1963).

Feminist philosophers have taken this critique of atomistic individualism further. All of the social contract theories imagine a society founded by men who have, as Hobbes puts it, sprung up like mushrooms, separate and independent. This, as feminist philosophers have pointed out, is a gross distortion of history. The reality, of course, is that all are born of mothers, into human groups. We are born dependent, and remain interdependent through our lives. Thus our freedom can be understood only in the context of this interdependence (Jaggar 1983; Benhabib 1992; Held 1993; Fraser and Gordon 1994; Irigaray 1985; Kittay 1999; Weir 2013). If the freedom of elite men in the social contract was founded on the exclusion of women (Pateman 1988) and raced others (Mills 1997) and the freedom of the atomistic individual is founded on defensive denial of connection to others, then real freedom can only be found through solidarity struggles attentive to all forms of interlocking oppressions (Mohanty 2003).

It remains true, however, that many feminist struggles for freedom are struggles for liberal individual freedoms. In modern Western philosophical and legal traditions, individual freedom is most often construed in terms of rights. And Western feminism has a long history of struggles for equal rights.

Yet the legacy of rights is problematic for feminists. In the modern liberal tradition, individual rights were conceived as rights to *privacy*, and specifically as the rights and freedoms of male household heads to exercise authority, over their private property, which was understood to include women, children, and servants—household chattel. One way of dealing with this is to argue that the rights and freedoms historically accorded to white propertied males should be extended to all individuals. Moreover, this inclusion of those formerly excluded can transform the nature of rights. Susan Okin argues for a reconception of human rights to include specific women's rights, such as rights to protection from violence and abuse (Okin 2000). Thus the nature and scope of rights are transformed: whereas rights have traditionally protected men's right to privacy, construed as freedom from interference of the state in the private realm, once women's rights are recognized, the private realm, and men's authority within it, are no longer protected from legal intervention. Critics argue that this formulation of a global feminism fighting for universal women's rights fails to attend to transnational relations of power, taking elite Western women as the privileged subjects of feminist politics, "who [see] themselves as 'free' in comparison to their 'sisters' in the developing world" (Grewal 2005: 142).

It is important to note that many local, national and transnational struggles for women's rights have not focused on rights to privacy or rights to non-interference but have been directed toward public civil and political rights: feminist suffrage movements worldwide have fought for the right to participate in democratic political life, including rights to vote and run for public office, and feminist movements fight for rights to freedom of speech and assembly, freedom from involuntary servitude, and equality in public places, as well as economic, social and cultural rights. Yet women's legal rights in the United States are still often framed in the language of privacy and noninterference: the historic *Roe vs. Wade* ruling in 1973 granted the right to abortion on the basis of a woman's right to privacy. Catharine MacKinnon has argued that abortion is construed as a private privilege, not a public right, in the United States: the state has no obligation to provide access to abortion, or public funding (MacKinnon 1987). The focus on abortion rights has typically neglected the interests of poor women and women of color, who have been subject to programs of forced sterilization in the

United States and elsewhere. Activists have worked to shift the discourse to focus more broadly on reproductive freedom (Fried 1990). Still, rights to privacy are invoked and have been upheld in rulings that corporations and individuals are free to withhold access to contraception and to discriminate on the basis of sexuality. (In contrast, the Supreme Court ruled in 2015 that bans on gay marriage contravened constitutional guarantees of equality as well as liberty.) And the right to privacy is granted selectively: the power of the state to intervene in the private realm increases the vulnerability of the poor and oppressed to regulation of their private lives.

Many feminist theorists draw on socialist and Foucauldian theories to argue that the focus on individual rights problematically constructs individuals as free choosers unencumbered by social contexts and relations of power. Legal rights mask substantive inequalities and oppression. Many argue that the language of individual rights is specific to modern European cultures, and draw on postcolonial theory and critical legal studies to point out that the legacy of rights is entangled with the legacy of colonization. Focusing on cases in India, Nivedita Menon argues that the feminist focus on rights has achieved little in the way of substantive change (Menon 2004). Yet Patricia Williams asserts the importance of rights as the mark of citizenship for African Americans (Williams 1991).

Some feminist political theorists argue that theories and struggles for freedom need to shift from demands for individual rights to practices of participation—and hence from demands for protections of privacy and non-interference to agonistic practices of public freedom. Yet these arguments must also confront the legacy of the public/private split in republican arguments for public freedom. As has been noted, the freedom of male citizens to participate in the public realm has historically been dependent upon the labour of women and slaves in the private realm. The affirmation of the public/private split reappears in the work of republican theorists like Hannah Arendt, who argued that freedom can be found only in action free from necessity—and hence free from labour, as well as the private realm of the household (Arendt 1958).

Second-wave liberal and socialist feminists often located freedom in the public realm of work, calling for women's liberation through escape from the household into paid work (e.g., Friedan 1963). While they differ as to the location of the public realm (Arendt's argument was a pointed critique of the Marxist faith in freedom through work) both the call for freedom through participation in political life and the call for freedom through entering the workforce share a faith in freedom from the private realm that can leave women's exploitation in the household unchanged: women in the workforce and in political life still typically bear most of the responsibility for childcare and housework. And conversely, the belief that freedom can be found only in escape from the household perpetuates the repudiation of everything associated with femininity: the body, children and relationships, our animality and mortality (e.g., Beauvoir 2010 [1949]).

Working-class women have known all along that the workforce is not a realm of freedom. As bell hooks points out, for black women and for poor and working-class women working in factories or in white homes, paid work is not liberation.

> Historically black women have identified work in the context of family as humanizing labor, work that affirms their identity as women, as human beings showing love and care . . . . In contrast to labor done in a caring environment inside the home, labor outside the home was most often seen as stressful, degrading, and dehumanizing.
>
> (hooks 1984: 134)

Drawing on the Hegelian-Marxist tradition, on feminist theories of relational identity, and particularly on the "love and justice tradition of Black America" Patricia Hill Collins and Cynthia Willett offer accounts of freedom situated in relationship and rooted in home. Hill Collins draws on Toni Morrison's *Beloved:* for the ex-slaves Sethe and Paul D, freedom is "a place where you could love anything you chose" (Collins 1990: 182). Willett draws on the slave narratives of Frederick Douglass to argue that this freedom is rooted in "home," understood not as ownership of property but as a source of connection with others and a nurturing of spirit (Willett 2001).

Many first-wave and second-wave feminists argued that women's liberation would require the socialist restructuring of households to eliminate the public/private split (Firestone 1970; Gilman 1996 [1898]), but this argument has generally been ignored in practice. Increasingly, the work of care for children and households, along with care for the elderly, sick, and disabled, is "passed on" from capitalist economies to private households, from private households to contracted labor, from men to women, and from women to other, poorer women. Thus "global care chains" are part of a system of interlocking oppressions in which migrants and women of color do most of the world's care work and domestic work for little or no pay, so that a privileged few can be "free" (Hochschild 2002; Weir 2005). Real freedom, then, would require transnational feminist solidarity to resist interlocking oppressions, with the recognition that no one is free when others are enslaved.

The Subject of Freedom and Its Discontents: Contemporary Feminist Philosophies of Freedom

In *The Second Sex*, Simone de Beauvoir famously argued that the "drama of woman" lies in the contradiction between each woman's aspiration to be a free subject and the demand that she conform to social ideals of womanhood. Women in this situation oscillate between two opposed ideals: as human individuals, we aspire to freedom; as women, we are expected to fulfil the conventions peculiar to the second sex. What would it mean then for women to be free? Is being a woman fundamentally opposed to being free?

For Beauvoir, freedom required self-transcendence. "Every subject posits itself as a transcendence concretely, thorough projects; it accomplishes its freedom only by perpetual surpassing towards other freedoms; there is no other justification for present existence than its expansion towards an indefinitely open future" (Beauvoir 2010 [1949]: 17). Beauvoir linked individual freedom to a universal struggle for liberation, arguing that freedom is the aim of human existence, and that the freedom of the individual is bound up with the freedom of all. "To will oneself free is to will others free" (Beauvoir 2010 [1949]: 73). Thus Sally Scholz notes that for Beauvoir an individual's freedom presumes solidarity with others (Scholz 2005: 51). In *The Second Sex*, Beauvoir argued that if women are to liberate themselves from their situation as the second sex, they must commit themselves to the collective struggle for women's liberation. They must "posit themselves authentically as Subjects," both individually and collectively as a "we" (Beauvoir 2010 [1949]: 8).

Thus Beauvoir points feminist philosophies of freedom in two directions: individual freedom and women's collective freedom. In what follows I shall discuss critical responses to these two directions and articulations of other possibilities for freedom in feminist philosophy.

Individual Freedom

Many feminist theorists continue to frame individual freedom in liberal terms as capacity for choice. For bell hooks "Being oppressed means the absence of choices" (hooks 1984: 5). But feminist theorists situate and contextualize this capacity within social relations of power. Nancy Hirschmann argues for a conception of feminist freedom that prioritizes the capacity for choice, but argues that such a conception must address both the external and internal conditions of choice, and the relations between them, in patriarchal societies stratified by systems of race and class, and further argues that feminist freedom requires the capacity to participate in reshaping those conditions: in order to formulate choices women must have meaningful power in the construction of contexts of choice (Hirschmann 2003). Shay Welch argues for a feminist theory of social freedom as the freedom "to choose and act with and through other community members" and " to partake in the construction of the community's values, norms, and institutions that shape one's own daily life" (Welch 2012: 23).

In their focus on choice, these theorists follow Isaiah Berlin's argument that the essence of freedom is negative freedom: the capacity to act without constraint or interference. Thus freedom requires the absence of obstacles to the exercise of choice (Berlin 2008). But they also contend that freedom cannot be only negative. Hirschmann argues that her attention to contexts of choice to address the issue of power relations distinguishes her approach from models of negative freedom.

> Like classic negative-liberty theorists, I maintain that the ability to make choices and act on them is the basic condition for freedom. However, like positive-liberty theorists, I maintain that choice needs to be understood in terms of the desiring subject, of her preferences, her will, and identity. For subjectivity exists in social contexts of relations, practices, policies, and institutions that affect and shape desires, will, and identity.
>
> (Hirschmann 2003: 30)

For Hirschmann, there are three ways in which theories of positive freedom challenge or expand the negative conception of freedom: (1) they are concerned with the "positive" provision of the conditions necessary to take advantage of negative liberties; (2) they focus on "internal barriers" to realizing my true or higher self; (3) they focus on the social construction of the choosing subject (Hirschmann 2003: 6–14). Charles Taylor argues that positive freedom is an "exercise concept," focusing on self-realization, and the achievement of a substantive end or condition of freedom, whereas negative freedom is an "opportunity concept," focusing on unconstrained action with no specification of an end (Taylor 1985). Kantians argue that positive freedom or autonomy is a proceduralist principle according to which one follows one's own will or law, in relation to an ideal. Other theorists argue that positive freedoms identify specific substantive rights. Berlin's account of positive freedom ranges among a number of different conceptions of freedom, including self-mastery, rational alignment with an ideal and with a general will, substantive freedom, and collective participation in democratic governance. Amartya Sen proposes a model of "development as freedom," emphasizing the ways in which poverty and oppression limit human freedom, and focusing on the role of specific rights and opportunities that foster human capabilities to achieve substantive freedoms (Sen 1999). Martha Nussbaum draws on Sen's work to argue that freedom requires the ability to exercise a specific substantive set of capabilities, and argues that specifying these capabilities as normative ideals is essential for advancing global women's freedom (Nussbaum 2000). Republican theorists including Hannah Arendt point out that all of these are liberal individual freedoms, and argue that positive freedom is participation in public life and democratic governance, while postcolonial and anticolonial theorists argue for collective resistance to colonization.

Poststructuralist theorists argue that even when liberal theories of individual freedom attend to the contexts of individual choice, they do not adequately address Foucauldian critiques of the individual as the subject of power. If the individual is deeply constituted through relations of power, then it makes no sense to advocate the liberation of the individual. Our desires, ideals, and choices, and the very concept of the individual, are all produced through regimes of power. This produces the paradox of the subject:

> Subjection consists precisely in this fundamental dependency on a discourse we never chose but that, paradoxically, initiates and sustains our agency. . . . "Subjection" signifies the process of becoming subordinated by power as well as the process of becoming a subject.
>
> (Butler 1997: 1–2)

Thus any call for the liberation of the subject, or the freedom of the individual, confronts the paradox of freedom: the individual who is supposed to be liberated is itself an effect of relations of power. How then can poststructuralist feminist theorists advocate individual agency and resistance to oppression?

Poststructuralist and queer theorists draw on Michel Foucault's distinction between liberation and freedom. For Foucault, the call for liberation of individuals and their desires relies on the repressive hypothesis, the belief that "all that is required is to break these repressive deadlocks and man will be reconciled with himself, rediscover his nature or regain contact with his origins, and re-establish a full and positive relationship with himself" (Foucault 1997: 282). Freedom, Foucault argues, is possible only in and through relations of power. He does affirm the struggles of colonized peoples for liberation from domination by their colonizers, but argues that this practice of liberation will not be enough to define "the practices of freedom that will still be needed if this people, this society, and these individuals are to be able to define admissible and acceptable forms of existence or political society" (Foucault 1997: 282).

Foucault thematizes multiple conceptions of freedom: agonistic politics of contestation and struggle; practices of critique, questioning, experiment, testing of limits; ethics of care of the self and aesthetics of existence, emphasizing bodies and their pleasures rather than individuals and their desires, in relations of humans with themselves and with each other.

Judith Butler argues that resistant agency can be exercised through subversive citations of norms, through performances that, intentionally or not, question and transform social norms. For example, drag performances expose the fact that all gender performances are forms of drag, that gender is not an essence but a social construct, constituted through repetitive citations of gender norms. Thus gender norms can be denaturalized and displaced by citations that invariably fall short of or challenge those norms (Butler 1990).

Postcolonial feminist theorists agree that the liberal individual is a specific historical and cultural production, but emphasize the imposition of this ideal on colonized peoples. While some believe that some ideal of individual freedom will be found in all societies, others argue that it is inappropriate to generalize this provincial ideal beyond modern European cultures. Saba Mahmood argues that poststructuralist feminists' affirmations of agency as resistance and subversion of norms actually reassert the liberal ideal of individual freedom. Like liberals, poststructuralist feminist theorists and cultural anthropologists conceive of agency only within the binary terms of subordination or resistance to norms. Mahmood argues, then, for a conception of agency entailed "not only in those acts that resist norms but also in the multiple ways in which one *inhabits* norms" (Mahmood 2005:15). Drawing on Foucault's ethics of the care of the self, Mahmood analyzes Islamic women's piety movements in Cairo to show how the agency of the participants is produced through practices of inhabiting norms.

Though she draws on Foucault, Mahmood does not distinguish between individual liberation and freedom. And not all liberal theories construe individual freedom as resistance to norms. While Mahmood articulates it in terms of embodied practice, the conception of agency as a practice of inhabiting norms is actually indebted to Kant, and aligns with Taylor's conception of positive freedom as realizing an ideal. Thus we can understand feminists to be oriented toward realizing an ideal of freedom. Serene Khader argues that Mahmood fails to distinguish between those practices that entail sexist oppression and those that do not: a transnational feminism does not depend on identifying freedom with individual critical agency, but must focus on the content of the practices (Khader 2016). Weir argues that the women in the piety movement are engaged in practices of freedom as practices of belonging—a conception of freedom that can be found in many religious and spiritual practices, both Western and non-Western, and exemplified in Islamic and Indigenous feminisms (Weir 2013). There are many diverse practices and conceptions of freedom, and not all are reducible to dominant Western conceptions of individual freedom. We need to beware of the assumption that all struggles for and practices of freedom are attempts to realize the kinds of freedom with which Western Europeans are already familiar.

From Women's Liberation to Feminist Practices of Freedom

While first- and second-wave feminists identified with a women's liberation movement, the claim to a collective social identity of "women" has been extensively criticized. Critics point out that theories and movements for women's liberation have failed to acknowledge differences and power relations among women (hooks 1984; Anzaldua 1987; Mohanty 2003). Others argue that the identity "women" depends on a claim to sameness or essence constituted through a hetero-patriarchal binary logic of exclusion (Rubin 1975; Riley 1988; Butler 1990). Thus the identity politics of women's liberation are regarded not as a politics of freedom but a politics of oppression, and as self-defeating affirmations of the very identities that colonize us (Brown 1995). Many advocate shifting our collective struggles to coalitions that do not rely on any claims to identity (Reagon 1983). As Chandra Mohanty writes, "the unity of women is best understood not as a given . . . it is something that has to be worked for, struggled toward—in history" (2003: 116). Nivedita Menon echoes this argument: "the creation of 'women' as subject should be understood to be the *goal* of feminist politics, not its starting point" (2004: 21). Transnational feminist theorists avoid making universal claims about women, arguing that feminists must collectively address sexism in the context of critiques of imperialism and interlocking oppressions (Mohanty 2003; Jaggar 2014; Khader 2016).

Linda Zerilli argues that feminist theorists have been overly preoccupied with what she calls the "subject question," which includes both questions about individual subjects and their agency, and questions about the category of women as the subject of feminism. Zerilli argues that feminists need to follow Arendt in shifting the question of freedom outside its current subject-centered frame, as a way to escape "our current entanglement in the paradoxes of subject formation and the vicious circle of agency" (Zerilli 2005: 12) To avoid these paradoxes and entanglements, we need to shift to a practice of freedom that focuses on the "who"—the "unique disclosure of human action," in contrast to the "what"—the identity or substance (Zerilli 2005: 13). According to Arendt, freedom is action in the context of plurality: we act always in relation to different and diverse others in a common world (Arendt 1958). Feminists, Zerilli argues, need to shift from our introspective preoccupation with our subjectivity and agency and step into what Arendt calls the "abyss of freedom"—to practice political freedom through practices of world-building. Thus Zerilli, with Bonnie Honig, affirms an agonistic performative feminism that involves critique and contestation, and participation in practices of freedom in collective and public spaces (Honig 1992). Zerilli takes the Milan Women's Bookstore Collective as an example of this practice: the women in the collective are creating feminist space to practice free relations among women. This involves the free practice of affirming community with and accountability to other women—in Beauvoir's words, of saying "we"—through engaging in struggle with each other in a politics of sexual difference directed toward transforming the given reality.

Queer theory and practice has opened up new possibilities for freedom, questioning and destabilizing fixed identities of sex, gender, and sexuality, and engaging the imagination to create techniques for thinking and acting differently. Butler's conception of gender as performance has inspired arguments for performing genders differently, and for transforming gender.

As Shannon Winnubst writes: "to queer is to create"—to practice freedom in a space of endless contestation and excessive possibilities. To inhabit and confront this space requires, as bell hooks writes, decolonizing our imaginations. "To live in the world queerly is then to live in the world transformatively, with an eye always toward how relations of bodies and pleasures can be multiplied and intensified . . . to veer off the rails of utility and reason" (Winnubst 2006: 148). Thus queer politics are techniques for transformation "from the pain of anxiety to the exuberance of joy" (Winnubst 2006: 200).

Jana Sawicki argues for a queer feminism: "an eccentric, provocative and unruly feminist practice, one able to risk, challenge, and transform itself, any static sense of its beloved objects and self-understandings, its sense of temporal and spatial orders" (Sawicki 2013: 75). Queer feminisms draw on Foucault's understanding of thought as a "critical (and ethical) practice designed to loosen our attachment to present ways of thinking and doing" and thus to open up possibilities for experiment, for thinking and living otherwise (Sawicki 2013: 75). As Sawicki notes, Eve Sedgwick offers a methodology: a shift from "paranoid readings" that obsessively unmask and expose systems of domination to "reparative readings" that depend on curiosity, creativity, and imagination, attending to the ways in which selves and communities flourish, to open up possibilities for pleasure, joy, excitement. While paranoid readings are focused on the binary of desire and lack, reparative readings open up "other ways of knowing, ways less oriented around suspicion, that are actually being practiced" provoking and sustaining affects of surprise and hope (Sedgwick 2003: 144). While some see these strategies as insufficiently political, Sawicki suggests that a political practice needs to create something to be free *for* (2013: 85). And to the critiques that reparative motives are merely about pleasure (merely aesthetic) and are frankly ameliorative (merely reformist) Sedgwick responds, "What makes pleasure and amelioration so 'mere'?" (2003: 144) In fact queer and feminist political activism, from Emma Goldman to Act Up to PussyRiot, has often worked through creative practices that engage the imagination and that multiply and intensify relations of bodies and pleasures.

In this spirit of openness and curiosity, Western feminist philosophers need to learn more about non-Western and Southern conceptions and practices of freedom. By attending to diverse Indigenous, African, Asian, Middle Eastern philosophies and practices of freedom, we might detach from our habits of thinking about what freedom is, and create new connections and alliances.

For example, Indigenous anticolonial struggles draw on traditions of freedom in connection to "all my relations," including other humans, the ancestors, and nonhuman persons, and on practices of freedom as collective joy and love enacted in danced rituals as sources of solidarity and resistance to colonization. How might these be connected to queer practices of freedom of bodies and pleasures, Islamic feminist struggles for gender equality within an ideal of freedom in union with the divine, African American freedom songs, and Buddhist practices of cultivating joy? All of these diverse practices pursue freedom from oppression within a theory and practice of freedom in relationship, rather than negative freedom from interference. How might connections with all such diverse movements and practices of freedom change feminist politics and philosophies of freedom in the twenty-first century?

Related Topics

Feminism, philosophy and culture in Africa (Chapter 4); feminist engagements with social contract theory (Chapter 7); feminism and the enlightenment (Chapter 8); introducing black feminist philosophy (Chapter 10); Native American chaos theory and politics of difference (Chapter 30); feminist theory, lesbian theory, and queer theory (Chapter 31); through the looking glass (Chapter 32); feminist and queer intersections with disability studies (Chapter 33); feminist intersections with environmental and ecological thought (Chapter 35); feminist conceptions of autonomy (Chapter 41); Latin American feminist ethics (Chapter 52); feminism and liberalism (Chapter 52).

References

Allen, Paula Gunn (1986) "Who Is Your Mother? Red Roots of White Feminism," *Sinister Wisdom* 25(1984): 34–36.
Anzaldúa, Gloria (1987) *Borderlands/La Frontera*, San Francisco, CA: Aunt Lute.
Arendt, Hannah (1958) *The Human Condition*, Chicago, IL: University of Chicago Press.
Beauvoir, Simone de (2010 [1949]) *The Second Sex*, trans. Constance Borde and Sheila Malovany-Chevallier, London: Vintage.
Benhabib, Seyla (1992) *Situating the Self: Gender, Community and Postmodernism in Contemporary Ethics*, New York: Routledge.
Berlin, Isaiah (2008) "Two Concepts of Liberty" and "From Hope and Fear Set Free," in Henry Hardy (Ed.) *Liberty*, Oxford: Oxford University Press.

Brown, Wendy (1995) *States of Injury: Power and Freedom in Late Modernity*, Princeton, NJ: Princeton University Press.

Butler, Judith (1990) *Gender Trouble: Feminism and the Subversion of Identity*, New York and London: Routledge.

——(1997) *The Psychic Life of Power: Theories in Subjection*, Stanford, CA: Stanford University Press.

Collins, Patricia Hill (1990) *Black Feminist Thought: Knowledge, Consciousness, and the Politics of Empowerment*, London: HarperCollins.

Firestone, Shulamith (1970) *The Dialectic of Sex: The Case for Feminist Revolution*, New York: Morrow.

Folbre, Nancy (1994) *Who Pays for the Kids? Gender and the Structures of Constraint*, New York: Routledge.

Foucault, Michel (1997) (*Ethics*) *Essential Works of Michel Foucault*, Ed. Paul Rabinow, New York: The New Press.

Fraser, Nancy and Gordon, Linda (1994) "A Genealogy of 'Dependency': Tracing a Keyword of the U.S. Welfare State," *Signs* 19(2): 309–336.

Fried, Marlene Gerber (1990) *From Abortion to Reproductive Freedom: Transforming a Movement*, Boston, MA: South End Press.

Friedan, Betty (1963) *The Feminine Mystique*, New York: W.W. Norton.

Gilman, Charlotte Perkins (1996 [1898]) *Women and Economics*, New York: Harper & Rowe.

Gordon, Lewis (1995) *Bad Faith and Antiblack Racism*, Amherst, NY: Humanity Press.

Grewal, Inderpal (2005) *Transnational America*, Durham, NC and London: Duke University Press.

Grinde, Donald A. and Johansen, Bruce E. (1991) *Exemplar of Liberty: Native America and the Evolution of Democracy*, Los Angeles, CA: American Indian Studies Centre, UCLA.

Held, Virginia (1993) *Feminist Morality: Transforming Culture, Society, and Politics*, Chicago, IL: University of Chicago Press.

Hirschmann, Nancy J. (2003) *The Subject of Liberty. Toward a Feminist Theory of Freedom*, Princeton, NJ: Princeton University Press.

Hochschild, Arlie Russell (2002) "Love and gold," in Barbara Ehrenreich and Arlie Russell Hochschild (Eds.) *Global Woman*, New York: Metropolitan Books, 15–30.

Honig, Bonnie (1992) "Toward an Agonistic Feminism: Hannah Arendt and the Politics of Identity," in Judith Butler and Joan W. Scott (Eds.) *Feminists Theorize the Political*, New York: Routledge, 215–235.

hooks, bell (1984) *Feminist Theory: From Margin to Center*, Boston, MA: South End Press.

Irigaray, Luce (1985) *Speculum of the Other Woman*, trans. Gillian C. Gill, Ithaca, NY: Cornell University Press.

Jaggar, Alison (1983) *Feminist Politics and Human Nature*, Lanham, MD: Rowman & Allanheld.

——(Ed.) (2014) *Gender and Global Justice*, Cambridge and Malden, MA: Polity.

Khader, Serene (2016) "Do Muslim Women Need Freedom?" *Politics and Gender* 12(4): 727–753.

Kittay, Eva (1999) *Love's Labor: Essays on Women, Equality, and Dependency*, New York: Routledge.

MacKinnon, Catharine (1987) *Feminism Unmodified*, Cambridge, MA: Harvard University Press.

Mahmood, Saba (2005) *Politics of Piety: The Islamic Revival and the Feminist Subject*, Princeton, NJ: Princeton University Press.

Marx, Karl (1963) *Karl Marx: Early Writings*, Ed. and trans. T. B. Bottomore, New York: McGraw-Hill

Menon, Nivedita (2004) *Recovering Subversion: Feminist Politics Beyond the Law*, Delhi/Urbana, IL and Chicago, IL: Permanent Black/ University of Illinois Press.

Mills, Charles (1997) *The Racial Contract*, Ithaca, NY: Cornell University Press.

Mohanty, Chandra Talpade (2003) *Feminism without Borders: Decolonizing Theory, Practicing Solidarity*, Durham, NC: Duke University Press.

Nussbaum, Martha (2000) *Women and Human Development: The Capabilities Approach*, Cambridge: Cambridge University Press.

Okin, Susan Moller (1989) *Justice, Gender, and the Family*, New York: Basic Books.

——(2000) "Feminism, Women's Human Rights, and Cultural Differences," in Uma Narayan and Sandra Harding (Ed.) *Decentering the Center: Philosophy for a Multicultural, Postcolonial, and Feminist World*, Bloomington, IN: Indiana University Press, 26–46.

Oksala, Johanna (2005) *Foucault on Freedom*, Cambridge: Cambridge University Press.

Pateman, Carole (1988) *The Sexual Contract*, Stanford, CA: Stanford University Press.

Reagon, Bernice Johnson (1983) "Coalition Politics: Turning the Century," in Barbara Smith (Ed.) *Home Girls: A Black Feminist Anthology*, New York: Kitchen Table, 356–368.

Riley, Denise (1988) *"Am I That Name?" Feminism and the Category of "Women" in History*, Minneapolis, MN: University of Minnesota Press.

Rubin, Gayle (1975) "The Traffic in Women: Notes on the 'Political Economy' of Sex," in Rayna R. Reiter (Ed.) *Toward an Anthropology of Women*, New York: Monthly Review Press, 157–210.

Sawicki, Jana (2013) "Queer Feminism: Cultivating Ethical Practices of Freedom," *Foucault Studies* 16: 74–87.

Scholz, Sally (2005) "Sustained Praxis," in Sally Scholz and Shannon M. Mussett, (Eds.) *The Contradictions of Freedom*, Albany, NY: SUNY Press.

Sedgwick, Eve Kosofsky (2003) *Touching Feeling: Affect, Pedagogy, Performativity*, Durham, NC and London: Duke University Press.

Sen, Amartya (1999) *Development as Freedom*, New York: Knopf.

Taylor, Charles (1985) "What's Wrong with Negative Liberty," in *Philosophy and the Human Sciences: Philosophical Papers vol. 2*, Cambridge: Cambridge University Press, 211–229.

Tully, James (1995) *Strange Multiplicity: Constitutionalism in an Age of Diversity*, Cambridge: Cambridge University Press.

Weir, Allison (2013) *Identities and Freedom: Feminist Theory between Power and Connection*, New York: Oxford University Press.

Welch, Shay (2012) *A Theory of Freedom: Feminism and the Social Contract*, New York: Palgrave Macmillan.

Willett, Cynthia (2001) *The Soul of Justice: Social Bonds and Racial Hubris*, Ithaca, NY: Cornell University Press.

Williams, Patricia J. (1991) *The Alchemy of Race and Rights*, Cambridge, MA: Harvard University Press.

Winnubst, Shannon (2006) *Queering Freedom*, Bloomington, IN: Indiana University Press.

Zerilli, Linda M.G. (2005) *Feminism and the Abyss of Freedom*, Chicago, IL: University of Chicago Press.

54

FEMINISM AND POWER

Johanna Oksala

Introduction

Power is a pivotal concept for feminist theory. While feminists strongly disagree on a host of issues, most of them take it for granted that feminism is at least somehow concerned with power relations between men and women. Whether they use the word "oppression," "subjection," "subordination," or "domination," the key claim is that these power relations are problematic—illegitimate or unjust. As a political project, feminism aims to alter, subvert, or eradicate them; as a theoretical project it aims to expose and understand them.

Power is a highly contested philosophical concept, however, not just in feminist philosophy, but in critical social and political theory more generally. While some philosophers have cast doubt on the possibility of there being some entity called "power" that could be usefully studied or systematically defined, others have argued that any objective, theoretical definition of power is impossible because our conceptions of power are themselves shaped by power relations (see e.g., Foucault 1982; 1991; Lukes 2005 [1974]). They contend that ultimately all conceptions of power are an outcome of political contestation and struggle, and depending on how we conceive of power, we may end up with very different views on its legitimacy and desirability, and hence its concrete political implications. As Steven Lukes formulates this:

> [H]ow we think of power may serve to reproduce and reinforce power structures and relations, or alternatively it may challenge and subvert them. It may contribute to their continued functioning, or it may unmask their principles of operation, whose effectiveness is increased by their being hidden from view.
> (Lukes 2005 [1974]: 63)

Accepting such a politicized view of power does obviously not preclude the importance studying it—on the contrary. It is vital that feminists take part in the political contestation over the meaning of power in order to endorse conceptions of it that are theoretically and politically effective for the attempts to resist male domination.

In this chapter, I will provide a critical overview of the most common ways of understanding power in feminist theory. I will begin by examining the distinction between two broad theoretical models—power-over and power-to—and I will discuss some of the feminist attempts to appropriate these models. I will then look at systemic accounts of power and focus on Marxist and poststructuralist approaches. I will discuss Michel

Foucault's conception of power in particular, as it is arguably the most influential approach to power in contemporary feminist philosophy. I will conclude by considering some of the consequences of the feminist views on power for the crucial question of resistance.

Power-Over and Power-To

The most common way of defining power is to understand it simply as a capacity to get someone else to do what you want them to do. Robert Dahl's influential definition, for example, states "A has power over B to the extent that he can get B to do something that B would not otherwise do" (1957: 202–203). This "intuitive view" of power underlies most feminist accounts of gender oppression: in patriarchal societies men generally have the capacity to exercise power over women through various means ranging from physical coercion to subtle forms of discrimination and belittling.

The most extreme form of power over someone is arguably slavery, and for the early feminist writers such as Mary Astell and Mary Wollstonecraft, slavery and the abolitionist debate provided a model for theorizing power (Astell 1996; Wollstonecraft 2001). Astell, a contemporary of John Locke, asked sarcastically: "if all Men are born Free, how is it that all Women are born Slaves" (Astell 1996: 18). Wollstonecraft's major polemic A Vindication of the Rights of Women also adapts the terms of contemporary political debate on slavery. Throughout the eighteenth century, feminist writers railed against marriage as a form of slavery. The power relations between men and women were viewed as relations of domination and coercion similar to the relations between slave owners and slaves. Until late into the nineteenth century the legal and civil position of a wife resembled that of a slave. Like a slave, she was her husband's possession in the sense that she had no legal existence apart from him, and he was also entitled to punish her physically.

By the time the second-wave feminist movement emerged in the 1960s and 1970s, the legal and civil position of women in most nations had dramatically improved, yet the power imbalances between men and women seemed to persist. The theoretical model of master/slave remained central in many of the radical feminist accounts of gender oppression at the time. The imbalance between power and powerlessness was understood as definitional for what it meant to be a man or a woman. In other words, the key feminist claim was that the categories of men and women were not just politically neutral descriptions, symmetrical and complementary, but in a gendered social order such as ours being a woman was only possible as a being subordinated to men. As the American legal theorists, Catharine MacKinnon provocatively put it: "women/men is a distinction not just of difference, but of power and powerlessness . . . power/powerlessness *is* the sex difference" (1987: 123). Sexuality became the flashpoint of the radical feminist analyses. It was not just a central arena of male domination; sexuality itself was understood as a form of power.

> A woman is a being who identifies and is identified as one whose sexuality exists for someone else, who is socially male. Women's sexuality is the capacity to arouse desire in that someone . . . Sexual objectification is the primary process of the subjection of women . . . Man fucks woman; subject verb object.
>
> (MacKinnon 1983: 533)

The political philosopher Carole Pateman's seminal book *The Sexual Contract* (1988) also relies on the master/slave model for understanding how male domination becomes constitutive of the meaning of the gender difference itself. She examines critically the story of the social contract, perhaps the most celebrated story of modern philosophy hailing universal freedom as the guiding principle of our historical era. Pateman contends that only half of that story is ever told: standard commentaries do not mention that women were excluded from the contract. The naturally free and equal individuals who people the pages written by social contract theorists are a disparate collection, covering "the spectrum of Rousseau's social beings to Hobbes' entities reduced to matter in motion," but what they have in common is that they are all male (Pateman 1988: 41).

In other words, the theory states that, if relations of subordination between *men* are to be legitimate, they must originate in a contract. Women were not party to the contract, they are subject to it: the contract established not only men's political freedom, but also their political right over women and their bodies—essentially the right of a master over a slave. Pateman argues that the significance of this position is not limited to a bit of poor philosophical reasoning by philosophers long dead. The structures of our society and our everyday lives still incorporate features of a patriarchal conception of marriage and family. Husbands obviously no longer enjoy the extensive rights over their wives that they still possessed in the mid-nineteenth century. However, aspects of conjugal subjection linger on, both in cultural attitudes, and in the legal jurisdictions of the many countries that refuse to admit that rape is possible within marriage, for example.

The problem with the master/slave model for theorizing women's subordination is that it makes it difficult to account for women's agency and resistance. Feminist theory clearly calls for a conception of power that does not view women solely as helpless victims of overbearing male power, but recognizes their specific strengths and strategies of resistance. A further problem concerns the desirability of such power: if feminists want women to gain more power, is the power of a master over a slave really the kind of power they want? Do they want to exercise more power if power means seeking hierarchical control, causing others to submit to one's will or limiting and putting down another person?

These problems have prompted many feminists to criticize views of power that conceive it only negatively, as power over somebody. They have sought to develop instead alternative accounts of power that define power as a positive capacity to act, as a power to do something. They have turned to the thought of the political philosopher Hannah Arendt for help, for example (see, e.g., Hartsock 1983; Honig 1995). Arendt offers a classic definition of a positive conception of power when she defines it as "the human ability not just to act but to act in concert" (Arendt 1970: 44). Her key idea is that power is never a means to something else, but an end in itself and should therefore be sharply distinguished from such related concepts as authority, strength, force, and violence. Power is essentially the shared ability to bring about change, to collectively and creatively transform and shape the world.

Feminists from various other theoretical backgrounds such as ecofeminism and maternal feminism have also argued that feminists need a conception of power that is integrally tied to the feminist idea of empowerment. Feminists should theorize power as a capacity to positively transform oneself and others. Jean Baker Miller (1992: 241–243), for example, argues that it is a convenient myth that women do not and should not have power. If we re-think power as the capacity to produce a change, then it is clear that women, in their traditional role as mothers and caretakers, have invariably exercised power to foster the growth of others. "This might be called using one's power to empower another—increasing the other's resources, capabilities, effectiveness, and ability to act" (Miller 1992: 242). The problem is that we are not accustomed to include such effective action within the accepted notions of power and therefore end up overlooking the strengths that women have demonstrated all through history. In other words, the fact that women are often reluctant to take or exercise power *over others* does not indicate that women have a problem; it indicates that there is a problem in our understanding of power, as well as in our relationships with each other in patriarchal society (see also e.g., Held 1993).

Feminists working in the liberal tradition also usually understand power as a positive social good, a resource or a capacity that should be equally distributed among individuals in society. The problem that liberal feminists seek to combat is the unequal distribution of power among men and women, and their political aim is to create equal opportunities for women to acquire more political and economic power. Betty Friedan (1968: 454), the author of the feminist classic *The Feminine Mystique* (1963), for example, argued that women "need political power" meaning equal access to political institutions (on liberal feminist approaches, see also, e.g., Okin 1989).

Whether we understand power as power-over or power-to both of these approaches suffer from an important oversight, however. Their focus is on individual women's capacities and/or their relationships to individual men. This means that they have difficulties accounting for the systemic or structural aspects of power. Liberal feminists' understanding of power as a resource or a capacity, for example, does not seem to recognize sufficiently the relational and contextual character of power. Women's lack of power cannot be understood in isolation and independently of their relationships to men in a patriarchal society. Feminist critiques of liberalism have foregrounded the insight that any critical social theory that begins with an isolated individual is bound to lead to absurd political consequences. People are always members of communities, and only their fundamental social bonds and familial ties make individual interests and goals possible. Liberal rights thus falsely equate emancipation with protected isolation (on feminist critiques of liberalism, see e.g., Elshtain 1981; Young 1990; Brown 2005).

When power is understood as power-over or a relationship of domination, on the other hand, this view also seems to leave the systemic or structural constraints out of the picture. It is obviously important to acknowledge that power relations are ultimately always exercised between individual subjects, but in order to understand how they function and why they persist, it is often not very helpful to focus on the motives or intentions of the individual actors. Instead it is crucial to examine the larger societal structures, rationalities and norms that make the actions of the individual actors possible and intelligible. Amy Allen (1996: 267) formulates this idea by arguing that an adequate feminist theory of power should include both the micro-level and the macro-level analyses. The micro-level analysis would examine a specific power relation between two individuals or groups of individuals. The macro-level analysis, on the other hand, should focus on the background to such particular power relations. It must examine the cultural meanings, practices, and larger structures of domination that make up the context within which a particular power relation is able to emerge. A feminist analysis of power relations that remained solely on the micro level would be seriously inadequate because power relations studied in isolation from their cultural and institutional context can be easily perceived as anomalies, and not as part of a larger system of domination such as sexism (Allen 1996: 268).

Socialist Feminist Approaches

Socialist feminists have readily appropriated this imperative to focus on the macro level in their analyses of power. They have emphasized the necessity to study the systemic aspects of capitalism in particular. When attempting to understand such diverse contemporary feminist issues as the feminization of poverty, the rapid growth of the sex industry in the global South or the care deficit in the global North, it seems apparent that feminists need a critical analysis of global capitalism and its implications for gender oppression.

Marx's important contribution in his major work *Capital, Volume 1* was to bring to light how behind the supposedly free relations of exchange between individual capitalists and workers laid deeper structures of exploitation. For Marx, an obvious problem with the idyllic picture that the defenders of the "free market" were portraying was that the worker and the capitalist were not in a symmetrical situation when they came to exchange their products—labor power for money. The capitalist was not forced to buy anything because he was in a position to wait, move his factory elsewhere, or reinvest his money in something else. The worker, on the other hand, could not wait. He constantly had to sell his labor power if he wanted to survive, because in a capitalist system all other means of making a living had been eradicated. Marx argued that a society of landless wage laborers with nothing but their labor power to sell was an historical outcome of the social upheaval that followed the breakdown of feudalism. It was not a result of some natural inequality of talents and preferences—some people did not freely choose to become workers and some capitalists. Deliberate and violent political acts, such as the appropriation of common resources and property legislation favoring rich landowners, led to the accumulation of property and raw materials into the hands of a few and made it necessary for the vast masses of landless peasants to sell their labor power. In other words, in the new commercial society organized on the principles of private ownership and monetary exchanges new kinds of power relations were established between people: behind the supposedly free relations of exchange lay a structural, institutionalized compulsion for the worker to sell his labor power to the capitalist.

Feminist thinkers appropriating the Marxist framework have argued that the structural domination of the working class by the capitalist class was analogous to the domination of women by men in a patriarchal society. Women formed an oppressed class in relation to men in capitalism because they had been forced to bear the responsibility for social reproduction—the daily, intergenerational, social and biological reproduction of the workforce. While capitalism was also exploiting women's labor power through varied forms of waged labor, women were still expected to do another shift at home for free. They were expected to do housework, clean, cook, and so on, but they were also mainly responsible for social reproduction in a much broader sense: the socialization of the young, the maintenance of social bonds and production and reproduction of shared meanings and values (for some pioneering Marxist-feminist work on social reproduction, see e.g., Vogel 1983; Dalla Costa and James 1997).

The imposition of social reproduction on women has been effectively disguised either as a woman's free choice, or as her natural propensity, however. Marxist-feminists insisted that the care work women did at home had to be finally recognized as a systemic condition indispensable for capitalism: it was materially producing and forming capitalism's human subjects, the exploitable workers the capitalist economic systems needs in order to function properly and to continue to generate wealth. Historically, capitalism's social organization thus rests on a structural division between the private, familial, female sphere of reproduction and the public, male sphere of production. As Nancy Fraser writes:

> With capitalism . . . reproductive labor is split off, relegated to a separate, "private" sphere, where its social importance is obscured. And where money is the primary medium of power, the fact of its being unpaid seals the matter: those who do this work are structurally subordinate to those who earn cash wages, even as their work also supplies necessary preconditions for wage labor.
>
> (Fraser 2014: 8)

In the 1970s, feminist theory in Western Europe was to a large extent dominated by Marxism and the parallel questions of class and gender oppression. However, the Marxist-feminist attempts to model gender oppression on the model of class oppression suffered from various theoretical problems and became progressively marginalized in the 1980s and 1990s. While effectively exposing forms of exploitation and alienation, Marxist theory tended to theorize power relations in terms of class antagonism between capital and the proletariat. Women did not form a unified class with similar interests and needs, however. Instead the intersections of class, gender, and racial oppression seemed to call for more specific and historically varied analyses than what was allowed by the framework of class antagonism.

Poststructuralist Feminist Approaches

At this theoretical and political crossroads Michel Foucault's conception of power opened up completely new avenues for feminist theory. Although Foucault had little interest in the feminist politics of his time, his theorization of the various historical rationalities and technologies of power has both opened up new resources for feminist critique, as well as being controversial among feminists. The feminist body of work appropriating Foucault's analysis of power that exists today is exceedingly large and diverse (see e.g., Sawicki 1991; McNay 1992; McWhorter 1999; Heyes 2007; Oksala 2016).

Foucault insisted that one should not start by looking for the center of power, or for the individuals, institutions or classes that rule, but should rather construct a "microphysics of power" that focuses on the extremities: families, workplaces, everyday practices, and marginal institutions. One has to analyze power relations from the bottom up and not from the top down, and to study the myriad ways in which the power relations operate in different but intersecting capillary networks (Foucault 1978: 94–96).

The idea of a microphysics of power resonated strongly with the feminist credo that personal was political. The second-wave feminists saw it as vitally important to expose power relations in what was considered the private sphere, and not only in what was considered the public and properly political sphere. The feminist establishment of sexual politics as a central area of struggle required a conception of power that was able to account for its capillary forms in everyday practices and habits. Feminist theorists appropriated the idea of a microphysics of power by studying the different ways that women shape their bodies, for example—from cosmetic surgery to dieting and eating disorders. They analyzed these everyday feminine practices as disciplinary technologies in the service of patriarchal, normalizing power. These normative practices train the female body in docility and obedience to cultural demands, while at the same time they are often paradoxically experienced in terms of "power" and "control" by the women themselves (see, e.g., Bartky 1988, 2002; Bordo 1989, 2001).

Apart from the idea that power is always relational, capillary, and diffuse, Foucault's conception of power also provided another major insight for feminism: power relations are productive of the subjects embedded in them. His perhaps most important theoretical contribution for feminist theory has been his idea of *productive power*, the idea that power does not operate primarily through repression, prohibition, and censorship, but is essentially productive. Being a subject, a socially recognized individual with intelligible intentions, desires and actions, is only possible within the power/knowledge networks of a society. Individuals do not enter the public, political arena as fully formed subjects who then demand rights and represent interests. The supposedly personal or private aspects of their being are already traversed by power relations, which not only restrain them, but produce them as certain kinds of subjects. In other words, the subjects over whom the power network is defined cannot be thought to exist apart from it.

The consequences of the idea of productive power for feminist theory were momentous: it formed the starting point of what has undoubtedly been the most influential appropriation of Foucault's thought for gender theory, namely Judith Butler's *Gender Trouble* (1990). The book opens with troubling questions: If we accept Foucault's argument about productive power and acknowledge that subjects are produced by power relations, does this not imply that the subject of feminism, "women," is produced by the very same oppressive power relations that it aims to theorize and eradicate? Would "women" even exist if society was not structured by sexist power relations? Who are the subjects that feminism aims to liberate?

Butler thus takes on Foucault's idea of productive power and asks what the consequences of this idea are for feminist politics. She insists that it implies that it is not enough to try to include more women in politics or to seek to represent their interests more effectively. We have to ask more fundamentally who these women are: how the very identity and the category of women are constituted through practices of power. This implies reconsidering the viability of feminist identity politics. The problem is not merely that the category of women denies the differences between women and thereby inadvertently privileges one group of women. More fundamentally, we have to pose critical questions about the desirability of embracing an oppressive identity that excluded women from politics in the first place.

It is no exaggeration to say that *Gender Trouble* caused a paradigm shift in the way that the intertwinement of power, feminist emancipation and the female subject was theorized. It was subjected to extensive feminist commentary, and Butler responded to the criticism in the books that followed *Gender Trouble* (Butler 1993; 1997; 2004).

Foucault's views on power and Butler's appropriation of them have also been formative for the key ideas behind queer politics: the identities of gay and lesbian— as well as of heterosexual—are not essential or authentic identities, but are culturally constructed through the power relations regulating the "healthy" and "normal" expressions of sexuality. This does not mean that homosexuality does not "really" exist. Just because something is constructed through practices of power does not mean that it is not real. People are defined by and must think and live according to such constructions. This idea does have important consequences for how we conceive of resistance, however, as I will show in the last section (on projects delineating "queer feminism" with the help of Foucault's work, see, e.g., Winnubst 2006; Huffer 2010; Sawicki 2013).

Power and Violence

In my own work (Oksala 2012) I have argued that Foucault's conception of power and the way that he theoretically distinguishes it from violence can also be helpful for feminist attempts to theorize gendered forms of violence such as domestic violence. It is my contention that a Foucauldian approach to gendered violence accomplishes two things: it refuses to explain men's violence against women in terms of inherent male aggression, yet it makes it possible to argue that it is not just incidental, but has structural and macro-level political aspects.

Foucault explicitly distinguished power from violence and denied that the essence of power would be violence. In his seminal essay "Subject and Power" from 1982 he poses the classic question of political philosophy—the same one as Hannah Arendt did in *On Violence*, for example—namely whether violence is simply the ultimate form of power (Foucault 1982: 220). He also follows Arendt in his negative reply, and puts forward an oppositional view of the relationship between power and violence. They are opposites in the sense that where one rules absolutely the other is absent. Foucault distinguishes power from violence by arguing that a power relationship is a mode of action that does not act directly and immediately on others, but rather acts upon their actions: it is a set of actions upon other actions. This means, first, that the one over whom power is exercised is thoroughly recognized as a subject, as a person who acts. Second, he or she must be free, meaning here that when faced with a relationship of power, "a whole field of responses, reactions, results, and possible inventions may open up" (Foucault 1982: 220). Violence, on the other hand, acts directly and immediately on the body. It is not an action upon an action of a subject, but an action upon a body or things.

Foucault's view here seems, at first glance, to explicitly support a gender-neutral view on violence: men have power over women in our society, but their power is not based on or upheld by violence. To exercise power is not to physically determine the conduct of passive objects, but to govern actions. A more careful reading of Foucault's writings on power and violence complicates the picture, however. He argued that even though power relations were essentially fluid and reversible, what usually characterized power was that these relationships had become stabilized through institutions. This means that the mobility of power relations is limited, and that there are strongholds that are difficult to suppress because they have been institutionalized in courts, codes, and so on. In other words, the power relations between people have become rigid (Foucault 1997: 169).

Patriarchal power, or power of men over women in our society, provides clear examples of institutionalized and rigid power relations or states of domination. The ongoing feminist struggles have made it obvious that the subordination of women is difficult to eradicate because it is often codified in economic and institutional structures. The fluidity and reversibility of the individual power relations between men and women have, in many cases, been effectively blocked. In a situation in which a woman is unable to leave her violent husband because of economic reasons and child care arrangements, for example, the power relation is clearly a form of domination that is, furthermore, linked with violence (Oksala 2012: 70–71).

Moreover, Foucault's analyses of governmentality open up a wider perspective on the issue of gendered violence (Foucault 2007; 2008). The practices and institutions of power are always enabled, regulated, and justified by a specific form of reasoning or rationality. The analytics of power technologies concentrates not only on the mechanisms of power, but also on the rationality that is part of the practices of governing. It is important to point out that while practices of power have rationality, so do practices of violence. Foucault repeatedly emphasized that there was no incompatibility between violence and rationality, but what is most dangerous about violence is its rationality (Foucault 2001: 803).

On this basis we could argue that what is most dangerous about gendered violence are those aspects of it that make it look like perfectly rational behavior. Even though male domination and male violence against women should not be theoretically conflated, feminist analysis must study the extent to which rationalities upholding male domination and those supporting forms of male violence against women are interrelated, mutually supportive, or even identical. When a form of rationality according to which a husband's responsibility is to provide for but also to control his wife and children is coupled with the acceptance of physical force as a means of control, for example, the patterns of domestic violence are set. From a Foucauldian perspective, therefore, it is important to take seriously the feminist insight that inequality between men and women is a key factor in explaining phenomena such as domestic violence. Domestic violence is effectively depoliticized when it is viewed in gender-neutral terms and reduced to an individual pathology. What is required is a careful analysis of the functioning, maintenance, and legitimacy of the power technologies on which it rests (Oksala 2012: 71).

Resistance

The key problem with systemic accounts of power seems to be how to account for agency and resistance. If subjects are always caught up in large social and economic structures such as capitalism and patriarchy that operate with deeply ingrained systemic logics, there seems to be very little that the subjects can do in order to affect change. Moreover, if we accept Foucault's claim that power is constitutive of the subject itself, we seem to be unable to distinguish genuine resistance from conformity: agency, autonomy, and resistance appear to be merely illusions or power's clever ruses.

For Foucault, power does not form a deterministic system of overbearing constraints, however. Because it is understood as an unstable network of practices, where there is power, there is resistance. What makes his position contested—and original—is precisely the way he understands the relationship between power and resistance. He forbids us to think that resistance is outside of power and also denies that we could ever locate it in a single point: "there is no single locus of great Refusal, no soul of revolt, source of all rebellions, or pure law of the revolutionary" (Foucault 1978: 95). To view the relationship between power and resistance as external would mean misunderstanding the relational character of power. Because power is not something that an individual acquires, holds or gives away, its existence depends on resistance: since power exists only in a relation, resistance must be located in these very same power relations.

The aim of feminist politics becomes more complicated than liberation from patriarchal power and the affirmation of one's true gender identity: resisting power entails questioning and even denying the identities that are imposed on us by making visible their cultural construction and dependence on the power relations that are operative in society. The goal is not a discovery of an identity, but its critical deconstruction.

In sum, an adequate understanding of power is crucial for any feminist theorizing of gender subordination, as well as the attempts to transform it. We have to recognize that even our innermost selves are always constituted in social and political practices incorporating gendered power relations. Without an adequate acknowledgment of how widespread and systematic power relations are and how profoundly they constitute the subjects' interests, desires and capacities for critical reflection we will not be able to understand the extent and the recalcitrance of gender oppression. However, we also have to maintain an adequate understanding of agency and feminist resistance. Conceptions of power that fail to account for the possibility of some measure of resistance will make it impossible to theorize feminist transformations—transformations of the self as well as political transformations. Moreover, our theoretical understanding of resistance has to translate into concrete practices of resistance. Feminism as a political project must aim at profound social transformation, not merely at some quantitative gain such as increase in women's power, political rights, or social benefits, for example. It has to aim to also change who we are and how we relate to each other.

Related Topics

Introducing Black feminist philosophy (Chapter 10); personal identity and relational selves (Chapter 18); speech and silencing (Chapter 23); feminist conceptions of autonomy (Chapter 41); feminism, structural injustice, and responsibility (Chapter 49); feminism and liberalism (Chapter 52); feminism and freedom (Chapter 53); feminist approaches to violence and vulnerability (Chapter 55).

References

Allen, Amy (1996) "Foucault on Power: A Theory for Feminists," in Susan Hekman (Ed.) *Feminist Interpretations of Michel Foucault*, University Park, PA: The Pennsylvania State University Press, 265–282.

Arendt, Hannah (1970) *On Violence*, New York: Harcourt Brace & Co.

Astell, Mary (1996) *Political Writings*, Ed. Patricia Springborg, Cambridge: Cambridge University Press.

Bartky, Sandra (1988) "Foucault, Femininity and the Modernization of Patriarchal Power," in Irene Diamond and Lee Quinby (Eds.) *Feminism and Foucault: Paths of Resistance*, Boston, MA: Northeastern University Press, 61–85.

——(2002) *"Sympathy and Solidarity" and Other Essays*, Lanham, MD: Rowman & Littlefield.

Bordo, Susan (1989) "The Body and the Reproduction of Femininity: A Feminist Appropriation of Foucault," in Alison Jaggar and Susan Bordo (Eds.) *Gender/Body/Knowledge*, New Brunswick, NJ: Rutgers, 13–33.

——(2001) "Feminism, Foucault and the Politics of the Body," in Caroline Ramazanoglu (Ed.) *Up against Foucault: Explorations of Some Tensions*, London: Routledge, 179–203.

Brown, Wendy (2005) *Edgework: Critical Essays on Knowledge and Politics*, Princeton, NJ and Oxford: Princeton University Press.

Butler, Judith (1990) *Gender Trouble*, London and New York: Routledge.

——(1993) *Bodies That Matter: On the Discursive Limits of Sex*, London and New York: Routledge.

——(1997) *The Psychic Life of Power: Theories in Subjection*, Stanford, CA: Stanford University Press.

——(2004) *Undoing Gender*, London and New York: Routledge.

Dahl, Robert A. (1957) "The Concept of Power," *Behavioral Science* 2: 201–215.

Dalla Costa, Mariarosa and James, Selma (1997) "Women and the Subversion of Community," in Rosemary Hennessy and Chrys Ingraham (Eds.) *Materialist Feminism: A Reader in Class, Difference, and Women's Lives*, London and New York: Routledge, 33–40.

Elshtain, Jean Bethke (1981) *Public Man, Private Woman*, Princeton, NJ: Princeton University Press.

Foucault, Michel (1978) *The History of Sexuality, Volume 1: An Introduction*, trans. R. Hurley, London: Penguin.

——(1982) "The Subject and Power," in Hubert L. Dreyfus and Paul Rabinow *Michel Foucault: Beyond Structuralism and Hermeneutics*, Hemel Hempstead: Harvester, 208–226.

—— (1991) *Discipline and Punish: The Birth of the Prison*, trans. Alan Sheridan, London: Penguin.

—— (1997) *Ethics, Subjectivity and Truth: Essential World of Foucault 1954–1984, Volume 1*, Paul Rabinow (Ed.) New York: The New Press.

—— (2001) *Dits et écrit II, 1976–1988*, D. Defert and F. Ewald (Eds.) Paris: Gallimard.

—— (2007) *Security, Territory, Population: Lectures at the Collège de France 1977–1978*, Michel Senellart (Ed.) Basingstoke: Palgrave Macmillan.

—— (2008) *The Birth of Biopolitics: Lectures at the Collège de France 1978–1979*, Michel Senellart (Ed.) Basingstoke: Palgrave Macmillan.

Fraser, Nancy (2014) "Behind Marx's Hidden Abode: For an Expanded Conception of Capitalism," *New Left Review* 86: 1–17.

Friedan, Betty (1963) *The Feminine Mystique*, Harmondsworth, UK: Penguin.

—— (1968) "Our Revolution Is Unique," in Kenneth M. Dolbeare and Michael S. Cummings (Eds.) *American Political Thought*, 5th ed., Washington, DC: CQ Press, 450–455.

Hartsock, Nancy (1983) *Money, Sex, and Power: Toward a Feminist Historical Materialism*, Boston, MA: Northeastern University Press.

Held, Virginia (1993) *Feminist Morality: Transforming Culture, Society, and Politics*, Chicago, IL: University of Chicago Press.

Heyes, Cressida (2007) *Self-Transformations: Foucault, Ethics and Normalized Bodies*, Oxford: Oxford University Press.

Honig, Bonnie (Ed.) (1995) *Feminist Interpretations of Hannah Arendt*, University Park, PA: Penn State University Press.

Huffer, Lynne (2010) *Mad for Foucault: Rethinking the Foundations of Queer Theory*, New York: Columbia University Press.

Lukes, Steven (2005 [1974]) *Power: A Radical View*, London: Macmillan.

MacKinnon, Catharine (1983) "Feminism, Marxism, Method, and the State," *Signs* 8(4): 635–658.

—— (1987) *Feminism Unmodified: Discourses on Life and Law*, Cambridge MA: Harvard University Press.

McNay, Lois (1992) *Foucault and Feminism: Power, Gender, and the Self*, Cambridge: Polity Press.

McWhorter, Ladelle (1999) *Bodies and Pleasures: Foucault and the Politics of Sexual Normalization*, Bloomington, IN: Indiana University Press.

Miller, Jean Baker (1992) "Women and Power," in Thomas E. Wartenberg (Ed.) *Rethinking Power*, Albany, NY: SUNY Press, 240–248.

Okin, Susan Moller (1989) *Justice, Gender and the Family*, New York: Basic Books.

Oksala, Johanna (2012) *Foucault, Politics, and Violence*, Evanston, IL: Northwestern University Press.

—— (2016) *Feminist Experiences: Foucauldian and Phenomenological Investigations*, Evanston, IL: Northwestern University Press.

Pateman, Carole (1988) *The Sexual Contract*, Stanford, CA: Stanford University Press.

Sawicki, Jana (1991) *Disciplining Foucault: Feminism, Power, and the Body*, London and New York: Routledge.

—— (2013) "Queer Feminism: Cultivating Ethical Practices of Freedom," *Foucault Studies, Special Issue: Foucault and Feminism* 16: 74–87.

Vogel, Lise (1983) *Marxism and the Oppression of Women: Toward a Unitary Theory*. New Brunswick, NJ: Rutgers University Press.

Winnubst, Shannon (2006) *Queering Freedom*, Bloomington, IN: Indiana University Press.

Wollstonecraft, Mary (2001) *A Vindication of the Rights of Woman*, New York: Random House.

Young, Iris Marion (1990) *Justice and the Politics of Difference*, Princeton, NJ: Princeton University Press.

55

FEMINIST APPROACHES TO VIOLENCE AND VULNERABILITY

Elizabeth Frazer and Kimberly Hutchings

Introduction

Considerations of violence and vulnerability are central to feminist philosophy. This is unsurprising given, not only that these are heavily gendered concepts, but also that gendered experiences of violence and vulnerability affect the lives of contemporary women and men across the world. For these reasons, feminist philosophers have wanted to address ontological, phenomenological, epistemological, and ethico-political questions about violence and vulnerability. In doing so, they have developed philosophical insights into a range of topics, from the fundamental nature of the Western philosophical imaginary, to the production of the gendered subject, to the ethics of war and peace, to the nature and meaning of structural and symbolic violence. It is not possible to deal adequately with all of this work here. In what follows, we will focus on two areas of debate within feminist philosophical work on violence and vulnerability: first, how violence and vulnerability are and should be conceptualized; second, feminist responses to normative questions about the ethics of political violence.

Conceptualizing Violence and Vulnerability

At first glance, violence and vulnerability make for a straightforward conceptual pairing. To be vulnerable is to be able to be wounded, and the most obvious form of violence is a physical act of wounding, or what Elaine Scarry refers to when describing war as a contest of "injuring and out-injuring" (Scarry 1985: 63). This is certainly an understanding of the two concepts that feminist philosophers have used, often in order to draw attention to acts of wounding that have not traditionally been the focus of philosophical debate. In a collection of essays on philosophical perspectives on violence against women, the editors ask: "How can there be an elaborate historical discourse on just war theory and no theory of rape or wife beating?" (French, Teays, and Purdy 1998b: 1). Feminist philosophers have brought domestic and sexual violence onto the philosophical agenda as phenomena that need to be understood and evaluated as much as other forms of violence such as war fighting or torture.

However, the introduction of these topics into philosophical debate opened up problems with conceptualizing violence. To the extent that mainstream analytic philosophy has been concerned with questions of violence and vulnerability, mostly within the context of debates between deontological and consequentialist approaches in applied ethics, it has tended to treat violence as a form of intentional action with specifiable consequences. On this view, violence is a tool that can be reliably used to fulfil certain purposes for an individual or collective actor. In contrast to this instrumentalist view, feminist philosophers have been sensitive to the embodied and embedded nature and experience of domestic and sexual violence, including the significance of psychological, as much as physical, wounding and injury. They have also been sensitive to the gendered social structures and discourses through which such violence may be rendered meaningful and legitimate, or even invisible, to perpetrators and victims alike. This has focused feminist attention on the meaning of violence/vulnerability as a conceptual pairing and inspired phenomenological work on violence, in particular from the perspective of the vulnerable feminized subject. It has also led to re-conceptualizations of violence as importantly structural and discursive/symbolic.

Feminist phenomenologies of violence have unpacked the experience of vulnerability and pointed to a whole host of ways violence can exceed the terms of descriptions that focus on the immediate results of particular physical acts of violence. Susan Brison courageously put her own experience of being the victim of murderous sexual assault onto the philosophical agenda in order to demonstrate the limitations of standard philosophical treatments of violence: "for the first several months after my attack, I led a spectral existence, not quite sure whether I had died and the world went on without me, or whether I was alive but in a totally alien world" (Brison 1998: 17). Her work drew attention to the world-destroying effects of violence on victims, going far beyond material damage. When this was taken into account it became much more difficult to, for example, engage in consequentialist ethical calculation in which the pleasures of the rapist were balanced against the pains of the victim (Brison 1998: 14). This kind of contribution not only enriched philosophical understandings of the meaning and implications of sexual violence, it allowed for comparisons of sexual violence with other forms of violence, such as terrorism and torture (Card 2007; 2010). Moreover, it opened up a range of questions about the nature and production of gendered subjectivities, and in particular the relation between vulnerability and the feminine.

The concept of structural violence was originally used in the neo-Marxist work of Johann Galtung. In Galtung's case it was used to refer to ways in which people were materially damaged through poverty and deprivation under capitalism, as opposed to through intentional, individual action (Galtung 1975). Feminist work developed the concept of structural violence in a somewhat different way, to refer to the system of patriarchal domination of men over women, masculine over feminine, that produces and legitimates gendered violence and vulnerability, and in which direct, physical violence or the threat of violence is an element in the system of norms that reproduces the structure. This structural violence could be traced in the ways in which gendered subjects were socialized to be manly or womanly, so that inflicting and suffering violence were presumed as part of set gender roles. For example, Susan Brownmiller (1975) identified rape as underpinning systems of male domination from primordial times. She argued that patriarchy was essentially a protection racket based on men's sexual predatoriness and women's fear. Catharine MacKinnon argued that violence against women was underpinned by a system of male domination in which men were the norm and women counted as less than human: "A kind of war is being fought unrecognized in a conflict that one suspects would be seen as such if men were not the aggressors and women the victims" (MacKinnon 2006: 272). Both Brownmiller and MacKinnon saw the prevalence of rape in warfare as demonstrating the ways in which sexual violence was not a matter of individual pathology, but should be understood as integral to the systematic domination of men over women. Other kinds of violence against women, from genital mutilation to the abortion of female foetuses to so-called "honor" killings were seen as part of the same pattern (French, Teays, and Purdy 1998a; Dobash and Dobash 1998). In this respect, individual violences and vulnerabilities could not be understood or addressed without reference to structural violence.

Structural violence could be identified in material inequalities between men and women, which deprived many women of the power to escape from violent relationships. It could be found in social, legal, and political arrangements that perpetuated men's power over women, including the power to attack and physically control them. Feminist legal theorists pointed to the longstanding (until very recently) feature of many legal systems in supposedly liberal countries that rendered rape within marriage a legal impossibility. And also to the problems surrounding the issue of "consent" in relation to sexual violence, and the ways in which women's testimony was routinely devalued inside and outside of the courts (Pateman 1988; Kazan 1998; MacKinnon 2006). For many of these theorists, one could trace a direct link between woman's less than human status in Western traditions of thought and routine domestic and sexual abuse. One could also trace a direct link—a continuum—between routine everyday sexual and domestic violence and the organized violence of war, including systematic sexual violence.

Feminist work on structural violence pointed to the importance of discourse to the perpetuation of patriarchy and to the relative silence of philosophy on the subject of gendered violence. This led to the development of concepts of discursive or symbolic violence. These terms referred to modes of legitimating structural and physical violence through ideological gendered systems of valuation. Discursive and symbolic violence rendered direct physical violence against women unremarkable. It included ways in which domestic and sexual violence were justified in terms of nature (sexual violence is a manifestation of biological drives), privilege (control over women is a matter of male entitlement) or desert (she asked for it). It also included the host of everyday ways in which women and the feminine were denigrated and their victimization thereby rendered simultaneously as part of common sense expectations and invisible. In this respect, feminist philosophers identified immanent links between the ways in which violent men justified their violence as acts of love, marital commitment or constructive correction (Lundgren 1998), and the ways in which philosophy, even in its critical Marxist variants, naturalized violence against women and therefore did not feel the need to subject the phenomenon to political critique or ethical justification.

We noted above that "violence" tended to figure in analytic philosophy solely in instrumental terms, as a tool to be used for either good or bad ends. In contrast to this, structuralist and poststructuralist philosophy used the concept of violence to capture the primordial conditions of subjectivity, language, and law. Gendered binary oppositions associate masculine with active, perpetrator, feminine with passive, victim; these generate and engender discourses and practices that valorize violent masculinities and that legitimate violence against women. This is much more than ideology in the classical Marxist sense. Rather, these categories are given to subjects as a condition of their agency—the embodiment of gender is non-optional if a subject is to enter into the intelligible world of symbols and meaning. This non-optionality is, itself, a primary violence—in its deepest sense this is what "symbolic violence" refers to. Looking at things this way puts gender at the root not only of sexual and domestic violence but of all forms of physical, structural, and discursive violence. Feminist philosophers reacting to and building on Lacanian insights demonstrated that the way in which the subject was produced through incorporation into the symbolic order was premised on the violent expulsion of the feminine. For thinkers such as Irigaray and Kristeva, symbolic violence therefore had a deeper meaning than as one element in a threefold combination of physical, structural and discursive gendered violence; and deeper than the justificatory function that legitimates physical and psychological violence. Here symbolic violence takes on primary philosophical and political importance.

Although their arguments are not the same, Jantzen and Reineke both relate the ubiquity of violence in Western history and thought to the exclusion of radical other-ness, exemplified by the inability to conceptualize what falls outside of binary oppositions between masculine and feminine, violent and vulnerable. Jantzen traces the gendered violence of the Western symbolic order back to the Greeks' naturalization of mortality and the fear of death as the grounding feature of human existence:

> From militarization, death camps and genocide to exploitation, commodifica-tion and the accumulation of wealth, from the construction of pleasure and desire to the development of terminator genes, from the violence on the streets to the heaven obsessed hymnody of evangelical churches, preoccupation with death and the means of death and the combat with death is ubiquitous. It is a necrophilia so deeply a part of the western symbolic that it emerges at every turn.
> (Jantzen 2004: 5)

Following Kristeva, Reineke argues for the need to think about symbolic and embodied gendered violence as part of a single sacrificial economy of violence in which the scape-goating of women is historically repeated in phenomena such as the European witch hunts (Reineke 1997).

Most feminist work on violence recognizes that structural and symbolic violence are part of what violence means. Nevertheless, for some feminists, the turn to symbolic vio-lence, in particular in work influenced by psychoanalysis, undermines feminist engage-ments with the lived experience of physical violence. It collapses too much under the umbrella of the concept of violence and focuses too much attention on discourse and language. And it thereby detracts from feminist attempts to bring specific gendered violences and vulnerabilities onto the philosophical agenda. Moreover, its holistic approach to the meaning of violence for feminists makes it difficult to unpack the pre-cise links between different aspects of violence and seems to make an escape from sym-bolic violence and its gendered violent consequences extremely difficult. Jantzen argues for the denaturalization of death and violence in the Western philosophical and politi-cal imaginary, and its replacement with a "poetics of natality," in which the maternal principle of life-giving underpins the symbolic order. Reineke argues for the embrace of Kristeva's category of the "uncanny" as a way to escape the sacrificial economy of vio-lence. But it is not clear how the deconstruction and reconstruction required could be played out in practice in a world still dominated by all of the violences that these think-ers trace back to the Western symbolic order. The distinct, more materialist, positions of thinkers such as Brownmiller, which trace gendered violence back to a pre-historical protection racket are similarly overwhelming and appear to make escape and resistance next to impossible.

There are, broadly speaking, two kinds of response to the analyses of feminist philosophers who make, in Reineke's terms, a gendered economy of violence fundamental to the world we inhabit. The first response challenges the focus of feminist philosophers on women or other feminised actors as the *victims* of violence, particularly sexual violence. Responding specifically to Brownmiller, Burton argues that the latter, in helpfully demonstrating the systematic nature of violence against women also, much less helpfully, generalizes women's position as one of fear and victimhood. For Burton, the focus on victimhood potentially undermines women's capacity for resistance in ways that are effectively complicit with masculinist identifications of feminine with vulnerability. She argues for more philosophical attention to be paid to women's capacity for agency and resistance, including the capacity to fight back (Burton 1998). From this point of view, the focus on women's victimization perpetuates a long-term bias in the Western philosophical tradition against women's agency and autonomy, and arguably an equally long-term silence about women and other feminized actors as practitioners, not just victims, of violence.

The idea that women's capacity to resist or fight may be tied to women's capacity for autonomy opens up a new set of questions in feminist philosophy in relation to violence. In the work of thinkers such as Brownmiller or MacKinnon, it is clearly the case that vulnerability, meaning vulnerability to violence, is a bad thing, a source of fear and, for Brownmiller, the origin of women's oppression by men across all times and places. In these analyses, violence and vulnerability go together historically, phenomenologically, and ethically, and are explicitly identified with the feminine/women. In contrast to this, Bar On (2002: 149–166) explores how feminized bodies are reproduced as violent bodies, in the context of discussing the production of her own embodied existence as a young Israeli and practitioner of Martial Arts. She refers back to Beauvoir's discussion of how the upbringing of girls and boys divides at the point at which adolescent boys undergo a "real apprenticeship" in violence and girls cease to participate in physical games (Beauvoir 1997a: 353). Beauvoir emphasizes how the embodied experience of fighting enables the boy to feel that his will impacts on the world. Bar On draws attention to ways in which violence may be experienced as positively liberating for women, and yet is also part of the story of the gendered economy of violence, both in helping to reproduce nationalist, patriarchal structures of power and in being identified and experienced as transgressive. The association of women with the use of violence, whether to resist an attacker or sustain identification with a nationalist project, displaces the terms of the violence/vulnerability binary analytically and normatively. It associates violence with the feminine by disturbing a necessary link between the feminine and vulnerability and by potentially re-valuing violence as a positive affirmation of autonomy.

However, from the point of view of other feminist philosophers, this kind of response is mistaken because it keeps the masculinist hierarchy in place by continuing to privilege violence over vulnerability. Bar On's own analysis draws attention to how gendered structural and symbolic violence is perpetuated through the participation of women as well as men, in the enforcement of normative expectations through physically violent as well as other means. An alternative response accepts neither the inescapability of a gendered economy of violence nor the revaluation of violence from a feminist perspective. Instead, it challenges the dominant way of conceiving the meaning of *vulnerability* as the correlate of violence. For these feminist thinkers, it is the myth of a link between violence and *invulnerability*, celebrated by Western ideals of the autonomous masculine subject that is the problem. The way beyond the gendered economy of violence is to recognize the absurdity of the idea of *invulnerability* and to start from *vulnerability* as the common and prior condition of the production of the human subject.

We find this move in a range of distinct feminist philosophical positions. For example in various versions of maternalist and care ethics (Ruddick 1990; Held 1993; 2006) and in work more influenced by continental and psychoanalytic feminist philosophy (Cavarero 2007; Butler 2004, 2009). This work extends the meaning of vulnerability beyond vulnerability to violence. In being paired with "invulnerability," we come to understand vulnerability as much more broadly to do with the permeability of the boundaries between embodied subjects, the inherent relationality of subjects, and the capacity of subjects to be affected in general, not only through violent assault (Mackenzie 2014). Thought about in this way, vulnerability has become foundational for some feminist ethical and political theorizing. For example, Fineman's work building on her influential article, "The Vulnerable Subject" (Fineman 2008; Fineman and Grear 2013) and a developing focus on vulnerability within feminist applied ethics and bioethics (Mackenzie, Rogers, and Dodds 2014). The latter literature has strong links with feminist accounts of relational autonomy as well as with the ethics of care. It rejects the rather generalized account of vulnerability to be found in Fineman's work and seeks to conceptualize vulnerability in ways that distinguish between vulnerability as a general ontological condition shared by all, and vulnerability as specific to situations of liability to harm. This is in order to show how different moral obligations follow from different aspects of vulnerability and to underline the point that vulnerability is neither good nor bad in itself (Dodds 2014; Mackenzie 2014).

Few feminist philosophers uncritically embrace the identification of autonomy with violence, or read vulnerability in wholly positive terms. In general, feminist thinkers remain convinced of the link between the devaluation of women in Western thought, and also in other cultural traditions, and their specific vulnerabilities to domestic and sexual violence, and identify a continuum between gendered violence in domestic contexts and the systematic violences of states and other collective actors. However, the questioning of the necessity of the link between the feminine and vulnerability to violence creates different kinds of possibilities for feminist normative judgment in relation to women's own violence and to organized political violence. Feminists remain united in their condemnation of sexual and domestic violence, but they are much less united when it comes to the moral and political judgement of war and resistant violence.

Feminism and the Ethics of Political Violence

Feminist philosophical arguments about political violence are always influenced by political context as well as by the philosophical presuppositions embedded in particular feminist positions. Feminist pacifist positions formulated in the 1980s were in part responding to an escalation of the nuclear arms race, and to developments such as the women-only peace camp at Greenham Common. They also intersected with the political construction of "violence against women" as a primary focus for feminist political organization and action, and the phenomena of sexual and gender violence, as we have seen, turned philosophical and ethical analysis away from a model of intentional physical action and its consequential injury or resistance, to a more complex model of structural and symbolic violence and hence the implication of violence in the very heart of identity and agency. More recently, feminist revisiting of just war theory has been largely a response to the growth of military humanitarian interventions since the 1990s, the "War on Terror," and specifically the wars in Afghanistan and Iraq. The ways in which state rhetoric has focused on women's human rights as a justification for various kind of intervention has provoked strong criticism from feminist activists and philosophers. In particular, feminist have been critical of military humanitarian intervention and the "War on Terror," which perpetuated a politics of rescue in which white Western men "save," in Spivak's words, brown women from brown men (Bar On 2008a).

At the beginning of the World War I, Western feminist movements were divided between nationalist and pacifist positions. In the work of Jane Addams, who embraced a pacifist position, one can identify themes in the analysis of war that have continued to work through feminist thought about war and other forms of organized political violence ever since (Addams, Balch, and Hamilton 2003). Addams challenged prevailing views about war by bringing gender into her analysis of nationalism, militarism, the logic of violence, and myths of chivalry and heroism. She was concerned about the structural effects of war on society in times of both war and peace, and how nationalist and militarist agendas were linked to the oppression of populations and in the gendered presuppositions and effects of war. Over the past century, feminist scholars have followed Addams by systematically demonstrating that gendered identities are fundamental to the meaning and practice of war (Elshtain 1987; Harris and King 1993; Kinsella 2011). Feminists have documented the gendered presuppositions and consequences of war, the ways in which war is embedded in and reproduces gendered political, economic, and ideological structures, and the continuum between the organized violence of the state and inter-personal violence at a domestic level. However, there has been no philosophical or political consensus as to whether the intimate links between organized political violence and gendered violence and oppression means that feminists must necessarily be pacifists (Frazer and Hutchings 2014).

Feminist pacifism has had different philosophical roots. Earlier Western feminists were inspired by Christian, deontological positions, following thinkers such as Tolstoy and later Gandhi. During the latter part of the Cold War, as part of the increasing importance of maternalist and radical feminisms, pacifism was linked to the valorization of feminine principles of life-giving and peace-making in opposition to the destructive logic of masculinist war-making. Some feminists made the case that feminism necessarily implied pacifism (Carroll 1987). Sarah Ruddick's work developed a philosophically sophisticated version of a maternalist, care ethics position on violence (1990; 1993):

> Caregivers are not, predictably, better people than are militarists. Rather, they are engaged in a different project. Militarists aim to dominate by creating the structural vulnerabilities that caregivers take for granted. They arm and train so that they can, if other means of domination fail, terrify and injure their opponents. By contrast, in situations where domination through bodily pain, and the fear of pain, is a structural possibility, caregivers try to resist temptations to assault and neglect, even though they work among smaller, frailer, vulnerable people who may excite domination.
>
> (Ruddick 1993: 121)

It is clear from the above quotation that Ruddick sees a different attitude towards *vulnerability* as fundamental to an alternative ethics of war. For Ruddick, both milita-rism and just war theory share a commitment to the expendability of concrete lives in abstract causes to which maternal thinking is inherently opposed. Ruddick claims that this means that the implication of maternal thinking is not just the rejection of war but the active embracing of peace politics, a fight against war that draws on the acknowl-edgment of responsibility and relationship and the specificity of need and obligations that are inherent in a proper understanding of the labour of caring (Ruddick 1990: 141–159). Although Ruddick argues that maternal thinking is aligned to the idea of non-violence, she is also insistent that it is sensitive to the specific contexts in which ethical dilemmas are embedded. For Ruddick, ethical judgment has to be on a case-by-case basis, but without ready-made principles of adjudication. Although the idea of maternal thinking is in principle non-violent, there are no universally applicable algorithms that can be applied to any given situation to render definitive answers to ethical questions, so that even the use of violence cannot be entirely ruled out a priori (Ruddick 1990: 138). Ruddick gives two examples of where it would be inappropriate to condemn violence out of hand, both of them are examples of resistant violence towards racist, militarist regimes in Nazi Germany and South Africa respectively.

Ruddick's reluctance to embrace a wholly pacifist position links her argument to an alternative feminist tradition of thinking about the ethics of resistant politi-cal violence, in which the arguments of Beauvoir and Arendt are more influential than care ethics. For both Beauvoir and Arendt, the circumstances of World War I and of anti-colonial struggles demonstrated that resistant violence was sometimes morally and politically required. In her *Ethics of Ambiguity*, Beauvoir examined con-sequentialist justifications of revolutionary violence. Although she demonstrated the problems with these kinds of moral calculations, she also argued that it was no more possible to rule violence out absolutely than it was to provide an ethical argument for its ethical or political necessity (Beauvoir 1997b). Her conclusions emphasized the importance of context and the impossibility of establishing a "pure" moral position on the question of the use of violence.

Arendt famously argued that violence could not be legitimate, but might in some cases be justifiable. It might be justifiable as being the only way to address an injus-tice at either individual or collective levels. For example, in an individual act of vio-lence to defend the vulnerable innocent, or in a just war against an enemy such as the Nazi regime. On the other hand, the use of violence could not be legitimate because it was ultimately a purely instrumental action, in contrast to genuinely political power, and the most likely outcome of the use of violence was more violence (Arendt 1969). Beauvoir's arguments about political violence were not formulated explicitly as part of her feminist philosophy, and Arendt famously distanced her own work from feminism. Nevertheless, these two philosophers, and Arendt in particular have been important for contemporary feminist philosophers, especially those influenced by postcolonial thought, who are convinced by the antithetical relation between feminist values and the use of violence, and yet reluctant to rule out political violence from the repertoire of feminist action altogether (Bar On 2002; Hutchings 2007).

This ambivalence about the relation between feminism and political violence has also been manifested in some feminist attempts to re-work just war theory (Peach 1994; Sjoberg 2006; Held 2008a; 2008b; Eide 2008). Virginia Held introduces the values of care as a supplement to more traditional, deontological, and utilitarian criteria, for the moral assessment of war. At one level, in the light of the feminist ethic of care the presumption against the use of violence as an effective way of responding to injustice is very strong and implies a commitment to developing alternatives to the use of violence: "We should seek to restrain rather than destroy those who become violent, we should work to prevent violence rather than wipe out violent persons, and we should contain violence as non-violently as possible" (Held 2008b: 4) Held also acknowledges that to the extent that one is making moral judgements about justice *ad bellum* and *in bello*, then one is neglecting the moral evaluation of all of the other aspects of warfare that feminist scholarship had brought to our attention, in terms of its material and ideological conditions and effects beyond the field of battle. Her response to this is to subsume the above concerns, specific to the ethic of care, largely to holistic or "long-term" evaluation, while admitting more familiar consequentialist and deontological moral principles as still adequate for the evaluation of moral dilemmas relating to immediate judgment and action before and during war.

Held attempts to operationalize the values inherent in care, grounded in a common vulnerability, while at the same time enabling feminist judgment about specific uses of organized violence, in particular for humanitarian ends. One obvious problem with her argument is the tension it perpetuates between the specifically feminist ethic of care and its orientation towards non-violence, and traditional consequentialist and deontological modes of moral theorizing. The two are only made compatible by assigning care ethics to long-term matters and just war theory to immediate judgments about specific uses of violence. Bar On, speaking from a non-pacifist position suggests another problem and criticises Held, not because Held is arguing that uses of violence may sometimes be justified in feminist terms, but because she attempts to do this by reference back to pure *moral* theory. Bar On argues that questions about the use of violence for political ends are fundamentally political questions and need to be open to political contestation, they are simply not resolvable at the level of philosophy (Bar On 2008b). The philosophical difficulties raised by Held's arguments reflect two broader problems encountered by feminists addressing the ethics of organized political violence: first, how specifically feminist insights are to be operationalized for the purposes of moral judgement; second, how feminists ought to think about the relation between ethics and politics when it comes to the judgement of political violence.

Although it is very differently grounded, Butler's recent work, in which she argues for a link between corporeal vulnerability and the appeal of non-violence, grapples with similar problems concerning the operationalizing of feminist insights for prescriptive purposes and the relation between ethics and politics in the judgment of violence. Butler responds to the first problem by rejecting the idea of a *necessary* link between the recognition of vulnerability and a normative ethics of non-violence. Nevertheless, following aspects of Levinas's ethics, she locates a "claim" of non-violence in the shared "precarity" of human existence (Butler 2009: 166–184). In this respect, Butler's notion of vulnerability means that we are all, as a primary condition of our embodied existence, open equally to violence and non-violence. However, this is a shared condition that is denied by violent responses, which shore up the fantasy of the invulnerability of the violent subject, and that is affirmed by non-violent responses, which recognize an underlying equality of exposure of all subjects regardless of power relations between them. In this respect, the role of ethics in Butler's writings on political violence is fundamentally bound up with politics, since there is no recognition of others outside of frames and power relations that produce us in different, including gendered ways. Rather than attempting to resolve feminist dilemmas about the judgment of political violence by seeking to generate prescriptive consequences from philosophical presuppositions, or by giving priority to ethics over politics, Butler leaves those dilemmas firmly in place.

Conclusion

In conclusion, we would like to suggest that the philosophical difficulties encountered by feminists in coming to ethical conclusions about the justice of various forms of political violence is precisely a reflection of the power of the insights feminists have generated into the nature and meaning of violence and vulnerability. In this respect, feminist work on violence and vulnerability acts as Butler argues non-violence acts, that is to say as a spanner in the works of the philosophical apparatuses through which violence has been made to appear necessary and legitimate in contexts from the bedroom to the battlefield (Butler 2009: 183–184). Once you start to unpack not only how violence is gendered, but also how violence reproduces gender, at all levels from that of subjective identity to that of the nation-state. And once you start to unpack the possibilities inherent in taking vulnerability rather than violence as a starting point for thought, it becomes much more difficult to reduce violence to a tool or to engage in any kind of cost-benefit analysis of its conditions and effects in any particular instance. This does not mean that feminists must be pacifists, but it does mean that feminists who are and are not pacifists both accept the impossibility of any clean resolution to questions about who has the right to kill or injure whom.

Further Reading

Bar On, Bat-Ami (2002) *The Subject of Violence: Arendtian Exercises in Understanding*, Lanham, MD: Rowman & Littlefield.

Butler, Judith (2009) *Frames of War: When Is Life Grievable?* London: Verso.

Card, Claudia (2010) *Confronting Evils: Terrorism, Torture, Genocide*, Cambridge: Cambridge University Press.

Cavarero, Alessandra (2007) *Horrorism: Naming Contemporary Violence*, New York: Columbia University Press.

French, Stanley G., Teays, Wanda, and Purdy, Laura M. (Eds.) (1998) *Violence Against Women: Philosophical Perspectives*, Ithaca, NY and London: Cornell University Press.

Scarry, Elaine (1985) *The Body in Pain*, Oxford: Oxford University Press.

Related Topics

Speech and silencing (Chapter 23); personal identity and relational selves (Chapter 18); psychoanalysis, subjectivity, and feminism (Chapter 19); feminist and queer intersections with disability studies (Chapter 33); aesthetics and the politics of gender: on Arendt's theory of narrative and action (Chapter 38); feminist ethics of care (Chapter 43); feminism, structural injustice, and responsibility (Chapter 49); feminism and power (Chapter 54).

References

Addams, Jane, Balch, Emily G. and Hamilton, Alice (2003) *Women at the Hague: The International Congress of Women and Its Results*, Chicago, IL: University of Illinois Press.

Arendt, Hannah (1969) *On Violence*, New York: Harcourt, Brace and World.

Bar On, Bat-Ami (2002) *The Subject of Violence: Arendtian Exercises in Understanding*, Lanham, MA: Rowman & Littlefield.

——(Ed.) (2008a) *Thinking About War*, Special Issue *Hypatia* 23(2).

——(2008b) "Military Intervention in Two Registers," *The Southern Journal of Philosophy* XLVI: 21–31.

Beauvoir, Simone de (1997a) *The Second Sex*, London: Vintage Press.

——(1997b) *The Ethics of Ambiguity*, Secaucus, NJ: Carol Publishing Group.

Brison, Susan (1998) "Surviving Sexual Violence: A Philosophical Perspective," in Stanley French, Wanda Teays, and Laura Purdy (Eds.) *Violence Against Women: Philosophical Perspectives*, Ithaca, NY and London: Cornell University Press: 11–26.

Brownmiller, Susan (1975) *Against Our Will: Men, Women and Rape*, New York: Simon & Schuster.

Burton, Nadya (1998) "Resistance to Prevention: Reconsidering Feminist Anti-Violence Rhetoric," in Stanley French, Wanda Teays, and Laura Purdy (Eds.) *Violence Against Women: Philosophical Perspectives*, Ithaca, NY and London: Cornell University Press, 182–200.

Butler, Judith (2004) *Precarious Life: The Powers of Mourning and Violence*, London: Verso.

——(2009) *Frames of War: When Is Life Grievable?* London: Verso.

Card, Claudia (2007) "Recognizing Terrorism," *The Journal of Ethics* 11: 1–29.

——(2010) *Confronting Evils: Terrorism, Torture, Genocide*, Cambridge: Cambridge University Press.

Carroll, Berenice A. (1987) "Feminism and Pacifism: Historical and Theoretical Connections," in Ruth R. Pierson (Ed.) *Women and Peace: Theoretical, Historical and Practical Perspectives*, London: Croom Helm, 2–28.

Cavarero, Alessandra (2007) *Horrorism: Naming Contemporary Violence*, New York: Columbia University Press.

Dobash, R. Emerson and Dobash, Russell P. (Eds.) (1998) *Rethinking Violence against Women*, Thousand Oaks, CA: Sage.

Dodds, Susan (2014) "Dependence, Care and Vulnerability," in Catriona Mackenzie, Wendy Rogers, and Susan Dodds (Eds.) *Vulnerability: New Essays in Ethics and Feminist Philosophy*, New York: Oxford University Press, 181–203.

Eide, Marian (2008) "The Stigma of Nation: Feminist Just War, Privilege and Responsibility," *Hypatia: Journal of Feminist Philosophy* 23(2): 48–60.

Elshtain, Jean Bethke (1987) *Women and War*, Brighton: Harvester Press.

Fineman, Martha Albertson (2008) "The Vulnerable Subject: Anchoring Equality in the Human Condition," *Yale Journal of Law and Feminism* 20(1): 1–23.

Fineman, Martha Albertson and Grear, Anna (Eds.) (2013) *Vulnerability: Reflections on New Ethical Foundations for Law and Politics*, Farnham, UK: Ashgate.

French, Stanley G., Teays, Wanda, and Purdy, Laura M. (Eds.) (1998a) *Violence Against Women: Philosophical Perspectives*, Ithaca, NY and London: Cornell University Press.

——(1998b) "Editor's Introduction," in Stanley French, Wanda Teays, and Laura Purdy (Eds.) *Violence Against Women: Philosophical Perspectives*, Ithaca, NY and London: Cornell University Press, 1–8.

Frazer, Elizabeth and Hutchings, Kimberly (2014) "Feminism and the Critique of Violence: Negotiating Feminist Political Agency," *Journal of Political Ideologies* 19(2): 143–163.

Galtung, Johann (1975) "Structural and Direct Violence: A Note on Operationalization," in *Peace: Research, Education, Action—Essays in Peace Research Volume 1*, Copenhagen: Christian Ejlers, 135–139.

Harris, Adrienne and King, Ynestra (Eds.) (1989) *Rocking the Ship of State: Toward a Feminist Peace Politics*, Boulder, CO: Westview Press.

Held, Virginia (1993) *Feminist Morality: Transforming Culture, Society and Politics*, Chicago, IL: University of Chicago Press.

——(2006) *The Ethics of Care: Personal, Political and Global*, Oxford: Oxford University Press.

—— (2008a) *How Terrorism Is Wrong: Morality and Political Violence*, Oxford: Oxford University Press.

—— (2008b) "Military Intervention and the Ethics of Care," *The Southern Journal of Philosophy* 46: 1–20.

Hutchings, Kimberly (2007) "Simone de Beauvoir and the Ambiguous Ethics of Political Violence," *Hypatia* 22(3): 111–132.

Jantzen, Grace (2004) *Foundations of Violence*, New York and London: Routledge.

Kazan, Patricia (1998) "Sexual Assault and the Problem of Consent," in Stanley French, Wanda Teays, and Laura Purdy (Eds.) *Violence Against Women: Philosophical Perspectives*, Ithaca, NY and London: Cornell University Press, 27–42.

Kinsella, Helen (2011) *The Image Before the Weapon: A Critical History of the Distinction between Combatant and Civilian*, Ithaca, NY: Cornell University Press.

Lundgren, Eva (1998) "The Hand That Strikes and Comforts: Gender Construction and the Tension Between Body and Symbol," in Rebecca Emerson Dobash and Russell Dobash (Eds.) *Rethinking Violence against Women*, Thousand Oaks CA: Sage Publications, 169–198.

Mackenzie, Catriona (2014) "The Importance of Relational Autonomy and Capabilities for an Ethics of Vulnerability," in Catriona Mackenzie, Wendy Rogers, and Susan Dodds (Eds.) *Vulnerability: New Ethics in Ethics and Feminist Philosophy*, Oxford: Oxford University Press, 33–59.

Mackenzie, Catriona, Rogers, Wendy, and Dodds, Susan (Eds.) (2014) *Vulnerability: New Essays in Ethics and Feminist Philosophy*, Oxford: Oxford University Press.

MacKinnon, Catharine A. (2006) *Are Women Human? And Other International Dialogues*, Cambridge, MA: Harvard University Press.

Pateman, Carole (1988) *The Sexual Contract*, Stanford, CA: Stanford University Press.

Peach, Lucinda J. (1994) "An Alternative to Pacifism? Feminism and Just War Theory," *Hypatia* 9(2): 152–172.

Reineke, Martha J. (1997) *Sacrificed Lives: Kristeva on Women and Violence*, Bloomington, IN and Indianapolis, IN: Indiana University Press.

Ruddick, Sara (1990) *Maternal Thinking: Towards a Politics of Peace*, London: The Women's Press.

—— (1993) "Notes Toward a Feminist Peace Politics," in Miriam Cooke and Angela Woollacott (Eds.) *Gendering War Talk*, Princeton, NJ: Princeton University Press, 109–127.

Sjoberg, Laura (2006) *Gender, Justice and the Wars in Iraq*, Lanham, MD: Lexington Books.

Scarry, Elaine (1985) *The Body in Pain*, Oxford: Oxford University Press.

56

FEMINIST PHILOSOPHY OF LAW, LEGAL POSITIVISM, AND NON-IDEAL THEORY

Leslie P. Francis

Feminist philosophy of law has been shaped by debates between liberal feminists who emphasize non-discrimination and equality of opportunity and more radical feminists who offer a variety of far-reaching criticisms of the law as a structure of patriarchal power. Among philosophers, these debates have taken place largely separately from the debates in philosophy of law over legal positivism and natural law theory: whether law as it is should be distinguished from law as it ought to be. Here, I argue the issues are deeply interconnected and feminist philosophy of law is better aligned with legal positivism. My argument has four steps: a brief methodological note about non-ideal theory, an account of the conceptual separation between law and morality advocated by legal positivists, a sketch of approaches to feminist philosophy of law, and two illustrative examples.

Just as there are many feminisms, there are many approaches to philosophy of law among feminists. There are also many issues in law and legal criticism that feminists have taken on. Critical legal studies, critical race theory, and disability studies raise some of these issues in alignment with feminists (see Crenshaw 1991; Harris 1990; Silvers, and Francis 2005; see also Botts (Chapter 28), Hall (Chapter 33), and Sheth (Chapter 29) in this volume. These are all important projects for the philosophy of law that could have been the subject of an essay on feminism and philosophy of law. I have chosen this particular set of issues in legal theory because they are at the core of many discussions in legal philosophy today, because their relevance to feminists has I believe been under recognized, and because they illustrate what feminist projects can contribute to legal theory and vice versa.

Non-Ideal Theory

Although the debates between legal positivists and natural law theorists are generally understood to be conceptual—how law is to be defined—they are, in my judgment, ultimately normative. Answers to questions such as what it is to have a legal system, to judge that a rule is a rule of that system, or to determine whether there is an obligation to obey some or all laws reach to deep questions about the legitimacy of political authority, the purpose of law, and the role of law in the lives of people who live under it. It is no accident that the renewal of the positivism-natural law debate occurred in the wake of the horrors of Nazism and the world's efforts to address it through the use of law in the Nuremburg tribunals. Nor is it an accident, as we will see below, that H. L. A. Hart's defense of positivism was shaped by his liberal view that the law should provide a framework within which different lives could flourish and that conceptual commingling of law and morality risked allowing judges unknowingly to inflict on others their views of what would be good for them. If there are any natural rights, Hart (1955) argued, there is an equal right of all to be free.

My argument about legal theory is shaped by my overall approach to normative questions. I am a non-ideal theorist in the sense that I think normative questions should be addressed from the recognition that natural or social circumstances are less than ideal, as John Rawls famously observed in A *Theory of Justice* (1971) in the midst of the civil rights movement (see Francis 2016).

While theorizing about justice for ideal circumstances, Rawls understood that different approaches might be needed where either natural or social circumstances were less than ideal. Rawls's theory of justice for ideal circumstances was soon confronted with objections rooted in non-ideal theory such as whether his views could be publicly justified to those with illiberal conceptions of the good (Freeman 2003: 29). And in his next book, *Political Liberalism* (1993), Rawls retreated to the idea that he was developing a theory of justice for a liberal society. But arguably he did not fully recognize the force of the challenge; Waldron points out (1999: 152–153) that Rawls understood the challenge to concern fundamental disputes about the good, not fundamental disagreement about justice itself.

For the discussion here, what is most important is how non-ideal theory approaches the role of law in pursuing justice under conditions of injustice. Concerning the project of justice, non-ideal theory treats issues such as how progress can best be made toward justice, what injustices take precedence to address, what strategies are likely to create new roadblocks to overcoming injustice, or what are the obligations of individuals or institutions when others continue to behave unjustly (Cohen 2000; Miller 2011). As I see justice, it is a matter of ongoing work at inclusion and flourishing: what next steps, at individual or social levels, will enable individuals in all their differences to do well at what matters to them? Law, as the primary social institution that does justice, plays a central role in this project.

Positivism and the Separation of Law and Morality

Since the Nazi era, a prominent—if not the prominent—theme in Anglo-American legal philosophy has been the debate over legal positivism. Legal positivists hold that law and morality should be understood as conceptually separate. On this "separation" thesis, "what is law?" is a different question from "what law ought to be." In adjudication, the separation thesis is manifest as the view that judges apply the law or, more controversially, have the authority that legislators do to make new law in difficult cases when existing law runs out. But when it occurs, judicial legislation should be recognized as such: judges are making new law rather than applying the law already on the books. They may have the authority to do this in a given society, just as legislators do—but whether they are exercising this authority appropriately is what must be critically examined.

Thomas Hobbes, holding as he did that justice is acting according to the requirements of covenant (in *Leviathan* 1651: Ch. XV), may have been the first proponent of legal positivism (see, e.g., Dyzenhaus 1991; Tucker 2013). The development of the tradition of utilitarian liberalism in Britain was an early setting for the fuller development of legal positivism, particularly in the writings of Jeremy Bentham and John Austin. The debate was rekindled in the wake of the Nuremberg trials, where the controversial question was whether punishment could be justified for those who had arguably followed Nazi law. H. L. A. Hart (1958) defended the separation thesis because he believed it would create clarity about what was at stake in deploying the force of the law against the Nazis accused of war crimes: the extraordinary, yet justifiable, use of the law as a statement of moral condemnation. The Nuremberg trials were not ordinary exercises of the legal process but a determination that the force of law should, ethically, be used to punish what the Nazis had done. In reply to Hart, Lon Fuller (1958) took the position that the most odious of Nazi commands were not law at all, because they violated what he termed the "internal morality of law." For Fuller, the aim of law was to enable people to engage in purposive activity; law must be constructed so as to enable people to conduct their lives in accord with it. This led Fuller to adopt a procedural version of natural law incorporating requirements such as consistency that were designed to evade the far-reaching moral commitments of earlier versions such as those associated with traditions in Catholic theology.

The canonical contemporary statement of legal positivism remains H. L. A. Hart's *The Concept of Law* (1961). In *Concept*, Hart distinguishes the conceptual question of whether there are logically necessary connections between what is law and what is morally right (no), from the historical question of whether the law has been influenced by morality (yes) and the ethical question of whether law can be subject to ethical critique (emphatically yes). What makes a precept a law is that it is recognized as such under the constitutional rules of the system in question. At bottom, whether there exists a legal system at all is a matter of fact: whether a sufficient number of those in relevant places in a society accept its basic constitutional structure.

In a famous debate with Lord Patrick Devlin, the British High Court Judge, Hart argued that the law should not be used to enforce morality. Hart's contribution to the debate, published as *Law, Liberty, and Morality*, argued for decriminalization of a number of what were thought to be victimless crimes, such as the voluntary sale of sex or homosexual sexual acts. Punishment of such consensual acts as crimes, Hart thought, amounted to an unwarranted imposition of conservative social values and could not be justified as legitimate protection of some from harm by others. Thus Hart's views about the nature of law were ultimately justified by his political liberalism (Lacey 2004).

Hart's views about adjudication are perhaps the most maligned of his views. For Hart, judges in applying the law need first to try to understand what the laws of a given system require. The laws may run out and there are problems of the penumbra where what the law requires is unclear. Prior adjudications may help with this interpretive task. But when the law runs out, faced with novel interpretive choices, judges must recognize that they are creating new law. Leaving judges to call on moral values in interpreting penumbral law—as though they were merely applying law—risks imposing the values of some, the judges, on others, in unrecognized fashion. This is so whether these values protect moral rights or traditional social mores.

The laws also may be evil, but if judges fail to apply them, they are stepping outside of the judicial role. If so, apartheid South Africa had a legal system that judges applied—despite the grievous immorality of these laws and the moral obligation to change. Hart did not hold the view that identifying law was the end of the matter. He thought that being clear about what the law is—to the extent that we can be clear—is an important first step in appreciating when we are making moral choices about law.

David Dyzenhaus (1991) criticized legal positivism for a politics of authoritarianism. But arguably Dyzenhaus attributes an overly strong form of majoritarianism to Hart, the view that judges must apply statutory law as enacted (Tucker 2013). Hart held a more complex view about how law was to be identified, in terms of the actual rule or rules for recognizing law in a given society. And he combined this ultimately descriptive account with the view that as a matter of political morality we would be more clear-headed if we recognized when judges were legislating and considered whether what they were doing was morally justifiable.

Hart's view about adjudication was also subject to the attack that instead of being authoritarian it could only account for the very small set of legal decisions in which the law's requirements were clear. Ronald Dworkin (1967) argued that Hart's view left most judges exercising a strong form of discretion, selecting new law unbound. This is not how most judges conceive of their roles, nor how judging should be conceived, Dworkin claimed (1967: 46). Instead, Dworkin argued, judges in applying the law call on a variety of principles, often moral, that have a dimension of weight; thus a murdering heir could not profit from his own wrong even though the statute of wills did not specifically provide for this case.

Separating law from morality as it does, positivism faces the challenge of explaining how law can carry obligatory force. Natural law theorists such as Dworkin or Fuller answer that it can do so because morality is endemic in law—and, if not, a coercive system is not law at all. Positivists before Hart, such as Hobbes (1651) or John Austin (1832) had identified law with sovereign commands. Critics of this view distinguished between being "obliged"—coerced—and being obligated. Hart's reply was to continue the project of identifying law as descriptive, not normative, but to say that the fundamental grounding of law was simply a matter of acceptance. Terribly bad laws, or legal systems that did not serve fundamental human interests, would not endure, he thought. The ultimate foundation of norm-governed behavior was social acceptance (Shapiro 2001). But the point of Hart's positivism was to create the space to recognize that such acceptance may be morally problematic. And feminist philosophers of law eagerly occupied this space.

Feminist Philosophy of Law

Interestingly, feminist legal theorists have paid little attention to the debates about legal positivism. They have focused elsewhere: on the critique of law as a system of patriarchal power, on civil rights and equality, on critical race and disability theory, and on problem areas such as abortion, rape, sexual harassment, or child custody and divorce.

Feminist philosophy of law has been informed by different approaches to feminism itself (Francis and Smith 2015). The so-called "first-wave" feminism of the late nineteenth and early twentieth centuries attempted to achieve political rights for women. These feminists were critical of how the law gave women unequal political and legal status. Establishing the right to vote was a critical step towards political equality. But legal status mattered, too, such as the rights to own property, to be licensed as a professional, and to enter into contracts, even as a married woman. Such deficiencies in status had been justified on views of the natural condition of women, a position rooted in a certain picture of natural law (Kimmel 1987: 266). For example, when Myra Bradshaw sought to be licensed as a lawyer in Illinois, she was met with the observation that the legislature could not have meant to allow women to practice law, because it was regarded as axiomatic that God had designed the sexes to occupy different spheres of action (*Bradwell v. State of Illinois*, 83 US 1380 (1873)).

The liberal feminism of the civil rights era aimed to establish non-discrimination in economic and social life as well: in education, in employment, and even in marriage and family formation and dissolution. These feminists sought both constitutional and statutory equality. Proposals for an Equal Rights Amendment finally bore fruit in 1972 when Congress adopted the Amendment and sent it to the states for ratification. The Amendment did not, however, succeed in receiving the necessary support of three-fourths of the states by the deadline of 1979. In the judgment of some commentators, many of its goals have been achieved through subsequent litigation and legislation. But assessing this claim is difficult, as goals changed, from formal to substantive equality and to the end of laws that although neutral on their face perpetuated inequality (Mayeri 2009).

Concomitantly, liberal feminists pursued efforts to move the Supreme Court to recognize women as a suspect classification so that any different treatment would require strict scrutiny. Cases such as *Reed v. Reed*, 404 US 71 (1971), struck down Idaho's preference for males as probate administrators in a conflict between the separated parents of a deceased son. The preference, the Court concluded, did not bear a rational relationship to the legislature's goal of reducing the workload of probate courts by eliminating a need for a hearing to determine the relative merits of the competing parties. The constitutional standard used in *Reed* was formally the rational basis test, not a more heightened test that would make it easier to strike down other statutes treating men and women differently. However, the Court, in this first case applying the equal protection clause to women, used a citation from a brief authored by then law professor and later Justice Ruth Bader Ginsburg to a case holding that states could not give in state residents tax advantages over out of state residents unless the difference has a "fair and substantial relation" to the legislature's purpose. (*F.S. Royster Guano v. Virginia*, 253 U.S 412, 415 (1920); see also Hirshman 2015)

In a succession of cases, many argued by Justice Ginsburg, the Court moved towards tighter scrutiny of statutes and regulations distinguishing men and women. Justice Ginsburg's goal as an advocate was to bring the law of sex discrimination under the "strict scrutiny" used for discrimination on the basis of race: that for different treatment to be justified, states must demonstrate a compelling state interest and treatment narrowly tailored to furthering that interest. In *Frontiero v. Richardson*, 411 US 677 (1973)—a case decided in the same year as *Roe v. Wade*—the Court rejected the military's assumption that wives were dependent on their male serviceman husbands for support but husbands were not so dependent on their female serviceman wives. But it did not adopt the strict scrutiny standard advocated by Ginsburg in an amicus brief filed on behalf of the ACLU. *Craig v. Boren*, 429 US 190 (1976), a further case presenting an equal protection challenge to a statute differentiating men and women, this time disfavoring men by setting their age for the sale of 3.2 beer at 21 while women could drink at 18, brought the Court to adopt an intermediate level of scrutiny. The state's rationale for the differentiation was traffic safety: that males of the relevant age were more likely to drive while intoxicated and to be killed or injured in alcohol related traffic accidents.

The Court applied what has been termed "heightened" (albeit not strict) scrutiny at the test that had been established in earlier decisions (429 US at 198). Although the Court assumed that traffic safety enhancement could be an important governmental objective, the statistics about males and females as drivers were insufficient to show that the gender-based distinction "closely serves to achieve that objective" (429 US at 200). This level of scrutiny—important objective, closely served by the state's distinction—is as far as women ever got towards constitutional equality.

So liberal feminists pursued statutory reforms as well in the effort to achieve social and economic equality. The initial important statute was the Equal Pay Act of 1963, which prohibited unequal pay for "for equal work on jobs the performance of which requires equal skill, effort, and responsibility, and which are performed under similar working conditions" (29 USC. § 206(d)(1)(2015)). The statutory language famously compromised between equal work and comparable work, a compromise that continues to be implicated in gender pay gaps today.

Other statutes followed quickly, most importantly the employment discrimination section of the Civil Rights Act in 1964 (Title VII) and the prohibition of discrimination based on sex in federally funded educational programs (Title IX) in 1969, and several amendments to Title VII including the Lily Ledbetter Fair Pay Act of 2009 (42 USC. § 2000e(5)(e)(3)(A)(2015)), which allowed women to challenge historical discrimination reflected in continuing pay disparities. Title VII, about which more below, prohibited discrimination in the terms or conditions of employment, a provision designed to rule out practices that while not singling out sex per se might have differing impacts based on sex. Despite their potential, disparate impact challenges to apparently neutral employment practices have had a troubled history. One of the ongoing difficulties in using disparate impact theories to counter inequality is the continuing failure of courts to recognize structural impacts on subordination. Radical feminists from the beginning challenged the structure of law, seeing it as the embodiment of patriarchy. Law itself is a form of dominance (Francis and Smith 2015). Legal systems in both structure and content reflect coercion and subordination, hallmarks of masculinity. Nowhere is this more apparent than in how the criminal law deals with sexual offenses. Rape law, the law of prostitution, and legalization of pornography reflect the dominance of masculinity (e.g., MacKinnon 1989).

Prostitution is an example of this disagreement between liberal and radical feminists. For many liberal feminists, if prostitution is a choice that is not coerced, it should not be prohibited. When prostitution threatens to blend into sex trafficking, to be sure, that should be prohibited. The potential inability to distinguish the voluntary sale of sex from trafficking is the concern that has led Sweden to criminalize the purchase, but not the sale, of sex (Crouch 2015) and the Netherlands to reconsider its toleration of prostitution (e.g., Bindel 2013; Dutch Ministry of Foreign Affairs 2012). Nonetheless, on the liberal view voluntary choices to sell sex, like voluntary choices to sell soap or labor power, should be legally permitted. To say that women—and their customers—should not engage in prostitution is a form of legal moralism, of exactly the kind criticized by Hart in *Law, Liberty and Morality*.

Radical feminist critics object that the choice of prostitution can never be voluntary in situations of economic distress or patriarchal subordination (e.g., Freeman 1989–1990). Moreover, they claim that the commodification and objectification of women's bodies found in prostitution—or in other practices of bodily commodification such as surrogate reproduction—violates human dignity and is thus harmful even if apparently consensual (e.g., Dickenson 2017). Their view, they argue, is not unjustified moral condemnation of prostitution but rooted in an understanding of pervasive sexual dominance.

Pornography is another example of how radical and liberal feminists are divided in how to address the dominance model of sexuality in law and society. Feminists such as Catharine MacKinnon opposed pornography (especially violent pornography) as the symbol of the dominance model. MacKinnon and Andrea Dworkin developed a model anti-pornography statute for jurisdictions to enact, a statute that was held to violate the First Amendment in *American Booksellers v. Hudnut*, 771 F.2d 323 (7th Cir. 1985). The proposed statute was much criticized as moralistic—although explicitly not by Ronald Dworkin, who saw the issue in terms of the importance of freedom of expression (see, e.g., MacKinnon, reply to Dworkin 1994; Duggan, Hunter, and Vance 1993).

The debates between liberal and radical feminists are related to, but not the same as, the disputes between positivists and natural law theorists. The former debate criticizes how law may be used, with liberal feminists arguing that it should be used to further equality in economic and civil rights and radical feminists that it should be stripped of patriarchal dominance. The latter debate is about what law is, that it is separate from morality. In the view of the positivists, only when we separate law from it is from law as it ought to be, can we see clearly what is at stake in debates about what law ought to be. To explore this point further, I now turn briefly to two examples, sexual harassment and abortion.

Sexual Harassment

When Title VII of the Civil Rights Act, the section on employment discrimination, was introduced, sex discrimination was an apparent afterthought to race, color, religion, or natural origin. Sex was added as a category in the last days before the bill's passage, perhaps to try to defeat the bill or more likely because of advocacy of gender equality (e.g., Freeman 1991).

Whether or not sex was an afterthought to Title VII, the statute did little to explain what the right to non-discrimination in employment meant in several employment contexts relevant to women. While it prescribed non-discrimination in the "compensation, terms, conditions, or privileges of employment" (42 USC. § 2000e-2(a)(1) (2016)), it said nothing further about the myriad of workplace rules, apparently neutral but in practice making work difficult for women, such as the failure to provide leave time for pregnancy.

And employers continued to fire women for becoming pregnant. In 1974, the Supreme Court held that mandatory unpaid leaves for pregnant schoolteachers violated the Fourteenth Amendment because they imposed arbitrary and irrebuttable presumptions about women's fitness to work (*Cleveland Board of Education v. LaFleur*, 414 US 632 (1974)). The Court's analysis rested in due process, not equal protection; the reasoning was that the requirement to quit work unduly burdened women's constitutional freedom of reproductive decision-making, the same liberty that had been the basis of the abortion decision the previous year. In 1978, Congress amended Title VII to add to the definition of discrimination because of sex different treatment "on the basis of pregnancy, childbirth, of related medical conditions . . ." (42 USC. § 2000e(k)) (2016)). The Pregnancy Discrimination Act did not, however, require accommodations for pregnancy—accommodations that are still largely unavailable today.

Thus Title VII's prohibitions of employment discrimination still do not extend to many workplace practices that, in Martha Minow's (1991) phrase, "make all the difference" for genuine workplace equality.

Nor did Title VII explain what was meant by conditions of employment. Early on, however, in race and ethnicity cases, courts determined that hostile work environments were discriminatory. In the words of one court:

> This language [of Title VII] evinces a Congressional intention to define discrimination in the broadest possible terms . . . But today employment discrimination is a far more complex and pervasive phenomenon, as the nuances and subtleties of discriminatory employment practices are no longer confined to bread and butter issue.
>
> (*Rogers v. EEOC*, 454 F.2d 234, 238)

But these were race, not sex cases. MacKinnon is generally credited with "inventing" the theory of workplace sexual harassment (Caplan-Bricker 2012). MacKinnon is indeed the first person to crystallize the concept of sexual harassment and argue that it was a violation of Title VII, but whether she "invented" the concept is another matter. MacKinnon's own description of the process of generating sexual harassment law is that it was "judge-made" (2002: 813), a claim that can be taken simplistically to imply that in finding a cause of action for sexual harassment under Title VII judges were legislating.

If judges were legislating in recognizing sexual harassment as a cause of action, however, they would be vulnerable to the criticism that they were stepping out of the judicial role to implement their own values, no matter how defensible those values were. A concomitant vulnerability is that acceptance of the theory could be seen as moralizing, imposing the values of some onto others. Not surprisingly, women who claimed sexual harassment were seen as overly sensitive or prudish. These kinds of criticisms were levelled against the development of sexual harassment law, but they are based on a misunderstanding of it as a matter of judges illegitimately imposing their values on the law.

There is, however, a way to see the theory of sexual harassment as far more defensible as a matter of legal theory. Sexual harassment, like other forms of discrimination in the workplace denies women equal work opportunities. Vicki Schultz (1998) explains in powerful detail how both quid pro quo harassment (harassment that takes the form of coercive offer exchange of supposed favors) and hostile environment harassment (harassment that creates an unwelcoming workplace) excludes women from entire categories of employment. Sexual advances by superiors, firehouses full of girlie posters, or ridicule directed at performance, all signal to women that they should not be present in the hostile workplace. Understanding sexual harassment as sexualized oppression—as the dominance theory of MacKinnon does—is both under and over inclusive, according to Schultz. It is under inclusive because it encourages courts to devalue forms of harassment that are not explicitly sexual, finding harassment for crude sexual advances but not for more delicate flirting or non-sexual ridicule. It is over-inclusive because it suggests that workplaces should be sexually pure. Instead, Schultz contends, harassment, sexual or not, should be understood as a form of workplace inequality created by a hostile environment.

Seeing sexual harassment as a discriminatory condition of employment places it centrally within the scope of Title VII. Rather than "invented," the theory is developed from within Title VII. It is thus not a case of judges legislating, but of judges implementing what the legislature has enacted. What judges do in interpreting Title VII—in understanding its prohibitions—is consider how various fact situations closely resemble the clear cases of inequality already recognized as Title VII violations. The novelty of the theory of sexual harassment was not that it was new law, but that it brought new insight into what workplace conditions were genuinely exclusionary.

Abortion

The Supreme Court's decision in *Roe v. Wade*, 410 US 113 (1973), is one of the most controversial in its history. In the decision, the Court determined that reproductive liberty, characterized as privacy, is a fundamental constitutional right that can be limited only by a compelling state interest. This interpretation of due process liberty was characterized as a form of substantive due process, reading substantive rather than procedural liberties into the Fourteenth Amendment's protection. It was thus maligned as the justices imposing their own values in distrust of democracy (Ely 1980).

There is, however, another way of reading *Roe*: that it could, and should, have been decided as a matter of equal protection. Abortion restrictions deny women reproductive control, with consequent difficulties for their ability to achieve in education, work, or other pursuits. Justice Ginsburg has staunchly defended this view. In an essay published while she was serving on the United States Court of Appeals for the District of Columbia Circuit, she wrote that *Roe* had become a "storm center" because the Court both "ventured too far" and "presented an incomplete justification for its action" (Ginsburg 1985: 376). The Court's inadequacy, she said, was that it had treated abortion as a matter of due process liberty, not as a matter of sex discrimination (Ginsburg 1985: 386).

Justice Ginsburg's jurisprudence is generally seen as "minimalist" in the sense that she seeks to carve judicial reasoning closely to existing law (e.g., Siegel 2009). In this commentary on *Roe*, and in many other writings, she applies such minimalism to explain the problems with the Court's due process approach.

In her arguments for an equal protection approach to abortion, Justice Ginsburg harbors no illusions about whether this could have avoided the controversy *Roe* generated (Ginsburg 1985). Abortion is an issue that reaches to the very basic and contested issue in moral theory, that of the status of the fetus. What an equal protection analysis can do, however, is change the legal theory terms of the debate, for it locates the question of abortion squarely within evolving equal protection doctrine. This is a positivist, not a natural law theory approach. And like the positivist approach to sexual harassment law as a matter of workplace equality, it shows how abortion jurisprudence can be defended without courting the charge that judges are in activist fashion imposing their own values.

Conclusion

Let me return briefly to my initial methodological remarks about non-ideal theory. Both the sexual harassment and the abortion examples suggest how the positivist approach to adjudication can further progress toward gender justice and justice more generally. The understanding that sexual harassment is a form of employment discrimination located exclusionary workplace practices squarely within the statutory prohibition of Title VII. Seeing reproductive liberty as a matter of women's ability to participate in economic life constructs it as a matter of progress toward inclusive justice. Similar points might be made about disability civil rights or other civil rights.

Now, abortion opponents may raise an objection at this point: what about inclusion of the fetus, is that not also needed for progress towards justice? Here, positivism has a response that natural law theory may not. The history of feminist jurisprudence in the US is the gradual achievement of political, economic, and social equality for women. Viewing the abortion cases as equal protection cases locates them within this equality project as legally constituted. There is no question whether women are citizens entitled to equal status under law. Fetuses have not been so recognized; to argue that they should be is to advance a moral critique of contemporary law. Natural law theory, as the Court's opinion in *Gonzales v. Carhart* illustrates, confuses on just this point: it is not a continuation of an ongoing equality project, but an argument for a new one.

All too frequently, positivists have failed to develop their theory in the progressive ways suggested by the sexual harassment and abortion examples. There are forms of positivism that have imposed literalist strictures on statutory and constitutional interpretation or that have been myopic about structural inequality. Some positivism was associated with the logical positivists' skepticism of normative theory—a position that Hart took pains from the beginning to disavow. Robin West (2011) takes contemporary positivism to task for failing to develop what she calls "a sustained tradition of censorial jurisprudence." Nonetheless, positivism has theoretical resources for legal development and criticism that are critical to furthering inclusive justice.

Related Topics

Feminist theory, lesbian theory, and queer theory (Chapter 31); the genealogy and viability of the concept of intersectionality (Chapter 28); critical race theory, intersectionality, and feminist philosophy (Chapter 29); feminism and liberalism (Chapter 52).

References

Austin, John (1832) *The Province of Jurisprudence Determined*, London: John Murray.

Bindel, Julie (2013) "Why Even Amsterdam Doesn't Want Legal Brothels," *The Spectator* February 2 [online]. Available from: www.spectator.co.uk/2013/02/flesh-for-sale/.

Caplan-Bricker, Nora (2012) "How Title IX Became Our Best Tool Against Sexual Harassment," *The New Republic*, June 21 [online]. Available from: https://newrepublic.com/article/104237/how-title-ix-became-our-best-tool-against-sexual-harassment.

Cohen, G. A. (2000) *If You're an Egalitarian, How Come You're So Rich?* Cambridge, MA: Harvard University Press.

Crenshaw, Kimberlé (1991) "Mapping the Margins," *Stanford Law Review* 43(6): 1241–1258.

Crouch, David (2015) "Swedish Prostitution Law Targets Buyers, but Some Say It Hurts Sellers," *The New York Times*, March 14 [online]. Available from: www.nytimes.com/2015/03/15/world/swedish-prostitution-law-targets-buyers-but-some-say-it-hurts-sellers.html?_r=0.

Dickenson, Donna (2017) "The Commodification of Women's Reproductive Tissue and Services," in Leslie P. Francis (Ed.) *Oxford Handbook on Reproductive Ethics*, New York: Oxford University Press, 118–140.

Duggan, Lisa, Hunter, Nan D., and Vance, Carole S. (1993) "False Promises: Feminist Anti-Pornography Legislation," *New York Law School Law Review* 38: 133–162.

Dutch Ministry of Foreign Affairs (2012) *Dutch Policy on Prostitution* [online]. Available from: www.minbuza.nl/binaries/content/assets/minbuza/en/import/en/you_and_the_netherlands/about_the_netherlands/ethical_issues/faq-prostitutie-pdf--engels.pdf-2012.pdf.

Dworkin, Ronald (1967) "The Model of Rules," *University of Chicago Law Review* 38: 14–46.

—— (1986) *Law's Empire*, Cambridge, MA: Harvard University Press.

Dyzenhaus, David (1991) *Hard Cases in Wicked Legal Systems: South African Law in the Perspective of Legal Philosophy*, Oxford: Clarendon Press.

Ely, John Hart (1980) *Democracy and Distrust*, Cambridge, MA: Harvard University Press.

Francis, Leslie P. (2016) "Applied Ethics: A Misnomer for a Field?" Presidential Address to the Pacific Division of the American Philosophical Association, *Proceedings and Addresses of the American Philosophical Association* 90 (November): 40–54.

Francis, Leslie P. and Smith, Patricia (2015) "Feminist Philosophy of Law," *The Stanford Encyclopedia of Philosophy* Summer 2015 [online]. Available from: http://plato.stanford.edu/archives/sum2015/entries/feminism-law/.

Freeman, Jo (1991) "How "Sex" Got Into Title VII: Persistent Opportunism as a Maker of Public Policy," *Law and Inequality: A Journal of Theory and Practice* 9(2): 163–184.

Freeman, Jody (1989–1990) "The Feminist Debate Over Prostitution Reform: Prostitutes' Rights Groups, Radical Feminists, and the (Im)possibility of Consent," *Berkeley Women's Law Journal* 5: 75–109.

Freeman, Samuel (2003) "Introduction," in Samuel Freeman (Ed.), *The Cambridge Companion to Rawls*, Cambridge: Cambridge University Press, 1–64.

Fuller, Lon L. (1958) "Positivism and Fidelity to Law: A Reply to Professor Hart," *Harvard Law Review* 71(4): 630–672.

Ginsburg, Ruth Bader (1985) "Some Thoughts on Autonomy and Equality in Relationship to *Roe v. Wade*," *North Carolina Law Review* 63: 375–386.

Harris, Angela (1990) "Race and Essentialism in Feminist Legal Theory," *Stanford Law Review* 42(3): 581–616.

Hart, H. L. A. (1955) " Are There Any Natural Rights?" *Philosophical Review* 64(2): 175–191.

—— (1958) "Positivism and the Separation of Law and Morals," *Harvard Law Review* 71(4): 593–629.

—— (1961) *The Concept of Law*, Oxford: Oxford University Press.

—— (1963) *Law, Liberty, and Morality*, Stanford, CA: Stanford University Press.

Hirshman, Linda (2015) *Sisters in Law*, New York: HarperCollins.

Hobbes, Thomas (1651) *Leviathan*, Project Gutenberg [online]. Available from: www.gutenberg.org/files/3207/3207-h/3207-h.htm.

Kimmel, Michael S. (1987) "Men's Responses to Feminism at the Turn of the Century," *Gender and Society* 1(3): 261–283.

Lacey, Nicola (2004) *A Life of H.L.A. Hart: The Nightmare and the Noble Dream*, Oxford: Oxford University Press.

MacKinnon, Catharine A. (1989) *Toward a Feminist Theory of the State*, Cambridge, MA: Harvard University Press.

—— (2002) "The Logic of Experience: Reflections on the Development of Sexual Harassment Law," *Georgetown Law Journal* 90: 813–833.

MacKinnon, Catharine A., reply by Ronald Dworkin (1994) "Pornography: An Exchange," *New York Review of Books*, March 3 [online]. Available from: www.nybooks.com/articles/1994/03/03/pornography-an-exchange/.

Mayeri, Serena (2009) "A New E.R.A. or a New Era? Amendment Advocacy and the Reconstitution of Feminism," *Northwestern University Law Review* 103: 1223–1302.

Miller, David (2011) "Taking up the Slack? Responsibility and Justice in Situations of Partial Compliance," in Zofia Stemplowska and Carl Knight (Eds.) *Responsibility and Distributive Justice*, Oxford: Oxford University Press, 230–245.

Minow, Martha (1991) *Making All the Difference: Inclusion, Exclusion, and American Law*, Ithaca, NY: Cornell University Press.

Rawls, John (1971) *A Theory of Justice*, Cambridge, MA: Harvard University Press.

—— (1993) *Political Liberalism*, New York: Columbia University Press.

Schultz, Vicki (1998) "Reconceptualizing Sexual Harassment," *Yale Law Journal* 107: 1683–1803.

Shapiro, Scott (2001) "On Hart's Way Out," in Jules Coleman (Ed.) *Hart's Postscript: Essays on the Postscript to the Concept of Law*, Oxford: Oxford University Press, 149–191.

Silvers, Anita and Francis, Leslie, 2005. "Justice through Trust: Disability and the 'Outlier Problem' in Social Contract Theory," *Ethics*, 116(1): 40–76.

Siegel, Neil C. (2009) "Equal Citizenship Statute: Justice Ginsburg's Constitutional Vision," *New England Law Review* 43(4): 799–856.

Tucker, Adam (2013) "The Politics of Legal Positivism: A Reply to David Dyzenhaus," *Australian Journal of Legal Philosophy* 38: 74–101.

Waldron, Jeremy (1999) *Law and Disagreement*, Oxford: Oxford University Press.

West, Robin (2011) *Normative Jurisprudence: An Introduction*, New York: Cambridge University Press.

INDEX